Ars Notoria

ARS NOTORIA

THE NOTORY ART OF SOLOMON

A Medieval Treatise on Angelic Magic and the Art of Memory

Translated and Introduced by
MATTHIAS CASTLE

Inner Traditions
Rochester, Vermont

Inner Traditions
One Park Street
Rochester, Vermont 05767
www.InnerTraditions.com

Cataloging-in-Publication Data for this title is available from the Library of Congress

ISBN 978-1-64411-527-5 (print)
ISBN 978-1-64411-528-2 (ebook)

Printed and bound in China by Reliance Printing Co., Ltd.

10 9 8 7 6 5 4 3 2 1

Text design and layout by Debbie Glogover
This book was typeset in Garamond Premier Pro with Abbess, Arno Pro, Gill Sans MT Pro, Times New Roman, and Trajan Pro used as display typefaces.
Artwork on pages 28, 58, 64, 66, 132, and 144 re-created by Kenleigh Manseau

To send correspondence to the author of this book, mail a first-class letter to the author c/o Inner Traditions • Bear & Company, One Park Street, Rochester, VT 05767, and we will forward the communication.

CONTENTS

Ars Notoria *Version A*

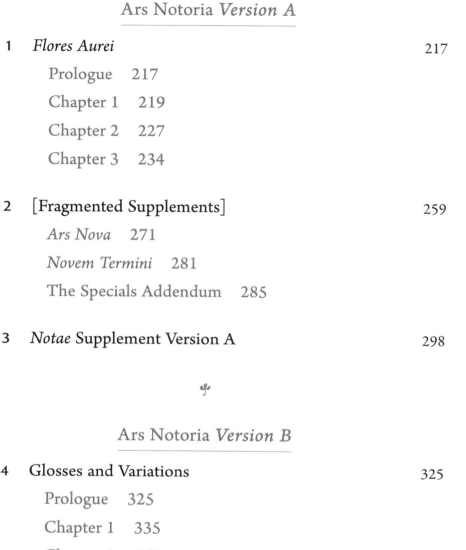

Ars Notoria *Version B*

Branches of the Ars Notoria *Tradition*

Appendices

A Note on the Translation

This Latin to English translation of the *Ars Notoria* and its derivative texts is based on Julien Véronèse's critical edition titled *L'Ars notoria au Moyen Age: Introduction et édition critique* published by Sismel–Edizioni Del Galluzzo (2007) and his doctoral dissertation, titled *L'Ars notoria au Moyen Âge et à l'époque moderne. Étude d'une tradition de magie théurgique (XIIe–XVIIe siècle)* (2004). This is a faithful translation of the Latin original, consulting Véronèse's work and some of the original manuscripts to provide the best reading in English. This English translation follows Véronèse's section numbering of the *Ars Notoria* and *Opus Operum*. New numbering of sections are introduced in the *Ars Brevis,* the abridged notory art attributed to Thomas of Toledo, and the *Ars Paulina*.

Translating the Latin texts of the *Ars Notoria* posed several unique challenges. About 60 percent of English is ultimately derived from Latin. My effort has been to follow the historical line of transmission from Latin to English as faithfully as possible without compromising the meaning of the word. For example, the Latin word *spiritus* is usually translated as "spirit," never "soul," thereby retaining the morphology of the word. As *spiritus* can also carry the sense of "wind," or "breath," sometimes this is translated as "spirited wind" or "spirited breath." In following the historical line of transmission from Latin to English, the reader will find certain English words in the translation which are now obsolete or have meanings that have changed (examples: *deprecation, exaudition, institution*). These obsolete English words are kept not just for the sake of diachronic linguistics but for retaining the original and best meaning of the Latin as well. All obsolete English words are explained in the footnotes. This work aims to provide the best reading experience, and this always trumps morphology. At times, the English translation is given with bracketed words, which are my own, to clarify further the meaning of the text.

For the sake of convenience, the masculine English pronouns "he," "his," and "him" are used in the text. Historically speaking, it was usually men who received a formal education during the Middle Ages, and thus it is men who would have been the target audience of the *Ars Notoria*. The Latin is sometimes ambiguous as to the gender of the ritual practitioner, though there are a few rare instances in which it acknowledges that the ritual practitioner could be either male or female.

In studying these texts, the reader will encounter a distinctly medieval perspective of how the mind-body complex operates through the senses. This medieval perspective is respectfully maintained in the English translation. Explanations are provided as footnotes on how the mind-body complex was thought about in medieval philosophy. Similarly, idioms peculiar to the Latin language are usually translated word-for-word to perserve the original meaning; again, footnotes are given to explain their meaning. No modern English idioms are introduced into the text.

The *Ars Notoria* contains strange words from "Greek, Hebrew, and Chaldean" which modern scholarship denotes as magical calls (*voces magicae*) or unknownable words (*verba ignota*). The *Ars Notoria* says they are prayers addressed to the Holy Trinity and angels, claiming that angelic names are contained therein. These strange prayers are given incipits—abridged shorthand names. These prayer incipits are based on the first few words of the prayer for the sake of clear identification, such as "*Helyscemath*," "*Rasay Lamac*," and "*Hazatam*." The *Ars Notoria* refers to the prayer incipits by their headwords (*capitula*). In the case of the first prayer, it is called *Helyscemath* (Version A, section 7). The Latin word *capitulum* (pl. *capitula*) is translated as "headword" (pl. "headwords") in these instances. Other occurrences of *capitula* are found in reference to certain sections of text or one of the three chapters of the *Flores Aurei;* these occurrences dictate that it is to be translated as "section" or "chapter."

There is a class of prayers called "Special prayers." This term also appears when describing others which are written within the *Ars Notoria*'s illustrations, referred to as "particular (*speciale*)." To avoid confusion, the latter are translated as "particular" or "adorning" prayers because they adorn the figure like an ornament.

The *Ars Notoria* claims that some of these strange prayers have received a partial Latin translation of their beginning or a summary; these Latin translations are called a "prologue." For example, the strange prayer *Lamehc Ragna* has the Latin prologue *Memoria irreprehensibilis*. In effect, this is a single prayer. As such, this book denotes these prayers and their Latin prologues with a forward slash—for example, *Lamehc Ragna / Memoria irreprehensibilis*.

There are minor discrepancies in the prayer incipits found between the short (A) and long (B) versions of the *Ars Notoria*. For example, the prayer incipit of section 16 in Version A has *Rasay, Lamac,* whereas in Version B, the prayer incipit is *Assaylemaht*. However, these prayers are essentially equivalent for the purpose of understanding the text. In this particular instance, *Assaylemaht* may be a late recension of *Rasay Lamac*. In a few cases, an address to God or Jesus appears to have been added to the beginning of the incipit. For example, the prayer incipit of section 29 in Version A has *Ancor Anacor Anilos,* whereas in Version B, the prayer incipit is extended to *Iesu Dei Filius incomprehensibilis Ancor Anacor Anilos*. Again, the prayers are essentially equivalent. These discrepancies are indicated in the footnotes.

Version B contains extended commentary (glosses) on Version A, and the same sections are found in both versions. Where the two versions differ in content for a given section, then that special section is represented in Version B under its own section number, just as Julien Véronèse had already done in his critical edition. Rather than duplicate the wording of Version A, I have indicated where the repeated sections appear. For instance, "[1, 2, Version A]" precedes section 2 Gloss of Version B, and so on. For the most part, the prayers are written verbatim, but sometimes there are small discrepancies. These small discrepancies may have occurred for certain reasons: (1) the writer chose to use different words, (2) my choice or ordering the sentence in the act of providing the best English translation, or (3) Latin transcription errors. Latin transcription errors certainly happened, either by the original scribe, Véronèse, Lundy, or myself. Any errors spotted, I have corrected; these are marked in the footnotes in which I simply write down the correct Latin word. My corrections can be compared against the original manuscripts and Véronèse. Some errors may remain because I did not have access to all the extant manuscripts to verify the accuracy of a given transcription. In any case, if the original scribe made a transcription error, it was probably because he misread the text or his source was already corrupted, not because he decided to add his own flourish or agenda to the original text.

Lastly, the Latin word *nota* (pl. *notae*) is a technical term in the *Ars Notoria* denoting a certain kind of knowledge contained both within a *voces magicae* prayer and a pictorial figure. In other words, the *nota* is the hidden knowledge itself, which the operator seeks to acquire; the *nota*'s symbols, or "containers" as it were, are the prayer and the pictorial figure. The usage of the word *nota* sometimes leans toward one of its containers—either the prayer or the pictorial figure. The Latin word *nota* (pl. *notae*) occurs quite frequently throughout the *Ars Notoria,* especially in Version A. It was decided that it would be best to simply translate *nota* as one of its two senses, either "prayer" or "figure," as dictated by the particular context and circumstance which called for that particular sense. For all other instances in which both senses could be understood, the word *nota* is left untranslated.

Manuscripts of *Ars Notoria*'s era were presented without paragraph breaks to maximize the vellum on which they were written. Paragraph divisions have been added to render the text more readable. Headings have also been added for the reader's navigation. These headings are bracketed to indicate they are mine and not original to the Latin. The present volume uses rubrics throughout, placed according to Véronèse's critical edition. Any prayers intended to be spoken aloud during the ritual operations have been set in boldface.

Acknowledgments

I am grateful to my Latin teacher, Yola Lambert, who always encouraged me to read Latin, and also my college professors Ben Letson, Ph.D.; Ed Damer, Ph.D; and Fred Kellogg, Ph.D who provided me the educational foundation in understanding the religion and philosophy of the medieval world. This project would not have been made possible without the well-laid foundational work established by Julien Véronèse. I would also like to thank Stephen Skinner, Ph.D, for providing feedback at the early stage of this project. I appreciate Tim Lundy, Ph.D, for his Latin transcription of the *Ars Brevis* found in the Sloane 513 manuscript. I thank Rabbi Yosef M. Cohen for kindly offering to do a preliminary study and partial translation of *Melechet Muscelet M'Chochmat Shlomo*. Finally, I would like to thank the team at Inner Traditions for their hard work in making this book possible and accessible to readers around the world.

Matthias Castle
June 2023

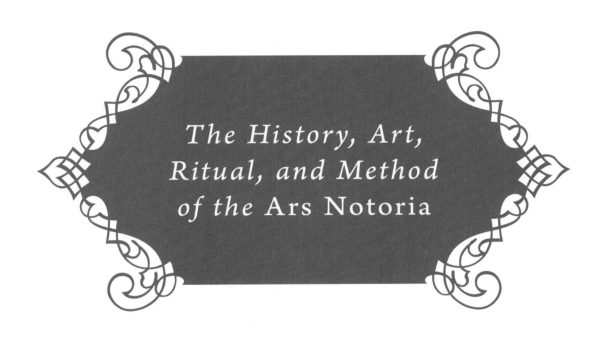

The History, Art, Ritual, and Method of the Ars Notoria

By Matthias Castle

That night God appeared to Solomon and said to him, "Ask what I should give you." Solomon said to God, ". . . Give me now wisdom and knowledge to go out and come in before this people, for who can rule this great people of yours?"

God answered Solomon, "Because this was in your heart and you have not asked for possessions, wealth, honor, or the life of those who hate you and have not even asked for long life . . . wisdom and knowledge are granted to you."

2 Chronicles 1:7–12, NRSV updated version

I.

The Mythical and Material Story of the *Ars Notoria*

King Solomon valued knowledge and wisdom over riches, honor, and vengence, knowing that if he wanted to govern his people well, he needed the necessary knowledge and wisdom to do so. Certainly, this story fascinated the minds of young boys studying in a Christian monastery or cathedral school during the Middle Ages. They might ask themselves: "What kind of knowledge will help me to achieve my goals in life?" The answer: a liberal arts education. Knowledge is the key to opening new opportunities, bestowing the capacity to lead others, and offers the means by which one can elevate one's social status.

Unfortunately for most young boys in school during the Middle Ages (for only boys were given a formal education), only the noble and wealthy were privileged to have access to at-home tutors and universities, including the oldest, the University of Bologna, founded in 1088. Moreover, books were often prohibitively expensive to produce and purchase, forcing the student to rely on his own memory of what his teachers had said. So much time was spent in lecture halls and studying all the key texts and their burdensome commentaries that acquiring an education was a challenging ordeal. Even so, gaining knowledge and the skills to debate one's peers became essential to advance in society's ranks. If one wanted to climb the societal ladder to a successful life, one had to gain an education—and that was no easy task.

What if there was a way to gain all the knowledge needed to succeed and excel in medieval society? Such an answer arrived in the form of an incredible thirteenth-century manuscript called the *Ars Notoria*. This mysterious handbook, supposedly passed through the hands of university students, describes the procedures of the notory art—a ritual involving strange prayers and figures that, if performed, would bestow on the dutiful practitioner the wisdom and understanding of King Solomon in a short amount of time. This claim was attractive to students who wanted a fast track to an education and to gain a career advantage. Yet, its contents were questionable, being a mix between Christian orthodoxy and heresy, such that it drew the attention and condemnation of the church and the famous theologian Thomas Aquinas, who branded it as "magic." Who would dare to risk his own Christian soul to gain knowledge from demons?

Yet, is Aquinas's accusation true? How much does the *Ars Notoria* resemble magical practices? Or are they perhaps late antique Hellenistic theurgic practices? Are the devotional prayers and fasts of Christian orthodoxy at the heart of the notory art, or are these practices just a Christian veneer? Who wrote it, and how did this handbook of prayers and figures survive in so many manuscript copies today, following the condemnation of the church?

The notory art contains bizarre prayers addressed to angels for the principal benefit of quickly acquiring all forms of knowledge, both earthly and divine. Supposedly governed by four angels and divinely revealed to King Solomon himself, the notory art also includes magical figures and a set of ritual instructions on how to implement both the prayers and the figures. The instructions entail that the operator lives a rigorously disciplined Christian life of devotion, chastity, fasting, and almsgiving to spiritually purify himself prior to beginning the practice of the notory art. Furthermore, he must be made worthy to receive a dream vision from an angel before even executing the operation proper. Once approved by the angel, he is to execute a complex procedure of ordered prayers to be given over the course of at least two months according to certain astronomical and astrological prescriptions. The operator is to dedicate himself to the inspection of certain figures, which will grant him the desired knowledge. The inspection of these magical figures involves the ancient art of memory so as to better retain the particular field of knowledge that is sought and studied.

Today, the *Ars Notoria* is considered to be the earliest representative of angelic magic in Europe. The book was expanded upon, taken apart, rewritten, expanded upon, and inspired the creation of several derivative texts. The book's contents appeared in the highly influential fourteenth-century magical text, the *Sworn Book of Honorius,* and in the *Opus Operum* of the German occult writer Heinrich Cornelius Agrippa, thereby entering the literary canon known as the Western esoteric tradition. While the *Ars Notoria* had only just begun to gain scholarly attention in the twentieth century from Lynn Thorndike, Jean Dupèbe, and Jean-Patrice Boudet, it was the French scholar Julien Véronèse who provided the first critical edition of the Latin text in 2007. The current book provides a complete English translation based on Véronèse's critical edition along with new original research and extensive commentary to unravel the mysteries that have shrouded the *Ars Notoria,* thus making it accessible to modern readers today.

THE MYTHICAL STORY OF THE *ARS NOTORIA*

The *Ars Notoria* offers a mythical origin story about its composition and how Solomon gained his famed wisdom and understanding; this secret account fills the gap in the biblical narrative of King Solomon, deceiving its readership into believing it has historicity. The story goes that during the night following Solomon's burnt offerings to God on Mount Gibeon before the First Temple was built (1 Kings 3:1–15; 2 Chronicles 1:1–13), the *Ars Notoria* relates how the angel Pamphilius revealed to Solomon a corpus of sacred writings that would later become known as "the most ancient Hebrew books," including such peculiar titles as *Eniclyssoe, Gemeliot,* and *Lengemath.* The *Ars Notoria* further suggests that Solomon compiled the contents of these books, then took extracts from those to write the *Liber Florum Caelestis Doctrinae* (*Book of Flowers of Heavenly Teaching*). The *Ars Notoria* explains:

> [Solomon] glorified the Lord in this [book] because he was inspired by the divine will to theology, and by the competence of the will, to suddenly receive certain kinds of prayers transmitted to him during the night of sacrifice to the Lord God [used] for the bestowing of greater things, he conveniently placed them in the corpus of the notory art, because they are holy, worthy, and revering the mysteries.[1]

1. *Ars Notoria,* section 38.

The *Liber Florum Caelestis Doctrinae* (*Book of Flowers of Heavenly Teaching*) is said to be a book of "a magnitude of qualities" containing strange prayers for acquiring knowledge supposedly composed from a subtle interweaving of the Greek, Hebrew, and Chaldean languages.[2] These strange prayers, or *voces magicae* (literally, "magical calls") or *verba ignota* (literally, "unknown words"), supposedly have their own secret grammar and syntax, appearing as incomprehensible words and syllables that sound like indecipherable speech. These prayers are said to list the names of angels who are called upon to help the invoker. It is said that the *Liber Florum Caelestis Doctrinae* was then passed down to the Greek philosopher Apollonius of Tyana, who provided many of these *voces magicae* a summary or partial translation into Latin, which he called "prologues." These prologues present petitions for memory, eloquence, and understanding, arranged according to Christian orthodox beliefs. In addition to these prologues, it is said that Apollonius made extracts from Solomon's writings, provided additional commentary, and placed these writings within his own edition, titled *Flores Aurei* (*Golden Flowers*). Eventually, the *Flores Aurei,* accruing further additions, became the *Ars Notoria.*

The later, longer version of the *Ars Notoria* presents the mythical origin story having occurred after the First Temple was built, saying:

> [W]e discover one among others, namely Solomon, whom the Most High chose beforehand, so that he was making a foundation of His own grace, wisdom, and knowledge in him; and thus, he sent to him some golden tablets by his own angel Pamphilius, in which were transcribed certain names of holy angels with prayers in Greek, Chaldean, and Hebrew. And together with those prayers were some figures depicted of a protracted and diverse manner, which the angel himself carried down in the same golden tablets above the altar of the temple that Solomon had built to God. He presented it to him, speaking about what those prayers were signifying and about what those figures were extending. And he was revealing the elements just as to a child, teaching him the method, form, and contents of the operation. But Solomon, having received the angelic command, accepted that golden book

2. For understanding what is meant by "a magnitude of qualities," see chapter IV, "The Art of Memory."

with great devotion. He proceeded, following the angelic mandate in that holy work, reading the prayers one by one at their [designated] times, according to the lunar months, never exceeding beyond the mandated form, just as the angel had ministered to him. Thus, by divine grace, having finished the work, he received all knowledge and possessed all wisdom thenceforth.[3]

Solomon receives the *Ars Notoria* from the angel Pamphilius.
BnF Latin 7153, f. unnumbered, front matter
(Version B manuscript).

---

3. *Ars Notoria,* Prologue Gloss, page 325.

There is a further mythical origin story for how Solomon received a portion of the text called the *Ars Nova* (*New Art*)—ten prayers that can be said on any day at any time and still bestow memory, eloquence, and understanding to the operator. This second divine revelation is said to have occurred after the Temple was built, saying:

> [W]hile the great king Solomon was offering an appeasing sacrament upon the golden altar in the sight of the Lord, he saw a book wrapped in a cloth, and ten prayers written in the book, and on each prayer a sign of a golden seal. And he heard in the spirit, "There are things that God has sealed and that he has closed off for a long period of time from the hearts of the unfaithful." The king did fear lest he was offending the Lord, and he guarded them.[4]

Elsewhere, we learn that the notory art is governed by four angels whose names are Hagnadam, Merabor, Hamiladei, and Pesiguaguol and who can bestow or take away the gifts of the art. The *Ars Notoria* provides two grave warnings about misusing the magical ritual known as the notory art. In the first, one of Solomon's house servants fails to heed the *Ars Notoria*'s instuctions to ritually purify himself before pronouncing the prayers. For this transgression, he is "made speechless and entirely without memory, blind and mute up to the hour of death. But [he] said in the hour of [his] death that four angels [who govern the notory art] who he had offended in so sacred a mystery by speaking presumptuously, [he] had endured daily the jailers and floggers, one of memory, the second of the tongue, the third of the eyes, the fourth of the ears. . . . For saying it in presumption is a sin, so it should be said just as it was taught."[5]

The second warning is given in a portion of the *Ars Notoria* that reads like a letter to an addressee who had questions about performing the ritual magic of the notory art. This vignette also tells the fate of King Solomon, which aligns appropriately with the biblical account, saying:

> And it is to be understood, just as you saw the *notae* of theology or philosophy and [their own] arts beneath [their own] contents themselves on

4. *Ars Notoria,* section 114a.

5. *Ars Notoria,* section 57.

> all those days, by no means should you laugh nor have fun, because one day while King Solomon was inspecting the forms of these same *notae,* perhaps drunk more than usual with wine, the Lord became angry with him and through his own angel he had spoken to him, saying, "Because you have despised my sacramental mystery, mocking and expressing contempt, I will take away from you a part of the kingdom and I will crush your sons before their own days," and the angel added, "The Lord prohibits you from entering his temple for eighty days, and God extends the observance to you, in order that you do penitence according to your sin." And with Solomon weeping and petitioning for mercy from the angel, the angel responded, "Your days are prolonged; however, innumerable iniquities and evils will come over your sons, and they will be snatched by an overcoming iniquity."[6]

These vignettes of the mythical origin story of the *Ars Notoria* offer the reader the ancient authority of King Solomon while also establishing divine approval to carry out the ritual procedures. Many readers might ask, "What mysteries could such a book contain, having been deemed so great that it was divinely revealed to God's chosen king, and yet so dangerous if misused?"

THE MATERIAL STORY OF THE *ARS NOTORIA*

Historically speaking, the *Ars Notoria* is a thirteenth-century medieval Latin handbook of prayers addressed to the Holy Trinity and angels for the purpose of quickly acquiring knowledge through the inspection of the magical figures. These prayers are used in conjunction with the magical figures to allow the operator to learn quickly the seven liberal arts[7]—grammar, logic, rhetoric, arithmetic, music, geometry, and astronomy—which make up the whole of medieval philosophy. Even the forbidden knowledge of the magical arts can be learned through the notory art. Such a book would have proved most useful to the aspiring student who sought to learn all his studies quickly, masterfully debate

6. *Ars Notoria,* section 134. The angel's response recalls 1 Kings 11:11–13 (NRSV).

7. The seven liberal arts were called "liberal" by the ancient Romans because they were considered to make a man capable of thinking independently, and these arts were reserved for learning by free men.

his peers with his newly acquired knowledge, and climb the social ladder to a life of honor and success.

The earliest surviving manuscript of the *Ars Notoria* is dated to around 1225 and is currently held at Yale University, specifically at the Beinecke Rare Book and Manuscript Library, belonging to the Mellon collection, and given the call number MS 1. This particular manuscript is identified as the *Ars Notoria, sive Flores Aurei* (*The Notory Art, or the Golden Flowers*), attributed to Apollonius of Tyana, and has eighteen parchment folios of text and images, beginning with the *Ars Notoria* text. It is written in the Gothica Textualis script using red, blue, and green inks for capital letters and brown ink for the regular text. At folio 10v, the thirty-four pictorial figures called *notae* are introduced, and the regular text column narrows down to the point that the words crowd around the figures. The binding is thought to be modern.

Julien Véronèse is credited with classifying about fifty extant *Ars Notoria* manuscripts. From a select few examplars, he established his 2007 critical edition of the original Latin text. He identified three main stages in the textual development of the *Ars Notoria,* which he classified into three categories: Version A, Version A2, and Version B.[8] It is essential to understand the key differences among Versions A, A2, and B.

Version A is the oldest and most primitive form of the *Ars Notoria.* Version A presents three main parts: (1) the *Flores Aurei* (*Golden Flowers*) of Pseudo-Apollonius of Tyana; (2) the Christian writer's letter containing a supplement answering the addressee's questions about performing the magic of the notory art, the ten prayers belonging to the *Ars Nova* (*New Art*), and the little treatise of nine prayers (called the *novem termini*); and (3) a late addendum of the Special prayers material from the *Flores Aurei* and its *Notae* Supplement (abbreviated as NS), which includes the pictorial figures called *notae.* In effect, the Christian writer's letter is sandwiched between two parts of the *Flores Aurei.* The *Flores Aurei* is fragmented and incomplete as a result of scribal redactions.

Véronèse also identifies a Version A2, which shows the transition period between Version A and Version B. It is marked by the astrological prescriptions (section 147), a penultimate chapter (*capitulum penultimum*) explaining

8. A complete list of the manuscripts can be found in appendix A1.

an operation about drinking rosewater tea and which recapitulates the entire notory art ritual procedure in a memorandum. Version A2 also shows the influence of the second-oldest derivative text, *Opus Operum*. *Opus Operum* perhaps acted as a mediatory between Version A and A2. The transition period between Version A to B begins around the middle to late thirteenth century.

In the fourteenth century, Version B arrives and may be thought of as the expanded edition of Version A. It contains all the same material as found in Version A and offers a series of lengthy glosses attempting to answer questions about the notory art, given what was already missing in Version A. During the Middle Ages, it was a common practice among scholars to provide extensive commentary to the text; in fact, university students were taught to write and comment upon important intellectual and cultural treasures. Version B is also characterized by new variant passages.

The table below explains the key differences between Version A and Version B. Because Version A2 presents such small changes which have already been mentioned, it is not represented in the following table.

DIFFERENCES BETWEEN THE VERSIONS

	Version A	Version B
Date	Thirteenth to fourteenth centuries	Fourteenth to sixteenth centuries
Text	*Flores Aurei*, the Christian writer's letter containing the supplement, the *Ars Nova* and the *novem termini*, and finally, the *Notae* Supplement	Everything in Version A plus the glosses and new variant passages that count for about 40 percent of the whole contents. Includes more prayers and figures. Quotes the *Opus Operum*.
Figures	The *Notae* Supplement contains simple figures.	The *Notae* Supplement includes ornate figures, containing mnemonic signs, accompanied by angels bearing crosses. Some figures are omitted or added.
The Duration of the Greater Ritual Procedure	Two months (reconstructed)	Four months

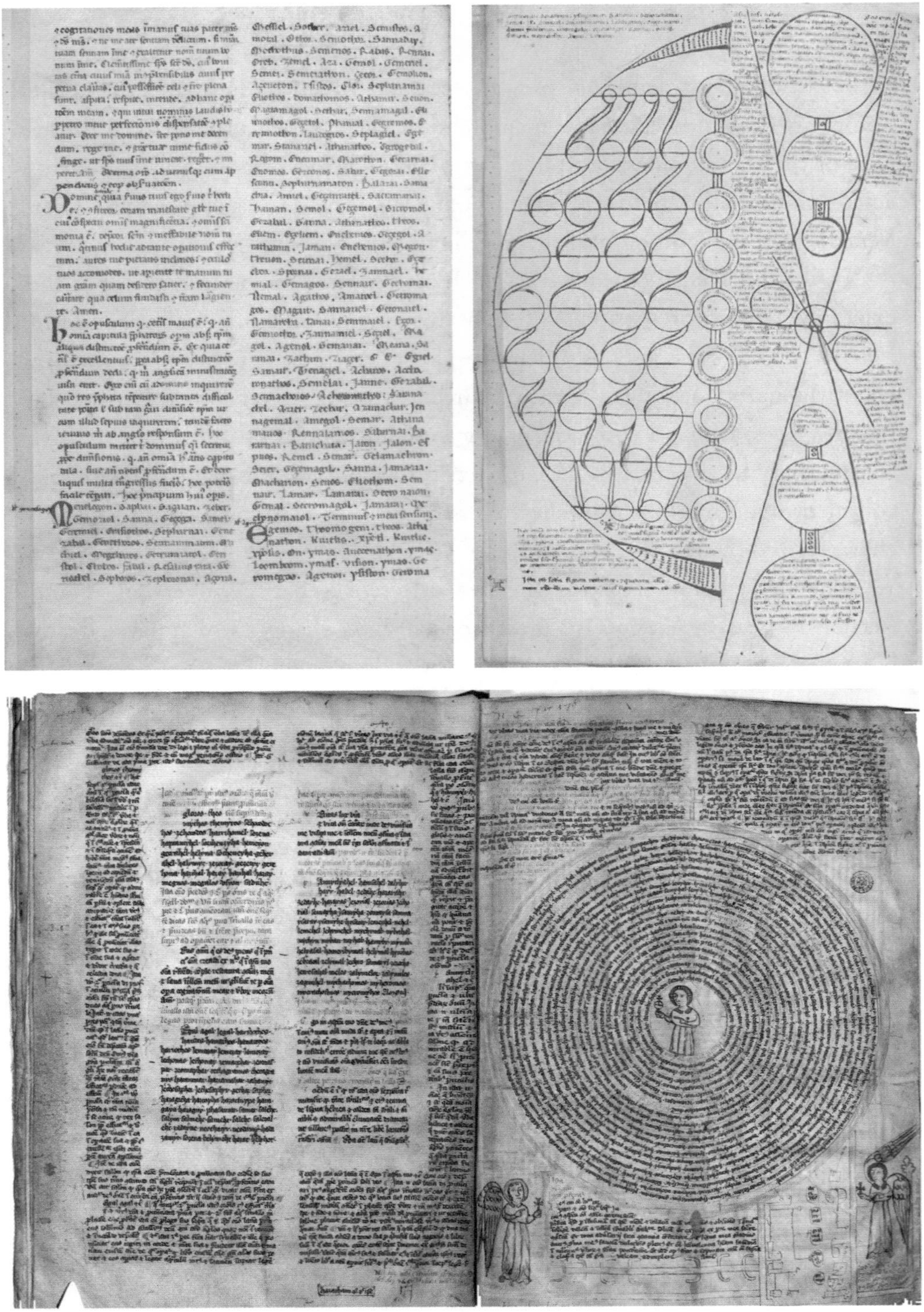

Top: Version A, folios from *Ars notoria, sive Flores aurei,* Mellon 1, Yale University, Beinecke Rare Book and Manuscript Library, c. 1225.
Bottom: Version B, folios from Bodley 951, University of Oxford, Bodelian Library.

Véronèse proposes a date and provenance of the *Ars Notoria* sometime between the second half of the twelfth century to the early thirteenth century in northern Italy; it likely circulated at the University of Bologna, which had a good reputation for educating students in law, rhetoric, and letter writing (*ars dictaminis*), fields intimately related to the ritual magic of the *Ars Notoria*. The Christian writer of the fragmented letter, if he was indeed a legislator (*lator*),[9] may have been participating in the Italian resurgence of Justinian the Great's *Corpus Juris Civilis* of Roman law and the art of shorthand writing, which previously had been dormant for a long time, going as far back as the sixth century. In chapter IV, "The Art of Memory," the connection between the legal profession, particularly the notary art, and the magical practice of the *Ars Notoria* is explored.

The *Ars Notoria* shows strong influences from the Latin West, referencing Pythagoreanism,[10] Neoplatonism,[11] classical education, and the literary medieval genre called "*speculum* literature."[12] Lying underneath this distinctly European mantle is a hidden Arabic and Byzantine Greek character found in the source material referenced in the *Ars Notoria*. The Arabs are responsible for the transmission of ancient Greek philosophy and medieval Byzantine thought to the Latin West, and this very transmission occurred through the Syriac and Greek languages. Such source material was probably made available by the Arabs through Arabic-to-Latin or Greek-to-Latin translation.

Specifically, these sources include the divinatory arts of chiromancy, geomancy, genethlialogy, onomancy, and perhaps even the positive portrayal of the neo-Pythagorean philosopher Apollonius of Tyana, the supposed author of

---

9. *Ars Notoria,* section 115. The original Latin text could also have been erroneously transcribed here, but I have not been able to verify it in either case.

10. Pythagoreanism is a pre-Socratic Greek school of philosophy and religious practices founded by Pythagoras, whose influence permeates the Western tradition.

11. Iamblichus and Pseudo-Dionysius the Areopagite.

12. Latin, *speculum,* meaning "mirror." Speculum literature sought to contain encyclopedic knowledge of a certain subject matter within a single instruction manual. For the most relevant titles of speculum literature and time period, see *Speculum Astronomiae* (*Mirror of Astronomy*), *Speculum Maius* (*Great Mirror*) by Vincent of Beauvais, *Speculum Fidei* (*Mirror of Faith*) by William of Saint-Thierry, *Speculum Stultorum* (*Mirror of Fools*) by Nigel de Longchamps, *Imago Mundi* (*Image of the World*), *Speculum Ecclesiae* (*Mirror of the Church*) by Honorius Augustodunensis, and *Speculum Religiosorum* (*Mirror of the Religious*) and *Speculum Ecclesiae* (*Mirror of the Church*) by Edmund of Abingdon.

astral magic treatises and, of course, the *Flores Aurei.*[13] It is difficult to determine whether these sources were available in their original Syriac, Greek, or Arabic languages or translated into Latin when they came into the hands of the notory art author.

If there ever was a Greek original of the *Flores Aurei,* then it is conceivable that the author might have known these sources in their original language. The Pseudo-Apollonius *Book of Wisdom* (Greek, *Biblos Sophias;* Arabic, *Miftah al-hikma*), a twelfth-century Greek astral magic treatise based on the Arabic version titled *Kitāb al-ṭalāsim al-akbar* (*The Great Book of Talismans*), might attest to a possible Greek version of the *Flores Aurei,* calling it Pseudo-Apollonius's book on scholasticism. The passage reads:

> Listen, my son, because I will show you the mystery of wisdom, that is unknown, and hides many things about propitious moments and times, hours, days and nights, along with their names and virtues, and about the true wisdom that is hidden in them. I will reveal to you, from a knowledge that God gave me, those *Apotelesmata* [talismans] with which everything that God created on earth can be enchanted. This consists of four books that I wrote—more precious than gold and gems: one on astronomy, another on astrology, the third on scholasticism (σχολαστική), and the fourth—the most precious of them all—in which there are great and fearful signs, wonders and mysteries of power; in other words, about the enchantment of all the creatures created and moved by God. If someone, approaching this book, wants to be successful in these wonders, he must abstain from any bad actions, as well as from conversation and intercourse with women.[14]

As tantalizing as this passage may be for a Greek original of the *Flores Aurei,* no such manuscript survives. Moreover, this passage does not quote the contents of the book of scholasticism to verify its contents. For now, the best hypothesis remains Véronèse's proposal.

---

13. These sources are referenced in the *Ars Notoria,* Version A, section 71. One of the medieval chiromantic treatises of the time shares a mythical telling of the Arab proponent of chiromancy as Manaeus the Sacrean. Geomancy has its origins in the Afro-Islamic tradition, being translated from Arabic into Latin. The divinatory arts of genethlialogy and onomancy are based on Arabic and Syriac sources.

14. Raggetti, "Apollonius of Tyana's Great Book of Talismans," 155–82.

Finally, the *Ars Notoria* contains Solomon's *voces magicae,* prayers which are supposedly written in Greek, Hebrew, and Chaldean,[15] and this claim might suggest a connection to the Greek magical tradition via the sequence of unintelligible vocables known as *Ephesia grammata* (the "Ephesian words," named after their earliest found inscriptions upon the pedestal of the statue of Artemis in Ephesus). The presence of these diverse cultural influences on the *Ars Notoria* is quite remarkable.

The *Ars Notoria* is written in Medieval Latin with a few words from Greek or Latinized Greek. The *voces magicae* or angelic names bear a misleading and false appearance to Hebrew, Greek, Syriac, and Arabic.

The Latin prayers called "prologues" appear to Christianize the questionably Byzantine Greek and Hermetic origins of the *Flores Aurei*. Obviously, there is influence from Christian orthodoxy and monasticism, including religious practices such as fasting, almsgiving, confession, and prayer. Yet, there is an attitude of tolerance for fringe beliefs and practices, making the *Ars Notoria* markedly unorthodox in its magio-religious approach. Some readers might see some commonalities in Hekhalot literature, which formed in Byzantine Palestine and Sassanian or early Islamic Babylonia (c. 500–900 CE), as an influence on the *Ars Notoria,* but there is not enough convincing evidence for this to be considered seriously.

ORIGIN OF THE TITLE

The titles of both Solomon's *Liber Florum Caelestis Doctrinae* (*Book of Flowers of Heavenly Teaching*) and Apollonius's *Flores Aurei* (*Golden Flowers*) share the key Latin word *flos* (plural *flores*), meaning "flower," and likely refers to the term *florilegia,* or "gathering of flowers," a poetic term for a collection of extracts taken from a treatise. Pseudo-Apollonius explicitly states that his *Flores Aurei* was composed from select extracts and quotations from Solomon's writings to which he added commentary; likewise, Pseudo-Solomon's *Liber Florum* is supposedly composed from select extracts from "the most ancient Hebrew

---

15. "Chaldean" means the Syriac language, also called Syriac Aramaic. The Chaldeans established the Neo-Babylonian Empire in 626 BCE. When the empire fell to the Persians in 539 BCE, the word "Chaldean" was passed on to the astrologers and astronomers of the Persian Achaemenid Empire. These were the Magi, the priests of Zoroastrianism, which gave us the word for "magician."

books," which, according to the mythical origin story, were revealed to Solomon by the angel Pamphilius. However, the composition of Solomon's *Liber Florum* is merely hypothetical, as there are no extant manuscripts with this title nor any identified as such. There are other works in religion, science, and philosophy that follow the "flowers" literary genre, including the contemporaneous Hermes's *Flores,* or *Centiloquium* (c. 1262), which is about astrology.

For Apollonius's *Flores Aurei,* the "golden" part of the title might just be about valuing the select extracts from Solomon's writings as "gold." Alternatively, it may also be an alchemical reference in which the soul is transformed into gold through ritual and prayer. The rationale for such an alchemical reference might be derived from the eighth-century Arabic treatise attributed to Apollonius titled *Kitab Balaniyus al-Hakim fi'l-'llal, Kitab Sirr al-khaliqa wa-san 'at al-tabi'a* (*The Book of Balinas the Wise: On the Causes, or, the Book of the Secret of Creation*) in which Apollonius is said to have discovered a statue of Hermes Trismegistus, the mythical author of Hermetic and alchemical texts, seated upon a golden throne. By this discovery, Apollonius is claimed as heir to the alchemy in which an alchemist strives to transform gross matter into gold. This same text might have been known to the compiler of the *Ars Notoria,* who would claim Apollonius as its second-greatest authority.

The *Ars Notoria* says of its name, "it is to be called a notory [art] . . . because it teaches [through] incomprehensible [language] the knowledge of all things out of writings with some [of the] shortest *notulis*."[16] The *Ars Notoria* has nothing to do with *notoriety* or *notorious.* The English noun and adjective come from the Latin adjectival form, *notorius,* and the perfect passive participle *notus,* both originating from the verb *nosco, noscere, novi, notum,* "to know." The word *notory* is an adjective coming from the word "note" (originating from the Latin noun *nota, notae;* also, consider the verb *noto, notare, notavi, notatum,* "to note" or "to mark"). The phrase *notory art* might also bring itself into confusion with the civil or legal work of the notary, although this seems deliberate. In fact, the title "notory art" likely references the genre of the *ars notaria,* instruction manuals for executing notarial formulas and instruments. The spelling for the notarial trade varied between "notory art," and "notary art," adding to the con-

16. *Ars Notoria,* section 20b.

fusion. In fact, the twelfth-century author of the *Ars Notoria Notarie* (*Notory Art of Shorthand*) conflates the two, using both *ars notoria* and *ars notaria*.[17] Modern spellings now denote the notory art (from the *Ars Notoria*) as "notory," and the notarial trade as "notary." In the present book, the lowercase use of *ars notoria* (notory art) refers to the ritual magic practice and not to the book itself. In chapter IV, the historical association between the two arts, the *Ars Notoria* and the notary art, is explored.

The *Ars Notoria* further elaborates on its title:

> For let us see firstly and principally about the title of this book. Therefore, it is to be understood, that this book is rightly called "the notory art," because it is comprehended beneath certain brief *notae*—namely, the prayers—and similarly, it is called "notory," because it [is contained] through the very art (that is, through the virtue of prayers' headwords, *notae,* and figures, which are contained in the very art), the *notitia* is given to the faithful and the good worker in it how he is able to acquire memory retaining in all things heard, eloquence in all things retained eloquently to one making the offering and conserving perpetually for memory, and the integrated and perfected knowledge and all the wisdom of all the liberal, mechanical, and exceptive arts. Also, this book is able to be rightly called "the art of memory" in the right manner, because through [the book] itself, just as it is said above, memory is to be acquired in all sciences heard, having been retained through memory, and this is the true title of the book.[18]

HISTORICAL AND FABLED ATTESTATIONS

The oldest surviving manuscript is dated to 1225, but the first attestation of the *Ars Notoria* comes roughly fifty years earlier, in the popular twelfth-century *Historia Scholastica,* a biblical abridgment and gloss of the Bible, written around 1173 by the French author Petrus Comestor (d. 1178). Petrus writes that Moses did a forty-day fast in the wilderness and thus acquired the *Ars Notoria*. This is also voiced later by Nicholas Oresme (c. 1320–1382), a French Scholastic philosopher, writing in his *Le livre de divinacions,*

17. See Haines, *The Notory Art of Shorthand* (*Ars notoria notarie*), 35.
18. *Ars Notoria,* section 126b gloss.

which was translated into Latin as *De Divinationibus* (*On Divinations*).[19] In 1310, Pietro d'Abano (also known as Peter of Abano, c. 1257–1316), an Italian astrologer and professor of medicine in Padua, says in his *Lucidiator astrologiae* (*Elucidator of Astrology*) that the "fortunate book" (*fortunati liber*) called the *Ars Notoria* was condemned by the Franciscan friar Alexander of Hales (c. 1185–1245).[20]

During the Middle Ages, the Roman poet Vergil of Naples (70–19 BCE), author of the Latin epic poem the *Aeneid,* was reputed to be a magician who used the *Ars Notoria.*[21] Historically speaking, this is an anachronistic claim, since an ancient Roman could not have possessed a medieval treatise on angelic magic. Nevertheless, the medieval imagination produced fantastical tales of "Vergil the magician" that later became known as the Vergilian tradition. Although the Vergilian tradition is extensive and complex, its discussion will be limited here. An exploration of the Vergilian tradition in Germany, England, and Italy will reveal, in part, the extent of the influence of magic and the *Ars Notoria* in medieval Europe.

The Vergilian tradition begins with *The Chronicle of Ralph Niger*[22] that says, "At this time,[23] the secrets of Aristotle of Athens are discovered, in which Virgil found the notary art (*artem notariam*) that he burned afterward according to Valerius Maximus."[24] In all likelihood, Niger meant that this notary art of Aristotle (*Ars Notaria Aristotelis*) belonged to the shorthand writing tradition of the secetary, not the magical art tradition. However, the storytellers of the "Vergil the magician" legend who were reading Niger must

---

19. Thorndike, *A History of Magical and Experimental Science,* vol. 3, p. 419.

20. Paris, BnF Latin 2598, f. 101r.

21. The Roman poet's name is spelled either as Vergil or Virgil.

22. Ralph Niger (c. 1140–1217), an Anglo-French theologian and English chronicler, was a student of John of Salisbury. He was part of Thomas Becket's entourage during Becket's exile in France in the early 1160s. Gervais visited Ralph Niger between 1177 and 1183 at the court of Henry the Younger; Gervais mentions the Ralph Niger quotation above in his *Universal Chronicle* (c. 1190).

23. That is, during the lifetime of Ovid, the Roman poet who lived during the reign of Augustus (43 BCE–18 CE).

24. My translation from the Latin found in *Radulfi Nigri Chronica: The Chronicles of Ralph Niger,* edited by R. Anstruther (London: n.p., 1851), 108. Valerius Maximus was a first-century Latin author of the *Factorum ac dictorum memorabilium libri IX* (*Nine Books of Memorable Deeds and Sayings*), which was one of the most popular schoolbooks during the Middle Ages.

have misinterpreted him, thinking of the magical art instead. This misunderstanding would conclude that the medieval *Ars Notoria* was, in fact, so ancient that Vergil had practiced its craft. This medieval misunderstanding might have been thought to be supported by Macrobius's (fl. c. 400 CE) ancient literary work, *Saturnalia,* which said that Vergil's poetry "contained all human knowledge." Similarly, this misunderstanding might have been propagated by John of Alta Silva, a late twelfth-century monk in Lorraine, who wrote in his *Dolopathos,* also called the *Historia Septem Sapientium* (*History of the Seven Wise Masters*) that

> because Virgil loved the liberal arts so much, he had turned the amazing and indescribable sophistication of his genius to the composition of a small handbook, which enabled one to learn those vast subjects in a short time. In three years anyone could learn perfectly what he himself had been able to learn only with great labor.[25]

In Middle High German literature, the Vergilian tradition is found in Wolfram von Eschenbach's medieval romance known as *Parzival.* In that story, Klingsor, a knight and Count of Terra di Lavoro (a plain near Naples), is said to be a magician and nephew of Vergil, thereby making the association between magic and Vergil. The oldest version of Vergil in possession of a magic book is preserved in the German poems of the *Sangerkrieg* (also called the *Wartburgkrieg*), which describes a legendary minstrel contest at the Wartburg castle in Thuringia in the year 1207. The description of the magic book in the *Sangerkrieg* is that the book contained "*grossen noten* (large notes)," a possible reference to the *notae,* or magical figures, found in the *Ars Notoria.*[26] There are two thirteenth-century expanded versions of Vergil's journey to a magnetic mountain to acquire the magic book, and they are, first, *Zabulon's Buch,* which the *Sangerkrieg* poems describe, and second, *Reinfried von Braunschweig.* There is also another version that derives from *Reinfried von Braunschweig,* which is falsely ascribed to Heinrich von Mügeln (d. c. 1372), a German royal poet.[27]

25. Ziolkowski and Putnam, eds., *The Virgilian Tradition,* 840.

26. Comparetti, *Vergil in the Middle Ages,* 317.

27. Ziolkowski and Putnam, eds., *The Virgilian Tradition,* 988–90.

Vergil's journey to the magnetic mountain describes a certain magician named Zabulon (or Savilon) who kept his gold, silver, and magic books in a treasure house on top of a magnetic mountain. Vergil sails to the magnetic mountain with Venetian nobles in search of these riches, and there he finds a devil imprisoned in a glass container.[28] After Vergil grants the devil's freedom, the devil reveals to him the secret cave where the magic book of Zabulon can be found. The devil explains how to secure the magic book from an iron figure which has been rigged with a booby trap, saying:

> *"I'll reveal to you how you'll patronize all arts.*
> *Nearby me lies a book*
> *About which, Virgil, I want to tell you. So, hear:*
> *With it you will be superior to all clerics.*
> *It stays by me*
> *And you will take*
> *What Zabulon wrote with his own hands."*

The devil goes on to say:

> *"An iron figure stands nearby*
> *Which has hidden the text for a full thousand years.*
> *That it was made by magic means*
> *No one can doubt*

28. There are two other versions about Vergil and glass containers. One comes from the tenth-century John of Salerno, who wrote *Vita Sancti Odonis,* in which Odo dreamed of a pot of snakes (read: spirits) that he believed belonged to Vergil. The other story comes from the thirteenth-century historian Jan Enikel of Vienna and recorded in his *Weltchronik* (*World Chronicle*). Jan Enikel recounts that while Vergil was chopping in his vineyard, he discovered a glass bottle. He conversed with the devils imprisoned within the glass bottle. The devils begged him to release them from the bottle, and in exchange they will teach him the art of magic. Vergil agreed, gaining the full knowledge of magic. What these stories allude to might be a thirteenth-century proto-source of the *Ars Goetia,* which is a magical handbook about summoning demons, now preserved only in seventeenth-century English manuscripts. The *Ars Goetia* also parallels these stories in that King Solomon had imprisoned demons within a brass vessel and then cast it out to sea; this mythical account hints at Arabic origins. Alternatively, these stories might allude to other magical texts within the Pseudo-Solomonic tradition circulating during the medieval period. Jan Enikel's full account is published in Ziolkowski and Putnam, eds., *The Virgilian Tradition,* 926–32.

A [magical] letter lies in its head,
From which it gets its force
It grasps strongly a stick in its hands:
I give you the power to control all this."
[Vergil] broke the figure without any effort.
Cunningly the book was in Virgil's hands
And he took it with him over the sea.[29]

Zabulon's Buch[30] shows strong parallels to the *Arabian Nights* story of the third dervish named Ibn Khadib. In the *Arabian Nights* story, Ibn Khadib is shipwrecked on the Magnetic Mountain, falls asleep, and has a dream instructing him to dig a hole, where he will discover a bow of brass and three magically inscribed lead arrows. The dream tells him to shoot the statue of a brass horseman, which would then fall into the sea. As a result, the waters would rise and a brass man with a lead tablet on his chest would arrive in a boat to ferry him to the Sea of Safety. When Ibn Khadib wakes up, he does as the voice in his dream instructed and everything happens as it was told, except he becomes injured, losing an eye.[31] In comparing *Zabulon's Buch* to the *Arabian Nights* story, the spirit would be parallel to the instructing voice from the dream, the magically inscribed letter in the head might be representative of the bow and magically inscribed arrows, and the iron figure a substitute for the brass horseman.

The *Reinfried von Braunschweig,* written after 1291, describes a young Athenian prince and astrologer named Savilon, born of a Jewish mother and a pagan father, who was the first man to understand astronomy, astrology, and necromancy. By observing the stars, he predicts the birth of Jesus Christ.[32]

---

29. Zironi, "Disclosing Secrets, 119–20. See also Tunison, *Master Virgil,* 24–32.

30. Ancient Greek ζάβολος (*zabolos*), a descendant of διάβολος (*diabolos*), meaning "the devil." The Latin is spelled *Zabolus* or *Zabulus*. Thus, the story's title is *The Devil's Book*. Alternatively, Zabulon is a misreading or mistransliteration of the name Savilon.

31. The Munich manual of magic describes a ceremony for conjuring a flying horse and includes a cautionary tale about maintaining spiritual purity and also suffering the loss of an eye. The same ceremony is also found in the *De nigromancia* or *Thesaurus spirituum* ascribed to Roger Bacon. Kieckhefer, *Forbidden Rites*, chapter 3.

32. Tuczay, "The Book of Zabulon," 400.

Savilon's mother expresses distress at the idea of the Jewish people being lost and convinces Savilon to use magic as a countermeasure to prevent the birth of Jesus Christ.[33] Savilon, knowing that it is impossible to subvert the course of the stars, takes a series of security measures to delay the birth of Jesus Christ for as long as possible. The first of these security measures against the astrological prediction involves Savilon writing down certain magical words and characters on parchment, rolling it up, and hiding it in a cave on a magnetic mountain; he even hides one of the magical letters in his own ear. Second, he hides three of his magic books within the cave wall, then binds his soul to a spirit imprisoned within a bottle; the bottle rests just outside the cave. Savilon makes his final resting place in a chair. At the foot of his chair lies a fourth book which is physically chained to the cave wall. The magic book acts as the physical link between Savilon and the spirit imprisoned inside the bottle. Savilon sits down, entering a death-like state of suspended animation, holding a hammer in his hand which triggers as part of a booby trap for any thief who would try to steal the magic book.[34]

After twelve thousand years pass, and the birth of Christ draws near, Vergil arrives on the magnetic mountain, finds the spirit imprisoned in the bottle, and safely recovers the magic book. Neither *Zabulon's Buch* nor the *Reinfried von Braunschweig* clearly identifies Vergil's magic book as the *Ars Notoria;* however, the English tradition does.

The English clerk Gervase of Tilbury (c. 1154–c. 1222) wrote *Otia Imperialia* (*Recreation for an Emperor,* 1209–1214), an example of speculum literature, which came to be known as the *Liber de Mirabilibus Mundi* (*Book on the Marvels of the World*). In it, Gervase tells the tale of an English scholar who unearthed Vergil's bones and discovered the *Ars Notoria:*

> In the reign of Roger [II, (1095–1154)] of Sicily, a certain scholar, an Englishman by birth, came before the king to ask a favor of his generosity. And when the king, noble by birth and by nature, gained knowledge that some favor was being asked of him, he answered: "Seek what favor you

33. Tuczay, "The Book of Zabulon," 402.
34. Tuczay, "The Book of Zabulon," 408.

wish, and I will grant it to you." Now, the petitioner was a famous writer, extremely well versed in the trivium and quadrivium, a devoted student of medicine, and most adept at astronomy. He says, therefore, to the king that he would not ask for ephemeral pleasures, but rather for something that in the eyes of men would be considered valueless, namely, the bones of Vergil, wherever they could be found within his kingdom's bounds. The king agreed, and the scholar, armed with letters from the king, made his way to Naples, where Vergil on many occasions put to work the power of his intelligence. When he presented the letters, the people were willing to obey, for, since they were ignorant of the location of the grave, they gladly agreed to what they believed must be considered impossible. Eventually, however, by applying the resources of his art the scholar discovered the bones beneath a mound in the center of a certain mountain where no sign of a breach was recognizable. The area was dug up, and with a great deal of effort the mound excavated in which was found the body of Vergil whole and entire, and at his head a book in which was written an *ars notoria* with other writings related to its study. The bones and the ashes were removed and the book taken away by the scholar. . . . When the scholar was asked what he had intended to do with the bones, he answered that he would put them to use for spells because at his questioning the bones would have revealed the whole art of Vergil himself, and he also put forward that this could be brought to a successful conclusion by him, if he were given the use of the bones for forty days. Therefore, taking only the book away with him, the scholar departed, and, by the kindness of the venerable John of Naples, cardinal [1158–1183] under Pope Alexander [III, 1159–1181], we have seen some extracts from the very book and have made experiments satisfactorily establishing their infallibility.[35]

Obviously, Gervase is reflecting on the prevalent Vergilian tradition, and this story demonstrates that the *Ars Notoria* was already gaining a reputation as a handbook of magic in the early thirteenth century in Naples. In

35. Ziolkowski and Putnam, *The Virgilian Tradition,* 409–11. Gervase is also cited by the notary and teacher of the arts, Domenico Di Bandino (1335–1418), who wrote an encyclopedic work titled *Fons Memorabilium Universi* (Wellspring of Things Memorable in the Universe); see also Ziolkowski and Putnam, *The Virgilian Tradition,* 303–21.

fact, it may be that Gervase's use of *ars notoria* was not referring to the book itself but to the entire notory art tradition. Gervase studied and taught canon law in Bologna where he encountered both arts, the notory art of magic and the art of shorthand writing. He may also have conflated in his mind the magic of the notory art with the legendary nigromantic magic of the Vergilian tradition.[36]

The fourteenth-century *Cronaca di Partenope* (Chronicle of Naples) relies upon Gervase but explains that Vergil acquired his learning from a book taken from the burial site beneath the head of the philosopher Chiron by which "he became most learned and trained in necromancy and in the other sciences."[37] In addition to the notory art's promise to teach necromancy, it is no surprise that the notory art becomes associated more generally with this magical practice. This concludes the study of the Vergilian tradition.[38] Other attestations of the *Ars Notoria* will now follow.

Gervase's tale is referenced by the author of the *Ars Notoria Notarie* (*Notory Art of Shorthand*), a late thirteenth-century epistle addressed to King Henry III (reigned 1216–1272), which presents an exposition on a unique cipher based on Tironian notes. The treatise references the *Ars Notoria,* saying:

---

36. Ziolkowski and Putnam, *The Virgilian Tradition,* 851. For more information about medieval legends regarding Vergil, see Ziolkowski, "Virgil the Magician," 59–75. See also Spargo, *Virgil the Necromancer.* See also Comparetti's *Vergil in the Middle Ages.* Furthermore, Gervase was a contemporary with Wolfram von Eschenbach, but there is no evidence of any direct contact between the two men. During a stay in Naples, Gervase was informed by his former teacher in Bologna, Giovanni Pignatelli, at that time archdeacon of Naples, about "what great wonders Virgil performed in this city." Zironi, "Disclosing Secrets," 115.

37. Ziolkowski and Putnam, *The Virgilian Tradition,* 952. "The philosopher Chiron" might actually refer to the fabled Greek centaur Chiron. Chiron was considered the wisest and most righteous of all the centaurs, having shared his knowledge among many famous characters of Greek mythology (Homer, *Iliad* xi.831). Linking Vergil to the Greek centaur might indicate that the magical tradition is Greek and necromantic. It seems plausible that the German Vergilian tradition received knowledge of the Greek and necromantic arts via Arabic transmission, including the *Arabian Nights.* Such knowledge would have included the portrayal of King Solomon as a conjurer of spirits.

38. As for Vergil, there are stories of magic that abound about him in Naples, making him something of a local hero, and these stories may show Byzantine influence, especially with the inclusion of automatons, a key point that is discussed in the fifth figure of theology. See chapter V.

> The false and unnecessary disputations which have been uttered concerning this art—such as that Virgil invented it, or that Blessed Gregory was so consumed with it that, having become proficient in this art in seven days, he made his skill most evident by revealing the seven liberal arts, and many others which no serious listener accepts—I have demolished, vehemently and boldly, not only through reason but also through authentic documentation, so that I have left absolutely nothing behind through which any further criticism may arise.[39]

The author accepts that both the notarial trade and the *Ars Notoria* are called a "notory art" but clearly differentiates the two arts, saying he opposes the *Ars Notoria* and had made arguments against it in the other two books he wrote but are now lost to us. If the modern scholar John Haines's hypothesis is correct that Edmund of Abingdon (c. 1174–1240), the archbishop of Canterbury, is the author of this work on shorthand writing, then the "Blessed Gregory" might be Pope Gregory IX (papacy 1227–1241) who appointed him as archbishop. The author of the *Ars Notoria Notarie* says that he is a lapsed monk who became devoted to the "notory art," and he experienced a dream vision of Saint Thomas Becket (1119–1170), a former archbishop of Canterbury, which led to his healing and recovery from a personal sickness.[40]

A contemporary to the author of the *Ars Notoria Notarie,* Michael Scot (1175–c. 1232), the mathematician and court astrologer to Emperor Frederick II, mentions the *Ars Notoria* in 1236. Michael Scot likely encountered the manuscript while in Toledo, writing in his *Liber Introductorius:*

> But when astronomy is one science and more noble than the rest of the seven liberal arts, having established their indispensable veracity as seven in number, [astronomy] is useful and delectable for all enthusiastic men to be wise by that which is the art of utility, necessity, and delectable in many, and they are to be employed for many as the healer for the weak, the kings and barons for mercantile agendas on account of their roads and

39. Haines, *The Notory Art of Shorthand,* 109.
40. Haines, *The Notory Art of Shorthand,* 36–38.

> mercantile trades, sailors on account of the diversity of air and sea, alchemists, necromancers, and *the workers of the notory art,* and on account of other constellations.[41]

The *Ars Notoria* is also attested in the Latin treatise titled the *Virgilii Cordubensis Philosophia* (*Philosophy of Virgil of Corduba*), translated from the Arabic in the late thirteenth century by a cleric in Toledo and now preserved in a 1753 manuscript. It tells the story of Virgil of Corduba, who became well versed in many subjects, including the most obtuse, such that scholars of Toledo went to Corduba to visit him. When they came, Virgil explains that he had come to learn so much through speaking with the spirits of the notory art, "which some call necromancy, but we '*refulgentia* (shining lights).'"[42] The text lists the number of teachers of Corduba[43] who gave instruction in a variety of subjects, including the notory art:

> And three teachers used to read about nigromancy, and about pyromancy, and about geomancy. And one teacher used to read about the notory art, which is a sacred science, and accordingly, he ought to be holy, which he will want to read them; similarly, and they ought to be sacred, immaculate, and without sin, listening [to the teacher]. Otherwise, nothing of this sacred science itself ought to be sent out [of himself], unless he was without sin, because it is the angelic art, and the good and sacred angels composed and made them, and afterward the good and holy angels gave to the holy King Solomon and the angels themselves made Solomon a teacher in that holy science, and they imbued him in it, and it is this art, and holy science, because all these other [sciences] are to be known [through it], and through that [art] all the other sciences are to be known without some difficulty, without some defect, and without some diminution.[44]

41. Scot, *Liber Introductorius.* The translation and italics are mine.

42. Comparetti, *Vergil in the Middle Ages,* 319.

43. Corduba is a town in the southern province of Hispania Baetica, now Cordoba, Spain.

44. My translation from Biblioteca Nacional de Espana MS 6463, fol. 106v–108v.

BRANCHING OF THE TRADITION

The heyday of the *Ars Notoria* was in the fourteenth and fifteenth centuries, when Version B was well established. Version B had synthesized the *Flores Aurei* and its first derivative text, the *Ars Nova*.[45] During this time, other derivative texts were produced, and the notory art prayers were excerpted into other books. The derivative texts include the *Opus Operum* (*Work of Works*), the *Liber Florum Doctrinae Caelestis* (*Book of Flowers of Heavenly Teaching*) composed by the French Benedictine monk John of Morigny, the *Ars Brevis* (*Short Art*), the *Ars Notoria Abbreviata* (the abridged version by Thomas of Toledo), and *Ars Paulina* (*Pauline Art [of Seven Figures]*).[46] The early derivative texts certainly influenced the later ones; in fact, the *Ars Brevis* inspired its very own tributary text titled *De Arte Crucifixi*.

Four of the five derivative works of the *Ars Notoria* are translated from Latin to English for the first time here in this book under "Branches of the *Ars Notoria* Tradition." The mid-thirteenth century treatise titled *Opus Operum* is presented in chapter 6. The fourteenth century *Ars Brevis,* which draws from John of Morigny's *Liber Florum* and the *Ars Notoria,* is given in chapter 7. The fifteenth-century abridged version of the notory art attributed to Thomas of Toledo is given in chapter 8. Finally, the fifteenth-century *Ars Paulina [of Seven Figures],* whose figures are dedicated to the divine hypostases, is presented in chapter 9.

The *Liber Florum Caelestis Doctrinae* (*Book of Flowers of Heavenly Teaching*), a fourteenth-century Latin book of prayers written by the French Benedictine monk John of Morigny, has not been translated into English yet,

---

45. Harley 181, a sixteenth-century manuscript held at the British Library in London, contains a derivative text of the *Ars Nova* called the *Ars Memorativa* (f. 1–17). The *Ars Memorativa* begins with an English prologue which claims that this magical art can grant the operator the acquisiton of medical knowledge, saying, "If thou wilt be [powerful] in phisik and surgery, thou must begyn this arte, etc." The treatise then describes its ritual prescriptions, which are mostly derived from the *Ars Nova,* and immediately thereafter the work comes to an end.

46. There are two works titled the *Ars Paulina*. (See page 755). For the sake of clarity, I am making the distinction between the two works by extending the title of the fifteenth-century work of interest here. Another treatise titled *Peri Anacriseon* (or *Anacrisis*) attributed to the Majorcan hermit Pelagius may also have been influenced by the *Ars Notoria*. Forshaw, "The Occult Middle Ages," 43.

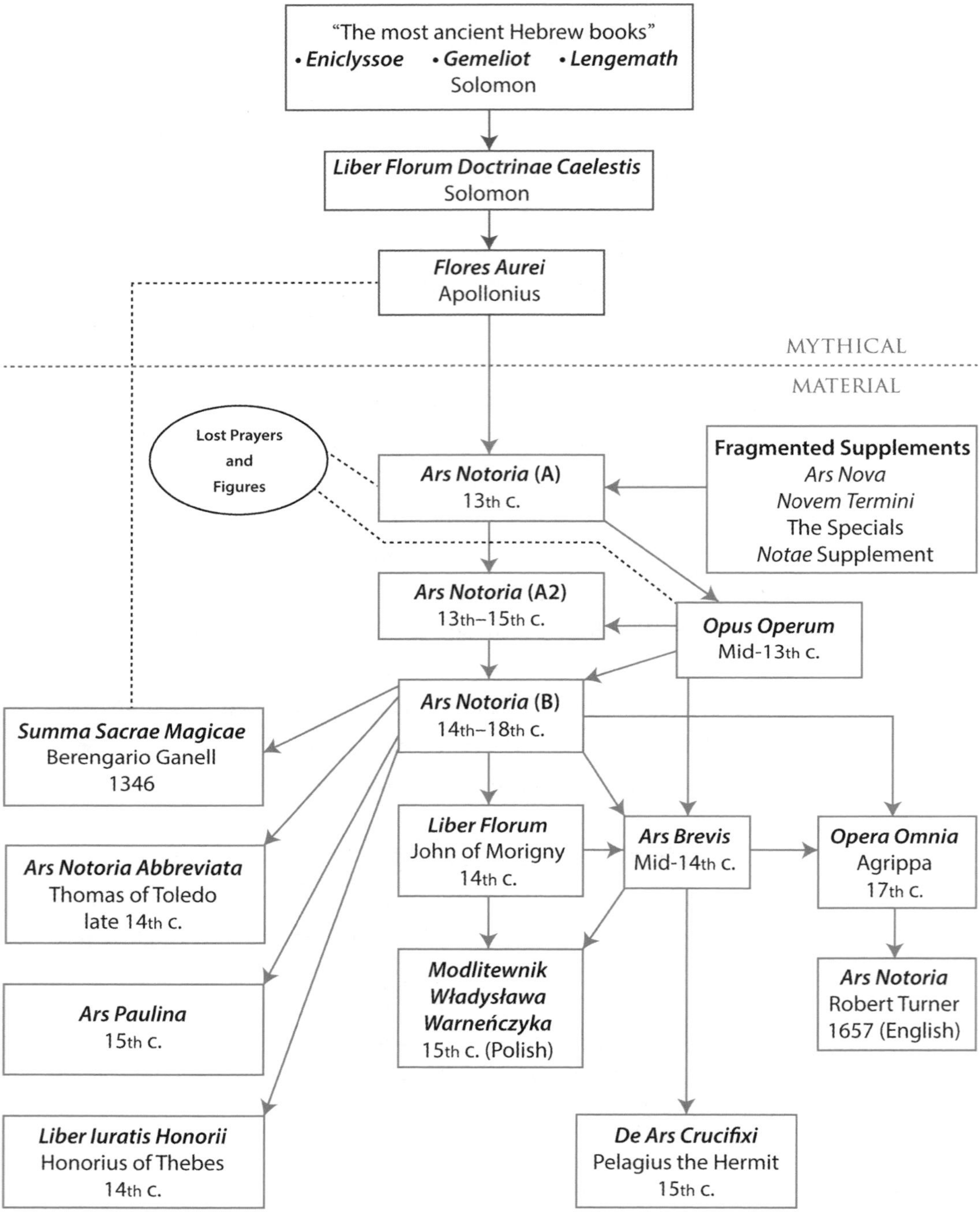

The Entire Notory Art Tradition. Texts framed in blue are part of the mythical tradition. Texts framed in red are historical, either extant on their own or by means of their insertion.

nor is an exhaustive study of its contents presented in this book.[47] Briefly stated, John of Morigny was fascinated by the *Ars Notoria,* and engaged in the magical arts. However, after his encounter with demons through its practice, he sought refuge in the Virgin Mary and ultimately rejected his former magical practice. Inspired by the Virgin Mary and a series of visions which he recorded in his book, he made adaptations to the *Ars Notoria,* creating his own version for the purpose of gaining knowledge of the liberal arts and improving one's memory and eloquence; John's work also features a book of figures.

The *Ars Notoria* exerted its influence on the world of magic, beginning with the fourteenth century magical treatises *Liber Iuratus Honorii* and the *Summa Sacrae Magicae.*[48] *Modlitewnik Władysława Warneńczyka,* the fifteenth-century prayer book belonging to the Polish king Wladislas Warnenczk contained notory art prayers repurposed for a ritual of crystallomancy. John Dee, the famous occultist of angelic magic, records his first scrying session with Edward Kelley in which he communicates with three angels, Anchor, Anachor, and Anilos, whose names are found in a notory art prayer.[49] The notory art prayer *Ancor, Anacor, Anilos* is ubiquitous among sixteenth- and seventeenth-century magical treatises, including the *Book of Oberon,* the *Heptameron,* and the *Ars Goetia* of the *Lemegeton.* Some of the magical figures would later be found in the seventeenth-century Hebrew text *Sepher Maphteah Shelomoh* (*Book of the Key of Solomon*).[50] Undoubtedly, the seventeenth-century composite Latin text found in Henry Cornelius Agrippa's *Opera Omnia* would have the most influence on the modern occult world following its own English translation in 1657 by Robert Turner of Holshott. Agrippa's own works on the Western esoteric tradition have had immeasurable influence, while Turner's translation made the

---

47. *Liber Florum* is too large of a tome to be included in this work, and the Latin text has been thoroughly researched and published by Claire Fanger and Nicolas Watson in a volume titled *Liber Florum Celestis Doctrine* (2015). A good companion volume for further study of John of Morigny is Claire Fanger's *Rewriting Magic* (2015).

48. Agreements between the *Ars Notoria* (Version B) and *Liber Iuratus Honorii* are detailed in appendix 3 of Skinner and Clark's *Ars Notoria.* Véronèse conclusively rules out an early date of 1228–1249 for the *Liber Iuratus,* for he has shown that the prayers in the London manuscript of the *Liber Iuratus* depend on Version B of the *Ars Notoria* (Véronèse, *Invoking Angels,* 116, n12). The *Summa Sacrae Magicae* also shows dependency on the *Ars Notoria* (Version B) according to my own study. Studies of the *Summa Sacrae Magicae* are currently in progress.

49. Peterson, *John Dee,* 26.

50. British Library, MS Oriental 14759, dating to 1700 or before.

notory art more widely accessible, still wielding influence into the twenty-first century. The Turner English translation has been reprinted in Joseph Peterson's 2001 *Lemegeton* and transcribed with additions from the British occultist and book collector Frederick Hockley (1809–1885), published by Teitan Press in 2015. Most recently, the Turner English translation by Skinner and Clark in 2019 was accompanied by the magical figures called *notae.*

The *Ars Notoria* was often found in the libraries of historic illuminaries and may have influenced their thoughts and magical practice. Among those known to be in possession of it are John Dee (1527–1608), the famed English magician of Enochian magic and court astrologer to Queen Elizabeth I; the Elizabethan astrologer Simon Forman (1552–1611); the English Paracelsian physician Robert Fludd (1574–1637); the Elizabethan playwright Ben Jonson (1572–1637); the astrologer William Lilly (1602–1681); the English antiquarian and astrologer Elias Ashmole (1617–1692); and the magician Dr. Thomas Rudd (1583–1656).

THE RECEPTION OF THE *ARS NOTORIA*

Despite its popularity among students, devout monks, and seekers of new religious experiences, the *Ars Notoria* was harshly rejected by many Christian writers and authorities. Such authorities condemned it as a book of magic.[51] The book was first condemned by William of Auvergne (c. 1180–1249), a bishop in Paris, in his *De Legibus* (*On Laws*).[52]

The famed Italian theologian Thomas Aquinas (1225–1274) condemned the practice of magic generally, but specifically mentions the *Ars Notoria.* Following the Christian theologian Augustine of Hippo, Thomas Aquinas perceived the practice of magic to gain knowledge and truth "by means of certain signs agreed upon by compact with the demons" as illicit. He quotes Deuteronomy 18:10–11: "Neither let there be found among you . . . anyone . . . that seeks the truth from the dead," which he says relies on the help of demons. Here, Aquinas makes a connection to the concept of necromancy, divination by consulting the dead by means of demonic assistance. It is implied that Aquinas

51. Magic and the *Ars Notoria* is discussed in chapter III, "The Knowledge of the *Ars Notoria.*"
52. *De Legibus* (1228–1230), chapter 24.

is interpreting that the names of angels found in the *Ars Notoria* are actually the names of demons, because he says that to acquire knowledge by magical means is inappropriate, and "therefore, it is unlawful to practice the notory art."[53] Thus, Aquinas erroneously classifies the *Ars Notoria* as belonging to the category of necromancy, an error perpetuated among the populace to this day.

Aquinas references the Book of Daniel in which Daniel and his three companions request to abstain from the royal rations of King Nebuchadnezzar of Babylon and only eat vegetables and drink water. In doing so, their abstinence brought them "knowledge and skill in every aspect of literature and wisdom; Daniel also had insight into all visions and dreams." Once Nebuchadnezzar spoke with these four young men, "he found them ten times better than all the magicians and enchanters in his whole kingdom."[54] Aquinas points out that the difference between the abstinence required in the notory art and that of Daniel and his companions is that Daniel and his companions' abstinence was in accordance with "the authority of the divine law . . . and hence as a reward for their obedience they received knowledge from God."[55] For Aquinas, the *Ars Notoria* is not divinely instituted by God, and, implicitly, there is a distinction to be made between miracles and magic.

In his 1267 text *Opus Tertium,* the English Franciscan friar Roger Bacon (c. 1219–1292) condemns the *Ars Notoria,* saying it should be outlawed.[56] The Italian hermit Augustinus Triumphus (1243–1328), belonging to the Order of Saint Augustine, wrote *Tractatus contra divinatores et Sompniatores* (*A Treatise against the Diviners and Dreamers*), addressed to Pope Clement V in 1310 and condemning the *Ars Notoria* for its method of dream incubation.[57]

Another act of condemnation came upon John of Morigny, author of *Liber Florum Caelestis Doctrinae.* John's *Liber Florum* was confiscated and publicly burned at the University of Paris in 1323. The *Grandes Chroniques de France,* a detailed historical record written at the abbey of St. Denis in Paris, presents

53. *Summa Theologica,* 2.2.96.1.

54. Daniel 1:17, 20.

55. *Summa Theologica,* 2.2.96.1.

56. Michael Camille, "Visual Art in Two Manuscripts of the *Ars Notoria,*" in Fanger, ed., *Conjuring Spirits,* 112.

57. Mitchell, "Cultural Uses of Magic in Fifteenth-Century England; Anderson, *The Discernment of Spirits;* Giglioni, ed., "*Tractatus contra divinatores et sompniatores,*" 5–111.

an account of this condemnation. The account appears to describe the Old Compilation of the *Liber Florum:*

> And in this same year [1323], there was a monk of Morigny, an abbey near Etampes, who through his curiosity and pride wanted to inspire and renew a condemned heresy and sorcery called in Latin *Ars Notoria*, although he hoped to give it another name and title. This science teaches the making of figures and designs, and they must be different from one another and each assigned to a different branch of learning. Also, they must be contemplated at particular times with fasting and prayers. And so, after contemplation, the branch of knowledge which one wants to have and acquire through this act of contemplation is bestowed. But one had to name and invoke various little known names, which were firmly believed to be the names of demons. Hence this science disappointed many and many were deceived by it. For nobody using this science had ever gained any benefit or received any fruit. Nonetheless, this monk condemned this science, even though he feigned that the blessed Virgin Mary had appeared to him many times, thereby inspiring him with knowledge. And so in her honour he had had many images painted in his book, with many prayers and letters, very richly in expensive colours, feigning that the Virgin Mary had revealed everything to him. After these images had been applied to each branch of learning and contemplated, once the prayers had been said, the branch of learning one was seeking would be bestowed."[58]

A series of condemnations against the notory art followed. Cardinal Francesco Zabarella (fl. late 14th and early 15th centuries), a student to the famous jurist John of Legnano (Italian: Giovanni da Legnano; c. 1320–1383), offers a testimony to the presence of the *Ars Notoria* circulating in the academic environment of the University of Bologna. He mentions the book in the context of defending his legal profession from accusations that it can be reduced to just memorization and lacks reasoning skills. Zabarella shares a rumor about his teacher, saying:

---

58. English translation quoted from Nicholas Watson, "John the Monk's Book of Visions of the Blessed and Undefiled Virgin Mary, Mother of God: Two Versions of a Newly Discovered Ritual Magic Text," Fanger, ed., in *Conjuring Spirits,* 164.

> And also, some [students] are said to be excited about practicing the notory art inasmuch as a short [amount of] time and without much labor, so that they may consider all things, [and] knowing the *genera,* they might advance, which, in fact, a certain [student practicing the notory art] mocked my illustrious, famous teacher, lord John of Legnano. Thus, when that one was speaking together [with my teacher and classmates] to say that the teacher himself had practiced through the notory art itself; "Truly," [John of Legnano] said, "they win that [debate], but know without understanding."

The cardinal goes on to condemn the *Ars Notoria,* saying, "For it is to be said the unknown names [*nomina ignota*] which are written in that place are not of angels, but of demons from which [the notory art is] to be rejected outright by a Catholic man and he is to beware."[59]

Giovanni da Fontana (c. 1395–1455), an Italian physician and engineer, mentions the *Ars Notoria* in relation to the angels who bestow knowledge to man, including those angels belonging to the twelve signs of the zodiac, which suggests he might have been influenced by the writings of Cecco D'Ascoli. Giovanni da Fontana prohibits his son from engaging in any such occult practices that the church condemns.[60] Nicholas Magni of Jawor (c. 1355–1435), a theologian and professor at Prague University, condemned the *Ars Notoria* in his *Tractatus de Superstitionibus* (*Treatise on Superstitions*).[61] Jacob of Juterbogk (c. 1381–1465), a German monk and lecturer on theology at the University of Erfurt, also condemned the *Ars Notoria* in his *Tractatus de Potestate Daemonum, de Arte Magica, de Superstitionibus et Illusionibus eorundem* (*Treatise on the Power of Demons, the Art of Magic, Superstitions, and Illusions*).[62] Other condemnations followed, including from Dionysius Carthusianus (named Lewis de Rickel, 1402–1471) in his *Contra Vitia Superstitionum* (*Against the Vices of Supersitions*)[63] and Thomas Ebendorfer of Haselbach (1387–1464).[64]

59. Véronèse, "L'Ars notaria au Moyen Age," section 4.4.1.3, pp. 256–59. The Latin-to-English translation is mine.

60. Thorndike, "An Unidentified Work by Giovanni da'Fontana," 31–46.

61. Véronèse, "L'Ars notaria au Moyen Age," book 2, section 6.3, p. 656.

62. Thorndike, *A History of Magic,* 4:285–87.

63. Thorndike, *A History of Magic,* 4:291–93.

64. Thorndike, *A History of Magic,* 4:295.

In 1456, German author and physician Johannes Hartlieb (c. 1410–1468) famously wrote an account of illicit magical arts, *Das puch aller verpoten kunst, ungelaubens und der zaubrey* (*The Book of All Forbidden Arts*). In it, he too condemns the *Ars Notoria,* saying:

> There is also the *Ars Notoria,* which enables a person to learn all the arts by means of certain words, figures, and characters. This art is only carried out by means of a bond with the evil devils, for the secret words bring about association and bond between the Devil and the human. Although this art entails fasting, prayer, and pure, chaste living, still it is forbidden and a sin, because beneath this show of goodness the evil devils conceal their seduction and misleading of poor humankind.[65]

During the northern Renaissance, the Dutch philosopher Erasmus (1466–1536) condemned the *Ars Notoria* in his *Colloquies,* stating that the art is fictitious and offers an empty promise of learning many things in just fourteen days. He describes its contents as having "various forms of dragons, lions, leopards and various circles and words written in them, some in Greek, some in Latin, and some in Hebrew, and other barbarous languages."[66] Lastly, the German Carthusian and author of the *Margarita Philosophica* (*Pearl of Philosophy*), Gregor Reisch (1467–1525), and the French novelist Charles Sorel, Lord of Souvigny (1602–1674), would both condemn the notory art but at the same time support the related art of memory.[67]

However, despite centuries of condemnation, the *Ars Notoria* and its derivative works survive, indicating that they were not actively sought out and destroyed by the church, especially when compared to other handbooks of magic. The notory art's survival may be due to its innocuous nature and the fact that it only has effects upon the operator, rather than upon others. In fact, the modern scholar Frank Klassen draws attention to its popularity among a scholarly community of monks at St. Augustine's Abbey at Canterbury. We know that the *Ars Notoria* (Version B) manuscript labeled as Bodley 951 was owned by a monk named Simon Maidstone, and the *Ars Brevis* manuscript Sloane 513

65. Kieckhefer, trans. *Hazards of the Dark Arts,* 36.
66. Erasmus, *The Colloquies of Erasmus,* vol. 2, 227–28.
67. Reinink and Stumpel, eds., *Memory & Oblivion,* 286.

was owned by the monk Richard Dove. A certain Michael Northgate was said to own a manuscript that included prayers extracted from the *Ars Notoria* that were intended for devotional practice; by extracting the prayers, this removes them from the original context of magic and the ill-reputed Pseudo-Solomonic corpus.[68]

Other possible uses aside, the manuscript tradition shows that the *Ars Notoria* enjoyed its height of popularity in the fourteenth century, with its practitioners seeking the promised rapid attainment of a classical education in the seven liberal arts. However, as the European institution of education changed, the notory art's value for its outdated education paradigm diminished, leading to its sharp decline by the mid-seventeenth century.

68. Klaasen, *The Transformations of Magic,* 89–113.

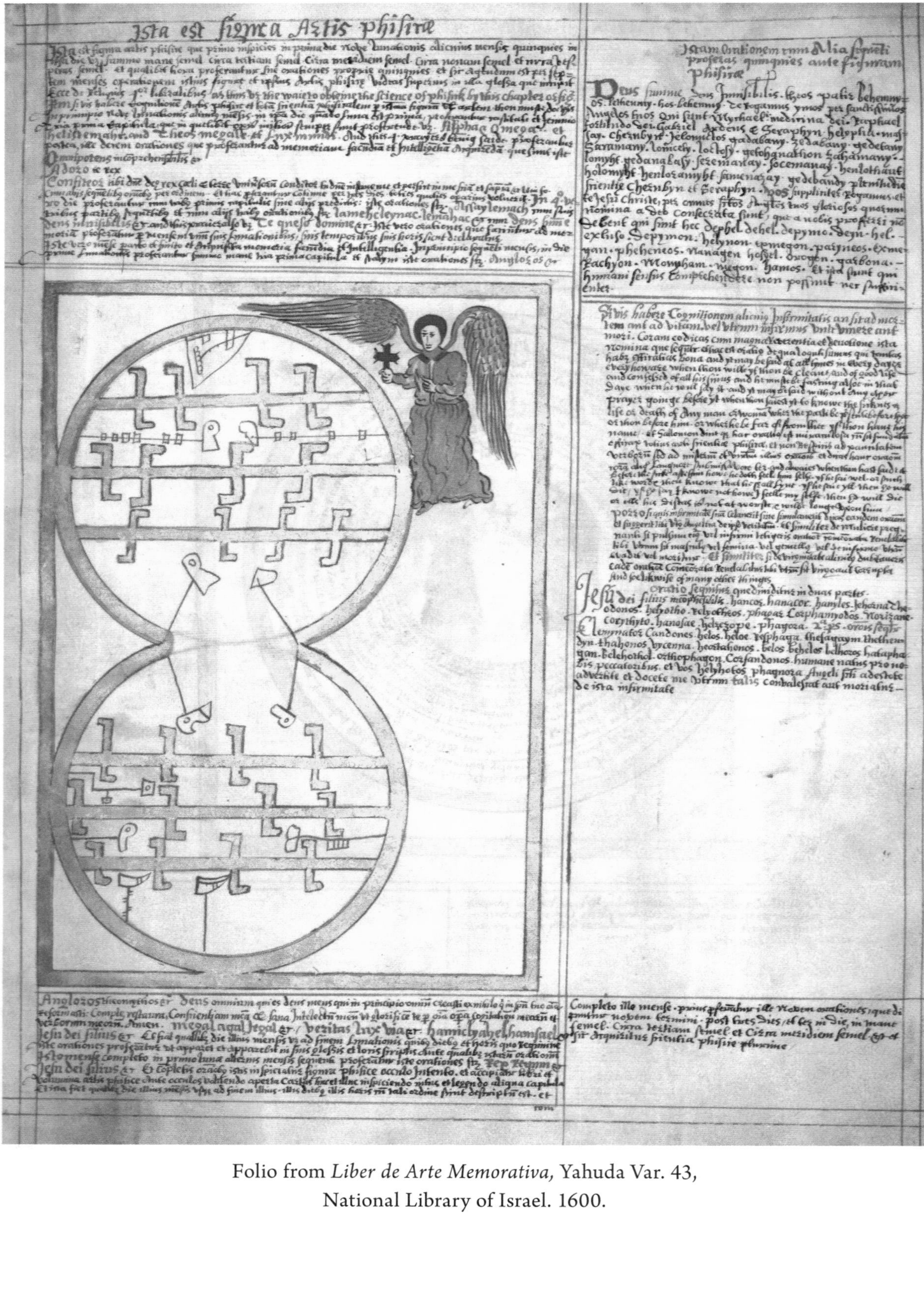

Folio from *Liber de Arte Memorativa,* Yahuda Var. 43,
National Library of Israel. 1600.

II.

Elements of the *Ars Notoria*

The *Ars Notoria,* though simple in its original presentation, has a complex structure, made even more complicated through redactions and assumed knowledge. While some of these qualities are shared with scholarly or occult works of its time, much of the *Ars Notoria* is quite unusual. For the reader to properly navigate the text, this chapter serves as an introduction to its basic outline, unique terminology, and textual problems before approaching the source text.

The *Ars Notoria* presents three rituals—greater, lesser, and those of the *Ars Nova*—by which a person may attain knowledge, virtue, or mental faculty. The basic ritual elements of the *Ars Notoria* are the prayers and the figures, both of which are called *notae.* The greater and lesser ritual procedures of the *Ars Notoria* consist of strange prayers referred to in the text as "Greek, Chaldean, and Hebrew" words. These *voces magicae* are not words in any one of these languages but rather magical calls joined together by means of grammatical zeugmas. The Greek word *zeugma* means "a yoking together." For instance, the first prayer of Version A is *"Hely, Semat, Azatau, Hemel, Samit, Theon."*[1] *Hely* is a corruption from transliterations of the Aramaic word for God, *alaha* (ܐܠܗܐ), into Greek and then into Latin. The Aramaic shares linguistic heritage with the Hebrew word for God, *elohim.* The function and construction of these prayers is further explored in chapter IV, "The Art of Memory." Each prayer has a further abridged shorthand name based on its incipits—the first few words of the prayer. The *Ars Notoria* calls them headwords (*capitula*). In the case of this first prayer, it is called *Helyscemath.*

As the *Ars Notoria* reinforces, reading these words as language or even

1. Refer to page 222, Version A.

understanding them is impossible; rather, they stand in for, and contain the full potency of, all the words of power contained within. In fact, the prayers are said to contain so much virtue and efficacy that they embody the "illuminating rays of the entire philosophy."[2] Although the *Ars Notoria* makes this claim, it is probably more accurate to state that these strange prayers petition the angels who, being impassioned by the prayers of this secret language, are the actual agents who bestow the desired knowledge.

The prayers are divided into two main groups—the Generals and the Specials, which are described in more detail in the following section. These barbarous prayers are often, but not always, accompanied by Latin prayers called prologues, which provide a partial explanation of the strange prayers.

Each prayer is also connected to certain *notae,* the mysterious illustrations and figures assigned to various fields of knowledge. The term *nota* can simply refer to the figures, but it also can mean a certain knowledge of something. Thus, in the *Ars Notoria, nota* has numerous meanings, referring to the images, the *voces magicae* that accompany them, and the knowledge to be gained from the combination thereof.

The prayers are recited and the figures are inspected according to certain days of the lunar month. The greater ritual procedure must be approved by an angel who will visit the operator and who will either grant or deny the operator permission to proceed with the ritual proper. These figures are not to be confused with the magical sigils or seals associated with certain spirits as found in other necromantic texts. These figures, called *notae,* are claimed to contain the occult virtue by which knowledge is attained through their inspection by applying the art of memory during ritual. The *notae* are explored in detail in chapter V, "Analysis of the Figures."

The *Ars Notoria* also presents lesser ritual procedures in which only a single prayer is offered for a particular purpose such as to gain eloquence, to know the prognosis of a sick patient, or for managing business affairs.

The *Ars Notoria* also contains a set of ten prayers known as the *Ars Nova,* which are prayers not bound to certain times of the month and promise to offer the operator the attainment of memory, eloquence, and understanding with applications for learning the liberal arts.

---

2. *Ars Notoria,* section 3 gloss.

The original scribes of the *Ars Notoria* manuscripts utilized different-colored inks for various reasons. Red ink in particular was used to add decoration, indicate special headings, or emphasize a particular passage. This red text is referred to as a rubric. There are variations in rubric placement among individual manuscripts, and the logic of the original scribe is not always clear. Today, the term *rubric* is still in use in the Catholic Church to describe the parts of the liturgy performed, as opposed to spoken.

Later manuscripts of Version B introduce a new component—glosses. This expanded commentary was added to later manuscripts to give a more concrete explanation of how the rituals function and clearer instructions on how to perform them. Version B is also more prolific in its usage of prayers containing additional *voces magicae* that are not included in the text but written within the figures. To distinguish these prayers from the prayers that are offered "before" the figures, and because they adorn the figures like ornaments, I have termed them "adorning prayers," though the text calls them a "particular" (*speciale*) prayer of a given *nota.*

THE PRAYERS OF THE *ARS NOTORIA*

As mentioned, the *Ars Notoria* presents three basic ritual forms in which to offer the prayers for certain effect: (1) the greater ritual; (2) the lesser rituals; and (3) the *Ars Nova* (*New Art*). Although "greater" and "lesser" rituals are not terms employed as such in the *Ars Notoria,* they are helpful in distinguishing which ritual procedure one is speaking about. What I denote the "greater ritual" procedure is the central ritual procedure the *Ars Notoria* expounds upon for the purpose of acquiring knowledge of "all the arts and all scientific literature" quickly. According to Version B, the greater ritual utilizes all the prayers. A "lesser ritual" consists of a single prayer that holds a special virtue or purpose outside of gaining knowledge of all the arts and sciences; there are only four such prayers. The *Ars Nova* has a role within the greater ritual but can also stand alone as a ritual procedure itself.

The two groups of prayers are the Generals and the Specials. The prayers of the Generals establish the operator's journey down the "first road" of knowledge, which consists of gaining memory, eloquence, understanding, and the stability of these three. The Generals are divided into five sequences which lend themselves easily enough to the principles of the art of memory (e.g., visualized as five landmarks along a road or in a building). The mnemonic signs are not always immediately apparent. The bracketed numbers in the following paragraphs indicate in which section that particular prayer can be found in the *Ars Notoria*.

The first sequence is called "the first three headwords" (*tria prima capitula*); a headword is a shorthand for the prayer incipit and indicates that the entire prayer is to be read aloud. The first sequence consists of three prayers, and they are *Helyscemath* [7], *Theos Megale* [10], and *Lux mundi* [11].

The second sequence is called "the triumphals," consisting of four prayers, and they are *Assaylemaht* [16], *Lamehc Leynac* [22], *Deus summe Deus* [24], and *Te quaeso Domine* [25]. Solomon gave the prayer *Assaylemaht* two special titles, which are the "light of the soul" and the "talent of happiness." Solomon describes it as being "inexpressible to human senses themselves." Apollonius called it the "mirror of wisdom" and the "image of eternal life." The prayer *Lamehc Leynac* is called the "queen of languages."

The third sequence consists of *Iesu Dei Filius* [29a], which, strangely, is not mentioned in the glosses as having a role in the greater operation of the notory art. Only Version B adds to the third sequence the prayer *Eleminator Caudones* [29b].

The fourth sequence is *Lamehc Ragna* [34], and its Latin prologue is *Memoria irreprehensibilis* [36]. This sequence is called the "crown jewel of the lord." Version B supplies another prayer, *Semeht* [35, variant 5].

The fifth sequence is the prayer *Hazatam,* which is divided into four parts with each part having its own Latin prologue. The prayer *Hazatam* is called the "sign of the grace of god." The fifth sequence consists of *Hazatam* [43] / *Confirma* [47]; *Agloros* [50] / *Deus omnium* [51]; *Megal* [52] / *Veritas lux et vita* [53]; and *Hanuyrlyhahel* [54] / *Ego in conspectus* [55].

There are two prayers that bridge the two categories of the prayers of the Generals with those of the Specials. From the mysterious book *Lengemath,* there is the Greek, Hebrew, and Chaldean prayer *Gemoht Gehel* [62] and its Latin prologue, *Omnipotens sempiterne Deus* [64]. It is a prayer of eloquence, and it is called the "renewal of languages" and "the last of the Generals and the first of the Specials." The other prayer is *Semoht Lamen* [69], which is called "the prologue to the Generals and the Specials." The prayer *Lux veritas* is the preamble to the prayers of the Specials.

The Specials consist of certain prayers that are assigned to certain fields of knowledge; each field of knowledge is assigned a certain number of *notae*. In the hierarchy of knowledge, theology and philosophy stand at the summit. Philosophy itself consists of the seven liberal arts. In conjunction with the liberal arts, the operator is taught moral virtues as found in the *nota* of chastity;the *nota* of justice, peace, and fear; and the *nota* of reprehension and taciturnity. Lastly, the Specials instruct the operator in the exceptives, or the divinatory magics, through the use of the four *notae* of the general sciences. According to the gloss, the four *notae* of the general sciences can also provide instruction about "some natural or moral science, or in any science of philosophy, or any kind of science which is contained beneath a greater or lesser philosophy."[3] The prayers of the Specials are listed with their respective field of knowledge. Furthermore, some *notae* have their own particular prayers written within them, usually a prayer containing angel names, or *voces magicae*. For the sake of clarity, I have chosen to label those prayers written within the *notae* as "adorning prayers," though the text simply calls them the "particular" prayer of a given *figure*. For a complete listing of the prayers assigned to their respective *notae,* see chapter V, "Analysis of the Figures."

Some prayers are assigned to more than one *nota,* and in *Ars Nova,* those prayers of astronomy and theology also serve the general functions of acquiring memory, eloquence, and understanding. The reasoning for these occurrences likely indicates redaction in the manuscript tradition; the reasons could be any number of things, with the best guess being simply a scribal error and confusion on the allocation of prayers to *notae* over the course of transmission in the written tradition.

Certain prayers are said to hold special virtues and to provide an additional function. These are considered the lesser rituals of the notory art. *Te quaeso Domine* serves three additional functions: (1) to gain certainty and knowledge about a dream vision you had; (2) to experience a prophetic vision of danger; and (3) to know the location of an absent person. It is to be said thrice in the evening with great reverence and with obsequiousness.[4] *Iesu Dei Filius* is a prayer for diagnosing disease and prognosticating the patient's outcome, whether he moves toward life or death. The prayer is said to have efficacy whether the

3. *Ars Notoria,* section 87 gloss.

4. *Ars Notoria,* section 26.

patient is present or at a distance. The prayer also helps discern the truth of whether a patient is feigning or concealing an illness. The prayer is said to reveal whether a woman is pregnant and whether a person is a virgin. *Lamehc Ragna* is to be said before giving a long speech, when studying writings, or when one is in danger of fire, earth, and beasts.[5] The prayer *Hazatam* may also provide a deeper understanding of theology, knowing the effects of heavenly and earthly things.[6]

The *Ars Nova* consists of ten prayers, and they are *Omnipotens incomprehensibilis, Adoro te rex regum, Confiteor, Otheos, Pie Deus, Pie Pater, Extollo sensus, Omnium regnorum, Deus vivorum, Profiteor,* and *Domine quia ego servus.* These prayers are not bound to the special timing of the lunar months, providing a convenience to the operator.

The prayers called the nine *termini* are *Genealogon, Geolym, Agenos, Genathores, Semathymoteham, Gerogueguos, Magnus Maguol, Remolithos,* and *Hamolehon.* According to Version B, they mark the beginning and end of certain rubrics of prayers at certain times during the greater ritual of the notory art.

OUTLINE OF THE *ARS NOTORIA*

The following outline lists the parts of the *Ars Notoria* along with a brief description of each. The section numbers are presented next to each part.

Flores Aurei, *the Prologue (sections 1–3)*

The prologue introduces the book title, *Flores Aurei,* and the supposed author, Apollonius of Tyana. The book is understood to be a florilegium, or collection of excerpts, from King Solomon's *Liber Florum,* which itself is a condensed version of the "most ancient Hebrew books" divinely revealed by the angel Pamphilius. The *Flores Aurei* provides Pseudo-Apollonius's commentary upon Solomon's writings and explains certain magical experiments which will grant the operator an understanding of all arts and sciences. The Iranian prophet Mani[7] and Euclid of Thebes are said to have tested these magical experiments.

5. *Ars Notoria,* sections 34 and 38.

6. *Ars Notoria,* sections 39, 43, and 49.

7. Version A2 manuscripts substitute the name Mani for Ptolemy (c. 100–c. 170), the famed Greek astronomer and author of the *Almagest.*

Flores Aurei, *Chapter 1 (sections 4–19)*

The occult virtue and efficacy of the *voces magicae* prayers are discussed, explaining that these prayers are *notulae* (little notes) whose secret language human reason cannot comprehend (4–6). The General prayers are introduced, which consist of seven sequences of prayers. They are subdivided into three main groups: (1) the preamble; (2) the prayers, which increase the mental faculties of memory, eloquence, understanding, and the stability of these three; and (3) the prayers that are concerned with a "theurgic" theology which entails working with the angelic powers. The first sequence is called "*tria prima capitula* (the first three headwords)"; namely *Helyscemath*, *[Ph]os Megal[os]*, and *Lux mundi*. The reader is given the admonition not to ponder or translate the words. It is explained that *Lux mundi* is the Latin prologue, or partial translation of the beginning of the strange prayer *[Ph]os Megal[os]* (7–13). The second sequence of General prayers, called "the triumphals of the liberal arts," is introduced with the prayer *Rasay Lamac*, named the "mirror of wisdom" and "the light of the soul." The second sequence is also called the "special introduction" to notory art because the General prayers are only offered on certain auspicious days of the lunar month. The first lunar month is explained, showing the auspicious days as being multiples of four (14–19). The second sequence of prayers is split between chapters 1 and 2; it consists of two prayers, *Rasay Lamac* and *Lemaac Salmaac*. Chapter 2 explains that the General prayers are divided into two groups. The first group (*Rasay Lamac*, *Lemaac Salmaac*, and *Theos Pat[e]r*, including their Latin prologues) are to be offered on the auscipious days of the first month. The first group offers the necessary mental faculties to acquire knowledge; that is, it prepares the intellect for the coronation and resplendor for gaining extraordinary intelligence (*Rasay Lamac*), eloquence (*Lemaac Salmaac*), and memory (*Theos Pat[e]r*). *Helyscemath* and *[Ph]os Megal[os]* (and its Latin prologue, *Lux mundi*) act as a preamble to the first group, having the occult virtue of preparing the soul, memory, and intellect for the ritual proper; not belonging to the "special introduction," these prayers are not bound to any prescribed timing but instead are expected to be offered at the beginning of ritual practice.

Flores Aurei, *Chapter 2 (sections 20–31)*

The notory art rests at the pinnacle of the hierarchy of knowledge because one can learn all the sciences through it (20b). The Latin word *nota* (pl. *notae*) is introduced as a technical term denoting a certain kind of knowledge contained both within a *voces magicae* prayer and a pictorial figure. In other words, the *nota* is the hidden knowledge itself, which the operator seeks to acquire; the *nota*'s symbols, or "containers" as it were, are the prayer and the pictorial figure. The usage of the word *nota* sometimes leans toward one of its containers—either the prayer or the pictorial figure (21). *Lemaac Salmaac,* the last part of the second sequence, also has an occult virtue which can be expressed in a lesser ritual for bestowing eloquence (21–23). The third sequence of the General prayers is introduced as *Deus summe Deus invisibilis Theos Pat[e]r,* and its Latin prologue, *Te queso Domine. Theos Pat[e]r* is said to be for the invocation of angels and bestows the mental faculty of memory (24–25). The second and third sequences conclude the first group of the General prayers, which are meant for gaining memory, eloquence, understanding, and the stability of these three.

Next, the text says, "Some things are divided hereafter," indicating that the General prayer sequences are split into two groups: the first through third sequences and the fourth through seventh sequences. Sequences 1–3 are assigned to the first month (the auspicious days which are listed as multiples of four), and sequences 4–7 are assigned to the second month (the auspicious days which are listed as multiples of three) (23). The fourth sequence of the General prayers is *Ancor Anacor Anilos,* which is also said to have two occult virtues, which can be expressed in two separate lesser rituals. The first occult virtue is for attaining visions of knowledge (26). The second occult virtue is for prognosticating the status of a person's health, including the outcome of an illness, whether a woman is pregnant, or whether a person is a virgin (29–30). A repeated warning is given not to translate or ponder the *voces magicae* prayers (31).

Flores Aurei, *Chapter 3 (sections 32–85)*

The text reiterates that the notory art rests at the pinnacle of the hierarchy of knowledge as "the art of arts and the science of sciences" (32). The prayer *Lamen Ragaa* and its Latin prologue, *Memoria irreprehensibilis,* is introduced as the fifth sequence of the General prayers. It also has the occult virtue of making the operator capable of learning and becoming an audacious, vivacious, and prudent speaker and defender of his ideas before his audience; in addition, it protects the operator from fire, earth, and beasts. The *Lamen Ragaa* prayer is said to have been thoroughly studied by Pseudo-Apollonius in a separate scroll, exploring its "magnitude of qualities" as it relates to Aristotle's philosophical theory of hylomorphism (33–36). Solomon's *Liber Florum Caelestis Doctrinae,* the condensed version of "the most ancient Hebrew books," which he received from the angels, is described (38). The second grouping of the General prayers (*Ancor Anacor Anilos, Lamen Ragaa, Hely Lehem,* and *Gemoht Gehel,* including their own parts) is said to be especially concerned with theology; that is to say, a "theurgic" theology working with divine and angelic powers, gaining authoritative power through one's faith, and acquiring divine justice over one's enemies. The notory art is not concerned with what is traditionally understood as contemplative theology or church doctrine but rather acquiring a "theurgic" theology in which the operator is communicating and working with angels as a means of participating in God's creation. The second grouping of the General prayers are collectively called the "Sign of the Mystery of God" (39). The second month is explained, showing the auspicious days as being multiples of three (40). The sixth sequence of the General prayers is given as *Hely Lehem,* which has four parts with each part having its own Latin prologue. They are *Hely Lehem* and its prologue, *Confirma; Agloros* and its prologue, *Deus omnium; Megal* and its prologue, *Veritas lux et vita;* and *Hely Latur Bael,* and its prologue, *Ego in conspectus* (39–56). The text explains that a portion of the knowledge gained through the notory art can be found on Earth (*Hely Lehem*), while the "golden" portion is found only in heaven (*Agloros, Megal,* and *Hely Latur Bael*) (49). The admonishing story of Solomon's house servant is told regarding what happens when the notory art is misused (57). The text briefly mentions that the arts and sciences are best learned at astrologically favorable times (58); this passage appears to reference section 147. The seventh and final sequence of the General prayers is *Gemoht, Gehel* and its Latin prologue, *Omnipotens sempiterne Deus;* and its second part, *Semot Lamen,* concludes the General prayers. The text transitions to speaking about the Special prayers and how the operator may pursue only one art at a time (59–70).

The introduction to the Special prayers begins by saying that each art and science has its own prayers and figures. There are seven liberal arts and seven exceptive arts. The seven liberal arts are grammar, logic/dialectic, rhetoric, arithmetic, music, geometry, and astronomy. The seven exceptive arts can be understood as the subdivisions of two natural sciences, or arts of divination, necromancy and astrology. Under necromancy, there is hydromancy and pyromancy (the author counts these as three arts). Under astrology, there is chiromancy, geomancy, genethlialogy, and onomancy (71). The text details the number of figures assigned to each of the three liberal arts (grammar, logic/dialetic, and rhetoric) by presenting the story of how King Solomon received them through his first divine revelation (72–76).

The text gives the instructions for the offering of the prayers belonging to grammar, specifically on the ordinary days of the lunar month, and the number of repetitions differs for three different divisions of the month. The first part of the month, from the first day to the fourteenth day, the prayers are to be recited 24 times. The second part of the month, from the fourteenth (or fifteenth?) to the eighteenth (or seventeenth?) day,[8] the prayers are to be recited 30 times. The third part of the month, from the eighteenth to the thirteenth day, the prayers are to be recited 37 (or 36?) times. The first figure of grammar is to be inspected 12 times from the first day to the fourteenth day. From the fourteenth (or fifteenth?) to the eighteenth (or seventeenth?) day, the first and second figures of grammar are to be inspected 20 (24?) times. From the eighteenth to the thirteenth day, all three figures of grammar are to be inspected (36 times?). The offering of prayers and the inspections of the figures are interspersed with intervals of rest and silence; in addition, the text points out that the Special prayers of grammar are offered in the same first month of the General prayers, which improve the mental faculties of memory, understanding, and perseverance (i.e., the first month, not the second month). The practice of the art of memory is implied during the inspection of the figures and the study of textbooks, which is explained in chapter IV, "The Art of Memory." Furthermore, the operator is advised not to fall into sin by neglecting the appointed ritual times and also abstaining from sins generally. Lastly, the operator is instructed to fast until evening on the first day of the inspection of the figures (77–81).

The preamble to the Special prayers, *Lux veritas,* is given (82). The instructions are given for all the prayers to be said before noon, to include the particu-

---

8. According to section 79, Solomon attests that the Special prayers are forbidden to be offered on the fifteenth, seventeenth, and ninteenth days of the month. These are Egyptian days and therefore are unlucky. The confusion of where to draw the dividing line between the first part of the month and its second part, marked in parentheses, may have arisen in Version B regarding whether these days are to have any prayers at all because the fifteenth and eighteenth days of the second month are considered auspicious; this should not matter, because the auspicious days are reserved only for the General prayers.

lar or "adorning" prayers of their own figures, to read aloud from the writing that is to be studied, and to pronounce them according to the specifications of each liberal art (83–84). The seven prayers of philosophy rule over the four liberal arts, and therefore, they are offered first before the prayers of any of the four liberal arts. The remaining Special prayers are dedicated to the second month, which has the auspicious days as multiples of three. The first four days of the second month are "to be venerated and revered more than the others following [Version B, sections 85/86 gloss]," probably due to the sacredness of the number four in the notory art (e.g., the four ruling angels of the notory art and their four scrolls written in the four interwoven languages and the second grouping of the General prayers, belonging to the second month, consist of four main prayers). The ritual instructions for the four liberal arts abruptly ends here (85). The *Flores Aurei* is missing any further ritual instructions or vignettes of Solomon and the angels regarding the prayers and figures of the quadrivium, the general sciences, the exceptives, philosophy, and theology (although the Christian writer preserves the seven prayers of philosophy in his letter, and the appended section safeguarded the prayers for arithmetic and geometry).

The Christian Writer's Letter (sections 85–127)

The Christian writer's letter is composed by an unknown Christian addressed to his unnamed companion to answer his questions about the notory art. Perhaps there was a time when the letter accompanied a copy of the *Flores Aurei*. Now the opening and closing of the letter are missing, probably to ensure anonymity as the letter and the *Flores Aurei* circulated among other practitioners. Now both the letter and the *Flores Aurei* are fragmented and harmonized into a single treatise known simply as the *Ars Notoria*. The Christian writer's letter is composed of three parts: (1) the supplemental material to the *Flores Aurei* called "the explement of the entire art" (105); (2) the ten prayers and ritual instructions of the *Ars Nova,* the first derivative text of the *Flores Aurei;* and (3) the nine prayers called the *novem termini*.

The Explement of the Entire Art (sections 85–109)

The explement answers the addressee's questions about the notory art, beginning with the figures belonging to philosophy, the general sciences, the seven exceptive arts which are classed under the general sciences, the four liberal arts, and "theurgic" theology (85–89). If the operator wishes to learn the four liberal arts, then the fifth prayer of theology, *Hosel* (104), is to be offered after the Special prayers of one of those arts (89).

Next, the explement moves on to the seven prayers of philosophy, explaining that these seven prayers are actually augmentations (*augmentationes*) of the five prayers of "theurgic" theology. The Christian writer reaffirms the medieval hierarchy of knowledge in that the seven prayers of philosophy contain beneath them the seven liberal arts and the seven exceptives (90). His assertion that the seven prayers of philosophy are augmentations of theology means that he views theology as the capstone to philosophy, which is a distinctly Christian perspective. He goes on to imply that the seven prayers of philosophy are to be said with any of the Special prayers of the four liberal arts and the seven exceptives. By deductive logic, this would mean to say that the seven prayers of philosophy precede any art belonging to the seven liberal arts or the seven exceptives on the ordinary days. Because he focused on the four liberal arts, the general sciences, and the seven exceptives, these then belong to the second month (logically, this must be certain since the first month has already been dedicated to the trivium). These details are explored further in chapter VI, "The Complete Ritual Procedures." The Christian writer presents the seven prayers of philosophy and their Latin prologues while subtly indicating their division into two groups (the first through fourth prayers and the fifth through seventh prayers) by interrupting the list of prayers with the teaching of the fourth prayer (97). The seven prayers of philosophy are as follows: (1) *Ezethomos* and its Latin prologue, *Domine Deus incomprehensibilis;* (2) *Domine Deus Sancte Pater* and its Latin prologue, *Deus semper via vita veritas;* (3) *Lemogethon* and its Latin prologue, *Vita hominum;* (4) *Rex regum;* (5) *Deus Pater immense [. . . magnitudo];* (6) *Gezomothon* and its Latin prologue, *Rex eterne Deus;* and finally (7) *Deus totius pietatis* (91–101).

The final section of the explement addresses the teachings of the *notae* of theology, but the letter must have been edited by another hand since only the teaching about the fifth and ineffable figure of theology is given (102–3). The explement gives the fifth prayer of theology as *Hosel* (104), followed by instructions to observe the new moons in the pronunciation of the *notae* with their own prayers. Also, he instructs his addressee to observe the fourth day of the (second) lunar month in the pronunciation of all the prayers of theology (105–6). The explement presents a miscellany of final thoughts on access to textbooks, the pronunication of the headwords,[9] the new magical experiment of death or life instituted by the Christian writer himself (28–30), and the possibility that new magical experiments can be performed according to the addressee's own angel, who visits him in dream visions (107). The explement closes with a discussion of the prescribed times for the prayers and figures, the occult virtues of certain prayers as lesser rituals, where in the text to begin the greater ritual, and the magical effect of the prayers of "theurgic" theology (108–9).

The *Ars Nova* (Sections 110–125)

The ritual instructions for the ten prayers of the *Ars Nova* are given, which can supplement the greater ritual of the *Flores Aurei* or stand alone. The ten prayers are (1) *Omnipotens incomprehensibilis;* (2) *Adoro te rex regum;* (3) *Confiteor;* (4) *Otheos* and its Latin prologue, *Pie Deus;* (5) *Pie Pater;* (6) *Extollo sensus;* (7) *Omnium regnorum;* (8) *Deus vivorum;* (9) *Profiteor;* and (10) *Domine quia ego servus* (110–25).[10] The ten prayers do not require any prescribed times, unlike most of the *Flores Aurei* prayers, but do require spiritual purification through the abstinence of sin (111). The Christian writer claims that these ten prayers are the proems (*proemia*) to the *voces magicae* prayers found in the *Flores Aurei.* He answers his addressee's unclear question about two of the headwords of philosophy. He claims to have received the *Ars Nova* as a sacrament from God through an angelic vision (112a). The operator is to prepare for the beginning of the work for six weekdays, while fasting for three days beforehand, for a total

9. The addressee's question might have been about whether to pronounce the headwords which are found in the beginning rubrics of the original and now lost *Flores Aurei.* The original layout of the *Flores Aurei* might have presented just the headwords in the rubrics, only to present the prayer in its entirety next to its magical figure farther below in the text. Alternatively, or in addition, the addressee's question may have been about the identity and/or placement of the astronomy and theology prayers belonging under philosophy (112a).

10. The magical figures belonging to astronomy and theology were transmitted from Version A to Version B. When Version B received the figures but not their respective prayers, the Version B scribe decided to insert this lacuna with the *Ars Nova* prayers. Thus, the *Ars Nova* prayers take on a dual function in Version B. The *Ars Nova* prayers newly assigned to the five figures of astronomy, from first to fifth, are as follows: (1) *Confiteor,* (2) *Extollo sensus,* (3) *Omnium regnorum,* (4) *Domine quia ego servus,* and (5) *Profiteor.* The *Ars Nova* prayers newly assigned to the five figures of theology, from first to fifth, are as follows: (1) *Omnipotens incomprehensibilis,* (2) *Adoro te rex regum,* (3) *Pie Deus,* (4) *Pie Pater,* and (5) *Deus vivorum.*

of nine days. The mythical account of how Solomon received the *Ars Nova* is given (114a). The *Ars Nova* promises the similar principal benefit of gaining knowledge, just like the *Flores Aurei* does (114b).

The Little Work of the *Novem Termini* (Sections 126–27)

The prayers called the *Novem Termini* are a separate little treatise which was also divinely revealed to the Christian writer. He claims his angel told him that it can be offered before all the prayers and figures of the notory art, and even if he passed over much of the times, by saying these novem termini he would retain the occult virtue that he was accruing in ritual, and therefore, he would still be successful in acquiring the desired knowledge. In effect, the *novem termini* are like a security measure or safety net in the event of forgetting or neglecting the prescribed times of the *Flores Aurei*. There are short descriptions to some of the *novem termini* that suggest that they also have their own occult virtue; these virtues might resemble human needs and desires found in other medieval charms and spells. The *novem termini* are as follows: (1) *Genealogon,* (2) *Geolym,* (3) *Agenos,* (4) *Genathores,* (5) *Semathymoteham,* (6) *Gerogueguos,* (7) *Magnus Maguol,* (8) *Remolithos,* and (9) *Hamolehon.*

Flores Aurei, ***a late addendum (Sections 128–46)***

There is a late addendum of the *Flores Aurei,* and it contains the prayers belonging to the trivium, the prayers of arithmetic and geometry, another Latin prayer belonging either to the first philosophy or the general sciences, and Version A2 material. The three prayers belonging to grammar are given—namely, (1) *Domine Sancte Pater [. . . imperfectum],* (2) *Respice Domine,* and (3) *Creator Adonay.* The ritual instructions remind the reader to observe the times. Also, the "adorning prayers," or those *voces magicae* prayers written within the figures, are addressed (128–32). The text mentions certain signs found in the figures. These signs are said to give the definitions for each art, just as expressed in the first divine revelation between Solomon and the angel in sections 72–76 (133). Definitions can be found in Version B figures, which might further support the premise that this addendum is, indeed, a late recension in the historic composition of the *Flores Aurei.* The topic of signs and definitions is explored further in chapter V, "Analysis of the Figures"; the reader might want to study the four wheels associated with the two figures of logic/dialectic first. The number of figures assigned to each art and science is given, followed by the admonishing story of how God punished King Solomon for getting drunk and mocking the magical figures (134). This story about King Solomon is classed as Version A2 material. The prayers belonging to the two figures of logic/dialectic are given—namely, *Sancte Deus* and *Heloy clementissime*—followed by instructions to the operator, who is blind or has poor eyesight, to practice the art of memory by visualizing the figures in his mind's eye. Additional comments are made about the figure of awe (which probably refers to the first figure of philosophy), the figure of chastity, and the figure justice, peace, and fear, but the text tells us these prayers, which number fifteen, are lost and some writing has gone unfinished. The text instructs the operator to give "the highest reverence" to the third prayer and figure of philosophy (135–37). Next, the four prayers belonging to rhetoric are given—namely, (1) *Omnipotens et misericors Pater,* (2) *Unus magnus,* (3) *Usyon,* and (4) *Reverende.* The prayer *Gezomanai,* situated between the second and third prayers of rhetoric, is a misplaced General prayer belonging to the second sequence of the General prayers following *Rasay Lamac* (138–42).[11] Next, the prayer for the first figure of geometry—namely, *Deus iustus iudex*—is given (143). Subsequently, the prayers for the first figure and the half figure of arithmetic—namely, *Deus qui omnia numero* and *Mediator omnium*—are presented (144–45). Lastly, the prayer *Omnipotens sapientiae* is given (146).[12]

Astrological Prescriptions and Epilogue (147)

Instructions are given on calculating whether a lunar month is embolismic as well as instructions for studying certain arts and sciences under certain astrological conditions involving the position of the Moon in certain zodiac signs as well other favorable astrological factors.

11. The original arrangement of the *Flores Aurei* probably had the General and Special prayers next to one another to explain the ritual instructions for the first month, but then also the figures would have immediately followed the prayers within the text. When the text was reworked, consequently, the arrangement of the prayers recorded in a new manuscript might have preserved this arrangment of the first two prayers of rhetoric, followed by the *Gezomanai* General prayer, then the last two prayers of rhetoric. Notice *Azelechias* [. . . *regi Salomoni*] and *Scio enim* are not listed here. The *Gezomanai* prayer of Version A is equivalent to the *Hanazay* prayer of Version B, as both belong to section 140.

12. According to Version B, this prayer belongs to the second *nota* of geometry. Version A does not have a second nota of geometry; the first *nota* of geometry has been duplicated in Version B, creating two *notae.*

Notae *Supplement*

The figures are presented pictorially. In Version B manuscripts, the figures are accompanied by their respective prayers and rubrics.

PROBLEMS WITH THE TEXT

As already mentioned above, the *Ars Notoria* consists of multiple parts, which all have been reworked by later scribes. The redaction of these parts has led to several problems which have plagued the text and its ritual practitioners for centuries. Such redactions likely inspired the later derivative texts in an effort to revive and renew the notory art tradition. These textual problems are explored here.

Misidentified or Incorrectly Numbered Notae

In several manuscripts, there are misidentified or incorrectly numbered *notae,* but these are confidently corrected in the present work based on comparative analysis and deductive logic. See appendix A1 for details.

Difficulty Following the Ritual Instructions

Historically speaking, the greatest barrier to performing the *Ars Notoria* has been following the complex and arduous ritual instructions. Version A has incomplete and missing ritual instructions, prayers, and figures, due to redaction. Version A is missing Solomon's preludes and teachings regarding the four liberal arts and the seven exceptives. It is also missing the original prayers for astronomy; theology; music; the general sciences; the exceptives; medicine; justice, peace, and fear; and reprehension and tactiturnity. Such problems led to questions and confusions, such as those expressed by the unnamed addressee in the Christian writer's letter. Furthermore, such problems needed answers. Version B attempts to answer such problems by providing lengthy explanatory glosses for each section, harmonizing the *Flores Aurei* with the *Ars Nova* and *novem termini,* and assigning *Ars Nova* prayers to the missing prayers for astronomy and theology. Version B's result made the ritual procedure twice as long, making its glosses intimidating to some and cumbersome for others. Moreover, in making these big changes, Version B erroneously doubled some of the figures and made other minor mistakes, such as the mistaken identity of the figure of music and creating a figure of chastity. See chapter VI, "The Complete Ritual Procedures" for more details.

The Christian Writer's Letter

The Christian writer's letter is a hypothesized source of the *Ars Notoria*. The letter is thought to have once accompanied a full copy of the original *Flores Aurei,* which circulated in northern Italy. At some point, both the *Flores Aurei* and the letter were reworked, causing the opening and closing of the letter to be omitted for the sake of preserving anonmity from Christian authorities in consideration of the work's illicit contents. This led copyists to embed the letter in the *Flores Aurei,* placing it just prior to the introduction of the four liberal arts. The reworking of the *Flores Aurei* and the letter led them both to a fragmented state. The evidence for the existence of the Christian writer's letter is fourfold: (1) the letter acknowledges an addressee and his questions, and it even acknowledges itself as an explement (i.e., a supplement in section 105); (2) references are made to outside sources and portions of the original *Flores Aurei,* which are now missing; (3) the writer is a Christian because he adopts certain Christian attitudes, such as those expressed in the letter itself, the *Ars Nova* prayers, and the belief that theology is the capstone to philosophy in the hierarchy of knowledge; and (4) the letter's content causes dissonance between the first and second portions of the *Flores Aurei*.

The existence of the letter's addressee is acknowledged in phrases such as "Those supplements are of those that you postulated . . . because you have postulated something of the mystery of the *notae,*"[13] "However, the headwords (about which you doubted or perhaps are still uncertain of),"[14] and:

> These are the preambles of their prayers before those, yet I wanted to place them [separate] from those you doubted, as one to one, placed in its proper order, making them clear apart from any distinction. These are those about which you doubted, either [of the two] headwords of philosophy (with everything below its own contents apart from the rest) ought to be offered . . . and I know the matter mentioned beforehand above you determined to regard more crafty.[15]

---

13. *Ars Notoria,* section 102.

14. *Ars Notoria,* section 107.

15. *Ars Notoria,* section 112a.

In addition, the letter writer would reference notory art material not found in the *Ars Notoria,* revealing a number of lacunae in the text.

Lacunae and Writing Left Unfinished

Lacunae are places in a text where content is evidently missing. They can also indicate the number of redaction layers; that is, the archaeological layers from the earliest to the latest. The fragmented letter reveals five lacunae, informing what might have been found in the original *Flores Aurei.* These can be identified by observing mismatched cross-references within the text, such as incorrect indications of what has preceded or is to follow a certain passage.

First, in section 85, it seems as though the four liberal arts might receive an introduction, but then section 86 interrupts with a mention of "[t]he seven *notae* of philosophy that you saw with the sciences below them." This interrupting statement shows a lacuna for the four liberal arts and the middles sciences contained within them. This is a significant loss of material. Second, a hint of a lacuna is found in section 85, which says, "the *nota* of awe, that you know, just as we said to you," but this is contrary to what is found earlier in the text as this is the first mention of the *nota* of awe. Third, section 86 says, "it must be pronounced just as you heard in the part," showing an assumption that the reader was already introduced to the instructions about the fifth *nota* of theology. Fourth, the prayers belonging to the four figures of the general sciences are missing. Section 87 says, "from the *notae* of the general [sciences] . . . you will be able to work just as it is said above." Again, this is the first mention of the four *notae* of the general sciences. Fifth, following the prayers of philosophy, section 102 promises the teachings of the *notae* of theology, but they are all missing except for the fifth *nota*. This concludes the five lacunae revealed by the Christian writer's letter.

Next, there are those instances in which the writing of the notory art goes unfinished. First, in the second portion of the *Flores Aurei* (sections 128–47), sections 132 and 136 say that a supplement containing the adorning prayers within their figures is to accompany the *Ars Notoria* but that it went unfinished. This supplement is what I call the *Notae* Supplement (NS), and it contains the figures, the prayers, and the rubrics. Second, another lacuna is found at section 136. After introducing the third *nota* of philosophy as the *nota* of sorrow, it says, "You will recite six other *notae* as it will be seen shortly," but this promise is never fulfilled as the entire text ends abruptly after the prayer attributed to the *nota* of awe (i.e., the first *nota* of the general sciences). Third, in the *Notae* Supplement, the *notae* of music; chastity; justice, peace, and fear; and reprehension and tactiturnity are found in Version A, but the text fails to eloborate, and it does not give their prayers (section 136). Fourth, section 19 reads, "[This prayer] is the first form of the notory art itself, and it is situated above the manifested quadrangle *nota*." The text is indicating that the prayer is positioned within the text just above a quadrangular figure, but none of the Version A manuscripts examined here present any figures near this section of text. This suggests that there was an older recension of the text in which prayers were positioned over the figures, rather than the present form, which places all the figures at the end of the treatise.

Prayers Which Are Missing, Incorrectly Assigned, or Newly Added

In Version B's attempt to rectify the problems plaguing Version A through the harmonization of its parts, Version B encountered its own set of problems. In Version B, section 126c gloss, there is a section listing thirty-two prayers that has problems. The section divides these thirty-two prayers effectively into two sets of prayers: first, the set of eighteen prayers, and second, the set of fourteen prayers.

The first group of eighteen prayers is assigned to the three liberal arts. The eighteen prayers are:

Lux, veritas (the preamble, section 82)
Domine sancte Pater [. . . imperfectum] (first grammar, section 128)
Respice Domine (second grammar, section 129)
Creator Adonay (third grammar, section 130)
Sancte Deus (first logic/dialectic, section 135)
Heloy clementissime (second logic/dialectic, section 137)
Omnipotens et misericors (first rhetoric, section 138)
Adonay, which may equate to *Hanazay* (first rhetoric, found only in Version B, section 140)
Unus magnus (second rhetoric, section 139)
Usyon omnium (second or third rhetoric, Version A, section 141; Version B, section 139 gloss)

Azelechias [. . . regi Salomoni] (second rhetoric, found only in Version B, variation 7)
Scio enim (third rhetoric, found only in Version B, variation 8)
Reverende (fourth rhetoric, section 142)
Deus qui omnia numero (first arithmetic, section 144)
Mediator omnium (half arithmetic, section 145)
Deus iustus iudex (geometry, section 143)
Omnipotens sapientiae (general sciences, or first philosophy, section 146; second geometry, found only in Version B, section 146 gloss)
Adoro te rex regum (second *Ars Nova* prayer and second theology according to Version B, section 116)

The second group of fourteen prayers is assigned to the four liberal arts and includes the thirteen prayers of philosophy and the single prayer, *Hosel,* which belongs to the fifth figure of theology (section 104). They are as follows:

Ezethomos and its Latin prologue, *Dominus Deus [incomprehensibilis]* (first philosophy, sections 90–91)
Domine [Deus] sancte Pater and its Latin prologue, *Deus, semper via* (second philosophy, sections 92–93)
Lemogethon and its Latin prologue, *Vita hominum* (third philosophy, sections 94–95)
Omaza and its Latin prologue, *Rex regum* (fourth philosophy, variation 10 and section 96)
Deus Pater immense [. . . magnitudo] (fifth philosophy, section 98)
Gezomothon and its Latin prologue, *Rex eterne Deus* (sixth philosophy, sections 99–100)
Deus totius pietatis (seventh philosophy, section 101)
Deus Pater immense [. . . misericordissme] (music, NS 69)

The first problem is that not all eighteen prayers belong to the three liberal arts of grammar, logic, and rhetoric; the disciplines assigned to the prayers are marked in the parentheses. The second problem is that Version B adds the new prayers, *Azelechias [. . . regi Salomoni]* and *Scio enim,* to rhetoric. The rationale for this is unknown; perhaps Version B is drawing from another source in the vein of the Version A tradition, which has not survived. The third problem is a matter of unknown, misidentified, or incorrectly assigned prayers, including *Adonay, Omnipotens sapientiae,* and *Adoro te rex regum.* The ritual use of the eighteen prayers may be that only the select prayers of the chosen discipline are to be offered, rather than all eighteen, as instructed. This is presumptuous, as it is never clearly stated as such in Version B. The glosser makes it plain elsewhere that not all the liberal arts are meant to be studied altogether as he has laid out the specific operations of each art in section 126; besides, the premise that only a single art or science is studied at any one time had already been established in Version A.

The fourteen prayers, as a single unit, draws from the Christian writer's letter, which emphasizes the importance of how the prayers and figures of theology rule over philosophy. In this case, the only remaining prayer of theology, the fifth, named *Hosel,* is intended to follow the Special prayers. In chapter VI, "The Complete Ritual Procedures of the *Ars Notoria,*" a discussion of how the seven prayers of philosophy rule over the seven liberal arts is explored in the reconstruction of Version A.

A SOURCE HYPOTHESIS

Considering all the problems which the text presents, what are the possible sources and composition of the *Ars Notoria*? This is a difficult question to answer. Yet, here I will venture into the realm of speculation and wonder, as I propose a source hypothesis for the *Ars Notoria*. First, there might have been a Greek original of the *Flores Aurei*. The first proposition necessitates that a translation would have been made from Greek to Latin. At this stage, it is difficult to guess if the Christianization of the *Flores Aurei* began right away or in a later recension, because no Greek original survives. In any case, the *Flores Aurei* became fragmented during the Christianization of the text, having lost its original form and material, including the loss of certain prayers and figures. The Christianization of the text includes the Latin prologues, the possible mention of the *Speculum Astronomiae* (section 19), and the Christian writer's letter, which would also have contained the *Ars Nova* and *novem termini*. There is also a hint of a certain scribe's own voice speaking of Apollonius in the third person, but its placement in this hypothesis is uncertain. There appears to have been a recovery and harmonization

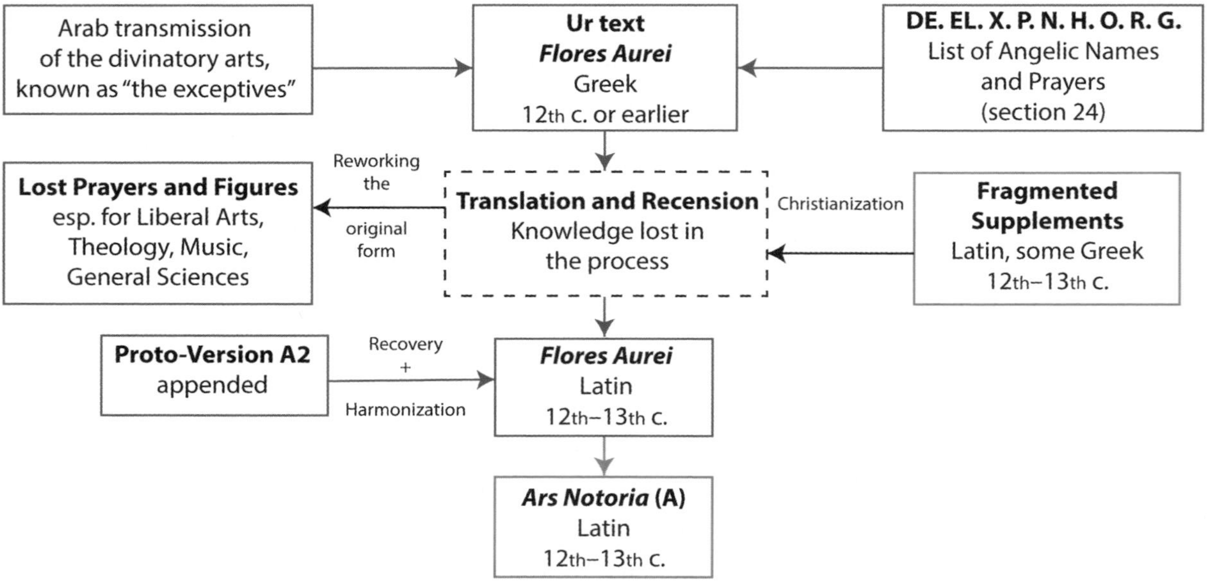

A source hypothesis of the *Ars Notoria.* Texts framed in blue do not exist on their own, but are evidenced as separate sources by examination of Version A. Texts framed in red are extant. The dashed black frame indicates a hypothesized intermediate stage.

stage, in which a later portion of the *Flores Aurei* was appended to the text (proto-Version A2) and the entire *Flores Aurei* melded together with the Christian writer's letter, reworking the material into its present form as the *Ars Notoria.*

A HYPOTHESIZED RECONSTRUCTION OF THE ORIGINAL *FLORES AUREI*

If there ever was an original Greek *Flores Aurei,* then its ordered form (*compositus figura*) probably looked different from its present form. Based on the clues presented in Version A, the original text was probably more orderly and structured, especially in regard to the prayers according to Solomon's instructions (section 8). The basic format would have included Solomon's prelude (*praeludium*) followed by a rubric on the timing and offering of the prayers (section 32b). Because both General prayers and Special prayers were offered in a single month, it is likely these two classes of prayers were discussed together, not separate as they appear today. This would explain why the General prayer *Gezomanai* ended up sandwiched between the second and third rhetoric and also explain the sequence of figures following the placement of the second figure of rhetoric in the manuscripts and the loss of the third figure in Version A (but was preserved in Version A2). After Solomon's prelude, the prayer's headword would be introduced, placed just above the figure (section 19; section 32b "the arts each have their own *nota* arranged and marked beforehand with the figures"). The full text of the prayer was probably introduced later on in the text. Thus, the original body of the text was interspersed with the figures rather than them all being collected as an addendum at the end. If Peterson's preliminary assessment of the *Summe Sacrae Magicae* is correct about it preserving an older tradition, then there were probably several more *voces magicae* prayers in the original text but were later omitted.[16] The original Greek *Flores Aurei* probably would not have contained any Latin prologue prayers either as such Christianization would doubtfully have interested an Arab translator who held an interest in the astral magic of Pseudo-Apollonius of Tyana.

16. Peterson, *Liber Trium Animarum,* 1.

Folio from *Liber de Arte Memorativa,* Yahuda Var. 43, National Library of Israel. 1600.

III.

The Knowledge of the *Ars Notoria*

The *Ars Notoria* did not grant knowledge instantly to the practitioner after he had performed the ritual; in fact, the *Ars Notoria* explicitly states that the practitioner must study his school textbooks and go to his university classes over the course of the months-long ritual. How was education taught during the Middle Ages? What knowledge was sought out by a practitioner of the *Ars Notoria*? To answer these questions, it is important to understand the history of Western European medieval knowledge, how it was taught in the medieval institutions of learning, and what fields of knowledge were studied.

Western European medieval knowledge was largely inherited from the Greco-Roman world of the Roman Empire. The two predominant languages of learning were Greek and Latin, but when the Western Roman Empire collapsed in 476, the West witnessed the decline in those who were fluent in Greek. After the death of the philosopher Boethius (c. 477–524 CE), called "the last of the Romans and the first of the Scholastic philosophers" and who was fluent in both Greek and Latin, Europe essentially lost access to the knowledge of the ancient Greek world and entered an age of intellectual darkness. For the next thousand years, Latin became the lingua franca of learning, and Boethius's works became school textbooks and a cornerstone of the foundation of education in the West. Following the rise and expansion of Islam beginning in the eighth century, Arabic scholars took an interest in the Greek sciences and began translating those old manuscripts into Arabic and performing scientific experiments and making great discoveries. By the twelfth century, the city of Toledo became the hub for classical learning as Arab translators took those Greek manuscripts that were translated into Arabic and began translating them into Latin. Thus, the School of Toledo translators made a great contribution to Western Europe's rediscovery of ancient Greek thought and, most importantly, the works of the great philosopher Aristotle, whose thought would permeate classical learning for many years to come.

As for the institution of medieval education, Christian monasteries and cathedral schools provided formal education, and thus the Catholic Church governed and curated the inherited knowledge of the pagan Greco-Roman world. In doing so, the Catholic Church had the difficult task of balancing between disseminating ancient pagan knowledge and Christian doctrine, between orthodoxy and heresy. The pinnacle of medieval education resided in the universities, reserved for the wealthy and privileged, and where the *Ars Notoria* most likely circulated first. At the time of the *Ars Notoria,* the European universities that had been established were Bologna (1088), Oxford (c. 1096), Paris (1150), Cambridge (1209), Salamanca (1218), Padua (1222), and Naples Federico II (1224). Based on Véronèse's proposed date and provenance of the *Ars Notoria,* the handbook of magic likely passed through the university halls of Bologna and Padua first.

Access to books was limited due to the intensive time and labor involved in their production, so students would go to lectures to take notes and listen to their master teach and read from a book. Students had to rely on their memory in order to recall their newly gained subject material. The ancient Greeks provided a mnemonic technique called the method of places (Latin *loci*), which is discussed in detail in chapter IV. Schoolmasters promoted the principles of morality and virtue in training their students. Those students who excelled in memorizing classical knowledge and who could speak about it well to others were seen as virtuous, with a promising future of success. The exemplary student embodied virtues of prudence, fortitude, temperance, and justice and had a love for wisdom, demonstrating his knowledge and skills in debates with peers and hoping to receive the honor of being called a true philosopher.

ORGANIZING KNOWLEDGE

During the Middle Ages, creating taxonomies of knowledge and compiling encyclopedic treatises were popular preoccupations among intellectuals. Such enterprises were attempts to chart the very nature of knowledge itself, like a cartographer exploring the natural world. If knowledge could be schematized, then it could be understood, and therefore progress would be made in epistemology, or the theory of knowledge. The taxonomies of knowledge varied but were primarily based on two models of philosophy—the Platonic-Stoic model and the Peripatetic model.

The Platonic-Stoic model, following the work of the Greek philosopher Plato and the Stoic philosophers, was divided into three branches—natural philosophy, ethics, and logic. The Peripatetic model, following the work of the Greek philosopher Aristotle, was divided into two main branches—the theoretical and the practical. The theoretical was subdivided into the sciences—natural, mathematical, and divine (or metaphysics). The practical was subdivided into what today resmembles the social sciences and philosophy—political science, household management (i.e., economics), and moral science. Again, the taxonomies of knowledge varied from one writer to another, sometimes expanding on the thought of his predecessor or making contradictory statements; in any case, these taxonomies were not held rigidly. The philosopher Boethius, following the Peripatetic model, established the elements of the quadrivium (arithmetic, music, geometry, and astronomy) under mathematical science for the Western intellectual tradition.

The Seven Mechanical Arts

Medieval society classified a group of skilled activities under the term "mechanics" or "mechanical arts" *(artes mechanicae)*, also called adulterate or vulgar arts, because they required physical labor to perform them and as such were looked down upon by the upper classes. The mechanical arts were understood to be practiced by those of an inferior social status. Since late antiquity, these arts were considered unbecoming of a free man and thus ranked below the seven liberal arts. Johannes Scotus Eriugena (c. 815–c. 877), an Irish theologian and Neoplatonist philosopher, wrote his commentary on Martianus Capella's allegory in which he makes the first mention of the seven mechanics, though he does not identify them.[1]

According to Hugh of St. Victor (c. 1096–1141), a Saxon canon regular

1. Hansson, ed., *The Role of Technology in Science,* 14.

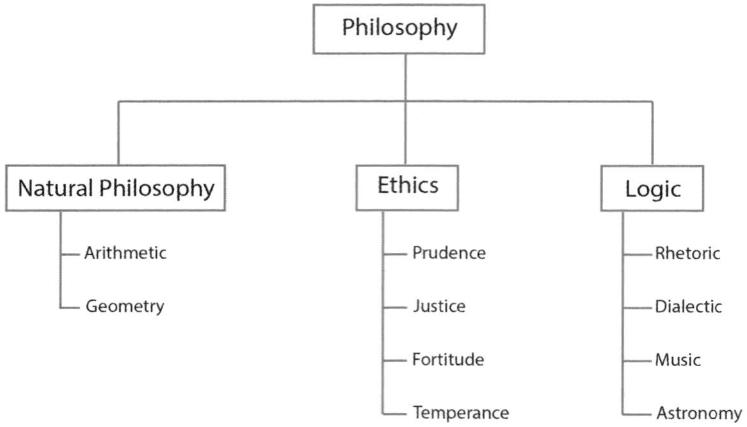

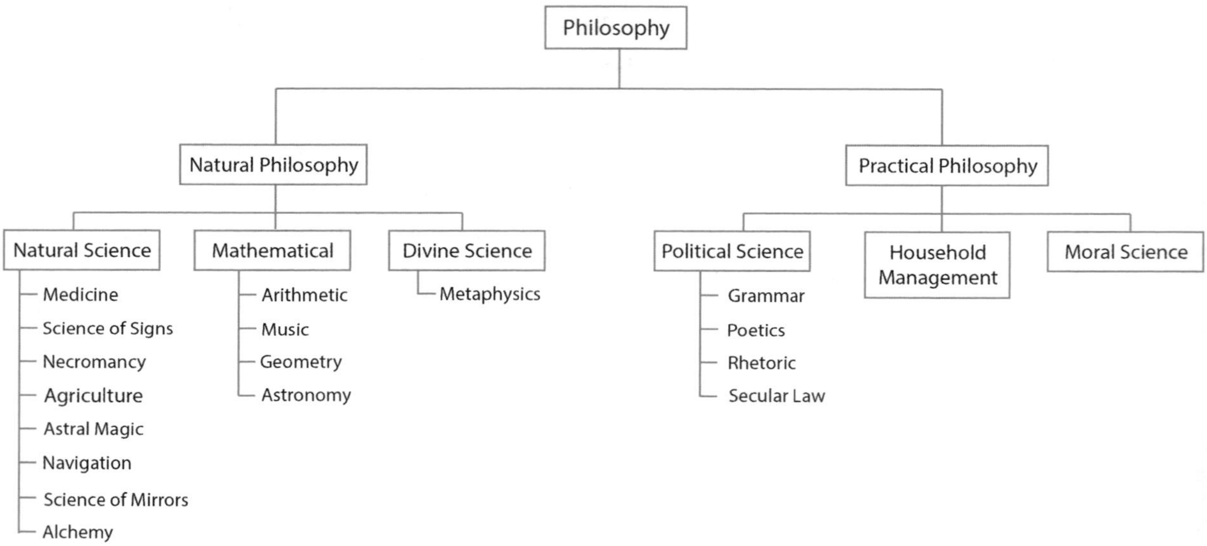

Top: The Platonic-Stoic and Peripatetic models of philosophy, Alcuin of York (Platonic-Stoic). *Bottom:* Dominicus Gundissalinus (Aristotelian). Gundissalinus says that logic is both part and instrument of philosophy and that grammar, poetics, and rhetoric are the "sciences of eloquence." Thomas Aquinas and others would debate the placement of "the middle sciences" (*scientiae mediae*), those sciences that were mathematically based sciences but dealt with natural subject matter, including the science of mirrors (i.e., optics), harmonics (i.e., music), mechanics (i.e., the science of weights and measures, parts, and joints), and astronomy. Although astronomy was considered part of the quadrivium, it also was thought to belong to the middle sciences for its mathematical demonstrations.

and theologian on mystical theology, the seven mechanics are concerned with the artificer's product, which borrows its form from nature. He draws a parallel and contrast between the seven liberal arts and the seven mechanics, in which he identifies the mechanics as follows: tailoring (*lanificium*), agriculture (*agricultura*), warfare (*armatura*), navigation (*navigatio*), hunting (*venatio*), medicine (*medicina*), *and* theatrics (*theatrica*).

Hugh of St. Victor's terminology is not to be confused with the actual art of working with mechanical parts; that is, the study of weights, measures, parts, and joints. This is important to keep in mind when reading the *Ars Notoria,* because its usage varies between Pseudo-Apollonius of the *Flores Aurei* and the Christian letter writer. The Christian letter writer thinks of the mechanical arts as the practical arts listed by Hugh of St. Victor, indicating that the practical arts cannot be learned through the notory art (section 90). In contrast, Pseudo-Apollonius of the *Flores Aurei* uses the phrase *mechanical arts* in reference to his own idiosyncratic term, *the exceptive arts* (sections 32a, 71, and 87), which are the seven kinds of divination (necromancy, hydromancy, pyromancy, chiromancy, geomancy, genethlialogy, and onomancy). Pseudo-Apollonius views the exceptive arts as practical or mechanical in the sense that they have constructive and functional applications, classed under the natural sciences."

Taxonomy within the Ars Notoria

The *Ars Notoria* contains a composite and unique taxonomy of knowledge, which proves elusive to classification and is even internally contradictory. It is unclear whether theology as a subject of study was original to the *Flores Aurei* or a late addition associated with the textual material of the *Ars Nova,* because its substantive material is found only in the *Ars Nova* material and any other mention of it has been redacted. If theology as a subject of study was a late addition, then philosophy would take its place in the first tier, adding support to a non-Christian, Greek-origin hypothesis for the *Flores Aurei.* For the *Ars Notoria,* the trivium is accepted, as is Boethius's quadrivium, as making up the seven elements of philosophy in Version A, but in Version B the quadrivium is altered to consist of medicine, music, arithmetic, and astronomy/astrology.

The *Ars Notoria* follows the Peripatetic model when delving into the "general sciences" (*generalia*), possibly analogus to the thirteenth-century

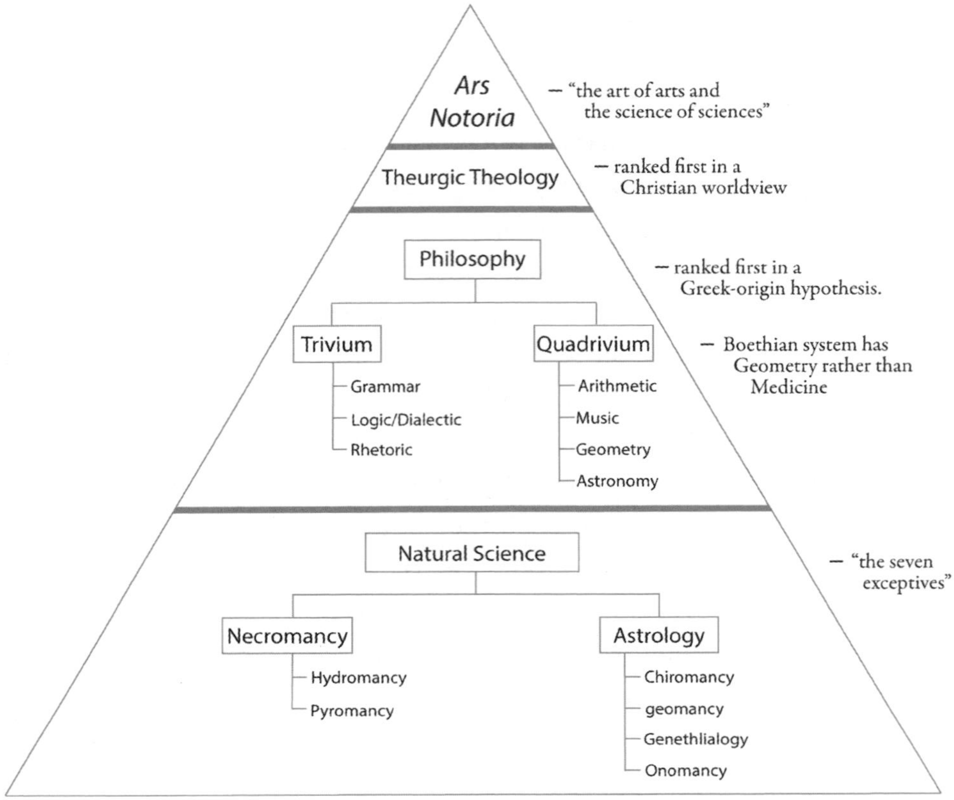

The taxonomy of knowledge according to the *Ars Notoria*

English philosopher Robert Grosseteste's subalternate sciences, which rest between the natural sciences (*physica*) and the mathematical sciences (such as arithmetic and geometry). Grosseteste's subalternate sciences included optics, music, and astronomy. Sometimes the field of mechanics, or the science of weights, was included.

The *Ars Notoria* may indicate that the general sciences are divided among the natural sciences, the mathematical sciences, and the exceptives. The *Ars Notoria* does not make this division explicit, often conflating them, understanding them to belong to a single category. In all likelihood, the author of the *Ars Notoria* would have classed the mechanical and the exceptive arts under the natural sciences. The seven exceptives are best thought of as having two main divisions—necromancy and astrology. Necromancy, along with hydromancy and pyromancy, consists of the first three exceptive arts. Astrology is subdivided into four arts: (1) chiromancy, (2) geomancy, (3) genethlialogy, and (4) onomancy. Altogether, the exceptives consist of seven magical arts of divination to predict the future and to know what is past and present, effectively mirroring the seven liberal arts. Below we will explore the divisions of knowledge as presented by the *Ars Notoria,* as well as the context and information a practitioner would be intending to learn through its ritual.

PHILOSOPHY, THE LOVE OF WISDOM

Generally speaking, the pinnacle of knowledge was philosophy, which set out to discover the truth of any matter, leading the student into a life of wisdom and virtue. However, the church fathers Clement of Alexandria and Augustine of Hippo would come to argue that philosophy served Christian theology; in making this assertion, the church symbolically asserts Christianity's triumph over pagan religion while also declaring the church's governance over the institution of education.

Now, philosophy itself, belonging to the first tier of knowledge, was divided into the seven liberal arts. The seven liberal arts are grammar, logic/dialectic, rhetoric, arithmetic, music, geometry, and astronomy. They are divided into two groups, the trivium ("three roads") and the quadrivium ("four roads"). The trivium is considered the lower division, which is encountered first in the classroom, and consists of grammar, logic/dialectic, and rhetoric. The quadrivium is the upper division, consisting of arithmetic, music, geometry, and astronomy. Boethius coined the word *quadrivium,* believing that "it was impossible to achieve the summit of perfection in the disciplines of philosophy unless one approached this noble wisdom by a kind of fourfold way."[2] The seven liberal arts were so called by the Roman orator Cicero because they were the knowledge and skills of a free man who had political freedom and citizen's rights, as well as being an elite member of society. The cognitive skills gained from a liberal arts education belonging to the ruling class were contrasted against the mechanical or productive arts belonging to the lower class. These arts became

---

2. *De Arithmetica,* Migne LXIII, 1079D, as cited in Boethius, *The Consolation of Philosophy,* xvii.

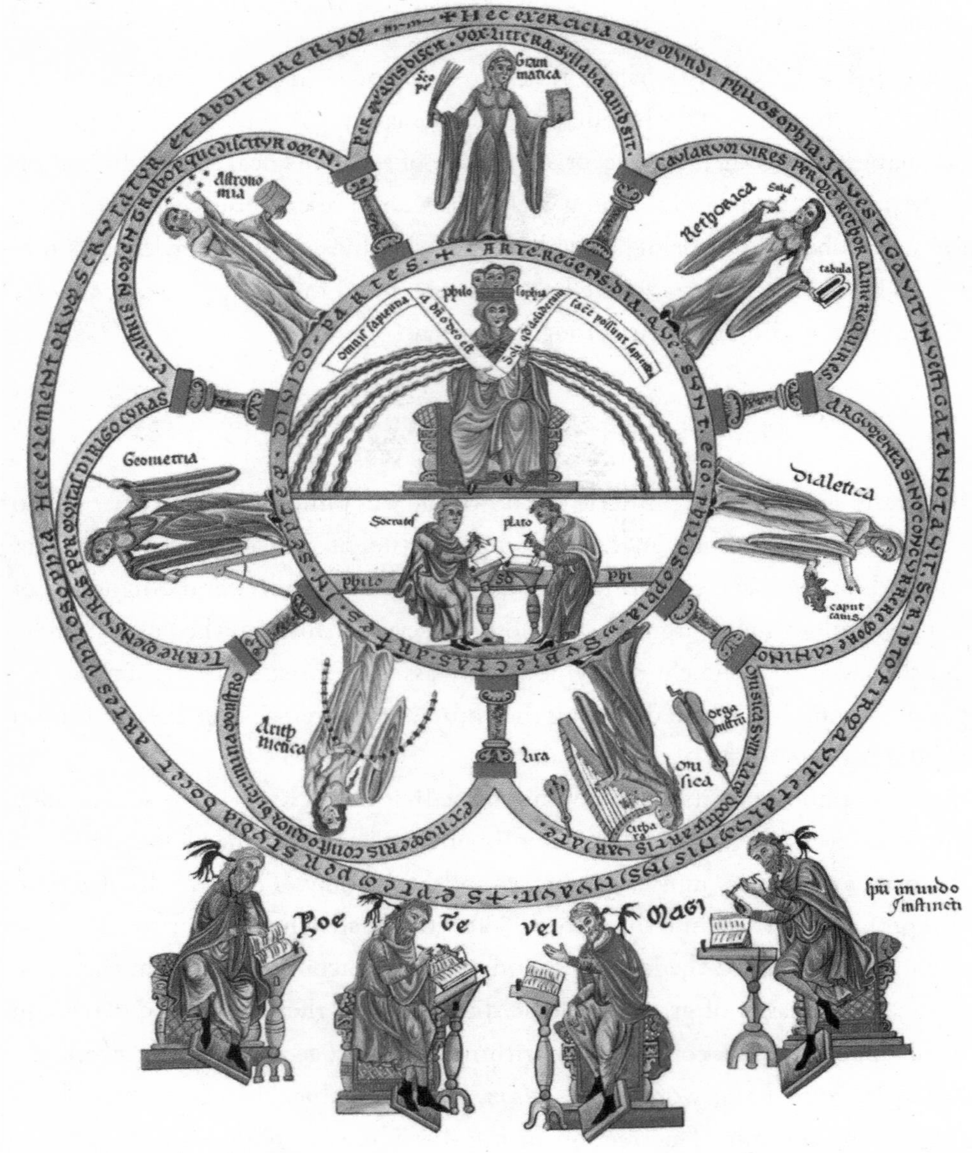

Philosophia et Septem Artes Liberales (*Philosophy and the Seven Liberal Arts*) as illustrated in the *Hortus Deliciarum* (*Garden of Delights*). Philosophy is personified as a queen who sits in the center of a circle that symbolizes a rose. She wears a crown with three heads representing the Platonic-Stoic divisions of philosophy. The scroll she holds reads, "All wisdom is given from the Lord God; the wise alone are able to make that which they desire." She is encircled with an inscription that reads, "I, Philosophy, having subjected the arts, divide [them] into seven parts, which are a divine ruling by the [Philosophical] Art." Beneath the queen sit Socrates and Plato. Surrounding the queen in a circle are seven rose petals, or archways, in which there is a single personification of each of the seven liberal arts.

known as the seven mechanical arts, or adulterine arts,[3] and belong to the second tier of knowledge.

In medieval society, this two-tier scheme of knowledge received wide acceptance; however, in the twelfth-century illuminated manuscript called the *Hortus Deliciarum* (*Garden of Delights*), compiled by Herrad of Landsberg, there is an illumination called *Philosophia et Septem Artes Liberales* (*Philosophy and the Seven Liberal Arts*) that illustrates knowledge that has been excluded and forbidden from the accepted taxonomy. The illumination depicts the personifications of Philosophy and the seven liberal arts within a grand wheel, and existing outside and below this wheel are magicians and poets sitting at desks. Beyond the influence of Philosophy, these magicians and poets have black crows sitting upon their shoulders and representing unclean spirits, cawing into their ears the forbidden knowledge of magic and poetry (i.e., fabled fictions) as they write.

THE TRIVIUM: GRAMMAR, LOGIC, AND RHETORIC

The trivium consists of the language arts—grammar, logic/dialetic, and rhetoric—and provides the entry point to a classical education. Martianus Capella (fl. c. 410–420), the Latin author of *De Nuptiis Philologiae et Mercurii* (*On the Marriage of Philology and Mercury*), was one of the earliest and most influential developers for the institution of education during the Middle Ages. *De Nuptiis* tells the story of the seven liberal arts in an entertaining manner, keeping the medieval student interested in what he was learning. It describes an allegory of Apollo, who unites Mercury with the personification of Philology in a wedding ceremony; the invited guests are the personified handmaidens of the seven liberal arts who teach their art or science and perform their talents for the audience of the Olympian deities. His work was based on the first-century BCE Roman scholar Marcus Terentius Varro's now lost *Disciplinarum Libri IX* (*Nine Books of the Disciplines*), which was an encyclopedia of the liberal arts based on Greek sources; Varro included medicine and architecture, but these arts were demoted by later authors. The subjects are discussed in an overview here, while the details that are illustrated as related pictorial figures called *notae* are examined in chapter V.

3. Lind, "Why the Liberal Arts Still Matter," 52–58.

The Ars Grammatica *(Art of Grammar)*

Latin was the language of learning, so studying grammar was the first step to acquiring a classical education. Capella says grammar has four functions: (1) to read, (2) to write, (3) to comprehend, and (4) to apply critical thinking. The foundation of learning Latin grammar was taught by studying the works of the Roman grammarian Aelius Donatus (fl. mid-fourth century CE), the Latin grammarian Priscian Caesariensis (fl. sixth century CE), and their commentators. In addition, the art of grammar (*ars grammatica*) was studied by making analyses of the poems of Vergil, Horace, and the texts on rhetoric.[4]

Logic and Dialectic, the Art of Reason and Debate

The medieval curriculum placed great emphasis on the study of logic, seeing it as the foundation of the trivium. With the rediscovery of Aristotelian works on logic in the mid-twelfth and thirteenth centuries, it became even more important among scholars in the universities at the time of the *Ars Notoria*.

Aristotle lists ten different ways of describing something: (1) substance, (2) quantity, (3) quality, (4) relation, (5) activity, (6) passivity, (7) time, (8) place, (9) position, and (10) state. Once things are defined, the next step is making statements about them that are called propositions and that form the basic elements of an argument. Every proposition has a subject and a predicate. The predicates are divided into five parts—genus, species, difference, property, and accident—according to how they relate to the subject.

These categories would be described by the Greek Neoplatonist philosopher Porphyry (c. 234–305 CE) in his *Isagoge* (*Introduction*) as a scale. Boethius's Latin translation of the *Isagoge* would become the student's introductory textbook on logic throughout the Middle Ages. Boethius also supplied an illustration of Aristotle's "scale of being" (*scala praedicamentalis*), which became known as the Tree of Porphyry. This type of visual representation likely informed some of the imagery of the figures found in the *Ars Notoria*.

All propositions are meant to either affirm or deny something. By deductive logic, one might affirm a series of propositions to lead to a particular conclusion. Aristotle's categorical syllogism consists of three propositions—two premises and a conclusion. An example of a categorical syllogism is as follows:

4. See appendix A8, "Annotated Bibilography of Medieval Scholarship."

Socrates is a man.
All men are mortal.
Therefore, Socrates is mortal.

Also illustrated in this example are the two kinds of terms—universal (men) and particular (Socrates). Aristotle established four kinds of categorical

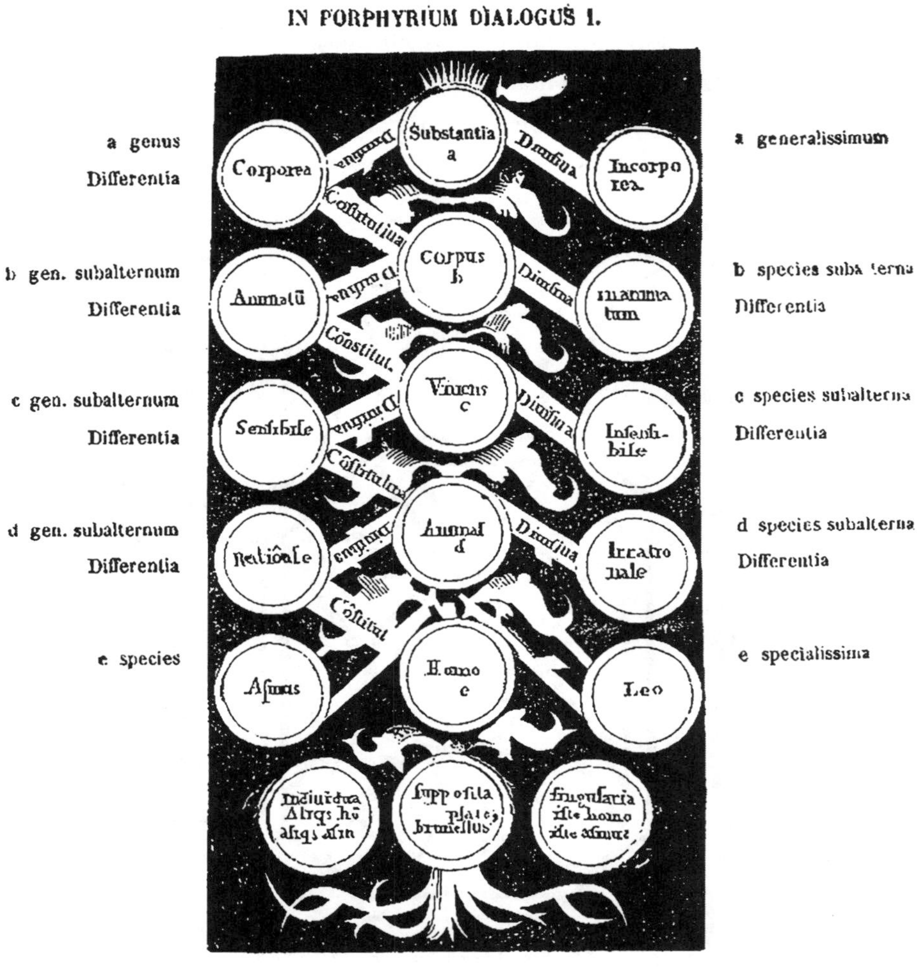

The Tree of Porphyry from Boethius's commentary on Porphyry's *Isagoge.* At the top is "substance," which branches into "corporeal" and "incorporeal," which leads to "body," which branches into "inanimate" and "animate," which leads to "single [living being]," which branches into "sensible" and "insensible," which leads to "animal," which branches into "irrational" and "rational," which ends with "human," which some tree diagrams give specific names such as Socrates or Plato.

propositions using the qualifiers "all," "some," and "no" to assert a relationship between two different categories. Boethius was the first to illustrate the four categorical propositions in the square of oppositions as seen in the figure below. Today, modern notation uses these four vowels to represent each of the four categorical propositions.

The four categorical propositions are:

Universal affirmation (A): All men are animals.
Universal negation (E): No man is an animal.
Particular affirmation (I): Some men are animals.
Particular negation (O): Some men are not animals.

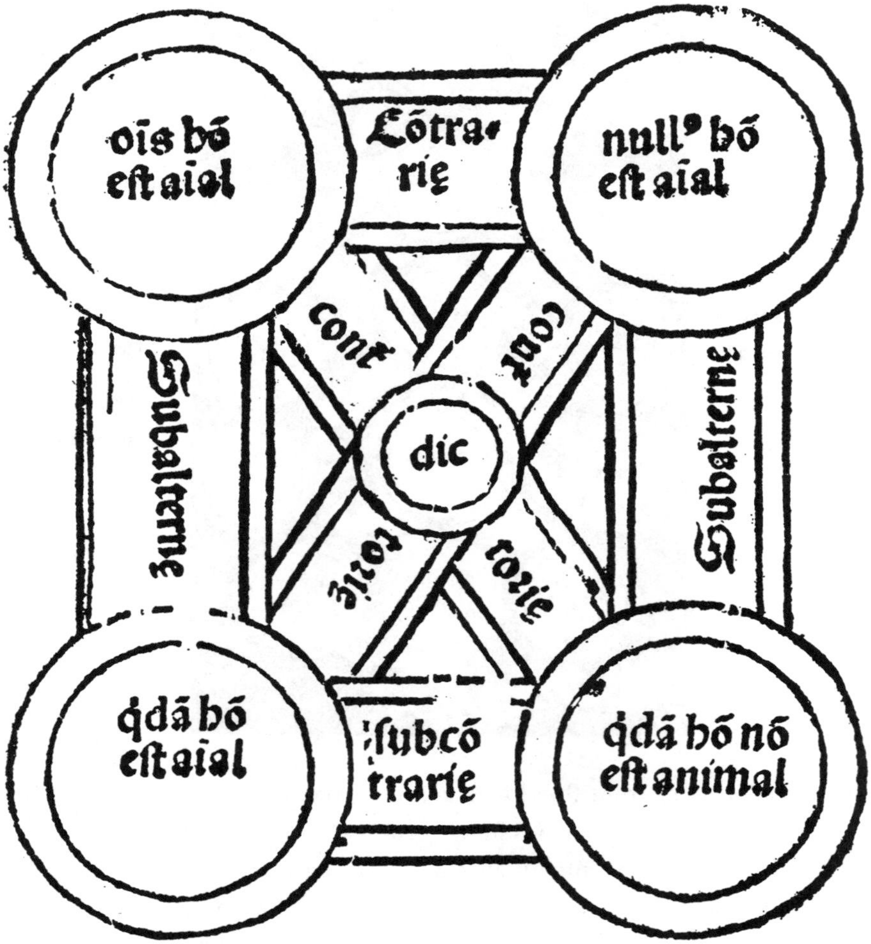

The square of oppositions

The medieval logicians summarized their understanding of the syllogism by the maxim *dictum de omni et null,* meaning "of all and none," which says that whatever is affirmed or denied of a whole must be affirmed or denied of a part.

Aristotle also mentions that propositions make claims about what *necessarily, possibly,* or *impossibly* is the case; these propositions are called *hypothetical.* Aristotle gives the example of a hypothetical sea battle that will or will not occur tomorrow. He says the necessary truth of such a proposition does not make the conclusion of either alternative to be necessarily true. Moreover, he says that one's personal belief about what will happen in the future does not determine whether the individual propositions are true.

Rhetoric, the Art of Persuasion

Rhetoric is the art of eloquence and persuasive speech, and, according to the Roman lawyer and philosopher Cicero, its highest purpose is to bring positive influence to political decisions made by the state for the good of its people, including the founding of cities, the forging of alliances, and bringing an end to wars. In rhetoric, there are three types of argument: (1) judicial (to accuse or defend), (2) demonstrative or epideictic (to praise or blame), and (3) deliberative (to persuade or dissuade).

A speech has five parts, called the five canons of rhetoric, and they are as follows: (1) invention, (2) disposition, (3) style, (4) memory, and (5) delivery. Invention is the discovery of valid arguments to render one's case plausible. The disposition is the arrangement of the arguments in proper order. The style is the proper expression of language used for the invented matter. Memory serves the orator in recalling the matter and words of his speech. The delivery is how the orator uses his voice, countenance, and gestures to convey his meaning.

Every controversial subject has a principal question about an issue (*constitutio*) in regard to a fact, a definition, the nature of an act, or the legal process. In court, the conflict of pleas from the two opposing parties determines the issue. Thus, there are four principal questions: (1) the conjecture about a fact regarding whether an event happened, (2) the definition of the action that happened, (3) the quality or nature of what happened, and (4) the translative issue in which a legal action is taken and ought to be transferred to another court or result in an altered plea. All other questions are subordinate to these. By identifying the issue and any related questions, the orator can begin to write and memorize his speech.

THE QUADRIVIUM: ARITHMETIC, MUSIC, GEOMETRY, AND ASTRONOMY

The quadrivium is built upon the foundation of the language arts. The quadrivium is considered the upper division of the seven liberal arts. For Boethius, the quadrivium is ordered on a continuum of pure mathematics to the natural sciences, from arithmetic (the study of number theory) to music (ratio and proportion) to geometry (the study of space, distance, shape, size, and position of figures) to astronomy/astrology (the study of celestial objects and phenomena moving through space and time while also making predictions about future events on earth).[5] Because Boethius's writings were the mainstay of the medieval curriculum, this was the order followed, establishing the tradition of classical learning for the sciences.

As with the trivium, the fundamentals of the quadrivium are explored here. Further detail on the connection with the figures will be given in chapter V.

Arithmetic, Number Theory, and Arithmology

For Boethius and the medieval world, the word *arithmetic* meant the study of number theory in which numbers or numeric ratios represented the foundation of reality, expressing the essence of things and originating from a divine source. Arithmetic was understood as a scientific pursuit involving philosophical and metaphysical questions and problems, more than just basic computation as it is understood today. Boethius's *De Arithemetica* (*On Arithmetic*) was the standard textbook for the medieval student, and is itself an adaptation of Nicomachus of Gerasa's *Introducción a la Aritmética* (*Introduction to Arithemetic*), which explains number theory. Number theory is the study of the set of positive whole numbers (1, 2, 3, etc.) and their relationship with one another.

Boethius's adapted work explores the definitions and properties of number, including their relationship to geometry. Nicomachus defines *number* as, "a limited multitude or a combination of units or a flow (or, series) of quantity made up of units; and the first division of number is even and odd."[6] He also

5. For the glosser of the *Ars Notoria,* strangely enough, the quadrivium consisted of "music, medicine, arithmetic, and astronomy," although there are *notae* for these as well as for geometry.
6. D'Ooge, trans., *Nicomachus of Gerasa,* 190.

Gregor Reisch, *Margarita Philosophica* (Pearl of Philosophy), 1503 woodcut titled *Allegory of Arithmetic*. On the left sits Boethius, using Hindu-Arabic numerals, while on the right Pythagoras is using an abacus. In the center is Arithmetic personified, holding two open books.

defines any *integer* as one half the sum of the two integers on each side of it in the natural sequence (e.g., 1, 2, 3, etc., excluding zero):

$$\frac{m = (m - 1) + (m + 1)}{2}$$

For Nicomachus, unity was highly regarded as the "natural starting point of all numbers." In this way, Boethius defines *number* as a stream of multitude (i.e., demarcated, delimited, and countable things, such as individual pebbles) which issue forth from a principal source or unity.

Nicomachus also drew upon the Pythagorean tradition of arithmology—the study of the esoteric significance of number. Martianus Capella echoes this ancient tradition by describing the significance of the decad (10) in the *tetractys* (a triangular arrangement of four rows), expressed as 1 + 2 + 3 + 4 = 10 (see figure, below). In Capella, Lady Arithmetic says, "The monad is unity, it alone is self-sufficient; from it, other things are generated; it alone is the seminal force of all numbers; it alone is the measure and cause of increases and the extent of losses. The monad is everywhere a *part,* and everywhere the *whole*."[7] Capella follows Boethius in defining *number* as a stream of multitude issuing forth from unities (i.e., the primary source) and returning to it. In other words, number is differentiated from the unit, the source of all numbers.[8] By understanding Nicomachus's definition of number and integer, it becomes clear why the *Ars Notoria* claims that there are one and a half figures (*notae*) belonging to arithmetic, rather than stating that there are simply two figures (*notae*).

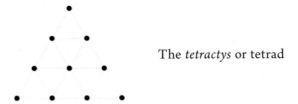

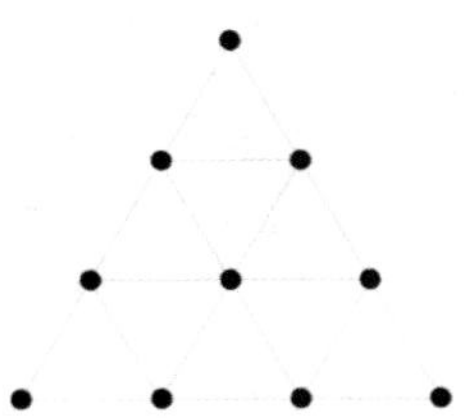

The *tetractys* or tetrad

7. Stahl, Johnson, and Burge, trans. and eds., *Martianus Capella and the Seven Liberal Arts,* Vol. 2, The Marriage of Philology and Mercury, No. 84, Records of Western Civilization, (New York: Columbia University Press, 1977), 276. Italics are mine.

8. D'Ooge, trans., *Nicomachus of Gerasa*. See also Waterfield, trans., *Theology of Arithmetic;* and Otisk, *The Definitions of Number in Boethius' Introduction to Arithmetic,* 14, 16–26.

Music, Harmony of the Celestial Spheres and the Soul

Music, or harmonics, was the study of number in time as proportions between musical intervals. Martianus Capella's principal sources for teaching his reader about music comes from the *Elementa Harmonica* (*Elements of Harmony*) by the fourth-century BCE Greek Peripatetic philosopher Aristoxenus of Tarentum and the three-volume work titled *Peri Mousikes* (*About Music*) by the Greek author Aristides Quintilianus (fl. late third or early fourth century CE). Aside from Capella, the Latin West's central textbook was Boethius's *De Institutione Musica* (*On the Institution of Music*), which was based upon another work by Nicomachus of Gerasa, *Manuel d'harmonique* (*The Manual of Harmonics*). The average student would learn about ancient Greek music theory, focusing on understanding the mathematical proportions rather than on playing a musical instrument.

In addition, it was thought that the classical seven planets each emitted a particular sound according to its size, speed, and position, although no one on earth could hear these sounds. A musical note was assigned to each of the planets as shown in the table below.

CLASSICAL PLANETARY HARMONICS

Planet	Pitch	Name Given by Nicomachus
Saturn	E	Hypate
Jupiter	F	Parhypate
Mars	G	Hypermese, or Lichanos
Sun	A	Mese
Mercury	B♭	Paramese, or Trite
Venus	C	Paranete
Moon	D	Nete

The musical notes assigned to the classical seven planets according to Nicomachus in *The Manual of Harmonics of Nicomachus the Pythagorean*, trans. Flora R. Levin

Aristides Quintilianus describes a very Platonic perspective of how the soul descends from the heavens to the earth and settles within the human body. The soul, pure and unadulterated, wanders among the heavenly spheres, joyful in the beauty of the cosmos, drawing to itself certain ethereal influences that are interwoven and bonded to the soul. As the soul descends to the earth, it becomes forgetful of the beautiful things of the cosmos, and it desires to enter into a body. Once the soul is embodied in the human figure, it exchanges its nonphysical form for matter, yet it retains the certain harmony of the celestial spheres that bonded to it in its wanderings so that when similar musical proportions are heard, the corresponding passions within the soul are moved at the same time.[9]

Macrobius's *Commentarii in Somnium Scipionis* (*Commentary on the Dream of Scipio*) also provides an explanation of the relationship between numbers and musical proportions in both the Platonic World-Soul and the human soul. Macrobius lists the two mathematical sequences from Plato's *Timaeus:* the even numbers (1, 2, 4, 8) and the odd numbers (1, 3, 9, 27) that form what would be called Plato's Lambda.[10] Macrobius explains Plato's Pythagorean cosmogony in which the Demiurge, the creator, made the World-Soul from a mixture of Sameness, Difference, and Existence whereby the Demiurge took a strip from this mixture and divided it into harmonic intervals consisting of these two mathematical sequences.[11] These two sequences are generated by multiplying

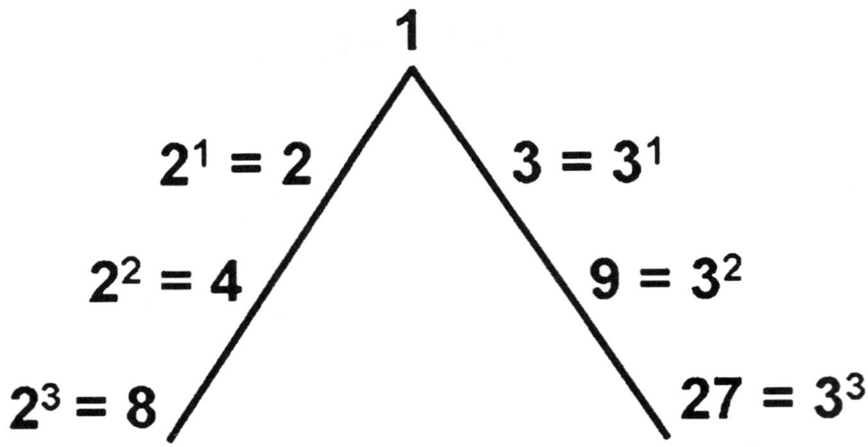

Plato's Lambda

9. Godwin, *Harmony of the Spheres,* 53.

10. Plato's Lambda is so called because it resembles the Greek letter *lambda.*

11. Stahl, trans., *Commentary on the Dream of Scipio,* 2.2.14.

1 by 2 and by 3 (see Plato's Lambda, opposite). These mathematical sequences show the ratios productive of the octave (2:1), the octave and a fifth (3:1), the double octave (4:1), the triple octave (8:1), the fifth (3:2), the fourth (4:3), and the whole tone (9:8); thus, by these harmonic intervals, a musical harmony is said to exist between the World-Soul and the human soul.[12]

Geometry, Measuring the Earth

Medieval geometry applied the principles in Euclid's *Elements* to measuring the earth's shape, size, dimensions, position, and regions, which consequently involved the study of geography. Medieval geometers understood that the earth was spherical, as maintained by the Greek philosopher Dicaearchus of Messana (c. 350–285 BCE), and made arguments for the case.[13] The circumference of the earth and the tilt of the earth's axis was first accurately calculated by the Greek geographer Eratosthenes of Cyrene (c. 276–194 BCE).

During the Middle Ages, people believed in a geocentric model of the universe in which the earth was stationary and sat at the bottom of the universe while the other planets orbited above; this is a belief inherited from the ancient Greco-Roman world and would carry on for centuries thanks to the Greek astronomer Ptolemy. The earth was divided into five terrestrial climates (*climata*), or circles (*circuli*), spanning the known world. In modern terms, these five zones are the Arctic Zone, the Northern Temperate Zone, the Equatorial Zone, the Southern Temperate Zone, and the Antarctic Zone. Only the two temperate zones were thought to be habitable. These five climates are illustrated in maps of the world (*mappae mundi*). Furthermore, the earth was understood to be divided into a Northern and Southern Hemisphere, and it was known, even then, that their seasons ran opposite to one another. Now, the known world consisted of four landmasses—Europe, Asia, Africa, and the Antipodes (a fourth unknown land). In practical matters, medieval geometers participated in land surveying and architecture, and the science (particularly spherical geometry) had further application in the study of astronomy.[14]

---

12. Levin, trans. and ed., *The Manual of Harmonics of Nicomachus,* 115.

13. Stahl, Johnson, and Burge, trans. and eds., *Martianus Capella,* 220–21.

14. Russo and Levy, trans., *Forgotten Revolution,* 273–77.

Astronomy and Astrology, Measuring the Heavens

For the medieval student, astronomy combined the study of music (i.e., harmonic intervals) and geometry. It was not just the study of the movement of the celestial spheres and knowledge of the constellations; it also included meteorology and celestial navigation. At the center of the universe was the immobile earth, which was thought to be surrounded by spheres of water, air, and fire. Beyond these were the rotating celestial spheres (i.e., the seven classical planets) set within a fifth element called aether, and beyond the planets lay the celestial sphere of the fixed stars. The principal circles of the heavens include: (1) the celestial equator, (2) the ecliptic, (3) the Tropic of Cancer, (4) the Tropic of Capricorn, (5) the Arctic Circle, (6) the Antarctic Circle, (7) the equinoctial colure, and (8) the solstitial colure, all of which are represented on an armillary sphere.

Prior to the twelfth century, astrological knowledge was largely known through Boethius's *Consolation Philosophiae* (*Consolation of Philosophy*) and Isidore of Seville's *Etymologiae* (*Etymologies*). Isidore made the distinction between superstitious astrology and natural astrology. "Superstitious" astrologers would cast horoscopes to predict the character and fate of a person, while "natural" astrologers predicted meteorological phenomena and assessed when to administer medicine to medical patients via what was called medical astrology.

Following the Arabic-to-Latin translation boom of the twelfth century, European Christians gained access to a great wealth of astrological treatises, with the most influential being Ptolemy's *Almagest* and the *Tetrabiblos*. Other important works include Albumasar's *Liber Introductorius Maior* (*Introduction to Astrological Prediction*) and his *De Magnis Coniunctionibus* (*On the Great Conjunctions*), Bernardus Silvestri's *Cosmographia,* Michael Scot's *Liber Introductorius* (*Introductory Book*), and Guido Bonatti's *Liber Astronomicus* (*Book of Astronomy*). The study of astrology would spread from the clergy to the courts and enter the universities.[15]

---

15. Forshaw, "The Occult Middle Ages," 34–38.

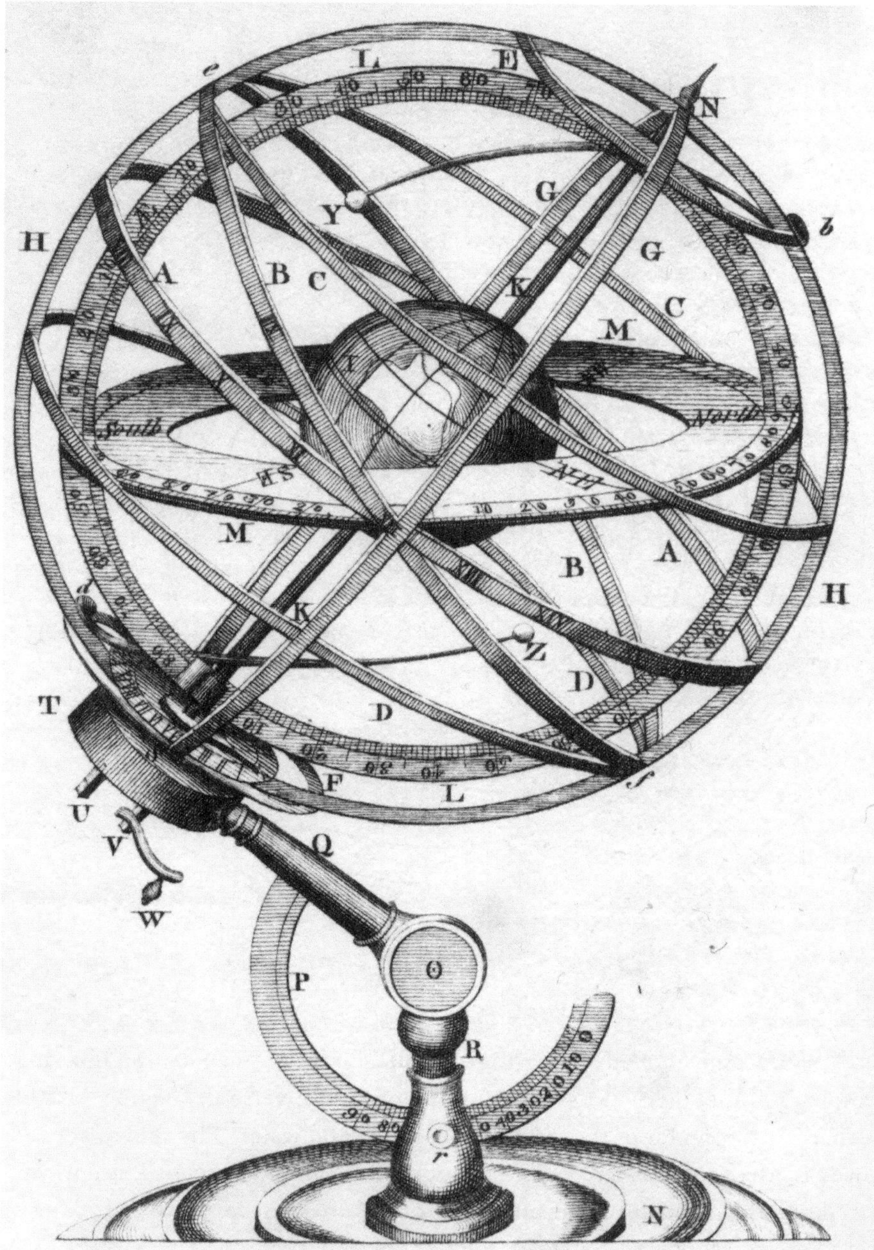

Armillary sphere. Presented by a Society of Gentlemen in Scotland, *Encyclopedia Britannica*, vol. 2, p. 681, from plate LXXXVII. (1) The celestial equator is labeled *A*; (2) the ecliptic is labeled *B*, which is the path of the Sun passing through the twelve zodiac signs; (3) the Tropic of Cancer is labeled *C*; (4) the Tropic of Capricorn is labeled *D*; (5) the Arctic Circle is labeled *E*; (6) the Antarctic Circle is labeled *F*; (7) the equinoctial colure is labeled *G*; and (8) the solstitial colure is labeled *H*.

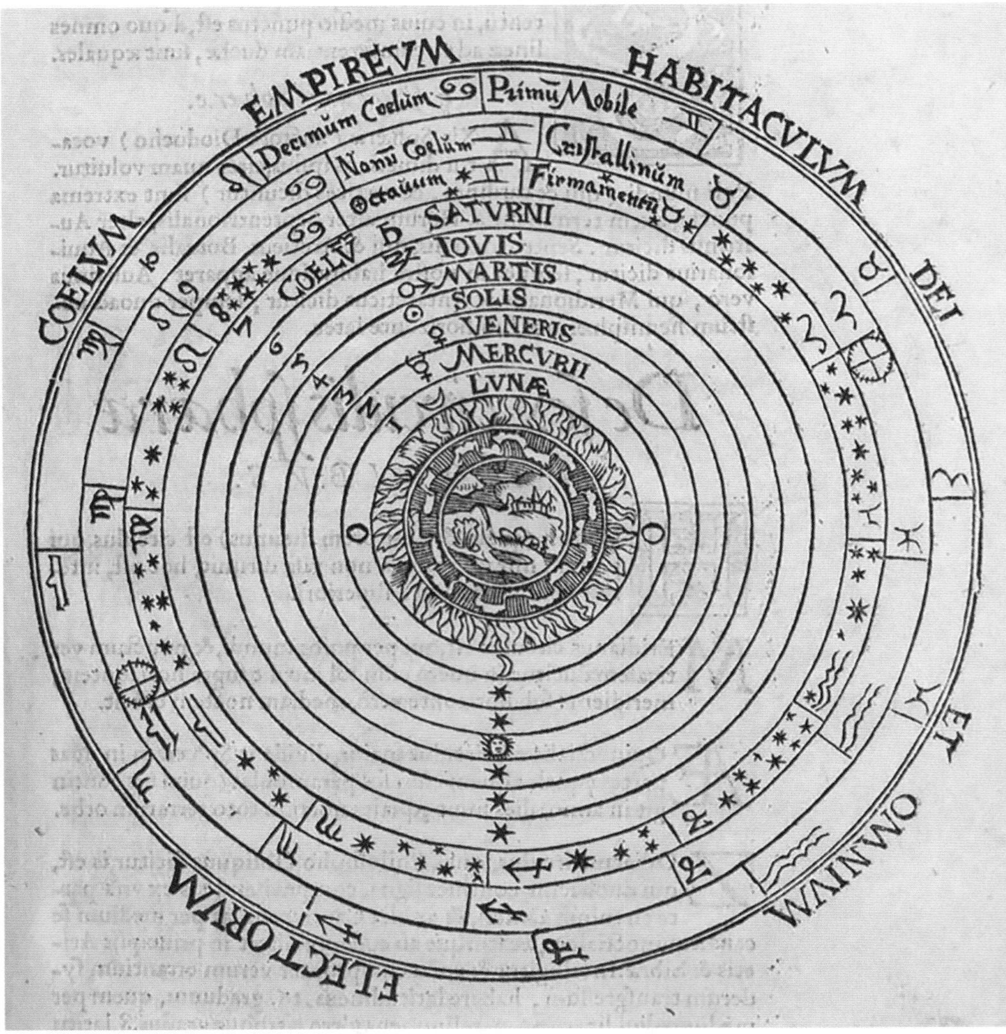

Peter Apian, *Cosmographia*, 1550 (Linda Hall Library of Science, Engineering, and Technology, Kansas City, Missouri). Model of the universe displaying Aristotelian influence. At the center of the universe lies earth and water. The sphere above is air, followed by the sphere of fire, where meteors and comets are seen. The surrounding celestial spheres from inner to outer are those of the seven classical planets: the Moon (*Lunae*), Mercury (*Mercurii*), Venus (*Veneris*), the Sun (*Solis*), Mars (*Martis*), Jupiter (*Iovis*), and Saturn (*Saturni*). The next outer sphere belongs to the firmament of fixed stars and the visible constellations. Due to the precession of the equinoxes, which creates the gap between the visible and the notional divisions of the twelve signs of the zodiac, medieval Christian astronomers designated another sphere, called the Crystallinum, which holds the eternal version of the zodiac. Beyond the known world lies the prime mover, or God.

MEDICINE, THE EIGHTH LIBERAL ART

In the classical era, Varro included medicine as one of the liberal arts, but it would be demoted by later authors.[16] Martianus Capella briefly mentions that the personifications of Medicine and Architecture stand by in waiting, "but since these ladies are concerned with mortal subjects and their skill lies in mundane matters . . . it will not be inappropriate to disdain and reject them."[17]

Medieval Europe inherited its medical theory of the four humors from the classic Greco-Roman world. The humoral theory states that there are four principal fluids of the human body—black bile, yellow bile, phlegm, and blood—that must be kept in homeostasis to be healthy. Any imbalance of these fluids would lead to disease. Just as Greek philosophy saw a decline and became intellectually stagnant in medieval Europe, so did the practice of medicine until new translations arrived thanks to Arabic scholars in the twelfth century. As the Arabs brought renewed interest in medicine with their translations and new discoveries, thereby elevating the social status of the medical practice at large, it is plausible that the *Ars Notoria* was influenced by this wave of new translations. It is shortly thereafter that the *Ars Notoria* emerges and medicine is included as a discipline for study.

The *Ars Notoria* holds interest in the prognostication of the medical diagnosis and provides prayer instruction dedicated to this art.[18] This same fascination with prognostication is further supported by the veiled Sphere of Life and Death, a prognostic tool used by medical practitioners, as the notory art's figure of medicine.[19] It seems quite probable that the *Ars Notoria*'s true author sourced the Sphere of Life and Death from the *Alchandreana* corpus, a tenth-century collection of astrological and prognosticative Latin texts, which was one of the first written collections of Islamic

16. The Greek word for *natural philosophy* (φυσική, *phusike*) would lose its classical meaning by the twelfth century. Then, the Latin word *physica* would become associated with medicine. The interaction between natural philosophy and medicine would carry on into the modern period. See Bylebyl, "The Medical Meaning of *Physica*."

17. Stahl, Johnson, and Burge, trans. and eds., *Martianus Capella,* 346.

18. *Ars Notoris,* sections 28–30.

19. See chapter IV, "Analysis of the Figures."

science to be acquired by Europeans.[20] This same *Alchandreana* corpus likely provides the source material for other divinatory practices mentioned in the *Ars Notoria*.

THEOLOGY, THE QUEEN OF THE SCIENCES

Clement of Alexandria (c. 153–220 CE), in his *Stromata* (*Miscellanies*), makes the case that classical learning proceeded from God and therefore acts as a preparation for the Gospel. He says that Philosophy serves Wisdom as her handmaiden, saying:

> The encyclical branches of study [i.e., music, geometry, grammar, rhetoric, etc.] contribute to philosophy, which is their mistress; so also, philosophy itself co-operates for the acquisition of wisdom. For philosophy is the study of wisdom, and wisdom is the knowledge of things divine and human; and their causes.[21]

Therefore, wisdom concerning divine things, understood here as theology, rules the seven liberal arts. For Boethius, theology is a subdivision of philosophy that deals with abstract ideas, which are motionless and capable of being separated from matter.[22] During the rediscovery of Aristotle, the question of the role of Greek philosophy and its relationship to Christian theology was raised. Theologians like Thomas Aquinas sought to make Greek philosophy subservient to Christian theology, thereby elevating theology to the royal position as queen of the sciences.

As far as the *Ars Notoria* is concerned, philosophy is indeed the handmaiden of theology. The *Ars Notoria* says that the seven prayers belonging to philosophy are actually augmentations of the five prayers of theology.[23] Thus, in the hierarchical structure of knowledge, theology reigns supreme as queen over philosophy, which itself consists of the seven liberal arts. A

---

20. See Juste, *Les Alchandreana primitifs,* 325–30, 386–87.

21. Clement of Alexandria, *Stromata,* 306.

22. Boethius, *On the Holy Trinity,* 2.66–67.

23. *Ars Notoria,* sections 90 and 102.

couple of the prayers belonging to theology suggest that the *notae* of theology were intended for the use of studying the Bible and attaining the gift of the Holy Spirit to speak in tongues; other prophetic, mystical, and visionary experiences may also be implied.[24] In fact, the *Ars Notoria* may be more interested in a "theurgic" theology, which involves communicating and working with angelic powers. There is no indication that the *Ars Notoria* references any specific theological writings or theologians to be singled out for the study of theology.

BEYOND THE SEVEN HEAVENLY VIRTUES

Developing moral character was another important part of the medieval education; it was rooted in virtue ethics, which asks, "How should we live?" The four classical cardinal virtues as identified by Plato and Aristotle are prudence, justice, temperance, and fortitude. These provided the basic moral compass for medieval students. Thomas Aquinas identified three theological virtues in citing 1 Corinthians 13 as faith, hope, and charity. Together, the cardinal and theological virtues created the seven Christian virtues.

The *Ars Notoria* also provides figures for three special virtues: (1) the figure of chastity; (2) the figure of justice, peace, and fear; and (3) the figure of reprehension and taciturnity.

Chastity: *Chastity* is defined as "refraining from any sexual conduct." Following the release of Pope Gregory's list of seven deadly sins in 590 CE, chastity was thought of as a Christian virtue in opposition to lust. The *Ars Notoria* says the figure of chastity was given to Solomon so that if the operator were to become aroused by sensual pleasure while performing the holy work, then he is to use it along with its two prayers. The text promises that by the prayers and the inspection of the figure "it will cease all the evil self-gratifications of libidinous pleasure from you, and you will be able to proceed safely in this holy work to acquire any knowledge."[25]

24. See chapter V, "Analysis of the Figures."

25. *Ars Notoria,* NS 140.

Justice, Peace, and Fear: The *Ars Notoria* describes the figure of justice, peace, and fear as having three virtues and three functions:

> [T]he first is the virtue of justice, the second is the virtue of possessing peace, the third is the virtue of expelling fear. But if you want to uphold true justice through yourself against others, or to obtain [it] at the hands of someone for another, or if you want to live peaceably, or to negotiate peace with some adversary, or if you want to go into some dangerous place without fear about which you doubt, or to impetrate some business without fear, [then] you must inspect this figure and its signs.[26]

Reprehension and Taciturnity: The *Ars Notoria* describes the figure of reprehension and taciturnity[27] thus:

> [I]f you propose and allege some knowledge or some serious claim[28] in the presence of others and you had publicly incited a powerful person, some judge, or principal authority, and you will have wanted to demonstrate [your knowledge or claim], and because you have so much grace that it is to be subject to you and it is consented to your statements,[29] and each [statement] that you allege and propose[30] is to be conceded to you in a brief amount of time, and [thus] they all become silent, [and] they do not say anything against you, nor do they reprehend [what] you have said.[31]

THE SEVEN EXCEPTIVES, OR THE FORBIDDEN ARTS

There are seven exceptives, which are seven magical arts of divination, that are listed in the *Ars Notoria:* hydromancy, pyromancy, nigromancy,[32] chiromancy,

---

26. *Ars Notoria,* NS 144.

27. Véronèse mistranslates and misunderstands this as the "note of self-mastery and silence," thinking the Latin word *reprehensio* referred to the rhetorical connotation that actually means "self-correction."

28. Or, legal case.

29. That is to say, the operator has so much grace from having performed the operation of the *Ars Notoria.*

30. That is to say, having said your argument or defense.

31. *Ars Notoria,* NS 148.

32. The term *nigromancy* literally means "black divination" or "black magic"; however, the word itself has a contentious history. For the *Ars Notoria* writer, it simply means necromancy.

geomancy, genethlialogy (*geonogia*), and onomancy (*neonegia*). This categorization of seven magical arts is particular to the *Ars Notoria*. The Roman author Marcus Terentius Varro (116–27 BCE) provides a list of divinations based on the four elements (*geomantia, hydromantia, aeromantia,* and *pyromantia*); it is the oldest known list of divinations and often quoted by later authors. Although Varro never explains the magical techniques employed in these divinations, his list appears to be concerned with interpreting the portents of natural phenomena (i.e., the disturbances of earth, water, air, and fire), such as earthquakes, the floating or sinking of cakes of barley meal cast into water,[33] blowing winds, and the flickering of flames.[34]

The *Ars Notoria*'s list omits aeromancy (*aeromantia*), indicating that Varro's list was not being followed. Rather, the *Ars Notoria* writer was classifying the divination of "the seven exceptives" as divided into two groups: (1) hydromancy, pyromancy, and nigromancy; and (2) chiromancy, geomancy, genethlialogy, and onomancy.

In the first group, the three divinations each receive their own brief descriptions. In the most basic terms, hydromancy is divination by water, pyromancy is divination by fire, and nigromancy (or necromancy) is divination by consulting the dead. The *Ars Notoria* writer says for summoning the evil dead,[35] "it is to be defined by *hydros*—water [and] *pyros*—fire." He says that hydromancy is employed to gain knowledge from "a ghost of standing or running water" and that necromancy involves "the sacrifice of dead animals," which are offered upon a sacrifical fire.[36] In this way, hydromancy and pyromancy are understood as serving the purpose of necomancy (i.e., hydromancy and pyromancy are subdivisions of necromancy).

In the second group, the four divinations belong "*sub astrologia*" (under astrology). In the most basic terms, chiromancy (another word for palmistry) is divination by the hand, and geomancy is divination by making points, either by stabbing the earth with a stick or making marks on a wax tablet with a stylus.

33. Pausanias, *Guide to Greece,* 3.23.8.

34. Plutarch, *Parallel Lives;* Cicero, *Pro Cluentio,* 19–22; Apuleius, *The Golden Ass,* 11–12; Pliny the Elder, *Natural History,* 18.84.

35. See the section on hydromancy on page 89 regarding scrying via water basins. Also, recall that in Betz, ed., *Greek Magical Papyri,* xiv, 1–92, certain ritual offerings are placed upon the brazier to attract the dead.

36. *Ars Notoria,* section 71.

Chiromancy establishes its astrological association according to one of the oldest treatises titled *Chiromantia Parva* (*Small Chiromancy*), which gives an elaborate description of the journey of the human soul passing through the cosmos and receiving imprints in the hand by the celestial powers, concluding, "Indeed, the celestial order above revealed the infallible ideas of which certain influence and signs of permanence pour through the lines in the hand."[37] Geomancy is associated with astrology, having a special astro-geomancy chart and many geomantic elements assigned astrological correspondences. Arguably, the two otherwise unattested terms *geonogia* and *neonegia* are corrupted and/or abbreviated Greek words mistransliterated into Latin for genethlialogy and onomancy, respectively.[38] Genethlialogy (Greek γενεθλιαλογία; Latin *genethlialogia*), better known as natal astrology, is the investigation of nativities, by which an astrologer makes a horoscope or birth chart for predictions about the good and bad fortunes of the person in question. Onomancy (Greek ὀνομαμᾰντείᾱ; Latin *onomamanteia*) is divination by a person's name. Onomancy takes the letters of a person's name, converts each letter into a numerical value, and then applies certain algorithms to determine the person's fate; because such computations involve the planets and lunar mansions, onomancy was classified under astrology.

Compared with the liberal arts and moral virtues, the magical arts of divination are much less studied. Therefore, historical background for each is given below.

Hydromancy, Pyromancy, and Necromancy

The *Ars Notoria* writer views hydromancy and pyromancy as the two main ritual procedures in conducting a necromantic rite in which the practitioner may converse with the dead. Hydromancy (Greek *hydromantia*) is understood as the ritual evocation of a spirit by scrying through water. This method has historical precedence in the Greco-Egyptian magical tradition in which a water vessel is used as the scrying medium[39] to induce a trance for the purpose of being able

37. Paris, BnF Latin 7420A, f. 132v, fourteenth century. There are other extant manuscripts of *Chiromantia Parva,* dating as early as the twelfth century; however, it is probably much older. My translation.

38. As mentioned earlier in this chapter, Western Europeans understood little or no Greek, so it has been commonly found in manuscripts that scribes mistranslated Greek.

39. Generally speaking, *hygromanteia* (Greek *hygros,* meaning "wet" or "moist") is divination by means of a water vessel. Other water vessels were used, and the ritual procedure was named according to them, including *gasteromanteia* (divination by a large water container) and

to communicate with a spirit, a god, or the deceased. To help facilitate this transition into trance consciousness and to call upon the spirit, incantations would be recited by a single practitioner. In the case of two individuals conducting the rite—usually the divining magician and a virgin boy scryer—the magician would whisper the incantations into the scryer's ear as the scryer stared at the water until a vision of a spirit appeared.[40] For the *Ars Notoria* writer, the other main ritual procedure in conducting a necromantic rite is pyromancy; that is, the construction of a sacrifical fire in which dead animals are offered to attract the dead.[41] In the oldest accounts of necromancy, the ritual offerings are pure-black sheep.[42] The two best examples of the evocation of the dead through hydromancy and pyromancy come from Homer's *Odyssey* and Statius's *Thebaid*. Aside from this, necromancy also encompasses the ritual procedures of the dream vision,[43] divination by the skull,[44] laying the restless dead,[45]

---

lekanomanteia (divination by a dish); see Skinner, *Techniques of Solomonic Magic,* 265–70, 273–75. In the Odyssey, Circe advises Odysseus to look "toward the gushing river" to communicate with the deceased Tiresias.

40. For an example of hydromancy in a necromantic rite, see Betz, ed., *Greek Magical Papyri,* xiv, 239–95. For predictions, see Apuleius, *Apologia* 42; for the evocation of a spirit for other various purposes, see Kieckhefer, *Hazards of the Dark Arts,* 54–55. On the mytho-historical origins of hydromancy as an evocation of a spirit by scrying through water, see Augustine, *De Civitate Dei,* 7.35.

41. For example, see Statius, *Thebaid,* bk. IV, ll. 455–61. See also Betz, ed., *Greek Magical Papyri* xiv, 1–92, as quoted in Ritner, "Necromancy in Ancient Egypt," 89–96.

42. Homer, *The Odyssey,* book 11, lines 24–36; Statius, *Thebaid,* bk. IV, ll 443–46, 461–67. See also Betz, ed., *Greek Magical Payri* II, 44–52, in which the brain of a black ram is offered.

43. For Aeneas's dream incubation in the cave of Avernus, see Virgil, *The Aeneid,* 6.1029–32. See also Ogden, *Greek and Roman Necromancy,* chapter 6. A dream vision (*oneiraiteton*) might also be understood as a visionary descent into the underworld (*katabasis*). For an example, Ogden argues that the mysteries of Trophonius involved dream incubation. See Pausanias, *Guide to Greece,* 9.39.4–14.

44. The necromancer summons a ghost to inhabit a skull for the purposes of acting as the necromancer's serving spirit and to speak prophecies. There may be a relationship between these necromantic talking skulls and the magical servant (also called a familiar spirit, or *paredros* as in the PGM) because the spirit or ghost of both operations come from the underworld. Examples include the head of Orpheus in Lesobos (Philostratus, *On Heroes,* 28.8–12) and Archonides's head (Aelianus, *Various History,* 12.8). For a most gruesome example, see Greer and Warnock, trans., *Picatrix* 2.12, 125–26 (a passage found only in the Liber Rebus Edition).

45. When the necromancer was faced with the restless dead who disturbed the living, he would "summon up and drive out ghosts"; see Ogden, *Greek and Roman Necromancy,* 98. For an example, see Ogden, *Greek and Roman Necromancy,* 6–7, 178–80. See also Alfaye, *Sit Tibi Terra Gravis,* 181–216.

curse tablets (*defixiones*),[46] and reanimation.[47] These necromantic practices may be associated or identified with the Greek magical art called *goeteia* (γοητεία), and someone who practices *goeteia* is called a *goes*. The supposed author of the *Flores Aurei,* Apollonius of Tyana, was denied experiencing the mystery cult of Trophonius because he was a necromancer (*goes*).[48]

In the same section, the *Ars Notoria* writer mentions books of necromancy attributed to Solomon, who has attained mythical status as a great magician commanding demons; those known and attributed to Solomon, dated from late antiquity to the medieval period are listed in appendix A7.

Chiromancy, Geomancy, Genethlialogy, and Onomancy

The second grouping from the *Ars Notoria* is chiromancy, geomancy, genethliaology, and onomancy, which are fields of knowledge classified "under astrology" (*sub astrologia*). Chiromancy, also called palmistry, is divination by the hand. The earliest attestation of chiromancy comes from Aristotle (384–322 BCE), who mentions that those who have one or two lines that extend through the whole palm will live a long life, while those whose two lines do not extend all the way across will live short lives.[49] Juvenal (fl. late first to early second century CE), the Roman poet known for his *Satires,* mentions the prevalence of chiromancy in his day, saying, "If [a woman] will be of an ordinary status, she will move in a circle around the [circus] promenade from both ends of the [chariot tournament] winning-posts and the fortune-tellers; she will consider [the fortune-tellers], and show her brow and hand to the fortuneteller, asking for numerous smacking of the lips for approval."[50] Aside from these brief attestations from antiquity about a chiromantic tradition, there are no surviving texts until the thirteenth century.

John of Salisbury (c. 1115–1180), an English author, mentions that in his day there were "chiromancers who are prophesying hidden things from the

---

46. Skinner, *Techniques of Graeco-Egyptian Magic*, 301–12. The practice of curse tablets did not survive into the Middle Ages.

47. For examples, see Lucan, *Pharsalia,* 6.637–827; Apuleius's *Metamorphoses* (or, *Golden Ass*), 2.28–29; Heliodorus of Emesa's *Aethiopica* ("Ethiopian Story," or "Theagenes and Chariclia"), 6.14–15, and Ovid's *Metamorphoses,* 7.234–93.

48. Philostratus, *Life of Apollonius,* 8.19.

49. Aristotle, *History of Animals* (*Historia Animalium*) 11.2

50. Juvenal, *Satires* 6.582–84. My translation.

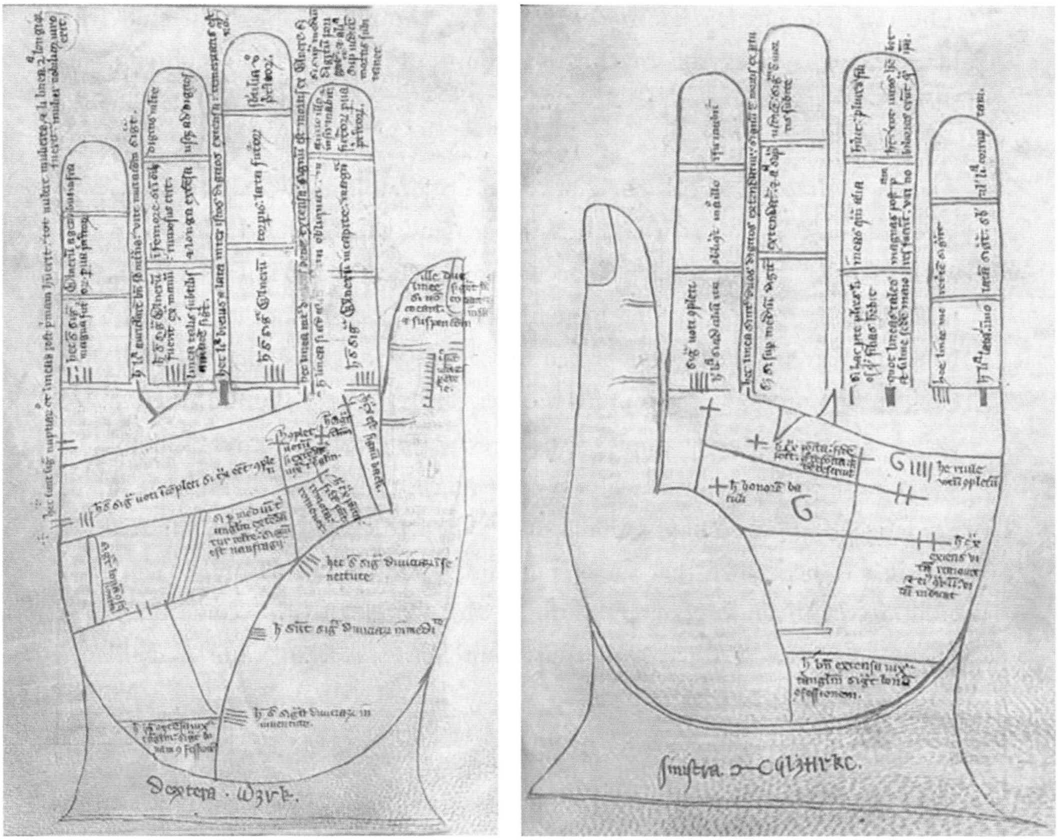

Dextra Viri, Sinistra Mulieris (*The Right Hand of a Man, the Left Hand of a Woman.*)
From thirteenth- or fourteenth-century treatise labeled as
Varia de astrologia et computo. Paris, BnF NAL 693, 95v–96r.

inspection of hands."[51] There are about a dozen medieval texts that establish the main Latin literary tradition of chiromancy, often untitled and falsely attributed to famous thinkers such as Ptolemy, Aristotle, and Adelard of Bath.[52]

---

51. John of Salisbury, *Ioannis Saresberiensis, Policraticus,* I.11–12. My translation.

52. Some of the most important chiromantic treatises include the one found in the Eadwine Psalter, Cambridge, Trinity College, MS R.17.I, f. 282r, thirteenth century; the *Chiromantia Parva* (*Small Chiromancy*), Paris, Bibliothèque Nationale, nouv. acq. lat. (NAL) 693, f. 95v–96r, thirteenth to fourteenth century; the *Dextra Viri, Sinistra Mulieris* (*The Right Hand of a Man, the Left Hand of a Woman*), London, British Library, MS Sloane 2030, f. 125–126r, twelfth to thirteenth century; and the two chiromancies bound together in the *Cyromancia Aristotilis cum Figuris* (*The Chiromancy of Arisotle with Figures*), published at Ulm in 1490, discussed in Thorndike, "Chiromancy in Mediaeval Latin Manuscripts," 674–706. See also Burnett, *Magic*

The twelfth-century *Chiromantia Parva*, thought to be translated from Arabic to Latin, gives the mythical account of the origins of chiromancy as follows:

> There was a certain religious anchorite[53] in Britain to whom God in his grace revealed these signs that would benefit men and women by an announcing angel. For his brother [was] preoccupied with death; for Hilarion,[54] that man devoted to God, having bent his knees to the ground, extended his hands to heaven for salvation, prayed so that the Lord surely might have disclosed a sign of life or death of his brother. Therefore, the Lord fulfilled his prayer. For getting up from prayer, he foresaw [in a vision] a kind of marble statue in his presence in which he discerned, the right hand of a man [and] the left hand of a woman sculpted, in which predicted signs are indicated. Yet, it is to be known that the certain discovered art is a natural [science] from a certain philosopher Edmund,[55] who a Saracen[56] had come before [Edmund] and was called Maneanus,[57] but Master Adelard translated this art from Greek into Latin.[58]

and Divination in the Middle Ages; Pack, "A Pseudo-Aristotelian Chiromancy," 189–241; and Roger A. Pack, "Pseudo-Aristoteles: Chiromantia," 289–320.

53. An anchorite is a religious ascetic who retreats from secular society to live in a cell within a church. Anchorites were known to exist between the eleventh and thirteenth centuries in England.

54. The anchorite's name is Hilarion, which is a name that recalls the fourth-century anchorite named Hilarion the Great. Hilarion the Great spent his life in the desert of Syria Palaestina according to the monastic lifestyle of Anthony the Great (c. 251–356).

55. Edmund of Abingdon (c. 1174–1240), the archbishop of Canterbury and university lecturer, has a chiromantic treatise, including "The Hands," copied by him, which is then recorded by the Harley scribe found in the Royal MS 12 C XII manuscript held in the British Library dated to the first half of the fourteenth century. The chiromantic treatise is accompanied by Edmund's *Speculum Ecclesiae* (*Mirror of the Church*) and hymns as well as a portion of a Latin copy of the *Secret of Secrets* and the *Liber Experimentus,* an astrological geomancy text translated from Arabic. The modern scholar John Haines suggests Edmund as a strong candidate for the authorship of the *Ars Notoria Notarie* (*Notory Art of Shorthand*), of which see below.

56. During the Middle Ages, Christians called those from Arabia by the term Saracens.

57. As Kieckhefer points out in his *Hazards of the Dark Arts,* the name Maneanus probably derives from the Latin word *manus,* meaning "hand." This Maneanus may refer to Yahya ibn al-Batriq (fl. 796–806 CE), the Syrian Christian translator who wrote the preface to the Arabic *Kitab Sirr Al-Asrar* (*Secret of Secrets*), telling the story of how the Pseudo-Aristotle chiromantic treatise was found near an altar of Hermes and then was quoted by John of Seville.

58. My translation.

Hartlieb confirms this account, saying that Mancius the Sorcerer invented chiromancy.[59] The other mythical origin story about chiromancy comes from John of Seville's Pseudo-Aristotle chiromantic treatise, which says:

> And I, [John of Seville], translated this book from the Arabic tongue into Latin and transcribed with many other good ones by the love of the Queen of Seville, elaborated from the book of Aristotle which he made for Alexander the Great, which in Arabic is called *Sirr Al-Asrar,* that is, *The Secret of Secrets,* in which many good Aristotelian tractates are transcribed on the principles by governance, which a certain translator, having been ordered by [his] master, and translated by great labor, in his Arabic translation, he said on that discovery thus, "Because it is ordered by the master, I am disembarking to seek diligently, and I believe had I not tarried to travel around the place and temple in which to discover philosophers who had concealed his secret writings. Eventually, because I arrived to one altar Hermes had set up, and in that place, I discovered a wise statue, and I directed my attention. And yet I dedicated myself to please all those powers, and I appeased the same [powers] by pleasant words, and it guided me to the place in which the many secrets of philosophy were concealed, and among others there I discovered a book written of gold letters, and I repatriated it carrying this to the master with delight." And after this I translated many good ones from Arabic into Latin and that *Secret of Secrets.*[60]

John of Seville's Pseudo-Aristotle treatise proclaims the mythical figure of Hermes Trismegistus, known to the Arabs as Idris, is the founder of chiromancy, which follows since Hermes represented knowledge of the sciences, including astrology and alchemy, which the Arabs had brought to the Latin West.

According to these chiromantic treatises, there are four principal natural lines of the hand: (1) the line of life (*linea vitae*), (2) the middle line (*linea mediana*), (3) the table line (*linea mensalis*), and (4) the base of the triangle (*basis trianguli*) (see figure on p. 94). Certain signs along or near these lines signify certain prognostications. From a medieval medicine perspective, the line of life corresponds to the heart, the middle line corresponds to the brain, the table line corresponds

59. Kieckhefer, *Hazards of the Dark Arts,* 75.

60. Pack, "A Pseudo-Aristotelian Chiromancy," 189–241. My English translation of the Latin.

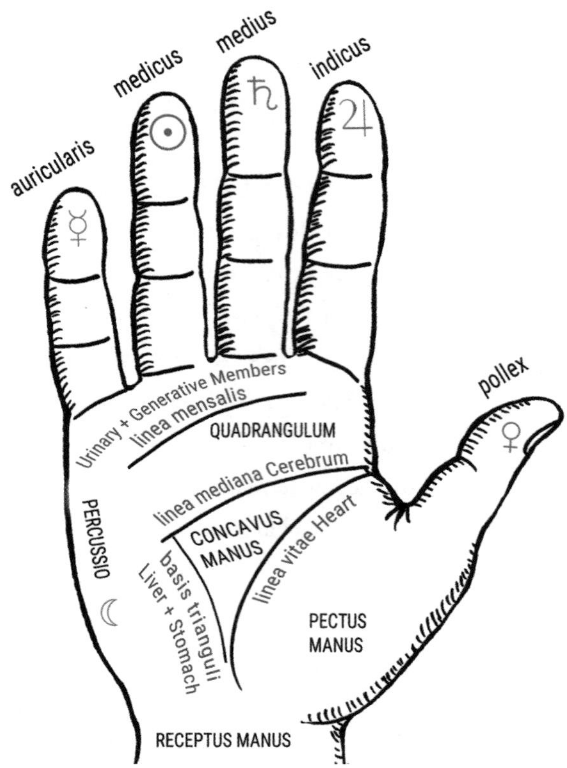

The chiromantic hand. The principal lines of the palm are four: (1) line of life (*linea vitae*), (2) the middle line (*linea mediana*), (3) the table line (*linea mensalis*), and (4) the base of the triangle (*basis trianguli*). The space between the table line and the middle line is called the quadrangle (*quadrangulum*). The line of life, the middle line, and the base of the triangle constitute the great triangle of the hand. The other features of the hand that were of interest to the chiromancer included the wrist (*rasceta*, or *receptus manus*); the hollow of the palm (*fovea*, or *concavus manus*); the chest of the hand (*pectus manus*), or the mount of the thumb or thenar eminence; and the hypothenar eminence, the "strike" (*percussio*) or "blow" (*ictus*) of the hand. The fingers are named from the little finger to the index finger (*auricularis, medicus, medius, indicus*), and the thumb is called the *pollex*. The mounds under the fingers, including the thenar eminence, the hypothenar eminence, and the concave of the hand, each correspond to one of the seven planets in astrology. The assignment of the planets sometimes differed from author to author (e.g., Mercury to the ring finger and the Sun to the little finger, which differs from the present figure). Lastly, certain organs corresponded to the four principal lines and held a certain prognostic significance according to Galenic medicine. Typically, the line of life corresponded to the heart, the base of the triangle corresponded to the liver and stomach, the middle line corresponded the the cerebrum, and the table line corresponded to the urinary system and generative members.

to the generative members, and the base of the triangle corresponds to the stomach and liver; however, these four principal lines and their signs have many different kinds of significations covering different aspects of life. Sometimes there are contradictions in these significations among the chiromantic treatises. The prognostications covered many topics, including marriage, children, family life, wealth, social life, and health. Some signs in the hand predicted good fortune, while others foretold bad luck, including how one might die.

Chiromancy was considered a subbranch or minor science to physiognomy, the art of discerning character traits from a person's physical appearance.[61] The most significant ancient and medieval works still extant on physiognomy include the Greek *Physiognomonica,* which is falsely attributed to Aristotle; a treatise from the second-century Greek aristocrat Polemon of Laodicea (preserved in a fourteenth-century Arabic translation); a Greek treatise written in two books by Adamantius the Sophist (fl. fifth century CE); a third- or fourth-century Latin treatise by an Anonymus Latinus; and Michael Scot's early thirteenth-century *Liber physiognomiae.*[62] Chiromantic texts were often accompanied by treatises on physiognomy, since chiromancy is essentially a physiognomy of the hand. By the fifteenth century, chiromantic texts would be found accompanying geomantic treatises.

Varro mentions geomancy in relation to the other three divinations—hydromancy, pyromancy, and aeromancy; together, these are the four elements of Greek thought (i.e, earth, water, fire, and air). For Varro, geomancy likely meant divination by the inspection of earthquakes and fissures, which the ancient Greeks interpreted as divine messages from the gods. For those living in medieval and Renaissance Europe, there was a different kind of geomancy called "the daughter of astrology" that meant a divination by making dots, lines, and figures in the earth, following a set of procedures according to binary arithmetic and certain rules of interpretation. The basis of geomancy consists of sixteen figures that are formed from dotted lines made in the earth (see figure, p.97). Geomancy, called "the science of sand" (*'ilm al-raml*), has North African and Arabic origins; the diviner would use a stick to draw lines and poke holes in the sand from which certain figures were

61. Hippocrates and Galen. See Evans, "Galen the Physician as Physiognomist," 287–98.
62. Boys-Stones, Elsner, Ghersetti, Hoyland, and Repath, *Seeing the Face, Seeing the Soul.*

made, then he would place them in a particular order on a chart, interpret the figures, and give his prognostication.[63] Ahmad ben 'Ali Zunbul (c. 1553) says the angel Gabriel taught the art of geomancy to Idris (the Arabic name for Hermes Trismegistus), who then passed it down to the Indian prophet Tum-Tum.[64] This is the kind of geomancy the *Ars Notoria* was referencing because this geomancy falls *sub astrologia* (under astrology).

Geomancy is largely credited as being first introduced into the Latin West by Hugh of Santalla (fl. twelfth century), who translated an Arabic treatise into Latin and titled it the *Ars Geomantiae* (*Art of Geomancy*), which was followed by the *Geomantia Nova* (*New Geomancy*). As Arabs translated many scientific works from Arabic to Latin, Plato of Tivoli, the twelfth-century Italian translator and astronomer, translated the *Questiones Geomanticae* or *Liber Arenalis* (*Geomantic Questions*) of Al-Fakini ibn Abizarch. Among the list of example questions one can propose to the art of geomancy, Al-Fakini ibn Abizarch says:

> In which science will he profit or advance in the most? If he will ask which [one]? Consider one and nine of the [house] signs; because if it was [Laetitia, then he would profit or advance in] the science of theology and law; if [Coniunctio], [then] it is a promising success in the science of arithmetic, geometry, sculpture, and especially silver and stones; and in like manner in necromancy, as they are images and incantations. If [Albus], in the knowledge of speaking, writing, verifying, and painting on white canvas or embroidering in white garments. If [Fortuna Minor], in natural philosophy. If [Greater Fortune], in geomancy. If [Acquisitio], in the science of the arts. If [Puella], in the science of [musical] instruments or the cithara[65] of this kind. If [Amissio] or [Coniunctio], in the musical art. If [Rubeus] or [Lesser Fortune], in the dialectic science.[66]

Another contributor to geomancy, Gerard of Cremona (1114–1187), trans-

63. After the computation of a geomantic reading, at the end of the chart there will always be three figures that help answer the querent's question. There are two witnesses and a judge. For example, two witnesses could be Tristitia and Puer, leading to a judge of Lesser Fortune.

64. Skinner, *Geomancy in Theory and Practice,* 33–37, 56.

65. The cithara is an ancient Greek instrument akin to the modern guitar.

66. Fludd, *Fasciculus Geomanticus,* 624–25. My translation.

The sixteen figures of geomancy. *Top row, from left to right:* Puer (Boy), Amissio (Loss), Albus (White), and Populus (People). *Second row, from left to right:* Fortuna Major (Greater Fortune), Coniunctio (Conjunction), Puella (Girl), and Rubeus (Red). *Third row, from left to right:* Acquisitio (Acquisition), Carcer (Prison), Tristitia (Sorrow), and Laetitia (Joy). *Bottom row, from left to right:* Cauda Draconis (Tail of the Dragon), Caput Draconis (Head of the Dragon), Fortuna Minor (Lesser Fortune), and Via (the Way).

lated an Arabic treatise into Latin called the *Liber Geomantiae de Artibus Divinatoriis qui Incipit Estimaverunt Indi* (*Book of Geomancy and the Art of Divination Which begins "They appraise . . . to be introduced . . ."*). It is commonly referred to by its incipit as *Estimaverunt Indi*.[67] Unlike Renaissance or modern forms of geomancy, the advent of geomancy into medieval Europe has received scant attention from scholars.[68]

Martianus Capella, author of *De Nuptiis Philologiae et Mercurii* (*On the Marriage of Philology and Mercury*), mentions the personification of genethlialogy, saying:

> In the course of this conversation between the Delian and Pallas, someone asked the names of the maidens. Phoebus then answered: "The first to appear will be Genethliace. She shares in the knowledge of the heavenly order and covertly declares the lots of Lachesis and the things to be produced in the approaching ages."[69]

67. Bodleian, Ashmole MS 4, ff. 49–70.

68. The study of medieval geomancy in the Latin West is an ongoing project. For the most current research on geomancy, see Alessandro Palazzo and Irene Zavattero, *Geomancy and Other Forms of Divination* (Firenze: Sismel – Edizioni del Galluzzo, 2017).

69. Stahl, Johnson, and Burge, trans. and eds., *Martianus Capella,* 894. From Greek mythology, the Delian refers to Apollo, the Olympian god of prophecy and poetry; Pallas is an epithet of Athena, the goddess of wisdom; and Lachesis is one of the Three Fates, or Moirai.

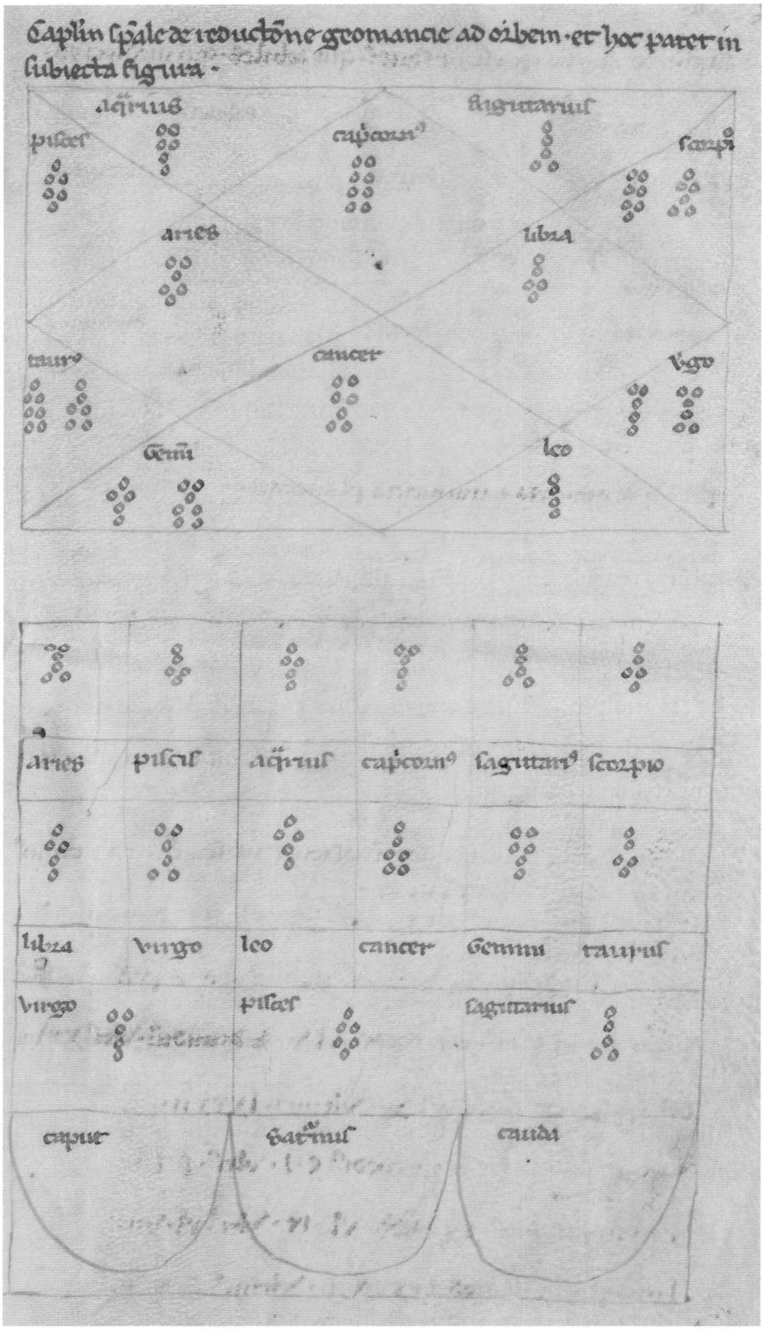

An astro-geomancy chart and a geomantic shield chart. At the top is an astro-geomancy chart and below is a geomantic shield chart from Pseudo-Ptolemy's *Archanum magni Dei de reductione geomanciae* (*The Great Secret of God about the Restoration of Geomancy*), copied between 1295 and 1315, Paris, BnF Latin 15353, f. 88r.

Genethlialogy, belonging to the branch of judicial astrology, was also known as natal astrology, which sought to prognosticate about a person's birth, age, physical appearance, temperament, education, and the stages of life development. Genethlialogy originated in Persia, consisting of writings in Pahlavi and Greek, which were translated into Arabic at the Abbasid court. Key figures and their works associated with genethlialogy include the eighth-century Jewish astrologer Mashallah ibn Athari's *Kitab mawalid* (*Nativities*); the Persian Abbasid court astrologer Albumasar's *Kitab mawalid al-rijal wa al-nisa* (*Book of Nativities of Men and Women*); the Persian astrologer Omar Tiberiades, who translated from Middle Persian into Arabic the *Pentateuch,* a didactic poem on Hellenistic astrology by Dorotheus of Sidon; and the Persian physician and astrologer Albubather, who wrote *De Nativitatibus* (*On the Nativities*). Some of these works were later translated into Latin.[70]

Both forms of divination, genethlialogy and onomancy, are executed in the *Alchandreana* corpus, a tenth-century collection of astrological and prognosticative Latin texts, which was one of the first written collections of Islamic science to be acquired by Europeans. The internal references in the *Liber Alchandrei* make it clear that the compilation is based on works reputedly addressed to Alexander the Great.[71] The *Alchandreana* corpus is a plausible source book which the *Ars Notoria* author knew. Because there is much literature available on genethlialogy, the constructing and interpreting of nativities, the scope of which exceeds the subject of this book, I will not delve into that subject here. However, its cohort, the divinatory art of onomancy, which so few know anything about, deserves attention for its prognosticating computations, which, interestingly enough, does not require any astronomical or astrological observations.

As mentioned previously, onomancy is a form of divination which takes the letters of a person's name, converts each letter into a numerical value, and then applies certain algorithms to determine the person's fate, often involving computations related to certain astrological elements. Onomancy may be conceived as

---

70. Saparmin, "History of Astrology and Astronomy in Islamic Medicine," 282–96.

71. Burnett, "Adelard, Ergaphalau and the Science of the Stars," in *Magic and Divination in the Middle Ages,* 140. The name Alhandreus is likely a corruption of Alexander the Great, according to Burnett, though Juste argues for the Muslim astrologer Al-Kindi (c. 801–873). The *Alchandrinus* or *Archandrinus* is also cited by Michael Scot in his *Liber Introductorius.*

the forerunner to modern-day numerology.[72] The onomantic method consists of four parts: (1) the question; (2) the names relevant to the question; (3) the algorithm for the computation of those names; and (4) the numerical result, what it means, and how it answers the question. In the late medieval world, all onomantic computations can be categorized into three types according to the numerical result: (1) the numerical value is either odd or even; (2) the numerical value of the remainder is distributed serially over a given ordered set (e.g., the 28 lunar mansions or the 7 classical planets), allotting one number for each element with the final distribution providing the result; and (3) the numerical value of the remainder corresponds to the same number in a results table.

Onomancy is dependent upon an alphabet that has a numerical value for each letter, such as Greek, Arabic, and Hebrew, for the algorithm to work properly. Latin does not have a numerical value for each letter, which posed a major problem for medieval scribes who wanted to translate a native onomantic prognostication device into Latin; this inevitably led to a lack of consensus on what numerical value ought to be attributed to any given Roman letter. The three types of onomantic computations which were likely known to the notory art practitioner include: (1) the literature which presented a series of questions answered by a numerical result as being either odd or even, (2) the horoscope in which the remainder is distributed serially over a given astrological set of elements, and (3) the results tables found in the Table of the Victor and Vanquished and the Sphere of Life and Death.

The first type of onomantic computation involves a variety of simple questions and their respective computations in which the numerical result is either odd or even. In the *Alchandreana* corpus, the onomantic algorithms based on the numerical result being odd or even answers questions about the following:

72. Onomancy, understood as a separate and distinct category of divination, did not develop until the sixteenth century; however, its early roots conceived this prognostic method as part of astronomy and astrology. See Edge, "Nomen Omen," 32. The twelfth-century astronomer Raymond of Marseilles, in the preface to his *Liber Cursuum Planetarum VII* (*Book of the Courses of the Planets*), would have classified these computation methods as part of the onomantic science (*onomica scientia*) under contemplative astronomy (*contemplativa astronomia*). Similarly, the tenth-century author of *Ut testator Ergaphalau,* who might have also authored a portion of the *Alchandreana* corpus, would have classified onomancy under astronomy. See Burnett, "Adelard, Ergaphalau and the Science of the Stars," in *Magic and Divination in the Middle Ages,* 138.

(1) marriage, (2) the sex of an unborn child, (3) the truth of a rumor, and (4) whether a certain woman is a prostitute. The first two questions are found in the *Alchandreana* and the twelfth-century medical compendium called the *Syriac Book of Medicines;* they are later transmitted into European Latin manuscripts of the fourteenth and fifteenth centuries,[73] and in fact, the German author and physician Johannes Hartlieb cites the first about marriage.[74] The excerpts for these two questions follow one another in a treatise of the *Alchandreana* corpus called *Quicumque* and are provided as follows:

> Also, if you want to know who is to die first, man or woman, compute the names of those and determine their number of letters and divide by nine. If it was an even number, the woman will bury the man in a tomb; if odd, the man will deposit [his] wife to the earth. If you want to know if a pregnant woman will give birth to a male or a female, compute the name of the female herself and the name of her younger son, which if she never had a son, compute the name of Mars, and add fifteen and divide by nine. If an even number remained, she will bear a male; if it was an odd number, she will bear a female. If what was asked of you happened in the feminine hour [i.e., Venus hour], she will bear a female. If in the masculine hour [i.e., Mars hour], she will bear a male.[75]

Other onomantic questions found in the *Alchandreana* corpus include questions about the following: (1) the matter of a theft,[76] (2) the recovery of a runaway slave,[77] (3) the return of an absent person, (4) the recovery of a stolen treasure,[78]

---

73. Edge, "Nomen Omen," 32–38.

74. Kieckhefer, *Hazards of the Dark Arts,* 51.

75. Juste, *Les Alchandreana Primitifs,* 504. The Latin-to-English translation is mine; my additions are made in the brackets. The hours referenced here are the planetary hours. According to astrology, the seven classical planets ruled over the hours of the day in succession following the Chaldean order. In addition, it is worthy mentioning that a few of these onomantic computations are also found within the twelfth-century medical compendium now called the *Syriac Book of Medicines* (BL Or. 9360) and published by E. A. Wallis Budge. See also Budge, *Syrian Anatomy,* 526–27, 625.

76. Juste, *Les Alchandreana Primitifs,* 470; see also Budge, trans. and ed., *Syrian Anatomy,* 525, 626.

77. Juste, *Les Alchandreana Primitifs,* 529–30; see also Budge, trans. and ed., *Syrian Anatomy,* 535–37, 541.

78. Juste, *Les Alchandreana Primitifs,* 530.

(5) the location of a treasure,[79] and (6) the outcome of a malady.[80]

The second type of onomantic computation involves the horoscope. Genethlialogy is combined with onomantic algorithms designed to determine the elements of the nativity (i.e., the lunar mansion, the zodiacal sign, the ruling planet at birth for a given person) so that other prognostics and judgments can be made. In the *Mathematica Alhandrei Summi Astrologi* (*Mathematics of Alhandreus, Supreme Astrologer*) a horoscope is calculated by first adding the person's name and his or her mother's name according to Hebrew letters (i.e., Hebrew gematria); this type of horoscope does not rely on the observation of the stars but instead on a calculation of numbers. Second, the total is divided by modular 28, which is the number of Arabic lunar mansions. Third, the remainder is distributed over the lunar mansions beginning with the first, Al-Nath (or, Al-Sharatain; i.e., Aries), allotting one per mansion until the numbers of the remainder run out. The zodiacal sign of birth corresponds to the sign that rules the lunar mansion in question (for example, if the mansion of birth is al-Nath, then the sign will be Aries).[81] To determine the planet of birth of a client, the numerical value of the letters of the name of the client is totaled and then the sum is divided by nine (or seven) and to distribute the reminder among the planets in the order Sun-Venus-Mercury-Moon-Saturn-Jupiter-Mars(-Sun-Venus).[82] As already stated, once these basic elements of the nativity are known, the astrologer is able to interpret and give his prognostication about his client's physical, mental, and moral characteristics, how many children he or she will have, including a prediction of his client's health status as it changes over the course of time, his term of life, and his manner of death.

The third type of onomantic computation is based on a diagram known as the Sphere of Life and Death. This is discussed in depth in chapter V under The Figure of Medicine.

---

79. Juste, *Les Alchandreana Primitifs,* 531.

80. Juste, *Les Alchandreana Primitifs,* 505, 533; see also Budge, trans. and ed., *Syrian Anatomy,* 531–41.

81. Juste, *Les Alchandreana primitifs;* see also Paris, BnF Latin 17868.

82. Juste explains that there are variations in the texts regarding numerical values and the planets allocated to remainders; the division made by nine is represented by including the two heavenly bodies provided within the parenthesis. See Juste, "Non-Transferable Knowledge," 517–29. See also Budge, trans. and ed., *Syrian Anatomy,* 620–21.

Magic and the Ars Notoria

The word *magic* has been difficult to define, having become burdened by a host of overlapping historical contexts. Modern scholars continue to debate its constitutive elements, scope, social contexts, and relationship to religion and mysticism.[83] For the purposes of this book, there are two proposed working definitions of Western magic as it relates to the *Ars Notoria*. The first definition proposed is magic as defined by its own constitutive elements, acknowledging the metaphysical world in which the practitioners operated, which is best thought of as the "insider's" definition of magic. These constitutive elements include three things: (1) the ritual procedures, (2) the spirits and the metaphysical world they inhabit, and (3) the practitioner's belief in his ability to interact with the spirits of the metaphysical world. In this definition, magic is the art and practice of certain ritual procedures, which assumes a particular metaphysical worldview, to attract and gain the assistance of nonphysical beings for accomplishing a particular aim.

In magic, there are certain ritual procedures to accomplish particular goals. There are ritual actions meant to draw and attract a spirit to the practitioner, such as ritual purification practices (e.g., prayers of penitence and fasting) and ritual offerings (e.g., prayers and animal sacrifice); unlike the magic of the *Ars Notoria,* there is even the ritual action of compelling or binding the spirit through spoken conjurations and ritual implements inscribed with special symbols. Other ritual actions include ways in which the practitioner may perceive and communicate with spirits (e.g., dream visitations by an angel or scrying through water as practiced in hydromancy). Typically, such ritual procedures involve sacred names, symbols, ritual implements, and auspicious timing, working under the assumption of a metaphysical worldview. A typology of magic can be gleaned from these basic elements, identifying magical practices based on their constitutive ritual procedures (e.g., prayers of invocation, dream visions).

The other consitutive element of magic involves the spirits and their metaphysical world. The class of nonphysical beings may include entities

83. See the following chapters in Sophie Page and Catherine Rider, eds., *The Routledge History of Medieval Magic* (New York: Routledge, Taylor & Francis Group, 2019): Richard Kieckhefer, "Rethinking How to Define Magic"; Claire Fanger, "For Magic: Against Method"; Bernd-Christian Otto, "A Discourse Historical Approach towards Medieval Learned Magic"; David L. d'Avray, "The Concept of Magic"; and Richard Kieckhefer, David L. d'Avray, Bernd-Christian Otto, and Claire Fanger, "Responses."

such as spirits, demons, angels, deities, and the dead; these entities inhabit certain parts of the metaphysical world (such as heaven, hell, and the earth), often set in a hierarchical structure to reflect an ordered world. A typology of magic can be made based on the spirits that are summoned from a particular region within a given metaphysical world (e.g., angelic magic versus chthonic, demonic, or necromantic magic); alternatively, the metaphysical world in which the practitioner operates may also be descriptive in the kind of magical tradition practiced (e.g., ancient Greek, Hermetic, or Christian). The last typology of magic is based on a mytho-historical personality who represents an actual historical lineage of magical texts, such as Hermes Trismegistus, King Solomon, and Apollonius of Tyana. This typology of magic reflects the historical record of magical texts; for example, the mythical narrative behind King Solomon is found in the *Testament of Solomon,* the *Liber de Umbris Idearum* (*Book from the Shadow of Ideas*), the *De Quattuor Annulis* (*Concerning the Four Rings*), the *De Novem Candariis* (*Concerning the Nine Pentacles*), and the *Ars Notoria* (*Notory Art*). The purpose of this typology is to trace the mythical narrative of a given personality.

From the insider's perspective, the magic of the *Ars Notoria* is classified according to the following elements: (1) the author attributions to the magical text, (2) the spirits and the metaphysical world they inhabit, and (3) the ritual procedures. The first two elements are best addressed together.

The two key personalities attributed to the *Ars Notoria* are Solomon and Apollonius of Tyana. According to the mytho-historical account, it is Apollonius of Tyana who is bringing a translation of excerpts and commentary of Solomon's writings to the "present-day" reader of the Middle Ages. What did medieval people know about Apollonius of Tyana? His biography was written in Greek, so it would have been inaccessible to the Latin West. The few scant patristic references hardly revealed much of anything about him, and what they did say was not favorable. During the twelfth century when the Arabs were transmitting numerous texts to the Latin West, there were Arabic and Greek astral magic treatises attributed to Apollonius of Tyana that were translated into Latin.[84] These astral magic treatises assert Apollonius as a great magician

84. See appendix A6 for more details regarding the magical texts attributed to Apollonius of Tyana.

and, more importantly, presents a narrative in which Apollonius is made the heir to Hermes Trismegistus, the Greco-Egyptian patron of magic, astrology, and alchemy. Thus, Apollonius of Tyana is depicted as the Arab-Hermetic figure who represents the repository of Hermetic magic during the Middle Ages. In addition, these treatises assume a Hermetic worldview in which Hermetic magicians call down spirits of celestial bodies to imbue talismans, brazen heads, and statues with their metaphysical energies at carefully calculated astrological times to accomplish a variety of tasks. Furthermore, in two texts from Hellenstic Judaism, the *Wisdom of Solomon* and Josephus's *Jewish Antiquities,* Solomon is portrayed as a Hermetic sage.[85] This stylized characterization of King Solomon as a Hermetic sage is also asserted by the fifteenth-century French Talmudist Jacob ben David Provençal, who says Solomon is given credit for the *Book of the Mystery of Nature* (an alternate title for *De Secretis Naturae,* which is actually attributed to Apollonius of Tyana), which contains the well-known passage about how Apollonius of Tyana discovered the statue of Hermes holding the Emerald Tablet and thereby asserting his inheritance of Hermetic magic.[86] Thus, for the medieval readers, the metaphysical world of the *Ars Notoria* presumes a Hermetic worldview based on the established reputation of Apollonius of Tyana as a Hermetic magician whose astral magic treatises were currently in circulation at the time. Mythologically, Apollonius of Tyana becomes the central figure of the *Ars Notoria* for two key reasons: first, his contributions of translation and commentary as the *Flores Aurei;* and second, he is the foremost magician in the Hermetic lineage, following Solomon historically and becoming the spiritual successor by discovering the hidden crypt containing the statue of Hermes Trismegistus and a cache of magical writings.

In short, the *Flores Aurei* presents a Hermetic worldview that was united or overlaid with a Christian worldview by the compiler of the *Ars Notoria*. Thus, a practitioner of the *Ars Notoria* operates within a Hermetic-Christian worldview inhabited by heavenly angels. The claim that the *Ars Notoria* operates within a Christian worldview is obvious—its prayers are addressed to the Christian Trinity; it references and imitates biblical passages; and it advocates for confession, Lenten fasting, and avoiding sin. In summary, the magic of the *Ars Notoria*

---

85. Torijano, *Solomon the Esoteric King,* 88–105.
86. Shavit, *An Imaginary Trio,* 156.

PRINCIPIVM·ET·FINIS·ET·PRETER·ME·NON·EST·DEVS
DEMONIA
F·DIDACVS
FECIT

Opposite page: The Great Chain of Being. Didacus Valades, *Rhetorica Christiana,* 1579 drawing. The Great Chain of Being has its origins in Homer's *Iliad,* book 8, and became a pervasive concept throughout the history of the Western tradition. At the top sits the Trinity (God the Father seated wearing a papal tiara, Jesus Christ resting in God's lap, and the Holy Spirit symbolized as a dove radiating from God's heart), with Mother Mary standing to God's right-hand side. In his right hand, God holds the "chain of being," which extends down through the entire world, ending with Satan at the bottom panel. The Trinity and Mother Mary are surrounded by the seven angels of the Apocalypse of John (Revelation), who offer incense. Beneath them are seven levels of reality; beginning from the top, they are: (1) the angels, (2) humanity with Adam and Eve in the middle, (3) creatures of the air, (4) creatures of the sea, (5) animals of the earth, (6) plant life and the earth itself, and (7) the infernal world ruled by Satan.

is classified according to its attributed authors of Solomon and Apollonius of Tyana and its adapted Hermetic-Christian worldview.

Lastly, the magic of the *Ars Notoria* is classified according to its ritual procedures. The *Ars Notoria* practitioner conducts the ritual in consideration of the prescribed astronomical and astrological times, performing ritual purification practices such as prayers of penitence and fasting to prepare himself to meet the angel; similarly, the ritual action of taking the angel names inscribed with saffron, then mixed into rosewater tea for drinking, is another means of infusing himself with the essence of the very angels with whom he seeks to contact. Next, he offers the *voces magicae* prayers to invoke and attract the angelic beings of the magical notory art; communication between the practitioner and the angel first occurs through a dream vision. The dream vision follows the biblical narrative of Solomon receiving a dream from God; thus, the practitioner may identify himself with Solomon, thereby seeking holy permission and initiation into the historic lineage of Solomonic magic. The mundane practice of the art of memory is then placed within the sacred context of ritual in which he studies his school textbooks and inspects the pictorical figures called *notae*. Thus, the magic of the notory art consists of three essential ritual procedures: (1) the preliminary ritual purification practices joined with the *voces magicae* prayers to attract the angels, (2) the dream visitation by the angel, and (3) practicing the art of memory with the figures.

The second working definition of magic considers the perspective of non-practitioners or outsiders; in this sense, magic becomes a pejorative word of condemnation, used as a weapon among religious leaders against their opponents of other competing religions. Historically, these non-practitioners are mainstream Christians who condemn certain ritual practices as "magical" and therefore are excluded from their traditional religious practice. Since the birth of Christianity, many Christian writers who were motivated to label a text as deviant or illicit (i.e., "magical") sought to make political and theological gains against those who promoted a different metaphysical worldview (e.g., Gnosticism, Manichaeanism); in doing so, they attempted to persuade their audience into their way of thinking about the world.[87] According to *Didascalicon* (*On the Study of Reading*), authored by Hugh of St. Victor, "magic is not accepted as a part of philosophy, but stands with a false claim outside of it: the mistress of every form of iniquity and malice." Oftentimes, opponents of magic did not truly understand or bother to understand the nuances of ritual magic procedures. This lack of interest or understanding led to mislabeling one kind of magic for another; for example, in the *Speculum Astronomiae* (*Mirror of Astronomy*), Albert Magnus condemns astral magic, calling it "necromancy" because it involves the offering of incantations and

87. Klutz, ed., *Magic in the Biblical World.*

voces magicae to demons; he associates certain "necromantic" texts with the procedures of astral magic that involve suffumigations and characters written upon a talisman. The misuse of the word *necromancy* is carried forward in time. In the *Book of All Forbidden Arts,* the German Christian Johannes Hartlieb (c. 1400–1468) confuses the issue by also attributing astral magic treatises to the category of "necromancy," saying:

> There are still more books on this [necromantic] art, such as Thabit [bin Qurra],[88] Ptolemy,[89] Leopold, [Duke] of Austria,[90] Arnold [of Saxony],[91] and all the books that have been written about images, which are many, telling how one at any particular time should fashion an image of the planets and stars, which have great power for love and harm, victory and fortune. All that is trumpery, for it involves a great deal of secret words, and characters and suffumigation and sacrifice, which is all unchristian.[92]

The outsider's definition of magic reveals the disdain and condemnation of its opponents as well as the ignorance of the ritual procedures and the metaphysical worldview in which spirits are said to reside and be able to interact with the human world.

---

88. *De Imaginibus* (*On Images*).

89. Among Ptolemy's pseudo-epigraphal writings were three astral magic treatises. The first treatise is *De imaginibus super facies signorum* (*The Making of Signs from Images Above*), a book of 46 chapters on the making and uses of talismans according to the 36 decans. It was likely translated from the Arabic by John of Seville (fl. 1133–1153), a member of the Toledo School of Translators. This work is now attributed to Albumasar (787–886 CE), the Persian Muslim astrologer, and preserved at Paris, BnF Latin 16204. Trithemius's *Antipalus Maleficiorum* (*Against the Underworld Swamp Waters of Malefic Spirits,* 1508) lists it as *Abenhali Liber imaginum mirabilium.* The second treatise falsely ascribed to Ptolemy is called *Liber de impressionibus imaginum, annullorum et sigillorum secundum facies duodecim signorum zodiaci* (*The Book on the Stamping of Images, Rings, and Making Sigils according to the Twelve Zodiac Signs*), preserved at St. Petersburg, Biblioteka Akademii Nauk, Q. 537. The third treatise falsely ascribed to Ptolemy is called *De XII annulis Veneris* (*On the Twelve Rings of Venus*). These last two treatises are also mentioned by Trithemius. See Juste, *Pseudo-Ptolemy, De imaginibus* and *Pseudo-Ptolemy, Liber de impressionibus.*

90. *Compilatio de Astrorum Scientia* (*Compilation on the Science of the Stars*). See Dykes, A Compilation on the Science of the Stars.

91. A German treatise that borrowed from the encyclopedic compendium of Bartholomeus Anglicus (before 1203–1272) called *De Proprietatibus Rerum* (*On the Properties of Things*). See Thorndike. *A History of Magic.*

92. Kieckhefer, trans. *Hazards of the Dark Arts,* 34–35.

THEURGY AND THE *ARS NOTORIA*

By naming Apollonius as the author of the *Flores Aurei,* the commentary on King Solomon's writings, the *Ars Notoria* invokes the magico-religious concept of theurgy and the art of memory in its ritual procedure.[93] The art of memory functions as an essential part of the inspection of the figures in the notory art tradition; this is explored in chapter IV, "The Art of Memory." Here, the magico-religious concept of theurgy is explored as an analog to understanding the magic of the *Ars Notoria.* Now, the key elements to the magic of the *Ars Notoria* are: (1) the *notae,* which are expressed as the *voces magicae* prayers and figures; (2) the dream vision of an angel who provides guidance and any additional instructions; (3) the art of memory for the inspection of the figures; and (4) the astronomical and astrological prescriptions. For the purposes of exploring the relationship between theurgy and the *Ars Notoria,* the key elements are the prayers, the figures, and the angels who communicate with the practitioner.[94] The magic of the *Ars Notoria* is grounded in both Iamblichian and Pseudo-Dionysian theurgy. But first, what is theurgy?

Theurgy (Greek *theourgia*) is a "work of the gods" (Greek *theion ergon*) by which man is transformed to a divine status; this transformation was thought to be accomplished through the Chaldean mystery rites that entailed invoking the pagan gods. In theurgy, the soul is thought to have descended into the body, and thus, the soul is perceived as having been imprisoned in the body and made separate from its divine source. The contemporary scholar Claire Fanger's definition of theurgy, which focuses on its functional traits, is adopted in this work. Theurgy involves rituals to bring about the soul's purification through invoking intermediary spirits (gods, angels, *daemons*), in which a revelatory or visionary experience is transmitted to the practitioner. Through these revelatory experiences, knowledge is gained, thereby perfecting the soul and allowing it to ascend and return to the divine source (known as achieving *henosis*).[95]

---

93. See appendix A6, which provides an excerpt from Apollonius's treatise on theurgic practices titled *On Sacrifices.* See chapter IV for the biographical sketch of Apollonius as an expert in memory recall.

94. Other magical traditions attest to the importance of astronomical and astrological timing in order to communicate with angels and spirits, but this feature is not discussed in great detail in this book.

95. Shaw, *Theurgy and the Soul,* 5.

Historically, the term *theurgy* belongs to the Egyptian and Greco-Roman religions, as hinted at in the *Chaldean Oracles* and Apollonius's *On Sacrifices* and then expounded upon by Iamblichus in *De Mysteriis*. The term *theurgy* is useful in describing those cultures whose religious practices have certain analogues that would have been recognizable to them; it is important to stress the term's usefulness so as not to be accused of naming another culture's religious practices as such.

Though its origins are shrouded in mystery, theurgic ideas were described in the *Chaldean Oracles,* then described by Iamblichus of Syria (c. 245–c. 325) in his *De Mysteriis* (*On the Mysteries*). These ideas were carried on by the Neoplatonists even when they faced a devastating blow to their ideas when Emperor Justinian the Great forced the closure of the Athenian Academy in 529 CE. At the emperor's command to never teach again, the Neoplationists chose exile in Persia. It is important to point out that Iamblichus is lacking substantive descriptions about the actual performance of theurgic rituals; however, he explains that certain ritual practices are revealed to humankind and become established by divine institution as a means for the ascension of the soul. He writes that theurgic ritual is not meant to influence the gods, saying that would be impossible. Iamblichus explains that humankind is faced with the problem of having an embodied soul that "becomes a stranger to itself" by being separated from its own immortal source, and therefore, the soul requires assistance from the gods to recover its lost divinity.[96]

Between the gods and the human soul stand a hierarchy of spirits who are ruled by the gods. Through divine mediation of the spirits and theurgic ritual, the human soul is able to transcend the world and return to its divine source. Theurgic ritual uses a symbol system that, divinely instituted, relies on the mythical stories by which the theurgist participates in a ritual reenactment that imitates the creation of the natural world. The creation story is about the emanations from the gods, to the intermediary spirits, to man, and to all of nature; therefore, there is an opportunity for the theurgist to perceive all of the natural world as a theophany.

The modern scholar Gregory Shaw describes Iamblichus's theurgic symbols (*sunthemata*) as a three-tier system that describes the key components of a

96. *De Anima* 223.31, as quoted in Shaw, "Neoplatonic Theurgy," 580.

ritual, ranked from lowest to highest. At the bottom, the material *sunthemata* includes stones, herbs, animals, and aromatics that correspond to the particular god invoked in accordance with that god's mythical account. Next, the intermediate *sunthemata* includes hieratic characters, signs, names, and musical compositions. At the top are the noetic *sunthemata,* which are immaterial abstractions such as numbers and mathematics. Thus, as the theurgist ritually harmonizes his soul to the correspondences of the natural world and cosmos (e.g., stones, herbs, animals, etc.), these correspondences awaken the knowledge within himself, and thus his soul progressively ascends through the heavens and unites with the divine source.[97]

Pseudo-Dionysius the Areopagite, a sixth-century Christian theologian and student of Neoplatonism, adapted theurgy within a Christian framework that would later influence the esoteric practices and mystical theology of medieval Christianity into the modern era. It is at the crossroads of theurgy, Neoplatonism, and medieval Christianity that the foundation for the adapted ritual practice of the *Ars Notoria* is derived.

Shaw argues that Pseudo-Dionysius the Areopagite borrows theurgic concepts and practices from Iamblichus, giving them a specific Christian expression. Pseudo-Dionysius the Areopagite (also known as Pseudo-Denys, fl. late fifth to early sixth century CE), a Christian theologian and philosopher of possible Syrian origins, wrote a Greek corpus of mystical writings. As a Christian, Pseudo-Dionysius perceives a Creator-and-Created cosmogony in which God rules the heavens and the earth. Between God and humankind are Christ, the nine choirs of angels, and the church. Christ's earthly mission was a ritual to save man from his fallen state.[98] Pseudo-Dionysius's symbol system also has three tiers, with the lowest rank being the sacred pictures of the scriptures used to educate the many lay Christians who were illiterate. Their only means of Christian education and worship was by going to church and learning through the sacred pictures that told biblical stories. The middle rank belonged to church liturgy and the Christian sacraments by which the soul makes its journey back to God through the process of *theosis,* which is the deification of the soul. The top tier is inaccessible to the human soul and belongs solely to the

---

97. Shaw, *Theurgy and the Soul.*

98. Luibheid and Rorem, trans. *Pseudo-Dionysius.*

angels who perform celestial worship of God. In the hierarchy, the church's role is to have priests transmit the deifying power of the sacraments to the laymen. Through the human soul's journey toward communion with God, the soul is participating in the new creation as established by the new covenant made through Christ. This new model of creation separates the human soul from nature and matter.[99]

The analogous components of Iamblichian theurgy to the Pseudo-Dionysian Christianized theurgy include two main elements: first, the ultimate goal of the soul's journey back to the divine (what theurgy calls *henosis,* in which the individual being "ascends" or merges with the One, and *theosis,* the Christian term, which Pseudo-Dionysius describes as the divinization of the soul), and second, the three-tier symbol system of Iamblichian theurgy and the ecclesiastical hierarchy of Pseudo-Dionysius.

For Pseudo-Dionysius, the path for the soul's return to God involves (1) the acquisition of divine knowledge, which culminates in an apophatic[100] and mystical understanding of God, and (2) the use of the symbols of the ecclesiastical hierarchy. The acquisition of divine knowledge involves a stirring of the soul in which the human senses and intellect are transcended, and the soul becomes divinized by uniting with a contemplated object. Pseudo-Dionysius says:

> We use whatever appropriate symbols we can for the things of God. With these analogies we are raised upward toward the truth of the mind's vision, a truth which is simple and one. We leave behind us all our own notions of the divine. We call a halt to the activities of our minds and, to the extent that is proper, we approach the ray which transcends being. Here, in a manner no words can describe, preexisted all the goals of all knowledge, and it is of a kind that neither intelligence nor speech can lay hold of it nor can it at all be contemplated since it surpasses everything and is wholly beyond our capacity to know it. Transcendently, it contains within itself the boundaries of every natural knowledge and energy. At the same time, it is established by an unlimited power beyond all the celestial minds. And if all knowledge

---

99. Shaw, "Neoplatonic Theurgy."

100. Apophatic (or negative) theology is a way of thinking and approaching God by speaking only in terms of what God is not. For Pseudo-Dionysius, God is transcendent and unknowable in such a way that nothing can be said about the divine essence of God since God is beyond beingness itself.

> is of that which is and is limited to the realm of the existent, then whatever transcends being must also transcend knowledge.[101]

By pursuing the truth of the mind's vision of a particular symbol in contemplation, the activities of the mind stop, and the soul is able to transcend human senses and intellect, thereby the soul becomes divinized and attains divine knowledge. This divine knowledge is transcendent, beyond being, but also contains within itself the boundaries of every natural knowledge (e.g., the liberal and mechanical arts). The acquisition of divine knowledge is pursued by the Christian's love of God and of things divine through the symbols of the ecclesiastical hierarchy. For Pseudo-Dionysius, theurgy is a participation in God's work (*theurgia*) through the church liturgy and the Christian sacraments, which are the symbols used for contemplation according to the ecclesiastical hierarchy.[102] Pseudo-Dionysius explains how the soul can be stirred up through the use of divine names and words, moving the attention away from the human senses and directing its energies to God:

> The truth we have to understand is that we use letters, syllables, phrases, written terms and words because of the senses. But when our souls are moved by intelligent energies in the direction of the things of the intellect, then our senses, and all that go with them, are no longer needed. And the same happens with our intelligent powers which, when the soul becomes divinized, concentrate sightlessly and through an unknowing union on the rays of "unapproachable light."[103]

Arguably, the blended Iamblichian and Pseudo-Dionysian theurgy provides the basis for the ritual procedure detailed in the *Ars Notoria*. The *Ars Notoria* is like Pseudo-Dionysius's theurgy in that it contemplates certain symbols called *notae,* the prayers and figures, for the attainment of knowledge. The *notae* are the working parts that are analogous to the divine names and words used in church liturgy and sacraments, which belong to Pseudo-Dionysius's second tier

---

101. Luibheid and Rorem, trans., *Pseudo-Dionysius,* "The Divine Names" (592C–593A), 53.

102. Luibheid and Rorem, trans., *Pseudo-Dionysius,* "The Ecclesiastical Hierarchy" (376A).

103. Luibheid and Rorem, trans., *Pseudo-Dionysius,* "The Divine Names" (708D), 80. The phrase "unapproachable light" comes from 1 Timothy 6:16.

of the ecclesiastical hierarchy. The *Ars Notoria* defines these three components of *notae,* figures, and prayers thus:

> Also, in this art [Apollonius] speaks about the *notae,* figures, and prayers, because in these three he establishes the entire art from where [in the text] it is to be understood what is a *nota,* what is a prayer, and what is a figure.
>
> The *nota* in this art is described thus: The *nota* is a certain cognition through the prayer and a superimposed figure, just like the *notae* of grammar, logic, and rhetoric; and of the other sciences, in those figures the prayer is written above. But the prayer is a sacramental mystery revealed and pronounced through the Greek, Hebrew, Chaldean, and Latin words.[104]

The *Ars Notoria* speaks of the virtues of the prayers, saying:

> For this you should pay close attention, and it is to be attended to and truly know that the entire mystery, the whole virtue and efficacy of this most holy operation consists in the prayers, within which the names of the holy angels of the living God, residing in the seats above, are named and invoked, and in the virtue of their figures and signs, because having invoked and named the holy angels of God with fasting and prayer, hope and faith, with the divine permission and virtue of God and his holy angels, which the angels have this grace from God who created them, the heart, mind, and all the senses, working [both] the interior and exterior [senses], are imbued and replenished with the divine knowledge of the Holy Spirit and the administration of the holy angels, and through them this most sacred work is being guided to an effect.[105]

The *Ars Notoria* often warns its reader to neither explain nor translate the foreign prayers. The text describes the angel Pamphilius warning Solomon, saying, "[H]is deed had the special justification of an angel carrying an irrefutable prohibition who said, 'See, you must not dare someone to explain or to translate about that, nor you, nor another after you. For it is a sacramental mystery. God heard your prayer not expressed in words by the [untranslatable] speech, and so may the

104. *Ars Notoria,* section 20 gloss.
105. *Ars Notoria,* NS 65.

intelligence, memory, eloquence, and of these three stable qualities be increased for you.'"[106] To explain or translate the prayers would alter their virtue, thereby losing their power. Similarly, the *Chaldean Oracles,* the spiritual and philosophical texts used by Neoplatonists, also seek to preserve the divine speech, which says, "'Do not change the *nomina barbara,*' that is, the names handed down by the gods to each race have ineffable power in the initiation rites."[107] Moreover, Iamblichus says, "And it is necessary that the prayers of the ancients, like sacred places of sanctuary, are preserved ever the same and in the same manner, with nothing of alternative origin either removed from or added to them."[108] As for the Latin prayers, they express the Christian atonement for sins and when recited alone, do not contain any special virtue.

The *Ars Notoria* imitates Pseudo-Dionysius's ecclesiastical hierarchy by stating that the Greek, Chaldean, Hebrew, and Latin prayers are "a sacramental mystery," belonging to the middle tier. The true author of the *Ars Notoria* does not intend to say that the notory art is a sacrament sanctioned by the church, but that these prayers are deemed a sacrament because (1) they were divinely instituted by God as revealed to Solomon, and (2) and it follows Pseudo-Dionysian thought, as already stated, "We use whatever appropriate symbols we can for the things of God." It is this second premise that, in part, places the *Ars Notoria* within an unorthodox and marginalized practice of the Christian tradition whereby it received condemnation by the church and others.

What makes the *Ars Notoria* especially unique are the "figures and their signs," which are divinely instituted as theurgic symbols. The "figures and their signs" might be categorized under the Iamblichian model as an intermediate *sunthemata* like characters and signs. Considering that many have geometric shapes and a certain number are allocated to certain fields of knowledge, the figures might even suggest the highest tier of the noetic *sunthemata,* which deals with numbers and what Shaw calls "the signatures of the intellect of the gods."[109] Both symbol sets entail a number of geometric figures meant for contemplation for

106. *Ars Notoria,* section 17.

107. Majercik, trans., *The Chaldean Oracles,* fragment 150, p. 107.

108. Iamblichus, *On the Mysteries* (259. 14–19).

109. Although Iamblichus does not go into detail about noetic *sunthemata,* there are hints about the theurgic secrets of geometric shapes rooted in pagan myth from the accounts of the tenth-century Baghdadi historian Al-Masudi and the sixth-century Byzantine administrator John the Lydian.

which the individual creates an image of the world (*imago mundi*) within himself, then offers it up to the divine with prayers. By analogy, the *Ars Notoria* may be called the "spritual successor" to Iamblichian theurgy for this reason.

For the *Ars Notoria,* the operator's quest for secular and divine knowledge is attained through the *notae;* that is, the recitation of the *voces magicae* prayers and the inspection of figures. When the operator has purified himself through confession, fasting, and chastity, he invokes the Holy Spirit and angelic choirs, who are the intermediary spirits of the celestial hierarchy. In his *Celestial Hierarchy,* Pseudo-Dionysius is credited with establishing the nine angelic choirs, grouped into three hierarchies: (1) Seraphim, Cherubim, and Thrones; (2) Dominions, Virtues, and Powers; and (3) Principalities, Archangels, and Angels. The *Ars Notoria* mentions these nine angelic choirs often in its prayers. Also, it is imperative that the reader understands that in theurgy, the spirits are called and persuaded by the prayers of the petitioner, never coerced or bound as chthonic spirits are in necromancy.

Although the *Ars Notoria* is silent on the matter, it seems that these divine hypostases would bring about the restoration and divinization of the soul through a Platonic remembrance of knowledge.[110] Such an implication seems plausible if it is understood that the magical foundation of the original *Flores Aurei* was rooted in Greek magic and thought, which was overlaid with a Christian veneer through the borrowing of Pseudo-Dionysian thought, which was prevalent and popular during the Late Middle Ages.

Even though the *Ars Notoria* presents an analog to theurgic rites, the greater ritual procedure of the notory art would more accurately be called a composite rite of magic, meaning it has multiple techniques and parts. The aforesaid *notae*—that is, the prayers and figures—are distinctly theurgic symbols in the context of magical practice. However, through the medieval and secular lens, the prayers appear akin to the notarial science of the legal notary and understood in terms of Aristotelian philosophy. Similarly, the figures resemble mnemonic diagrams for memorizing information related to the seven liberal arts and other disciplines; such mnemonic diagrams would necessitate the employment of the mnemonic principles and techniques found in the art of memory.

110. *Ars Notoria,* section 115, which is a prayer to God saying, "teach me in your truth, and restore my soul with knowledge according to your great mercy." See also Version B, section 32 gloss, which talks about God restoring the operator by virtue and instruction. The restoration of the soul through knowledge is a prominent theme in the *Ars Notoria.*

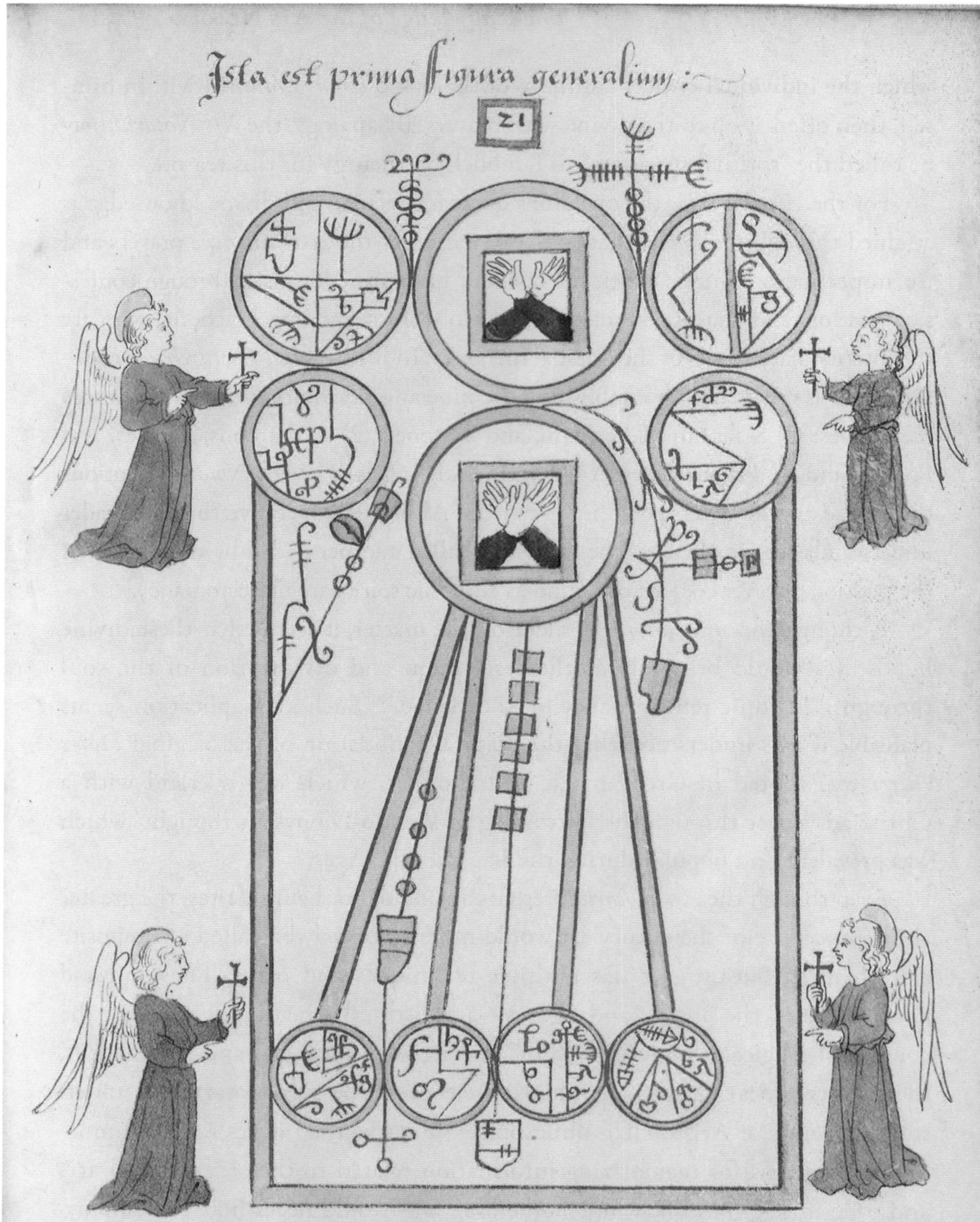

First figure of general sciences, from *Ars notoria de Salomone,*
BnF Latin 7153. 15th century

IV.

THE ART OF MEMORY

The notory art is also called the art of memory.[1] The art of memory is a number of mnemonic principles and techniques used to convert new information into impressions or images, which are then visualized and plotted along an imaginary and orderly route for optimal recall.

The exact origins of the art of memory are uncertain, with some claims going back to the ancient Egyptians and Pythagoreans. The Greeks claim Simonides of Ceos (c. 556–468 BCE), a lyric poet, was the founder of the art.[2] The primary classical sources for the art include the *Rhetorica ad Herennium* (book 3), Cicero's *De Oratore* (book 2.350–60), and Quintilian's *Institutio Oratoria* (book 11).[3] Aristotle also wrote about memory in his *De Anima* (*On the Soul*) and *De Memoria et Reminiscentia* (*On Memory and Reminiscence*). Aristotle and the prevailing medical tradition understood memory as a physical process involving both the brain and the heart. This association between memory and heart was embedded within Greek and Latin such that it carries on to this day as when people say they had something "memorized by heart."

The most thorough study of the art of memory to date has been done by Mary Carruthers. Frances Yates says memory training for religious purposes was advocated by Iamblichus, Porphyry, and Diogenes Laertius, who refer to Pythagoras as the originator of this teaching.[4] Thus, Apollonius, as a Neo Pythagorean, took his memory training seriously. He had a reputation for recalling what he had learned by memory. While on his travels, Apollonius met

1. *Ars Notoria,* Prologue Gloss, page 325.

2. Yates, *Selected Works,* 29.

3. Carruthers, *The Book of Memory,* 59–60.

4. Yates, *The Art of Memory,* 42.

an Indian who said to him, "Apollonius, I see that you are well-endowed with Memory, the god whom we honor most."[5] In another instance, Apollonius was so famous for his ability to recall information that he is said to have surpassed the Greek father of the art of memory, as Philostratus writes:

> Euxenus once asked Apollonius why he did not become a writer when his ideas were noble and his diction pure and alert. "Because I have not yet fallen silent," he answered. From then on, he considered himself bound to silence, though while he held his tongue, his eyes and mind read and stored away very many things in his memory. In fact, even when he was a hundred, he surpassed Simonides himself in power of recollection. He used to sing a hymn in honor of [the muse called] Memory,[6] in which he says that all things wither in time, but time itself is ageless and immortal thanks to memory.[7]

It is important to understand that the *Ars Notoria* assumes the medieval model of the soul in which the faculty of memory belongs to one of the five internal senses as described by the Persian philosopher Avicenna (980–1037). These senses are common sense, retentive imagination, compositive imagination, estimative power, and memory. The common sense receives and interprets the perceptions of the external senses. The retentive imagination stores these perceptions, and the compositive imagination processes them. The estimative power, or instinct, judges the "intentions" of the perceived objects, such as whether they be friendly or hostile, and these intentions are stored in the memory.[8]

The five external senses were enumerated by Aristotle as touch, taste, smell, sight, and hearing in his *De Anima* (*On the Soul*). Boethius speaks of four kinds of knowledge that are attained by the senses, imagination, reason, and intelligence.[9] What he means by intelligence (Latin *intelligentia*) consists of two faculties of the soul: understanding (*intellectus*) and reason (*ratio*). Understanding is the simple

---

5. Philostratus, *Life of Apollonius,* 3.16.4.

6. Apollonius follows the Greek tradition of honoring Memory as did Plato, who wrote, "As to what came next, Crito, how can I describe it to you beautifully? For it is no small task to recount thoroughly such an extraordinary wisdom. I therefore need to begin my description in the very same way as the poets—invoking the Muses and Memory." See Plato, *Euthydemus,* 275.

7. Philostratus, *Life of Apollonius,* 1.14.

8. Kärkkäinen, "Internal Senses."

9. Boethius, *Consolation of Philosophy,* book 5.

grasp of a self-evident truth, and reason is the step-by-step progression to prove a truth that is not self-evident. Both the internal and external senses, including the Latin terms, are found in the text and prayers of the *Ars Notoria*.

According to the *Ars Notoria,* the "first road" to knowledge entails gaining four qualities—memory, eloquence, understanding, and the stability of these three—which will aid the student down the paths of the trivium ("three roads") and the quadrivium ("four roads").

THE METHOD OF PLACES

Apollonius's renowned memory was achieved through the essential mnemonic technique called the method of places (Greek *topoi;* Latin *loci*). The method of places is a technique rooted in the imagination. Cicero compares memory to writing, saying:

> As to memory, which is in a certain manner the sister of writing; and though in a different class, greatly resembles it. For as it consists of the characters of letters, and of that substance on which those characters are impressed; so, a perfect memory uses *topoi,* as writing does wax, and on them arranges its images as if they were letters.[10]

The ancient authorities recommend that the student select a building, or shops along a street, or anything similar in which there a number of discrete places (*topoi*); in fact, they suggest a geographical area with which the student was very familiar, such as his hometown. This will function as the mental map upon which the student will place his newly acquired information. The method consists of the following three stages: imprinting, storing, and retrieval.

The imprinting stage: The newly acquired information to be remembered is encoded within an image. The ancient authorities use the metaphor of writing on a wax tablet or stamping a seal. Just as a stamp is pressed into hot wax, leaving a seal, so the mind imprints the image upon a place. Ancient authorities observed that the memory is best stimulated by images that are

10. "A Dialogue Concerning Oratorical Partitions," in Yonge, trans., *The Orations of Marcus Tullius Cicero.*

novel, exceptionally immoral, unbelievable, and laughable; in addition, the best images excite the senses for learning—visual, audio, and tactile. The mind fails to remember things that are ordinary, petty, and banal.

The storing stage: The storing stage is about organizing the contents of one's memory, and so the ancients used the metaphor of a storeroom or treasury. In Plato's *Theaetetus,* when talking about memory recall, Socrates compares the particular pieces of information to be recalled like domestic pigeons housed in a pigeon coop. Thus, the coop is the place (*topos*) where pigeons (i.e., the images) reside, and they are organized in a logical fashion. The author of *Rhetorica ad Herennium* recommends the use of architectural features in building one's own storeroom to aid memory. Buildings with columns are particularly helpful as the spaces between columns (*intercolumnia*) provide good backgrounds for things to be remembered. The background to each image ought to be well lit, having a contrast of color against the image, with the viewer seeing the image from a middle perspective, not too close nor too far. The backgrounds should be bare and simple and must not be too much alike but differ just enough to be clearly distinguishable from one another. A student might group images together within a single room. Alternatively, if there is a row or street of many images, he would mark every fifth image with a golden hand (a hand has five digits) and every tenth image with the face of his Roman friend Decimus (Decimus means "the tenth" in Latin). Thus, creating divisions helps to remember information.

The retrieval stage: The student takes an orderly mental walk-through of his chosen building or street, seeing each image he placed along certain landmarks and recounting the information imprinted in each image. The walk-through can be performed forward or backward, but never out of sequence.

The art of memory assists the student in learning quickly, though it takes practice, and each stage would be repeated several times to gain the full benefit for recalling information quickly and easily.

An example of location imagery used for mnemonic function can be seen in the figure opposite, a sample of a 1533 text, *Congestorum Artificiose Memorie* (*Collected Rules of the Art of Memory*). On the left, the streets of a town include the barber (*barbitonsor*), armorer (*bellator*), abbey (*abbatia*), bookseller (*bibliopola*), the slaughterhouses (*bovicidia*), and the herdsman (*bubulcus*); the streets of the town provide a good example of a mental walk-through. On the right, the abbey (*abbatial*) is divided into three areas—the courtyard (*aula*),

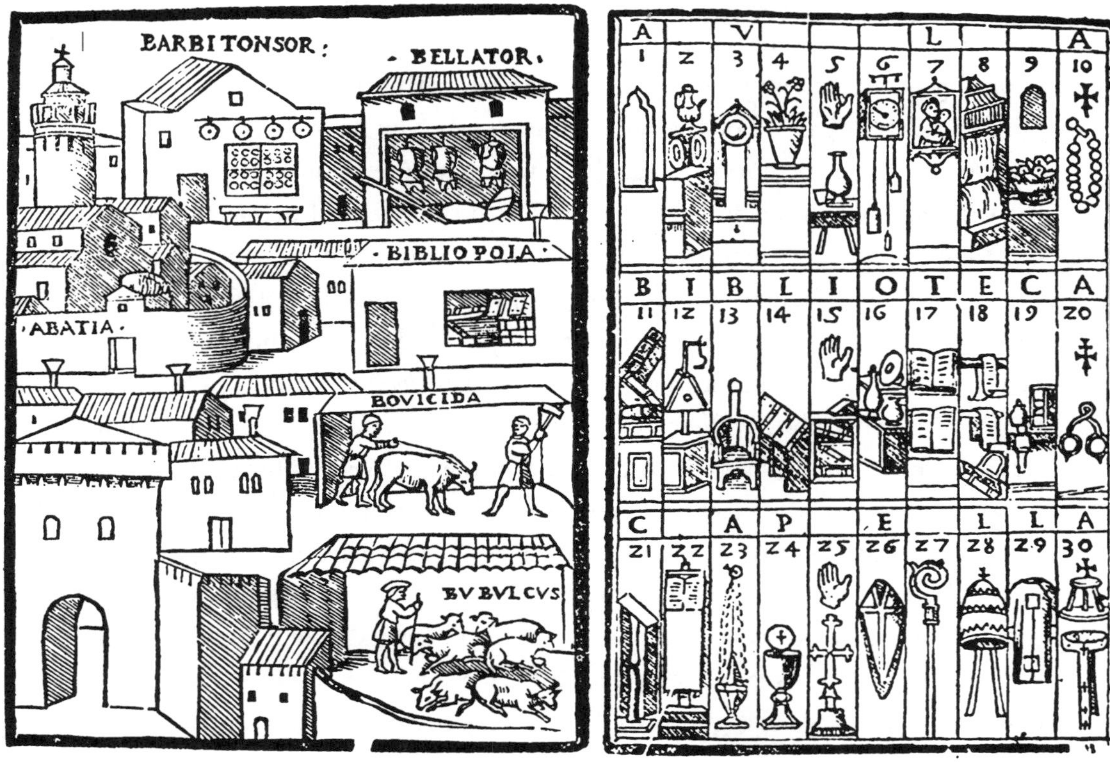

Pages from the *Congestorum Artificiose Memorie* (*Collected Rules of the Art of Memory*) by the German Dominican Johann Horst von Romberch, Venice, 1533

the library (*biblioteca*), and the chapel (*capella*). Ten places (*loci*) are designated within each of these three areas, including things such as a window, a pot of flowers, and a clock. Notice that Romberch follows the advice of the author of *Rhetorica ad Herennium* by placing a golden hand at every fifth place; for every tenth place, he marks it with a cross.

Concerning the imprinting stage, the *Ars Notoria* says, "[T]hey ought to be kept in memory if an impressed sign is to be made in the heart of those figures which are inspected."[11] For the storing stage, the *Ars Notoria* provides each art and science with a certain number of figures. For example, grammar has

11. *Ars Notoria,* NS 3.

three figures, logic two, and rhetoric four. The prayers are divided to aid the operator's memory, such as *Hazatam,* which has four parts; also, many of the adorning prayers, those prayers that are written within the figures themselves, are divided into parts. For the retrieval stage, the *Ars Notoria* relates the figures to the art of memory, saying, "[H]e may have the figures themselves and their significance in memory and in mind, and place [them] before the eyes of reason and intellect, which the eyes of the flesh cannot see."[12] Thus, whenever the *Ars Notoria* instructs the operator to inspect (*inspectio*) the figures (*notae*), what the operator must do is visualize the figure within his mind, using it as a memory palace that contains many discrete places (*loci*) within it. To be abundantly clear, when the *Ars Notoria* says to inspect the *notae,* it does not mean to scry. There are no instructions to be found in the *Ars Notoria* for using a bowl of water, flame, mirror, or crystal. This is purely a mnemonic technique.

Because the operator would visualize a figure and place his images within it, this became a highly individualized process. The art of memory itself is a very personal process, as certain places and images evoke strong emotions subjectively, and therefore provide better recall, for some, while not so for others. Likewise, the use of the figures would be a very personal matter; in fact, there may be some evidence of this personalization in regard to the signs (*signa*) found within the figures of Version B. These signs might very well indicate the places (*loci*) held in the memory of a notory art practitioner. Following the ancient authorities' advice about using architectural features, the notory art has certain figures that look like towers or columns suitable for an operator's memory palace. Yates suggests that the *Ars Notoria* was a poor descendant of the art of memory or a writing system of shorthand.[13]

ALLEGORY, SYMBOLS, AND PERSONIFICATIONS

One of the key principles of the art of memory states that the mind conceives of ideas as pictures and symbols, which, if organized coherently, can form a narrative. Thus, the literary device of allegory, a narrative and visual representation of a character or event that can be interpreted to symbolize a hidden signifi-

---

12. *Ars Notoria,* section 136.
13. Yates, *Art of Memory,* 15, 43.

cance, is a useful mnemonic tool. Similarly, personification, the literary device of taking an abstract idea and representing it as a person, can also aid memory. Such literary devices can be used to populate the imaginary locations (*topos*) that form the organizing principle of the art of memory.

Martianus Capella, the author of *De Nuptiis Philologiae et Mercurii* (*On the Marriage of Philology and Mercury*), describes personifications of the seven liberal arts in his allegory for the purpose of assisting the memory of young learners. In the figure on page 128, we can see an excellent example of allegory and symbol to represent substantial concepts. Capella's work describes an allegory of Apollo, who unites Mercury with the personification of Philology in a wedding ceremony; the invited guests are the personified handmaidens of the seven liberal arts who teach their art and science and showcase their talents for the audience of the Olympian gods. His work was based on the first-century BCE Roman scholar Marcus Terentius Varro's now lost *Disciplinarum Libri IX* (*Nine Books of the Disciplines*), which was an encyclopedia of the liberal arts based on Greek sources; Varro included medicine and architecture, but these arts were demoted by later authors. The following descriptions of the personifications and their symbols are given to each of the seven liberal arts as mnemonic devices to aid the medieval student.

Grammar: She is an old woman who carries an ivory box containing a pruning knife, black ink, and a red medicine made of fennel flower and goat hair. She also carries a writing tablet and a file containing the eight parts of speech. At her feet are three boys learning her art. The pruning knife, black ink, and red medicine are said to correct a student's pronunciation. Traditionally, Grammar's teacher is represented as Priscian.

Logic/Dialectic: She carries in her right hand a wheel with a set of patterns (*formulae*) inscribed on wax tablets, which are adorned with contrasting colors, and held on the inside by a hidden hook. In her left hand she holds a snake wrapped in coils. The shape of the wheel is chosen as a pedagogical tool for expressing word combinations in the propositions of a syllogism; by turning the wheel, one can easily view and generate new combinations to test their validity. In a persuasive argument, certain propositions are made appealing to an opponent. Once he accepts those propositions (following certain colored patterns or *formulae* on Lady

Logic's wheel), he must make certain admissions (the hook), leading to an unexpected and striking conclusion (the snake), which leads to his defeat. Traditionally, Logic's teacher is represented as Aristotle.

Rhetoric: A beautiful woman whose head is adorned with a helmet and wreathed with royal grandeur. She carries a sword, wearing a Roman *stola* adorned with light, devices, and figures and a belt made of colors and jewels. Capella has Rhetoric accompanied by two teachers—Demosthenes and Cicero.

Arithmetic: A stately woman from whose face shine rays of light representing both unity and infinity as exemplified by the Pythagorean decad. Her fingers flash like lightning at the speed of her counting. She wears a robe symbolizing pure numbers with an undergarment for numbers applied to material objects. Her symbols include a flaming torch and an abacus. Capella has Arithmetic accompanied by Pythagoras. In art, Lady Arithmetic is represented by Pythagoras or Nicomachus of Gerasa and then later by Boethius.

Music: Lady Music, also called Harmony, is accompanied by other young women; namely, Genethliace, Symbolice,[14] and Oeonistice.[15] These three prophetic personifications are symbolized by the sacrificial tripod that represents the triple time sequence of past, present, and future. Harmony is adorned with ornaments of glittering gold and wears a stiff garment of incised and laminated gold. In her right hand she carries a circular shield bearing the design of the orbits of the celestial bodies. In her left hand she holds golden musical instruments made by mortals. In art, Pythagoras or Tubal-cain is attributed to music.[16]

---

14. Symbolice means "symbolic" or "riddling," and she represents an oracle consulted about future events.

15. Oeonistice is the personification of the ancient diviners of augury (i.e., divination according to the flight of birds). Her symbols include the plumage of the white swan and the black crow, which represent omens that come to humankind by both day and night.

16. Tubal-cain, also known as Jubal, is said to be the inventor of the art of music and is mentioned in Genesis 4:19–22 (Septuagint) and Philo's *On the Posterity of Cain and His Exile,* which are the sources for the Old Latin translation of Flavius Josephus's *Jewish Antiquities* and which were ascribed to the fourth-century CE theologian Rufinus of Aquileia (345–410 CE). The passage reads, "[The children of Seth] also were the inventors of that peculiar wisdom, which is concerned with the heavenly bodies, and their order. And that their inventions might not be lost before they were sufficiently known, upon Adam's prediction that the world was to be destroyed

Geometry: In her right hand she carries a geometer's rod, and in her left hand she holds a globe of the celestial sphere. She wore a Greek peplos adorned with the heavenly orbits, dimensions, and intersections of celestial bodies and which included figures and measures.[17] Capella's Lady Geometry mentions Archimedes and Euclid as the principal teachers.

Astronomy: A maiden enclosed in heavenly light and surrounded by the seven planetary deities and the celestial sphere, decked in sparkling gems and shown with a starry countenance. She has crystalline golden wings and held a celestial navigation instrument and a book of astronomical calculations.[18] Capella mentions Eratosthenes, Hipparchus, and Ptolemy as representatives of Astronomy.

Boethius's written works had a profound influence on the medieval curriculum regarding the seven liberal arts, especially his *Consolation of Philosophy.* In the image on page 128, Boethius stands on the far left speaking to his "sovereign comfort," Lady Philosophy, who governs the personified seven liberal arts. The seven liberal arts, personified as ladies, follow Lady Philosophy in tow because all the arts seek the truth. From left to right, an inscription and symbol identify each of the liberal arts: Grammar holds an open book; Rhetoric holds a scroll perhaps of written decrees or a speech; Logic holds a patterned wheel featuring a cross at its center to represent fourfold divisions of logic; Music holds a sheet of musical notation; Geometry holds a set square; Arithmetic holds a scroll with

---

at one time by the force of fire, and at another time by the violence and quantity of water, they made two pillars: the one of brick, the other of stone: they inscribed their discoveries on them both: that in case the pillar of brick should be destroyed by the flood, the pillar of stone might remain, and exhibit those discoveries to mankind: and also inform them that there was another pillar of brick erected by them. Now this remains in the land of Siriad [i.e., Egypt] to this day," *Jewish Antiquities* 1.2.12–13. The Old Latin translation was used by later writers including Boethius and Isidore of Seville. The Old Latin translation is repeated in the twelfth-century *Glossa Ordinaria* (Ordinary Gloss), which is a collection of biblical commentaries.

17. The modern-day depiction of the wizard dressed in a robe adorned with stars and planets comes from this very image of Lady Geometry.

18. In the *Magical Calendar* (1620) the seven classic planets are assigned to the seven liberal arts as follows: Sun to grammar, Moon to logic/dialectic, Jupiter to rhetoric, Mercury to arithmetic, Venus to music, Mars to geometry, and Saturn to astronomy. However, a deeper examination of the extant literature shows that there was no formal consensus on which planets were assigned to which liberal art.

Philosophy Presenting the Seven Liberal Arts to Boethius.
Coëtivy Master (Henri de Vulcop?) (French, active c. 1450–1485); Paris, c. 1460–1470. The J. Paul Getty Museum, Los Angeles, Ms. 42, leaf 2v. Image courtesy of Getty.edu.

mathematical notations; and Astronomy holds an armillary sphere. All seven young women are well dressed in the popular fashion of the Burgundian court in the late fifteenth century. Lady Philosophy, as the senior member and leader of the group, wears an elaborate M-shaped kitelike headdress known as a *hennin* over a gold steeple-shaped cap.

Another example of personification is found in Gregor Reisch's *Pearl of Philsophy,* as seen on the facing page. The personification of Grammar leads a young boy to a building housing the other liberal arts. At the door, it reads *congruentia,* meaning "unity" or "harmony," and the first floor has the beginning grammar students learning from the Latin grammarian Aelius Dontaus. On the second floor, there are the advanced students of grammar learning from the Latin grammarian Priscian. On the third floor, from left to right, there is Aristotle for logic, Marcus Tullius Cicero for rhetoric, and Boethius for arithmetic. On the fourth floor, from left to right, there is Pythagoras for music, Archimedes for geometry, and Ptolemy for astronomy. On the fifth floor, from left to right, there is Pedanius Dioscorides for medicine and Seneca the Younger for morals. At the top, Peter Lombard represents theology.

Margarita Philosophica (*Pearl of Philosophy*), 1503,
woodcut titled *Typus Grammaticae* (Figure of Grammar).

THE ART OF MAGIC AND THE ART OF SHORTHAND WRITING

The entire confusion between the magical art described in the *Ars Notoria* and the notarial science may have begun with the fantastical tales surrounding the Roman poet Vergil and the Greek philosopher Aristotle during the Middle Ages. Returning to *The Chronicle of Ralph Niger,* the record of the Anglo-French theologian and English chronicler reads, "At this time [i.e., during the lifetime of Ovid, the Roman poet who lived during the reign of Augustus (43 BCE–18 CE)], the secrets of Aristotle of Athens are discovered, in which Virgil found the notary art (*artem notariam*) that he burned afterward according to Valerius Maximus."[19] This passage can be interpreted in a couple of ways.

The first interpretation is that the notary art of Aristotle (*Ars Notaria Aristotelis*) belonged to the shorthand writing tradition that is a part of the notarial science, not the magical art. The second interpretation is that "the secrets of Aristotle" meant esoteric and magical knowledge, which Vergil discovered while visiting in Athens; in this way, Vergil becomes the heir to the esoteric knowledge of Aristotle.[20] Because Vergil would have immediately understood the value of these secrets, he would have memorized them and then burned Aristotle's book so that no one else would know them.

But from where, according to legend, did Aristotle get his esoteric knowledge? The medieval author of the *Philosophy of Virgil of Corduba* (a different person named Virgil), explains that Aristotle traveled with his pupil Alexander the Great to the Temple of Jerusalem, where Aristotle discovered the many secret writings of Solomon.[21] One of the most popular books during the Middle Ages was the *Kitab Sirr Al-Asrar* (*Secret of Secrets*), falsely attributed to Aristotle and translated by John of Seville, containing esoteric knowledge. The text claims to be a letter sent by Aristotle to his pupil Alexander the Great

19. My translation of the Latin found in *Radulfi Nigri Chronica: The Chronicles of Ralph Niger,* edited by R. Anstruther (London: n.p., 1851), 108. Valerius Maximus was a first-century Latin author of the *Factorum ac dictorum memorabilium libri IX* (*Nine Books of Memorable Deeds and Sayings*), which was one of the most popular texts during the Middle Ages.

20. Such a story of discovery parallels that of Apollonius of Tyana, who discovered the secret crypt of Hermes Trismegistus and a cache of esoteric writings. See appendix A6.

21. Alexander the Great makes his own discovery of an esoteric text entitled *Kitab Thakhirat Al-Iskander* (*The Book of the Treasure of Alexander*). See appendix A6.

about many different topics; it was received as an authentic work of Aristotle. In the thirteenth century, the chapters that dealt with occult sciences began to circulate separately, including the book *Tabula Smaragdina* (*The Emerald Tablet*). The *Tabula Smaragdina,* describing the prime alchemical principle, originates from the Latin treatise *De Secretis Naturae* (*On the Secrets of Nature*), falsely attributed to Apollonius of Tyana; it was translated from an Arabic original by Hugo of Santalla in the twelfth century. *De Secretis Naturae* describes how Apollonius of Tyana discovered a crypt that concealed a statue of Hermes and his secret writings. Thus, Apollonius of Tyana becomes heir to the Hermetic writings of Hermes Trismegistus. To reconstruct the mythical lineage of the divergent esoteric texts presented here and elsewhere in this book, the first figure of esoteric and magical knowledge was Hermes Trismegistus. Hermes was followed by Solomon,[22] then Aristotle and Alexander the Great, then Vergil the Roman poet. Apollonius of Tyana, who discovers the vault concealing the statue of Hermes, has a direct link from Hermes himself; of course, Apollonius of Tyana is said to be the spiritual successor of King Solomon in regards to the notory art. These personalities become part of the narrative and heritage of the magico-religious and philosophical way of life called Hermeticism.

Does the notarial science actually have any relation to the magical art of the *Ars Notoria*? The short answer is yes, but it is a complicated matter involving not just the notarial science but also medieval philosophy and linguistics. Some background knowledge in each of these fields is necessary in order to begin to comprehend the relationship between the notarial science and the *Ars Notoria*. Valentin Rose and Charles Burnett were among the first scholars to suggest a link between the notarial science and the *Ars Notoria*.[23] The civil-law notary practiced the art of shorthand writing, which was essential to recording the words spoken by his high-ranking official in order to compose official documents. The art of shorthand writing is an ancient Roman system called Tironian notes, named after Tiro, Marcus Tullius Cicero's personal secretary. The writing system is based on a combination of "notes" (*notae*) and attached "strokes" (*titule*), tallying up to about five thousand symbols. A great resource for understanding Tironian notes is the late thirteenth-century

---

22. The relationship between Hermes and Solomon is explained in chapter III under the subheading "Magic and the *Ars Notoria,*" page 103.

23. Rose, "Ars Notaria," 303–26; Burnett "Give Him the White Cow," 1–30.

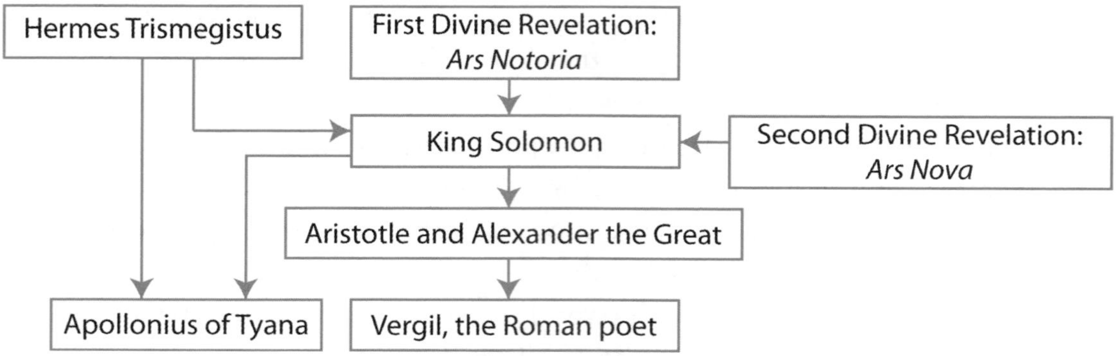

The lineage of mythical personalities in hermeticism.

At the top of the diagram is Hermes Trismegistus, the mythical figure and fountainhead of magic, astrology, and alchemy. The transmission of knowledge passed from Hermes to Apollonius of Tyana is told in the *De Secretis Naturae* (*On the Secrets of Nature*). The transmission of the notory art from King Solomon to Apollonius of Tyana has already been explored in chapter I. Virgil of Corduba relates the tradition of how Solomon's knowledge was transmitted to Aristotle, which is in accord with *Kitab Sirr Al-Asrar* (*Secret of Secrets*), the supposed letter of Aristotle to Alexander. *The Chronicle of Ralph Niger* tells how Vergil the Roman poet gained the notory art from Aristotle's writings.

treatise titled the *Ars Notoria Notarie* (*Notory Art of Shorthand*), which is written by an unknown author addressed to King Henry III of England. The work falls under the literary genre known as the mirror of princes, explaining the marvels of the shorthand system and the author's personal adaptation of the writing system to King Henry III. The anonymous author addresses the king, saying:

> We make note of your excellence, [King Henry III of England (reign 1216–1272)], for recently, in your days, the notory art was rediscovered by our humble selves through great and strenuous labor. This very art was ancient and, being most honored among the philosophers, in the past, it flourished until the time of Justinian the Great [reign 527–565] . . . after which it lay dormant for six hundred years and has remained completely unstudied up until our time.[24]

24. Haines, *The Notory Art of Shorthand,* 1.1.

Remarkably, the timing described here matches the same time in which the twelfth-century Italian renaissance of Roman law surged through Bologna, the very city that Véronèse proposes is the provenance of the *Ars Notoria*.[25] Justinian's *Corpus Juris Civilis* (*Body of Civil Laws*) was rediscovered, interestingly enough at the same time as the *Notae Tironinae* (Tironian notes). The rediscovery of the notarial science and law may have coincided with the Fourth Crusade in which Venetians pillaged the great libraries during the sack of Constantinople in 1204.[26] This also fits well with the advent of the *Ars Notoria*.

The *Notory Art of Shorthand* explains how the Tironian notes system compacted words into symbols, saying, "Indeed, this art does not deal with letters or syllables, but with figures of their parts which clearly designate their meaning, since the scribe does not make words, but symbols for words—symbols, that is, which completely express the words."[27] The English author John of Salisbury (1115/20–1180) says that the small *nota* holds wonderful "power . . . to generate a variety of compositions from relatively few elements."[28]

The *Notory Art of Shorthand* points out the two qualities of a *nota*—that is, the symbol and its brevity—saying, "There are two particular elements granting the greatest power to this speed: the note standing for the whole part, and the speed of the hand running tirelessly without obstacle."[29] The author, portrayed as the notary in his dialogue, explains the fundamentals of the notary art to his friend (the reader), who becomes bewildered, saying:

> **Friend:** Well, could anyone possibly exist with such a tenacious and perfect memory that he could remember all of them, if there were a hundred thousand times a hundred thousand parts?
>
> **Notary:** The answer is no. For the infinity of parts that you believe to be finite can be reduced to a very small number thanks to the compressing power of the notory art. And if you do not believe this, have a look at that

25. Similarly, theurgy and Neoplatonism went into decline after Justinian the Great closed the Academy in 529 CE. These religious and philosophical topics also reemerge in the *Ars Notoria*.

26. It is exciting to speculate at the possibility that the Venetians brought back with them a Greek original of the *Flores Aurei,* the Arabian story of the magnetic mountain, and other related sources, but there is no concrete evidence to support this.

27. Haines, *The Notory Art of Shorthand,* chapter 1.2.

28. Haines, *The Notory Art of Shorthand,* 8.

29. Haines, *The Notory Art of Shorthand,* chapter 1.8.

third book which contains the practice of the art's theory already covered in the two preceding ones. And what do you see?

Friend: I see only the written figures of primitive parts.

Notary: There is no need to put anything else! For both the primitive and the derivative part can be signified by one note, as the notory art teaches.

Friend: And these [Latin] parts can be contained within the space of a quarter-parchment, on one-fourth of a traditional folio?

Notary: Exactly right, on one-fourth. And would you believe that it is possible to learn this within only a few days' arduous work?[30]

The *Notory Art of Shorthand* lauds the shorthand system for its compactness, brevity, and ability to be learned quickly. The author goes on praising the notary art for its shorthand symbols and brevity, saying that Homer's epic poem, the *Iliad,* could fit inside a nutshell.[31] A professional notary examining the *Ars Notoria* would immediately recognize that the prayers of angel names containing *voces magicae* are like shorthand symbols, standing in for not just words but perhaps entire sentences and paragraphs. In other words, the *voces magicae* prayers encode lengthy prayers and angelic names into compact and short verses, which elicits the heavenly assistance in gaining secular and divine knowledge. On this account, the *Ars Notoria* would seem most impressive, and so its promise of being able to grant so much knowledge and to be learned rapidly would be very attractive.

Recall that the *Ars Notoria* defines *nota* as "a certain knowledge," which is represented through its two symbols: first, the pictorial figures, and second, the *voces magicae* prayers. Both the notary art of shorthand and the *Ars Notoria* agree that the two qualities of a *nota* are described as, first, written symbols that pack a great amount of information within them, and second, each symbol is very brief. The *Ars Notoria* says the magical art is like the art of shorthand because "it teaches [through] incomprehensible [language] the knowledge of all things out of writings with some [of the] shortest *notulis.*"[32] These *notulis* (little notes) are the *voces magicae* prayers. This is confirmed in Version B, which reads from the section 34 gloss, "Accordingly, Solomon called that book a scroll about

30. Haines, *The Notory Art of Shorthand,* chapter 6.1–2.

31. Haines, *The Notory Art of Shorthand,* chapter 7.

32. *Ars Notoria,* section 20b.

Figure 24. Tironian notes found in Isidore of Seville's *Lexicon Tironianum,* preserved in a tenth-century French manuscript written in Latin (British Library, Additional MS 21164). The large diagonal figure represents a stylus, which would be used for writing upon a wax tablet.

A wax tablet and bronze stylus in the medieval style. Photo by Steve Oser.

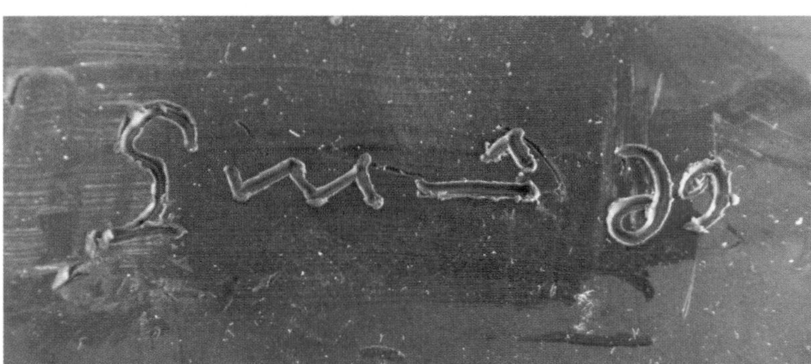

An example of Tironian notes carved into the wax, presenting the first line of Psalm 68 (KJV 69): *Salvum me fac, Deus.* Photo by Steve Oser.

the magnitude of quality, because in that scroll it has been declared of what kind and how great are the quantities and qualities of the most sacred Greek and Hebrew words and of the prayers of this book." Italics are mine.

Next, the philosophical and linguistical connection is made to the *Ars Notoria.* Solomon's *Liber Florum Caelestis Doctrinae* is said to be a book of "a magnitude of quality" containing the Greek, Hebrew, and Chaldean prayers for acquiring knowledge.[33] The "magnitude of quality" is a reference to the philosophical concepts presented in Aristotle's *Categories,* that would be commented upon by later medieval philosophers. Aristotle developed the philosophical theory which is now known as hylomorphism; Aristotle conceived every physical entity or substance (*ousia*) as a compound of matter (*hyle*) and immaterial form, with the generic form as immanently real within the entity. For example, Roman letters are the matter of syllables; the syllables express the accidental form. A substance (*ousia*) can have one or more accidental forms—that is, certain qualities such as number, time, place, action, and others—which Aristotle numerated. Matter undergoes a change in accidental form, whether that change becomes intensified (more) or remitted (less). Thus, the philosophical problem of intension and remission of accidental forms looks at how changes of degree within a given quality of nature occur—for example, how an object becomes hotter, or how the shade of a color changes.[34]

Interestingly, the *Ars Notoria* writer is applying this philosophical problem to the field of linguistics. For the *Ars Notoria,* the matter in this case, are the *voces magicae* prayers. According to the *Ars Notoria,* these prayers have undergone intensified changes in their word formation (morphology) and syntax because Solomon distorted the prayers by a subtle interweaving of the Greek, Hebrew, and Chaldean languages.[35] The process of word formation (morphology) involves the compounding of the words. A compound word consists of more than one lexeme; that is, a word or sign representing a unit of meaning. Compounding happens when two or more affixes, stems, or words are combined to make a longer word. For example, in Latin the word *adficio,* meaning "to influence," "to work upon," is a compound made up of *ad,* meaning "to" or "toward," and *facio,* meaning "to do" or "to bring about." The meaning of the compound may be similar to or different

33. *Ars Notoria,* section 34 and 34 gloss.

34. Can L. Loewe, "Gregory of Rimini on the Intension and Remission of Corporeal Forms," *Recherches de Théologie et Philosophie Médiévales* 81, no. 2 (2014): 273–330.

35. *Ars Notoria,* section 31.

First figure of geometry, from *Ars notoria Salamone,*
BnF Latin 7153. 15th century.

from the meaning of its components in isolation. The *notulis* are described in Aristotelian terms—"magnitude of qualities," "of which kind" (*genus*), and "how great" (*magnitudo*). The matter of magnitude directly references the philosophical problem of the intension and remission of accidental forms (i.e., qualities). The greater the compounding of a Greek, Hebrew, or Chaldean word with other affixes, the greater its intension or magnitude, and therefore compacts more meaning within it. In effect, the compounding of a word is the very process by which knowledge is encoded. Having been compounded, perhaps multiple times, the code becomes more complex, carrying greater meaning that, if translated or decoded, would contain many sentences. The reader of the *Ars Notoria* is often admonished to never translate or decode the prayers, because the attempt at such a translation would simplify (or remit) the compounded words, misconstruing them, and losing the original meaning.

In addition, the secret syntax of the *voces magicae* prayers has also undergone intensified changes. The syntax is changed through rhetorical schemes and figures of speech.[36] One type is a zeugma, the grammatical bridge between a word that governs two or more other words in such a manner that it applies to each in a different sense (e.g., He took *his weapon* and his *leave*). Zeugmas provide a great utility and efficacy in both meaning and brevity, thereby offering the opportunity for multiple and nuanced meanings and using fewer words to say them. Given how the *voces magicae* of the *Ars Notoria* can be modified through compounding and zeugmas, these strange words can increase the magnitude of the qualities of meaning. The more compounding of words and the linking through zeugmas, the greater compacting of meaning is conveyed through fewer words. Thus, the meaning of a few words becomes more complex and layered. In philosophical terms, the words are the matter while the accidental forms are the affixes (prefixes, suffixes, word stems) which are modified through compounding (morphology) and zeugmas (syntax), giving greater intension of meaning. The *Ars Notoria* compares the *voces magicae* prayers to the story of Daniel and the writing on the wall, saying:

> For this reason, because some of those Greek words are the names of holy angels and that they cannot be explained at all, but also among those names

36. *Ars Notoria,* section 8.

are placed some deprecations apart from angels in Hebrew, Greek, and Chaldean which were explained, particularly in Latin. But as yet [Solomon and Apollonius] had not explained those [deprecations] thoroughly on account of the prolixity of the exposition, because they would have been much too long if any words had been explained from them into Latin. Thus, because human sense is not able to understand those, neither to deduce for the purpose of an effect, nor are they able to be offered in so short hours of the day, just as it has been taught, because sometimes [Apollonius] comprehends only one Hebrew or Greek vocabulary word, explaining them into five- or six Latin-lettered vocabulary words, as an example is to be given in many places.[37] And just as it is read in the book of Daniel[38] concerning King Belshazzar of Babylon, who while he made a feast and drank with silver cups with his entire family, whose cups Nebuchadnezzar had carried out from the Jerusalem Temple praising their gods, and then, while they were doing so, there came into sight a certain hand writing on the wall, and all who stood by together seeing with the king, similarly seeing these words: *"Mane, Techel, Phares,"* which, translated into Latin, is "The Lord numbered your kingdom, it has been weighed on the scales and has been found wanting; your kingdom has been divided and given to the Medes and Persians."[39] For when these three vocabulary words (that is, *"Mane, Techel, Phares,"*) [are] comprehend[ed] into a Latin exposition as twenty-three vocabulary words, the prolixity was becoming too much in this art if any Greek, Hebrew, and Chaldean word would be explained in Latin.[40] And Solomon and Apollonius

---

37. Latin *vocabulum* and *vocabula* are given in this sentence. The sense is that Apollonius's own vocabulary or lexicon, those set of words known to him, limits his ability to not only recognize the Hebrew or Greek within the *voces magicae* prayers but also to translate those into Latin. The complexity of the Hebrew, Greek, and Chaldean prayers often leads to a Latin translation of several more words. The glosser says there is an example of a word count comparsion between the Hebrew, Greek, and Chaldean prayer *Phos Megalos* and its Latin translation, *Lux mundi.*

38. Daniel 5. The glosser follows Jerome's Latin translation from the Greek text by Theodotion.

39. Latin *Numeravit Dominus regnum tuum, appensum est in statera et inventum est minus habens, divissum est regnum tuum et datum est Medis et Persis.*

40. In this sentence, the Latin word *vocabula* carries the sense of the word as an instrument by means for communicating a meaning. The story of the writing on the wall illustrates how brief and efficient the Chaldean (Aramaic) language really is, and that when translated into Latin, it becomes long-winded, making the act of translation laborious, complex, and confusing. *Ars Notoria,* Version B, 12 gloss.

> explained thus, shorter and more remitted [words],[41] and the other words, just as they lay in the book given by the angel, Solomon and Apollonius dismissed on account of the prolixity of the exposition and the brevity of time in which they ought to be read and be pronounced, but where he says [it] in that same section.

Thus, a reasonable comparison of the *voces magicae* prayers can be made to the art of shorthand writing. A single compounded word from a *voces magicae* prayer is like a single Tironian note, which compacts more meaning than its constituent parts. This explains why the *Ars Notoria* advises the practitioner not to translate them, because first, he really would not understand them,[42] and second, the many layers of meaning would become lost in the decoding process. Also, the Latin prologues really do not convey the full meaning of the original but instead describe the first part of the strange prayer, and even then, the Latin does not fully express the depth and the nuances of the meaning which lies therein; hence, they are a "prologue," or a beginning.

To be clear, there are no Tironian notes in the *Ars Notoria* or its pictorial figures. The illegible characters in the figures of Version B are not specifically Tironian notes. They may represent personalized mnemonic devices but cannot be conclusively linked to the notary art of shorthand proper. It is conceivable that students made Tironian notes within the figures while attending university lectures, but we have no physical evidence for this. Tironian notes were ephemeral by nature, historically made on wax tablets that were often erased and became lost. The anonymous twelfth-century *Notory Art of Shorthand* is one of the few surviving works on Tironian notes that we have.

As we have seen, the art of memory is an essential step in the ritualistic inspection of the figures of the *Ars Notoria*. The art of memory was also an

41. Latin *leniora*. Solomon and Apollonius explained some prayers with "more remitted" words; that is, words that are less intensive in the philosophical context of hylomorphism. That is to say, they chose to explain or translate with simpler or shorter words. From a modern linguistic standpoint, this would be akin to translating from a synthetic language like Latin, which uses inflections to express word relationships in a sentence, to a more analytic language like English, which uses helper words and word order to convey the relationship of words in a sentence. More English words are needed to fully express Latin words.

42. Remember that Greek, Hebrew, Chaldean (i.e., Aramaic), and even Arabic, were foreign and exotic languages to readers of the Latin West.

important part of medieval education in which learning through allegory and symbols was necessary in a culture which conducted its dissemination of knowledge primarily through oral tradition and access to books was limited. Finally, the relationship between the notarial science and the magical tradition of the notory art is revealed through symbol and brevity; the notarial science has notes and strokes, and the notory art has prayers and figures. The relationship is further explained through Aristotelian philosophy, and the advent of the *Ars Notoria* is set within the historic context of the Italian resurgence of Justinian's law code, the rise and demand for notarial science education, and the revival of Tironian notes.

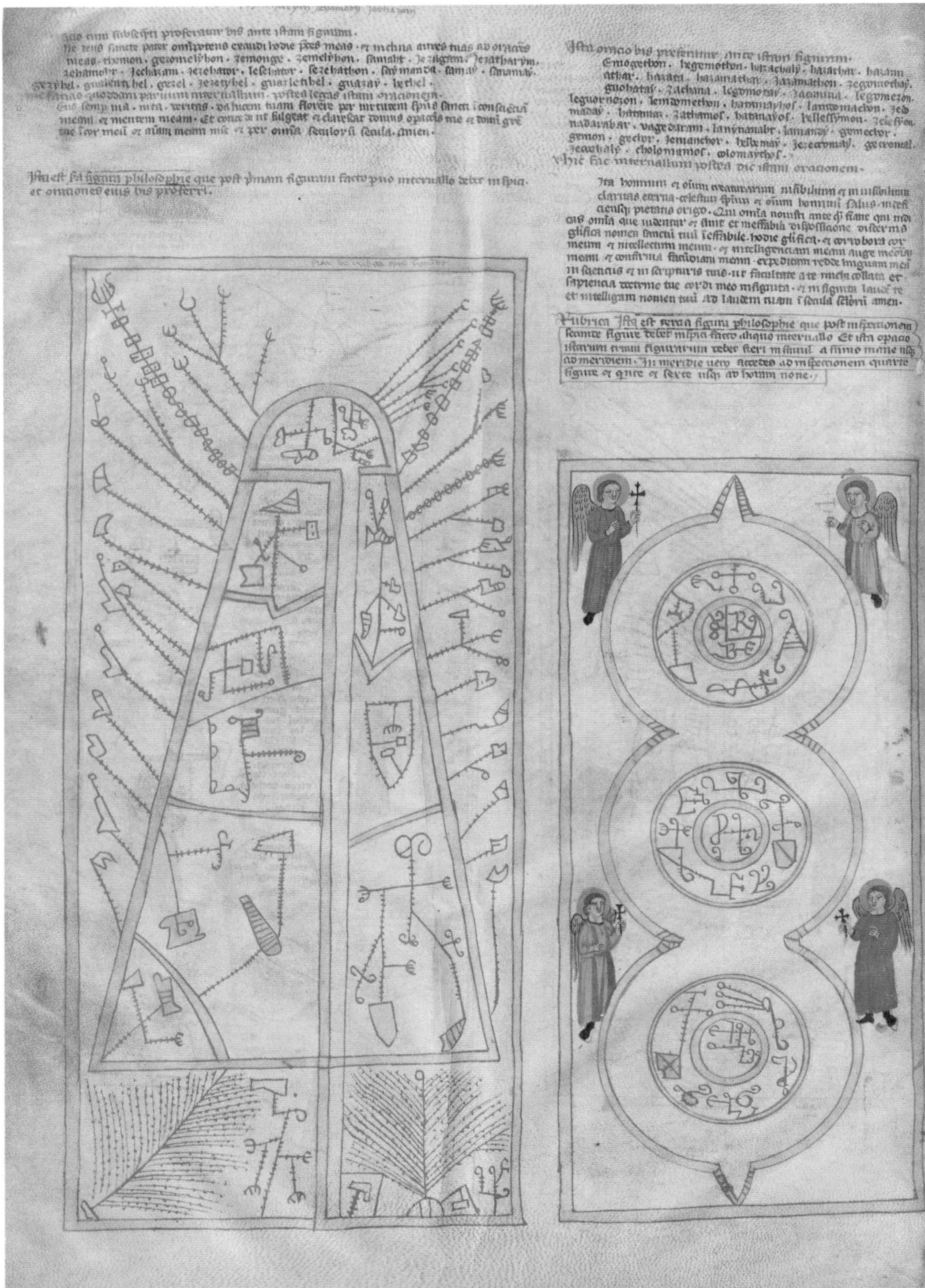

The second (*left*) and third (*right*) figures of philosophy, from *Sacratissima ars notoria,* BnF Latin 9336. 1360–1375.

V.

Analysis of the Figures

According to the *Ars Notoria,* a note (*nota*), a technical term which carries two senses, one of which refers to a hidden knowledge encoded within a figure (*figura*), specifically a pictorial representation assigned to a particular field of knowledge. The figure functions as a mnemonic device in practicing the art of memory as the practitioner studies his textbooks and then stores that new information through repeated *inspectiones* (inspections), or mental walk-throughs of the visualized figure. Following a complete analysis of all the examined *Ars Notoria* manuscripts, it has been determined that there are three figures of grammar; two figures of logic/dialectic; four figures of rhetoric; two figures of arithmetic; one figure of music; one figure of geometry; six figures of astronomy; one figure of medicine; four figures of the general sciences; seven figures of philosophy; five figures of theology; one figure of justice, peace, and fear; one figure of reprehension and taciturnity; one figure of chastity; and one figure of the exceptions (the seven arts of divination), for a total of forty figures.

The very nature of such figures is to convey knowledge. Although mysterious, the figures have five elemental forms—wheels, triangles, trees, columns or towers, and windows—which may reveal the secrets behind their design. Obviously, some figures combine these elemental forms.

Wheels. Wheels may show the contrary elements of ideas if positioned at the opposite spokes of a wheel, or the relationship of ideas between juxtaposed wheels, or both of these as the wheel is turned by the viewer. The "four signs of all knowledge" presented just before the figures of logic/dialectic in Version B are likely inspired by the pedagogical wheel and coiled snake held by Lady Logic

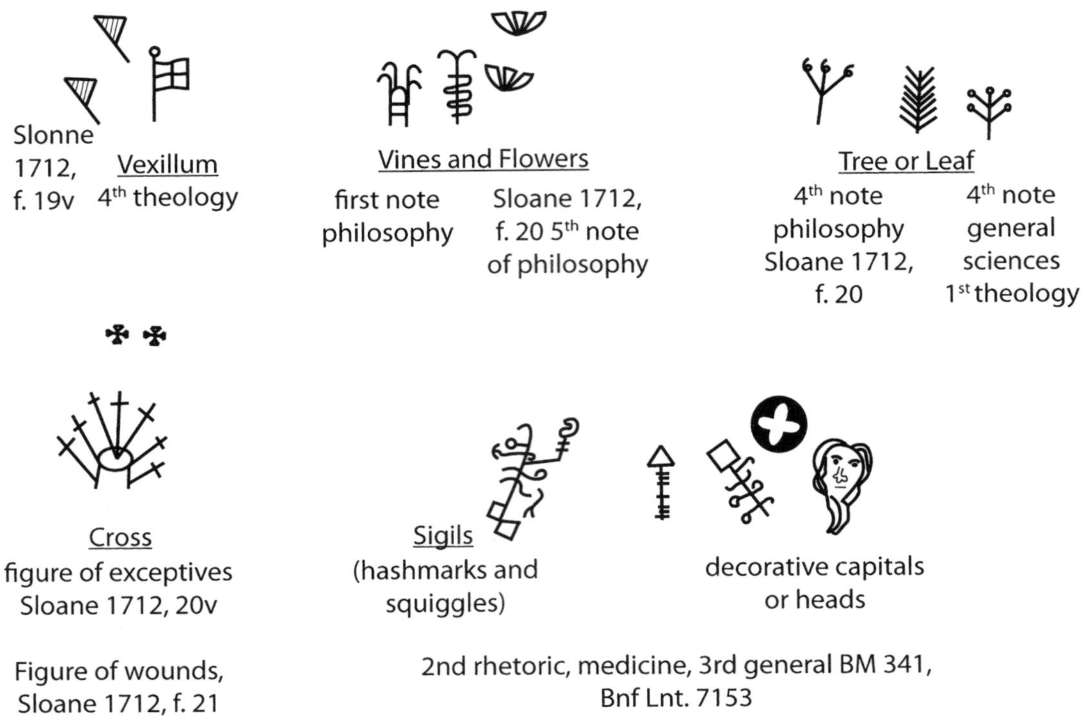

The small mnemonic signs found within the *notae*

that was used to teach students about the syllogism. Wheels are featured in nearly all the figures.

Triangles. Triangles show the importance of hierarchy, from the many to the one; alternatively, a triangle may show nesting, as in the study of logic in which one wishes to organize elements of something under *genera* (class) and *species* (kind). Triangles are featured in the figures of logic/dialectic and philosophy.

Trees. Trees show a central concept that begets other ideas, showing key relationships among ideas. The ideas are typological and therefore can ignore any ordered sequence of understanding. Tree diagrams are featured in the figures of logic/dialectic showing a key concept in the philosophical problem of universals, depicting the spectrum from the general to the particular; also, another figure of logic/dialectic has a tree diagram showing the elements of grammar. The figure of the exceptives has seven branches with crosses at their ends, likely indicating each of the seven forms of divination—hydromancy, pyromancy, necromancy, chiromancy, geomancy, genethlialogy, and onomancy. Trees are also featured in the figures of rhetoric, general sciences, philosophy, and geometry.

Columns or towers. The column consists of squares stacked upon one another in an elongated rectangular shape that could be topped by a capital. Columns indicate the division of types and ranking order of things. The classical writers of the art of memory recommend the use of columns to place an image of the thing to be remembered between them. The best examples are the fourth figure of the general sciences, the second figure of philosophy, the seventh figure of philosophy, and the second figure of theology.

Windows. Windows are framed pictures that show a scene. Examples of windows are the first and second figures of astronomy, which present a view of the night sky; another example is the fifth figure of theology, which reveals a strange vision of many objects and creatures.

There are various small signs in the figures, the symbolic meaning of which is not certain. These are probably mnemonic devices, which would be personalized to each operator as he amended the figure after each inspection and study session. The small signs are categorized in the figure on page 146.

There are some key differences between the figures found in Version A and Version B. Version A figures have simple designs, often made in a single-colored ink. Version B figures are more ornate with cursive mnemonic signs, decorated with multiple colored inks, and contain keywords within the figures themselves as they relate to the knowledge associated with that particular figure.

As the *Ars Notoria* transformed from Version A to Version B, the most striking changes are found in the figures of logic/dialectic, music, the first and second figures of the general sciences, and the figure of justice, peace, and fear. Conversely, there are strong similarities between the figure of music (Version A) and the figure of chastity (Version B), between the third figure of the general sciences and the third figure of philosophy. An examination of appendix A1 will yield an understanding of which figures were omitted and which ones were added from Version A to Version B; for example, the figure of exceptives is omitted, and Version B supplants it by instructing the operator to use the figures of the general sciences when studying the arts of divination. Version B erroneously duplicates the figure of geometry, creating a second figure of geometry; interestingly, Version B also seemingly recovers the lost figures of astronomy.

The figures are found at the end of the *Ars Notoria* in a section which I call the *Notae* Supplement (NS). Before there was Version A, it is hypothesized that the proto-version of the *Flores Aurei* presented the Special prayers in the body of the text followed immediately by their associated figures. This would have been done successively through each of the seven liberal arts and all the other disciplines. Following scribal rewrites and reworkings of the *Flores Aurei*, it is thought that the scribe decided to move all the figures to the very end of the treatise. This new arrangment of the figures is dubbed here as the *Notae* Supplement. Version A's *Notae* Supplement presents the figures, each with their own captions, but otherwise, there are no rubrics. Most of the figures are plain and empty, although a few have prayers written with them (i.e., the adorning prayers). Only Version A contains a single prayer not found elsewhere about a prayer that Solomon offered during his sacrifice of peacemaking to God.[1] Version B manuscripts, such as the Parisian Latin 9336 and the Oxford Bodley 951, include the Special prayers alongside their figures with rubrics and additions. Most of the figures contain adorning prayers as well. Unlike Version A, Version B explains when and how often the adorning prayers are to be offered during the greater ritual. Also, Version B often divides a single adorning prayer into multiple parts. These multiple parts are not detailed here in this chapter but can be found in Version B's *Notae* Supplement, which is translated from Latin 9336.

What follows is a step-by-step examination of each discipline's figures.

THE FIGURES OF GRAMMAR

According to section 74, the angel says that there are three figures assigned to three parts of grammar, and they are about:

> "the ordering [of letters, syllables, and words], the corresponding distinction—that is, the construction of the cases and the tenses—and the adjoining of themselves or the simple and compound forms and the successive declension of the parts *toward* the parts or *from* the parts [of speech] by a congruent and ordered division."

1. See page 307.

The angel explains that the first figure is about "the entire investigation of declining [nouns, adjectives, pronouns, and participles]." The prayer offered before the first figure of grammar is *Domine Sancte Pater [. . . imperfectum]*. Its adorning prayers are *Helyscemaht Scemoht* and *Deus cui omne cor bonum patet*. In Version A, the figure is depicted as a gyrus, which spirals out its arm from its center; other manuscripts depict it as a great wheel with concentric rings (see page 148).

In Version B, the first figure of grammar is also depicted as a great wheel but also has two additional rectangles attached at its inferior end: one contains mnemonic signs, and the other contains five wheels. These wheels are labeled with grammatical terms, from top to bottom, as follows: accidence (*accidens*), property (*proprium*), grammar (*grammatica*), genus (*genus*), and species (*species*).

Accidence (*accidens*), in the grammatical sense of the word, refers to the inflectional properties of a part of speech. The Roman Latin grammarian Donatus identified eight parts of speech: the noun, pronoun, verb, adverb, participle, conjunction, preposition, and interjection; note that adjectives, thought of as substantives, were classed as nouns. In Latin, the parts of speech which are generally thought to have inflectional properties are the noun, pronoun, verb, and participle. Donatus says there are six accidents, which are quality, comparison, gender, number, form, and case. For Donatus, quality refers to whether the noun is proper or common. An example of comparison is the positive "learned (*doctus*)," the comparative "more learned (*doctior*)," and the superlative "most learned (*doctissimus*)." Nouns and adjectives have a grammatical gender in Latin, whether they be masculine, feminine, neuter, or common. The number of nouns is either singular or plural. Nouns have either a simple form (e.g. *decens,* meaning "decent") or a compound form (e.g., *indecens,* meaning "indecent"). According to Priscian, nouns have five accidents: species, genus, number, form, and case. Priscian uses the Aristotelian logic terms, genus and species, which are found in the wheels of the rectangle. Genus (*genus*) means a class of things that differ in kind. Species (*species*) means a kind which is described by its genus (i.e., class) and its differentia (i.e., what make's the kind different from the rest of the group). For example, a human being is a species defined as an animal (*genus*) who can also speak a language (*differentia*). There are slight differences in which Donatus and Priscian understand accidents and classify the parts of speech, and it appears the scribe of Version B was following Priscian's approach more closely.

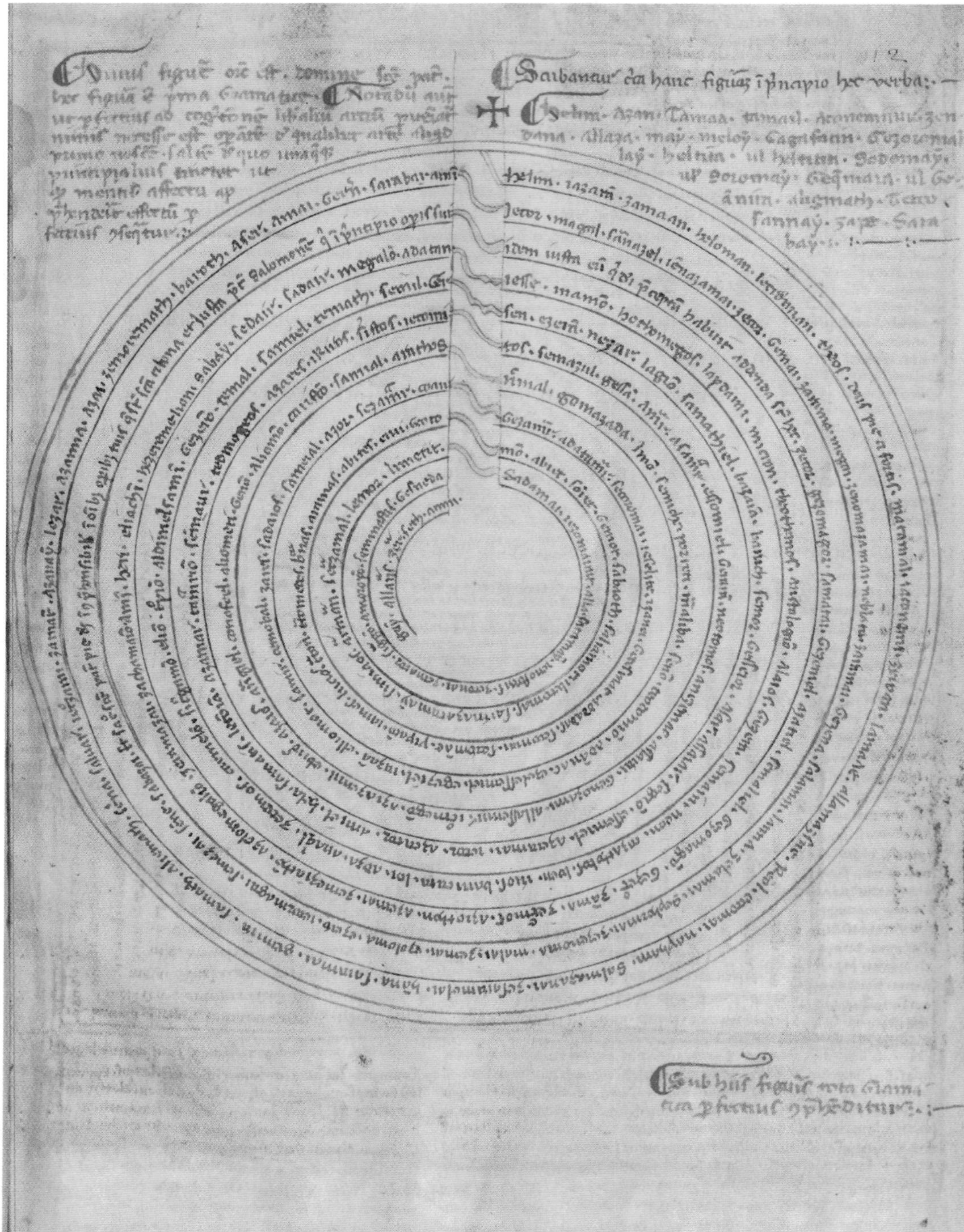

First figure of grammar, from *expositiones Apollonii ad cognitiones scientiarum quas Flores aureo appelavit*. BnF Latin 7152. 1239.

The next wheel contains the Priscian term *proprium,* which means a special property of a part of speech. According to Priscian, the noun signifies substance and quality, the verb signifies action and passion, the pronoun is to replace a proper noun, the adverb is to modify or qualify the verb, the preposition is to connect words in a composition, and the conjunction is to connect clauses together or coordinate words in the same clause.[2]

The next wheel contains the word *grammar* (*grammatica*), which is the set of rules for speaking correctly, and it is considered the origin and foundation of the liberal arts. According to Isidore of Seville, grammar has about thirty parts, which he lists as the eight parts of speech, articulate sound, the letter, the syllable, the metrical feet, accents, punctuation marks, critical signs, orthography, analogy, etymology, glosses, differences, barbarisms, solecisms, errors, metaplasms, schemata, tropes, proses, meters, fables, and histories.[3]

The angel explains that the second figure is about "the agreement of all the parts of the same order." In other words, a part of speech in a sentence, such as a noun, must be agreeable with its paired part, such as an adjective, in the same case. Both Greek and Latin are inflected languages, which means that certain parts of speech (such as nouns, adjectives, pronouns, and participles) have special endings which denote their meaning and relationship to the other parts of speech within a sentence. Depending on how the noun relates to the verb and other parts of speech in a sentence, it may take on different endings. These different endings of the same noun are called cases. In Latin, there are seven cases; these are the nominative, genitive, dative, accusative, ablative, vocative, and locative cases. For example, an adjective must agree with the noun it modifies in gender, number, and case. A participle modifies a substantive and agrees with the word it modifies in gender, number, and case. A pronoun agrees with its antecedent in gender, number, and person. Likewise, a verb must agree with its subject in person and number. The prayer offered before the second figure of grammar is *Respice Domine.* Its adorning prayer is *Otheos Iezehur.* The figure is depicted as a diamond within a square. The four sides of the diamond may coincide with these four pairings: (1) nouns and their adjectives, (2) verbs and their subjects, (3) participles and their substantives, and (4) pronouns and their antecedents (see page 150).

---

2. Priscian's *Institutiones* 2.18–21 as quoted in Copeland and Sluiter, *Medieval Grammar and Rhetoric,* 176–77.
3. Isidore of Seville, *Etymologies,* 42.

The angel explains that the third figure is about "the successive division must be had of all the simple and compound parts themselves." For example, the form of nouns are either simple (e.g., *potens,* meaning "powerful") or compound (e.g., *inpotens,* meaning "impotent"). There are four modes in which nouns are compounded: (1) an integral part with another integral part, (2) a corrupt part with another corrupt part, (3) an intergral part with a corrupt part, and (4) a mixture of many parts. The intergal part is the affix or stem which is kept intact. The corrupt part is the affix or stem which has become altered from its originally sourced word. Donatus provides examples of each of these four divisions, saying:

> How many modes are nouns compounded? Four: integral from two [parts], for example, [*sub* + *urban* equals] "suburban (*suburbanus*)," corrupt from two [parts], for example, "*efficax,* [meaning, "efficacious," which comes from *efficio,* "I make out," + *-ax*, "inclined to," and] *municeps* [meaning, "citizen," which comes from *munus,* "duty, service," + *-ceps,* "sharing"]; from integral and corrupt, for example, "*insulsus,* [meaning, "unsalted; bungling; insipid," which comes from *in-*, "not" + *salsus,* "salted; witty"]; from the corrupted and integral, for example, *nugigerulus,* [meaning "clothes-dealer (in female finery)" which comes from *nugae-*, "trifles" + *gerulus,* "a bearer, carrier; one who does something, a doer"]; sometimes from many things, for example, *inexpugnabilis,* [meaning "inexpugnable," which comes from *in-*, "not" + *ex-* denoting privation, + *pungo,* "fight," + *bilis,* "able"]; *inperterritus,* [meaning, "unterrified, dauntless" which comes from *in-*, "un" + *per,* "thoroughly" + *terreo* "frighten"].[4]

Now the figure consists of four wheels connected by lines, forming a diamond. Perhaps these four wheels correspond to these four modes in which nouns and other parts of speech are compounded. The prayer offered before the third figure of grammar is *Creator Adonay.* Its adorning prayer is *Principium Deus.*

In Version A2, there is a special figure of grammar, which might indicate the transitional development of the "four signs of all knowledge," which belong to logic/dialectic found in Version B. This special figure alone claims to provide

4. Aelius Donatus, *Ars Minor,* chapter 2. My translation.

the operator all knowledge of grammar, and its shape is shared in part with the figures of logic/dialectic (see page 153). From Version A2, the figure is a large rectangle divided into four triangles. Inside the bottom triangle there is a big circle that says, "Grammar is the science of letters" (*Grammatica est scientia literarum*). Five smaller circles stem from it, each containing a part of grammar, which are "letter" (*littera*), "syllable" (*syllaba*), "word" (*dictio*), "speech" (*oratio*), and "parts of the letter" (*litera partes*). Below this, there are eight little tree diagrams labeled as the eight parts of speech—noun, pronoun, verb, adverb, participle, conjunction, preposition, and interjection; each tree diagram has multiple branches with a single letter at its end, representing a mnemonic aid. These concepts are thoroughly treated in Priscian's *Institutiones Grammaticae* (*Institutions of Grammar*). At the bottom of the figure, there are four shapes—a pentagram, a square, a triangle, and a circle—that represent qualities of the Latin alphabet and draw directly from Aelius Donatus's *Ars Maior*.[5] The pentagram represents the vowels (*vocales*), *a, e, i, o, u*.[6] The square represents consonants that are mute. Mute letters cannot be pronounced by themselves and do not produce a syllable by themselves. There are nine of them: *b, c, d, g, h, k, p, q, t*.[7] The triangle represents the consonants that are semivowels (*semivocales*) which are seven, *f, l, m, n, r, s, x*.[8] The circle represents the two letters, *y* and *z*,[9] which are Greek letters used for loanwords. Inside the circle is the Greek sign of aspiration given as the letter *h*.

THE FIGURES OF LOGIC/DIALECTIC

According to section 75, the first figure of logic/dialectic is about adducing arguments eloquently, and the second figure is about responding prudently to another's argument or counterargument. The first and second figures of logic/dialectic show significant changes in their form and function from Version A to Version B.

---

5. Aelius Donatus, *Ars Maior*, I.2.

6. In BnF Latin 9336, the reason for the inclusion of the letter s may be that in meter it loses its force as a consonant.

7. BnF Latin 7152 has *b, c, d, f, g, t, q, p, k*. It adds f and omits *h*.

8. BnF Latin 7152 has *r, m, l, n, f, x*. The scribe omits *s*.

9. BnF Latin 7152 omits *z*.

The prayer offered before the first figure of logic/dialectic is *Sancte Deus.* Its adorning prayers are *Seguoht Semzyhony Zay Samarahc* and *Lectiones.* In Version A, the figure consists of a great wheel and inside it is four other wheels. Of those four, one is at its center while the other three have their centers intersected by the central wheel's circumference. See page 303.

The "figure of logic for developing dialectic skills," identified as 4a2, belongs to Version A2. This figure features an equilateral triangle divided in half. Below the triangle is a tree diagram of a central wheel labeled "dialectic," having six wheels extending out from it. The six wheels represent a key concept in the philosophical problem of universals, showing the spectrum from the general to the particular. Accompanying these figures are two other wheels: one wheel presents the four Aristotelian propositions as expressed in the square of opposition (see Figure 9; Figure 3.6?), and the other contains the elements of language. These two wheels would be used together in the formulation of an argument or syllogism against an opponent in a debate.

In Version B, the figures labeled 4a, 4a2, and 123a2 are joined together with minor changes. The 4a portion retains the great wheel but is now reduced to two wheels within it. Drawing from Boethius's commentary of Aristotle's *On Interpretation,* one of those wheels has the two opposing universal propositions from Aristotle's example, "Every man is an animal," and "No man is an animal."[10] A line divides this wheel, which is labeled "argument" (*argumentum*) and "solution" (*solutio*). The other wheel below it is surrounded by the phrase *Quidam homo est animal* (A certain man is an animal), and *argumentum solutio* (solution to the argument). A line divides this wheel, which contains the phrases *Omnis homo est animal* (Every man is an animal) and *Facundia scienda* (Eloquence which is to be known). Specifically, these two wheels express the practice of dialectical refutation, which would have been practiced by medieval students in debate class. By extension, these figures make reference to the Aristotelian works; namely, *Topics* and *Sophistical Refutations.* These wheels clearly reference section 75 of the *Ars Notoria.* The 4a2 and 123a2 portions are melded together. Below the downward-pointing triangle is the seven-wheeled tree

10. See Boethius's commentary on Aristotle's *On Interpretation* in these two separate modern editions—Smith, trans., *Boethius: On Aristotle, On Interpretation 1–3* and *Boethius: On Aristotle, On Interpretation 4–6.* Specifically, see pages 89–111 in Boethius's chapter 7 in *Boethius: On Aristotle, On Interpretation 1–3.*

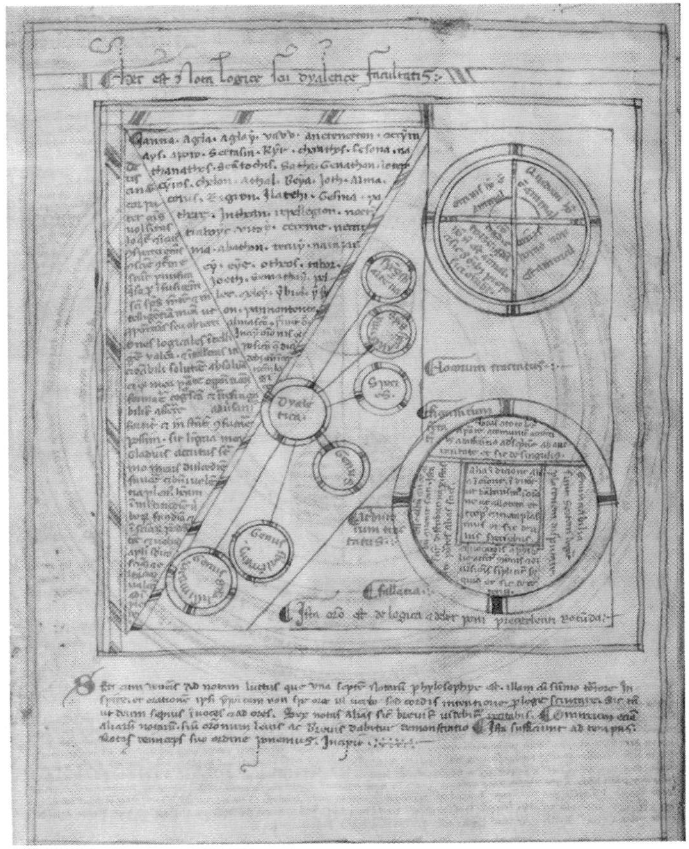

Top: Nota of Logic for Dialectic Skills from *Expositiones Apollonii ad cognitiones scientarum quas Flores aureos appellavit,* BnF Latin 7152. 1239. *Bottom:* First figure of logic/dialectic from *Ars notoria Salamone,* BnF Latin 7153. 15th century.

diagram that has now transformed into six wheels representing "letter" (*littera*), "syllable" (*syllaba*), "grammar" (*grammatica*), "parts of speech" (*dictio*), "syntax" (*oratio*), and "science" (*scientia*). The four parts of grammar are letter, syllable, parts of speech, and syntax, which was studied as a science.[11] Below these six wheels are rectangles containing the following grammatical keywords "[the eight] parts [of speech]" (*partes*), "noun" (*nomen*), "word" (*verbum*), "participle" (*participium*), "pronoun" (*pronomine*), "adverb" (*adverbium*), "conjunction" (*coniunctio*), "proposition" (*proposition*), and "interjection" (*interiectus*). Instead of little tree diagrams, there are small rectangular compartments that contain the letters for mnemonic aid.

Furthermore, Version B expands upon the subject matter of logic/dialectic by organizing it into four wheels known as the "four signs of all knowledge."[12] Two of the wheels are sourced from 4a2, another wheel from 123a2, and another wheel expands upon the elements of an argument. The "four signs of all knowledge" are now separated from the figures of logic/dialectic and act as a supplementary figure (see page 506–507). They are not to be read but simply held within one's memory.[13] The information they contain are considered the essential building blocks of the trivium.

In examining the four signs of all knowledge, the top circle has four divisions made by a cross, each containing a shape. The four shapes—pentagram, square, triangle, and circle—represent qualities of the Latin alphabet and draw directly from Aelius Donatus's *Ars Maior* as already mentioned above. The second circle is divided into three parts containing Aristotle's logic terminology sourced from his collected works known as the *Organon*. The left compartment contains three interconnected circles labeled "term" (*terminus*), "substance" (*substantia*), and "hypothetical" (*hypothetica*). The right compartment contains "categorical" (*categorica*), "proposition" (*propositio*), and "hypothetical"(*hypothetica*). The bottom compartment reads "leading" (*inducens*), "argument" (*argumentum*), "similar" (*similis*), "examples" (*exempla*), and "essence" (*essentia*).[14] The third circle contains the following grammatical keywords: "letter" (*littera*), "construction" (*constructio;* i.e., ordering of letters,

11. See the works of Alcuin of York.

12. NS 147.

13. NS 25.

14. See Aristotle's *Topics,* book 1.

syllabi, or words), "syntax" (*oratio;* i.e., ordering of words or sentences),[15] "parts of speech" or "word" (*dictio*), "syllable" (*syllaba*), "intransitive" (*intransitiua*), "transitive" (*transitiua*), "ditransitive" (*retransitiua*), and "reciprocal" (*reciproca*). These grammatical concepts are discussed at length in Priscian's *Institutions of Grammar.* The fourth and final circle contains an inner circle labeled "argument" (*argumentum*), which has four axles to create four divisions of the circle that contain examples of the four forms of the categorical statement from Boethius's *On Hypothetical Syllogisms,* his commentary on Aristotle's *On Interpretation.*

The prayer offered before the second figure of logic/dialectic is *Heloy clementissime.* Its adorning prayer is *Seguoht Semzyony Zahy Halamarym.* In Version A, the second figure of logic/dialectic is constructed from four circles, which are paired as two vesica piscis.[16] In Version B, the figure appears distorted, having two wheels joined together with the top, smaller wheel divided vertically in half.

THE FIGURES OF RHETORIC

The prayers offered before the first figure of rhetoric is *Omnipotens et misericors.*[17] Its adorning prayer is *Lemor Lemoyz.*[18] The first figure of rhetoric is a tree diagram. The central image of the figure consists of three interpenetrating circles, the center of each lying on the circumference of the other. Three other smaller circles extend from it, connected by arcing lines. Section 76 implies that the first figure of rhetoric is about "an ornate, neatly arranged, and florid locution."

The prayer offered before the second figure of rhetoric is *Unus magnus.*[19] Its adorning prayers are *Gezomanai, Habytay,* and *Potentia equalitas.*[20] The second

---

15. *Oratio* can also mean "speech." See Priscian, "On Construction," *Institutiones grammaticae,* books 17–18, as cited in Copeland and Sluiter, *Medieval Grammar and Rhetoric,* 178–79.

16. The phrase *vesica piscis* is Latin for "bladder of the fish." It is a geometrical symbol, being the almond-shaped opening formed of two interpenetrating circles, the center of each lying on the circumference of the other.

17. *Ars Notoria,* section 138, NS 41.

18. *Ars Notoria,* NS 44–48.

19. In Version B, *Unus magnus, Usyon omnium, and Azelechias [. . . regi Salomoni]* are assigned to the second *nota* of rhetoric (NS 49–51). *Gezomani* is a prayer belonging to the second *nota* of rhetoric according to Version A in section 140. In Version B under section 140, the equivalent prayer's incipit is *Hanazay.*

20. *Ars Notoria,* section 140, NS 54–55.

figure of rhetoric has a complex tree diagram of wheels, lines, and a grand semicircle. According to Section 76, the significance of the figure is about "a competent, discrete, and ordered judgment of cases or offices, witnesses, pleads, damages, and judgments." One could imagine that the figure is divided into two parts. One part is the grand semicircle which resembles a courtroom with seating on the outer rim, and the other part to the right is "the speaker," as it were, which contains five wheels in a vertical line and three wheels horizontally. The five wheels may reference the five canons of rhetoric, and the other three wheels may reference the three types of argument.

The prayer offered before the third figure of rhetoric is *Usyon omnium*.[21] Version B gives the adorning prayer *Hatanathel*.[22] Strangely, Version A does not supply the third figure of rhetoric, and this may have something to do with redaction in its early days of circulation and transmission. The third figure is found in Version A2 and Version B manuscripts. The third figure of rhetoric is a tree diagram that consists of a mandorla or wheel radiating six rays with each ending in a semicircle; the semicircles are labeled and are meant to represent the six-part structure of an argument as described by the author of *Rhetorica ad Herennium* (*Rhetoric for Herennius*) 1.4, and in Cicero's *De Inventione* (*On Invention*) 1.19. From left to right, the terms are:

introduction (*exordium*)
narrative (*narratio*)
division (*partitio*)
proof (*confirmatio*)
refutation (*reprehensio*)
conclusion (*conclusio*, or *finis*)

The exordium presents the argument's premise. The narrative states the facts. The division expresses the disagreements with one's opponents. The confirmation is the evidence provided to support the argument's premise. The reprehension is the part of the argument that shows the opponent's arguments are weak or wrong. The conclusion may appeal to the audience's pathos in order

21. *Ars Notoria,* section 141. In Version B, variant 8, the prayer offered before the third *nota* of rhetoric is *Scio enim;* see also NS 56.
22. NS 58–59.

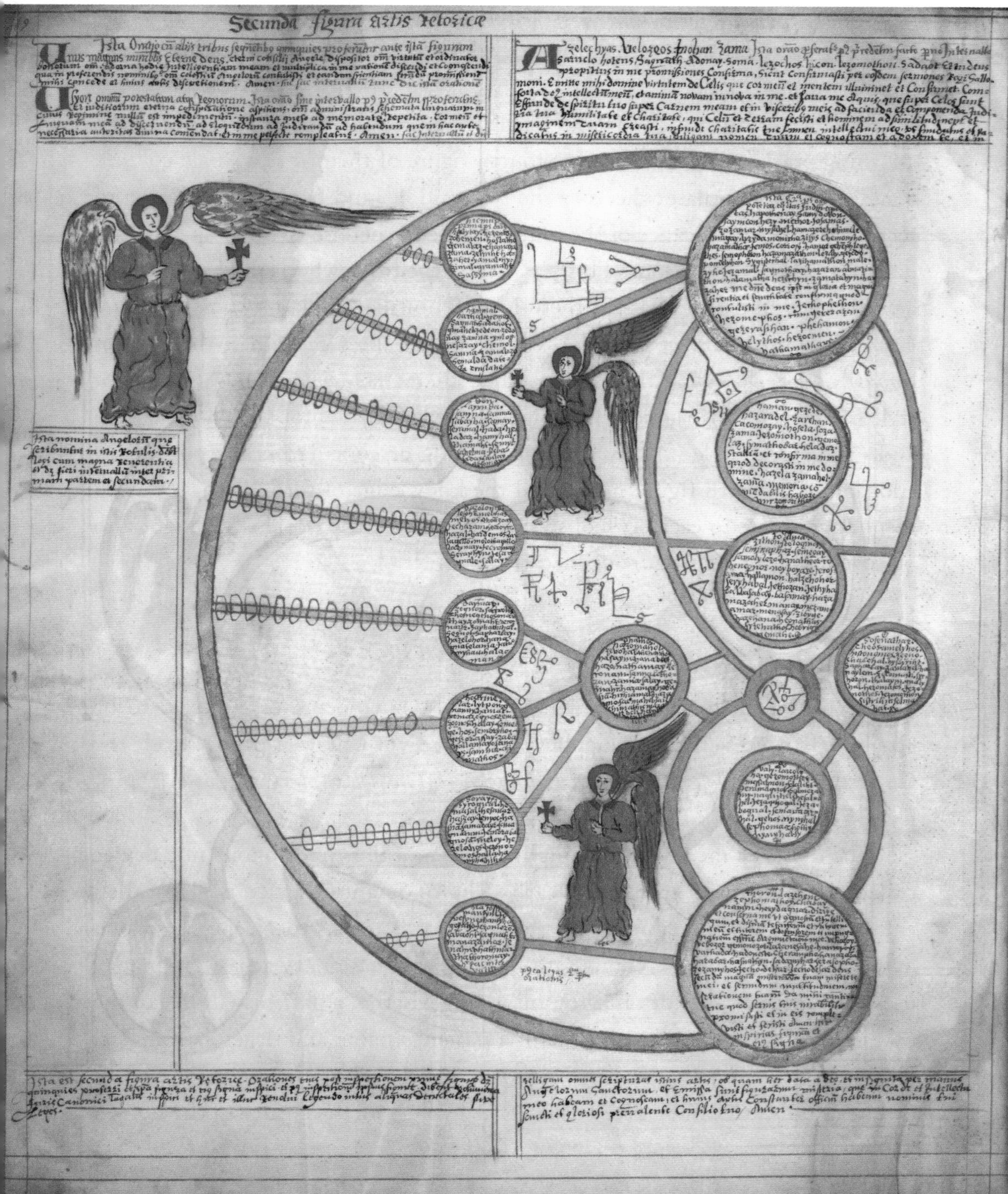

Second figure of rhetoric, from from *Liber de Arte Memorativa,* Yahuda Var. 43, National Library of Israel. 1600.

to side with one's argument. These elements follow what section 76 implies as belonging to the third figure of rhetoric which is "an ordered disposition of the same art of negotiation."

The prayer offered before the fourth figure of rhetoric is *Reverende*.[23] Its adorning prayer is *Senezemon*. The fourth figure of rhetoric is a single column containing three ornate wheels at the top, middle, and bottom. According to section 76, the significance of the fourth figure of rhetoric is "an eloquence and demonstration with reason." This phrase and the three wheels might be seen as a clue which points to what the rhetorician Quintilian explains in his *Institutio Oratoria* (*Institutions of Oratory*), which is that the Greeks had three styles (*modi*) of speech—what the Greeks called characters (*charakteres*): (1) a plain style (*ischnon*) for instruction; (2) a vigorous style (*hadron*) for a moving oration; and (3) a florid style (*antheron*) for a pleasing or conciliating discourse.[24] In addition, the fourth figure may entail the knowledge of formulating an argument appropriate to each style of speech. Recall that the florid style might also be covered in the first figure of rhetoric.

THE FIGURE OF MEDICINE

The figure of medicine appears in Version A, but no prayers are said to be attributed to it. Version B supplies the figure with prayers drawn from the General prayers, *Deus summe Deus invisibilis Theos Pat[e]r* and its Latin prologue *Te quaeso Domine* (sections 24–25).

The figure of medicine is a simplified form of the Greek onomantic device called the Sphere of Life and Death. The onomantic device is also called the Petosiris Sphere, named after the letter of Petosiris to Nechepso, which describes the onomantic computation.[25] The divinationary art of onomancy uses the device as a result table for answering whether a patient will live or die by calculating the numerical value of a patient's name and other astrological factors to determine his or her prognosis. The Greek tradition of the Sphere of Life and Death can be dated as far back as the fourth century in the Leiden

---

23. *Ars Notoria,* section 142, NS 60.

24. Quintilian, *Institutio Oratoria* 12.10.58.

25. The Sphere is also called the Sphere of Pythagoras, the Sphere of Apuleius, Columcille's Circle, and the Democritus's Circle.

Papyrus V and the *Greek Magical Papyri* (*PGM* XII.351); however, the earliest extant Latin tradition dates from the ninth century CE. The onomantic computation is detailed as follows:

1. Take the Greek name of the sick person and convert the letters of the person's name into their numerical equivalents. This second-century practice of adding up the numerical values of the Greek letters in a word to acquire the sum total is called isopsephy. See the table on page 161.
2. Add the number of the day of the Moon on which the patient first fell ill (a number between 1 and 30) and the number of the planetary weekday (each day has a corresponding number). See the table on page 161.
3. Add the number of the patient's name, the number of the lunar day in which the patient became sick, and the number of the planetary weekday[26] to acquire the grand total. Divide the grand total by the lunar month (30 or 29), according to modular arithmetic.
4. If the remainder is in the top sphere of the diagram, the patient will live. If the remainder is in the bottom sphere, the patient will die. The three lines or columns indicate whether the patient's recovery or death will be fast, moderate, or slow. See the figure on page 160.

For example, the Greek name Achilles (Αχιλλευς, Achilleus) is calculated as 1 + 600 + 10 + 30 + 30 + 5 + 400 + 200, which equals 1,276. The numbering of the days of the Moon begins with the new Moon (*noumenia*) counting as one; thus, if Achilles falls ill on the fourth Moon, then the number is four. If that day is a Monday, then that corresponds to the Moon which is 17 (see Planetary Correspondences on page 162). This brings the grand total to 1,297. If the grand total is divided by 30, then the quotient is 43, and the remainder is 7. The prognosticator then searches for the number 7 between the sections for life and death, and where the number is found is the predicted result for the patient.

---

26. One auxiliary table presents the numerical value of the Greek names of the planetary gods arranged according to the days of the week. See McCluskey, *Astronomies and Cultures,* 149.

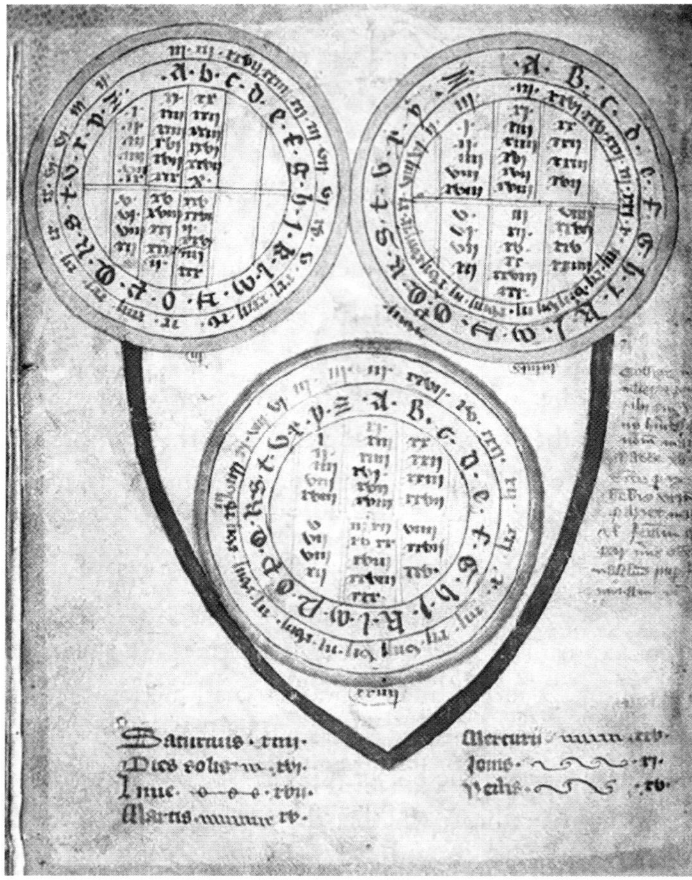

The Sphere of Life and Death, attributed to Bernardus Silvestris. Bodleian MS Digby 46, f. 107v. Late 14th century.

In BnF Latin 9336, the figure of medicine extracted here (see page 162) has two interlocking circles each containing three lines. Within a circle, there are four marks on each line, which, when added together equals 12. Taking the two circles together, adding all these marks together equals 24, which corresponds to the 24 letters of the Greek alphabet. Notice that each of these marks has a *keraia* (Greek, meaning "horn"), or a little hook, which is used to distinguish Greek letters from one another. When the onomantic device was translated from Greek to Latin, the Greek letters were deleted, only leaving behind the *keraia*. The *keraia* indicates that these marks do in fact leave a trace of the deleted Greek letters.

ISOPSEPHY

Value	Greek Letter		Value	Greek Letter		Value	Greek Letter	
1	Alpha	α	10	Iota	ι	100	Rho	ρ
2	Beta	β	20	Kappa	κ	200	Sigma	σ
3	Gamma	γ	30	Lambda	λ	300	Tau	τ
4	Delta	δ	40	Mu	μ	400	Upsilon	υ
5	Epsilon	ε	50	Nu	ν	500	Phi	φ
6	Digamma, Stigma	Ϝ, ς	60	Xi	ξ	600	Chi	χ
7	Zeta	ζ	70	Omicron	ο	700	Psi	ψ
8	Eta	η	80	Pi	π	800	Omega	ω
9	Theta	θ	90	Koppa	κ	900	Sampi	ϡ'

Isopsephy: the numerical values of the twenty-four letters in the Greek alphabet. In Greek, each unit was assigned a separate letter. The ones unit (1–9) was assigned the obsolete letter *digamma,* the tens unit (10–90) was assigned the obsolete letter *koppa,* and the hundreds unit was assigned the obsolete letter *sampi* (100–900); these three obsolete letters bring the total to 27 Greek letters. This table is not found in MS Digby 46, but the study of isopsephy is well documented.

PLANETARY CORRESPONDENCES

Planetary Weekday	Number
Saturn—Saturday	14
Sun—Sunday	16
Moon—Monday	17
Mars—Tuesday	15
Mercury—Wednesday	25
Jupiter—Thursday	11
Venus—Friday	15

The planetary weekdays and their corresponding numbers according to the table found in Bodleian MS Digby 46, fol. 107v, late fourteenth century. The planetary weekdays and their corresponding numbers would also vary from manuscript to manuscript.

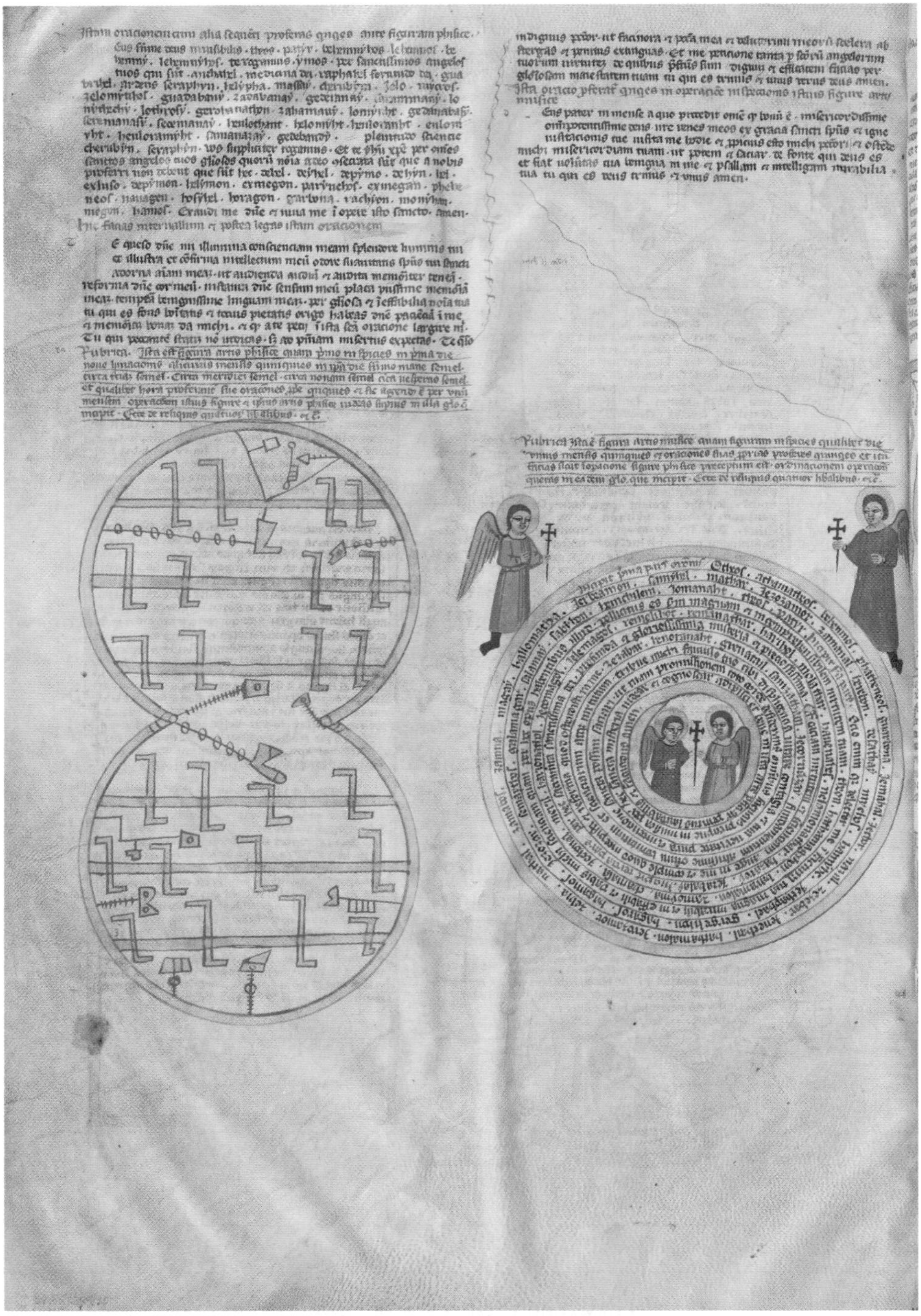

Figure of medicine (*left*) and the third figure of astronomy, which the scribe has mis-identified as the figure of music (*right*), from *Sacratissima ars notoria,* BnF Latin 9336. 1360–1375.

The inherent problem encountered during the transmission of the Sphere was the fact that the 23 letters in the Latin alphabet do not have corresponding numerical values like Greek does. As such, scribes ended up assigning numbers to Latin letters arbitrarily, resulting in a mix of different number–letter correlations found among multiple Spheres. This led to confusion among later scribes who tried to figure out which version was the "correct" original and gave reason to explain why the Sphere might have predicted rightly or wrongly in any given instance.[27]

THE FIGURE OF MUSIC

In Version A, the figure of music is a triangle which contains a square, and in that square there are two concentric rings. Version A does not supply a prayer of music. In Version B, the third figure of astronomy is mislabeled as the figure of music, receiving its own Special prayer and adorning prayer. As a result, the triangular figure becomes the figure of chastity in Version B. The triangular figure of music now identified in Version A likely represents Plato's Lambda, which expresses the Pythagorean musical scale.[28]

THE FIGURES OF ARITHMETIC

The two figures of arithmetic are images drawn directly from Boethius's diagram in his *De Institutione Arithmetica* 1.12.

Before explaining how the *Ars Notoria* derived its two figures from this diagram, it is important to explain what it is showing as this will help to understand why the author of the *Ars Notoria* chose to create the two figures as he did. It is worth quoting Boethius at length:

> If you look at the latitude where there is a middle point between two terms, you can join these terms, and you will find them to be double the median,

27. Jean-Patrice Boudet, *Entre science et nigromance,* 43. See also Edge, "Licit Medicine," 611–32 and Juste, "Non-Transferable Knowledge," 517–29.

28. See chapter III under the heading "Music, Harmony of the Celestial Spheres and the Soul" on page 77.

> as 36 and 20 make 56, half of which is 28, which is the term placed between them. Again, if you join 28 and 12, they make 40, half of which is 20, and 20 is found to be their middle term. But where there are two middle terms, the two extreme terms joined together are equal to the middle terms, as 12 and 36; when you join them together, they become 48. If you apply their middle terms to each other, that is 20 and 28, the sum is the same. Also, in another part of the latitude in the same order where numbers have been written down, in no way will the reasoning process differ. You will also note the same thing about the other numbers. This is done according to the diagram of the even times odd number, concerning the nature of which an explanation was given above.
>
> Again, if you look at the longitude, where two terms have one median, the product of the extremes multiplied gives the same total as the middle term multiplied by itself, for 12 times 48 gives 576. If the middle term, that is 24, is squared, it produces the same number, 576. Again if 24 is multiplied by 96, it makes 2304. Where, however, two extremities include two middle terms, the number produced by the multiplication of the outer extremities is the same as that produced by the multiplication of the middle terms. So, twelve multiplied by 96 makes 1152. The two middle terms, that is 24 and 48, if multiplied, give the same 1152. This is done in imitation of and in agreement with the even times even number, so the participation of this inborn property is recognized in the odd times even. The same reasoning process and description may be noted on the side of the longitude. For this reason, it is obvious that this number [odd times even] is produced from the two prior [even times even and even times odd] because it retains their properties.[29]

The author of the *Ars Notoria* divided Boethius's diagram in two, thereby creating the first figure of arithmetic as the central semicircle and the two smaller circles on either side. Interestingly enough, this new halved figure can be oriented in any of the four positions of Boethius's diagram, whether the top position is either longitude or latitude. This is most clearly seen in Version A figures. The prayer offered before the first figure of arithmetic is *Deus qui omnia numero*. Version B supplies an adorning prayer, *Azelechyas [. . . mensura]*.

29. Masi, *Boethian Number Theory,* 87–89.

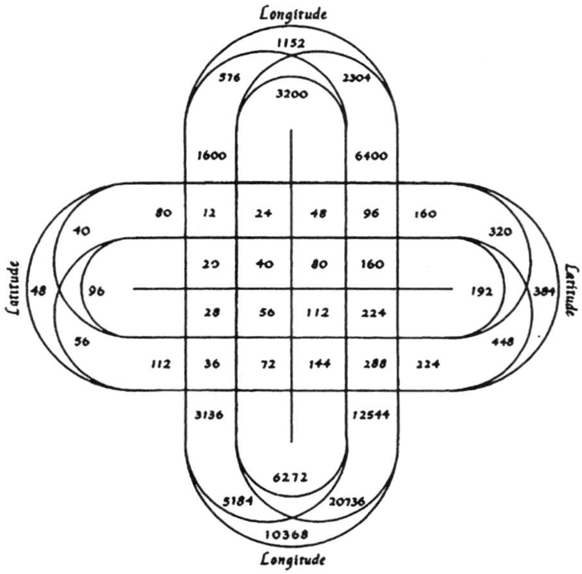

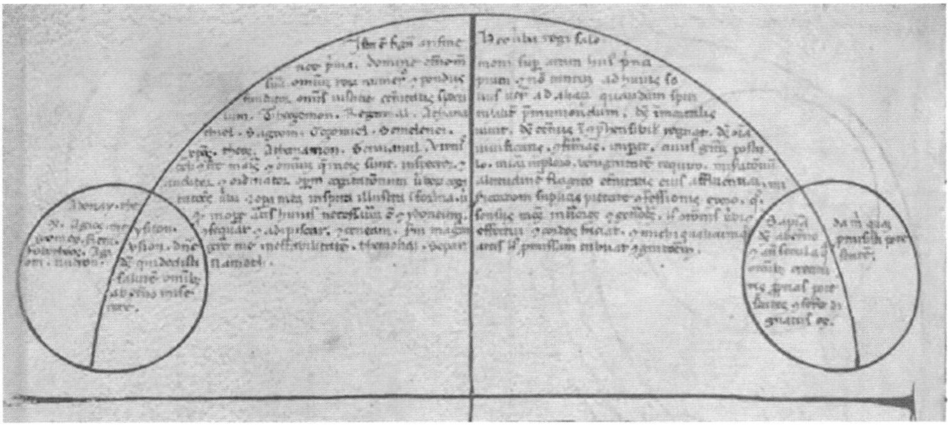

Top: Boethius's arithmetic diagram. The diagram relates the nature of odd numbers times even numbers in his *De Institutione Arithmetica.* Reproduced from Masi, *Boethian Number Theory,* 88. *Bottom:* First Figure of Arithmetic from Mellon I.

According to Clm 276, the first figure of arithmetic is also called the figure of awe, which is probably another misidentification made by the scribe.[30]

The half figure of arithmetic consists of the central 4 × 4 square of Boethius's diagram; however, the grid of numbers is now removed, leaving an

30. Clm 276, f. 13.

empty squared figure as seen in Version A. The prayer offered before the half figure is *Mediator omnium*. Version B supplies an adorning prayer, *Thoemy Gruheguon*. In some Version B manuscripts, either the adorning prayer or an image of an angel fills the empty squared figure.

The second figure of arithmetic is found only in Version B; it is made in error as a duplicate of the first figure. The second figure of arithmetic was then assigned the first figure of geometry's prayer, *Deus iustus iudex*. The second figure of arithmetic has the adorning prayers of *Habba Habebat* and *Thebel Ysaym*.

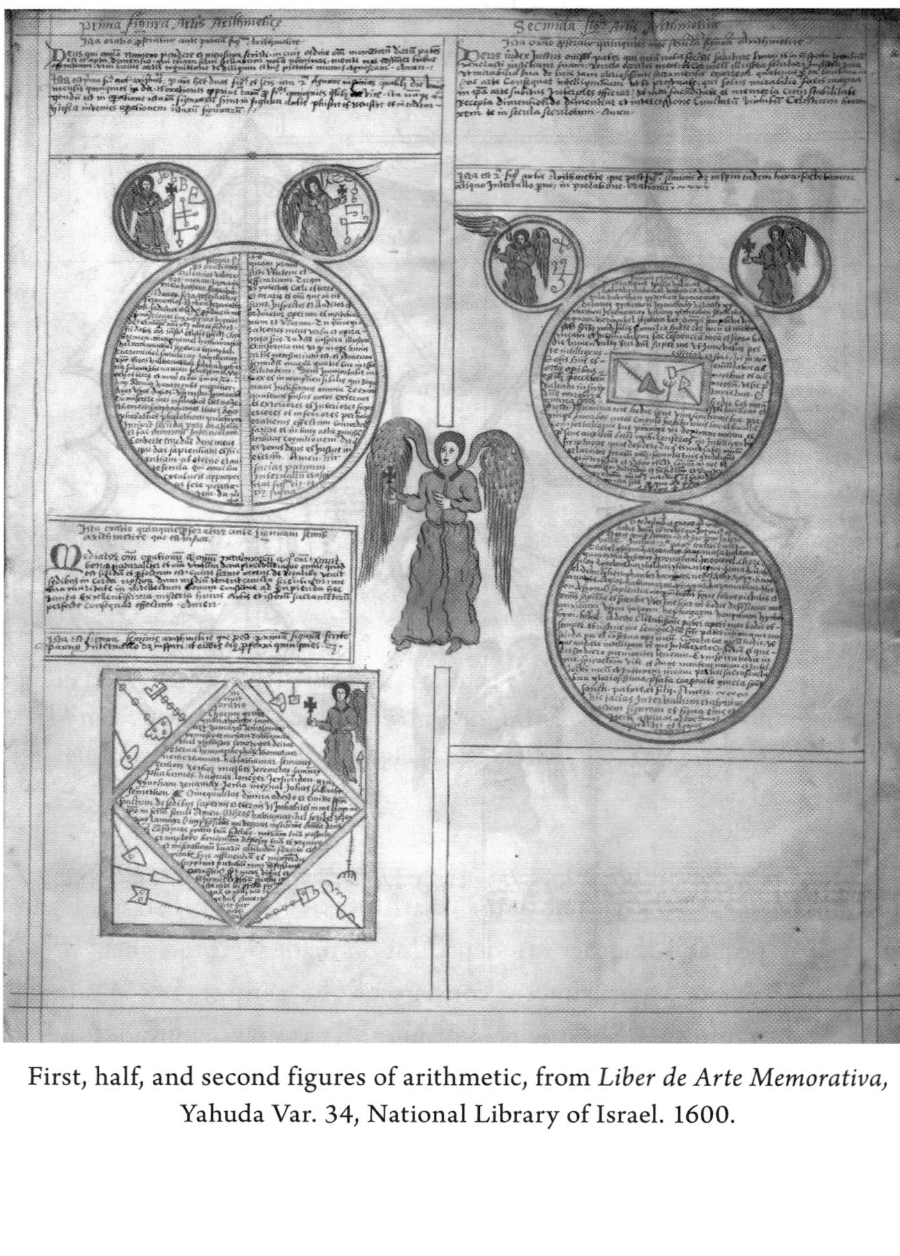

First, half, and second figures of arithmetic, from *Liber de Arte Memorativa*, Yahuda Var. 34, National Library of Israel. 1600.

THE FIGURES OF ASTRONOMY

All the prayers of astronomy are missing in Version A; the only figures belonging to astronomy found in Version A are the first and the third. The first is labeled "of wonders," and the third is labeled "of the moving stars." Version B borrows the *Ars Nova* prayers and newly assigns them to six figures of astronomy.

According to Version B, the prayer offered before the first figure of astronomy is *Confiteor tibi Domine.* The first figure of astronomy is a diamond-shaped window divided into four parts and has a semicircle on at the left and right points. The figure might suggest an understanding of the four quadrants of the sky based on the cardinal directions with the two semicircles referencing the Sun and/or the Moon for calculating times of the calendar. In Version A, there are crosses in the figure, perhaps indicating certain stars of the sky for the purpose of maritime navigation.

According to Version B, the prayer offered before the second figure of astronomy is *Extollo sensus.* The second figure of astronomy is found only in Version B. It is also a diamond-shaped window but divided into two parts, having three semicircles on the left and the right. The second figure of astronmy may be a duplicate of the first figure, and if so, may indicate that there were originally five figures of astronomy, not six.

The third figure of astronomy consists of concentric circles and is blank in Version A. Now this figure always precedes the figure of music in the list of figures of the *Notae* Supplement. This great wheel has been mistaken as a fifth figure of the general sciences, but according to the notory art, there are only four such figures. This great wheel has also been identified as figure "of the moving stars," which would identify it as the third figure of astronomy. It has been determined by deductive logic that this mysterious figure is indeed the third figure of astronomy. The Version B scribe has taken this figure of the great wheel with concentric rings and misidentified it as the figure of music. This scribal error leads to a duplication of the figure. In making such an error, the Version B perspective might be that the concentric rings correspond to the planets' course through the heavens, which makes the inaudible sounds resonate throughout the cosmos.[31] Version B scribe has filled

31. See chapter III under the heading, "Music, Harmony of the Celestial Spheres and the Soul" on page 77.

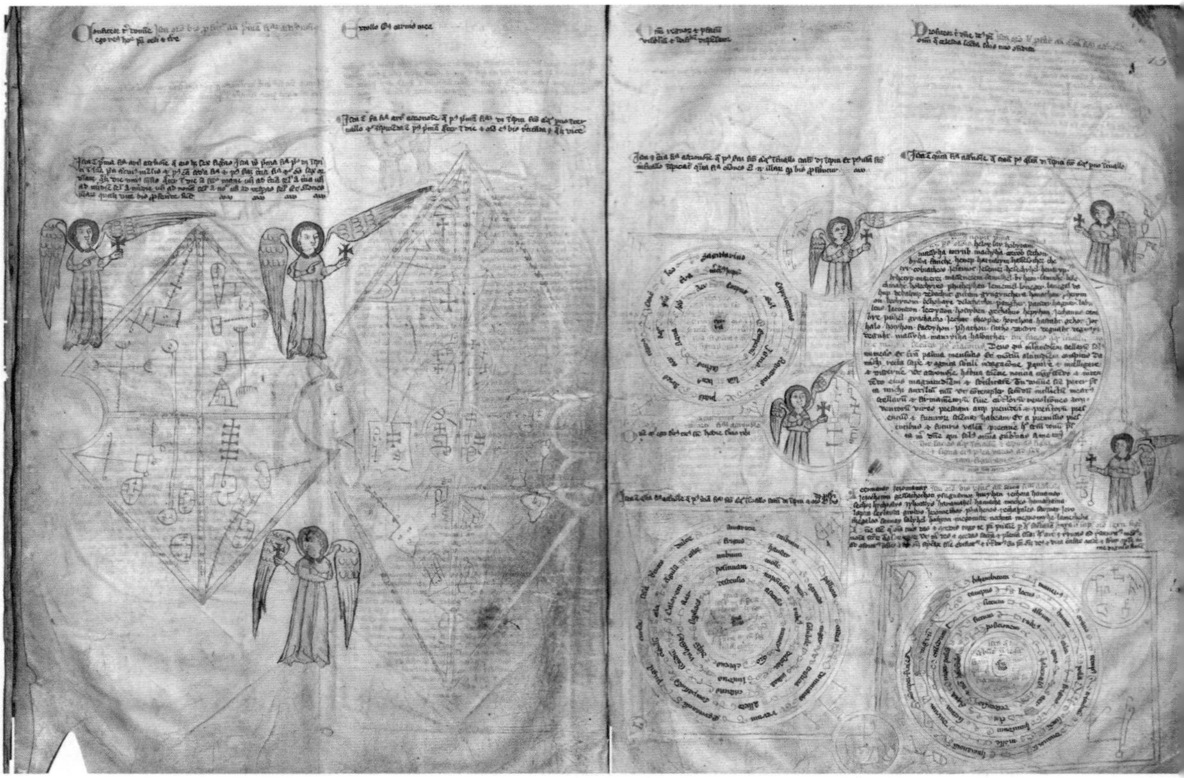

The first, second, third, and fourth figures of astronomy, from Bodley 951, Bodleian Library. Early 15th century.

in what has been erroneously thought to be the missing prayer of music with *Deus Pater immense [. . . misericordissime],* the prayer originally belonging to the seventh figure of philosophy. An adorning prayer, *Otheos Athamatheos,* is added.

The Version B scribe presents another copy of the great wheeled figure, identifying it as the third figure of astronomy, labeling "earth" (*terra*) at its center. The outermost ring lists the twelve zodiac signs, the middle ring lists the classical planets and their elemental qualities, and the innermost ring has the four elements, Saturn, and the Empyrean Heaven, which is the highest heaven and contains the element of fire according to medieval cosmogony. According to Version B, the prayer offered before the third *nota* of astronomy is *Omnium regnorum.*

According to Version B, the prayer offered before the fourth figure of astronomy is *Domine quia ego servus*. The fourth figure of astronomy appears only in Version B. There are five concentric circles that make up the fourth figure of astronomy. In the center it says "quality" (*qualitas*), and the outer rings have the following astrological and meteorological terms: "of clouds" (*nubium*), "of dimness" (*pallorum*),[32] "square" (*quara*), "lord" (*dominator*), "of the rest" (*rerum*),[33] "sickly" (*aegrotaticius*), "pugilist" (*pugil*), "a runner" (*cursor*),[34] "knowledge" (*scientia*), "virtues" (*virtutes*),[35] "melodious" (*dulce*),[36] "Notus" (*Auster*),[37] "sickness" (*aegritudo*), "black" (*niger*), "sorrow" (*tristitia*),[38] "whiteness" (*albedo*), "sympathy" (*compassio*), the "little tongue" or pointer of a measuring device (Latin *lingula*, Arabic *alidade*),[39] "warmth" (*calor*), "cold" (*frigus*), "gentle" (*molle*), "rough" (*durum*), "loosening" (*solubilis*), "favorable [winds]" (*secundus*),[40] "justice" (*iustitia*), "purity" (*castitas*), "red" (*rubeus*), "discolor," "judgment" (*iudicium*), "rubicund" (*rubicundus*), "air" (*aer*), "positive"

---

32. A description of the magnitude of stars and planets.

33. In astrology, there are five major aspects—conjunction, square, opposition, trine, and sextile—which describe the angle the planets make in relationship to one another as well as to the ascendant, midheaven, descendant, and lowest heaven within a horoscope. The "lord" (*dominator*) may mean the domicile lord in which each planet rules a zodiac sign.

34. The words *sickly, pugilist,* and *runner* describe the quality of a planet's movement (i.e., fast like a runner or slow like a sick person) or relationship with another planet (i.e., conflicting planetary natures) or even with the divining querent himself.

35. Astrology asserts that the celestial bodies hold certain virtues and can bestow knowledge to humankind.

36. A reference to the music of the planetary spheres.

37. The Anemoi are the ancient Greek wind gods of the four cardinal directions, of which Notus (Auster) is the south wind. The north wind is called Boreas (Aquilo). The west wind is called Zephyrus (Favonius). The east or southeast wind is called Eurus (Vulturnus).

38. In astrology, these are common characteristics associated with the planet Saturn.

39. The astrolabe, a disk-shaped instrument for making astronomical measurements. The main pointer, the alidade, was the ruler used for sighting during sky observation, for which the astrolabe can provide information about a particular portion of the sky and further calculations can be made. For this word usage and equivalency, see *Quia nobilissima scientia astronomiae,* a mid-fourteenth-century treatise (Cambridge University Library Gg. VI.3, ff. 217v–220v, and Oxford, Bodleian Library, Digby 57, ff. 130r–132v). See Falk, "Improving Instruments."

40. The words *warmth, cold, gentle, rough, loosening,* and *favorable,* describe the weather, winds, and seas for sailing ships; the word *secundus* is used here in its nautical sense. All these descriptives would suggest knowledge of using a mariner's astrolabe for navigation.

(*positivus*), "negative" (*impositivus*),[41] "Hebrew prayer" (*oratio Hebreus*), "disposition" (*dispositio*),[42] "superficies (*superfices*),"[43] "descent" (*descensio*), "ascendant" (*ascensio*),[44] and "number" (*numerus*).

According to Version B, the prayer offered before the fifth figure of astronomy is *Profiteor,* and it is the only figure of astronomy that has an adorning prayer, *Heloy Lay Hobidam,* which has a Latin prologue prayer, *Deus qui multitudinem*. Perhaps the adorning prayer and its Latin prologue are recovered source material from the original *Flores Aurei*. The fifth figure of astronomy appears only in Version B. There is nothing remarkable to say about the five wheels that constitute this figure; its number and arrangement of wheels remain a mystery. Perhaps these five wheels were not meant to be understood as a single figure, as Version B has presented it here, but were originally meant to represent all five figures of astronomy.

According to Version B, the prayer offered before the sixth figure of astronomy is *Iezomanay,* a *voces magicae* prayer. The sixth figure of astronomy is found only in Version B; it consists of concentric circles in which the center is labeled "quantities" (*quantitas*). Interspersed among the sigils in the circles are various terms such as "fortnight" (*bihebdomadalicus*),[45] "it is now the . . . day since,"

41. The positive zodiac signs of astrology are the fire triplicity (Aries, Leo, Sagittarius) and air triplicity (Gemini, Libra, Aquarius). The negative zodiac signs of astrology are the earth triplicity (Taurus, Virgo, Capricorn) and the water triplicity (Cancer, Scorpio, Pisces).

42. *Disposition* is a technical term in Arabic astrology. To use an example analogy, the planets are like lords of their domain, and when one planet, such as Mercury, is moving faster than another planet, such as Jupiter, and when Mercury perfects its aspect to Jupiter, then Mercury is "pushing its disposition" onto Jupiter, meaning Mercury is shoving its counsel onto Jupiter on how it ought to manage its affairs with the expectation that Jupiter will carry out Mercury's orders. The astrological concept of disposition was written in Arabic by the ninth-century Syriac astrologer of northern Iran named Sahl ibn Bishr. Five of his books on Greek astronomy and astrology were translated into Latin by John of Seville, and another book was translated by Herman of Carinthia. See Sahl Ibn Bishr, *The Introduction to the Science of the Judgments of the Stars*.

43. In geometry, a superficies is the two-dimensional magnitude surface that has length and width that forms the boundary of a solid.

44. The ascendant is the rising zodiac sign or the exact rising degree in a horoscope; it refers to the eastern horizon, where the Sun rises. The descendant is the opposite of the ascendant; it refers to the western horizon, where the Sun sets.

45. *Bi-hebdomada-licus,* a rare Greek loanword meaning "two weeks," from *hebdomad*. In astronomy, a lunar fortnight is half a lunar month.

(*nudius*), "[an astronomical] treatise" (*oratio*),[46] "three cubits" (*tricubitus*),[47] "number" (*numerus*), "time" (*tempus*), "place" (*locus*), "position" (*positio*), "superficies (*superficies*)," "humor (*humor*),"[48] "black" (*nigrum*), "white" (*album*), "red" (*rubeus*),[49] "gentle" (*molle*), "rough" (*durum*), "warmth" (*calor*), "cold" (*frigus*), "humid" (*humidum*), "dry" (*siccum*), "hot" (*calidum*),[50] "air" (*aer*), "earth" (*terra*), "water" (*aqua*), and "fire" (*ignis*).[51]

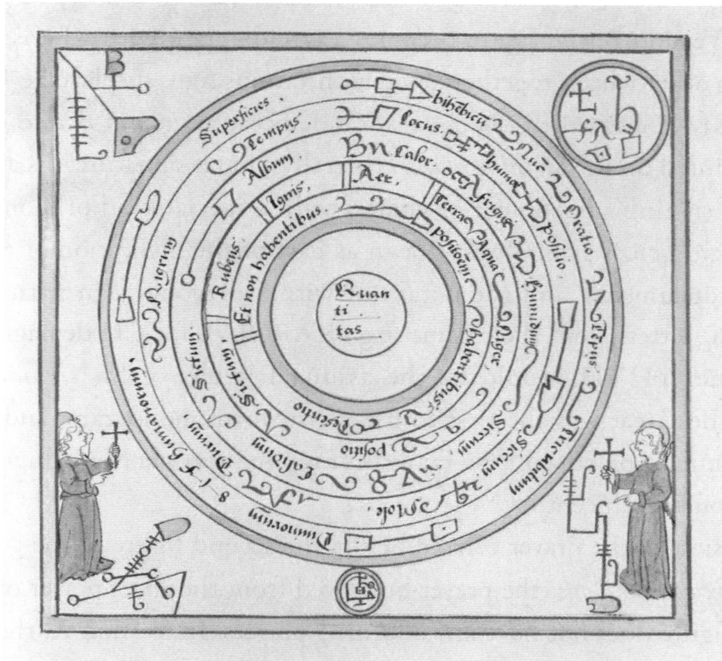

Sixth figure of astronomy, from *Ars notoria de Salomone,*
BnF Latin 7153. 15th century.

46. *Nudius* is a contraction of *nunc dius* (*dies*), suggesting a record-keeping of time. In the context of the notory art, it probably refers to the operator keeping track of the days for which prayers are to be offered.

47. Three cubits may have been a common measurement used during stargazing to mark the distance between stars.

48. Humorism is an ancient and medieval system of medicine based on four bodily fluids; namely, blood, phlegm, yellow bile, and black bile. Its inclusion here is probably in the context of medical astrology.

49. Venus is associated with white, Saturn is associated with black, and Mars is associated with red.

50. These are clearly meteorological terms.

51. The four classic elements of nature.

THE FIGURES OF THE GENERAL SCIENCES

In Version A, none of the figures of the general sciences have any prayers. In Version B, the prayer offered before the first figure of the general sciences is *Zedomor Phamanos,* and its adorning prayer is *Gedomor Phamazihon.* In Version A manuscripts, the first figure of the general sciences is a simple square with a cross or letter *x;* this image is expanded in Version B as a pair of crossed hands. In Version B, the figure becomes a tree diagram with wheels and lines connecting other wheels together along with various signs displayed everywhere. The gloss says, "it is called 'the *nota* of God,' because *signum manus* of God is to be imprinted on it." *Signum manus* (literally, "hand signature") is a medieval practice of signing a document or charter with a special kind of monogram or royal cypher; a cross symbol was drawn as part of the invocation or beginning of official documents, and the notary or witnesses would sign with a *signum manus* using letters from their name (e.g., KAROLVS for Charlemagne). Thus, God's name, YHVH, would be the assumed letters of his *signum manus.* Justinian the Great was the first to use a cruciform monogram, and it would become common practice in the Frankish Empire from the Merovingian period until the fourteenth century.[52]

In Version B, the prayer offered before the second figure of the general sciences is *Rex eterne Deus,* the prayer borrowed from the sixth prayer of philosophy. The figure does not have any adorning prayers. In Version A, the figure is a plain and empty wheel consisting of three concentric circles. In Version B, the figure is a great wheel divided in half horizontally with a pair of wheels above and below the line. Various mnemonic signs fill the figure. The significance of this figure is unknown.

In Version B, the prayer offered before the third figure of the general sciences is *Deus Pater immense [. . . magnitudo],* the prayer borrowed from the fifth prayer of philosophy. Its adorning prayer is *Iazer Hazacala.* The figure consists of three wheels stacked on top of one another in a vertical line. The gloss says one of the figures of philosophy (or the general sciences) is called "the *nota* of awe" and has an "angelic appearance" (*vultus angelicus*).[53] Presumably, the reference is to the

52. Garipzanov, *The Symbolic Language of Royal Authority,* 157–202.

53. *Ars Notoria,* section 103 gloss.

third figure of the general sciences as the three circles would correspond to the three spheres of the angels (first sphere: seraphim, cherubim, and thrones; second sphere: dominions, virtues, and powers; and the third sphere: principalities, archangels, and angels) as recorded in the writings of Pseudo-Dionysius. This figure bears a strong resemblance to the third figure of philosophy; because the general sciences fall under philosophy in the taxonomy of medieval knowledge and both third figure of each knowledge branch look alike, there may be confusion as to which figure receives this alternate title of "the *nota* of awe."

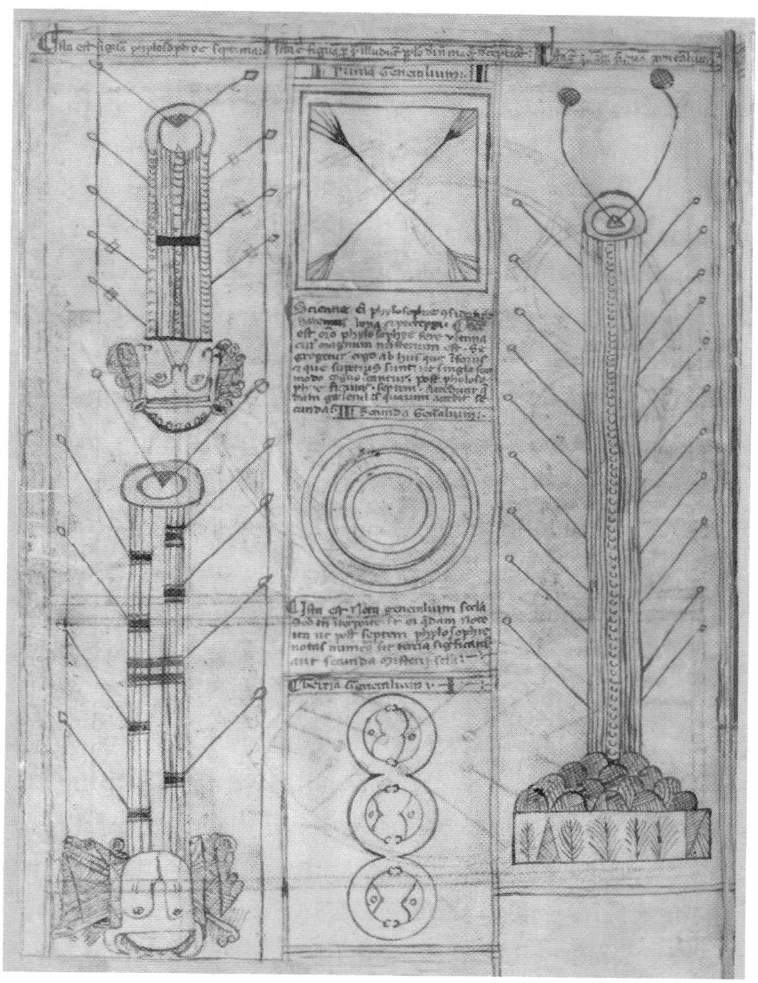

Seventh figure of philosophy (*left*); first, second, and third figures of general sciences (*center*); fourth figure of general sciences (*right*); from *Expositiones Apollonii ad cognitiones scientiarum quas Flores aureo appelavit.* BnF Latin 7152. 1239.

In Version B, the prayer offered before the fourth figure of the general sciences is *Deus totius pietatis,* the prayer borrowed from the seventh prayer of philosophy. The figure does not have any adorning prayers. In Version A, the figure is a tree diagram, and it does in fact resemble tree foliage and has little trees at its base. In Version B, the figure is further adorned with various mnemonic signs and wheels.

THE FIGURES OF PHILOSOPHY

The prayer offered before the first figure of philosophy is *Ezethomos* and its Latin prologue, *Domine Deus incomprehensibilis.* In Version B, its adorning prayers are *Themezehos Saguamal* and *Themon Gezomelyhon.* The first figure of philosophy is also called the *nota* of awe.[54] Assigned the identification label 25a, the figure is given the added title "inexpressible by men," presents a rectangular window in which the center has eight wheels stacked on top of one another; there are trees or other vegetation reaching out to the wheels from both sides. In each of the eight wheels are the following Greek letters: *alpha* (α, or the Hebrew *aleph,* א); *omicron* (ο); *iota* (ι); *tau* (τ, or instead of *tau,* the scribe used the Latin *t* to indicate the Greek *theta,* θ); and *gamma* (γ). These letters point to a special prayer which is said to have been offered by Solomon at his sacrifice of peacemaking to God on Mount Gibeon. The prayer contains *voces magicae* from these Greek letters which is meant to be sung like a song or glossalia.[55] The exact significance of this figure is unknown. Perhaps the eight wheels represent the seven planets and the Empyrean realm, with the plant life symbolizing heavenly paradise.

The prayers offered before the second figure of philosophy is *Domine Deus Sancte Pater* and *Deus semper via.* It does not have any adorning prayers. The second figure of philosophy is a column or tower diagram with lines extending out from its sides like a tree with branches. It is very similar in appearance to the fourth figure of the general sciences. Its significance is unknown.

The prayer offered before the third figure of philosophy is *Lemogethon* and its Latin prologue, *Vita homnium;* it does not have any adorning prayers.

54. BnF Latin 7152, f. 18.

55. See page 303. The inclusion of the Hebrew letters *aleph* and *gimel* would suggest that the scribe thought that Solomon was speaking the Hebrew sounds, not the Greek.

According to Version A2, the third figure of philosophy is also called the *nota* of sorrow.[56] The significance of this figure is unknown.

The prayer offered before the fourth figure of philosophy is *Rex regum*.[57] The fourth figure of philosophy is an isosceles-obtuse triangle filled with three trees in Version A. In Version B, the fourth figure appears as an isosceles-acute triangle topped with a wheel and filled with tree diagrams. The significance of this figure is unknown.

The prayer offered before the fifth figure of philosophy is *Deus Pater immense [. . . magnitudo]* and its Latin prologue, *Vita bonorum*. In Version A, the figure resembles a flower in which the central circle contains the Latin prologue *Vita bonorum,* which has seven semicircles, or flower petals, at its circumference. Beginning with the top petal at the twelve o'clock position and moving clockwise, the petals are listed as follows:

First petal: *potentia* (power), *vitus* (felloe or rim), *rex* (king)
Second petal: *fortis ut fons* (strength as a fountain), *deus* (god), *lux* (light)
Third petal: *ades* (you approach), *pax* (peace), *regnum* (kingdom)
Fourth petal: *tuas* (your), *visio* (vision), *factus* (having been made)
Fifth petal: *adiuvi* (I helped), *clairfica* (make famous), *mortem meam* (my death)
Sixth petal: *conditor lucis* (creator of light), *factor tenebrum* (maker of shadows)
Seventh petal: *misercordia* (mercy), *vita* (life), amen

The fifth figure of philosophy presents the reader with questions such as what is the meaning of one's life, how to fulfill one's vision and life goals, what legacy will one leave behind, and how to find God as one's strength through life's challenges. The first petal philosophically reflects upon the Wheel of Fortune (*Rota Fortunae*), a common medieval concept, viewing the rise and fall of power as typically illustrated by a king who moves around the wheel with the sayings, "I will reign," "I reign," and "I have reigned." The second petal suggests that God and spiritual brilliance act as an ever-flowing fountain of strength for the

56. BnF Latin 7152, f. 18v.

57. *Ars Notoria,* Section 96. In Version B, the prayer *Omaza* is also included (NS 109).

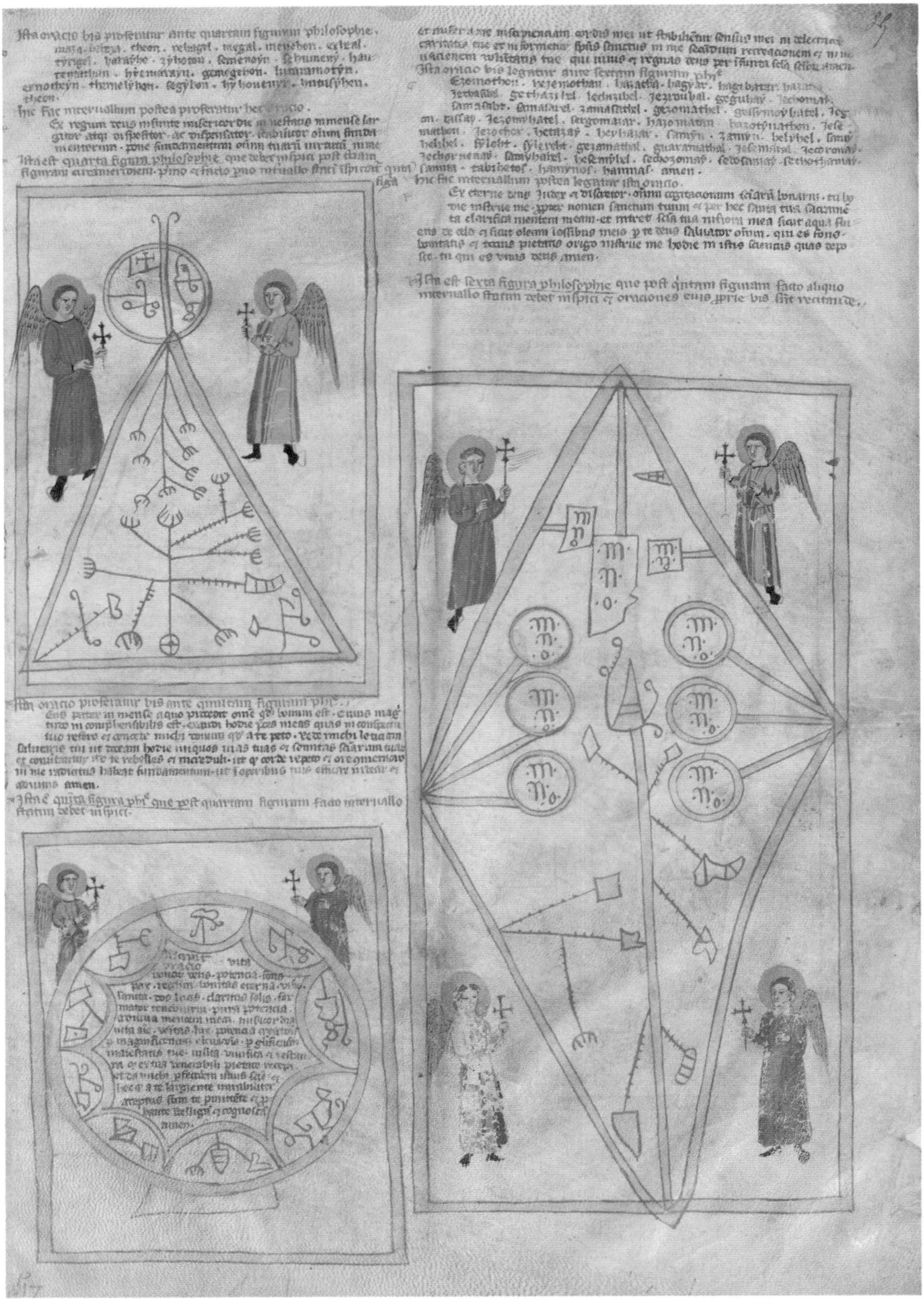

Fourth fifth, and sixth figures of philosophy (sixth also called the figure of awe, figure of god), from *Sacratissima ars notoria*, BnF Latin 9336. 1360–1375.

operator. The third petal suggests the reading, "You approach the kingdom of peace." The fourth petal suggests that the operator must have a vision of his life and make it manifest. The fifth petal says, "I helped make my death famous"—that is, having made his life's vision manifest, the operator has left a legacy, and his name will be remembered for it. The sixth petal makes a reference to God as the creator of light and darkness. The seventh petal might be advising the operator to have compassion and mercy for all life. In Version B, the words are substituted for mnemonic signs, and *Vita bonorum* is substituted for an angel.

The prayer offered before the sixth figure of philosophy is *Gezomothon* and its Latin prologue, *Rex eterne Deus.* The figure is a sort of tree diagram shaped like a mandorla or diamond, containing branches of wheels that point to the figure's center. Written within the wheels are the letters *m, n,* and *o.* The significance of this figure is unknown.

The prayer offered before the seventh figure of philosophy is *Deus totius pietatis.*[58] In Version A, the figure consists of two separate columns each with an upside-down head of a beast or man and sprouting branches (although Vatican Latin 6842, a Version A2 manuscript, does not have the upside-down heads). The significance of this figure is unknown. In Version B, the figure is unified with two wheels containing two kings, one upright and the other upside down, probably meant to symbolize the rise and fall of political power.

THE FIGURES OF GEOMETRY

The prayer to be offered before the first figure of geometry is *Deus iustus iudex.*[59] It does not have any adorning prayers according to the text, but in Version A there does appear to be a few *voces magica* therein (Zomodor, Zemanay, Lophares). In Version A, the figure is a semicircle divided in half; each half has two wheels, one big and one small. The big wheels each have a cross within them. The small wheels are joined by a single line. In Version A, the Greek letter *lambda* is grouped together in a few places.[60] The small mark below the *lambda,* a *keraia,* denotes the letter as a numeral sign. In Greek

---

58. In Version B, the prayer *Deus Pater immense [. . . misericordissime]* is also included (NS 116).

59. According to Latin 9336, a Version B manuscript, an additional prayer is also offered; namely, *Gemaht* (NS 119).

60. See Yale Mellon 1 and Munich Clm 276.

isopsephy, the letter-numeral system that assigned a numerical value to each letter of the alphabet, the *lambda* equals 30. Notice that the *lambda*s are grouped at angles and along the lines. Thus, three sets of *lambda*s equal 90, indicating the degrees of a right angle; these are placed at the angles. A set of six *lambda*s equal 180 degrees, which is a straight line. This calculation is known as geometric algebra and is explained in Euclid's *Elements*. In Version B, the four wheels are filled with mnemonic signs. Obviously, the entire figure is representative of Euclidean geometry.

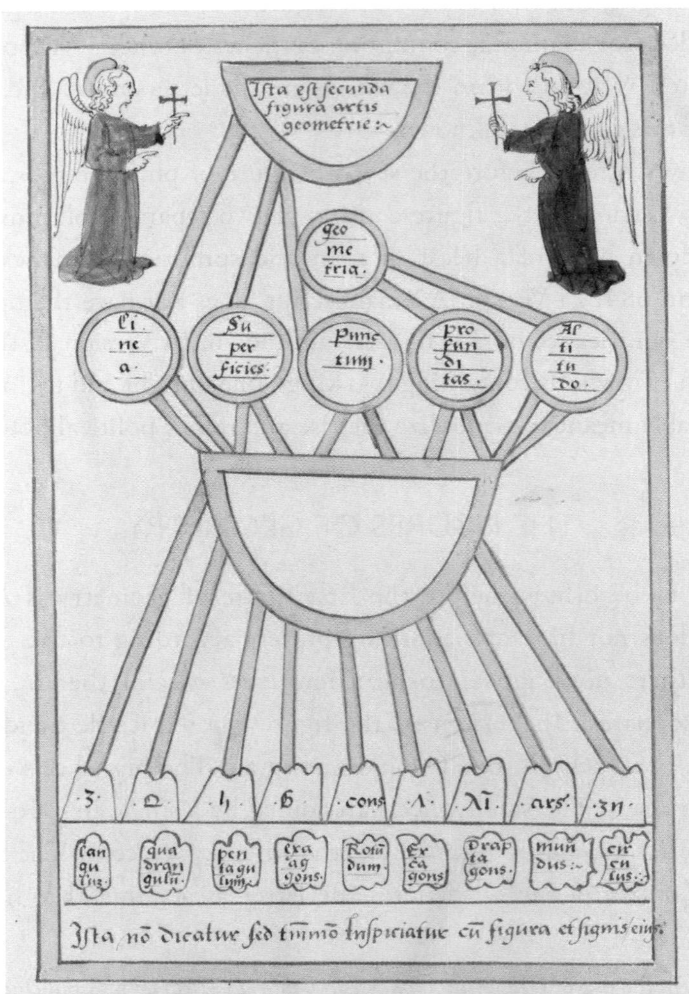

Second figure of geometry, from *Ars notoria de Salomone*, BnF Latin 7153. 15th century.

Version A2 witnesses a second figure of geometry, though its two semicircles might suggest it was the first figure of geometry just duplicated, then embellished as two tree diagrams. Version B says the prayer to be offered before the second figure of geometry is *Omnipotens sapientiae*. The adorning prayer is *Honoy Theon Hystym*. In BnF Latin 9336, the figure is presented as a tree diagram containing two semicircles, a group of circles, a rectangular base, and numerous lines branching out among these figures. Below the top semicircle is a circle labeled "geometry" (*geometria*) followed by five circles marked "line" (*linea*), "superficies" (*superficies*)," "point" (*punctum*), "depth" (*profunditas*), and "height" (*altitudo*). Beneath this is the other semicircle from which lines radiate below to the rectangular base that contains small irregular shapes in which are written mnemonic letters for remembering certain geometric knowledge. The bottom lists various geometric figures including the triangle (*triangulum*), quadrangle (*quadrangulum*), pentagon (*pentagonum*), hexagon (*hexagonum*), and sphere (*rotundum*). The list concludes with the world (*mundus*) and the circle, orbit, or calendrical cycle (*circulus*) in which the planets revolve around the world. These final two entries mark the entry point in which the 2-D realm of geometry enters the 3-D realm of astronomy. BnF Latin 7153 mentions that these geometric notions are not meant to be spoken aloud but only inspected during ritual. Most likely Boethius's lost work on geometry, which was based on Euclid's *Elements,* is the source of knowledge for this figure.

THE FIGURES OF THEOLOGY

In Version A, there are no prayers belonging to theology, but the five figures of theology are present. Version B supplies the five figures with prayers borrowed from the *Ars Nova*. According to Version B, the prayer offered before the first figure of theology is *Omnipotens incomprehensibilis*.[61] Version B adds the two adorning prayers, *Theos Hazamant Hel Hamyfodel* and *Heloy Adonay Sother Messias,* to the figure. The first figure of theology is a window diagram shaped by like an elongated diamond, having a point at the top, three semicircles on each side, and a semicircle at its bottom. Inside the window are a cross, four flags, and tree or plantlike figures. In Version B, the figure is diamond-shaped with a single semicircle on each side, resembling more like

61. *Ars Notoria,* section 115, NS 126.

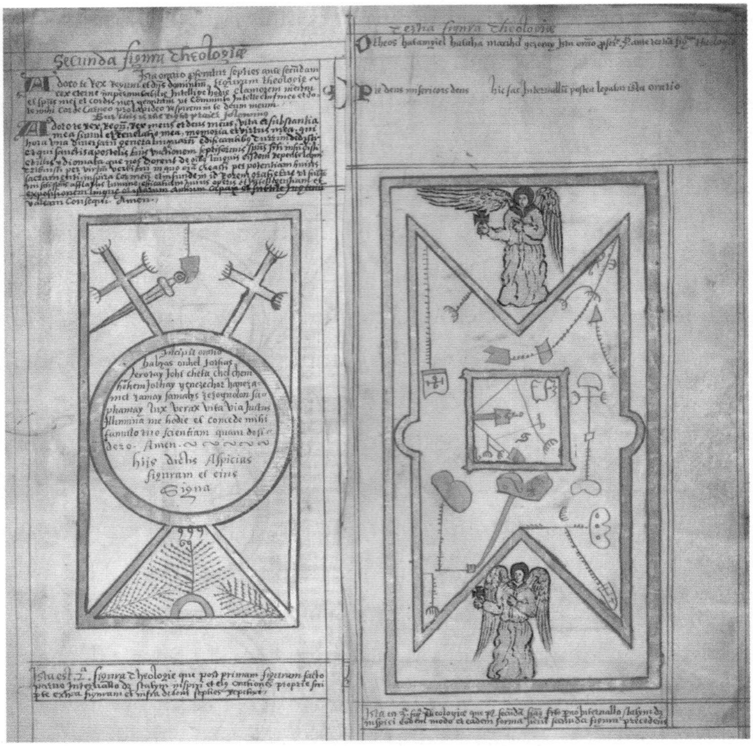

Second and third figures of theology, from *Liber de Arte Memorativa,* Yahuda Var. 34, National Library of Israel. 1600.

the first figure of astronomy. The significance of this figure is unknown.

According to Version B, the prayer offered before the second figure of theology is *Adoro te regum;* its adorning prayer is *Habyas Rihel.* The second figure of theology resembles a tower with a zigzag road leading from its base to the capstone where there are three flags and a sword. At its base might be plant life. An indication as to what this figure might mean comes from Version B's variation 9 prayer. The petitioner requests the gift of speaking in tongues just as the apostles had received from the Holy Spirit as recorded in chapter 2 of the Acts of the Apostles. Such a request would be consistent with the notion of a "theurgic" theology rather than a contemplative theology. The three flags may represent the Holy Trinity who resides in heaven, overlooking the Tower of Babel, just as it is described in the variation 9 prayer. If so, the flag with the sword might represent the Son who has a sword coming out of his mouth as in the Revelation 1:16 and 19:15. The figure's zigzag road and flags might also provide mnemonic uses.

According to Version B, the prayers offered before the third figure of theology are *Otheos* and *Pie Deus*.[62] It has no adorning prayers. The third figure of theology is an irregular polygon with another small one within its center. Version A adds tree figures within it, while Version B adds various mnemonic signs. The significance of this figure is unknown.

According to Version B, the prayer offered before the fourth figure of theology is *Pie Pater*. It has no adorning prayers. The fourth figure of theology is a wheel with four semicircles within it. In Version A, one pair of semicircles contains three flags, while the other pair contains a single tree diagram. Version B supplants the flags and trees with various mnemonic signs. The significance of this figure is unknown.

According to Version A, the prayer offered before the fifth figure of theology, also called the ineffable *nota,* is *Hosel*.[63] Version B contradicts this information, stating that *Deus vivorum*[64] is the prayer belonging to the fifth figure. It has no adorning prayers. The fifth figure of theology is a window diagram shaped by twenty-four "nooks" (*anguli*) at its border. Within the window is a vision of swords, candelabra,[65] birds in flowering trees, and winged serpents.[66] The entire fifth figure of theology recalls the imagery found in Solomon's temple according to the *Targum Sheni*. The *Targum Sheni* is a Byzantine midrash, Aramaic translation, and elaboration of the

62. *Ars Notoria,* sections 118–19, NS 132–33.

63. *Ars Notoria,* section 104.

64. *Ars Notoria,* NS 135.

65. Candelabra, also called a candle tree, might recall the Jewish menorah found in Solomon's temple.

66. The inclusion of winged serpents may represent King Solomon's summoned demons. The image may be inspired by the Greek historian Herodotus's passage that reads, "There is a place in Arabia not far from the town of Bouto [Buto] where I went to learn about the winged serpents. When I arrived there, I saw innumerable bones and backbones of serpents: many heaps of backbones, great and small and even smaller. This place, where the backbones lay scattered, is where a narrow mountain pass opens into a great plain, which adjoins the plain of Aigyptos [Egypt]. Winged serpents are said to fly from Arabia at the beginning of spring, making for Aigyptos; but the ibis birds encounter the invaders in this pass and kill them. The Arabians say that the ibis is greatly honored by the Aigyptoi [Egyptians] for this service, and the Aigyptoi give the same reason for honoring these birds." Herodotus (c. 484–425 BCE), *Histories,* 2.75.1–4. Classical writers such as Cicero, Pliny the Elder, Aelian, Isidore of Seville, and others are dependent on Herodotus's account. See also Isaiah 14:29, 30:6 and Lucan's *Pharsalia* 6.677 for passing references.

Book of Esther dating widely from the fourth century to the eleventh century and might show dependency upon the tenth-century Byzantine treatise titled *De Ceremoniis* (*Book of Ceremonies of Constantine VII Porphyrogennetos*).[67] It is worth quoting the *Targum Sheni* at length for its description of Solomon's temple:

> This is Solomon, the great king, who made his great royal throne covered with fine gold from Ophir, overlaid with beryl stones, inlayed with marble, it was overlaid with samargel, carbuncle, diamonds, and pearls, and all kinds of precious ones. For no king was one made like it, or were any of the kings able to produce one similar to it. Now this was the workmanship of his throne: twelve lions of gold stood upon it, and opposite them were twelve eagles of gold, a lion opposite an eagle and an eagle opposite a lion, they were arranged opposite each other. . . . The sum of all the lions was seventy-two. Now the top of the throne where the king's seat was located, was round. It had six steps, for it is written: "then the king made a great throne of ivory, the throne had six steps" (1 Kings 10:18). Thus, on the first step lay a golden ox and opposite it lay a golden lamb. On the third step lay a golden panther and opposite it lay a golden suckling kid. On the fourth step lay a golden eagle and opposite it a golden peacock. On the fifth step lay a golden cat and opposite it a golden hen. On the sixth step lay a golden hawk and opposite it a golden bird. Now on the top of the throne stood a golden dove, grasping a golden hawk in its claw. So likewise, with all the nations and (speakers of all) languages in the future be delivered into the hand of Israel. Now at the top of the throne was located a golden lampstand set in proper order in its arrangement of its lamps (and) with pomegran-

67. In the *De Ceremoniis* there is a description of an actual throne of Solomon at the Byzantine court in the Great Triklinos of the Magnaura Palace, the hall where the emperor and his officials received foreign embassies. Moreover, there is an eyewitness account of the Ottonian diplomat Liudprand of Cremona, who says, "In front of the emperor's throne there stood a certain tree of gilt bronze, whose branches, similarly gilt bronze, were filled with birds of different sizes, which emitted the songs of the different birds corresponding to their species. The throne of the emperor was built with skill in such a way that at one instant it was low, then higher, and quickly it appeared most lofty; and lions of immense size . . . coated with gold seemed to guard him, and, striking the ground with their tails, they emitted a roar with mouths open and tongues flickering." See Boustan, "Israelite Kingship, Christian Rome, and the Jewish Imperial Imagination," 167–82.

> ates, (and) with its ornaments, (and) with its snuffers/ashpans (and) with its cups and with its lilies. Now at one side of the lampstand were standing seven golden branches, upon which were portrayed the seven Patriarchs of the world, and these are their names: Adam, Noah and the great Shem, Abraham, Isaac, and Jacob, and Job among them. Now at the other side of the lampstand were standing seven other branches, upon which were portrayed the seven pious ones of the world and these are their names: Levi, Qehat (Kohath), Amram, Moses, Aaron, (and) Eldad and Medad, as well as the prophet Haggai among them. Now at the top of the lampstand was a golden vessel filled with pure olive oil, whose light supplied the lights of the lampstand, and upon it were portrayed the high priest. From the large basin proceeded two golden clusters, upon which were depicted the two sons of Eli—Hophni and Pinchas. Now within the two golden clusters there proceeded from the large basin upon which were portrayed the two sons of Aaron—Nadav and Abihu—as well as two golden seats, one for the high priest and one for the deputy high priest. Towards the top of the throne were set seventy golden thrones, upon which sat the seventy (members of the) Sanhedrin, dispensing justice before King Solomon. Now two dolphins were on either side of King Solomon's two ears in order that he should not become frightened. Above the top of the throne were set twenty-four golden vines, which provided shade for King Solomon.[68]

The Dutch philosopher Erasmus mentions lions, leopards, and dragons when talking about the notory art, and it seems likely he was thinking about the highly illustrated fifth figure of theology. Certainly, the dragons would equate to the winged serpents. Although not found in our selection of examined manuscripts, the lions probably represent the twelve golden lions on the six steps of the temple, each facing a golden eagle as described in 1 Kings 10:18–20, 2 Chronicles 9:17–19, and the *Targum Sheni*. Erasmus also mentions leopards, which might equate to the "panther" opposite the suckling kid and the "cat" opposite the hen as described in the *Targum Sheni*.

The *Targum Sheni* goes on to describe that a golden serpent lay coiled

---

68. Fine, *Art and Judaism in the Greco-Roman World,* 105–6. The modern scholar Ra'anan Boustan believes such a description of Solomon's throne room, and others like it, developed from the environs of Constantinople itself, further supporting a Byzantine origin for the *Ars Notoria*.

near the throne. There is said to be a mechanism within the throne that animated the various golden animal statues that would assist Solomon to be seated upon his throne, and a dove, perched above the throne, would fetch the scroll of the Law from the Ark of the Covenant and bring it to him when he oversaw judgments before the people. Also, there were palm trees that would move to provide shade to Solomon. Thus, from this description and that from the Bible, many of the illustrations might be explained concerning the birds in the trees, the candelabra, serpents, flowers, vines, and Erasmus's attested animals. All these would be representative of a heavenly paradise that is most suitable to theology. The swords were likely representative of King David and King Solomon and the prophesied kings to come, namely Rehoboam, Hezekiah, Manasseh, Amon, and Josiah, but alas for Solomon, this prophecy did not come to pass.[69] The significance of the number 24—that is the 24 nooks of the figure—can be found simply in the 24 vines; also, the number is a doubling of 12, such as the 12 lions and 12 eagles present on both sides of Solomon's throne. There are 6 steps leading up to the throne of Solomon; the number 6 might represent the 6 days of creation, and according to *Genesis*, on the sixth day God created man. Six times 12 gives 72, which is another symbolic number in Judaism.

THE FIGURE OF CHASTITY

In Version A, there is no figure or prayer of chastity. Version B has erred in its identification of the figure of chastity. The Version B scribe took the triangular figure of music found in Version A and labeled it as the figure of chastity. Version B asserts that the prayer to be offered before this triangular figure of chastity is *Lamahel Mysub* and its accompanying Latin prayer, *Domine Sancte Pater [. . . misericordia]*. It is not given any adorning prayers. The Version B figure of chastity is a triangle that contains a square and in this square are two concentric rings. See "The Figure of Music" (p. 162) and "The Figures of Astronomy" (p. 168) for more details.

69. Hirsch, Price, Bacher, Seligsohn, Montgomery, and Toy, "Solomon," in Singer et al., eds., *The Jewish Encyclopedia,* 436–48.

THE FIGURE OF JUSTICE, PEACE, AND FEAR

Version A does not supply any prayers for this figure. It has no adorning prayers. In Version A, the figure of justice, peace, and fear is a wheel, and inside of it is a symmetrical design of four scrolls on the left and another four on the right. The significance of the figure is unknown, although the two columns of scrolls might suggest a declaration or accusation versus a response—if one were to imagine a judicial court setting.

In Version B, the prayer to be offered before the *nota* of justice, peace, and fear is *Heloy clementissime Hel Ianazay,* and its Latin prologue is *Domine Deus scio quia in conspectu*. In Version B, the figure is depicted quite differently, showing two wheels joined by an isosceles-acute triangle, with the uppermost wheel topped with a pair of crosses. There is a horizontal line which divides the figure near the point of the downward pointing triangle. Inside the figure are various mnemonic signs. It is not clear how this *nota*'s stark change occurred over the course of time from Version A to Version B, nor is its significance made manifest.

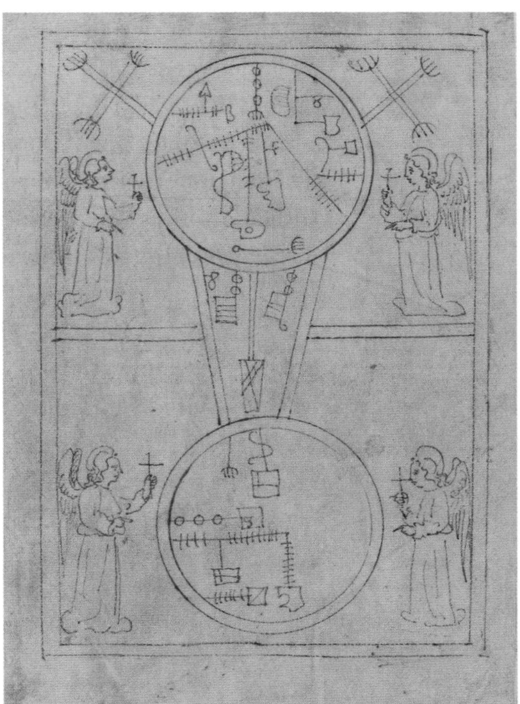

Figure of justice, peace, and fear, from *Sacratissima ars notoria,* BnF Latin 7154. 16th century.

THE FIGURE OF REPREHENSION AND TACITURNITY

Version A does not supply a prayer for this figure. In Version B, the prayer to be offered before the *nota* of reprehension and taciturnity is *Ezomathon Zehimochor* and its Latin prologue, *Ecce Domine Deus.*[70] It has no adorning prayers. The figure of reprehension and taciturnity (*figura reprehensionis et taciturnitatis*) is so called for its magical ability to silence others when the operator persuasively speaks the truth or share some great knowledge in the courtroom or debate class.[71] It has nothing to do with self-mastery as Julien Véronèse translates it. The figure of reprehension and taciturnity is a diamond-shaped window made by semicircles along its borders, and inside are groupings of arrows pointing toward its empty center. Perhaps the arrows are meant as a threatening sign to anyone who would dare speak against the operator's words.

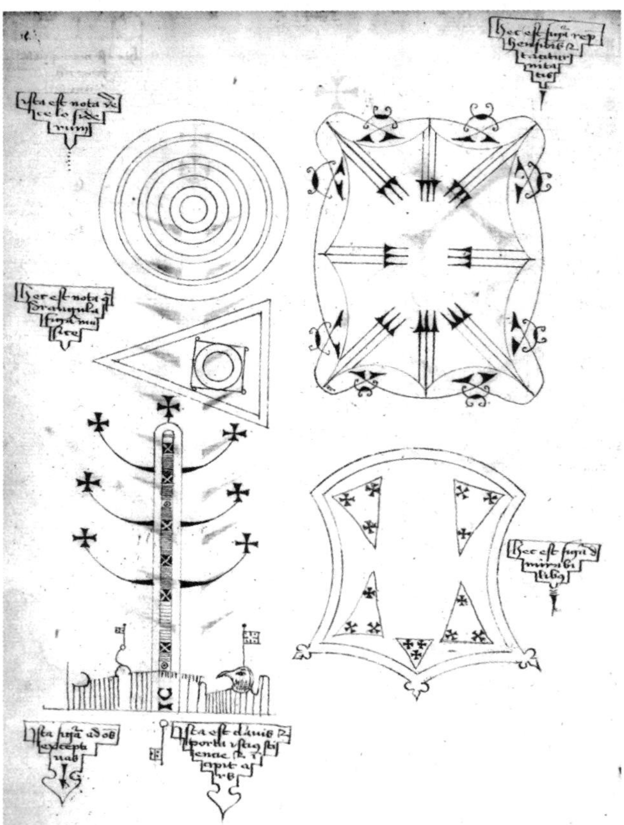

There are two columns of five figures. In the left-hand column, beginning at the top, there is the third figure of astronomy called "the nota of the moving stars" consisting of concentric rings. Next, there is the triangular figure of music. At the bottom is the figure of the seven exceptives. In the right-hand column, there is the figure of reprehension and tactiturnity. Below it, there is the first figure of astronomy called "the figure of wonders." from *Flores Aurei,* Clm 276, Bayerische Staatsbibliothek. Late 15th century.

70. *Ars Notoria,* NS 145–46.
71. See *Ars Notoria,* NS 148.

THE FIGURE OF ALL EXCEPTIVES

The figure of all exceptives is a tower set upon a landscape. The tower has seven crosses springing from its sides, and it has a wheeled capstone. A flag stands on both sides of the tower, and one flag stands upside down on the horizon like a mirror reflection of the tower itself. The figure is only found in Version A, and there are no instructions or prayers given for it there. Version B tells the operator who wishes to study the seven arts of divination to use the four figures of the general sciences.

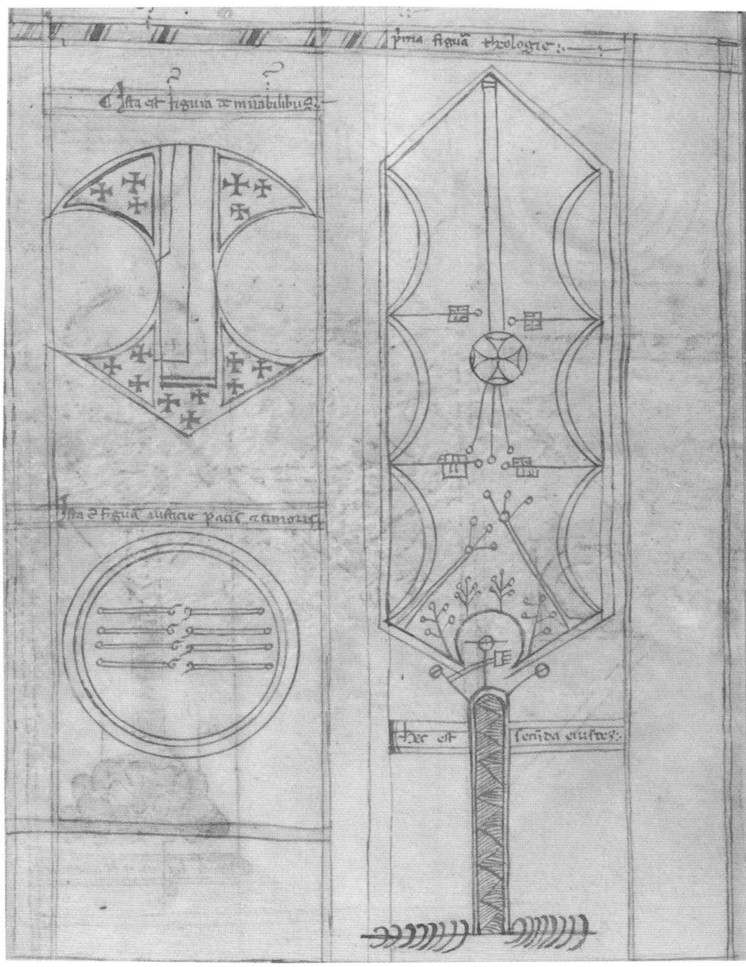

The figure of all exceptives (*lower right*), along with the figure of reprehension and taciturnity, from *Flores Aurei,* Clm 276, Bayerische Staatsbibliothek. Late 15th century.

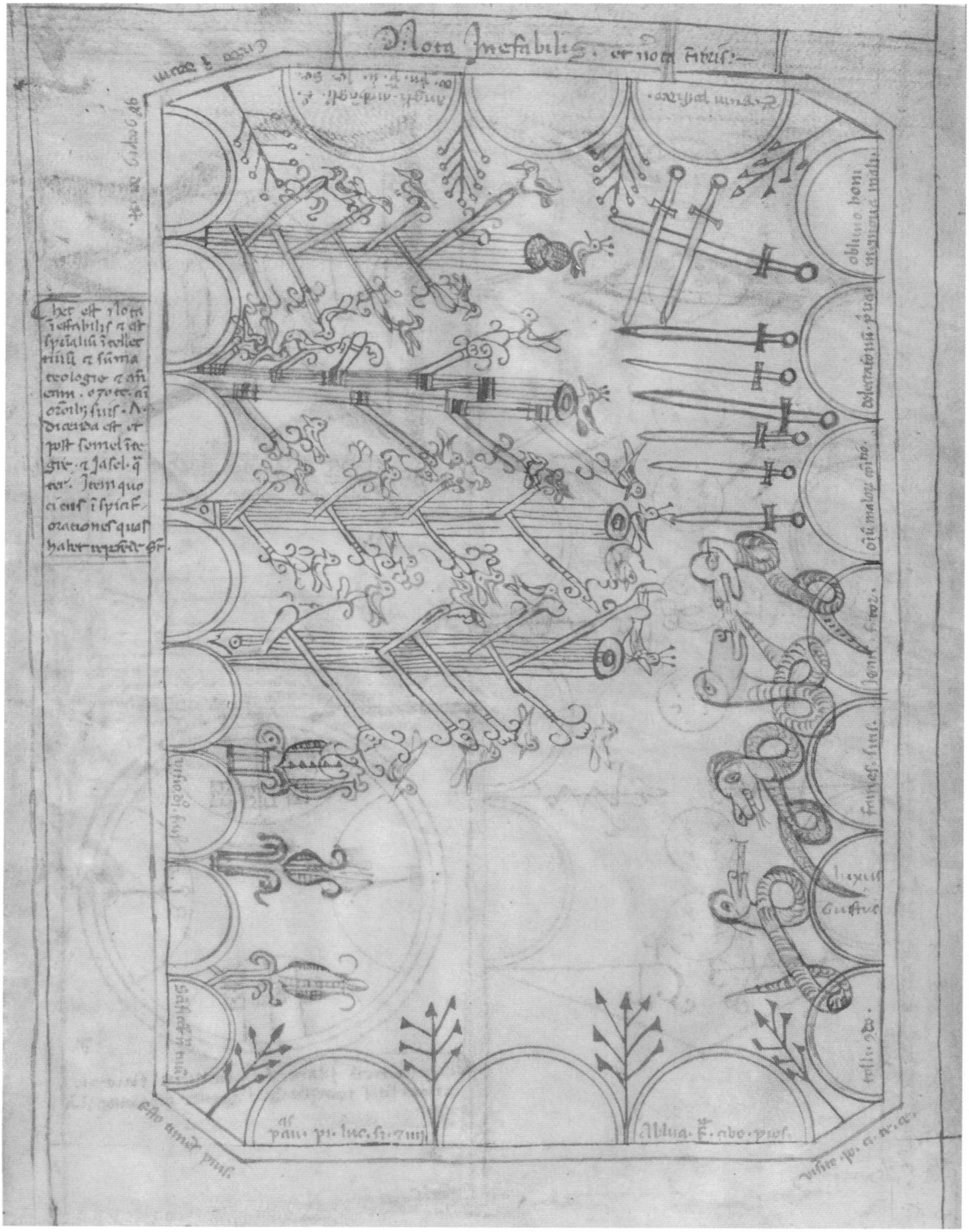

Fifth figure of theology, also called the *Ineffavle Nota,* from *Expositiones Apollonii ad cognitiones scientarum quas Flores aureos appellavit,* BnF Latin 7152.

VI.

The Complete Ritual Procedures

This chapter explores the ritual procedures of the *Flores Aurei* (*Golden Flowers*), the *Ars Nova* (*New Art*), and the supplement composed by the Christian letter writer. The *Flores Aurei* has two types of rituals. In this book, the central months-long ritual meant for the attainment of knowledge is called "the greater ritual." The other ritual type is the short rituals involving the General prayers used for their own occult virtue; here they are collectively called "the lesser rituals." Both A and B versions of the *Ars Notoria*'s ritual procedures are studied here. The *Ars Nova* is studied both as a stand-alone ritual in contrast to the *Flores Aurei* and also as a harmonized portion of the *Ars Notoria* (Version B). The supplement of the Christian letter writer provides ritual instructions that were either original to the *Flores Aurei,* to himself, or a mixture of both. The little work of the *novem termini* is so brief that its description and ritual procedure have already been explored in chapter II, "Elements of the *Ars Notoria*."

THE GREATER RITUAL OF THE *FLORES AUREI,* VERSION A RECONSTRUCTED

Because the *Flores Aurei* survives only in a fragmented state, it is difficult to discern what the ritual procedures truly are. A reconstruction of the ritual procedures of Version A is necessary to piece together what might have been prescribed in the original text. The following reconstruction is informed by clues detected within Version A, and then also consulting the ritual framework expressed in Version B (particularly the second, third, and fourth months). What emerges from this reconstruction is a mathematical beauty of number, proportion, and complementary parts, accentuating the principal significance of the number seven.

The greater ritual is divided into multiple parts. First, there is the division of time into months, days, and hours. The greater ritual is hypothesized to have spanned just two lunar months based on the evidence that only two months are ever mentioned in which there are certain auspicious days for the recitation of certain prayers. The first lunar month lists the auspicious days as the fourth, eighth, twelfth, sixteenth, twentieth, twenty-fourth, twenty-eighth, and thirtieth (section 15). There are eight auspicious days, and those days are multiples of four. The second lunar month lists the auspicious days as the first, third, sixth, ninth, twelfth, fifteenth, eighteenth, twenty-first, twenty-fourth, twenty-sixth, twenty-ninth, and thirtieth (section 40).

In the second month, there are twelve auspicious days, and those days are multiples of three. From this alone, it is clear that the month is divided into ordinary days and auspicious days. Moreover, the heading to section 14 reads, "How he will have eloquence in all the sciences within one month . . . " This would suggest that a single month is used as a ritual framework for all the sciences (explained further below). The next clue follows the *Lemaac Salmaac* prayer, which reads, "Some things are divided hereafter that in the beginning of the month ought to always be said . . ." (section 23). The key phrase here is "in the beginning of the month," signaling that each month is divided. By consulting Version B, it can be inferred that each month is divided into half, having days 1–15 and days 16–30 ("For on the other days of that month . . . up to the fifteenth day," and also, "And it is to be done thus concerning these from the fifteenth day of the lunar month up to the end . . ." section 126f gloss). Lastly, the day is divided into four parts, or canonical hours for prayer—prime, terce, nones, and vespers ("four times for the circular course [of the day]," section 15). In summary, the timing of the greater ritual consists of two months in which each month is divided in half (days 1–15 and 16–30). The first month has eight auspicious days, and those days are multiples of four. The second month has twelve auspicious days, and those days are multiples of three. Finally, the day is divided into four canonical hours for prayer.

Next, the greater ritual divides the prayers into two categories: the General prayers and the Special prayers. The General prayers consists of seven sequences of prayers which are for the purpose of developing the operator's mental faculties. These seven sequences are further subdivided into two groups. The first group consists of sequences 1–3, and they are for the purpose of gaining memory, eloquence, understanding, and the stability of these three (the first sequence functions as a preamble for the ritual proper). The second group consists of sequences 4–7, and they are "concerned with theology"; that is, for the purpose of developing the operator's capacity to communicate with the angelic powers. The Special prayers are associated with certain fields of knowledge and their respective magical figures. Those fields of knowledge are organized according to a hiearchy in which philosophy, residing at the summit of the hierarchy, is composed of the three liberal arts (grammar, logic/dialectic, and rhetoric) and the four liberal arts (arithmetic, music, geometry, and astronomy). In a the notory art, philosophy "rules over" the seven liberal arts.

Because philosophy "rules over" the seven liberal arts, its own Special prayers are divided into two groups—the first, second, third, and fourth prayers are assigned to the first month and the fifth, sixth, and seventh prayers are assigned to the second month. Version B has only retained the second portion of this reconstruction—that is, the recitation of the fifth, sixth, and seventh prayers of philosophy—which prefaces the operation of the specific art or science the operator wishes to obtain (126f gloss).

The Special prayers of philosophy are offered first, then the Special prayers of the liberal art follow on any ordinary day. Traditionally, the three liberal arts are learned first, then the four liberal arts are second. Because the three liberal arts are learned first, they are assigned to the first month. Similarly, the four liberal arts are assigned to the second month. The *Flores Aurei* informs us that only a single liberal art is learned one at a time (section 68). Thus, it is conceivable to reconstruct that the original framework of the *Flores Aurei* dictates that one of the three liberal arts (grammar, logic/dialectic, and rhetoric) is learned in the first month, then one of the four liberal arts (arithmetic, music, geometry, and astronomy) is learned in the second month. Or perhaps, the first month, as a ritual framework itself, is repeated for each of the three liberal arts. This would take a total of three months, assuming the operator was successful in acquiring each art successively. Then the operator proceeds to the second month to learn the four liberal arts, repeating that ritual framework for each art, and if successful, this would take a total of four months. The other fields of knowledge, such as the general sciences and the exceptives, belong under the umbrella of the four liberal arts in the medieval hiearchy of knowledge and therefore would belong to the second month's ritual framework. The pursuit of a single art is called an experiment (section 2). Now the division of the Special prayers over the two months has been established. It is also important to mention that the Special prayers are assigned to the ordinary days (section 78a).

Similarly, the seven sequences of General prayers are divided into two groups: sequences 1–3 and sequences 4–7 (Version A, section 23, reads, "Some things are divided hereafter . . ."; that is, after the third sequence of *Theos Pater* and *Te queso Domine*). Sequences 1–3 are assigned to the first month (the multiples of four) and sequences 4–7 are assigned to the second month (the multiples of three). Version B parallels the division of the General prayers, making the split between the second and third months. Now the General prayers are assigned to the auspicious days (Version A, sections 14–17). If Version B, section 40 gloss, is any indication of how many times each General prayer is to be offered, then it follows that a General prayer belonging to the the first month (the multiples of four) would be offered as many times as corresponding to that day's number. In other words, the General prayer offered on the fourth day would be offered four times; likewise, the same prayer offered on the eighth day would be offered eight times, and on the twelfth day it would be offered twelve times, and so on. Furthermore, the offering of the prayers are divided over the course of the day's four canonical hours.

Now each month is divided into half (days 1–15 and days 16–30), although the accounting of the Egyptian Days—the fifteenth, seventeenth, and nineteenth days—give a false impression that the month is divided into three parts (sections 78–79). What is actually happening here is that the scribe expresses uncertainty about how the Egyptian Days, those unlucky days in which the Special prayers are forbidden to be offered according to Solomon's instructions, align with the two-part month in consideration of the auspicious days. This confusion is carried forward into Version B about where to draw the dividing line between the first part of the month and its second part. The fifteenth day of the second month is considered auspicious, and the fifteenth day is an Egyptian Day, but this should not matter because the auspicious days are reserved only for the General prayers. Version B follows the instructions for the format of a first half and second half of the month. Now, there is no indication that the General prayers of either month are affected by the one-half division of the month because they are offered on auspicious days.

Now, the offering of the Special prayers of the liberal arts and the inspection of their figures are performed on the ordinary days of the month. In considering the two-part division of the month, the inspection of the figures of a given liberal art is roughly divided in half, depending on the number of figures. For example, the general sciences have four figures. The first and second figures are inspected in the first half of the month, and the third and fourth figures are inspected in the second half of the month (Version B, section 87 gloss).

Now the number of times the inspection of the figures and the offering of the Special prayers of the liberal arts are to be conducted on the ordinary days depends on the particular instructions of any given liberal art. The ritual instructions for acquiring the art of grammar has already been summarized in chapter II, "Elements of the *Ars Notoria,*" and the original text is found in sections 77–81. How these numbers for the offerings and inspections are calculated are not demonstrated. Also, there are instructions for fasting until evening on the first day of the inspection of the figures belonging to grammar, but nothing more is said. Because Version A perserves only the ritual instruction for the art of grammar, this reconstruction ends here.

Complements and Symbolism, Reconstructed Version A

Throughout the Version A reconstruction, there is a pervasive theme in which one thing is divided into two parts, and those parts complement one another. Philosophy is divided into the three liberal arts and the four liberal arts. The prayers of philosophy are divided into two sets of sequences (1–4 and 5–7). Because the prayers of philosophy rule over the liberal arts, the first month has sequences 1–4 ruling over the trivium and the second month has sequences 5–7 ruling over the quadrivium. Thus, the sequences 1–4 of philosophy, totaling four, plus its three liberal arts, equals seven. Complementary, the sequences 5–7 of philosophy, totaling three, plus its four liberal arts, equals seven. Notice that the first month, which has auspicious days in multiples of four, is assigned to the three liberal arts; again, four plus three equals seven. Likewise, the second month, which has auspicious days in multiples of three, is assigned to the four liberal arts; again, three plus four equals seven. The two months and their prayers of philosophy and the seven liberal arts complement one another.

The prayers are divided into the General prayers and the Special prayers. The General prayers are subdivided into two sets of sequences (1–3 and 4–7). The Special prayers are subdivided into the fields of knowledge. Notice that the General prayer sequences (1–3, totaling 3) plus its assignment to the first month (multiples of 4 as "4") equal seven; likewise, the General prayer sequences (4–7, totaling 4) plus its assignment to the second month (multiples of 3 as "3") also equal seven.

The days of the month are divided in ordinary days and auspicious days. Each month is divided in half (days 1–15, 16–30) and each day is divided into four main hours for the purpose of distributing the offering of prayers and the inspection of the figures. There are eight auspicious days of the first month given as multiples of four (4, 8, 12, 16, 24, 28); because there are not 32 days in a month to fit the pattern, day 30 is the last day. There are twelve auspicious days of the second month given as multiples of three (3, 6, 9, 12, 15, 18, 21, 24); however, in order to achieve a total of twelve days, the pattern is altered at the end, giving day 26 and day 29 but ending rightly with day 30. Thus, both months have to make an exception to the rule of multiples: the first month cannot do day 32 because the number of days within a month is usually calculated by 30, and the second month cannot achieve the twelve days within the month by its multiples of three. The exception or remainder to the rule of multiples is the number two. In conclusion, the reoccurrence of the number two is found in two months, two parts of a month, and two remainder days.

Next, each day is naturally divided into morning and evening; the morning is divided into two hours (prime, terce) and the evening is divided into two hours (nones, vespers), giving a total of four hours for the offering of prayers. There are four hours of the day, which might have been chosen to align with the fourfold symbolism expressed in the divine revelation of the notory art, including the four ruling angels, Hagnadam, Merabor, Hamiladei, and Pesiguaguol, who carry the four scrolls (section 15).

The number of times a General prayer is offered on an auspicious day equals the corresponding number of that day (e.g., four times on the fourth, eight times on the eighth, etc.). The formula for the number of times a Special prayer is offered on an ordinary day is not certain. In any case, the motif of complements is felt across the entire reconstruction of the greater ritual.

THE LESSER RITUALS OF THE *FLORES AUREI*

Certain General prayers are said to hold certain occult virtues which function outside of the greater ritual procedure. These are considered the lesser rituals of the notory art. They are not bound by any certain time restraints, and their execution is brief.

1. *Lemaac Salmaac,* called the "queen of languages," has the occult virtue for bestowing eloquence (sections 21–23).
2. *Deus summe Deus invisibilis Theos Pat[e]r* and its Latin prologue, *Te queso Domine,* have the occult virtue to invoke angels and bestow the mental faculty of memory (sections 24–25).
3. *Ancor Anacor Anilos* is a prayer which has two occult virtues, which can be expressed in two separate lesser rituals. The first occult virtue is for attaining visions of knowledge (section 26). The second occult virtue, which is a new magical experiment supposedly instituted by the Christian writer himself (section 107), is for diagnosing disease and prognosticating the patient's outcome, whether he moves toward life or death. The prayer is said to have efficacy whether the patient is present or at a distance. The prayer also helps discern the truth of whether a patient is feigning or concealing an illness. The prayer is said to reveal whether a woman is pregnant and whether a person is a virgin (sections 28–30).
4. *Lamen Ragaa* and its Latin prologue, *Memoria irreprehensibilis,* can be said before delivering a long speech, when studying writings, or when one is in danger of fire, earth, and beasts (sections 34 and 38).
5. *Gemoht Gehel* is a prayer of eloquence from the lost book called *Lengemath.* Its Latin prologue is *Omnipotens sempiterne Deus,* and its second part is *Semot Lamen.* The prayer is intended to persuade a director, president, patron, or bishop to look favorably upon the operator's

request. The *Flores Aurei* claims that its effect is as quick as when Jesus called his disciples to follow him (section 60).

The other General prayers might also be considered to function on their own, but no further details are offered in the *Flores Aurei*. The *Summe Sacrae Magicae,* on the other hand, does describe the occult virtues of each of these General prayers plus others not found in the *Flores Aurei*.

THE CHRISTIAN WRITER'S LETTER

The Christian writer's fragmented letter may be divided into three parts: (1) the explement of the entire art, (2) the *Ars Nova,* and (3) the little work of the *novem termini*. The letter is intended as supplementary material meant to accompany the *Flores Aurei*. The explement answers the addressee's questions about the notory art, beginning with the figures. When reading the explement, the reader realizes that certain information which is referenced is missing, and the addressee's comments and questions are not always felt nor does the letter writer elaborate any further. These hints and fragments leave the reader wanting to know more about what was said between the two. The author says that the seven prayers of philosophy are to be said seven times on each of their own days; he specifically mentions days seven, seventeen, and twenty-seven of the lunar month. According to Version B, section 87 gloss, days seven and seventeen are days forbidden in the offering of the prayers of philosophy. The figure of God, which is thought to correspond to the first figure of the general sciences, is to be inspected on the new Moon, but nothing else is explained. There are incomplete ritual instructions regarding the prayers of theology for "whenever you want to investigate about a great theology through a more satisified love." The ritual instructions for the prayers of the general sciences does appear to coincide with Version B, section 88 gloss. What the Christian writer says about the four liberal arts is strikingly different from what is found in Version B. If the operator wishes to learn the four liberal arts, then the fifth prayer of theology is to be offered after the Special prayers of each one of those arts (section 89). The Christian writer asserts that the seven prayers of philosophy are augmentations of the five prayers of theology (section 90). He says that the first, second, third, and fourth prayers of philosophy must be offered first before offering the prayers of the general sciences (the prayers of the general sciences are missing). What he says about the seven days, which lead up to the lunar month for the operation of theology, coincides with the ritual instructions given in Version B, section 97 gloss. The Christian writer warns his addressee: "[W]hatever came to you through a vision, you must keep secret and guard, and when the great angel of the Lord appeared to you bearing the sign of the cross on a stand, guard ineffably the words which he has shown written to you" (section 103). He says that the *Hosel* prayer is to be given after the *notae* of all the arts, and it is to be said four times (section 104). He also instructs his addressee to observe the fourth day of the lunar month in the pronunciation of all the prayers of theology (sections 105–6). He says that even inspecting just half a figure and repeating the prayers of theology five times can confer the effect of learning what is written within the great books of contemplative theology (section 109).

THE *ARS NOVA* (*NEW ART*)

The *Ars Nova* is the second divine revelation of King Solomon whose principal benefit is to gain knowledge (section 114a). The Christian writer claims that the ten prayers of the *Ars Nova* are the proems (*proemia*) to the *voces magicae* prayers found in the *Flores Aurei*. None of these ten prayers require any special observation of time, unlike most of the *Flores Aurei* prayers. There is a nine-day ritual preparation in which the operator conducts a fast for three days and abstains from sins. After the fast, he is expected to maintain ritual purity for six days before beginning the ritual proper. Of the ten prayers, the first three prayers belong to the trivium, and the next four prayers belong to the quadrivium. The Christian writer also states that *Ars Nova* prayers may be used in conjunction with the *Flores Aurei* prayers, but it is not necessary (114b). The prayers may be offered as often as desired whether secretly or openly. The ten prayers and their purposes are as follows:

1. *Omnipotens incomprehensibilis* "is valid for almost all headings and *notae*."
2. *Adoro te rex regum* for understanding.
3. *Confiteor* for stability of the mind.
4. *Otheos / Pie Deus* is "great for accomplishing all good work."

5. *Pie Pater* may bring clarity to the internal and external senses.
6. *Extollo sensus* brings "constancy of morals" and instills virtues within the operator.
7. *Omnium regnorum* brings "the restoration of ingenuity and the subtlety of intellect."
8. *Deus vivorum* comes "from the purity of confession and the impetration of the grace of God with respect to understanding."
9. *Profiteor* presents the seven gifts of the Holy Spirit.
10. *Domine quia ego servus* is meant for "the observation of both the [New and Old] testaments with their appendices."

THE GREATER RITUAL OF THE *ARS NOTORIA*, VERSION B

The greater ritual of the *Ars Notoria* (Version B) harmonizes the ritual instructions from multiple sources into one whole. The Version B scribe's main sources include the *Flores Aurei,* the *Ars Nova,* and the *novem termini.* Essentially, Version B uses two ritual models—the *Flores Aurei* and the *Ars Nova.* From these, the ritual components were examined and divided across four months, thereby extending the duration of the ritual in order to harmonize all these parts. The ritual components of all these parts are studied below. By harmonizing and expanding the notory art, the Version B scribe erred in doubling ritual instructions, having inconsistent usage of the original ritual frameworks, and burdening the practitioner with cumbersome glosses and recapitulations.

In addition, the Version B scribe found problems with the fragmented *Flores Aurei* as it lacked certain prayers and figures. New prayers were assigned or borrowed from elsewhere and given to those figures which lacked prayers. Those astronomy and theology figures which had no prayers were assigned the *Ars Nova* prayers. These new changes are recognized in the footnotes of the English translation of Version B and appendix A2.

The key glosses of Version B that inform the structure of the greater ritual are those in sections 126a–f. These glosses lay out the skeletal framework of the entire greater ritual procedure. The basic outline of the greater ritual procedure is laid out in the following five phases, whose titles are not found in the text but are given here for easy identification.

Phase 1: Fifteen Days of Penitence
Phase 2: Three-Day Opening Ritual Procedure
Phase 3: Interim Period
Phase 4: Operation for Obtaining a New Science
- The First Lunar Month
- The Second Lunar Month
- The Third Lunar Month
- The Fourth Lunar Month

Phase 5: Three-Day Closing Ritual Procedure

Each phase is explored in detail here.

Phase 1

The Fifteen Days of Penitence is a preliminary stage in which the operator purifies himself in preparation for the upcoming ritual procedure. In this phase, the operator performs confession, fasting, and giving alms to the poor for the first twelve days. The number fifteen might draw from the *Ars Nova* ritual model in which there are three days of fasting followed by six days of ritual purity, for a total of nine days. The first nine days would satisfy the ritual requirement of the *Ars Nova*. The next six days of ritual purity may also be modeled after the *Ars Nova* in that the first three days are for fasting. This brings the total number of days to twelve. The final three days, a Friday, Saturday, and Sunday, are likely the preparatory days to align with the lunar month, modeling after the *Flores Aurei* ritual model.

Phase 2

The remaining three days begins phase 2, the Three-Day Opening Ritual Procedure. Phase 2 is Days 13, 14, and 15. It is imperative that Day 13 be a Friday.[1] Ideally, the three-day opening ritual would be set closest to the new Moon. Only about once a year does a new Moon occur on a Friday, so it is safe to assume that there will be a few days between phase 2 and the beginning of the lunar month; these extra days belong to phase 3. In certain instances, it seems the glosser(s) mistakenly assumed phase 2 would begin on the new Moon, which, as already said, is rare and unlikely.

---

1. *Ars Notoria,* section 126e gloss.

Day 13, Friday

At lauds, the saffron and rosewater tea is made. At prime, the operator drinks the tea and recites *Bonitatem, etc.,* four times. The tea should be drunk only once a day and only at prime. The following prayers are offered at prime, terce, and sext: The preamble *Alpha et Omega* and the *prima tria capitula* ("first three headwords")—that is, *Helyscemath, Theos Megale*—and its Latin prologue, *Lux mundi.*[2] These first three headwords are also called the first sequence of the General prayers and are recited once. After an interval of silence, the ten prayers of the *Ars Nova* and the *novem termini* are recited once. Smaller intervals can be made between any prayers. During the course of the morning, the operator should fast on bread and water and eat nothing until after the prayers at sext. Then, the operator may eat Lenten food.[3] The operator must keep away from mortal sin and practice chastity.[4]

Day 14, Saturday

At lauds, the saffron and rosewater tea is made. At prime, the operator drinks the tea and recites *Bonitatem, etc.,* four times. The tea should be drunk only once a day and only at prime. The following prayers are offered at prime, terce, and sext: The preamble *Alpha et Omega* and the first three headwords are recited once. After an interval, the ten prayers of the *Ars Nova* and the *novem termini* are recited once. Smaller intervals can be made between any prayers. During the course of the morning, the operator should fast on bread and water and eat nothing until after the prayers at sext. Then, the operator may eat fish and Lenten food. The operator must keep away from mortal sin and practice chastity.

Day 15, Sunday

At lauds, the saffron and rosewater tea is made. At prime, the operator drinks the tea and recites *Bonitatem, etc.,* four times. The tea should be drunk only once a day and only at prime. The following prayers are to be offered once at prime, terce, and sext. The preamble *Alpha et Omega* and the first three headwords are recited once. After an interval, the ten prayers of the *Ars Nova* and the *novem*

---

2. *Ars Notoria,* sections 7, 10, and 11.

3. *Ars Notoria,* sections 126a gloss and 126e gloss. In contrast, the text of variation 1 gloss instructs the operator to fast on bread and water for the entire thirteenth day.

4. *Ars Notoria,* section 126c gloss.

termini are recited once. Smaller intervals can be made between any prayers. After the prayers of the sext hour, the operator is permitted to eat fish or meat. Alms are to be given to three or more poor people.[5] The operator must keep away from mortal sin and practice chastity. At night, the operator goes to sleep in hopes of receiving a dream visitation from one of the four ruling angels of the notory art who will provide instruction on proceeding with the operation. If it is a failed outcome in which no angel appears or the angel says not to proceed, then the operator is not to proceed any further. The operator is redirected to returning to phase 1. Otherwise, if the operator receives permission from one of the four ruling angels, then he is to proceed to phase 3.

Phase 3

The Interim Period is the time between Sunday night and the first day of the new Moon. It is quite rare for the calendar month to align with the lunar month; thus, this is called the Interim Period. In this period, the operator may pray the preamble *Alpha et omega,* the Special prayers of the chosen science to be obtained,[6] and the ten prayers of the *Ars Nova* on any day and any night as many times as desired before entering phase 4. Alternatively, the operator may pray the *novem termini* any time but never on the same day as the ten prayers of the *Ars Nova.*[7] It is not necessary to drink the saffron and rosewater tea. The operator must guard himself against mortal sins such as extravagance, intoxication, perjury, theft, murder, and the like. The operator must attend school and study at this time, and fasting up until noon is optional.[8]

Phase 4

Phase 4, the Operation for Obtaining a New Science, is the heart of the entire ritual procedure. Phase 4 consists of a four-month period that details certain

5. *Ars Notoria,* section 126a gloss. Symbolically, to give alms to three poor people would reflect the three days described here. At section 126e gloss, the operator is instructed to give alms to at least nine poor people.

6. "The Special prayers of the chosen art or science to be obtained." The gloss lists thirty-two Special prayers; however, it seems likely that only those Special prayers belonging to the chosen art or science to be obtained are intended to be recited here. This is also true of the phrase as it is presented in the first and second months.

7. *Ars Notoria,* section 126c gloss, 126d gloss, and 126f gloss.

8. *Ars Notoria,* section 126f gloss.

ritual instructions to follow for each month. Each month has its own unique instructions. To understand how and why each month's ritual instructions are different, it is necessary to study the ritual formulas that the Version B scribe sought to harmonize.

The Ritual Formulas of Version B

The Version B scribe constructed certain ritual formulas to be executed at certain times during the greater ritual. Those ritual formulas are as follows:

1. The *Alpha et Omega* prayer (Version B, variation 1), the *prima tria capitula* (*Helyschemat, Theos Megale,* and its Latin prologue, *Lux mundi,* taken from the *Flores Aurei*) are the preambles to the offering of all other prayers. They are not bound to any time restraints.
2. The ten *Ars Nova* prayers and the *novem termini* stand as one of the main ritual models in Version B. The ten prayers of the *Ars Nova* and the *novem termini* are said to be offered on separate days, never together. This may be because the Version B scribe is reflecting the division found between the General prayers which are only offered on auspicious days and the Special prayers which are only offered on ordinary days as found in the *Flores Aurei*. Thus, this division can be expressed in a single month, designating auspicious days and ordinary days. The *Ars Nova* ritual model spans the first two months; this execution may reflect the *Flores Aurei* ritual model of two lunar months (the first month having eight favorable days and the second month having twelve favorable days). According to the *Ars Nova,* the ten prayers ought to be offered before the *Flores Aurei* prayers and figures; the Version B scribe fulfills this requirement by having the *Ars Nova* prayers and *novem termini* executed in a two-month model prior to the *Flores Aurei* model. The Version B scribe creates an overlap of the two ritual models in its own second month of a new four-month ritual model.

3a. The General prayers, belonging to the *Flores Aurei,* are roughly executed in four parts only on auspicious days during the four-month ritual. The *prima tria capitula* (the first three headwords) acts as a preamble, so it is always executed first before any ritual formula; it accompanies the *Ars Nova* ritual model in the first month, and it is the only General prayer permitted to be offered on any day. In the second month, *Assaylemaht* and its Version B variants, *Lamehc Leynac* and *Deus summe Deus invisibilis Theos Pater* and its Latin prologue, *Te queso Domine,* are offered. The Version B scribe errs in the first half of the third month by omitting the General prayer *Ancor Anacor Anilos* and instead repeats *Deus summe Deus invisibilis Theos Pater* and its Latin prologue, *Te queso Domine,* again. The first half of the third month also has *Lamehc Ragna* and its Latin prologue followed by *Hazatam* and its four parts. The second half of the third month presents the final General prayer *Gemoht Gehel* and its Latin prologue and its second part.

3b. Section 40 gloss presents a ritual procedure for how many times the General prayers are to be offered on any of the twelve auspicious days in the third lunar month. This ritual procedure is found only in Version B. Oddly enough, this same ritual procedure is not given to the General prayers, which are to be offered on the eight auspicious days of the second lunar month.

4a. Version B has grouped the 32 Special prayers of the *Flores Aurei* and divided them into two groups: first, the 18 prayers, which belong to the three liberal arts; and second, the 14 prayers of philosophy, which belong to the four liberal arts, which brings the total to 32. *Hosel,* the fifth prayer of theology, draws from the Christian writer's letter in which he describes theology as the capstone to philosophy and how it ought to always be offered after the other Special prayers of the chosen science. These 14 prayers are to be offered before the inspection of the figures of the four liberal arts; yet, the glosser also acknowledges that these prayers are to be pronounced singularly in their own particular operations. The 32 prayers, taken all together, may be offered with the preamble *Alpha et omega* and the ten prayers of the *Ars Nova* on any day and any night as many times as desired during the interim period (phase 3); this instruction may be interpreted literally, or that the operator selects the chosen art and its prayers from the 32-prayer collection and just offers those select few.

4b. The 13 prayers of philosophy:

> "which always have to be offered before some figures are to be inspected, and it seems that there are thirteen—that is, five in that place and eight above—and there it says that there are seven; it is true that there are thirteen separately, but they are not, unless the seven are offered jointly" (102 gloss).

Version B acknowledges the division of the prayers as five[9] and eight, but always instructs the operator to use all thirteen prayers together, except for once instance. The one instance is in the fourth month in which only the five prayers are to be offered just prior to the particular operation of an art. This singular instance corresponds well to the reconstructed Version A ritual, which declares that the division of the prayers, as five and eight, has two separate ritual functions. Version B acknowledges this division's purpose by using the latter five prayers in the second lunar month of the *Flores Aurei* ritual model but ignores the first eight prayers which would apply to the first lunar month of the *Flores Aurei* ritual model (i.e., the month of eight favorable days, which is Version B's second month).

4c. The 18 prayers of the Specials. The 18 prayers "should be pronounced in the first seven days before the inspection of the figures of the three liberal arts." The eighteen prayers are those beginning with *Lux veritas* and ending with *Adoro te rex regum.* They are presented in chapter II, "Elements of the *Ars Notoria*." The last five of these prayers bear no relationship to the trivium. Again, the instruction to offer all 18 prayers together and at once may be interpreted literally, or that the operator selects the chosen art and its prayers from this 18-prayer collection.

---

9. The fifth, sixth, and seventh prayers of philosophy, plus *Deus Pater immense [. . . misericordissime],* the prayer belonging to music. Version B strangely includes this prayer belonging to music; Version A does not contain *Deus Pater immense [. . . misericordissime].*

HARMONIZING THE RITUAL MODELS AND THEIR FORMULAS, VERSION B

In summary, Version B has combined the *Ars Nova* ritual model with the *Flores Aurei* ritual model; in doing so, the Version B scribe has essentially taken the two-month ritual model of the *Flores Aurei* and doubled it, dividing its ritual formulas and those of the *Ars Nova* across four months. The idea that a single month is divided into auspicious days and ordinary days is not always explicitly stated but does appear to exist in each of the four months. The same may be true of the idea that a single month is also divided into first and second halves (i.e., days 1–15 and 16–30) or, at least, in the execution of the *Flores Aurei* ritual model in Version B's second and third months. Consequently, these divisions affect the distribution of the prayers, which has led to confusion, ignorance, and error of their original purpose when Version B harmonized the material.

The first and second months of Version B present the *Ars Nova* ritual model, which utilizes the ten prayers plus the *novem termini*. The ten prayers are always offered on days separate from the *novem termini*. These first two months also include the Version B ritual formula of the 32 prayers (or the select prayers of the chosen art of study) of the *Flores Aurei*. The second month blends the *Ars Nova* ritual model and the first half of the *Flores Aurei* model. The second month presents the *Flores Aurei* ritual model of utilizing the first part of the General prayers and the lunar month of the eight auspicious days (the eight days are in multiples of four). The Version B scribe finalizes and seals this use of the *Ars Nova* ritual model in the second month.

Now the two-lunar month model of the *Flores Aurei* is executed in the second and third months. The divison of the month into days 1–15 and days 16–30 is ignored in the second month but present in the third month. This is probably because the *Ars Nova* prayers had already occupied the ordinary days of the second month, leaving no room for the prayers of philosophy and their subordinate prayers and figures of the three liberal arts (as proposed in the reconstruction of Version A).

The division of the month into days 1–15 and 16–30 is introduced in the third month, but its execution is inconsistent. As already mentioned, the division is ignored entirely in the second month. Now, in the third month the division affects the General prayers but not the Special prayers. This brings into question the original purpose of dividing a month into two halves. What does happen in the third month is the excecution of the second part of the General prayers and their lunar month of the twelve auspicious days (the days are in multiples of three). Among the second, third, and fourth months, the General prayers are divided into four sets (excluding the first three headwords, which act as a preamble to any beginning): (1) in the second month, there is *Assaylemaht, Hazaylemaht, Lemath Sebauthe,* and *Lamehc Leynac* (as the second sequence) and *Deus summe Deus invisibilis Theos Pater* and its Latin prologue, *Te queso Domine* (as the third sequence); (2) in the first half of the third month, there is *Deus summe Deus invisibilis Theos Pater* and its Latin prologue, *Te queso Domine* (as the third sequence), which is repeated again, and there is *Lamehc Ragna* and its Latin prologue, *Memoria irreprehensibilis* (as the fifth sequence), and *Hazatam* and its four parts (as the sixth sequence); (3) in the second half of the third month, there is *Gemoht Gehel* and its Latin prologue, *Omnipotens sempiterne Deus,* and its second part, *Semoht Lamen* (as the seventh sequence); and (4) in the fourth month, *Gemoht Gehel* and its Latin prologue and second part are offered again. This fourfold division of the General prayers appears inconsistent and erroneous. The fourth sequence, *Ancor Anacor Anilos,* is completely forgotten. Also, the third and seventh sequences are both repeated twice. Omissions and doublets suggest scribal errors, and that is exactly what happens here.

In the third month, on the ordinary days, the operator is to offer the preambles followed by the thirteen prayers belonging to philosophy. The Special thirteen prayers of philosophy are offered, but they are not divided in the third month. Only in the fourth month are the Special thirteen prayers of philosophy divided into two parts (1st–4th prayers and 5th–7th prayers). The first part is ignored, and only the second part is executed in the third and fourth months as a distinct ritual formula, just prior to the offering of the Special prayers of a given liberal art or science. Version B carries out the remaining ritual procedure of the *Flores Aurei,* the inspection of the figures, in the fourth month. The particular operations of each art are conducted, one at a time, in the framework of this fourth month. In other words, if only one art were studied in the course of the four-month ritual, then it would take just over two years to learn seven disciplines! Finally, another inconsistency arises in Version B's fourth month in which the Egyptian Days are ignored for grammar (section 78 gloss) but acknowledged for rhetoric (79 gloss). What follows are the complete ritual procedures of Version B's harmonized four-month ritual as it is described in the glosses.

First Lunar Month

The operator selects the appropriate prayers and figures for the desired science to be obtained. The preamble *Alpha et omega,* the first three headwords, and the Special prayers of the chosen art or science to be obtained may be offered with either the ten prayers of the *Ars Nova* or the *novem termini* on any day and any night. However, the ten prayers of the *Ars Nova* must not be prayed on the same days as the *novem termini.*[10]

It is optional for the operator to drink the saffron and rosewater tea; if he does, it must be done at prime and only once, as previously instructed. It is also optional for the operator to fast. The operator is advised to live piously, not to dismiss school or work, and to pursue his studies.

Second Lunar Month

Every day of the second month, at lauds, the saffron and rosewater tea is made. At prime, the operator drinks the tea and recites *Bonitatem, etc.,* four times. The tea should be drunk only once a day and only at prime.

Similar to the first lunar month, the operator offers the following prayers once; namely, the preamble *Alpha et omega,* the first three headwords, and the Special prayers of the chosen science to be obtained. These may be spoken with either the ten prayers of the *Ars Nova* or the *novem termini* on any day and any night. However, the ten prayers of the *Ars Nova* must not be prayed on the same days as the *novem termini.*[11] The operator is not to fast or dismiss his studies or occupation. These actions are to be carried out for the first three days of the second lunar month. The second month concludes the *Ars Nova* ritual model; although it is not made explicit, the offering of the ten prayers of the *Ars Nova* and the *novem termini* may have been thought to be offered on the ordinary days of the second lunar month. The glosser does not introduce or define the division of auspicious days and ordinary days here, although he does

10. *Ars Notoria,* section 126c gloss, section 126d gloss.

11. *Ars Notoria,* section 126c gloss, section 126d gloss.

introduce the eight favorable lunar days for the General prayers next. He does not introduce the division of the first half and second half of the month until the third month.

The eight favorable lunar days are the 4th, 8th, 12th, 16th, 20th, 24th, 28th, and 30th. On the eight favorable lunar days, the operator must carry out the following instructions. In the early morning, the saffron and rosewater tea is made, and the operator drinks and recites *Bonitatem, etc.,* four times. The preamble *Alpha et omega* and the first three headwords (i.e., the first sequence of the General prayers) are offered once. After an interval, the operator recites the the second sequence of the General prayers; namely, *Assaylemaht, Hazaylemaht, Lemath Sebauthe,*[12] *Lamehc Leynac,* and the third sequence of the General prayers, *Deus summe Deus invisibilis Theos Pater* and its Latin prologue, *Te queso Domine,* once in the early morning, and at terce, sext, and vespers. The operator must fast on Lenten food on those eight days and not eat until after sext[13] or the evening.[14] If the operator cannot fast until the evening, then he must make an additional effort to pray these same prayers at another time during the day as often as he can. The operator is instructed to live soberly, piously, and cleanly in those eight favorable lunar days.

Third Lunar Month

Every day of the second month, at lauds, the saffron and rosewater tea is made. At prime, the operator drinks the tea and recites *Bonitatem, etc.,* four times. The tea should be drunk only once a day and only at prime.

The third lunar month is divided in auspicious days and ordinary days. The first half of the month has nine ordinary days, and the second half also has nine ordinary days. There are twelve favorable days.

The first half of the month has the shortest ritual formula for the ordinary days. The ordinary days are Days 2, 4, 5, 7, 8, 10, 11, 13, and 14, and on these days the operator must offer the preamble *Alpha et omega,* the first three headwords, and the thirteen prayers belonging to philosophy once in the early morning, once at terce, and once at sext, for a total of three times.

---

12. Notice that the Version B scribe has included its very own variant prayers, *Hazaylemaht* and *Lemath Sebauthe* (Variation 3 and 4).

13. *Ars Notoria,* section 126d gloss.

14. *Ars Notoria,* section 126f gloss.

The second half of the month extends the ritual formula for the ordinary days. The ordinary days are Days 16, 17, 19, 20, 22, 24, 25, 27, and 28, and on these days the operator must offer the preamble *Alpha et omega,* the first three headwords, and the thirteen prayers belonging to philosophy once in the early morning, once at terce, and once at sext, for a total of three times a day. The operator may not eat until after noon. Essentially, the division of the month into two halves has no real effect on the ritual procedure as the same prayers and their offerings are the same. This is strange and suspicious. Why bother mentioning the division at all? What was its original purpose, and why is it being kept?

Next, there are twelve favorable lunar days of the third month. Those favorable days are: Days 1, 3, 6, 9, 12, 15, 18, 21, 23, 26, 29, and 30. On these twelve favorable days, after the preamble *Alpha et omega* and the first three headwords have been offered and an interval is made, the operator recites the third sequence of General prayers again: *Deus summe Deus invisibilis Theos Pat[e]r* and its Latin prologue, *Te quaeso Domine.* Then, the fifth and sixth sequences of General prayers: *Lamehc Ragna* and its Latin prologue, *Memoria irreprehensibilis,*[15] and *Hazatam* and its Latin prologue, *Confirma, Agloros* and its Latin prologue, *Deus omnium, Megal* and its Latin prologue, *Veritas lux et vita,* and *Hanuyrlyhahel* and its Latin prologue, *Ego in conspectus.*[16] These General prayers are offered in the early morning once, at terce three times, at sext three times, and at nones three times. This takes place on Day 1.[17]

These same General prayers follow the rubric laid out in the section 40 gloss, which gives instructions on what days and hours the General prayers are to be offered and how many times. The twelve favorable days are the same as those days found in the section 40 gloss, in which the prayers are to be offered as many times as the number of the day. For example, on

---

15. Notice that the fourth sequence of the General prayers, *Ihesu Dei Filius incomprehensibilis Ancor Anacor Anilos,* and its second part, *Eleminator Caudones,* are missing. Plus, the third sequence of the General prayers is repeated, being offered in the second and third months. This repetition may signal an error in the scribe's ritual instructions.

16. The third sequence of the general prayers is not included here.

17. According to 126f gloss. This passage then references the section 40 gloss, which contradicts how many times the prayers are to be offered at each hour. The section 40 gloss says the prayers are to be offered in the early morning once and then again at terce once. Then the prayers are to be offered at noon three times and then at nones three times.

Day 3, the prayers are offered three times; on Day 6, the prayers are offered six times; on Day 9, the prayers are offered nine times, etc. (Strangely, the rubric described in section 40 gloss is not mentioned to be applied to the lunar month of eight auspicious days. For example, on Day 4, the prayers might have been prayed four times, etc.) On Day 15, a favorable day, after the third, fifth, and sixth sequences of the General prayers are offered, just as it is said above, the operator should make an interval of silence, then the operator offers the seventh and last General prayer—namely, *Gemoht Gehel* and its Latin prologue, *Omnipotens sempiterne Deus,* and its second part, *Semoht Lamen*—fifteen times, in the early morning three times, at terce three times, at sext three times, at nones three times, and at vespers three times. Next the glosser's words are contradictory, saying:

> [A]nd having made some interval, you must successively offer the other prayers just like on the second day, of which the first begins *Ezethomos, etc.*, with the others through the following order. And it is to be done thus concerning these from the fifteenth day of the lunar month up to the end, except those twelve days in which the other prayers are offered."

On the one hand, the glosser is saying that the thirteen prayers belonging to philosophy are to be offered on Day 15, a favorable day, and on the other hand, he is saying that the thirteen prayers ought to be offered on the ordinary days in the second half of the month. Up to this point, the instructions are clear to keep the General prayers and Special prayers offered on separate days (i.e., the General prayers have the favorable days and the Special prayers have the ordinary days). Thus, it would appear correct to say that the thirteen prayers of philosophy belong to the ordinary days, and this is probably what is actually intended.

The operator may not eat meat until after noon. In those twelve favorable lunar days, the operator is to be fasting on Lenten food, and he may assign an hour of eating or if he is able, to finish the operation before he eats.

Fourth Lunar Month

The fourth lunar month is for the inspection of the figures for the science the operator desires to obtain. The operator must retreat to his home and not leave during the fourth month. He may be accompanied by his associate or master, but the associate must not observe the operator while he is practicing the notory art. His associate may bring him food and drink, and his master may help instruct him, such as in the pronunciation of the prayers. The operator must fast every day of the fourth month on Lenten food. Every day of the fourth month, in the early morning, the saffron and rosewater tea is made. The operator drinks the tea and recites *Bonitatem, etc.,* four times. The rosewater tea should be drunk only once a day and only in the early morning.

The operator offers the preamble *Alpha et omega* and the first three headwords once in the early morning. Then, after an interval, the operator recites the General prayer *Gemoht Gehel* and its Latin prologue, *Omnipotens sempiterne Deus,* and also its second part, *Semoht Lamen,* once. This ritual formula effectively closes the General prayers. After an interval, the operator opens a new ritual formula by reciting the following five prayers once, which are prayers belonging to the fifth, sixth, and seventh figures of philosophy—namely, *Deus Pater immense [. . . magnitudo], Gezomothon, Rex aeterne Deus, Deus totius pietatis,* and, oddly, the prayer belonging to music, *Deus Pater [immense . . . misericordissime].*[18]

After these five prayers, the operator is directed to follow the instructions per the operation of the specific art or science he wishes to obtain. In each of these operations, the operator must offer the preamble *Lux veritas* once before any prayers that are specific to a certain art or science. Version B asserts that each liberal art operation has its own particularities in ritual. These particularities include the number of prayers and figures each art has, how many times the prayers are to be offered, how many times the figures are to be inspected, and how these ritual procedures are dispersed over the first and second half of the fourth month.

The glosser assumes the operator will follow through the hierarchy of knowledge, beginning with the study of grammar and ending with theology. The custom operations include instructions for learning the following: (1) grammar; (2) logic/dialectic; (3) rhetoric; (4) medicine; (5) music; (6) arithmetic; (7) astronomy; (8) geometry (instructions presented only in NS 119–25); (9) philosophy; (10) the general sciences (although the text suggests that each

18. Version B refers to these as the "five prayers."

one must be learned individually); and (11) theology. The specific ritual steps for learning each subject matter are as follows:

- Grammar: section 78 gloss
- Logic/dialectic: section 80 gloss
- Rhetoric: section 79 gloss
- The four liberal arts: sections 85–86 gloss
- The general sciences: section 87 gloss
- The mechanical arts: section 88 gloss
- Theology: section 97 gloss

Phase 5

The "Three-Day Closing Ritual Procedure" consists of three days in which the *novem termini* are to be offered just as it was done in the Three-Day Opening Ritual Procedure. The gloss does not specify that the ten prayers of the *Ars Nova* must also be offered, but they certainly must be if the operator has sinned.

The *novem termini* are offered after the completed operation of some acquired science.[19]

Contingency Plans for an Unexpected Outcome

There are contingency plans for unexpected outcomes during the ritual procedure. If the operator sins or neglects a portion of the greater ritual, whether by missing some hours or days or prayers, then the operator will lose his acquired knowledge. If this happens, he is to recite the ten prayers of the *Ars Nova* (see section 126a gloss). If the operator sins or angers God, he will lose his acquired knowledge. If this happens, he ought to pray the ten prayers of the *Ars Nova* and the *novem termini* through one month (see section 126c gloss).

19. *Ars Notoria,* section 126c gloss.

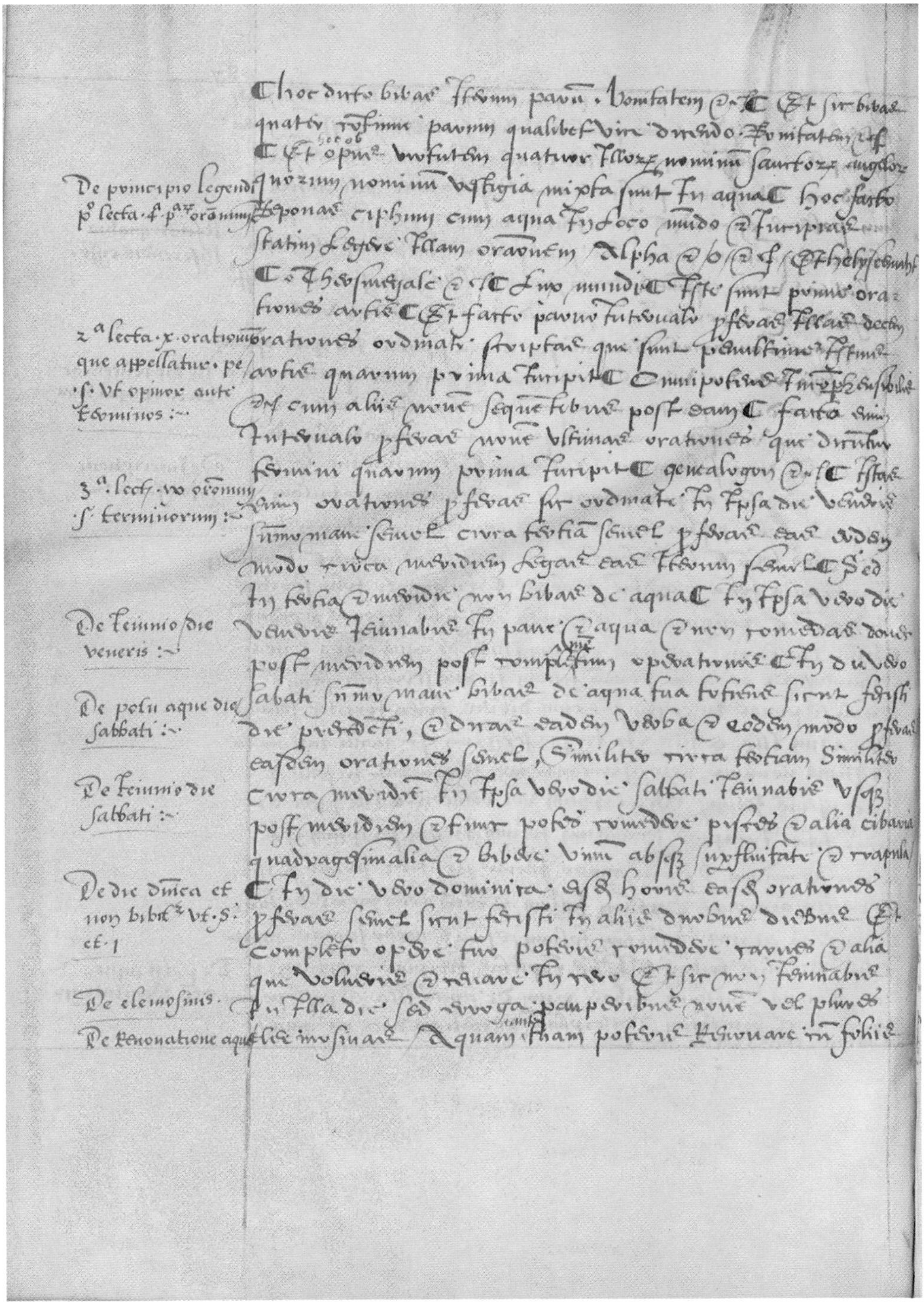

Folio from *Ars notoria de Salomone,*
BnF Latin 7153. 15th century.

Ars Notoria *Version A*

13th–14th Centuries

1

FLORES AUREI

Attributed to Apollonius of Tyana

[Prologue]

[1] *Here begins the preface, or requirements, which the great Apollonius*[1] *called the* Flores Aurei (Golden Flowers), *for the erudition and understanding of all sciences and natural arts generally, rightly, and properly. This is composed and tested by the highest authority of Solomon,*[2] *Mani,*[3] *and Euclid.*[4] *Behold, it begins.*

[2] I, [Apollonius of Tyana], justly called master of the arts (especially the nature of the liberal arts), who is regarded by many to possess a treatise of knowledge of astronomy or astrology[5] by which a person may be able to have the compendious

---

1. Apollonius of Tyana (15–100 CE) was a neo-Pythagorean Greek philosopher and a reputed magician. See appendix A6.

2. King Solomon of Israel (reigned 970–931 BCE) was renowned for his wisdom and built the Temple in Jerusalem during biblical times. A portrayal of King Solomon as a magician developed in the Greco-Egyptian and Arab worlds, which was reinforced by the appearance of the magical treatise called the *Testament of Solomon*. See appendix A7.

3. Mani (216–274 CE) was the Persian founder and prophet of Manichaeanism, a religion teaching a complex dualistic cosmogony of good and evil powers in conflict with one another. Manichaeanism was once a great world religion but then became heavily persecuted, and most of its writings are now lost. See appendix A3.

4. Euclid of Thebes, the father of Honorius and a magician, who is mentioned in the fourteenth-century handbook of magic called the *Liber Iuratus Honorii* (*Sworn Book of Honorius*). See appendix A3 for thoughts on these authorship attributions.

5. Philostratus, *Life of Apollonius,* 3.41. According to Philostratus, Apollonius of Tyana had written four books on astrology. Also, there are astral magic treatises falsely attributed to him. See appendix A6.

and competent understanding of the experiments of the [magical] arts;[6] by which he may be able to have the nature of the proper times [to conduct these experiments], whether the rest [of those times are] to be divided into a [strong and] weak nature competently, or by which days or which hours, and [when the experiments] of men must be begun or ended;[7] [and] how a man ought to conduct the course of [his] life's moral disposition.[8] First, I chose certain teachings of the spiritual sciences to be excerpted, [and those others that] are mentioned shall be expanded upon in the subsequent order with respect to each and every one.[9]

[3] Therefore, do not be astonished at what [things] will be taught or what you are about to understand in the subsequent little treatise, as you may ponder a little miracle more than the customary examples of learning. For some [parts of the treatise], I obstruct the astonishing things for you, hereafter. Having read the extracts out of the most ancient of Hebrew books we mentioned before, and whatever you will have understood (although strange with regard to language), ponder that you knew about a little miracle that would be granted to you from the Lord your God.

The prologue ends. The wonder of the author concerning so much virtue of this art.

---

6. According to the notory art, each of the liberal arts has an experiment assigned to it which involves the offering of prayers and the inspection of certain pictorial figures for the purpose of gaining knowledge of those liberal arts. These experiments have their foundation in astronomy and astrology (see section 20b), so it is fitting that Apollonius of Tyana, the alleged author of astrological treatises and astral magic texts, would be the presenter of the notory art.

7. Section 147. It is said that certain lunar months act as gates by which the holy angels' *magna potentia* "great power" provide the desired efficacy and knowledge to the operator. Pseudo-Apollonius says the reader will know how to competently divide these lunar months according to the certain zodiac signs that rule over each liberal art.

8. The notory art instructs the operator in spiritual purification practices such as fasting and abstaining from sin.

9. That is to say, Pseudo-Apollonius has selected certain passages from "the most ancient of Hebrew books" and expands upon them in his present treatise, the *Flores Aurei (Golden Flowers)*, following an order. Presumably, Pseudo-Apollonius intends to follow the order of the material laid out in these "most ancient of Hebrew books," but there is no way of knowing the truth of this assertion since these works are lost.

[Chapter I]

[4] Since I myself am astonished at any words able to have so much virtue concerning the original treatise set forth.[10]

[5] For the efficacy of some words is so great, that when you read them [below], they might augment your eloquence [so] suddenly and unexpectedly [that it is] almost as if you will have been made from a speechless person to an eloquent one. Yet, how this arises [whether] out of his moral disposition [or elsewhere], will be demonstrated to you fully in the following [chapters]. But now we discuss the particulars that are at hand.

[6] *Also, of the virtue*[11] *of this art.*
Therefore, concerning the notory art, certain *notulae*[12] are manifested to us with their writings of whose virtue human reason cannot comprehend. For it is the first *nota,* [*Hely Semat,*][13] whose meaning is from a distorted Hebrew, which although it may be comprehended with the fewest words, nevertheless it does not lose the virtue in the expression of the mysteries. For its virtue is so great, it produces inestimable wonder in anyone who beholds it.

[7] For these are the words. These words, with the following prayer, [*Phos Megalos*], and with the [Latin] prayer [*Lux mundi*], which is its

10. Véronèse has made this its own section, most likely due to Version B's glossing, but in Version A it could be seen as one continuous statement with the end of section 3.

11. Virtue has a meaning of an occult or metaphysical power. The power of the experiments of the notory art are imbued by the visitation of the angels. The secret language in which the notory art prayers are recorded is said to contain an occult virtue because it originates from the divine source, and therefore designates it as a divinely revealed language.

12. Latin, *notulae* means "little notes" or "little marks."

13. The Latin word *nota* (pl. *notae*) is a technical term in the *Ars Notoria* denoting a certain kind of knowledge contained within a strange prayer consisting of magical calls (*voces magicae*) and a pictorial figure. In other words, the *nota* is the hidden knowledge, which the operator seeks to acquire; the *nota*'s symbols, or "containers" as it were, are the prayer and the pictorial figure; the usage of the word *nota* sometimes leans toward one of its containers—either the prayer or the pictorial figure. In this instance, the word *nota* denotes the first prayer identified by its incipit, *Helyscemath,* which is the first strange prayer found in section 7. The word *nota* is first defined in section 21. See chapter II.

explanation,[14] of those which are to be said in the prolation[15] or investigation of any writing.[16]

Hely, Semat,[17] Azatau, Hemel, Samit, Theon.

[8] Solomon first wanted the form [of the prayers] ordered thus, so that every [form was] to lack a translator, knowing so great the subtlety of Chaldean, Hebrew, Greek, and Arabic with the profundity of an extracted speech, so that no one is able to explain the scheme[18] of the entire speech. But that is its own efficacy, [just as] Solomon reveals the status of wisdom's splendor in the book *Eniclyssoe*.[19] But our friend and predecessor Apollonius,[20] with the few and remaining [students], was given those manifestations of science; they explained, saying, "These more profound mysteries are not to be offered as words without great faith."

---

14. Also called a prologue. See Version B, 10 gloss, for definition of a prologue Latin prayer.

15. *Prolation* can have two meanings here: the pronunciation of speech and the emission of divine speech. The theological sense is now obsolete in modern English.

16. The ritual procedure of the *Ars Notoria* involves the student reciting certain prayers followed by the study of his school textbooks. When investigating his textbooks, the student would read aloud its words.

17. *Hely Semat,* the first prayer of the "first three headwords" (*tria prima capitula*) that make up the first sequence of the General prayers. The "first three headwords" consist of *Helyscemath, Phos Megalos,* and *Lux mundi.*

18. Latin *schematae* comes from the field of rhetoric and includes figures of speech that involve the manipulation of syntax and sounds by an orator to create a persuasive effect upon his audience. There are several figures of speech, including zeugma and syllempsis (including their related figures of diazeugma, hypozeugma, prozeugma, and mesozeugma), hypozeuxis, anadiplosis, anaphora, epanalepsis, epizeuxis, paronomasia (also known as a pun), schesis onomaton, paromoeon (i.e., alliteration), homoioptoton, homoeoteleuton (i.e., rhyme), polyptoton, polysyndeton, and asyndeton. These figures of speech make the speech strange and incomprehensible to humankind, and thereby increase the "magnitude of qualities" supposedly present in Solomon's *Liber Florum Caelestis Doctrinae* (see section 35). For more on these figures of speech, see chapter IV on the philosophical theory of hylomorphism as it is applied to linguistics. The inclusion of such figures of speech might suggest that these strange prayers would be persuasive to the angels who listen to them.

19. *Eniclyssoe* is an unidentified work attributed to Solomon. The book is also spelled as either *Eliosse, Vemeliose, Gromeliosse,* or *Yndeneliosse.*

20. Notice here that another scribe is narrating, not Pseudo-Apollonius. This scribal addition indicates that Version A is a late recension of *Flores Aurei,* which would have been written entirely in the first-person as Pseudo-Apollonius.

[9] *Instruction for the investigation of the writings concerning the preceding and succeeding prayers.*

If he wanted to investigate or to offer the beginning of any writing, or any eloquent writing,[21] which he must offer diligently with that prayer, [*Phos Megalos,*] (which having prefaced the above words of the [composed] form,[22] in the morning, in the name of God the Most High, or in the prolation of the writing itself) which is from the Hebrew, Chaldean, and Greek distorted speech, subtly and wonderfully illuminated, then [the prayer's own speech] is to be extended through the [Latin] exposition summarily, which is this.[23]

[10] *The first prayer, [Helyscemath,] is to be said with the following words.*

[Ph]os, Megal[os],[24] Patir, Ymos, Ebel, Eber, Helioth, Gezeiel, Salatial, Sadim, Helgyo, Megis, Micron, Esel, Gecor, Granal, Semaranxai, Gelsemana, Arasamion, Sale, Patir, Agion, Atanas. Amen.

[11] *Truly, of this prayer [Phos Megalos], this [prayer, Lux mundi,] is a part and summary to the aforementioned explanation. Still, you must not ponder every word which could be explained thus.*

The description and explanation of the preceding prayer [is written here].

O light of the world,[25] O immeasurable God, O Father of eternity, the bestower of wisdom, knowledge, and all spiritual grace; O pious and inestimable dispenser, knowing all things before they happen, making the light and

---

21. That is, any writing belonging to philosophy, theology, the seven liberal arts, or any other art or science. Also, the notory art can help with one's rhetoric in making an eloquent speech.

22. That is, the book's format presents the Hebrew, Chaldean, and Greek prayer and its Latin "prologue" prayer preceding the pictorial figure. This format can be seen in the *Notae* Supplement of BnF 9336.

23. That is to say, there is a pair of prayers spoken together. One prayer is written from the Hebrew, Chaldean, and Greek speech, and the other is the "explanation," or elsewhere called the "prologue," which is written in Latin and is just a partial translation or summary of what the Hebrew, Chaldean, and Greek prayer actually says. Pairings of prayers appear frequently throughout the notory art.

24. *Phos Megalos,* the second prayer of the first three headwords (*tria prima capitula*) that make up the first sequence of the General prayers. The first two words, "Theos Megale," here might be corrupted Greek, *phos megalos,* meaning "great light," followed by the Greek or Latin *pater,* meaning "father." Thus, "the Great Light, the Father" is an epithet for God the Father.

25. *Lux mundi,* the third and final prayer of the first three headwords (*tria prima capitula*) that make up the first sequence of the General prayers. Compare the wording to John 8:12.

the darkness, send forth your hand and touch my mouth, and make that . . .[26] as a sharpened sword for the purpose of explaining my words eloquently. Make my tongue, as a chosen arrow[27] for the purpose of pronouncing that by memory. Send forth your Holy Spirit into my heart[28] to perceive and to retain within my soul and to meditate within my conscience, by the oath of your co-heir;[29] that is, through your right-hand. Inspire, teach, and instruct piously, holy, mercifully, and gently, the coming in and going out of my senses[30] and my thinking. Let your instruction teach and correct me continuously up to the end. Let your highest counsel help me through your infinite mercy. Amen.

[12] Still, you must not ponder because every word of the aforesaid prayer[31] must be [as long as an entire] speech translated into Latin, with some words of the prayer itself containing more sense[32] and mystical profundity within themselves. As a matter of fact, we acknowledged the writings referencing from the authority of Solomon himself [that] the prayer itself is by no means capable to be explained through the sense of the human condition.[33]

[13] As a matter of fact, it is necessary to say that the distinct particulars themselves of astronomy, astrology, or the notory art are to be said in the manner, place, and time themselves, and ought to be worked from them, according to the disposition of the times.[34]

[14] *What should be observed for which these [precepts] are to be taught within one month in the art he will have eloquence in all the sciences.*

---

26. Here and other times throughout, an ellipsis acts as an empty placeholder for the operator to insert the desired knowledge to be gained.

27. Compare the wording of this section to Jeremiah 1:9 and Isaiah 42:9.

28. During Aristotle's time, it was thought that memory was held in the brain and the heart. By the medieval era, it was understood as residing within the brain, but the metaphor of knowing a thing "by heart" continued onward.

29. That is, Jesus Christ.

30. The phrase "coming in and going out of my senses" makes reference to the medieval view of how the mind-body complex works.

31. *Phos Megalos.*

32. As in the sense or meaning of a word.

33. Section 17.

34. Section 15.

For there are certain forms or prayers that Solomon called by the Chaldean "*Helym*" (that is, "the triumphals of the liberal arts" and "the sudden and excellent efficacies of virtues"), and they are an introduction to the notory art, especially the beginning. Solomon constituted [the certain forms or prayers] out of those very ones, so that they must be offered following the determined times of the Moon and not without the consideration to a scheduled end date, because our master,[35] having copied [them] fully and competently, instituted [the following rule or teaching], saying, "Whosoever has offered these [prayers] according to the determined time and institution,[36] he may know eloquence in all things pronounced, having removed himself from every occasion that entire month to achieve much greater things than the ordinary, wonderfully and inestimably."[37]

[15] *Which times the prayers are to be said, and how the figures must be inspected [after] offering the triumphals by the times of the [days of the] Moon.*

For these are the introductory requirements of the notory art which should be offered either to the fourth [day of the] Moon, or eighth, or twelfth, or sixteenth, or twentieth, or twenty-fourth, or twenty-eighth, or thirtieth. From Solomon:

> We gave the four phases of the Moon[38] which are written by the four holy angels,[39] and the fourth Moon manifested to us, and the four [scrolls][40]

---

35. Notice that a scribe is narrating, not Pseudo-Apollonius. Thus, the following quotation comes from an earlier copy of the *Flores Aurei* (*Golden Flowers*).

36. Latin *instituto.* The English word *institution* comes from the Latin, which has lost this obsolete sense, meaning "that which institutes or instructs, especially a textbook or system of rules." For example, the Latin grammarian Priscian's famous work, *Institutiones Grammaticae* (*Institutes of Grammar, or the Instructions of Grammar*), became the standard textbook on the rules of Latin grammar during the Middle Ages.

37. The implied analogy here is a triumphal procession marching along the month's course of determined times. The Latin verb *profero, proferre, protuli, prolatum,* meaning "to offer," is used in relation to these prayers called "the triumphals." The verb has many senses, but its military sense means "to march forward," so this section might say, "Whosoever has marched forward these triumphal ones according to the determined time . . ."

38. This refers to the new Moon, first quarter, full Moon, and last quarter. The Latin here is *tempora,* literally "times."

39. The four angels of the *Ars Notoria* are Hagnadam, Merabor, Hamiladei, and Pesiguaguol. See Version B, section 126e.

40. Perhaps a reference to *Liber Florum Caelestis Doctrinae* (*The Book of Flowers of Heavenly Teaching*), *Eniclyssoe,* and *Gemeliot.*

unrolled and repeated to us by the angel, their law-carrier; and also, written and renewed four times for the circular course [of the day][41] showing to us the full eloquence from God, by asking through the entire four languages Chaldean, Greek, Hebrew, and Latin, having been evidently explained and to have efficacy of power in the four parts of the earth.[42] Also, [we gave] the four virtues of the human mind–intelligence, memory, eloquence and the stability of those three as the greatest to rule. For those [virtues] are from the aforesaid [prayers] that we just said, and so they are about to be referred.

[16] *This prayer [Assaylemaht], which is to be said over time in the designated hours,[43] is to increase intelligence, memory, eloquence, and mental stability. [It is] to be called the "mirror of wisdom," the "light of the soul," or that "ingenuity of felicity"[44] It ought to be said during silence and solitude, and it is general to all arts.*

Rasay, Lamac,[45] Azzaar, Gesemon, Releamic, Azaga, Elial, Sezior, Pamphilios,[46] Sicrogamon, Laupda, Iothim, Lezezae, Amor, Sichem, Egal, Geleton, Samagal, Halna, Alna, Alyos, Gemeonegal, Saramalaip, Zamiel, Sealalmaga, Esemedat, Gealfam, Silmial, Semalfay, Craton, Anagil, Panthomegos, Tingen, Amissiton, Sebarnay, Alimoo, Gennai, Sadraial, Neomail, Cristos, Sephacaphalmal, Azoron, Gezamael, Hayla, Semenai, Gellesmon, Baracata, Geennazai, Scealmagahal, Gezamai, Zerifaton, Gelimen, Acaciezai, Semmac, Sezorobal, Funasiel, Leoelmac, Sennatol, Ababeen, Ruophahos, Ydormasay, Negraen, Feramiec, Soon, Vehepoten, Invalliasenon, Innamos, Geramatos, Zefamar, Leem, Hecletamal, Agniol, Naratol, Semadaior, Necot, Maypissamat, Ragaal, Agamal, Fagamessim,

---

41. The four times of the day: prime, terce, nones, and vespers. See appendix A4.

42. The four cardinal directions—east, south, west, and north—in which the angels manifest through the gates according to the lunar month. See section 147.

43. Sections 17 and 19.

44. Seneca the Elder, *Controversiae,* III, 8 *Oratorum et rhetorum sententiae divisions colores.* Here Seneca the Elder calls the Roman poet Vergil "that ingenuity of felicity" (*illa felicitas ingenii*), which matches the same wording "*felicitatem ingenii*" used here.

45. *Assaylemaht,* the first prayer belonging to the second sequence of the Generals. The second sequence of the Generals is called the "triumphals," which consists of *Assaylemaht, Lamehc Leynac, Deus summe Deus,* and *Te quaeso Domine.*

46. The angel who gave the notory art to Solomon. See Version B, prologue gloss.

Theomogem, Rasalimacha, On, Lon, Hen, Sephizion, Arion, Usyon, Semension, Regon, Amen, Amen, Amen.

[17] *The teaching about the preceding.*
This is a holy prayer without any danger of sin from which Solomon affirmed "to be inexpressible to the actual human senses." He added, "Its explanation is more prolix than it is able to be considered by man, excepting its very secrets, which it is not permitted nor given to man to speak, [any] much more than of the same prayers in Moses's Pentateuch. For that reason, he left everything unexplained, because no one before has been able to comment to completion, summarily and shortly, out of so much of its magnitude of the prolixity of the prayer."[47] Nevertheless, his deed had the special justification of an angel carrying an irrefutable prohibition and who said, "See, you must not dare someone to explain or to translate about that, nor you, nor another after you. For it is a sacramental mystery. God heard your prayer of words, and so may the intelligence, memory, eloquence, and stability of these three be augmented for you by the determined days of the Moon either the fourth, or eighth, or twelfth, and the following in succession, just as it is written;[48] read the prayer diligently four times a day, believing it (from which it is said above without ambiguity) to increase [these faculties] suddenly and beyond human measure."

[18] *About the above prayer.*
This prayer is what Solomon [called] the "talent of happiness" and the "light of the soul"; the true master and our lord and also [his] predecessor,[49] called it the "mirror of wisdom." Moreover, I believe that prayer that is to be called by name "image of eternal life," although that efficacy is so great, is understood and comprehended by the fewest men or by just no one at all.[50]

---

47. In other words, no one has been able to fully comprehend or translate the entire *Rasay Lamac* prayer due to the complexity of its construction, by means of notarikon, zeugma, or other methods; as a result, only the Latin prayer can provide a partial translation.
48. Section 15
49. That is, Apollonius of Tyana. Notice that the other scribe is narrating again, not Pseudo-Apollonius.
50. The scribe offers his own special title, the "image of eternal life," to the prayer, which alludes to Christian eschatology of life after death.

[19] [This prayer] is the first form of the notory art itself, and it is situated above the manifested quadrangle *nota*.[51] In fact, in the defense of astronomy,[52] the angelic wisdom itself, having been well kept by a few, is wholly described to be the foundation in the notory art, specifically of science, and in [the foundation of] astrology, the *Mirror,* the ring of philosophy.[53] Still, [the *Assaylemaht* prayer] is not to be offered four times successively that early in the morning of the day,[54] but it is to be offered in the morning[55] once, and in around the third [hour] the second [time], and around the ninth [hour] the third [time], and around the evening [hour] the fourth [time]. This is the prayer that ought to be offered in secret while he is alone, and he must scarcely hear himself, and if he is able to be alone, [then] this is to be his condition, and if the necessity of some great [mundane] work came rushing [at you for that day], you will be able to say [it] twice by the morning and around the ninth [hour] twice.

---

51. The first form (*prima figura*) of the notory art is the second sequence of the General prayers, called the "triumphals of the liberal arts," which "march foward" according to the determined times of the Moon. The ordered form (*compositus figura*) of the notory art is said to be retained per Solomon's instructions according to section 8.

52. Latin, *in astronomiae exceptionibus.*

53. Here the Latin word *speculum,* meaning "mirror," is a reference to a certain literary treatise on astrology, having been given the description "the ring of philosophy," which evokes the imagery of the orbits of the celestial bodies. In the Middle Ages, speculum literature was a kind of literary genre with the aim of encompassing encyclopedic knowledge on a given subject. The word "mirror" (*speculum*) may be a shorthand for the thirteenth-century *Speculum Astronomiae* (*The Mirror of Astronomy*), which defends astrology as a Christian form of knowledge and surveys quantitiative astronomy and judicial astrology, having been written by an anonymous author and later misattributed to Albertus Magnus in 1339. The anonymous writer describes himself as "a certain man, a zealot of faith and philosophy," and his text was central to the debate about astrology during the Middle Ages. Sections 18 and 19 appear to be redacted by a scribe "Christianizing" the text, having offered his own special title to the *Assaylemaht* prayer and then possibly referencing the *Speculum Astronomiae,* which favors the harmonization of the Catholic faith with astronomy and astrology but also condemns the Pseudo-Apollonius corpus of astral magic treatises. The original *Flores Aurei* would not have mentioned the *Speculum Astronomiae,* because its condemnation of Pseudo-Apollonius's treatises runs contrary to its supposed authorship.

54. Latin *matutino diei.*

55. At prime (the first hour of daylight, typically around 6:00 a.m.). For more on the canonical hours, see appendix A4.

[Chapter 2]

[**20a**] *The first chapter ends. The second [chapter] begins. The description about the following and the notory art is called into question.*

And thus, having mentioned before certain [divinely revealed] signs or teachings about a certain introduction with respect to these that we are saying we gave, still they have that part that we mentioned above.[56] Nevertheless, before it must come to this, I[57] judge certain things to be fully necessary, and [the art] may also be attained more perfectly and clearly set forth according to its history. For as we said, some requirements of the notory art are made obscure and some clearly manifested.[58]

[**20b**] *How the notory art contains all the arts and all knowledge in itself.*

The notory art has a second book out of astronomy,[59] of which the foundation itself is a teacher and an efficacy. For it is to be understood that the notory art contains all arts and all scientific literature wonderfully, indubitably, and reasonably. On that account, it is to be called a notory [art] by Solomon, who testifies, because it teaches [through] incomprehensible [language] the knowledge of all things out of writings with some [of the] shortest *notulis*.[60] For thus, it is said in the treatise *Lemegeton:* "This [notory art] is the spiritual and secret experiments."[61]

---

56. Sections 14–15.

57. Pseudo-Apollonius is speaking.

58. Section 15.

59. The identity of the "second book out of astronomy" is uncertain; however, the writer may be making a reference to the thirteenth-century version of the *Lemegeton,* perhaps suggesting the book comes out of the same astronomical and astrological current as the notory art.

60. *Notulis,* "little notes."

61. Here, the *Ars Notoria* quotes *Lemegeton,* itself referencing the *Ars Notoria.* "Spiritual and secret experiments" is a reference to section 2, in which Pseudo-Apollonius describes the notory art as a collection of "experiments" based on "spiritual sciences." In addition, the Version B gloss for section 21 uses the same phrase, "secret experiments," when talking about the efficacy of Solomon's prayers that are said to be found in the *Lemegeton,* saying, "[the *Lamehc Leynac* prayer] is to be named in its own certain book, the *Lemogethon,* titled [as] the same prayer, because the prayer itself is exulting and special *of their own secret experiments.*" Moreover, section 20b does not make sense if the *Lemegeton* is referencing itself. Section 20b presents the earliest known statement about the *Lemegeton,* dating it to at least the thirteenth century. It is likely the thirteenth-century version differs from its extant seventeenth-century recension. Furthermore, the thirteenth-century version of the *Lemegeton* that cites the *Ars Notoria* here makes it clear that this thirteenth-century *Lemegeton* came before this Version A of the *Ars Notoria.* Thus,

[21] But what or by what reason the *notae* are to be called in the notory art, this is the reason.

What a nota *must be and concerning the nature of the following prayer.*

The *nota* is that acquisition of knowledge through the prayer and the figure[62] placed on top, but a mention should be made presently about the prayers and about the times of their figures.

About that prayer which is to be called the "queen of languages."

Among all these exulting prayers there is a certain one that King Solomon wished to call the "queen of languages" for the reason that it may take away a certain secret guard, an impediment of the tongue, and may bestow a wonder and skill for eloquence (according to how it must come before),[63] it is to be mentioned beforehand for a short time, according to the prayer. For the prayer is to be held in the mouth, as it is always taught in writing,[64] yet according to the distorted speech of Chaldean, which is permitted to be short, is of a wonderful efficacy, so that when you read aloud the writing, having remembered the prayer beforehand, you will not be able to refrain from speaking aloud [because of any incompetency to enunciate] what the mind and tongue advise you.[65]

[22] *For this is the prayer itself for the purpose of making the erudition of tongues.*[66]

---

the present Version A is not the original form of the *Ars Notoria;* Véronèse agrees with this latter statement (see his doctoral dissertation). Obviously, there must have been an earlier *Ars Notoria* in order for the thirteenth-century *Lemegeton* to cite it and reference Pseudo-Apollonius in section 2. Other indicators suggest the same; see chapter I. The various spellings for the *Lemegeton* in the manuscripts are as follows: *Lemogeton, Lemogetan, Demegeton,* and *Lemogedan.*

62. The definition of a *nota*.

63. The *Lamehc Leynac* prayer must come before the other General prayers in order to have its effect of eloquence upon the operator. In other words, the General prayers must be conducted in their proper order to have the desired effect.

64. That is, the enunciation of syllables to make words as taught in an educational setting.

65. Thus, the worker of the notory art recites the prayer first, then reads aloud a written passage from a book he wishes to learn from and study. In doing so, the virtue or power of the prayer allows the worker to speak well and confidently. The image of a queen instructing the worker might parallel the personifications of Lady Grammar and Lady Rhetoric. See chapter IV, "The Art of Memory."

66. Erudition is when a teaching is reflected upon and effaces all rudeness from the student; that is, smooths away all untrained speech behaviors.

This prayer is said to be the "queen of languages," which must be held in the mouth, and is to be taught or acquired in writing.

Lemaac, Salmaac,[67] Elmay, Gezagra, Raamaasin, Ezieregomial, Egziephiar, Iosamin, Sabach, Ha, A Em, Be, He, E, Sepha, Sephar, Ramar, Semoit, Lemaio, Pheralon, Amic, Phin, Gergom, Letos. Amen, Amen, Amen.

[23] *Likewise, concerning the aforesaid prayer and about the following ones, when they ought to be said.*

These are the words that are necessary to be held in the heart, and ought to be said in the beginning of the writings of the most secret of teachings, and they should not be kept silent, which the tongue and mind might have suggested reading to you. Some things are divided hereafter[68] that in the beginning of the month ought to always be said, and with the highest degree of veneration and sanctity, and before food and drink may be consumed.

[24] *This is the prayer for the invocation of angels, which is to be said in the beginning of the month.*[69]

Theos, Patir,[70] Heenminos, through your most holy angels, Elypha, Masan, Gelomioos, Gedehantrai, Sasaramana, Elomuid, and through your archangel, whose names are made secret by God, so that they ought not be offered by us which are these: DE. EL. X. P. N. H. O. R. G., and the rest, some of which are not sufficient to comprehend by human senses.[71]

---

67. *Lamehc Leynac,* the second prayer belonging to the second sequence of the General prayers.

68. The phrase "Some things are divided hereafter" describes part of the greater ritual procedure of the notory art according to Version A. The division parallels what Version B says about a division of the second sequence of the General prayers between the second and third months of the four-month ritual. See chapter VI, "The Complete Ritual Procedures of the *Ars Notoria*."

69. Again, the time frame of "the beginning of the month" parallels the call for certain prayers at the first half of the third month in Version B. See chapter VI, "The Complete Ritual Procedures of the *Ars Notoria*."

70. *Deus summe Deus invisibilis Theos Patyr,* this is the third prayer of the triumphals that comprise of the second sequence of the General prayers. The phrase, *Deus summe Deus invisibilis,* is a scribal interpolation added in Version B but presented here for the sake of clearly identifying the prayer by its incipit. The Greek and Latin has been reconstructed.

71. Compare to section 24 in Version B. The abbreviations may be for the following divine names: DE for one of these names—Deihel (Deyhel), Dehel, Depymo, or Dein (Deyn); EL for Hel; X for Exluso or Exmogon (or Exmegan or Exmegon); P for Parineos (Paryneos) or Pheheneos; N for Nauagen (or Navagen); H for Hosyel (Hosiel); O for Oragon; R for Rathion (or Rachion);

[25] *The prayer, the purpose of which is to be merited for memory, to be said above at any time.*

I beseech you,[72] O Lord, fortify my conscience with the brilliance of your light, illuminate and strengthen my understanding with the sweet scent of your Spirit, adorn my soul, in order that I may retain the knowledge of what is heard and is to be listened to from memory. Transform, O Lord, restore, O God, placate, O most pious one, open, O calmest one, my memory, and temper my senses, O most benevolent one, through your glorious and ineffable name, and you who are the fountain of goodness and the source of all piety. Have patience with me, and give me your memory, and because I have asked you to grant me in this holy prayer; and you who does not immediately judge a sinner, but pities him, awaiting his repentance, I, an unworthy sinner, beseech you to wipe away the filthiness of my crimes, sins, wickedness, and failures, and through so much of my petition of the angels and archangels from those I mentioned before, may you bring about virtue, worthiness, and efficacy through your glory and majesty, you who are the one and true God, Amen.

[26] *The teaching of the preceding prayer and virtue.*

For if you would have doubted about some great vision [and] what it might present, or if you want to see a great vision of danger at present or about to come, or if you will want to have certainty about an absentee anywhere, you may say this same prayer thrice in the evening with the highest degree of veneration, and you will see that which you requested.

[27] Behold, [we are] about to give some general teachings about everything; some, having been mentioned beforehand, we judged some great offices are to be contained in those.[73]

G for Garbona; and the rest is Monyham, Megon, Hamos (or Megonhamos). The abbreviated names may support the premise of an oral tradition and indicate that there was an earlier recension that had the names spelled out. See also appendix A5, which discusses *Melechet Muscelet.*

72. *Te quaeso Domine,* this is the fourth and final prayer of the triumphals that make up the second sequence of the general prayers.

73. The "great offices" (*magna officia*) refers to the the function of a prayer to have an efficacy outside of the greater ritual of the notory art; that is, the prayer offers an effect to the operator in a particular circumstance of need. Such an office is called a lesser ritual in this book. The writer says that a lesser ritual has just been mentioned earlier, pointing to sections 21–23.

[28] *The prayer for understanding many types of infirmities.*

For if you wish to have knowledge of someone with a sickness, whether it be for life or death,[74] if the sick man lies ill languishing, stand before him, and say secretly:

[29] *This is the prayer.*

Ancor, Anacor, Anilos,[75] Theodonos, Helyothos, Phagor, Ucor, Nacor, Thudonos, Helyethys, Phagor, holy angels appear, direct, and teach me.

[30a] Later you will ask him: "What do you think?" If he responds, "Good," or "I am recovering," or something like these, you know without a doubt that the infirm person is [prognosticated] toward life.[76] However, if he responds, "Worse," or "Bad," or something like these, you know without a doubt that the infirm person is [prognosticated] toward death. If, however, he does not respond, you know that very person will die in the near future. If, however, he responds: "I do not know," similarly, it is death, or the infirmity will be increased in severity. But if there is a child who is too young to respond to you, or an adult who, languishing severely, is not be able or unwilling to respond, after having said the prayer, [the answer] will come to you first in your mind, [then] you will know about the future.

---

74. See the Sphere of Life and Death discussed under the figure of medicine in chapter V, "Analysis of the Figures."

75. *[Iesu Dei Filius incomprehensibilis] Ancor, Anacor, Anilos* is the first prayer of the third sequence of the General prayers. The name and title, "Jesus, the incomprehensible Son of God," is a scribal interpolation added in Version B but noted here for the sake of clearly identifying the prayer by its incipit.

76. The writer is thinking about this hypothetical situation in terms of a prognostic tool called the Sphere of Life and Death, used by medieval doctors. Essentially, the tool consists of two spheres containing numbers meant for the application of onomancy, a form of divination by the interpretation of the letters of a person's name that are converted into a numerical value, calculated, and applied by a certain algorithm to determine the person's fate. The top sphere represents life, and the bottom sphere represents death. After calculating and converting a patient's name into a numerical value, that number is found in either the Sphere of Life or the Sphere of Death. One might visualize an imaginary axis between these two spheres that plots the position of the patient's illness. Thus, according to the Sphere, if a patient is recovering well and his number appears in the upper Sphere, then the illness is "inferior" to life. See chapter V.

[30b] *Of the nature and virtue of the preceding prayer.*

Further, if anyone feigned or concealed an illness, say the same prayer and the angelic virtue will advise you because [the angelic virtue] is from the truth itself. Specifically, if the sick person was distant, by having heard his name, similarly, for this [circumstance] you say this prayer and it will come to you in spirit immediately whether he ought to live or die. For if you feel the pulse of some sick person, the same prayer uttered in secret will suggest to you what kind or effect the illness has; and if you feel the pulse of a woman, you will know without a doubt if she was pregnant, and if it was a male or female, or if they were twins. But you will know that [truth] not from your own nature, but from the angels' office [which] is to lead and advise you wonderfully. But if you doubted concerning the virginity of anyone, the same prayer uttered without doubt advises you whether the person is a virgin.

[31] *Also, so that we might not look back upon the few words of the aforesaid prayer.*

This is the efficacy of the previous prayer, and this is contained within itself, from where Solomon said, "I received this new medicine created by God," and from where my teacher[77] [said]:

> This new learning of such an efficacious knowledge contains the quality and quantity of the entire foundation of the arts of scientific medicine, for which the rest is a miracle more splendid than dreadful, because [the prayers] are to be taught from God, some briefly, some lightly, [but] some truly burdensome and lengthy. But you, whenever you read it, do not look back upon the multitude of words, but praise the virtue of so great a mystery.

For Solomon distorted [the prayer] itself out of the subtlety of the notory art with the wonderful privilege of divine help. But because it is, indeed, so great, that we[78] have proposed evidently to constrain so many, and so much

---

77. Pseudo-Apollonius speaking of King Solomon.
78. Pseudo-Apollonius and Solomon.

under such a qualitative degree with brevity,[79] I judge some general prelude work, to be placed [as] necessary [and] first before the order, so that the mind of a hearer might be more strengthened and prevail.[80]

79. Another reference to the philosophical theory of hylomorphism as it is applied to the field of linguistics.

80. Pseudo-Apollonius says he has provided a translation of the *Ancor, Anacor, Anilos* prayer into Latin for which he calls a prologue (*proemium*) to help his reader have some understanding of the divinely revealed prayers. Unfortunately, the Latin prologue prayer is missing.

[Chapter 3]

[32a] Therefore, we must explain what is necessary for it to be possible for us to approach the greater things.

The third chapter begins, [and] according to it, that notory art is said to be the art of arts, because all the arts are inferred within it, and it teaches everything to any unskilled and illiterate a person with few words, and every nota *has its own office of the art to exercise, and because one* nota *of the art may not serve for another known art.*

For Solomon, the great composer of the notory art and the entire arts, having [the entire arts] contained within [it]—or to some extent participating in [sharing something with the notory art]—the teacher called that art as the greatest, [and] on that account, [he] called [it] "notory," because it is the art of arts and the science of sciences. For he comprehends all these liberal, mechanical, and exceptive arts within it, and he comprehends that in other arts by laborious and burdensome speeches, and also he comprehends [the arts] by the prolixity and fastidious of books to scrolls over a great span of time by whichever genius; in [the notory art] he comprehends with a few words, having been written with the smallest [*notae*]; the virtues of the angels are to be known with a subtle acuity by wonderful and unheard of words in a few and placid days by any unskilled and illiterate person.[81]

[32b] Therefore, may we receive, properly and worthily, an egregious gift (and it is so much an office), from which so many faculties, flowing from the Most High Creator, have been granted with the reason of a writing of the sciences. For although the arts each have their own *nota*[82] arranged and marked beforehand with the figures, and [the operator] has to practice the office with each and every *nota* of its art, the *notae* of one art will not be useful for the purpose of learning another art. Since it is a little difficult [to understand] that the prelude is said to be the corpus of the [notory] art in this small treatise,[83]

---

81. The author assumes a hierarchy of knowledge in which the notory art is positioned at the top and contains all the arts and sciences beneath it. See the taxonomy of knowledge on page 66.
82. Here the word *nota* denotes the prayer.
83. The prelude (*praeludium*) is the general teaching provided before each prayer and its figure as it was established first by Solomon (section 8). The prelude is not to be confused with the Latin prologue (Latin *prologus*) or the proem (Latin *proemium*). A Latin prologue is the summary or

let us explore that [corpus of teaching] because it is more necessary for each individual *nota* to be defined fully one by one for the purpose of acquiring the knowledge of the universal writings by divine influence.

[33] Truly we believe it suitable and useful for us and our posterity, and so that learning from some compendious treatises[84] and great and lengthy volumes can be done easily, we should inquire most diligently about the three most ancient books that were composed by Solomon.[85] In the first of these [books is to be found] that important [prayer],[86] which is to be understood that (having sent ahead the prayer before the following headword[87] in every long delivery of speech, nevertheless) it is to be used before the beginning of a speech, so that the first three words of the prayer, [*Lamen, Ragaa, Regiomal*], may be uttered secretly and at a suitable time.[88] But the succeeding parts of the prayer are to be said, especially when you inspect the unrolled scrolls[89] for the purpose of acquiring understanding of them. So, from then on, the prayer is to be said when you wish to clarify and resolve some serious sentence unknown and unheard of by you before, that suddenly it will be made fully and clearly known to you. Similarly, you will say the same prayer when someone says to you something serious and inopportune that is not in your ability to explain.

---

partial translation of one of the strange incomprehensible prayers. See Section 68.

84. That is, the many great treatises of men who wrote about the arts and sciences.

85. That is, *Liber Florum Caelestis Doctrinae* (*The Book of Flowers of Heavenly Teaching*), *Eniclyssoe,* and *Gemeliot.*

86. *Lamehc Ragna* is the first prayer of the fourth sequence of the General prayers. It is accompanied by its prologue, titled *Memoria Irreprehensibilis. Lamehc Ragna* is not a "Special" as belonging to the class of Specials that deal with the liberal arts. The meaning here is that the writer considers the prayer *Lamehc Ragna* as a very important prayer that can be utilized in a small ritual for a specific effect. I label these as "Lesser Rituals," contrasted against the all-encompassing "Greater Ritual" of the notory art.

87. The Latin prologue *Memoria irreprehensibilis.*

88. The prayer *Lamehc Ragna* / *Memoria irreprehensibilis* has a special utility for an orator in that it can be pronounced first before he gives a speech to an audience, thereby enhancing the speech's effect.

89. Although books were the primary depositories of knowledge in the Middle Ages, scrolls were still being used. Scrolls were useful for taking down notes in class because a student did not know how much material he had to write down for a given subject until he finished it. It was more convenient for the student to keep all his notes in a single scroll rather than using multiple sheets of parchment. In addition, a student's scrolls were often cheaper parchment offcuts, too small to be made into books, but easy to glue together and more portable than heavy books.

[34] *These words are to be said at the beginning of a long speech and follow the unrolling of folios, and this prayer is said to be the "crown jewel of the Lord," and it is to be said against danger from fire, earth, and beasts.*

Lamen, Ragaa,[90] Regiomal, Agalad, Craotad, Antonomos, Ledensazaia, Maratal, Momaton, Hosacro, Cogemal, Salaliel, Gessomami, Azarod, Begestar, Amal.

[35] This prayer is contained in the following passage of the first General *nota* of a treatise about every writing, of which we[91] have sufficiently completed the fiftieth part in a scroll about the magnitude of qualities of the same art, but certainly the unskilled hearer must not be wanting in the sacramental understanding of its admirable mystery; he must undoubtedly know its explanation to be [just] the beginning [of the prayer].[92]

[36] *The prayer that is called the explanation of the preceding [prayer].*

O irreprehensible memory,[93] O uncontradictable wisdom, O immutable efficacious God, the angels of eternal counsel, hold my heart with your right hand, may your memory, the scent of your ointment, and the sweetness of your grace fill up my conscience; strengthen my mind, O splendor of the Holy Spirit, by which the affection of the angels, with all the heavenly hosts, desire to behold your face without end, by the wisdom with which you made all things, by the intelligence through which you restored all things, by the steadfast blessedness through which you restored the angels,

---

90. *Lamehc Ragna* is the first prayer belonging to the fourth sequence of the General prayers. It is accompanied by its Latin prologue, *Memoria Irreprehensibilis*.

91. Pseudo-Apollonius and Solomon.

92. *Liber Florum Caelestis Doctrinae* (*The Book of Flowers of Heavenly Teaching*), *Eniclyssoe,* and *Gemeliot;* the name is given below in section 38. Pseudo-Apollonius claims to have composed his own version of the *Liber Florum Caelestis Doctrinae,* which explores the philosophical theory of hylomorphism as applied to the field of linguistics, rather than Aristotle's application of hylomorphism to nature. There are no extant manuscripts of the *Liber Florum Caelestis Doctrinae* as described here; there is no indication that it ever existed. However, John of Morigny, the fourteenth-century Benedictine monk who was inspired by the *Ars Notoria* and composed his own creative, although derivative version, called his work by the same name. For other hints to this mysterious and otherwise unknown text, see the gloss in section 34 of Version B and section 38. For an explanation on hylomorphism, see chapter IV.

93. *Memoria Irreprehensibilis.* This is the Latin prologue belonging to *Lamehc Ragna*.

by the love through which you aroused in the fallen man [who desires to return] back to the heavens, by the instruction you let Adam (who is worthy) be taught all knowledge: instruct, replenish, correct, and refresh me, so that I may become new in understanding your commandments and embracing knowledge for the salvation of my body and soul and of all the faithful who believe in your name, who is blessed forever and ever, amen.

[37] *The description of the preceding prayer and its explanation.*

For this is a certain little part of the explanation of the preceding prayer that every learned one who read in this most valuable art, has left unexplained, knowing that its explanation is never able to be sufficient for the human faculty.

[38] For this prayer is called by Solomon the "crown jewel of the Lord." He said, "Indeed, it helps against the danger[s] of fire, earth, and beasts, having been spoken with faith, believing." For it is said to have been carried forth by one of the four angels to whom it was given to [both] damage the land and the sea and to do good for the earth, sea, and trees.[94] Solomon called the *Liber Florum Caelestis Doctrinae* [(*The Book of Flowers of Heavenly Teaching*)][95] an example of the prayer. He glorified the Lord in this [book] because he was inspired by the divine will to theology, and by the competence of the will, to suddenly receive certain kinds of prayers transmitted to him during the night of sacrifice to the Lord God [used for] for the bestowing of greater things,[96] he conveniently placed them in the corpus of the notory art, because they are holy, worthy, and revering the mysteries; the Gentiles[97] (some not procuring from theology themselves) had despised Solomon, who having been taught beforehand by an angel, called [those divinely revealed prayers] the "Sign of the Mystery of God."[98] For this [*Liber Florum Caelestis Doctrinae*] is the complement of our dignity and salvation that is contained within them.

94. Revelation 7:1–3.

95. This book title is the one Solomon gave to the collection of prayers that would later enter into Pseudo-Apollonius' *Flores Aurei* and then even later, the *Ars Notoria*.

96. 1 Kings 3:4–5.

97. The word *Gentiles* may refer to both the ancient non-Jewish people and those without a god or a theology.

98. This story introduces the fifth sequence of the General prayers, which along with the sixth and seventh sequence, grant the operator mental faculties relating to theurgic theology.

[39] For these are the prayers in which our salvation is able to have great efficacy. The first important prayer is specifically about theology, which is to be learned, and memory steadfastly retained, and on that account, Solomon ordered the [divinely revealed] sign itself to be called "the Grace of God." For the grace of God is, as Ecclesiastes[99] said, "a spiritual thing in us that has inspired me to speak of everything from the cedar of Lebanon unto the hyssop that grows out of the wall."[100]

[40] *At which times and how often the prayer is to be said according to its efficacy and virtue.*

The first prayer ought to be offered once by the first Moon, and in the third [Moon] thrice, and in the sixth seven times, and similarly it ought to be said in the ninth, twelfth, fifteenth, eighteenth, twenty-first, twenty-fourth, twenty-sixth, twenty-ninth, and thirtieth seven times.[101] For the prayer that you have said by the determined day is of such virtue and of such efficacy, thus will the virtue of knowledge of theology be increased so much for you, just as if you desired, [then] you will hardly be able to keep silent about it and if before you were an unskilled person [or even just] an associate or your inferior or [someone] similar, having been understood by the same person and to know about the rest, so that [someone who knows you] might be suddenly struck with fear and love by those things from you, [then] you will be commended, and be made famous and proclaimed widely. Nevertheless see, that which you utter it by day, may you keep secret and may you live chastely. When you say [it] once, you must say it in the early morning.

[41] He carried that prayer, the same testifying angel, the commander of thunder, who always stands in the sight of the Lord, whose name is Pamphilius,[102] carried that prayer, and even whose sacrosanct prayer is a judgment, and even whose efficacy is to be bestowed, just as when you said it once, it is not necessary to say it anymore.

---

99. Refers to Solomon. It was commonly believed that Solomon wrote the book of Ecclesiastes; therefore, he was called by that name.

100. Not a direct quote, but it refers to 1 Kings 4:33.

101. Or, six times, according to Mellon 1 manuscript. These are the twelve favorable days of the Moon, which has a parallel with Version B's greater ritual procedure in its third month (except instead of the 24th day it is the 23rd day). See chapter VI, "The Complete Ritual Procedures of the *Ars Notoria*."

102. The angel who gave the *Ars Notoria* to Solomon.

[42] And it is to be said about the same prayer that its mystery is so great, for just as the heavenly spirit moves forward to some great divine-permitting agenda and bestowing power, and also, it has its own mystery to effect with an abundance, just as it exalts the tongue and the heart itself bringing forth so much inspiration, just like you know you have understood something new, great, and mysterious. This is the beginning of the prayer itself, which, it is necessary to be observed with so much consideration, just as we have said.

[43] *This is the prayer, of which it was said, of which there are four parts, and which the sign is called "The Grace of God," and it is particularly related to theology.*
Hely,[103] Lehem, Azatau, Iezoi, Iezar, and you angels whose names are written in the Book of Life, whose names are to be recited.

And this again, from the prayer.
Rasan, Lemar, Teviannaot, Setrai, Anachor, Iosiel, Elimot, Theodoni, Patene, Neos, Ataraim, Aziacor, Iesemonai, Amvosia, Caegilios, Zagael, Amen.[104]

[44] *The order in which the preceding prayer with its parts is said.*

This is the beginning of the aforesaid prayer, of which there are also four parts, but because something is to be said about the first, and also the other parts one by one, for that reason, we properly made that division between the beginning and its four parts.

[45] Truly [*Helma* and its Latin prologue] is what is to be said from the beginning. First, it should be understood[105] that this prayer, as we have said, is to be divided up, and that the words of the first part, that is, the beginning, are to be said before another part of the [*Hazatam*] prayer is to be said.

---

103. *Hazatam,* the first part of the four-part prayer of the fifth sequence of the General prayers.
104. The same prayer continues.
105. *Sciendum est* means "it should be understood," which is a phrase directing the reader's attention to a particular explanation or rule. The phrase is found in civil law books and is frequently used throughout the *Ars Notoria*.

[46] Helma,[106] Hebros, Eloa, Octomeges, Micustagil.

[47] *And in the Latin language these are to be added:*
O Abba,[107] O God, O God the Father, God the Son, God the Holy Spirit, strengthen,[108] solidify, and enlighten my memory, reason, and intellect for the knowledge, eloquence, and perseverance that is to be undertaken, known, and kept [in] all of the good writings.

[48] *The teaching concerning the aforesaid knowledge and its parts.*
That is the beginning of the prayer, which, as we have said, it is necessary to speak according to the prolations and according to the institutions themselves, on account of the forgetfulness of our memory, again, the practice was not being maintained continually, and the example to our sanctity, in which everything is efficacious.

[49] It follows also that subtle science which, (below, just as it is said above,)[109] is a sacrament of every mystery, and it is completed, having been finished mysteriously. For [Solomon] said about [the subtle science] itself, "just as we were knowing *that* heaven and *that* earth according to the earth of earthly things and according to the heaven of heavenly things, meanwhile [the subtle science] is being effected." The Lord said, "Your eyes beheld my unformed substance. In your book were written all the days that were formed for me, when none of them as yet existed."[110] For thus, it is to held in the teachings of God. "For we are not able to write everything, just like the Sun had [raced] that same course first,"[111] and our order [of prayers] is to be confirmed. For every writing [coming] out of God is not to be read, [and] God wanted to divide everything himself, even[112] this [prayer], and just as there are these which are only to be

106. The same prayer continues.
107. Aramaic for "father," or more informally "daddy." Compare to Mark 14:36.
108. *Confirma,* the Latin prologue of *Hazatam.*
109. Section 17.
110. Psalms 139:16 (NRSV).
111. 1 Esdras 4:34; 1 Esdras is an ancient Greek version of the Hebrew book of Ezra.
112. That is to say, the knowledge contained within the *notae* is both heavenly and earthly. Thus, the written works of men contain earthly knowledge and can be known, but the heavenly knowledge is a mystery that can only be known through carrying out the ritual of the notory art. This division

done before the next part. For the next part of the aforesaid prayer is called "the golden part";[113] thus, it begins.

Also from the same prayer.

So glorious, excellent, and competent [is this prayer] of all the consecrated supplication prayers, that it is defined to have a part in the heavens, so that it can by no means be defined in human tongues.

[50] *This is the beginning of the second part of the prayer.*

Agloros,[114] Theomiros, Seotodos, Azamos, Cozienna, Geerael, Alimud, Iezozai, Azai, Megalos, Amen.

[51] This is the second part of the prayer, about which something in particular must be said. For if you happen to say the prayer, you will say this as the second part:

This [prologue] prayer is to be said after the second part of the prayer.

O God of all things,[115] you who are my God, who in the beginning created all things out of nothing, who in your Spirit has restored all, fill, renew, and heal my understanding, so that I may glorify you through all my thoughts, words, and deeds.

[52] *And after you have said this, after an interval of half an hour, you will say the third part of the prayer, which is this:*

The third part of the said prayer.

Megal,[116] Ariotas, Lamazai, Ieconai, Zemazfar, Tetragramos, Aziamios, Azamair, Zecosaphor, Azacapasamar, Selot, Zadasamir, Amen.

---

of heavenly and earthly knowledge is decreed by God. Thus, the author is not able to write all the definitions of every mnemonic sign found in the pictorial figures called *notae*. See section 133.

113. The title, "the golden part," may be inspired by geometry's golden ratio by which the author here perceives the four parts of Hely Lehem as perfect and therefore golden. The first part is divided from the latter three parts.

114. *Agloros*, the second part of *Hazatam* called "the golden part."

115. *Deus omnium,* the Latin prologue of *Agloros*.

116. *Megal,* the third part of *Hazatam*.

[53] Having said this third part of the prayer, you will meditate about the writings that you will want to know and you next say:
The truth, light, and life[117] of all creatures, O God quicken me and strengthen my comprehension, and restore my conscience just as you did before with King Solomon.

[54] Having said these, you say the fourth part of the prayer, which is this:

This is the fourth part of the aforesaid prayer, that is, Hely[118]
Latur, Bael, Zedac, Azaras, Iezonal, Comaia, Ysaray, Iehemiehel, Mihinniaub, Zelmeal, Ietrozaal, Molos, Microtamos, Amen.

[55] For these aforesaid parts, you will add these according to what was defined and taught.

This [prologue] prayer is to be said after the fourth part of the prayer.
I speak these things in your presence,[119] O Lord God, at whose command all things are naked and open,[120] so that, when the error of unbelief is removed, your Spirit may help all things, vivifying my unbelief.

[56] *On the virtue and greatness of the preceding prayer.*
For it is to be understood that this entire prayer has been left unexplained; therefore, because its zeugma of speech is of such subtlety from the Hebrew and Chaldean languages [and] of such a subtle and admirable difficulty [with illumination],[121] having been distorted, so that it is by no means able to be translated freely in our office of locution. But the Latin words[122] that are joined to the parts of the aforesaid prayer, these are words that have been able to be translated out of the Chaldean speech into ours; yet, they are not from

---

117. *Veritas lux et vita,* the Latin prologue of *Megal Ariotas.*
118. *Hanuyrlyahel,* the fourth and final part of *Hazatam.*
119. *Ego in conspectus,* the Latin prologue of *Hanuyrlyahel.*
120. Hebrews 4:13.
121. Latin *elimatione* or *eluminatione.* The intended Latin word is probably *illuminatione.*
122. That is, the Latin prologue prayers *Confirma, Deus omnium, Veritas lux et vita,* and *Ego in conspectus.*

the prayer, but of every part of the aforesaid prayer, the headwords pertaining to the prayer.[123]

[57] For the prayer [*Hazatam*] itself is of so great a mystery, that, as King Solomon testifies, while his servant of the house, too drunk after the approach of a woman, by chance found this book, was uttering presumptuously the aforesaid prayer, and while not having yet finished [reading] its part, was made speechless and entirely without memory, blind and mute up to the hour of death. But [he] said in the hour of [his] death that four angels [who govern the notory art] who he had offended in so sacred a mystery by speaking presumptuously, [he] had endured daily the jailers and floggers, one of memory, the second of the tongue, the third of the eyes, the fourth of the ears. By this testimony, the same prayer was made more commendable for King Solomon. For it is so much the mystery of the prayer but rather that, whoever should wish to say it, should not say it presumptuously. For saying it in presumption is a sin, so it should be said just as it was taught.

[58] Given the general instructions regarding the conditions of all the [liberal, mechanical, and exceptive] arts we thought it necessary to define something about the precepts of the individual arts. But since we have mentioned something of the Sun's course,[124] it is necessary to explain what we mean regarding the course of the Sun. The Sun passes through the twelve signs in one year, and the Moon the same in one month, and the Holy Spirit inspires, makes abundant, and illuminates one and the same by the end, from where it is said, "just like the Sun has [raced] that course first"[125]—for *habeat*[126] is to be [grammatically] understood; but since this word is defective in [biblical] Hebrew, and even in Latin, we consider *debere* to be defective.[127] That is enough about the prayer itself.

---

123. In other words, the Latin prologues are not direct translations of the *voces magicae* prayers, but instead are composed by translating only a small portion of each headword in the Hebrew and Chaldean speech.

124. Section 49.

125. 1 Esdras 4:34.

126. The Latin present active subjunctive verb meaning "it has" or "it ought to have," as in "the Sun has" or "the Sun ought to have" or "the Sun must have."

127. The writer is indicating that the Latin verb *debere,* meaning "ought, "must," or "should," is a defective verb because it is a modal or auxillary verb: one that helps another verb in a sentence. For example, "*You ought* to carry your textbooks to school." There are very few modal verbs in Latin.

[59] *The teaching about the following prayer and its virtue.*
It is this second prayer, [*Gemoht Gehel,*] which is especially regarded by a certain [book called Lengemath], (although the other prayers have an efficacy about many things), it is to be understood [as something important], for it is a certain one, containing a Special [prayer] in itself, but nevertheless it is one of the General prayers, showing a certain general quality in itself and common to all the arts, just as God established all things, saying, "These things I give to you, so that you may observe and keep the law of the Lord; and who are those always assisting in the sight of the Lord and who see the Savior face-to-face night and day?"[128] This is, I say, that glorious, mystical, and intelligible prayer in which the mind, conscience, and tongue will be advised. It is so great, that it may keep itself according to the will of God who makes provision for all things created in his sight. But of the prayer itself, whose mystery is so glorious and sacramental, let no one presume to say something after excessive drunkenness or lust, for nothing must be said without fasting, except with the highest discretion.

[60] Whence Solomon said, "Let no one," he says, "presume to practice this prayer except at its determined times."

And if someone was meeting before the director[129] himself, whose memory having been composed from the prayer itself (and it is so salubrious), just like having read that biblical passage about [the apostles,] own intervention from which it is said, "Follow me, I will make you fishers of men,"[130] and it was said and done. We do not know from our faculty how the prayer itself is of such virtue and mystery, nor are we even able to know how he said it to his disciples, that [is], the prayer itself, as we have said, is such a mystery, like the great name of the Lord,[131] because there are many who pretend to know it,

128. Unknown citation. Compare to Revelation 7:15.

129. Or president, patron, protector, or bishop.

130. Matthew 4:19; Mark 1:17.

131. The Hebrew name of God is YHVH, which is commonly pronounced "Yahweh," but according to Jewish tradition, there is a secret pronunciation that allows its speaker to perform miracles. There is also a twenty-two-letter name of God and a seventy-two-letter name of God (this one derived from Exodus 14:19–21) called the Shem Ha-Mephorash, meaning "the explicit name," originating from the *Sepher Raziel* ascribed to Eleazar of Worms and having Geonic

and because although Jesus [who] discovered [the name of the Lord] in the temple and sewed it up [in his] flesh [in order] to perform miracles (they are deceived whosever composed [it]); nevertheless, so no one might dare to reveal that [prayer] of those [words] to be comprehended, for the purpose of how it is to be attained before, we consider some [individuals] to be declared on the outside [of this mystery].[132]

[61] *The order in which the prayer is to be offered.*

For it is the last of the Generals and the first of the Specials, containing each of them in itself, and since it has an important virtue and eloquence, it must be understood at what time, in what order, and in what parts it should be offered. At all times, except the fourteenth Moon and beyond,[133] this prayer is to be said each morning of the day after the particular prayers before a man becomes contaminated.[134] The prayer is to be said only once entirely without division, and yet there are divisions to be had in it. This is not because the prayer is divided in itself, but because so great and so glorious a name is written through the parts, and each part of the so great and so glorious name is to be said through to the ends. Thus, on account of our fragility and weakness, the most excellent name itself is not to be offered in its entirety all at once. Additionally, the elements (or syllables) of the name

---

sources. See Trachtenberg, *Jewish Magic and Superstition,* chapter 7.

132. The *Jewish Life of Jesus (Toldot Yeshu)* is an alternative biography of Jesus from a Jewish perspective, dated widely from the third to the eleventh centuries, that circulated in medieval Europe. The polemical text against Christianity has Aramaic and Hebrew origins, though it also exists in Judeo-Arabic manuscripts from the eleventh and twelfth centuries. The narrative depicts Jesus as an illegitimate son who practiced magic, seduced women, and, while exceptionally wise, was disrespectful to his elders and died as a false prophet. The reference here tells the story of a stone engraved with the ineffable name of God contained within the Temple of Jerusalem that was guarded by the priesthood and two brass lions. Whenever someone entered the Temple to learn the name, when he left, the lions would roar and he would forget the secret name. Jesus entered the Temple, learned the name, and wrote it down on parchment, cut open his thigh, placed the parchment inside the wound, and sewed it up. When he exited the Temple, the lions roared and he forgot the name; however, when he got home, he reopened his wound, took out the parchment, relearned it, and then used the name of God to perform his miracles. See Goldstein, "Early Jewish-Christian Polemic in Arabic," 9–42.

133. The month is divided in half. The scribe does not explain why *Gemoht Gehel* is not to be offered in the second half of the month. The reason may be because of a concern about the prohibition of offering certain prayers on Egyptian days. See Chapter VI, 'The Complete Ritual Procedures.

134. That is, before he breaks his fast and eats.

merit remembrance, and it is to be learned where they are placed, lest anyone presumptuously pronounce it, or, behaving through ignorance, do something with it that is not to be done.

[62] For this is the simple prayer of eloquence that Solomon and his descendants had called in that skillfully constructed [book] *Lengemath;*[135] that is, "the restoration or disentanglement of tongues." This is the beginning of the prayer up to the end.

A great prayer of general virtue to all the arts.

Gemot, Geel,[136] **Zabael, Gezezai, Azagra, Gezomai, Alla, Athanaton, Agyel, Azamiel, Athanayos, Ezomai, Cealragen, Ezenton, Gotha, Gezerebgal, Anabiac, Zadachial, Ezeden, Pellicitaros, Thyethis, Cremodios, Ziim, Gezeomiel, Ezerum, Zorol, Zarabiel, Samil.**

[63] *Also, the teaching about the preceding prayer.*

Behold, the story [about the great name of the Lord and its prayer, *Gemoht Gehel*], having been preserved in the writings of the wise sages of the world which, just as we have said,[137] is to be offered and performed with the utmost diligence. In fact, it can be offered every day if one was not impeded in crimes. But on the day [in] which you were impeded by the crimes, you will be able to remember it in your heart, and if you wanted to be favorably eloquent, [then] repeat it thrice, and if it was a misfortune or a secular business affair from where you wanted to take action, [then] you repeat the prayer once, and as much eloquence will be added to you as is needed; and if you will repeat [the prayer] twice, [then] a multitude will be prejudiced against you for speaking well, so great is the sacrament of the prayer. There is also another thing to be considered in the prayer—namely, that the prayer ought to be pronounced in such a way that a confession of the heart and mouth should precede it; however, it is to be pronounced once and without interruption, but it is to be pronounced in the early morning and [the Latin prologue prayer] is to be said after the prayer.

---

135. Or *Lengemat, Logemat,* or *Legenmat.*

136. *Gemoht Gehel,* the *Lengemath* prayer of eloquence.

137. Section 60.

[64] *This [prologue] prayer is to be said every day after the previous.*

O almighty, everlasting God,[138] and merciful Father, you who are blessed before all worlds, O eternal, incomprehensible, and unchangeable God, who has granted us the medicine of salvation, who through the omnipotence of your majesty has allowed us the ability to speak, denied to other animals, whose disposition is unfailing, whose nature is both eternal and of the same substance, as you God, you who are exalted above the heavens, in which the entire divinity dwells bodily, I deprecate[139] your majesty and I glorify your eternal omnipotence, virtue, and magnifience, and I deprecate, O my God, O ineffable wisdom, O life of the angels, entreating with an imploration of the highest and innermost intention, O God the Holy Spirit and the incomprehensible one, in whose sight the multitude of angels stand, I adjure and pray to you, so that through your holy and glorious name, and through the sight of your angels and through the heavenly Principalities may you bestow your grace and eloquence to me, and may you grant your comprehension, memory, and perseverance [to me], you who lives and reigns eternally one and threefold God, in the sight of all the heavenly Virtues, now both always and everywhere, amen.

[65] *Also, the teaching about the preceding prayer.*

Thus, having finished that prayer and those placed out of the necessity of speech, when you have some silence, it is to be placed beneath just like a mystery, and after you will begin the silence to say insofar as you wanted. After you will have the eloquence just as you wanted to have, use it sparingly for yourself, and do not bring it forth just because the tongue advised you.

[66] *The general teachings are given concerning the sciences to be had.*

That is the goal of the general teachings that are given to acquire memory, intelligence, and eloquence.

---

138. *Omnipotens sempiterne Deus,* the Latin prologue of *Gemoht Gehel.*

139. *Deprecate* is an obsolete term which means "to pray with a penitent voice," and a deprecation is a prayer. In essence, when the petitioner says, "I deprecate your majesty," it means "I pray to your majesty." This obsolete term has nothing to do with the modern expression of disapproval or to belittle someone. Both the verb and noun parts of speech of this word are found frequently throughout the *Ars Notoria.*

[The Specials]

[67] For all those things that have been mentioned above regarding the general teachings have been given [divinely revealed] signs, so that there may be an opportunity to understand and acquire the general teachings. Those that are [found] hereafter are what Solomon himself called "Specials." Behold, each art has a single authority.[140]

[68] *[Solomon] passes over with respect to any nota hereafter concerning the Specials.*

For after having given a sufficient explanation about the general teachings [of the notory art], and the prayers and advice[141] of the prayers are placed in which it is designated—what ought to be done about each prayer? But because we are to practice each art one by one, it is necessary in so far as what our authority and master set as an example for us to follow.[142] For Solomon said, "Before [the notory art] is to be illuminated with respect to each *nota* or the prayers marked before the *notae* of each art,[143] we have appointed a prelude to be given because it is a prologue or proem."[144] And again, the subsequent words of the same wise sage.

[69] *The Generals and Specials are to be learned by this prayer.*

---

140. See chapter III regarding illustrious and historic individuals associated with each liberal art. The author is hinting to his reader to visualize the historic figure associated with each art when performing the imprinting stage of the art of memory. For example, the reader would visualize Priscian for grammar, which is followed by a series of images for the notory art's teachings and prayers on the art of grammar.

141. Latin *auctoritates;* that is, the advice or counsel provided by Solomon called a prelude (*praeludium*).

142. Pseudo-Apollonius speaking in the first-person plural about himself, or he is including his reader with himself.

143. Here the word (*nota, notae*) refers to the figure or figures which immediately follow the prayers for a given art or science within the text. This format of introducing a liberal art, giving its prayer followed by its figure, has been lost in Version A. See chapter II on the textual changes that occurred in the *Ars Notoria*.

144. In other words, the prelude (*praeludium*) is the introductory teaching to the *nota;* that is, the prayer and its figure. Therefore, the prelude acts as a prologue or proem; the meaning here is in its common usage. The words "prologue or proem" are not to be confused with the technical term *prologus,* referring to a Latin prologue prayer which partially translates a strange prayer.

Semot, Lamen,[145] Gezeil, Samatial, Maaziol, Ezolca, Zinegos, Alzamiol, Memicros, Lemeloi, Zemenai, Zettronaum, Labdenadon, I, Iotha, Vau, Ziet, Omos, E, Elintomai, O, A, Ot, Alle, Semanai, Nataim, Iezaol, Magal, Iecramagai, Sennasadar, Iezama, Faffa, Iobat, Ammial, Zanagromos, Negorobalim, Longai, Izeremelion, Sicroze, Gramaltheoneos, Carmelos, Samiel, Gezesiot, Semornail, Amen.

[70] *A description of the preceding prayer and permission for learning the arts.*

King Solomon said, "This is the prayer of prayers and a special experiment, in which all things, whether general or particular, may be heard, known, and recollected by memory fully, perfectly, efficaciously," and before we arrive at the teaching of each and every art, it is necessary we explain how each art has separate figures.

[71] *How many arts there are.*

For there are seven liberal arts, and there are seven exceptive [arts] or seven mechanical [arts].[146] The first to be pursued are the seven liberal arts. Now the seven mechanical and exceptive arts are to be contained below the seven liberal arts. It is clear what the seven liberal arts are. Now, the seven mechanics are these: hydromancy, pyromancy, [and] nigromancy; under astrology, chiromancy, geomancy, *geonogia,* [and] *neonegia*.[147] Now, the mechanics are to be called quasi-adulterous.[148]

---

145. *Semoht Lamen* is the prologue to the Generals and Specials. It is spoken in the third and fourth months of the operation according to Version B.

146. The term *exceptives* comes from medieval grammar, which identifies those constructions that express exclusion. Here the term refers to the magical arts of divination that are excluded from the rest of knowledge; namely, the seven liberal arts. The Latin word *et,* which lies between *exceptive* and the Roman numeral vii, must have been a later scribal error since there are not a total of 21 arts mentioned here but only 14; that is, the seven liberal arts and the seven exceptive arts.

147. The terms *geonogia* and *neonegia* are not attested anywhere but are likely corrupted from a transliteration from Greek to Latin. The text indicates that they are four forms of divination classified under astrology—chiromancy, geomancy, genethlialogy, and onomancy. Chiromancy is divination of the hand and the lines of the palm. Geomancy is divination by making points in the sand, on a wax tablet, or on paper. Genethlialogy, more commonly known as natal astrology, is a method of divination by studying nativities (i.e., birth charts). Also under astrology was the form of divination called onomancy (or nomancy) that divined by the letters in a person's name. See chapter III on these disciplines for more details.

148. Here the author names the forms of divination as the mechanical arts, speaking generally

Description of hydromancy.

Hydromancy is the science of water, because certain knowledge might be had of great experiments by [water disturbed] in a rapid motion, or in a ghost of standing or running water.

Description of pyromancy.

Pyromancy is the science of fire, because [the old masters] saw its great efficacy for scientific experiments in fire and flame running and bending around.

Description of nigromancy.[149]

Nigromancy is allegedly about the sacrifice of dead animals. For *nigros* is defined as dead,[150] *hydros* is water,[151] [and] *pyros* is fire.[152] Therefore it follows: for nigromancy is allegedly the sacrifice of dead animals, who certain ancient masters[153] became accustomed to comprehending the mysteries without sin. For Solomon taught that any just person could read his five books of the art without sin, but two were counted as sacrilege, for the two books of this art cannot be read without sin.[154] For that reason—

---

that they are practical arts but reside outside the normative and accepted realm of human knowledge. The *Ars Notoria*'s idiosyncratic classification term *exceptive arts* seems to have originally been intended for these divinations. Hugh of St. Victor, in the appendix to the *Didascalicon,* says magic is false knowledge and therefore "excepting" it from the order of knowledge properly speaking. See chapter III as well as Fanger, "Sacred and Secular Knowledge Systems," 167–68.

149. Or *necromancy,* the magical art of conjuring the dead for consultation. See chapter III for more details.

150. The Latin word *nigros* means "black," not dead; however, the word *nigromancy* came to be synomous with necromancy (Greek νεκρομαντεία, *nekromanteía*; Latin *necromantia*), a word deriving from νεκρός (*nekrós*), meaning "dead," and μαντεία (*manteía*), meaning "divination." Nigromancy has also been defined as "black divination" or "black magic" although these two latter definitions may be contentious.

151. That is to say, the consultation of the dead was conducted by scrying using water basins (i.e., hydromancy). Greenfield suggests that demons were evoked into a basin of water and that this water basin, a key ritual instrument, was later dropped from the magical texts. See Greenfield, *Traditions of Belief in Late Byzantine Demonology,* 160–61.

152. Necromancy (*nekromanteia*) performed by the light of an oil lamp; that is, lecanomancy (*lychnomanteia*).

153. Ancient masters refers to the sorcerers (*goetes*) who practiced sorcery (*goeteia*), which is an art that bears a strong relationship with necromancy. The reference is likely made to those sorcerers of the ancient Greco-Roman world.

154. A possible reference to *Liber Razielis,* commissioned by Alfonso X of Castile (c. 1260),

because, concerning that art presently, enough has been said—we divert to the others.

[72] *Specifically concerning the liberal arts that are to be learned through the notory art.*

The liberal arts are seven, which [the operator] is able to know and to read each one without sin. For the great philosophy is containing them and a profound mystery within. All these arts are to be known wonderfully by the aforementioned art.

[73a] *How many* notae *any art has.*[155]

For grammar has only three *notae,* dialectic two, rhetoric four, and each with distinct and accessible prayers. But on what account grammar has three, dialectic has two, rhetoric has four *notae,* we know that affirmation and attestation from King Solomon himself. For he said:

> I, marveling and reflecting in my heart what and whence that knowledge came to be, an angel of the Lord brought to me a book in which figures and prayers were written, and he divided for me the *notae* and the distinct and accessible prayers of each art, (and as we said), it is necessary for me [to understand] about how many each [art has].

[The rest of the text] is joined below:

The teaching of the angel:

> Just as children proceed through some letters of the alphabet[156] to the great arts in a tedious and burdensome space of time, and thus, you will be moved forward toward all knowledge through these increasing virtues.

which contained books attributed to Solomon. See *Sepher Raziel: Liber Salomonis,* Karr and Skinner (Singapore: Golden Hoard, 2010). Alternatively, there were also other books falsely attributed to Solomon; see appendix A7.

155. Here the word *notae* refers to the pictorial figures in this section.

156. Latin *elementa quaedam litterarum,* meaning literally "some elements of the letters."

[**73b**] *Solomon's interrogation:*

> And when I was asking, "Lord, from where, how is this, and in what kind of manner?"

The angel's response:

> The angel responded, "The hand of the Lord is a sacramental mystery, and a better conscriptor through the virtue of the Holy Spirit, inspiring, making abundant, and illuminating thought than through handbooks or the inspection of a writing'; and again, the angel [said], "Look upon those *notae* often," he said, "with their prayers according to the determined time and arrangement itself just as they are arranged by God and not otherwise."

Having said these things, [the angel] shows King Solomon the book in which all these are to be offered in their times, he demonstrated [these things] most openly according to the vision of the Lord. Upon which Solomon, having heard and seen according to the word of the angel brought from God, did all these, and he left behind for us his succeeding authority, [Apollonius of Tyana]; we observe, after him, according to [our] ability.[157]

[74] *For this reason grammar has only three* notae:[158]

Behold, on what account the art of grammar has only three *notae* in the book of Solomon [called] *Gemeliot;*[159] that is, in the book of the art of God, which is the art of all other sciences, Solomon spoke when he was inquiring one by one [about each *nota*] with awe at the hands of the angel of God, saying, "O Lord, from where will this be bestowed on me, so that I may fully know why so many and so much of this art's *notulae* with the enumerated prayers and divisions are to be ascribed to having their own efficacy?"

---

157. Notice that a scribe is speaking and providing the quotation from his source, not Pseudo-Apollonius.

158. The meaning of *notae* as referring to the pictorial figures is carried through to section 81.

159. Another lost book of Solomon. Julien Véronèse proposes that the title is formed from the Latin transliteration of the Hebrew letters *gimel* and *yod*.

It is to be read [in that place that] the angel responded:

> The art of grammar, which is called the art of letters, has three by necessity: the ordering, the corresponding distinction, that is—the construction of the cases[160] and the tenses[161]—and the adjoining of [inflectional endings] to themselves or the simple and compound forms[162] and the successive declension[163] of the parts *toward* the parts or *from* the parts [of speech] by a congruent and ordered division, whose three *notae* are appointed so wisely. For example, through one [*nota*], the entire investigation of declining, through the second, the agreement of all the parts of the same order,[164] through the third, specifically, the successive division must be had of all the simple and compound parts themselves.

[75] *Why dialectic has two* notae.

Likewise, dialectic, which is to be called the form of the arts and a dual speech, has two by necessity: the science [1] of adducing arguments eloquently and [2] of responding prudently. On that account the High One of divine providence and piety appointed two *notae,* so that through the first [figure], of adducing arguments eloquently, and through the second [figure], they may acquire the hard work[165] of responding without ambiguity. Therefore, we have written three *notae* for grammar and two for dialectic.

---

160. Like Greek, Latin is a highly inflected language. Both have cases which provide certain endings to nouns, adjectives, pronouns, and participles to denote their relationship to other words in a sentence. Latin has seven cases: nominative, vocative, genitive, dative, accusative, ablative, and locative.

161. The verb tenses, which carry an accidental quality of time; that is, the six verb tenses (present, imperfect, future, perfect, pluperfect, and future perfect). The scribe is saying the noun must agree with its verb in time.

162. In Latin, inflected parts of speech can be simple or compound.

163. Declensions are grammatical variations of nouns, adjectives, participles, and pronouns. There are five declensions in Latin, each with certain endings based on case and number, which must agree with the other parts of speech in a sentence. A regular noun can have up to sixteen forms. Latin beginners are taught to decline a noun to learn its different forms and usages.

164. For example, an adjective agrees with the noun it modifies in gender, number, and case. Likewise, a verb agrees with its subject in person and number.

165. Latin *industriam,* meaning that the student may be able to acquire the ability to work hard at responding to his opponent in an assiduous, diligent, and conscientious manner.

[76] *Why rhetoric has four* notae.

Therefore, let us see why rhetoric has four *notae*.

Moreover, as the angel of the Lord said, "Four things are necessary: [1] an ornate, neatly arranged, and florid locution,[166] [2] a competent, discrete, and ordered judgment of cases or offices, witnesses, pleads,[167] damages,[168] and judgments; [3] an ordered disposition of the same art of negotiation, and [4] an eloquence and demonstration with reason. For the art of rhetoric, therefore, the sublimity of God appoints four *notae* with his glorious and holy prayers, sent reverently by the hand of the Lord so to speak, in order that each *nota* has every faculty in the aforesaid art, so that he may attend to the first *nota* of ornate, florid, agreeable, and neatly arranged locutions in the art; the second, he may discern judgment [about what is] just and unjust, ordered and disordered, true and false; and the third, he may dispose an arrangement according to offices, cases, and personas; [and] as for the fourth, he may distribute reason and the eloquence of subtlety without prolixity in all the works of the art itself."

The conclusion of the above prayers.

Behold, for this reason, every *nota* for grammar, dialectic, and rhetoric must be placed in each art thus. We will dispose of the other arts and their *notae* and in the proper place and time, just as we find them in the book of Solomon.[169]

---

166. Latin *ornatus locutionum concinnus et floridus*. The word *concinnus* is a term from cookery with the sense of cooking from different ingredients, and the word was used as a metaphor in rhetoric to express oratorical rhythm, verbal symmetry, and the phonetic effects of a speech's composition so as to attain an agreeable harmony of all its parts. Quintilian explains in his *Institutio Oratoria* (*Institutions of Oratory*) that the Greeks had three styles (*modi*) of speech—what the Greeks call characters (*charakteres*): (1) a plain style (*ischnon*) for instruction, (2) a vigorous style (*hadron*) for a moving oration, and (3) a florid style (*antheron*) for a pleasing or conciliating discourse. See *Institutio Oratoria* 12.10.58. Thus, the third style (*floridus*) is referenced here, meaning "a florid and ornate rhetorical style (*ornatus et floridus locutionum*)."

167. Or disputing or debating.

168. Or injury or financial loss.

169. Unfortunately, due to redaction of the text at some point, none of the other arts receive the same treatment as the trivium does here with the quotations from Solomon's book, which includes a description of each figure (*nota*). The reason for this is because of redaction to the text. The *Flores Aurei* is interrupted by a fragmented letter, beginning at section 85. This letter is

[77] *The* notae *are to be inspected or offered: at what times or [in] what state, and because to learn further [without proper instruction] otherwise . . .*[170] *Although, unless [the aspirants] do it according to anyone taught [in the notory art].*

Here we must pass over to another subject, so we may discuss at what times or in what state or in what manner the *notae* of those arts are to be examined, the prayers are to be offered, or the arts themselves are to be learned. If you are totally unskilled in the art of grammar and want to have knowledge of it, and if it has been bestowed upon you by God, (so that you may be able to have this work of works[171] and art of arts), [then] it must be known to you (with the utmost subtlety), that you do not presume to do otherwise than this book has instructed you. For the book will be a master to you, and the art itself will be a mistress to you.[172]

[78a] *Of the unskilled [students] who have learned nothing and how they ought to learn in addition to the above.*

For the *notae* of the art of grammar are to be inspected and its prayers to be offered thus. Therefore, on the first day of the Moon, the first *nota* is to be inspected twelve times, and its prayers are to be recited twenty-four times with the utmost veneration of sanctity; after taking short intervals and detailed inspection of the *nota,* the prayers are to be recited twice, and observed to be exceedingly free from mistakes. Thus, it is to be done, from the first day of the Moon up to the fourteenth, and from the fourteenth[173] up to the eighteenth, the first *nota* and the second are to be inspected twenty times and the prayers recited thirty times.[174] And having made and separated the intervals, and of

then compiled with another fragment of the the *Flores Aurei* appended at the end of the treatise (sections 128–47).

170. An ellipsis indicating that something bad would happen to the operator if he does not carry out the ritual instructions properly according to this book.

171. Latin, *opus operum,* this may be the source of inspiration for the title of the derivative text by the same name.

172. The book is given the masculine form for master (*magister*) since *liber* is a masculine noun, and the art is given the feminine form for master (*magistra*) since *ars* is a feminine noun.

173. *Quartam decimam.* According to the gloss in section 78, Version B, it should read "the fifteenth" (*quintus decimus*).

174. According to the gloss in section 78, Version B, the prayers are to be prayed six times in the early morning, seven times at terce, eight times at nones, and nine times at vespers for a total of thirty times.

this art's books placed before the eyes,[175] [scrolls] unrolled and inspected, from the [eighteenth[176]] day and above, all three *notae* are to be inspected one by one at a time for twelve days and the prayers are to be recited thirty-seven times.[177]

[78b] *For those who have learned further.*

Behold, from the *notae* of the art of grammar. However, if you have read in small amounts and desire to have the complete [education] of the books of this same art, then you must do this just as it is to be taught. However, [even if you do follow the teachings by reciting] the holy prayers [of the art of grammar] and the General [prayers] for the purpose of increasing the memory, understanding, and perseverance and these [pictorial figures] that are recounted above, you still must [not] fall into sin by neglecting the appointed time and hours. Again, for as long as you do this, be careful that it is a secret, and that you have only God as your witness. With these instructions, we now arrive at the notae.[178]

[79] *Concerning the inspection and prolation of the* notae *and the observation of hese.*

Truly it must be considered, however, that at the beginning of the inspection of all the *notae*—that is, on the first day—one must fast until evening, and if it is a child, [then] he must observe it until evening, if he is able; and if he cannot be compelled to fast by his own ability, [then] this is the precept we give from the art of grammar. The two *notae* of dialectic can be offered every day, except those days that are called Egyptian.[179] However, the four *notae* of the art of rhetoric are to be offered on those days on which it was established; that is, on any day except three days of the month—the lunar days fifteen, seventeen, and nineteen, and therefore it is forbidden to offer the prayers on these days,

175. That is, having divided one's study materials according to how the grammatical knowledge is divided according to each *nota*. See section 74.

176. According to the gloss in section 78, Version B, it should read "the seventeenth."

177. The manuscript reads *tricies septies* but ought to read *tricies sex[t]ies;* that is, thirty-six. Compare to Version B, NS 10.

178. The figures (*notae*) of the art of grammar are missing here. As the *Ars Notoria* was redacted and compiled anew, the figures were repositioned to the end of the treatise, which this book calls the "*Notae* Supplement." A comparsion between the *Notae* Supplement of Version A against Version B can be found in the appendix A2, "Magical Figures of the Ars Notoria."

179. A form of calendar prognostication, Egyptian days signify misfortune and bad luck. Certain activities were avoided on these days. See appendix A4, "Medieval Computations of Time."

because, as Solomon himself attests, the *notae* of all the arts except the *notae* of that art have been removed on those days. These precepts are to be observed courteously.

[80] *How the* notae *of dialectic are to be inspected [and the prayers to be recited].*
It is to be understood, however, when the *notae* of the art of dialectic are to be inspected, and their prayers are to be recited twenty times on that very day, and at intervals with the books of the same art of dialectic placed before one's eyes.

Also, concerning the notae *of rhetoric.*
The books of the art of rhetoric should be placed before our eyes when we look at the *notae* of the same art and when the prayers of the same art are recited as defined.[180] These are sufficient for the learning of those three arts.

[81] *How the sinner is abstaining from sin.*

[Abstinence from sin] must be achieved before one begins [inspecting] the first *nota* of the art of grammar. Some are to be inspected beforehand insofar as learning may be able to be had by the first, second, and third *notae;* it is necessary to consider and to know the beginning of the first *nota,* because on that day which the *notae* of either grammar or dialectic or rhetoric are to be inspected, it is necessary that he is to abstain and guard himself from all sin by the greatest willpower.

[82] Behold, having finished the Generals, the Specials begin at the beginning of the prayers, [that is] the words of Solomon according to the impetration[181] with respect to the Lord concerning the foregoing *notae* of the three arts.[182]

O light, truth,[183] way, justice, compassion, fortitude, patience, preserve, help, and have mercy, amen.

---

180. Section 79.

181. *Impetration,* an obsolete term once used in ancient Roman law and meaning "to obtain by request or entreaty."

182. The preamble prayer is associated with Solomon's impetration to the Lord, see section 73. The three arts are grammar, logic, and rhetoric.

183. *Lux veritas,* the first prayer given before the Special prayers of the *notae.*

[83] What we have said concerning the first three headwords must be pronounced before all General and Special *notae.*[184] Thus, when you say the prayers themselves on their specified days, if you want to work from the *notae* as has been shown beforehand to you, it is necessary that all the prayers be said once before noon for each day of the entire month, and yet, you must say the *notae*'s own prayers before each *nota,*[185] and when you want to begin writing, reading, or teaching, do as you have been told.

[84] *Of the recitation of a single art.*

It is to be understood, that if you want to know something from a single art, the prayers of that art are to be pronounced at their specified time. We have said enough concerning the three liberals.

[85] *This institution grants complete knowledge concerning the seven* notae *of philosophy.*

Behold, nothing in those *notae* is to be observed except in the first four days concerning the remaining four liberal arts.

---

184. Section 7.

185. Here *notae* is possessive, in which the knowledge possesses its own prayers. Therefore, the words *nota* and *notae* are understood as the knowledge contained in both the prayers and their figures. The phrase "you must say the *notae*'s own prayers (*orationes notis proprias dices*)" indicates the prayers. Next, "before each *nota* (*ante notas singulas*)" clearly indicates the pictorial figure.

2

[Fragmented Supplements]

The Explement of the Entire Art[1]

Of the seven notae of philosophy.

The seven notae of philosophy that you saw with the sciences below them[2] contained the lunar days seven, seventeen, and twenty-seven with the prayers, which are to be pronounced and repeated seven times for each of their own days.

Of the nota *of awe.*[3]

---

1. The *Flores Aurei,* which was about to introduce the prayers and figures of philosophy, the four liberal arts, and the general sciences, is abruptly interrupted by a fragmented letter sent to an unknown addressee who had questions about the *Flores Aurei.* The letter contains supplementary material about philosophy, the four liberal arts, and the general sciences, followed by the *Ars Nova* and the little book of nine prayers called the *novem termini* (nine ends). The opening and closing of the letter is missing; it appears to begin somewhere in its middle, seen here as starting at section 85 and ending at section 127. See chapter II about the historic origins and development of the *Ars Notoria.*

2. The verb "you saw" (*vidisti*) is the first indication of a lacuna, or text that is missing, as the reader has not yet encountered the *notae* of philosophy or the sciences contained below them in the hierarchy of knowledge (i.e., the quadrivium, the general sciences, or even medicine). This lacuna and the others that follow are one indicator that this is no longer the original *Flores Aurei* but another text entirely.

3.Latin, *nota terroris.* The *nota* of awe is an alternate title for either the first figure of philosophy or the third figure of the general sciences. *Terroris* can also mean fear or dread. To understand this title in its Judeo-Christian context, consider Proverbs 1:7, which reads, "The fear of the Lord is the beginning of knowledge." In the biblical sense, fear means having great reverence for God; also, because God is all-powerful, it is prudent to be a little fearful of God's might. Likewise, the "*nota* of awe" must confer reverence and fear upon its viewer.

And the prayer of awe,[4] that you know, just as we have said to you,[5] is to be pronounced with silence and dread, but it is a holy sacrament.

Of the nota *of God.*[6]

But the *nota* of God, whose title I appointed, is to be inspected and repeated always in the neomenia, that is; in the new Moon.[7]

[86] *For your protection in the* notae *of the four liberals.*
It is to be understood concerning the prayers of the four liberals, that when you pronounce those very prayers, you should live chastely and soberly during their [appointed] days.

Of the ineffable nota.[8]

But the *nota,* having twenty-four nooks with its sign,[9] and has its own fullness and perfection with respect to the Old and New Testaments. Nevertheless, it must be pronounced just as you heard in the part thus.[10] Yet, this stands firm by itself because whenever you repeat it, all the prayers, (which theology has), are to be recited twice, even though the prayers must come together, [and] every prayer is to be pronounced one at a time, one by one, just as we have said. Truly, just as we have said to you, whenever you want to investigate about a great theology through a more satisified love, repeat the prayer that we said, and pronounce the rest of the other prayers of theology with [their] times just as you wanted, having so much of the sacraments for the efficacy.

---

4. Latin *nota temporis et terroris* ("the prayer of time and awe") is the special title given by Mellon 1.

5. The letter writer is making a reference to an earlier part of his letter about the *nota* of awe that is now missing. In this small passage, the meaning of *nota* refers to both the prayer and its pictorial figure.

6. The first figure (*nota*) of the general sciences.

7. The first mention of the "new Moon" has *neomenia* (from the Greek *noumenia*) and the second has the Latin *nova Luna*.

8. The fifth figure (*nota*) of theology.

9. There are twenty-four nooks or angles (*angulos*) along the perimeter of the figure (*nota*). The sign is the cross of Jesus Christ. In Version B, angels are depicted each holding a cross, surrounding the figures.

10. The part referenced here is missing from the text. It indicates that the text is redacted and there must be a lacuna somewhere. See chapter II, "The Mythical and Material story of the *Ars Notoria*."

[87] *Of the exceptive and mechanical arts.*

And from the *notae*[11] of the general [sciences] and their prayers, you must know that whenever you want to know [something] about the exceptives or the adulterine [arts],[12] you will pronounce a general [science] *nota* itself and its prayers ten times for each day, having made intervals,[13] and having inspected the books of those arts, just as it is said about the others, and by whatever day you wanted, you will be able to work just as it is said above.[14] Before, however, you wanted to work that something perfectly within the art itself, you knew everything which is to be said in the first three headwords; that is, the prayers themselves, you say for seven days, seven times each day,[15] having made intervals, and to have read over and inspected the books of all the arts which you wanted, [then] afterward to work in the arts just as you wanted, and just as it is said for you.

[88] *It is necessary to pronounce from the prayers of the three headwords just like [it is to be performed] before each* nota.

Now, the initial knowledge given is from all the *notae*[16] and from the

---

11. Here the meaning of *notae* refers to the pictorial figures and is carried through to the first part of section 88.

12. The letter writer uses the word *adulterinis* as synomynous with the exceptives and the mechanical arts. Because these all fall under the category of the *generalia* (i.e., the general sciences), which are those middle sciences situated between the natural sciences and the mathematical sciences in the Aristotelian model of philosophy (see chapter III), then the mechanical arts here are the practical arts of science, including the exceptives of necromancy and astrology and their sub-sciences (see section 71); indeed, the science of weights, measures, and machines with moving joints and parts (also called "mechanical") is included as a middle science. Excluded are the seven mechanical arts as listed by Hugh of St. Victor (i.e., tailoring, agriculture, warfare, navigation, hunting, medicine, and theatrics).

13. Version A does not supply enough information, so it is necessary to consult Version B to help reconstruct what might have been in the original instructions of Version A. Section 88 gloss explains that the first and second prayers for the general sciences are to be said five times from morning to noon; likewise, the third and fourth prayers belonging to the general sciences are to be said five times from noon to the evening. Thus, altogether the prayers are pronounced ten times for each day of that lunar month.

14. Here is another lacuna. See chapter V, "Analysis of the Figures."

15. Section 88 gloss explains that the first seven days prior to the beginning of a lunar month are meant for the first three headwords (i.e., *Helyscemath, Phos Megalos,* and *Lux mundi*), followed by other prayers, and ought to be said seven times by any day.

16. Here the meaning of *notae* refers to the prayers, and this sense is carried through to the end of the section.

headwords belonging to [all] the prayers, and it is almost completed, and just as you have the completion of them. You will know this because in pronouncing the general prayers, or the *notae* themselves, the prayers of the [first] three headwords are [also] to be pronounced.[17]

[89] Behold [we now speak] of the remaining four other liberal arts that are to be described. If you want to have a complete knowledge of them, you must do so in this way: you say the fifth prayer of theology after the prayers of each *nota*. This is enough for you to understand and know. And also, you must know the prayers of the three headwords that ought to be pronounced before each *nota* of every art, just as it was determined, [and] how to protect [yourself] and perform [the work].

[90] There are these [seven] augmentations[18] of the [five] prayers[19] to which the *notae* of all the liberal and exceptive arts, except the mechanics,[20] belong and are ascribed specifically to theology.[21] For they are to be proclaimed in this way, so that when you repeat and inspect each *nota* of each art and its prayers, you must say the prayers themselves.

This first prayer is useful for whichever art, for it is to be said for all seven arts whenever you have said these prayers, inspected their notae, *and specifically [offered them] for the purpose of theology.*[22]

---

17. The first three headwords (i.e., *Helyscemath, Phos Megalos,* and *Lux mundi*). This passage does not specify any class of prayer, but is referring to the prayers overall.

18. The seven prayers belonging to philosophy.

19. The five prayers of theology that are: *Omnipotens incomprehensibilis; Adoro te rex regum; Otheos,* with its Latin prologue, *Pie Deus, Pie Pater;* and *Hosel* (Version B has *Deus vivorum*).

20. Here the letter writer mentions the mechanical arts, which are those practical arts associated with artisans and often involve manual labor (i.e., tailoring, agriculture, warfare, navigation, hunting, medicine, and theatrics). According to the letter writer, the mechanical arts are not part of the notory art's curriculum nor are they associated with theology. This is a different sense of the word *mechanic* than previously used in section 87.

21. In section 102, the writer further explains that he views the seven prayers of philosophy (sections 90–101) as augmentations of the five prayers of theology; therefore, he views them all under the discipline of theology. This is a distinctly Christian view that Lady Philosophy is the handmaiden to Theology, because it was understood that all wisdom proceeds from God. Thus, the study of wisdom was the study of theology.

22. What follows are the seven prayers attributed to philosophy.

Giezeomos, Azaiatan, Ezenotes,[23] Zamazaiaton, Ezenogor, Gromonai, Ziphararin, Fabogeton, Seremial, Sicramazan, Achonamathos, Ethelemiaton, Zanna, Zazai, Gizithios, Megalon, Cratruit, Amen.

[91] *That is part of the same prayer's exposition.*

O Lord the incomprehensible,[24] invisible, immortal, intelligible God, whose appearance the angels, archangels, and heavenly hosts desire to see ardently, for whose majesty I exercise my ability eternally and continually, adoring him, the living God, forever and ever, amen.

[92] *This is the second prayer [of philosophy to be said] before all the individual* notae, *the exposition of same.*

O Lord God, holy Father[25] almighty, hear my petitions today and incline your ears to my prayer,[26] Semon, Gezomelion, Samac, Gezacarin, Zeamiot, Lezeator, Sannamai, Gezeel, Gezietiel.

[93] *This is the end of the second prayer [of philosophy].*

O God, always the way, the life, and the truth,[27] let the light of the Holy Spirit flourish in my conscience and my mind that the gift of your working may shine and illuminate my heart and my soul now and forever and ever, amen.

[94] *This is the third prayer [of philosophy], which is to be said before the* notae.

Leomagoton,[28] Azacar, Azannacar, Zegomathai, Zachavo, Legemozon, Lempodomoton, Acheraos, Eliesion, Nadelabor, Lammandi, Gemecor, Ellemai, Gezetromai, Colomanos, Amen, Amen.

---

23. *Ezethomos,* the first prayer belonging to the first *nota* of philosophy.
24. *Domine Deus incomprehensibilis,* the Latin prologue belonging to the first prayer of philosophy.
25. *Domine Deus Sancte Pater,* the prayer belonging to the second *nota* of philosophy.
26. Psalm 5 (NRSV).
27. *Deus semper via vita veritas,* the Latin prologue belonging to the second *nota* of philosophy.
28. *Lemogethon,* the prayer belonging to the third *nota* of philosophy.

[95] *This is the end of the same prayer.*

O life of [man[29] and] all creatures visible and invisible, O God, O eternal brightness of the heavenly spirits, the unfailing salvation of men, and the origin of piety, who knows all before they are made, who judges all things that are seen, and yet are not, and all things that are unseen, and yet are, you discern with an ineffable disposition; may I glorify your ineffable holy name in my heart, strengthen my understanding and my intelligence, augment my memory and strengthen my eloquence, deliver my tongue expedite in the sciences and in your [holy] scriptures, so that having been conferred with the faculty from you, and the wisdom of your teaching, marked in my heart, may I praise and acknowledge you and love your name forever and ever, amen.

[96] *This is the fourth prayer [of philosophy].*

O King of kings,[30] O God of infinite mercy, immense bestower and disposer of all lasting foundations, lay the foundation of your virtues within me, and take away the foolishness of the heart, so that my senses are made firm in the love of your charity, and my spirit be formed in the restoration and renewal of your will; you who live and reign, God, forever and ever, amen.

[97] *The teaching of the fourth prayer [of philosophy].*

These are the prayers that ought to be offered, and are always to be given together whenever they are offered. The remaining four liberal [arts] are necessary, but they are particularly pertinent to theology.[31] When you want to pronounce the general [science] *nota* or the *nota*[32] of some liberal art with its own prayers, you must say those first four prayers together once a day. However, when you want to practice with respect to the *notae* of theology, just as we said,[33] you must say the same prayers before each and every *nota* seven times,

---

29. *Vita hominum,* the Latin prologue to *Leomegoton.*

30. *Rex regum,* the prayer belonging to the fourth *nota* of philosophy. Oddly, this prayer does not contain any *voces magicae.*

31. Latin *theologiam.* The text reads "theology," but it is best understood as "philosophy" as the passage is speaking about the seven prayers belonging to philosophy.

32. Here *nota* refers to the prayers, and this sense is carried through to the end of the section.

33. Again, the Christian letter writer views philosophy as subservient to theology. The "*notae* of theology" (*notis theologiae*) to which he refers are those belonging to philosophy. See section 85.

and if you want to learn or to demonstrate[34] some science, such as by repeating, versifying, singing, instrumentalizing, or by other [acts] of this kind, you are to rehearse that science. First rehearse the prayers themselves, so that you might read them wherever. If a boy is of lesser undertstanding, read before him, so that he rereads after you word for word. If he has greater understanding, let him read them seven times for the seven days, and if you want to offer the general [science] *nota* with its prayers, offer the same prayers, and it will be of much benefit to you. For the virtue is of the prayers themselves. If perhaps they are to be said before everything, and even a long speech, some of them are said to have great efficacy. Solomon said of those prayers, "No one must presume to say those prayers alone, except on account of the offices to which they are established."[35]

[98] *The fifth prayer [of philosophy] begins.*

O God the immeasurable Father,[36] from whom proceeds all that is good, whose magnitude of mercy is incomprehensible, hear my prayers that I bring before your sight today, and deliver the joy of your salvation to me today, so that I may teach the disadvantaged the way of your knowledge, and may the rebellious and the unbelievers be converted to you, so that what I recall with the heart and the mouth, I remember. Having been rooted in me, it has a foundation, so that I may be regarded as efficacious and as having been helped in your works, amen.

[99] *The sixth prayer [of philosophy] begins, before the prayers themselves [which] belong to the* nota *of awe or the* nota *of God, [those prayers] having been recited five times.*[37]

---

34. Or teach. This meaning carries on through the rest of the sentence.

35. Section 60.

36. *Deus Pater immense [. . . magnitudo],* the prayer belonging to the fifth *nota* of philosophy.

37. In consulting Version B for further clarification of this passage, what might be intended here is that which is found in Version B's fourth month in which the operator offers the ritual formula of the five prayers belonging to the fifth, sixth, and seventh *notae* of philosophy once before commencing the operation of the four general sciences. In that operation, if the operator is working from the early morning up to noon, then the first and second figures are to be inspected (the first *nota* of the general sciences which has been identified as the *nota* of God) and the prayers offered five times. Also, in that same operation, if the operator is working from noon up to the evening, then the third and fourth figures are to be inspected (the third *nota* of the general sciences then

Gezomaton,[38] Agiathar, Iezaziel, Gechonai, Samasaiel, Gezomiatel, Segomazar, Azomaton, Gezacor, Eiazar, Samin, Elielsilot, Gezamatar, Gechorozamai, Samiel, Esemiel, Sochozamai, Sanna, Rabiathos, Aminos.

[**100**] *This is the end of the same prayer.*

O [God the] eternal king,[39] the judge and discerner of all things, the one who acknowledges the good sciences, instruct me today through your holy name and through these holy mysteries, make my mind illustrious, so that your knowledge, just like water, enters into my innermost being, just like oil in my bones,[40] through you, O God, the Savior of all, amen.

[**101**] The seventh prayer begins, which is the end of the prayers and their supplement,[41] especially with respect to the ineffable *nota* that is the last of theology, having twenty-four nooks. This is the beginning of the prayer; but it must be understood first that although it is applicable to all the *notae,* it is especially applicable to the ineffable *nota*.

The prayer begins.

O God, the creator of all piety[42] and the foundation of all things, the eternal salvation and redemption of the people,[43] the inspirer of sciences and the immense bestower of the arts, from whose office mercy comes, so that you may still deem us worthy, your servants of the sciences, to inspire [personal] growth, for whom you granted to me, a miserable sinner, to know the mystery; guard my soul and free my heart from the thoughts of this depraved world and the incitements of every libidinous pleasure or fornication within me; extinguish and repress forcefully, so that I may be delighted in your sciences and arts, I may be delighted in them, and

---

being identified as the *nota* of awe) and the prayers offered five times.

38. *Gezomothon,* the prayer belonging to the sixth *nota* of philosophy; see also NS 113.

39. *Rex aeternae Deus,* the Latin prologue belonging to the prayer of the sixth *nota* of philosophy; see also NS 114. Latin Prayer, JP p. 153.

40. Psalms 109:18 (NRSV).

41. Latin *explementum*. See page 271, footnote 60 for the letter writer's analogy of geometry to the notory art.

42. *Deus totius pietatis,* the prayer belonging to the seventh *nota* of philosophy.

43. Or the parish (perhaps in the global sense).

give to me the petition of my heart, so that I may love you, having been strengthened and exalted in your glorification, and the power of the Holy Spirit may be increased in me through your salvation and the reward of the faithful for the salvation of my soul and body, amen.

[102] *The prayer is set forth. The teachings of the* nota *for the first, second, third, fourth, and fifth of theology begin.*[44]

Those seven prayers, which we have set forth, are the augmentations of the remaining prayers, and they ought to and are able to be spoken before all the *notae* of theology,[45] but nevertheless, they are to be pronounced, especially before the ineffable *nota,* as we have said. Those supplements[46] are of those you asked about and the sufficiency to which we direct you to test along with the observation and authority of Solomon. Behold, because you have postulated something of the mystery of the *notae,* and you have this, especially concerning the ineffable *nota.*

[103] *The design of the ineffable* nota.

The explanation of the swords, flowers, trees, birds, candelabra, and serpents is given in the figure itself in its nooks through the forms. Solomon received this *nota* of peacemaking depicted on a golden folio[47] from the Lord, and he heard from the Lord, "Do not doubt or be alarmed, and this is a great sacramental mystery for all," and the Lord added, "When you have inspected that *nota* and read its prayers, observe the commandments that are given above, and inspect what you have read diligently." Still, take heed for yourself in the *nota* of awe, in the *nota* of God, and in the ineffable *nota,* so that whatever you inspected and whatever came to you through a vision, you must keep secret and guard, and when the great angel of the Lord appeared to you bearing the sign of the cross on a standard, guard the words which he has ineffably shown written to you, and whatever appeared to you in all

44. The teachings of the prayers (*notae*) for the first, second, third, and fourth of theology are missing.

45. The letter writer reaffirms his perspective that the seven prayers of philosophy are an extension of the five prayers of theology.

46. Latin *explementa.* For the analogy of geometry as it relates to the instruction of the notory art, see page 271, footnote 60.

47. That is, a golden page from the divinely revealed book of the notory art.

these *notae* similarly, observe with the utmost attention,[48] and pronounce the prayers, just as it is said thus: say and repeat at the two determined hours.[49] Still, you have the parts of the great prayer as far as it has been taught; divide and make intervals, just as it was said to you above. After you have said them, act wisely and chastely on that day. But if you do anything unchaste, [then] some danger is imminent. There is something greater that we marvel at from certain other *notae* and their prayers, and [those greater things] come into being through [the *notae*] themselves, which is to be considered in the Specials.

[**104**] *These are the ineffable words of the prayer to the fifth* nota *itself.*

Hosel,[50] Aziatol, Gerner, Gezamier, and they are given after the *notae* of all arts, and they are to be said four times, especially to theology.

[**105**] This is the explement of the entire art,[51] but because it is necessary to say or declare something more fully about the explement of the entire work, we must complete it more clearly, having mentioned it beforehand. I have shown the given and *almost* perfect knowledge of all the initial arts. Behold, on what account have I said "almost"? Indeed I have said ["almost"], because some flowery and neatly arranged institutions of this work remain still further, the first of which is this.

[**106**] When you want to work from all the arts generally, just as it has been demonstrated above, and diligently observe the new Moons[52] in the pronunciation of the *notae* with their own prayers. Also, you will observe the fourth Moon in the pronunciation of all the prayers of theology. Whenever the fourth Moon

48. The angel who appears within one's dream vision will present important words and instructions to the operator in which he is to say and follow; therefore, it is imperative that the operator pays attention lest he forgets upon awakening.

49. See Version B 97 gloss about the noon hour and the ninth hour.

50. The prayer belonging to the fifth *nota* of theology.

51. The explement is the remainder of subtracting an angle from a full circle. His commentary represents the explement. Following Boethius and ancient grammarians, the letter writer is using an analogy of geometry to the instructions given for the notory art. The full circle represents the entire instruction on the art, and his commentary acts as a supplement to it. He continues the analogy by saying he must complete the circle; that is, finish his commentary.

52. *Neomenias,* from Greek.

is in efficacious position for an urgent work, look into the books more acutely, and you may listen to the writings themselves.[53]

[107] Moreover, it is to be understood that if you will not be able to have the books on hand, or if there were no opportunities given to you for [the books] themselves to be inspected, [then] on that account the effect of the operation will not be less. However, the headwords (about which you doubted or perhaps are still uncertain of) are to be pronounced as it has been said, just as it is taught in the books above. Furthermore, you must know this, because we have instituted the holy words which are to be said before the deathbed of the sick for the purpose of an experiment of death or life,[54] and also, if you wanted to do nothing else from the entire corpus of the art than to be able to test the above, and if you wanted, you will be able to attempt making an experiment when and as often as you want according to the [angelic] vision.[55]

[108] There are these which are to be done and observed especially when you wanted to work from theology besides those which are instituted to you briefly, no day is to be observed. Also, all those times are an agreement for the *notae*[56] and prayers from which a definition of the times is not given. However, that [institution of the times] remains in that place for the pronunciation of the three liberal arts or the operation of the *notae* themselves; by chance, if you pass over the previous institution on some day, [and] if you will be able to observe the rest [of the hours], even if you were passing over two [hours], on that account, the work will not be made void; and observe the days of the Moon rather than the hours in greater numbers, from where Solomon says, "If you passed over the hours in one day or two, you must not be deterred with terror thenceforth," and just as it has been defined to work from the general headings, that is enough on these things. However, you must not forget any occasion and the words I have proposed to you which are at the beginning of making speeches or readings

53. That is, in the form of university lectures. The "urgent work" refers to section 147.

54. Sections 28–30 and footnote there.

55. The instructions for attaining the first angelic vision through dream incubation referenced here is missing from the text. It indicates that the text is redacted and there must be a lacuna somewhere. Clearly, the letter writer had access to a now lost portion of the *Flores Aurei*. See chapter II, "Elements of the Ars Notoria." For the gloss(es) on the angelic vision, see page 459.

56. Here the word *notae* refers to the pictorial figures.

which are to be read, acquired and taught,[57] for through them they have an effect, and you will be able to work frequently the sacramental words of the [angelic] vision. But if you wanted to begin the work from the whole corpus of the art as it has been defined, recite it from the heading from which the definition is given according to the situation.

[109] *Instruction.*

Likewise, it is to be understood that you will be able to work so much through them concerning theology. Yet, inspect half a *nota*[58] and repeat the prayers of theology above five times. And if you stopped [offering and inspecting] the rest from the entire work, [then] this will be able to confer the effect of the great writings for you. Indeed, it is necessary that you have the *nota,* having the twenty-four nooks, with their own prayers always in memory, and just as we said to you above, which you saw in the prognosticating angel through the vision; keep it under your safekeeping and under the battle with the faithful.[59]

---

57. That is, the prayers belonging to the lesser rituals.

58. Here the word *nota* refers to the figure, and this sense is carried through to the end of the section.

59. In other words, the letter writer is admonishing his addressee to not share his visionary experiences with anyone and to keep it secret, especially in the ongoing religious or spiritual battle between the faithful believers (such as the practitioners of the notory art) and evil forces or other religious opponents. The phrase *sub custodia tua* (under your guard) recalls the more well-known phrase for secrecy, *sub rosa* (under the rose).

[Ars Nova]

[110] *The New Art of Solomon begins.*
There are these [prayers] that are a supplement[60] to the preceding work. This [is the] beginning of the secret prayers that Solomon called the *Ars Nova.*

[111] For those prayers can and should be said before all things especially and before all things generally. Even if you wanted to work without the other headings from the prefaced [notory] art, you will be able to have great knowledge in any art by saying the prayers themselves in [their proper] time and order. In the prayers themselves neither the days nor the times nor the Moon are to be observed, but nevertheless, it especially ought to be observed that that those prayers are offered on which days, it is to be observed from sins, criminal offenses, lechery, gluttony, and especially, superfluous oaths. Something is to be preceded before [presenting] these [prayers], which is to be mentioned beforehand of a fuller and more complete knowledge of the prayers themselves is to be had, whence Solomon said in the golden book, "I did fear those prayers that I was about to offer, lest I was offending the Lord, and I established for myself the time in which I should begin in order to live more chastely and work more virtuously with them."

[112a] These are the preambles of their prayers before those, yet I wanted to place them [separate] from those you doubted,[61] as one to one, placed in its proper order, making them clear apart from any distinction. These are those about which you doubted, either [of the two] headwords of philosophy (with everything below its own contents apart from the rest) ought to be offered, and they can be offered by the measurement of the times. Indeed, they can, and just as we mentioned beforehand, they are able to do so in this way. But this is to be understood, but if, following the intention[62] which, I believe has been collated for you by God, and I know the matter mentioned beforehand above you determined to regard more crafty, there are few or none to be doubted from

60. Latin *explementum.*

61. Section 107.

62. The intention of God and the angel who appeared to the letter writer, who now communicates about the prayers to the addressee.

those [given] to you hereafter. However, I have not placed the end [of the text] for you, for which I established the end, having corrected writings according to the [angelic] vision, you may not question.[63]

[**112b**] *Instruction.*

If by chance you want to begin an affair so exalted and so necessary, I believe when you have six weekdays for the beginning of this work (as it is disposed by you yourself), it is good to perform fasting for three-days beforehand, whether the desires are good or bad of this volition are to be shown divinely.

[**113**] For these [preparations] were instituted in ancient times of religious observance before every good operation. But if there is some other thing about which you are doubting, having had full consideration of the effect of the first three or four subsequent liberal arts, and if you considered and pronounced the prayers, headings, and *notae* according to how it was described above, and if you neglected something unknowingly, you will be able to be reconciled by the spiritual virtue of the subsequent prayers.

[**114a**] For these are the prayers about which the Lord said to Solomon, "See, for example, if you presumptuously or unknowingly transgressed against the sacrament of those prayers, [then] you must speak more reverently and subtly." And the great angel said about the prayers themselves, "This is a sacrament of God because it is sent to you through my hand." According to the parable, while the great king Solomon was offering an appeasing sacrament upon the golden altar in the sight of the Lord, he saw a book wrapped in a cloth, and ten prayers written in the book, and on each prayer a sign of a golden seal. And he heard in the spirit, "There are things that God has sealed and that he has closed off for a long period of time from the hearts of the unfaithful." The king did fear lest he was offending the Lord, and he guarded them.

[**114b**] It is not the will of God for the prayers themselves to be said by the unfaithful nor to be worked from themselves, but by he who wants to acquire

63. The letter writer keeps his own visionary experience of the angel secret and will not share it with his addressee.

some great or particular matter of knowledge in the arts or in some art. If he is not able to possess the work above,[64] he may say these prayers to every and whichever time he will want, the first three for the three liberal arts especially each one for each, or generally all three for the three, just as they are said; that is, you may say [according to] whichever time you will want, and the four subsequent ones for the four subsequent liberal arts to a similar manner. And by chance, if you had the entire corpus of the art, [then] you will be able to pronounce the prayers without some definition of the times themselves, before each art and before the prayers and their *notae* as often as you want to pronounce fully, secretly, plainly, and yet for you, [the operation] must be lived soberly and chastely in the pronunciation of them.

[115] *This is the first prayer that, along with the following, is valid for almost all headings and notae.*

O all-powerful, incomprehensible,[65] indivisible God, I adore your holy name today, I am an unworthy and most miserable sinner, extolling my understanding and my reason at your holy temple of heavenly Jerusalem, and I stand before you today, O my God, showing you, my God and my creator, and myself, your rational creature, I call upon your renowned clemency, so that the Holy Spirit may visit my infirmity today. O Lord my God—who bestowed upon your servants, Moses and Aaron, your efficacious teaching through the alphabet of letters of the outer laws—today confer on me the grace of a superior sweetness by which you stirred up your servants the prophets. And just as you were able to bestow the teaching on them quickly, extend the knowledge to me, a proposer of law,[66] as much as I desire, and cleanse my conscience of dead works, and cleanse my heart to be understood, open, and extend my understanding in the right way, you who has deemed worthy to create me in your image and likeness; listen to me in your justice, and teach me in your truth, and restore my soul with knowledge according to your great mercy, just like walking within a multitude of your mercies, may I

64. That is, the *Flores Aurei.*

65. *Omnipotens incomprehensibilis,* the first prayer of the *Ars Nova.*

66. *Lator,* meaning "someone who proposes a law," or "a bearer," or "law-carrier." These all describe the duties of a notary, a legislator, or other legal professional. The petitioner identifies the parallel between his legal profession with that of the law-giver Moses and Aaron the high priest.

take delight in your great works; may I please you in the admiration of your commandments, so that according to the work of your grace, having been helped and restored, you will exalt my heart and my conscience, having been cleansed, I may trust in you, and feast sumptuously in your sight, and may I exalt your name because it is good in the sight of your holy ones; sanctify me today, so that I may live in faith, perfected hope, and constant charity, learning as much as I desire, having attained an exulted knowledge, having been strengthened [and] illuminated, may I love you and may I get to know you, and may I know and I will have prudence and I will understand [things] about your secrets which you permitted to be known by men; O Jesus Christ, the only begotten Son of God, to whom the Father gave everything in hand before the ages, give to me today on account of your glorious, ineffable, and holy name, the provision[67] of the soul and of the body, a suitable and sharp-witted, unfettered, loose, and fluent tongue, so that whatever I will ask in your mercy and will be dispensed, and may all my actions stand rooted and strengthened in your pleasure; open to me, O Lord the God and the Father of my life, open to me the fountain you opened to the first man, Adam, and that you opened to your servants Abraham, Isaac, and Jacob for the purpose of understanding, discerning, and judging; accept, O Lord, for me this day the petitions and prayers of all your saints and all the heavenly hosts, so that I may be constantly taught by all your writings.

[**116**] *The second prayer for understanding.*

I adore you, O King of kings[68] and Lord of lords, O eternal unchangeable king, understand today the cry of my spirit and the groaning of my heart, so that you will change my understanding and you will give me a heart of flesh instead of stone; O my Lord and Savior may I breathe you in. O Lord, wash my interior [self] with your new spirit, and place your good holy understanding for my poor understanding of the flesh, and take away what is evil from me, changing me into a new man, so that the love with which you restored me with your salvation, and may it yield an increase to my intelligence; O Lord, listen for my prayer today, which I cry out to you, and open the eyes

---

67. Latin *instrumentum*. NS 126 reads *nutrimentum* (nourishment).

68. *Adoro te, rex regum,* the second prayer of the *Ars Nova*.

of my flesh and mind, so that by considering, understanding, and guarding the wonders from the scriptures of your laws, vivified in your justifications, may I prevail in the sight of devils, the adversaries of the faithful; O Lord my God, listen to me, and be propitious to me, you who formed me, show me your mercy today, and offer to me the vessel of salvation, so that I may drink and be satisfied from the fountain of your grace, you who are God, as having obtained the psalm[69] with understanding from the scriptures, and I will understand in an immaculate way, so that the grace of the Holy Spirit may come and rest within me, amen.

[117] *The third prayer for stability of mind.*

I confess[70] to you today, I the accused and unworthy, O God the Father of heaven and earth, creator of all visible and invisible creatures, the dispenser and bestower of all virtues and good graces, you conceal your knowledge and wisdom from the proud and the false, humble my heart today, and make my understanding and my mind stable, make my conscience love you, and stamp the light of your countenance over me today, O Lord, so that I may be made absolutely restored and understanding in your commandments and cleansed from the dead works of my sins, and may I prevail in the holy scriptures; O most merciful and all-powerful God, test me, burn my kidneys and my heart[71] today, and visit me today, O grace of the Holy Spirit, by the fire of your visitation, and gird my loins[72] with the fortitude of your steadfastness, and give the pastoral staff of confirmation[73] in

---

69. The second *nota* of theology may be intended to study and know biblical scriptures such as the Psalms. One interpretation is that the phrase "and I will come to know . . . with understanding and knowledge" actually presented an ellipsis for the operator to fill in his request.

70. *Confiteor,* the third prayer of the *Ars Nova.*

71. Psalms 26:2 (Vulgate). The kidneys and the heart both represent the essence or psyche of a person according to the ancient Hebrews. The phrase "burn my kidneys" means that the petitioner is asking God to burn away his impure passions by means of a test. See Eknoyan, *The Kidneys in the Bible.*

72. A Hebrew idiom commonly found throughout the Bible, meaning to prepare oneself for action, hard labor, or combat. In biblical times, the tunic, flowing down to the ankles, would be gathered up by folding and knotting the fabric at the waist.

73. The pastoral staff or crosier is a staff with a hooked end similar to a shepherd's crook and carried by a bishop to represent his religious authority. The crosier comes from the Staff of Moses, which Moses used in performing miracles as recorded in the Old Testament. Here, the writer petitions God to make him knowledgeable in bibical law just like Moses.

my right hand concerning the writings of your laws, and direct my mind in your teachings, and strengthen my spirit in the work of your hands, so that by rooting out the vices and filth of my sins I may prevail and be made stronger in the joy of your mercy; O Lord, inspire me today, a breath of life,[74] and increase my mind, my understanding, and my reasoning through the Holy Spirit and constancy, so that having been exercised, my spirit may be made strong and vigorous in the works of your scriptures. O Lord, see and consider the labor of my mind today, and let your will be kind to me, and send to me the Holy Spirit, a comforter to the earth, from heaven, so that she may fortify me with a perpetual stability for the present and common [time], and may she confer upon me in understanding the help which I desire for my defense, amen.

[118] *The fourth prayer which is a great one of Solomon for accomplishing every good work.*

Otheos,[75] Athamaziel, Gezomi, Saziel, Sazamai, Geternamai, Salathiel, Gozomiel, Megal, Nathamian, Iamazair, Sephonai, Mois, Ranna, Zaramaen, Gezonomai, Amamin, Delot, Azememelot, Chades, Baruc, Semor, Gezeron, Malaparos, Ellamai, Merai.

[119] O pious God,[76] O merciful God, O gentle God, O all-powerful God, make me to believe all things [are] possible today,[77] help my incredulity, and have mercy on me today, just as you pitied the penitent Adam, to whom you conferred knowledge suddenly through your many mercies, confer to me today through your omnipotent mercy as much knowledge as I desire, so that, pleased with the magnificence of your works, I may perceive the efficacy and virtue of your powers; O most gracious Father, attend to my work, and instruct me, benevolently; O most gentle one, always the only begotten Son of God, favor and strengthen me; O Holy Spirit the first God to God, breath [and] make firm my work today, and teach me, so that I may walk in the scriptures of God, and may I glo-

74. Latin *spiraculum vitae.* Genesis 2:7 (Vulgate).

75. *Otheos,* the fourth prayer of the *Ars Nova.*

76. *Pie Deus,* the Latin prologue to the fourth prayer of the *Ars Nova.*

77. Mark 9:22 (Vulgate).

rify his outflowing grace in abundance, and the impetus of the river of his most holy ones, let the city of my heart[78] rejoice in the faith of the scriptures, restore hope of knowledge's efficacy, may it replenish with the charity of abundance, may his overflowing mercy vivify with an eternal clarity; O Lord God, I ask [that] your grace be within me, and may it always remain within me in many ways; O Lord, satisfy my soul by your piety of your ineffable clemency, and strengthen my heart today, so that I will understand what I hear or what I read, and what I have understood I will guard, and what I will have guarded may I retain in memory, through this aforesaid holy sacrament, and with the uniting grace of the Father, Son, and Holy Spirit, amen.

[120] *The fifth prayer with respect to much strengthening of the five internal or external senses.*[79]

O holy Father,[80] O merciful Son, O gentle Holy Spirit, threefold and one inestimable God, I adore, I invoke, I deprecate your holy name and your superabounding equity to the extent you may forgive, allow, and have mercy on me, a presumed miserable sinner, and may I step out upon the office with knowing the science efficaciously from the literature, [and] may it invigorate and strengthen within my senses; O Lord, open my ears powerfully so that I may hear, wipe away the dirt from my eyes so that I may see, enlarge my ears so that I may hear, strengthen my hands so I may work, strengthen my feet so that I may walk, clear out my nostrils and mouth so that I may smell and sense, and may I speak pleasingly to you always to the honor of your name, that is blessed in the ages.

[121] *The sixth prayer on the constancy of morals and the acquisition of virtues.*

---

78. Latin *civitatem cordis.* A phrase is found in the commentary on the Parable of the Prodigial Son in the thirteenth-century *Gesta Romanorum* (Deeds of the Romans), which is a Latin collection of moral stories. The *Gesta Romanorum* drew from Valerius Maximus's *Factorum ac Dictorum Memorabilium Libri IX* (Nine Books of Memorable Deeds and Sayings), the first-century collection of short stories about morality.

79. The five internal senses are common sense, retentive imagination, compositive imagination, estimative power, and memory. The five external senses are sight, hearing, touch, taste, and smell. See chapter IV.

80. *Pie Pater,* the fifth prayer of the *Ars Nova.*

I lift up the senses[81] of my body and soul to you today, O Lord God, and I lift up my heart to you, so that my sorrow may be pleasing in your sight, and my words and deeds be pleasing in the sight of your house,[82] and may your great, all-powerful mercy shine out today within my viscera, and may my mind be expanded in order to be worked efficaciously in all things, and may your eloquence thicken in my mouth [like honey], and may your grace sprout forth in my heart, so that what I read, inspect, or hear, just as Adam understood, I may understand, just as Abraham guarded, I may guard, just as Jacob remembered, I may remember, so that, having been founded and rooted in the virtue of your scriptures, I may glorify the foundation of your mercy [which] was acquiring me, and having been delighted in the works of your hands, may I guard, having attained the justice and peace of mind and body steadfastly; O Lord, the plenary of your Spirit, working the grace within me, may I rejoice to have surmounted the visible and invisible enemies and their opposing snares and cunning.

[122] *The seventh prayer concerning the restoration of intelligence and the subtlety of intellect.*

O disposer and dispenser of all kingdoms[83] or visible or invisible powers, O Lord God, the orderer of all volitions, O Lord, O good spirit of total judgment, dispose today the weak and feeble dominion of my mind, and order today your volition in goodness and delightfulness, and dispense to me your manifold grace in benevolence, and propitiously grant to me, not looking back to the multitude of my sins, . . .[84] which I desire, considering, understanding, and retaining the effect in memory, and accommodate your grace to my senses, and visit me with the visitation

---

81. *Extollo sensus,* the sixth prayer of the *Ars Nova*. See also the prayer belonging to the second *nota* of astronomy at NS 84.

82. Latin *populi,* which literally means "your parish." Because it is commonly thought that the church is the house of God, the scribe chose to use the ecclesiastical meaning of *populi* for "parish." Alternatively, *populi* could mean God's people, referring to his company of angels.

83. *Omnium regnorum,* the seventh prayer of the *Ars Nova*. See also the prayer belonging to the third *nota* of astronomy at NS 85.

84. The operator would insert his desired area of study for this prayer here.

of your Spirit, so that I have contracted,[85] out of the stain of the flesh or out of the Fall of sin from birth, your ineffable divine power, that piety may abolish, which in the beginning you wanted to create heaven and earth, and that restores with a great and spiritual compassion, which you deemed worthy to call back man, having lost the first [original] state [of being] in consequence of lost grace, and because the judgment of Satan snatched away the senses and the faculty of comprehension from me, may the sense of the Lord and his wisdom restitute me, entering [me] from end to end strongly, and disposing all things sweetly, how I, an unworthy and miserable sinner, having been strengthened in your works, effect clear sight, eloquence, and subtlety in these which I desire, to the threefold and sevenfold of the Father, Son, and the Holy Spirit, by bestowing, uniting, and administrating grace, amen.

[123] *The eighth prayer about the purity of confession and the impetration of the grace of God with respect to understanding.*

O God, lord of the living[86] and the maker of abundance of all invisible creatures to all beings everywhere, each with a mixed constitution [of the elements], each of every one, bestowing a faculty according to its own nature, and recompensating the abundance of heavenly grace for the equality of the merits of angels and men, pour out the grace of the Holy Spirit into my heart and soul today, and multiply the gifts of the Holy Spirit within me, and strengthen within me the inner man, and make me fruitful by the dew of your grace by which you instructed the angels, inform me with the generosity which you have taught your faithful from the beginning, so that the sevenfold gifts of grace of your Holy Spirit may be worked within me, and let the waters above Jerusalem irrigate the cistern of my conscience and the fountain of my soul with force, flowing from Lebanon. Let them replenish and overflow with the charity which you came upon the waters of your majesty from heaven, confirm the great things of this sacrament within me.

---

85. That is, the act of making a legally binding contract (i.e., the covenant between God and humanity).

86. *Deus vivorum,* the eighth prayer of the *Ars Nova.*

[124] *The ninth prayer of the sevenfold grace of God, an exemplar for the renewal of the sevenfold grace of the Holy Spirit.*[87]

Today I confess to you,[88] O Lord God, the Father of all, you who reveals the secrets of heaven to your servants, and I humbly deprecate your majesty, so that you may be the king and prince of my thoughts today, and may my thoughts be directed in your sight and my actions prevail in sight of the heavenly hosts, I cry out to you today, O God, hear my cry, I groan to you, accept the groaning of my heart, today I entrust my spirit, my soul, and my thoughts into your hands; O my Father and my God, may I not feel myself abandoned by you, but may I feel your mercy within me, and let your good name be exalted in me. O most gracious God the Holy Spirit, whose goodness is eternal, whose mercy is incomprehensible, whose clarity is perpetual, whose possessions are of the entire heavens and earth, breathe, look upon, and attend to this, my work, and what I accomplish in your praise with honor, may it be completed in your perfection with a dispensation. Teach me, O Lord, I place myself within you to be taught, guide me, O Lord, and fasten the faith of your grace into me, so that your Spirit may conquer, reign, and rule over me, amen.

[125] *The tenth prayer for the purpose of the observation of both the [New and Old] Testaments with their appendices.*

O Lord, because I am your servant,[89] I serve you today, and I confess in the presence of your glorious majesty, in whose sight all magnificence and every sanctimony exist, and I deprecate your holy and ineffable name; today incline your pious ears and adjust your eyes to such an effect of the operation, so that opening your hand with grace as much as I desire, satisified and more abundant with the charity with which you made heaven earth with abundance, amen.

---

87. The seven gifts of the Holy Spirit are wisdom, understanding, counsel, fortitude, knowledge, piety, and reverence of God. They originate from Augustine of Hippo and have their biblical basis in Isaiah 11:1–2.

88. *Profiteor,* the ninth prayer of the *Ars Nova.*

89. *Domine quia ego servus,* the tenth prayer of the *Ars Nova*. See also the latter half of the adorning prayer belonging to the first *nota* of rhetoric at NS 45 and the prayer belonging to the fourth *nota* of astronomy at NS 86.

[*Novem Termini*]

[126] *This is the little treatise that is greater than the rest, because before all the headings of the prefaced works I gave [that] which is to be offered apart from any distinction of the times, [just as] it was understood by the administration of the angel.*

For when I inquired of the Lord how I would be able to manage the aforementioned things [that is, the prayers, their divided parts, and their Latin prologues,] (under such difficult placements or under such burdensome measurement of times),[90] so that when I inquired about it more often, having performed a fasting at length, a response came from the angel, "This little treatise the Lord sent to you with the secret of its own measurements, because it is to be offered before all the headings or before the *notae* of this art, and if you pass over much of the rest,[91] [then] you will be able to manage this easily."

[127a] *This is the beginning of this work [First Terminus].*

Genealogon, Saphal, Sajazan, Zeber, Gemoziol, Sanna, Gezoga, Samiel, Geremiel, Erasiothos, Sepharnai, Genezebal, Genethoros, Semaminarim, Malachiel, Magraros, Getrumatol, Geristos, Thebos, Febal, Resalkrara, Genatel, Sepheros, Zephoronai, Azona, Messiel, Sother, Aziel, Semistos, Amotal, Othor, Femethor, Sannadai, Morothothiel, Semenos, Rabas, Rennai, Oreb, Somel, Aza, Gemol, Gemeziel, Semei, Semeiaton, Zecor, Gemolin, Remelech, Gennai, Eliothos, Domathomos, Athamir, Senon, Magra, Magol, Sethar, Senamagol, Eliomothos, Gezetol, Phamal, Geremos, Eremiothon, Laudagios, Sephaciel, Egernar, Stanatiel, Athanathos, Egrogebal, Rogon, Enezimar, Marothon, Gecarnai, Enemos, Gezconos, Sabar, Gegozai, Elesercti, Sepharnamaton, Balazai, Samahiar, Amiel, Gezamatel, Sacramanai, Aman, Semol, Gezemol, Sacromol, Gezobal, Sanna, Athanathos, Theos, Eliem, Ezeliem, Euchenes, Megenthenon, Sennai, Hemel, Sechor, Ezechor, Sephornai, Gazael, Samirael, Hennal, Semagos, Semair, Gecornai, Nemal, Agathos,

---

90. The "difficult placements" refer to how complicated the *Ars Notoria* text has laid out the prayers and the "burdensome measurement of times" refer to the complex rubric of the entire ritual procedure.

91. That is, the days and hours missed by the operator out of neglect or error.

Amathos, Gecromages, Magait, Sannaziel, Geconail, Namarcha, Thanai, Seeagel, Ezor, Gemiothor, Lanamiel, Seziel, Magos, Agenol, Semanai, Menna, Saranai, Latham, Liazel, Egeiel, Saman, Tanaziel, Atharos, Atharenathos, Sennael, Azier, Zechar, Azanachar, Lennagemal, Amegol, Semor, Athamanos, Rennalamos, Sabarnai, Baruchata, Ialon, Espuos, Remel, Semar, Gelamacron, Seger, Gezemagil, Sanna, Iamazia, Iezion, Ogozion, Gerolegos, Ammos, Avir, Matharion, Senes, Eliothon, Sennair, Lamar, Lamarai, Secronaion, Gemal, Secromagol, Iamarai, Seconomaios.

[127b] *The terminus and the boundary limit of the senses [Second Terminus].*

Agenos, Themogemtheos, Athanathon, Kyrieleyson, Christeleyson, Kyrieleyson,[92] **on Ymas, Avethenaton, Ymas, Loomboom, Ymas, Usyon, Ymas, Geromegos, Agenor, Ysiston, Geromagol, Aziamal, Latham, Sennaar, Geconaal, Gacramagal, Gezero, Genomeli, Neomenos, Hennagel, Ganna, Gethennanos, Semenael, Otheios, Athazios, Sepharnemenemos, Thomothonai, Lamazamamin, Lamiar, Agramos, Genoramos, Semma, Magil, Amagron, Semmagaron, Semir, Arrannas, Ramoth, Anarannai, Ioye, Christos, Amiristos, Charachees, Ruchanos, Geros, Saleth, Seramamarin, Iasol, Salem, Alleluya, Theos, Phobos, Alleluya, Aristos, Reemruos, Alleluya, Samici, Siloth, Allegenomai, Methonomos, Geconomai, Zanathoros, Sannamarathos, Genoulos, Genasar, Senanaser, Sennacherub, Iamaneziel, Sechoizomiel, Thaman, Mathar, Azamathar, Zechonomathar, Samia, Esara, Samaiair, Enaziatel, Samaiel, Agenozoron, Samach, Abisanaac, Endontingehen, Azamaguen, Lemorach, Semmariaton, Zaguan.**

[127c] *Out of place.*[93] *[Third Terminus].*

Apozothos, Naamalathos, Ezachairalathos, Genozababal, Lemach, Almailemach, Sechozamial, Rabasadail, Semmaziel, Gechomazial, Logos, Patir, Genomicros, Sennazsamar, Azamiatol, Gemotron, Laudothes, Faron, Deconpentamias, Decapende, Dialnelathos, Samiarim, Ienathalai, Sazaman.

---

92. Greek *kyrie eleison,* meaning "lord have mercy," a common phrase in the psalms, and *Christos eleison,* meaning "Christ have mercy," both of which form a part of Christian liturgy.

93. The scribe is indicating that this *terminus* is out of order in the sequence or misplaced entirely.

[127d] *Fourth Terminus.*

Semaziotheos, Trathopanos, Geramiel, Garomamonas, Sephomeron, Geblathor, Ecidron, Zamastasis, Anasthasion, Olitos, Ostision, Gezabal, Samathiel, Semirramot, Sathatlos, Lemelian, Saphoronegon, Zaamirael, Geristosomeros, Othon.

[127e] *Fifth Terminus.*

Iadalemon, Nagera, Nanuogos, Sanagiar, Elaph, Ornoolnotheo, Indoo.

[127f] *Sixth Terminus. These four [termini], with the Lord's Prayer, [are to be spoken] for the purpose of the restriction of blood.*[94]

Lemal, Ragam, Sobsaron, Eriegil, Rognon, Negal, Hemel, Gemot, Sagnnar, Chalapalos, Genoyamel, Garazmaziel, Gezachar, Sathamianes, Mathelagios, Uriel, Phahangor, Iathomegon, Sarat, Sazaisach, Eramelitotum, Ezaladna, Usiem.

[127g] *[Seventh Terminus.]*

Geronegos, Semanator, Sazanachozai, Lamathias, Sennaziel, Taquiol, Zamrael, Karion, Karistomemon, Saromonai.

[127h] *[Eighth Terminus.]*

Decapendos, Meramalathon, Sabrnael, Seramalael, Nagathamal, Endamios, Regamatal, Sazanazel, Theogeros, Amazai, Eenelios, Zachamanes, Theomegos, Labdalnelion, Gerozion, Othemeigalon, Gezomegalon, Gethoromonai, Elzachamel, Azabanos, Amiaron, Labdafomalion, Usilogion, Eleis, Ymon, Microzion, Theos, Elothoi, Saramazai, El, Lamathiamon, Lagaii, Lomeziel, Lannos, Azamothon, Themathanathon.

[127i] *[Ninth Terminus.]*

Magnus, Magol, Naziatol, Saziathos, Ebonothon, Sepharnaiaton, Gemoriel, Sezamel, Lehathon, Bazios, Lannazamarathon, Labamegal, Sagemicros, Egemeziol, Samalegoron, Anomos, Gratomessios, Sothron,

---

94. The heading suggests that these *voces magicae* prayers were either once used as an incantation to stop a bleeding wound or such an occult virtue was later attributed to it.

Zenegessephd, Chelael, Zephastamos, Amaragios, Sannaziel, Getramatiol, Azagal, Azaganamar, Sennagel, Secastologion, Genologos, Agenolothogos, Serozomai, Iaminaramos, Remelithos, Christomeliel, Azimeros, Samal, Azaramagos, Gelemiel, Gezonomegal, Anachristos, Gemotheon, Samot, Eliemon, Ialamiim, Aminos, Gezelias, Sacarai, Gehezamarai, Theos, Agios, Yskiros, Athanatos,[95] amen.

95. Greek *theos,* meaning "god"; *agios,* meaning "holy"; *ischyros,* meaning "strong"; and *athanatos,* meaning "immortal."

[The Specials Addendum][96]

[128] *About the first.*

This is part of the prayer of the first *nota* with those [other adorning prayers],[97] which are written within it, about which it is to be done as in the art of grammar according to the rest.

O Holy Lord, the almighty Father,[98] all-powerful, eternal God, in whose sight all things are visible and invisible, the foundations of all creatures, whose eyes have seen my imperfections, whose ears hear all things, whose charity is the heavens and the earth full with sweetness, who saw all things before they are made,[99] in whose book all days are formed and men inscribed; today look over me, your servant, subjected to you with [his] whole heart, mind, and [ritual] operation through your Holy Spirit; strengthen, bless, and protect my present-day actions, and illuminate this inspection or repetition[100] with the constancy of your visitation.

[129] *This [here], from the second prayer of the same art.*

O Lord God,[101] O gentle Father, the disposer of all eternal virtues, look upon my [ritual] operations; O inspector and judge, consider today the actions of angels and men, so that your admirable promise may deem worthy to fill virtue[102] within me suddenly, to so much a working efficacy

---

96. The fragmented letter has ended. The *Flores Aurei,* having lost material, resumes, beginning the Special prayers with the first prayer belonging to the art of grammar. The treatise's original format has been altered, repositioning the pictorial figures from underneath their respective prayers to the very end of the treatise. This addendum is likely not original to the first part of the *Flores Aurei* but rather taken from another copy of the *Flores Aurei,* dated to a time after the first part but prior to the *Opus Operum.*

97. To identify those prayers that are to be spoken before the *nota* and those prayers that are written within the figure, I have named the latter as the "adorning prayers," because they adorn the figure, giving it an ornate appearance. Also, those prayers that are to be spoken before the *notae* are never instructed to be written within the figure. Here the scribe seems to have either mistaken the nine *termini* for the six parts of the adorning prayer belonging to the first *nota* of grammar, or he is referencing a portion of text that is no longer extant in our manuscripts.

98. *Domine Sancte Pater [. . . imperfectum],* the first prayer given before the first *nota* of grammar.

99. Or done or finished.

100. The operator may insert either the word *inspection* or *repetition* according to which step of the ritual procedure he is performing at that moment.

101. *Respice Domine,* the prayer belonging to the second *nota* of grammar.

102. Instead of virtue, the operator might insert his desired area of grammatical study.

within me, [that] I may glorify your glorious name to you in a mouth of love according to your praise, amen.

[**130**] *This is the third [prayer] of the art of grammar.*
O Lord, creator of all visible and invisible creatures,[103] O Lord God, O most holy Father, dwelling eternally in the enclosed light before the beginning of the world,[104] ineffably ordering all things and governing the incomprehensible piety of your eternity, I approach with supplicating words, so that the promise and reminiscence of the sciences with stability[105] of this sacramental and mystical work within me may illuminate through your holy angels, the efficacy, consideration, and memory with your holy one[106] within me.

[**131**] *The instruction about all things.*
This is the full and clear knowledge by which the *notae* of the art of grammar are to be discerned, and how they ought to be offered, or at what times, or by which discretion they are to be correctly and properly revealed; indeed, we said above concerning the prolation or the inspection of the *notae* and the prayers.[107] Now, truly [the ritual procedure] is to be divided in some respects, because although the action is in part from the times, nevertheless, I judge it must be performed from the others their same parts of things.[108]

[**132**] For I, Apollonius, attaining the authority of Solomon, arranged to guard his work and observances, just as it is said about the three *notae* of the art of grammar, The times are to be observed thus.

---

103. *Creator Adonay,* the prayer belonging to the third *nota* of grammar.
104. In the Middle Ages, the cosmos was perceived as orbs, and the highest heaven where God, the saints, and the elect dwell was an invisible immobile orb called the empyrean orb, which enclosed the entire universe.
105. Instead of *promissio scientiarumque reminiscentia cum stabilitate,* the operator might insert his desired area of grammatical study.
106. That is, the Holy Spirit.
107. Section 79.
108. Pseudo-Apollonius is describing the adorning prayers written within the pictorial figures. Pseudo-Apollonius indicates that these adorning prayers are divided into parts, separated by intervals of silence.

He certifies about the following [prayers to be written within the figures].

But it is not yet understood—the prayers to be written [within the figures]—but it is to be demonstrated fully about themselves in the following work.[109]

Concerning the written notae.

But still, [the prayers] that are written in those three *notae* are not prayers, but rather like definitions of those *notae,* for the Greek, Hebrew, Chaldean, etc., writings are to be comprehended within the *notae* through themselves. Still, these are to be written [within the figures], which cannot be understood by Latin readers; none ought to be offered on any day, except on those days which was established by King Solomon, (that is, on those days which the *notae* are to be inspected, but on those days, always following the day after the *nota* is inspected on the first day). After the second day itself, which [the Latin prologues] are [placed] after a written *nota*[110] [in the text] they are recited themselves, and yet these [prayers] which are, themselves, Latin, are able to be offered on those days the *notae* are to be inspected.

[133] *How many* notae *of dialectic there are.*

Also, the *notae* of the art of dialectic are two, but at what times they ought to be offered is said in part, but hereafter [the art of dialectic] is to be called Circius [based on its two parts, argument and response] from [which they] themselves [make a circular motion with each other].[111] Behold, [the art of dialectic] is to be turned toward the rest [of the liberal arts]. But it is be understood that even those things that are written within the *notae* of the art

109. The addendum describing "the prayers to be written [within the figures]" (i.e., the adorning prayers) apparently went unfinished; although, the intended addendum might be what is now found in Version B. Version A presents a few figures containing adorning prayers but no instructions are given. Version B expounds upon the adorning prayers as seen in the "*Notae* Supplement" of BnF Latin 9336, f. 18r–28v.

110. That is, the adorning prayer.

111. Of the classical compass winds, for which there were twelve for the Greeks, Circius is the north by northwest wind. Circius is also spelled as "Cercius" in Hispania, which is the spelling provided in the original text. Aulus Gellius (c. 125–after 180 CE), the Roman author and grammarian, says that Circius was a local wind of Gaul known for its dizzying, circular motion. Thus, the writer is drawing a parallel between the circular nature of logic/dialectic and the Circius wind, which further alludes to the circle of patterns held in the right hand of Lady Dialectic in Martianus Capella's allegory. See Gellius, *Attic Nights,* 2.20.22, 28–29.

of dialectic[112] can be offered on all the days on which the *notae*[113] of the same art are inspected.

About the Latin writing.

Also, it is to be understood: the Latin writing itself, according to the antiquity of the Hebrews,[114] is not able to be offered except on those days which we have said. Nevertheless, it must be understood: these are to be pronounced in no other manner, unless preceded by a confession. Still, these are to be considered, so that, apart from some occasion thus, everything must be done just as they are said. For Solomon thenceforth said, "All those teachings should be done just as they were given, but from the rest that follow below is to be done otherwise."

A mention is made about the remaining sciences.

For when you saw the first *nota* of dialectic, repeat with your hand and your heart the sign that was in the first *nota,* and from those [signs] a definition will be given thus in every *nota* of every art except those arts [that do not contain signs].[115]

[134] Also, we will give the definitions for each art and their *notae,* just as it is defined in the book of Solomon:[116] geometry has one *nota;* arithmetic one and a half; but philosophy has seven [along] with the arts and sciences beneath its own contents;[117] theology has five *notae.* But still, these are more perilous and serious for this reason: they are not serious because they are pronounced seri-

112. The adorning prayers which are "written within the figures (*notae*)."

113. Here *notae* refers to the figures.

114. *Eniclyssoe,* see section 8.

115. In Version A, the first *nota* of logic/dialectic is labeled 4a as found in chapter V and appendix A2. Within the great wheel are four other wheels. There are supposed to be signs in these the four wheels, but those signs are not found in the extant manuscripts belonging to Version A. However, Version B supplies these four wheels and their signs which act as mnemonic devices to help the student recall any given definition (*definitio*) about a logic/dialectic concept to which any given sign refers.

116. The book of Solomon mentioned here is *Eniclyssoe,* see section 8. The definitions for each art and their figures are never given in this addendum. They are missing.

117. That is, the general sciences, including the seven exceptives of necromancy (which contains hydromancy and pyromancy) and astrology (which contains chiromancy, geomancy, genethlialogy, and onomancy). Other middle sciences such as the science of mirrors (i.e., optics) and the science of weights, measures, and machines (i.e., mechanics) were included in this category.

ously, but they are serious because they have a serious efficacy. Music has one *nota;* medicine has one *nota;* therefore, each one is to be offered only on the determined days.

For your protection.[118]

And it is to be understood, just as you saw the *notae* of theology or philosophy and [their own] arts beneath [their own] contents themselves on all those days, by no means should you laugh nor have fun, because one day while King Solomon was inspecting the forms of these same *notae,* perhaps drunk more than usual with wine, the Lord became angry with him and through his own angel he had spoken to him, saying, "Because you have despised my sacramental mystery, mocking and expressing contempt, I will take away from you a part of the kingdom and I will crush your sons before their own days," and the angel added, "The Lord prohibits you from entering his temple for eighty days,[119] and God extends the observance to you, so that you do penitence according to your sin." And with Solomon grieving and petitioning for mercy from the angel, the angel responded, "Your days are prolonged; however, innumerable iniquities and evils will come over your sons, and they will be snatched by an overcoming iniquity."

[135] *About the first nota of the second art [i.e., the dialectic].*

O holy and pious God,[120] the indissoluble concord of an argument, you who wanted to stabilize the sky and earth, the sea, the abyss, and everything that is in them, in whose sight all reason and speech subsists, through these precious sacraments of your angels, give me . . .[121] as much as I desire, and I believe the knowledge of this art without the fear of ambiguity.

---

118. Véronèse identifies the following passage as a key part of Version A2, the intermediary between Versions A and B.

119. It is well known that certain numbers have a symbolic value in the Bible. For example, forty years represents a generation or a man's life. Thus, it would seem that the eighty days mentioned here could represent two generations (i.e., eighty years), one for each of Solomon's sons, Menelik I, the first emperor of Ethiopia, and Rehoboam, the king of the Kingdom of Judah. What the angel said came to pass as the United Monarchy of Israel collapsed during a rebellion, dividing the country into the Northern Kingdom of Israel and the Southern Kingdom of Judah as given in the accounts of 1 Kings and 2 Chronicles.

120. *Sancte Deus,* the prayer of the first *nota* of logic/dialectic.

121. The operator would insert his desired area of dialectic study for this prayer here.

[136] *Instruction.*

This is the prayer of that *nota,* like those which are written, (that is, in figure placed above or around the figure itself), should be read with the utmost sagacity just as it is determined in the consideration of the figure itself. Likewise, it is to be understood that if [the operator] had any of the eyes impeded or any infirmity, such that he may not be healthy [enough] to inspect the aforementioned figures with his eyes, (just as it happens with the eyes of the elderly or those who are blinded), [then] he may have the figures themselves and their significance in memory and in mind, and place [them] before the eyes of reason and intellect, which the eyes of the flesh cannot see, whence Solomon said, "The mind and intellect are the memory of the eyes and the sight."

Furthermore, we read before night-time, indeed, [during] the day [about] the aforesaid king himself [and] the figures, having been sent from the Lord through the holy angel, have been known and reflected upon in his mind and repeated the significations in his heart,[122] from where it has been committed to memory more often with consideration than by the inspection of the external eyes at the determined hours and the observed teachings with veneration, [and the figures] are to be read with the intervaled prayers.

Also, it is to be noted that what we are calling the *nota* of awe[123] ought not to be offered on any day, except on account of the greatness and fear of danger, and the *nota* of chastity[124] ought to be offered only for the great fear of lechery, and the prayer of friendship ought to be offered for the fear of odium, and similarly, the prayer of love for the favor of love.[125] For the prayers from which manner we speak are contained beneath the *notae,* but they each do not have their own *notae.* These prayers are fifteen [in number], each one having its own respective virtues, but just as it is said above about the *notae,* some still remain to be finished.[126]

---

122. Latin *novisse mente replicasse et corde significatas revolvisse.* This phrase also evokes the meaning of visualizing the unrolling of a scroll and memorizing it.

123. Or the *nota* of terror. See section 85.

124. In Version A, there is no *nota* of chastity. For Version B, the *nota* of chastity is found at NS 137–40.

125. The prayers of friendship and love are likely made in reference to those prayers belonging to the *nota* of justice, peace, and [expelling] fear. Version A has the *nota,* but no prayers are assigned to it. Version B has the *nota,* but it looks strikingly different, and it supplies a prayer and Latin prologue at NS 141–44.

126. In reference to the apparently unfinished addendum, see section 132.

Now the first *nota* of the art of dialectic is written, as the second follows, but when you came to the *nota* of sorrow, which is one of the seven *notae* of philosophy,[127] inspect that with the highest reverence and the prayer placed before itself, not always by mouth or by word, but read through [it] and scrutinize with the intention of the heart, so that you often invoke and adore God. You will recite six other *notae* as it will be seen shortly.[128] Furthermore, a swift and short demonstration will be given of all the other *notae,* or prayers, that [text near you] will be sufficient for now. We place the *notae* next in their own order. The second *nota* of dialectic begins.

[137] *From the second* [nota] *of the same art [of dialectic].*

O most merciful HELOY,[129] the creator, inspirer, and reformer of all good volitions, the endorser and ruler of the jaws, look favorably upon my mind and my most glorious deprecation with intention, so that what I ask[130] out of humility just as it is promised by you to me may you grant to me from your majesty with abundance.

---

127. Latin *notam luctus.* The third *nota* of philosophy according to BnF Latin 7152.

128. This promise is left unfulfilled in the latter portion of the *Flores Aurei* (sections 128–46) as this text is missing, but the other six prayers (*notae*) of philosophy are presented in the fragmented letter section (sections 82–125). See chapter V, "Analysis of the Figures."

129. *O Heloy clementissime,* this prayer belongs to the second *nota* of logic/dialectic. See also NS 33. On the divine name Heloy, see the eleventh-century abbot of Pomposa Abbey of northern Italy named Wido (d. 1047) who wrote *On the Names of Christ (De Nominibus Christi),* saying that the Hebrews had ten names for God, and Wido provides the Greek and Latin equivalents. The Hebrew names are as follows: (1) Hel ("strength," Greek *ischikros;* Latin *fortis*); (2) Elohim ("gods,"); (3) Heloe (or Heloy, meaning "god," Greek *theos;* Latin, *deus*); (4) Sabaoth ("divine power" or "virtue of medicine," Greek *dunamis;* Latin *dynamidia* or *virtutum*); (5) Helion ("the highest" Greek *ipselos;* Latin *excelsus*); (6) Eheieh Asher Eheieh ("I am that I am," from Exodus 3:14, Greek *O esti,* literally, "O you are!"); (7) Adonai ("lord," Greek *kyrios;* Latin *dominus*); (8) Yah is the short form of God's name, YHVH; (9) YHVH, which are "unpronounceable" (Greek *anekphoneton*), is called the "four-letter name" (Greek *Tetragrammaton*), in which each Hebrew letter is explained as YOD ("the beginning," *principium*), HE ("the Passion," *passio*), VAU ("life," *vita*), and HE ("life of the Passion," *passionis vitae*); and (10) Shaddai. Although only a few appear in the *Ars Notoria,* many of these names are found in later treatises on magic. See Pitra, *Spicilegium Solesmense complectens Sanctorum Patrum,* 448. See also Tanner, *Medieval Elite Women and the Exercise of Power,* 191.

130. Throughout this the operator would insert his desired area of study here.

[138] *This concerning the first* nota *of the art of rhetoric.*
O almighty and merciful[131] Father, the orderer of all creatures, just judge, eternal king of kings and Lord, who gave eloquence and deemed worthy to confer knowledge wonderfully to your holy ones; you who judges and discerns all things, today illuminate my heart today with your brilliance, so that I may understand and know considerately what I greatly wish for[132] in the teachings of this art.

[139] *This, from the second [*nota*] of the same art [of rhetoric].*
O one, great,[133] wonderful, eternal God, O angel of the eternal plan and disposer of all virtues, and furnisher and disposer, adorn my understanding today, and multiply within me discerning the reason and cognition that you conferred on Adam in offering the names of all the creatures, grant me the same knowledge and every art of this judgment, nod [your] assent [to grant me] the discretion,[134] according to your promise.

[140] *This is the second* nota *of the art of rhetoric.*
Gezomanai,[135] Sezachoton, Yson, Eag, Marbariornai, Gethora, Namai, Iecoal, Ysaramael, Amathamathos, Labdagrothos, Chorometai, Amen, Fababbenos, Gerocagalos, Merataiel, Sannai, Saliel, Othion, Megocristos, Amen, Lemoros, all these [names] are given from God given to King Solomon, they are a mystical and plenary sacrament for the restoration of memory, the confirmation and fortification of understanding, the edification of morals, and the retribution of all knowledge of the writings, which you, O Father, God of all things and

---

131. *Omnipotens et misericors,* this prayer belongs to the first *nota* of rhetoric.
132. The operator would insert his desired area of rhetorical study here.
133. *Unus magnus,* this prayer belongs to the second *nota* of rhetoric.
134. The operator would insert his desired area of rhetorical study here.
135. *Gezomanai* is a misplaced General prayer belonging to the second sequence following *Assaylemath;* this proposed new assignment is based on the order of prayers found in the *Summa Sacrae Magicae,* book 4, folio 10. The prayer's misplacement is indicated by the *voces magicae,* the petition for memory and understanding, and the doubling assignment of two prayers to the second's position for rhetoric. There are also other coinciding indicators of redaction of text and figures in the manuscripts. Here, *Gezomanai* is mistakenly said to belong to the second *nota* of rhetoric and modified accordingly at its end; its parallel in Version B is the same prayer whose incipit is *Hanazay,* which is also found at the gloss for section 140 and NS 42.

the life of all creatures, may you deem worthy to fill . . .[136] within me suddenly.

[141] *This [here], from the third of the same art [of rhetoric].*

O Usyon[137] of all powers, kingdoms, and eternal judgments with the conspicuous pronunciation of all things, administrating the zeugma of languages, in whose regime nothing is a impediment, I beg you, give this mystery . . . [to me],[138] my heart and my tongue, having recounted or repeated [it], quickened for the purpose of discerning, judging, speaking well, and arranging, which the divine authority commits to be filled within me in this necessary art.

[142] *This, from the fourth of the same art [of rhetoric].*

O revered and powerful one,[139] with all the angels and archangels and all the heavenly creatures, as well as those infernal and terrestial, from whose magnificence of plenitude comes, so that us worthy ones may serve you, whose powers which, you made man from the four parts of the world out of flesh and bones and soul and spirit according to your image and likeness, give me the knowledge of this art, strengthening me in the faculty of knowledge itself.

[143] *This, from the* nota *of geometry.*

O God, just and all-powerful judge,[140] who has made known to us your salvation so that you might reveal your justice in the sight of the nations; open my eyes and instruct my heart in the salvation of your justice, so that, considering the wonders of your glorious sacramental mysteries, how I will gain so much understanding through them in this art, as you provide, you alone who does great wonders within us, knowing the art itself, and may I be made an interpreter suddenly, so that in it, I may be measured by the received faculty, memory, and stability which is measured

136. The ellipsis represents the empty space in which the operator would insert his desired area of rhetorical study for this prayer.

137. *Usyon omnium,* this prayer belongs to the third *nota* of rhetoric.

138. The ellipsis represents the empty space in which the operator would insert his desired area of rhetorical study for this prayer.

139. *Reverende,* this prayer belongs to the fourth *nota* of rhetoric.

140. *Deus iustus iudex,* this prayer belongs to the first *nota* of geometry.

out, and by the intercession of all the heavenly hosts, may I honor you forever and ever, amen.

[144] *This is about the art of arithmetic.*

O God, you who has made all things by number,[141] weight, and measure,[142] out of whose number, not even the hair of a man's head falls or escapes, in whose order of [mathematical] points, moments, minutes or days, opening and have opened the measurement, for which you alone count the stars, bestow a efficacy to my mind constantly, so that I may love in the knowledge of this art and acknowledge the gift of your piety, amen.

[145] *This is the half* nota *of the same art.*

O mediator[143] of all operations[144] and creatures, from whom all good things and all gifts of virtues naturally proceed, from whom [proceeds] every thing that is unbroken and perfect, whose almighty discourse comes from the royal seats [of the angels] while they kept the whole silence in our hearts, the middle ratio,[145] and my understanding[146] about love for the purpose of perceiving this mystery of so much consternation and to such an excellent degree, so that through these porismatic sacraments[147]

---

141. *Deus qui omnia numero,* this prayer belongs to the first *nota* of arithmetic.

142. Wisdom of Solomon 11:21.

143. *Mediator omnium,* this prayer belongs to the half *nota* of arithmetic.

144. Véronèse notes that in some texts, this word is *operantium,* which has a meaning of performing a mathematical operation, rather than *operationem,* which would give a more general sense of work or operation.

145. See Boethius's diagram about the definition of number involving the ratios of equality and inequality in chapter V, page 165.

146. Wisdom of Solomon 18:14–15.

147. The porismatic sacraments are the *notae* of arithmetic. Euclid of Alexandria wrote the now lost treatise titled *Porisms.* This is known to us through the Greek mathematician Pappus of Alexandria (c. 290–350 CE), who wrote in his *Synagoge* (Collection) about porisms, saying, "All of them are in form are neither theorems nor problems, but of a type occupying a sort of mean between them, so that their propositions can assume the form of theorems or problems, and it is for this reason that among the many geometers some have assumed them to be of the class of theorems, others of problems, looking only at the form of the proposition." A porism is a proposition deduced from some other demonstrated proposition such that the proposition uncovers the possibility of finding conditions to make a certain problem capable of many solutions; Jones, ed., trans., and commentary, *Pappus of Alexandria,* 94. Hogendijk makes the case that there was a lost Arabic translation of Euclid's *Porisms;* see Hogendijk, "On Euclid's Lost Porisms," 93–115.

I may obtain a sudden perfection and efficacy in this art.[148]

[146] *This, from the first of philosophy with respect to the* nota *of awe.*
O all-powerful lover of wisdom[149] **and knowledge in whom there is no sin, the master, instructor of every spiritual discipline and, O Lord, through your glorious angels and archangels, through the Thrones and Dominions, through the Principalities and Powers, through the Virtues, Cherubim, and Seraphim, through the twenty-four elders,**[150] **through the four living creatures,**[151] **and through all of the heavenly army, I adore, deprecate, invoke, request, supplicate, implore, and revere, glorify and exalt your holiest, terrible, and gentlest name, and I beseech you, so that, today you illuminate my heart abundantly and strongly by the light of the Holy Spirit and the grace of your visitation.**[152]

---

148. The petitioner is making comparisons between God and his creation with numbers and the rules of mathematics. Many consider the Persian mathematician Muhammad ibn Musa al-Khwarizmi (c. 780–850) the founder of algebra. The word "algebra" comes from the Arabic *al-jabr,* meaning "reunion of broken parts," for which comes from the title of his book, *The Compendious Book on Calculation by Completion and Balancing,* which was translated into Latin by Robert of Chester, who was working in Hispania in 1145. Al-Khwarizmi introduced the method of reduction and balancing a quadratic equation in which like terms are canceled on both sides. Thus, the petitioner compares God's creation as an "unbroken" and "perfect" equation. In this cosmic equation, "good things" and "the gifts of all virtues" come and go, and also, part of God's calculations of creation are placed within the hearts of humankind while the other part is kept hidden by the angels as a "consternating mystery," which humankind must go out to discover through sacraments and restore balance to the cosmic equation and himself. This prayer might belong to the third *nota* of the general sciences. It might be called "the first one"; that is, the first prayer of two which is listed first in the section 99 heading and would be offered from noon to evening in the operation of the four general sciences. See page 267, section 99, footnote 45. Also, the gloss in section 103 says that the third *nota* has an "angelic appearance" and it would seem to follow that angelic choirs are mentioned here in the prayer. See chapter III, "The Knowledge of the *Ars Notoria*" under the heading "Problems with the Text."

149. *Omnipotens sapientiae* is the prayer belonging to the general sciences. The general sciences "are contained beneath" philosophy. According to Version B, this prayer belongs to the second *nota* of geometry.

150. Revelation 4:4.

151. Ezekiel's vision of the living creatures are cherubim having four faces—that of a man, a lion, a cherub, and an eagle as described in Ezekiel 1 and 10. The same four animals are referenced again in Revelation 4:6–8, appearing as a lion, an ox, a man, and an eagle.

152. The gloss in 146 and NS 122 erroneously assigns this prayer, *Omnipotens sapientiae,* to the second *nota* of geometry.

[Astrological Prescriptions]

[147][153] We said above about the termini of the notory art regarding reading the prayers and inspecting the notae. It now remains to be said how the aforesaid lunar months are to be found, but it must afterward be observed that, lest there be any deception on account of lunar month embolisms,[154] we must proceed in this manner. When we arrive at the epacts[155] and the regular months, which for the epact days are nineteen [year of the Metonic cycle] and for the regular [months] twelve, and which also make up the embolism—that is, the excess—if the numbers of epact days and regulars represent thirty, there will not be an embolismic lunar month; if it increased beyond, it will be embolismic. Having left behind thirty, we must enter upon that insofar as it has been increasing the calculating above, it will be so many as one, two, and the rest, and this you arranged which is to be computed in the calends[156] of that month of which regulars with the epact year of the present, and thus, through the order concerning the rest of the epacts and regulars. But it is to be understood insofar as all the lunar months ought to have everything in calculation of thirty [days], specifically the common year of thirty [days for a month, having twelve months in a year], following the first moon from September, having selected the beginning and the rest, as we marked in the aforesaid notory art.

The aforesaid lunar months are also the gates of the holy angels in which the holy angels descend [to earth] by the order of the Creator and his great power, and particularly the great angel of God who descends through the eastern gate; the second gate is southern,[157] the third western, [and] the fourth northern. When you wanted theology or astronomy, the Moon must be put in

---

153. According to Véronèse, section 147 is a late addition and distinct to Version A2. It does not always appear at the end of the manuscript but sometimes somewhere in the middle.

154. Or intercalation.

155. The epact (Latin *epactae,* from Greek *epaktai hemerai,* meaning "added days") is the number of days by which a solar year exceeds twelve lunar months, usually by eleven days; it is also used in computations to determine the date of Easter.

156. The first day of every month in the Roman calendar.

157. The Latin here is *Affricalis,* meaning "African" and thereby referring to the southern direction and wind.

a fiery sign,[158] or it must be in the [zodiac] sign of the working master;[159] for grammar or logic, it must be in Gemini or in Virgo, and the same applies for philosophy and rhetoric, arithmetic and geometry; for music, in Taurus or in Libra; for astrology, in Aries or in Gemini, and in the hours of the lords of the aforesaid ruling houses,[160] [the planets] must not be malefic[161] or retrograde[162] and free from evil and in every good place.[163] For all the celestial powers and the choir of angels themselves rejoice[164] in their designated lunar months, days, and hours.

The *Ars Notoria,* of Solomon, Mani, and Euclid [of Thebes], ends.

---

158. The fiery signs are Aries, Leo, and Sagittarius.
159. It is not clear to which zodiac sign of the working master's natal chart is intended here. The best guess is the ascendant sign, the zodiac sign that is ascending on the eastern horizon at the moment of one's birth, as it has the greatest expression and meaning in a natal chart. Although, there are other signs to consider—the descendant, the Sun, and the Moon.
160. Each zodiac sign is ruled by a planet. The Moon rules Cancer. Mercury rules Gemini and Virgo. Venus rules Taurus and Libra. The Sun rules Leo. Mars rules Aries and Scorpio. Jupiter rules Sagittarius and Pisces. Saturn rules Capricorn and Aquarius. The intended meaning of "hour" is of the window of time in which the planet resides within the zodiac sign it rules. This is not to be confused with planetary hours; if it did, that would run contrary to the prescribed canonical hours of prayer detailed in the gloss.
161. Mars is the lesser malefic, and Saturn is the greater malefic. A malefic planet is unfavorable.
162. A planet is retrograde when is has the illusionary appearance that it is moving backward in the night sky. In astrology, this is unfavorable as the planet's functioning powers or attributes will be weakened.
163. In choosing an astrological election for taking a certain action, the astrologer will be mindful of the placement of the planets such that they exhibit their attributes the best when placed in their favored signs and favored relationship to other planets in the chart, which are called aspects. The instructions given are fundamental to any student of astrology.
164. "Rejoice" is a technical astrological term meaning that a planet exhibits its attributes best when residing within the sign it rules.

3

NOTAE SUPPLEMENT VERSION A

Mellon 1

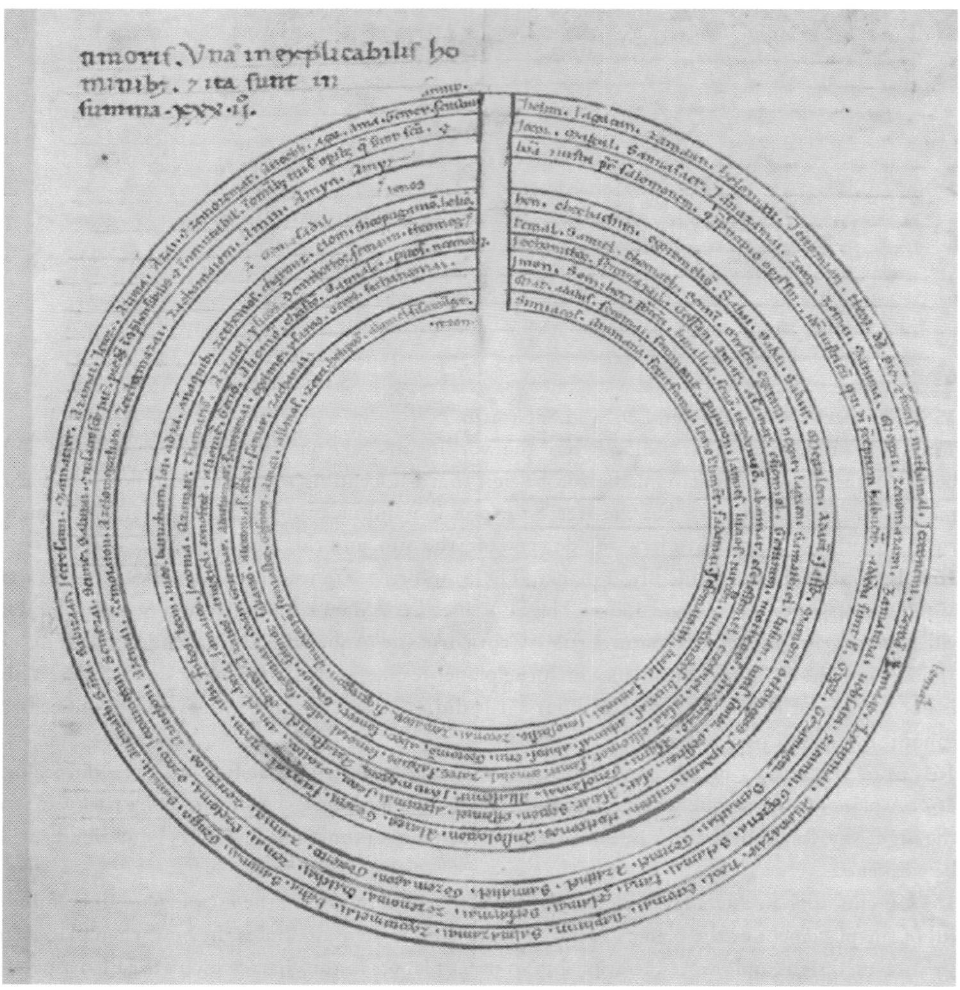

The first figure of grammar,
from New Haven, Yale University, Mellon, MS 1, f. 10v.

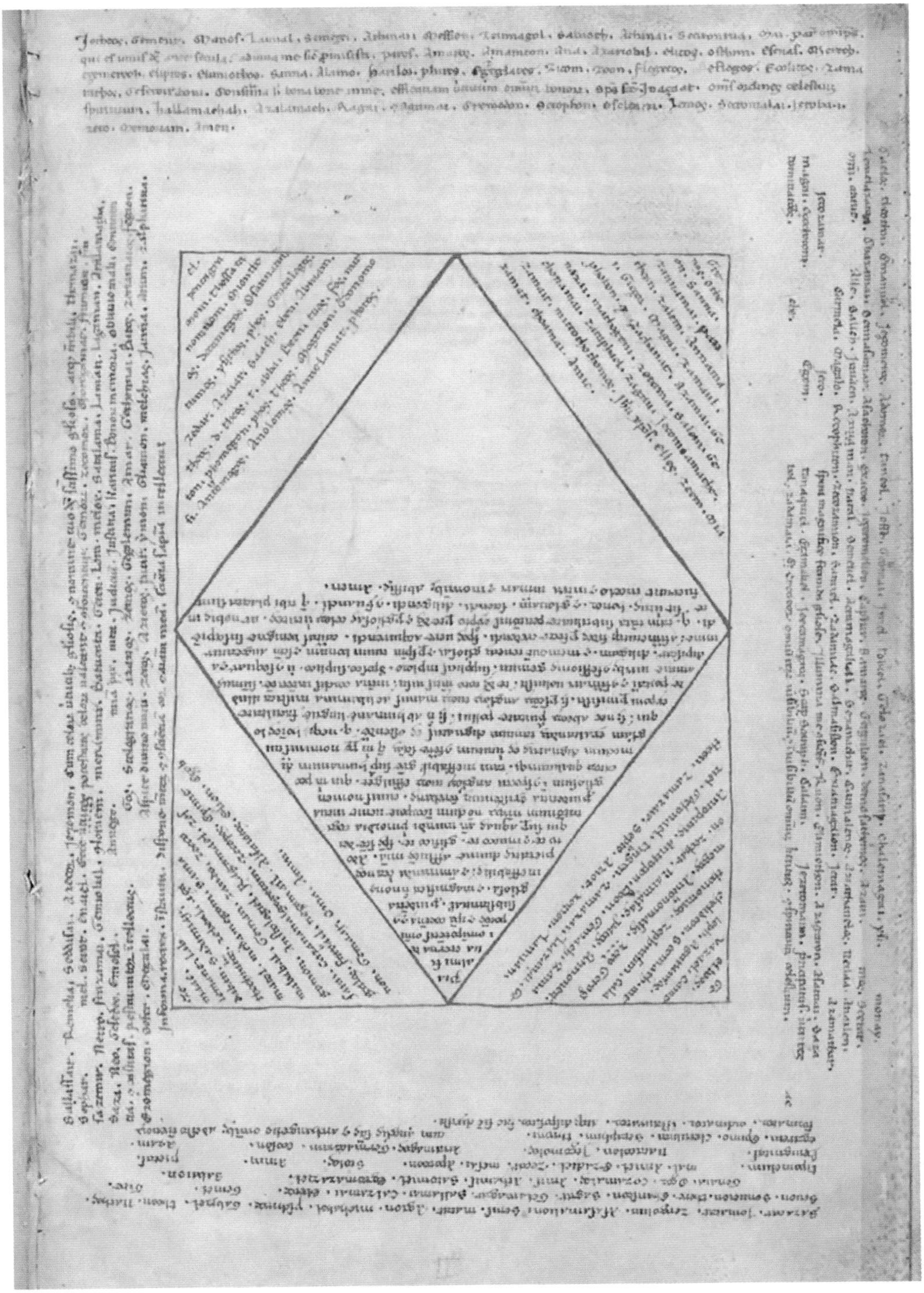

The second figure of grammar,
from New Haven, Yale University, Mellon, MS 1, f. 11.

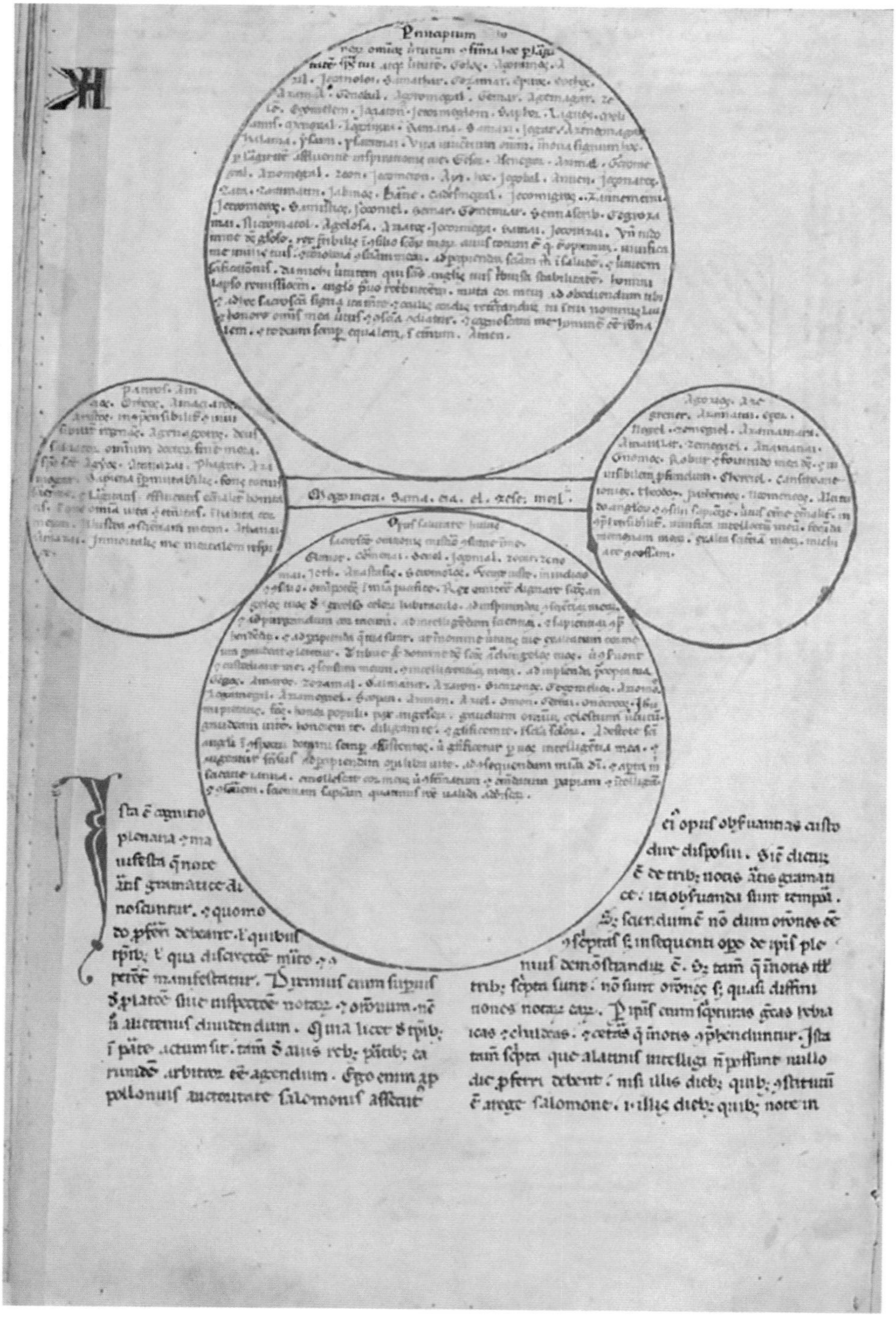

The third figure of grammar,
from New Haven, Yale University, Mellon, MS 1, f. 11v.

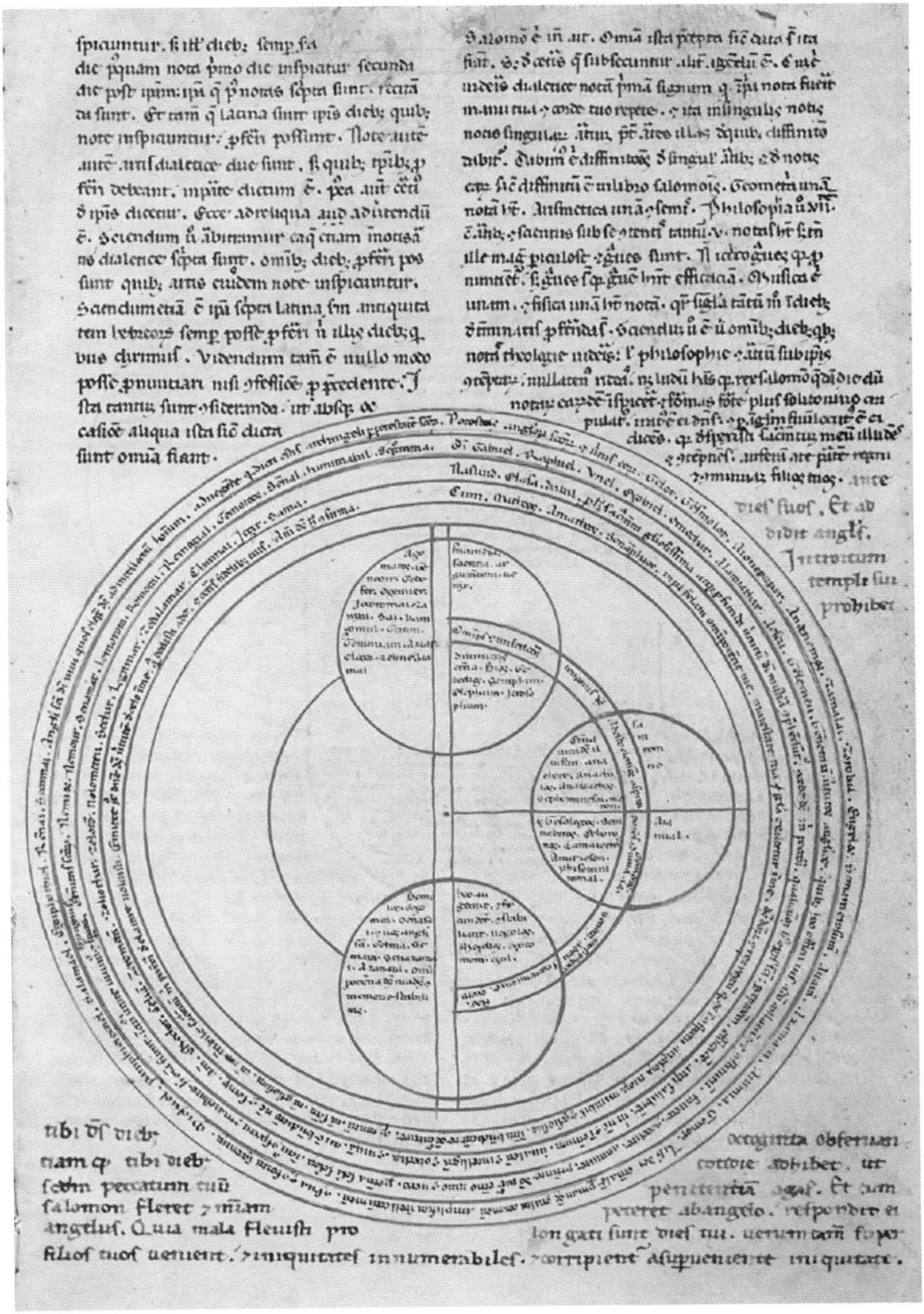

The first figure of logic/dialectic,
from New Haven, Yale University, Mellon, MS 1, f. 12.

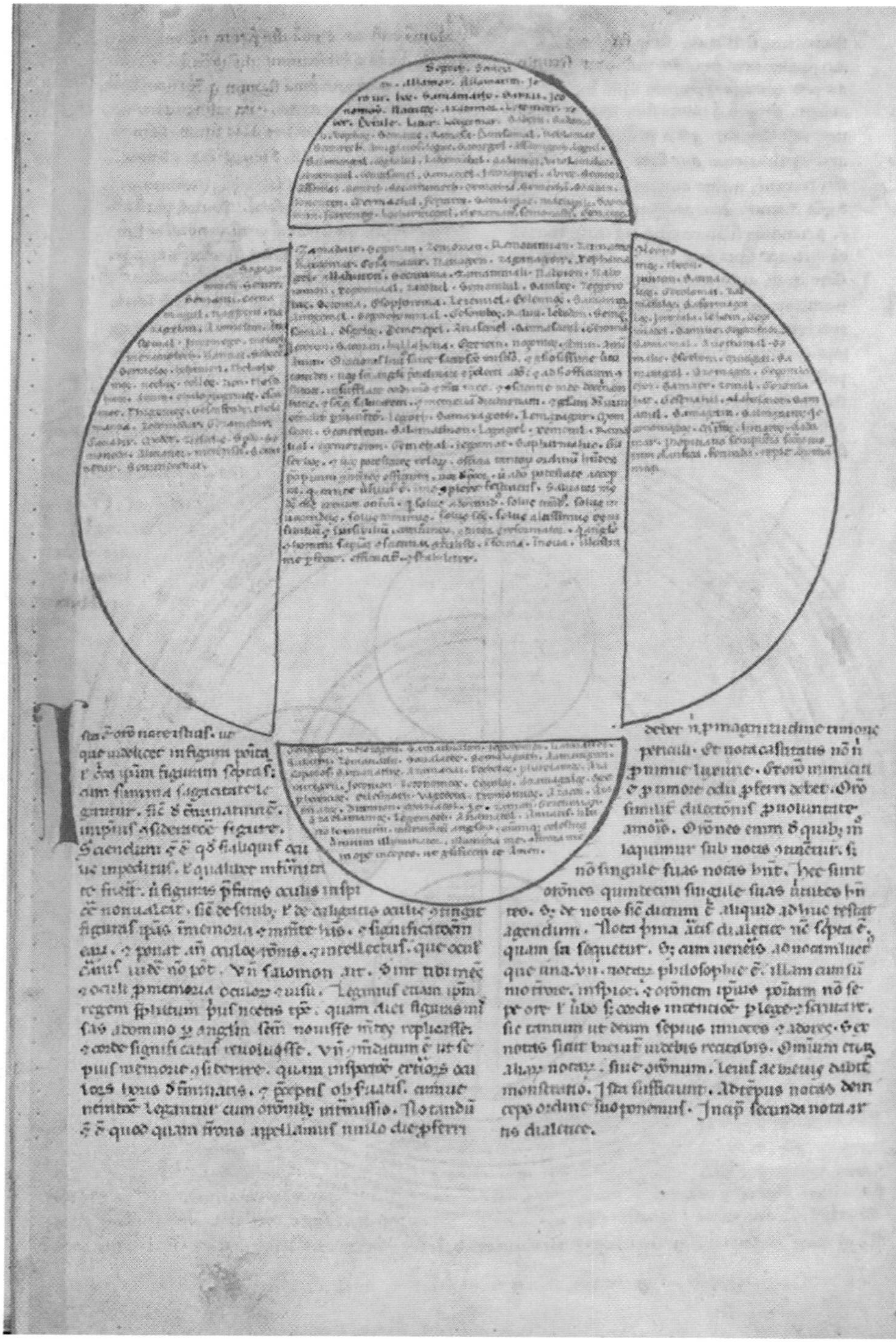

The second figure of logic/dialectic,
from New Haven, Yale University, Mellon, MS 1, f. 12v.

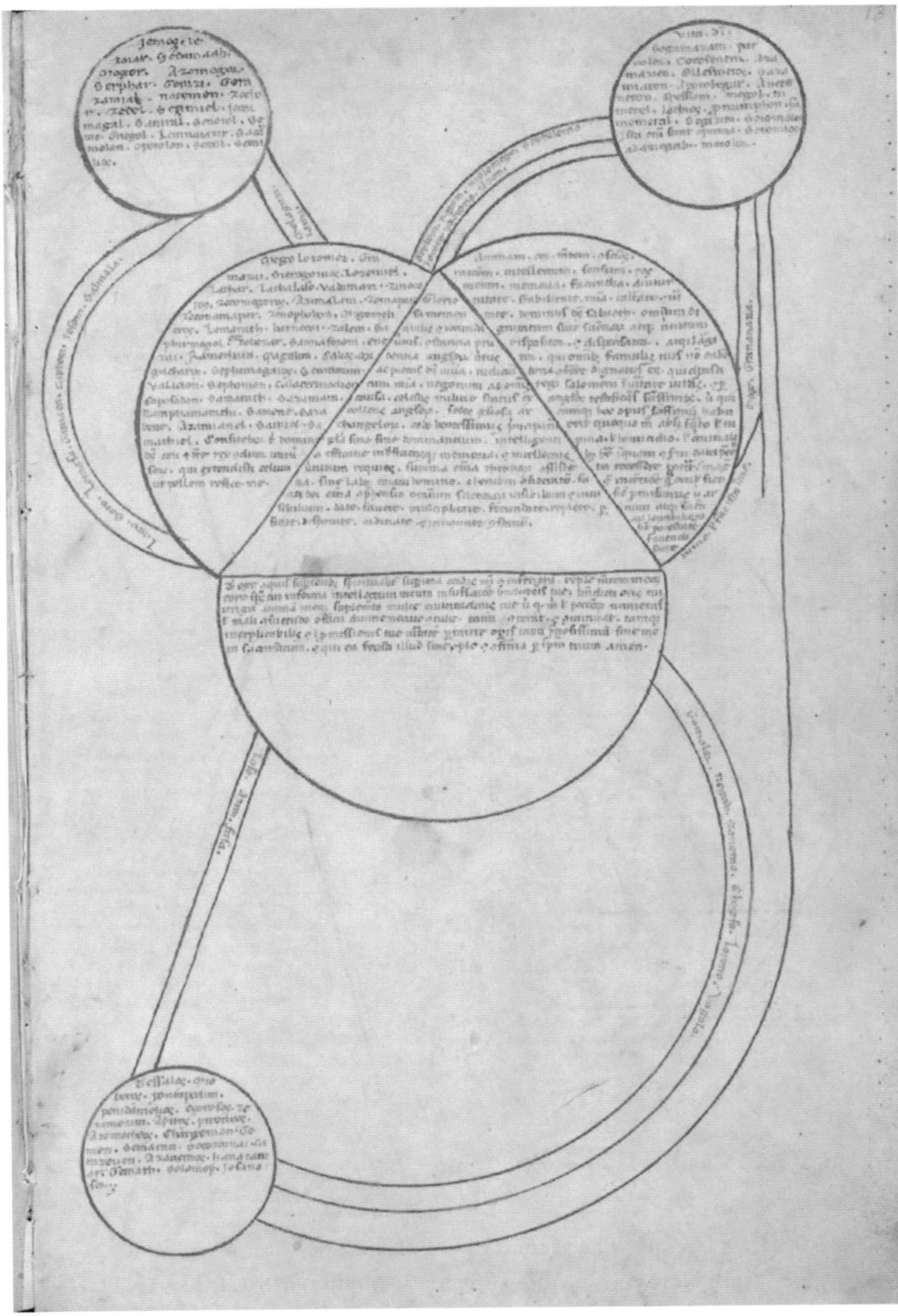

The first figure of rhetoric,
from New Haven, Yale University, Mellon, MS 1, f. 13.

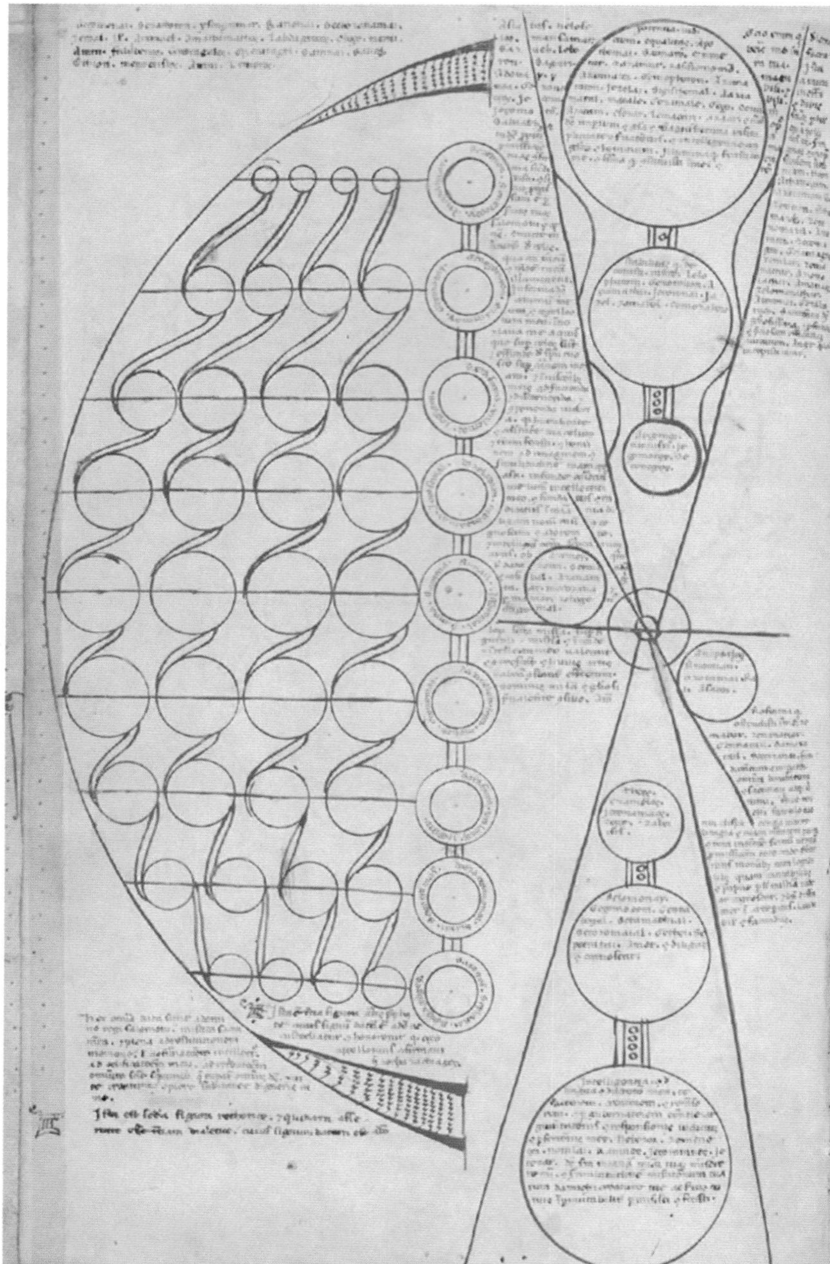

The second figure of rhetoric,
from New Haven, Yale University, Mellon, MS 1, f. 13v.

[**Notice the absence of the third figure of rhetoric from Mellon. It is found in Version A2 in BnF 7152 and Sloane 1712.**]

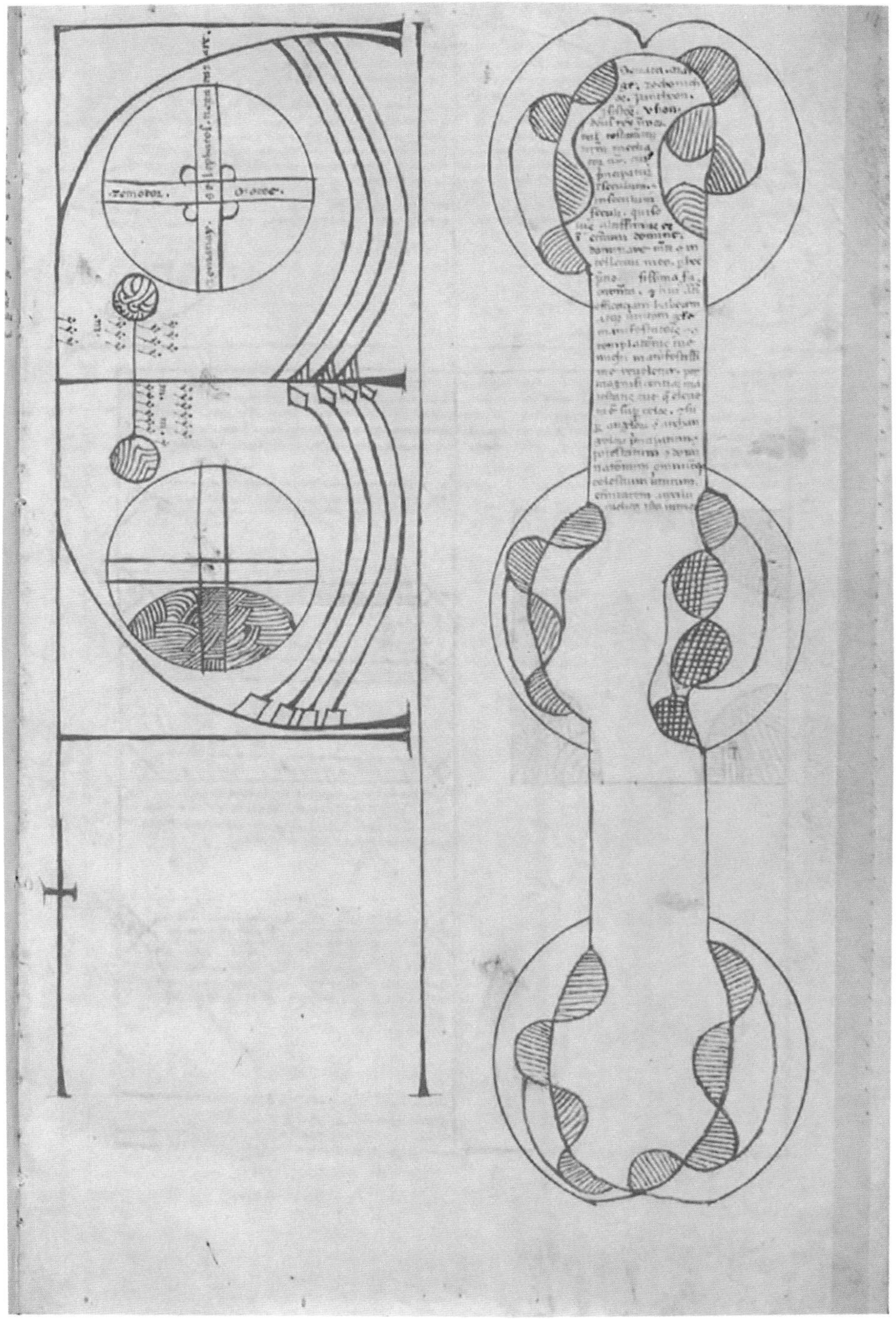

The first figure of geometry (*left*) and the fourth figure of rhetoric (*right*), from New Haven, Yale University, Mellon, MS 1, f. 14.

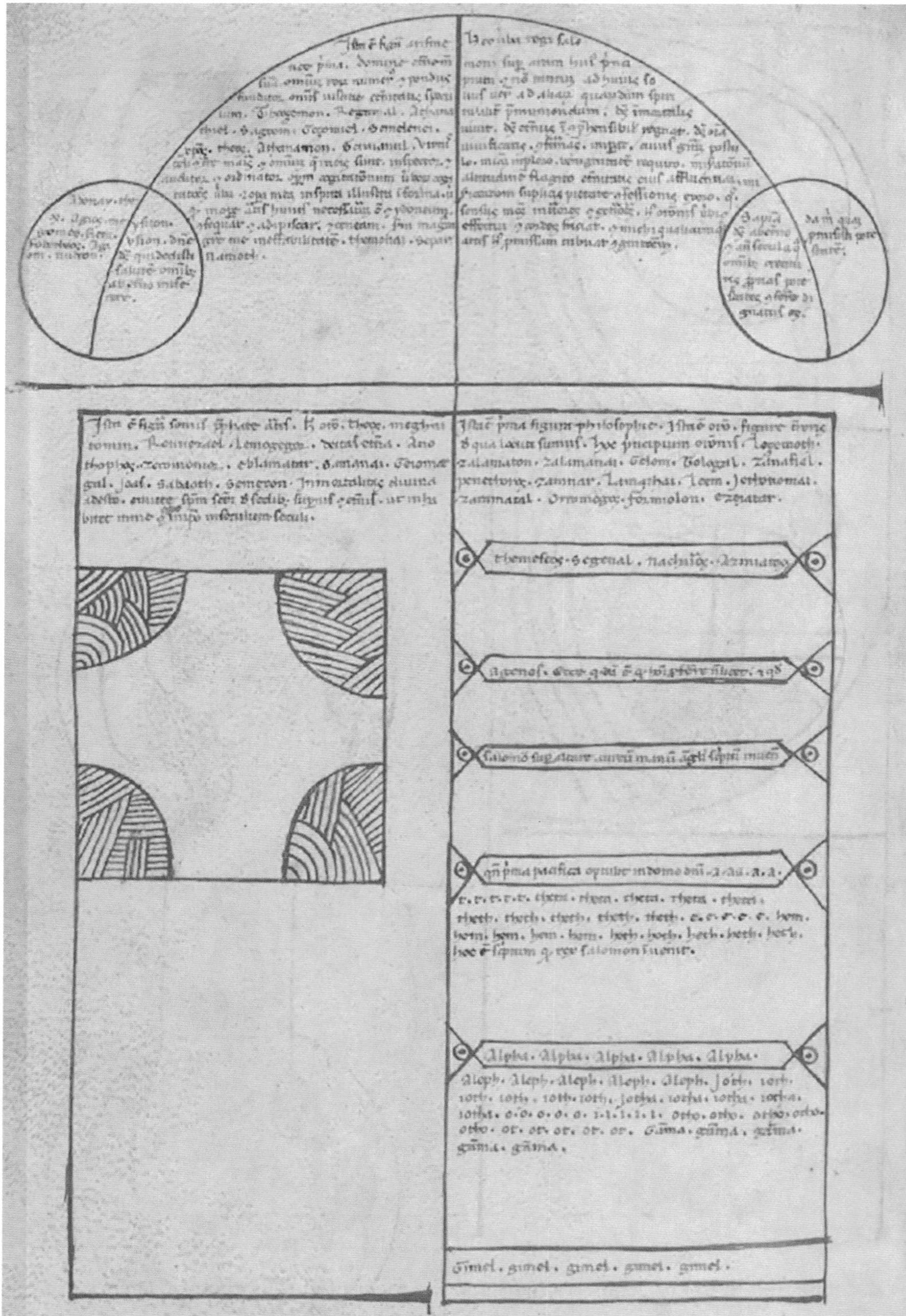
Alpha. Alpha. Alpha. Alpha. Alpha.
Gimel. gimel. gimel. gimel. gimel.

The first figure of arithmetic is depicted as a semicircle with a circle at each of its ends (*top*). Below the first figure of arithmetic are two columns. The half figure of arithmetic is a simple square with hash markings at each of its corners (*bottom, left-hand column*). There is prayer which Solomon supposedly offered during his sacrifice of peacemaking to God which contains *voces magicae*. The prayer in the bottom right column is associated with the first figure of philosophy, but that figure does not appear on this folio. Additionally, Version A has a rubric of special prayers for the first figure of philosophy. It reads: These two figures and the prayer of Solomon are from New Haven, Yale University, Mellon, MS 1, f. 14v.

This [figure here] is the first philosophy, and that [below] is the prayer, and it is the figure of awe of which we had spoken. This is the first part of the prayer: Lezemoth, Zalomoton, Zalamanay, Gelora, Tonagal, Xanafial, Penetores, Zainnai, Lemarai, Leui, Ieconamai, Zaramatal, Orivmofor, Unolon, Eziatai.

[The second part of the prayer] Themetheos, Segenal, Vacharig, Azauuachos, Agenos.

Behold, a certain *nota* that is to be offered to mankind by which it came to Solomon above the golden altar by the hand of an angel.

[This prayer below] is to be offered seven times in peacemaking in the day of the Lord.

A. A. A. A. T. T. T. T. Theta. Theta. Theta. Theta. Theta. Thet. Thet. Thet. Thet. Thet. E. E. E. E. E. E. Hem. Hem. Hem. Hem. Hem. Hec. Hec. Hec. Hec. Hec.

This [prayer] that Solomon discovered out of seven hundred.

Alpha. Alpha. Alpha. Alpha. Alpha.

Aleph. Aleph. Aleph. Aleph. Aleph.

Ioth. Ioth. Ioth. Ioth. Ioth. Iotha. Iotha.

Iotha. Iotha. Iotha. O. O. O. O. O. I. I. I. I. I.

Otho. Otho. Otho. Otho. Otho. Ot. Ot. Ot. Ot. Ot.

Gamma. Gamma. Gamma. Gamma. Gamma. Gimel. Gimel. Gimel. Gimel. Gimel.

The rubric indicates that the "certain *nota*" is the first *nota* of philosophy. Here, the *nota* is associated with the time in which Solomon entered the Temple and stood before the golden altar performing penance for his house servant who disrespected the notory art . . . However, the timing is conflated with the biblical account, 1 Kings 3, in which Solomon made an offering in peacemaking to the Lord on Mount Gibeon before the Temple was built; the *Ars Notoria* claims that is the time in which Solomon received the golden book of the notory art. Thus, the rubric above suggests that the *voces magicae* prayer that is to be offered seven times in peacemaking is the same prayer Solomon offered on Mount Gibeon.

The second figure of philosophy (*left*), the third figure of philosophy (*center*), and the fourth figure of philosophy (*right*), from New Haven, Yale University, Mellon, MS 1, f. 15.

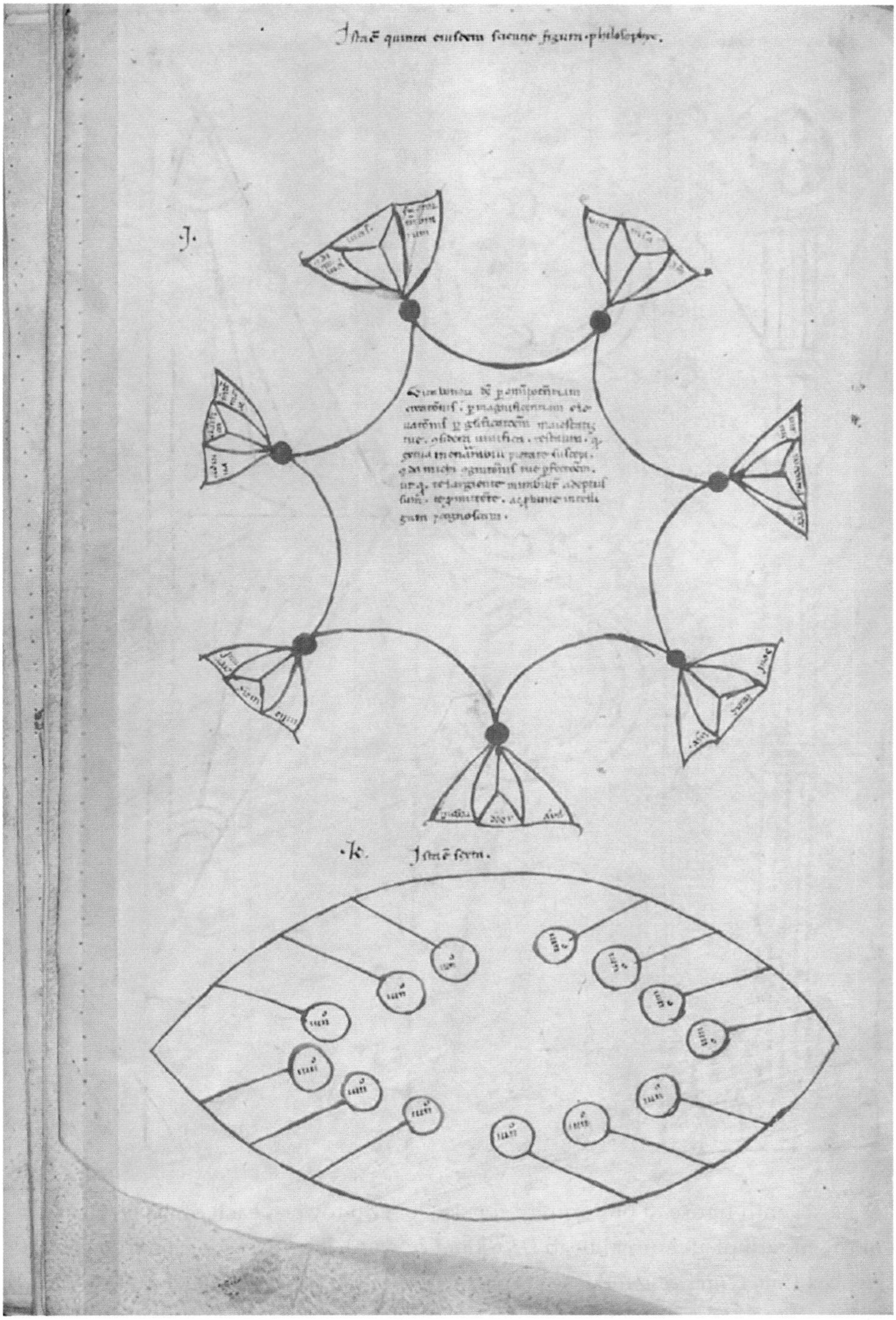

The fifth figure of philosophy (*top*) and the sixth figure of philosophy (*bottom*), from New Haven, Yale University, Mellon, MS 1, f. 15v.

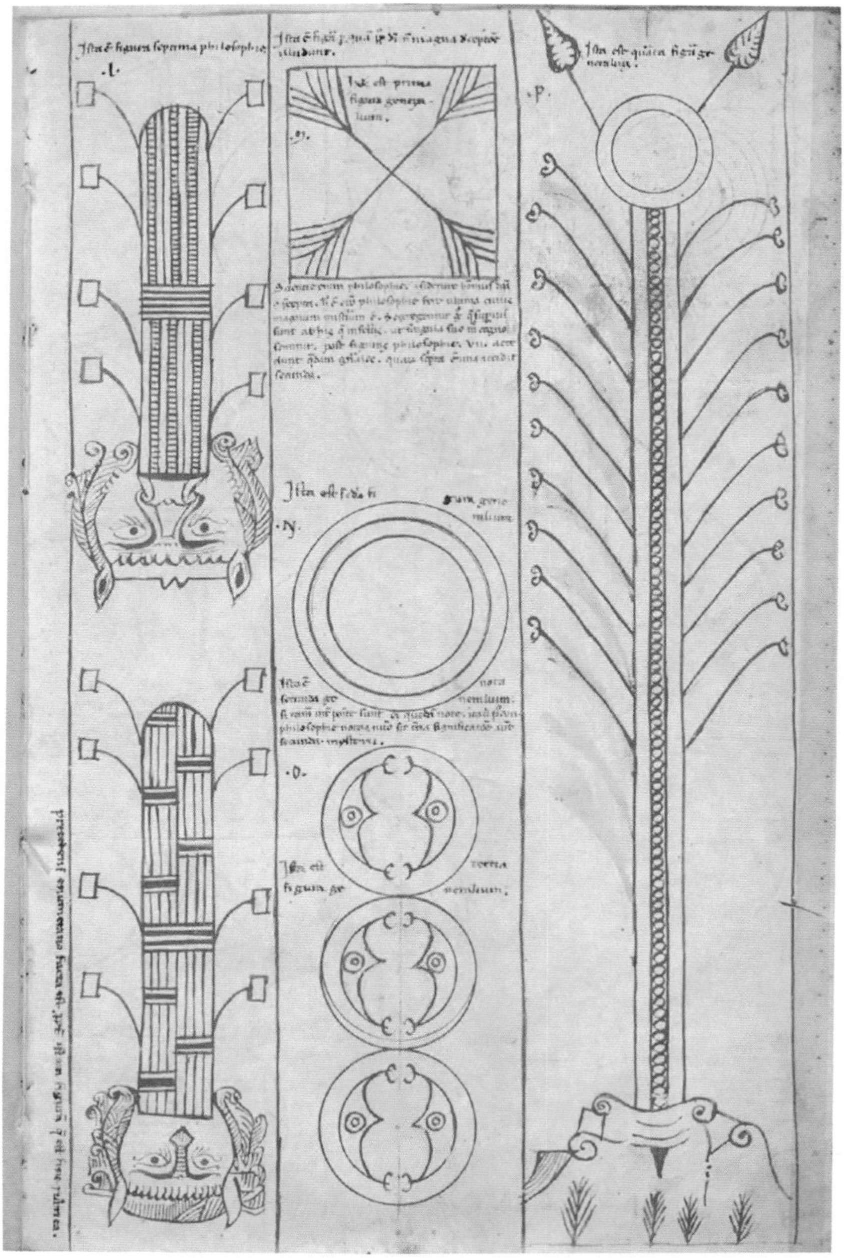

The seventh figure of philosophy consists of two towers, each of which rise out of the mouth of an animal head (*left-hand column*). The first figure of the general sciences (*top, center column*), the second figure of the general sciences (*center, center column*), and the third figure of the general sciences (*bottom, center column*). The fourth figure of the general sciences (*right-hand column*). These five figures come from New Haven, Yale University, Mellon, MS 1, f. 16.

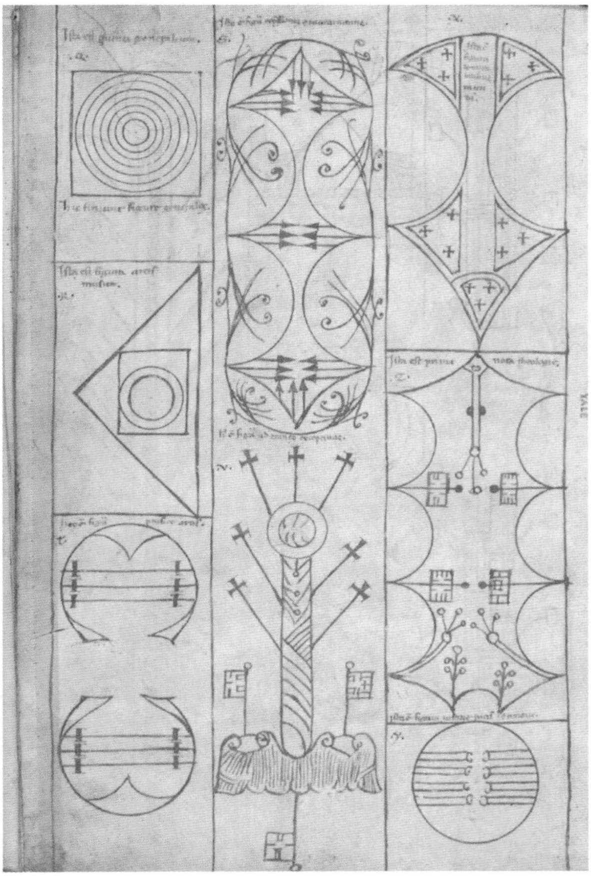

Mislabeled as the fifth figure of the general sciences, the figure of concentric rings is, in fact, the third figure of astronomy as informed by Clm 276, f. 17v, which has the same figure, reading "*Ista est nota de caelo siderum*" (This is the figure of the stars of heaven). This astronomical figure is further verified with the similar figure found in Version B manuscripts. There is no fifth figure of the general sciences according to the text of the *Ars Notoria*, indicating that this labeling was made in error (*top, left-hand column*). The figure of music likely draws its inspiration as a triangular shape from Plato's *lambda* (the Greek letter λ) as described in the dialogue of *Timaeus* (*center, left-hand column*). The figure of medicine presents a concealed vestige of the Sphere of Life and Death (*bottom, left-hand column*). The figure of reprehension and taciturnity (*top, center column*). The figure of exceptives which is meant for the seven forms of divination (*bottom, center column*). The first figure of astronomy, which is called here "*de mirabilibus mundi*" (of the wonders of the world) (*top, right-hand column*), the first figure of theology (*center, right-hand column*), and the circular figure of justice, peace, and fear (*bottom, right-hand column*). These eight figures come from New Haven, Yale University, Mellon, MS 1, f. 16v.

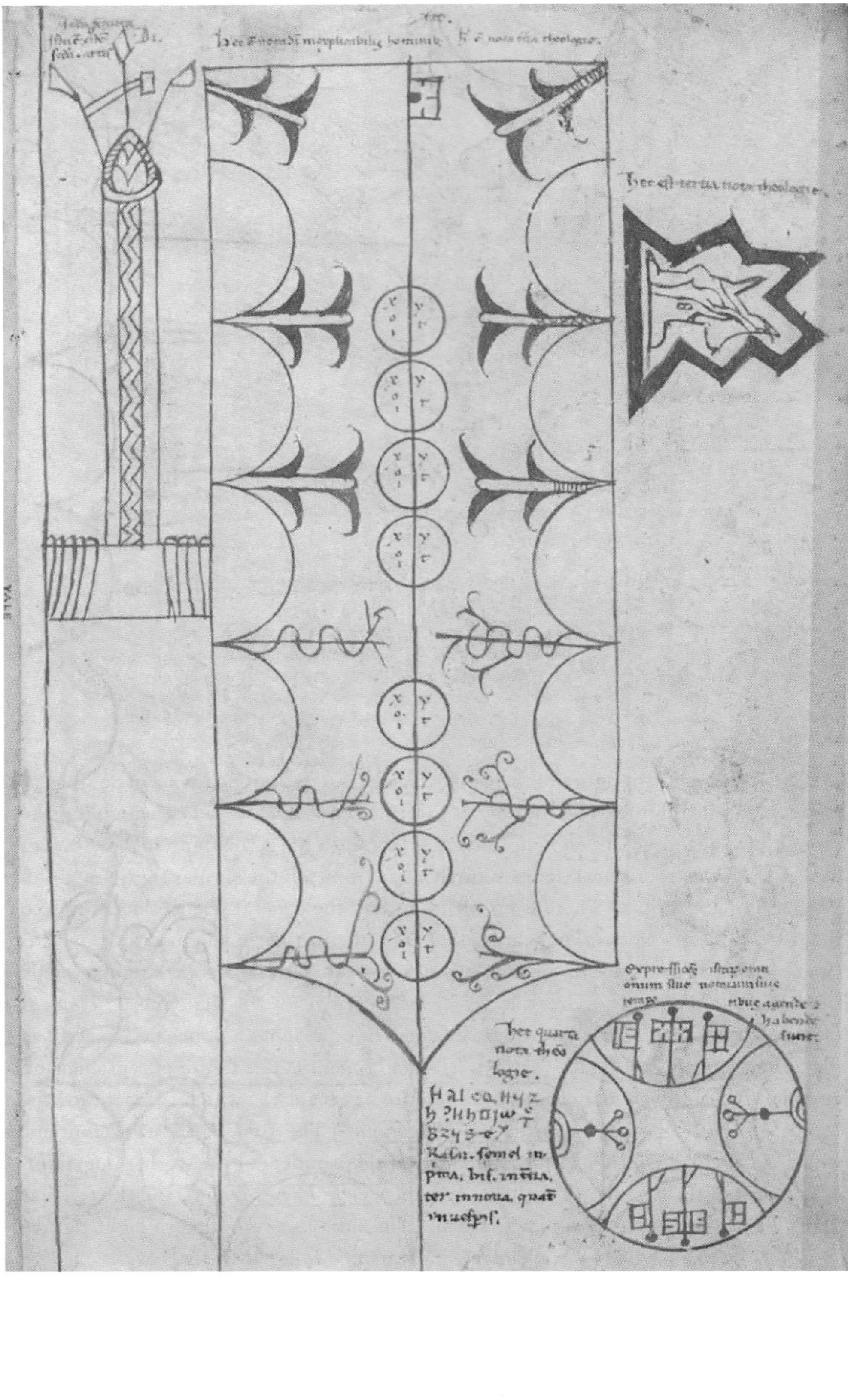

The second figure of theology appears as a tower with a zigzag path leading up to the top in which three banners are placed at its pinnacle. Although simplified here, examination of the same figure in other manuscripts suggests that these three banners represent the Holy Trinity (Son, God, and Holy Spirit, from left to right). The far left banner has a sword protruding from it, indicating that it is the Son as depicted in the Apocalypse of John (Revelation 1:16 NRSV) (*top, left*). The first figure of philosophy is a window figure, displaying an view of heavenly paradise with trees and vegetation. There are eight wheels which contain the letters "xoiyt," which may represent the *voces magicae* from the prayer of Solomon, which is associated with this figure (the prayer of Solomon is mentioned on page 309 and appears in the figure on page 308), (*center of the folio*). The third figure of theology (*top, right*). The fourth figure of theology (*bottom, right*). These four figures come from New Haven, Yale University, Mellon, MS 1, f. 17.

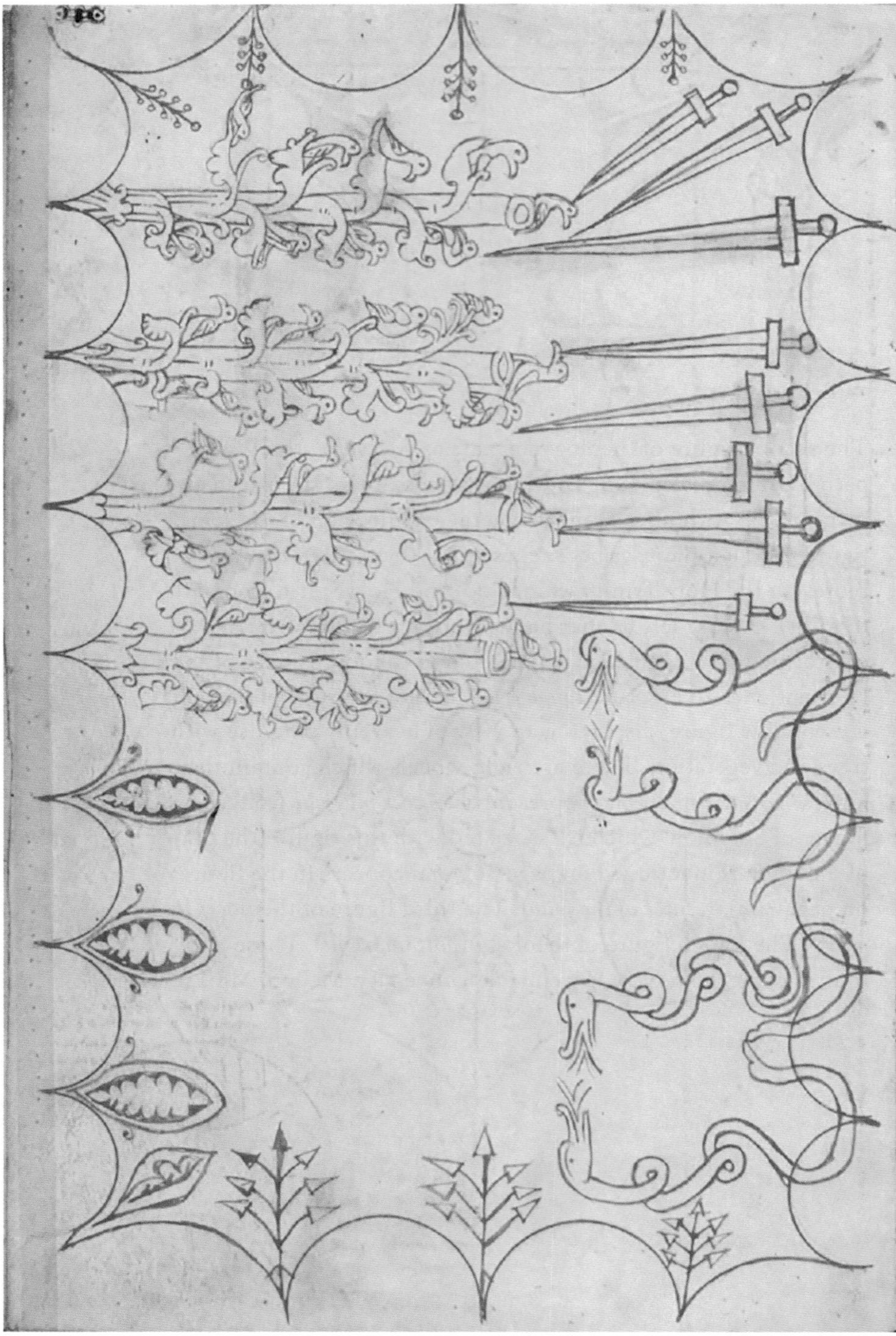

The fifth figure of theology, also called the ineffable *nota,* from New Haven, Yale University, Mellon, MS 1, f. 17v.

Selection of Version A Folios

The following selection of folios show diverse presentations of the *Ars Notoria* across several extant Version A manuscripts.

Plate 1: Sloane 1712, an example of Version A2

Plate 2: BnF Latin 7373, a copy of Euclid's Elements that features the first figure of rhetoric

Plate 3: BnF Latin 7373, a copy of Euclid's Elements that features the first figure of rhetoric

Plate 4: CLM 276

Plate 5: CLM 276

Plate 6: Klosterneuburg, Augustiner-Chorherrenstift, CC 221

Plate 7: Klosterneuburg, Augustiner-Chorherrenstift, CC 221

Plate 8: BnF Latin 7152

Plate 9: Mellon 1

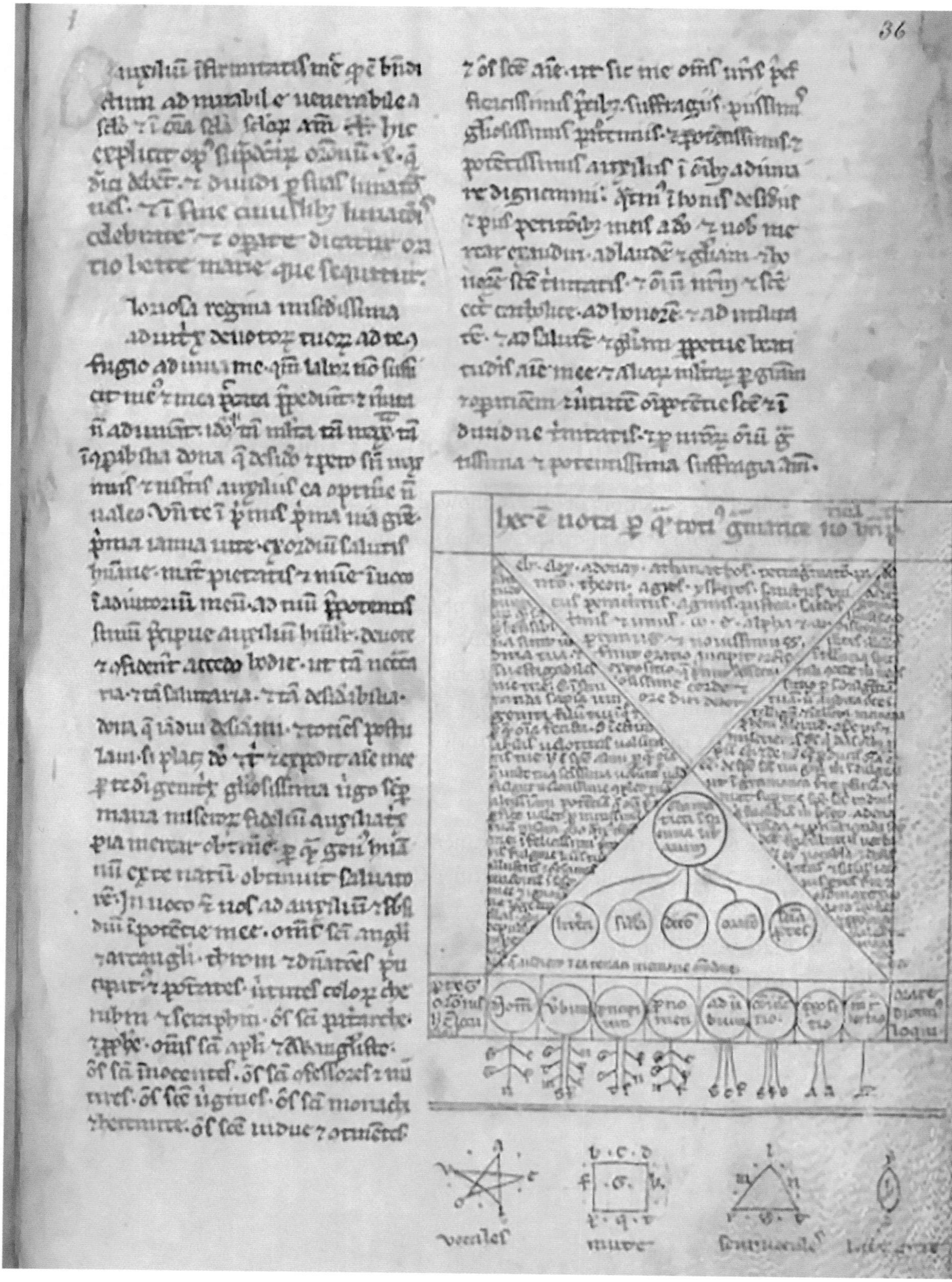

Plate 1

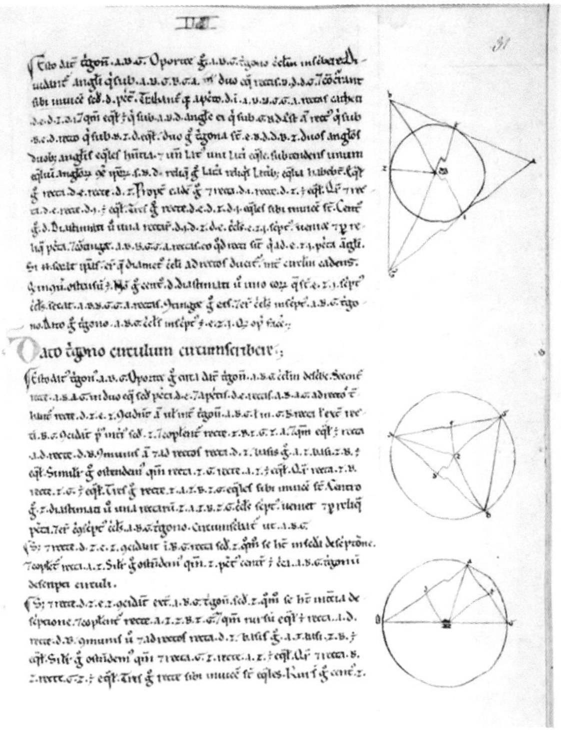

Plate 2

Plate 3

Plate 4

Plate 5

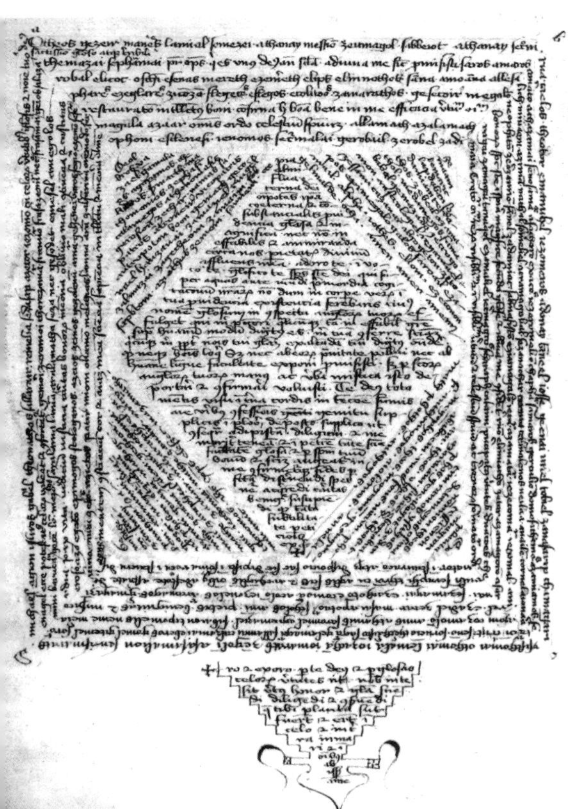

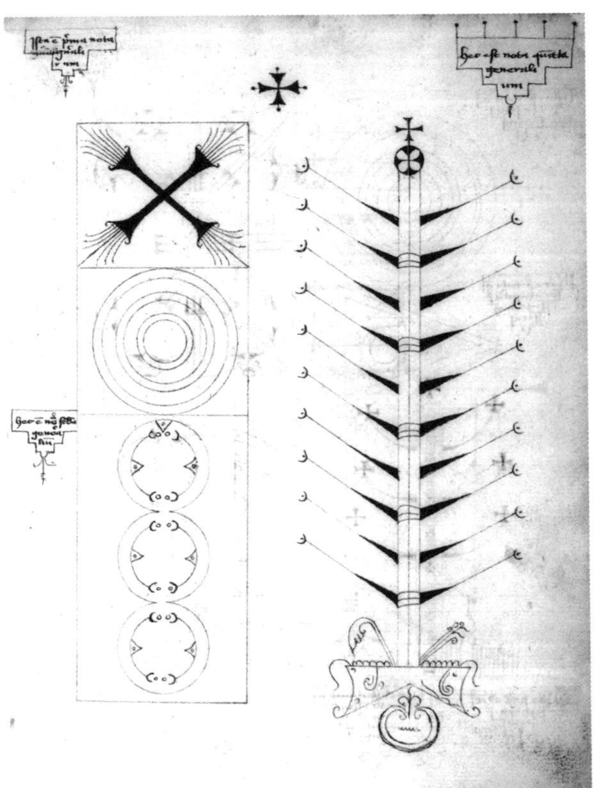

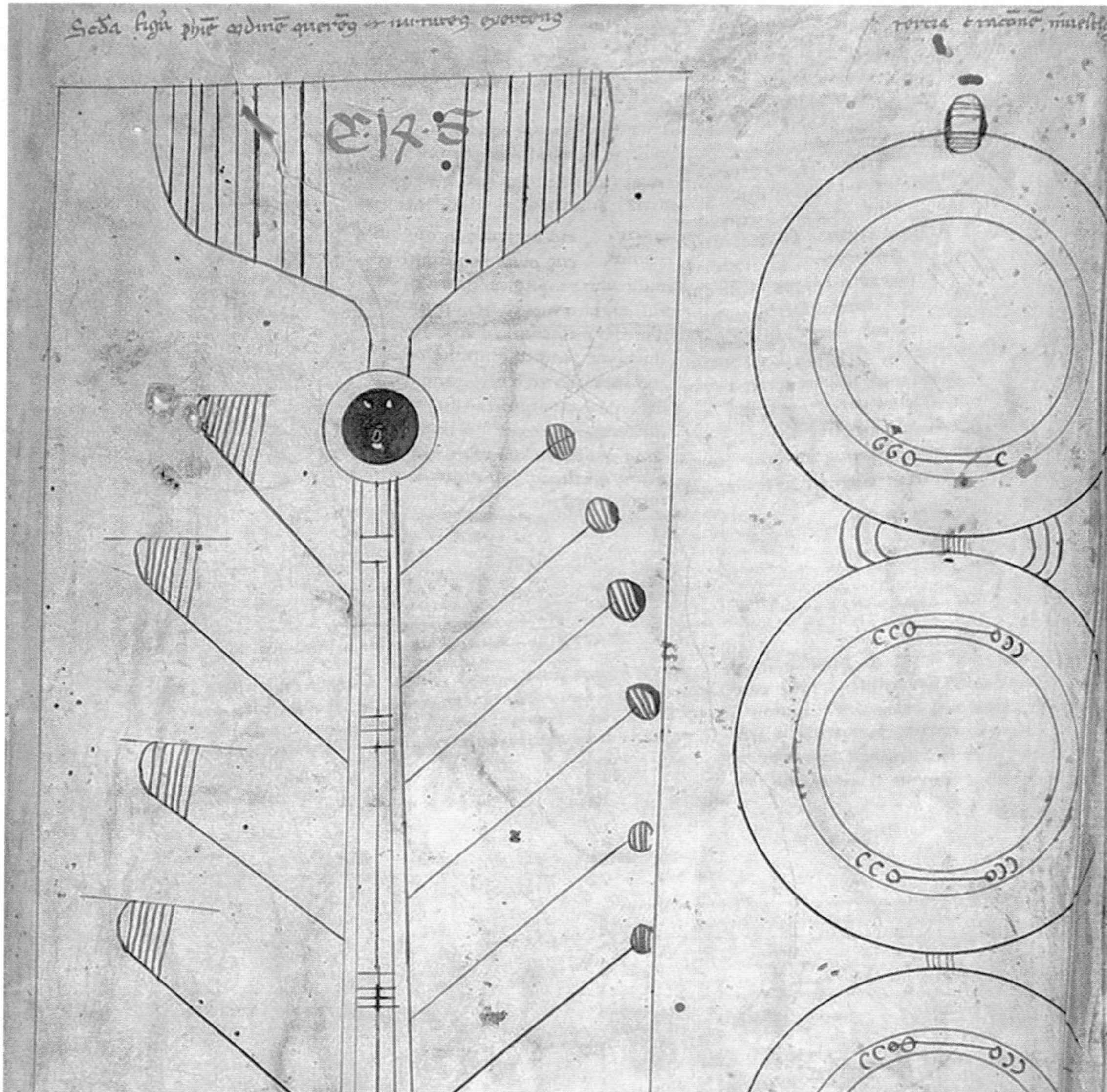

Plate 6

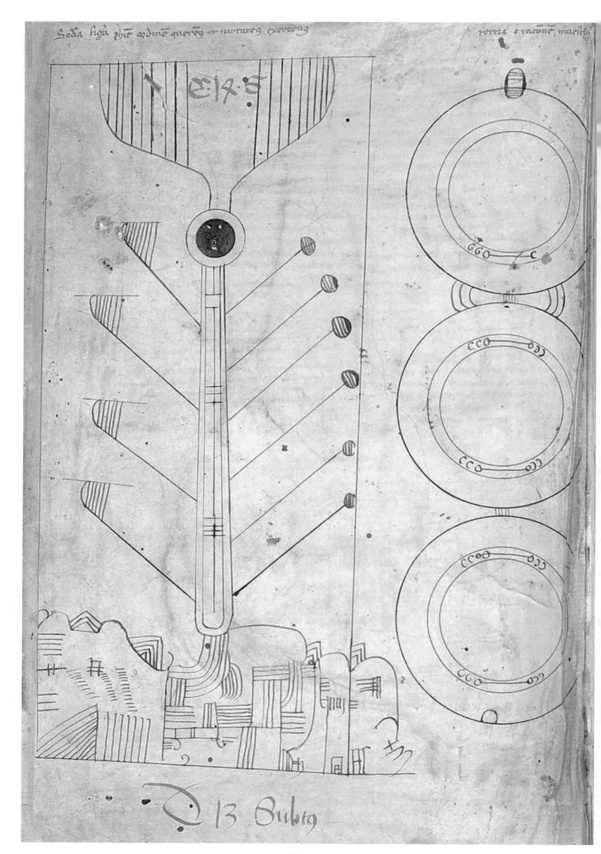

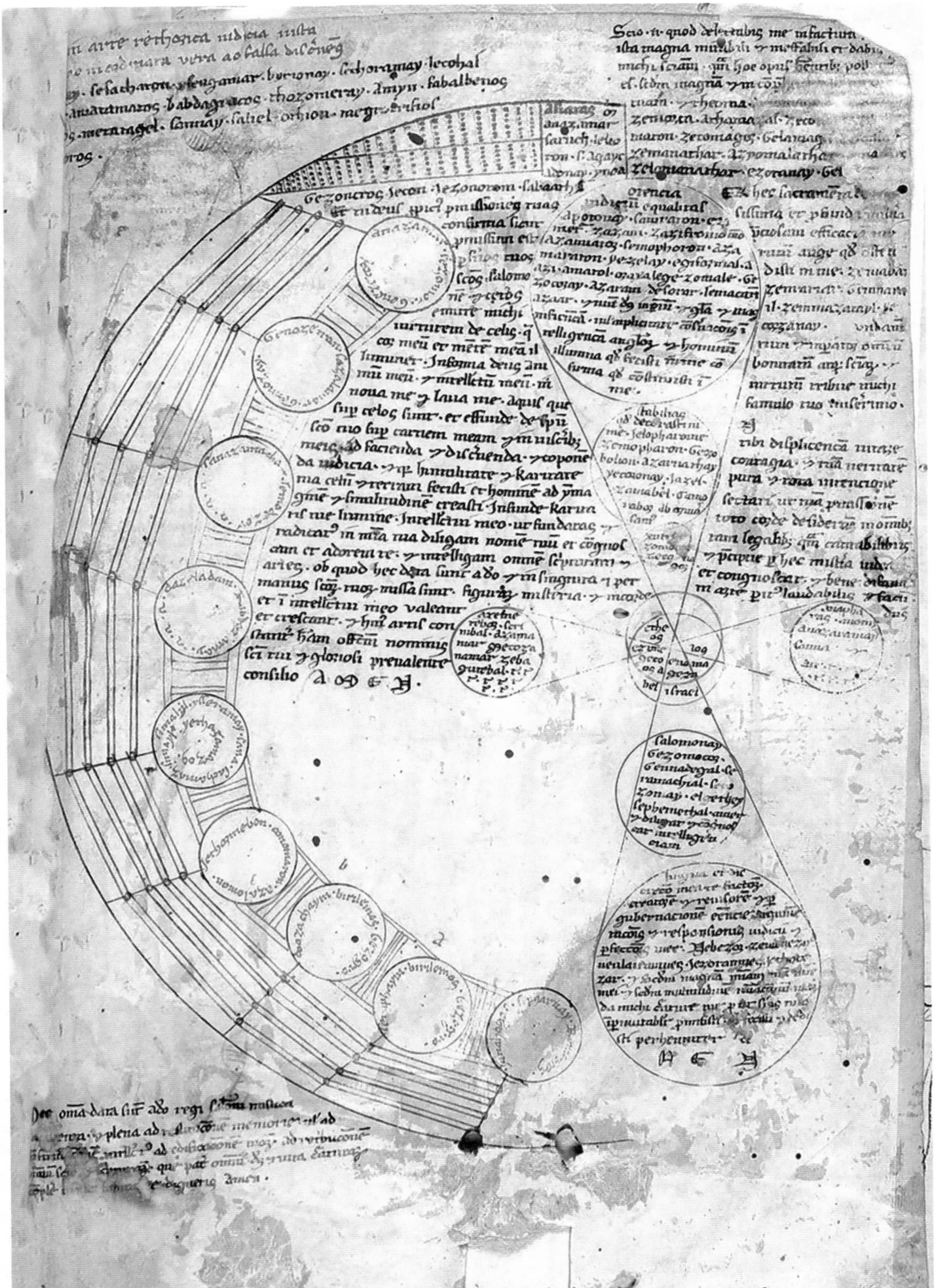

Plate 7

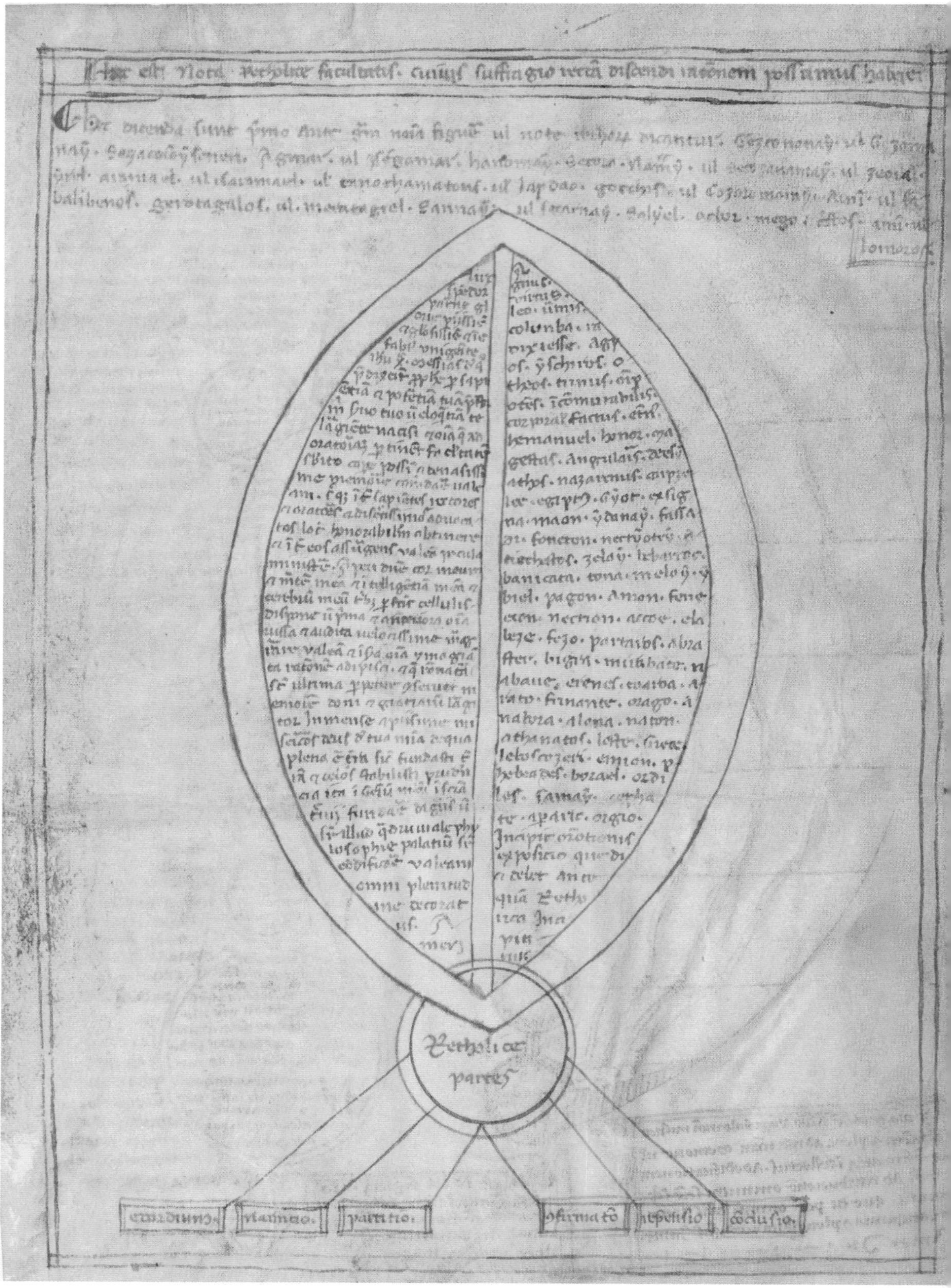
Hec est Nota Retholice facultatis. cuius suffragio veram discendi rationem possumus habere
Retholice partes
exordium
narratio
partitio
confirmatio
conclusio

Plate 8

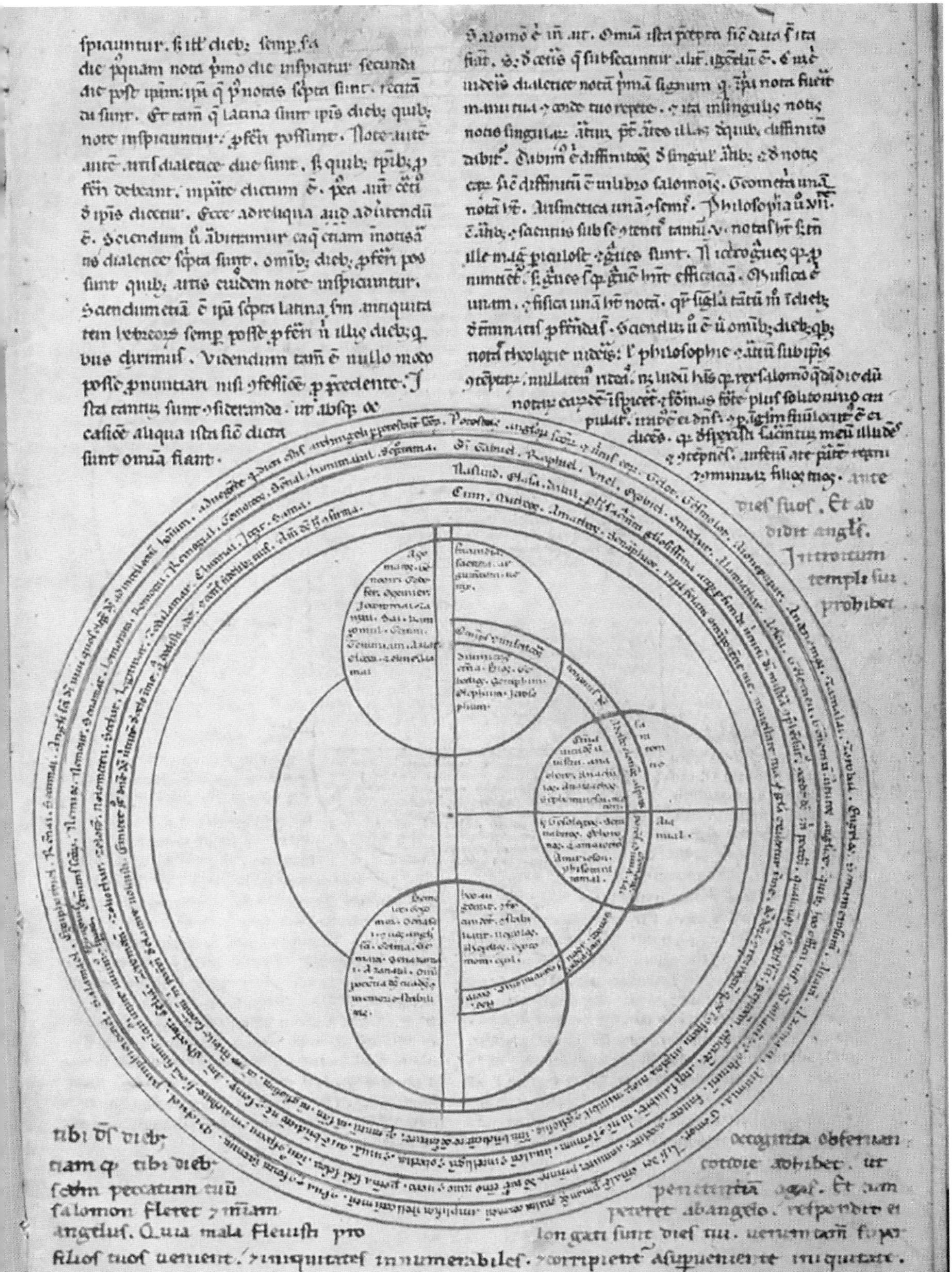

Plate 9

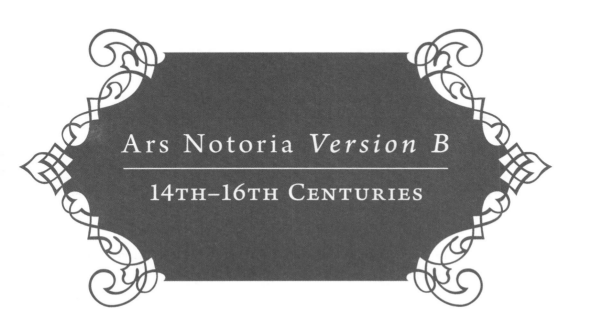

Ars Notoria *Version B*

14th–16th Centuries

Version B contains extended commentary (glosses) on Version A, and the same prayers are found in both versions. Rather than duplicate the wording of Version A, a bracketed mention indicates where the repeated sections appear.

Rubrics in Version B follow the Latin, with the exception of the repeated Version A prayers. Although the rubrics occasionally differ from Version A to Version B, for easier visual reference, bracketed mentions are all black.

4

Glosses and Variations

[Prologue]

In the name of the holy and indivisible Trinity. The most sacred notory art begins, which the Most High Creator, through his angel above the altar of the Temple, ministered to Solomon while he was praying on a certain night,[1] *so that through it, he would be able to acquire and possess all the liberal sciences, mechanics, exceptives, and their faculties in a brief period of time, and in offering the mystical words of the holy prayers and invoking the names of the holy angels which are contained within them, he would be made the foundation in every science and wisdom.*

[Prologue Gloss] *In nomine sancte et individuae Trinitatis, etc.*[2] The name of the Most High Creator is to be invoked at the beginning of the operation of that most sacred notory art, so that it may be undertaken from the beginning, middle, and end, which is a beginning without a beginning, an end without an end, and from Him all things were created out of nothing. Therefore, when the Most High was establishing man as a worthy creature among all created things, (namely, within the lower world), [the Most High] transferred all the others to be under his rule, and enlightened him as a more worthy creature by the natural virtues. And it pleased the Most High, such that he had loved man so greatly that he had formed him in his own image and likeness, so that the

1. See depiction on page 7 from the front matter of BnF Latin 7153.

2. These are the opening words of the section being glossed as written by the medieval scribe for the purpose of identification, in this case the Prologue. The entire content is found under the same section number in Version A. The actual Version B manuscripts have all the content of Version A plus these glosses.

worthy *prae ceteris*[3] himself might be worthy to be illuminated with virtues; from whom when the Most High Maker was forming man alone, he wanted the science of natural virtue itself to be taught and all wisdom to be illuminated, and thus the Lord established him master above all other creatures, and commanded all creatures should obey man himself, and rendered him trained with all knowledge and wisdom and making him, among other things, wise.

And although the first man[4] himself had perfectly illuminated all the wisdom of the Most High, yet we find that not only did he minister his own grace, wisdom, and knowledge to [Adam] alone but to many others, we discover one among others—namely Solomon, whom the Most High chose beforehand, so that he was making a foundation of His own grace, wisdom, and knowledge in him; and thus, he sent to him some golden tablets by his own angel Pamphilius, in which were transcribed certain names of holy angels with prayers in Greek, Chaldean, and Hebrew. And together with those prayers were some forms depicted of a protracted and diverse manner, which the angel himself carried down in the same golden tablets above the altar of the Temple that Solomon had built to God. He presented it to him, speaking about what those prayers were signifying and about what those figures were extending. And he was revealing the elements just as to a child,[5] teaching him the method, form, and contents of the operation. But Solomon, having received the angelic command, accepted that golden book with great devotion. He proceeded, following the angelic mandate in that holy work, reading the prayers one by one at their [designated] times, according to the lunar months, never exceeding beyond the mandated form, just as the angel had ministered to him. Thus, by divine grace, having finished the work, he received all knowledge and possessed all wisdom thenceforth.

Then after Solomon, Apollonius, having been called a philosopher to whose hand, through God's grace, came before this most sacred art, elucidated, in part, the Greek, Hebrew, and Chaldean prayers into Latin. He explained as much

3. *Prae ceteris,* literally "in front of the others," is a rank or a grade given to a candidate. Universities will give the highest honorary title, *laudabilis prae ceteris,* to students, meaning "commendable over others." Saint Augustine calls Paul of Tarsus the *prae ceteris* of the apostles (*Confessions* 7.21). Here the glosser is referring to the laborer of the notory art.

4. *Proto-plaustrum,* literally "the first wagon," is an epithet for Adam.

5. In other words, he was revealing the elements to Solomon just as a teacher would instruct a child about the letters of the alphabet.

of those as he could more simply and concisely, and many, on account of the difficulty and long-windedness of their expositions which they have in themselves, he dismissed thoroughly, just as he found it written in Solomon's book.[6] But in that most sacred art, which is called the notory art by Solomon and elsewhere the art of memory, the most sacred mystery contains it within itself, because nothing else is to be contained within itself except the most sacred deprecations[7] of the orations among those names of the holy angels are to be named residing in the presence of the Highest, and in having deprecated, they are to be invoked.

By having recounted those prayers and by having deprecated with invocations the names of the holy angels in their own proper times, keeping to their own lunar months, it will be explained and clearly shown in the following headings [that] you will be able to acquire the memory, the grace in speaking well,[8] a persuasive eloquence,[9] and both the understanding and mental stability which is first to be gained in this work, which the above said have with respect to these particular prayers which you will find their own distinctions and orders in this summary.

Having possessed and acquired those aforesaid first, any knowledge of the seven liberal arts, mechanics, and exceptives will be able to be possessed,

---

6. According to the gloss, Apollonius explained some of the Greek, Hebrew, and Chaldean prayers through the partial Latin translations, called "prologues" because they provide just the beginning part of those prayers (see the gloss of section 10). Apollonius left some prayers without a Latin prologue because either their Latin translations would be too long and laborious to write out or offer as prayers, or their complexity was too great for even Apollonius to comprehend. The *Ars Notoria* explains that the Greek, Hebrew, and Chaldean prayers hold an occult virtue which human reason cannot comprehend (sections 6, 12, 17, 35, 37, 49, and 56); this incomprehensible quality of the prayers reflects the Greek magical formulas called the *ephasia grammata,* which also has a list of unintelligible words and syllables spoken in magical rites. In section 11, the *Ars Notoria* expresses the same admonition as found in theurgic writings, warning, "'Do not change the *nomina barbara* [barbarous names]'; that is, the names handed down by the gods to each race have ineffable power in the initiation rites." See Majercik, *The Chaldean Oracles,* fragment 150.

7. As mentioned in footnote 139 on page 247, the archaic use of the word "deprecation" or "deprecate" as a noun, verb, or participle is all but obsolete in a religious context. The word simply means a prayer or to pray.

8. *Facundia,* usually translated as "eloquence." However, in this context it specifically refers to the grace in speaking well.

9. *Eloquentia,* usually translated as eloquence. However, here it means specifically to speak well and be persuasive. The glosser most certainly would have been familiar with Quintilian, who makes this distinction in the prologue of his *Institutio Oratoria* (*Institutes of Oratory*).

acquired, and retained by memory with respect to having particular [virtues], having recounted beforehand the headings and prayers. But in acquiring the sciences, it is necessary to inspect these figures above their descriptions and assignments for one month, and to offer their prayers at their own [designated] times, their own lunar months and assigned hours, and according to the mandates assigned here to rule his life.

What prayers are necessary for these things mentioned above, and at what times and in which lunar months the prayers ought to be said and the figures ought to be inspected, and how he ought to rule his own working life, and [how] to proceed through the order in this holy work will be fully and perfectly explained in the following headings in their own places.

[Variation 1] Alpha and Omega, O almighty God, the beginning of all things without a beginning, the ending without an end, hear today my prayers. O most pious one, neither repay me according to my iniquity nor according to my sins, O Lord my God, but according to your mercy, which is greater than all visible and invisible things. Have mercy on me, O Wisdom of the Father, Christ, the light of the angels, the glory of the holy ones, the hope, the harbor, and the refuge of sinners, the originator of all things and redeemer of human frailty, who holds the weight of heaven and earth, the seas and mountains in the palm of your hand. O most pious one, I deprecate and entreat you, [being] one with the Father, may you illuminate my soul with the ray of light of your most Holy Spirit, may I be able to progress far in this most sacred art, so that I may prevail with respect to the renown of such knowledge and any of all the arts and wisdom, memory, eloquence, intelligence, and intellectual virtue to come before your most Holy Spirit and your name; and you, who are my God, who in the beginning created the heaven and the earth, and all things out of nothing, who restores, fills, and restores all things in your Spirit, make my intellect sound, so that I may glorify you through all works of my thoughts and my words. O God the Father, strengthen my prayer, and augment my intellect and my memory for the knowledge of all writings, the memory, the eloquence, and the perseverance, which is to be undertaken, known, [and] retained, you who lives and reigns through the infinite age of ages, amen.

[Variation 1 Gloss] *Alpha et Omega, Deus omnipotens, etc.* This prayer is the first prayer of that most holy art, and for that reason [it] is described in the beginning, because it ought to be pronounced and offered before the other prayers are offered, and having finished [it] in an operation[10] of any hour of the day, [and] having offered all the prayers similarly once, it is to be offered again from *Alpha et Omega,* because it is the beginning and the end; and thus having said that prayer first, the three following headwords, which are *Heliscemaht, etc.; Theos, Megale, etc.; Lux mundi, etc.,* are to be said afterward.[11]

And after these three headwords have been said there are these nine prayers that are called the *novem termini.*[12] They are the last prayers of the text of this art and should always be offered throughout the three days before the beginning of this work. Having completed any operation, the same prayers themselves are to be offered through the three days.[13]

And such reason is how they ought to always be offered first at the beginning of any operation, similarly and at the end, because these prayers are of such great virtue and efficacy that as long as they are offered through the three days before the beginning of that month in which the operator ought to begin, having done a fasting on bread and water on the first day of those three and having made confession beforehand, and on the other two days let him fast on Lenten food, [then] it will be revealed to the operator in those three nights spent in sleep, through an angel in a vision, to what end he will be able to come before with respect to this work and what effect he will obtain thereafter, and whether he is worthy to undertake so great work.[14]

Similarly, if the work, having been completed and having been executed in the proper order according to the precepts, the said prayers are to be offered through the three days, just as it is said. So great is the virtue and efficacy that

---

10. The operation for each art or science which the operator may pursue to acquire. These are listed in section 126 gloss.

11. This gloss adds *Alpha et Omega* as a new preamble to the *tria prima capitula*, the first three headwords.

12. See sections 126–27. Variation 1 gloss goes on to briefly sketch out the greater ritual discussed in chapter VI and section 126 gloss.

13. The operation of the three days has an opening and a closing to the central part of the entire operation. See glosses of Section 126e–f.

14. Compare to section 126e gloss.

they conserve the acquired memory and eloquence first, and another science having been acquired through that art by memory.

And if they are omitted in the operation owing to some negligence or some sin, and those prayers are offered (just as it is said), all things shall be restored and brought back to their effect through their virtue, and they are conserved firmly; and the entire work is conserved, from beginning to end, having been judged a firm, stable, and perpetual memory. Likewise, if for some reason—for example, having drunk to extravagance, having committed theft, or murder, or despair, or any other mortal sin thus—then he will have surrendered the knowledge gained through this holy art to forgetfulness at some time (like within the course of a year or two). Then [the operator] must fast for three days, just as it is said: the first day on bread and water, and in the other two days on Lenten food. And the aforementioned prayers are to be said on any day of those three days, thrice in a day—namely, once in the morning, once around the third [hour], once around noon[15]—and on those three days of the following month; after those three days he is not [required] to fast, which is to be done except through the eight days in the month separately[16] and not through the successive order (just as it is to be found in the text and in the glosses below and on Lenten food), and this is to be done when the prayers are to be offered, which they ought to be offered in those days. And thus this prayer *Alpha et Omega* should always be offered once before any [other] prayers are offered, and having finished the prayers it should be offered again, and thus, whichever above science is to be worked—for memory, eloquence, understanding, or some other efficacy and knowledge—[it is] always to be offered first, and similarly again at the end of any operation.

Also, it is to be understood that three things are to be inspected in this wondrous art—that is, the *nota,* the form,[17] and the prayer. And what *nota* is described in the art itself? Truly, the form is to be learned accordingly in this art. Specifically, the form is that sacramental and ineffable prayer which

15. See appendix A4, "Medieval Computations of Time."

16. Section 15.

17. Latin *figura*. The same Latin word is used in the remainder of this small paragraph. The form is the manner in which the strange names and words are ordered; the form is important because it has a great magnitude of qualities (see Section 17). The form (*figura*) is called Solomon's ordered form (*compositam figuram*) in section 8.

cannot be explained through the human sense of reason.[18] And the prayer is a deprecation for the atonement of one's sins, which is not to be attempted in a voice of deprecating[19] but to be read aloud [in a voice] pleasantly bursting forth; therefore, that art consisted in these entire three things. And the *nota* contains within itself the prayer and the form, from where [it is says in the text] every thing is a cognition in this art through the prayer and the form[20] and following the precepts given from God through the angel to be worked.

> Also, it is to be understood [that] the greatness of this work is a mystery and an inestimable sacrament to the human mind. And in this very work it is to be very much considered that nothing ought to be done in it beyond the proper form of the institution.[21]

For the first and particular commandment in this art is to believe firmly, because in all the commandments of God, faith comes before God in praying. The second is to have a great desire and volition to begin the work and to advance beyond that knowledge over which the operator sets out to operate. For it is written thus over the determination of this place.[22]

Whosoever will have read the prayers of this most sacred art presumptuously, or will have learned or taught of this science, or has tried with derision, or who will have practiced in a disgraceful manner, or will have practiced theft, robbery, perjury, or some other malice, let him know he himself will have no effect to gain in the aforesaid art, but also:

> Let him know that, without doubt, he will have incurred not only corporal but also spiritual detriment.[23] For the *prae ceteris,* having observed in the work itself, is the work,[24] wishing to have the cognition of this art, ought

18. The *Assaylemaht* prayer, see section 17.

19. That is, a penitent voice.

20. Latin *orationem et figuram*. This phrase is from the Version A Turin manuscript E.V. 13, section 5, fol. 8rb rather than Véronèse's critical edition. *Figuram* refers to Solomon's ordered forms of the prayers, rather than a pictorial figure.

21. Excerpt from *Opus operum,* section A.

22. Section 5 gloss.

23. Section 57.

24. The operator is the work; the notory art is the means for personal and spiritual transformation.

to study himself with so much faith, so much taciturnity, and chastity with fasting while he is in the work itself, and never will [the cognition] have been a vision except that it ought to reveal something to him in this art by some compulsion or occasion."[25]

And these commandments are especially expressed here, so that anyone sees to them beforehand does not incur some danger from the abovesaid things in this holy operation. And thus let no one exceed the form of this document if he wants to attain to some good end of this art. For it is to be understood that in this most holy art all the sciences, licit and illicit, are comprehended in the prayers, figures, and *notae,* and through them they are able to be posssessed and acquired just like the trivium—namely, grammar, logic, [and] rhetoric—and these fields of knowledge have their own particular *notae* and figures. Similarly, the quadrivium—namely, medicine, music, arithmetic, and astronomy[26]—have their own particular *notae* and figures. Other mechanical and exceptive sciences, such as geomancy, nigromancy, and the rest of the sciences, do not have particular *notae* or figures but [instead] are contained under the *notae* of philosophy and the general sciences.[27] It is to be understood that with respect to having acquired memory, eloquence, understanding, and mental stability of those there are particular prayers here which do not necessarily have *notae* or figures, which all will be openly revealed in the following headings through the order.

[1, 2, Version A]

[2 Gloss] *Ego, Apollonius, etc.*[28] In this section it is shown that Apollonius, after Solomon, was [the next] teacher and philosopher in the liberal arts through that most sacred art. Also, he was asserting that the nature of the liberal arts was spiritually granted to him, and he gave an erudition of those working in them, and he inserts their own expositions in that place, which he calls the

25. "For the *prae ceteris . . .* occasion." Paraphrased excerpt from *Opus Operum,* section A.
26. Notice that the glosser excludes geometry from the quadrivium but includes medicine.
27. For understanding the hierarchy of knowledge, see chapter II.
28. These are the opening words of the section being glossed as written by the medieval scribe for the purpose of identification. The entire content is found under the same section number in Version A. The actual Version B manuscripts have all the content of Version A plus these glosses.

Flores Aurei, in that place, and he confirms that art by the primary authority of Solomon, followed by his own particular authority. And it is to be understood that Apollonius was the first [authority] after Solomon to whose hand this most sacred art came; and thus, when that art seemed to him too obscure on account of the Greek, Chaldean, and Hebrew words, it pleased him when he had explained and translated into Latin the Greek, Chaldean, and Hebrew prayers mixed among the names of the holy angels, and yet, he did as much as he could. But because some Greek, Hebrew, and Chaldean prayers were having so much prolixity in themselves, which is to be explained in Latin, and because it was much too difficult to explain everything for them, some he dismissed explaining, among those, just as it is said, there are certain names of the holy angels of whose office is to administer so much grace for the worker in that art through their invocation [and] whose names are not able to be made intelligible in Latin. And thus Apollonius dismissed those holy names and some prayers mixed among them just as he found [them] in the book of Solomon.[29] Likewise, he teaches in that place[30] under what condition and under what direction of life,[31] and in which [solar] months,[32] which lunar months,[33] and which hours of the days the operator ought to be working and to be investigating it himself in that holy work, and under which hours that work ought to begin and similarly, to end.[34]

[3, Version A]

[3 Gloss] *Nemireris ergo, etc.* This removes the doubt of nonbelievers because these holy words can have so much virtue and efficacy in offering them, and it says, "Do not wonder," because it is not to be marveled at nor should you be astonished at that most sacred gift, because it is granted by the Most High Creator in this holy art, in which Solomon wanted first, and after him others confiding in themselves to be the illuminating rays of the entire philosophy,

29. Prologue Gloss.
30. Section 2.
31. About the rule of life, see section 81.
32. About the solar months, see section 147.
33. About the lunar months, see sections 15 and 40.
34. About the times the operator ought to work, see sections 77–80.

because that which has been granted by God and given by all [the others] is to be believed and to be held in awe and not to be doubted nor admired, because the Most High himself created all things out of nothing from his Word alone, and on account of this, it says in that place: "Do not wonder," but consider it just as a miracle you are able to have so much wisdom in merely offering such short and subtle words which will be described in this holy art. And thus, you must not have less faith but [instead] a greater amount in offering the Greek, Chaldean, and Hebrew names than in offering the Latin prayers, because those names, which according to the right order, are to be offered for the purpose of acquiring memory; they firmly offer, minister, and administer the same grace working in the other sciences thus.

[Chapter I]

[4, Version A]

[4 Gloss] *Ego siquidem de propositis, etc.* In that same [prologue] section approving this art, he shows himself to have worked in this holy work, while he says in that place: "I myself am astonished at any words able to have so much virtue, etc." And he inserts in that place the general and particular precepts close to all the sciences which are to be acquired, and he says that just as there are different sciences to be acquired through this art, there are different lunar months and different hours of different [solar] months necessarily selected and ascertained beforehand, and different prayers which are to be offered and different *notae* and figures which are to be inspected.

Just as in acquiring memory, there are particular prayers to their own particulars coinciding in those particular lunar months and particular hours in which they ought to be offered, and similarly, the prayers which are made for the purpose of speaking well, the eloquence of persuasion, and the understanding have their own particular hours in which they ought to be offered.[35] Also, there are some prayers which are called "Generals" in this art, which generally pertain to acquiring all sciences, just like the first prayer, *Alpha et Omega,* is [a General], and [so are] the first three headwords[36] and the last nine prayers that are called "the *novem termini,*" which are always to be offered at the beginning of any work, and similarly must be repeated in completing the work. As a matter of fact, there are some other prayers which are similarly called "the Generals" which are always to be offered in acquiring some knowledge; and those number forty-two in Latin [altogether], which are able to be offered on all days [and] all hours without any other prayers, you will find the form and method of those prayers are to be pronounced declared in their own glosses.[37]

---

35. These are the General prayers which have their own lunar months and hours for the purpose of attaining improved faculties for memory, eloquence, understanding and the stability of these three.

36. The first three headwords (*tria prima capitula*) are *Helyscemath* and *Phos Megalos* and its Latin prologue, *Lux mundi.*

37. The glosser is making three distinctions among what he calls the "General" (*generales*) prayers. First, there are those prayers with their own lunar months and hours for the purpose of attaining improved faculties for memory, eloquence, understanding, and the stability of these three; beginning with *Assaylemaht* and ending with *Semoht Lamen,* there is a total of ten General

[5, Version A]

[5 Gloss] *Est enim tanta quorundam, etc.* In this section it is to be shown how much grace [and] how much virtue pleased the Most High to be created in such short prayers in offering them, and this Apollonius repeats in the text, so that the operator is strong enough, believing more, and has a stronger faith while it is to be worked in this most sacred art, offering so much as the most sacred short words. He also shows how much virtue [and] how much efficacy those most sacred prayers contain in themselves, so that when he will have read with devotion according to the teachings given in working with themselves, he will have offered them, reading sweetly, and not trying, because he will suddenly and unexpectedly acquire the memory, eloquence, and understanding and the stability of these three, because he offers the particular prayers[38] of whatever efficacy in their own hours, and [the virtue of these prayers] will be added to [the operator's mental faculties] in so much memory [and] eloquence that he will hardly be able to keep silent about those virtues, if he had firmly believed in offering them, because God alone created all things by the Word, and God is the Word itself, and in the beginning was the Word,[39] and every sacrament stands in the Word and faith. Therefore, let the operator believe he is able to acquire and possess so much wisdom [and] so much knowledge in offering these most sacred prayers, proceeding in the work according to the precepts given in this art—that is, with hope, faith, and a great desire—because they are necessary for any worker in this art who wishes to have so much wisdom and to obtain so much knowledge.

---

prayers (including the Latin prologues as being considered separate prayers). Second, there are those General prayers offered at the beginning and the end of any work, which include the *Alpha et Omega* prayer, the *tria prima capitula,* and the *novem termini,* which total thirteen. Third, there are the Generals which are to be offered in acquiring some knowledge, which likely refers to the Special prayers assigned to the seven liberal arts among others. Counting the *voces magicae* prayers and their Latin prologues as separate prayers plus the preamble *Lux veritas,* then all the prayers of grammar, logic, rhetoric, philosophy, medicine, music, arithmetic, astronomy, geometry (including *Omnis sapientiae,* which is mistaken by Version B as belonging to a second figure of geometry), and theology do reach a reckoning of the glosser's computation of forty-two. Notice that this reckoning excludes the prayers belonging to chastity; justice, peace, and fear; reprehension and taciturnity; and the prayers written within the figures (which in this book are called "adorning prayers" because they adorn the figures).

38. That is, the General prayers for acquiring memory, eloquence, and understanding and the stability of these three.

39. John 1:1.

[Variation 2] *That subsequent division is about this notory art. Specifically, this art is divided into two parts. It places the General* notae *and prayers in the first part but the Specials in the second. But first let us come to the Generals, which are necessary for acquiring the sciences of the trivium, quadrivium, theology, and the other sciences ([i.e.] the mechanical arts and the exceptives), which you undoubtedly obtain the sciences with the operation of these prayers and the other Specials, if you pronounce them just as it is proper.*

[6, Version A]

[6a Gloss] *De notoria igitur arte, etc.* In this art Apollonius makes certain divisions, because first, he divides that art into two parts, and in the first part—that is, at the beginning of that art—he places the particular [General] prayers for the purpose of acquiring memory, eloquence, and understanding. In the second part, he places the Special prayers pertaining to the specific sciences, as in the sciences of the trivium and quadrivium, and in another place, with respect to theology. He also places the general science prayers with respect to the general science *notae* with those prayers to each *nota*. All the liberal, mechanical, and exceptive sciences are able to be acquired without sin, just like nigromancy and the other similar ones.

[6b Gloss] *De notoria igitur arte, etc.* Apollonius says that this art is called "the notory art" for a reason, because an astonishing effect is to be shown wonderfully and inestimably to the prudent operator in the work itself with some notae and compendious prayers, and thus, truly speaking, this art is "'the art of arts and the science of sciences,' because it grants so much efficacy in the operation and the order of the prayers of the liberal arts and the other sciences, so that as much of its utility expands out of them human reason may extend beyond the faculty,"[40] and for that reason it is entitled to such an excellent name, because more fitting words are not to be found elsewhere.

[7] **Helyscemaht, Hazaram, Hemel, Saduc, Theon, Heloy, Zamaram, Zoma, Iecromaym, Theos, O God, pious and strong, Hamathamal, Iecronamay, Hala, Zanay, Hacronaaz, Zay, Coluaphan, Salmazay, Zaihal, Geromelam,**

---

40. *Opus Operum,* section A.

Haymasa, Ramay, Genzi, Samath, Helyemaht, Semay, Selmar, Iecrosamay, Iachat, Lemar, Harana, Hamany, Memothemaht, Hemelamp, and you, O holy Father, pious God, and incomprehensible in all your works, which are holy, just, and good, Megal, Hamechor, Semassaer, Zamathamar, Geogremay, Megus, Monorayl, Hamezeaza, Hillebata, Maramai, Iehenas, Gehemia, Malamay, Sephormay, Zemenmay, Melas, Hemay, Hemesna, Iecormay, Lemesey, Senosecary, Zemaher, Helcamay, Calion, Tharathos, Usyon, Gezethon, Seminathmas, Zesahas, Thaman, Helomany, Hamel, amen.

[7 **Gloss**] *Helyscemaht, Hazaram, etc.* Here Apollonius makes a mention about the first three headwords, which are to be offered at the beginning of any writing or for acquiring knowledge, yet, while they are being offered, having made some interval among themselves.[41] And let he who offers them be first confessed, fasted, and chaste, and let them be offered first early in the morning, which the three headwords are these *Helyscemat, etc.; Theos, Megale, etc.; Lux mundi, etc.* These prayers have so much mystery and virtue in them because in their pronunciation he is being administered to work in some science and virtue of the invocation of the holy names of the angels by the grace of our Lord Jesus Christ, [which] the four angelic administators gave to him in his own work,[42] one of whom suggests to him through a vision during the night while he sleeps, what he is about to do in his work and what effect he will obtain within himself, [and] while from there he begins to work for the purpose of acquiring memory and eloquence, which are to be acquired first, and afterward for the purpose of acquiring some knowledge of the seven liberal or mechanical arts, [and] these three headwords with the first preceding prayer[43] are always to be offered before all the other prayers. And they are written at the beginning of the art, because they are "the first way"[44] and the beginning to those to be had, which are to be acquired first in that art; namely memory, eloquence, and understanding. Also, they are the way and the beginning to acquiring all of the

41. The glosser is indicating that an interval of silence is to be given between the offering of each of those prayers. Intervals of silence are an essential part of the greater ritual according to Version B.

42. Namely, Hagnadam, Merabor, Hamiladei, and Pesiguaguol. See section 126e gloss.

43. *Alpha et Omega*.

44. Latin *prima via*. As *trivium* literally means "three ways," or "three roads," so memory, eloquence, and understanding are called "the first way" or "the first road."

other liberal and mechanical sciences—namely, in the inspection of the figures and *notae* of those sciences—which are to be acquired first; these first three headwords are to be offered before the prayers[45] of their own *notae* are offered [and] which are to be inspected. Likewise, it is to be understood that whatever field of knowledge has its own particular *notae* and figures, and specifically the seven liberal arts, which are grammar, logic, rhetoric, medicine, music, arithmetic, and astronomy.[46] Thus, theology has its own particular *notae* and figures, but other sciences are contained under the [four] *notae* of the general sciences and [the seven *notae* of] philosophy.

[8, Version A]

[8 Gloss] *Quam Salomon, etc.* In this place it says that the preceding prayer—namely *Helyscemaht*—is the first prayer among all the other prayers, and the angel ministered to Solomon about it first over the altar of the Temple, written on those golden tablets, and taught to him how he must always offer it at the beginning of any science. And while Solomon had done so he suddenly found so much efficacy and subtlety in offering them, the most holy names and words are contained in it under that [Greek, Chaldean, and Hebrew] form which he had received from the angel, prohibiting him or anyone else to presume to be able to interpret [or translate] from that, or anyone after him that was to be promoted to a higher status [in the notory art],[47] accustomed to a better memory, eloquence, and understanding; from where Solomon wonderfully commends this prayer and speaks much about its efficacy in a certain book of his which he composed himself after the operation of this most sacred art, which is called the *Idea of Solomon*[48] (that is, "the wisdom of Solomon" or "the splendor of wisdom"). So great is the power of this prayer in offering it for efficacy in anything whatsoever that human reason scarcely apprehends it, and this is what he said about this first prayer that is called "the first headword" in this art.

---

45. That is, the prayers belonging to the seven liberal arts, philosophy, and theology.
46. Strangely, geometry is omitted, but medicine is included, in this listing of the seven liberal arts.
47. Latin *promovebatur*. The sense is anyone who had advanced in their studies of the notory art.
48. Véronèse cites Thorndike, who says this book, perhaps of Arabic origins, titled *Idea Salomonis et Entocta*, is known in the first half of the thirteenth century from the astrologer Michael Scot and the bishop of Paris, William of Auvergne. The book is identified as *De Quattuor Annulis* (*Concerning the Four Rings*).

[9, Version A]

[9 Gloss] *Siquis initium, etc.* This [section] makes a mention about a certain teaching that Apollonius presents to the operator in this most sacred work: how in the beginning of his own operation he ought to have it, and how he ought to conduct and rule his own life, and how he must see beforehand the hours of the days and the lunar months assigned to the occasion; namely, in which he ought to begin this work and to offer his own prayers, and especially those first three headwords, which are always to be offered and bursting forth pleasantly at the beginning of any science which is to be acquired. Therefore, when you come to these prayers—that is, when you want to begin to work for some [specific] mental faculty—the name of the Lord is to be invoked first because at whatever kind of beginning of any work, hope, awe, and faith is to be invoked. Likewise, having received confession at the beginning just as it is said, you will be able to guard better in proportion [to your confession], you must guard against criminal sins, and a great deal stronger against mortal [sins], and, above all sins, you must guard against lechery, inebriation, [and] to the lesser [sins][49] from the beginning of the work until it is thoroughly finished; and on the first day of the beginning [of the work], it is best to fast on bread and water, "unless it was the Lord's day, and then you will not fast but expend nine alms"[50] either in bread or in nine denarii for the poor.[51] But if it was a day to be fasting, [then] you will fast with the greatest devotion. "Also, you ought to know [that] this work is to be done in a solitary, clean, and remote place away from human company,"[52] for you do not call some [people] coming over to you at the beginning of your work; you must dismiss the morally imperfect.[53]

49. Latin *ad minus.* A reference to the Latin idiom *a maiori ad minus,* meaning "from the greater to the lesser." Here the glosser is listing the greatest sins down to the lesser ones. The Latin idiom itself has the legal sense of the form of an argument in which one argues first from one's best points.

50. "unless . . . alms," *Opus Operum,* section D(b).

51. The denarius was the standard Roman silver coin, denoting its value as ten asses, or assarii (the Roman bronze or copper coin). The denarius was in use during the Late Roman Republic and Empire. The denarius is also mentioned numerous times in the New Testament, and it is likely this biblical context is intended as the glosser's archaic style for regarding almsgiving as a Christian act of virtue.

52. *Opus Operum,* section D(b).

53. In other words, the operator must take a retreat from society to properly perform the greater ritual without any outside disturbances.

Also, if you were less knowledgeable and do not understand the form of this art, you may be able to have a master teacher who may teach you this doctrine or the book's form of another field of knowledge better than you, but you ought not to have another associate with you in the pronunciation of the prayers.[54] Also, it is permitted to you to have a servant who gives you the necessary nutritional provisions in the assigned hours in which you ought to eat, yet he must never be present with you while you proceed in the work reading the prayers, yet the master teacher can be with you who may instruct you and teach you [how] to read the prayers, whether Greek or Latin, competently. Also, if you do not know [how] to read the prayers, the master teacher is able to read [first], and you after him, but it is necessary that the master teacher must be of good faith toward you, which he does not do for the sake of derision. Therefore, a teacher of good conscience and faith must be acquired before the beginning of the work. And if you can oblige him through a sacrament, [then] you must oblige [him], so that he acts in good faith and he reveals [your work] to no one.

Also, if by chance some invited visitor was coming over to you in the action of the work, as you were stopping the reading [to answer the door], on account of this, you must not become irate or disturbed, but immediately you must administer (or you send through your servant) ten almsgivings for ten poor individuals, and you must return to the location [of the ritual working] and read in that place [within the book] where you stopped.

> But if working out of temerity or fear, he committed some [error or sin], unless it was revealed out of the process through a vision, [then] the work is to be done a second time from the beginning. Also, especially if the worker falls asleep during the very action of the work, such is human frailty, just as it was revealed to him through the vision according to this, it must be done, his work is to be repeated from the beginning of this day. Furthermore, if he falls into infirmity during the work itself, if the work has proceeded up to the middle, if he did not hear a prohibition through a vision, having recovered a state of health, [then] he follows the beginning [where he left off]. And if he has accomplished less than half, unless it was revealed to him by a spirit, [then] the work will be repeated from the beginning. In

54. For the idea of having a master teacher, see *Opus Operum,* section E.

addition, working by whatever means necessary to remain at [his] place, if he had moved,[55] [then] the work is relinquished; retiring it, he must complete [it], having retaken [it from its very beginning,] to remain with the proper mental faculty. For whatever reason, if he fell into criminal sin, especially [while] working in the work itself, [then] he must not presume to proceed in the work, unless his penitence has been completed first. For criminal sins are dissimilar, especially if he has lapsed into misery[56] or frailty creeping along with respect to lechery before he proceeded in the work, he must complete a full penitence,[57] unless it was revealed to him in a vision what he ought to do. For concerning whatever criminal sin that has befallen him, penitence must be done first, unless an alleviation was made to him through a vision. For thus, from the twentieth day and beyond up to the completion of the work, it is always to be done with the utmost devotion through the three hours (that is, from morning until noon, from noon to the evening [hour], from the evening [hour] to after twilight). For on all the days from the twentieth day and beyond to those [latter] days the work is done, the visions will appear at night after twilight. And note them all, and accordingly, do what was shown to you in them. And accordingly, do what was revealed to you in the visions for the consummation of the entire work.[58]

Therefore, it is to be understood that according to what was revealed to you in the night by the angelic voice, if for some reason, you dismissed something in the work, [then] it is to be done as has been said. Also, you ought not to reveal your vision to anyone under any circumstance. And so, if you have acquired some mental faculty with so much labor after having completed the operation and you have lost or particularly put to forgetfulness through some fault, you must say for one month on any day in the early morning the first prayer, [that is, *Alpha et Omega*,] the first three headwords, and the last nine prayers which

---

55. Or move away from, or sell.

56. Latin *miseria*. The archaic sense of greed or avarice is likely meant here, like a greedy person who is called a miser. Although, it could also mean an affliction that has befallen the operator in which case the affliction is perceived as God's punishment for the operator's sins.

57. That is, a promise to God and oneself to not fall into sin.

58. In other words, certain sins might be permitted by the angel to alleviate the worker from his toils in doing the ritual work; or the angel knew such sins would happen despite the worker's best efforts due to his human frailty. Passage is paraphrasing *Opus Operum,* section D(b).

are called "*termini,*" just as it is written in the first gloss of this art,[59] similarly in the gloss near the text of the aforesaid nine prayers which are written at the end of the text of this book, whose first prayer begins *Genealogon.*[60]

[10] *Here begins the second headword [prayer—namely Phos Megalos—belonging to the first three headwords], which, after the first, and having made a short interval, ought to be pronounced with the Latin prayer which follows, which is the third headword, and those first three prayers are to be called "the first three headwords" that are to be offered at any beginning. Similarly, you should pay attention to that because all words of the preceding prayers are not able to be expounded in Latin.*
[Ph]os, Megal[os], Pat[e]r, [Vehe]m[en]s,[61] Hebrel, Haboel, Heroy, Habey, Elyhot, Hety, Hebeot, Letiel, Iezey, Sadaz, Salasiey, Salacial, Salatelli, Samel, Sadamiel, Saday, Helgion, Helgiel, Lemegos, Mycron, Megos, Myheon, Legines, Muthon, Mycohyn, Heel, Heseli, Iecor, Granal, Semhel, Semobohat, Semeltha, Samay, Geht, Gehel, Rasahanay, Gelgemana, Semana, Harasunihon, Salepatir, Ragyon, Salera, Thurigium, Hepatyr, Usyon, Hatamas, Hotonas, Harayn.

[10 Gloss] *[Ph]os, Megal[os], Pat[e]r, etc.* Here begins the second headword of this art, which ought to be offered immediately after the first headword, yet having made a short interval after that one, and having said that second headword, another short interval is to be made before its prologue is offered. The prologue is that Latin prayer which follows (that is, *Lux mundi,*); [then] *Deus [Pater] immense [. . . magnitudo], etc.,*[62] which the prayer [*Lux mundi*]

59. That is, Variation 1 Gloss.

60. Section 127c.

61. The original text reads, "Theos, Megale, Patyr, Ymos." This is a reconstruction of the Greek and Latin meaning "O Great Light, vehement Father." If *theos megalos* is the original intention of the writer, then it would mean "O Great God," but this is doubtful, being a late scribal redaction. If Ymos and its variant spellings are not Latin and meant to be a part of the *voces magicae,* then it would just be a Greek reconstruction meaning "O Great Light the Father."

62. *Deus Pater immense [. . . magnitudo]* is the prayer belonging to the fifth figure of philosophy, which leads to the prayers of the sixth and seventh figures of philosophy. Together, these three prayers of philosophy rule over the four liberal arts in the second month according to the reconstructed greater ritual of Version A. In Version B, the fifth, sixth, and seventh prayers belonging to philosophy (and *Deus Pater [immense...misericordissime],* the prayer belonging to music) are

is the explanation of some Greek diction of that prayer about which it speaks here; (that is, *[Ph]os, Megal[os], etc.*). Certain names of the holy angels are to be invoked in this prayer which they always have to be invoked and deprecated at whatever beginning of acquiring any mental faculty.

And it is to be understood that wherever Greek, Chaldean, and Hebrew prayers are to be found in this art, for the most part and in certain places throughout the whole, they are the names of the holy angels who have the virtue and are able to administer grace to the working operator in this art for some efficacy, naming and invoking the said names and deprecating with the greatest devotion. And Solomon explained some words of those prayers first. But Apollonius, expounding some things and extracting as much explanation with more subtlety about the prayers as he could (that is, the deprecations mixed between the names of the holy angels), and in this art those Latin prayers called "prologues" (that is, the explanations made from the Greek [and] Chaldean into Latin).

Nevertheless it is not yet understood, what any Greek, Hebrew, and Chaldean words are to be expounded just as they are placed through the order, and similarly, the entire Latin prayer may not be the sole explanation of any Greek, Hebrew, and Chaldean expression, but it is some part of the prayer's explanation, just as [Apollonius] has been able to extract and extort a shorter [explanation], because so many prolixities were in certain prayers that, if they were to be thoroughly explained in Latin according to what are placed in the letters, human sense would never [or] barely be able to apprehend them, nor [would they] be able to be offered in such short hours as is necessary.[63] From where [in the text][64] it is to be understood that when this most sacred art was first delivered to Solomon through the angel, there were no Latin prayers in that place but only those names of the holy angels, which were completely unknown by any human being, and at that time Solomon was working according to the angelic command thus, explaining nothing about them, but after the operation [Apollonius] explained some in Latin. Similarly, Apollonius, coming after Solomon, working in the same art, explained [the prayers] as much better and more succinctly as he could, so that we and others coming after them,

---

said in the fourth month just before the operator begins the particular operation of a given art or science.

63. See Prologue Gloss, footnote 7.

64. Section 73.

would not dismiss such a most holy and most sacred mystery on account of ignorance of the forbidden Greek, Hebrew, and Chaldean words; and thus, it pleased God and those [others coming after them], that so much mystery was revealed to us through the Latin language, and they wanted that most sacred art through which such great knowledge and wisdom can be acquired, [an art which] was becoming lost on account of ignorance and negligence, and investigated by some as having little value.

[11, Version A]

[11 Gloss] *Lux mundi, Deus [Pater] immense [. . . magnitudo], etc.* This Latin prayer, which is called a "prologue" because it was extracted from some Greek, Hebrew, and Chaldean words which are contained in the preceding prayer—namely, *[Ph]os, Megal[os], etc.*—is the most sacred prayer and important deprecation to God, and for this reason, it is appropriated to God alone, so that it may please him, and may he pour out his compassion, and may he help the faithful working in this most sacred art for some efficacy, which his most holy angels, whose names are called and invoked in the preceding prayer, whose office it is to pour out his grace to the operator with God's permission to deliver an effect. But even this Latin prayer is an explanation of the preceding particular prayer. On the same day and in the same hour, having finished the preceding prayer, [and] having made some short interval, it ought to be pronounced as like the space of one Lord's Prayer and always at the beginning of any efficacy which is to be acquired, and these [instructions] are sufficient for the purpose of presenting about those first three headwords, which are always to be offered in the beginning.

[12, Version A]

[12 Gloss] *Nec tamen putes, etc.* In this section it says, repeating those Greek names which are described in this art, [that it] cannot entirely be explained in Latin. For this reason, because some of those Greek words are the names of holy angels and that they cannot be explained at all, but also among those names are placed some deprecations apart from angels in Hebrew, Greek, and Chaldean which were explained, particularly in Latin. But as yet [Solomon and Apollonius] had not explained those [deprecations] thoroughly on account of the prolixity of the exposition, because they would have been much too long if any words had been explained from them into Latin. Thus, because human sense is not able to understand those, neither to deduce for the purpose of an effect, nor are they able to be offered in so short hours of the day, just as it has been taught, because sometimes [Apollonius] comprehends only one Hebrew or Greek vocabulary word, explaining them into five or six Latin-lettered vocabulary words, as an example to be given in many places.[65] And just as it is read in the book of Daniel[66] concerning King Belshazzar of Babylon, who while he made a feast and drank with silver cups with his entire family, whose cups Nebuchadnezzar had carried out from the Jerusalem Temple praising their gods, and then, while they were doing so, there came into sight a certain hand writing on the wall, and all who stood by together seeing with the king, similarly seeing these words: "Mane, Techel, Phares," which, translated into Latin is "The Lord numbered your kingdom, it has been weighed on the scales and has been found wanting; your kingdom has been divided and given to the Medes and Persians."[67] For when these three vocabulary words (that is, "Mane, Techel, Phares") [are] comprehend[ed] into a Latin exposition as twenty-three vocabulary words, the prolixity was becoming too much in this art if any Greek, Hebrew, and Chaldean word would be explained in Latin.[68] And Solomon and Apollonius explained thus, shorter and more remitted [words],[69]

65. Latin *vocabulum* and *vocabula* are given in this sentence. The sense is that Apollonius's own vocabulary or lexicon, those set of words known to him, limits his ability to not only recognize the Hebrew or Greek within the *voces magicae* prayers but also to translate those into Latin. The complexity of the Hebrew, Greek, and Chaldean prayers often leads to a Latin translation of several more words. The glosser says there is an example of a word count comparsion between the Hebrew, Greek, and Chaldean prayer *Phos Megalos* and its Latin translation, *Lux mundi*.

66. Daniel 5. The glosser follows Jerome's Latin translation from the Greek text by Theodotion.

67. Latin *Numeravit Dominus regnum tuum, appensum est in statera et inventum est minus habens, divissum est regnum tuum et datum est Medis et Persis.*

68. In this sentence, the Latin word *vocabula* carries the sense of the word as an instrument by means for communicating a meaning. The story of the writing on the wall is meant to illustrate how great the long-windedness of the Chaldean (Aramaic) language really is, making it too laborious, complex, and confusing to translate it in its entirety into Latin.

69. Latin *leniora*. Solomon and Apollonius explained some prayers with "more remitted" words; that is, words that are less intensive in the philosophical context of hylomorphism. That is to say, they chose to explain or translate with simpler or shorter words. From a modern linguistical standpoint, this would be akin to translating from a synthetic language like Latin, which uses inflections to express word relationships in a sentence, to a more analytic language like English, which uses helper words and word order to convey the relationship of words in a sentence. More English words are needed to fully express Latin words.

and the other words, just as they lay in the book given by the angel, Solomon and Apollonius dismissed on account of the prolixity of the exposition and the brevity of time in which they ought to be read and be pronounced, but where he says [it] in that same section.

[12 Gloss, version Kr/C1].[70] *Nec tamen putes, etc.* In this section it says that the Greek, Hebrew, and Chaldean prayers that are described in this holy art are not thoroughly explained in Latin from word to word, because one part or only one vocabulary word of Greek or Hebrew or Chaldean conveys so much within it for a Latin explanation, because if any Greek vocabulary word were to be explained into Latin, [then] there would be such prolixity in those that the human intellect would never be able to understand them, nor in such short hours of the day, just as it has been established to offer them, because one Greek or Hebrew or Chaldean word comprehends sometimes five or six words of Latin explanation within it; for example, you have in the Passion of our Lord Jesus Christ: when he said, "Hely Lamazatabani," this is, "God, my God, why have you forsaken me?"[71] Behold, that the two Greek words convey a Latin explanation into six vocabulary words, and thus, the Greek prayers have remained unexplained in Latin, for the most part, and this is what it says there.

[13, Version A]

[13 Gloss] *Necessarium est, etc.* Some precepts are to be placed, which are necessary for anyone wanting to work in this holy art; namely, that he has a great desire to begin the work, to lead that beginning to an effect. Also, that he firmly believes he is able to acquire that faculty for which he labors by virtue of the holy Greek and Latin words which are to be offered. Also, that he leads a good life in the action of the work having done so with confession and penitence beforehand. Also, that the place is such that some tumultous

---

70. Kr = Kremsmünster Abbey Library, CC 322. C1 = Bernkastel-Kues, the Library of St. Nikolaus Hospital, 216.

71. Mark 15:34, which quotes Psalms 22:1 (NRSV). The Gospel of Mark has the Aramaic phrase *Eloi, Eloi lema sabachthani?* In the next sentence, the glosser mistakes this Aramaic phrase for a Greek one. As a side note, it is worth mentioning that the name for God used here, *Hely,* is a corruption from transliterations of the Aramaic word for God, *alaha* (ܐܠܗܐ), into Greek and then into Latin. The Aramaic shares linguistic heritage with the Hebrew word for God, *elohim.*

disturbance coming over [to his place] in which the operation is performed does not perturb him, as it is necessary for him to dismiss [any] work already begun [which had been interrupted]. Also, that he offers the names of the holy angels devoutly, cleanly, and chastely, and read the other Latin prayers as often as he should according to their own lunar [days of the] months [and] their own arranged and determined hours according to their own divided sections in the art. Also, it is to be understood that all the prayers of this art are good and most holy as in Greek as well as Latin, but there are some of those which have a greater virtue in them than others, and present a greater efficacy to the operator while he offers and reads them according to what he ought to do. Likewise, there are certain prayers which present a great efficacy through them, but some do not, from [where in the text] these prayers which are at the beginning of this art—*Alpha et omega, etc.,*[72] *Helyscemaht, etc., Theos, Megale, etc., Lux mundi, etc.,*[73] *Assaylemaht, etc.,*[74] *Azaylemaht, etc.,*[75] *Lemaht, etc.,*[76] *Deus summe, Deus invisbilis, etc., Te queso, etc.*[77]—are the way, the beginning, and the entire foundation of the entire efficacy of this art,[78] without those preamble [prayers] he is not able to achieve an effect in any faculty. From those, Solomon established and taught a special mandate that they are not to be offered without faith, a term, and an established time by any means.[79] But I will declare how they have to be offered and at which times in the following sections. But these are attended to for a perfect memory if they are offered in the established order.

[14, 15, Version A]

[15 Gloss] *Hec enim sunt expositions, etc.* In this section it explains and shows the assigned lunar [days of the] months and the hours of the days of those months in which these following prayers ought to be offered—namely, *Assaylemaht, etc.,*

---

72. See Variation 1 and Variation 1 Gloss.
73. The first three headwords. See sections 7 and 10–11.
74. Section 16.
75. Variation 3.
76. Section 22.
77. Sections 24–25.
78. Section 19.
79. Section 60.

Azaylemaht, etc., Lemahc, etc., Deus summe Deus, etc., Te queso, Domine, etc.—with the preceding [prayers of the first] three headwords, which always ought to be offered first, and it says that, seeing beforehand, it is the fourth [day of] the Moon in which they are to be offered first, the second in the eighth, the third in the twelfth, the fourth in the sixteenth, the fifth in the twentieth, the sixth in the twenty-fourth, the seventh in the twenty-eighth, the eighth in the thirtieth, and thus it is apparent that these prayers do not have to be offered on any day of the month, but only during [these] eight days in the month.

Specifically, Solomon calls those prayers "triumphals" on account of their virtue, because by this [virtue] the operator discovers through those [prayers] the first effect with respect to all the other faculties to be acquired and without which he could not discover from where [in the text it says] these prayers are the way and the foundation with respect to attending to all the other faculties of the sciences,[80] and since the other prayers were delivered to Solomon before, Solomon placed them in the beginning of this art, which it was revealed to Solomon through the angel carrying those to him what kind of an efficacy he might obtain from them, if in those days, in those abovesaid hours, he may offer them four times in a day—that is, once in the morning, once around the third [hour], once around noon, once around the evening [hour]—which prayers, having been said thus, present a good memory for retaining all things heard, and expedite eloquence in retaining all things for those who do the offering, [and] a refined understanding in learning more about all the sciences.

But in those days in which they are offered he ought to be doing a Lenten fast and to live chastely and devoutly, and confession must always precede in any beginning of any month. This is in that first month in which these prayers ought to be offered, similarly in the other months in which the other prayers ought to be pronounced for the purpose of acquiring other efficacies and faculties. But in the very same month in which these prayers ought to be offered and said from those, a mention is made here, some other prayers ought to be pronounced and said—that is, on all the other days of the month, except those eight on which these prayers are offered—on which the other days he is not to do a fast, yet [the operation] is to be lived chastely and devoutly.

80. Section 19.

The prayers, which are *Omnipotens, incomprehensibilis, etc.,*[81] *Confiteor tibi Deus, etc.,*[82] with the others following successively up to that place: *Hoc est opusculum, etc.*[83] But these prayers are able to be said on all days, at all hours, before and after meals. Nevertheless, when they are offered first in the morning, the first three headwords ought to be said once first, and the [first three] headwords are always offered once at any time before the other prayers of this art are to be offered, and this, before he who works eats, and you must attend to all these things well, and see beforehand the beginning of the work thenceforth, if you endeavor to come before an effect.

[16] *For this following prayer is an invocation of the names of some holy angels, yet among them are certain deprecations in Greek, Hebrew, and Chaldean which they are able to be explained with difficulty and prolixity. This prayer is called "the splendor"*[84] *and "the mirror of wisdom," and it ought to be read once on any day in the morning, once around the third [hour], once around noon, once around evening in every [favorable day of the] lunar month.*[85]

Assaylemaht,[86] **Rasay, Semaht, Azahat, Haraaht, Lemehc, Hazabat, Hamac, Hamae, Gessemon, Grephemyon, Zelamye, Relamye, Hazaca, Hamatha, Hazaremehal, Hazanebal, Hehal, Zebial, Seziol, Semyphor, Hamyssiton, Tintingon, Tintingethe, Hamissirion, Sebarnay, Halimohc, Alymion, Gemays, Halmihoc, Sadayl, Heomayl, Neomayl, Cristos, Chiothos, Sepha, Caphamal, Paphalios, Sicrogramon, Laupdam, Laupta, Iothym, Baupada, Iochym, Iochiletha, Lezahemor, Iemeamor, Locahemor, Sycromegal, Haemor, Giselector, Gihelerehon, Glereleon, Gamaggay, Semagar, Somalgay, Semasgey, Balna, Harethon, Iesamahel, Gememahel, Hay, Hala, Hela, Iemay, Semethay, May, Semnay, Geles, Syney, Ielesemoy, Lesmay, Samenay, Bariacrata, Cariacteta, Tharihem, Socalmata, Getymay,**

81. Section 115. The first prayer of the *Ars Nova*.

82. Section 117. The third prayer of the *Ars Nova*; curiously, the glosser skipped over mentioning the second prayer, *Adoro te rex regum*.

83. Section 126.

84. Section 8 reads, "Solomon reveals the status of wisdom's splendor in the book *Eniclyssoe*."

85. That is, those favorable days of the lunar month which are listed in Section 15.

86. The *Assaylemaht* prayer has three parts *Assaylemaht, Gezemanay,* and *Sathamar*. See page 352, footnote 87.

Socalina, Socamagal, Halgezamay, Balma, Hailos, Halos, Zaynos, Ienevegal, Sarimalayp, Zarmalayp, Sacramalayp, Tamyel, Thamahel, Sachabinel, Sathabinal, Samal, Maga, Samalauga, Sammaga, Sacalmagu, Sylymal, Salmana, Saguaht, Silymythu, Semalsay, Gahyht.

Gezamanay, Sabal, Zegaphaton, Zahanphaton, Iezemo, Iezelem, Zozelimem, Hatanatos, Hathanatay, Semaht, Semnahc, Zemahet, Iezorabel, Cherorab, Hel, Gerozabal, Crathon, Hariabal, Hariagal, Hanagay, Hariagil, Parithomegos, Samazihel, Symasyhel, Leosemnaht, Leosamaty, Themiathol, Gemnatol, Iemyzatol, Hebalthe, Helabee, Hamissithon, Sebanay, Halmyx, Gemayl, Sadayl, Nebomayl, Cristolepha, Caphamal, Hazaron, Gezamel, Haymal, Hayhala, Sememay, Gehesmoy, Thariacta, Iennazay, Zohauphaton, Ielezamen, Hatanatay, Gemaht, Iezomabel, Haynosiel, Halabehen, Hebaiohe, Halabeht, Ebalohe, Rubos, Phabos, Phelihor, Phobos, Ydolmassay, Predolmssay, Pholihor, Negioggen, Negmather, Pharamnee, Faranehc, Scomicopoten, Sohomythepoten, Himaliasenon, Ynnamos, Manyhas, Geromay, Iemay, Getamazy, Passamaht, Theon, Beht, Bon.

Sathamar, Haginol, Naragal, Semozihot, Nerochinay, Raguaty, Ragualy, Ranal, Ragahal, Haginal, Hagamal, Phagomossyn, Phagamesynz, Domogentha, Theomogen, Theromogen, Salmatha, Salamaht, Zalamatha, Hon, Bolon, Lialon, Sephizimu, Sapynon, Sepizihamon, Hamon, Harion, Usyon, Gemession, Sepha, Halymix, Sebanay, Hamyssichon, Tyntygren, Hacion, Regon, Bon, Lon, Usion, amen.

[**16 Gloss**] *Assaylemaht, etc.* In this place a mention is made about this most holy prayer, which is the first prayer of this art, having an efficacy for acquiring memory, a provoking eloquence, an augmenting understanding, and with their following parts and with the first three headwords coming before. But some of the most precious names of the holy angels are contained in this prayer, whose effect is to administer the aforesaid efficacy, among whose names are certain Greek, Chaldean, and Hebrew deprecations which are most difficult and too prolixious to be explained in Latin, and thus on account of too much prolixity of the Latin words, those words have remained thoroughly unexplained. But it is to be understood that, however much [the Greek, Chaldean, and Hebrew prayer] is unexplained and unknown in Latin, nevertheless, it administers so much virtue and so much efficacy to the Latin worker ignorant of them, like Greek, Hebrew, and Chaldean, who acknowleges them in their own idiom, and on account of this, the virtue of the holy names, which are unknown and unexplained among all, which in their invocation and their pronunciation have great virtue and the greatest sacrament, contained in them. But this prayer, on account of its own sanctity, virtue, and efficacy that Solomon found in it, he calls "the splendor" or "the mirror of wisdom," because, through the splendor of its virtue, having been enlightened, he had all that wisdom he acquired.

For this prayer, on account of its prolixity, is divided into three parts,[87] yet it is the same one prayer, but in order that it may be offered better with some short intervals and without so much labor, because it would become troublesome for so many Greek names to be offered at once without a pause for some breath, it was ordered to be divided by the angel, and for this reason those divisions were made. For so much efficacy was discovered in it, first by Solomon, second by Apollonius, that any one of them named it in different ways. For Solomon, as I said before, called it "the splendor of wisdom" and "the mirror," and elsewhere he called it the "felicity of ingenuity." But Apollonius calls it "the image of eternal life," from where [in the text] that is the prayer itself, which is the way and foundation to acquiring all the sciences and without which, briefly speaking, no knowledge or other efficacy is able to be acquired through this art.

It is to be seen beforehand and chosen of the month in which it ought to be offered to one's pleasure, and thus when it was the fourth [day of] the Moon in the early morning, having said the first three headwords first once, it is to be offered. This is the reason why in the first day of the lunar month it is not to be offered like the other prayers, because in the fourth [day of] the Moon the angel appeared first to Solomon, and [the angel] taught him it then to offer [it]; and Solomon said and claimed the angel from then on to have said to him about this prayer, because in the pronunciation and invocation of

87. The *Assaylemaht* prayer has three parts, but they are never explicitly identified in section 16 or its gloss. Only Variation 3 and Variation 4 identify themselves as the second and third parts, respectively. Thus, according to these variant passages, the three parts, named after their own first headwords, are *Assaylemath, Gezamanay,* and *Sathamat.*

the holy names of the angels, the four angelic administrators are to be sent pronouncing it to him in four virtues, of which one is administering memory, another eloquence, indeed the other understanding, but the fourth conserves and strengthens the acquired stability of the three virtues. The angel also prohibited Solomon thus, saying, "See, you must not dare someone to explain or to translate about that, nor you, nor another after you."[88] because it is the prayer itself, which is "the light of the soul," and it is the "first way"[89] with respect to acquiring every efficacy. For it is the angelic wisdom itself and the foundation of this art.[90]

But the prayer itself, with its own parts, has its own form, manner, and lunar days of the month and particular hours, and how it ought to be pronounced in which hours. For he who offers it must confess first and have a secret place in which he offers it alone, and with great devotion and he invokes with a low voice those sacred names of angels which are written in that place and without any associate.

And if by chance someone was coming over to the operator without his knowledge or invitation during the operation, on account of this [disturbance], he must not dismiss it [i.e., the pronouncing the prayer], finishing up to the end, but he must complete it perfectly; since on account of this [disturbance], the prayer does not lose its mystery nor the operator his own work, but on account of the disturbance, having been made to the operator on account of someone coming over, it is to be repeated again in the same hour in which [the visitor] arrived, coming over. From [this gloss] summarily, if someone arrived in the morning in the same hour (that is, in the morning [hour]),[91] [then] it is to be said twice; if in the third [hour], [then] that same [instruction]; if in the ninth [hour], [then] that same [instruction] similarly; if in the evening, [then] it is to be reiterated twice similarly.

Solomon said about this prayer after its very own experiment, "This is a holy prayer without danger of any sin, which Solomon affirmed to be "inexpressible" to human senses themselves,"[92] neither could the deprecation of words be able

88. Section 17.

89. Section 7 gloss.

90. Section 19.

91. Latin *in mane.* The glosser is emphasizing the canonical hour, prime.

92. Section 17.

to be explained thoroughly into Latin; and if any were to be expounded, [then] so great the prolixity of the Latin prayers would become that they were not able to read in any opportune time.

Solomon also says, and especially in the following section, that those names which are in the prayer are so great and so much a secret that it is not permitted for a person to speak it except in the operation itself, and whoever wants to offer such secrets must confess and live chastely down to the lesser [actions of daily life][93] before he begins through the nine days [of a new lunar month] and he fast on the day in which he offers it, and which he did it thus, having finished the prayer of words in the day itself, God heard [the operator's] own prayer if he believed firmly what is said about that prayer.

[Variation 3] *The second part of the preceding prayer begins, in which, having made some short interval, it should be offered in a lowered voice with affection.*

Hazaylemaht Lemaht Azat Gessemon,[94] Thelamoht, Hazab, Habacal, Haebal, Sezior, Sicremogal, Gigere, Mogal, Gielotheon, Somagoy, Haphiles, Pamphilos, Sicragramon, Laupda, Iothym, Halual, Haylos, Halna, Genenogal, Samanlay, Tacayhel, Thamiel, Secalmana, Hesemelas,

---

93. Latin *ad minus*. See section 9 gloss, foonote 732.

94. *Hazaylemaht Lemaht Azat Gessemon* is described as the second part of *Assaylemaht* according to Version B. Although Version B does not acknowledge that Variation 3 has more than one part, Ganell's version does, asserting that it has three parts, which are *Lemath Azach Gessemon Hazaylemath Lemath*, *Gelyor Synoy Bariatahtha*, and *Lemach Sebauthe*. In Variation 3, *Hazaylemath Lemath Azat Gessemon* and *Gelior Synoy Bariathata* are present; for Ganell, these are the first two parts. Variation 4, presented below and whose headwords are *Lemahc Sebauthe,* matches Ganell's third part. Thus, Ganell's *Lemath Azach Gessemon Hazaylemath Lemath* prayer has three parts: *Lemath Azach Gessemon Hazaylemath Lemath, Gelyor Synoy Bariatahtha,* and *Lemach Sebauthe*, thereby agreeing with Variation 3 and Variation 4 of Version B. *Rasay Lamac* (section 16, Version A) appears to have a mix of angelic names, which are found later in the prayers *Assaylemaht* (section 16, Version B) and *Hazaylemaht Lemaht Azat Gessemon* (Variation 3, Version B). Also, *Rasay Lamac* has four special prayer titles assigned to it (sections 16, 18), of which Ganell only acknowledges a single title to each (*Assaylemath* as the mirror of knowledge, *speculum scientiae,* and *Lemath Azach Gessemon Hazaylemath Lemath* as the light of the soul, *lumen animae*). The conflation of titles in *Rasay Lamac* (section 16, Version A) strongly suggests a conflation of the prayers as well (i.e., copying separate parts as a single prayer at least twice or more, leading to duplication of angelic names and confusing the number of parts to any single prayer), thereby further complicating the transmission of these angelic names from its earliest beginnings to its later recensions.

Hezomelaht, Gethasam, Cechalsam, Soylmon, Caibaiol, Semalsay, Crathon, Hanaguyl, Pancomnegos, Tyngeny, Hamissitoy, Sebarnay, Hassymilop, Thenaly, Soday, Henaly, Halaco, Meahil, Crihitos, Sepha, Caphanal, Hazaron, Cezamahal, Haila, Seramnay, Gelior, Synoy, Bariathata, Gehemizay, Iecrafagon, Legilime, Haramatay, Senac, Gremyhazay, Sothal, Magaal, Iezamai, Zehemphagon, Hasyhezamay, Legelyme, Hatama, Ieyzobol, Gerozabal, Symaliel, Seymaly, Seyhel, Leosamaht, Gemihatal, Halebre, Tyhophagros, Theos, Phabos, Ycolmazay, Nogen, Pharameht, Neyhaben, Saratihar, Ierasiay, Hinaliha, Sememamos, Gezamay, Iecremay, Passamaht, Thagayl, Hagamal, Fugamesy, Phagamesym, Themegeman, Zemegemary, Salamatha, Zalamothono, Bon, Lon, Sepizihon, Harion, Usion, Semession, Thegon, Amen.

[Variation 3 Gloss] *Hazaylemaht, Lemaht, etc.* Here begins the second part of the preceding prayer; that is, *Assaylemaht,* which, although divided into parts, is still the same prayer, and should be offered together on the same day and in the same hour, nevertheless, having made some short interval in offering them.

But in this second part,[95] there are certain names of the holy angels among which are some that are not permitted to man to speak or offer, except in the proper operation, on account of the sanctity and virtue which they possess. But this is an unexplained little part,[96] which Solomon dared not to attempt to explain on account of the angelic prohibition, nor [did] anyone after him; and no one ought to read them in having been tempted thus, because just as the angel prohibited Solomon, and Solomon, transcribing the angelic commandments, wrote the same [in his book], and prohibited his own followers to not attempt the same thing.

There is also so much virtue and sanctity in these prayers because having recalled the first three headwords, which are always offered at the start of any beginning [ritual procedure]. So much memory [and] so much eloquence is increased for offering these, that human nature is admired over this. Yet, it is not understood that only these prayers ought to be offered just for these

95. Variant 3.

96. Latin *particula,* meaning "little part," refers to the second headword of the three-part prayer *Hazaylemaht, Lemaht.*

efficacies alone but also that other prayers having the same efficacy are to be offered with these both before and after, just as it was ordered in this summary.

But truly these are the way and the foundation, and they have a greater virtue and they are a greater efficacy than the other prayers which are offered for this efficacy, because having finished these prayers in the obligated manner, God heard the voice and the prayer in deprecation, and [the operator] discovers the grace to acquire memory, eloquence, and understanding, he who pronounces them. Therefore, when there are many prayers of different kinds in Greek, Hebrew, Chaldean, and many in Latin which are called "prologues" in this most sacred art, because they have been extracted from some Greek words intermixed among names of angels, and it is to be understood that just as there are different arts and different words are contained [within those prayers], thus they have different efficacies and are to be read for different efficacies, and are offered in different lunar months and at different hours and days. Also, is to be understood that some of these prayers have greater virtue and greater efficacy than others, and those names which are said to be in Greek, Chaldean, and Hebrew have to be pronounced with greater reverence and greater solemnity than the Latin prayers, because the entire virtue of this art consists within these names.

Also, there are some of those prayers, which reading through them, present to the offering no efficacy, just like the first three headwords, which are always to be offered in any beginning [ritual procedure], which if [some of those prayers] are to be offered through [the first three headwords, and] they present no efficacy, and without those other prayers spoken, they are of no value.

Also, there are some prayers which have an efficacy for the purpose of acquiring memory through them, but others only for eloquence, indeed, others for memory and eloquence together, moreover, others for unloosing an impeded tongue, certainly others for the stability of acquiring the efficacies of both; and thus, they have diverse efficacies and they have to be pronounced at different times.

But those prayers that both bring in memory and loosen an impeded tongue when said, although they are not different but the same one prayer; still, they have to be pronounced at different hours of the day so as to acquire these two efficacies, that is, for one efficacy, that is, for acquiring memory, it should be offered in the morning; but for acquiring eloquence, it should be said in the evening, and this on the same day.

For there are other prayers in this art which have the most sacrosanct virtues and efficacies in them, which without the first three headwords and without some other prayers adjoined to them, they are able to say and be offered on all days [and] at all hours of the day. However, he who wants to offer them must have a good life, and having confessed from all his sins, living cleanly and chastely, and he must be fasted on that day in which he offers them.

Accordingly, those prayers pertinent to acquiring the physical science are the prayers *Ihesu Dei Filius, etc.; Eleminator, Caudones, etc.; angeli sancti, etc.*[97] But these prayers and others you will see are ordered in their own places and in their own sections; and thus, in this art there are such sacrosanct prayers which have so much virtue that through them they are able to be possessed of such efficacy as said above and knowledge to be acquired and to be retained in memory, if they are offered in the correct manner.

[Variation 4] *Here follows the third part of the prayer, which, having made an interval after the aforesaid [prayers], it ought to be pronounced.*

Lemahc, Sebauthe, Helitihay, Gezogam, Romasym, Hegeto, Gozimal, Exihophiam, Sorathym, Salachaam, Besapha, Saphrem, Hacubam, Samyht, Senaioho, Phetaloym, Harissim, Gengeos, Lethos, amen.

[Variation 4 Gloss] *Lemahc, Sebauthe, etc.* Here begins the third and last little part of that most holy preceding prayer, which is *Assailemaht, etc.* But this prayer, which is the last little part, contains in itself the greatest virtue and holiest mystery, although it is the shortest in words, and on account of this virtue, the holiest mystery, and the sanctity of the names of the holy angels which are to be invoked in it. For itself, having finished the second little part, which is *Azaylemaht, etc.,* it ought to be pronounced, nevertheless, having made some short interval among themselves, with great affection and the greatest veneration, obedience, and solemnity, yet according to the period of time of long or short days in which it is to be offered.

---

97. Sections 29a–29b. The glosser is pointing out the special virtue of the third sequence of the General prayers; such an application of this special virtue is called a lesser ritual in this book. The third sequence of General prayers is not to be confused with the Special prayer and its figure for medicine.

But Solomon called this prayer, on account of its virtue, subtlety, and efficacy, the "felicity of ingenuity," after the operation itself. But after Solomon, Apollonius, seeing and cognizing the virtue and efficacy of the prayer itself through an effect, named the very prayer "the light of the soul." For those most holy words, which are read in it, are of so great of a mystery and so great a virtue, if according to what is taught, they are to be offered, that [his] heart, soul, and volition of offering are to be illuminated in so much through the holy angels whose names are recited, and he is to be increased in so much memory itself that he retains everything heard and observes what is retained in memory.

For this prayer with its little parts in themselves comprehends how much virtue and of what kind of efficacy is unknown to the human race. For Solomon established a special commandment regarding this prayer, saying that no one may presume to offer this prayer,[98] unless he offers *Alpha et Omega* first, then the first three headwords; that is, *Helyscemaht, etc.; [Ph]os, Megal[os], etc.; Lux mundi, etc.*

Also, that this last little part is not to be offered, unless the first and second part are offered first. And again, the first, second, and third parts are not able to be offered, unless, having been heard in confession is first and having received penance for [one's] sins, and at the beginning of the work with good intention, they are able to be offered, having for their efficacy and he is to be fasting, clean, and chaste on the very day when they are to be offered, not for the sake of testing and proving the holy words and their efficacy, but with devotion and veneration, with affection and desire, faith and solemnity, in their own lunar months, days, [and] hours, just as it is perfectly declared from those above in the gloss of the first part.

[17, 18, 19, Version A]

[19 Gloss] *Ispa vero est artis notaries, etc.* In this section Apollonius makes a further mention of the very same prayer—namely, *Assaylemaht, etc.,* with its two divisions, and says that the prayer itself is the first form (that is, the prayer in the notory art itself).[99] It shows this is it, because it is the way and founda-

---

98. Section 60.

99. The first form (*prima figura*) of the notory art proper begins with the *Assaylemaht* prayer; that is, the prayer, having its three divisions, belongs to a series of prayers called the Generals,

tion of the entire efficacy of all the sciences which are contained in the notory art, [and] no one is able to achieve an effect without that prayer, because it presents a memory for retaining all that has been heard, yet with the other prayers spoken which are made for the purpose of acquiring memory. But the very prayer is common to acquiring all sciences heard, just like in the seven liberal and mechanical arts.

From where [in the text] Solomon calls it "an angelic wisdom" in a certain book of astronomy, because it was first delivered to him through the angel, and because the invocation of the names of the holy angels which are contained in them gives so much wisdom for the worker; in another certain book of astrology, [the prayer] is called the "ring of philosophy," because the entire philosophy is betrothed through it,[100] and these are sufficient about this prayer, since it is the foundation of the entire art.

---

which are bound to certain prescribed lunar months, days, and hours. This first form (*prima figura*) is also called the ordered form (*compositus figura*) of the notory art, which is retained per Solomon's instructions according to section 8.

100. The glosser presents the metaphor reminscient of Capella in that the worker is to be betrothed to Lady Philosophy (or Lady Astronomy) herself, as in a wedding ceremony. The glosser misreads the text as referring to the prayer as "the ring of philosophy" rather than interpreting this descriptive title as belonging to the book called the *Mirror* that is, *Speculum Astronomiae* (*Mirror of Astronomy*).

[Chapter 2]

[20, Version A]

[**20 Gloss**] *Praelibatis igitur quibusdam, etc.* Therefore, within the preceding sections sufficient teachings and adequate definitions are given about the lunar months, times, and hours of the days in which that most sacrosanct preceding prayer—namely, *Assaylemaht, etc.,* with its two little parts—have to be read and offered, and how often and in what hours [*Assaylemaht* and its little parts] are to be offered.

Now in this section are placed the necessary teachings to those three prayers that follow, which are *Lamehc, [Leynac] etc.; Deus summe Deus [invisibilis], etc.; Te queso, Domine, etc.,* and it says that this first prayer—namely, *Lamehc, [Leynac] etc.*—contains the holiest names of the holy angels within it, which having been invoked and named in the right order, call forth a wonderful eloquence to the one making the offering. But others that follow bring in memory. Truly, these prayers have diverse efficacies, and thus they are to be said separately and at different times and hours of the day, just as it will be declared in the glosses of any of those prayers.

But in this same place Apollonius says that in this notory art all fields of knowledge are contained, such as the liberal [arts], as well as the mechanical and the exceptive [arts], and he shows the reason why this art is called "notory," and he says that is called "the notory art" because with some of the most shortest *notae* (that is, the prayers), memory, eloquence, and understanding is to be brought in, and through the same cognition of any knowledge it is able to be acquired and possessed.[101] Also, in this art he speaks about the *notae,* figures, and prayers, because in these three he establishes the entire art from where [in the text] it is to be understood what is a *nota,* what is a prayer, and what is a figure.

The *nota* in this art is described thus: The *nota* is a certain cognition through the prayer and a superimposed figure, just like the *notae* of grammar, logic, and rhetoric; and of the other sciences, in those figures the prayer is written above. But the prayer is a sacramental mystery revealed and pronounced

101. Section 20b.

through the Greek, Hebrew, Chaldean, and Latin words. For there is a figure in which the various and diverse signs are protracted, and no prayer is described within the figure, just like in the fifth figure of theology swords, serpents, birds, candlesticks, and the like are inscribed, but the figure is called a form.[102] Also, in some places it is able to be called a prayer, just like the Greek, Hebrew, and Chaldean *notae,* from where this prayer *Lamehc [Leynac], etc.,* is able to be called a *nota,* and the other similar prayers, all the liberal and exceptive fields of knowledge are able to be acquired and retained in memory through those *notae* and their figures. But this is to be understood that all efficacies and all sciences about which we have spoken are not able to be acquired or possessed together and at once in one month alone. But just as there are different efficacies and different sciences, so there are different prayers, *notae,* and figures; and for these different lunar months, different [solar] months, different days and hours, are to be employed in a similar way for the purpose of offering prayers and inspecting the *notae* and figures of their arts, and this is what it says.

[21, Version A]

[21 Gloss] *Inter istas tamen orations, etc.* In this section mention is made about this most holy prayer that follows—namely, *Lamehc, Leynac, etc.*—with the other two following prayers. But Solomon said before this prayer is to be of greater efficacy and virtue among all other prayers of this art for the purpose of acquiring eloquence, and for this reason, Solomon himself called this prayer the "queen of languages" for the reason that [it has] its own efficacy, because its principal virtue

---

102. The Prologue Gloss reads, *"Et pariter cum illis orationibus erant quaedam figurae depictae diversimodae protractae,"* meaning "And together with those prayers were some figures depicted of a protracted and diverse manner." The glosser correctly comprehends that there are two main components of the notory art which consists of the prayers and the figures but fails to understand that the passages he is reading are about the prayers having a certain form; that is, their magnitude of qualities. The glosser confuses the pictorial figures (*figura, -ae*) with the ordered form (*compositus figura*) of the prayers. He unwittingly asserts that the pictorial figures, like the fifth figure of theology (*figura*), is called a form (*forma*), using his own word, *forma,* to clarify the meaning. Nowhere in the *Ars Notoria* are the figures called forms (*forma, -ae*). Section 8 declares that the prayers were instructed to be kept in a certain ordered form (*compositam figuram*) by Solomon. Section 19 asserts that the *Assaylemaht* prayer has a certain form (*figura*). The glosser has misunderstood those passages about the prayers having a certain form. See also Variation 1 Gloss, which has a parallel passage.

is to disentangle the tongue of the one offering it and to dissolve his impediment, which if it is offered in the right order and according to the precepts assigned there, [then] it suddenly presents a wonderful eloquence to the one making the offering, and for that reason, Solomon placed it among all the other prayers of this art, performing for acquiring a more special and excellent eloquence, and in a certain one of his books, which is called the *Lemogethon,* he titled [this] same prayer, speaking about it, because this very prayer is excellent and special, [having] its own secret experiments.[103] Specifically, that prayer, just as I said before, returns an encumbered, slow-witted, lisping, and stammering tongue into an expedited, freed, and acute one, and it returns things heard and retained in memory to the one offering it eloquently, if [offered] in the right order and in a good manner, just as it is shown, will be shown, and offered to this [end].

[22] *This prayer which follows is a certain invocation of the names of holy angels of God and calls forth eloquence, and it ought to be said at the beginning of the assigned writings*[104] *[and] it is always to be offered at the beginning of the month first.*
Lamehc, Leynac, Lemahat, Semahc, Selmahat, Helmay, Helymam, Helmamy, Helmy, Helymamy, Zezecta, Zezegra, Zezegata, Gezegata, Zezegam, Remasym, Themaremasym, Ieranyha, Phuerezo, Gramyhal, Zetegomyal, Hezerogamyal, Heziephiar, Hezoperbiar, Iosaytyn, Zosatyn, Iosany, Gosamyn, Salaht, Salacoham, Salatehen, Salacanbel, Hen, Hemben, Hahena, Henbezepha, Bosephar, Saphar, Hemphar, Thamar, Sahaletremar, Hafartytimar, Tymal, Tyrimar, Namor, Seminhot, Semohit, Zemihoc, Semoiz, Lemayhon, Lemahac, Phetalon, Hamyht, Phetalonamye, Zamye, Zamiht, Prihity, Phihey, Haphyn, Gergeon, Gergohen, Ierchon, Lochios, Lothos, Semyhot, Lemahat, Zemohit, Lemayho, Phetalon, Hamys, Pheralon, Hamye, Hamyht, Phetiogergion, Lecton, Gerohen, Cochios, Lethos, amen.

[22 Gloss] *Lamehc, Leynac, etc.* This is the most sacrosanct prayer, about which we have spoken above in the preceding two glosses [and] which has so much of a most

103. The glosser says the prayer is found in the thirteenth-century version of the *Lemegeton*. See also section 20b.
104. Those writings which are assigned for the study and practice of gaining eloquence, such as the works of Cicero.

excellent virtue within it, because it renews and expedites the impeded tongue; it is called the "queen of languages" by Solomon. In this most sacrosanct prayer are the most sacred names of the holy angels among which are certain deprecations mixed in the Chaldean tongue, and on account of the subtlety of the speech, words, and their prolixity, they were not explained nor translated into Latin. But it is this which he calls forth eloquence still, with the other offered prayers which follow; namely, having the first three headwords said first which are to be acquired in any mental faculty, [and] having said [those], there are [others], which are *Alpha et omega, etc.; Helyscemaht, etc.; [Ph]os, Megal[os], etc.; Lux mundi, etc.* Having said those first three headwords first, this prayer is to be said and the other two following, still having made some interval between them, and this, having begun in the early morning on the first day of a new lunar month, [and] having been continued on each day of the lunar month up to the end of said lunar month always once in the early morning, and if they were to be said twice, [then] a greater efficacy is to be found in them. Having said those three prayers, those ten Latin prayers are to be said and ought to be said, which are performed for the purpose of memory, eloquence, and understanding, of which the first begins *Omnipotens, incomprehensibilis, etc.,* the second begins *Adoro te, rex regum, etc.,*[105] and the others following up to that place: *Hoc est opusculum, etc.*[106] And thus these prayers are to be offered together on any day of the lunar month up to the end for acquiring memory, eloquence, and understanding. Again, this prayer with the two following has the noblest efficacy. But if you have any doubt about some great vision, what it portends[107] to be, or about some present or future danger, or if you want to know the certainty of how [the current situation] stands with someone who is absent,[108] [then] it is to be done in this way: first, you must confess and you must do a Lenten fast on the very same day, and you must say the first three headwords of this art with great devotion in the late evening hour,[109] and having immediately made a

105. The ten prayers of the *Ars Nova* from sections 115 to 126.

106. Section 126.

107. Originally, the Latin reads *pr[a]etendat,* however, it has been corrected to *portendat,* meaning "portends," as it makes more sense in this context.

108. See section 26, which describes the efficacies for the prayer *Te quaeso Domine.*

109. Latin *hora serotina,* has the general meaning of an evening hour without specifying which one. Typically, the glosser specifies actions taken at vespers (Latin *vespers*), the canonical hour, which is translated throughout the gloss as "the evening hour." See appendix A4, "Medieval Computations of Time."

short interval, you say these three prayers once or twice, and you will go to bed and you will see in a vision all the things mentioned above because it ought to bind to you, and this is the efficacy of this most holy prayer.

[23, Version A]

[24] *These are those sacred and mystical words of which we have spoken for the purpose of calling forth memory:*
O most high God, O invisible God, Theos, Pat[e]r,[110] Gehemnos, Lehemnyhos, we ask you, Ymos, through your most holy angels who are Michael (that is, "the house of God")[111] Gabriel (that is, "the strength of God") Raphael (that is, "the medicine of God") Seraphim (that is, "the burning one") Cherubim (that is, "the fullness of knowledge"),[112] Helypha, Masay, Cherubyn, Ielonucios, Gadabany, Zedabanay, Gederanay, Saramany, Loniteci, Lotrosi, Gerohanathon, Zahamany, Lomyht, Gedanabasy, Seremanay, Secemanay, Heulothant, Helomyht, Heuloramiht, Samanazay, Gedebandy, by the fullness of knowledge, we humbly ask you, O Cherubim and Seraphim, and you, O Jesus Christ, through all your glorious holy angels, whose names are consecrated by God, which no mortal is permitted to pronounce, which are these: Deyhel, Dehel, Depymo, Deyn, Hel, Exluso, Depymon, Helynon, Exmegon, Paryneos, Exmegan, Pheheneos, Navagen, Hosiel, Oragon, Garbona, Rachion, Monyham, Megon, Hamos, and those are which human sense cannot and will not be able to comprehend.

[**24 Gloss**] *Deus summe, Deus invisibilis, etc.* In the preceding section it has been shown properly concerning the preceding prayer—that is *Lamehc [Leynac], etc.*—which has one most excellent efficacy in particular; that is to say, that it expedites and renews the impeded and slow tongue and administers eloquency in improvisation to the one making the offering, just as it has been said in the preceding gloss.

---

110. *Deus summe Deus invisibilis Theos Pat[e]r,* the prayer belonging to the third sequence of the General prayers.

111. The writer is mistaken. The Hebrew name "Michael" means "he who is like God."

112. The writer is referencing Pseudo-Dionysus, *Celestial Hierarchy* 7.1. Actually, the etymology of the word is as follows: from the Akkadian (*karabu/kuribu*), Hebrew (*kerub*), and ancient Greek (*cheroub*), meaning "blessing, blessed."

Now mention is made in that very place about that most holy prayer which is the most sacred invocation through the names of the holy angels which are invoked there. That prayer, although it is the shortest, has the greatest virtues and provides the most sacred efficacies. In that prayer there are certain holy and most sacred names that it is not permitted for anyone to offer or speak about them, except in the proper operation itself proceeding according to the order, and whoever would have offered them in the operation itself, let him first be well confessed from all his sins thoroughly; he will become better. And having received penitence, in this very work, he must live cleanly and chastely, and on the very day when he will have offered them, he must do a fast on Lenten food. Specifically, this prayer, [*Deus summe Deus invisibilis Theos Pateyer,*] ought to be pronounced after the preceding prayer [*Lamehc Leynac*], having made a short interval, and having completed and finished that, its prologue, which is the subsequent Latin prayer—namely, *Te queso, Domine, etc.*—is to be offered immediately after the slightest interval.

> "Here we want to show what an interval must be in this art. Accordingly, an interval is the proper period of time of one Lord's Prayer, that is, the period of time in which *Our Father*[113] would be able to be said once. However, while someone is working, having foreseen there are times, days, and hours,and according to the prolixity or brevity of days, it is necessary that the intervals be made longer or shorter, where if [the operation] of prayers is proceeded in wintertime, [then] it is necessary to make short intervals on account of the shortness of days and hours; but if it is to be offered in summertime, [then] intervals are able to be made greater, and similarly, according to the size and shortness of the prayers which are to be offered on any day, the intervals ought to be estimated, and it is made evident thus what is an interval and now the prayers have to be made in [their] pronunciation in this work."[114]

Specifically, this prayer has two virtues and efficacies in its pronunciation, and accordingly, because it has several and diverse efficacies, in a similar manner it has different hours of the day in which it ought to be offered for its own

113. Matthew 6:9–13; Luke 11:2–4.

114. Paraphrase from *Opus Operum,* section D(a), indicated by the scribe as a quote.

universal efficacy. Therefore, if that prayer is to be offered for memory and eloquence, having said the first preceding prayer with the other antecendents, it is to be offered in the early morning, just as it has been taught. But if for some other efficacy, such as for the purpose of having prescience of some vision about some present or future danger, or concerning someone who is absent from him, [then] that prayer, with the preceding and subsequent ones, is to be offered in the evening before he goes to bed, [and] the one who offers it and does it, just as it has been taught, will discover in that efficacy that he seeks it. Thus these prayers are to be offered at different hours of the day for their own different efficacies.

However, it is to be understood that when these three prayers are to be offered, one day for memory and eloquence, at the beginning of studying the writings, by no means should they to be offered for those others of their own efficacies on the very same day, from when it is to be offered for one efficacy in that day, it ought never to be offered for some other [efficacy], except for only one [efficacy] alone. Therefore, any hour in which someone will have offered these prayers, let him not be in mortal sin, and if he has been confessed and he says them with devotion, while living chastely, [then] he reads them with faith and strength. And if he does so, [then] he will discover the true effect in all the efficacies of these holy prayers which he selects.

[25, Version A]

[25 Gloss] *Te quaeso Domine mi, illumina, etc.* This Latin prayer, which is the prologue of a particular preceding prayer and the explanation of the prayer itself, because from some Greek and Chaldean words which are mixed among the most sacred names of the holy angels, which are to be deprecated, having invoking them, so that so much efficacy is carried out to an effect, [*Te quaeso Domine*] should be pronounced, having finished the preceding prayer, [*Theos Pater*], [and] having made a short interval between the same. That Latin prayer, although it contains good and sacred words within it, was not bestowing the same efficacy to the one offering it, through them if it is to be offered without the preceding others thus, [then] the other two preceding [that is, *Lamehc Leynac* and *Deus summe Deus invisibilis Theos Patyr*] were made thus, [and] if they were pronounced first, from where it is to be noted in this place[115] that the Latin prayers which are contained in this art, if they are to be offered for the purpose of acquiring some efficacy through them without the other Greek, Hebrew, and Chaldean ones, and they were showing little or no virtue or efficacy to the operator, and in this it is to be understood that those Greek, Hebrew, and Chaldean words, especially the most sacred names of the holy angels which are invoked and deprecated among them, undoubtedly they have this work to bring to effect and to bestow to the good and faithful worker all those efficacies and virtues.[116] Also, it is to be understood that the Latin prayers are their own prayers and humble supplications [made] in the presence of the true God. But the other Greek, Hebrew, and Chaldean ones are deprecations [composed] among the holy angels, who by divine permission have to minister all the efficacies and virtues in this holy work.

[26, 27, 28, Version A]

[28 Gloss] *Si enim volueris habere, etc.* In this place he makes a mention about the most sacred prayer, which is the shortest in words and the most holy in its own mystery, whose efficacy and virtue is the most probative in medical science, and of this Solomon said after the experiment of this very prayer, discovering and seeing its efficacy and virtue, "I received this new medicine created by God, . . . which . . . is a miracle more splendid than dreadful."[117] Therefore, this very prayer contains within it so great an efficacy in the medical art, just as I said and many other different efficacies that I will number there.

Therefore, if you wanted to test the experiment of this prayer in the medical art, you must perform [it] thus. First, if you are in some mortal sins and you confess to others, and on the very day when you want to experience this prayer, you must do a fast on Lenten food, living chastely, and assisting in the presence of someone weak or someone languishing on their deathbed thus, you say the following prayer, which is divided into two parts, in a low voice three times with great reverence, humbly and devotedly invoking those names which are

115. Sections 22 and 24. See also the section 24 gloss.

116. In other words, the Latin prayers present small or no virtue or efficacy by themselves. The Greek, Hebrew, and Chaldean prayers are the active agents for bringing about an effect.

117. Section 31.

contained there,[118] and [the outcome] will immediately be announced to you, and suggested by the virtue of the angels whether that infirm person ought to recover or die.

Also, this prayer has another efficacy which is such. For if you want to know about some woman, whether she is pregnant, doubting about her whether she truly is, stand in her presence, and offer the same prayer, just as it has been said above, and it will be revealed to you if she is or not, and if it is a male or a female that she conceived.

It also has another such efficacy. For when you want to know about some young woman whether she is a virgin or corrupted, doubting about this very [young woman], you must stand before her, and you recount the same prayer in the same manner, and [the truth] will be suggested to you by an angelic voice about knowing the truth.

Also, if you want to acquire perfect knowledge in the medical art, you mention the first three headwords of this art, which are to be mentioned first in acquiring any knowledge, and you mention after the prayers for administering memory, eloquence, and understanding, the very same prayer about which we are speaking here is to be mentioned after those first ones, and afterward the *nota* of the medical art is to be inspected according to their own times, days, and hours determined by him,[119] as I will clearly show in its proper place. This short prayer, which is *Ihesu Dei Filius, etc., Eleminator, Caudones, etc.,* with the two preceding, has those efficacies and virtues we have mentioned. However, it is not necessary to say the first three headwords or the other prayers for the other preceding efficacies, except in acquiring the medical science, and this is what it says there.

[29a] *Here begins the very prayer about which we have spoken, which has such good efficacy.*

Jesus, Son of the incomprehensible God, Hancor, Hanacor, Hamylos, Iehorna, Theodonos, Helyothos, Heliotheos, Phagor, Corphamodos, Norizane, Corithico, Hanosae, Helse, Zope, Phagora.

---

118. Sections 29a and 29b.

119. That is, God who commissioned Solomon to follow the angelic mandate about the determined times for conducting the greater ritual of the notory art. See section 73b.

[29a Gloss] *Ihesu Dei Filius, etc.* This is the prayer about which we spoke in the preceding section which has so many and more efficacies and is the entire foundation of the medical art, and the principle by which this very science is able to be acquired and to be had perfectly. For about this prayer Solomon said he had received and discovered the true efficacy of its virtue, which although it is the shortest in pronunciation of words, it has wonderful efficacies within the virtue of its mystery, and presents them to the worker who offers them in the precise order. For in its pronunciation certain names of holy angels are offered and invoked, having deprecated [them], whose office it is, and the virtue and gift is given to them by God, to reveal to the one offering them the truth of those efficacies, which he has an appetite to know. If, however, it is offered with great reverence, great veneration, devout obsequiousness, and in a low voice in the presence of a sick person or other persons[120] of whom he wishes to know the truth, [then] it will be revealed thus through this prayer by the angelic virtue what he is going to do or what he complains about this [matter] in the future.

This prayer ought to be offered three times in the presence of the aforesaid persons, standing before them, not moving until it is offered thrice, and having begun, the prayer ought not to be interrupted by mixing in other words until it is completed thrice. For this prayer—namely *Ihesu Dei Filius, etc.*—although it is divided into two parts, is still a single prayer, and it ought to be said at the same time before offering [it], let it inspire him, but he must be able to make some minimally timed interval. For in the prolation of this prayer no lunar month, time, or hour is to be seen beforehand, because it is able to be pronounced and offered on all days and all hours of the day. However, he who offers it must be fasting [and] chaste, saying it thrice reverently and devoutly. Also, if he who wants to have an understanding of the medical art and to acquire and to possess the entire [and] complete medical science, at the beginning of a new lunar [day of] some month, in the very day when the Moon is first, the first three head-words are to be offered—namely, *Alpha et omega, etc.; Helyscemaht, etc.; Theos, Megale, etc.; Lux mundi, etc.*—which are always to be offered at any beginning.[121] Having said those, those ten prayers are to be offered, which have to be offered for the purpose of acquiring memory, eloquence, and understanding,

120. Or lords or dignities.

121. Notice that the glosser is including the preamble prayer, *Alpha et Omega,* as belonging to those initial prayers called "the first three headwords" (*tria prima capitula*).

which prayers are *Omnipotens, incomprehensibilis, etc.; Adoro te, rex, etc.; Confiteor tibi, etc.,*[122] with the others following through the order, and these are to be offered successively over three days as often as the operator will want to do so. But on the fourth day they are to be offered with the first three headwords without the aforesaid others, these prayers, *Assaylemaht, etc.*, with its own three parts,[123] and with the other three following, *Lemahc, etc.; Deus summe, Deus, etc.; Te queso, Domine, etc.* Specifically, those prayers which make for the purpose of memory are to be offered for one month according to their lunar months, times, [and] hours, just as it has been declared in their own sections. But this month has been completed and finished, and memory, eloquence, and understanding have been acquired, in the beginning of the following month, on the first day of the lunar month, the first three headwords are to be offered in the early morning, and immediately these prayers are to be offered—*[Hazatam, etc.; Confirma, etc.;] Agloros, etc.; Deus omnium, etc.; Megal, etc.; Veritas, lux, via, etc.; Hanuyrliael, etc.; [Ego in conspectus, etc.;]*[124] [and finally] *Ihesu Dei Filius, etc.*—and let it be thus on any day of that month up to the end of the lunar month. The prayers are to be offered according to those days, hours, and that regimen, [as] it appears and will be appear in the glosses in their written passages before each of these prayers. Having completed that month, on the first Moon of another month, these other prayers are to be offered up to the end, which are *Ezethomos, etc.; [Domine Deus incomprehensibilis, etc.;] Domine Deus Sancte Pater, etc.; Deus, semper via et vita, etc.; Lemogethon, etc.; Vita omnium, etc.; Rex regum, etc.;*[125] *Ihesu Dei Filius, etc.*, and having completed those prayers, the figure of medicine is to be inspected with an intention, and the books and scrolls of the medical art are to be placed before the opened eyes, by rolling documents this way and that, by looking within and reading some sections, and these may be done on any day of that month up to the end, during those days [and] during those hours, with such an order, just as it has been described in the

122. The ten prayers of the *Ars Nova*.

123. The three parts of the *Assaylemaht* prayer are designated by the first headword of each part, which are *Assaylemaht, Gezamanay,* and *Sathamar* (section 16, Version B).

124. These prayers belong to the General prayers, though this sequence excludes *Hazatam* and its Latin prologue, *Confirma,* and the Latin prologue *Ego in conspectus,* which belongs to *Hanuyrliael.* Perhaps these omissions are an oversight.

125. These are the first four prayers belonging to philosophy, including their own Latin prologue prayers.

glosses placed juxtaposed to the aforesaid prayers. And having completed that month, those nine prayers, which are called the *novem termini,* are to be said over the three days and thrice in a day: once in the morning, once around the third [hour], once around noon, and the science of medicine is to be acquired fully and perfectly thus.

[29b] *The other part of the prayer follows that is one and the same.*
Eleminator, Caudones, Helos, Heloc, Resphaga, Thefagaym, Thethendyn, Chahonos, Vicenna, Heortahonos, Belos, Behelos, Belhoros, Hataphagan, Belehothol, Orthophagon, Corfandonos, having been born human for us sinners, and you holy angels, Helyhothos, Phaguora, aid, guide, and teach me whether he or she may recover or die of this infirmity.

[30, 31, Version A]

[Chapter 3]

[32, Version A]

[32 Gloss] *Disseramus ergo, etc.* In this section Solomon shows, first, the reason why this most holy work is called the notory art, [and] second, he wants to show how much virtue [and] how much efficacy the art itself contains and comprehends within it.[126] Therefore, this book is called a notory art, because it is that through which all arts, all liberal and mechanical sciences, can be acquired and possessed in a short period of time. And thus, this work is called the art of arts and science of sciences by Solomon, because it is contained beneath some brief notulis.[127] For the efficacy of this art is so great, since having read the Greek, Chaldean, Hebrew, and Latin prayers in their own times, days, and hours according to the precepts of the art, and inspecting the figures of the sciences on account of the virtue of the holy words, and the invocation of the names of the holy angels and their deprecation are administered to the operator in [the art]—memory, having heard all things in [his] memory, retaining by memory, eloquence in all things retained eloquently in the offering, a crafty intellect, and all the sciences, as much as the licit as the illicit, all these things are to be kept by the successive order written above. And thus, through this most sacred art, which is the shortest in the most sacred and most efficacious operation and prolation of words, the sacraments of those words and the aforesaid efficacy of the sciences can be acquired and possessed in a short time, which in studying and learning even the least of the sciences another is not able to apprehend during the life of a man; and thus it pleased the Most High Creator who created all things, and wanted to provide for all created things, and especially man whom he had molded with respect to his own likeness, [God] pleased to restore that very man, having been graced with virtues and documents, through these most sacred words, which were becoming contained in this art, and he is able to have been illuminated in all the sciences in a brief period of time, which sciences to another manner he would not have been able to be graced in reading, learning, and studying, when the life of a man is very

126. Section 32a, "[Solomon] called [it] 'notory,' because it is the art of arts and the science of sciences. For he comprehends all these liberal, mechanical, and exceptive arts within it . . ."

127. Latin *notulis,* meaning "little notes"; that is, the minute meanings of the words found in the *voces magicae* prayers composed of Greek, Chaldean, and Hebrew.

short and has an insufficient nature to accepting and retaining so many virtues, efficacies, [and] sciences necessary to him.

Therefore, let every faithful and devoted good person rejoice to study this most sacred art and with good works bring it to an effect, because God himself did not want only Solomon to administer the virtues themselves, but any other good faithful one who was laboring in this holy work, because with God there is no favoritism, but he pours his gace upon him who he finds worthy and faithful, and he administers suddenly the aforesaid efficacies and their sciences with the virtue of the holy words of that art. Accordingly, the prayers and the figures or *notae* are in that art; it is to be known from those that each and every one has its own special office to exercise, and it must be remembered that the *nota* of one art does not profit to the acquisition of another art, nor can it help or have any efficacy in acquiring any other science, except for that one alone for which it is designated. And thus, the divine on high foresaw that he would assign their own special prayers and figures to every one of the sciences. And thus, because certain arts are nobler and more difficult than others, so [Solomon] established and wrote down the nobler and more difficult *notae* and figures and appointed and described many others, whence there are some for the liberal arts that have three *notae,* some two, some four, some more, some fewer, and the reason why some arts have more or fewer than others we will assign and show in the written glosses in their own special sections in which mention will be made of the figures and *notae* of each particular science or art. Therefore, it is necessary for anyone wanting to begin such a most sacred work and to bring it to him who wants it to be accomplished that he is prepared to receive such a gift from the Most High Creator; that is, that before he may enter upon such a work to begin with he must be cleansed through confession from sins and become as better as possible and be faithful and strong in faith, firmly believing that the most holy words written in this book have so much virtue and to be able to have and to acquire through the same words that efficacy, that knowledge for which it is pleasing to him to work. Therefore, let him say the prayers of this art in their own lunar months, their times, their assigned days and hours, nothing exceeding beyond the form of this document. Accordingly, he must live chastely during the operation, he must govern his life honestly up to the end of the words of that art, and thus he will attain so much knowledge [and] so much wisdom just as it is said, and so any good worker in this art will obtain the grace from the Holy Spirit.

[33, Version A]

[33 Gloss] *[I]llud enim nobis necessarium est, etc.* In this section are placed some special precepts which are properly pertinent to the operation of that following prayer, which is *Lamehc, Ragna, etc.,* which prayer contains more efficacies and virtues within it in having been pronounced in the right order, just as it has been taught. But the teaching of the operation of this very prayer is as such. Therefore, when someone wanted to proceed with respect to the operation of this art, first, just as it has been said above, the first three headwords are to be offered, which they are always to be offered in any beginning for the purpose of acquiring some special efficacy. After reading and speaking the [first] three headwords, that most sacred prayer is to be pronounced with its own headwords, of which the beginning is *Assaylemaht, etc.,* and having made some interval to an immoderate amount, this prayer with its own particular part is to be offered with great reverence. For this prayer is necessary and more than useful with respect to acquiring the knowledge of all the writings; thenceforth, having read and pronounced the prayers which administer memory, eloquence, and understanding according to their own lunar months, times, days, and hours, the worker might have wanted to proceed according to the order of this book with respect to acquiring some knowledge of the seven liberal arts. This prayer is to be offered after the preceding prayers in the same days and hours in which those prayers are offered. Likewise, until [the operation] is to come before the inspection of the figures of any art, similarly, this prayer ought to be offered before the prayers of these very figures are offered. And this is to be understood that whenever and wherever this prayer is offered so often, and at the same hour, its prologue, which is *Memoria irreprehensibilis, etc.,* is to be offered, having made some short interval. Also, this very same prayer is able to be pronounced for certain other efficacies. Therefore, if someone who was less knowing about some question of some science that perchance, he would otherwise never had heard of, he was uncertain about, and he wished to solve and to enucleate that question[128] to them, hav-

128. The word "enucleate" is archaic English, having been derived from the Latin *enucleare,* meaning "to explain," perhaps in a more logical and detailed manner. In the Parisian manuscript labeled Latin 9336, *enucleare* acts upon the accusative *illam qu[a]edam,* meaning "that certain thing"; however, the Bodley 951 manuscript has *illam questionem,* meaning "that question," which is the chosen reading here.

ing been made [known] suddenly in the presence of everyone, [then] he must offer this very same prayer then at a secret time with great reverence and devotion, and after its very own prologue, and immediately having finished the prayer, God heard his deprecation and administered grace to him in solving the question and responding fully and perfectly. Still, it is to be understood that before such a sudden efficacy is to be found in this prayer, that it is to be offered first during one month with the other preceding prayers, just as it has been said in its own determined days and hours, and thus concerning the rest, the worker himself will suddenly discover this efficacy any time in this operation, having offered it once.

Also, we find from this prayer that it is able to be pronounced for another efficacy, which the efficacy is, as it were, similar to the previous one. Therefore, [the text] says that if he who offered that very same one successively through the month with the other preceding prayers, and by chance, it was through some [amount of] time among others, which they must pronounce it presently, and they must oppose some serious and inopportune science, which he may not be able to explain fully about the nature of its own ingenuity with this prayer, having been remembered with great affection and devotion, it will be recalled to him suddenly over this truth through the virtue of the holy angels, whose names, having been declared, are recited within it, and this is what it says about this prayer.

[34] *This is the prayer, about which we have spoken, and it is a wonderful prayer, whose first part is explained in the scroll about on the magnitude of quality of this art. The prayer begins:*

Lamec, Ragna, Ragaha, Ragya, Ragiomal, Ragiomab, Haguaht, Hoguolaz, Exhacdodan, Heracdodoz, Hantonomos, Hethaenehc, Hemones, Iothe, Lothem, Sezayha, Sazaratha, Hensazacha, Serayl, Marab, Mynachil, Maratal, Mayratal, Brihamothon, Tahamachon, Leprodoz, Lephorys, Leprohoc, Lephozrys, Hesacro, Hesacohen, Corquenal, Thoremal, Guoiemal, Valayhol, Salayl, Salayz, Salayhor, Galayz, Salquyhel, Gessydomy, Gessenazy, Iessonay, Hazoroz, Hazarob, Tharahal, Bostyhal, Hamol, Hamal.

[34 Gloss] *Lamehc, Ragna, etc.* This is that most sacred prayer about which we have spoken in its own preceding section in which we show its efficacies and virtues fully and perfectly. But in this most holy prayer, certain names of the holy angels are to be invoked, having been deprecated, which having been invoked beforehand with confession and devotion sent beforehand with faith, all the abovesaid efficacies are to be administered to the prudent and good worker.

Since Solomon, found this prayer on account of its very subtlety, virtue, and efficacy, which in themselves, while he offered it according to the angelic mandate, he compiled out of those [prayers], one great book,[129] explaining first about the very virtue and efficacy, which contains within it, and in the very same scroll he wanted to declare, to show, and to narrate the virtues of the Greek, Hebrew, and Chaldean words which are contained in this most sacred art following what is conscribed within the prayers. Accordingly, Solomon called that book a scroll about the magnitude of quality, because in that scroll it has been declared of what kind and how great are the quantities and qualities of the most sacred Greek and Hebrew words and of the prayers of this book.

Still, I do not say that Solomon has explained in Latin all the Greek, Hebrew, and Chaldean words which are described in the prayers, and especially the names of the holy angels which are not to be thoroughly explained, but particularly some words he did explain, which in having deprecated and invoked the names themselves in Latin, and compiled in that volume, because so great is the subtlety, so prolixious, and so burdensome in the exposition of any vocabulary word that scarcely or never could they have been able to explain in Latin, and although Solomon himself had explained a few out of the very words with respect to [those] words, still he compiled a certain great, burdensome, and prolixious scroll out of those.

But this very prayer, on account of its subtlety and efficacy, which he made use of, he called the "crown jewel of the Lord," because just as a jewel (that is, a precious stone), having been placed within some crown illuminates that, and makes it splendid, so this most sacred prayer, placed and written below among the other prayers written in this book, illuminates and makes it resplendent, augmenting their virtues and efficacies as long as it is pronounced with these at the same time in this right order. Therefore, this prayer, having been recalled secretly and devotedly, illuminates and makes resplendent the heart and mind

---

129. *Liber Florum Doctrinae Caelestis.*

of the one offering it in its lunar months, its days, its hours with the other aforesaid prayers.

But on the very day on which this very prayer ought to be offered, its prologue (that is, the Latin prayer written after it, which is *Memoria irreprehensibilis, etc.*), [is] to be pronounced, yet having made some short interval, and this very prologue is offered with great devotion and the obsequiousness of veneration. The prologue is a proper deprecation and a true impetration in the presence of God, so that the words of the preceding prayer may be led to an effect.

[35, Version A]

[Variation 5] **Semeht, Segahat, Raguaht, Reloymal, Hagualaz, Exhacor, Hanchomos, Lezen, Sarayl, Marab, Brihamathon, Lephez, Hyesacto, Thoemay, Salayhel, Agessomay, Hararothamal.**

[Variation 6] *This tells about the end of these prayers. For this preceding prayer is contained in the following place, having been abridged for the first prayer of the Generals, we sufficiently explained the greater part of its explanation in the scroll about the magnitude of qualities of the same art, but not about the sacramental understanding of the prayer itself from the [ritual] process, the hearer was having to be inept, admiring the mystery. This he knows undoubtedly and most certainly about some words of the aforesaid prayer itself to be in a Latin exposition. For these are some sections of the excerpts of the prayer itself. The prologue begins.*[130]

[36, 37, 38, Version A]

[38 Gloss] *Haec enim oratio a Salomone, etc.* In this section [Solomon] makes mention again about the aforesaid most holy prayer [*Lamec Ragna*], which makes it so much a virtuous and most sacred mystery, just as it is said. And again, it is said [the prayer] contains [such a mystery] within itself, and [Solomon] places in that] certain efficacies in the Specials, which the [book] contains within those [certain kinds of prayers]. Similarly, certain times are assigned, certain lunar [days

130. *Semeht Segahat* is offered as an alternative to *Lamec Ragna*.

of the] month, and coinciding hours in which this most holy prayer ought to be offered and read. Since Solomon first placed its efficacies and because [the text] says it ought to be pronounced at the beginning of all studied writings, just as it has been declared in the preceding gloss. Also, it has other efficacies and virtues; therefore, if someone was in some danger like in earth, fire, or water, or in danger of beasts, lions, or similar things, and he offered this prayer devoutly with hope and faith, and he will invoke the holy names of the angels who are summoned in the prayer with reverence, having been deprecated, [then] he will be safe in relation to these aforesaid dangers, nor will any of them be hurtful to him. But if someone was in these dangers and he wanted to pronounce this prayer, [then] it is not necessary to offer the first three headwords nor the other prayers, except this one, nor is it necessary to provide for such danger an offering in them nor to see beforehand the times, lunar months, other days, or hours of the aforesaid dangers in a state of fear, but still he must be fasting and chaste, he who offered it.

But in other efficacies, the times, lunar months, days, and hours are to be seen beforehand, which we will assign in the following gloss on that section: *Oratio autem in prima Luna, etc.*[131] Solomon recounts about this prayer that he received it through a certain angel, of those four in number, who have authority to serve and damage the earth, sea, and trees.

Also, Solomon calls this very prayer elsewhere an example of the *Liber Florum Doctrinae Caelestis* on account of the efficacies and virtues which he discovered in having offered it himself. Also, out of the mystery and virtue of this very prayer Solomon asserts he suddenly received the knowledge of theology through the divine grace of God, because he offered it in the beginning of the theological writings, just as it was taught by the angel to him, not exceeding the form of the document. He also recounts that this very angel singularly carried down this prayer to him, and while Solomon himself was reading this prayer on a certain night, seeing its very efficacies and virtues, he placed it among other prayers in this notory art, and he named it "the sign of the sacred mystery." For this prayer, having been offered thus, wonderfully preserves and commits to memory the knowledge of theology acquired through this art, if it is offered once in the morning for every determined day after having acquired the knowledge, [then] he who will have offered it must, nevertheless, be fasting, chaste, and devout.

---

131. Section 40.

[39, 40, Version A]

[40 Gloss] *Oratio autem in prima Luna, etc.* In the preceding sections it has been declared satisfactorily, entirely, and perfectly concerning the virtues and efficacies of the preceding prayer—that is, *Lamehc, Ragna, etc.,*—and with its prologue, *Memoria irreprehensibilis, etc.* Accordingly, in this section he assigns and shows the certain times, certain lunar month, certain days, and certain hours in which this most excellent prayer is to be offered.

For all its efficacies, except for that guarding against dangers, this prayer is always be offered in the beginning of the month (that is to say, when the Moon is first) because, in this art, we call the first or new Moon the beginning of the month, and so on that day when the Moon is first, the prayer is offered first; that is to say, once in the early morning, once around the third [hour], thrice around noon, [and] thrice around the ninth [hour].

But on the following day it is never offered.

On the third day, it is to be offered thrice, once in the early morning, once around noon, [and] once around the ninth [hour].

But from the third day up to the sixth day, it should not be offered.

Accordingly, on the sixth day, it is to be offered six times, twice in the early morning, twice around noon, [and] twice around the ninth [hour].

But from the sixth day up to the ninth day, it is not to be offered.

Accordingly, on the ninth day, it is to be offered nine times; that is to say, thrice in the early morning, thrice around noon, [and] thrice around the ninth [hour].

But from the ninth day up to the twelfth day it is not to be read.

On the twelfth day, it is to be offered twelve times; that is to say, thrice in the early morning, thrice around noon, thrice around the ninth [hour, and] thrice around the evening.

Accordingly, from the twelfth day up to the fifteenth day, it is not to be offered.

But on the fifteenth day, it is to be offered fifteen times; that is to say, thrice in the early morning, thrice around the third [hour], thrice around noon, thrice around the ninth [hour, and] thrice around the evening [hour].

From the fifteenth day up to the eighteenth day, it is not to be read.

Similarly, on the eighteenth day, it is to be offered fifteen times; that is to say, thrice in the early morning, thrice around the third [hour], thrice around noon, thrice around the ninth [hour, and] thrice around the evening [hour].

From the eighteenth day up to the twenty-first day, it is not to be offered.

On the twenty-first day, it is to be offered thrice in the early morning, thrice around the third [hour], thrice around noon, thrice around the ninth [hour, and] thrice around the evening [hour].

From the twenty-first day up to the twenty-third day, it is not to be read.

On the twenty-third day, it is to be read thrice in the early morning, thrice around the third [hour], thrice around noon, thrice around the ninth [hour, and] thrice around the evening [hour].

From the twenty-third day up to the twenty-sixth day, it is not to be offered.

On the twenty-sixth day it is to be offered thrice in the early morning, thrice around the third [hour], thrice around noon, thrice around the ninth hour, and thrice around the evening [hour].

Accordingly, from the twenty-sixth day, it is not to be offered up to the twenty-ninth day, on which day it is to be offered thrice in the early morning, thrice around the third [hour], thrice around noon, thrice around the ninth [hour, and] thrice around the evening [hour].

On the thirtieth day, which is the consummation and completion of that lunar month, this very prayer is to be offered fifteen times on this very day; that is to say, thrice in the early morning, thrice in the third [hour], thrice around noon, thrice around the ninth [hour, and] thrice around the evening [hour].

For these are the lunations, days, and hours, in which, and not in others, this most sacred prayer ought to be pronounced with the other prayers adjoined to it, just as there are the first three headwords and others adjoined to them, just as it has been declared in the preceding gloss.

For in those days in which this prayer is prohibited to be read and to be offered, the first three headwords and the other prayers ought to be read and offered, [having been made][132] for the purpose of memory, eloquence, and understanding, just as it has been declared above.

For this very prayer, as we said before, is of such efficacy and so great virtue, and those most holy names of the most holy angels of God have such a glorious mystery in them, which are invoked, having been deprecated, in the prayer, that on those days in which you pronounced it, just as it has been taught, you will be inspired forward [toward your goal] by the virtue of the angels to the knowledge which you are acquiring, and especially with respect to the knowledge of theology, so much so that you will scarcely be able to keep silent when you begin speaking about that knowledge.

And it is to be understood that whoever offered it first ought to be confessed, and on that day in which he works from it, he is to be fasted and be cleaned, and thus, having made an effect, it will be found on this very same day. For [these words] must suffice with respect to presenting these things about this prayer.

[41, 42, Version A]

[43] *Rubric: And this is the beginning of this very prayer, in which there is so much efficacy, and it is necessary to be preserved and to busy one's self with so much consideration, just as we have said. For this is the prayer about which we have spoken, how it is necessary to pronounce with great humility and devotion.*

Hazatam, Hyhel, Hehelilem, Chelyhem, Hazagatha, Agriraztor, Hyzguor, Hazahetam, Iesay, Zezor, Iezar, Ysayl, and you angels, of whose names are written in the Book of Life and they are recited in that place: Rasaym, Boros, Helsa, Heremegos, Myretagyl, Resaym, Lemay, Lemar, Rasamen, Lemar, Themamoht, Ythasym, Iemamoht, Chemamoht, Secray, Socthac, Sehan, Hanatar, Than, Sechay, Helymaht, Ioroyhel, Helymoht, Sathamaht, Helymyhot, Iosey, Theodony, Zasamaht, Pharene, Panetheneos, Phateneynehos, Haraman, Theos, Hathanaym, Hanatayhar, Hatanazar, Basyaccor, Iesenemay, Iasamana, Iesamanay, Hazyhaccor, Hamynosya, Zezaymanay, Hamos, Hamynos, Hiatregilos, Tahegilihos, Zaguhel, Zatahel.

---

132. The Latin word *facientes* has been corrected to *faciendae* for perfect tense agreement.

[**43 Gloss**] *Hazatam, Hyhel, etc.* In this place a mention is made about a certain most holy prayer, which prayer has four parts or four divisions, and this is the reason why it is divided into four parts, because it was carried down by four angels, since each prayer was carried down to Solomon singularly by each of the four aforesaid angels. And similarly, on account of the burdensomeness of the vocabulary words which are contained in them, it was necessary that [*Hazatam*] should be divided in parts, so that some interval is able to be made between them, lest in pronouncing them, with so many and such weighty names in the very pronunciation thereof without any interval, it would be burdensome to the human nature of the one offering them, even though having pronounced one without the other parts, by itself alone would not administer any efficacy or even minimal effect to the one offering it. Accordingly this prayer, having been offered with its parts, has several good efficacies and virtues, just as the antecending prayer whose beginning is *Lamehc, Ragna, etc.,* has the same ones. But this prayer—that is, *Hazatam, etc.,* for acquiring some perfect knowledge—ought to be pronounced for moral incontinence[133] immediately after that precedent one, yet having made some interval, which has to be pronounced at the beginning of the studied sciences.

As a matter of fact, this prayer has other efficacies, having been pronounced with its parts, because in its pronouncation according to what ought to be pronounced, it has to excite [its efficacies], and affect[134] the heavenly spirits—that is the holy angels—whose names are recited in this very prayer and in its parts, and having invoked them, they are deprecated, I say, it excites them with respect to doing that great matter that is required of them, having been deprecated. For this prayer ought to be pronounced from the beginning of a new lunar month up to the end with the others preceding for the first efficacy at the same times, on the same days, at the same hours, and as often as the prayer *Lamehc, Ragna, etc.,* is to be pronounced. For some efficacy—that is to say, in order that he may inspire the heavenly spirits to some great matter—[the prayer] ought to be pronounced only once in a day; that is, once in the early morning. And he

133. That is, for a lack of moral or sexual restraint.

134. The Latin word *promoveo, promovere, promovi, promotum* is the choice word in this section for describing the prayer's effect on the heavenly spirits; it means "to move, affect, excite, and inspire."

who offered it for whatever efficacy it may be, he must first be confessed and be fasting, chaste, and devout on that day in which he wanted to offer it, and he who offered it in this way knows that that most sacred mystery, since it is contained within it, is through the virtue of the holy angels who have this gift to lead to an effect, the heart, mind, and all the natural senses of the one offering it will be exalted, because a new mystery will be understood, having known and acquired the new knowledge for himself, because this prayer, having been offered thus, just as it has been said, presents an efficacy to the one offering it with respect to receiving and retaining the knowledge of all the good writings. But in this prayer in which certain names of the holy angels are contained, just as I have said, are mixed and interposed certain Hebrew and Chaldean deprecations to the holy angels, and although they are not explained entirely, still some Latin words are mixed among those Greek words, so that all fear and error, on account of ignorance of the Greek and Chaldean words, is to be cast off by the ignorant. For this prayer ough to be read in a low voice, having bursted forth the words in a plain manner, humbly and devoutly, in hope and faith, and with a great office of veneration. For that must suffice concerning this first part of this most holy prayer.

[44, 45, Version A]

[46] *This is the division of the prayer among the other parts:*
Hyhelma, Helma, Heymac, Henma, Hytaratas, Hemyna, Hytanatheys, Helsa, Hebos, Hyebros, Helca, Hagasa, Hoctomegos, Mycrotagil, Mycragon, Myharegyn.

[47, 48, 49, Version A]

[50] *This is the beginning of the second part of this prayer, which presents so much virtue and so much efficacy to the one pronouncing it, just as it has been said above:*
Agloros, Theomythos, Themyros, Sehotodothos, Zehotodos, Hacrihamel, Sozena, Haptamyhel, Sozihenzyha, Hemya, Getrahel, Helyna, Sotheneyhya, Geherahel, Halymyz, Zezoray, Gezetyz, Gerehona, Hazihal, Hazay, Hazihal, Hazay, Meguos, Megalos, Usyon, Saduhc.

[50 Gloss] *Agloros, Theomithos, etc.* Here begins the second little part of these prayers in which the little part, although it is the shortest in words, there is so much of the most sacred mystery in offering the most sacred words and names of the holy angels which are contained within it, and in the pronunciation of those words and names which are contained in this prayer, both in the preceding and in the subsequent one are supplied so much memory, eloquence, subtlety of ingenuity for the purpose of taking and retaining that knowledge beyond which it works, since it is admirable to obtain so much knowledge by human reason so perfectly and completely, and so great a virtue and so much efficacy is to be found within it and in its other parts because those have been pronounced once. He who pronounces them finds them in his own heart and mind, and he knows and divides [those] which are earthly and heavenly gifts. But the second little part ought to be pronounced for moral incontinence after its own first prayer, yet having made some short interval between those very two. Also, between these two parts is placed a certain middle [prayer] that is pronounced in Latin (which the Latin is a certain prayer or deprecation before God alone, whose divine grace permits the holy angels whose names are recited) [and] has so much grace [and] so much efficacy to lead through to an effect. But in this little part are so many precious names, and [the prayer] contains so much mystery in it that King Solomon, on account of the efficacy and virtue [which] he discovered in it in his own operation, and on account of its excellence, he called the prayer itself "the golden part." Also concerning this prayer, Solomon said that having recalled beforehand and pronounced this very prayer according to his own order, time, and established term, the holy angels receive in heaven the deprecation of the one offering it, from where [in the text] Solomon said that the prayer itself has a part consecrated in the heavens.[135] As if he might say, having finished with the prayer, God hears the prayer for moral incontinence by the one offering it, and this is enough said about this second little part.

[51, Version A]

[52] *Rubric: And after you have said the aforesaid prayer, having made some*

---

135. Section 49.

interval following this prayer, which is the third part of the prayer, you must read it, bursting forth sweetly:

Megal, Agal, Iegal, Harihothos, Handos, Hanathos, Hanatoyas, Hariothos, Lemazay, Iemezay, Lamezay, Lethonas, Iechonay, Zemazphar, Zeomaspar, Zeomaphar, Tethagramos, Thetagramys, Hatammar, Haziamyhos, Hazamahar, Zahamayr, Iechosaphor, Zethesaphyr, Gethor, Saphor, Hazagitha, Hazacapha, Hazactuypa, Haragaya, Hazaguy, Phasamar, Samar, Saleht, Salym, Salmehc, Samehc, Salehc, Salezaleht, Zadayne, Neochatyr, Neodamy, Hadazamyr, Sozena, Belymoht, Hazac, Helyhot.

[**52 Gloss**] *Megal, Agal, etc.* Here begins the third little part of the prayer which is of such efficacy and virtue, having said and pronounced the first and the second part, having made some short interval in the prolation of them, this is to be offered with its following prologue, which is a certain Latin prayer pertaining only to God the Most High, who created the holy angels, whose names are recited here and having been invoked, they are deprecated, and having finished this third part thus, an interval is made, and he who pronounces them, thinks in his heart and mind, and he must see beforehand that knowledge and the material of the same science from which he works, and place the books of this very science before his own eyes, and open them, and read within them a little, and he begins to read for moral incontinence the Latin prayer which follows; namely *Veritas, lux, via, etc.,* which the Latin prayer is not drawn out from the preceding Greek prayer, but was placed and added there, so that God himself, in whose hand all things exist by his divine-permitting grace picks out to strengthen, through his most sacred angels, that memory, that eloquence, and that understanding for acquiring that knowledge for which he works in offering said prayers. And having finished this Latin prayer thus, and having made some short interval, the fourth part of the prayer, which is *Hanuyrylyhahel, etc.,* is to be offered. But having pronounced and finished these four parts, just as it has been shown in a convenient and competent manner in its own glosses, he will be administered so much memory, eloquence, [and] understanding for pronouncing those by the grace of the Holy Spirit for the purpose of having that knowledge which he requires and foresaw to acquire and to have, because human nature will be able to and such is able to be reputed as the greatest miracle, having been given by God, and this is what it says about the third little part of the prayer.

[53, Version A]

[54] *Rubric: Indeed, the three parts, just as it has been said, having mentioned [it] beforehand, you will pronounce the following prayer after those, having made some interval, which is the fourth and last part of these prayers:*
Hanuyrlyahel, Hamsahel, Dalyhir, Hayr, Hahel, Zedahc, Hazaraht, Zedayhc, Hazayas, Iezorial, Zezorias, Iechorial, Semayha, Ysamyha, Zamaysa, Samna, Ysaray, Ysamyhe, Hysatay, Lemeyhel, Nehel, Lemehel, Iehymehel, Mychynab, Nybahal, Mychyn, Myban, Myhab, Hamyby, Mynab, Helyasal, Homeribymal, Helymal, Hymbas, Zebracal, Zelymal, Iecro, Samaryl, Zezocha, Iecrosahal, Melos, Zalymelor, Zalymilos, Zaguhel, Mychathomos, Myheromos, Mycrachosmos, Nytromyhos, amen.

[54 Gloss] *Hanuyrryliahel, etc.* Here begins the fourth and last little part of the aforesaid prayers. For in this last part is such a most sacred mystery and so much virtue asserted by Solomon that is admirable for human nature if it is pronounced, just as it has been taught with its preceding little parts. For in this prayer, which is the shortest, there are certain names of the holy angels among which there are certain Hebrew and Chaldean words which are said to be prayers or deprecations pertaining to said angel names, which the words were particularly explained in Latin, which the exposition is that Latin prayer, which is *Ego in conspectus tuo etc.,* which the prayer is a certain proper deprecation pertaining solely to God. For this Latin prayer ought to be pronounced after the antecedent prayer, having made some short interval between them. Therefore, it is to be understood that these four prayers about which we have spoken are the most sacred prayers, and the most excellent mystery is contained within the prolation of these very words and they ought to be pronounced with great devotion, hope, faith, and reverence without mortal sin, and just as Solomon testifies, it pleased the Most High God, so that the virtue and sanctity of these four prayers was being understood miraculously. From where [in the text] King Solomon places a certain example here about this, saying that one day while he had been absent from his house for whichever of his business affairs, and he had dismissed his book in which these four prayers were written forgotten outside his strongbox; someone came, his amicable and family servant came, and entered the chamber of the king, and finding the book by chance, he opened the book, and began to read the first prayer of these four; namely, *Hazatam, etc.* And thus, he himself, now being sated and drunk on wine, and similarly after having approached a woman, unclean and full of other sins, while he was now near the end of the aforesaid prayer, the book fell from his hands and immediately he had been made mute, blind, and deaf and lost sense, memory, and understanding, those which he used to have at first, and thus he had been made demented and he remained in this way up to the hour of his death. But at the hour of his death, it pleased God, as he himself was explaining in detail to Solomon how it had fallen to him according to his lot for [this] reason in this way, so that the virtue and sanctity of these holy prayers may be known, and he spoke and recounted how he had entered the king's chamber and how he had taken the book and opened it, having been drunk and unclean, and he had begun to read those prayers, and how he had lost the four natural senses, having scarcely finished the first part. But now, in the hour of his death, he said that he was seeing four angels above him who used to flog [him] and had scourged [him] from that hour in which he begins to read up to that time, saying that each of the said angels used to have their own proper office in flagellating the senses which he had lost. But a certain one of them had flagellated him in eloquence and speech, and thus he was made mute, but another had flagellated in light and clarity of the eyes and thus he was made blind, but another had flagellated him in hearing, and thus he had been made deaf, and the fourth had scourged him in memory and understanding, and thus he had been made insane. And thus, he shows through this example that in these four prayers are the four names of the angels written, which are the principal angels, and they have greater power than the other angels in this operation whose names are similarly written there, by whose virtue and power this work is brought to an effect, whose very angels he had offended, by naming their names, having been drunk and unclean, from where [in the text it reads that] King Solomon, when he heard this, was stupefied, and admiring and revering well, he established a special mandate over these prayers that he himself kept the mandate humbly and devoutly, and he says thus that anyone must not presume to read nor pronounce these four prayers of which the four angels are the administrators, unless [he] has been maintained first with confession and with fasting, chastity, reverence, hope, and faith; and let anyone beware not to offend those most holy angels whose names are recited in those [prayers] in the correct operation, and if anyone performs [those prayers] successively, having been uttered presumptuously in the pronunciation itself, [then] he would be able to incur bodily danger. For in which days, in which hours [the prayers] ought to be offered is declared in the gloss of the first part—namely, *[H]azatam, etc.,*—and it has been sufficiently said here about those four prayers.

[55, 56, 57, 58, Version A]

[58 Gloss] *Datis ergo praeceptis, etc.* In this place it says that in the preceding sections and their glosses there are satisfactorily, fully, and perfectly given general precepts for the introduction of the operation and pronunciation of all the preceding prayers—that is to say, how it must be proceeded first in the beginning of this most sacred art, how the worker ought to conduct his life, in which lunar month he ought to begin, in which days and hours the antecedent prayers ought to be pronounced, and in which [days and hours the antecedent prayers ought] not [to be pronounced]. But in this present section it says that certain other singular teachings are necessary for beginning and acquiring each art. This is because in learning the seven liberal arts and acquiring their sciences through this art, the times, months, and their [zodiac] signs are to be seen beforehand in which the said knowledge of the liberal arts are to be acquired and in which operation of the liberal arts especially is to be begun. But at what times, in which months, and under which [zodiac] signs, it is to be begun for any knowledge of any art, in that section below through the two documents placed [there] that begins *Diximus superius, etc.,*[136] we will show entirely and perfectly.

[59, 60, Version A]

[59/60 Gloss] *Haec est oratio sancta, etc.* In the preceding sections a mention has been made and a corresponding order given of all the prayers which generally are made for memory, eloquence, and understanding. But in this place a mention is made about a certain most holy prayer with its own prologue and its following little part, which is a particular prayer for acquiring eloquence, the

---

136. Section 147.

beginning of this prayer is *Gemoht, Gehel, etc.*[137] But this prayer contains within it such a glorious mystery and such a glorious virtue and sanctity of a certain most glorious name, our Lord Jesus Christ, because the name is said to have written with his own hand while he was in the Temple among the Jews, because in the pronunciation of this very most sacred name and of the other holy names of his angels that are to be invoked, having been deprecated, in this very same prayer, God hears the pronunciation of this very prayer, and he administers as much eloquence as is necessary for him. Therefore, having been seen beforehand, in these [holy names] there are two [parts], although it contains only one particular virtue; that is to say, eloquence.

First, therefore, [the operation] is to be lived for the purpose of acquiring eloquence, memory, etc. At the beginning of the pronunciation, the first three headwords are to be offered, which are always to be read in any beginning. But afterward, the following prayers are to be offered after the written sections, which are made for acquiring memory, etc., just as it has been written above in their own sections. But after those prayers, this most holy prayer with its two divisions is to be spoken on those days, in those hours, in the same term, and in the same order, just as the preceding prayers with which it ought to be offered.

Second, it is to be understood that this prayer, although generally it has to be pronounced with the others, is still able to be pronounced by itself singularly for the same efficacy, and if it is pronounced singularly by itself, [then] it is to be done concerning it in this way. First, therefore, before it is itself pronounced, the first three headwords are to be offered, which having been said are always in any beginning. But reading those sections, having made some interval, this prayer is to be offered. But having finished the prayer, an interval is made and then its prologue is to be read; namely, *Omnipotens, sempiterne Deus, etc.*

Having finished the prologue, an interval is made, then the following prayer, which is *Semoht, Lamen, etc.,* is to be said. But having finished this prayer, those ten prayers are to be read which are made for the purpose of eloquence, memory, etc., which are written below after these near the end of this book, but the first of those begins *Omnipotens, incomprehensibilis, etc.,* the second begins *Adoro te, rex, etc.,* the third begins *Confiteor tibi, etc.,* and all ten are to be spoken up

---

137. The *Gemoht Gehel* prayer has two parts: *Gehmoht Gehel* (section 62) and *Semot Lamen* (section 69). Its Latin prologue is *Omnipotens sempiterne Deus* (section 64).

to the end, thus of those the last is *Domine, nunc quia ego servus tuus, etc.*[138] Indeed, this prayer about which we are speaking here, having been pronounced with these prayers once in the early morning for one month, only administers eloquence to the one making the offering, but not so much if it were being pronounced with those antecendent prayers which are written after the first three headwords, just as I have declared above in their own glosses.

Nevertheless, it is to be attended to that if the first three headwords are to be offered and afterward the following prayers—namely, *Assaylemaht, etc.*—and the others successively after it, which ought to be offered for the purpose of acquiring memory and eloquence, then this prayer ought not to be pronounced with them on the first day of the month, nor the second, nor the third, up to the fourteenth [day of the] Moon. But on the fifteenth [day of the] Moon, having read the other prayers and having finished at the same hour, this prayer is to be offered first and not before any day [before the fifteenth day] up to the end of the lunar month, and this is what it says in this section.

[61, Version A]

[62] *This is the simple prayer of eloquence which Solomon and his descendants called "Lenguamaht" in Greek, which they called "the restoration of tongues" in Latin. For this prayer is the beginning concerning the faculty of eloquence and its virtue. The prayer itself begins:*
Gemoht, Gehel, Helymoht, Hemeb, Sabahel, Zerothay, Zabahel, Gerozay, Hebel, Crosay, Hamagra, Hacyhagra, Ragen, Seromay, Zehez, Hezehengon, Iezomay, Hemehegon, Hamagrata, Cezozoy, Gesomnay, Hezehenguon, Iethomay, Halla, Hathanathon, Hagiel, Hatamyhel, Hamamyhel, Hacanayos, Ozamyhel, Hathomas, Hecohay, Zemohay, Hecozomay, Thealgetha, Theal, Regon, Hagem, Iezeragal, Zehalragem, Geht, Zeregal, Hamabihat, Hezegon, Gethage, Madyhachios, Zachalchios, Zadanthyos, Exhedem, Pallacharos, Zallachatos, Thelchis, Crehodyos, Zezcechyam, Pallicitacos, Nechy, Delchys, Heremodyos, Helmelazar, Helyne, Iazar, Haron, Gezero, Mymyhel, Henthon, Hermelazar, Sython, Genython, Hezemyhel, Heymemy, Helmelazar, Cromymyhel, Exheruz,

138. These are the ten prayers of the *Ars Nova* (sections 115–25).

Zorol, Mothora, Rabyhel, Samyb, Lamely, Melyon, Sarabyhel, Samyl, Tamyl, Samyhel, amen.

[62 Gloss] *Gemoht, Gehel, etc.* This is that most sacrosanct prayer of which we made some mention in the preceding section, but because no full or complete mention of it had been made. In its own proper place, we want to show and to demonstrate fully its virtue and efficacies. Therefore, it is to be understood that this most sacred prayer or deprecation has more efficacies, uses, and belonging to any science, one of those virtues is especially attributed to it, namely, to increase and to bestow eloquence to the one offering it, which are to be acquired in school or study in some science, however, as long as it is offered in the correct order and the right times. But another, wonderful and excellent efficacy is found in it, whose mystery is as such.

Therefore, if someone was preoccupied by some great and serious business in the presence of some great director[139] or king or some other public figure, and that business is not able to lead to an effect by any counsel, [then] this prayer with its following prologue, which is the Latin prayer—namely, *Omnipotens, sempiterne Deus, etc.*—[which] he has in his memory (that is, he knows them by heart if it is possible for him), and he offers them secretly in the presence of the director himself before he arrives for the purpose of expounding his own business, and if he was not able to offer them by heart, he has them written in some schedule, and just as it was better he offers [it] secretly with great devotion, assisting in the presence of the chief [director], and if they were pronounced in the right way, [then] he who offers them will impetrate, through the virtue of the names of the holy angels, who, having deprecated them, are invoked so much grace on the side of him in the presence of [the director] who is to be incited to his own business, which is to be brought thoroughly into effect.

For it is to be understood that this prayer (namely, *Gemoht, Gehel, etc.*) and the other following prayer (namely, *Semoht, Lamen, etc.*) are the same, but there is a certain division between them and between [them] is placed that Latin prayer—namely, *Omnipotens, sempiterne, etc.*—which the Latin prayer is a certain deprecation pertaining solely to God, so that his holy angels who are invoked with his divine permission, preside over and accomplish that business to lead to an effect expeditiously and freely. Again, that division is placed

139. Or president, patron, protector, or bishop.

between the two Greek [prayers] themselves, so that there may be some interval between them, because so many names were becoming burdensome to offer and to read together without some interval, from where [in the text] Solomon put in that place an interval between those names below, which was coming together to be made an interval.[140] Therefore, let the first prayer be read up to the Latin prayer, and let a short interval be made in that place. Afterward, let the Latin prayer be offered and let there be a shorter interval. Finally, let the other Greek prayer be read, and thus these three prayers are to be offered for any of the two efficacies said above. Therefore, let them be read with great veneration, obsequiousness, and with devotion, [and] with hope, faith, and a confession coming before, and having received penitence humbly for all his sins.

But on the very day in which they are to be offered for whichever efficacy, he who offers these very prayers must be fasting and living chastely and cleanly. But on the preceding day, while he wants to offer those very ones for some efficacy on the following day, he must fast on bread and water, and be on guard against mortal and criminal sins, and especially against drunkenness and lechery, and this especially on the preceding day and on the very day in which the prayers are to be offered. But if the other preceding prayers are offered for acquiring eloquence, just like the first three headwords and the others that follow, are just as it is declared above in the preceding section, they ought to be first before these are offered to be pronounced at their times, their lunar [days of the] month, their days, their hours assigned above, and thus. Thus the preamble prayers, having been memorized beforehand, (these three prayers from which we made this mention) are to be offered once by the early morning.

And Solomon said that if someone offers them twice in the early morning successively, so much eloquence might be administered to him [to the degree] that the abundance of his own eloquence and speech hinders him,[141] from where [in the text] it suffices that they be offered for acquiring eloquence once in a day.[142] But if for some efficacy—that is, for expediting some serious business matter—it requires them to be offered, otherwise [if not for such a

140. Section 61.

141. In other words, the divinely acquired gift of eloquence will oppose the practitioner's natural tendency to speak and enunciate poorly.

142. Section 61, although the glosser's description is more detailed. The glosser may be fabricating these details or referencing the material found in the now lost *Lengemath*.

business matter, then] they are to be offered in a softer [voiced] manner.

Therefore, he must fast first on the preceding day on bread and water and he is to be confessed and be fasted and chaste on the following day, assisting in the presence of the judge, director,[143] or prince, let him say them twice, reverently and devoutly, without any other prayers. They can also be said and offered for this business matter on any day, at any hour, in any place, still [he must be] clean, fasting, and chaste.

But these prayers, on account of the wonderful efficacy of eloquence, administers to the one who speaks them, Solomon named *Lenguamaht* in the Hebrew speech, that same [*Lenguamaht*] sounds in Latin as "restoration of tongues," because by restoring the stammering tongue and the slow manner of speaking they restore them in all things heard eloquently to the one making the offering, if they are offered according to the above-mentioned order. But the great name of our Lord God is written in those prayers among the other names of the holy angels of God, just as Solomon asserts that name, God himself[144] wrote by his own hand in the Temple, [the very Temple] in which he was found when his own mother was searching for him, and it is said many miracles have been made in that place,[145] just as it was said above.

For it is prohibited by Solomon for anyone to presume to offer those prayers for the sake of temptation[146] nor up to this place, except in the very proper operation of this very art; that is to say, for acquiring eloquence or for another efficacy already mentioned above. But those three prayers are the last of this book's first part,[147] which with all the preceding prayers, read and pronounced in their own times, their own days, their own determined hours in time and constitution, and nothing is exceeded beyond the commanded form; [the prayers] add memory in everything heard [and] retained by memory, [they also add] eloquence to the one making the offering in everything retained eloquently, [and they add] an understanding of both with a [mental] stability, and this is because it says so up to this place.

[63, 64, 65, Version A]

143. Or president, patron, protector, or bishop.

144. That is, Jesus Christ, called "God" here based upon the doctrinal belief in the Trinity.

145. Luke 2:41-52.

146. Section 60.

147. The first part belonging to the General prayers.

[69] Semoht, Lamen, Iezael, Salmacyhal, Zamatyhel, Salmatyhel, Mahazihol, Zamazyhal, Hezcleaz, Mahatyholen, Hezole, Helzoleaz, Megos, Hemol, Hemnole, Mechos, Hazamegos, Halzamyhol, Alsamahol, Alzamoy, Menmamycros, Menomycros, Zoly, Marayhathol, Zolmazachol, Zelymanyhatol, Zolmatha, Zachol, Zolmycratol, Zemeney, Iemenay, Lameley, Zethemalo, Zechenorau, Labdayo, Lodoho, Zabday, Hothon, Ladaiodon, Lapdayhadon, Iothanau, Hyzemuzyhe, Hyzthancyhe, Iotha, Vahu, Zyhof, Zihanacyhe, Phomos, Zeherem, Zehe, Zyhehelmos, Hyehanacyhe, Homos, Hessycamal, Hessyromal, On, Thehesibotha, Magal, Hesyhota, Mycho, Haipha, Husale, On, Us, Flum, Tals, Hallemassay, Alesemony, Salemanasay, Helemazay, Zazyro, Semanay, Nachayro, Nachauz, Gemaol, Ieculmassay, Gemahol, Iezemalo, Magul, Gehamas, Senadar, Iezama, Salpha, Secramagay, Iehermagay, Zehetyn, Semasadayr, Iehyr, Ramagay, Geiama, Salpha, Gemama, Zyhemehama, Supha, Iohec, Iohabos, Haymal, Hamanal, Chanocromas, Iobohc, Hamynal, Zanogromos, Nyzezoroba, Nygerozoma, Negero, Robaly, Negora, Hohalym, Nycheromachum, Tholymtay, Colomay, Loynar, Cholumgay, Zenolozyhon, Zenomelihon, Samyhel, Gyhety, Sycrozegamal, Thonehos, Carmelehos, Samel, Gehys, Zesyhor, Iezolnohyt, Phicorse, Gramaht, Theonehos, Carmelos, Samihel, Sermanay, Gozesior, Semarnayl, Zarmacyhayl, Heliozo, Tahel, Samayl, amen.

[69 Gloss] *Semoht, Lamen, etc.* In this place we make mention of this most holy prayer, which is the last little part or division of the preceding prayer—namely *Gemoht, Gehel, etc.*—of which those who pronounce the said prayers in the correct order with the preceding others administer to the one offering them memory, eloquence, and a complete and perfect understanding. Specifically, this prayer of this art—namely of the Greek, Hebrew, and Chaldean prayers, which the prayers administer to the one offering them the abovesaid efficacies (that is, memory, eloquence, and understanding, etc.) is not able to be acquired or possessed completely and perfectly any knowledge of the seven liberal arts and of other mechanical [arts] without those aforesaid efficacies to be acquired first and foremost.

Also, it is to be understood that up to this place, general and singular precepts have been given separately, singularly and generally, sufficient enough for the operation of the General and Special prayers, and which the same prayers are called "Generals" because they have been given before all the liberal, mechanical, and other sciences that are contained in this art. All the aforesaid prayers, which have been written are from the beginning of this book up to this place, are to be pronounced first before [Solomon's prelude or precept] is able to be reached with respect to acquiring any knowledge of the aforesaid arts.

But among those abovesaid prayers, which all are composed for acquiring memory, eloquence, understanding, one is a most holy prayer, placed and written, which should not be offered with the aforesaid prayers for the now aforesaid efficacies, because it has its own important efficacies and it is pertient to physical science, just as it is to be seen fully above in its own section and gloss. Specifically, that prayer begins *Ihesu Dei Filius, etc.,* with its own little part following; therefore, with the above, evidently from the beginning up to this place,[148] it is given a sufficing definition and a sufficient precept, [and it is given] special and general [rules] from the Special and General prayers.

Now, about the rest we will make a mention about the seven sciences of the liberal arts and of the other mechanical [arts] and about their prayers and figures, but first and foremost, about the science of grammar and its figures; second, about the science of dialectic and its figures; third, about the science of rhetoric and its figures; fourth, the science of the four liberal arts and their figures, which there are the four arts of music, medicine,[149] arithmetic, and astronomy.

Specifically, this most holy prayer is a prayer that contains a most sacred mystery within itself by virtue of the holy angels whose names are invoked in reciting this very prayer. For nothing was extracted from this prayer in Latin, and thus, it does not have any prologue on account of its difficulty and prolixity. Therefore, this prayer is to be offered, having finished the antecedent prologue, having made some short interval on the same day [and] at same hour, and just like the preceding prayer, which is its first part, it is to be offered chastely, devoutly, and with great reverence, just as is contained in the preceding gloss.

---

148. Sections 28 gloss to 29b.

149. Latin *physica* means "natural philosophy" in the classical Greco-Roman sense. Although by the Late Middle Ages when the Arabs translated Greek medical texts that would become accessible to Europe, the term came to mean "medicine." Strangely, the glosser excludes geometry from the four liberal arts (i.e., the quadrivium) and substitutes in its place the art of medicine.

[70a] *About this prayer King Solomon said, "This is the prayer of prayers and a special experiment, by which all things whether singular, particular, or general may be heard, known, and recollected by memory fully, perfectly, and efficaciously."*

[66, 67, 68, Version A]

[70b] *Here it says how each art has its own proper* notae *and figures:*
As we come before the singular ones, specifically before the teaching of each art, it is necessary that we discuss how each art has its own *notae*.

[71, Version A]

[71 Gloss] *Artes vero liberals sunt septem, etc.* From the beginning of this art, mention has been made of special and general prayers that have their own virtue and efficacy to administer to someone pronouncing them, as was taught, memory, eloquence, understanding, and its [mental] stability.

Now in this place mention will be made of the seven liberal arts, their *notae,* figures, and the particular and regular prayers pertinent to those arts themselves, from where [in the text] it is to be understood that there are seven liberal arts that are divided in two—namely, into the trivium and quadrivium—and the seven mechanical arts. Specifically, the trivium is grammar, logic, and rhetoric. Accordingly, the quadrivium is music, medicine, arithmetic, and astronomy.[150] Specifically, the mechanics are these: hydromancy, pyromancy, nigromancy, chiromancy, geomancy, [and] *neonegia*.[151]

Also, any art of the seven liberal arts has its own prayers and its own *notae* and figures. Specifically, grammar has three *notae* or figures, and any figure of those three has its own Hebrew, Greek, and Chaldean and Latin prayers in which are contained the most sacrosanct names of holy angels who are deprecated, having been invoked there. Specifically, logic has two important figures and four other signs divided by the figures, which the figures have their own particular prayers. Specifically, rhetoric has four figures, any of those

150. Strangely, geometry is missing from this list, having been substituted with medicine.

151. *Neonegia*. Likely a corrupted Greek word for onomancy. Notice that the seventh mechanical art, *geonogia,* likely another corrupted Greek word for genethlialogy, the astrological practice of casting nativities, is missing from this list. See chapter III.

four has its own separate Latin, Greek, Hebrew, and Chaldean prayers.

Specifically, music has one figure and its own prayers, which ought to be pronounced before the figure itself; that is, having inspected it. Medicine has one and its own prayers. But astronomy has six figures, any of which has its own prayers which always ought to be pronounced before them with the inspection of those.

But in the other sections in which a mention is made about the arts themselves, and of others, and their figures, I will show more completely [and] singularly about each art and each of those figures, just as it is concerning theology and philosophy, and their sciences and figures.

Also, concerning the mechanical arts and their figures; that is, [the mechanical arts] are comprehended beneath these figures. But of those mechanical arts, there is a certain one which is called nigromancy,[152] about which it is not permitted to work through this art on account of sin because [sin] is to be worked in it by sacrificing to malignant spirits. But yet, Solomon says that in nigromancy there are seven books. Five of those can be read with minor sin and through those, working the science of nigromancy. But two of those are altogether prohibited to be worked, if any of those was worked, he commits sacrilege by offering sacrifices to malignant spirits, because without a sacrifice dedicated and presented to the spirits themselves no one is able to work from those two books, and whoever offers a sacrifice of human blood or other bodily matter to demons offends God and denies him, and [God] is to be angered with him mortally and he loses his own soul entirely, unless he evades it through carrying out penitence. For that reason, those two books were especially prohibited, and although it may be a sin to work from those [five books] in which it is not necessary to sacrifice, still it is less of a sin than from those [two books], but of what kind are those five books about which it is not a great sin to work without those two from which it is the greatest sin I now omit, because it is not good to make any mention about that science, and especially in this book in which there are pure things and sacraments of God and the holy angels, and these things are sufficient with respect to presenting.

152. *Nigromantia*. The glosser extends the Greco-Roman word sense of "necromancy," consulting the dead, to include the conjuring of malignant spirits. See NS 65. See chapter III.

[72, Version A]

[72 Gloss] *Artes vero liberals sunt septem, etc.* Here he says that there are seven liberal arts, which are able to be learned, read, taught, and acquired through working this most sacred art without any sin. But the other arts, which are these: nigromancy, geogenia,[153] and the others, which are contained under the greater philosophy are able to be possessed, acquired, and taught through this most certified art, but not without sin. Therefore, since there are seven liberal arts, and they can be learned, known, read, taught without sin, it was pleasing to the Almighty, so that any of those seven arts are attributed their own notae and figures; and according to that, he was attributing [the prayers and figures] to each art, and especially to the trivium, namely, grammar, logic, and rhetoric, in which it is not a sin for learning.

[The Almighty] wanted to show good reasons and to explain through the elements of letters[154] why so many *notae* [and] so many figures were corresponding to any art, and they were necessary to be appointed neither more nor less; therefore, Solomon recounts thenceforth so that we may receive an example of having faith in the operation of this art, how he had the foundation and the knowledge of this book (that is, [the foundation and knowledge] of the prayers and figures), and how this holy work was sent to him; and he says that one night, while he was asking God in a good and holy prayer, an angel of God appeared to him, carrying to him a book written with prayers and figures, telling him how would be able to acquire and possess knowledge and wisdom through that book written with prayers and figures, and the angel showed him the prayers and taught him the manner for offering [them], and showed him the *notae* and figures to each designated art, and taught him the manner and form for inspecting them.

For Solomon, having been astonished and stupefied over this, received the book, and looking within this very [book], he saw the prayers, he looked at the *notae* and figures described there, thinking and wondering at [it] admirably, he doubted, and he scarcely believed that in offering those brief prayers and in inspecting those few *notae* and figures and their signs he would be able to acquire and possess so much knowledge [and] so much wisdom in such a brief

153. *Geogenia*. Likely a corrupted Greek term for genethlialogy. See chapter III, "Knowledge of the *Ars Notoria*."

154. That is, learning the basics.

period of time; the angel is said to have responded to Solomon, "Do not be surprised, doubt or become frightened, because the great mystery of the Lord that was sent to you by him is the most sacred mystery, and all holy gifts proceed from his hand, therefore do just as I enjoin and command you."

Then Solomon, being comforted, asked the angel, saying, "O my Lord, what kind of significance do these *notae* [and] these figures have? Why place them in front [of oneself for the offering]? To what purpose are they assigned with respect to these known arts and their sciences? To what purpose are they especially assigned, only three figures to the art of grammar, and two [figures] and those four signs to the art of dialectic, and four [figures] to the art of rhetoric, distinctly and separately in this way, for any of those three arts?"

Then the angel said to Solomon, "God, seeing in advance, he who foresees all things and wants to provide for all things, it pleased him, and it is pleasing, that with respect to knowing the art or science of grammar (which the art is a science of letters through which it is necessary to learn the letters, the other arts, and their sciences), is assigned three figures, no more nor less, to the operation of acquiring this very knowledge; because for this reason, in this grammatical science, three are concurrent by necessity: the first of which is the order of letters, the second, the distinction of speech, [and] through the third, the construction of [Latin] cases and all other [inflectional endings] adjoined to them, and thus, through the virtue of the prayers and through the virtue of their signs, figures, and those names of the holy angels which are described below these figures, if the prayers are offered in their times and these figures inspected [according to] the order and properly, as it is said elsewhere in this book, the knowledge and wisdom of the entire art of grammar will be had firmly, fully, and perfectly, in such a brief period of time; and this is the obvious reason why grammar has only three notes, no more no less."

[73, 74, 75, Version A]

[75 Gloss] *Dyalectica vero, etc.* Having said and shown entirely and perfectly in the preceding gloss about grammar's order, invention,[155] and

---

155. The inventive procedure is finding out what to say using one's given inventory of grammatical knowledge and vocabulary; in other words, using one's own lexicon.

apposition[156] of its three figures, now we speak about the order and invention of the art of dialectic and the apposition of its two figures with its signs.

Therefore, after the announcement and demonstration made by the angel to Solomon about the art of grammar and its prayers and figures, the same Solomon wanted to be certain about the figures and their signs [and] why only two figures belonged to the art of dialectic, neither more nor less, to which the angel is said to have responded,

> Just as I told you, Solomon, that three figures are necessary for the art of grammar, for the reason why three are necessary, similarly, I say to you that in the art of dialectic there are two apposite figures with their own four signs, because only two are necessary to them for that reason.
>
> Dialectic is, therefore, a subtle art which informs the sciences of all the other arts, and it is called a "dual discourse," that is, the knowledge which is pertinent to only two persons and not more; that is, the opponent and the respondent. Since, therefore, dialectic is a dual discourse and it is pertinent to only two—that is, the opponent and the respondent—two [figures] are to be understood as necessary to occur in it.

Therefore, the first is necessary in it (that is, the fluency of adducing arguments) [and] the second is the foreknowledge to respond, and thus since only those two are necessary in dialectic, it was necessary as divine providence was providing for them in two figures, and thus [the divine providence] assigned and described to it, acquiring the highest science, providing only two figures.

But those four signs are common and useful for acquiring the art of grammar, dialectic, and rhetoric, and after the inspection of the three figures of grammar, the two of dialectic, and the four of rhetoric they ought to be inspected once and the impression of the signs in the mind and heart ought to be committed to memory.

For through those two figures and through the virtue of the holy prayers

---

156. *Apposition,* in its grammatical sense, is the grammatical construction in which one noun or noun phrase is usually placed adjacent to another as an explanatory equivalent, having the same referent stand in the same syntactical relation to the rest of a sentence. For example, "Helena, my youngest daughter." Thus, the glosser is speaking of the figures as explanations or definitions of their own respective arts.

and the names of the holy angels which are described below the figures having been named, they are to be invoked, and perfect knowledge is to be gained for anyone working faithfully in this art, that is, by pronouncing the prayers written above and by inspecting these very figures in their own times, days, and hours, just as it has already been said above.

[76, Version A]

[76 Gloss] *Quaerere ergo recthorica, etc.* A good and true solution is given above through the angel to Solomon why grammar has only three figures, [and why] dialectic [has] two, neither more nor fewer.

Now let us speak about how many figures rhetoric has why they have neither more nor fewer. For Solomon, while he had been sagaciously inquiring about the figures of the art of grammar and dialectic with great diligence from the angel, he inquired about the figures of the art of rhetoric, and he said, "O Lord, tell me why four figures are in apposition to the art of rhetoric, since there are only three in grammar, [and] only two in dialectic."

To which the angel responded:

> O friend, four are necessary in the science of rhetoric. For the first is the necessity of ornate, florid, and neatly arranged locution. Second is an ordered, competent, and discreet judgment. Third, is the discrete composition and disposition of their offices, of litigating, of damages, of buyers and vendors and of their business negotiations. And fourth is necessary, a good understanding, truthful eloquence, and subtlety to inspecting and cognizing about the causes of litigations without prolixity. Therefore, these four things are necessary in the art of rhetoric. Therefore, since four are necessary in this science, [which] the the Most High Divine One provided, who provided for all things and will always provide to appoint, to design, and describe these four figures of the science, so that through these figures and their signs, and the holy names of the blessed angels, which are written in the same figures described, and having been named, are invoked, by the virtue of God and their angels, their own blessed and holy prayers are able to be administered so much knowledge of any good and faithful operation through a brief period of time.

Therefore, the prayers are to be read first which ought to be read for the purpose of acquiring these first three sciences just as it is said above, and afterward it is proper [that] the figures of the said arts are to be inspected by the correct order.

[77, 78, Version A]

[**78 Gloss**] *Sicut enim notae grammaticae inspiciendae sunt, etc.* In the preceding sections it has been said and defined how many figures any art of the seven liberal arts has and what explanation is given [as to] why [there are] so many and not so many; first about grammar, second about dialectic, third about rhetoric; of these the first, namely grammar, has three figures; dialectic has two, rhetoric has four.

Now in this present section it makes a mention first about the figures of the art of grammar—that is, which times, days, [and] hours of the day these three figures ought to be inspected and the prayers themselves are to be offered. It is to be understood, therefore, that before one arrives at the inspection of the figures of the art of grammar, so that through it, the inspection, he is able to have a perfect efficacy with respect to having the perfect knowledge in the art of grammar itself, but in this very operation of this very art it is to be done first in this way.

Accordingly at the beginning of this operation, the operator who desires such knowledge ought to have [it] through this art to acquire it, so that he has a good will and a great desire for acquiring and performing the teachings of the art, that is to say, first, to be confessed with a pure heart and not feigned and having received penitence, he must have the will to abstain from sins by that hour down to the minute[157] while he will be in this operation and in the beginning of any month, that is, in the first day of a new lunar month, he must offer the first three headwords, which are to be offered at the beginning of acquiring any knowledge.

And afterward, the assigned and written prayers for the purpose of acquiring a perfect memory, eloquence, and understanding in their own times, their days, and their determined hours [listed] above, and the other prayers after those, which they do with respect to memory following just as it has been established, he must offer and read them according to the order; therefore, while all

157. Latin idiom, *adminus,* which literally means "to the lesser," and it is translated here as "down to the minute" because it is used as an expression about time.

the prayers which always ought to be said and read beforehand for acquiring any knowledge, they had to be said and read in order to acquire the knowledge of the art of grammar.

Then the first day of the month is to be seen beforehand—that is, of some new lunar month—the operator should remain alone somewhere permitting[158] in some secret and remote place away from the noise of people, and sitting in that place let him hold the book open with the figures before him, and in the early morning of the very day, he must say these prayers, *Deus Pater immense [. . . magnitudo], etc.; Gezomothon, etc.; Rex aeternae Deus, etc.; Deus totius pietatis, etc.;*[159] *Deus Pater immense [. . . misericordissime],* once.[160]

Thus, having said these, he must speak the particular prayer which is written above the figure which is *Lux, veritas, vita, etc.,* and having spoken it, the prayers[161] and those names of the holy angels[162] which are written below the figure, having been recalled and invoked, are to be offered. The prayer is spoken which is [positioned] below the figure, which is *Deus, cui omne [cor] bonum, etc.,*[163] and thus, having spoken and read those prayers through the order twice, the very first figure is inspected once, and having inspected the figure, having made some interval, its own particular prayers[164] are to be recited twice, and again the figure is to be inspected,[165] and thus it is to be done concerning this very figure, because it may be able to be inspected thrice by the early morning

---

158. Latin *sinente.*

159. These prayers belong to the fifth, sixth, and seventh *notae* of philosophy.

160. *Deus Pater immense [. . . misericordissime]* belongs to the art of music according to NS 69.

161. That is, the three prayers belonging to the art of grammar (*Domine Sancte Pater [. . . imperfectum], Respice Domine,* and *Creator Adonay*).

162. That is, the adorning prayers of the first *nota* of grammar, *Helyscemaht Scemoht, Benon, Henelic, Harastologion,* and *Iana* (NS 4–8), in which each adorning prayer is placed within one of the rings of the five-ringed wheel. Version B manuscripts place *Deus cui omne cor bonum patet* (NS 9) within the left-hand box below the great wheel. For the second *nota* of grammar, the adorning prayers are *Otheos Iezehur, Pehangryes, Rebelleos, Heloy Emanuhel,* and *Zemoham Lemaryht* (NS 12–16). For the third *nota* of grammar, there is *Principium Deus, Panthac Panthos, Ageryos, Hagenozoy,* and *Opus salutare* (NS 19–22).

163. NS 9. See the first figure of grammar on page 489, where the prayer is placed just below the great wheel.

164. NS 4–8.

165. That is to say, the first figure is inspected once, then the adorning prayers are recited once, then the first figure is inspected a second time, an interval is made, and then the adorning prayers are recited for a second time, and then the first figure may be inspected for a third time.

up to the third [hour] in this way, and the particular prayers to be offered twice each time of a sole inspection, from the third [hour] up to noon thrice, from noon up to the ninth [hour] thrice, from the ninth [hour] up to the evening [hour] thrice, and thus any day from the beginning of a lunar month up to the fifteenth day this figure is to be inspected twelve times, and on each inspection of the same prayers of the figure are to be offered twice.

Accordingly on the fifteenth day in the early morning, just as you did on the other preceding days concerning the prayers, you must do so in this way, that is, having spoken about the five prayers once, and having said those five,[166] offer the prayers of the first and second figures six times, and inspect the same first figure once, and immediately having made some short interval after the inspection of the first figure, you must inspect the second figure. And thus these two figures are to be inspected together on this very day twenty times; that is to say, five times from the early morning up to the third hour or close to it, from the third [hour] up to noon five times, from noon up to the ninth [hour] five times, from the ninth [hour] up to twilight of the night[167] five times. And it is to be done thus concerning these two figures on the very fifteenth day, and similarly as often on the sixteenth [day], and in the same hours and in the first hour of inspection, that is to say, when the first and second figures are to be inspected five times, the prayers of those ought to be offered six times from the morning up to the third [hour]. In having made the inspection, [the prayers] ought to be offered seven times from the third [hour] up to noon, [then] the prayers ought to be offered eight times from noon up to the ninth [hour] during the very inspection of the figures, [then] the same prayers ought to be offered nine times from the ninth [hour] up to twilight at the time of the very inspection, and thus on the fifteenth day and the sixteenth [day], the first and second [figures] ought to be inspected twenty times and the prayers of the figures ought to be pronounced thirty[168] times.

---

166. Presumably, the prayers belonging to the fifth, sixth, and seventh *notae* of philosophy, which are *Deus Pater immense [. . . magnitudo], Gezomothon, Rex eternae Deus, Deus totius pietatis,* and *Deus Pater immense [. . . misericordissime]* (Variation 11).

167. Latin *crepusculum*. According to Bede, in his *On Times,* "it is also called dusk which is that uncertain light between light and darkness, for we call what is uncertain '*creper*.'" Bede, *On the Nature of Things,* 108.

168. Latin *tres decies* literally means "three tens"; that is in Roman numerals "XXX" or thirty (*triginta*).

But on the seventeenth day and on all the other days following of that whole lunar month, the first figure ought to be inspected twelve times first, [then] the second [figure] second, and the third [figure] third on any of those, just as it has been taught concerning the first figure on the first day of the lunar month, and the particular prayers of those three figures ought to be pronounced twenty times. Therefore, on the seventeenth day, the first, second, and third figures are to be inspected thrice, beginning from the early morning up to the third [hour], from the third [hour] up to noon thrice, from noon up to the ninth [hour] thrice, from the ninth [hour] up to twilight thrice, and the particular prayers of those three figures may be repeated five times in any hour of the inspection, and thus from the seventeenth day up to the end of the lunar month these three figures of the art of grammar are to be inspected twelve times, and their own particular prayers are to be offered twenty times on any of those days.

For this is to be understood that on the first day of the operation of the figures of any art whose knowledge he wishes to acquire and possess this very work through this [notory] art, he ought to fast on the very day until that entire operation of that day is completed, and having completed [it] with the prayer, he must not eat meat, except Lenten food. But on other days, it will be good if he is able to fast on any day until that whole operation is completed, and then in the evening he may eat meat and other things which are pleasing to him. But if he is not able to fast up to that hour, he must see beforehand some hour [to be made available] for himself in the day in which it is not necessary for him to inspect the figures nor read the prayers, and then he may eat, but [the food] must be Lenten food, and thus, fasting must be done in the inspection of the figures of any art.

Also, it is to be understood that after the inspection of any of the figures of any knowledge, just as the books and scrolls of those fields of knowledge ought to stand before the eyes of the operator and they ought to unroll the scrolls, reading some chapters within here and there with respect to the book, and these are necessary to the operation of the figures of any art.

[79, Version A]

[79 Gloss] *Notae autem quattuor artis rectoricae, etc.* It has been said above about the order of the prayers and the inspection of the figures of the art of grammar and the art of dialectic.

Let us now examine through the order concerning the operation and the order of the prayers and the inspection of the four figures of the art of rhetoric, which is one of the three liberal arts, and which is an art which contains canon and civil law and any knowledge of florid and ornate speaking within it. Therefore, if through this most holy art—that is to say, by offering the holy prayers which are contained within it, and naming the names of the holy angels which are described in this very [notory] art, and inspecting those four figures which are attributed to these fields of knowledge, through the divine hand—it is to be done thus:

First, observe a good conscience, hope, and a desire for working, a confession is to come before all else in this art, and having received penitence, you ought to guard against sins as much as you are able to minimize[169] while you are intending to work, and especially while you are in the operation itself. And when the time arrives in which you want to work with respect to having this knowledge—that is to say, with respect to one of those or to the knowledge of civil law, the knowledge of canon law, or florid and ornate composing or speaking—you must see beforehand the beginning of that month in which you want to work (that is, the first day of the new lunar month) and on the very day you begin to offer the first three headwords in any beginning of any science to be acquired are to be pronounced, and having read these, the prayers are to be offered, which having been prolated, just as it has been said, are attended to memory, eloquence, understanding, and the [mental] stability of each. Having prolated and read these, the other following prayers are to be said through the order according to their times, days, [and] hours, just as it has been said above, therefore, having read all the prayers, which ought to be read for the purpose of acquiring memory and eloquence are to be seen beforehand with respect to the inspection of any figures of any art.

Then the first day of the lunar month is to be seen beforehand, and in the early morning of that very day, the figures of rhetoric are to be placed open before the eyes, and the books and scrolls of the laws or decrees, and having opened the decrees out of another part. Then these five prayers ought to be offered once: *Deus Pater immense [. . . magnitudo], etc.; Gezomothon, etc.; Rex aeterne Deus,*

169. Latin idiom *adminus,* which literally means "to the lesser," and it is translated here as "to minimize"; that is to say, to reduce the severity and number of sins to milder and fewer sins as much as possible.

etc.; Deus totius pietatis, etc.; Deus Pater immense [. . . misericordissime].[170]

Having said those prayers once, the prayers written above the first figure and below the figure are to be spoken five times, and having read those, this very figure and its signs are to be inspected with an open and attentive eye, and after the inspection of that first figure, the prayers of the second figure are to be offered five times, and having spoken and read those, this very figure and its signs are to be inspected, and after the inspection of these two figures, those scrolls which you have are to be unrolled, and you may read within some laws or decretals and the decrees here and there, and thus these first two figures of the art of rhetoric are to be inspected once in the early morning up to the third [hour], and the prayers of any one [of those] are to be offered five times.

But from the third [hour] up to noon, prior to having made some interval again, the prayers of the first [figure] are to be offered five times, and again the figure ought to be inspected, and having made a short interval, the prayers of the second figure ought to be offered five times, and this very figure is to be inspected, and after the inspection, unroll the scrolls again and read a little something within.

But having inspected these first two figures thus, having made an interval, the other two figures—namely, the third and fourth—are to be inspected, and thus: first, the third figure is to be inspected once from noon up to the ninth [hour], and its particular prayers are to be read five times, and having made a short interval, the prayers of the fourth figure are to be offered five times, and having read these, the figure itself and its signs are to be inspected, and after the inspection of these two figures, the scrolls are to be unrolled and read here and there, just as it has been said above.

But from the ninth [hour] up to the evening [hour], the prayers of the third figure are to be repeated five times again, and the figure is to be inspected again, and then the prayers of the fourth figure are to be read, and the figure is to be inspected just the same, and after the inspection of these figures, the scrolls are to be unrolled and read within here and there, and thus it is to be proceeded through the order for the operation of the figures of the art of rhetoric and with respect to the pronunciation of the prayers of these very figures on any

170. These five prayers belong to the fifth, sixth, and seventh figures of philosophy. The last also belongs to music, according to Version B (NS 69).

day of the entire lunar month on which this operation is to be begun, excepting three days of that month, namely, the fifteenth, seventeenth, and nineteenth days. Specifically, on those three days these figures are never to be inspected nor their prayers to be offered, because on those days [the notory art] was offered to Solomon through the angelic hand.

But on other days of the entire month the first and second figures ought to be inspected twice a day, from the morning up to the third [hour] once, from the third [hour] up to noon once. But the third and fourth figures ought to be inspected twice through them on the same day, from noon up to the ninth [hour] once, from the ninth [hour] up to the evening [hour] once, and the particular prayers of any figure ought to be pronounced five times during any inspection.

And it is to be done in this way in this operation with fasting, just as in the operation of the figures of the art of grammar and dialectic. Indeed, these [words] are sufficient for the erudition of the operation of the figures of the three liberal arts; namely, grammar, logic, and rhetoric.

[80, Version A]

[80 Gloss] *Sciendum est autem quod notae dialecticae, etc.* In the preceding section the full and complete teaching about the operation of the three figures of the art of grammar and the prolation of their prayers is given; that is to say, by which times, which days, which hours, and how often in a day the figure of grammar ought to be inspected and their prayers offered.

For in this present section we will give the teaching about the operation of the figures of the art of dialectic and about the prolation of their own particular prayers; that is to say, according to which times, days, hours, and how often these two figures of dialectic ought to be inspected and their own prayers ought to be pronounced. Therefore, when you want to come before the operation of the art of dialectic, so as to obtain the complete knowledge of this very art, it is to be done in this way, just as it has been said in the preceding section, with respect to acquiring the knowledge of the art of grammar; that is, by having said confession and received penitence, the first three headwords are to be offered first and the other prayers which are to be offered for the purpose of acquiring memory, eloquence, and understanding, all the other prayers which ought to be offered in all the fields of knowledge which are to be acquired before [the operation] is to come to the inspection of any of the figures of any art, having spoken and read all these prayers according to their own times, days, and hours through the order, just as it has been said above.

The beginning of the month is to be seen beforehand, that is, on the first day of that new lunation of that [calendar] month, specifically, in the first day of that new lunar month, having opened the book of figures, the other five prayers[171] are to be spoken once which are to be said in the inspection of the figures of the art of grammar.

Having said those, the particular prayers of the first figure of dialectic and the first Latin [prayer] which is described above the figure are to be offered, and after that, those which are written below the figure are to be said five times;[172] and having said those, this very first figure is to be inspected, and having made some short interval, the particular prayers of the second figure of dialectic are to be offered five times;[173] and having read those, this very figure and those four signs[174] which are described near the figure are to be inspected.

And thus, it is to be done concerning these two figures from the first day of the lunar month up to the end of any day four times. Therefore, from early morning up to the third [hour] the first and second figures are to be inspected once and the prayers of any [of those] which is to be offered five times, and from the third [hour] to noon once, and from the ninth [hour] up to the evening [hour] once, and thus, on any day the two figures must be inspected four times and the prayers offered twenty times, that is to say, five times at any one inspection.

But on these days of a lunar month, two days are excepted which are called "Egyptian days," on which days these two figures are not to be inspected nor are their prayers to be offered. Therefore, it is to be seen beforehand and to

---

171. *Deus Pater immense [. . . magnitudo], etc.; Gezomothon, etc.; Rex aeterne Deus, etc.; Deus totius pietatis, etc.; Deus Pater immense [. . . misericordissime],* of which these first four prayers belong to the fifth, sixth, and seventh figures of philosophy. The last prayer belongs to music, according to Version B (NS 69).

172. *Seguoht Semzyhony Zay Samarahc* and its two parts, which are *O aeternitas seculorum* and *Gerarauht Hazirelochon*. Then there is *Lectiones nostras* and its second part, *Deus qui corda gentium illustras*. Then there is the adorning prayer *O altitudo divitiarum*.

173. *Seguhot Semzyony Zahy Halamarym* and its four parts, *Othomyhos Samarithy, Germogon Nezologon, Zemal Iezemaht, Guamathomen Semezemary.*

174. The fours signs of all knowledge. See the figure on page 509 and chapter V, page 506.

beware about those two days, because in those days Solomon said the angel carried down those two figures to him, and these [words] are sufficient concerning these two figures of dialectic.

[81, 82,[175] Version A]

[82 Gloss] *Lux, veritas, vita, etc.* In the preceding sections—that is to say, from the beginning up to this place—a full mention is to be made about the written and given prayers for the purpose of memory, eloquence, and understanding, and about all the others which ought to be pronounced for acquiring knowledge of any art before [the operation] is to come before the inspection of the figures of all the arts, and about the regular [Special] prayers which ought to be offered before the particular prayers[176] of the figures themselves.

Now we speak about the Special prayers[177] which especially ought to be pronounced before these very figures; that is, before the written prayers below the figures are to be offered. Therefore, it is to be understood that this prayer, *Lux, veritas, vita, etc.,* ought to be pronounced first in the inspection of all the figures of any art before the particular prayers of the figures are to be offered. For at the beginning of the inspection of the first figure of grammar the first is to be offered, and after that, the particular prayer of the figure itself, which is *Domine sancte Pater, etc.,* is to be offered, and after that, the prayers written below the figure itself—namely, *Helyscemaht, [Scemoht etc., Benon Zihazamay, etc., Henelic Sasmiha, etc., Harastologion, etc., and Iana Agla Aglay,] etc.*[178]—are offered, and after those, the prayer written underneath the figure which is *Deus, cui omne bonum, etc.,*[179] is to be read.

And thus, in all the other figures to be inspected, this prayer, *Lux, veritas, etc.,* is the preamble before the particular prayers of these very figures are to be read. For it is to be understood that this Latin prayer, *Lux, veritas, etc.,* and the other Latin prayers which are written above the figures to be inspected, and

175. Beginning with section 82, Véronèse reorders the text to follow the order of the ritual instructions. I have opted to present the sections in their original order.
176. Latin *orationes proprias.*
177. Latin *orationibus specialibus.*
178. NS 4–8.
179. NS 9.

other Latin prayers which are written in this holy art were discovered and written at the hands of Solomon and Apollonius with respect to the impetration of divine grace, so that with the divine grace itself permitting, the holy angels, whose names, having been named, are invoked, would bring this most holy work to an effect, whose only names with other Hebrew, Chaldean, and Greek prayers with the figures were carried down to Solomon through the angelic hand, and these [words] are sufficient for presenting [the teaching] in this place.

[83, Version A]

[83 Gloss] *Quae de primis tribus capitulis, etc.* It has been said above in the preceding sections concerning about certain prayers which are eighteen in number,[180] of which the first begins *Lux, veritas, etc.,* with the others following successively after it, which the prayers have to be pronounced twice in the operation of this [notory] art—that is, once before noon—especially while he works for the purpose of acquiring memory and eloquence, and again any one of those ought to be offered once before any figure of any art, just as [it is] written above in any teaching, although it is described and repeated of these prayers.

But now remembering again the present [matter] in this section, it says that the first three headwords of this art, which are the first prayers of this book, ought to be pronounced once before the aforesaid prayers are to be offered; and similarly, they are always to be pronounced before the other prayers are to be offered for acquiring any efficacy, and this is what it says there.

180. According to section 126c gloss, the eighteen prayers are (1) *Lux veritas* (the preamble), (2) *Domine Sancte Pater [. . . imperfectum],* (3) *Respice Domine,* (4) *Creator Adonay* (the three prayers belonging to grammar), (5) *Sancte Deus,* (6) *Heloy clementissime* (the two prayers belonging to logic/dialectic), (7) *Omnipotens et misericors,* (8) *Adonay* (or *Hanazay*), (the two prayers belonging to first figure of rhetoric), (9) *Unus magnus* (the prayer belonging to the second figure of rhetoric), (10) *Usyon omnium* (the prayer belonging to the third figure of rhetoric) (11) *Azelechias [. . . regi Salomoni]* (the prayer belonging to the second figure of rhetoric), (12) *Scio enim* (the prayer belonging to the third figure of rhetoric), (13) *Reverende* (the prayer belonging to the fourth figure of rhetoric), (14) *Deus qui omnia numero,* (15) *Mediator omnium* (the two prayers belonging to arithmetic), (16) *Deus iustus iudex* (the prayer belonging to geometry), (17) *Omnipotens sapientiae* (unattributed prayer), and (18) *Adoro te rex regum* (the second prayer belonging to theology). These eighteen prayers are listed in the Parisian manuscript BnF Latin 9336, f. 10v–11v.

[84, 85, 86, Version A]

[85/86 Gloss] *Ecce de reliquis quattuor liberalibus, etc.* It has been said above in the preceding sections and handled competently enough about the three liberal arts—namely, grammar, logic, and rhetoric—how to acquire knowledge of any of them, the prayers which ought to be offered, just like the first three headwords and prayers which are applied to memory, eloquence, and understanding in their prolation, and the other prayers which ought to be offered through the order in this holy operation, and how, after the operation's prolation of all the prayers, the figures of any of these three arts ought to be inspected, and how often, and their prayers are to be offered, and what months especially are to be chosen for the inspection of these very figures.

Thus, in this place, it is necessary as we speak about the other four liberal arts through the order (that is, medicine, music, arithmetic, and astronomy), how the prayers of these arts are to be offered and at which times and during which hours, and how the figures of these arts are to be inspected with respect to acquiring knowledge of any of these arts.

We see to medicine first. For if you want to acquire the art or the science of medicine through this field of knowledge, [then] first, the first three headwords are to be offered, and the prayers are to be offered which are applied to memory, eloquence, and understanding according to their times and hours, just as it is determined above concerning those and the other prayers which ought to be offered through the order in the operation of any field of knowledge which is to be acquired, which, until [the moment] is to come before the inspection of the figure, which the art has only one figure.

Therefore, when you arrive at the inspection of the figure of medicine, on the very first day of the month in which you begin to inspect the figure, you will fast in Lenten food nor may you eat until the operation of that day is completed, and so in the early morning of that day you will begin to offer the first three headwords, and having pronounced those once, you offer those eighteen prayers once, of which the first begins *Lux, veritas, etc.*[181]

Having said these once, you must offer the particular prayer of the figure five times, and having done this, you must inspect its figure and signs with great

181. The eighteen prayers come from section 126c gloss. See page 415, footnote 188.

devotion and intention of the heart, and after the inspection of the figures, you must unroll the scrolls of the art of medicine, reading within some chapters here and there, and thus it is to be done five times on the very day concerning these very prayers and this very figure; that is to say, it is to be done once, beginning in the early morning, once around the third [hour], once around noon, [once around the ninth hour, and once around the evening hour].[182] For it is to be done thus, concerning the inspection of the figure of the art of medicine and concerning the pronunciation of the prayers on any day of that entire lunar month up to the end of the month.

Attend to this because the first four days of the month of this very operation is to be venerated and revered[183] more than the others following, and on that account, this [operation] is to be fasted on Lenten food in those days, and until the entire operation of those days is completed, and thus until after the evening [hour]. But on the other days of the month you are able to eat and drink at whatever hour it pleases you, and whatever foods you want, still you will eat once in a day, but on all the other days of this operation and any other, it is to be lived chastely, soberly, and it is to be guarded against drunkenness and especially lechery, and this is the teaching of the operation of the inspection for the figure of the art of medicine for the purpose of acquiring its knowledge.

We speak about the operation of the art of music; that is, how its figure ought to be inspected and its prayers ought to be offered. Therefore, if you want to work on the figure of music, so that you have perfect knowledge of it, [then] you must do so in this way, just as it is written in the operation of the figure of the preceding art of medicine.

In the operation of the figures of the art of arithmetic, it is to be done in this way, and to be performed, just as it is written in the operations of the arts of medicine and music. Therefore, from the first day of the month up to the end the two and a half figures of arithmetic are to be inspected five times on any day, and the particular prayers of the figures which are written above and below the figures ought to be pronounced five times before any figure, still having first spoken the first three headwords once, and the other eighteen prayers, which

182. Restored from NS 68.

183. Latin *timendi,* meaning "feared" but translated as "revered" based on the biblical concept of the fear of the Lord.

are to be said before the figure of the arts of medicine and music, and this is the operation of the figures for medicine, music, and arithmetic.

Regarding the operation of the six figures of astronomy it is to be worked differently from medicine and music, because on the first day of the lunar month, it is to be begun from the early morning up to the third [hour], and all six figures are to be inspected once and the particular prayers of the figures themselves are to be recited twice, from the third [hour] to up noon once, specifically from noon up to the ninth [hour] once, from the ninth [hour] up to the evening [hour] once, and any time their particular prayers are offered twice. But the first three headwords and the other eighteen prayers which ought to be offered first, as the particular prayers of the figures are to be offered only once in the morning on any day. It is to be done in this way concerning the figures of astronomy up to the end of the lunar month of any day, [the particular prayers of the figures are to be offered a total of] four times.

This is to be attended to [by the operator], but if it is to be seen beforehand through the seven days with respect to the inspection of any figure of any of these arts, [then] those eleven Latin prayers, which are the last prayers of this art, of which the first begins *Omnipotens incomprehensibilis, etc.,*[184] are to be offered twice on any day. Many [of these prayers] call forth memory and eloquence for the purpose of that knowledge which is to be acquired for its efficacy. Some figures are to be inspected,[185] and these are to be attended to and kept.

[87, Version A]

[87 Gloss] *De notis autem generalium, etc.* It has been said above in the preceding sections about the figures of the seven liberal arts, how they are to be inspected through the order and according to which months, times, days, hours, and how often.

---

184. That is, the ten prayers belonging to the *Ars Nova*. The glosser counts eleven based on the fourth prayer, *Otheos,* and its Latin prologue, *Pie Deus,* being two separate prayers.

185. The glosser is speaking of those *Ars Nova* prayers which bring in memory and eloquence to the operator, yet these prayers do not have their own figures for inspection. However, there are the figures of astronomy and theology, whose original *Flores Aurei* prayers have been lost, and it is these figures which become newly assigned to the magical system of the *Ars Nova*.

Now it is to be said about the other seven exceptive or adulterine arts;[186] that is to say, how the knowledge of any of these arts is able to be acquired and possessed through this art, and which prayers and figures we ought to work regarding them. Therefore, when you want to work some natural or moral science, or in any science of philosophy, or any kind of science which is contained beneath a greater or lesser philosophy, it is to be done in this way.

First, concerning the first three headwords and the prayers which apply to memory, eloquence, and understanding, just as it has been said in acquiring the other seven liberal arts, and about the other prayers of these arts up to the inspection of their own figures.

Therefore, when you want to work for the purpose of acquiring some knowledge of the seven exceptive arts which are to be contained beneath the seven liberal arts, and having completed the proper operation of the prayers, and you want to come before the inspection of the particular figures of these arts, the first day of the new lunation of any [calendar] month has been selected, and on that very morning the seven figures of philosophy are to be placed before the eyes, and then these thirteen prayers, are to be read with great devotion, which are written here once, of which the first begins *Ezethomos, etc.,* and thus, all the following ones after it up to the end.[187]

But having read those, that other prayer, *Lux, veritas, vita, etc.,* is to be read once, and after that, the particular prayer of this very figure and the names that are written in the first figure are to be read twice.[188] Having said those [prayers], the figure itself and its signs should be inspected reverently. But having inspected the first figure, [then] having made some interval, *Lux, veritas, etc.,* it is to be offered again, and the first prayer of the second figure[189] [is to be offered] twice, and the second figure and its signs is to be inspected

---

186. Latin *septem artibus exceptivis et adulterinis.* "Exceptive" meaning those arts which are excluded from the socially accepted fields of knowledge. "Adulterine" meaning those arts which are spurious or illicit like necromancy, or otherwise those arts which are mixed with other arts, following under the category of the "general sciences" or "middle sciences," such as the science of mirrors, harmonics, the science of weights and measures, and astronomy.

187. *Ezethomos* up to *Deus totius pietatis* are those twelve prayers (including *Omaza Beheza,* which is only found in Version B) belonging to philosophy. *Deus Pater immense [. . . misericordissime]* (Variation 11) brings the total number of prayers to thirteen. For the mention of the thirteen prayers, see also sections 88 gloss, 97 gloss, and 102 gloss.

188. *Themezehos Saguamal* (NS 103). See the figure on page 314.

189. *Domine Deus Sancte Pater / Deus semper via.*

immediately; but having made an interval, *Lux, veritas, etc.,* is to be read again, and the particular prayer of the third figure[190] [is to be offered] twice, and then the third figure and its signs are to be inspected. For the operation of these three figures ought to be performed in this way, just as it has been said, from the morning until noon.

But at noon [hour] you will begin to read the thirteen prayers once, just as you did in the morning, and afterward *Lux, veritas, etc.,* and the particular prayer of the fourth figure[191] twice, and then you must inspect this very figure and its signs, and having made an interval, you inspect the fifth and its signs having always offered their own particular prayers twice. For the operation of these three[192] are done thus, from noon up to the ninth [hour].

But around the ninth [hour] you must offer the thirteen prayers themselves with the greatest devotion, and then through the order *Lux, veritas, etc.,* and any particular prayer of those six figures and the particular prayer of the seventh figure of philosophy.[193] All these are to be offered twice, and then you must inspect the seventh figure itself and its signs with the greatest obligatory service of veneration, and after the inspection of the figure, you must unroll the scrolls of that art for which you work, reading some chapters within here and there, and then you may rest on that day.

But on the following day and on all the other days of the entire lunar month, except two—namely, on the seventh and the seventeenth day—it is to be done thus concerning of these seven figures, just as you did on the first day.

Accordingly, on the seventh day, the first three figures are to be inspected twice from morning to noon, and all the aforesaid prayers are to be recited twice, specifically from noon up to the ninth [hour]; the other three figures are to be inspected twice in the same manner, and the very same prayers are to be

190. There is no adorning prayer of the third figure of philosophy.

191. *Omaza* and its prologue *Rex regum.*

192. The glosser has forgotten to mention that the sixth prayer *Gezomothon* and its prologue, *Rex aeterne Deus,* is also to be offered twice, an interval is to be made, and then followed by the inspection of the sixth *nota* of philosophy.

193. There appears to be only two adorning prayers among the seven figures of philosophy. *Themezehos Saguamal* (NS 103) is the adorning prayer belonging to the first figure of philosophy. *Vita bonorum* (NS 112) is the adorning prayer belonging to the fifth figure of philosophy, and it is found only in Version B.

read twice; all the aforesaid thirteen prayers, *Lux, veritas, etc.,* and the particular prayers of those very seven figures[194] are to be repeated thrice, specifically from the ninth [hour] to the evening [hour], and the seventh figure itself is to be inspected thrice; that is to say, once in any pronunciation of the prayers, and it is to be done thus concerning these figures on the seventh day and in a similar manner on the seventeenth day.

But after the inspection of the ultimate figure on any day, the scrolls of that science for which this very operation is made, ought to be unrolled. For in the operation of these figures you ought to live chastely and honorably and to conduct a life in almsgiving and fasting, just as it has been said in the operation of the figures of the seven liberal arts, and these which pertinent to the seven *notae* of philosophy, for the seven exceptive arts, and the others which are contained under philosophy.

[88, Version A]

[88 Gloss] *De notis omnibus iam initialis, etc.* Having spoken about the figures of the seven liberal arts and of the seven exceptives.

Now we speak in order about the seven mechanical or adulterine arts, that is, under which figures they are comprehended, and how their proper operation comes to be. Therefore, the first operation is some such thing of the aforementioned arts to be acquired, how it is the other liberal and exceptive arts are to be acquired, that is to say, first, to offer the first three headwords and prayers which bring in memory, eloquence, etc., and the other prayers of this art through the order by their own times, their own [days of the] lunar months, [and] their own hours, just as it was said above, with respect to the inspection of the figures. Also, the figures beneath those to be comprehended are the four figures of the general sciences to these seven mechanical arts.

Therefore, when you want to come to the inspection of the four figures of the general sciences, the first through seven days, you must say the first three headwords with the other eighteen prayers,[195] which ought to be said in acquiring the other arts on any day seven times, of which the

194. That is, the adorning prayers. See page 419, footnote 201.

195. The eighteen prayers come from section 126c gloss. See page 415, footnote 188.

first prayer of which begins *Lux, veritas, etc.,* with the others following in order.

For having finished those seven days, on the first day of the new lunar month of some [calendar] month after those seven days, these thirteen prayers, presented here, are to be offered in the early morning, the first of which begins *Ezethomos, etc.,* with the others following in order once, and having made a short interval, *Lux, veritas, etc.,* is to be said, and after that particular prayer, the prayer of the first figure of the first general [science],[196] and the holy names written below the figure,[197] is to be said once; having made an interval, *Lux, veritas, etc.,* is to be offered again, and the special prayer of the second figure[198] [should be offered] once, and then the first and second figures and their signs should be inspected with great intention.

Having done this, *Lux, veritas, etc.,* and the prayer of the first figure must be reiterated once, and this very figure ought to be inspected, and having made an interval, that prayer *Lux, veritas, etc.,* and the prayer of the second figure ought to be reiterated, and then the second figure and its signs is to be inspected. It is to be done thus concerning these two figures, from the morning up to noon five times, and the prayers' own particular ones are to be repeated any time once, five times.

From noon to evening, the third figure should be inspected and the fourth one after the other in order five times, and their prayers[199] should be offered five times, just as you did from morning to noon for the first figure and the second. Thus, it is to be done from noon to evening concerning the third and fourth figures, and thus it is to be done of these four *notae* of the general sciences on any one day up to the end, and it is to be done thus, one must live and abstain in this operation just as in the others preceding. Also, the books and scrolls of that art for which these figures are to be inspected [and] some chapters always ought to be unrolled and read within,

---

196. In Version A, the prayers of the general sciences are missing. Version B supplies the first prayer, *Zedomor Phamanos,* as belonging to the first figure of the general sciences (see NS 91).

197. That is, *Gedomor Phamazihon* (see NS 93).

198. As the remaining three prayers belonging to the general sciences are missing, Version B fills these three empty slots with the prayers from philosophy. This is a logical editorial decision on the part of the scribe since the general sciences are "contained underneath" philosophy in the Aristotelian hierarchy of knowledge. The prayer *Rex aeterne Deus,* taken from the sixth of philosophy, is assigned to the second figure of the general sciences, which is referenced here.

199. The third prayer, *Deus Pater immense [. . . magnitudo],* taken from the fifth *nota* of philosophy, is assigned to the third figure of the general sciences. The fourth prayer, *Deus totius pietatis,* taken from the seventh *nota* of philosophy, is assigned to the fourth figure of the general sciences.

and this is the operation of the four figures of the general sciences through the order.

[89, Version A]

[90] *These are the augmentations of the prayers which the* notae *of all the liberal and exceptive arts, except the mechanical arts, correspond,*[200] *and, especially the* notae *of theology, are to be ascribed. For these are to be pronounced thus before each* nota *of each art, as long as you inspected the figures and you offered their prayers, of which the first prayer begins:*

Ezethomos, Iezemomos, Hazalathon, Azaython, Heutyvethel, Hezemethel, Hezemtynethel, Zamay, Zathon, Hamayzathon, Zamayzathon, Hezemeguer, Zecromanda, Iechomantha, Iaraphay, Zaraphamy, Phalezethon, Phabogethon, Seremyhal, Sacramyhal, Zeremyhal, Sacramazan, Iethemathon, Sacramazaym, Secranal, Satramathan, Iezemyhalathon, Hathecyhachos, Ieteley, Mathan, Acheriathos, Zay, Mazay, Zamma, Zazay, Guyguthehyo, Gigithios, Guarihos, Megalon, Senegalon, Heratruhyc, Crarihuht, Heracryhuz.

[91, Version A]

[92] *This prayer should be offered before the second figure of philosophy:*

O holy Lord, the almighty Father,[201] listen to my prayers today, and incline your ear to my prayers,[202] Chemon, Gezomelyhon, Zemonge, Zemelyhon, Samaht, Gezagan, Iezehator, Lesehator, Sezehathon, Saymanda, Samay, Sanamay, Gezihel, Gualentyhel, Gezel, Iezethyhel, Galetyhel, Gazay, Hetyhel.

[93, Version A]

---

200. That is to say, the liberal and exceptive arts belong under philosophy in the Aristotelian hierarchy of knowledge. The mechanical arts, which include those practical arts such as tailoring, hunting, and agriculture, have no place in philosophy. The prayer *Ezethomos* and those found in the following sections up to section 101, belong to philosophy. For the Christian writer, philosophy is the "handmaiden to theology"; therefore, he says that philosophy's prayers and figures belong under theology's prayers and figures.

201. *Domine sancte Pater [. . . exaudi],* the prayer belonging to the second *nota* of philosophy.

202. Psalms 5 (NSRV).

[94] *This prayer should be offered before the third figure of philosophy:* **Lemogethon, Hegemothon, Hazatay, Hazathar, Hazamathar, Hazata, Hazamathar, Hazamathan, Zegomotay, Gohatay, Zachara, Legomotay, Iachamna, Legomezon, Legornozon, Lemdomethon, Hatanayos, Lamdomathon, Iegomaday, Hatamaz, Zachamos, Hatanayos, Hellessymon, Zelesyon, Vaderabar, Vagedarem, Lanynanaht, Lamaudy, Gemechor, Guomon, Gehor, Ienamthor, Helbemay, Iezecromay, Gecromal, Ietrahaly, Cholomanos, Colomaythos.**

[95, Version A]

[Variation 10] *This should be offered before the fourth figure of philosophy:* **Omaza,[203] Beheza, Theon, Megal, Menehon, Exheal, Tyrigel, Harapheyhoton, Semenoyn, Sehumeny, Hantemathan, Hyemarayn, Gemegehon, Lucharanotyn, Exnotheyn, Themelyhen, Segyhon, Hyhouenyr, Hatusyhen, Theon.**

[96, 97, Version A]

[97 Gloss] *Quae orations quattuor, etc.* It has been fully discussed above about the prayers and figures of the seven liberal, the seven mechanical, and the seven exceptive arts. Now with respect to presenting [the rest] according to the order it is to be said concerning theology and the operation of the five figures of theology.

Therefore, if you want to work to acquire a perfect knowledge of theology, which the knowledge contains within it the Old Testament and the New Testament, the prayers of this art is to be offered in the beginning through the order by their own lunar [days of the] months, their own days, and those hours, just as it is said above with respect to acquiring the other arts, up to the operation of the figures.

For it is to be understood that when you want to work with respect to the figures of theology, that first, through seven days, you ought to offer on any

203. *Omaza,* the prayer belonging to the fourth *nota* of philosophy.

day once the first three headwords and afterward those eighteen prayers,[204] of which the first begins *Lux, veritas, etc.,* with the others through the following order, and having made an interval, those thirteen prayers which are here are to be offered, of which the first begins *Ezethomos, etc.,* and the others following through the order.

Having completed these seven days thus, on the first day of the new lunar month after those seven days, in the early morning, you must offer those thirteen prayers seven times, and having made an interval, *Lux, veritas, etc.,* and the particular prayer of the first figure of theology is to be offered seven times, and then the figure itself and its signs are to be inspected with great devotion. Having said these thus, [and] having made some interval, reiterate the aforesaid prayers all the same with the particular prayer of the second figure, and then you must inspect the second figure and its signs. But having been inspected the following figure thus, the very same prayers are to be reiterated seven times with the particular prayer of the third figure, and then the third figure and its signs is to be inspected, for it is to be done thus concerning these three figures to be inspected from the early morning to noon.

But in or around the noon [hour], the aforesaid thirteen prayers and that prayer *Lux, veritas, etc.,* and the particular prayer of the fourth figure is to be reiterated seven times, and then this very fourth figure is to be inspected, and having made an interval, these very prayers and all the particular prayers of the four figures with the particular prayer of the fifth and last figure of theology must be read again seven times. For then this very figure and all its signs is to be inspected with the greatest devotion and humility, because the most sacred mystery is contained in the figure itself. For those two figures ought to be inspected thus, and the prayers to be offered from noon up to the ninth [hour]. For the operation of those five figures ought to take place in this way during the entire lunation of one month on any day.

But the operator ought not eat nor drink, especially wine, until the daily work is completed—that is, until after the ninth [hour]—for then he may eat fish or other Lenten food, and not meat. But no one is to attempt that operation after excessive drinking or after lechery.

Also, it is to be understood that after the inspection of the fifth figure

204. The eighteen prayers come from section 126c gloss. See page 415, footnote 188.

the scrolls of theology ought to be unrolled and some chapters ought to be read here and there, just as it has been said above in the other sciences to be acquired.

For this is the end of the operation and completion of all the figures of this most sacred art, by which the art and all the figures of the aforesaid field of knowledge can be acquired, had, and retained in memory; the operation is to done through the order in this way thus, just as it is taught.

[98, Version A]

[98 Gloss] *Deus Pater immense, etc.* Although generally this prayer has to be offered for all arts, both liberal as well as exceptive and mechanical, still, singularly and especially, it ought to be offered with the other prayer *Lux, veritas, etc.,* before the fifth figure of philosophy, and after its pronunciation, this very figure and its signs ought to be inspected.

[99] *This particular prayer is to be pronounced before the sixth figure of philosophy:*

Gezomothon, Ezomathan, Hayhata, Hagyar, Hagihatar, Hayhata, Lethasihel, Gethazyhel, Lechizihel, Geziduhal, Geguhay, Gethonay, Samasaht, Samasarel, Zamasathel, Gezomathel, Gessyhomyhatel, Iogomassay, Iezomyhatel, Sergomazar, Hazomatan, Hazotynathon, Iesomathon, Iezechor, Heyhazay, Heyhazar, Samy, Zamy, Samyn, Helyhel, Samyelihel, Syloht, Sylereht, Gezamathal, Guaramathal, Iesematal, Iecoronay, Iecornenay, Samyahel, Hesemyhel, Sechozomay, Sedosamay, Sechothamay, Samia, Tabibatos, Hamnos, Hamnas, amen.

[99 Gloss] *Gezomothon, etc.* This prayer, which is a most sacred invocation of the names of the holy angels, whose invocation and deprecation, this most sacred gift given by God, is brought to an effect with the subsequent Latin prayer, although, generally, it has to be offered for seven days before the operation of the figures of whichever art; still, it is pronounced singularly and especially over the sixth figure of philosophy, and after its very pronunciation the figure itself and its signs are to be inspected.

[100, Version A]

[100 Gloss] *Rex eterne Deus, etc.* This Latin prayer is a certain deprecation before God, so that his divine grace may send the holy angels named in the preceding prayer to bring this work to an effect, together with the preceding, still having made some interval between them, it ought to be pronounced before the sixth figure of philosophy; and after its pronunciation, this very figure with its own signs and forms is to be inspected.

[101, Version A]

[101 Gloss] *Deus, totius pietatis, etc.* This most holy prayer, which is the deprecation of the one working in this most sacred notory art addressed to God the almighty, ought to be pronounced together with the other subsequent prayer, still having made some interval between them in the inspection of the seventh preceding figure of philosophy, still that other prayer which is *Lux, veritas, etc.,* ought to be pronounced.

[Variation 11] *In this way the following prayer with the preceding ought to be pronounced together always and everywhere:*
O God the immeasurable Father, from whom proceeds all that is good, O most merciful, almighty God, burn my kidneys out of the grace of the Holy Spirit, and visit me today with the fire of your visitation, and be propitious to me, show your mercy to me, so that I may drink and be satisfied[205] from the fountain, you who are God, and let your good will be done within me, and I may sing about and understand your wonders, you who are God threefold and one, amen.[206]

[Variation 11 Gloss] *Deus Pater immense, etc.* This Latin prayer ought to be pronounced after the preceding prayer, having made some interval, and after this very pronunciation, the seventh and ultimate figure of philosophy and its very signs with its strange things ought to be inspected, and after the inspection

205. Latin *satier.*
206. *Deus Peter immense* [. . . *misericordissime*], another prayer belonging to the seventh *nota* of philosophy. See also NS 69 and 116. This prayer is not found in Version A.

of this very figure, the scrolls of this knowledge ought to be unrolled for which this seventh figure of philosophy is to be inspected.

[102, Version A]

[102 Gloss] *Orationes istae septem, etc.* It says here that there are seven prayers, which always have to be offered before some figures are to be inspected, and it seems that there are thirteen—that is, five in that place[207] and eight above[208]—and there it says that there are seven; it is true that there are thirteen separately, but they are not, unless the seven are offered jointly.[209]

From where [in the text] the first prayer of these seven which begins *Ezothomos, etc.,* with its Latin [prayer] following, are not only one,[210] since *Domine Deus sancte Pater, etc.,* with the other following—namely, *Deus, semper via, etc.*—are said to be one and the same.[211] Similarly, *Lemogethon, etc.,* and the following prayer *Vita hominum, etc.,* are one and the same,[212] *Omaza, Beheza,*

207. The five prayers of philosophy (*Deus Pater immense [. . . magnitudo], Gezomothan* and its Latin prologue, *Rex aeternae Deus, Deus totitus pietatis,* and *Deus Pater immense [. . . misericordissime]*) are found at sections 98–101 and NS 69. Notice that *Deus Pater immense [. . . misericordissime]* fulfills two functions in Version B; it is a prayer of philosophy and it is also the prayer belonging to music according to NS 69. The prayer *Deus Pater immense [. . . misericordissime]* does not appear in Version A nor does Version A present a prayer belonging to music. These five prayers are also known as the fifth, sixth, and seventh prayers of philosophy (including *Deus Pater immense [. . . misericordissime],* according to Version B).

208. The eight prayers of philosophy (*Ezethomos* and its Latin prologue, *Domine Deus incomprehensibilis; Domine Deus Sancte Pater* and its Latin prologue, *Deus semper via vita veritas; Lemogethon* and its Latin prologue, *Vita ominum;* and *Rex regum* and its accompanying prayer, *Omaza Beheza*) are found at sections 90–96. Notice that *Omaza Beheza* is found only in Version B. These eight prayers are also known as the first, second, third, and fourth prayers of philosophy. The division between the five and eight prayers is significant for the greater ritual procedure, establishing a division in time and a division of what prayers belonging to what arts and sciences are "contained" beneath philosophy. See chapter VI for details.

209. There are seven prayers of philosophy if the reckoning excludes the Latin prologues, which are really just partial or summarily translations of the strange speech. The seven prayers are: (1) *Ezethomos,* (2) *Domine Deus Sancte Pater,* (3) *Lemogethon,* (4) *Rex regum,* (5) *Deus Pater immense [. . . magnitudo],* (6) *Gezomothan,* and (7) *Deus totitus pietatis.*

210. *Domine Deus incomprehensibilis.*

211. These two prayers belong to the second part of philosophy.

212. These two prayers belong to the third part of philosophy. The Version A incipit of the Latin prologue is *Vita omnium,* but at NS 107 and through the glosses of Version B the incipit is *Vita hominum.*

etc., and the other following *Rex regum, etc.,* are the same prayers,[213] and thus, we have four prayers from the eight above.[214]

Deus Pater immense [. . . magnitudo], etc., is one prayer through them, and it ought to be said through them.[215] *Gezomothon, etc.*, and the other following—namely, *Rex aeterne, etc.*—are one and the same prayer;[216] and they have to be said together. *Deus totius pietatis, etc.,* and the other following—namely, *Deus Pater immense [. . . misericordissime]*—are the same prayers, and they ought to be pronounced together,[217] and thus from these five, we have three,[218] from where it is said well in the text: *Orationes, istae septem, etc.,* and this is what is said in the present place.

[103, Version A]

[103 Gloss] *Ecce quia de misterio notarum, etc.* Above in the preceding sections a certain definition is given about the pronunciation of the preceding prayers and about the inspection of all the figures of each art through the order: the first, about the three figures of the art of grammar; the second, about the two figures of the art of dialectic; the third, about the four figures of the art of rhetoric; the fourth, about the figure of medicine, the fifth, about the figure of music, the sixth, about the figure[s] of arithmetic; the seventh, about the figures of astronomy; the eighth, about the figures of philosophy; the ninth, about the figures of the general sciences, the tenth, about the figures of theology.

But in this section there is made a certain separate mention about certains

---

213. These two prayers belong to the fourth part of philosophy.

214. The four prayers are: (1) *Ezethomos,* (2) *Domine Deus Sancte Pater,* (3) *Lemogethon,* and (4) *Rex regum.* These are the first, second, third, and fourth prayers of philosophy forming the first division of philosophy in the greater ritual procedure.

215. This prayer belongs to the fifth part of philosophy.

216. These two prayers belong to the sixth part of philosophy.

217. In Version A, *Deus totius pietatis* stands alone as the seventh prayer of philosophy. In Version B, *Deus Pater immense [. . . misericordissime]* is joined with *Deus totitus pietatis* as belonging to the seventh part of philosophy.

218. The three prayers, excluding their accompanying prayers, are: (1) *Deus Pater immense [. . . magnitudo],* (2) *Gezomothan,* and (3) *Deus totius pietatis.* These are the fifth, sixth, and seventh prayers of philosophy forming the second division of philosophy in the greater ritual procedure.

figures of the aforesaid figures, which the figures have a greater mystery and a stronger sacrament than other figures among them, and for that reason they possess and contain within themselves a greater sacrament, that they ought to be inspected with so much more greater diligence, humility, reverence, devotion, and abstinence than the other figures, from where [in the text] we see how many of these figures there are, and of what kind; of those, one is from the figures of the general sciences, and it is called "the *nota* of God,"[219] because the *signum manus* of God[220] is to be imprinted on it. Indeed, the other *nota* is one of the figures of philosophy, and that figure is called "the *nota* of awe," because an angelic appearance is described by its own impression in that [figure].[221] Accordingly, the other figure is one of the figures of theology and it is the last, and that figure is called "the ineffable *nota,*" because there are twenty-four nooks impressed in that [figure], diverse species of diverse things and diverse signs are depicted, dividedly and separately, in these nooks, just as in some nooks swords are drawn, and this is in the first upper nooks; but in others, serpents are depicted, but in others candlesticks, but birds in others, trees in others, and as such this figure is called "ineffable." Therefore, these three figures are to be inspected in any operation of their own with the greatest veneration of duty, devotion, chastity, [and] abstinence; and their prayers are to be offered in a similar manner.

---

219. The first figure of the general sciences.

220. The *signum manus* (literally "the sign of the hand") is the medieval practice of signing a document with a special kind of monogram or royal cypher. At the end of important documents, officials and witnesses would sign with a *signum manus,* often in the form of a cross, called a "cross-signature." As for the monogram of a ruling monarch, the terminals of each bar would be marked with a letter, forming a ligature. Thus, the glosser is pointing to the first figure of the general sciences, which contains a cross-signature and hinting that at its ends would be the Hebrew name of God, called the Tetragrammaton (i.e., יהוה, transliterated as YHWH and pronounced as Yahweh). The practice bears some resemblance to the staurogram in Early Christian studies.

221. The third figure of the general sciences. The glosser says it is "one of the figures of philosophy," and in doing so, he may be conflating philosophy and the general sciences together since the general sciences fall under the domain of philosophy. The first and three figures of the general sciences are likely highlighted in the fragmented letter because of their first position in the two-part division of the operation of the general sciences. The first division of the general sciences includes the first and second figures for inspection from morning to noon. The second division includes the third and fourth figures for inspection from noon to evening. See 88 gloss.

For the great angel of the Lord[222] carried down to Solomon in his operation those figures singularly howsoever through him [i.e., the angel], and of those [Solomon] enjoined to him whatever was necessary in the inspection of any of those. Therefore, when one night Solomon was inspecting the first four figures of theology which the angel had carried down together to him, admiring much over them and doubting to work in them, the angel of the Lord descended to him and said to him, "Do not doubt or be afraid, behold, the Lord sends to you this ineffable figure in which is contained a greater sacrament to all the other four figures, behold it transcribed in this golden folio."

And again, the angel said to him:

> See beforehand and observe the command first given to you in the operation of the first four figures, and follow what has been taught to you to work with them in this way. Therefore, when you come to the operation of this ineffable figure, diligently inspect the figure itself and its signs, and with great reverence and chastity, without lechery, without drunkenness, in those days [and] in those hours, just as it has been taught to you in the operation of the other four figures. For in those days on which you inspect this figure, in no way may you mock, nor have fun, nor after approaching a woman, nor after drunkenness.

From where [it is said in the text:] One day while Solomon was working, he was forgetful of the angelic commandment, and was more drunk with wine than usual, inspecting the figure and its signs, he began to think in vain, and he mocked [it], and immediately the Lord had become angry with him, and [the Lord] sent back the very angel through whom he had commanded that figure to him. Saying to him, thus: "Because you despised my sacramental mystery, mocking and expressing contempt, I will take away[223] from you a part of your kingdom and diminish[224] your sons before their own days. Also, the Lord prohibits you entrance to his Temple." Indeed Solomon, upon hearing the angelic words, saddened and angry, wept bitterly, and kneeling on his bare knees before

---

222. "For the great angel . . . nor after drunkenness." This passage may be a quotation from a lost Version A or A2 source.

223. Latin *aufera[m].*

224. Latin *diminuam.*

the altar of the temple, petitioned mercy from God, and thus the angel, sent by the Lord God, had returned and said to him:

> Because you wept bitterly and petitioned mercy from the Lord, God has mercy on you, and your days and your sons are prolonged, but they will be diminished by an overcoming iniquity, and they will sustain many evils and serious iniquities on account of the sins which they will commit. But the Lord prohibits you entrance to his temple for an entire eighty days and nights, in order that you may perform penitence over this, because you have been found deliquent against God and his commandment.[225]

Also, the angel said about the rest:

> You must not presume to exceed the precepts of God given in this holy prayer, but you must guard them strongly, and if an angel carrying a standard in his hand appears as someone to you in a vision during the night while asleep, do not doubt or be afraid or reveal it to anyone, but the precepts which he will have given to you and the letters which he will have shown to you, you must guard and retain, concealing [them], because it is the most sacred sacramental mystery of God and his holy angels, and whatever works through these figures and whatever is to be pronounced through the most sacred prayers which are written there.[226]

On hearing these things, Solomon following [and] observing from that hour, the angelic commandment, he had firmly continued to follow the operation of this art, and this [angelic commandment] ought to be made with reverence and held in the inspection of these three figures[227] more than in the other figures. Still, in the operation of any figure of any art devotion, rever-

---

225. The passage from "From where [it is said in the text that] one day while Solomon was working . . ." to ". . . because you have been found deliquent against God and his commandment" is transmitted in a more condensed form by the Vatican Library manuscript, Latin 6842, fol. 15v (14th century). See section 134 under the heading "For your protection," which Véronèse asserts as a passage characteristic of what he calls Version A2.

226. This seems to be the end of the quoted lost source.

227. The *nota* of God (first *nota* of the general sciences), the *nota* of awe (third *nota* of the general sciences), and the ineffable *nota* (fifth *nota* of theology).

ence, and chastity, it ought to be applied, and this is what it says in this present section, and similarly, it is to be touched upon in certain other preceding sections from this material. For it is worth noting that in the inspection of the figures of any art when the Moon is [in the] fourth [day] the scrolls of that knowledge for which the operation is performed ought to be unrolled and inspected more subtly and more intensely and to read some chapters within here and there, and this command has been submitted to Solomon by the angel who always appeared to him on the fourth Moon of his operation.

[**104a**] *For these following words are the ineffable names of God, and they are to be offered, especially before the ineffable* nota *of theology:*
Hosel, Iesel, Haziatol, Iosel, Anchiatar, Hazatol, Hasiatol, Gemor, Gezamihor, Namachar, Senales, Iole, Caro, Theos, Lothos, Genos, Halla, Samihel, Ramay, Sacharios, Logos, Patyr, Saraht, Iotho, amen.

[**104b**] *These aforesaid words were given so that they may be read after the* notae *of all the arts, four times with the preceding prayers, and especially before the* notae *of theology and after the inspection of the figures.*

[105, 106, 107, 108, 109, Version A]

Ars Nova

[110, 111, Version A]

[111 Gloss] *Orationes enim istae, etc.* In this place a mention is made about certain prayers, which are are ten in number, of which the first begins *Omnipotens, incomprehensibilis, etc.,* with the others following. Therefore, when it pleased the Most High to provide for his creatures, so that through his own most holy sacraments, his own virtue, and his own holy angels, [the operator] is able to be illuminated in all knowledge and wisdom in a brief period of time, and knowing and acquiring his [desired] knowledge over any art, he was pronouncing certain, proper, and special sacraments with respect to having these, and [the Most High] demonstrated to him the manner, form, time, and the hours with respect to offering these, and thus [the Most High] assigned his particular prayers and particular figures to each art thus.

But God himself, who knew and wanted all things, and it pleased [him] to give humankind free will, knowing good and evil, and working to one's pleasure over them, seeing that King Solomon, to whom he revealed such a sacrament, failed in his operation, and he saw him, the negligence in his sacraments, and exceeded the angelic mandate and the precepts given to him by God for the completion of the entire operation, just as is demonstrated in the preceding gloss,[228] God himself, having mercy on him and [his] other successors desiring to work in this holy work, and to reconcile himself and the others, wanted to reveal the failure of this operation on account of his negligence. From where [in the text it says] God himself wished to reconcile through the same sacrament Solomon with whom he was pleased to give all knowledge and wisdom through his most sacred sacraments and his holy angels, and to reveal through the same [sacrament] his negligence and his failure of the operation.[229]

Therefore, he commissioned Solomon himself the ten prayers written in Hebrew, Chaldean, and Greek, which the prayers are only pertinent to God himself alone, excepting only one [of the ten prayers], in whose pronunciation certain names of the holy angels are invoked, whose deprecations and invocations

---

228. Section 103 gloss.
229. Section 134.

[are] to God, [such that] they [would have][230] to lose the work with extraordinary effect on account of some negligence [so as] to reduce the effect. Indeed, the angel brought these ten prayers which follow the writings in a certain book enveloped in muslin[231] on the altar of the Temple, while Solomon himself sacrificed to God, to reconcile him in this holy operation for some fault of his own previously lost, and the book was sealed with a golden sign, and Solomon heard the voice of the angel saying to him: "There are these things which the Lord has pointed out to you and which he has excluded from the hearts of infidels."

Then Solomon took the book, opened it, and saw the prayers, but fearing, he did not want to offer them, and he did a fast lasting three days and he conducted [for himself] a chaste life, and on the fourth day—namely, in the sixth holy day of the week[232]—he began to offer these ten prayers with great devotion, fearfully[233] and humbly, and he offered them thrice through one month on any day, once in the early morning, once around the third [hour], once around noon, and thus, he was offering them, fasting, chastely, and with great devotion. But after Solomon seeing so much sacramental mystery and so much virtue in them, that on account of their very operation he had recuperated whatever he had lost on account of his own delinquence, fault, and negligence in his own operation; and nine of them which were pertaining to God himself alone; having deprecated them, he translated into Latin. This is because he enucleated them in so much [detail] that they are translated into the Latin language. But he could not translate that prayer[234] in which the names of angels are invoked, because the names of the holy angels are not able to be changed, nor was Solomon himself knowledgeable of what it was, because he was thoroughly ignorant of these very names, as a matter of fact, he was ignorant on account of [his] incredulity working in this holy art.

---

230. Corrected the Latin from *habent* to *habeant*.

231. The book of ten prayers is the *Ars Nova*. The Italian merchant Marco Polo (1254–1324) was the first to describe muslin, which he said was made in Mosul, Iraq. Marco Polo, *The Most Noble and Famous Travels,* 28.

232. That is, the Sabbath.

233. That is, reverently.

234. The prayer referenced here is unknown. A plausible candidate is *Hosel* (section 104, Version A), a short list of angelic names associated with the fifth and ineffable figure of theology, because the letter writer of the *Ars Nova* places a strong emphasis on theology; however, it must be said that *Hosel* is never explicitly mentioned in Version B.

These ten prayers are to be offered for one month thrice in a day, once in the early morning, once around the third [hour], and once around noon. For whenever more [prayers] are to be offered in a day, the more they perfect [the operation and the operator]. For in pronouncing these prayers there is no day, time, or hour to be seen beforehand; nevertheless, they are to be offered devoutly with chastity, reverence, and abstinence from all sins.

Also, these prayers ought to be pronounced with the inspection of all the figures of any art. For example,[235] if you want to work on any knowledge of the three liberal arts, on the inspection of any figure of these very arts, [then] the first three of these ten are to be offered; that is to say, one each for a figure. But if the operation is to be done for acquiring some knowledge of the four liberal arts, [then] you must offer the fourth, fifth, sixth, seventh, and eighth prayer each singularly over a single figure, and thus they are to be offered before the particular prayers of the said figures.[236] Also, these—namely, the fourth, fifth, sixth, seventh, and eighth prayers—ought to be offered singularly over the figures of theology, which are five. Still, this is to be understood that all ten ought to be pronounced together through the order before the ineffable *nota,* which is the fifth and ultimate figure of theology.

Also, if you passed over some hours or a day or two in the operation, or if you dismissed some headwords or prayers on account of some overcoming impediment, [then] you must offer these prayers at any hour of the day and night more often as you can, with devotion and chastity, and you will be reconciled in your work. And even if you did not have any prayers of this most sacred art except only these ten prayers, and you offered them devoutly and chastely at any hour, day and night, while it was allowed to you, [then] the memory and understanding is administered to you with respect to retaining the knowledge of that art for which you study and labor, for the purpose of learning more knowledge which you desire, and such is the effect, just as it is as written of these ten following prayers.

[112, 113, 114, 115, Version A]

---

235. Latin idiom *verbi gratia*.

236. That is, the adorning prayers written within the figures.

[115 Gloss] *Omnipotens, incomprehensibilis, etc.* This is the first prayer from the ten about which all things is made a mention in the preceding gloss in which it is fully discussed about its virtue, its efficacy, and the correct operation of those very [prayers]. For this prayer is able to be pronounced all together at once with the others following and singularly through them. For if you want you may offer these prayers before the beginning of an operation of this art[237] and its efficacy, and they ought to be offered together. Similarly, after the completed operation if you pass over some hours, days, or prayers, [then] you must offer those very ones together for one hour. For this prayer, having been prolated with the nine others following, is useful for memory, eloquence, and understanding and the [mental] stability of those three. However, this first Special prayer[238] is for acquiring eloquence. For this prayer has to be offered singularly through them before any figure of any art—that is to say, before the first figure of that art—whose knowledge is to be acquired. This prayer is a particular prayer which ought to be pronounced over the first figure of theology; still, having pronounced that prayer, *Lux, veritas, etc.,* first, and after the pronunciation of those very two prayers, those most sacred names of the holy angels ought to be offered, which are described in the figure itself; and after the prolation of those very names of angels, the figure and its signs ought to be inspected by an attentive eye, and after the inspection of the first figure, it is to be repeated for the second figure.

[116, Version A]

[116 Gloss] *Adoro te, rex regum, etc.* This is the second prayer of those abovesaid ten prayers, which, if it is offered with the preceding prayer, [then] it has the same efficacy as the first; however, it ought to be pronounced, having made some short interval, and having prolated to such a manner, the operation applies to pronounced them with the others together, just as it is taught well and through the best eloquence, speaking and offering all things which he studied, knew, and retained. For this prayer, [*Adoro te, rex regum, etc.,*] ought to be pronounced through them without the preceding [prayer—that is, *Omnipotens incomprehensibilis, etc.*—] over the second figure of theology and over the second figure of any of the three liberal

237. The *Ars Nova.*
238. *Lux veritas.*

arts; for after its pronunciation over the *nota* of theology, the figure itself and its signs ought to be inspected. Nevertheless, it is to be understood that the names of angels which are written in this very figure ought to be pronounced with great reverence, and its figure and its very signs ought to be inspected with great diligence both to be designated in the heart and in the mind.

[117, Version A]

[117 Gloss] *Confiteor tibi ego reus, etc.* This is the third prayer of the ten, which if it is to be offered generally with the two preceding and with the other subsequent ones together, [then] it administers to the one offering it an expedited eloquence for speaking and offering knowledge which has been acquired from memory, and it strengthens the stability of the mind for retaining the knowledge which he has learned with perpetual and strong stability. For this prayer ought to be pronounced singularly without the other nine before the third figure of any art whose knowledge is to be acquired and before the particular prayers of this very figure are to be offered. Also, this prayer is the particular prayer of the first figure of the art of astronomy, from [where in the text it says] this very prayer ought to be pronounced in the inspection of this very figure. Still, that other which is *Lux, veritas, vita, etc.,* comes before [it]. For having pronounced these two prayers, this very figure and its signs are to be inspected, and it is to be repeated immediately after the inspection of this very first figure, yet having made some interval with respect to the inspection of the second figure of astronomy.

[118] *These names of the holy angels, having been pronounced, make this work lead to a good effect:*
Otheos, Hatamagiel, Hatahamarihel, Gezoray, Gezozay, Iezoramp, Gezozay, Saziel, Sazamay, Iezoramp, Sazamanp, Sacamap, Zachamay, Iecornamas, Iecornampda, Salatihel, Gezomiel, Zarachiel, Megal, Nathama, Nechamiham, Sazamaym, Sephonaym, Lazamayr, Mehis, Ramna, Hamamyl, Zamamyn, Sihel, Deloht, Hamamyn, Hazemeloht, Iazameloht, Moys, Ramna, Secozam, Hanasithonea, Seronea, Zaramahen, Sacramohen, Iegonomay, Zegomaym, Iezenomay, Zaramohen, Chades, Bachuc, Iazemeloht, Haruho, Semor, Gizethon, Malaparos, Palapathas, Helatay, Helacnay, Mechay, Meray.

[118 Gloss] *Otheos, Hatamagihel, etc.* This most holy prayer is the fourth prayer of ten, which the prayer contains the most sacred mystery within it, in whose pronunciation the most sacred names of the blessed angels are invoked, having been deprecated, whose divine office is to lead through to an effect by divine permission in presenting this most holy work with invocation and deprecation. Accordingly, this prayer, having been pronounced ordinarily together with the three preceding, and with the other subsequent ones on any day, just as it has been said above, administers for the good and faithful operator the completion of his entire work. Also, this prayer ought to be pronounced with the other subsequent ones together before the first figure of any of the four liberal arts and before the particular prayers of this very figure are to be offered. Also, it is to be understood that this holy prayer with the subsequent one is the particular prayer which ought to be pronounced before the third figure of theology, still, the other which is *Lux, veritas, etc.,* comes before [it]; and after the pronunciation of them, this very figure and its signs is to be inspected, just as it has been taught, and afterward it is to be repeated for the inspection of the fourth figure and its signs.

[119, Version A]

[119 Gloss] *Pie Deus misericors, etc.* This Latin prayer, having been pronounced together and ordinarily with the preceding four [prayers] and with the other subsequent ones, just as it has been said above, gives strength to the five external and internal senses of the faithful worker on any day and night and every hour, so that he may be able to proceed to work his own beginning of the work to the end. For this prayer always ought to be pronounced together after the preceding Greek prayer, and both are to be counted together as only one prayer among these ten, hence whenever and wherever this very preceding prayer is to be pronounced, this prayer, [*Pie Deus misericors, etc.,*] ought to be pronounced after it, having made the shortest interval, and thus this, with the preceding one is a particular prayer, which ought to be pronounced before the third figure of theology.

[120, Version A]

[120 Gloss] *[P]ie Pater misericors, etc.* This is the fifth prayer of the ten, and having been pronounced ordinarily together with the four preceding and the other subsequent ones, it provides for the operator the subtlety of ingenuity and the strength of his own five external and internal senses, so that the work conserves his own stability and firmness. For this prayer has to be pronounced before the second figure of any of the four liberal arts, before the particular prayers of those very figures are to be offered. Also, this prayer is a particular prayer which ought to be pronounced singularly through them before the fourth figure of theology, and after its pronunciation this very figure and its signs ought to be inspected, imprinted, and held in the mind by memory.

[121, Version A]

[**121 Gloss**] *Extollo sensus carnis mee, etc.* This is the sixth prayer of ten, which having been pronounced together and orderly with the five preceding and with the other subsequent ones, refines the sense and the austerity of the heart to the one offering it. For this prayer generally has to be pronounced before the third figure of any of the four liberal arts once before the particular prayers of the figure itself are to be offered. Also, this prayer especially ought to be offered before the second figure of astronomy. Still, that *Lux, veritas, etc.,* comes before [it], and similarly, it is to be understood that this very particular prayer of the fifth figure of theology, which the figure is called the "ineffable *nota.*" But this is to be seen beforehand because the preceding prayers, which are five, all ought to be pronounced together with that before the said ineffable *nota,* which is the fifth and ultimate figure of theology; and after the pronunciation of those very ones, the figure itself and its signs is to be inspected with great reverence and humility; and after the inspection of this very figure, the scrolls of theology are to be unrolled, inspected, and reading some chapters within here and there.

[122, Version A]

[**122 Gloss**] *Omnium regnorum, etc.* This is the seventh prayer of ten. For this prayer is to be pronounced together and orderly with the first six preceding ones and with the other subsequent ones, and it provides a subtlety of ingenuity to the operator in this art and to the one who pronounces it, and it restores that subtlety and ingenuity. This prayer has to be pronounced generally before the fourth figure of any of the four liberal arts once before the particular prayers of the figure itself are to be offered. Also, this very prayer especially ought to be pronounced without the others before the third figure of astronomy (still, that prayer *Lux, veritas, etc.,* is to be offered first); afterward this prayer and this very figure with its signs is to be inspected after their very pronunciation.

[123, Version A]

[123 Gloss] *Deus, vivorum dominator, etc.* This is the eighth prayer of ten. Specifically, this prayer, having been pronounced together and ordinarily with the first seven preceding ones and the other subsequent ones, augments memory, elucidates eloquence, and gives understanding to the one who pronounces it; and it is to be understood that this prayer is more particular and special before the fifth figure of theology than that other [prayer], *Extollo sensus, etc.,* whence during the inspection of that fifth figure, the first, second, third, and fourth prayers—that is to say, they are to be offered before the first, second, third, and fourth figures of theology—ought to be offered ordinarily and together before this fifth figure of theology; and after those four, this ultimate prayer is to be offered.

[124, Version A]

[124 Gloss] *Profiteor hodie, etc.* This prayer is the ninth prayer of ten, which the prayer, having been prolated successively and ordinarily together with the eight preceding ones, infuses the grace of the Holy Spirit into it with the pronunciation. For this prayer ought to be pronounced singularly through them before the fourth figure of astronomy, because it is its very own prayer. Still, this is to be attended to, because the seventh of these prayers, which is *Omnium regnorum, etc.,* and that other, *Lux, veritas, etc.,* ought to be pronounced once before this fourth figure of astronomy, and after this prayer and those prayers have been read and pronounced in this way, this very figure with its signs are to be inspected and to be held within the mind.

[125, Version A]

[125 Gloss] *Domine, quia ego servus, etc.* This is the tenth and ultimate prayer of these prayers from which we have made a mention in the preceding sections. For this prayer, having been pronounced together and orderly with the other nine preceding prayers, augments the memory and the understanding, and makes subtle the durable ingenuity for the one offering it. This prayer is particular to the fifth figure of astronomy, and ought to be pronounced through them singularly without the other nine during the inspection of the figure itself. For after the pronunciation of this prayer and the other—namely, *Lux, veritas, etc.*—he ought to be observe this very figure with its signs, and after the inspection of this very figure, the scrolls of astronomy ought to be inspected and unrolled, reading some chapters within. Therefore, these ten prayers, which the angel of the Lord presented to Solomon, have so much efficacy, virtue, and mystery in them, just as we have said above, because with having read and pronounced together and orderly on any day, any night, and any hour, living chastely and honestly, they grant memory, augment eloquence, accrue understanding, make ingenuity subtle, [and] call forth the grace of God for working in some field of knowledge through this most holy operation of this art. And in this way these prayers are able to be read and pronounced on all days, at all hours of the day and night, both with fasting and without fasting, nevertheless they are not to be offered after lechery, drunkenness, perjury, nor after some mortal sin, because he who offers them would find no good, but rather evil, in the pronunciation of them. And this is the efficacy and the only operation of these ten prayers, without the other prayers of this art joined with itself, and especially the Greek prayers, in which are the names of the holy angels, which the prayers have their own particular times, days, and hours in which they ought to be pronounced with fasting and chastity, and this is the knowledge given of these ten prayers.

[126, Version A]

[126a Gloss] *Hoc est opusculum quod ceteris maius est, etc.* A full mention has been made above in the preceding sections from the beginning of this work up to this place from the sections, prayers, and the figures of those and what days and which hours they ought to be pronounced, the figures to be inspected, and how, and when, and under what special kind, and for what reason, and for what necessity they were made for Solomon through the angel.

[Solomon Receives the *Ars Nova*]

But in this section, it is to be said and understood about these last nine prayers, (which all nine prayers are invocations of the names of holy angels)[239] what efficacy they have, and how, and when, and for what reason, and for what kind of necessity they were presented last to Solomon. And again, it is to be understood at which times, on which days, and in which hours they ought to be offered. Therefore, when on the same night Solomon, who said the preceding prayers[240] that were delivered to him by an angel and sealed with a golden seal, just as it has been said above, looked back upon the prayers. [He was] thinking and doubting about their operation, the other headwords, and the preceding prayers, how he could pronounce so many headwords [and] prayers under such a brief period of time and retain all the precepts given to him by memory, and especially doubting more how, after the operation of the art, he could be able to commit to memory perpetually any acquired knowledge, when it is impossible for him to always guard against mortal sins on account of nature to excite [the senses], and if possible, yet difficult. On account of this, it pleased the Most High, knowing the thoughts of men, to apply a remedy over this, and then at that very same hour, [the Most High] commissioned Solomon these nine prayers,[241] through this very same angel who had ministered to him the ten preceding prayers, by saying and ordering him in this way:

> Because you think, doubt, and admire to acquire and to possess so much knowledge and so much wisdom through such prayers and sacraments, having been pronounced in such short days and hours, just as it is mandated by God to you, and especially, because the more you doubt to lose the acquired knowledge and wisdom on account of some overtaking sin, and this most holy work,[242] having been acquired with so much labor, fades away on account of some negligence, the Lord sends to you this most sacred mystery in which are contained his most sacred names, and his holy angels, about which it is to be worked, undertaken, and obeyed accordingly in this way.

239. The *novem termini*.

240. The ten prayers of the *Ars Nova*.

241. Again, the *novem termini*.

242. That is, the perpetual knowledge gained.

Therefore, when you want to come before the beginning of some field of knowledge, and you doubt you are not able to proceed continuously with respect to pursuing your work or to lead through to an effect in such a short period of days and hours, [then] it is to be done in this way.

[On Day 13, Friday]

On one Friday of any [calendar] month, make a fast on bread and water,[243] but first you must be well confessed in proportion as you will be able to be better [successful in your operation] through some days,[244] and on this very Friday early in the morning, you must offer those ten preceding prayers once, successively and orderly, just as it has been said above, having made some interval for moral incontinence, you must offer these nine prayers, and make a short interval between each prayer once in the early morning, once around the third [hour], once around noon, and thus thrice in a day.

[On Day 14, Saturday]

But on the Sabbath you must say the same prayers in the same hours, and at the completion of the hours and on reading the prayers, you must fast, but nevertheless you may eat Lenten foods.

[On Day 15, Sunday]

Accordingly, on the Lord's Day you must offer the prayers at the very same hours, and having completed the midday hour, you may eat what pleases you, either fish or meat, but give alms to three or more wandering poor. And thus, on that night of the Lord's Day, it will be revealed to you by an angel to which end and effect you ought to come before the beginning and proposed work, and

---

243. Not just any day, but on a Friday of the calendar month. There is an interim period between the first stage of spiritual purification and the ritual proper, which begins on the lunar month. Thus, it is preferable to calculate the Friday of any given calendar month to be close to the beginning of a lunar month. The lunar months are reserved for the special operations given for each art and science. For calculating a lunar month, see 126e gloss.

244. See "Fifteen Days" in section 126e gloss.

thus in this very night spent in sleep, the Lord will minister to you through his holy angel.

[On Account of Sin or Error in the Operation]

Also, having finished your operation and having completed that knowledge in the right order, which you have acquired and retained in memory through the aforesaid operation, and you have offered eloquently, [but if][245] you have lost [that knowledge] on account of some overcoming sin, or by chance, you passed over some more days and hours in your operation, or you might have passed over some headwords and prayers which is to be read, [then] you will be able to reconcile your work through these ten prayers and lead [it] through to a pristine state.

[The Prayers of the Three-Day Opening Ritual Procedure]

Therefore, if you wish to work from these, you must do so in this way for such a case after the operation. On a certain Friday, just like at the beginning of the operation, you must offer those ten preceding prayers once in the early morning, and having made an interval, you must offer these nine, specifically around the third [hour] similarly, [and] around noon similarly. But on the Sabbath and the Lord's Day, you must do that same thing because it is taught to you above in this gloss regarding the [proper] beginning of the work [which is] about to to begin.

[The First Lunar Month]

But having completed these three days, on the first day of the next [lunar] month of those three days—that is to say, when the Moon is first—you said these very same prayers, which in those three days, having been pronounced in the same hours, and as many times, just as you did on the aforesaid three days,

245. Reconstructed Latin *quodsi.*

and thus, you must do so from those on any day of the entire lunation that month, and it is to be lived soberly, chastely, and without any mortal sin, especially without the approach of a woman, drunkenness, and perjury, and it is to be fasted on any day up to which it is to be completed in those three hours of the day in which the operation is performed—that is to say, until after noon—and then you are able to eat whatever pleases you, whether meat, fish, or other [foods]. Still, it is to be guarded against superfluity and ebriation on point, and this is the operation of these prayers before the beginning of the work of this art with respect to avoiding any doubt and to avoid incredulity of its completion, and, similarly, after the operation of the art with respect to recuperating some lost efficacy on account of some negligence or sin, such as memory or eloquence or some acquired knowledge.

[The *Novem Termini,* the Boundaries of the Ritual]

For these nine prayers are spoken and called *termini*—namely, "boundaries," because the entire operation of that most sacred art is set and stands between those *novem termini*—because at the beginning of the operation of this most holy art they ought to be pronounced before any headwords or prayers are offered. Similarly, having perfected, intergrated, and completed the operation of this art, [the *novem termini*] ought to be pronounced in the same manner, just as we said above, and this is the efficacy and the operation of those nine prayers of this notory art.

[The Compendium of the Glosses]

[126b Gloss] It is mentioned above in the preceding written sections and glosses from the beginning of this book up to this place, separately about the operation of this art through its own parts and about the operation, and about the efficacy and virtue of the headwords and prayers of the *notae* and figures of that art, and because he is scarcely able to gather together and collect all the above written [material] scatteredly and separately by a fragile nature when he was going astray in the work, for this reason, we wanted to collect the first operation, the efficacy and virtue of all the headwords, and all the prayers, *notae,* and figures of the entire book in this place through the order under a compendium.

[The Five Parts of the Compendium]

And first, let us make mention of the name of the title[246] of this book; second, about how the order of the headwords of the prayers of the art are described through the order in this art; third, what kind of efficacy they present to those who offer them; fourth, which [prayers] ought and are able to be pronounced by themselves without the others and which [are] not [able to be pronounced] without the others; fifth and last, we speak about the entire order of the operation of this art under the compendium, collecting all the aforesaid sections on how and in what manner [the operation] is to be proceeded through the order in this holy work for the purpose of having all the aforesaid efficacies, and with respect to all the sciences of the seven liberal arts, the seven mechanical [arts], and the seven exceptives, and acquiring perfectly and retaining perpetually the entire philosophy.

[The Compendium, Part I: The Name of the Title of This Book]

For let us see firstly and principally about the title of this book. Therefore, it is to be understood, that this book is rightly called "the notory art," because it is comprehended beneath certain brief *notae*—namely, the prayers—and similarly, it is called "notory," because it [is contained] through the very art (that is, through the virtue of prayers' headwords, *notae,* and figures, which are contained in the very art), the *notitia* is given to the faithful and the good worker in it how he is able to acquire memory retaining in all things heard, eloquence in all things retained eloquently to one making the offering and conserving perpetually for memory, and the integrated and perfected knowledge and all the wisdom of all the liberal, mechanical, and exceptive arts. Also, this book is able to be rightly called "the art of memory" in the right manner, because through [the book] itself, just as it is said above, memory is to be acquired in all sciences heard, having been retained through memory, and this is the true title of the book.

---

246. *Intitulatio,* a technical term used by notaries meaning "title," which is used in the protocol for writing medieval documents for the pope, emperor, or other high-ranking officials. Such a document would contain the *invocatio, intitulatio,* and *pertinentia. Intitulatio* is chosen for the glosses rather than *titulus, tituli.*

[The Compendium, Parts 2 and 3: The Order and the Efficacy of the Prayers]

[126c Gloss] But now we must speak about the order of the headwords and prayers, and which prayers are Specials, and which are Generals, and for which efficacy they are to be read, just as they are written in the book.

Therefore, at the beginning of this art, a certain prayer whose beginning is *Alpha et omega, etc.,*[247] is written. For this prayer should always be pronounced first at the beginning of any efficacy of any field of knowledge which is to be acquired, and having completed the operation and acquired some efficacy, [the prayers] are offered just as they would be pronounced for memory, eloquence, or acquiring another field of knowledge. This prayer should be offered first; similarly, this very prayer ought to be pronounced, and twice in any operation thus (that is, before and after) at any time and at any hour, having finished the particular prayers of that efficacy.

For the three prayers that are called "the first three headwords," the first of which begins *Helyscemaht, etc.;* the second begins *[Ph]os, Megal[os], etc.;* the third *Lux mundi, etc.,*[248] follow after this very prayer. But those three headwords generally ought to be pronounced in the beginning of any operation for acquiring some efficacy with the other premable prayer first; namely, *Alpha et omega, etc.*

For after the pronunciation of the first prayer and the three headwords, certain prayers which follow through the order should be pronounced, and they are six in number, of which the first begins *Assaylemaht, etc.;* the second begins *Azaylemaht, etc.;* the third *Lemahc [Sebauthe], etc.;* the fourth *Lamehc [Leynac], etc.;* the fifth *Deus summe Deus [invisibilis], etc.;* the sixth *Te queso, Domine, etc.*[249] Accordingly, these prayers are specifically offered for the purpose of acquiring memory, eloquence, and understanding. For these six prayers are only offered in the month through the eight days four times a day, once in the early morning, once around the third [hour], once around noon, and once around the evening.

---

247. *Alpha et omega* is found in variation 1 gloss.

248. These three prayers consist of the first sequence of prayers found at sections 7, 10, and 11.

249. *Assaylemaht* (section 16), *Azaylemaht* (variation 3), *Lemahc Sebauthe* (variation 4), *Lamehc Leynac* (section 22), *Deus summe Deus invisibilis* (section 24), and *Te queso Domine* (section 25). Variation 3 gloss states that *Azaylemaht* is the second part of *Assaylemaht*. Variation 4 gloss explains that *Lemahc Sebauthe* is the third part of *Assaylemaht*.

But the days on which they are offered are these: therefore, the first day on which those prayers are to be offered—the first is the fourth day of the month, (that is, on the fourth day of the Moon); second, they are offered on the eighth day; third, on the twelfth; fourth, on the sixteenth; fifth, on the twentieth; sixth, on the twenty-fourth; seventh, on the twenty-eighth; the eighth, or the last, on the thirtieth day. For he who pronounces these [prayers] must live chastely and honestly, and let him fast on any day of those eight days on Lenten food and not eat until after the evening,[250] because then the operation of that day is finished.

For after those prayers, a certain prayer follows which is divided into two parts, which is a certain experiment of the Special by itself, and it is able to be said without the other prayers, which the prayer begins *Ihesu Dei Filius, etc.,* and its part begins *Eliminator, Caudones, etc.*[251] The efficacy of this prayer is manifold, just as it is described the above in its own section,[252] and, just as it is said, it is able to be offered by itself without the others.

After these prayers follow some other prayers through the order which have an important virtue and efficacy for the purpose of acquiring eloquence and with respect to pronouncing them eloquently which the aforesaid prayers are committed to memory. For the first of those prayers begins *Lamehc, Ragna, etc.;* the second, *Semeht, Seguat, etc.;* the third, *Memoria incomprehensibilis, etc.;*[253] and these three prayers are offered, just as was it is declared in their own proper sections, present a good understanding and subtlety of ingenuity in learning the sciences heard [e.g., from a private teacher or in the lecture halls of a school].

Indeed, following after these, some other most holy prayers, which by themselves with the first three headwords, have to be pronounced through one month, and this is to be acquired for some perfect knowledge of an art, and after their very operation in the following month it is to be seen beforehand with respect to the inspection of the figures of that art whose knowledge is to be desired to be obtained. For these prayers are twelve in number, of which the first begins *Hazatham, Hihel, etc.;* second, *Hyelma, Helma, etc.;*

---

250. At 126d gloss, which speaks about the second month, it says the operator can break fast after noon.

251. This two-part prayer is found at sections 29a and 29b.

252. Sections 30–31. See also 28 gloss and 29a gloss.

253. *Lamehc Ragna* (section 34), *Semeht Seguat* (Variation 5), *Memoria Irreprehensibilis* (section 36).

third, *Confirma, consolida, etc.;* fourth, *Agloros, etc.;* fifth, *Deus omnium, etc.;* sixth, *Megal, Agal, etc.;* seventh, *Veritas, lux, via, etc.;* eighth, *Hanuirliahel, etc.;* ninth, *Ego in conspectus, etc.;* tenth, *Gehot, Gehel, etc.;* eleventh, *Omnipotens, sempiterne Deus, etc.;* twelfth, and last, *Semoht, Lamen, etc.*[254] For these prayers should be pronounced at the beginning of the operation of the knowledge to be aquired of any art in their own days [and] their own hours, just as it is described and perfectly declared above in their own proper sections.[255]

As a matter of fact, some other prayers follow in order, which are thirty-two in number, of which the first begins *Lux, veritas, etc.;*[256] second, *Domine sancte Pater [. . . imperfectum], etc.;* third, *Respice, Domine, etc.;* fourth, *Creator Adonay, etc.;*[257] fifth, *Sancte Deus, etc.;* sixth, *Heloy clementissime, etc.;*[258] seventh, *Omnipotens et misericors, etc.;* eighth, *Adonay, etc.;* ninth, *Unus, magnus, etc.;* tenth, *Usyon omnium, etc.;* eleventh, *Azelechias [. . . regi Salomoni], etc.;* twelfth, *Scio enim, etc.;* thirteenth, *Reverende, etc.;*[259] fourteenth, *Deus que omnia, etc.;*

---

254. *Hazatam Hyhel* (section 43, Version B), *Hyhelma Helma* (section 46, Version B), *Confirma* (section 47), *Agloros* (section 50, Version B), *Deus omnium* (section 51), *Megal* (section 52, Version B), *Veritas lux via* (section 53), *Hanuyrlyahel* (section 54, Version B), *Ego in conspectus* (section 55), *Gehot Gehel* (section 62, Version B), *Omnipotens sempiterne Deus* (section 64), and *Semoht Lamen* (section 69, Version B).

255. This passage concludes the General prayers.

256. *Lux veritas* (NS 1) is to be said before all the Special prayers.

257. These three prayers belong to grammar. *Domine Sancte Pater [. . . imperfectum]* (section 128), *Respice Domine* (section 129), *Creator Adonay* (section 130).

258. These two prayers belong to logic. *Sancte Deus* (section 135) and *Heloy clementissime* (section 137).

259. *Omnipotens et misericors* (section 138) is the prayer belonging to the first figure of rhetoric. *Adonay, etc.,* is an unidentified prayer; however, it may correspond to *Gezomani* (section 140) and its equivalent, *Hanazay* (section 140, Version B), which may be actually the second little part of the General prayer, *Assaylemaht,* misplaced among the prayers of rhetoric based on the original ordering of passages of the primitive *Flores Aurei;* it is spelled *Gezamanay* in section 16, Version B. The mentioning of *Adonay, etc.,* is a clue consistent with this intrepretation of an early redaction of the *Flores Aurei;* see page 294, footnote 143 in section 140, Version A. The proposed redaction leads to further confusions among the prayers of rhetoric in Version B. *Unus magnus* (section 139) is the prayer belonging to the second figure of rhetoric. *Usyon omnium* (section 141) is the prayer belonging to the third figure of rhetoric. *Azelechias [. . . regi Salomoni]* (variation 7; NS 51) competes with *Unus magnus* for the position of being the second figure of rhetoric. *Scio enim* (variation 8; NS 56) competes with *Usyon omnium* for the position of being the third figure of rhetoric. There is also an abridged form of *Scio enim* found at NS 72, in which it belongs to the figure of music as the second part of the adorning prayer *Otheos Athamatheos* (NS 71). *Reverende* (section 142) is the prayer belonging to the fourth figure of rhetoric.

fifteenth, *Mediator omnium, etc.;*[260] sixteenth, *Deus iustus, etc.;* seventeenth, *Omnipotens sapientiae, etc.;*[261] eighteenth, *Adoro te, rex regum, etc.;*[262] nineteenth, *Ezethomos, etc.;* twentieth, *Dominus Deus [incomprehensibilis], etc.;* twenty-first, *Domine [Deus] sancte Pater, etc.;* twenty-second, *Deus, semper via, etc.;* twenty-third, *Lemogethon, etc.;* twenty-fourth, *Vita hominum, etc.;* twenty-fifth, *Omaza, Beheza, etc.;* twenty-sixth, *Rex regum, etc.;* twenty-seventh, *Deus Pater immense [. . . magnitudo], etc.;* twenty-eighth, *Gezomothon, etc.;* twenty-ninth, *Rex aeterne Deus, etc.;* thirtieth, *Deus totius pietatis, etc.;*[263] thirty-first, *Deus Pater immense [. . . misericordissme], etc.;*[264] and thirty-second, *Hosel, Iehel, etc.*[265]

For these prayers specifically should be said during the seven days before [the operation] is to arrived at the inspection of some figures of any art, and especially, eighteen of the those first prayers should be pronounced in the first

260. These two prayers belong to arithmetic. *Deus que omnia numero* (section 144) and *Mediator omnium* (section 145).

261. *Deus iustus iudex* (section 143) is the first figure of geometry. *Omnipotens sapientiae* (section 146) is the first prayer, or at least the Latin prologue, belonging to the general sciences. In Version B, the prayer is misassigned to a duplicated figure of geometry, thereby creating a second figure of geometry. Notice also the transposition of the ordering of arithmetic and geometry between Version A and Version B. Such transposition may account for minor redactions at certain stages of the development of the *Ars Notoria* manuscript tradition; it may also account for how the Clm 276 manuscript misattributed the special title, *notae terroris* (the nota of awe), of *Omnipotens sapientiae* to the first figure of arithmetic on folio 13r.

262. *Adoro te rex regum* belongs to the second figure of theology. Strangely, the other prayers belonging to theology, the first, third, and fourth, are not present in this list.

263. These twelve prayers belong to philosophy. *Ezethomos* (section 90) and its Latin prologue, *Domine Deus incomprehensibilis* (section 91), together form the first prayer of philosophy. *Domine Deus Sancte Pater* (section 92) and its Latin prologue, *Deus semper via* (section 93), together form the second prayer of philosophy. *Lemogethon* (section 94) and its Latin prologue, *Vita hominum* (section 95), together form the third prayer of philosophy. *Omaza Beheza* (Variation 10) and its Latin prologue, *Rex regum* (section 96), together form the fourth prayer of philosophy. *Deus Pater immense [. . . magnitudo]* (section 98) is the fifth prayer of philosophy. *Gezomothon* (section 99) and its Latin prologue, *Rex aeternae Deus* (section 100), together form the sixth prayer of philosophy. *Deus totius pietatis* (section 101) is the seventh prayer of philosophy, but it is only the first of two parts according to Version B.

264. *Deus Pater immense [. . . misericordissime]* (NS 69) has the dual function of serving as the second part of the seventh prayer of philosophy and also being the sole prayer to music. This is true only for Version B.

265. *Hosel* (section 104a) is the prayer belonging to the fifth figure of theology. The glosser does not acknowledge *Deus vivorum* as the fifth prayer of theology as BnF Latin 9336 does at NS 135.

seven days[266] before the inspection of the figures of the three liberal arts,[267] but the remaining fourteen[268] before the inspection of the figures of the four liberal arts.[269] Similarly, any of those have to be pronounced singularly by itself while the very figure of that art (over [the place in] which they are described [in the text]) is inspected, just as it is described above in their own proper sections and glosses.

Also, if these aforesaid prayers[270] with the other ten that follow[271] are to be offered through one [calendar] month before it is proceeded with respect to any operation of this art[272] on any day and any night, [then] it will be a good, useful, and most holy operation, and it will be administered to the one who pronounces them by the grace of God and the subtlety of ingenuity and the good intention to follow through on the work. For these prayers ought to be offered on any day and night at all hours, not dismissing to pronouncing them for his own pursuits, but rather to learn and to listen to that knowledge from the master teacher from whom he wishes to work through this art. And it is to be understood that however many more are offered during the day and night, the more beneficial and proficient they become, and they administer greater efficacy to the one offering them. For in the operation of these [prayers] one must live chastely and soberly, because no one may presume to offer them in this way after having approached a woman nor after having made some mortal sin on the very day.[273]

Accordingly, some other most holy prayers follow which are eleven in number, of which the first begins *Omnipotens, incomprehensibilis, etc.;* second, *Adoro*

---

266. The eighteen prayers are those beginning with *Lux veritas* and ending with *Adoro te rex regum*. Notice that the last five of these prayers bear no relationship to the trivium.

267. That is, the trivium which consists of grammar, logic, and rhetoric.

268. The fourteen prayers are those beginning with *Ezethomos* and ending with *Hosel*. These are the prayers belonging to philosophy, except for *Hosel,* which is associated with theology. None of these Special prayers are assigned specifically to any one of the four liberal arts.

269. That is, the quadrivium, which consists of arithmetic, music, geometry, and astronomy. For more on this problematic section, see chapter V.

270. The thirty-two prayers.

271. The ten prayers of the *Ars Nova*.

272. This is the interim period of the ritual procedure. The operator is to pray during any calendar day or night, for so many days, up to the first day of a lunar month that is planned ahead for the operation to obtain a new science.

273. This passage concludes the Special prayers.

te, rex regum, etc.; third, *Confiteor, etc.;* fourth, *Otheos, etc.;* fifth, *Pie Deus, etc.;* sixth, *Pie Pater, etc.;* seventh, *Extollo sensus, etc.;* eighth, *Omnium regnorum, etc.;* ninth, *Deus vivorum, etc.;* tenth, *Profiteor, etc.;* and eleventh, *Domine, quia ego servuus, etc.*[274] For these prayers, although they may be eleven separately, yet there are not, but only ten, because that prayer which is *Otheos, etc.,* with its following prologue, which is *Pie Deus, etc.,* are not [two] but only one prayer, because that prologue is an exposition of the particular preceding prayer.

For those ten prayers ought to be offered in three ways in the operation of this art. Indeed, at the beginning of this operation, with the other nine Greek prayers which follow have to be made on three days, just as it is described in the gloss of those *novem termini* which are called *termini.*[275] Also, these prayers should also be offered through one month with the other thirty-two prayers which precede these ten. Also, these prayers should also be offered singularly before the figures of theology and astronomy, just as it is written above in their own proper glosses.[276] For these offered prayers, by whatever means they are offered, administer memory, eloquence, understanding, and the subtlety of ingenuity, and they administer the grace of the Holy Spirit to the one pronouncing them. For after these ten prayers are divided, the nine most holy prayers which are called *termini,* and they are the last prayers of this art up to the figures.[277]

---

274. The ten prayers of the *Ars Nova.*

275. Sections 127a through 127i.

276. In the *Flores Aurei,* the original prayers of astronomy are missing. To solve the problem of the missing prayers, the glosser decides to newly assign the *Ars Nova* prayers to astronomy. These new assignments are *Confiteor tibi Domine ego reus, Extollo sensus, Omnium regnorum, Domine quia ego servus,* and *Profiteor;* this assignment of five prayers may indicate that there were originally just five figures of astronomy in the *Flores Aurei.* The Version A manuscripts give an imperfect presentation of the figures of astronomy, certainly not adding up to six. BnF Latin 9336 assigns the prayer *Iezomanay* (NS 90) to the sixth figure of astronomy. Notice that these *Ars Nova* prayers do not petition God or the angels for knowledge of astronomy. The glosser refers the reader to 85/86 gloss for astronomy. The glosser also assigns *Ars Nova* prayers to theology which are these: *Omnipotens incomprehensibilis, Adoro te rex regum, Otheos/Pie Deus, Pie Pater,* and *Deus vivorum.* The *Ars Notoria* has retained the prayer *Hosel* as belonging to the fifth figure of theology; thus, for Version B, *Deus vivorum* and *Hosel* now compete for the fifth position of theology. Furthermore, the glosser's list of thirty-two prayers, which includes *Adoro te rex regum* and *Hosel,* may indicate a retention of the assignment of these prayers as belonging to theology in an older and lost recension of the *Flores Aurei.* The glosser refers the reader to 97 gloss for theology.

277. This passage concludes the prayers of the *Ars Nova* and the *novem termini.*

[The *Novem Termini* at the Beginning and the End of the Ritual. Also, If You Will Have Lost the Knowledge Because of Some Sin or the Anger of God.]

For those nine prayers ought to be pronounced twice in the operation of this art. Firstly, they should be pronounced at the beginning of the operation with the other ten preceding prayers through the three days with fasting and chastity, just as it is described in their own glosses, and just like the pronounciation through those three days, it is to be announced to the one making the offering through the angel from sleeping at night, [and] he ought to come beforehand to that end, [i.e., the dream vision of the announcing angel, in order to come] to the proposed work.[278] Secondly, [the nine prayers] should be offered after the completion of the operation of some acquired science, and they should be offered for three days thus, just as they should be offered in the beginning, or if, by chance, on account of some sin, or on account of the anger of God, you would have lost the knowledge which you had acquired, [then] these nine prayers with the other ten preceding them which are be offered through one month, just as it is described above and perfectly declared in their own proper sections and their own proper glosses, and they are to be offered in one month thus, [and] you will have recuperated the lost knowledge and the grace of God, and again you will have committed the said knowledge to your pristine memory.

And thus, you have the order of all the headwords and the prayers of the whole art, up to the figures, and their efficacy and their number, and the whole operation of the book, [kept] beneath [this very] compendium, through this [very] gloss up to the figures. For the headwords and the prayers of this art up to the figures are seventy in number separately; and here the end is made about the operation of those and the quantity, efficacy, and quality.

[The Compendium, Parts 4 and 5: The Method of the Entire Operation]

[126d Gloss] For this is to be attended to because if you want to work in the proper order through this art, and you wanted to completely acquire and pos-

---

278. A restatement of what has already been described above in 126c gloss.

sess some knowledge of the seven liberal arts or of the other arts, it is necessary for you and anyone wishing to work in this art to work for four months.

[The Interim Period and the First Month]

Specifically, in the first month, these last nine prayers[279] with the others[280] preceding are to be said during the three days, just as it was said, and in those very three days, those preceding prayers[281] those ten [more][282] ought to be said in the other hours of the day in which these nine are not to be read. But on the other days of that entire month, those prayers preceding those ten, which are thirty-two in number, are to be said with the same ten or last nine prayers at any day until the end of the lunar month of all hours of the day and night when you want.[283] And in this first month it is not necessary for you to dismiss your business affairs or your pursuits, neither is it necessary for you to fast but to go to school frequently.

[The Second Month]

Specifically, in the second month, the very same prayers are to be said through the three days just as in the first month, and on the fourth day—that is, when it is the fourth [day] of the Moon—the prayers which are made for the purpose of memory, eloquence, and understanding (namely, the first three headwords and the other prayers[284] that follow in order) are to be said, just as it is said above. But in this second month, similarly, it is not necessary to dimiss your pursuits or your other business affairs, except it is necessary to see beforehand certain hours of the day in which those prayers should be pronounced through

279. The *novem termini*.

280. The ten prayers of the *Ars Nova*.

281. The ten prayers of the *Ars Nova*.

282. A scribe is confused by the phrase "those ten," thinking it meant there were ten more prayers to be added here; hence, the scribe added the word "more." Actually, the phrase "those ten" refers to the ten prayers of the *Ars Nova*.

283. That is to say, in the remaining days of the lunar month, the operator is to pray the thirty-two prayers and the ten prayers of the *Ars Nova* of any hour of any day or night. This is a restatement of what is found above in 126c gloss.

284. The other prayers are the *novem termini* and the ten prayers of the *Ars Nova*.

the eight days,[285] just as it was described in their own proper glosses, nor will you fast in the same month, except on those eight days in which those very prayers are to be read, and after noon, you will be able to eat all the foods that you want except meat.[286]

[The Third Month]

In the third month, the first three headwords are to be pronounced and the other prayers which ought to be pronounced for the purpose of acquiring that perfect knowledge for which this operation is performed. But in that third month, similarly, you must not dismiss your pursuits, but that month while you will be able to listen earnestly [and] studying the readings of knowledge for which you will work, and you must see beforehand certain hours in which you ought to work, and you will fast on certain days in that month, just as it will be described in the glosses of those prayers above, which should be read at that time.

[The Fourth Month]

But in the fourth month, it is to be seen beforehand with respect to the inspection of the figures of the art of that science whose knowledge you desire to obtain. Accordingly in this fourth month, you will not go out of the house during the entire month in which you perform the operation of the figures, except in the evening if you will have completed the day's operation, and this is how no one may impede you during the day while you work, and you will fast any day of that month on Lenten food, and I will briefly demonstrate the whole operation of this art, and of the prayers and figures, under the compendium in the subsequent gloss without any scruple.

[126e Gloss] Having said and shown well and sufficiently in the preceding gloss about the title of that most sacred art, and about the order of all the head-

285. The eight lunar days are the fourth, eighth, twelfth, sixteenth, twentieth, twenty-fourth, twenty-eighth, and thirtieth. See section 126c gloss.

286. At 126c gloss, following the mentioning of the eight lunar days, it says the operator breaks fast after the evening.

words and prayers which are described in it through the order, and about the virtue and efficacy of those, and about the months, how many are necessary to complete the operation of acquiring any science.

[Calculating the First Day of a Lunar Month]

In this place, beneath the brief compendium, we must speak about the method and form of the operations of the first, second, third, and fourth months—namely, what kind of lunar [day of the] any [calendar] month is to be seen beforehand with respect to beginning—and we speak about what things are necessary for the worker who wants to proceed in this holy art. Therefore, first, it is necessary for you if you want to work in this most holy art to see beforehand and to think about when the Moon is first[287] according to astronomy, but still, you must not be deceived, [because] you must know this that when the Moon is first announced in church it is called the third [day] according to astronomy, and just two days before the Moon is seen and is said to be the first [day] in church you ought to see beforehand and elect it,[288] and in this such a lunar [day of the] month this most holy work is to be begun, except on the three days in which only the last nine prayers called *termini* ought to be offered.

[Fifteen Days of Penitence]

Accordingly, with respect to beginning such a most sacred work you must see beforehand some month in which it will be best for you to begin working, and before that month which you have elected, for fifteen days or thereabouts, you go to confession with great hope, faith, and desire and insofar as you are better able to confess and repent from sins, and you must begin to take action about the penitence has enjoined something to you, just like doing a fast, if you have or were able to restitute another person by almsgiving, [if] you are not able to implement them, that with respect to presenting them, [then] you must have

287. That is, a new Moon.

288. An ecclesiastical new Moon is the first day of a lunar month, which is equated with a new crescent Moon. The ecclesiastical new Moon can be any day from the day of the astronomical new Moon to two days later. An ecclesiastical full Moon is the fourteenth day of the ecclesiastical lunar month. An ecclesiastical lunar month contains 29 or 30 days.

good will to implementing and to accomplishing [them], and if the entire penitence enjoined to you, [then] may you be able to accomplish [it] agreeably before you must begin this work, [then] it will be better. Nevertheless, it does not punish you beforehand if you do not perform it, since you have the volition while you will be able to carry out [this operation].

[The Operation of the Three Days]

But having received the penitence, you must appoint only four leaves of olive, date palm, or bay (whatever you have), and you should have one new glass cup, and you must place these leaves in the cup, and keep it, and store it in some clean place until the next Friday near the new Moon of the month of in which you propose to start working.

[On Day 13, Friday]

Specifically, on that very Friday, at the dawn of the day, you must take up your four leaves, and with saffron mixed with rosewater in some new vessel, you must write on one leaf this name [here] "Hagnadam," with one new quill pen (when that was not being used to write other things), and place [it] on any clean part upon the writing tablet; afterward, on another leaf you write this name [here] "Merabor," and you place it next to the other leaf; on the third leaf you write this name [here] "Hamiladei," and you place it next to the other leaves through the order; on the fourth leaf you write this name [here] "Pesiguaguol," and you place it next to the other leaves through the order.

Having done these things in this way, fill your cup from the clear, pure, and clean water, and take the first leaf on which you wrote the first name and place it in the cup, and with the fingers strongly rub the leaf with water on that side on which the name is written in such a way that no vestiges of the name remain behind or appear visible on the leaf, and then you throw the leaf out of the cup wherever you want. Having done this with the first leaf, you must take the second leaf on which the second name is written, and in a similar manner, you must do just [what] you did with the first. Next, you must take the third leaf, and this you do the same with that. Next, you must take the fourth leaf, and in a similar manner, you must do with that just as you did with the other three.

Having completed these, you must take the cup and with great devotion drink a little from that water, and after the drink you say once, "Teach me goodness, discipline, and knowledge, because I have believed in your commandments."[289] Having said this, you drink a little again, and you say *Bonitatem, etc.,* and thus, you drink a little four times successively, each time saying *Bonitatem, etc.,* and according to this, the virtue of those four names of the holy angels whose names are a mixed vestige in the water.

[The Prayers Offered on that Friday]

Having done this, store the cup with water in a clean place and immediately begin to read those prayers *Alpha et omega, etc., Heliscemaht, etc.; [Ph]os Megal[os], etc.; Lux mundi, etc.*[290] These are the first prayers of the art, and having made a short interval, you must offer those ten prayers of the order which are written as the penultimate of that art, the first of which begins *Omnipotens, incomprehensibilis, etc.*[291] With the nine others following after it, indeed, having made a short interval, you must offer the last nine prayers, which are called *termini,* of which the first begins *Genealogon, etc.*[292] For you will say these prayers of the order thus, on that very Friday in the early morning once. Around the third [hour] you must offer them in the same manner, you must read them once again around noon, but on the third and noon [hours] you must not drink from the water. Specifically, on that very Friday you will fast on bread and water, and you must not eat until after noon; that is, after the completion of the operation.

[On Day 14, Saturday]

Specifically, on Saturday morning you must drink from your water as many times as you did on the preceeding day, and say the same words and the same

289. *Bonitatem, etc.* Psalms 119:66 (NRSV). The Latin text is translated here to suit the author's goal of learning the seven liberal arts, philosophy, theology, etc.; however, the psalm, in its own historic context, suggests a translation that would reflect a focus on learning God's commandments. The NRSV Bible provides the following English translation: "Teach me good judgment and knowledge, for I believe in your commandments."

290. That is, *Alpha et Omega* and the first three headwords.

291. That is, the ten prayers of the *Ars Nova.*

292. Sections 127a through 127i.

way you offer the same prayers once, similarly around the third [hour], and similarly around noon. On the very day you will fast until noon, and then you are able to eat fish and other Lenten foods, and to drink wine without superfluity and drunkenness.

[On Day 15, Sunday]

Specifically, on the Lord's day you offer the same prayers once at the same hours just as you did on the other two days, and having completed your work, you will be able to eat meat and other things you want and to dine in the evening, and thus you will not fast on that day, but pay out to nine poor people or more almsgiving.

[Re-creating the Saffron and Rosewater Tea]

You will be able to re-create your water with the leaves in any morning of those three days if you want to make it the same way as you did on the first day, or you will be able to drink from the very same if you want on those three days, but you must not drink from it except only in the early morning of any day in the beginning of your work. Also, you must know that you will be able to re-create the leaves, the cup, and the water on any day of the week of any month in the early morning in your operation—that is, in any beginning of your work—or if you wish you will be able to re-create the aforesaid thrice in any week (namely, Monday, Wednesday, and Friday) and always in the early morning before the beginning of your work.

The first operation of the three days at the beginning of this work ends [here].

[The Interim Period]

[**126f Gloss**] But these three days, having been completed thus, just as it is said, another is to be made, because on the other days following those three days if some are left over up to the New Moon of that month in which you ought to ordinarily begin working, you will read and offer *Alpha et omega, etc.,* and *Omnipotens, incomprehensibilis, etc.,* with the other nine prayers[293] written after

293. The ten prayers of the *Ars Nova*. Recall that in gloss 126d it says that the ten prayers of the

them, on any day as often as it will be pleasing to you, and in those hours in which you will be able to intend [to do so].

For in these days in which you offer these prayers, any hour is not to be seen beforehand, but they are able to be said day and night, before lunch and after lunch, neither is it necessary to have the aforesaid water nor to drink from that, but one is to be guarded against mortal sins like lechery, drunkenness, perjury, theft, murder, and similar actions.

Also, you ought to enter school and to hear about that knowledge for which you want to work in the subsequent months.

Still, you must know that, but if you are able to speak the order [of the prayers] on those days, all the prayers together, on any day on the same hours, drinking from the water and doing just as you did in the first three days, it would be much more profitable to you; it is not needed to fast on those days on account of this except up to noon, and then you are able to eat meat and all the other things which are pleasing to you.

[The Angelic Vision]

For this operation of these three days and of the others following, if any [of those days] are up to the beginning of the ordered work,[294] having been finished thus, just as we have said, [then] it shows and reveals to the worker through an angelic vision whether he is worthy to begin such a work and to what end he will be able to arrive, and if he ought to proceed to the following operation. Therefore, if it is prohibited to him according to the angelic vision to dismiss the work, [then] it is to be dismissed, and he ought not to proceed any further, and he ought to consider if he might be in any sin from which he was not confessed; for if it is instructed to him, he must keep secret the mandate and he is not to reveal that vision to anyone, but he may proceed in the work under these circumstances just as the art instructs.

Ars Nova are kept separate from the *novem termini* following the three-day ritual part.

294. The ordered work consists of the operations conducted in the lunar months. The angelic vision may occur at the end of the operation of the three days or even during the interim period just before the first day of the lunar month (i.e., the new Moon).

[The Greater Ritual Begins]

The first operation of the first month begins:
On the first day of the new lunar month, following after the aforesaid first operation, in the early morning you should have another four leaves, new and fresh, as you had before, and you must write on them the same names of the [same] order just as you did on Friday, when you began, and erase [them] in water, and drink from it four times just as before and say the same words, and after drinking you begin to say these prayers in the name of your God *Alpha et omega, etc.;*[295] *Helyscemaht, etc.; Theos, Megale, etc.; Lux mundi, etc.,*[296] which are prayers in the beginning of the order, and having made a short interval, you must offer all those prayers following together just as they are placed through the order up to those nine prayers following which are called "the *novem termini*";[297] of those prayers—that is, those you ought to read—the first begins, *Lux, veritas, etc;* second, *Domine sancte Pater, etc;*[298] and all others of the order written up to that place which I had said before.[299] For you may say these prayers on any day of that month as often as you will be able, at all hours of the day and night in which you will be able, and it is not necessary to have from the water nor to drink from that except once a day (that is, in the early morning), nor is it to be fasted on any day. Also, you must go to school and listen attentively about that knowledge for which you are working, and it is to be done thus from these prayers in that month until the end of the lunar [days of the] month of that [calendar] month.

The second operation of the second month begins:
For on the first day of the new lunar month of the second month following, the operation is to be done differently. Therefore, in the early morning of that first day of the lunar month you have prepared your four leaves,[300] the cup, and the

295. Variation 1 gloss.
296. The first three headwords (sections 7, 10–11).
297. The *novem termini,* meaning "the nine ends," which refers to their last placement within the order of the prayers and the greater ritual as a whole, can be found at sections 127a through 127i.
298. The thirty-two prayers mentioned in section 126c gloss.
299. The other prayers include the General prayers from *Assaylemaht* to *Semoht Lamen,* as mentioned in section 126c gloss.
300. Véronèse says this passage was to be written in the margin as indicated by a reference sign in the text, but the folio was cut. He says he follows BnF Latin 7153.

water to be re-created again, and you must do them in the proper order just as you did above, and drink from the water, and say *Bonitatem, etc.,* four times, and after drinking you may begin to read *Alpha et omega, etc.; Helyschemaht, etc.; Theos Megale, etc.; Lux mundi, etc.; Lux, veritas, vita, etc.; Domine sancta Pater, etc.,* and all those other prayers following and of the order after them, written up to the last nine prayers,[301] just as it was said in the preceding month. All these prayers you say as often as you will be able at all hours of the day and of the night through the three days—that is to say, on the first, second, and third day of the new lunar month—and in those three days you will not fast nor dismiss your studies nor your other business affairs.

Accordingly, on the fourth day in the early morning you must drink from the water you re-created just as you should, and after drinking you must read with the greatest devotion, hope, and faith, these prayers once *Alpha et omega, etc.; Helyschemaht, etc.; Theos, Megale, etc.; Lux mundi, etc.* Having said these, having made some interval with a humbled pronunciation, you must offer these prayers which follow, of those the first is *Asseylemath, etc.; Hazaylemaht, etc.; Lemath [Sebauthe], etc.; Lamehc [Leynac], etc.; Deus summe Deus [invisibilis], etc.; Te queso, Domine, etc.*[302] Having said and read these prayers once, you can go to school to hear your lectures, but you must see beforehand, so that you return to [your] home sometime before the third [hour], and around the third [hour] you must read the same prayers once again, specifically, around noon once, or between noon and the ninth [hour] once, around the evening [hour] once, and it is to be done thus concerning these very prayers on the very fourth day. Indeed, in a similar manner and form, the same prayers are to be said after the fourth day on the eighth day and not before, just like on the twelfth day, just like on the sixteenth day, just like on the twentieth, just like on the twenty-fourth, just like on the twenty-eighth, [and] just like on the thirtieth day. Therefore, these aforesaid prayers ought to be pronounced four times a day during the eight days of that month. But on any of those eight days it is to be fasted on Lenten foods, and you should not eat until any daily operation is completed; that is, after the evening. And it is to be lived

301. The *novem termini.*

302. See section 126c gloss. The last two Latin prayers, *Deus summe Deus* and *Te queso Domine,* may not have been intended to be spoken in the second month. Rather, we see these two prayers are to be said on the favorable lunar days in the third month. See the text below.

in those eight days more soberly, chastely, and cleanly than on other days.

For on all other days of that month, except those eight, those prayers which are to be said once in the early morning, which they have been said on the first day of the month and in the other hours of the day and night to one's pleasure, since how many more are to be offered so much more are all the Latin prayers beneficial. Also, it is to be understood since those prayers which are to be read in those eight days only, they should not be read on the other days, and the other prayers which are to be read on other days are not be read in those eight,[303] yet, you can read them well if you wish, and you can read day and night, but if you cannot, [then] it does not happen as you wish. Also, if you cannot fast during those eight days until after the evening [hour, then] you must see beforehand any hour in which it is not necessary for you to read those prayers, and this is the proper operation of these prayers in the second month.

The operation of the third month and the last prayers begins:

Having completely finished these in the first day of the new lunar month of the third month following, re-create your leaves, the water, and the cup, and make from these just as you did above, and drink from that and say *Bonitatem, etc.*

Then you begin to read *Alpha et omega, etc.; Helyscemaht, etc.; Theos, Megale, etc.; Lux mundi, etc.* Having said these, this prayer, which in the preceding month was offered last with its own prologue, which the prayer is *Deus summe Deus invisibilis, etc.; Te quaeso, Domine, etc.,* is to be offered again,[304] and having made an interval, this prayer, *Lamehc, Ragna, etc.; Memoria irreprehensibilis, etc.,*[305] is to be offered, and, having made a short interval, you must offer these others: *Hazatham, etc.; Hyelma, etc.; Confirma, consolida, etc.;*

303. The prayers to be read only on the eight days (4th, 8th, 12th, 16th, 20th, 24th, 28th, and 30th) include *Alpha et Omega, Helyscemaht, Phos Megalos, Lux mundi, Assaylemaht, Azaylemaht, Lemahc Sebauthe, Lamehc Leynac, Deus summe Deus invisibilis,* and *Te quaeso Domine.*

304. The doublet of the offering of *Deus summe Deus invisibilis* and its Latin prologue, *Te quaeso Domine,* in the second and third months may signal a scribe's misunderstanding and/or redaction to the original *Flores Aurei.*

305. *Lamen Ragna* and its Latin prologue, *Memoria irreprehensibilis,* is the fifth sequence of the General prayers. Notice the glosser omitted the fourth sequence, *Iesu Dei Filius,* and its second part, *Eleminator Caudones,* whether intentionally or neglectfully.

Agloros, etc.; Megal, etc.; Hanuiriahel, etc.; Ego in conspectus tuo, etc.[306] For you must offer these prayers just as it is said in the early morning of that first lunar month once, around the third [hour] you must offer them thrice, around noon thrice, around the ninth [hour] thrice, and it is to be done thus on the very first day of these prayers.

Specifically, these prayers have to be offered on certain days of the month and not in all, which days are days of the lunar month, the first, the third, sixth, ninth, twelfth, fifteenth, eighteenth, twenty-first, twenty-third, twenty-sixth, twenty-ninth, and thirtieth day, which is the last day of the lunar month, and thus they ought to be offered through the twelve days in the month and no more, and on which hours of the day and how often they are offered on any day; you may see in the gloss that begins: *Oratio autem in prima Luna, etc.*[307] For on these twelve days it is to be fasted on any day on Lenten food, and assign yourself a hour of eating in which it is not necessary to read, or if you can first complete the operation of the day before you eat.

For on the other days of that month, except those twelve up to the fifteenth day, you must offer once in the early morning of any day *Alpha et omega, etc.; Helyscemaht, etc.; [Ph]os, Megal[os], etc.; Lux mundi, etc.,* and having made an interval, you must offer these following prayers: *Ezethomos, etc.; Domine Deus incomprehensibilis, etc.; Domine Deus sancta Pater, etc.; Deus semper via, etc.; Lemogethon, etc.; Vita hominum, etc.; Omaza, etc.;*[308] *Deus Pater [immense . . . magnitudo], etc.; Gemozeton, etc.; Rex aeterne, etc.; Deus totius pietatis, etc.; Deus Pater immense [. . . misericordissime], etc.*[309]

You must offer these prayers thrice in a day, once in the early morning, once around the third [hour], and once around noon, and you may not eat until after noon, but then you may eat whatever meat and other provisions you want.

But on the fifteenth day, having said those prayers once in the morning,

306. The sixth sequence of the General prayers are listed here from *Hazatam* and its Latin prologue, *Confirma* to *Hanuyrlyhahel / Ego in conspectus*. Notice that the Latin prologue, *Deus omnium,* which belongs to *Agloros,* is missing. Likewise, notice that the Latin prologue, *Veritas lux et vita,* which belongs to *Megal,* is also missing.

307. Section 40 gloss.

308. *Rex regum* is missing.

309. The prayers belonging to philosophy.

having made some interval after that prayer which begins *Hanuirihabel, etc.,*[310] say that one written following after that very one which begins *Gemoht, Geel, etc.,* with the other two following, *Omnipotens, sempiterne Deus, etc.; Semoht, Lamen, etc.,* of the order; and having made some interval, you must successively offer the other prayers just like on the following day, of which the first begins *Ezethomos, etc.,* with the others through the following order. And it is to be done thus concerning these from the fifteenth day of the lunar month up to the end, except those twelve days in which the other prayers are offered.

Specifically, on those twelve days, after any operation of any hour of any day, you must inspect the scrolls of that knowledge for which you are working and look inside reading some chapters here and there. All these prayers you must offer with great devotion, because these are the keys of the trivium and quadrivium, and this operation is of all the prayers of the entire work for acquiring memory, eloquence, and understanding and to acquiring the foundation of any knowledge.

The fourth operation of the fourth and last month up to the operation of figures begins:

Having finished all these fully, perfectly, and completely and just as it is said, it is to be arrived at with respect to the inspection of the figures of this art for whose knowledge you have labored so much. Therefore, on the first day of the new lunar month keep [your] house secret and far away from the noise of people, may you not be impeded by some [people], and you have with you your servant who administers to you and provides your necessities; however, he must not be with you while you will be in your operation; that is to say, when you pronounce and read your prayers and inspect their figures and signs. However, if you were less knowledgeable and ignorant of the art and its operation, you have a master teacher who can teach and instruct you, but it is not permitted for you to have another associate, ergo you are alone and no one knows the location in which you are working with respect to the figures, unless you are able to have your servant and your master teacher, if anyone.

And on the very day, at the dawn of the day, re-create your four leaves and

---

310. The fifteenth day is a favorable day, so the operator would have pronounced from the third sequence of General prayers; namely, *Deus summe Deus invisibilis* and its Latin prologue, *Te queso Domine,* up to *Hanuiriahel* and its Latin prologue, *Ego in conspectus.*

write the names mentioned above on them, and keep a cup full with water, and do just as you did in the other months, and drink four times, saying, *"Bonitatem et disciplinam et scientiam doce me, etc.,"* and while you said thus, reading these prayers once in the early morning, *Alpha et omega, etc.; Helyscemaht, etc.; Theos, Megale, etc.; Lux mundi, etc.*

Having read these, having made some interval, you read the prayers *Gemoht, Gehel, etc.; Omnipotens, sempiterne Deus, etc.; Semoht, Lamen, etc.*[311]

Having said these, having made some interval, you must offer these others: *Deus Pater immense [. . . magnitudo], etc.; Gezomothon, etc.; Rex aeterne Deus, etc.; Deus totius pietatis, etc.; Deus Pater [immense . . . misericordissime], etc.;*[312] *Lux, veritas, vita, etc.*[313]

Having read these once, the prayers of the particular figures or the figures which are written within and outside the figures are to be offered, and those particular prayers of the figures are to be read as often as it is described in the glosses of the teaching of any art.[314] For these prayers named above ought to be offered on any day [and] on any hour in the operation of the three liberal arts.

[Operation of the art of grammar figures:]

Therefore, if you want to work with respect to the figures of the art of grammar, you must see beforehand that gloss which begins *Sic enim notae gramaticae, etc.,*[315] and proceed to the inspection of the figures and their operation just as it is written there. However, no mention is made there about the three prayers which are to be appointed to the present teaching,[316] which they ought to be offered in the inspection of the figures of the art of grammar.

---

311. These prayers were added at the end of the ordinary days from Day 15 to Day 30 of the third month.

312. The prayers for the fifth, sixth, and seventh figures of philosophy. Recall that Version B is special in that it has *Deus Pater immense [. . . misericordissime]* as being paired with *Deus totius pietatis* as the seventh prayer of philosophy.

313. *Lux veritas,* the prayer given before the offering of the Specials.

314. That is, the prayers adorning the figures, which are often written within the figures. See page 303 in which they are written "outside" the figures, usually presented after the figures.

315. Section 78 gloss.

316. Section 78 gloss does not specifically name the three prayers belonging to the art of grammar, which are *Domine Sancte Pater [. . . imperfectum]* (section 128), *Respice Domine* (section 129), and *Creator Adonay* (section 130).

Operation of the dialectic figures:

Specifically, if you want to work with respect to the figures of dialectic you must see beforehand the other gloss following which begins *Sciendum est autem quod notae dialecticae, etc.,*[317] and there you will find the order and operation of the figures of the art of dialectic.

Operation of the art of rhetoric figures:

For if you want to work in the art of rhetoric and to proceed to the inspection of the figures these preceding prayers are to be said once in the early morning, and after them the prayers of the particular figures of this very art [of rhetoric] are to be offered, and those four signs which are placed and written before the two figures of the art of dialectic.[318] You must see beforehand the ordering of the operation's four figures of the art of rhetoric in that gloss which begins *Notae autem quattuor artis rectoricae, etc.*[319] For this is the order and operation of the figures of the three liberal arts, ergo, you must see beforehand the aforementioned glosses, and you do this just as it is written here and there, and thus you will obtain the perfect knowledge of the said arts.

Operation of the other figures of the four liberal arts:

For if you want to work in the other four liberal arts and to work from their figures as from the art of medicine, music, arithmetic, and astrology, on the morning of the first day of the lunar month, first having made the leaves and water just as it is said above, the prayers *Alpha et omega, etc.; Helyscemaht, etc.; Theos, Megale, etc.; Lux mundi, etc.,* are offered once, and having made some interval, the [prayers] *Gemoht, Geel, etc.; Omnipotens, sempiterne Deus, etc.; Semoht, Lamen, etc.,*[320] are to be read once, and having made an interval, the [prayers] *Lux, veritas, etc.;*[321] *Deus sancta Pater, etc.; Respice, Domine, etc.;*

---

317. Section 80 gloss.

318. Latin *quattuor signa,* meaning "the four signs," are seen on page 509. The four signs do not have their own prayers; however, they may have been referenced here for their valued information in presenting a logical argument which can be useful when composing and presenting a persuasive and rhetorical speech. For an analysis of the signification of these four signs, see chapter V, pages 155–58.

319. Section 79 gloss.

320. The seventh sequence of the General prayers (sections 62, 64, and 69).

321. *Lux veritas* is given first before the special prayers.

Creator Adonay, etc.;[322] *Sancte Deus, etc.; Heloy clementissime, etc.;*[323] *Omnipotens [et misericors], etc.; Hanazay, etc.,*[324] are to be said once, and the others of the following order written after them, of which the last is *Adoro te, rex regum, etc.*[325] Having said these prayers once thus, the particular prayers of the figures are to be said as often as they are described in their own proper glosses, which are written successively and orderly, after those three liberal arts, of which the first begins *Ecce de reliquis quattuor liberalibus, etc.*[326] For in those written glosses you will see successively the order and operation of the figures of the four liberal arts, except for the three prayers which are placed in this location,[327] and not the other, because in the book it speaks separately and specifically about any section from its own proper material, but here, [in the book we speak] generally, ergo, you see beforehand those glosses which show the operation of the figures of the four liberal arts and you work from them just as it is written there and in that place.

On the operation of the [seven] general figures [of philosophy]:

But if you want to work from the general *notae,* [then] you must do it in the way just as it is taught in the others above, and you must see that gloss which begins *De notis autem generalium, etc.,*[328] and do just as it is written here and there.

On the operation of the [four] figures of [the general sciences classified as] the mechanical arts [which includes the exceptive arts]:

For if you want to work from the figures through which the seven sciences of the mechanical arts are to be acquired, [then] you must do just as it is said in the others, and you must see beforehand that gloss which begins *De notis autem omnibus iam initialis, etc.*[329]

---

322. The three prayers belonging to grammar.

323. The two prayers belonging to logic/dialectic.

324. These two prayers belong to rhetoric. Notice that *Hanazay* takes the second position; compare this order to the order of section 126c gloss, which has *Omnipotens et misericors* and *Adonay.* See page 447, footnote 265.

325. From *Lux veritas* to *Adoro te rex regum,* there are eighteen prayers, the first portion of the thirty-two prayers listed in section 126c gloss.

326. Section 85/86 gloss.

327. The seventh sequence of the General prayers.

328. Section 87 gloss.

329. Section 88 gloss.

On the operation of the figures of theology:
But if you want to work from the figures of theology, you must see beforehand the gloss which begins *Que orations quattuor artibus, etc.*[330]

[About the *Notae* Supplement]

For in these ordered, written, and successive glosses, you see the order and operation of all the figures of the seven liberal arts, the seven mechanical and exceptive [arts] in the book. But pay close attention to this, because [the glosses] are in the operation of whatever figures and whatever art. It is to be fasted on Lenten food on any day in which he is working. Also, after the pronunciation of all the prayers of whichever figure, he ought to open the scrolls of that knowledge for which you are working, yet before inspecting the figure itself and its signs. Also, you ought to read some sections within [that scroll]. Also, after the inspection of those figures on which you are working, you ought to inspect once those four signs which are written before the figures of the art of dialectic.[331] Also, in all the aforesaid operations, having performed and finished in this way the prayers and figures through the three days after the completed operation, you must say the first three headwords once, and having made some interval, you say those last nine prayers which are called *termini* with those other preceding ten thrice in a day, once in the early morning, once around the third [hour], and once around noon, and this is done for the conservation of the acquired knowledge. But in those last three days, you will fast on Lenten food, and you must not eat until that daily work is completed; that is to say, until after noon.

[Closing Summary]

And you, O creature of God, who works in this holy art, and you accept the audacity for working, living chastely, and with the greatest faith and devotion offer the Latin and Greek prayers, especially because they are invocations of the holy names of heavenly angels, whose office is to intercede in this holy work and to administer the operation. And if you did thus, just as it is taught in

330. Section 97 gloss.
331. See page 465, footnote 324.

the teachings of that art, [then] you will have the memory for retaining everything heard, the eloquence in all things, having been offered eloquently, the wisdom and knowledge of the seven liberal arts, the seven mechanical and exceptive [arts], and the entire philosophy through this most sacred art—that is, offering the prayers successively and orderly, just as it is said—and you have inspected the figures of the said arts, [and] you will be able to acquire, have, and retain [the arts] in memory in a brief period of time, because it is made worthy to present to you, he who lives and reigns through the infinite age of ages, amen.

The teachings of the entire operations of all the figures of that highest art of memory ends [here]. Thanks be to God, amen.

[*Novem Termini*]

[127a] *The first terminus begins, and these last nine prayers Solomon received by the angelic hand on the altar:*

Genealogon, Renealogon, Benealogon, Saphay, Sazayham, Saphya, Zede, Zemoziham, Zemozihel, Sanamam, Samna, Geguogual, Samyhel, Ieremyhel, Horacihotos, Hetha, Syhothos, Sepharaym, Henemos, Genozabal, Iemerabal, Hethemel, Genothoram, Genorabal, Semyha, Semna, Mynarom, Imnathon, Geristol, Hymacton, Chalos, Phabal, Resaram, Marachiel, Naracheos, Ietriuancho, Iezihathel, Sephoros, Thesirara, Zepharonay, Hazana, Messyhel, Sother, Hazihel, Semythros, Chiel, Hamacal, Hacor, Zemothor, Sanaday, Morochochiel, Semenos, Sacabis, Themay, Horel, Remay, Renay, Zemel, Haza, Gemol, Zemelaza, Gomol, Iemezihel, Zemey, Zemeihacon, Zechor, Helychos, Semey, Semie, Hiacon, Iechor, Meholym, Hazenethon, Semase, Mepathon, Zemolym, Systos, Heloy, Semegey, Manos, Helypos, Hemychopos, Geys, Seray, Sephec, Sephamanay, Helyhothos, Cherobalym, Hazenethon, Hysistos, Domengos, Iemyrobal, Samanathos, Semaham, Behenos, Megon, Hanythel, Iothomeros, Ielamagar, Remeleht, Genay, Demathamos, Hathamyr, Seryhon, Senon, Zaralamay, Sabayhon.

[127b] *The second terminus begins:*

Geolym, Hazenechon, Ysistos, Heloy, Sephey, Manay, Helyhotas, Ierobalym, Remalet, Genay, Hehyhotos, Domatamos, Hatamyr, Seryhon, Hamynyr, Senoz, Magamagol, Sechar, Senam, Magel, Hel, Helymothos, Helseron, Zeron, Phamal, Iegromos, Herimyhoton, Lautamos, Haramaton, Laudamos, Lanaymos, Sephacyhel, Sephazihel, Hagenalys, Legenale, Hegernar, Stanazihel, Stancihel, Hathanathos, Hegregebal, Rogor, Heremynar, Heneryman, Marochon, Marathon, Iecharnaym, Henemos, Iezeduhos, Gezconos, Sabam, Geguaray, Helychithym, Helestimeym, Sepharma, Mathar, Saphar, Manatham, Bezay, Samay, Sephay, Sihamathon, Balazayr, Samamar, Hamyhel, Marmamor, Henemos, Iegohomos, Samar, Sabar, Hamyhel, Gezamahel, Sacramay, Iezamathel, Hamansamol, Hamazamoly, Geromol, Gezemon, Sycromal, Iezabal, Samna, Zama, Hathanathos, Theos, Helyhene, Zelym, Helyhem, Hezelym, Crymemon, Henethemos,

Gegeuol, Hemchemos, Iamam, Harachanam, Megon, Meguonthemon, Sirmay, Hethemel, Hemel, Sechor, Helsechor, Sofornay, Behelchor, Sesalihel, Thanahel, Homyhal, Iezahel, Zemahel, Homal, Guomaguos, Semayr, Iechor, Nomemal, Gehamguo, Genayr, Iecorname, Malyhaguathos, Hachamol, Iecromaguos, Maguarht, Noynemal, Haguathos, Hamathalys, Iecoraguos, Sammazihel, Ieconayl, Hesuogem, Thocorym, Mynamtha, Namaytha, Thanaym, Rauvara, Sanayhel, Hemnogenton, Lanamyhel, Gehemguor, Gemyhothar, Lamnamyhel, Sezihel, Magob, Samanay, Haganal, Mena, Ferymay, Sarramay, Lanamyhel, Guohemguor, Gemothar, Lamnamyhel, Sezyhel, Magol, Samanay, Haganal, Mena, Ferymay, Saranay, Lanamyhel, Guohenguor, Gemothar,[332] **Lamnamihel, Sezihel, Maguob, Samanay, Hagamal, Mena, Ferymay, Sarramay, Latham, Lihares, Lethan, Agihel, Nathes, Samayr, Liazer, Egihel, Thanazihel, Hataros, Tazayhel, Hataraz, Hacacho, Harona, Semyday, Hacca, Choharon, Semelay, Iamyhe, Iazabal, Laverechabal, Iammeze, Chabal, Sumachoros, Hacoronathos, Sathanahel, Hariham, Zachar, Harachar, Haziher, Zechar, Hazyhem, Hazacar, Locragemar, Hazanachar, Hameguar, Semal, Gehem, Negemar, Hemeguol, Semam, Hatamanos, Hatymayros, Retyhamos, Hamogual, Semar, Temnalamos, Sebranay, Sebamnay, Baruchata, Ialon, Hespuhos, Ramel, Semal, Renylsemar, Ielamacron, Ielama, Crymysayber, Seger, Sayher, Ierologuos, Iegemaguolon, Geremaguosam, Hamynos, Iamozyha, Iozyhon, Iacuoziha, Haguozyo, Ierologuos, Hazeogihon, Hamynos, Hamyr, Macharyhon, Machanon, Senos, Helyhothon, Zenos, Semiar, Lamar, Lamaral, Secronalon, Gemal, Secromaguol, Sacromehal, Lamagil, Lamayl, Secoham, Sochoyro, Mayhol, Sacromoguol, Genos, Theomegen, Nycheos.**

[127c] *The third terminus begins:*

Agenos, Theomogentheos, Hathanathos, Kyrihel, Ypolys, Ypile, Kariel, Cristopholys, Hon, Ymasyhor, Ymas, Harethena, Chenathon, Leonbon, Boho, Usyon, Geromeguos, Hagenoy, Hysithon, Geromagol, Hagyhamal, Latham, Zarihamal, Seriar, Phechonahal, Geconahal, Lacramagual, Sehar, Sehan, Iezeron, Genomoly, Ienomos, Iezoro, Nomeros, Henahihel, Gemehagate, Ienuha, Iechenmahos, Myhayhos, Semana, Hahel, Semahel,

332. Notice the repetition of this series of names, whether intentional or scribal error.

Hoteyhos, Hatazayhos, Saphar, Nemenomos, Hoeyhos, Hataz, Hayhos, Seyha, Chomo, Chomotanay, Laman, Sanamyr, Lamuhar, Lamanazamyr, Leunar, Hagramos, Generamosehc, Senyha, Exhagal, Hamagron, Semaharon, Semyr, Haramna, Mamagil, Haramatha, Mothana, Ramay, Iose, Ramaht, Hanaramay, Iole, Christus, Hamyristos, Hamyrrihos, Charothos, Carotheos, Ruchanos, Geros, Ielos, Salehc, Semamarym, Iasol, Salem, Schunamaym, Hallehuma, Haristeyz, Bohem, Ruhos, Halla, Samyey, Siloht, Samyhel, Hallenomay, Samychy, Methonomos, Iethonomos, Geconomay.

[127d] *The fourth terminus begins:*

Genathores, Sanamacathos, Guanathores, Zanothoros, Genomos, Ienazar, Semna, Marachos, Senather, Sematheher, Senachar, Cherub, Iamam, Exihel, Chublamam, Hesihel, Sethey, Semylihel, Zomyhel, Genocomel, Thanyham, Machar, Hacay, Hazanacay, Theos, Hamanacar, Hazanehar, Theconay, Chihatar, Theothen, Namacar, Semiales, Samyha, Hesata, Semialy, Hesamen, Semiahes, Sarcihate, Nazihatel, Hanazihathel, Pamylihel, Haziathel, Hagenoron, Haienozem, Haienorozom, Samaht, Samohc, Habisninahc, Hendon, Habisanahat, Tyngehen, Tragohem, Hazamgery, Hazamaguem, Lemehot, Hasomgery, Iemoyhoc, Semyha, Rihahathon, Semymarihaton, Semynar, Zihoton, Zaguam, Horay, Honethe, Hoparothos, Nahamala, Rothos, Hazata, Helralatos, Horecha, Horalotos, Haralo, Lothos, Geno, Zabahal, Lemaht, Hezetha, Lematalmay, Halmay, Iemalys, Sethomatal, Halmarlemaht, Sechamazal, Rabasadayl, Semnaziel, Semachiel, Iechom, Hagihal, Genomychos, Samihas, Ienemeros, Samma, Zasamar, Hazamyha, Sanar, Hasamyha, Hazaymam, Thaguoro, Laudochepharon, Thagromathon, Landothes, Pharon, Decarpe, Medihos, Decarpenridihos, Decapothen, Duhemelathus, Decaponde, Dihamelathos, Semyharyht, Samyhan, Genathely, Zazamar, Sazamar, Myremoht, Sacharios, Iemyliham, Sacrehos, Saphorenam, Saphoro, Megon, Hassahamynel, Hazaa, Myrahel, Gerizo, Ieristo, Symithos, Hothos, Hymycros, Otheos.

[127e] *The fifth terminus begins:*

Semathymoteham, Zemathiotheos, Hesapopa, Hezaphopanos, Gramyhel, Garamanas, Saphomoron, Gelbaray, Ieblaray, Hecidiham, Henzan,

Hezidiam, Canazpharys, Hanathesyon, Canastphasis, Holythos, Hosstyhon, Samatyhel, Zamayhel, Semyramoht, Sachanos, Gecabal, Hostosyon, Lemeliham, Saphara, Negon, Zaramyhel, Zamyrel, Geriston, Symyhoros, Hocho, Hadalomob, Vagem, Nagenay, Megos, Naymogos, Semazihar, Helaph, Herlo, Holopheo, Helepherno, Lopheo, Hornobahoteo, Indehc, Heribegyl, Roguohon, Indocricib, Vegal, Neguabel, Memoht, Hemel, Gemoht, Saguanar, Thalapalos, Zenozamyhel, Iesagat, Genoz, Hamel, Guaramaziel, Gerathar, Sathamyhanos, Sahamuham, Guamazihel, Mathelaglilos, Ieraguaht, Sathamyham, Hurihel, Phalomagos, Phabomgros, Iocho, Megom, Saraht, Sazaysac, Heramylithos, Carmelythos, Hezaladuha, Hezeladam, Hysihel, Hemal, Usyon, Lamal, Raguam, Sablachom, Sabsatom.

[127f] *The sixth terminus begins:*

Gerogueguos, Ieronehos, Samanachor, Sazanacoray, Zamachoray, Sanatyhel, Lamamathios, Sanazyel, Thamyquyol, Zararahel, Kyrion, Zamynel, Kyrys, Cromemon, Karistomenon, Sacronomay, Soromono, Hestympandos, Ietham, Panydos, Methalamathon, Merasamaty, Sabarna, Hehihama, Guathamal, Hemdamyhos, Thega, Myhabal, Teguamathal, Chathanathel, Tehogethos, Tehoguos, Savanazyhel, Theoguos, Canazay, Theneloyhos, Zenelyhos, Cachaliel, Theomeguos, Labdamylon, Laudamelyhon, Geroyhon, Ierocyhon, Lapda, Mezyhon, Homen, Samal, Samothya, Homy, Samal, Samazyho, Sachamenay, Samohaya, Sathomonay, Geromazihel, Lamohaytha, Guomazihel, Hoccho, Macalon, Hothomegalon, Zezomegalon, Guocazamanay, Hazatamel, Hazabanas, Iechco, Tynogualem, Sehor, Gehoraya, Haramanay, Harathatihel, Hasabamoht, Hamython, Lapdas, Hazatham, Thihel, Hazabanos, Hamathon, Hamalilihon, Samalyhon, Usyologyhon, Legyn, Heleys, Hymon, Matytilon, Theos, Helotoy, Saramazili, Samachily, Helamon, Thyhamon, Hel, Lamothiamon, Lagay, Lemechiel, Semezihel, Laymos, Lanof, Hazamathon, Themohan, Thanaton, Theon, Natharathon.

[127g] *The seventh terminus begins:*

Magnus, Maguol, Nazihatol, Sazihathos, Helyam, Mathon, Saphar, Nazathon, Gemegihel, Iemorihel, Sanayhel, Sazanyel, Saramel, Semyhel, Sezymel, Lebathon, Iarathon, Loratham, Basyhas, Lamnazo, Ronala, Mathathon,

Rasyhos, Layna, Chezo, Laymatham, Labynegual, Scomycros, Bazihos, Lamua, Labunegas, Herezemyhel, Pheamycros, Negemezyhal, Samalaguoram, Hanamyhos, Hanomos, Gracosihos, Gracomessyos, Sotyron, Genozepha, Chelahel, Zepastanelyos, Zepastonomos, Hamarazyhos, Hamarizihos, Senazihel, Geramatiel, Iecramatihol, Hasaguar, Hasagry, Paramyhot, Hapasyry, Haranamar, Senales, Haza, Guanamar, Semiagel, Secastologyhon, Genaguolos, Hagenolo, Thegos, Sozor, Hamay, Seroguomay, Serosamay, Iamaramos, Remolythos, Lammaramos, Zenon, Ierolen, Zabay, Perypaton, Harihac, Hananyhos, Crascosyhos, Graguomoysyhos, Sochiron, Genozempha, Zelahel, Zephastanehos, Hamaristihos, Senazihel, Geramatihel, Pazamyhol, Haphasy, Zinhazamanar, Senasel, Secaschologyhon, Genaguolos, Hegenole, Thegos, Sorozamay, Sozor, Hamay, Iamaramos, Zelyhon, Iezolen.

[127h] *The eighth terminus begins:*
Remolithos, Ypomelihel, Hazimelos, Samal, Hazaramagos, Gelomihel, Gezeno, Megual, Hanacristos, Hanaypos, Gemothehon, Samahot, Helyhemon, Hyalamum, Salamyhym, Hamynos, Gezelyhos, Sarcharay, Sartamy, Gechora, Maray, Iechozamy, Ieguoram, Myhamy, Theos, Agyos, Crehamnos, Ykarros, Hathanathos, Probyhos, Meguon, Hatazmazay, Hecoy, Urihel, Ielozihel, Saryb, Rogay, Halomora, Sarahihel, Harachathiel, Hechamazihel, Sezamaguay, Iechar, Hazaz, Zeleham, Zarapha, Iany, Yhesu Christe, Theos, Agios, Ykiros, Hathanatos, amen.

[127i] *The ninth and last terminus begins with the two prologues following:*
Hamolehon, Halugeon, Habhel, Migromeonathos, Hanatigal, Haglareon, Grinelam, Hebmothios, Heugene, Damigal, Thoregol, Symelon, Genoht, Hamam, Gedomoz, Phamazahos, Semelios, Gezamamym, Samarachy, Rehezobor, Ierdomoz, Vegel, Hanamay, Samay, Samistihos, Hagelos, Menoy, Hazena, Magar, Hamiros, Hazeton, Sycazomos, Secray, Hamizai, Hasamathar, Ysaramay, Nemeneos, Messelon, Genes, Sahal, Magalos, Ieleglola, Relegloma, Semaray, Iezara, Themar, Semesaht, Gerbohos, Nezologon, Mazihatol, Iezabamiham, Iezebachel, amen.

[Variation 12] *The first prologue of the said prayers begin and they ought to be said together:*

O God, creator of all things,[333] you who created all things out of nothing, you who created for the ordering all things step by step [and] wonderfully, and in the beginning, you founded heaven and earth, it is in your Son through whom all thing are made, in whom all things are, to whom all things are finally returned, you who are called the Alpha and Omega, and you are [the Alpha and Omega]! O Lord, I beg you, [as] an unworthy sinner, so that I may be able to see beforehand swiftly the desired end in this most sacred art, and may I prevail not to lose such a gift made for me by driving out my sins; O Lord, according to that ineffable compassion of yours, of which it is said, "the Lord has not made us according to our sins and nor will he repay us according to our iniquities."[334]

[Variation 13] *The second and last prologue of the aforesaid nine prayers begins and it ought to be offered last:*

O Wisdom of God, the incomprehensible Father,[335] O most merciful Son, repay me through your ineffable mercy your final gifts of knowledge; O Lord, you who are to bestow the worthy a gift to wonder at the manner of all the sciences, not looking upon our wicked deeds and deliquent actions, but mercifully providing a future gift for posterity. O most merciful one, I deprecate and entreat you, how long you open your hands to me, a most worthless sinner, an abundance, and in this art you bestow to me such an end through which your hand of generosity is bestowed powerfully onto me, so that, on account of this, I may prevail to spring back from my impious way and be able to walk devoutly onto the paths of your light, and thenceforth, command me to give others an example through which all who see and hear me are able to spring back from [their] vices, and to praise you through the entire age of ages, amen. May the name of the Lord be blessed from this now and forever, amen.

---

333. The prayer *Conditor omnium* is found in Agrippa's *Opera Omnia* (page 649, dated c. 1620) and also the derivative *Tractatus Artis Notoriae,* Amsterdam, Bibliotheca Philosophica Hermetica, M 242, fol. 25–26, 79–80, dated to the 17th century.

334. Psalm 103:10 (NRSV).

335. The prayer *O sapientia Dei Patris incomprehensibilis* is also in Agrippa's *Opera Omnia* (page 649, dated c. 1620) and also the derivative *Tractatus Artis Notoriae,* Amsterdam, Bibliotheca Philosophica Hermetica, M 242, fol. 80–81.

[Variation 14] *The General and Special prayers of the most sacred notory art and [the art of] memory ends through the operation of which a perfect memory is to be brought within [oneself] in all sciences heard, having been retained by memory, eloquence in all things retained, having been offered eloquently, the ingenuity and the understanding in learning and comprehending the sciences, and the [mental] stability in acquiring all the aforesaid [qualities] in their own hours [and] their own times, just as the teachings of the order [of the prayers and operations] are offered above.*

[Variation 15] *Now the figures are to be divided through the order of any art. Firstly, the seven liberal arts, namely, grammar, logic, rhetoric, medicine, music, arithmetic and astrology. Secondly, the figures of general sciences and philosophy are to be divided which are pertient to the seven mechanical arts, the exceptives, and similar [arts]. Thirdly, the figures of theology follow. Fourthly, and lastly, three figures follow, of which the first is the figure of chastity, the second of justice and peace, and the third and last the figure of reprehension. All the sciences of any of the abovementioned arts are to be acquired perfectly through their inspection, the proper operation, the pronunciation of their own proper and preceding prayers, and you will have a firm and stable foundation in them, because he, the Most High One, who attributed so great a gift to Adam and King Solomon, deemed it worthy to grant, he alone who lives and reigns, amen.*

[128, Version A]

[128 Gloss] *Domine sancte Pater, etc.* This prayer ought to be pronounced after that prayer *Lux, veritas, etc.,* during the inspection of the first figure of the art of grammar. Having made some short interval, the prayers written below the figure and the following prayer after those ought to be pronounced, and the figure and its very signs are always to be inspected.

[129, Version A]

[129 Gloss] *Respice, Domine, etc.* This Latin prayer ought to be pronounced after that other *Lux, veritas, vita, etc.,* during the inspection of the second figure, and after that, the prayers written below the second figure of the art of grammar are to be offered, and then, having finished those prayers, the figure itself is to be inspected, just as it has been said above.

[130, Version A]

[130 Gloss] *Creator Adonay, etc.* This Latin prayer ought to be offered before the third figure of the art of grammar. Still, *Lux, veritas, vita, etc.,* comes before that prayer, and after these the prayers written below the figure are to be offered, and having finished those, [the operation] is to come before the inspection of this very figure, and there ought to be some interval between the prayers which are to be read above the figure and those which are to be read below the figure.

[131, 132, 133, 134, 135, Version A]

[135 Gloss] *Sancte Deus Pater, etc.* It has been said above about the prayers which are pertinent to the inspection of the three figures of the art of grammar. Now it is to be said about those which are especially pertinent to the figures of the art of dialectic. Therefore, this prayer *Sancte Deus, etc.,* is to be pronounced before the first figure of the art of dialectic, still the other *Lux, veritas, etc.,* comes before [it], and after them, the prayers written below the figure are to be offered; nevertheless, let there be some interval between the prayers themselves; and having offered those, this very figure with its signs is to be inspected.

[136, 137, Version A]

[137 Gloss] *Heloy clementissime, etc.* This prayer ought to be pronounced before the second figure of dialectic; and having finished that, the prayers written below the figure ought to be offered, having made a short interval, and afterwards this very figure with its signs is to be inspected.

[138, Version A]

[138 Gloss] *Omnipotens, misericors, etc.* This Latin prayer with the following holy names of angels ought to be pronounced before the first figure of the art of rhetoric, nevertheless, the other prayer *Lux, veritas, etc.,* comes before [it], and having said these, [and] having made some interval, the prayers written through the order below the figure are to be offered,[336] and then this very figure and its signs are to be inspected, just as it has been taught.

[139, Version A]

[**139 Gloss**] *Unus, magnus, etc.* This prayer together with the other two following prayers, that is, *Usyon omnium, etc.* and *Azelechias, etc.*, ought to be pronounced before the second figure of the art of rhetoric; but having prolated first the other prayer *Lux, veritas, etc.,* For those four prayers, having been prolated, the prayers written below the figure[337] are to be offered, and following those, yet having made a short interval and after [that], the figure itself with its signs are to be inspected.

[**140**] *This prayer is to be offered together after the preceding one:*
Hanazay, Sazahoran, Hubisenear, Ghu, Hyrbaionay, Gymbar, Zonayl, Selchora, Zelmora, Hyramay, Lethohal, Ysaramel, Hammatha, Mathoys, Iaboha, Gechors, Cozomerag, Sozomeraht, Hamy, Phodel, Denos, Gerothagalos, Melyha, Thagahel, Sechamy, Salihelethon, Mecogristes, Lemenron, Hathaguon, Amyhon.

[**140 Gloss**] *Hanazay, etc.* In this prayer certain names of the holy angels are invoked in its prolation, which names ought to be read more devoutly when naming them than the other preceding Latin prayers, and that prayer *Hanazay, etc.,* should be pronounced, after a short interval, after the antecedent Latin prayer before the first figure of the art of rhetoric,[338] and after this prayer, the prayers written below the figure,[339] and having finished the prayers, the figure itself with its signs are to be inspected.

---

336. According to Version B, *Hanazay* (section 140, Version B) follows *Omnipotens et misericors* as belonging to the first figure of rhetoric. The adorning prayers of the first figure of rhetoric include *Lemor Lemoyz Iecholor* (NS 44–48), which has five parts (*Lemor Lemoyz Iecholor, Confiteor tibi Domine Deus rex celi et terra, O maiestas ineffabilis, Formator rerum Deus,* and *O gloriosa*).

337. The adorning prayer of the second figure of rhetoric is *Habytay,* which has a second part, *Potentia equalitas* (NS 54–55).

338. *Omnipotens et misericors,* the first prayer belonging to the first figure of rhetoric.

339. The adorning prayers of the first figure of rhetoric.

[141, Version A]

[Variation 7] *This prayer with the two preceding ought to be offered together:* **Azelechias,[340] Velozeos, Mohan, Zama, Saruelo, Hotehus, Saguaht, Adonay, Soma, Ienozothos, Hychon, Iezomothon, Sadahot, and you, O propitious God, strengthen in me your promises, just as you strengthened King Solomon through the same words, send to me, O Lord, the virtue from heavens that may strengthen my heart and illuminate my mind, strengthen, O God, my understanding and my soul, renew . . .[341] within me and wash me with the waters which are above the heavens, and pour out . . .[342] from your Spirit onto my flesh and in my viscera for the purpose of performing in accordance to your commandments and reconcile your judgments with the humility and charity with which you made heaven and earth, and created and formed man in your image and likeness, infuse the light of your brillance into my intellect, so that having been founded and rooted in your mercy I may love your name, and I may know and adorn you, and understand all the writings of this art, for this reason, how much these things are given and marked by God, and sent forth through the hands of the holy angels are a mystery of these figures, for which I may have and know all things in my intellect, my heart, and my mind, and may I constantly have the effect of your holy name, [having and knowing] . . . of this art,[343] and for the most glorious plan prevailing, amen.**

[Variation 7 Gloss] *Azelechias, Velozeos, etc.* In this prayer there are at the beginning certain names of holy angels which are to be named and invoked in the inspection of the second figure of rhetoric, which angels have to administer to the worker the grace for acquiring knowledge by inspecting the figure itself and its signs, and after these very names is a certain Latin prayer which is the impetration and deprecation addressed to God the almighty that it may please

---

340. *Azelechias [. . . regi Salomoni],* a prayer belonging to the second figure of rhetoric, which is only found in Version B (see also NS 51). This prayer follows *Unus magnus* (section 139).

341. The ellipsis represents the placeholder for which the operator would insert his desired area of study in rhetoric.

342. Another ellipsis to be filled in by the operator.

343. Another ellipsis to be filled in by the operator.

him and his angels of his divine grace by bestowing that most sacred gift that was granted to Solomon to bring forth to an effect. This prayer, after the other preceding two, having made some interval, is to be offered more devoutly than the other prayers before the second figure of the art of rhetoric, and immediately after this very prayer, the other names of the angels which are written below the figure[344] are to be offered.

[Variation 8] *This prayer is to be offered before the third figure of rhetoric:*
For I know,[345] because I am delighted for myself in the making of your wonderful and ineffable greatness, and you will give me the knowledge [of] . . .[346] (which you, [the petitioner], are promised that) for enduring through this work, according to your great and incomprehensible virtue, Theon, Haramalon, Zamoyna, Chamasal, Iethonameryl, Haryonachor, Iecomagol, Gelamagos, Remolyhot, Remanathar, Hariomolathar, Hananehes, Velomonathar, Hayozoroy, Iezabaly, through these most sacred, most glorious, profound, and most precious mysteries of God, augment the most precious efficacy, virtue, and knowledge within me and complete [that] . . . which you began, and reform [that] . . . which you showed within me, Zamabar, Henoranaht, Grevatyl, Samazatham, Iecornazay, O foundation, O Most High of all the goodness, the sciences, and virtue, bestow to your servant, [who] displeases you to avoid moral contagions, and may I be able to be satisifed[347] with your pure truth and holy intention, so that desiring your promise with all [my] heart in all things as much as laws as well as decrees, especially through these holy mysteries may I be understood and known to obtain . . . , and may I be well perfected in this art [and] thoroughly praiseworthy and eloquent, amen.

[Variation 8 Gloss] *Scio enim, quia delector, etc.* This holy prayer, whose beginning

344. The names of the angels consist of the adorning prayer *Habytay,* which has a second part, *Potentia equalitas* (NS 54–55), which belong to the second figure of rhetoric.

345. Latin *Scio enim,* this prayer belongs to the third figure of rhetoric (see also NS 56). *Scio enim* competes against *Usyon omnium* for the position as the second prayer belonging to rhetoric in Version B.

346. The ellipsis represents the placeholder for which the operator would insert his desired area of study in rhetoric. Three other ellipses follow, which are to be filled in by the operator.

347. Latin *satiari,* meaning "to be satisifed."

is a certain Latin invocation and deprecation before God, whose middle is an invocation and deprecation of the holy names of the blessed angels administering in this field of knowledge, whose end is a certain supplication in Latin addressed to God the almighty, so that it may please him through its virtue and the holy angels to bring forth this work from beginning to the desired end; [the prayer] ought to be pronounced before the third figure of the art of rhetoric, that other prayer, which is *Lux, veritas, etc.,* comes before [it], and after that prayer, having made an interval, that prayer which is written below the figure[348] is to be offered, and this very figure with its signs is to be inspected thus.

[142, Version A]

[142 Gloss] *Reverende, potens, etc.* This Latin prayer ought to be offered before the fourth figure of the art of rhetoric, that other prayer which is *Lux, veritas, etc.,* comes before [it]. Having said these, [and] having made a short interval, those names of the holy angels written below this very figure[349] ought to be pronounced by invoking the same names with the greatest obligatory service of veneration, whose angels have in their power the divine grace mediating this knowledge of canon and civil law to bring forth into effect. Indeed, having prolated these, the figure itself ought to be inspected by an open and attentive eye, and similarly, its signs, and after the inspection of this very figure, the scrolls of the art of rhetoric are to be unrolled, reading within some laws or other decretals or decrees here and there, and this is what is said in this place.

[143, Version A]

[143 Gloss] *Deus, iustus iudex, etc.* After the inspection of the half figure of arithmetic, this prayer, having made a short interval, ought to be pronounced with the other *Lux, veritas, etc.,* coming before [it], and having pronounced these, those holy names written below the figure with the subsequent Latin prayer ought to be pronounced and the figure itself ought to be inspected with

348. The adorning prayer *Hatanathel Sarihel* and its second and final part, *Genomythos Vehamal,* belong to the third figure of rhetoric (NS 58–59).

349. The adorning prayer *Senezemon Zenezemor* and its second and final part, *Hely Theos Iesaram,* belong to the fourth figure of rhetoric (NS 62–63).

great diligence, and after the inspection of this figure, the scrolls of the art of arithmetic are to be unrolled, reading some chapters within here and there. This same prayer ought to be pronounced before the first figure of the art of geometry.

[144, Version A]

[144 Gloss] *Deus, qui omnia numero, etc.* It has been said above about the Special prayers of the figures of the three liberal arts; namely, grammar, logic, and rhetoric. Now it is to be said about the prayers which ought to be pronounced above the two and a half figures of arithmetic. Therefore, this prayer, which is *Deus, qui omnia numero, etc.,* ought to be pronounced after that other which is *Lux, veritas, etc.,* in the inspection of the first figure of the art of arithmetic, and having read that, [and] having made some interval, those prayers that are written below the figure[350] ought to be pronounced through the order, and then the figure itself with all its signs ought to be inspected.

[145, Version A]

[145 Gloss] *Mediator omnium, etc.* After the inspection of the first figure of arithmetic, this prayer ought to be pronounced before the half figure of arithmetic, [and] that other prayer which is *Lux, veritas, etc.,* comes before [it]; and having finished that, [and] having made a short interval, that prayer written below the figure[351] ought to be pronounced, and the names of the angels which are written in the beginning, having been invoked and offered with great devotion, and the figure itself ought to be inspected with great understanding.

[146, Version A]

[146 Gloss] *Omnipotens sapientiae, etc.* This prayer, after the inspection of the first figure of geometry, having made some interval, ought to be pronounced before the second figure of geometry, still that one which is *Lux, veritas, etc.,*

---

350. The only adorning prayer belonging to the first figure of arithmetic is *Azelechyas [. . . mensura]* found at NS 76.

351. The adorning prayer *Thoemy Gruheguon* (NS 78) belongs to the half figure of arithmetic.

comes before [it]; and having prolated those, the prayers written below the figure[352] are to be pronounced, having made some interval, and then the figure itself is to be inspected, and after its inspection, the scrolls of that art are to be unrolled, reading chapters within here and there.

[**Variation 9**] *This prayer ought to be spoken before the second figure of theology:* **I adore you, O king of kings[353] and my God, and together my substance and my revelation, my memory and virtue, who at one time gave different kinds of languages to the builders at the tower,[354] and who poured an unction of the sevenfold [gifts of] Holy Spirit upon your holy apostles, and those idioms which they would teach us,[355] you granted through the virtue of your word in which you created all things from all the tongues you repeat the same to speak,[356] through the power of this sacrament, inspire my heart and pour in that dew of your grace, so that having breathed on the efficacy of this operation with the light of your Holy Spirit suddenly, I may be able to follow [with the Holy Spirit] the understanding and expedition of the tongue and this capable art and subtle ingenuity, amen.**

[**Variation 9 Gloss**] *Adoro te, rex regum, etc.* This Latin prayer ought to be pronounced in the inspection of the second figure of theology, having first spoken and read the five prayers[357] which ought to be pronounced first at the beginning of inspecting any figure of any art, and that other prayer, *Lux, veritas, etc.;* and having pronounced all these prayers thus, those most holy names ought to

---

352. There are two adorning prayers, *Honoy Theon* and *Iazen Hezachaly* (NS 124–25), which belong to the second figure of geometry, which is only found in Version B.

353. *Adoro te, rex regum,* the prayer belonging to the second *nota* of theology.

354. Tower of Babel. Genesis 11:1–9. See also the analysis of the second figure of theology in chapter V.

355. A possible reference to the individual teachings of the apostles, whose stories and missions are recorded in the New Testament apocrypha, including works such as the Acts of Peter, the Acts of Andrew, the Acts of Thomas, the Acts of Philip, and so on.

356. Glossolalia, or the speaking in tongues, is a blessing of the Holy Spirit upon the apostles, which is recorded in chapter 2 of the Acts of the Apostles. Thomas Aquinas said the gift of tongues was the ability to speak every language in order for the apostles to perform their missionary work. See *Summa Theologica,* question 176.

357. *Deus Pater immense [. . . magnitudo], etc.; Gezomothon, etc.; Rex eterne Deus, etc.; Deus totius pietatis, etc.; Deus Pater immense [. . . misericordissime].* These are the prayers belonging to the fifth, sixth, and seventh *notae* of philosophy.

be pronounced which are described within the figure itself, still having made some interval, and having said those, the figure itself with all its signs is to be inspected.

[**147**] *This says how different months are to be elected following the operation of different arts:*

We said above about the *termini* of this notory art in which the prayers are to be read and the *notae* are to be inspected. Now it remains to say how the aforesaid lunar months are to be inspected and to be discovered. But then it is not to be understood, [if] by chance, there may be deception.[358] Still, in the aforesaid [notory] art, I noted the lunar months which are in power and the gates of the holy angels in which the gates the holy angels descend by virtue of the Creator and his great power, and especially the great angel of the Lord who descends through the eastern gate. For there are certain months which are more useful for beginning this work than others.

Therefore, when you want to work on theology or astronomy in a fiery sign[359] or in the sign of a working master[360]—that is, beneath your [sign[361]—then] you may begin. Specifically, if [you begin] in grammar or logic, [then] the sign must be Gemini or Virgo; but if [you begin] in medicine or music, [then] it must be Taurus or Libra. If [you begin] in rhetoric, philosophy, arithmetic, or geometry, [then] it must be Gemini or Cancer, [but if] for the astrological art,

---

358. See 126e gloss, which explains how to avoid deception by properly calculating the first day of a lunar month.

359. The four classical elements and their characteristics are fire (hot and dry), earth (cold and dry), air (hot and wet), and water (cold and wet). In astrology, these elemental attributions are assigned to four groups of three zodiac signs each called, a triplicity. The fiery signs are Aries, Leo, and Sagittarius. The earthy signs are Taurus, Virgo, and Capricorn. The airy signs are Gemini, Libra, and Aquarius. The watery signs are Cancer, Scorpio, and Pisces.

360. It is not clear to which zodiac sign of the working master's natal chart is intended here. The best guess is the ascendant sign, the zodiac sign that is ascending on the eastern horizon at the moment of one's birth, since it has the greatest expression and meaning in a natal chart. Although, there are other signs to consider—the descendant, the Sun, and the Moon.

361. The operator's zodiac sign (whether ascendent, descendant, Sun, or Moon) must be superior to the zodiac sign of his master. That is to say, the order of the zodiac signs begins with the Sun in Aries and ends in Pisces. So if the operator's zodiac sign is Libra, then if the master's zodiac sign is Scorpio, then the operator may work in Scorpio for either theology or astronomy. But if the same operator has a master whose sign is Virgo, then the operator cannot work in the master's sign because it precedes his own.

[then] it must be Aries or Gemini, and these days are fortunate and free from malice and remain in a good place. For then all the heavenly powers and choir of angels rejoice[362] in these very lunar months and in those determined days and hours.

[147 Gloss] *Diximus superius, etc.* Above in the preceding written sections from the beginning up to here, shown through in their own sections about the virtue of the prayers of this most sacred art, and about the manner and form of their pronunciation and their operation, and the teaching of the operation, how the figures of all the arts (and especially the three liberal arts) ought to be inspected, and how often the prayers ought to be offered, and in which times, days, and hours these abovesaid ought to be worked.

In this present section, certain times of the year are assigned; that is, certain months whose lunar months are more useful to the operation of this most sacred art. Therefore, it is to be understood when in this holy art there are many prayers having diverse efficacies, under whose operation and prolation of different fields of knowledge of different arts are to be comprehended, and in the pronunciation of those, many and different names and divisions of the holy angels residing in supernal seats are named and invoked, to whom the holy angels have to administer by their virtue granted to them by God to the operator in this art for acquiring some knowledge and following as consequence the grace, the wisdom for which you labor, because the offices of the angels whose names are invoked in the prayers is the knowledge for which they are invoked to bring forth an effect.

Therefore, it is to be understood that, just as there are different fields of knowledge of different arts and in any of those the names of different angels which are to be acquired are to be invoked, of whom some have to administer to the operator grammatical knowledge, to another dialectic knowledge, to another rhetorical knowledge, to another theological knowledge, to another astronomical knowledge, and thus from each field of knowledge, in this way different times of different months are to be seen beforehand more than others to acquire these fields of knowledge, because, accordingly, they are different,

---

362. *Rejoice* is a technical astrological term meaning that a planet exhibits its attributes best when residing within the sign it rules.

because those holy angels whose names are to be invoked and deprecated for the purpose of administering the knowledge of the art of grammar have certain times and certain months in which they rejoice more than in other months, and then it is better to invoke them at [their] times [rather] than in other times in order to have the grace of those [angels].

But other angels who have to administer other liberal and mechanical sciences similarly have their own months in the year in which they rejoice, enjoy, and are more benevolent in those months more than in others [with regard to] pouring out their grace upon the one who works and invokes their names; hence, if you want to work for acquiring knowledge of the art of grammar or to acquire knowledge of the art of dialectic, [then] you must see beforehand those months in which that [zodiac] sign reigns, because the sign is said to be of Gemini and the sign of Virgo. But in that month in which the sign is Gemini to which it is called the month of May,[363] you begin to work for the purpose of acquiring knowledge of the art of grammar. But if you want to acquire the art of dialectic you must see beforehand the month of August in which month the sign of the Sun rules in Virgo.[364] But if you want to work in the art of rhetoric, you must see beforehand the month of May[365] in which the Sun is in Gemini.

If you want to work in medicine or music the sign of the Sun must be in Taurus, and thus, in the month of April.[366] But if you want to work for music, similarly, the sign of the Sun must be in Libra, and thus, in the month of September.[367] But if you want to work for theology and astronomy in a fiery month—that is to say, you must begin to work under a fiery sign—and thus, in the months of June, July, and August[368] or under your sign, the same sign of that month under which you were born. But if you want to work for arithmetic, geometry, or philosophy, [then] you must elect June in which the

363. Latin *Maius*. Under the tropical zodiac, the Sun is in Gemini from May 20 to June 20.

364. Under the tropical zodiac, the Sun is in Virgo from August 22 to September 22.

365. That is, the month of June.

366. Under the tropical zodiac, the Sun is in Taurus from April 19 to May 20.

367. Under the tropical zodiac, the Sun is in Libra from September 22 to October 22.

368. In the astrological sense, the only fiery sign of these months is Leo, which, under the tropical zodiac, the Sun is in Leo from July 23 to August 22. In a meterological sense, these are the summer months in the Northern Hemisphere and so would be designated as "fiery" months. For the medieval reader, astrology and meterology were studied together along with astronomy.

Sun is in Cancer.[369] Indeed, if you want to work for some knowledge of the mechanical arts, you must see beforehand the month of March in which the Sun is in Aries[370] or in April in which the sign of the Sun is in Gemini.[371] For these months are to be elected before the other months by reason of the names of holy angels which are to be invoked for the acquiring any knowledge, because at those times these heavenly powers rejoice who have to lead this work to an effect.

Nevertheless, in any month of the year any worthy person of both a good life and good conduct is able to begin this holy work and bring it to the best end. But it is better to begin this work in those months by reason of the power of the angels and by reason of the length of those days and hours. For it is to be attended to because it is to be said about electing these months for the purpose of the operation of said arts of the figures. This is to be seen beforehand in those months for the inspection of the figures of those arts for which these said months are elected. But another operation which is performed for acquiring memory, eloquence, and understanding and for the other prayers which are to be offered through the order before [the operation] is to come before the inspection of the figures is able to be done in any month of the year in which it pleases you more. But for the purpose of the inspection of the figures of the arts which are to be elected, these abovesaid months are [placed] before the other months,[372] and this is the knowledge given for the operation of all the liberal and mechanical arts.

369. Under the tropical zodiac, the Sun is in Cancer from June 20 to July 22.

370. Under the tropical zodiac, the Sun is in Aries from March 20 to April 19.

371. During the month of April, the Sun is either in Aries or Taurus.

372. That is, given priority.

5

Notae Supplement Version B

BnF Latin 9336

[NS 1] *This prayer ought to be offered first before this [first] figure [of grammar] and before all the other figures of this art.*

Light, truth,[1] *life, way, justice, compassion, fortitude, patience, preserve and save me, and have mercy on me.*[2]

[Grammar]

[NS 2] *This following prayer ought be pronounced immediately, after the antecendent, having made a short interval, after the preceding:*

O Lord, holy Father the almighty,[3] **eternal God, in whose sight all invisible things are the foundations of creatures, whose eyes have seen my imperfection, whose ears hear all things, whose charity is the heavens and earth filled with sweetness, you who saw all things before they were made, and who sees before they are made, in whose book all days are formed and men inscribed in it; O Lord, today look over your servant, subjected to you**

1. *Lux, veritas,* the first prayer spoken before all the Special prayers. See section 82.
2. Many of the *Ars Notoria* prayers imitate or allude to biblical passages. *Miserere mei [deus]* references Psalm 51 (NRSV), one of the penitential psalms used in Jewish and Christian liturgy.
3. *Domine Sancte Pater [. . . imperfectum],* the prayer belonging to the first figure of grammar. See section 128.

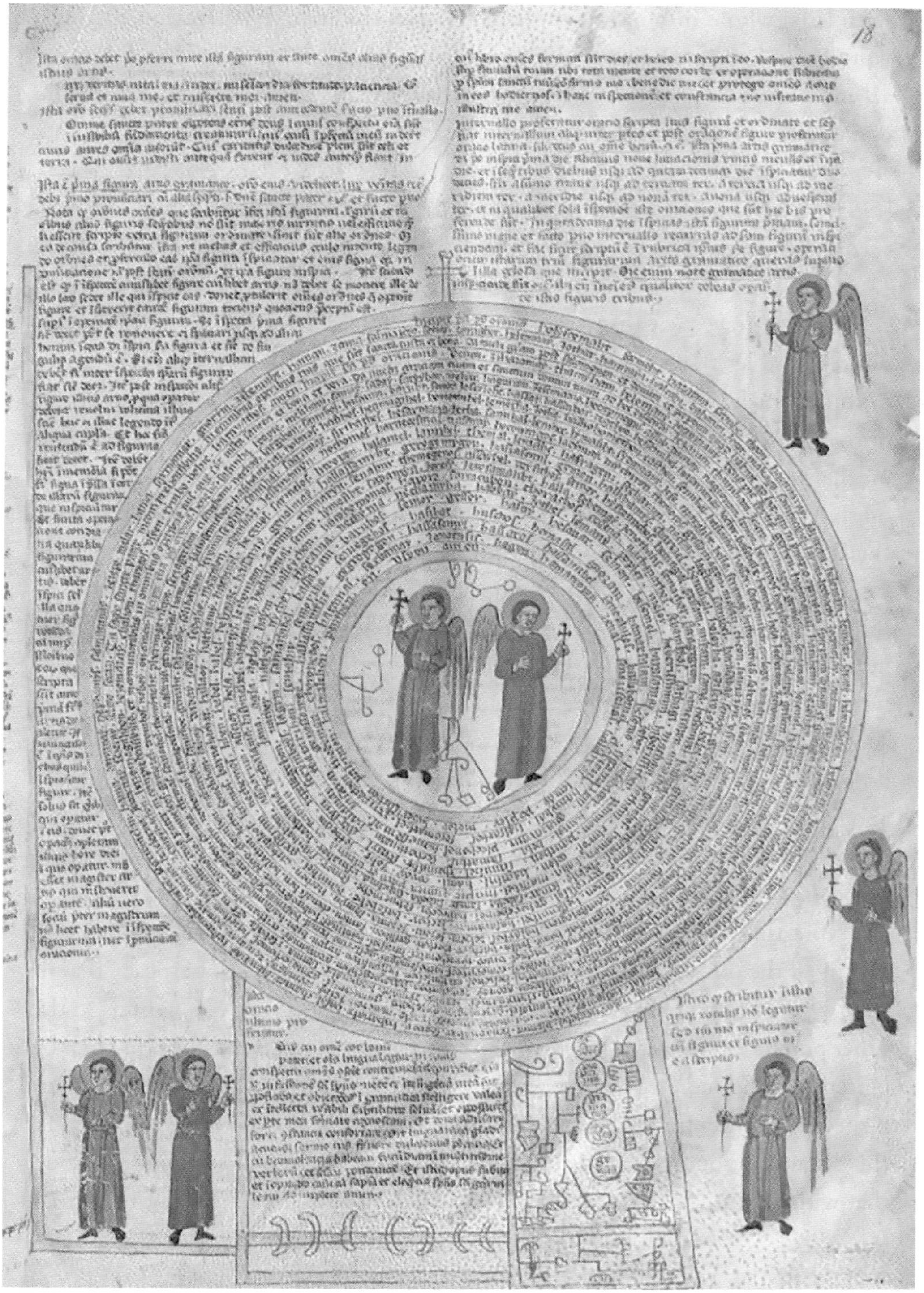

The first figure of grammar (1b)

with [his] whole mind and whole heart, and the [ritual] operation through your Holy Spirit. O Lord, strengthen me, bless me, O Lord, and protect all my present-day actions. Illuminate me in this inspection and with the constancy of your visitation, amen.

[NS 3] This is the first figure of the art of grammar. Its prayer (namely, *Lux, veritas, etc.,*) ought to be pronounced first with the others following (namely, *Domine Sancte Pater* [. . . *imperfectum*], etc.,) and having made a short interval, the written prayer within the figure and of the order [of the prayers], is to be offered, and let there always be some interval between the parts, and the Latin prayer (namely, *Deus, cui omne bonum, etc.*[4]) is to be offered after the prayer of the figure. This first figure of the art of grammar ought to be inspected first on the first day of any new lunar [day of] one month, and on this very day and on the following days up to the fifteenth day, it is to be inspected twelve times—that is, from in the early morning up to the third [hour] thrice, from the third [hour] up to noon thrice, from noon up to the ninth [hour] thrice, from the ninth [hour] up to the evening [hour] thrice—and these prayers, which are here, are to be offered twice in any single inspection, in the fifteenth day, you must inspect this first figure once in the early morning, and having made a short interval, you may return to the second figure which is to be inspected, and do just as it is written in the rubric of the second figure itself, you may inquire about the operation of those three figures of the art of grammar above in that gloss which begins Sicut enim notae gramaticae artis inspiciende sunt, etc.[5] For you will find there how you ought to be working from these three figures.

Note that all the prayers which are written below this figure in the gyre[6] and in all the other figures following are not of a greater virtue or efficacy than if they were written outside of the figure of the order [of the prayers], just as in the other prayers, but they are written below it for a reason, so that the prayers can be better read and more effectively with an attentive eye and the figure and its signs inspected and in offering them, because this very figure ought to be inspected in the pronunciation or immediately after the prayer. Also, it is to be understood that with the inspection of any figure of any art, [the figure] ought not to remind

---

4. NS 9.

5. Section 78 gloss.

6. Latin *gyrus,* which comes from the Greek γῦρος, meaning "circular or spiral form."

him of that [art generally], but; he must impart [some new information] concerning that very place,[7] he who inspects these [places within the figure] as long as he has offered all the prayers which are corresponding to the figures, and he inspected the same figure as often as it is taught above in the operation of those very figures, but inspect the first figure just as it is proper, he is able to remind himself, and to take a [mental] walk-through up to the other hour in which he ought to inspect the second figure, and it is to be done thus concerning each one. For if some interval ought to be made between the inspection of these very figures, let it be done just as it is proper. Also, after the inspection of the last figure of that art for which he works the scrolls of that science ought to be unrolled, and read within some chapters here and there, and having done this, [the operation] is to be returned to the figures, just as it is proper.[8] Also, they ought to be kept in memory if an impressed sign is to be made in the heart[9] of those figures which are inspected, and having finished the daily operation of any figures of any art those four round signs ought to be inspected once with the impressions of those which are written before the first figure of the art of dialectic.[10] Also, it is to be fasted on the very days in which the figures are inspected. Also, anyone who works alone in them until after the completed operation of that hour of the day in which he works, unless he was a master teacher of the art who was instructing the operator, but another associate, besides the master, is not permitted to attend the inspection of the figures or the pronunciation of the prayers.

[NS 4] *The first part of the prayer begins:*

Helyscemaht, Scemoht,[11] Hazatam, Saduhc, Theon, Hazamaray, Iazaram,

---

7. In other words, the operator is to impress new grammatical information at certain points along the gyrus of the first figure of grammar. Then as long as he has offered all the prayers corresponding to the figures, he may carry out the steps according to the art of memory.

8. The method of loci is applied here. After the operator has performed his mental walk-through of the figure, he reads new information from his scroll, and then visualizes that new information in the form of images and then by inspecting the figure, he places those new images along certain places or landmarks within his own mental mirror image of the notory art figure. See chapter IV.

9. That is, the mind. The same metaphor for describing memory is found in Plato's dialogue *Theaetetus,* indicating that the art of memory dates back to ancient Greek times. See chapter IV.

10. See page 508.

11. *Helyscemaht Scemoht,* the adorning prayer (*oratio propria*) written within the figure, consists of five parts and belongs to the first figure of grammar. *Helyscemaht Scemoht* is found written in the outer ring of the *gyrus*. See the figure on page 487.

Helomani, Iemiher, Saraty, Helmasachon, Helamam, Iecromiham, Theos, O pious and strong God, Hamathamal, Halcronemeha, Pherant, Hencronahar, Secroga, Hahanahe, Basal, Chamay, Sabnazay, Hestromelar, Nehol, Segeromelan, Hama, Zaramay, Nephamys, Salmatanay, Iezepo, Melar, Harna, Sarmamar, Guorym, Zehemaht, Haman, Zama, Salmaiero, Somay, Zamaher, Heltamay, Iothar, Hammya, Halcahi, Bahatim, Iecor, Maliaga, Sanitucahel, Layma, Hethacay, Zoconozay, Zarama, Hevagas, Zomon, Zamyn, Haym, Manather, Neblata, Zamamy, Ieculas, Halzamay, Zezenoma, Malay, Chumay, Hozelo, Maieron, Iethy, Soymagay, Zemezay, Zemaze, Bauzan, Hezelerma, Iecornay, Sezeray, Selmo, Secazi, O holy one, the incomprehensible Father, you who are holy in all your works, just and good, give me the grace, the gift, and the teaching after Solomon which he had in respect to this . . . ,[12] who in the beginning of your work had your spirit, gift, and grace with respect to having this . . ., Zegor, Zeramagor, Iezamam, Gezemel, Zachiel, Zamahel, Gozemagon, Guzoharo, Gamecomos, Gamazechomos, Hazethon, Hazomay, Zemoyhachon, Hazogamalihon, Iezomazay, Chalion, Tharatos, Usyon, Tymbo, Bohic, Hatanathos, amen.

[NS 5] *The second part of the prayer begins:*

Benon, Zihazamay,[13] Thamyham, Helomany, Iecromany, O pious [and] strong God, Gethon, Hatanamal, Hacuhemy, Zezoham, Iame, Iecormay, Crethomayr, Hachor, Naphamy, Zezoma, Melar, Heimia, Charanamay, Zeruhy, Zymaht, Hachmaht, Samna, Ysebasa, and you, O God the savior, the incomprehensible and immutable Father, for who there is justice, sanctity, goodness, and truth in all your works, give me your grace and your holy gift for learning these . . . ,[14] Iezaram, Thanuham, Iezero, Iezimagos, Gemalym, Semanay, Iezemel, Helphachiel, Samiha, Hamihel, Gezemago, Iezero, Thumcha, Meromas, Hassibocon, Adonay, Zemolathon, Hazomegelihon, Gecazamay, Crithamahion, Zamolizo, Hemmeleos, Gemezel, Tromhos, Neboy, On, amen.

---

12. An ellipsis is provided for the petitioner to fill in the blank with the desired knowledge of grammar. Another ellipsis follows for the same purpose.

13. *Benon Zihazamay,* the second part of the particular or adorning prayer belonging to the first figure of grammar. This part is also found within the *gyrus* of the figure.

14. An ellipsis is provided for the petitioner to fill in the blank with the desired knowledge of grammar.

[NS 6] *The third part of the prayer begins:*

Henelic, Sasmiha,[15] Hecrore, Meliham, Samay, Saday, Sathyhar, Mehar, Hagaram, Iesemamo, Hecapmegas, Assub, Damay, Tiagroram, Hemon, Hectemos, Haristologion, Halaros, Gessera, Samayn, Nehon, Cathagelihos, Bacharnas, Harihethata, Hadissera, Harthimathil, Helzenos, Carthulehon, Hesronsihon, Tropon, Hion, Hassamihal, Gezechon, Samna, Themas, Semaihel, Thomynoht, Phermigeriham, Seriagersam, Cisareham, Nechay, Largihon, Samihel, Basaram, Baruht, Semor, Ieseyloht, Hassar, Hassaihar, Degehon, Hessemihel, Hasaramay, Iechor, Basebahe, Hamihel, Hela, Iechoram, Iechomany, Hazamany, Thamariha, Semahit, Samayr, Theomegios, Hasibacdel, Iesahal, Cemoritheos, Nithosemagar, Geslermo, Hemal, Hasamal, Iesemon, Iesamyn, Nothomos, Hamecesmal, Nasaray, Gemolomas, Hamason, Iachosemithon, Hasihamezin, Hobiros, Hasihos, Heamagihel, Homothihel, Lemecha, Iotha, Halliohomethon, Casthen, Semihal, Hasiathos, Hassor, Sachamihar, Corloge, Zamar, Hada, Hatamar, Secoromay, Hesacre, Ysaray, Theripachon, Iabymehc, Dachies, Draco, Tyrochonides, Litrahas, Hatamas, Habiroseruhit, Iecro, Chemihon, Naburechi, Samthoc, Gemaht, Salynohc, Solihathon, Ieromasephil, Samihal, Sacramay, Sirihathos, Hesarmana, Ietha, Samihal, Lemhoc, Lymasiht, Sydamany, Iese, Maraliht, Hella, Seramay, Hithonathasi, Sehemos, Sehamor, Siacrathon, Hamotrophon, Chomynthis, Stiganehas, Hamy, Halla, Vathier, Thethay, Gessihon, Samyn, Chenas, Hen, Halathin, Iecho, Semelihan, Sabay, Daday, Saday, Sedahc, Megalon, Admihaz, Iessemamyn, Nochomos, Harnecesmal, Nasaray, Hoconnigos, Ladymay, Mychiron, Themocos, Gessemagon, Malazi, Theon, Hamazyn, Usyon, amen.

[NS 7] *The fourth part of the prayer begins:*

Harastologion, Halayhos,[16] Zehem, Iezem, Iezoma, Samyn, Nechon, Cathapleos, Lechmos, Barnehachat, Hallaoy, Hathamy, Hachmyl, Hecenos, Sarmelos, Litropon, Halamel, Lamihel, Themal, Lemahc, Hasragenz, Secharam, Nochar, Laglon, Samihel, Barasabay, Semor, Geserchor, Hasaro,

15. *Henelic Sasmiha,* the third part of the particular or adorning prayer belonging to the first figure of grammar. This part is also found within the *gyrus* of the figure.

16. *Harastologion Halayhos,* the fourth part of the particular or adorning prayer belonging to the first figure of grammar. This part is also found within the *gyrus* of the figure.

Hassyhar, Legihon, Hessermihel, Hasaramay, Iechor, Basebehe, Hamihel, Gesseram, Nechemos, Lihen, Habel, Hahel, Helymac, Hassaray, Genolmay, Hallassemyht, Gerogemygon, Hasiasemil, Gemon, Hallihamys, Charizel, Hemihal, Holoyha, Adiserozos, Behemol, Gemassadym, Ymos, Perrosisel, Gehocchemol, Habrechi, Sehucmehc, Semor, Sabihaham, Assciorum, Asseior, Hela, Samatys, Lethomam, Zamna, Thamaryn, Senahur, Themegenos, Assayhel, Deysithos, Semor, Hystomichos, Hemagal, Gessam, Mihara, Sama, Hesemihel, Hassaramay, Haboremas, Thebily, Semar, Saholla, Samar, Sahella, Sahelma, Ysmahor, Hathemona, Hechalama, Hisimahol, Bathomana, Hechalamal, Semor, Lymesiht, Sadamya, Ieresy, Ierosamaliht, Halla, Sehemay, Ienothalis, Semachor, Sicragegecon, Hamerapon, Cimastis, Genehos, Hamon, Halla, Massihel.

[NS 8] *The fifth and last part of the prayer begins:*
Iana, Agla, Aglay,[17] **Haym, Halleychon, Hacohomonos, Haporo, Sarcacuhon, Chorachos, Cessena, Nachanathos, Sehamthos, Sathagi, Matham, Iotham, Thiros, Celon, Hacahil, Hacal, Coxay, Ioht, Ietheam, Repellegehon, Nather, Nathey, Nychor, Therama, Nechyma, Nechamyha, Habbay, Iothes, Lemany, Popley, Meloy, Heberissimum, Hiberissither, Panmon, Pantheon, Samihel, Themaht, Semyl, Gersym, Serymboys, Lagym, Samathihel, Bassaham, Baruhos, Semor, Gessor, Hasay, Hesanar, Sehion, Hesemel, Harasamay, Iehor, Hesehacor, Hamel, Hela, Samathis, Sechothuam, Hasamay, Thatarihon, Semahir, Semoriho, Semegehos, Hasihat, Huschos, Hemasal, Guozam, Hamarsalam, Hesomo, Sygamazym, Guazaram, Plechonos, Havessemas, Hisarai, Genossoiray, Hallassamyht, Gegrogogon, Hassasemyl, Hassaros, Hassamihel, Senophilos, Hallihomel, Chariozil, Hamyhal, Halsathos, Seromathel, Peripathon, Thedymon, Choronedos, Hatamas, Sechamay, Ienotasis, Hagon, Hamatropon, Zenas, Senazisehas, Hallareas, Lemay, Popley, Meloy, Hibericlichon, Pahimon, Halmalehon, Panthon, On, Usyon, amen.**

17. *Iana Agla Aglay,* the fifth and last part of the particular or adorning prayer belonging to the first figure of grammar. This part is also found within the *gyrus* of the figure.

[NS 9] *Let this [sixth and] last prayer be offered:*
O God, to whom every good heart is open,[18] and every tongue speaks, in whose presence all consciences tremble, I beg you purify my mind and my understanding through the infusion of the Holy Spirit, so that I might be able to comprehend the propositions and objections in grammar, and having understood [how] to reason, I may solve with a subtlety,[19] and may I learn to form oppositions out of my part, and to strengthen the gift against stronger adversaries with constancy;[20] may my tongue be a sharpened sword,[21] my speech full of sweetness with favor, and may I have eloquence in a multitude of words and the weight of the sciences with benevolence, and may I be able to accomplish this work by a sudden and unexpected fortune with the wisdom and eloquence of the grace of the Holy Spirit, amen.

That which is written in these five wheels is not to be read but only inspected with the figure and signs written in it.[22]

[NS 10] *This prayer is to be offered six times [before this first] figure and after this, the prayers of this very figure, [the second figure,] is to be offered:*
O Lord God,[23] O gentle Father of all eternal things, the disposer of all virtues, look upon [and] consider my activities today, you who are the inspector and judge of the actions of men and angels, so that the grace of your admirable permission may be deemed worthy suddenly to implement

18. *Deus, cui omne cor bonum patet,* the last adorning prayer belonging to the first figure of grammar. The prayer is found outside and below the *gyrus* within a polygon.
19. In other words, to solve a problem with an exact precision with respect to its details.
20. This passage describes the Scholastic method of disputation, made popular during the Middle Ages, in which teachers and students would engage in formalized debates, about any given topic to discern what truths can be known. Aristotelian logic governed the rules for the debates, and there was also the requirement of citing known authorities of any given topic (e.g., Donatus and Priscian for grammar). For example, the teacher would offer a proposition about grammar and the students would make objections or refutations against it. The teacher would then make a counter argument against the students and then the students would, in turn, provide their own counter arguments against the teacher. This is also known as the dialectic method in which reasoned arguments are made in search of the truth.
21. Compare the wording to Psalms 57:4 and 64:3 (NRSV).
22. This statement contradicts the instructions given in 126f gloss that says the adorning prayers are to be spoken as part of the operation.
23. *Respice, Domine Deus,* the prayer belonging to the second figure of grammar. See section 129.

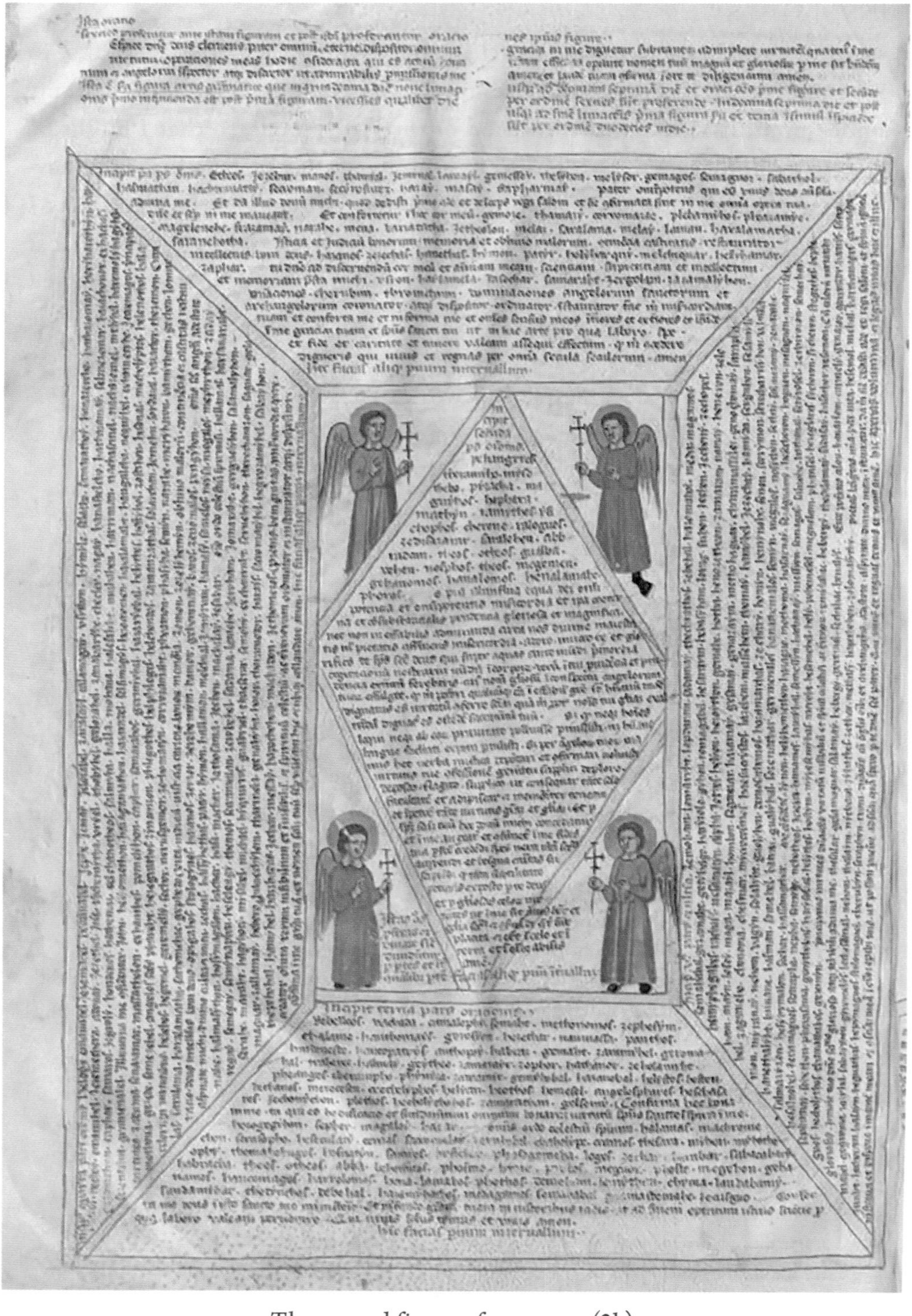

The second figure of grammar (2b)

(virtue)[24] within me, inasmuch as your great and glorious name is blessed by me, amen, and strengthen your praise in the mouth of those who love you, amen.

[NS 11] *This is the second figure of the art of grammar, which is to be inspected on the fifteenth day of the new lunar month after the first figure [of grammar] twenty times on any day up to the seventeenth day, and the prayers of the first figure and the second [figure] are to be offered through the order six times on the seventeenth day; and afterward, the first figure, second, and third are to be inspected together through the order twelve times in a day up to the end of the lunar month.*

[NS 12] *The first part of the prayer begins:*

Otheos, Iezehur,[25] Manos, Thamyal, Iemynal, Lamayl, Gemessey, Thesyhon, Secroman, Secryosutez, Hazay, Masay, Sapharmay, O Father the almighty, you who are the one God before the ages, help me, and give that gift to me which you gave to Adam[26] first and afterward to King Solomon, and they are to be confirmed[27] thus within me by all your works; O Lord, may they always remain within me, and may my heart be comforted[28] in this, Gemoze, Thamazy, Corromazae, Plebamyhos, Pheazamye, Magelenehc, Frazamay, Narahe, Mena, Bariatatha, Ietheolon, Melaz, Saralama, Melay, Laman, Haralamatha, Saranehotha, justice and judgment of good things, memory and the forgetfulness of evil things, abstinence, chastity, O God the restorer of good intellect, Hazanos, Zezechas, Hanethas, Hymon, Patyr, Holyharquy, Melchiquar, Helyhamar, Zaphar, O Lord, present to me, with respect to my discerning heart and soul, the knowledge, wisdom, understanding, and memory, Usyon, Haylamela, Iasochar, Samaraht, Zergolam, Zazamalyhon, O Dominions, O Cherubim, O Thrones, O Dominions, O crowner and disposer of the holy angels and

---

24. The word *virtutem* may be a placeholder for whatever quality the petitioner desires to entreat from God.
25. *Otheos, Iezehur,* the adorning prayer, consisting of five parts, belongs to the second figure of grammar. *Otheos Iezehur* is found in the top bar along the rectangular figure. See the figure on page 494.
26. That is, the first man.
27. Latin *confirmata* has an additional meaning of strengthened.
28. Latin *confortetur* also has an additional meaning of strengthened.

archangels, O ordainer, O restorer, show me your mercy, strengthen me, and inform me and all my internal and external senses, and infuse into me your grace and your Holy Spirit, so that in this art for which I labor, I may prevail to obtain an effect with hope, faith, charity, and awe, that you would deem worthy to grant to me, you who lives and reigns forever and ever, amen.

You must make a short interval here.

[NS 13] *The second part of the prayer begins:*
Pehangryes, Theramyho,[29] Mysotheho, Pyzacha, Maguyhos, Hophara, Mathyn, Ramythos, Ysichophos, Cherene, Raloguos, Zedisazarar, Saralehen, Abbradam, Theos, Otheos, Gualba, Vehen, Nosphos, Theos, Megemen, Gehanomos, Hanalomos, Henalamahc, Phoros, O pious one, O nourishing river, the horse of God the almighty and the mercy of the almighty,[30] and the very co-eternal and consubstantial prudence,[31] the glorious and the magnificent, and also admiring the ineffable around us, the divine majesty or piety overflowing with mercy, I adore, invoke, and glorify you, O God the Holy Spirit, who was carrying the truth of the thoughts of our nakedness in body, within your providence and wisdom, before the primoridal world, above the waters, whose glorious name shines forth in sight of your angels, because for me, a sinner, for the sake of whatever kind of ineffable grace, you who are deemed worthy to confer upon the human race the knowledge of virtues on account of exalting the glory of your name, you who are deemed worthy to show me your sacrament, but because you did not permit men to speak nor to have polluted them[32] by their depravity, nor did you conduct them to be explained for the purpose of the faculty of the human tongue, but you wanted these mystical words to be carried down and to be strengthened through the hands of your angels;

---

29. *Pehangryes Theramyho,* the second part of the adorning prayer belonging to the second figure of grammar. This part is found in the diamond at the center of the figure. See the figure on page 494.

30. Epithets of the Holy Spirit.

31. A reference to the Trinitarian doctrine.

32. The mystical words of the prayers.

I deplore, earnestly pray, entreat, [and] supplicate a confession with a supplicant lamentation for your virtue, so that I may obtain and acquire the faculty of so much knowledge, grasp [it] in memory, and procure so much grace and glory of virtue, and that this gift granted to me and augmented within me through your Holy Spirit, and your faith is to be strengthened within me for believing perfectly, true hope acquiring this knowledge, and admiring the beneficial charity, that I entreat so much subtlety of a petition[33] through you, O God, and through the glorious virtues of heaven, so that the virtue, honor, and glory is within me, knowing and conserving, those things which are pleasing to you, and they will be in heaven and on earth and in every abyss, amen.

You must offer these prayers in the order just as you make some short interval through the parts and between any part.

[NS 14] *The third part of the prayer begins:*

Rebelleos, Vachada,[34] Camalephy, Semaht, Methonomos, Zephesym, Chalame, Hanthomays, Gorosyon, Hezethar, Naumassa, Pantheos, Hindoneste, Hantopatrys, Anthopoy, Habraz, Gemaht, Zaramyhel, Geromahal, Traherez, Halmay, Geytheo, Zamazayr, Zophor, Hathanor, Zeholamyht, Pheanges, Cherampho, Phynyza, Zamarayr, Gemyhobal, Hazanobal, Helystos, Hosten, Hechanos, Merecesen, Crechelyphos, Helyan, Heothos, Hemesel, Angelosphares, Heschasares, Iechonychon, Plethos, Hecholychohos, Zamaratham, Gelsemy, strengthen this good within me, you who are the edification and foundation of all good virtues; O Holy Spirit, inspire within me, Hozogegyhon, Sepher, Magaloy, Hazar, the order of all the heavenly spirits, Halamas, Machromechon, Serasopho, Heseculaty, Cemas, Sacromalay, Zerubehel, Chahelype, Cramos, Thesara, Myhon, Myhotheophy, Themahehugos, Hosuatyn, Samyos, Hysichar, Phosegemeha, Logos, Zechar, Harabar, Sahacabary, Habracha, Theos, Otheos, Abba, Behemnos, Phosmo, Hyne, Prohos, Meguon, Phoste, Megehon, Gehanamos, Hancomagos, Haryolomos,

---

33. Or, so much of a detailed petition.

34. *Rebelleos Vachada,* the third part of the adorning prayer belonging to the second figure of grammar. This part is found along the bottom bar of the figure. See the figure on page 494.

Hena, Lamahos, Phothos, Demeham, Lemythan, Chyma, Landabamy, Sandamyhar, Thetynchos, Debehal, Hazamyhathos, Medagamos, Semahabal, Guamastemahc, Iecusguo, strengthen me, O God, in this your holy ministry, and infuse your grace into my viscera, so that I may be able to arrive before the desired end of this knowledge for which I labor, you alone who lives threefold and one, amen.

You must make a short interval here.

[NS 15] *The fourth part of the prayer begins:*

Heloy, Emanuhel,[35] Iezemares, Heccanahel, Iephe, Iemay, Ielozabel, Zarasayl, Calamagay, Usython, Hymyle, Selatho, Samarathoy, Hanazereho, Hathazomay, Heryharothyn, Haychapos, Hechoy, Emanuhel, Iezemethera, Adonay, Iesethel, Iose, Thehemytha, Uryel, Thobyhel, Gelozahel, Zanabaryhc, Checler, Nagay, Hanastelcho, Hathazamay, Selmezemar, Hazachonor, Exhachos, Gezomolyon, Caphar, Samaros, Iegroly, Hondenos, Hathemaz, Celchanotheos, Salmyha, Halla, Mohana, Halesalyht, Muhahen, Harriman, Nachasemel, Nachazemel, Melyhel, Haremolyhagyha, Sezenachat, Gramenahel, illuminate me audaciously, Iohir, Helyomethon, Hazagamathon, Hazaradel, Selsimagys, Hezocromen, Hazalamaht, Hangalcha, Nequyhel, Exhametyhc, Iecremagos, O Principalities [and] Hosts,[36] Zadama, Senazamar, Massatholon, Exhauthes, Pomelyhon, Caphar, Samarahos, Germyohal, Hazaryobal, Helythos, Hostyhol, Zostihon, Hesonas, Mechelyptos, Helenothos, Halamothona, Gezede, Semezehel, O holy angels, Phareht, Hezegrathos, Zynconzon, Phlegothes, Helphleges, Hechondos, Zamanzathas, Solarcham, Iemehiz, Sordazal, Hazathor, Thezemon, with the virtues of the heavens, Helehos, Hegemel, Geremelly, Sechor, Nerusgemor, Zethomatyn, Corrozamaht, Pheamon, Phasyha, Semyn, Narahe, Meryharon, Bamytham, Gechon, Lomnelas, Saralama, Haralamatha, Sathomehac, Gephedo, life, judgement, justice, charity,

---

35. *Heloy Emanuhel,* the fourth part of the adorning prayer belonging to the second figure of grammar. This part is found along the left-hand sidebar of the figure. See the figure on page 494.

36. The Principalities and Virtues were two orders of angels. See page 117.

memory of goodness, Zemon, Zozelyhemyn, the forgetfulness of evil things, abstinence and chastity, restoration, O God, good intellect, O God, Opigahos, Stologynos, Hazanos, Zemor, Zerehemym, Hamor, Gehemnay, Baros, Zenomalos, Pengyhon, all holy angels will arrive to assist[37] me, having been clothed and initiated by the divine,[38] Zechas, Hassyhethas, Patyr, Hymon, Hallamon, Melchial, Iamyrum, Hamasy, Samelos, Neysa, Megalos, Mephython, Zadaynahc, Halmasython, Hosymagalon, Hachar, Hasa, Machar, Iethosama, Iechon, Machalay, Iesabar, the order of all the heavenly spirits, Hallamas, Harsanaraht, Regay, Semegay, Semynaphaz, Heseleagy, Themos, Secramalan, Zerobehel, Sadama, Lamehc, Ieroham, Iomaraht, Gerguolyhon, Sasamalyhon, Seruhc, Maraht, Hagyhoty, Mysahel, Michael, Hyquirros, Guabriel, Thacserar, Semohy, Exchauruht, Servehyhon, Therechamzon, Saguar, Gelamaguar, Zallamay, Hebero, Havechylem, Tharinela, Genahyha, Hozor, Thoramodor, Harays, Sacromatyhel, Hegrozamyhel, Sabayhon, Thephehohal, Hamyhel, Hazihadas, Iechar, Messay, Hapochohon, Machadon, Iethomezos, the piety, benevolence, mercy, [and] peace, O Creator of all visible and invisible things, the celestial and terrestrial spirits, the ordainer, restorer, and disposer, strengthen within me your grace and may I always be able to praise highly your holy name here and everywhere, amen.

You must make a short interval here.

[NS 16] *The fifth and last part of the prayer begins:*

Zemoham, Lemaryht,[39] Lapdaram, Sadamay, Thechrathos, Zebehal, Hazomahol, Medaz, Magamos, Semahabal, Gezamaht, Getyhelgo, Haryzolo, Gyhon, Remagahel, Hesaraym, Lorag, Suhon, Iechon, Iechony, Zechopes, Hemyphegabes, Rachays, Vesamatyn, Alpha, Iothos, Helyon, Hezoython, Gemahe, Hotha, Henozetheon, Zamaram,

---

37. Latin *aspirate* can also mean "to breathe upon" or "infuse" the petitioner with a divine energy or life force.

38. Latin *cultu et initu* evokes the imagery of the Greco-Roman mystery religions, and perhaps also Luke 24:44–49, in which the resurrected Christ advised his disciples to "stay here in the city until you have been clothed with power from on high" (NRSV).

39. *Zemoham Lemaryht,* the fifth part of the adorning prayer belonging to the second figure of grammar. This part is found along the right-hand sidebar of the figure. See the figure on page 494.

Namay, Heneron, Zeleham, Mayn, Losey, Maga, Mazayl, Hombon, Segamar, Hazamay, Gesamay, Genazaym, Methohaguar, Charamassalez, Genochomay, Saraphahel, Zagameho, Chonoma, Chesmar, Mycrocosmos, Haesucrystos, Lazehem, Massehem, Thomay, Hamyhel, Iezochay, Hamyda, Serguhon, Sesamylymon, Myranay, Nehom, Vagyn, Solalyht, Guolyhon, Demosathemos, Hazamarchas, Zechary, Homyn, Hemynohc, Senon, Scorymon, Serecharisyhon, Vehalla, Hanethalyht, Huvane, Hasman, Semehel, Hatraz, Gualyhal, Sozenathar, Germenalos, Hanathemalos, Semyn, Megalos, Nosython, Sethay, Salmezamy, Zenadahc, Salmazyzon, Hesyhymalon, Sechar, Hassamathar, confiding in me, Lynon, Helyhomethon, Hazaguo, Mothoma, Hasarnay, Sezaguamy, Heschoron, Hoguon, Mesaguon, Naquyhel, Hesalnohel, Ieramaguos, Scarapha, Nepha, Somora, Nehotheos, Iezera, Hamamos, Lamyhal, Semessyn, Hathanay, Messyon, Semagos, Salnohc, Hathanal, Setyrosel, Zethirozon, Semechay, Sephamay, Sohethon, Pharasama, Genythobas, Harysobal, Helythos, Hostym, Myhesemyhas, Meroht, Hesemehel, Hely, Pohemesel, Meguolam, Phansel, Hezeglares, Sychoron, Sycheron, Stegethes, Hepheguos, Hecholythos, Thamathahos, Gezemyn, O Principalities, Virtues, Dominions, of the visible virtues and of celestial and also terrestrial spirits, Remylahac, Hebergy, Thesalamay, Sadasay, Hasathor, Resomon, with the glorious virtues of the heavens, in your name, O Lord, the most holy, glorious, and terrible one, help me, Thesalar, Gelamaguar, Salamay, Hebergy, Geremel, Sechihac, Henalys, behold, the Powers of the heavens, Hanaylem, Carmely, Genazor, Gerandor, Hamys, Sacromahel, Gegroma, Zazyhel, Sabaython, Gyromelys, Lethosamal, Nehom, Thalaym, Nychaza, Zybathes, Zethar, Methasy, Hapethehon, Zolomasythy, piety, benevolence, peace, life, Hesemol, Mehal, Barthamagos, Germagaziraht, Hechoram, Hasaym, Heguathas, Hepymaguos, Stolomaguol, the Cherubim, Seraphim, Thrones, Dominions, arrive with all the Angels and Archangels; O restorer, assist[40] with a divine reciprocity, give to me just as you gave to Adam and King Solomon, and restore and dispose within my mind and my conscience a fiery form in all your works, so that I may be able to attain the

40. Latin *aspirate*. See page 501, footnote 43.

knowledge which I await from you, O holy Lord the Father, who lives and reigns threefold and one, amen.

You may open this scroll and read within here and there.[41]

[NS 17] *This prayer must be offered before this figure, and after that, the prayers of this figure are to be offered:*
O Creator, Lord[42] of all visible creatures, O most pious Father, who dwells eternally in the enclosed light, and before the beginning of the world, ineffably [disposing] all things and governing your eternity, I approach [your] incomprehensible piety with supplicating words, so that . . .[43] of this sacramental and mystical work within me, may illuminate the power, efficacy, and good consideration through your holy angels, and make abundant the memory within me through the names of the holy angels, and may your holy works illuminate the reminiscence of all the sciences within me with [mental] stability, amen.

[NS 18] *Rubric: This is the third and last figure of the art of grammar, which, after the first and second figures, is to be inspected twelve times a day on the seventeenth day—that is, from the morning [hour] up to the third [hour] thrice, from noon up to the ninth [hour] thrice, from the ninth [hour] up to the evening [hour]*[44] *thrice—and after the inspection of this figure, the scrolls of the art of grammar are to be unrolled and read within here and there.*

[NS 19] *The first part of this prayer begins:*
O God the foundation[45] of all good and holy virtues, strengthen the Holy Spirit and virtue through abundance, Thehel, Hazethamos, Hatylleomony, Samchar, Sezamar, Hezelem, Hezemelos, Lamar, Samacharthe, Lorchiaton,

41. The writer is directing the operator to study his books on grammar.

42. *Creator Adonay,* the prayer belonging to the third figure of grammar.

43. The ellipsis represents an empty placeholder in which the operator would insert his desired area of grammatical study.

44. These canonical hours are *prime, terce, nones, and vespers,* respectively. See appendix A4 for the canonical hours.

45. *Principium Deus,* the adorning prayer, consists of four parts and belongs to the third figure of grammar. This first part is found in the top wheel of the figure. See the figure on page 502.

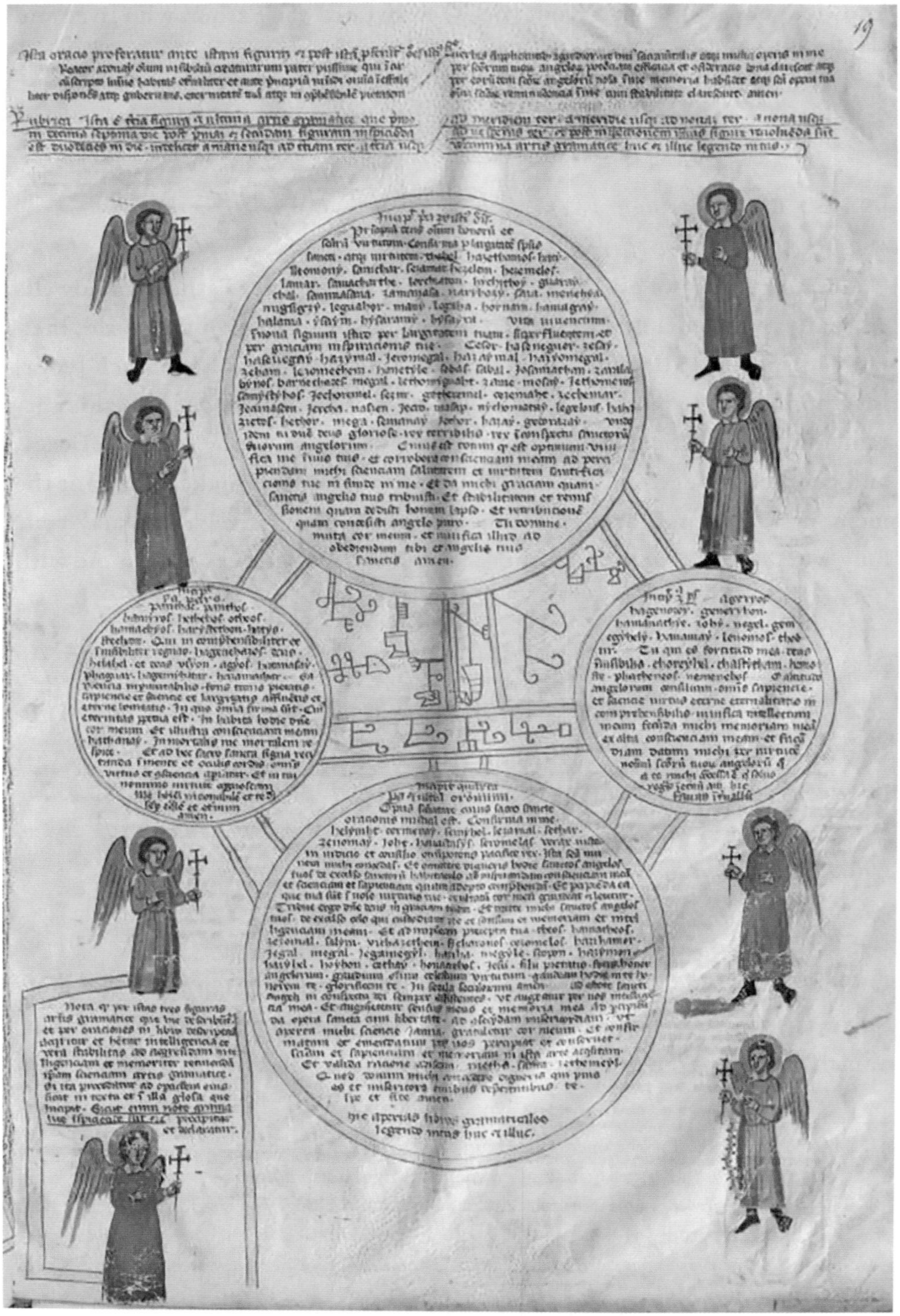

The third figure of grammar (3b)

Hychithoy, Guaraychal, Sammasana, Zamanasa, Naryhozy, Saza, Menehya, Migsigzy, Leguahor, Many, Legaha, Hornam, Hamagay, Halama, Ysaym, Hysaramy, Hysayra, O life of the living, renew this sign through your overflowing abundance and through your grace of inspiration, Cesor, Haseneguor, Zesay, Hasenegay, Hazymal, Ieromegal, Hazaymal, Hazyomegal, Zeham, Lezomechem, Hanetyle, Sobas, Sabal, Iosamatham, Zaralabynos, Barnechades, Megal, Lethomyguaht, Zame, Mosay, Iethomeros, Samystyhos, Iechoremel, Sezur, Getheremel, Cezemaht, Zechemar, Iecunascen, Iercha, Naszen, Iecro, Masap, Nychomatay, Legelons, Hahazictos, Hethor, Mega, Semanay, Iechor, Hazay, Gecorazay, from you, O Lord God, the glorious king, the revered king,[46] in sight of your holy angels, whose entire being exists because it is the best, vivify me in your ways, and strengthen my conscience towards comprehending the knowledge [given] to me; infuse within me the salvation and the virtue of your sanctification, and give me the grace which you bestowed upon your angels, and the [mental] stability and the forgiveness that you gave to the Fallen man,[47] and the retribution which you have granted to a pure angel; O Lord, change my heart and quicken it to obey you and your holy angels, amen.

[NS 20] *The second part begins:*

Panthac, Panthos,[48] Hamyros, Hethehos, Otheos, Hamachyos, Harystethon, Hatys, Stecham, you who reigns incomprehensibly and invisibly, Hagenehazos, God, Helahel, and God Usyon, Agyos, Hatanasay, Phaguar, Hagemyhatar, Hazamachar, O immutable wisdom, the fountain of all piety, wisdom, knowledge, affluent abundance, and eternal goodness, in whom all things are firm, whose eternity is perpetual; O Lord, inhabit my heart today and illuminate my conscience, Hathanay, look upon the mortality of my immortal self, and with respect to these most sacrosanct

---

46. Latin *terribilis rex,* literally means "terrible king," but the sense comes from the biblical concept of having "fear of the Lord," which really expresses an awe-inspiring reverence for God. See page 416, footnote 191.

47. The Fallen man refers to humanity as a whole who has entered a state of sinfulness after the biblical Fall and explusion from the Garden of Eden according to the book of Genesis.

48. *Panthac Panthos,* the second part of the adorning prayer, belongs to the third figure of grammar. This second part is found in the left wheel of the figure. See the figure on page 502.

signs which are to be recited in the mind and eyes of the heart,[49] let every virtue and conscience be opened, and by the virtue of your name may I get to know myself as a reasonable man and know you as God always equal and eternal,[50] amen.

[NS 21] *The third part begins:*
Ageryos, Hagenozoy,[51] Generyhon, Hamanathye, Zohy, Negel, Gemegyhely, Hamamay, Lenomos, Thobur, you who are my fortitude, O invisible God, Chereyhel, Chastytham, Hemoste, Phatheneos, Nemenehos, O High One of the angels, O Council of Every Wisdom and Knowledge, O Eternal Virtue of the Incomprehensible Eternity, vivify my understanding, make fruitful to me my memory, exalt my conscience and the eloquence given to me through the virtue of the names of your holy angels which is granted to me from you, you alone who reigns in eternity, amen.

You must make an interval here.

[NS 22] *The fourth and last part of the prayer begins:*
O Salvific Work,[52] whose sacrosanct prayer is a mystery, strengthen in me, Helymht, Cormenay, Semyhol, Lezamal, Sethar, Zenomay, Ioht, Hanastasys, Seromelas, truthful, just in judgment and counsel, almighty, peaceable king, may you grant these holy gifts to me, and may you deem worthy to send out today your holy angels from the highest dwelling of the holy ones for the purpose of inspiring my conscience, and choosing knowledge and wisdom rather than comprehending and perceiving it which are yours in the name of your virtue. May my heart rejoice and be glad; ergo bestow, O Lord God, to me your grace, and send to me your holy angels from the highest heaven who may guard me and my sense, memory, and intelligence,

---

49. The figures are to be visualized like roadmaps or buildings in the practice of the art of memory.
50. "Equal and eternal" is a reference to the Trinitarian doctrine of the Athanasian Creed.
51. *Ageryos Hagenozoy,* the third part of the adorning prayer, belongs to the third figure of grammar. This third part is found in right wheel of the figure. See the figure on page 502.
52. *Opus salutare,* this is the fourth and last part of the adorning prayer belonging to the third figure of grammar. This fourth part is found in the bottom wheel of the figure. See the figure on page 502.

and may I implement your precepts, Theos, Hamatheos, Zezomal, Salym, Vichazethem, Sycharonos, Cezomelos, Hazihamor, Iegal, Megal, Iegamegyl, Haziha, Megyle, Scopon, Hazymon, Hazyhel, Hoyhon, Cethay, Honacrehos, O Jesus, the Son of piety, the fountain, the honor of the angels, the joy of all the celestial virtues, may I rejoice in you today, may I honor you, may I glorify you in the age of ages, amen. Be present, holy angels, always assisting in the sight of God, so that my intelligence may be augmented through you, and may my sense and memory be augmented to perceiving the holy works with liberty [and] to obtaining mercy, so that the door of knowledge, having been opened to me, my heart may give praise, and having been strengthened and emended through you, may [my sense and memory] perceive and conserve the knowledge, wisdom, and memory acquired in this art and I will learn with valid reasoning, Metha, Sama, Zethemeyl, what a gift you might deem worthy to grant me, you who are pious and merciful to all the hopeful and faithful ones deprecating you, amen.

Here you may open the grammar books reading within here and there.

[NS 23] *Note that, through these three figures of the art of grammar which are described here and through the prayers decribed in the book, intelligence is to be acquired and had and true stability for acquiring understanding and retaining in memory the very science of the art of grammar, if it is to be proceeded accordingly to its operation, just as it is to be understood and declared in the text and in that gloss, which begins* Sicut enim *notae* gramaticae inspiciende, etc.[53]

53. Section 78 gloss.

[Logic]

[NS 24] *This prayer ought to be offered five times first before this figure and after this prayer the prayer written below the figure is to be offered five times:*
O holy God the Father,[54] and the indissoluble argumentation of the heart,[55] you who wanted to stabilize the sky, the earth, the sea, the abyss, and everything that is in them, in whose sight all reason and speech subsists through these precious sacraments of your angels, give me that . . . ,[56] which I desire and believe—that is, the knowledge of this art without malignant intent—amen.

[NS 25] *Rubric: These four-wheeled figures are the four signs given by God, through which the operation and the memory of all letters are given,[57] and for that reason, they ought to be inspected once and to be held in the memory always at the end of the inspection of the last figure of any art, for this which is written in these four signs ought not be read but only be inspected and held in the memory.*

[NS 26] *Rubric: This is the first figure of the art of dialectic, which on the first day of the new lunar month of any [calendar] month, it ought to be inspected first and its prayers offered five times, and having made a short interval, the prayers of the second figure ought to be offered five times by inspecting the second figure itself; and it is to be done thus, concerning these two figures during one month on any day four times, from the early morning up to the third [hour] once, from the third [hour] up to noon once, from noon up to the ninth [hour] once, [and] from the ninth [hour] up to the evening [hour] once, you may inquire about the order of these figures in that gloss which begins:* Sciendum est autem quod notae dyalecticae, etc.[58]

---

54. *Sancte Deus Pater,* the first prayer belonging to the first figure of logic/dialectic. See section 135.

55. Latin *cordis.* Compare against its parallel word, *concordia,* in section 135.

56. The ellipsis represents the placeholder for which the operator would insert his desired area of logic/dialectic study.

57. The four-wheeled figures are called "the four signs of all knowledge" at NS 149. The Latin *litterarum,* translated here as "letters," may not refer to just the letters of the Latin alphabet but also the knowledge of dialectic literature both of which are depicted within these four signs. See chapter V for the analysis of these four signs.

58. Section 80 gloss.

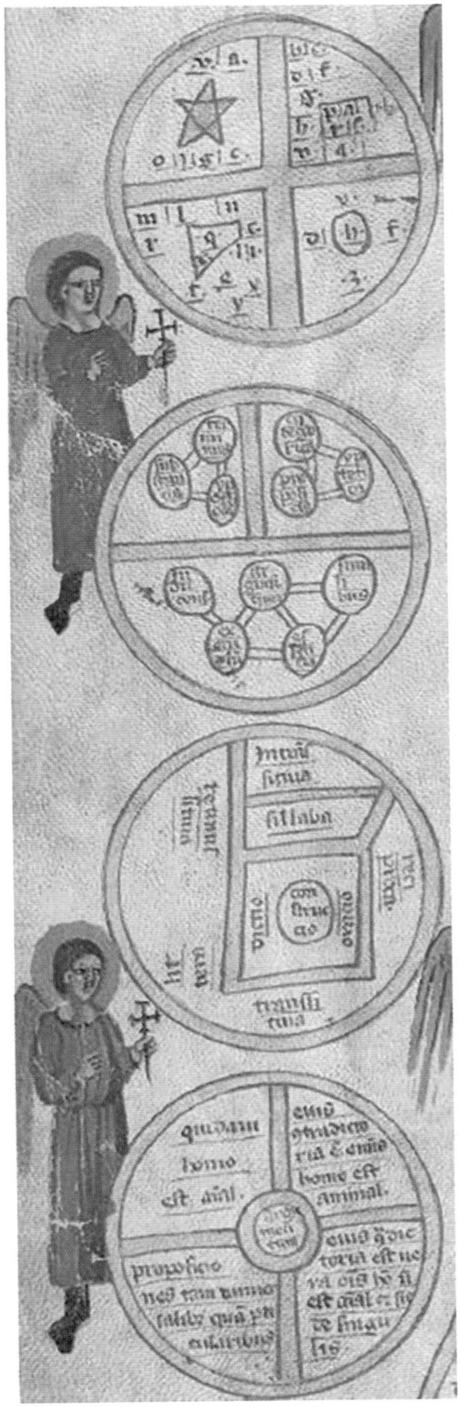

The four signs of all knowledge—a detail of the first figure of logic/dialectic (4b)

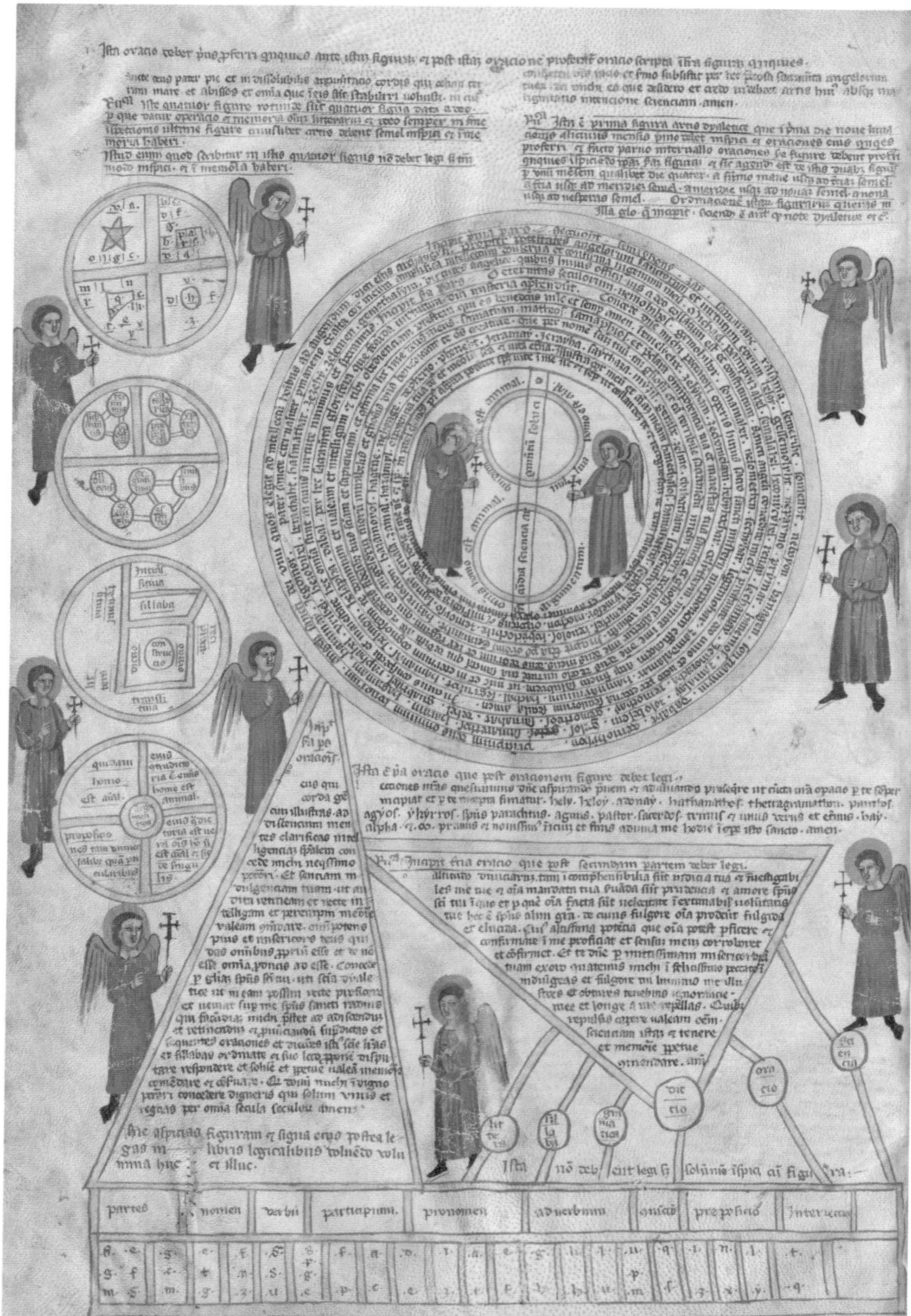

The first figure of logic/dialectic (4b)

[NS 27] *The first part begins:*

Seguoht, Semzyhony, Zay, Samarahc,[59] Rasama, Semeriht, Somenht, Neboyon, Banagen, Sonnamym, Dabaht, Gemohyhon, O God, the beginning of all good things, O holy angels of the living God whom he elected for the purpose of augmenting the understanding among men, you are called archangels, on account of the powers of the holy angels and their virtues, Heloy, Gessemolyht, Nepaymo, Prymar, Hanemos, Zamalay, Zolobelem, Gelos, Samarethos, Haram, Hagamam, Haramay, Iegomor, O holy Father, everlasting eternally, exalt my heart, amplify [my] understanding, conserve and strengthen my ingenuity, Michael, Pamphizahel, Semalahel, Heconyches, Renay, Lechamay, Iemoracha, Remothay, Gemotheos, Sarnahat, Dehel, Guabrihel, Raphahel, Urihel, Hezobihel, Berachaht, Hasmathar, Zezehy, Zelemen, Gemethasym, the angelic virtues to which the law of this office and the constitutum[60] is conferred by God, O holy angels, grant me with presenting the true and living God through the eternal age of ages, amen. In whose sight and majesty all these things are, in whose virtue we live and hope.

[NS 28] *The second part begins:*

O Eternity of the Ages,[61] Nemohihos, Gemohihor, Sonamaher, Nelomethen, Sechyhar, Legamohar, Zamdalamar, Hamnaymuum, Hachal, Segruhot, Hamanas, Helmon, Helapha, Dabal, through these sacraments, [these angels] comprehend the glorification and the fruitfulness of the virtues of the Lord's mysteries; O Lord, grant me, a sinner, the beginning, efficacy, and the salubrious end to the mysteries of this sacrosanct work, so that now and forever I may know and understand you Lord, and present to you obedience, you who are blessed now and always, amen. Hemelyehoc, Zelyham, Zechomelam, Hebyhochar, Celytheym, O Lord God, send into me your holy virtue from heaven, which you gave to Adam and the rest of your faithful the knowledge and wisdom, and strengthen this within

---

59. *Seguoht, Semzyhony, Zay, Samarahc,* the adorning prayer consists of three parts and belongs to the first figure of logic/dialectic. This first part is found in the outer ring of the great wheel, or *gyrus,* of the figure. See the figure on page 508.

60. Latin *constitutum,* an agreed arrangement.

61. *O aeternitas seculorum,* the second part of the adorning prayer belonging to the first figure of logic/dialectic. This second part is found in the great wheel of the figure. See the figure on page 508.

me; O my God, Samathan, Matheos, Samaphios, and may your almighty splendor and your holy and glorious majesty be exalted in me, O my God; O God of gods and king of kings, you who are the wonderful and glorious Lord of your angels, may all creatures praise you which you wanted to declare to me, a sinner, through your holy name so much glory and such a revered sacramental mystery,[62] amen.

[NS 29] *The third part begins:*

Gerarauht, Hazirelochon,[63] Hazamoyos, Hagene, Nehonge, Depherio, Pheneht, Ieramay, Ierayha, Saythaza, Myzil, Gerahc, Zelme, Chibatham, Lassehuthos, Gememthes, Hevolos, Hobyclochihe, Zemoyso, Lamay, Lenasa, Zamal, Hazamyl, your almighty power, O God, and the holy memory, and the eternal life, illuminate my heart and my soul, Hanethalos, Hamacihathos, Sepha, Lymesor, Mechon, O almighty and merciful God, attend to me, a pious gentle sinner, today, now and always, breathe powerfully the spirit of life into me now and always, so that I may praise you and recognize you as God my savior and declare your holy works to all who love you, amen.

[NS 30] *This is the first prayer which ought to be read after the prayer of the figure:*

O Lord, we ask [you to] assist to come before and help to attend our readings,[64] so that our whole operation may always begin through you, and having begun, it is finished through you, Hely, Heloy, Adonay, Hathanathos,[65] Thetragramathon,[66] Panthos,[67] Agyos,[68] Yhyrros,[69]

62. Latin *terribile sacramentum,* literally means "a terrible sacrament," but again, the sense is based on the biblical concept of "fear of the Lord" in which the sacrament is meant to inspire awe and reverence of the divine power contained within the sacrament.

63. *Gerarauht Hazirelochon,* the third part of the adorning prayer belonging to the first figure of logic/dialectic. This third part is found in the great wheel of the figure. See the figure on page 508.

64. *Lectiones nostras,* the adorning prayer consists of three parts and belongs to the first figure of logic/dialectic. This first part is found in the space between the great wheel and the downward pointing triangle. See the figure on page 508.

65. *Hathanatos,* Greek word meaning "immortal."

66. *Tetragrammaton,* Greek word for the Hebrew four-letter name of God, Yahweh.

67. *Panthos,* a corruption or abbreviation of the Greek word *Pantocrator,* meaning "almighty."

68. *Agios,* Greek word meaning "holy."

69. *Ischyros,* Greek word meaning "strong."

Paraclete,[70] the lamb, the shepherd, the priest, threefold and one, the true and eternal one, Hay, Alpha and Omega, the first and the last, the beginning and the end, help me today in this holy work, amen.

[NS 31] *The second part of the prayer begins:*
O God, you who illuminates the hearts of the people,[71] you clarify the minds of the learned, grant me, a most worthless sinner, a special intelligence, and may I sense your indulgence,[72] so that having heard [something worth remembering], I may retain and understand [it] correctly, and having erased [something from memory], may I be able to commit [it back] to memory; O almighty, pious, and merciful God, you give your own being to all things, and being present, bring forth everything from non-existence; grant, through the glory of your Holy Spirit, the advantage of dialectic knowledge, so that I may be able to progress rightly within it, and may the ray of the Holy Spirit come over me, who presents me the eloquence with respect to learning further, retaining, and pronouncing the abovesaid and following prayers and sayings of this [dialectic] science, the letters and syllables of the order and its own place to propose, to dispute, to respond, to solve, and may I be able to commit and to conserve perpetually to memory, because you deemed worthy to grant the gift to me, an unworthy sinner, you alone who lives and reigns through all the ages of ages, amen.

Here you may inspect the figure and its signs after you read in the logic books by unrolling the scrolls here and there.

---

70. *Paraclitus,* (Greek: παράκλητος and the Latin *paracletus*), which is the Paraclete or the Holy Spirit, often translated as "the advocate" or "the helper."

71. *Deus qui corda gentium illustras,* the second part of the adorning prayer belonging to the first figure of logic/dialectic. This second part is found in the upward pointing triangle located on the left-hand side of the figure. See the figure on page 508.

72. Latin *indulgentiam.* In the Catholic faith, an indulgence is a remission of the punishment of sin; a pardon. Here the petitioner is simply asking God for a pardon of his sins and a reduction of time spent in postmortem punishment. During the Middle Ages, the Roman Catholic Church affirmed that the sacrament of penance did not wipe away the stain of sin through absolution alone but that the sinner had to face temporal punishment for his offense. After death, the sinner had to temporarily suffer in purgatory, a metaphysical and intermediate place of torment, until all his debts of sin had been paid to God.

[NS 32] *Rubric: The third prayer begins, which ought to be read after the second part:*

O the depth of riches [of the wisdom and knowledge of God],[73] so incomprehensible are your judgments and unsearchable your ways,[74] and keeping all your commandments are the prudence and love of your Holy Spirit, in whom and through whom all things, having been made, are your volition with an inestimable swiftness, this is a spirit you went[75] with grace, from whose effulgence all things go forth flashing and lucid, whose most highest power, which every one is able to advance and strengthen within me, is beneficial, and strengthens and fortifies my sense; and I entreat you, O Lord, through your most gentle mercy, to what point you indulge[76] me, a most misfortunate sinner, and illuminate me with the effulgence of your luminosity, and obstruct the darkness of my ignorance, and repel [it] far away from me, after which, having been repulsed, may I be able to capture and grasp all this knowledge and to commit [it] perpetually to memory, amen.

[NS 33] *This prayer ought to be offered five times before this figure:*

O most gentle Heloy,[77] the creator, inspirer, and informer of all good volitions, the approver and ruler of the jaws, O glorious Father, look favorably upon my mind and my deprecation with intention, as I deprecate, entreat, and request out of humility and devotion, hope and faith, just as it is promised by you to me through the deprecations of your holy angels, grant me . . .[78] from your magnificence with abundance, you who lives and reigns through the infinite ages of ages, amen.

---

73. *O altitudo divitiarum,* the third part of the adorning prayer belonging to the first figure of logic/dialectic. This third part is found in the downward pointing triangle of the figure. See the figure on page 508.

74. Compare against Romans 11:33 (Vulgate), *O altitudo divitiarum sapientiae et scientiae Dei quam inconprehensibilia sunt iudicia eius et investigabiles viae eius.* The bracketed text is restored from this New Testament passage. The Romans passage draws from Isaiah 40:28.

75. Latin *isti,* the second-person singular perfect active indicative of *eo,* meaning "you went," is a correction taken from the Bodley 951 manuscript, folio 10v. Véronèse reads *alim,* an unidentified or nonsensical word, from BnF Latin 9336, folio 19v.

76. Latin *indulgeas,* in the sense of pardoning or permitting. See footnote 78, below.

77. *Heloy, clementissime,* this prayer belongs to the second figure of logic/dialectic. See also section 137.

78. The ellipsis represents the placeholder for which the operator would insert his desired area of dialectic study.

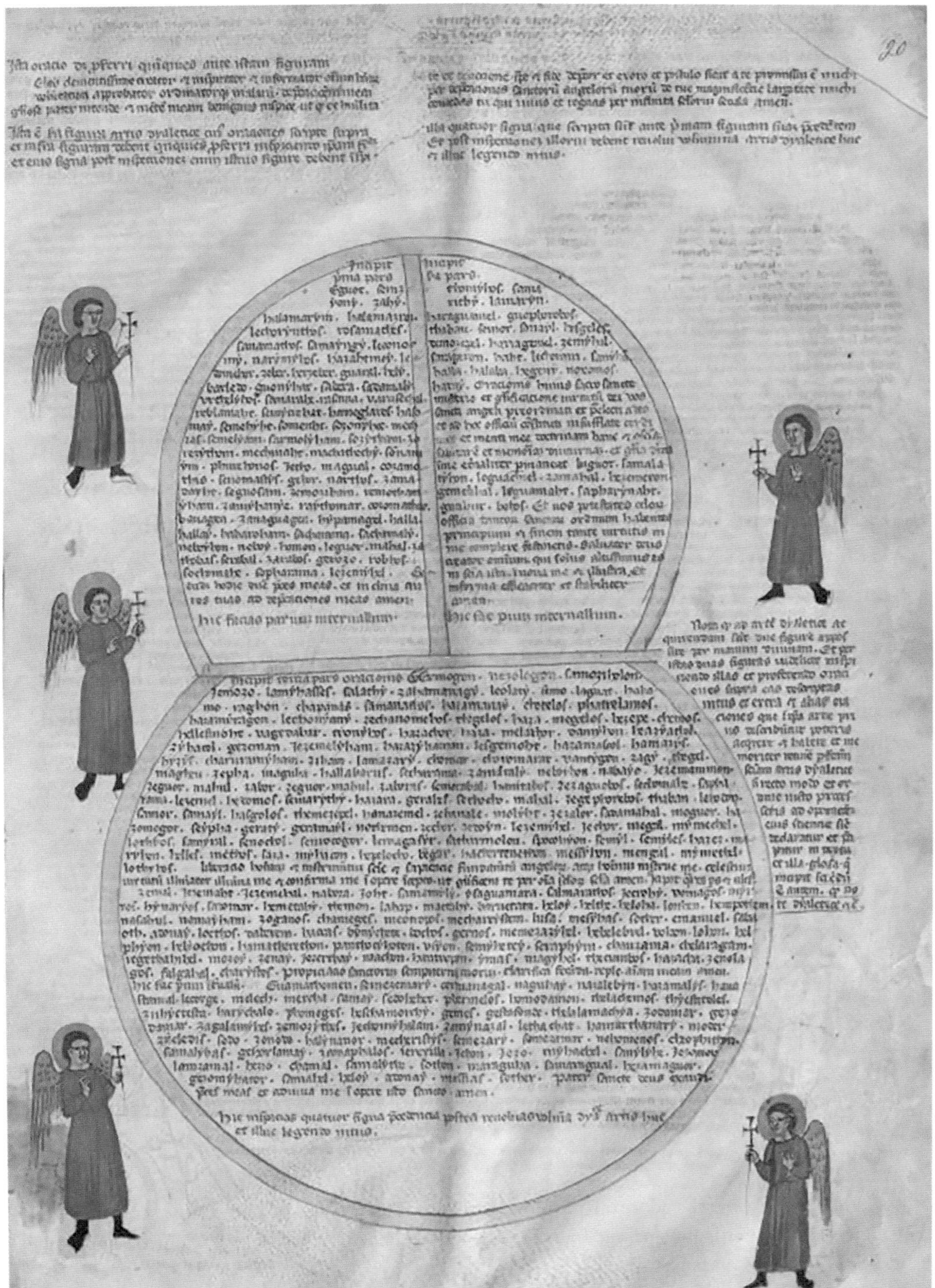

The second figure of logic/dialectic (5b)

[NS 34] This is the second figure of the art of dialectic, whose written prayers above and below the figure ought to be offered five times, having inspected this very figure and its signs; for after the inspection of this figure, those four signs which are written before its own preceding first figure ought to be inspected, and after the inspection of those, the scrolls of the art of dialectic ought to be unrolled reading within here and there.

[NS 35] *The first part begins:*
Seguoht, Semzyony,[79] Zahy, Halamarym, Halamazrez, Lechorynthos, Rosamathes, Sanamathos, Samayngy, Leconomy, Narymyhos, Hazahtmoy, Ledomehor, Zeber, Herzeber, Guaral, Helybarledo, Guonyhar, Sabera, Sadamaly, Urthelyhoi, Samarahe, Rasama, Varusechal, Reblamaht, Semytrehat, Hameglares, Hasomay, Semehyht, Somenht, Sozonyhec, Mechias, Semelyam, Sarmolyham, Sozytham, Zorezythom, Mechinaht, Machathechy, Sonamym, Phurehonos, Ietho, Magual, Cozamothis, Senomastys, Gehor, Narthos, Zamadayht, Segnuosam, Zemoziham, Remothamyham, Zamyhanye, Raythomar, Cozomathar, Bavagen, Zanaguagen, Hypamagel, Halla, Hallay, Haharoham, Sacharama, Sachamaly, Neboyhon, Neboy, Homon, Leguor, Mahal, Zathobas, Serabal, Zarabos, Gerozo, Robhos, Sochomahe, Sopharama, Lezemyhel, O Lord, hear my prayers today, and incline your ears to my deprecations, amen.

Here you must make a short interval.

[NS 36] *The second part begins:*
Othomyhos, Samarithy,[80] Lamaryn, Haraguamel, Guophorobos, Thabau, Semor, Sanayl, Hesgeles, Demozepel, Hariagemel, Zemyhal, Sarageron, Haht, Lechoram, Sanyham, Halla, Halaba, Hegeny, Noromos, Haray, the mystery of this sacrosanct prayer and the glorification of God's virtues, you

---

79. *Seguoht Semzyony,* the adorning prayer consists of four parts and belongs to the second figure of logic/dialectic. This first part is found in the top circular part of the figure on the left-hand side. See the figure on page 513.

80. *Othomyhos Samarithy,* the second part of the adorning prayer belonging to the second figure of logic/dialectic. This second part is found in the top circular part of the figure on the right-hand side. See the figure on page 513.

holy angels, preordained and elected beforehand by God to this office of the constitutum, insufflate[81] this teaching to my heart and my mind and a salutary conscience and long-lasting memory, and may the divine glory remain within me eternally, Luguot, Samalatyhon, Loguachiel, Zamahal, Hezemeron, Gemelihal, Leguamaht, Spharynaht, Guabur, Bohos, and you powers of the heavens, the offices of so many holy orders, having the beginning and end of so much virtue, hasten to complete . . .[82] within me, O God the savior, creator of all things, who alone is the highest in this knowledge, renew, illuminate, and instruct me efficaciously and firmly.

Make a short interval here.

[NS 37] *The third part of the prayer begins:*

Germogon, Nezologon,[83] Samoziholon, Iemozo, Lamyhasses, Salathy, Zahamanagy, Leolaty, Semo, Laguat, Hahamo, Raghon, Chapamas, Samanathos, Hazamanay, Chetelos, Phatrelamos, Hazamyragon, Lechonyany, Zechanomehos, Thegelos, Haza, Megelos, Hezepe, Chemos, Hellesmoht, Vagedabar, Tronyhos, Hazachor, Haza, Melachor, Damyhon, Heazyathol, Zyhacol, Gezeman, Iezemelyham, Hazazyhaman, Lesgemoht, Hazamascol, Hamazys, Hyzys, Charuramyham, Ziham, Lamazary, Chomar, Choromarar, Vantygon, Zagy, Thegel, Magheu, Zepha, Maguha, Hallabarus, Secharama, Zamaraly, Neboyhon, Nabayo, Iezemammon, Zeguor, Mahul, Zabor, Zeguor, Mahul, Zaboras, Semorabal, Hamtabos, Zezaguobos, Sechomahr, Sapharama, Lezemzl, Hedomos, Semarythy, Hazara, Gerahes, Sechocho, Mahal, Zegephorebos, Thaban, Lehodon, Samor, Samayl, Hasgolos, Themezepel, Hanazemel, Zehanale, Molyht, Zezalor, Sadamahal, Moguor, Hazomogor, Seypha, Geraty, Geramayl, Nothemen, Zechor, Zedoyn, Lezemyhel, Iechor, Megal, Mymechel, Lothyos, Samyral, Senochol, Senrocogor, Lemagasyr, Satharmolon,

---

81. Insufflate is the ritual practice of breathing or blowing life force energy for the purpose of bestowing a blessing or driving away evil.

82. The ellipsis represents the placeholder for which the operator would insert his desired area of dialectic study.

83. *Germogon Nezologon,* the third part of the adorning prayer belonging to the second figure of logic/dialectic. This third part is found in the bottom circular part of the figure. See the figure on page 513.

Spocohyon, Semyl, Semyles, Hazez, Maryhen, Helles, Methos, Saza, Myhacon, Hepelocho, Begar, Hachertenethon, Messyhon, Mengal, Mymethel, Lothyhos, O the liberation of men and the instrument of knowledge and wisdom, O the foundation of angels and men, instruct me . . .[84] **Of the heavenly virtues, O illuminator, illuminate me and strengthen me in the work undertaken, so that i may glorify you throughout all the ages of the ages, amen.**

[NS 38] *The fourth and last part begins:*

Zemal, Iezemaht,[85] **Iezemehal, Naboza, Ioht, Samamyly, Ysaguamara, Salmarathos, Iecrohy, Vomagos, Myrros, Hynaryos, Sadomar, Hemetahy, Themon, Lahap, Mactaby, Baructata, Heloy, Helthe, Heloba, Louhen, Hempothem, Nasahul, Namayham, Zoganos, Chameges, Meotropos, Mechareystem, Lusa, Mesyhas, Sother, Emanuel, Sabaoth, Adonay, Locthos, Daberem, Hacras, Bynychete, Bochos, Gernos, Memezazyhel, Hebelebrel, Vohon, Lohon, Helphyon, Helyochon, Hamatherethon, Panthocyhoton, Usyon, Semyhetey, Seraphim, Chauzama, Chelaragam, Regethahihel, Mozoy, Zenay, Iezerthay, Machon, Hantropon, Ymas, Magyhel, Thecumbos, Hazacha, Zenolagos, Falgahal, Charystos, O the propitiation of your eternal holy ones, clarify, make fruitful, and replenish my soul, amen.**

[NS 39] *Make a short interval here.*

Guamathomen, Semezemary,[86] **Cormanagal, Naguhay, Nazalebyn, Hazamalys, Havastamal, Lecorge, Melech, Mercha, Samay, Sedohehet, Phermelos, Homodamon, Thelachemos, Thyestiteles, Zuhyctesta, Harychalo, Phomeges, Heschamorchy, Gemes, Gestafonde, Thelalamachya, Zodamar, Gezodamar, Zagalamyhes, Zemozythes, Iechomyhalam,**

---

84. The ellipsis represents the placeholder for which the operator would insert his desired area of dialectic study.

85. *Zemal Iezemaht,* the fourth part of the adorning prayer belonging to the second figure of logic/dialectic. This fourth part is found in the bottom circular part of the figure. See the figure on page 513.

86. *Guamathomen Semezemary,* this is either a subcomponent of the fourth part or an unrecognized fifth part of the adorning prayer belonging to the second figure of logic/dialectic. This part is found in the bottom circular part of the figure. See the figure on page 513.

Zamynazal, Lethachat, Hamarthanary, Moderzycledis, Sodo, Zonodo, Halynanor, Mecheristys, Semezary, Somezamar, Nehomenos, Cheophithon, Samalyhas, Gehorlamay, Zamaphalos, Ierexilla, Iehon, Iezo, Myhachel, Sanylyhe, Iezomor, Lamzamal, Hezio, Chamal, Samalythe, Sothon, Maraguha, Samaragual, Hezamaguor, Gezomyhator, Samahel, Heloy, Adonay, Messias, Sother, O God the holy Father, hear my prayers and help me in this holy work, amen.

You must inspect the preceding four signs here, afterward you may unroll the scrolls of the art of dialectic and reading within here and there.

[**NS 40**] Note that with respect to acquiring the art of dialectic, there are two figures apposite by the divine hand, and through these two figures—that is, inspecting them and offering the [adorning] prayers above them (having been transcribed within and without [the figure]) and the other prayers which are described first within this very art—you will be able to acquire, possess, and retain in memory the perfect knowledge of the art of dialectic, if you proceed to the operation of its science in the right manner and proper order, just as it is declared and taught in the text and that gloss, which begins *Sciendum est autem quod notae dyalecticae, etc.*[87]

87. Section 80 gloss.

[Rhetoric]

[NS 41] *This prayer is to be offered first before this figure, having said first that [prayer]* Lux, veritas, etc.:

O almighty and merciful Father,[88] the orderer of all creatures, the eternal judge, the king of kings and the Lord of lords, you who are wonderfully deemed worthy to confer eloquence and knowledge to your holy ones, who adjudicates and discerns all things, today illuminate my heart with effulgence of your brilliance, so that I may understand and know . . .[89] which are considered in this art, and what I greatly wish for in the teachings of this art, amen.

[NS 42] *These names are to be offered after the preceding prayer:*

Hanazay,[90] Sazahoron, Ubisevehar, Ghu, Hyrbaionay, Gynbar, Zonayl, Selchora, Zelmora, Hyramay, Iethobal, Ysaramahel, Hamathamathohys, Iaboha, Iechors, Cozo, Meralx, Sozomeraht, Hamy, Phodel, Denos, Gerotha, Gualos, Mehiha, Taguahel, Sechamay, Salihe, Lethon, Mecho, Gristes, Lemenron, Hatagon, amen.

[NS 43] *This is the first figure of the art of rhetoric. For in the first day of the new lunar [days] of any [calendar] month in the early morning these prayers which are written above the figure and below the figure are to be offered five times, having always inspected the figure itself, and after the inspection of this first figure, the prayers of the second figure following are to be offered five times, having always inspected the second figure itself, and it is to be done thus concerning these two figures from the early morning up to the third [hour], and then an interval is to be made. From the third [hour] up to noon the same prayers of both figures are to be reiterated five times, and these very figures are to be inspected. But at*

---

88. *Omnipotens et misericors Pater,* the first prayer belonging to the first figure of rhetoric. See section 138.

89. The ellipsis represents the placeholder for which the operator would insert his desired area of study in rhetoric.

90. *Hanazay,* the second prayer belonging to the first figure of rhetoric. *Hanazay* equates to the prayer *Gezomanai,* as inferred by other sections of the *Ars Notoria*. Also, in the other sections, *Hanazay* is assigned to the second figure of rhetoric, not the first. Furthermore, *Gezomanai* appears to be a misplaced General prayer. See sections 126c gloss (page 447, footnote 265), 126f gloss, 140 (Versions A and B), and 140 gloss.

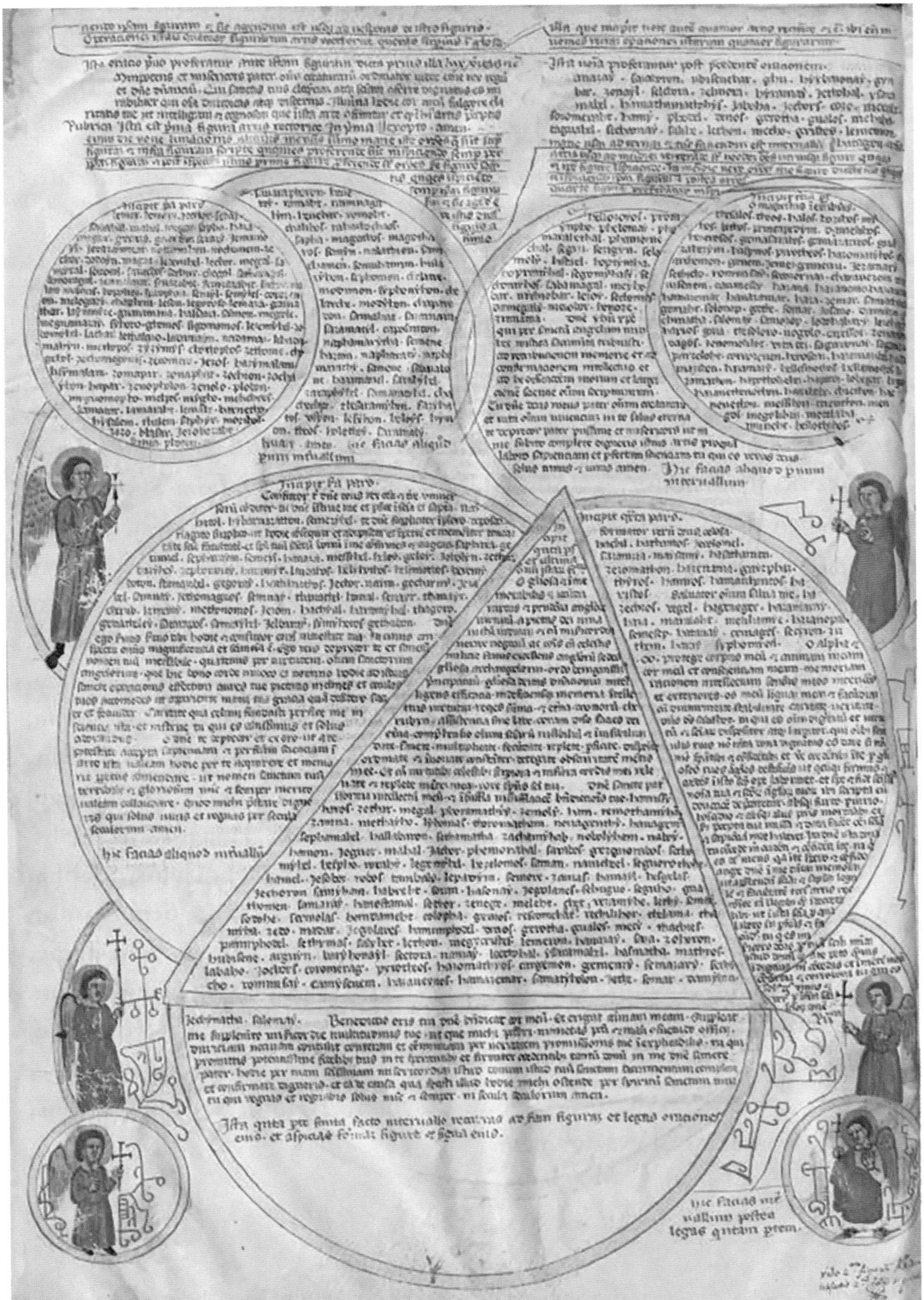

The first figure of rhetoric (6b)

noon the prayers of the third figure are to be said five times and having inspected this very figure, and afterward the prayers of the fourth figure are to be offered, having inspected the figure itself, and it is to be done thus up to the evening [hour] concerning these figures. You may inquire about the operation of those four figures of the art of rhetoric above in that gloss which begins: Notae autem quattuor artis rectorice, etc.[91] *For you will find there the right operation of these four figures.*

[NS 44] *The first part begins:*

Lemor, Lemoyz, Iecholor,[92] Seday, Sadahal, Mahal, Megor, Sapha, Hazamagor, Gerazy, Guorfar, Serazy, Iemamoyl, Ierazammar, Nothemiham, Nochomem, Zechor, Zodoyn, Magar, Lezemihel, Lechor, Megal, Samyral, Sonocol, Sanechos, Sechur, Chogol, Satharagol, Semoragol, Zennalazir, Senazabic, Iemzazahit, Sachor, Malon, Malozis, Hopolioz, Spocophon, Semyl, Semyles, Corozenon, Melogazy, Chaphem, Leson, Legoroso, Lemaza, Gamathar, Laymnyze, Guanamana, Halsava, Salmon, Megole, Meguamazay, Syhoro, Ghomos, Sigomomos, Lezemyhel, Zobomyhel, Lathar, Lethalazo, Ladamayn, Nadamaz, Lihada, Mahyn, Methopos, Zyzymys, Chothophos, Zethome, Chogelos, Zothomegonis, Zecomero, Iezos, Hazymalam, Lisymalam, Zomapar, Zonaphat, Zochion, Zochayhon, Hapar, Zenopholon, Zenolo, Plobon, Myguomopho, Melpos, Mygho, Melichros, Lamatar, Lamaraht, Lemahe, Barnetho, Hysalem, Thalem, Saphyr, Mozihol, Zezo, Blasar, Iezobezaht, Semia, Photon, Savaraphoron, Henetoy, Ramaht, Raminagalym, Henchar, Romoht, Chalilos, Rahachochaos, Sapha, Magathos, Magotharos, Semyn, Nalathion, Samichamen, Semuhamin, Hulazyhon, Sephomon, Chelatre, Modimon, Syphonyhon, Chelarche, Modihon, Chaparedon, Samahat, Sazamara, Sazamatyl, Caposandon, Naphamarytha, Semenehazam, Napharaty, Naphamarathy, Samene, Sabazabone, Hazamanel, Sarahyhel, Zaraphyhel, Samaratyhel, Chacheclipe, Thesaramyhon, Sazyhatos, Usyon, Lesyhon, Heloys, Hymon, Theos, Holethoy, Saramaty, Lyvazy, amen.

---

91. Section 79 gloss.

92. *Lemor, Lemoyz, Iecholor,* the adorning prayer, consisting of five parts, belongs to the first figure of rhetoric. This first part is found in the small wheel on the left-hand side of the figure which then spills over toward the center space next to the arcing line. See the figure on page 519.

You must make another short interval here.

[NS 45] *The second part begins:*
I confess to you, O Lord God, king of heaven and earth,[93] creator of the universe, O Lord, instruct and perfect me in the knowledge and wisdom, Nayhatol, Hybarnazathon, Semezyhel, O Lord, I implore suppliantly to you, I pray earnestly to you, I entreat you, I supplicate you, so that today I may know, obtain, impetrate, and grasp by memory the faculty of so much knowledge, and may you strengthen and augment the good things of your Holy Spirit within me, Saphara, Getumel, Sepharaym, Semeyl, Hanaza, Messyhel, Heloy, Geloy, Ieholyn, Zethor, Hazyhey, Zephoranay, Haramyt, Laudahos, Helyhothos, Helymothos, Heremyboton, Stamazihel, Gegoray, Hathanathos, Iechor, Naym, Gecharny, Iezabel, Samnay, Iethomaguos, Semnay, Thanathel, Homal, Senayr, Thanayr, Cherub, Lamany, Methonomos, Iezom, Hachyal, Haramyhal, Thagoro, Genatheley, Sacarapos, Samatyhel, Ielbaray, Symyhoros, Gethubon, O Lord, I, your servant,[94] speak to you today and confess before your majesty, in whose sight every magnificence and sanctity exists, I, a guilty person, deprecate you and your ineffable holy name, inasmuch as, through virtue of all the holy angels, who I invoke and name here today with a good heart, incline your pious ears and adjust your eyes to the effect of this holy operation, so that opening your hand with grace the sacred and fruitful . . . which I desire,[95] you who poured the heavens with charity, perfect and instruct me in this knowledge, you who are the highest and alone is to be worshiped; O Lord, I deprecate and entreat you, so that having received the wisdom and perfect knowledge in this art from you with authority I may be able to acquire and to commit . . .[96] perpetually to memory, so that I may be able to rightly

93. *Confiteor tibi, Domine Deus, rex celi et terra,* the second part of the adorning prayer which belongs to the first figure of rhetoric. In the figure, this second part is found in the semicircle on the left-hand side of the triangle. See the figure on page 519.
94. This portion of the prayer bears strong resemblance to *Domine quia ego servus* found at NS 86, belonging to the fifth note of astronomy and the tenth prayer of the *Ars Nova* at section 125.
95. Psalm 145:16. The adjectives "sacred and fruitful" (*sacer et fecunder*) modify whatever desired knowledge about the art of rhetoric the petitioner would fill in for the ellipsis.
96. The ellipsis represents the placeholder for which the operator would insert his desired area of

praise your revered,[97] glorious, and holy name, now and always, because you deemed [it] worthy to present to me, you alone who lives and reigns through the ages of ages, amen.

You must make some interval here.

[NS 46] *The third part begins:*

O ineffable majesty,[98] Thesalos, Theos, Halos, Hozihos, Myhos, Bethos, Pemtapedym, Damelihos, Hezerosos, Gemasarahos, Gamazaziros, Guazahezym, Haspiros, Pirotheos, Hazomatyhos, Charchemon, Genem, Iemez, Gemenzi, Iezamary, Sethicho, Romimsay, Secozornaz, Charavezem, Cauvisenem, Caumesey, Hazana, Hazanemo, Hazavemo, Hamazemar, Havazamar, Haza, Zemar, Samathiholos, Gemaht, Solonop, Gethe, Somar, Zosano, Damihon, Gechmatha, Salonay, Samozop, Lodohahary, Lezohary, Harios, Gaza, Thesoloro, Nogolo, Capessor, Zonomorol, Dagos, Ienomolihot, O life of God, Sagazamay, Sagamazo, Parzeloht, Corrozeven, Herosem, Hazamizihel, Hassamazihen, Hazamazy, Hellesmothos, Hellemechos, Sazamathon, Hapotholiehez, Haperoz, Lobegar, Begar, Hazanethenothon, Hatuhehe, Chiethon, Hacuevethon, Messihon, Menthon, Mengol, Megolihuz, Metelaha, Muneht, Hellothihos, Hellozoyos, Promynpho, Phelomay, Phamarahethal, Phamomechal, Segizi, Sezigyn, Selomoly, Histael, Hoptymha, Hoprimyhal, Segomyhasy, Sechomyhos, Sabamagal, Meyhobar, Nychiobar, Lezoy, Sechomys, Damegaly, Meiobor, Honoze, Zimiama, O Lord Jesus Christ, who bestowed this mystical sacrament[99] through your holy angel to the retribution of memory, and to the strengthening of the intellect, and to the edification of morals, and the generosity of all written knowledge; O Lord my God, the Father of all creatures, and life of all living things, I deprecate the eternal salvation in you; O most pious and merciful Father, I deprecate you, so that you may deem

---

study in rhetoric.

97. Latin *terribile.* See foonote 1115.

98. *O maiestas ineffabilis,* the third part of the adorning prayer which belongs to the first figure of rhetoric. This third part is found in the small wheel on the right-hand side of the figure, which then spills over toward the center space next to the arcing line. See the figure on page 519.

99. Note that here the *Ars Notoria* is described as a Christian sacrament.

worthy to suddenly fill . . . of this art[100] within me for which I labor the wisdom and perfect knowledge, you who are solely the true God, threefold and one, amen.

You must make some short interval here.

[NS 47] *The fourth part begins:*

O God, the creator of things,[101] Celosa, Hachil, Hathamos, Iecolomel, Sazamzia, Maysamy, Hasathaman, Zezomathon, Hazenama, Gayzphaz, Thyros, Hamros, Hamatihantos, Haristos, save me, the savior of all beings, Hazechios, Vegel, Hageneger, Hazamaray, Haza, Maralaht, Melihamye, Hazanopal, Semesep, Hatanay, Cemagos, Secyron, Zuthem, Haray, Syphomyon, O Alpha and Omega, protect my body and my soul, my heart and my conscience, [my] memory, reason, [and] understanding, my internal and external senses, my mouth, my tongue and eloquence with long-lasting stability, charity, [and] truth; O Lord God of Hosts,[102] you who are the disposer and bestower of all of worthy things, virtues, and sciences, you who deemed worthy to give so many gifts not to all your servants, but only to those hoping and confessing and truly believing in you, testifying through your glorious angels, so that whosoever labors firmly and believing in this holy work, and [whosoever] deprecated your most holy name and your holy angels, written in that very place with devotion, hope, and faith, and without theft, perjury, murder, and without other mortal sins, and it was being done according to your precepts, having been sent and given to he who was having all the knowledge and wisdom thenceforth; in this way, O Lord, may you grant me these gifts, believing and confiding in you, you who are my God, because I hope and confide in you; O Lord, augment so much memory within me, so that I may apprehend the legal knowledge and wisdom, and the entire [mental] faculty of the art of rhetoric, so much in

---

100. The ellipsis represents the placeholder for which the operator would insert his desired area of study in rhetoric.

101. *Formator rerum Deus,* the fourth part of the adorning prayer which belongs to the first figure of rhetoric. In the figure, this fourth part is found in the semicircle on the right-hand side of the triangle. See the figure on page 519.

102. The original text reads *Dominus Deus Sabahot [Sabaoth].*

laws as well as in decrees, so that in this knowledge for which I labor I may be perfect and eloquent, you who are the merciful God, this gift that I ask of you by your holy mercy, although you grant [it] to me, an unworthy one, and you fortify and strengthen my mind, you alone who are God, living and true through the infinite ages of ages, amen.

You must make an interval here after reading the fifth part.

[NS 48] *The fifth and last part of the prayer of those figures begins:*
O glorious,[103] immemorable, and pleasant virtue and prudence of the angels' virtues, the living just judgment from the piety of God, and the truthful statesman with the mercy and the common cause of the heavenly army, the excelling status of the Angels, the glorious seat of the Archangels, the benevolent order of the Principalities, the glorious divinities of the Dominions, understanding the efficacy and unfailing memory, the understanding of the Virtues, the highest and eternal rest of the Thrones, the Cherubim, assisting without fail, before the Lord, the face of the eternal God, the comprehension of all the visible and invisible sciences, give, favor, multiply, make fruitful, replenish, perfect, dispose, order, and renew constantly and detect the obscurity of my mind, and with the heavenly virtues above and below reveal to my heart, and replenish my mind with the dew of your Holy Spirit,[104] O Lord the Holy Father, inform my intellect and insufflate your benediction with insufflation, Hamissyharos, Zothar, Megal, Phoramathys, Zemoly, Ham, Remothamyham, Zamma, Methayho, Lyhomas, Thoromatham, Novagenthy, Havageny, Sephamahel, Hallabaron, Sethamatha, Zachamyhab, Nobolyham, Naboy, Hamon, Ieguor, Mahal, Iachor, Phemorabal, Sarabos, Gezguorabos, Sochomyhel, Hespho, Rorahy, Legemyhel, Hezelomos, Saman, Namcheel, Seguorothoht, Hamel, Iesoboz, Robos, Tambaly, Lepadym, Semore, Zamas, Hamayl, Hesgelas, Iechoron,

---

103. *O gloriosa,* the fifth and last part of the adorning prayer which belongs to the first figure of rhetoric. This fifth part is found in the central triangle of the figure. See the figure on page 519.
104. The phrase "dew of the Holy Spirit" (*ros sancti spiritus*) is a special phrase used by the Christian monk John Cassian (c. 360–435) in his *De Institutis Coenobiorum* (*Institutes of the Coenobia;* see 6.17, 5.14.2), which explains the organization of monastic communities of the Desert Fathers of Egypt. See Humphries, *Ascetic Pneumatology,* 26.

Samyham, Hanostamal, Sethor, Zenege, Meleht, Chet, Vezamyhe, Lethy, Semay, Sodohe, Scrinolas, Homdameht, Colopha, Gemos, Rescomehat, Rechilihor, Thelama, Thamyha, Zedo, Madar, Iegolares, Hamimphodel, Denos, Gerotha, Gualos, Mecy, Thachies, Pamphodel, Sethymas, Salyhet, Lethon, Megocristes, Lemeron, Hanazay, Saza, Zohoron, Hubisene, Arguyn, Baryhonayl, Sectora, Namay, Lecchohal, Ysaramahel, Hasmatha, Mathyos, Labaho, Iochors, Coromegar, Pyrotheos, Hazomathyos, Cargemon, Gemenzy, Semazary, Sethycho, Rommisay, Camysevem, Hazaveynos, Hamazemar, Samatyholon, Iethe, Somar, Damyhon, Iechynatha, Salomay, O Lord, may the blessing of your mouth bless my heart and raise my soul, may it supply me with the supplement of the multitudes of your mercies,[105] so that it conferred to me, a sinner, who [has] an excess of sin, bad habits of duty, and a harmful austerity, having been bruised and broken into small pieces[106] through the truth of your inexplicable promise, you who promised the most powerful to your faithful ones, hoping and believing firmly in you, such a gift within me; O Lord the Holy Father, you deemed worthy to fulfill that gift through your most holy mercy and to strengthen your holy sacrament today, and you who made it for a reason, show me that . . .[107] today through your Holy Spirit, you who reigns and will reign alone, now and always in the ages of ages, amen.

Having finished this fifth part, [and] having made an interval, you may return to the second figure and read its prayers and inspect the shape of the figures and its signs.

[NS 49] *This prayer, with the other three following, is to be offered five times before this figure:*

O one,[108] great, wonderful, eternal God, O angel of the eternal plan, O disposer, composer, and orderer of all virtues, adorn my understanding

105. Psalm 51 (NRSV).

106. A metaphorical reference to ascetic or self-mortification practices including, fasting, waking, repetitive genuflection during prayer, wearing penitential robes (*cilicium*) and girdles (*cingulum, catena*), and self-flagellation.

107. The ellipsis represents where the operator would insert his desired area of study in rhetoric.

108. *Unus magnus,* a prayer belonging to the second figure of rhetoric. See section 139.

today, and multiply within me reason to discerning cognition that you conferred on your creatures in offering the names of your heavenly angels, and grant me the same knowledge according to your promise, and give me (the discernment)[109] in this art, amen.

[NS 50] *This prayer is to be offered without an interval after the preceding one:* **Usyon,[110] of all powers, kingdoms, and eternal judgments with a conspicious concord, administering the zeugma of all languages, in whose regime you will give no impediment, I beg [you] to restore . . . ,[111] having recounted and repeated [it within] my heart and my tongue for the purpose of discerning, being eloquent, judging, and to having it, which the divine authority entrusts to the necessary in this art, and it is to be completed perfectly within me, amen.**

[NS 51] *This prayer is to be offered after the preceding one, having made a short interval:*

Azelechias,[112] Velozeos, Mohan, Zama, Sarvelo, Hoteus, Saguaht, Adonay, Sozo, Zezomochos, Zezonochos, Hychon, Iezomochon, Sadohoc, and you, O propitious God, strengthen in me your promises, just as you strengthened King Solomon through the same words, send to me, O Lord, the virtue from heavens that may strengthen my heart and illuminate my mind, strengthen, O God, my understanding and my soul, renew . . .[113] within me and wash me with the waters which are above the heavens, and pour out . . . from your Spirit onto my flesh and in my viscera for the purpose of performing in accordance to your commandments and reconcile your judgments with the humility and charity with which you made heaven and earth, and cre-

---

109. The petition may specify the discernment of something in particular here.

110. *Usyon omnium,* a prayer belonging to the second figure of rhetoric. See section 141.

111. The ellipsis represents the placeholder for which the operator would insert his desired area of study in rhetoric.

112. *Azelechias [. . . regi Salomoni],* a prayer belonging to the second figure of rhetoric found only in Version B. See also Version B, Variation 7. Compare its opening words to those found at NS 76.

113. The ellipsis represents the placeholder for which the operator would insert his desired area of study in rhetoric. Two more ellipses are to be filled in later within this same prayer by the operator.

ated and formed man in your image and likeness, infuse the light of your brillance into my intellect, so that having been founded and rooted in your mercy I may love your name, and I may know and adorn you, and understand all the writings of this art, for this reason, how much these things are given and marked by God, and sent forth through the hands of the holy angels are a mystery of these figures, for which I may have and know all things in my intellect, my heart, and my mind, and may I constantly have the effect of your holy name, [having and knowing] . . . of this art, and for the most glorious plan prevailing, amen.

[NS 52] *This is the second figure of the art of rhetoric, whose prayers ought to be offered five times after the inspection of the first figure, and this very figure and its signs are to be inspected, and after the inspection of this very figure, the canon or civic scrolls of the law*[114] *ought to be inspected and are to be unrolled, reading here and there within some decrees or laws.*

[NS 53] *These names of the holy angels which are written within these wheels ought to be offered with great devotion, and they ought to be made [having] an interval between the first and second part.*

[NS 54] *This is the first prayer:*
Habytay,[115] **Sezemen, Zohemen, Hoslatho, Gemolaz, Thamaza, Lazaher, Ramal, Hyzymal, Germahc, Gemez, Saguat, Sadahot, Germahel, Zodehon, Zedonay, Symacobar, Iemodonay, Zamna, Samna, Zamalezo, Semalda, Datheladam, Treslahedom, Layruda, Samna, Zamna, Sabayha, Samay, Saramay, Semal, Hada, Heladaz, Sabara, Saday, Saulay, Sozomai, Dazoloinon, Iesoht, Melyhos, Thomazohay, Hardemos, Lassagello, Molathagello, Seraphyn, Iezamale, Salay, Daymahy, Mathay, Zomaht, Recorznazay, Saphathihal, Seguoht, Sapharbay, Ba, Zelohor, Hamna, Guale, Lama, Guahycihamal, Remazoguos, Zema, Soguos, Halay, Zabera, Hallamays, Samnays, Samma, Chymathos, Sorar, Syrogual, Hasnam,**

114. Scrolls were better suited for archiving laws and decrees than books.

115. *Habytay,* the adorning prayer, consisting of two parts, belongs to the second figure of rhetoric. This figure has two columns of wheels. In the left-hand column of wheels, the first part of the *Habytay* prayer is distributed across these eight wheels. See the figure on page 528.

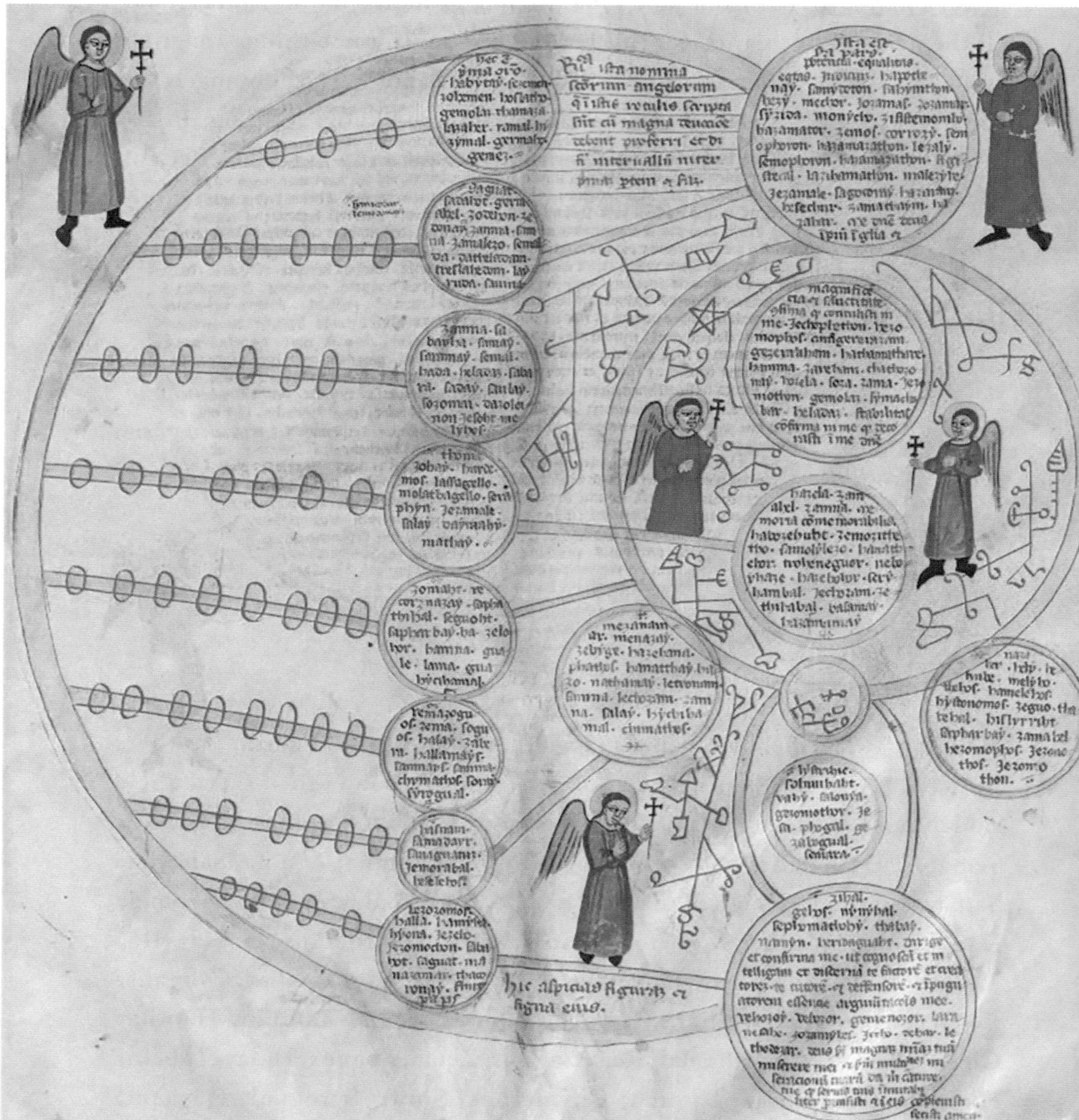

The second figure of rhetoric (7b)

Samadayr, Sanaguatuz, Iemorabal, Heselehos, Bezozomos, Halla, Hamyha, Hyona, Iezeho, Iezomochon, Sabahot, Saguat, Manazamar, Thacoronay.

[NS 55] *The first part ends. This is the second part:*

O power, equality,[116] **equity, judgment, Hapothenay, Samydoton, Sahymthon, Hezy, Mechor, Iozamas, Zozamar, Syzida, Monycho, Zisistemoniho, Hazamator, Zemos, Corrozy, Semophoron, Hazamazathon, Sigistecal, Lazihamathon, Malezyhe, Iezamale, Sagocoray, Hazaram, Hesechur, Zamachaym, Hazahar, strengthen me, O Lord God, in glory, magnificence, and sanctity, who has conferred . . .**[117] **within me, Iechophethon, Hezomophos, Cumgererazam, Gezeraliham, Hathamathare, Hamma, Zareham, Chathozonay, Hozela, Soza, Zama, Iezomothon, Gemolaz, Symachobar, Heladaz, O stability, strengthen . . . within me what you have adorned within me, O Lord, Hazela, Zamahel, Zamna, O commemorable memory, Habozehuht, Zemozithetho, Samolylezo, Hanathehor, Troheneguor, Neboyhaze, Hazehohor, Seryhambal, Iechozam, Zethihabal, Basamay, Hazamamay, Mezanamar, Menazay, Zebyge, Hazehana, Phathos, Hanatthay, Hazo, Nathamay, Letronam, Samna, Lechozam, Zamna, Salay, Hychihamal, Chimathos, Nazaher, Hely, Hehube, Melyho, Thehos, Hamelehos, Hystonomos, Zeguo, Tharehal, Hislyrriht, Sapharbay, Zamahel, Hezomophos, Iezonothos, Iezomothon, Lystrihic, Solimihaht, Vahy, Salonya, Gezomothor, Iesa, Phogal, Gezabogual, Semara, Zibal, Gehos, Nynyhal, Sephomathohy, Thabay, Namyn, Heridaguaht, guide and strengthen me, so that I may know and understand and discern you, the maker and the creator, you, the tutor, the defender, and the assailant of my essential argument, Vehozoy, Vebozor, Gemenozor, Laranesahe, Iozamyhes, Ietho, Dehar, Lethodezar, O God, have mercy on me according to your great mercy, and according to the multitude of your mercies,**[118]

---

116. *Potentia, equalitas,* the second part of the adorning prayer which belongs to the second figure of rhetoric. This second part is distributed across seven of the ten wheels, which line up like a column on the right-hand side of the figure. See the figure on page 528.

117. The ellipsis represents the placeholder for which the operator would insert his desired area of study in rhetoric.

118. Psalm 51 (NRSV).

give me, your creature, what you immutably promised to your servants, and you have accomplished and made [it] within them, amen.

You must inspect this figure and its signs here.

[NS 56] *This prayer is to be offered five times before the third figure of rhetoric with the other following [which] is written below the figure:*
For I know[119] that I am delighted in your great, wonderful, and ineffable making, and you will give me the knowledge which you have promised through this work according to your great and incomprehensible virtue, Tehon, Hathamagihon, Haramalon, Zamayma, Camasal, Iechonameryl, Haryhonachor, Iechomagel, Ielamagos, Remolyhot, Remanachar, Hariomolathay, Hanahenes, Velomonathar, Hazoroy, Iezabaly, augment the most precious and efficacious virtue and knowledge within me through these most sacred, glorious, and profound mysteries of God, and complete what you began, and reform what you showed within me, Zemabar, Henotanaht, Grenatayl, Samazatham, Iechornazay, O deepest foundation of all goodness, the sciences, and the virtues, bestow . . .[120] to your servant, [who] displeases you, [so as] to avoid moral contagions, and may I be able to be satisfied[121] with your pure virtue and holy intention, so that desiring your promise with all [my] heart in all fields of knowledge, as much as in the laws as the decrees, especially through these holy mysteries, having become adept and established [in the community], may I be understood and known, and thus, [also adept and established] in this art; O Lord, that I may be thoroughly accomplished, praiseworthy and eloquent, amen.

[NS 57] *This is the third figure of the art of rhetoric, which after the inspection of the second figure, ought to be inspected around noon first, and after this, having*

---

119. *Scio enim,* the first prayer belonging to the third *nota* of rhetoric. The *Per haec sacramenta sanctissima Dei* prayer belonging to music (NS 72), agrees almost verbatim with the latter portion of the *Scio enim* prayer here. See also variation 8.

120. The ellipsis represents the placeholder for which the operator would insert a moral virtue or quality befitting of avoiding moral contagions.

121. Latin *satiari,* meaning "to be satisifed."

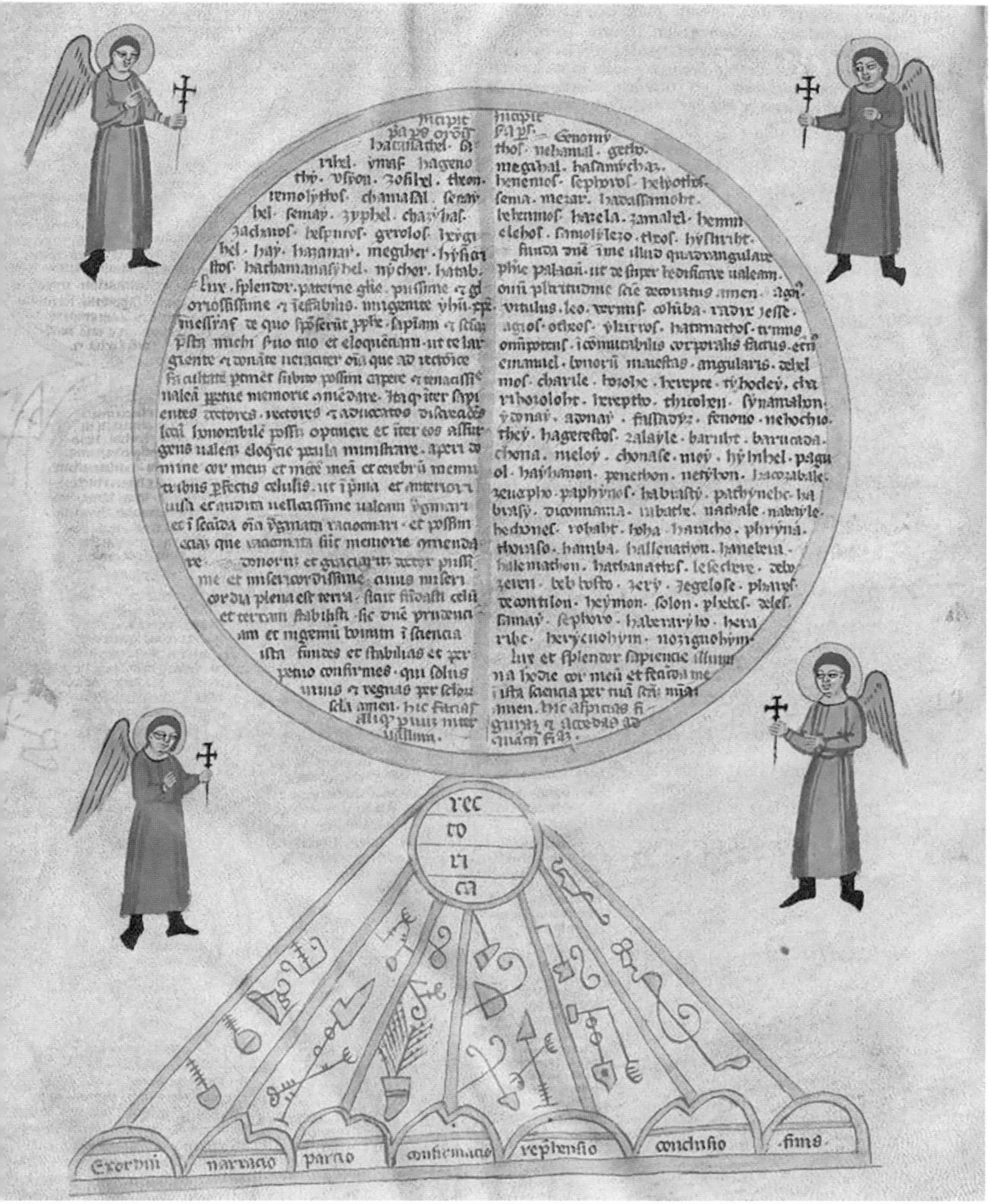

The third figure of rhetoric (8b)

made a short interval, the fourth figure is to be inspected with its signs. For the prayers of those particular ones over any figure are to be offered five times.

[NS 58] *The first part of the prayer begins:*

Hatanathel, Sarihel,[122] Ymas, Hagenothy, Usyon, Zosihel, Theon, Remolythos, Chamasal, Senayhel, Semay, Zyphel, Chazyhas, Zacharos, Hespuros, Gerolos, Heygihel, Hay, Hazanay, Megiher, Hysicristos, Hathamanasyhel, Nychor, Hatab, O light, O splendor of the paternal glory, O most pious, most glorious, ineffable, and the only begotten Jesus Christ, the Messiah, about whom the prophets were promising, present the wisdom, knowledge, and eloquence to me, your servant, so that, by bestowing and truly giving all things which are pertinent to the faculty of rhetoric, I may suddenly be able to understand and be able to most tenaciously to commit to memory perpetually. So that among the wise doctors [of philosophy], rectors, advocates, and judges I may be able to obtain an honorable place, and rising up among them, I may be able to minister drinking cups of eloquence. O Lord, open my heart, my mind, and my brain to the three perfect cells, so that in the first and anteriorly [positioned cell], may I be able to imagine things seen and heard most swiftly, and in the second all imagined things to be reasoned, and may I even be able to commit to memory those things which have been considered;[123] O most pious and most merciful doctor [of philosophy] of the gifts and graces, whose entire mercy is the earth, just as you founded the sky and established the earth thus, O Lord, may you lay the foundation of prudence and good ingenuity

---

122. *Hatanathel Sarihel,* the adorning prayer, consisting of two parts, belongs to the third figure of rhetoric. This first part is found in the left-hand side of the top wheel of the figure. See the figure on page 531.

123. According to the *Anatomia Magistri Nicolai Physici* (*The Anatomy of Master Nicolaus,* ca. 1150–1200), the brain is divided into three cells (*cellulae*): one for imagination (*phantastica*), located anteriorly; another for reason (*logistica*), located in the middle; and the other for memory (*memorialis*), located posteriorly. The ancient philosophers called the brain the temple of the spirit since its process reflected the functions of the three chambers of a temple. In the first temple chamber, called the *vestibulum,* declarations were made in law cases. In the second temple chamber, called the *consistorium,* the declarations were sifted. In the third temple chamber, the *apotheca,* the final sentence was given. Likewise, the brain gathers ideas, considers them, and then comes to a reasonable conclusion, which is committed to memory.

in this knowledge, and may you strengthen . . . and . . .[124] perpetually, you alone who lives and reigns through the ages of ages, amen.

You must make another short interval here.

[NS 59] *The second part begins:*

Genomythos, Vehamal,[125] Getho, Megihal, Hasamychaz, Henemos, Sephoros, Helyothos, Sema, Mezar, Hadassamoht, Behemnos, Hazela, Zamahel, Hemmelehos, Samolylezo, Theos, Hysliriht, O Lord, establish that quadrangular palace of philosophy within me, so that I may be able to build upon [it],[126] having been decorated to every beauty of knowledge, amen. O lamb, O bull calf, O lion, O worm,[127] O dove,[128] O root of Jesse, Agios, Otheos, [Agios] Ykirros, [Agios] Hatanathos,[129] threefold,

---

124. The first ellipsis represents the placeholder for which the operator would insert his desired area of study in rhetoric, and the second ellipsis represents the placeholder for which the operator would insert his desired knowledge, which is to be committed perpetually to memory.

125. *Genomythos Vehamal,* the second part of the adorning prayer which belongs to the third figure of rhetoric. This second part is found in the right-hand side of the top wheel of the figure. See the figure on page 531.

126. The quadrangular palace of philosophy is a reference to the metaphor of the one who practices the art of memory as an architect, and the quadrangular palace of philosophy represents his imagined palace, which stores the images of things to be remembered. The metaphor of the architect is expressed in Peter Abelard's commentary on Aristotle's *De Interpretatione,* the Christian mnemonic tradition which cites Paul of Tarsus's First Letter to the Corinthians 3:10–11 ("like a skilled master builder I laid a foundation, and someone else is building on it . . . For no one can lay any foundation other than the one that has been laid; that foundation is Jesus Christ") and ultimately traces its origins to architectural mnemonics as described in *Rhetorica ad Herennium.* See Copeland and Sluiter, *Medieval Grammar and Rhetoric,* pages 25–26.

127. A title given to Jesus Christ, who sang Psalm 22 during the crucifixion in which he calls himself a worm as it is written at verse 7, "But I am a worm not a man."

128. The bull calf and lion are two of the living creatures, or cherubim, that make up Ezekiel's vision (see Ezekiel 1 and 10). The other two living creatures are a man and an angel; it is possible the author is alluding to man by way of the worm reference in Psalm 22:6, and the dove may be representative of the Holy Spirit or an angelic being. These creatures are also prominent in Merkabah literature and mentioned in Revelation 4:6–8.

129. This Greek phrase translates as "O Holy God, O Strong One, O Immortal One," which forms the first portion of the Trisagion prayer. The Trisagion prayer may have its origins in the angelic cry recorded in Isaiah 6:3 or Revelation 4:8; also, there is an origin story that says during the reign of Theodosius II of Constantinople (408–450), an earthquake happened and a child shouted the phrase. The Trisagion prayer is a hymn sung in the Divine Liturgy of the Eastern Orthodox Church; it was also sung on Good Friday in the Latin Church as well as part of the Liturgy of Hours.

almighty, immutable, made corporeal, O eternal Emmanuel, the [quad] angular majesty of the good,[130] Dehelmos, Charile, Hozohe, Herepte, Tyhocley, Charihozoloht, Herephto, Thicohen, Synamahon, Ydonay, Adonay, Fassadyz, Fenono, Nehochio, They, Hagestestos, Zalayle, Baruht, Barucada, Chona, Meloy, Chonase, Moy, Hyhihel, Paguol, Hayhanon, Penethon, Netyhon, Hacozabale, Zevopho, Paphynos, Habrasty, Pathynehc, Habrasy, Dicomiama, Rabathe, Nathale, Nabayle, Hechones, Rohaht, Hoha, Haracho, Phryna, Thoraso, Hamba, Hallenathon, Hanebera, Halemathon, Hathanathos, Lesechere, Debozeren, Bebbosto, Zery, Iegelose, Phares, Decontilon, Heymon, Solon, Phebes, Deles, Samay, Sephoro, Haberaryho, Herarihc, Herycuohym, Noziguohym, O light and splendor of wisdom, illuminate my heart and make me abundant in this knowledge through your holy mercy today, amen.

You must inspect this figure and advance to the fourth figure.

[NS 60] *This prayer is to be offered five times before this figure:*
O revered and powerful God,[131] ruling over the higher angels and archangels and all the celestial creatures as well as the infernal and terrestrial ones, from whose magnificence of plenitude comes, so that us worthy ones may serve you, whose power reigns over the four parts of the world, you who formed man in your image and likeness from bones, soul, and spirit, give me the knowledge of this art, strengthening me in the faculty of this very knowledge, amen.[132]

[NS 61] *This is the fourth figure of the art of rhetoric, which, after the third figure, having made a short interval, ought to be inspected, and its prayers written above and below are to be offered five times. For after the pronunciation [of the prayers] of this figure and its own proper inspection, the books of rhetoric ought to*

130. A reference to Jesus Christ as the cornerstone. See Parable of the Bad Tenants (Matt 21:33–46; Mark 12:1–12; Luke 20:9–19).

131. *Reverende,* the prayer belonging to the fourth figure of rhetoric. See section 142.

132. Where the word *scientia* (knowledge) appears in this prayer, it is likely a placeholder for which the operator may replace it with his own personal request for a certain kind of knowledge about the art of rhetoric.

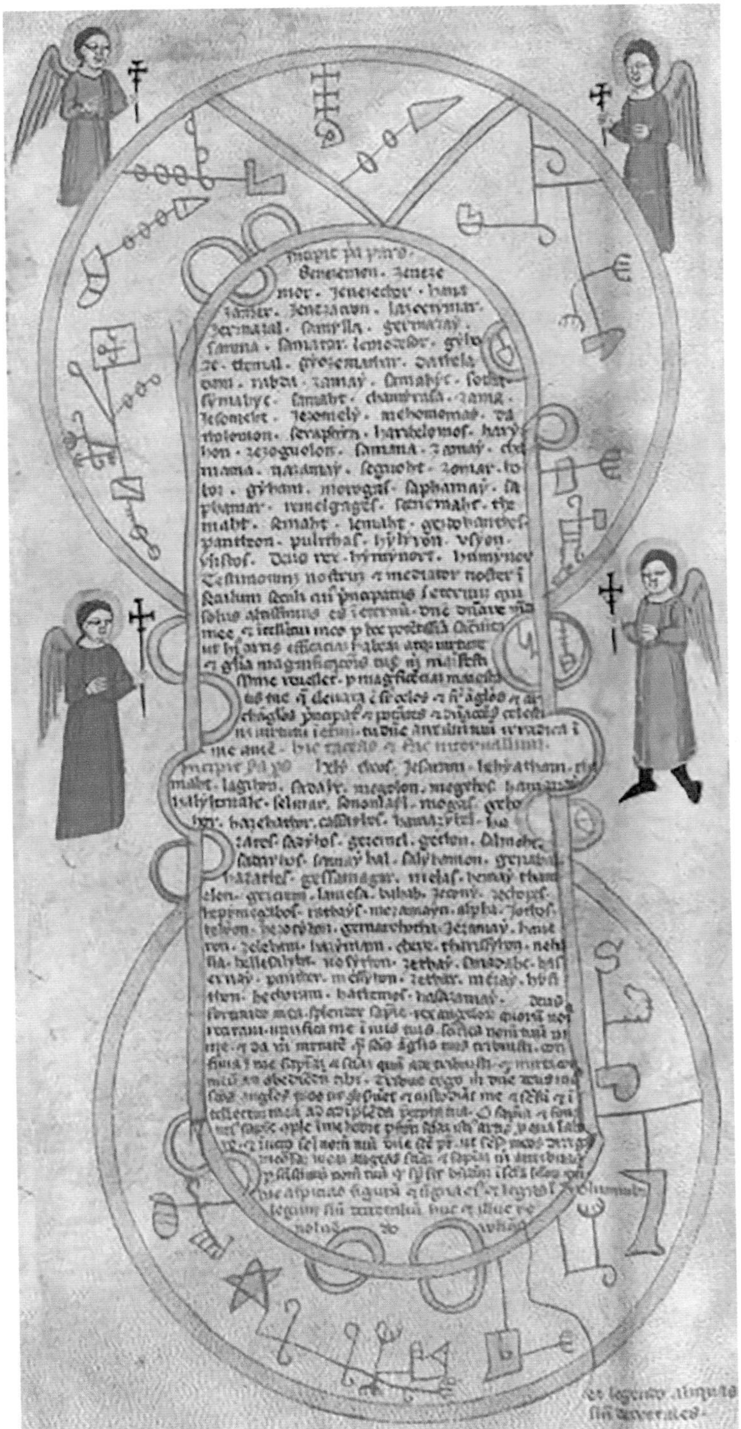

The fourth figure of rhetoric (9b)

be opened and the scrolls unrolled here and there and to read within some chapters here and there, having spread [them] out [before you].

[NS 62] *The first part begins:*
Senezemon, Zenezemor,[133] Ienezechor, Hanazamer, Ienezacron, Lazoctymar, Iermazal, Samylla, Germazay, Samna, Samatar, Lemodesor, Gyhoze, Themal, Gyozemathar, Datheladam, Rabda, Zamay, Samahyc, Sotha, Symahyc, Samaht, Chamyrasa, Zama, Iesomeht, Iezomely, Mehomomay, Datholomon, Seraphyn, Harihelomos, Haryhon, Zezoguolon, Samana, Zamay, Chamama, Nazamay, Seguoht, Zomar, Hoboz, Gyham, Morogas, Saphamay, Saphamar, Remelgages, Scenemaht, Themaht, Semaht, Lemaht, Gezdohanthes, Pantheon, Pulithas, Hylyron, Usyon, Ylistos, O God the king, Hymynort, Humynor, our witness and our mediator in the age of ages, whose sovereignty [is] in the eternal realm, you alone who is the highest in the eternal realm, O Lord, rule my mind and my intellect through these most powerful sacramental mysteries, so that I may have the efficacy and the virtue of this art, and the glory of your magnificence will be most manifestly revealed to me through the magnificence of your majesty, which is elevated above the heavens and above the Angels and Archangels, the Principalities and the Powers, and the Dominions of the celestial virtues in the eternal realm, you, O Lord, root within me your help, amen.

Here you may keep quiet and make an interval.

[NS 63] *The second part begins:*
Hely, Theos, Iesaram,[134] Hehyatham, Thamaht, Lagihon, Sadayr, Megolon, Megehos, Hamanay, Halyhemahc, Selmar, Sonomayl, Mogas, Gehohor, Hazehathor, Cassayhos, Hamazyhel, Hazates, Sadyhos, Gezemel, Gethon, Salmoht, Sadayhos, Samayhal, Salyhamon, Genabal, Hazathes, Gessamagar, Melas, Hemay, Thamelon, Gezerem, Lamesa, Bahab, Iecony, Zechopes,

---

133. *Senezemon Zenezemor,* the adorning prayer, consisting of two parts, which belongs to the fourth figure of rhetoric. This first part is found in the top portion of the figure. See the figure on page 535.

134. *Hely Theos Iesaram,* the second part of the adorning prayer which belongs to the fourth figure of rhetoric. This second part is found in the bottom part of the figure. See the figure on page 535.

Hepymegabos, Rathays, Mezamayn, Alpha, Iothos, Helyon, Hezotyhon, Gemarehotha, Iezamay, Haneron, Zeleham, Hazymam, Chere, Tharissyhon, Nehalla, Hellesalyht, Nosython, Zethay, Sanadahc, Hasernay, Panther, Messyhon, Zethar, Mezay, Hysithon, Hechoram, Hathemos, Hasazamay, O God my fortitude, O splendor of wisdom, O king of the angels whose names I recited, vivify me in your ways, sanctify your name within me, and give me the virtue which you have bestowed to your holy angels, strengthen within me the wisdom and knowledge which you bestowed to Adam, and transform my heart for the purpose of obeying you, ergo bestow to me, O Lord my God, your holy angels, so that they may observe and keep me and my sense and my intellect to implementing your precepts; O wisdom and fountain of total wisdom, complete within me today the perfect knowledge of this art for which I labor and invoke your holy name, O Lord the Holy Father, in order that you may guide my senses, augment my memory, [and] attribute knowledge and wisdom to me, through your most holy name, which may always be a benediction in the ages of ages, amen.

[NS 64] *Here you must inspect the figure and its signs, and you must read here and there in the scrolls of laws or decrees, having unrolled the scrolls and reading some laws or decrees.*

[NS 65] Note that to this point because the perfect intelligence, memory, and eloquence is able to be had, acquired, and retained in memory with respect to having the knowledge of the art of rhetoric, which is the knowledge which provides the manner of ornate and florid speaking and which contains within itself the knowledge of canon and civil law, some of the most holy prayers and the four figures have been sent and presented by God through the angel to King Solomon, so that through their prayers any good person is able to speak ornately and floridly, and wisely and discreetly, and to pronounce and to read those sciences which he had acquired through this holy art and through the commandment and gift of the Lord, which operation, if you begin and finish well and perfectly, just as it teaches and declares in the text and in that gloss, which the gloss begins *Notae autem quattuor artis rectorice, etc.*,[135] you will acquire and

135. Section 79 gloss.

have a florid and ornate manner of speaking in all the sciences of dictamen[136] and lectures, and you will be able to acquire the perfect knowledge in both canon and civil law, and without any doubt to retain [it] and commit [it] to memory perpetually.

For this you should pay close attention, and it is to be attended to and truly know that the entire mystery, the whole virtue and efficacy of this most holy operation consists in the prayers, within which the names of the holy angels of the living God, residing in the seats above, are named and invoked, and in the virtue of their figures and signs, because having invoked and named the holy angels of God with fasting and prayer, hope and faith, with the divine permission and virtue of God and his holy angels, which the angels have this grace from God who created them, the heart, mind, and all the senses, working [both] the interior and exterior [senses], are imbued and replenished with the divine knowledge of the Holy Spirit and the administration of the holy angels, and through them this most sacred work is being guided to an effect. It is to be understood that these same prayers, in which the names of the holy angels are unknown, were carried away and sent only with the figures and their signs from God through the angel to Solomon and presented to him, and not the Latin prayers which are now apposite[137] in this art, because some Greek, Hebrew, and Chaldean words which were said in Latin for the prayers were translated by the successors of Solomon and Apollonius, so that some sinner who was attempting to undertake such a sacred work with ignorance and sin might find a greater grace in the presence of God.

Also, it is to be understood that, just as it was promised by the Almighty Creator, it is still permitted, and especially for Solomon and after him, the many others like Apollonius, Ptolemy,[138] and Vergil[139] to constrain

136. The *ars dictaminis* is the art of letter writing performed by notaries for the purpose of church and state business. In Italy, the rise of political organization led to the increased demand for chanceries and notaries to write up official documents. Adalbertus Samaritanus (c. end of the eleventh century and probably died before 1150), working in Bologna, published the first *ars dictaminis* manual around 1120 and titled *Praecepta dictaminum* (*Teaching the Art of Letter Writing*).

137. That is to say, the Latin prayers are now next to or in apposition to the unknown prayers.

138. Claudius Ptolemy (c. 100–170), Greek mathematician, astronomer, and astrologer who wrote two widely influential texts titled the *Almagest* and the *Tetrabiblos*. During the Middle Ages, Ptolemy had gained a legendary reputation as a magician as three astral magic treatises were later and falsely attributed to him. See page 109, footnote 89.

139. Vergil (70–19 BCE), the ancient Roman poet who wrote three famous poems titled the

malignant spirits and to congregate them by naming and invoking them, by naming their names so that they might obey [the magicians] and satisfy their desires, so that they would be able to bind and to enclose them, having offered to them various kinds of sacrifices, because it is an evil, most serious, and dangerous thing to work. For many it is to be believed strongly because it is permitted by God, and having been given to ask him his name, having been named, and to ask his own holy angels, having named their names with the good operations, with confession, with fasting, chastity, hope, and faith and by doing all good works, so that working in this holy operation for the sake of having the knowledge from God, [the believers] may return to leading a good life, and they may have graciousness and kindness, with respect to acquiring first the grace of God and the holy angels, and afterward the knowledge and wisdom, because it is licit of anyone to deprecate God and his holy angels without sin with respect to acquiring such graces.

Eclogues, the *Georgics,* and the *Aeneid*. During the Middle Ages, legends and fantastic tales arose of Vergil's reputation as a magician. See chapter I.

[Medicine]

[NS 66] *He must offer this prayer with the others following five times before the figure of medicine:*

O highest God, O invisible God,[140] Theos, Pat[e]r, Behemnyhos, Lehemnos, Behemny, Lehemnyhos, we ask you, Ymos, through your most holy angels who are Michael, the medicine of God, Raphael, the fortitude of God, Gabriel, the ardent Seraphim, Helypha, Massay, Cherubim, Ielo, Mycros, Zelomytihos, Guadabany, Zadabanay, Gederanay, Sarammany, Lonythechy, Lothrosy, Gerobanathon, Zahamany, Lomynht, Henloranht, Enlomyht, Henloramyht, Samanazay, Gedebandy, the plenitude of knowledge, Cherubim, Seraphim, we suppliantly ask you and you, Jesus Christ, through all your glorious holy angels whose names are consecrated by God, which ought not to be offered by us, which are these: Dehel, Deyhel, Depymo, Dehyn, Hel, Exluso, Depymon, Helymon, Exmegon, Parynehos, Exegan, Pheheneos, Navagen, Hosyhel, Horagon, Garbona, Rachyon, Monyham, Megon, Hamos, hear me, O Lord, and help me in this holy work, amen.

[NS 67] *You must make an interval here and then read this prayer:*

I beseech you,[141] O my Lord, illuminate my conscience with the splendor of your light, and illuminate and strengthen my understanding with the sweet scent of your Holy Spirit, adorn my soul, so that I may hear [that] which is to be heard, and having heard, I may grasp [it] by memory; transform, O Lord, my heart, restore, O Lord, my sense, placate, O most pious one, my memory, temper, O most benevolent one, my tongue through your glorious and ineffable name, you who are the fountain of goodness and the origin of all piety.[142] O Lord, have patience with me and give me a good memory, and because I have asked you to grant me . . .[143] in this holy prayer, you who does not judge a sinner immediately, but having pitied

---

140. *Deus summe Deus invisibilis* is the prayer belonging to the figure of medicine. See section 24 in which the prayer belongs to the General prayers.

141. *Te queso Domine* is the Latin prologue to *Deus summe Deus invisibilis*. See section 25.

142. Latin *fons bonitatis et totius pietatis origo*. An epithet of God found in the Gregorian Sacramentary. The same epithet is found at NS 94 and 114.

143. The ellipsis is a placeholder for the operator to insert his own desired area of knowledge concerning medicine. Another ellipsis for the same thing follows later in the prayer.

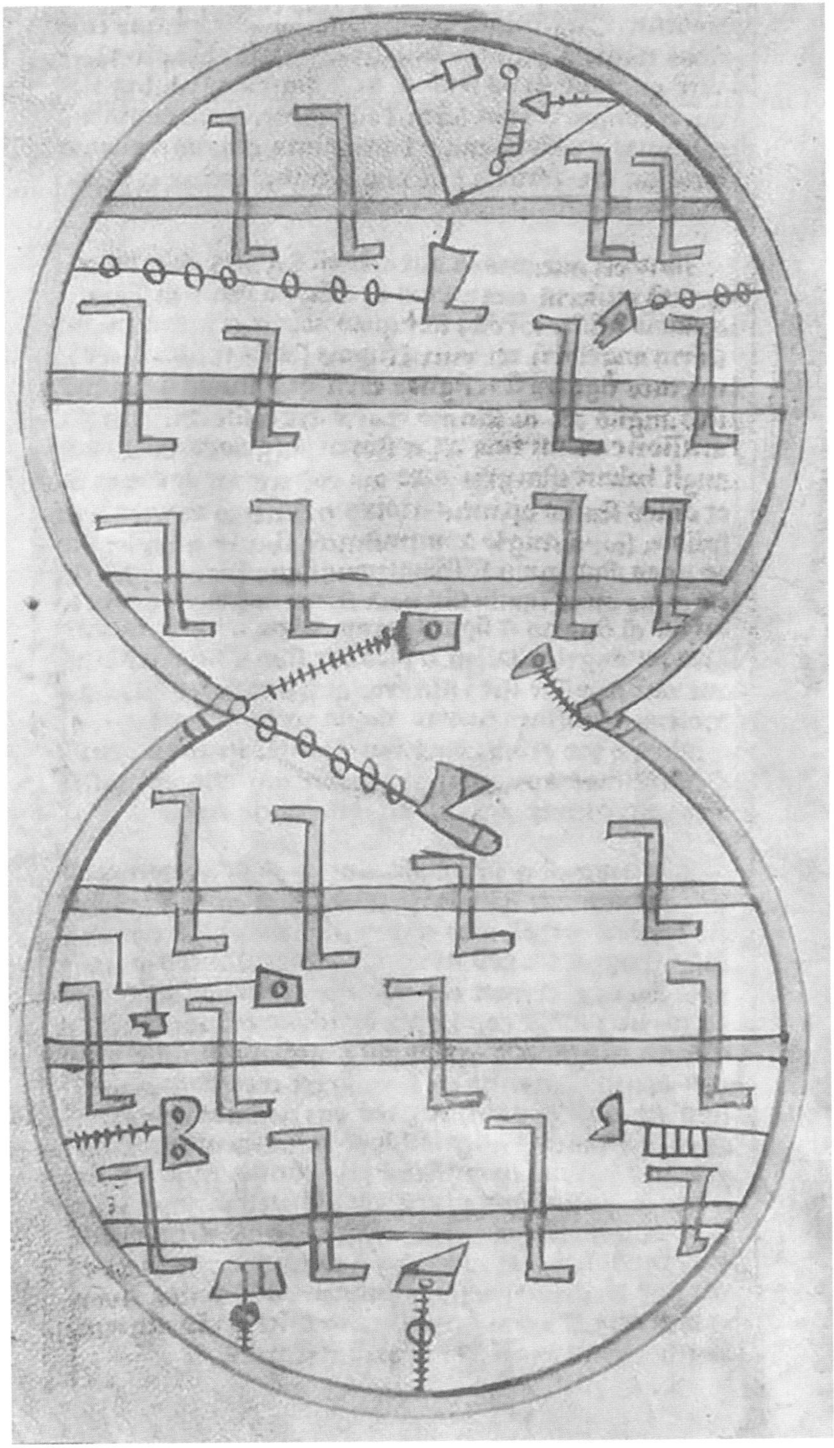

The figure of medicine (10b)

[him], awaits [his] penitence; I, an unworthy sinner, beseech you, O Lord, to wipe away and thoroughly extinguish my crimes, sins, and the wickedness of my failures, and with my petition so much virtue from which I am made worthy and efficacious beforehand through your holy angels, you make . . . through your glory and majesty, you who are threefold and one, the true God, amen.

[**NS 68**] *This is the figure of the art of medicine, which you will inspect first in the first day of the new lunar [day of] any month five times in that very day: once in the early morning, once around the third [hour], once around noon, once around the ninth [hour], and once around the evening [hour], and their own particular prayers are to be offered at any hour five times, and it is to be done thus through a one-month operation of this figure, and you may see about the art of medicine above in that gloss, which begins:* Ecce de reliquis quattuor liberalibus, etc.[144]

144. Section 85/86 gloss.

[Music]

[NS 69] *This prayer is to be offered five times in the operation of the inspection of this figure of the art of music:*

O God the immeasurable Father[145] from whom proceeds every thing that is good, O most merciful and almighty God, burn my kidneys[146] out of the grace of the Holy Spirit, and visit[147] me today by the fire of your visitation[148] and be propitious to me, a sinner, and show me your mercy, so that I may drink and satisfy [myself] from the fountain, you who are God,[149] and let your kind will be done within me, and may I sing and understand your wonders, you who are God, threefold and one, amen.

[NS 70] *This is the figure of the art of music, which you will inspect the figure on any day of one month five times, and you will offer its own particular prayers five times, and you must do so in this way just as it is taught in the operation of the figure of medicine. You may inquire about the order of the operation in the same gloss, which begins:* Ecce de reliquis quattor liberalibus, etc.[150]

[NS 71] *The first part of the prayer begins:*

Otheos, Athamatheos,[151] Behemnos, Phatheneos, Guarbona, Iemahal, Iechor, Nazal, Zezebar, Ienechail, Hathamalon, Ierozamor, Zehia, Nathal, Zamabos, Zamna, Magay, Hallomatha, Ierbeamon, Samyhel, Mathar, Iezozamor, Zamanal, Herebon, Desathay, Mychos, Hamyhc, Iethaphael, Gergelihon, Hagaros, Hagamos, Iezozar, Semaythos, Galamagar, Salamay, Sabyhon, Hemchilem, Iomanaht, Theos, Patyr.

[NS 72] *The second part begins:*

---

145. *Deus Pater immense [. . . misericordissime]* is the prayer belonging to music. See also Variation 11 where the same prayer is attributed to the seventh *nota* of philosophy.

146. Psalm 26:2 (Vulgate). See section 117, page 277, footnote 80.

147. Or punish. This translation would support the preceding request for a divine testing.

148. Compare similar phrasing from the *Ars Nova* prayer *Confiteor* in section 117.

149. Compare similar phrasing from the *Ars Nova* prayer *Adoro te rex regum* in section 116.

150. Section 85/86 gloss.

151. *Otheos Athamatheos,* the adorning prayer, consisting of three parts, which belongs to the figure of music. The first part is found in the outer ring of the figure. See the figure on page 544.

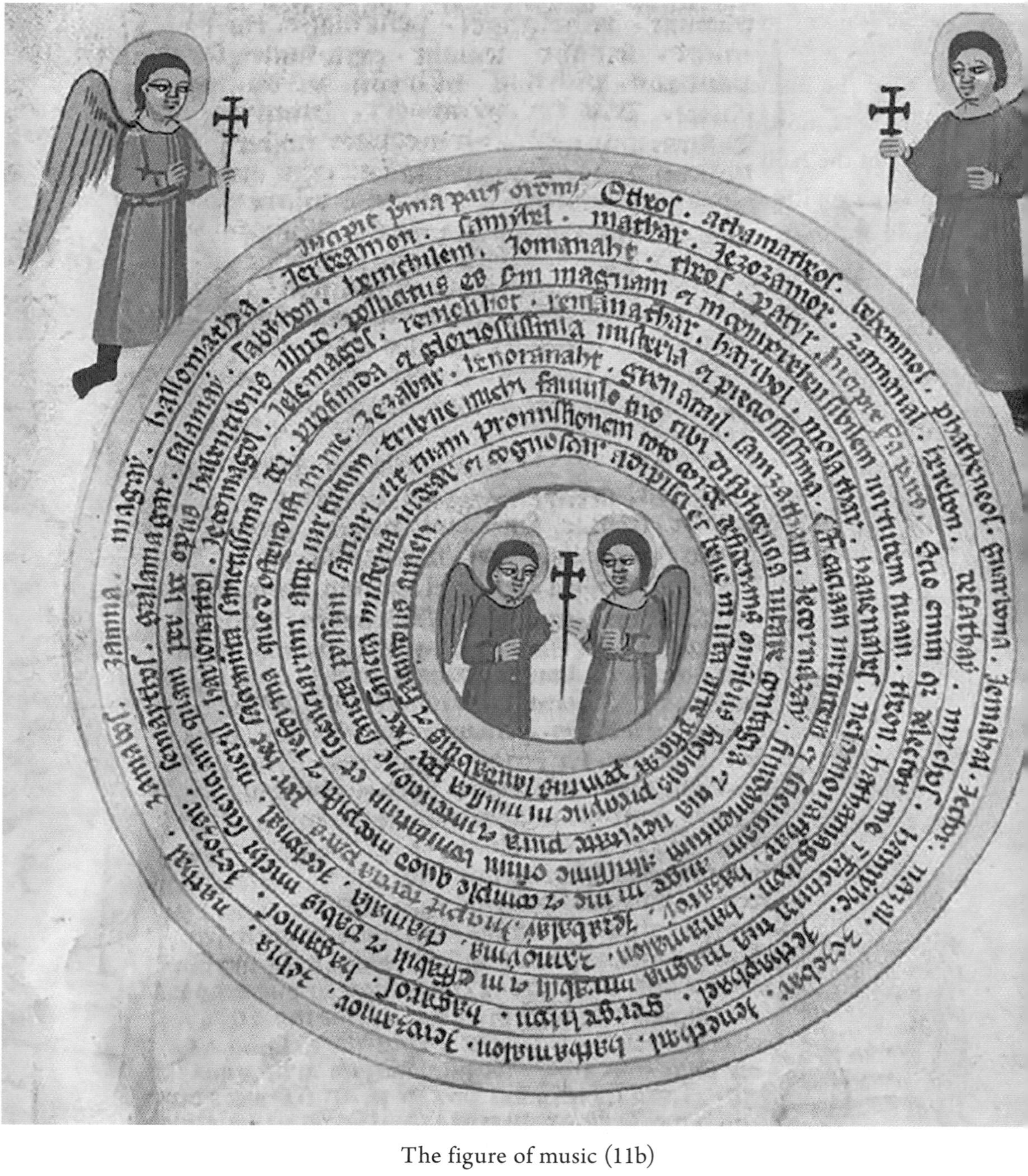

The figure of music (11b)

For I know[152] because I am delighted for myself in your great, wonderful, and ineffable work, and you will give me the knowledge [of] . . . (which you, [the petitioner], are promised that) through enduring this work, according to your great and incomprehensible virtue, Theon, Hathamagihon, Haramalon, Zamoyma, Chamasa, Iechonal, Meril, Harionathol, Iecomagol, Ielemagos, Remolihot, Remanathar, Harihol, Molathar, Hanenahes, Nelomonathar, Hazaroy, Iezabalay.

[NS 73] *The third part begins:*

Through these most holy sacraments of God,[153] the profound, the most glorious, and the most precious mysteries, augment the efficacy, the virtue, and the knowledge within me, and complete what you began and transform what you have shown within me, Zezabar, Henoranaht, Grenatail, Samzatham, Iecornazay, O foundation, O Most High of all goodness, the sciences, and virtue, bestow . . .[154] to your servant, [who] displeases you, [so that] I may be able to be satisifed with your pure truth and holy intention, so that desiring your promise with all [my] heart in all fields of knowledge, especially in music, through these holy mysteries, may I be understood and known to obtain . . . , and may I be well perfected in this art, thoroughly praiseworthy and eloquent, amen.

152. *Scio enim* is the second part of the particular prayer, *Otheos Athamatheos,* which belongs to the figure of music. Compare against *Scio enim* belonging to the third figure of rhetoric at NS 56. This second part is written within the figure, following the first part.

153. *Per haec sacramenta sanctissima Dei,* the third part of the *Otheos Athamatheos* prayer belonging to music. The *Scio enim* prayer (NS 56) shares almost verbatim the latter portion of this prayer here. This third part is written within the figure, following the second part and closest to the center.

154. The ellipsis is a placeholder for the operator to insert his own desired area of knowledge concerning music. A second ellipsis follows to be filled in by the operator.

[Arithmetic]

[NS 74] *This prayer is to be offered before the first figure of arithmetic:*
O God, you who has made all things by number,[155] weight, and measure,[156] out of whose number, weight, and measure every head of man desiring . . .[157] will be elevated, in whose order of all moments or days is extending and opening a dimension, for you alone who count and name the names of the stars, bestow an efficacy to my mind constantly, so that I may love you in the knowledge of this art and acknowledge the gift of your piety, amen.

[NS 75] *This is the first figure of the art of arithmetic, which the art has two and a half figures. Therefore, you must inspect these figures on any day of one month fives times in a day, and their particular prayers five times at any time. For it is to be done in this way in the operation of these figures, just as in the figure of the art of medicine and music, and you will find the operation of those figures in the same gloss.*[158]

[NS 76] *The first prayer begins:*
Azelechyas, Velozeos, Mohan, Zama, Sarvelo, Hotheus, Seguahat, Adonay, Soza, Zezomothos, Iezonochos, Hichon, Iezomothon, Sadahot, and you, O propitious God, strengthen in me your promises,[159] you who are God, and the measure of all things, the number, the weight, and the founder of all justice, the mirror of eternity, Cherzomon, Cheaguamal, Hathamachihel, Rathamathel, Segehora, Tezomihel, Theromychel, Sameleney, Zamchemey, Christus, Theos, Athana, Saliha, Hachanasalma, Thenamnon, Senazemyl, the virtue of the heavens, earth, and sea and all things which are in them,

---

155. *Deus qui omnia numero,* the prayer belonging to the first figure of arithmetic. See section 144.
156. Wisdom of Solomon 11:20.
157. The ellipsis is a placeholder for the operator to insert his own desired study of arithmetic.
158. Section 85/86 gloss.
159. Compare these opening words to the opening of the *Azelechias [. . . regi Salomoni]* prayer (NS 51). *Azelechyas [. . . mensura],* the adorning prayer here, belongs to the first figure of arithmetic and can be found in the left-hand side of the large wheel of the figure. See the figure on page 547.

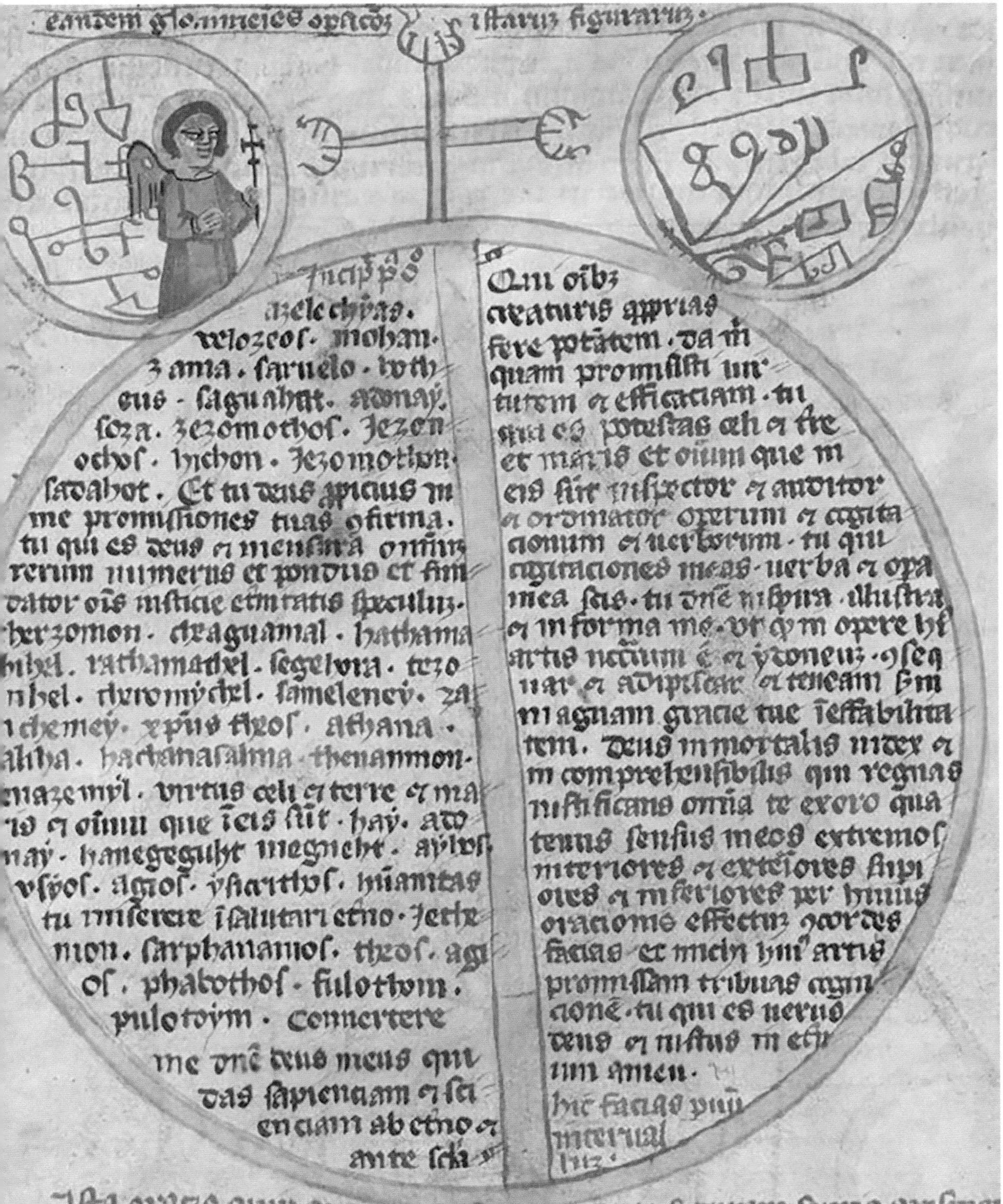

The first figure of arithmetic (12b)

Hay, Adonay, Hanegeguht, Megneht, Ayhos, Usyos, Agios,[160] Ysicrithos,[161] have mercy on humanity in eternal salvation, Iethemon, Sarphanamos, Theos, Agios, Phabothos, Fulothon, Pulotoym, convert me, O Lord my God, who gives wisdom and knowledge from eternity and before the ages, you who makes entirely appropriate the power [given] to all creatures, give me that virtue and efficacy you promised, you who are the authority of the heavens, earth, sea, and of all things which are in them; O inspector, listener, and orderer of thoughts, words, and works, you who know my thoughts, words, and works; O Lord, inspire, illuminate, and inform me, so that I may obtain and acquire what is necessary and suitable in the work of this art, and may I grasp . . .[162] according to the greatness of your ineffable grace; O God, the incomprehensible and immortal judge who reigns justifying everything, I entreat you to the extent that you make concordant the boundaries of my senses,[163] [both] the external and internal, the superior and inferior, through the effect of this prayer, and bestow unto me the promise of cognition of this art, you who are the true and just God in eternity, amen.

You must make a short interval here.

[NS 77] *This prayer is to be offered five times before the half figure of arithmetic:*

O mediator of all[164] operations and all creatures, from whom all good things exit naturally and the gifts of all good virtues proceed, from whom everything is unbroken and perfect, whose every word is new and comes from the royal seats [of the angels] into our hearts, while the middle [class of angels][165] were keeping the whole [of creation] silent,[166] you alarm the middle ratio within

---

160. Greek, meaning "O Holy One."

161. Probably corrupted Greek for *ischyros,* meaning "O Strong One."

162. Another possible ellipsis which acts as a placeholder for the operator to insert his desired area of studying arithmetic.

163. Latin *sensus meos extremos.*

164. *Mediator omnium, etc.,* the prayer belonging to the half figure of arithmetic. See section 145.

165. In the Christian angelology of Pseudo-Dionysius the Areopagite, the middle class of angels includes the Dominions, Virtues, and Powers.

166. Wisdom of Solomon 18:14–15. Also, notice the poetic contrasts of the macrocosm (creation),

me by your charity [and] good understanding with respect to perceiving these . . . ,[167] such excellent mysteries of this art and of these sacraments; may I gain the perfect effect, amen.

This is the half figure of arithmetic, which ought to be inspected after the first figure, having made a short interval, and its prayers are to be offered five times.

[NS 78] *The prayer begins:*
Thoemy, Gruheguon,[168] Thomyn, Samazy, Zamazal, Lemoseguor, Lemozeger, O eternal divinity, Hemmothe, Fase, Thomornor, Neche, Thamar, Heblatamar, Semanay, Iecho, Megal, Iohas, Sabahot, Semethon, O divine equality, come and send out the Holy Spirit from the eternal thrones above, so that he[169] may dwell within me and I in him in the age of an age, amen, Otheos, Hathamagihel, Sezihel, Zezozay, Lamayr, O incomprehensible one who reigns justifying everything, O God, you who strengthens your grace for your faithful ones, I implore and call for your mercy, I pray earnestly and require your benevolence, and I entreat the height of your compassion, the affluence of your eternity, and I beg for the piety of a kneeling mercy with confession, may you direct and strengthen my senses to such an extent, and grant me the perfect knowledge in this art through your holy piety and grace, amen.

Make an interval here, and inspect the figure and its signs, then read in the scrolls of the art.

---

the whole number, being kept silent by the angels while the microcosm (man), middle ratio or half part, is awoken by God, thereby creating balance in the cosmic equation. See Boethius's *De Institutione Arithmetica* for more details on understanding medieval arithmetic.

167. A possible ellipsis, which acts as a placeholder for the operator to insert his desired area of studying arithmetic.

168. *Thoemy Gruheguon,* the adorning prayer which belongs to the half figure of arithmetic and can be found in the diamond located in the center of the figure. See the figure on page 547.

169. In Latin, each noun has a grammatical gender and *spiritus,* the word for "spirit," is assigned the masculine gender. In Greek, the word for "spirit" (πνεῦμα, *pneûma*) is neuter and in Hebrew (רוּחַ, *rūaḥ*) is feminine.

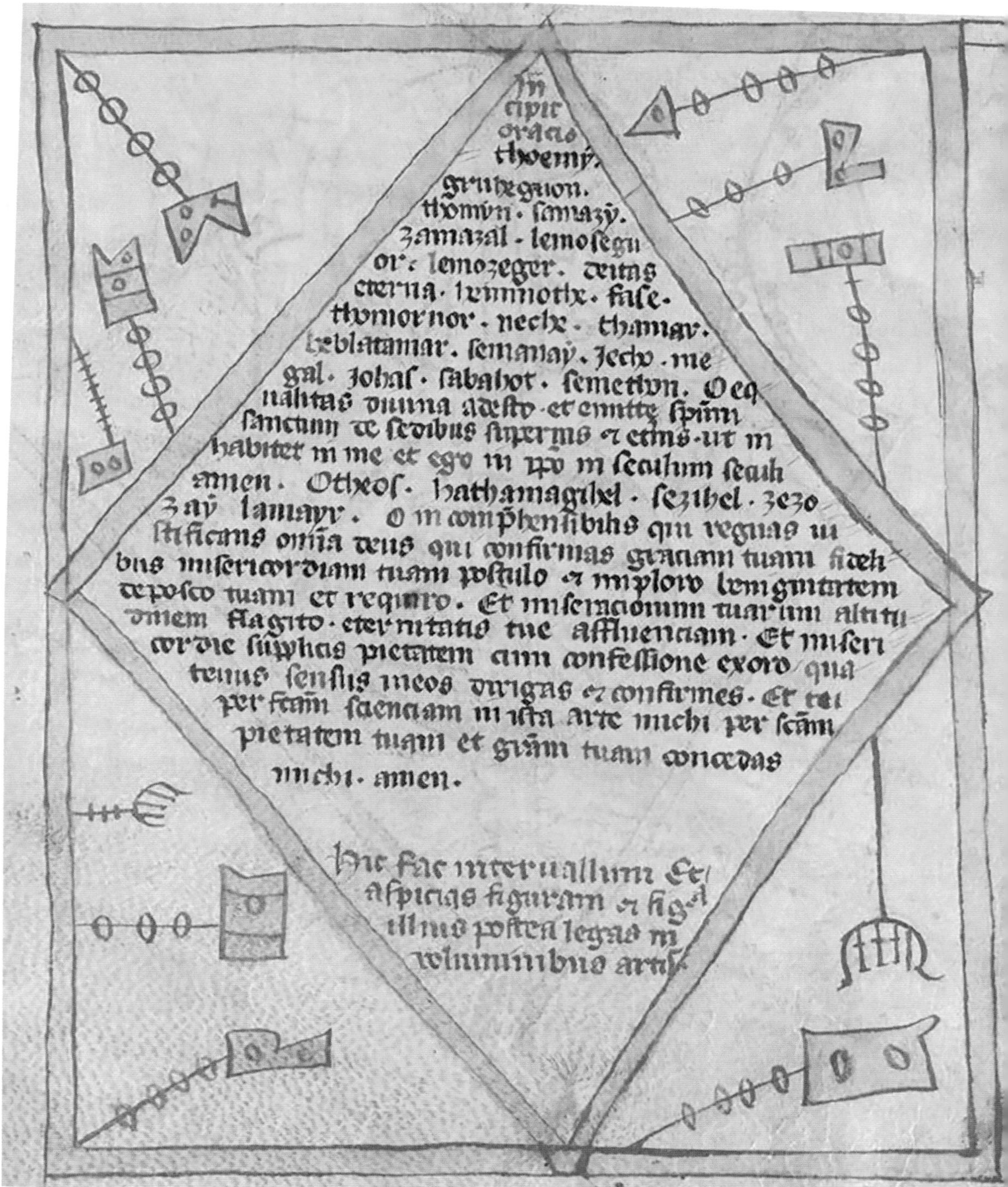

The half figure of arithmetic (13b)

[NS 79] *This prayer is offered five times before the second figure of arithmetic:*
O God, O just judge,[170] O almighty Father, who has made known to us your salvation, and you revealed your justice in the sight of the nations; open my eyes and illuminate my heart in your salvific justice, so that I may expound about the wonders of your most glorious sacramental mysteries, how I will gain so much understanding through them in this art, as you provide [them], you alone who does great wonders, may I be made effective interpreting . . .[171] suddenly in this art, so that, I measure out the precepts[172] within it, having been measured out with fruitfulness, memory with stability, and with the intercession of all the heavenly virtues, may I honor you in the ages of ages, amen.

This is the second figure of the art of arithmetic, which ought to be inspected after the half figure at the same hour, still having made some interval in the prolation of the prayers.

[NS 80] *The first part begins:*
Habba, Habehat,[173] Habrac, Habracal, Habracha, Habratala, Habrion, Githechon, Iegonomay, Helamy, Gichechon, Soza, Cheagamal, Thezomihel, Segehora, Heht, O almighty everlasting God, O trustworthy Holy Spirit, humble my heart and mind today, make my conscience intelligible, and sign the light of your countenance over me today, so that, having been made new through you, I may be made effective knowing . . . and made stable in your commandments, and having been cleansed from all dead works and from the works of my sins, so that I may be able to . . .[174]

---

170. *Deus, iustus iudex,* the prayer belonging to the second figure of arithmetic. Here this prayer is attributed to arithmetic, but originally the prayer is assigned to the first figure of geometry in Version A (section 143, NS 120). See also chapter V regarding the figures of arithmetic and geometry.
171. An ellipsis which acts as a placeholder for the operator to insert his desired area of studying arithmetic.
172. Latin *recepta,* corrected to *praecepta,* meaning "precepts" or "teachings."
173. *Habba Habehat,* the adorning prayer, consisting of two parts, which belongs to the second figure of arithmetic. The first part is found in the large central wheel of the figure. See the figure on page 552.
174. A possible ellipsis to be filled out by the operator. Two other ellipses follow in this prayer, which seems to indicate that they are to be filled in by the operator concerning a desired knowledge for theology and virtue, not arithmetic.

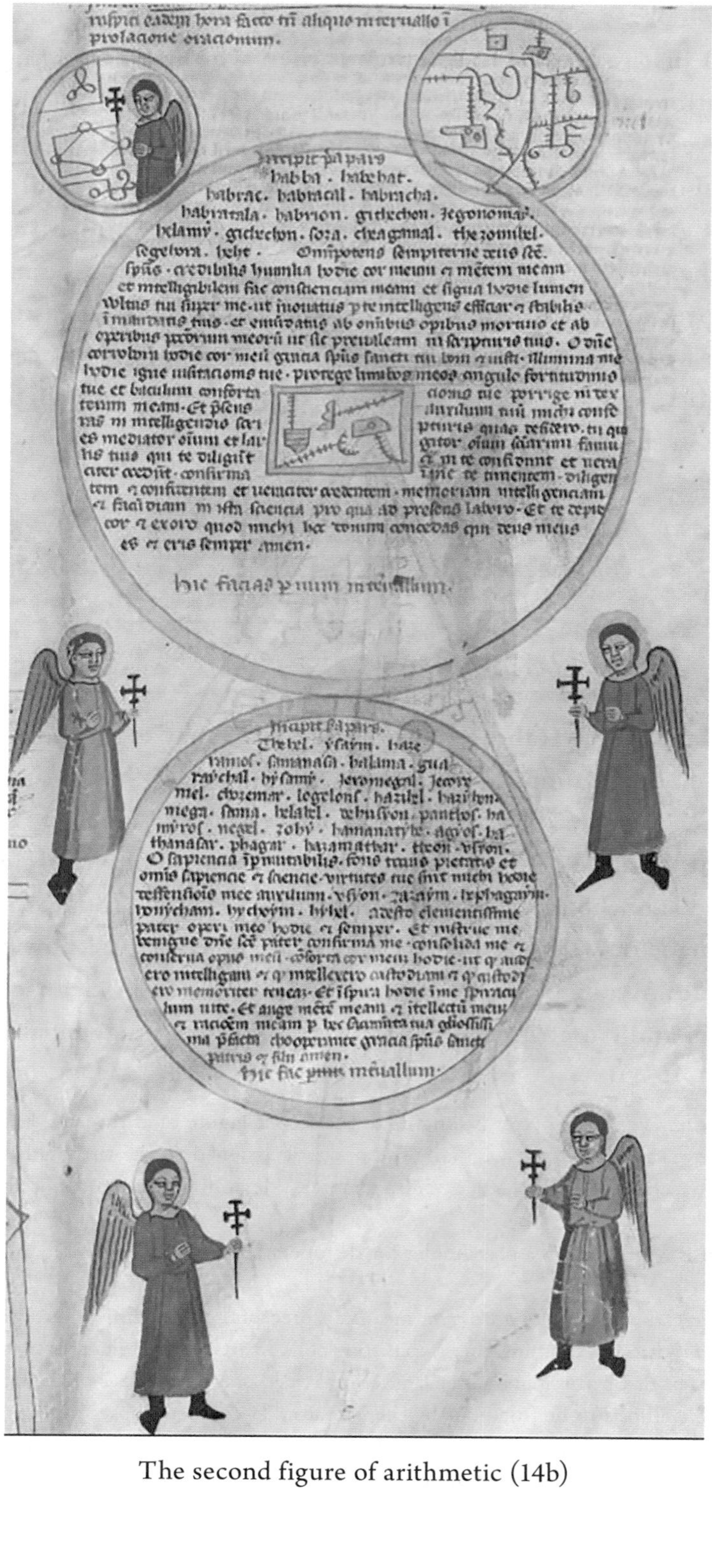

The second figure of arithmetic (14b)

thus in your Scriptures; O Lord, strengthen my heart today; illuminate me today with the grace of your good and just Holy Spirit; by the fire of your visitation, defend my loins with the cincture of your fortitude,[175] and extend the pastoral staff of your strength to my right hand, and presenting your help to me, confer [that] . . . which I desire in understanding the Scriptures,[176] you who are the mediator of all things, and the bestower of all fields of knowledge to your servants who love you and confide and truly believe in you, strengthen . . . within me, revering, loving, and confiding in you, and truly believing the memory, understanding, and eloquence in this science for which I am presently laboring towards,[177] and I deprecate and beg you that you grant me this gift, you who are my God and always will be, amen.

You must make a short interval here.

[NS 81] *The second part begins:*
Thehel, Ysaym,[178] Hazeramos, Samanasa, Halama, Guaraychal, Hysamy, Ieromegal, Iecoremel, Chozemar, Logelons, Hazihel, Hazyhon, Mega, Sama, Helahel, Dehusyon, Panthos, Hamyros, Negel, Zohy, Hamanathyhe, Agyos, Hathanasar, Phagar, Hazamathar, Theon, Usyon, O unchangeable wisdom, fountain of total piety and your virtues of every wisdom and knowledge are to me an aid to my defense today, Usyon, Zazaym, Hephagaym, Honycham, Hychoym, Hyhel, O most gentle Father, be present at my work today and always, and instruct me, O benevolent Lord the Holy Father, strengthen me, make me solid, and conserve my work, comfort my heart today, so that I may understand what I will have heard, and keep what I will have understood, and hold on to [that] which I will have kept in

175. This phrase may be derived from or inspired by the vesting prayers in which the cleric puts on vestments and his cincture as part of a liturgical rite.

176. Compare the wording from "humble my heart today" (*humilia hodie cor meum*) to this point here against *Confiteor,* the third prayer of the *Ars Nova* (section 117).

177. The desire for gaining memory, understanding, and eloquence of a certain kind of knowledge reflects the purpose and design of the *Ars Nova.*

178. *Thehel Ysaym,* the second part of the adorning prayer belonging to the second figure of arithmetic. This second part is found in the bottom wheel of the figure. See the figure on page 552.

memory, and today inspire . . .[179] within me, a little breath of life,[180] and augment my mind, my understanding, and my reasoning[181] through these, your most glorious sacramental myteries, having perfected the grace of the Holy Spirit, Father, and Son with cooperation, amen.

Make an interval here.

---

179. An ellipsis to be filled in by the operator for whatever area of study in arithmetic he desires to obtain.

180. Latin *spiraculum vitae.* Genesis 2:7 (Vulgate).

181. Compare the wording from "today inspire . . ." (*inspira hodie*) to this point here against *Confiteor,* the third prayer of the *Ars Nova* (section 117) and also NS 82.

[Astronomy]

[NS 82] *This prayer is to be offered twice before this figure:*

O Lord, I confess to you[182] today, I, the accused, O God the Father of heaven and earth, creator of all visible and invisible creatures, and the dispenser and bestower of all virtues and good graces, who keeps your wisdom and your knowledge from the arrogantly superior and reprobate, humble my heart today, and make my understanding stable, and my mind firm, and augment my understanding and my conscience, so that I may love and understand you; O Lord, sign the light of your countenance over me today, so that having been made prosaically new, I may be made effective knowing . . .[183] and made stable in your commandments, and having been made prosaically new and cleansed from all dead works and from my sins, may I be able to . . . in your Scriptures; O most merciful and almighty God, test me and burn my kidneys,[184] strengthen my heart, and illuminate with grace of the Holy Spirit, and visit me by the fire of the grace of your visitation, and illuminate my mind and gird my loins with the fortitude of your stability, and place your staff of strength into my right hand, and make me educated in the Scriptures of your knowledge, and direct my mind in your doctrines, and strengthen my spirit in the work of your hands, so that having eradicated the vices and sordid actions of my sins, I may prevail and be made stronger in the delight of your mercy; O Lord, today inspire me, a little breath of life,[185] and augment my mind, my understanding, and reasoning through the firmness and constancy of the Holy Spirit, so that my spirit, having been excited, may be strengthened and augmented in the works of your writings; O Lord, see and consider today the labor of my mind, and let your volitions be made kind within me, and from

---

182. *Confiteor tibi,* the first prayer belonging to the first figure of astronomy. Compare the strong word agreements to section 117 and NS 80.

183. An ellipsis to be filled in by the operator concerning some desired knowledge. The prayer's context suggests the ellipsis ought to be filled in with a desire to know something about theology; however, the prayer is assigned to astronomy here. There are two additional ellipses to be filled in by the operator, which also suggest that they ought to be filled in with a desire to know something about theology, not astronomy.

184. Psalm 26:2 (Vulgate). See section 117, page 277, footnote 80.

185. Latin *spiraculum vitae.* Genesis 2:7 (Vulgate).

heaven, send to me the Holy Spirit, a comforter to the earth, so that he may fortify me with a perfect stability, and presenting help to me, may he confer . . . in understanding the Scriptures which I desire, which are a help to my defense, amen.

[NS 83] *Rubric: This is the first figure of the art of astronomy, which has six figures. In fact, this first figure ought to be inspected first in the first Moon of any month, and after it, the second figure, and after the second, the third, and in this way all six of the order on any day of one month four times a day: once from the early morning up to the third [hour], once from the third [hour] up to noon, once from noon up to the ninth [hour], and once from the ninth [hour] up to the evening [hour], and the prayers of any of those are to be offered twice at a time.*

[NS 84] *This prayer is to be offered twice before the second figure:*
I extol the senses of my body[186] and my soul to you today, O Lord my God, and I lift up my heart to you today, so that my lamentations may be pleasing to you today, O Lord, and they may be manifest in your sight, and may my words and my work be pleasing in the sight of your house,[187] and may your omnipotence and your mercy shine today in my viscera, and may my mind be expanded more efficaciously from the beginning for the purpose of working in all my works, and may the eloquence thicken in my mouth [like honey], and may your grace germinate within my heart and mouth, so that what I will have read or heard, just as Adam understood, may I understand thus, just as Abraham kept [in his memory], may I keep [in memory], just as Jacob recalled in memory, may I recall thus,[188] so that having been founded in your Scriptures with virtue and rooted in your mercy I may glorify [you], having aquired the strong foundation of your mercy, and having been delighted in the works of your hand, may I adopt, obtain, and keep the justice and peace of my mind and body steadfastly; O Lord, the

---

186. *Extollo sensus,* the prayer belonging to the second figure of astronomy. See section 121.
187. Literally "your parish." Since it is commonly thought that the church is the house of God, the scribe chose to use the ecclesiastical meaning of *populi* for "parish." Alternatively, *populi* could mean "God's people," referring to his company of angels.
188. The writer presents the three practical steps in the art of memory—imprinting, storing, and retrieving—through the Jewish patriarchs, thereby linking the art to the Judeo-Christian tradition. For more on the art of memory, see chapter IV.

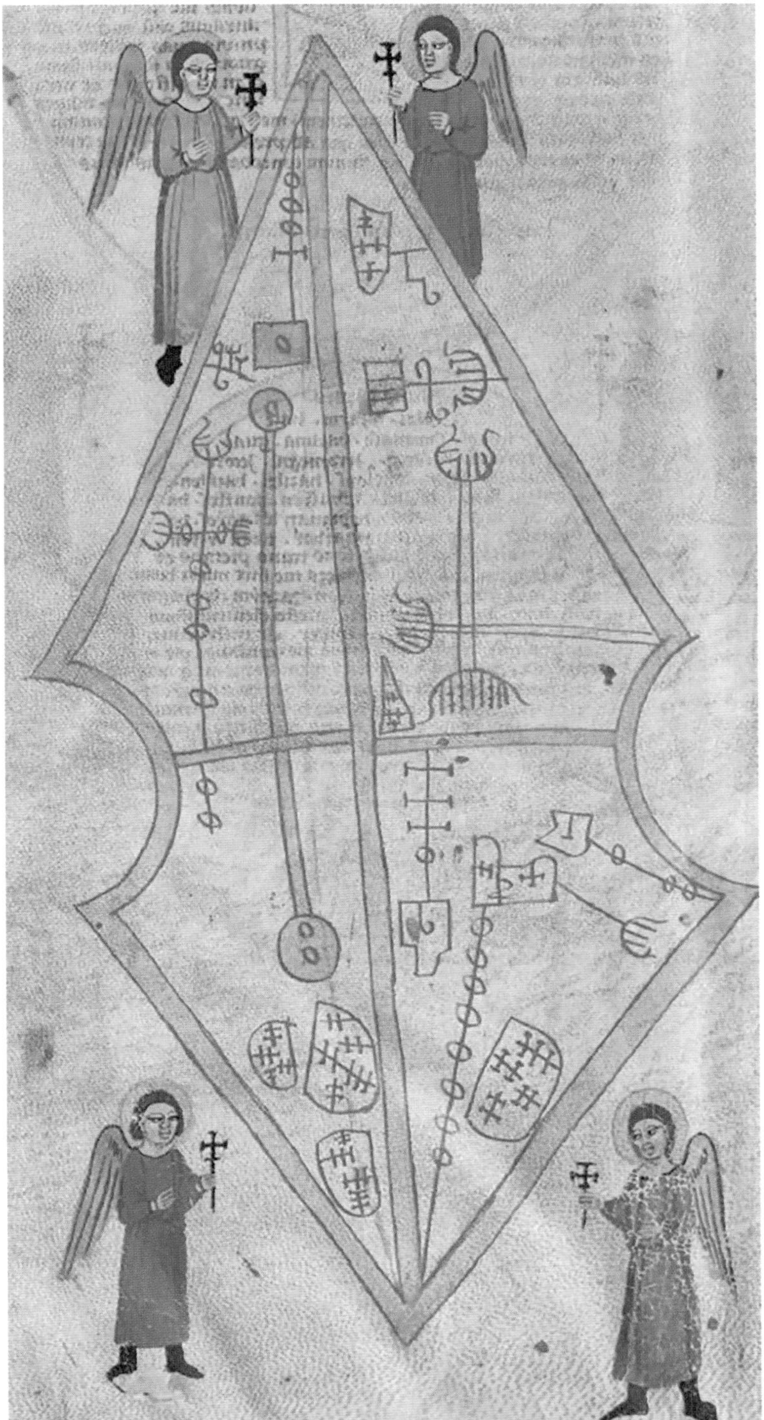

The first figure of astronomy (15b)

plenary of your Holy Spirit, working the grace in me, may I rejoice to have surmounted the visible or invisible enemies and their opposing snares and cunning, amen.

This is the second figure of the art of astronomy, which ought to be inspected after the first figure, having made some short interval, and it is to be inspected thus after the first four times in a day, and its prayer is to be recited twice at any [one] time.

[NS 85] *This prayer is to be offered twice before the third figure of astronomy:* **O dispenser and disposer of all kingdoms[189] and visible and invisible powers, O God, and orderer of every volition, O Lord, dispose and vivify your good spirit today, O Lord, deride[190] and order my debilitated power, my weakness, the debilitation of my mind, and my volition in [doing] good works, and in having pleased you, and bestow propitiously to me your multiform grace in the benevolence of [your] dispensation, not looking back on the multitude of sins, but bestow to me . . . , which I desire, strengthen for me the reason for thinking, understanding, and retaining in memory, and accomodate my effect with your grace to my senses, and visit me with the visitation of the Holy Spirit, as I have contracted[191] your ineffable divine power, [that] piety may abolish, whether out of the stain of the flesh or because out of the birth of sin from the Fall, which in the beginning you wanted to create heaven and earth, your mercy may restore that great spiritual compassion, which you deemed worthy to call back the lost man, having lost the pristine status with respect to grace, of whom the judgment of Satan has snatched away the sense of faculty and intellect; O Lord, whose sense and wisdom, reaching from end to end, and disposing all things strongly and mercifully and sweetly, restitute all my eloquent senses within me, so that I, an unworthy and miserable sinner, having been strengthened in all your works, in these things[192] which I desire, may I be**

---

189. *Omnium regnorum,* the prayer belonging to the third figure of astronomy. See section 122.

190. Latin *subsanne,* meaning "to deride."

191. That is, the act of making a legally binding contract (i.e., the covenant between God and humanity).

192. Instead of saying "these things" (*hiis*), the operator may specify his desired area of knowledge here.

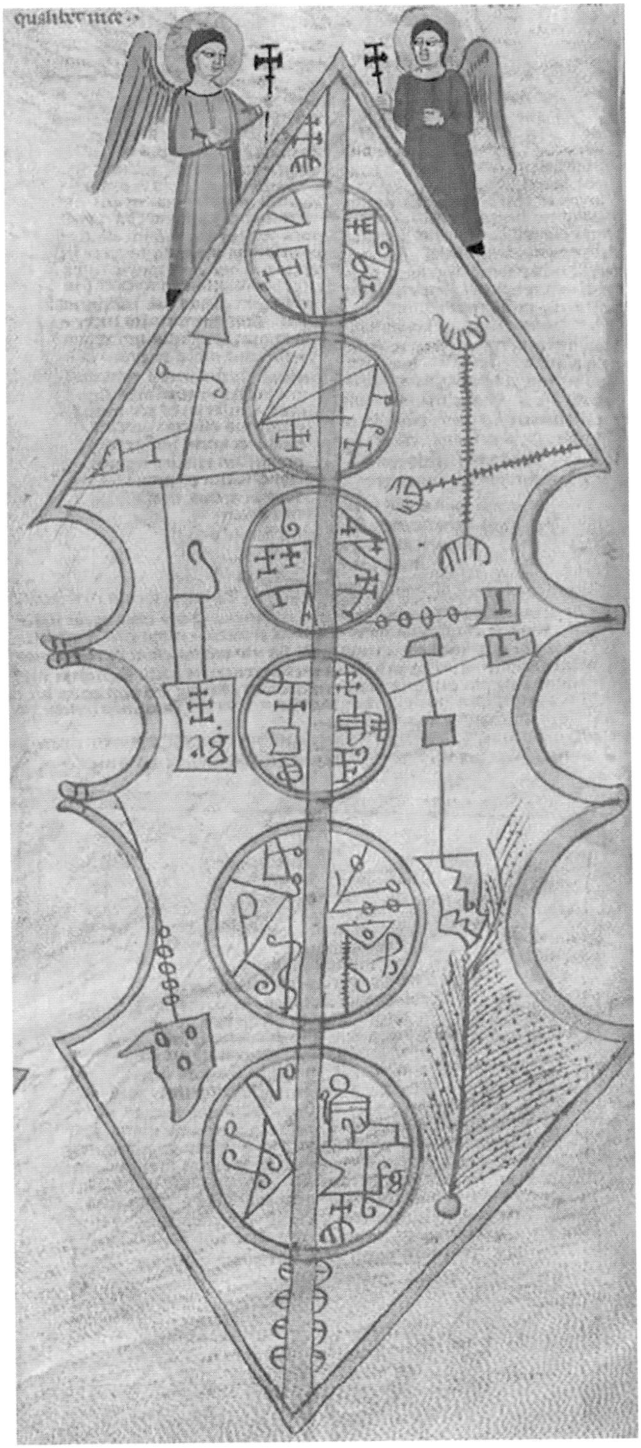

The second figure of astronomy (16b)

made effectively subtle, perspicuous, and eloquent, by the threefold and sevenfold of the Father, Son, and the Holy Spirit with geneosity, may I be made effective by God, presenting, cooperating, and administering his most holy grace, he who lives and reigns threefold and one, amen.

This is the third figure of astronomy, which after the second, having made some interval, it ought to be inspected immediately, and after this, having made an interval, the fourth figure is to be inspected, and even the prayers of those are always to be offered twice.

[NS 86] *This prayer is to be offered twice before the fourth figure of astronomy:* **O Lord, because I, your servant,[193] am talking to you today, and I am confessing in the presence of your glorious majesty, in whose sight every thing is a magnificence and sanctity, I deprecate your holy and ineffable name; incline your ears of piety and adjust your eyes to such an effect[194] of my operation, so that opening your hand with grace . . . , which I desire, more satisified and abundant,[195] you who founded heaven and earth with charity and brillance, most pious [and] generous Father, you who lives and reigns threefold and one, amen.**

This is the fourth figure of astronomy, which after the third, having made some interval, ought to be inspected immediately, and its prayer ought to be repeated twice.

[NS 87] *This prayer is to be offered twice before the fifth figure of astronomy:* **Today I confess[196] to you, O God, the Father of all, who has shown the secrets of heavenly and earthly things to your servants, I deprecate you suppliantly and I entreat your majesty that, so that, just as you are the king and prince of my thoughts and all other things, today you must hear my prayers**

---

193. *Domine quia ego servus,* the prayer belonging to the fourth figure of astronomy. See section 125. See also the latter half of the adorning prayer belonging to the first figure of rhetoric at NS 45.

194. The operator may specify what kind of effect he desires here.

195. Psalm 145:16, recalling its use as a blessing prayer before meals in a monastery setting. Compare to NS 45.

196. *Profiteor,* the prayer belonging to the fifth figure of astronomy. See section 124.

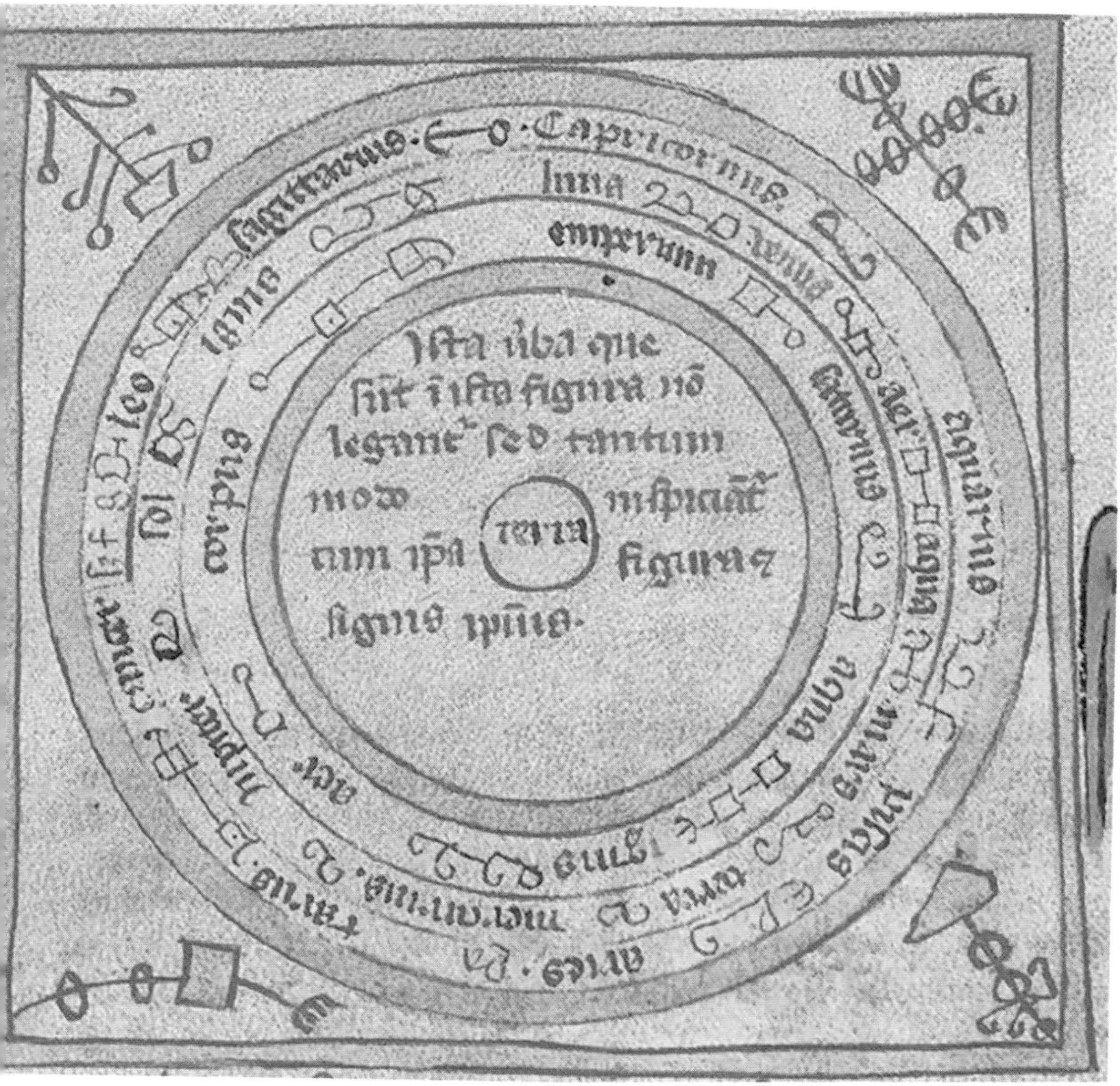

The third figure of astronomy (17b)

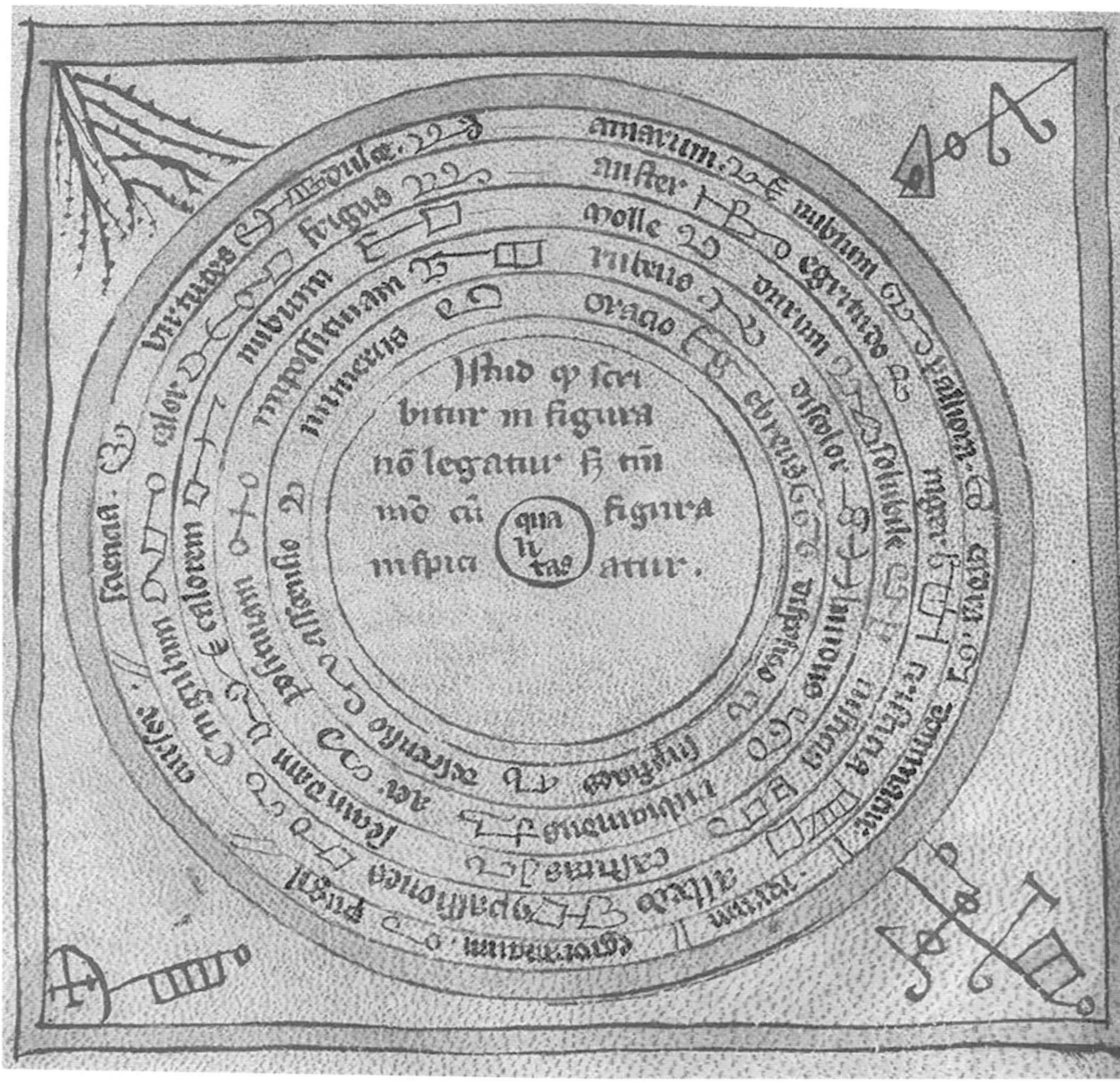

The fourth figure of astronomy (18b)

and may my operations be directed into your sight, and my actions may in the sight of the heavenly virtues I cry out to you today, O my God, now hear my cry, I groan to you, today hear the groaning of my heart, and I entrust my spirit, body, and soul and my thoughts into your hands, O my Father and my God, and may I not feel abandoned by you, but may I feel your mercy within me, and may your name be exalted within me, O most gracious God the Holy Spirit, whose goodness is eternal, whose mercy is incomprehensible, whose clarity, perpetual, whose possessions are of the entire heavens and earth, breathe into and look upon me, O Lord, and to this, my operation, and grant me what[197] I desire in your praises with honor [and] devotion, and may every perfection be completed within me of by divine dispensation; teach me, O Lord, because I place myself within you to be taught; guide me, O Lord, and infuse and fasten your grace [and] faith into me, so that the Holy Spirit may come and reign me and rule over me, amen.

This is the fifth figure of astronomy, which ought to be inspected immediately after the fourth, having made some a short interval.

[NS 88] *The first part begins:*

Heloy, Lay, Hobidam,[198] Massyha, Corrub, Machia, Corrob, Sethon, Bilba, Muche, Henep, Harnatym, Hassesothez, Thechir, Chezir, Cobratheos, Iesemoht, Iesemez, Hezechihel, Henaryp, Henaryp, Lihetyp, Mazerez, Mavenerem, Samuhel, Byhem, Samuhc, Belechynat, Helechires, Phitepham, Lememel, Loneger, Lanegel, Vahup, Debahup, Debachuc, Gictara, Gyngynchara, Honatam, Phetymon, Bechynom, Helohayhe, Delochator, Panger, Hanger, Pander, Hagar, Labulchus, Lecondon, Locohiston, Hostihen, Gechahus, Hepyhon, Iechanus, Cambre, Puhel, Grachaho, Iethac, Thophe, Horehora, Hastaht, Gehoht, Iothalo, Hotyhon, Facoyhon, Phathon, Satho, Dandiz, Deguaht, Degayz, Deguht, Massyha, Manzyha, Halbate.

---

197. The operator may specify what kind of astronomical knowledge he desires here; again, keep in mind these *Ars Nova* prayers were originally written with the intent of gaining theological knowledge and general improvement in memory, understanding, and eloquence, but that they are substituted in Version B manuscripts for gaining astronomical knowledge.

198. *Heloy Lay Hobidam,* the adorning prayer, consisting of two parts, which belongs to the fifth figure of astronomy. This first part is found in the upper part of the central wheel of the figure. See the figure on page 564.

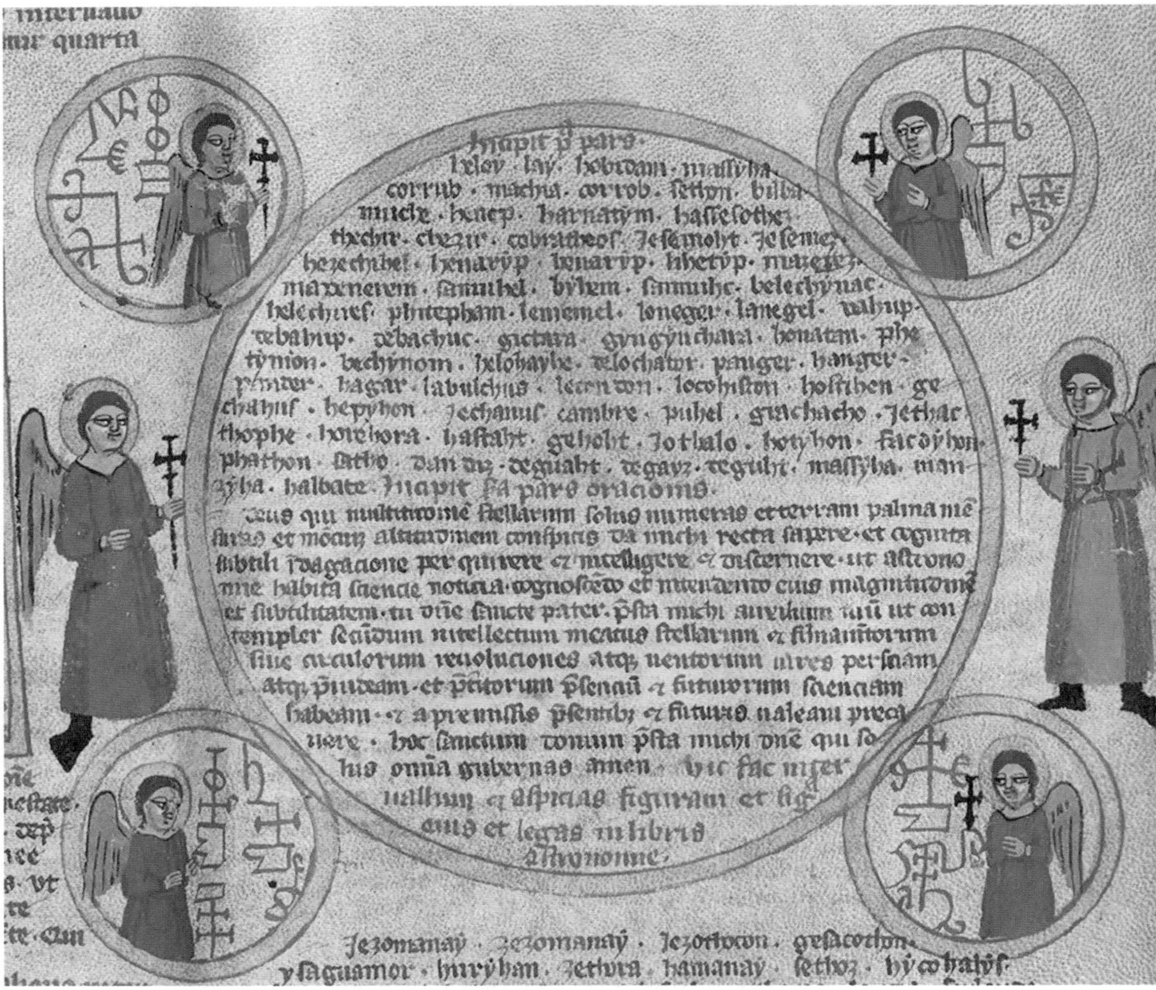

The fifth figure of astronomy (19b)

[NS 89] *The second part of the prayer begins:*
O God, you alone who counts the multitude of stars,[199] measures the earth with the palm,[200] and considers the height of mountains, give me the right way to be wise, and having recognized [it] in an accurate investigation to inquire, to understand, and to discern, so that having kept the notion of the knowledge of astronomy, in thinking and understanding its magnitude and subtlety, you, O Lord the Holy Father, present me your aid, so that I may contemplate according to understanding the passage of the stars and the firmament, or the revolutions of the orbits, and the forces of the winds; and may I know of past events, foresee [future events] and [have] prescience; and may I have knowledge of the present and future, and may I be able to guard against things sent beforehand into present and future [moments]; present this holy gift to me, O Lord, you alone who governs all things, amen.

Make an interval here, and you must inspect the figure and its signs, and you may read in the books of astronomy.

[NS 90] *This prayer must be offered twice before the sixth figure of astronomy:*
Iezomanay,[201] Zezomanay, Iezothocon, Gesacothon, Ysaguamor, Huryhan, Zethora, Hamanay, Sethoz, Hycohalys, Zihocalys, Haramahel, Hamacha, Mathes, Hamathama, Lapda, Serlanda, Grobos, Ieromethay, Phahenos, Rechagales, Sarmay, Ierothegalos, Seimay, Salyhel, Hochihon, Mogonyste, Nochytha, Megomyhe, Lamethehamyn, O Lord the Holy Father, you who gives and grants all your things, I ask of you, O most pious Father, through the most sacred names of your holy angels, so that you might give and grant me the sacred and entire knowledge of this art, and may you recall to the

199. *Deus qui multitudinem stellarum,* what might be the Latin prologue of the preceding *Heloy Lay Hobidam* prayer belonging to the fifth figure of astronomy; however, the scribe is presenting this as the second part of the adorning prayer *Heloy Lay Hobidam*. In either case, this prayer appropriately reflects the desire for gaining astronomical and astrological knowledge. It is not found in either Version A or the *Ars Nova*. The prayer can be found written within a figure of astronomy accompanying the *Opus Operum* in Clm 30010, f. 15r.

200. In medieval Europe, the human palm was used as a unit of measurement.

201. *Iezomanay,* the prayer belonging to the sixth figure of astronomy. This prayer is found only in Version B.

mind with respect to the restoration of memory, the strengthening of the intellect, and to the edification in all the writings of [this] science, and the retribution which you, O Father the God of all things and the life of creatures, you who are deemed worthy to grant and to complete suddenly . . .[202] in me, amen.

This is the sixth figure of astronomy, which after the fifth figure, having made an interval, it ought to be inspected immediately and its prayers to be offered twice.

---

202. The operator may specify what kind of astronomical knowledge he desires here.

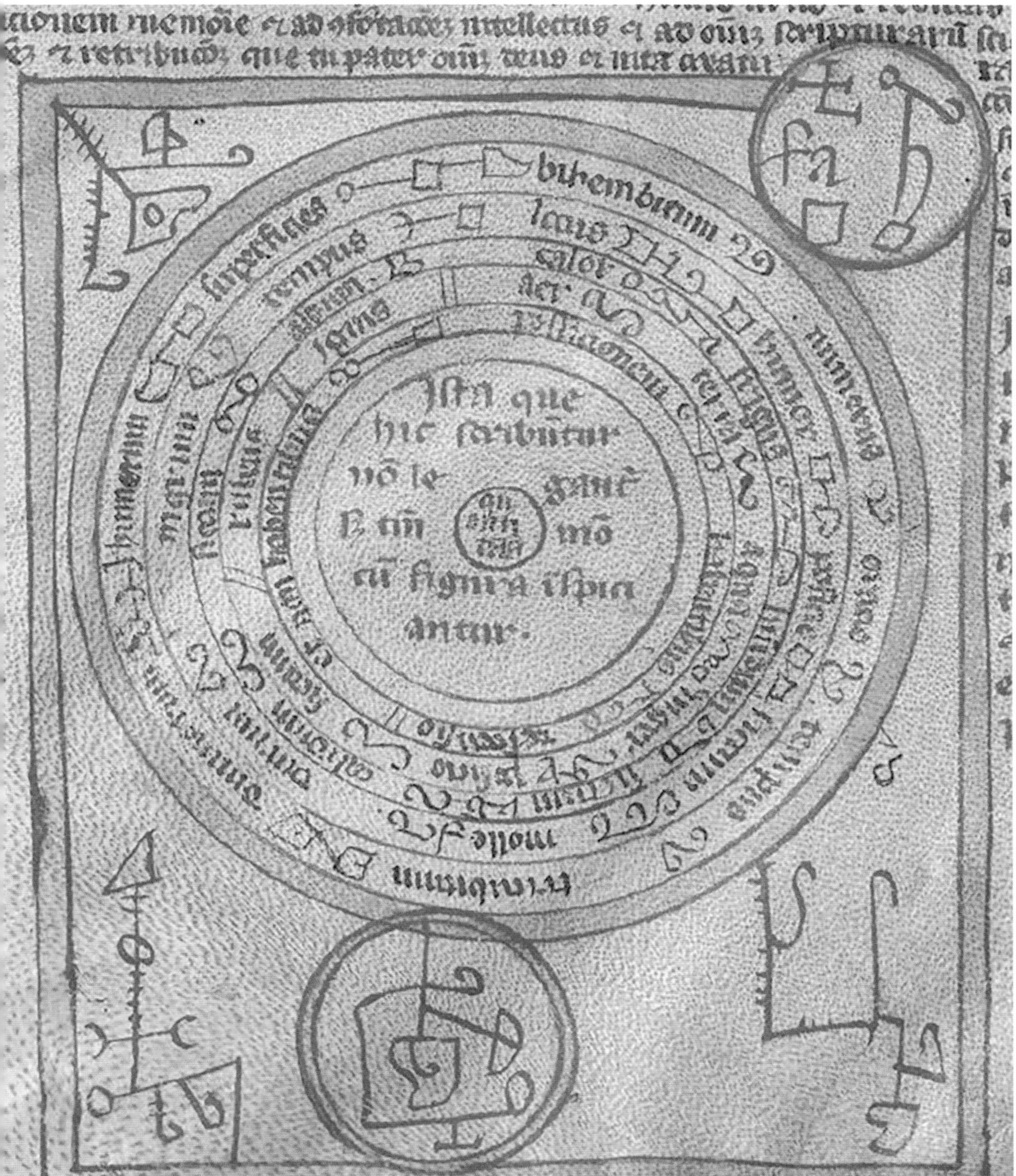

The sixth figure of astronomy (20b)

[The General Sciences]

[NS 91] *This prayer ought to be offered five times before the first figure of the general sciences:*

Zedomor, Phamanos,[203] Samalos, Schothono, Mechuroht, Halmethy, Samalos, Sabeht, Phamazihos, Scothomo, Hochiothom, Semelyhos, Zamaro, Genotharam, Guohacroham, Hysicomam, O God the immortal king, our witness, our meditation, and our mediator, whose rule [is] in the age of ages, you alone who are the highest in eternity, O Lord, govern my mind and my understanding through these, your precious sacraments, so that I may have the efficacy of this art, the glory of virtues, and the mercy of your haste and your contemplation made most manifest to me, pull back . . .[204] through the magnificence of your majesty, which is elevated above the heavens, and through your holy Angels and Archangels, the Principalities, Powers, Dominions, and of all the celestial Virtues, establish the eternity of your counsel within me, amen.

[NS 92] *Rubric: This is the first figure of the general sciences, of which there are four. Specifically, this first figure ought to be inspected first on the first day of the new lunar [day of] any month first in the early morning once, and having made an interval, the second ought to be inspected immediately, and having inspected the second, it is to be reiterated exactly like the first, and these two figures are to be inspected thus on any day from morning to noon five times, and their particular prayers are to be repeated five times.*

[NS 93] *This figure is to be called the nota of God.*
The prayer begins:

Gedomor,[205] Phamazihon, Thonochio, Thoyn, Semehoz, Thamaro, Cahem, Tezemaht, Ysoma, Magos, Samaha, Zabra, Iechor, Mahara, Hazeramos, Pander, Iesezmor, Phodigena, Gemaht, Meioboz, Herayp, Debachuc,

---

203. *Zedomor Phamanos,* the prayer belonging to the first figure of the general sciences. This prayer is found only in Version B.

204. The ellipsis is a placeholder for the operator to fill in what knowledge of the general sciences he desires God to reveal to him.

205. *Gedomor,* the adorning prayer belonging to the first figure of the general sciences, which is written within the figure.

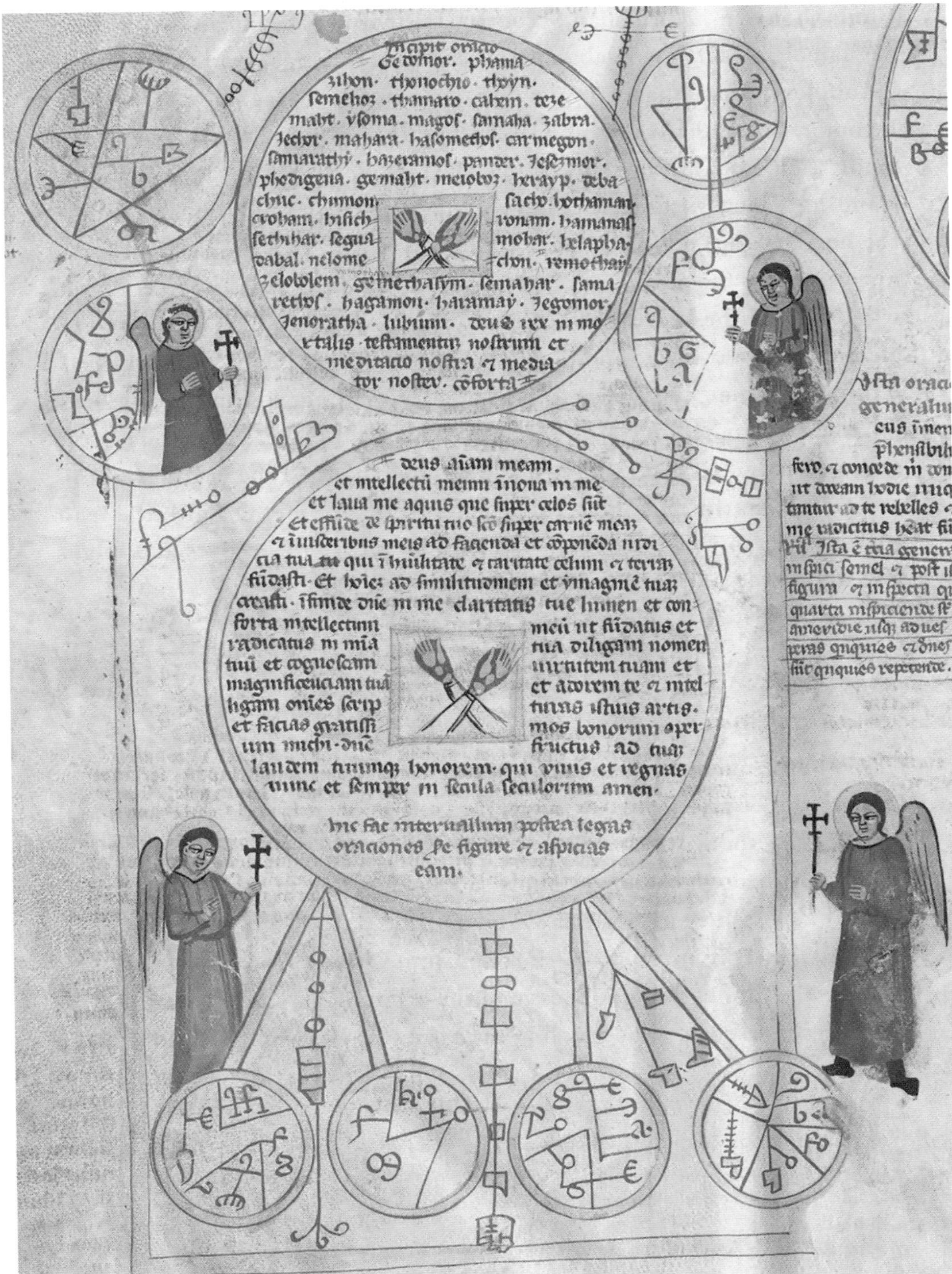

The first figure of the general sciences (21b)

Chumon, Sacho, Hothaman, Croham, Hisichronam, Hamanas, Sethihar, Seguamohar, Helapha, Dabal, Melomechon, Hachai, Seguoht, Remothay, Zelobolem, Gemethasym, Semahar, Samarethos, Hagamon, Haramay, Iegomor, Ienoratha, Lubium, O God, immortal king, our testament, our meditation, and our mediator, strengthen, O God, my soul and my understanding, renew within me, and wash me with the waters which are above the heavens, and pour . . . from your Holy Spirit over my flesh and into my viscera for the purpose of making and composing your judgments, you who founded the heavens and the earth in humility and charity, and created man in your image and likeness, O Lord, infuse the light of your brilliance within me and strengthen my understanding, so that having been founded and rooted in your mercy I may love your name, know your virtue and your magnificence, adore you, and understand all the writings of this art, and make the most grateful of good works for me, O Lord, the fruit with respect to you and your praise and honor, you who lives and reigns now and always in the ages of ages, amen.

Make an interval here, then you must read the prayers of the second figure and inspect it.

[NS 94] *This prayer is to be offered before the second figure of the general sciences:* **O God the eternal king,[206] judge, and discerner of all good thoughts, instruct me today on account of your holy name, and make my mind illustrious through these, your holy sacraments, and may your knowledge [about] . . .[207] enter my innermost being, like water flowing from heaven and like the oil in my bones,[208] through you, O God, the savior of all, you who are the fountain of goodness and the origin of all piety,[209] instruct me today in these sciences for which I pray earnestly, you who are the one God, amen.**

---

206. *Rex aeterne Deus,* the prayer belonging to the second figure of the general sciences. Compare it to the prayer belonging to the sixth figure of philosophy (section 100 and NS 114).

207. The ellipsis is a placeholder for the operator to fill in what knowledge of the general sciences he desires to acquire.

208. Psalm 109:18 (NRSV).

209. Latin *fons bonitatis et totius pietatis origo.* An epithet of God found in the Gregorian Sacramentary. The same epithet is found at NS 67 and 114.

This is the second figure of the general sciences, which ought to be inspected immediately after the first figure, still having made some short interval between them.

[NS 95] *This prayer ought to be pronounced before the third figure of the general sciences:*

O immeasurable God, from whom proceeds all that is good, whose magnitude[210] is incomprehensible, hear my prayers which I bring before your presence today, and grant me the gift because I ask [for] . . .[211] from you, deliver the joy of your salvation to me, so that today I may teach the disadvantaged your ways and the paths of your sciences, and may the rebellious and unbelievers be converted to you, so that what I recall with the heart and the mouth, I remember; having been rooted within me, it has a foundation, so that I may be regarded as efficacious and as having been helped in your works, amen.

[NS 96] *Rubric: This is the third figure of the general sciences, which after the preceding two, ought to be inspected once first around noon, and immediately after this, having made some interval, the fourth figure ought to be inspected, and having inspected the fourth once, it is reiterated with respect to this, and thus, these two, the third and the fourth [figures], are to be inspected from noon up to the evening [hour] five times, and the prayers are repeated five times.*

[NS 97] *The prayer begins:*

Iazer, Hazacala,[212] Gemor, Iechanyhon, Cheta, Chet, Chehem, Het, Alpha, Helepa, Iotha, Pozohoht, Guama, Gymelt, Tahu, Lamaht, Vahu, Hecamos, Hasym, Mohys, Thoym, Maguos, Hysiconam, Gedomor, Samalos, Semelihon, Hazeramos, Moyf, Phabam, Ieleht, Iohot, Zetrama, Samal, May, Hephy, Phanos, Nypho, Haphety, Iethos, Meioboz, Croham, Hisicroman, Iegomor, Zelobolem, Hathalmai, Lechnos, Salathy, Zehamanathy, Iegomor,

---

210. *Deus [Pater] immense . . . magnitudo,* the prayer belonging to the third figure of the general sciences. Compare it to the fifth prayer belonging to philosophy (section 98 and NS 111).

211. The ellipsis is a placeholder for the operator to fill in what knowledge of the general sciences he desires to acquire.

212. *Iazer Hazacala,* the adorning prayer belonging to the third figure of the general sciences, which is written within the figure.

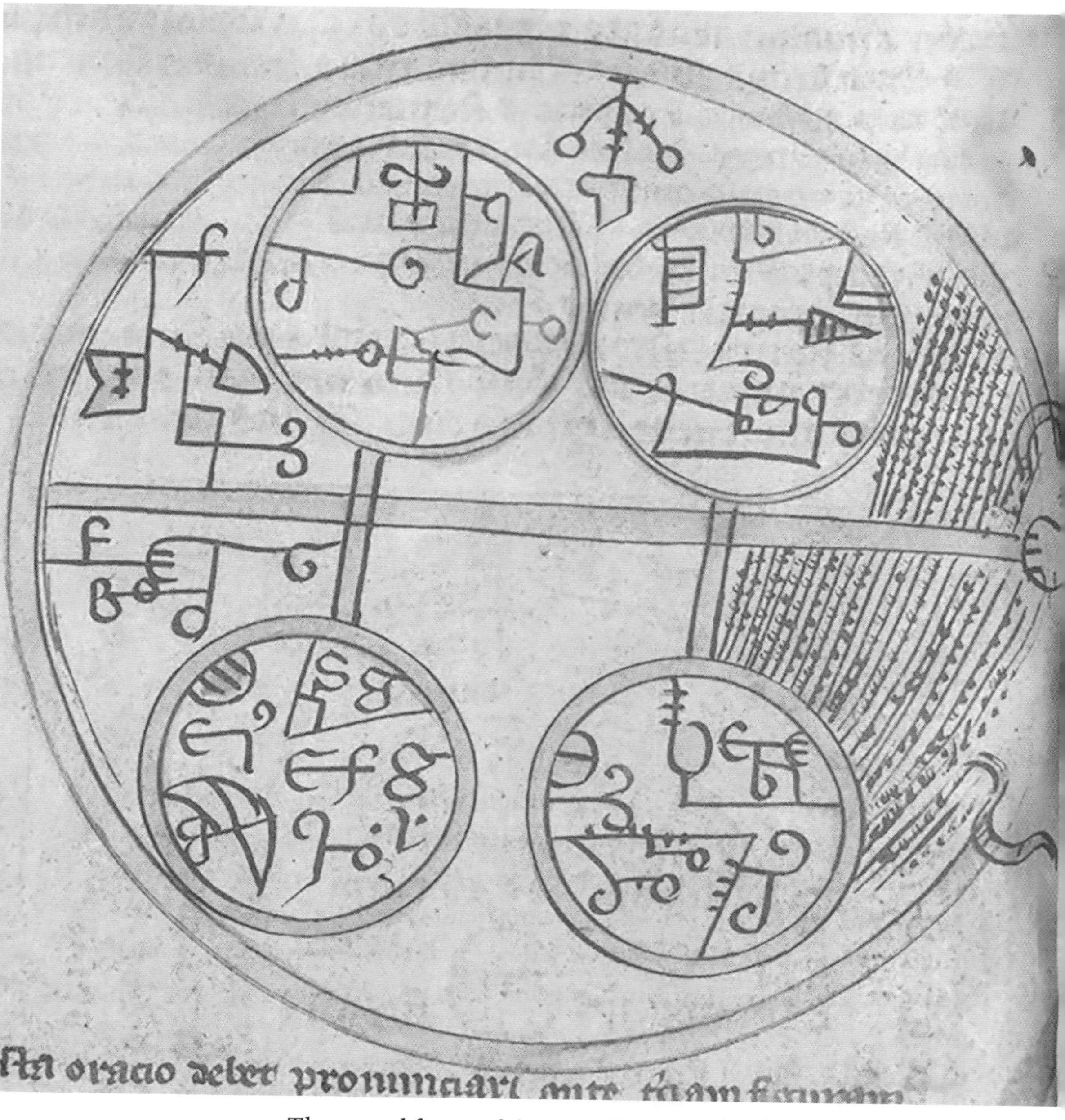

The second figure of the general sciences (22b)

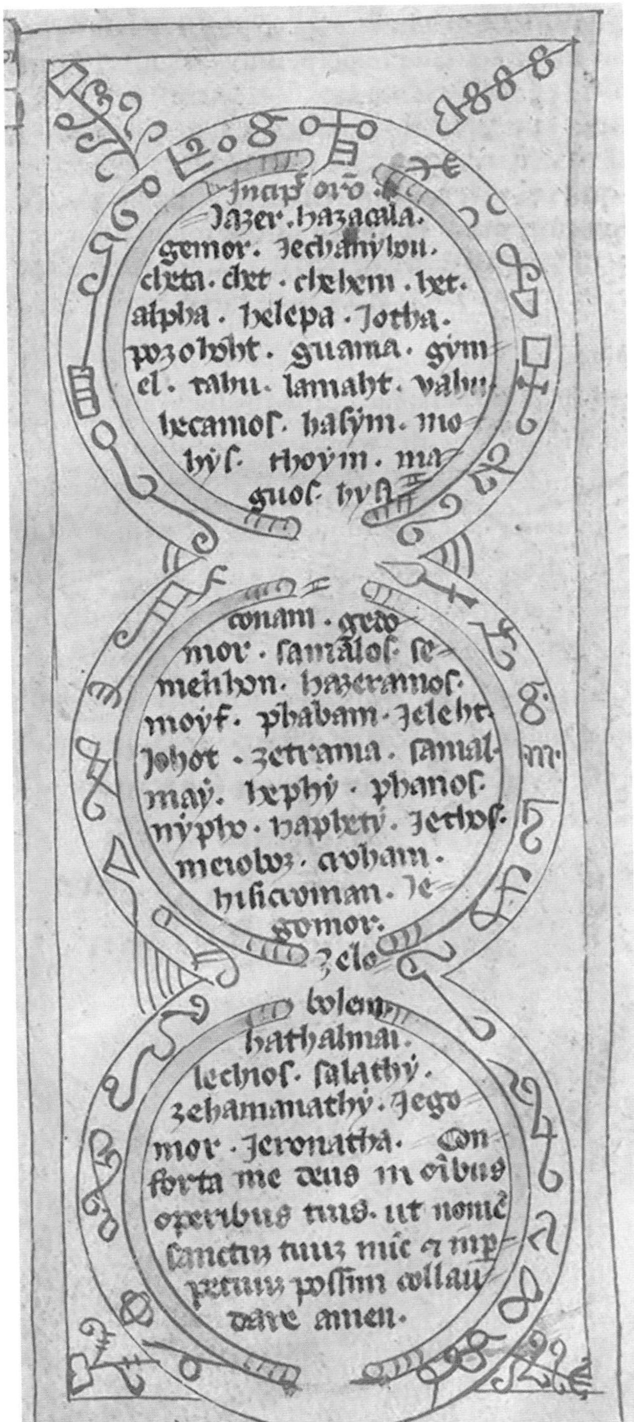

The third figure of the general sciences (23b)

Ieronatha, strengthen me, O God, in all your works, so that I may be able to praise your holy name now and in perpetuity, amen.

[NS 98] *This prayer ought to be offered before the fourth figure of the general sciences:*

O God, the [creator] of all piety[213] and the foundation of all things, the eternal salvation and redemption of the people,[214] inspirer of all graces, and the immense bestower of all the arts and sciences, from whose office and mercy comes, so that you may deem us so worthy, your servants of the sciences, to inspire [personal] growth, for whom you granted to me, a miserable sinner, to know the way by means of your sacrament; O Lord, defend my soul and free my heart from the thoughts of this depraved world, the incitements of a libidinous pleasure with a voluptuous gratification, and every desire of fornication within me; extinguish and repress all these things forcefully, so that, having understood your sciences and arts,[215] I may be delighted in them, and may you give to me the petition of my heart, so that I may love you, having been strengthened and delighted in your glorification, and the virtue of the Holy Spirit may be augmented within me through your salvation and the remuneration of the faithful in the salvation of my soul and my body, amen.

[NS 99] *Rubric: This is the fourth and last figure of the general sciences, which ought to be inspected immediately after the third figure, having made some interval, and its own particular prayer to be offered at any time. You may inquire about the order of these figures in the text, in that gloss, which begins* De notis omnibus iam initialis, etc.[216]

---

213. *Deus totius pietatis,* the prayer of the fourth figure of the general sciences. Compare it to the prayer belonging to the seventh figure of philosophy (section 101 and NS 115). The Latin word *actor,* meaning "agent who does something," is corrected here as *auctor,* meaning "creator."

214. Or the parish (perhaps in the global sense).

215. Latin *artibus.*

216. Section 88 gloss.

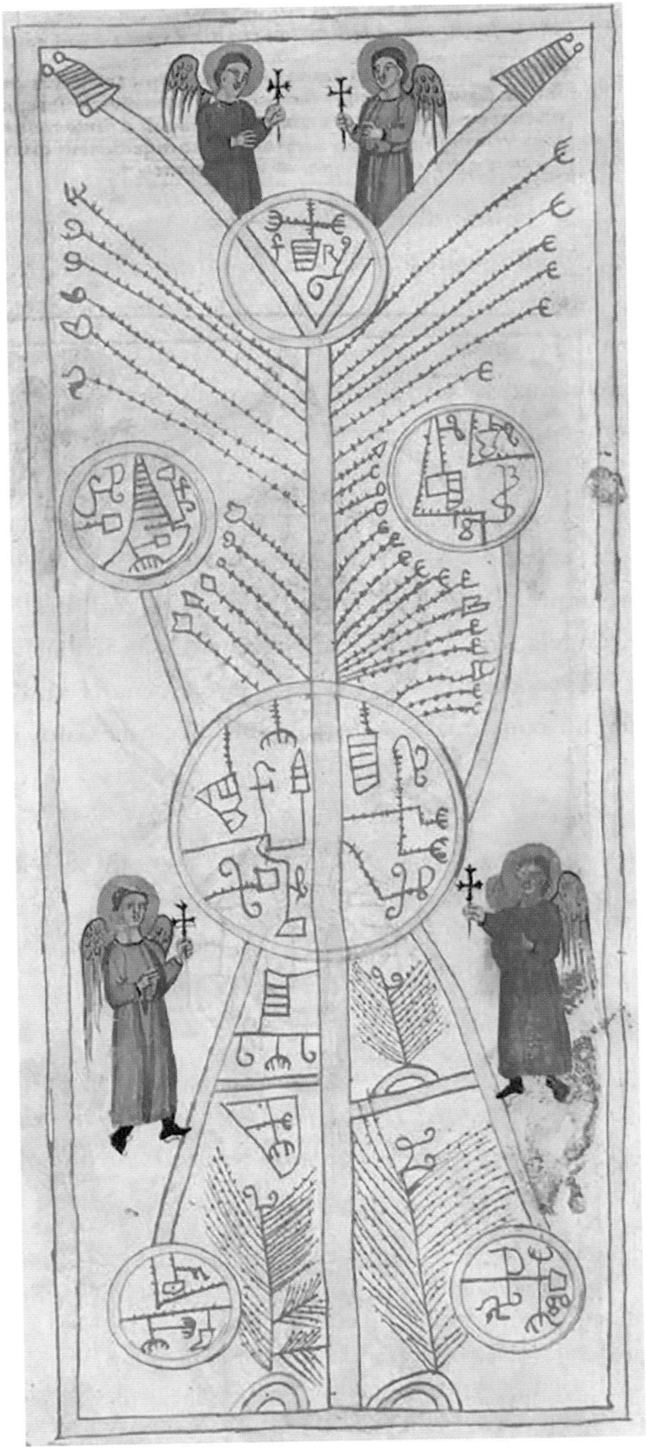

The fourth figure of the general sciences (24b)

[Philosophy]

[NS 100] *This prayer is to be offered twice before the first figure of philosophy:* **Ezethomos,[217] Iezemomos, Hazalathon, Azaython, Hentynechel, Hezemethel, Hezemtynechel, Zamay, Zathon, Hamayzathon, Zamazathon, Hezemeguer, Zecromanda, Iechomantha, Iaraphay, Zaraphamy, Phalezethon, Phabogethon, Seremybal, Sacramyhal, Zeremyhal, Sacramazan, Iethemathon, Sacramazaym, Secranal, Satramathan, Iezemyhalathon, Hathechihathos, Ieteley, Mathan, Hacheriathos, Zay, Mazay, Zamma, Zazay, Giugutheyo, Gygithios, Guaryhos, Megalon, Sevegalon, Heracruhyc, Craryhuc, Heracryhuz.**

[NS 101] *You must make one short interval here and afterward this prayer is to be read:*
O Lord the incomprehensible, invisible, immortal, and intelligible God,[218] whose face the angels, archangels, and heavenly hosts ardently desire to see, [the] . . .[219] of whose majesty I desire to adore eternally and I exercise for my ability [to] . . . continually, adoring you, the one God, in the ages of ages, amen.

[NS 102] *Rubric: This is the first figure of philosophy, of which there are seven in number. For this first figure ought to be inspected first on the first day of the new lunar [day of] any month once in the early morning and its own particular prayers to be offered twice, and immediately having made an interval, the prayers of the second figure are to be offered twice and this very figure is to be inspected, and [having made an interval, the third figure and its signs are to be inspected,] the operation of these [first] three figures is to be performed in this way from the early morning up to noon; from noon up to the ninth [hour is][220] the operation of*

---

217. *Ezethomos,* the prayer belonging to the first figure of philosophy. See section 90.
218. *Domine Deus incomprehensibilis,* the Latin prologue belonging to the first prayer of philosophy. See also section 91.
219. The ellipsis represents a placeholder for the operator to fill in the desired quality or philosophical knowledge of God he wishes to acquire. The second ellipsis represents another placeholder for taking action in that quality as an infinitive verb. For example, the operator who desires to adore God's "rational intelligence" would like to exercise his ability "to reason."
220. Latin *sit,* meaning "is." The Latin word *sit,* appears again in the next clause.

The first figure of philosophy (25b)

these [latter] three [figures];[221] *but from the ninth and last [hour is] the operation of the seventh and last figure. You may inquire about the operation of [the first set of] these three figures in the gloss that begins* De notis autem generalium, etc.[222]

[NS 103] *These names which are written in these eight wheels are to be read continuously and orderly without any interval:*

Themezehos, Saguamal,[223] **Nahemnan, Nahenamos, Hacgenos, Iemoze, Molyht, Zalomotay, Zalamar, Gelon, Romagal, Zalamar, Iezaphial, Penethetoy, Zammar, Lamathay, Lemnon, Iechanomay, Laramathal, Hazomon, Phormolon, Hozey, Tay, Cheta, Zarasamy, Phalezethon, Cheta, Chet, Haseht, Sehot, Chec, Heht, Hee, Hehem, Hem, Aleph, Ioht, Ioht, Iotha, Hecho, Hetha, Hoht, Guamina, Hehel, Hel, Heloy, Ymas, Hihoht, Hymnel, Sadhuc, Theon, Usyon, Zathana, Iezomelyhon, Saday, Iezomelihon, Iezel, Thazata, Saocamal, Ietheloy, Machon, Senegualon, Zeremyhal, Usihel, Sacramyhal, Lamen, Hazay.**

Make an interval here.

[NS 104] *This prayer, [*Domine Deus Sancte Pater,*] with the subsequent one, [*Deus semper via vita veritas,*] is to be offered twice before this [second] figure [of philosophy]:*

O Lord God, Holy Father[224] **almighty, hear my prayers today and incline your ears to my prayers,**[225] **Themon, Gezomelyhon, Zemonge, Zemelyhon, Samaht, Iezagam, Iezathamym, Zehamoht, Iezagam, Iezatharym, Iehamoth, Iechazam, Iezatharym, Zehamoht, Iechazam, Iezehator, Lesehator, Sezehaton, Saymanda, Samay, Sanamay, Gezyhel, Gualentihel, Gezel, Iezetyhel, Guazletihel, Guazay, Hethel.**

---

221. That is, the operation of the fourth, fifth, and sixth prayers and figures of philosophy.

222. Section 87 gloss. The operation of philosophy may be understood as having three distinct parts: (1) the first set of three figures (namely the first, second, and third), (2) the second set of three figures (namely, the fourth, fifth, and sixth), and (3) the seventh figure of philosophy.

223. *Themezehos Saguamal,* the adorning prayer belonging to the first figure of philosophy, which is written across the eight wheels of the figure. See the figure on page 577.

224. *Domine Deus Sancte Pater,* the prayer belonging to the second figure of philosophy. See section 92.

225. Psalm 5 (NRSV).

[NS 105] *Here you must make some short interval, then you must read this prayer:*
O God, always the way, the life, and the truth,[226] give your light to flower within my conscience and my mind through the virtue of the Holy Spirit, and grant . . . ,[227] so that it may shine [upon] . . . , and may your house of operation[228] be illuminated, and the gift of your grace illuminate . . . within my heart and my soul, now and through the ages of ages, amen.

This is the second figure of philosophy, which ought to be inspected after the first figure, having made a short interval, and its prayers are to be offered twice.

[NS 106] *This prayer is to be offered twice before this figure:*
Lemogethon,[229] Hegemothon, Hazachaly, Hazathar, Hazamiathar, Hazata, Hazamathar, Iazamathon, Zegomothay, Guohatay, Zachana, Legomotay, Iacamna, Legomezon, Lehornozon, Lemdomethon, Hatamayhos, Lamdomachon, Iedomaday, Hatamaz, Zathamos, Hatanayos, Hellessymon, Zelesyon, Nadarabar, Vagedaram, Lanynanaht, Lamandy, Gemechor, Gemon, Gechor, Iemanchor, Helbemay, Iezeocomay, Gecromal, Iecrohaly, Cholomamos, Colomaythos.

[NS 107] *Make an interval here, then say this prayer:*
O life of man[230] and all visible and invisible creatures, O eternal brightness of the heavenly spirits, the unfailing salvation of all men, and the origin of piety, who knew all things before they are made, who judges all things that are to be understood, you discern with an ineffable disposition; may I glorify your ineffable holy name. Today, glorify and strengthen my heart, my

---

226. *Deus semper via vita veritas,* the prayer belonging to the second figure of philosophy. See section 93.
227. An ellipsis, which represents a placeholder for the operator to fill in with his desired area of philosophical study. The second ellipsis may indicate the philosophical problem the operator is looking to answer or from which to draw a conclusion. The third ellipsis represents the same desired area of philosophical study.
228. "Your house of operation" (*domus operationis tuae*) is a poetic description of the operator himself.
229. *Lemogethon,* the prayer belonging to the third figure of philosophy. See section 94. Compare the first name to the book *Lemegeton.*
230. *Vita hominum,* the Latin prologue prayer belonging to the third figure of philosophy. See section 95.

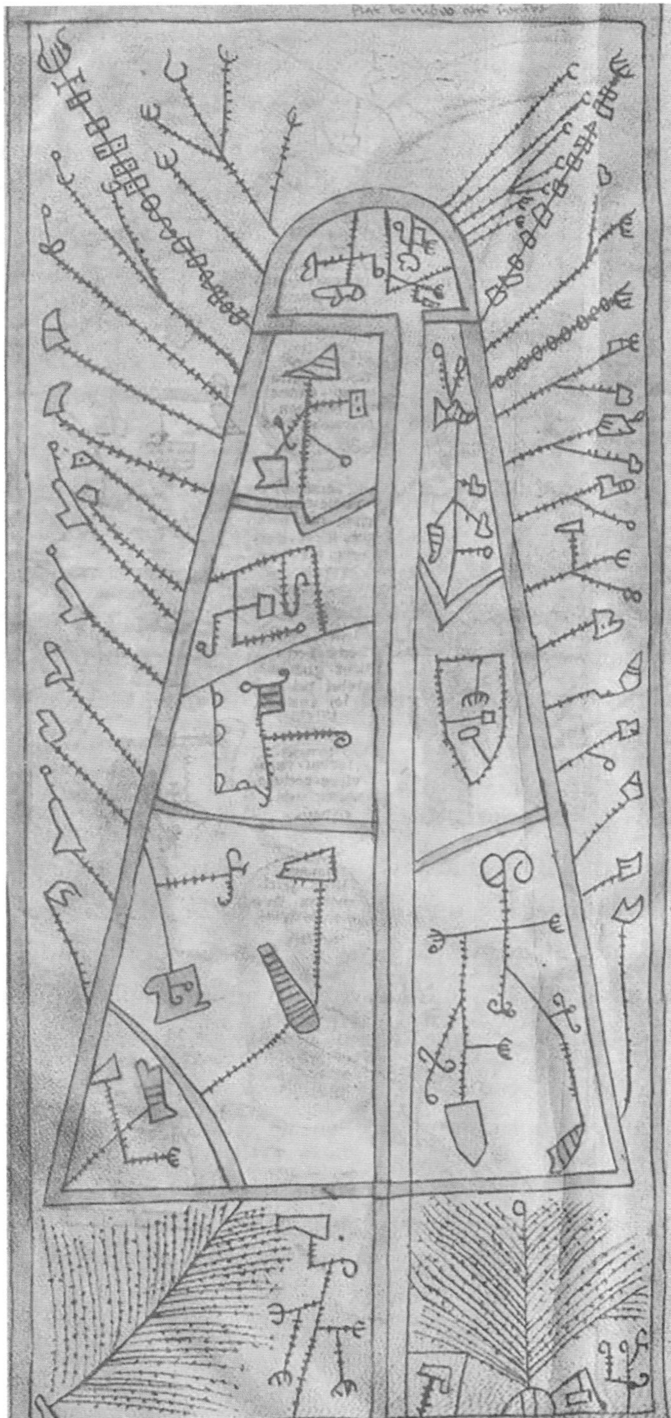

The second figure of philosophy (26b)

understanding, and my intelligence; augment my memory and strengthen my eloquence, render my tongue expedite in the sciences and in your [holy] Scriptures, so that having been conferred with the faculty from you, and having been decorated [as with an insignia] the wisdom of your doctrine upon my heart, and having been decorated, may I praise you and may I know your name with respect to your praise in the ages of ages, amen.

[NS 108] *Rubric: This is the third figure of philosophy, which, after the inspection of the second figure, ought to be inspected, having made some interval, and this operation of these three figures ought to be made at the same time from the early morning up to noon, but at noon you will undertake to the inspection of the fourth, fifth, and sixth figures up to the ninth hour.*

[NS 109] *This prayer is to be offered twice before the fourth figure of philosophy:*
Omaza, Beheza,[231] Theon, Rehagel, Megal, Menehon, Exheal, Tyrigel, Harayhe, Zyhoton, Semenoyn, Sehumeny, Hautemathan, Hyemarayn, Gemegehon, Lutaramotyn, Exnotheyn, Themelyhon, Segyhon, Hyhovenyr, Hutusyhen, Theon.

[NS 110] *Make an interval here, then this prayer is to be offered:*
O King of kings,[232] O God of infinite mercy, bestower, disposer, and dispenser of an immense majesty, the stabilizer of all foundations, lay the foundation of all your virtues in me and take away from me the insipidity of my heart, so that my senses may be stabilized in the delight of your charity, and the Holy Spirit may be informed within me according to the recreation and renewal of your will, O God, you who lives and reigns through the infinite ages of ages, amen.

This is the fourth figure of philosophy, which ought to be inspected after the third figure, first around noon, and having immediately made a short interval, the fifth figure is to be inspected.

---

231. *Omaza Beheza,* the prayer belonging to the fourth figure of philosophy. This prayer is only found in Version B.

232. *Rex regum,* the prayer belonging to the fourth figure of philosophy. See section 96.

The third figure of philosophy (27b)

The fourth figure of philosophy (28b)

[NS 111] *This prayer is to be offered twice before the fifth figure of philosophy:*
O God the immeasurable Father, from whom proceeds all that is good, whose magnitude[233] is incomprehensible, hear my prayers which I bring before your sight today, and grant me the gift that I ask from you, deliver the joy of your salvation to me, so that today I may teach the disadvantaged your ways and the paths of your sciences, and may the rebellious and unbelievers be converted to you, so that what I recall with the heart and mouth, I remember; having been rooted within me, it has a foundation, so that I may be regarded as efficacious and as having been helped in your works, amen.

This is the fifth figure of philosophy, which after the fourth figure, having immediately mad an interval, ought to be inspected.

[NS 112] *The prayer begins:*
O life of good things,[234] O God, the power, the fountain, the peace, the kingdom, the eternal goodness, the holy vision, the gift of light, the brightness of the sun, the creator of darkness, pure power, help my mind, the mercy, the life of the soul, the truth, the light, the power of the creator, through the magnificence of your elevation, through the glorification of your majesty, visit, vivify, and restore what I have received out of your venerable piety, and give me the perfection of this knowledge, and these things[235] which I am wonderfully adept from your generosity, may I recognize and understand . . . by your permission and approval, amen.

[NS 113] *This prayer must be read twice before the sixth figure of philosophy:*
Gezomothon,[236] Hezemothan, Hazatha, Hagyar, Hagibatar, Hazatha, Iethasihel, Gethazihel, Lechizihel, Iezroubal, Geguhay, Iechomay, Samasaht, Samasarel, Zamasathel, Gezomathel, Gessymoyhatel, Iegon,

233. *Deus Pater immense . . . magnitudo,* the prayer belonging to the fifth figure of philosophy. See section 98. The same prayer is assigned to the third figure of the general sciences (NS 95).
234. *Vita bonorum,* the adorning prayer of the fifth figure of philosophy is written within the center of the figure; it is only found in Version B. See the figure on page 585.
235. This part of the prayer could be adapted to suit the specific knowledge and mental faculties which are particular to the operator's work. The ellipsis which follows is meant to be filled in by the operator regarding the desired area of philosophy study.
236. *Gezomothon,* the prayer belonging to the sixth figure of philosophy. See section 99.

The fifth figure of philosophy (29b)

Tassay, Iezomyhatel, Sergomazar, Hazomatan, Hazotynathon, Iesemathon, Iezochor, Hetazay, Heyhazar, Samyn, Zamyn, Helyhel, Samyhelihel, Syloht, Sylereht, Gezamathal, Guaramathal, Iesematal, Iecoronay, Iechornenay, Samyhahel, Hesemyhel, Sechozomay, Sedosamay, Sechothamay, Samna, Tabihetos, Hamynos, Hamnas, amen.

[NS 114] *Make an interval here, afterward this prayer is to be read:*
O God the eternal king,[237] judge, and discerner of all thoughts of the good sciences, O Lord, instruct me today on account of your holy name, and make my mind illustrious through these, your holy sacrament, and may your knowledge [about] . . .[238] enter my innermost being, like water flowing from heaven and like the oil in my bones,[239] through you, O God, the savior of all, you who are the fountain of goodness and the origin of all piety,[240] instruct me today in these sciences for which I pray earnestly, you who are the one God, amen.

This is the sixth figure of philosophy, which after the fifth figure, having immediately made some interval, ought to be inspected and its particular prayers are recited twice.

[NS 115] *This prayer with the subsequent one is to be offered twice before this figure:*
O God, the creator of all piety[241] and the foundation of all things, the eternal salvation and redemption of the people,[242] the inspirer of all nations, the immense bestower of the graces and of the sciences of all the arts, from whose office and mercy comes, so that you may deem us so worthy, your servants of the sciences, to inspire [personal] growth,

---

237. *Rex aeterne Deus,* the prayer belonging to the sixth figure of philosophy. See section 100. The same prayer is assigned to the second figure of the general sciences (NS 94).
238. The ellipsis is a placeholder for the operator to fill in what knowledge of philosophy he desires to acquire.
239. Psalm 109:18 (NRSV).
240. Latin *fons bonitatis et totius pietatis origo.* An epithet of God found in the Gregorian Sacramentary. The same epithet is found at NS 67 and 94.
241. *Deus totius pietatis,* the prayer belonging to the seventh figure of philosophy. See section 101. The same prayer is assigned to the fourth figure of the general sciences (NS 98).
242. Or the parish (perhaps in the global sense).

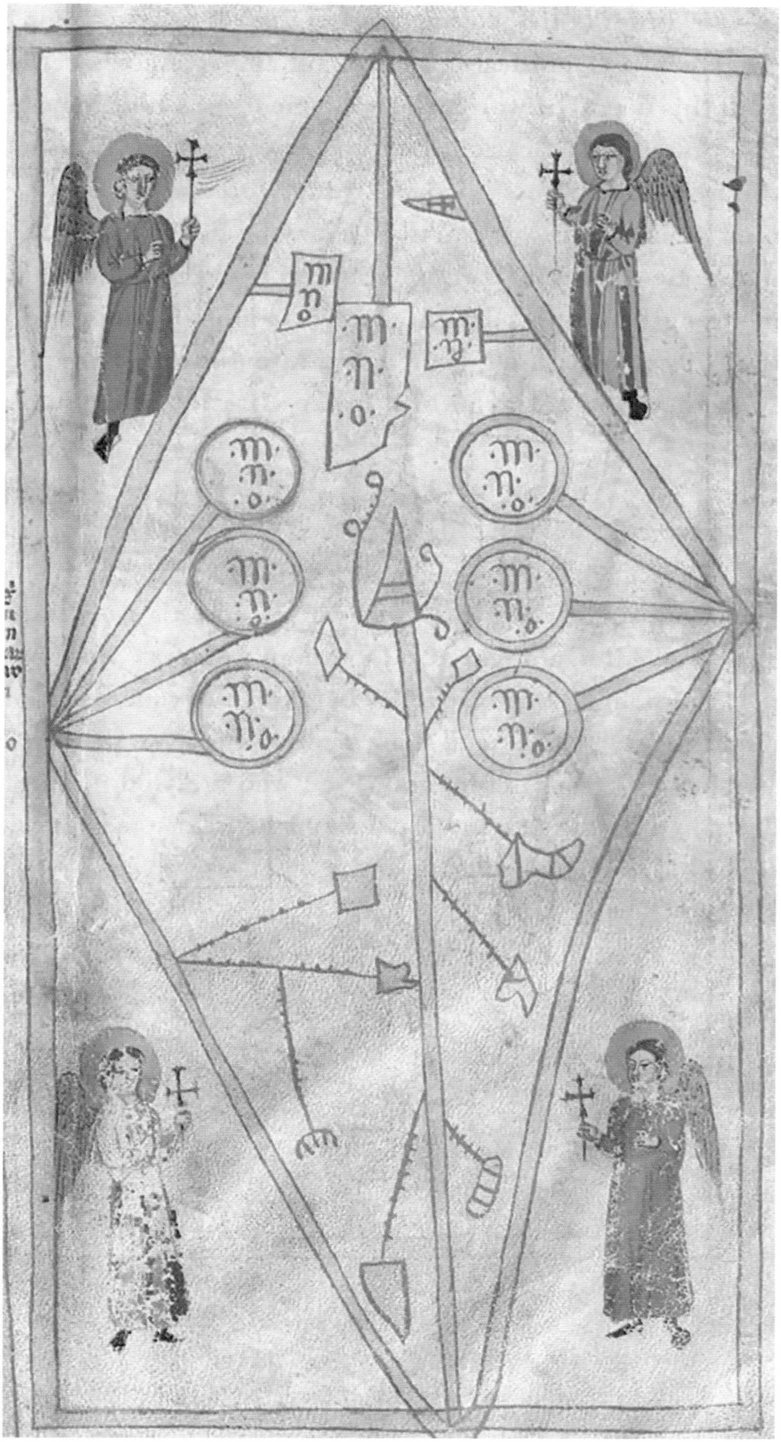

The sixth figure of philosophy (30b)

and even you, who granted to me, a miserable sinner, to know the way of your sacrament; O Lord, defend my soul and free my heart from the thoughts of this depraved world, the incitements of a libidinous pleasure with a voluptuous gratification, and every desire of fornication within me; extinguish and repress all these things forcefully, so that, having understood your sciences and arts,[243] I may be delighted in them, and may you give me the petition of my heart, so that I may love you,[244] having been strengthened and delighted in your glorification, and the virtue of the Holy Spirit be augmented within me through your salvation and the remuneration of the faithful in the salvation of my soul and my body, amen.

[NS 116] *This prayer should be offered immediately after the preceding without an interval:*

O God the immeasurable Father,[245] from whom proceeds every thing that is good, O most merciful, almighty God, burn my kidneys[246] out of the grace of the Holy Spirit, and visit[247] me today by the fire of your visitation[248] and be propitious to me, a sinner, and show me your mercy, so that I may drink and satisfy [myself] from the fountain, you who are God,[249] and let your kind will be done within me, and may I sing and understand your wonders, you who are God, threefold and one, amen.

[NS 117] *Rubric: This is the seventh and last figure of philosophy and the angel named it, "the* nota *of awe."*[250] *Accordingly, this figure ought to be inspected with awe and with the greatest devotion after the other six figures, around the ninth [hour] of the very day of the new lunar [day of the] month. You may*

243. Latin *artibus.*

244. Latin *diligante* has been corrected to *diligam t[a]e,* meaning "I may love you."

245. *Deus Pater immense [. . . misericordissime],* another prayer of the seventh figure of philosophy. Compare it against the prayer belonging to music (NS 69).

246. Psalm 26:2 (Vulgate). Section 117, page 277, footnote 80.

247. Or punish. This translation would support the preceding request for a divine testing.

248. Compare similar phrasing from the *Ars Nova* prayer *Confiteor,* in section 117.

249. Compare similar phrasing from the *Ars Nova* prayer *Adoro te rex regum* in section 116.

250. Compare against section 85 and footnote 25 (page 158) where the epithet the *nota* of awe is identified with the third figure of the general sciences.

The seventh figure of philosophy (31b)

inquire about the order of these seven figures in that gloss, which begins: De notis autem generalium, etc.[251] *For there you will find the operation of the figures of philosophy.*

[NS 118] Note that the seven figures of philosophy are working to this end, and for this reason they were sent from the Most High through the angel, so that any art of the seven exceptive arts[252] which are contained under the seven liberal arts, whether some moral or natural science, or whatever other science which is contained under a greater or lesser philosophy, is able to be acquired and to be possessed perfectly in a short period of time through the inspection of those very ones and the prolation of their own prayers, and through the operation of this most sacred art to be offered eloquently and ornately and to be retained in memory, which you will be able to obtain all the abovesaid, if following what is instructed in the gloss, which begins: *De notis autem generalium, etc.*[253] if you follow [it] and have worked [it] properly. You should pay attention because that seventh figure of philosophy, which is last, ought to be inspected with a greater veneration, obsequiousness, devotion, and humility than the other preceding six, yet anyone ought to be inspected in hope and faith, with devotion and humility, and the prayers of these very figures is to be offered in the same manner.

251. Section 87 gloss.

252. That is, the seven exceptives, which are hydromancy, pyromancy, nigromancy, chiromancy, geomancy, genethlialogy, and onomancy. See section 71 and the introduction.

253. Section 87 gloss.

[Geometry]

[NS 119] *This prayer with the subsequent one is to be offered thrice before the first figure of geometry:*
Gemaht, Semanay, Iohas,[254] Phares, Nerguazathe, Zeguomor, Moche, Zechamay, Cortozo, Semachia, Machym, Hesel, Halyhacol, Gemoy.

[NS 120] *Make a short interval here and then you must read this prayer:*
O God, O just judge,[255] O almighty Father, who has made to us the promise of your salvation, and you revealed your justice in the sight of the nations, open my eyes and illuminate my heart in your salvific justice, so that I may expound about the wonders of your most glorious sacramental mysteries, how I will gain so much understanding through them in this art, as you provide [them], you alone who does great wonders, may I be effective interpreting . . .[256] suddenly in this very art, so that, I may measure out the precepts[257] with eloquence and memory with stability within it, and with the intercession of all the heavenly virtues, may I honor you in the ages of ages, amen.

[NS 121] *Rubric: This is the first figure of geometry, which ought to be inspected on any day thrice from the first day of a new lunar [day of] one month up to the end, once in the early morning, once around the third [hour], once around noon, and then, having made a short interval, the second figure is to be inspected.*

[NS 122] *This prayer is to be offered thrice before the second figure of geometry:*
The dignity of every wisdom and [the giver *or* lover] of knowledge[258] to

254. *Gemaht Semanay Iohas,* the prayer belonging to the first figure of geometry. This prayer is found only in Version B.
255. *Deus iustus iudex,* the prayer belonging to the first figure of geometry. See section 143.
256. An ellipsis which acts as a placeholder for the operator to insert his desired area of study.
257. Latin *recepta,* corrected to *praecepta,* meaning "precepts" or "teachings."
258. *Omnipotens sapientiae* belongs to the second figure of geometry according to Version B. See section 146, where the prayer belongs to the general sciences. Latin *Omnis sapienti[a]e decus et scienti[a]e donator. Dator,* a noun meaning "the giver," may be intended rather than the verbal command *donator.* Compare against *Omnipotens sapientie sive scientie amator* in section 146; scribal errors may have occurred here. Notice that *sive* may be interpreted as *decus* and *amator* for *donator* in medieval script.

The first figure of geometry (32b)

those in which sin does not exist, you, O Lord, the master and instructor of every spiritual discipline, through your Angels and Archangels, through the Thrones and Powers, Principalities and Virtues, through the Cherubim and Seraphim, through the twenty-four elders,[259] through the four living creatures,[260] through the every military unit of the heavenly army, I adore, invoke, request, revere, glorify, and exalt your most calm, terrible, most holy, holy name, and behold, I beseech you, O Lord, so that today you may illuminate my heart, having been made abundant and strengthened by the light of the Holy Spirit and the grace of your visitation, you who are threefold and one, amen.

[NS 123] *Rubric: This is the second figure of geometry, which after the first figure, ought to be inspected, yet having made some short interval; for these two figures ought to be inspected at the same time thrice on any day, one after another, and their prayers are to be offered thrice.*

Say this prayer after the preceding one without an interval.

[NS 124] *The prayer of the holy angels of God begins:*
Honoy, Theon,[261] Hystym, Patynton, Helectethon, Hares, Helyeram, Helsemona, Hesacnahyos, Hubene, Gemelihon, Ierilon, Balachalixon, Getham, Syhasta, Rethym, Honycam, Hepycto, Mamyha, Pryhanaday, Ypozoziha, Zasaym, Sayha, Phametoha, Panchamom, Hycohamym, Trabrasym, Bresem, Thabuhel, Humyhor, Collinays, Phara, Exihegelem, Cezclephay, O Lord, send forth the Holy Spirit from the seats above, so that [the Holy Spirit] dwells within me and I in him, now and always, amen.

You must make an interval here, and then you must read the following prayer.

---

259. Revelation 4:4.
260. Revelation 4:6–8. The four living creatures are the ox, lion, eagle, and man, which comes from Ezekiel 1:5–28.
261. *Honoy Theon,* the adorning prayer, consisting of two parts, which belongs to the second figure of geometry, which is found only in Version B. This first part is written within the top semicircle of the figure. See the figure on page 594.

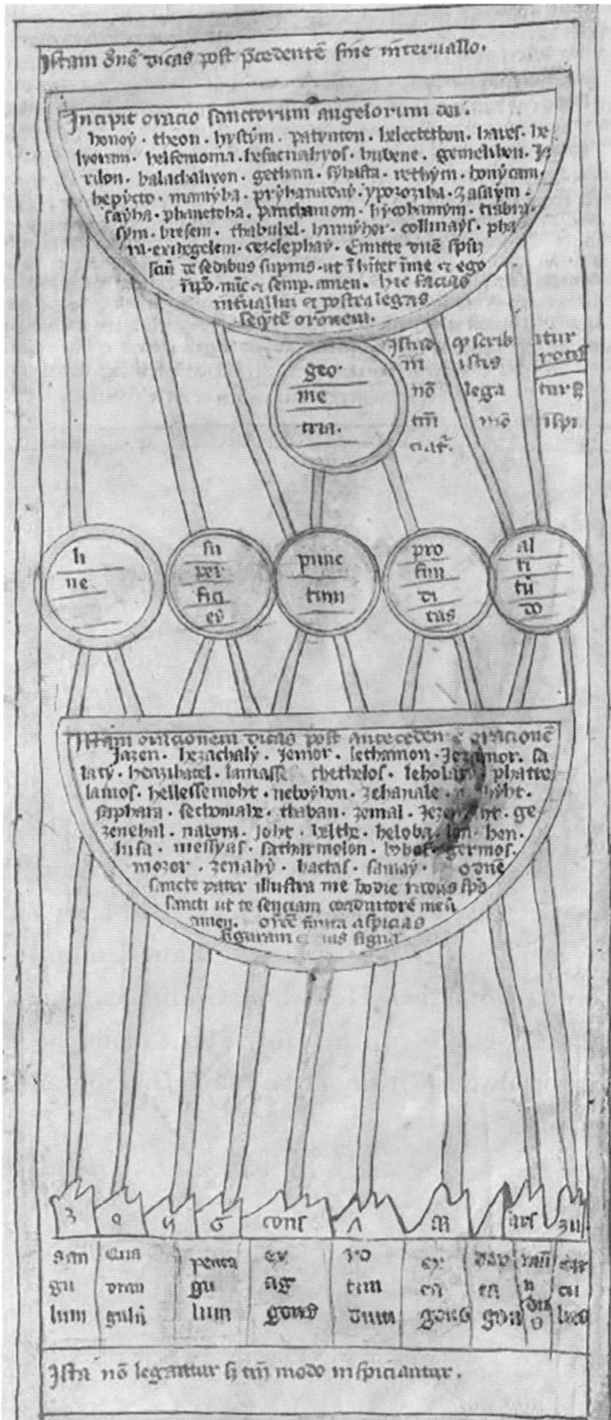

The second figure of geometry (33b)

[NS 125] *Say this prayer after the antecedent prayer:*
Iazen, Hezachaly,[262] Iemor, Lethamon, Iezamor, Sataty, Heazihatel, Lamasse, Thethelos, Leholaty, Phatrelamos, Hellessemoht, Neboyhon, Zehanale, Mohyht, Saphara, Sechomahe, Thaban, Zemal, Iezemoht, Gezenehal, Nabora, Ioht, Helthe, Heloba, Lon, Hen, Hisa, Messyas, Satharmolon, Bohos, Germos, Mozor, Zenahy, Hactas, Samay, O Lord the Holy Father, illuminate me by the rays of the Holy Spirit today, so that I may feel you as my coadjutor,[263] amen.

Having finished with the prayer, you must inspect the figure and its signs.

262. *Iazen Hezachaly,* the second part of the adorning prayer which belongs to the second figure of geometry. This second part is written in the bottom semicircle of the figure. See the figure on page 594.

263. The term *coadiutorem,* or "coadjutor," is a title qualifier indicating that the holder shares the office with another person, with powers equal to the other in all but formal order of precedence. It also holds a specific religious context about church officials' duties and the order of succession. Thus, the petitioner is asking for God's assistance so that he may feel like God is working in partnership and cooperation in accomplishing the work of the notory art.

[Theology]

[NS 126] *This prayer is to be offered seven times before the first figure of theology:* **O almighty, incomprehensible,[264] invisible and indivisible God, I adore your holy name today, I, an unworthy and most miserable sinner, extolling my prayer, understanding, and reason to your holy temple of heavenly Jerusalem, and I stand before you today, O my God, showing you, my God, my creator, my salvation, and I, a rational creature, call upon your glorious clemency today, so that the Holy Spirit may visit my infirmity today; O Lord my God, who conferred upon your servants, Moses and Aaron, your efficacious teaching through the elements of the letters[265] of the outer laws, today confer on me the grace of your superior sweetness with which you instructed to your servants, and which you investigated the same [laws] through the prophets with an investigation, just as you wanted to confer a short doctrine to them, extend to me the doctrine of the science[266] which I desire, and cleanse my conscience from dead works, and send my heart down the right path, and open [it] at once to understanding, and distill my understanding in a holy way; O Lord my God, you who are deemed worthy to create me in your image and likeness, listen to me in your justice, and teach me in your truth, and replenish my soul in your knowledge according to your great mercy, so that [walking] in the multitude of your mercies[267] I may take delight in your great works and may I satisfy your commandments in [my] administration [of them],[268] and according to the work of your grace, having been helped and restored, you will exalt [my] heart and my conscience, having been cleansed, I may confide in you, and feast sumptuously in your sight, and may I exalt your name because it is good; O Lord, sanctify**

264. *Omnipotens incomprehensibilis,* the prayer belonging to the first figure of theology. See section 115.

265. Latin *litterarum elementa,* meaning "the basics" or "the fundamentals."

266. This phrase may be adapted by the operator to specify what he desires to learn. Also, a scribal error may have occurred here in which *lator,* meaning "a proposer of the law," became *doctrinam,* meaning "doctrine" or "teaching."

267. Psalm 51 (NRSV). This clause has been slightly reconstructed to make grammatical sense and also to reflect what was most likely the original meaning found in section 115.

268. Section 115 has "may I please [you] in the admiration of your commandments" (*complaceam in admiratione mandatorum tuorum*).

me today in the sight of your holy ones, so that I may live in faith, perfected hope, and constant charity, learning as much as I desire, having attained an exulted knowledge, having been strengthened and illuminated, may I love you and may I get to know you, may I understand the knowledge, wisdom, and intelligence from your Scriptures, which you promised everyone everything which to is to be known, and may I have it firmly and may I retain it in memory; O Jesus Christ, the only begotten Son of God, whom the Father has given all things into [your] hands before the ages, give to me, O Lord, on account of your glorious, ineffable, and holy name, the proper nourishment for body and soul; O Lord, present to me the gift that I ask for and a perspicacious, free, expedite, and fluent tongue, so that whatever I ask in your mercy and truth will be dispensed according to [your] will, and may my every prayer and action stand rooted and strengthened in your good pleasure; open, O Lord my God and the Father of my life, the foundation of the knowledge which I desire; open to me, O Lord, the fountain which you opened to the first man,[269] Adam, and you who opened to your servants Abraham, Isaac, and Jacob, for the purpose of understanding, discerning, and judging, accept my prayers and orations today, O Lord of all the holy angels and all the holy heavenly hosts, so that I may be efficaciously teachable of all your Scriptures constantly, amen.

[NS 127] *Rubric: This is the first figure of theology, which this field of knowledge has five figures. Specifically, this first figure ought to be inspected once, first on the first day of the new lunar [day of the] month, and its particular prayers to be offered seven times, and having made a short interval, the prayers of the second figure are to be offered seven times, and this very figure is to be inspected once. [But having been inspected the following figure thus, the very same prayers are to be reiterated seven times with the particular prayer of the third figure, and then the third figure and its signs is to be inspected.] For it is to be done thus concerning these three figures once on any day of one month from the early morning up to noon.*

---

269. *Protoplaustrum,* literally "the first wagon," though in the ecclesiastic sense means "first man."

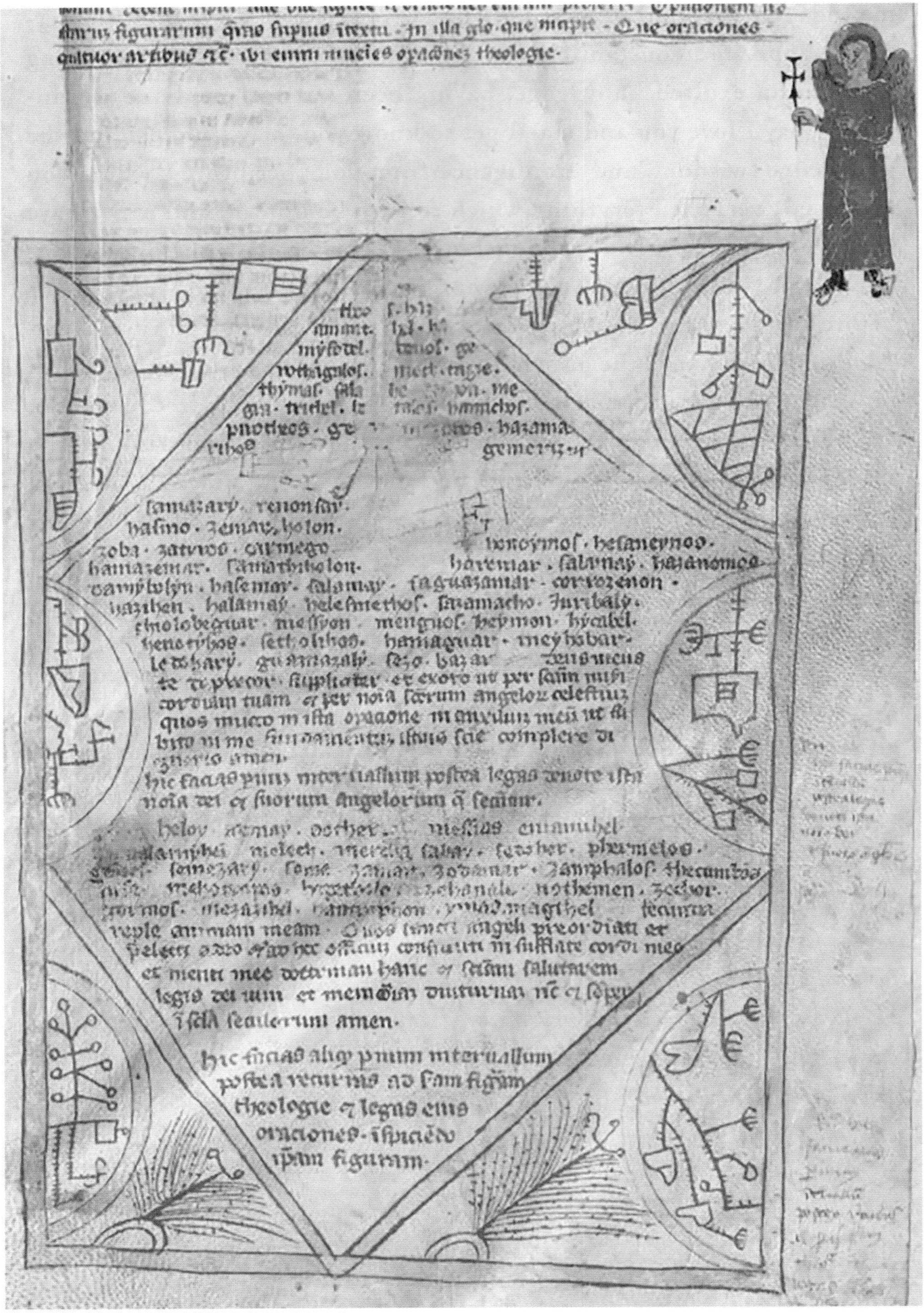

The first figure of theology (34b)

The other two figures ought to be inspected and their prayers are to offered from noon up to the ninth [hour]. But you may inquire about the operation of those figures above in the text [and] in that gloss, which begins "Que orations quattuor artibus, etc."[270] *For there you will find the operation of theology.*

[NS 128] Theos, Hazamant,[271] Hel, Hamyfodel, Benos, Gerothagalos, Mechitagie, Thymas, Salahe, Zechon, Megra, Trichel, Hetalos, Hamichos, Pirotheos, Gemozoros, Hazamarihos, Gemeriz, Samazary, Renonsay, Hasino, Zemar, Holon, Zoba, Zatyros, Carmego, Honoymos, Hesaneynos, Hamazemar, Samathiholon, Haremar, Salanay, Hazanomos, Damybolyn, Hasemar, Salamay, Saguazamar, Corrozenon, Hazihen, Halamay, Helesmethos, Sazamacho, Iuribaly, Chiolobeguar, Messyon, Menguos, Heymon, Hycabel, Henotyhos, Setholihos, Hamaguar, Meyhobar, Ledohary, Guamazaly, Sezo, Bazar, O my God, I suppliantly deprecate and entreat you, so that through your holy mercy, and through the names of your heavenly [and] holy angels, whom I invoke to help me in this operation, so that you may deem worthy to suddenly complete the foundation of this knowledge[272] within me, amen.

[NS 129] *You must make a short interval here, then you must devoutly read these names of God and of his angels which follow:*

Heloy, Adonay, Sother,[273] Messias, Emanuhel, Melech, Merchasahay, Sedoher, Phermelos, Semezary, Some, Zamar, Zodamar, Zamphalos, Thecumbos, Mehothopos, Hepetholo, Zehanale, Nothemen, Zechor, Gormos, Mezazihel, Hantrophon, Ymas, Magihel, make abundant, replenish my soul, O you holy angels, preordained and pre-elected by God and appointed to this office, insufflate my heart and my mind with that

---

270. Section 97 gloss.

271. *Theos Hazamant,* the adorning prayer, consisting of two parts, which belongs to the first figure of theology. This first part is written within the top portion of the figure. See the figure on page 598.

272. "The foundation of this knowledge" (*fundamentum istius scienti[a]e*) may act as a placeholder for the operator to specify what kind of theological knowledge he desires to acquire.

273. *Heloy Adonay Sother,* the second part of the adorning prayer which belongs to the first figure of theology. This second part is written within the lower portion of the figure. See the figure on page 598.

doctrine and salvific knowledge of the law of the living God and a long-lasting memory, now and always in the ages of ages, amen.

You must make some short interval here, then you must return to the second figure of theology, and read its prayers, having inspected this very figure.

[NS 130] *This prayer is to be offered seven times before the second figure of theology:* **I adore you, O king of kings[274] and Lord of lords, O unchangeable eternal king, hear my cry and my spirit and the groaning of my heart, so that you will change my understanding, and give me a heart of flesh for a stone; O my God and my salvation, may I breathe you in; O Lord, wash my interior [self] with your new spirit for the understanding of my flesh I want instead; O Lord, place your good holy understanding within me, and take away from me what is evil, changing me into a new man, and you who has transformed the world, transform me with love, and may your holy salvation grant me an increase of good intelligence; O Lord, listen to my prayers today, which I cry out to you, and reveal to my eyes of flesh and my mind, considering, understanding, and guarding the wonders from the Scriptures of your laws, so that, having been vivified in your justifications, I may prevail in the sight of the devil, the adversary of the faithful; O Lord my God, listen and be propitious to me, you who formed me; O Lord, show me your mercy today, and offer me the vessel of salvation, so that I may drink and be satisfied from the fountain of your grace, you who are God, so that . . .[275] from the Scriptures which I desire and having obtained [it] today, I may sing with understanding, and know and understand, and may I stand in the immaculate way, and may the Holy Spirit come today with grace from heaven and rest within me, amen.**

This is the second figure of theology, which after the first figure, having made some interval, ought to be inspected immediately, and its own particular prayers written outside and below the figure ought to be repeated seven times.

---

274. *Adoro te rex regum,* the prayer belonging to the second figure of theology. See section 116.
275. The ellipsis acts as a placeholder for the operator to fill in his desired area of theological study.

The second figure of theology (35b)

[NS 131] *The prayer begins:*
Habyas, Rihel, Iochas,[276] Lorothay, Ioht, Chetha, Chel, Chem, Hehem, Iothay, Genezechor, Hanezamoht, Zamay, Samalys, Zezoguolon, Saphamay, the light, the truthful one, the life, the way, the just judge, illuminate me today and grant me, your servant, the knowledge[277] which I desire, amen.

Having said these, you may inspect the figure.

[NS 132] *This prayer is to be offered seven times before the third figure of theology:*
Otheos, Hatamagiel,[278] Hataha, Marihel, Gezothay, Iezoramy, Gezozay, Sazihel, Sazamay, Iezoramy, Sazamap, Sacamay, Zachamay, Iechor, Namas, Iechormada, Salatihel, Iezommyel, Zarachiel, Megal, Nathama, Nachamyham, Sazamaym, Sephollaym, Lazamayr, Sephonay, Nathama, Lamazayr, Mehys, Ramna, Hamamyl, Zamamyn, Syhel, Deloht, Hamamyn, Hazemeloht, Iazameloht, Mohyramna, Sechoram, Iechonomay, Zegomaym, Zezenomay, Zaramohen, Hanasithoneha, Seroneha, Zaramahem, Sactomohem, Chades, Bachuhc, Iazemeloht, Haruho, Semor, Gizechon, Malaparos, Palapathas, Helatay, Helacnay, Mechay, Meray.

[NS 133] *Let there be a short interval here, then this prayer is to be offered:*
O pious God[279] and merciful God, O gentle, almighty God, giving all things, make me believe all things [are] possible today, and help my incredulity today, and have mercy on me today, just as you pitied the penitent Adam, to whom you conferred knowledge of the arts to him, having approached [you], through your almighty [and] multiple mercies, confer to me today through your omnipotence and your mercy the knowledge which I desire, so that, having been delighted in the magnificence of your works, I may prevail to obtain the efficacy of the knowledge which I desire by the

---

276. *Habyas Rihel Iochas,* the adorning prayer, written within the wheel of the figure, belongs to the second figure of theology.

277. The word "knowledge" (*scientiam*) here may be replaced with the specific area of theological knowledge which the operator desires to acquire.

278. *Otheos Hatamagiel,* this prayer belongs to the third figure of theology and it is found only in Version B. This is not an adorning prayer; it is either a recovered prayer from the original *Flores Aurei* or a newly fabricated one. If original, then *Pie Deus* would be its Latin prologue.

279. *Pie Deus,* the prayer belonging to the third figure of theology. See section 119.

power of your virtue; O most gentle Father, be present today in my work and instruct me; O benevolent, nourishing, most gentle, and only begotten Son of God, strengthen me, breathe into me the Flame of the Holy Spirit; O God the Holy Spirit, strengthen my work today and teach me, so that I may walk in your Scriptures, and may I glory in the multitude of your effluent grace, so that the impetus of the Holy Spirit's river rejoices in the city of my heart[280] in the faith of the Scriptures and in hope of the holy efficacy for which I labor, and replenish and restore my heart with the generosity of charity, and vivify the rays of the Holy Spirit and fortify [them] with the eternal charity of flowing mercy, and may it not be vacant within me; I beg you, O Lord my God, by your grace, but may it remain always and be multiplied within me; O Lord, heal my soul with a gentle piety, you who [are] inestimable and ineffable and strengthen my heart today, so that I may understand what I will hear, and I may guard what I will understand, and I may retain in memory what I will guard, through these aforesaid most sacred sacraments with the cooperating grace of the Father, Son, and Holy Spirit, amen.

This is the third figure of theology, which after the second figure, having made a short interval, ought to be inspected immediately in the same manner and in the same form.

[NS 134] *This prayer is to be offered before the fourth figure of theology:*
O pious Father[281] and merciful Son, O gentle God the Holy Spirit, O inestimable and ineffable king, O threefold and one God, I adore you, I invoke you, and I deprecate you and your holy name, and your superabounding equity working all things to the extent that you may forgive, indulge,[282] and have mercy on me, a presuming miserable sinner and the

---

280. Latin *civitatem cordis*. A phrase is found in the commentary on the Parable of the Prodigial Son in the thirteenth-century *Gesta Romanorum* (Deeds of the Romans), which is a Latin collection of moral stories. The *Gesta Romanorum* drew from Valerius Maximus's *Factorum ac Dictorum Memorabilium Libri IX* (Nine Books of Memorable Deeds and Sayings), the first-century collection of short stories about morality.

281. *Pie Pater,* the prayer belonging to the fourth figure of theology. See section 120.

282. Latin *indulgeas,* in the sense of pardoning or permitting. See page 512, footnote 78.

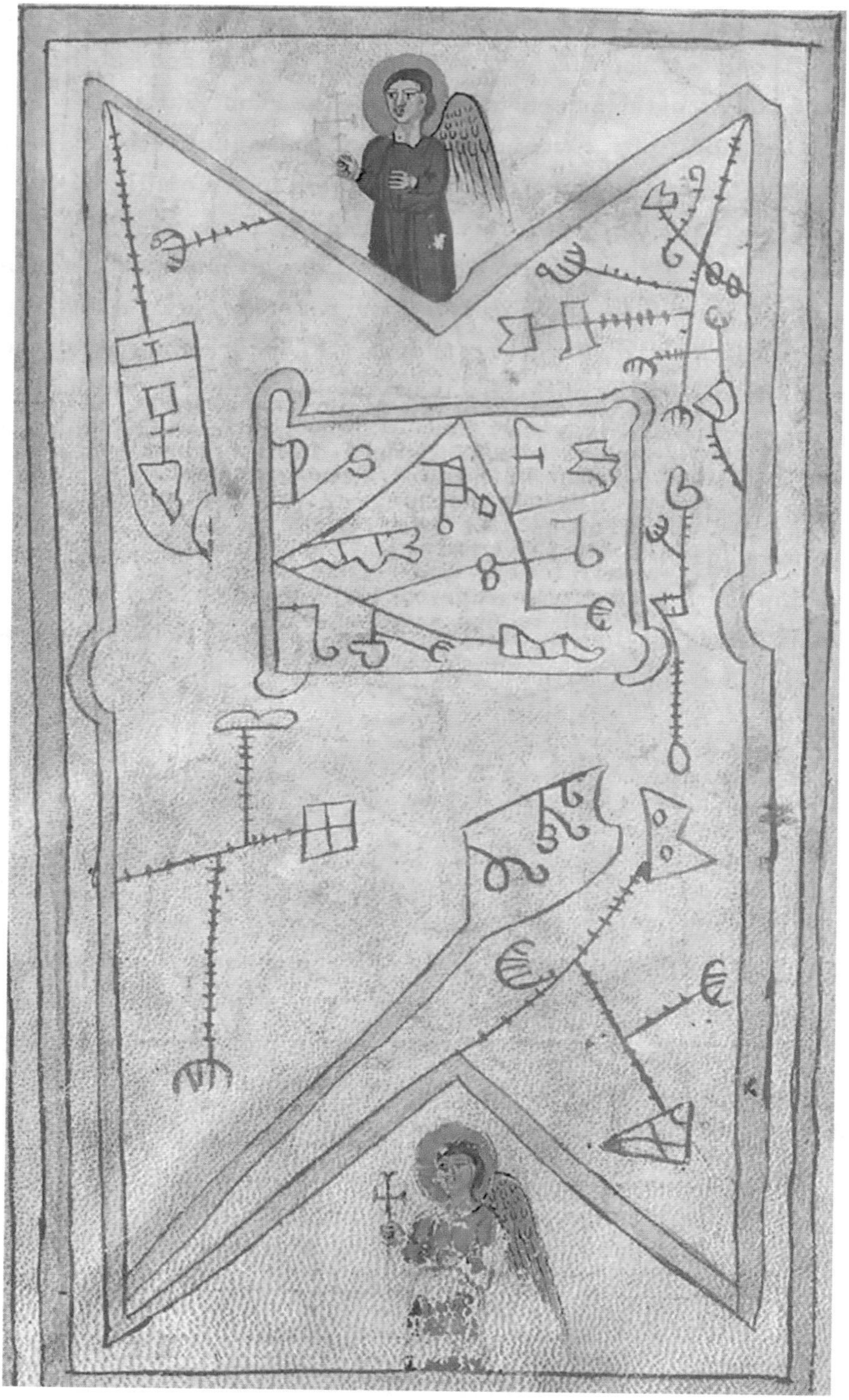

The third figure of theology (36b)

office that I undertook, may I perceive and know . . .[283] within me, having thought about the literature; and you, O my Lord, may the knowledge which I desire invigorate and strengthen . . . efficaciously within me; O Lord, open . . . within me,[284] open my ears potently, so that I may hear, strengthen my hands, so that I may work, wipe away the dirt of my eyes, so that I may see, enlarge my ears, so that I may hear, strengthen my feet, so that I may walk, free my nostrils and my mouth, so that I may smell and feel and speak pleasingly to you, now and always to the honor of your name because it is a benediction in the ages of ages, amen.

This is the fourth figure of theology, which after the other preceding figures, ought to be inspected, that is, first around noon once, and its own particular prayer ought to be said seven times.

[NS 135] *This prayer with the others preceding ought to be read seven times before this figure:*

O God the lord of the living[285] and all visible and invisible creatures, administrator and the maker of abundance, granting all things to all [and] each thing for every one according to its own faculty, pour into me the abundance of heavenly grace for the quality[286] of the merits of angels and men, and may the grace of the Holy Spirit illuminate my heart and my soul today; O Lord, multiply the gifts of the Holy Spirit within me, and strengthen and renew my interior man, and make me fruitful in the dew of your grace by which you instructed the angels; inform me of your wisdom with generosity, you who has taught your faithful ones from the beginning, so that the sevenfold gifts of graces and the gifts of the Holy Spirit may work within me, and the waters of the higher river of Jerusalem, flowing

283. The ellipsis acts as a placeholder for the operator to fill in his desired area of theological study. The same is meant for the second and third ellipses.

284. These last three sentences are corrupted, beginning with *et officium* and ending at *apperi in me.* See Véronèse, *L'Ars Notoria,* pages 80 and 289, especially the critical apparatus.

285. *Deus vivorum,* the prayer belonging to the fifth figure of theology according to BnF Latin 9336; the *Hosel* prayer found in the *Ars Notoria* (Version A, section 104) competes with *Deus vivorum* for the same fifth position belonging to theology (see Version B, section 126c gloss and footnote 271 on page 448).

286. Perhaps the operator may specify what kind of "quality" (*qualitate*) he desires.

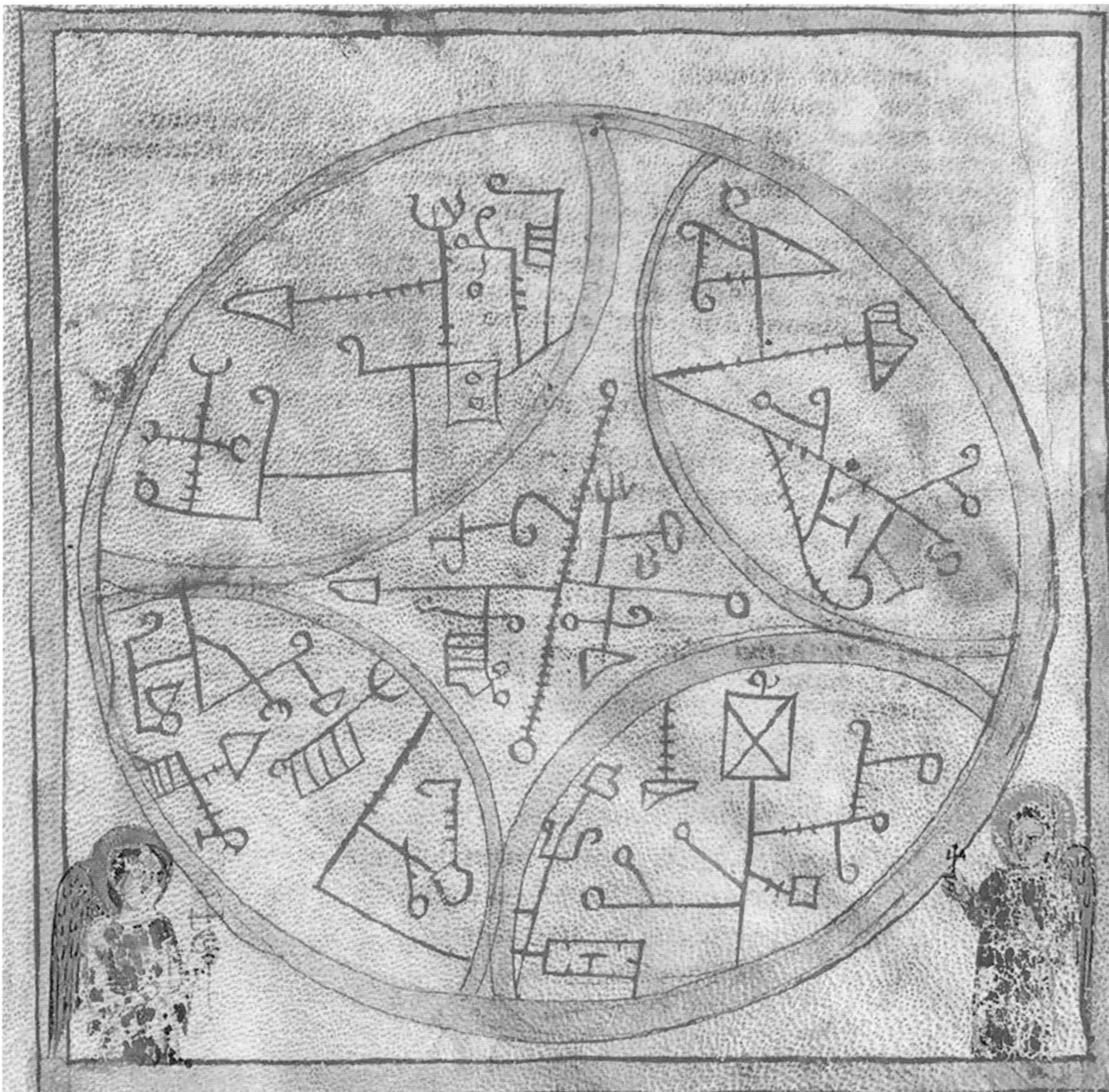

The fourth figure of theology (37b)

with force, may irrigate, replenish, and abound the cistern of my conscience and the fountain of my soul; you who came with charity from heaven over the waters,[287] strengthen the mighty works of your majesty of this pure sacrament within me, amen.

[**NS 136**] *Rubric: This is the fifth and last figure of theology, and it is called the "ineffable* nota.*" For this very figure, after the inspection of the fourth figure, having made a short interval, it ought to be inspected first around noon up to the ninth [hour], and its own particular prayer with all the other prayers of the four figures ought to be read seven times. For this figure ought to have twenty-four nooks with strange things and its own signs.*

287. Genesis 1:2 (NRSV).

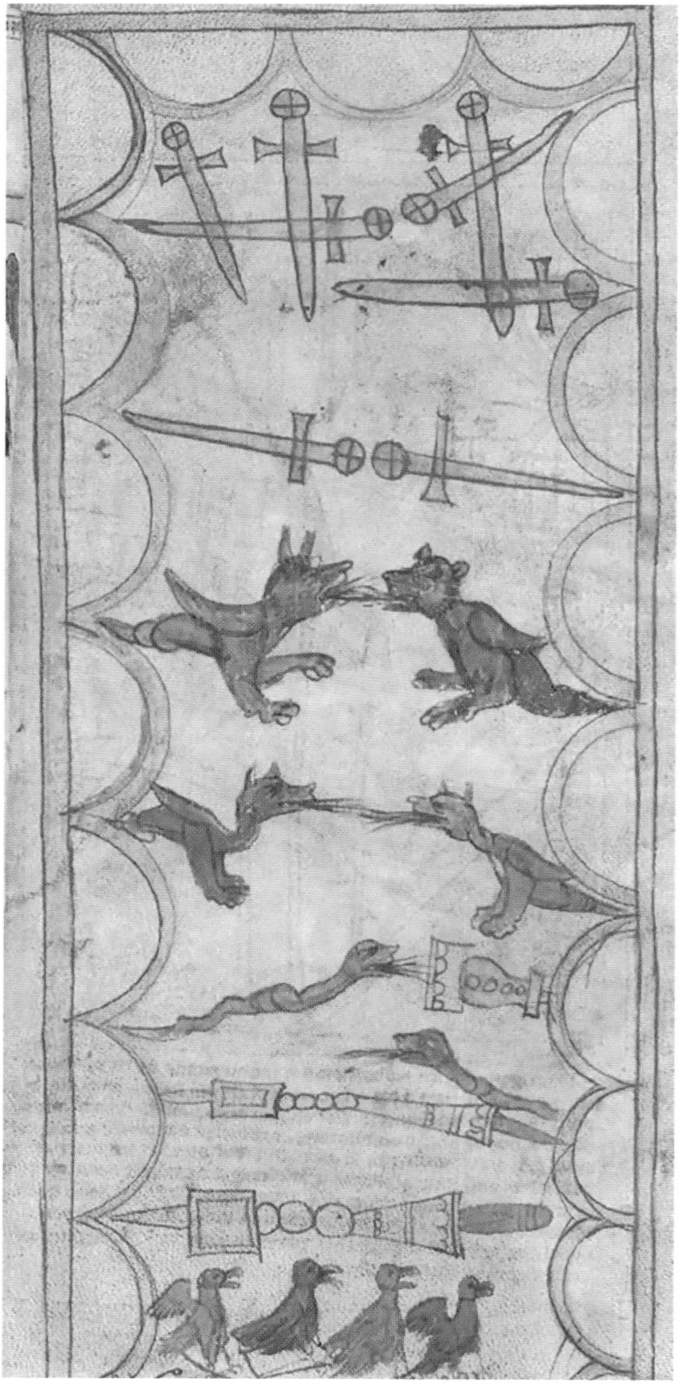

The fifth figure of theology (38b)

[Chastity]

[NS 137] *This prayer ought to be offered twice before the figure of chastity:*
Lamahel, Mysub,[288] Monoy, Sychemas, Thozohar, Ridihec, Phasguor, Hisurohor, Behehuc, Iamynyhec, Mopullo, Hamysym, Chalazel, Hazachar, Iazihol, Ieramon, Seht, Hamor, Thecha, Chet, Chet, Hem, Ioht, Iotha, Halay, Hel, Hon, Helyhon, Heht, Cheht, Hestelbus, Monoy, Sevaza, Iero, Cheleht, Hafphechit, Tymemoraht, Zybic, Samel, Hathytheyhe, Nophelety, Heplaz, Mopullo, Hallothar, Myseht, Styhyc, Hella, Sebellay, Saduhc, Theon, Fountain, Light, Hachita, Hihel, Samaray, Hon, Thehec, Tau.

[NS 138] *Make an interval here, then say this prayer:*
O Lord the Holy Father,[289] the almighty eternal God of inestimable mercy and immense piety; Jesus Christ, the most pious founder, restorer, and regenerator of the human race; the Holy Spirit, the Paraclete [and] lover of all the faithful ones, you who suspended the rock with three fingers, having balanced it in weight and the hills in a balance,[290] you who make inscrutable and mutable things, and you alone who makes great wonders,[291] when there is nothing which is able to resist your will, whose ways [are] unsearchable,[292] defend my soul and free my heart from the thoughts of this depraved world, extinguish and repress the incitements of a libidinous pleasure and every fornication within me, so that, having understood your arts,[293] I may be delighted, and the virtue of the Holy Spirit be augmented within me through your salavation and the remuneration of the faithful in the salvation of my soul and body, amen.[294]

---

288. *Lamahel Mysub,* the prayer belonging to the figure of chastity, which is found only in Version B. This is not presented as an adorning prayer; in this case, *Domine Sancte Pater [. . . misericordiae]* may be the intended but unspoken Latin prologue as its contents appropriately exhibit the petitioner's desire to remain chaste.

289. *Domine Sancte Pater [. . . reparator],* the prayer belonging to the figure of chastity, which is found only in Version B. Compare it against the prayer with the same incipit as found in section O of *Opus Operum,* as well as Agrippa's *Opera Omnia* (c. 1620), page 659.

290. Isaiah 40:12 (Vulgate), *quis adpendit tribus digitis.* The *Ars Notoria* has *qui . . . apprehendisti* which has been corrected here to *qui . . . appendisti,* meaning "you who suspended."

291. Psalm 136:4 (NRSV).

292. Romans 11:33, which in turns draws upon Isaiah 40:28. See also NS 32.

293. Latin *artibus.*

294. The latter portion of this prayer derives from the *Deus totius pietatis* prayer (section 101, NS 98, and NS 115).

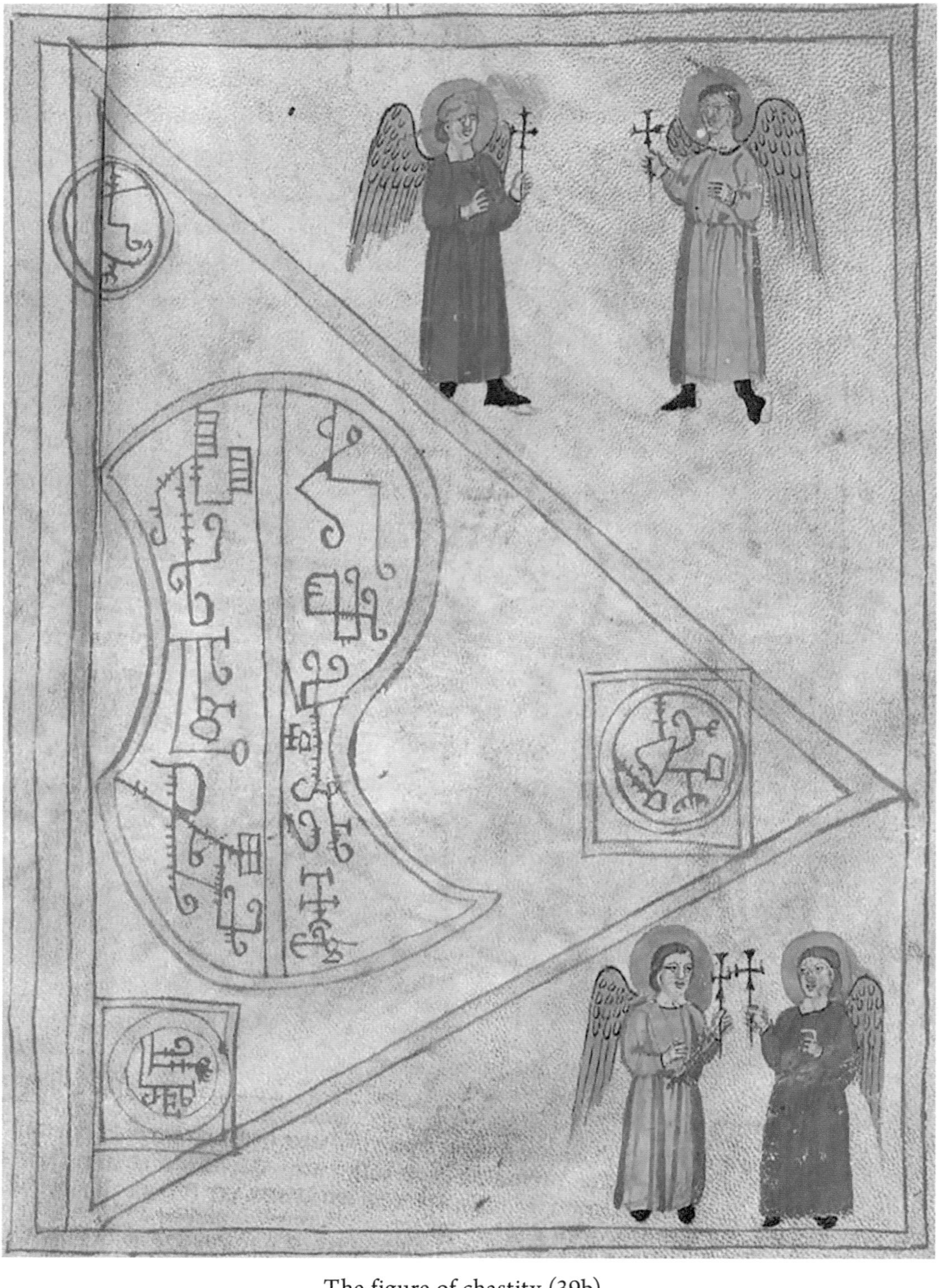

The figure of chastity (39b)

[NS 139] *Rubric: This is the figure of chastity. Indeed, this figure ought to be inspected first on the day of a new lunation of any month twice in a day up to the end of the lunar month, once in the early morning [and] once around noon; and the first three headwords and all the prayers of the figures of theology ought to be said five times, once at any time; and these two prayers after those ought to be said twice.*

[NS 140] Note that the figure of chastity was given and sent to Solomon to this end, so that if an operator of this art was especially aroused by a libidinous pleasure while he was in this holy work and while he was pronouncing the mystical words of the holy prayers and was inspecting the forms of the figures and their signs, [then] he would inspect this figure of chastity twice every day through the one month before he began this most sacred work, and would pronounce the prayers attributed to them; if you inspected that figure just as it is said, and you offered the prayers just as it is taught in its rubric, [then] it will cease all the evil self-gratifications of libidinous pleasure from you, and you will be able to proceed safely in this holy work to acquire any knowledge which will have pleased you more, and you will have obtained the grace of God and will remain chaste.

[Justice, Peace, and Fear]

[NS 141] *This prayer with the following is to be offered twice before the figure of justice, peace, and fear:*
O most gentle Heloy, Hel, Ianazay,[295] Hon, Rechanathas, Hoscymos, Hysmaly, Lamahel, Moynysa, Senzaraht, Revetha, Horabesy, Bey, Heonesa, Chenon, Mabu, Chomyhe, Rabohely, Nygehitha, Hyllohc, Zympnymos, O Father, whose name is On and Hel.

[NS 142] *Here you make an interval, then this prayer is to be offered:*
O Lord God, I know[296] that the angels of the world are scarcely found in your sight, nor is the infant of one day on earth without sin; O Lord, you alone who are justice, peace, and true concord, have mercy on me, and convert the hearts of my enemies, you who do not want the death of a sinner, but so that he may live, and be converted into a better person; O Lord, do for me what I desire, and convert the hearts of my adversaries, so that I may praise you, the everlasting Lord, now and in the ages of ages, amen.

[NS 143] This is the figure of justice, peace, and fear. Specifically, this figure is to be inspected first on the first day of the new lunar [day of] any month twice in a day, once in the early morning [and] once around noon; and those prayers are always to be offered, which they are to be offered before the figures of philosophy as often as they are offered in their operation, and after those prayers, these two prayers are to be offered twice before this figure and this very figure and its signs are to be inspected.

[NS 144] Note that this figure of justice, peace, and fear has three virtues in it: the first is the virtue of justice, the second is the virtue of possessing peace, the third is the virtue of expelling fear. But if you want to uphold true justice through yourself against others, or to obtain [it] at the hands of someone for

---

295. *Heloy clementissime Hel Ianazay,* the prayer belonging to the figure of justice, peace, and fear. This prayer is not to be confused with the *Heloy clementissime* prayer, which belongs to the second figure of logic/dialectic.

296. *Domine Deus scio,* this prayer may be the intended but unspoken Latin prologue belonging to the figure of justice, peace, and fear. The contents appropriately exhibit the petitioner's desire to attain justice, peace, and concord with his enemies.

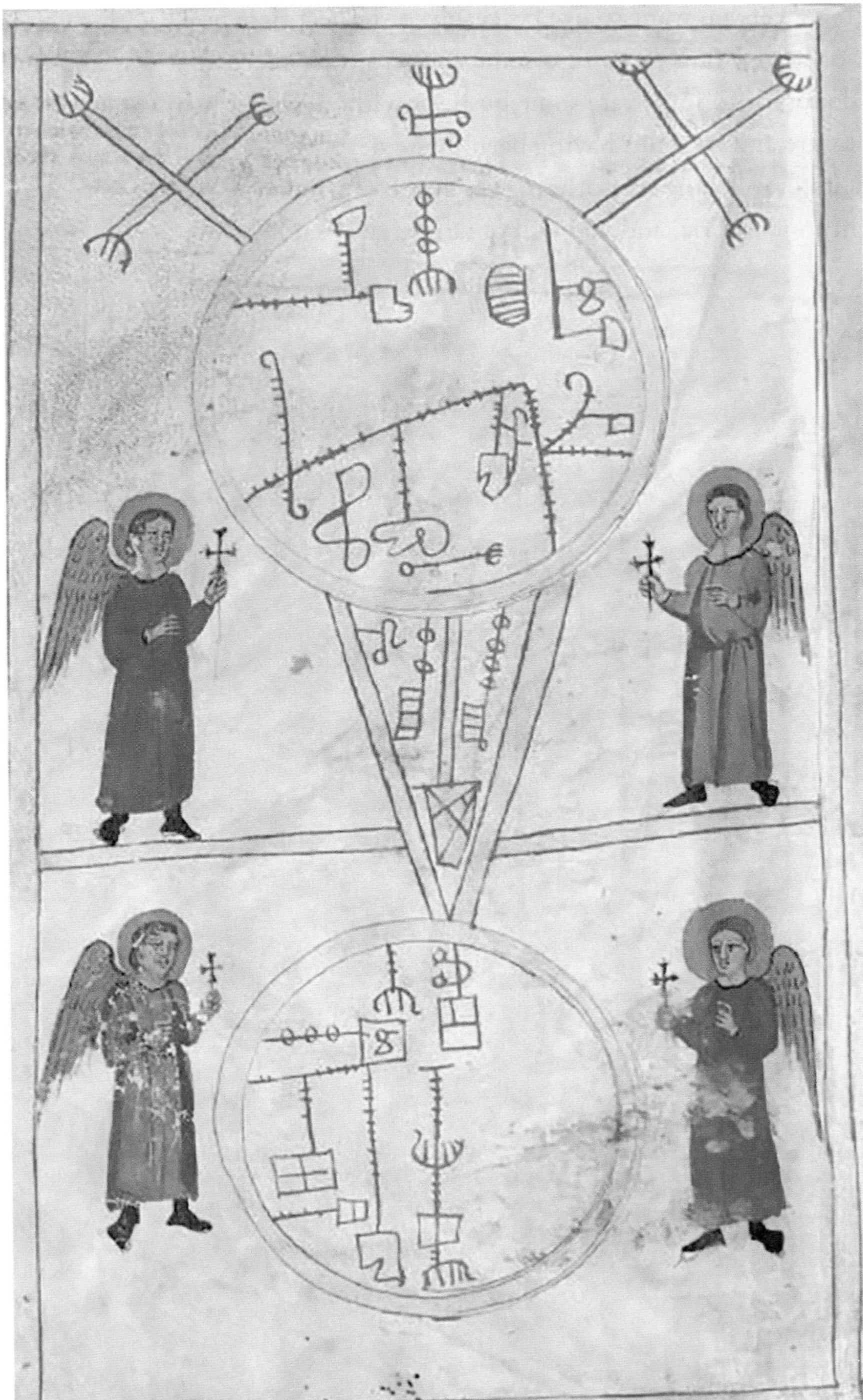

The figure of justice, peace, and fear (40b)

another, or if you want to live peaceably, or to negotiate peace with some adversary, or if you want to go into some dangerous place without fear about which you doubt, or to impetrate some business without fear, [then] you must inspect this figure and its signs, having been living devoutly and chastely, and you must offer its prayers and the others, which are pertinent to them as often as it is taught in its rubric, and you will obtain what is said above.

[Reprehension and Taciturnity]

[NS 145] *This prayer is to be offered with the following before the figure of reprehension:*

Ezomathon, Zehimochor,[297] Sephecuc, Sesohu, Taymehanohc, Seneht, Seher, Geherba, Senersay, Mychedey, Lehusyo, Chalara, Orthynoht, Nygeycha, Cohozopra, Phelyp, Hebeht, Rabohesy, Iasel, Haschaly, Iemorz, Lechamon, Hahechamor, Cetheym, Iotha, Thohar, Vahy, Hel.

[NS 146] *Let there be a short interval here, then this prayer is to be offered:*

Behold O Lord God,[298] most pious founder and restorer of the human race, I, your servant and your son ([or] maidservant),[299] the work of your most merciful hands, your bought and redeemed one, I stand before you before the sight of your immense piety, groaning, crying out, deprecating, and asking insistently with all [my] heart with affection, so that, hoping in respect to my merits, you may amplify [the size of] a gift of heavenly benediction to me, a miserable sinner out of your great mercy, confiding in me; may you make firm your grace of consolation, so that [the grace of the Holy Spirit] has heard [me], having been taught eloquence from the holy Scriptures, [the grace of the Holy Spirit] has sensed my mellifluous words in his mouth, and [the grace of the Holy Spirit] has understood and heard me, [so that] the wise sages understand [me], becoming gentle, superb, submissive with taciturnity and humility, and [the wise sages] sense my words [addressed] to them [as] a mellifluous and pleasing [speech demonstrating] your benefits with an exhibition, having been desired [by everyone], you who lives and reigns now and in eternity, amen.

[NS 147] *Rubric: This is the figure of reprehension and taciturnity. Accordingly, this figure ought to be inspected twice, once in the early morning, once around noon, first on the first day of the new lunation of any month on any day of that month, and the first three headwords and the prayers which are to be offered before*

---

297. *Ezomathon Zehimochor,* the prayer belonging to the figure of reprehension and taciturnity, which is found only in Version B.

298. *Ecce Domine Deus [. . . empticius],* this prayer may be the intended but unspoken Latin prologue belonging to the figure of reprehension and taciturnity.

299. The practitioner supplies either "son" or "maid" when speaking the prayer based on his or her sex.

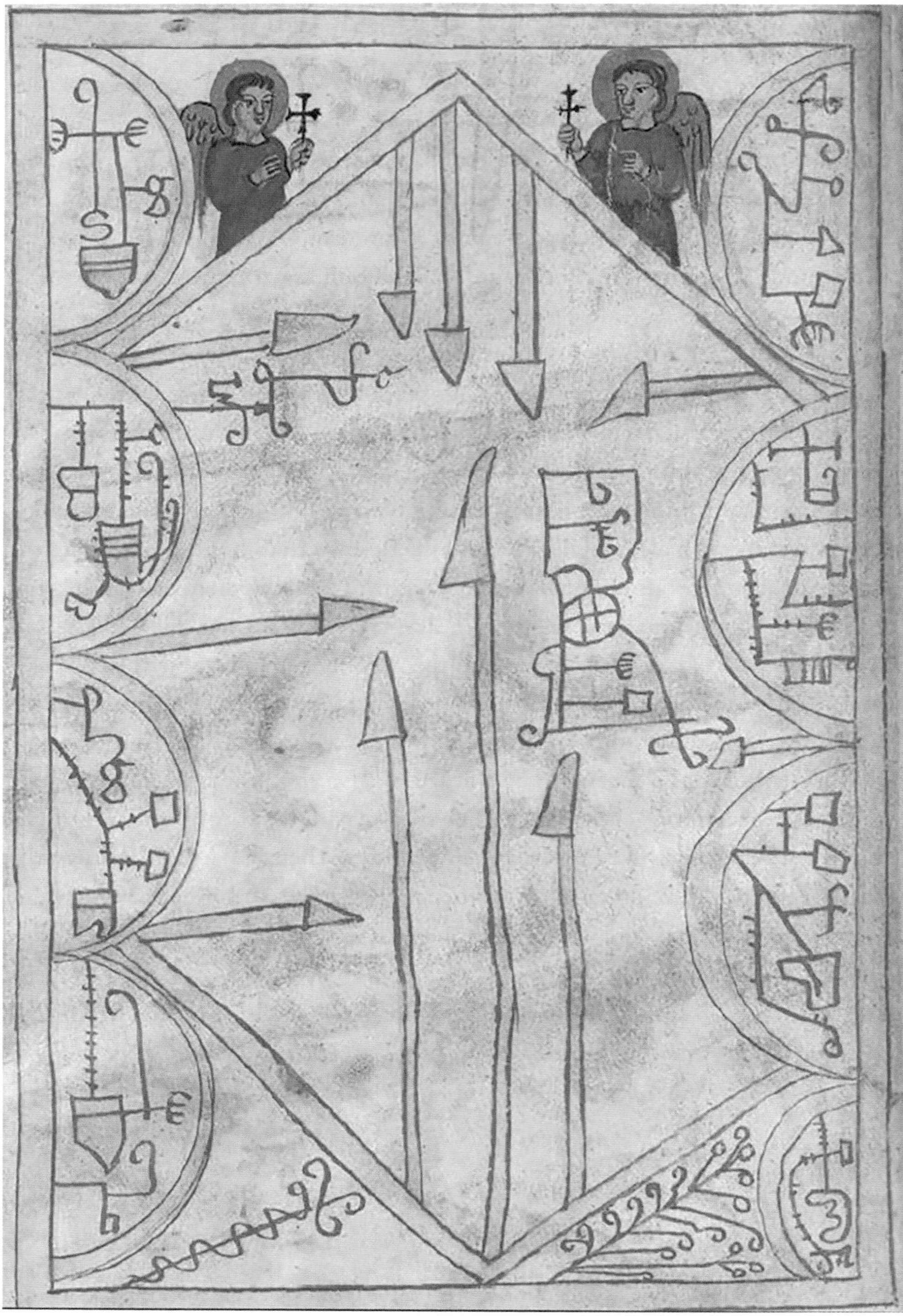

The figure of reprehension and taciturnity (41b)

the figures of the general sciences ought to be offered once on any day and at any time, and this very figure and its signs are to be inspected.

[NS 148] Note that this figure of reprehension and taciturnity is working to this [end] and for this reason, it was given by God and was discovered, but if you propose and allege some knowledge or some serious claim in the presence of others and you had publicly incited a powerful person, some judge, or principal authority, and you will have wanted to demonstrate [your knowledge or claim], and because you have so much grace[300] that it is to be subject to you and it is consented to your statements, and each [statement] that you allege and propose is to be conceded to you in a brief amount of time, and [thus] they all become silent, [and] they do not say anything against you, nor do they reprehend [what] you have said.

You must inspect this figure twice on any day for one month, and say its own prayers, and the other prayers which ought to be said above it, just as it is taught in its own rubric, and you will accomplish all the abovesaid things, just as it is said.

[NS 149] *Rubric: The seven figures of the liberal arts, the seven mechanical [arts], the figures of the general sciences, theology, all of philosophy, the figures of chastity, [of] justice, peace, and fear, and [of] reprehension, which are forty-one in number without the four signs of all knowledge, which are written before the first figure of dialectic.*

Selection of Version B Folios

The following selection of folios show diverse presentations of the *Ars Notoria* across several extant Version B manuscripts.

Plate 1: BnF Latin 7153
Plate 2: BnF Latin 9336
Plate 3: Yahuda Var. 34
Plate 4: BnF Latin 7153
Plate 5: Bodley 951
Plate 6: Bodley 951

300. From having performed the operation of the *Ars Notoria*.

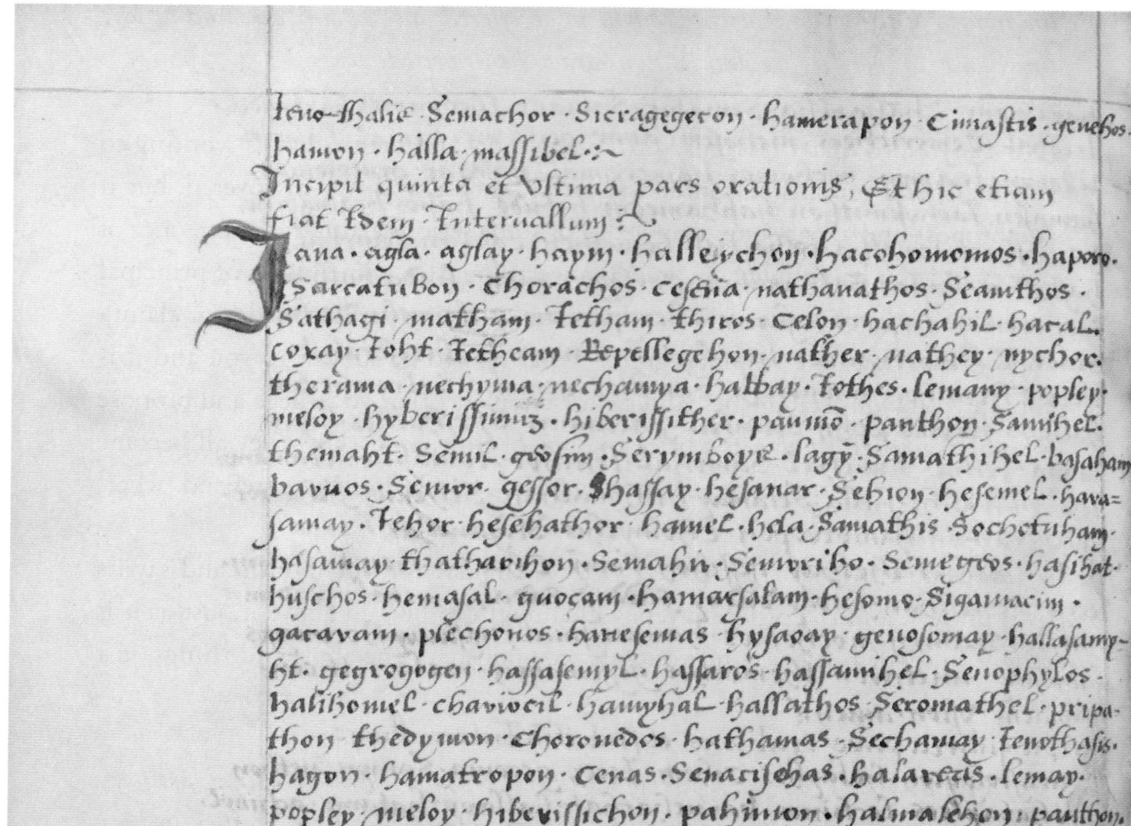
Ieno-thalie · Semathor · Sicragegeron · hamerapon · Cimastis · genehos.
hamon · halla · massibel ·:~
Incipit quinta et ultima pars orationis, Et hic etiam
fiat idem interuallum:~
Iana · agla · aglay · haym · halleychon · hacohomemos · hapoco.
Sarcatuboy · Chorachos · cestia · nathanathos · Seamthos ·
Sathagi · matham · tetham · thiros · celon · hachahil · haral.
coxay · toht · tetheam · Repellegthon · nather · nathey · nychor.
therama · nechyma · nechamya · halbay · tothes · lemany · popley ·
meloy · hyberissimuz · hiberissither · paumo · panthon · Samihel.
themaht · Semil · gerosim · Serymboyre · lagy · Samathihel · basaham
bavuos · Semor · gessor · hassay · hesanar · Sehion · hesemel · hara=
samay · tehor · hesehathor · hamel · hela · Samathis · Sochetuham ·
hasamay · thatharihon · Semahin · Semriho · Semetros · hasihat ·
huschos · hemasal · guocam · hamarsalam · hesoms · Sigamacim ·
garavam · plechonos · hanesemas · hysaoay · genosomay · hallasamp-
ht · gegrogogen · hassasemyl · hassaros · hassamihel · Senophylos ·
halihomel · chaviocil · hamyhal · hallathos · Seromathel · pripa-
thon · thedymon · Choronedos · hathamas · Sechamay · tenothasis.
hagon · hamatropon · cenas · Senarisehas · halaretis · lemay.
popley · meloy · hibevissichon · pahimon · halmalehon · panthon.
on · Vsyon · Amen ·:~
Hic aspicias primam figuram:~ ·1·
Ista oratio ultima proferatur post omnia:~
Deus cui omne cor bonum patet et omnis lingua loquitur in cuius
conspectu omnes conscientie contremiscunt · purifica quese per infu-
sionem sancti spiritus, mentem et intelligentiam meam ut ypositiones
et obiectiones in gramatica intelligere valeam Et intellecta ratio-
nabili subtilitate soluam Et oppositiones ex parte mea formare
cognoscam · Et dona aduersarij fortius constantia confortare, sit
lingua mea gladius acutus sermo meus fauore dulcedinis plenus
et cum beniuolentia habeam facundiam in multitudine verborum.

Plate 1

Plate 2

Tertia figura artis retorice
Rhetorica
Exordium
narratio
finis

Plate 3

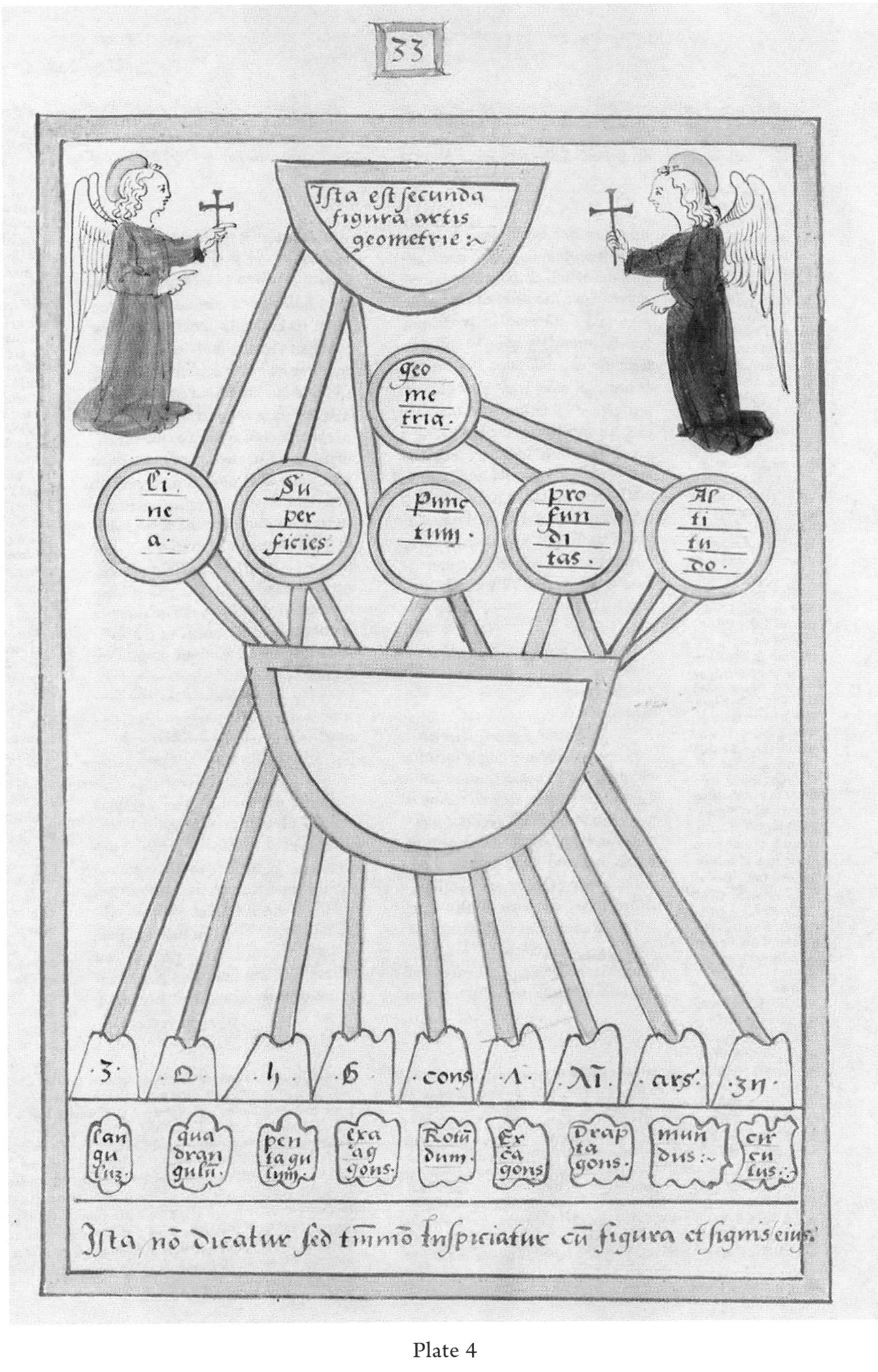
33
Ista est secunda figura artis geometrie :~
geo me tria.
Li ne a.
Su per ficies.
Punc tum.
pro fun di tas.
Al ti tu do.
cons
ars.
qua dran gulū
pen ta gu lum.
exa ag gons.
Rotū dum.
Drap ta gons.
mun dus :~
cir cu lus :
Ista nō dicatur sed tm̄mō Inspiciatur cū figura et signis eius.

Plate 4

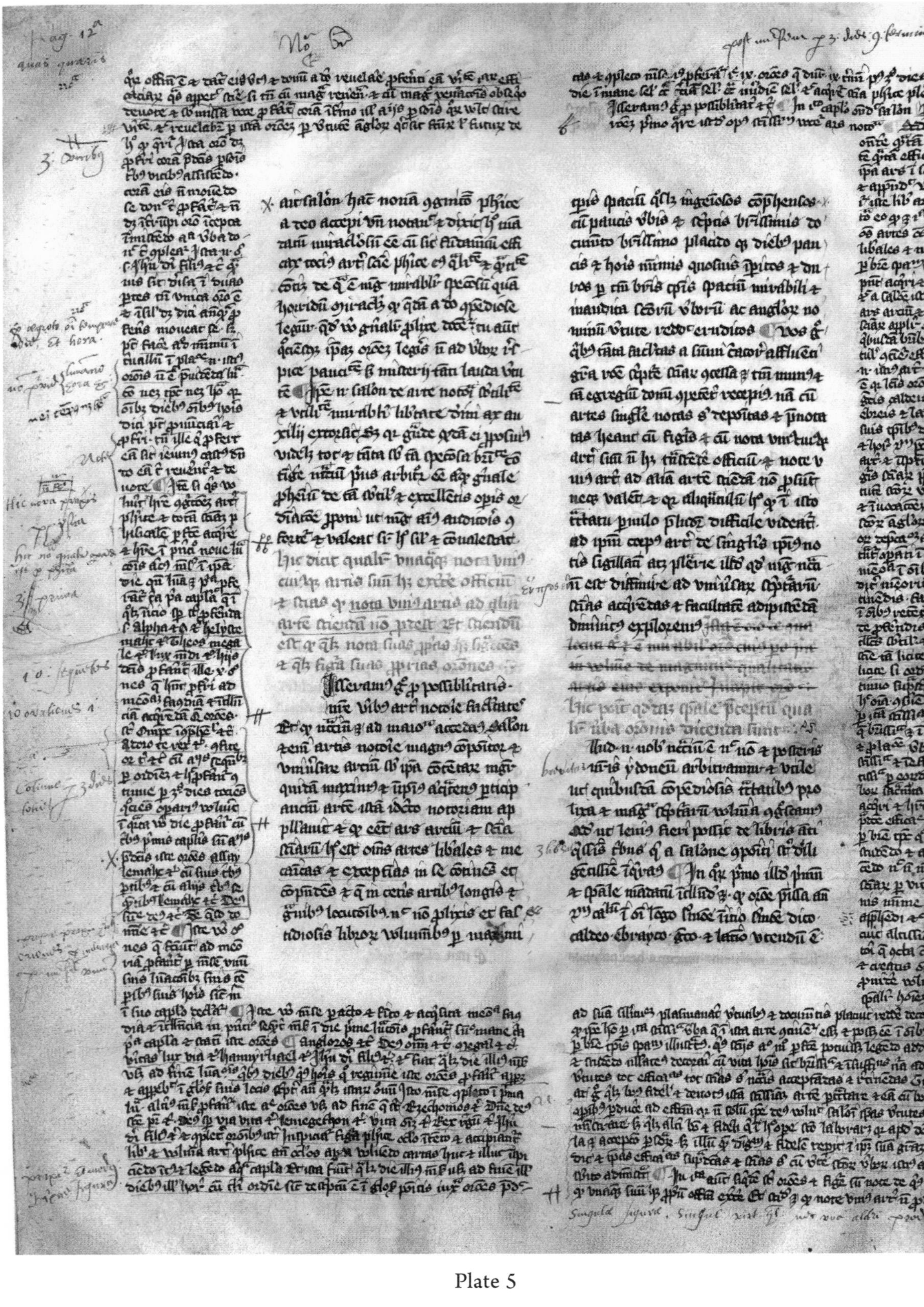

Plate 5

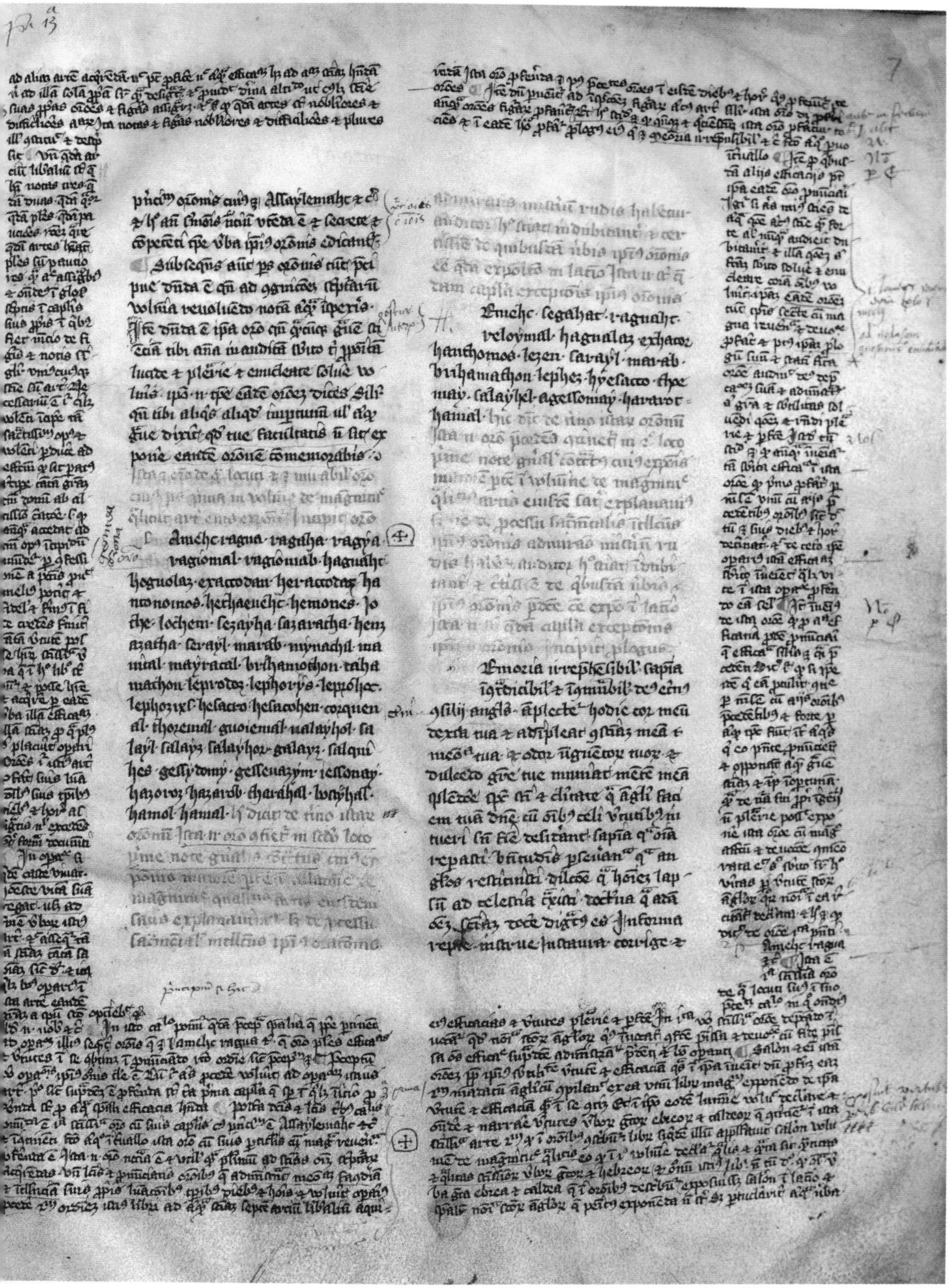

Plate 6

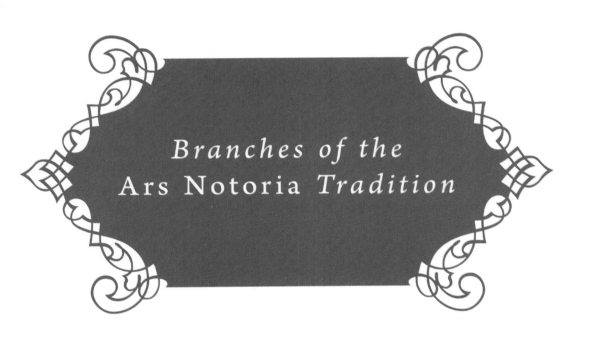

Branches of the Ars Notoria *Tradition*

6

Opus Operum (Work of Works)

13th–15th Centuries

The *Opus Operum* (*Work of Works*) follows the *Ars Nova* as the next derivative text in the *ars notoria* genre and tradition. The *Opus Operum* may have its title inspired by the *Ars Notoria* (section 77, Version A) in which the *Ars Notoria* describes itself as a "work of works and art of arts" because it is the best instrument for attaining all knowledge since it rests at the pinnacle of the hierarchy of knowledge.[1] Thus, the *Opus Operum* adds another ritual operation to the *ars notoria* corpus of writings for attaining a great amount of knowledge in a short period of time. In fact, the opening line of the *Opus Operum* identifies itself as a "new art" (*ars nova*), the successor to the ten-prayer ritual operation of the *Ars Nova*. Unlike the *Flores Aurei* and the *Ars Nova,* there is no mythical origin story in the *Opus Operum*. The *Opus Operum* was written by an unknown mid-thirteenth-century author from northern Italy.

The text presents a three-month prayer regimen of thirty-two prayers, including both *voces magicae* prayers and Latin prologue prayers. Each *voces magicae* prayer has two Latin prologues, one at the beginning and one at the end, following in the *ars notoria* tradition that a strange prayer partly translated or summarized in Latin is known as a "prologue" (*prologus*). The prayer regimen begins with the preamble *Summe Deus Pater piissime,* which is said five times and functions much like the preambles *Alpha et Omega* and *Lux veritas* in the *Ars Notoria*. There is a total of ten fields of knowledge or

1. For more information on the medieval view of the hierarchy of knowledge, see chapter III.

mental faculties which are to be acquired, and three prayers are assigned to each, which are offered over the course of three lunar months. The first prayer is for improving one's mental faculty of memory (*Domine Sancte Pater [. . . summum bonum], Aleph Alche, Beatitudinum*). The second prayer is for eloquence (*Creator omnium, Behenna, Ecce Domine Deus meus [. . . infinite]*). The third prayer is for understanding (*Ecce Domine Deus meus [. . . auxilium], Hemmenna Halla, Domine Sancte Pater [. . . institutor]*). The fourth prayer is for perseverance (*Gaudium angelorum, Cnesa Ospulmo, Ha Ha Ha Domine Deus [. . . inveniuntur]*). These first four prayers are to be offered in the first lunar month. When compared against the prayer regimen of the *Ars Notoria,* these equate to the "first way" or the General prayers for memory, eloquence, understanding, and the stability of these three.

The fifth, sixth, and seventh prayers are to be offered in the second lunar month. The fifith prayer is for particular sciences, probably like the general or middle sciences (*In te sperantium, Luna Boson, Raaf cogitationum*). The sixth and seventh prayers are for the study of medieval philosophy involving metaphysics, logic, and epistemology; the metaphysical problem of universals (*Legifer altissime, Gymel Pomahuhac, Misericrdissime miserator miserabilis*) and particulars (*Naturalis, Gymel [. . . Sehepmet], Pater noster [. . . sanctificas]*) asks a range of questions that date back to Plato, Aristotle, and Boethius. When compared against the prayer regimen of the *Ars Notoria,* these roughly equate to the Special prayers for learning philosophy, the general sciences, and logic/dialectic.

The eighth, ninth, and tenth prayers are to be offered in the third and final lunar month. The eighth prayer is for prose and neume (*Quem omnes caelestes, Estachion Elaf, Rex regum [. . . gubernator]*). The ninth prayer is for the secret cognition of poetic meter—that is, Latin prosody which studies poetry and its laws of meter—(*Sanctus sanctus sanctus Dominus Deus Sabaoth, Anuen Negena, Sancte sanctorum [. . . abyssus]*). The tenth and last prayer is for the completion of the entire operation and the knowledge to be acquired therein (*In honore omnipotenis Dei, Zemon Tehet Nepehet, Tehet Zai Patrem*). At the end of each lunar month, the prayer of the Blessed Virgin Mary is to be offered (*Gloriosa regina angelorum*). When compared against the prayer regimen of the *Ars Notoria,* the eighth and ninth prayers roughly equate to the study of grammar, which included the study of Latin prosody. The tenth prayer and that of the Blessed Virgin Mary roughly equates to the *novem termini,* which seals the ritual operation. The prayers are intended to attract angels who appear in visions to the operator with special instructions for attaining the desired knowledge. Final details on the ritual operation of the *Opus Operum* are found in sections B, D(a), D(b), and E.

There are six figures (also called *notae,* after the *Ars Notoria*) found in the *Opus Operum,* and they are as follows: the *nota* to acquire all parts of grammar (123ab); the *nota* of logic for dialectic skills (4ab); a third *nota* of rhetoric (8ab); a first *nota* of arithmetic (12ab); a second *nota* of geometry (33b); and a third *nota* of astronomy (17b). Strangely, the *Opus Operum* does not provide any instructions for the inspection of the *notae,* nor does it even acknowledge their presence. Regardless, the reader will notice that the *Opus Operum* plays a mediating role in these six figures as they are transmitted from Version A to Version B of the *Ars Notoria* (see appendix A1). The evidence indicates that *Opus Operum* not only derives from the *Ars Notoria* but was often copied alongside it in the same manuscript.

The *Opus Operum* text which has been studied here comes from five manuscripts, which are as follows:

1. London, British Library, Sloane 1712, f. 22vb–37, circa 1250.
2. Leiden, Universiteitsbibliotheek, Vulcanius 45, f. 1–11v, circa 14th century.
3. Vatican, Biblioteca Apostolica, Latin 6842, f. 1–8r, circa 14th century.
4. Munich, Bayerische Staatsbibliothek, Clm 276, f. 26rb–39ra, circa 15th century.
5. Munich, Bayerische Staatsbibliothek, Clm 30010, f. 1–16, circa 14th century.

The *Opus Operum* is translated from Latin into English for the first time here based on Julien Véronèse's critical edition (2007); Véronèse's textual edition is based on the first four manuscripts listed above. There are variations in the spellings of the angelic names and *voces magicae,* and all such variations are not accounted for in Véronèse's work. Thus, only a single spelling for each is found in the present English translation. The fifth manuscript, Clm 30010, is newly discovered, and its images are presented here for the first time. Some of the *Opus Operum* figures are also found in the following two manuscripts, although the *Opus Operum* text is absent in them:

1. Paris, Bibliotheque nationale de France, Latin 7152
2. Turin, Biblioteca Nazionale, E.V. 13

Only three manuscripts are known to present the figures with the text. Those include Vulcanius 45, Sloane 1712, and Clm 30010.

There are other extant manuscripts of the *Opus Operum*, but these have not been thoroughly studied. They are also follows:

1. Vienna, Österreichische Nationalbibliothek, Cod. 15482, f. 1–14v (fragment), circa 13th–14th centuries.
2. Oxford, Bodleian Libraries, Jones 1 [Bodleian 8908], f. 6–85v, year of 1601.
3. Munich, Bayerische Staatsbibliothek, CLM 17711, f. 332r–376v (composite), c. 17th century.

It is quite plausible other copies exist, waiting to be discovered by future researchers.

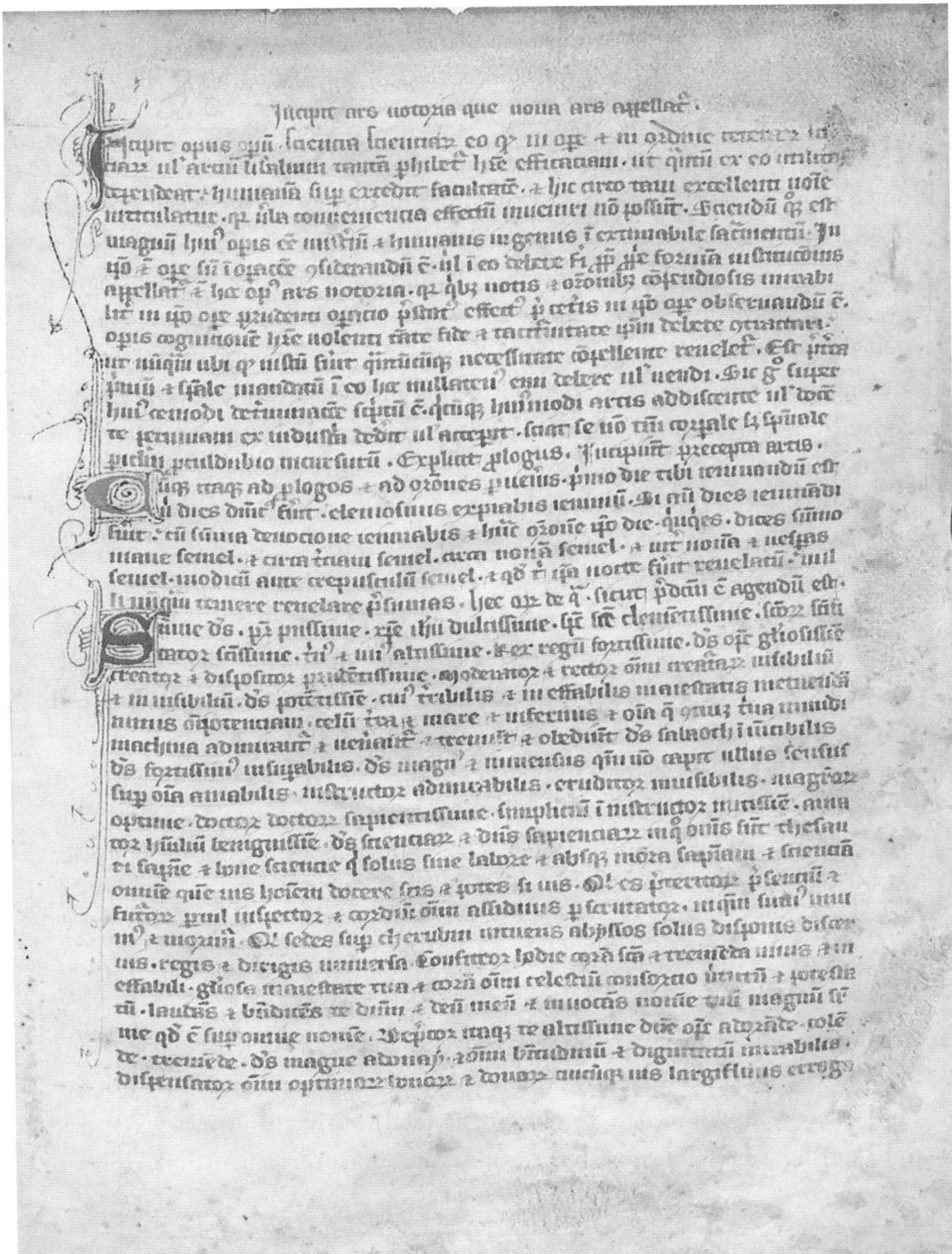

The incipit of the *Opus Operum* from the Munich manuscript at the Bayerische Staatsbibliothek, Clm 30010, f. 1

Opus Operum

[A] *In the name of the most holy and indivisible Trinity of the Father and of the Son and of the Holy Spirit. An* ars notoria *begins, which is called a new art.* The *Opus Operum* begins, the science of sciences, because it is said to have so much efficacy in the work and in the order of the rest of the sciences or the liberal arts, because how much usefulness derives from it, it exceeds beyond human capacity, and for that reason, it is entitled to such an excellent name, because more fitting words cannot be found effective for it. Also, it is to be understood [that] the greatness of this work is a mystery and an inestimable sacrament to the human mind. And in this very work it is to be very much considered that nothing ought to be done in it beyond the proper form of the institution. And also, this work is called a "notory art" because by certain *notae* (that is, the compendious prayers) an effect is wonderfully presented to the prudent operator in this very work. Also, it is to be observed of the work [that] the *prae ceteris,* wanting to have knowledge in this very work, ought to have drawn to himself so much faith and taciturnity, so that [the happenings of the operation] are never to be revealed, except that it was lawful by whatsoever means with a compelling condition.[2] Moreover, there is a first and special commandment in it: this [new art] ought not be bought or sold. Thus, ergo, it is written over the determination of this place, "Whoever has given or received money out of hard work for the purpose of learning or teaching this art, knows that he himself will undoubtedly incur not only bodily, but also, spiritual danger."[3]

The prologue ends. The teachings of the art begin.

[B] Therefore, when you arrive at the prologue and the prayers, [the operation] is to be fasted on the first day, unless it was the Lord's Day. But if it is the Lord's Day, you will expiate by almsgiving [and] fasting.[4] But if it was a day to be fasting, you will fast with the utmost devotion. You must say this prayer

---

2. In other words, the operator (called here the *prae ceteris*) is to keep the happenings of the operation secret unless a special circumstance or law requires otherwise.

3. Compare against the *Ars Notoria,* Version B, variation gloss 1.

4. It appears that no matter what day it is, the operator will be fasting.

five times a day: once in the early morning, once around the third [hour], once around the ninth [hour], [and twice] between the ninth [hour] and the evening [hour], [such that] a little interval [is made] once before twilight and once after twilight. And what was revealed to you in that very night, you must presume to reveal [it] to no one at any time heedlessly.

[C] *This is the prayer about which, just as it is said before, is to be done:*
O highest God, O most pious Father,[5] O sweetest Jesus Christ, O most gentlest Holy Spirit, the most holy sanctifier of the holy ones, the Most High [as] threefold in one, the strongest king of kings, the almighty God, the most glorious creator and dispenser, the most prudent moderator and rector of all visible and invisible creatures, the almighty God, whose terrible and ineffable majesty, the almighty exceedingly feared, the heavens, the earth, the sea, and the infernal realms and everything, which contains the triple world machine[6] is to be admired and venerated, [and] they tremble and obey,[7] O invisible God Sabaoth,[8] O strongest and insuperable God, O great and immeasurable God, whom not any sense can capture, O instructor lovable above all, O admirable invisible teacher of

5. *Summe Deus Pater piissime,* this prayer is also found in both long and short versions in the *Ars Brevis,* sections 57–L2.1.

6. Latin *trina machina mundi.* Lucretius, the first-century BCE Roman poet, in his *On the De Rerum Natura* (*Nature of Things*) 5.91–96, says, "As to what remains, so that I don't delay you any further with promises, first look to sea, earth, and sky; their triple nature, their three bodies, Memmius, their three kinds so dissimilar, their three textures, a single day will give over to destruction, and the mighty form and *machina* of the world, held up through many years, shall fall down into ruin." Lucretius probably drew upon Plato's *Timaeus* in which the world is viewed as an artificial system designed by the divine demiurge. See Taylor, *Lucretius and the Language of Nature,* 108–9. Also, Sacrobosco, author of *De Sphaera Mundi* (*On the Sphere of the World*), said the order of the world machine was disrupted when there was an eclipse of the Sun during the crucifixion of Jesus (Mark 15:33; Matthew 27:45; Luke 23:44–45). Sacrobosco, reading Pseudo-Dionysius's seventh letter, had put these words into the mouth of Pseudo-Dionysius, saying, "Either the god of nature suffers, or the whole machine of the world has come undone." See Burton, Hollman, and Parker, *Nicholas of Cusa,* 345. See also John of Sacrobosco, *On the Sphere,* 465.

7. Here ends the agreed portion of *Summe Deus Pater piissime,* which is found the *Ars Brevis,* section 57.

8. Hebrew, meaning "God of Hosts."

erudition [and] the best masters,[9] O most wisest doctor of doctors,[10] the instructor of the simple [and] most gentle people, lover of the most benevolent [and] humble people, O God of the sciences and Lord of wisdom, in whom are all the treasures of wisdom and good sciences, who alone wants to teach humankind the wisdom and knowledge of all things what you know and are able to do so if you want without labor and without delay, you who are the vigilant watcher of the past, present, and future, and the assiduous investigator of the hearts of all, through whom we are, we live, and we die, who sits above the Cherubim looking upon the abyss,[11] you alone dispose, discern, rule, and direct the universe.

I confess today in the presence of the most holy and very tremendous one and with your ineffably glorious majesty, and in the presence of all the celestial consortium of the Virtues and Powers, praising and blessing you; O Lord and my God, and invoking your great name above me because it is above every name; therefore, I deprecate you, O almighty Lord of the highest, who is the adored, honored, and revered[12] God, the great Adonay,[13] † admirable dispenser of all beatitudes and dignities, generous dispenser of all the best gifts to whomever you want, so that you would graciously, abundantly, and permanently deem it worthy to pour over me today the multiple gifts of the grace of the Holy Spirit, and now you, most clement Lord himself, who deemed worthy to create Adam, the first man, in your image and likeness, having been deemed worthy to send and to strengthen . . . ,[14] and you want this . . . within me today because you worked wonderfully into your faithful people from the most splendid temple of the heavens, of the light-flowing grace of your almighty ineffable majesty.

O most high, most benevolent, eternal, [and] glorious king, send out to

---

9. A medieval title given to university teachers of the liberal arts.

10. As in a doctor of philosophy from a university, not necessarily a medical doctor.

11. Daniel, Prayer of Azariah and Song of the Three Holy Children 3:54 (Vulgate).

12. Latin *tremendae,* meaning "fearful, terrible," from which the English words "tremble" and "tremendous" originate. Again, following the biblical concept of fear of the Lord, this is best translated as "revered."

13. Hebrew *Adonay,* meaning "Lord."

14. The ellipsis is a placeholder for the operator to insert his desired gift of the Holy Spirit and/or desired mental faculty or knowledge. A second ellipsis for the same thing follows.

me . . .[15] today, from the admirable, most holy, and glorious seat of your majesty's dominion, the multiple benediction of your sevenfold grace:[16] the spirit of wisdom and understanding, the spirit of counsel and fortitude, the spirit of knowledge and piety, and the spirit of the fear and love of you,[17] with respect to knowing, loving, and always doing most freely your incomprehensible will in all things, and with respect to investigating and understanding, to venerating and admiring well your holy mysteries and your occult wisdom, which are fitting for you to manifest, which are latent, and your faithful people are expedient to know, so that I may be able to investigate and to comprehend the profound benevolence and ineffable sweetness of you mercy, immeasurable piety, and divinity.

And now you, the most merciful Lord himself, who once blew the little breath of life[18] into the making of the first man, may you deem it worthy to infuse gently and permanently a complete, true, subtle, persistent, swift, correct, and perfect understanding in all things, an unfailing memory, a vivacious, tenacious, and efficacious eloquence, and the mellifluous, ignited, expedited, and flowing grace of the Holy Spirit within my heart today, so that from the multiplicity of your benedictions and from the abundantly flowing bounty of the many gifts of your graces copiously spoken and permanently endowed, henceforth, I will despise all things which is to be held in contempt; and you, the only God of all, you who are the true, highest, and ineffable good of every thing, I will ardently love, glorify, honor, praise, adore, bless, and exalt you above all things, the king of kings and the Lord of all lords, and may there always be a praise to your magnificent and tremendous omnipotence in my mouth at any time [with]

---

15. The ellipsis represents a possible placeholder for the operator to insert his desired knowledge or mental faculty; alternatively, the anonymous author of the *Opus Operum* chose to insert his own desired mental faculties of the seven gifts of the Holy Spirit, which is placed just after the phrase "from the admirable, etc." In Latin, the seven gifts could be placed in either position.

16. At the end of the *Ars Brevis,* there is a prayer which begins with the opening epithets to God from *Unus magnus* (*Ars Notoria,* section 139), and then the rest of the prayer borrows from this very section—*Opus Operum,* C—beginning with "the mutliple benediction of your sevenfold grace" and ending with "in my mouth at any time [with] the sweetest ardor."

17. These are the seven gifts of the Holy Spirit. Fear of the Lord means having awe and reverence for God.

18. Latin *spiraculum vitae.* Genesis 2:7 (Vulgate).

the sweetest ardor; and may[19] the most maddening, sweetest, and beatific love of your vehemently and permanently enflame endlessly within my heart and within my soul and in eternity in the presence of you, you who are the almighty God of all things, the highest peace, the true wisdom, the insatiable sweetness, the inestimable pleasantness, the ineffable joy, the blessed satiety and glorious end of all good things and beatific desires, for whom he was, is, and always will be from eternity, the invincible virtue, the impassible salvation, the inextinguishable splendor, the benediction and clarity, the honor, the praise and venerable glory, before and beyond all the times of the ages, amen, amen, amen.

[D(a)] *The other special teachings of the work begin, which are to be concluded after the present prayer.*

But before coming to the work itself, it is very much to be considered in this way, so that [the teachings] are ordered to every occasion, [and] after having been placed, ought to be observed. It is to be taught first that the work itself, with the prologues and their prayers, is to be done twice on the first day of the Moon, once in the early morning and once at the evening [hour]. And on the second day, once in the early morning, once at noon, and once at the evening [hour]. And on the third day, once in the early morning, once around the third [hour], once around the ninth [hour], and once at the evening [hour]. And on the fourth day, this very work is to be performed with the utmost reverence four times, just like on the third day, and at those same hours [as] on the third [day]. And on the fifth day, this very work is to be done five times, once in the early morning, once around the third [hour], once after noon, once after the ninth [hour], and once at twilight. Accordingly, on the sixth day, this very work is to be done six times, once in the early morning, having made an interval of about one hour once, [then] once after the third [hour], once after noon, once after the ninth [hour], and once at twilight. And on the seventh day, the aforesaid work is to be reiterated[20] seven times, once at matins,[21] having made a little interval once, [then] once around the third

19. Lightly reconstructed to *in ore meo suavissimo ardor.*

20. Latin *reiterandum.*

21. Latin *matutinus.* It is not clear if the text refers to the canonical hour of matins (around 2:00 a.m.) or more generally speaks of the early morning time period. Alternatively, other

[hour], once after noon, once after the ninth [hour], once around the evening [hour], and once at twilight. On the eighth day, the distinguished work is to be done eight times, twice in the early morning with little intervals, twice in the first [hour] up to the third [hour], twice between noon and the ninth [hour], twice in the evening [hour] up to twilight. And on the ninth day, the aforesaid work is to be done nine times, thrice in the early morning with little intervals, thrice from the first [hour] up to noon with greater intervals, thrice in the ninth [hour] up to the evening [hour] with greater intervals. And on the tenth day, the aforesaid work is to be increased; that is, it is to be done ten times, four times in the early morning up to the third [hour], four times from the third [hour] up to the ninth [hour], and twice from the ninth [hour] until after twilight.

However, since a question will be able to be made about the intervals, it is to be understood that an interval, while brief, is like the period of time of having said three Lord's Prayers, but while a lengthened one is to be defined as the period of one hour in this work according to the measurement of the days of summer and winter; that is, the intervals are to be noted according to the prolixity.

But on the eleventh day, the prefaced work is to be done eleven times, once in the early morning, thrice between the third [hour] and noon, thrice between noon and the ninth [hour], thrice between the ninth [hour] and the evening [hour], and once at twilight. On the twelfth day, it is to be done just like in the eleventh, except that it is to be done twice at twilight. And on the thirteenth day, four times from the morning up to the third [hour] with intervals, four times from the third [hour] up to the ninth [hour], four times from the ninth [hour] up to twilight, always with intervals, and once after twilight once. On the fourteenth day, five times from the morning up to the third [hour] with equal intervals, five times from the third [hour] up to the ninth [hour], and four times from the ninth [hour] up to twilight. The fifteenth day is to be done just like the fourteenth day, except that from the ninth [hour] to after twilight it is to be done five times. On the sixteenth day, six times from the morning up to noon with intervals, six times from noon up to a little after the ninth [hour, and] four times from after the ninth [hour] to after twilight. On the seventeenth

instances of the "early morning" (*summo mane*) could be a reference to the canonical hour of matins.

day, six times from the morning up to noon, six times from noon up to a little after the ninth [hour], and five times from the ninth [hour] up to twilight. The eighteenth day is just like in the seventeenth day, except that it is to be done six times from the ninth [hour] to after twilight. And on the nineteenth day, it is to be done six times from the morning up to noon with the necessary intervals, six times from noon up to after the ninth [hour], and seven times from after the ninth [hour] to after twilight. And on the twentieth day, from the early morning up to the ninth [hour] it is to be done ten times with the necessary and distinct intervals, and ten times from the ninth [hour] to after twilight.

[D(b)] And thus, you will approach up to the day of the completion of the lunar month. And of the lunar month, the proper time is a period of thirty days. Also, it is to be understood, as it has been shown beforehand, from the beginning of the prefaced work on the third, sixth, ninth, and twelfth days and thus, it is to be fasted for three more days up to the completion of the work, unless it was the Lord's Day. And if it was the Lord's Day, alms are to be given. Also, you ought to know [that] this work is to be done in a solitary, clean, and remote place away from human company, except the company of a doctor of the work;[22] by chance, if he will be present to assist and will want to intercede. But if, by chance, someone comes over unexpectedly to you, having been invited, during the action of the work, [then] you will be able to expiate by giving ten alms. But if working out of temerity or fear, he committed some [error or sin], unless it was revealed out of the process through a vision, [then] the work is to be done a second time from the beginning. Also, especially if the worker falls asleep during the very action of the work, such is human frailty, just as it was revealed to him through the vision according to this, it must be done, his work is to be repeated from the beginning of this day. Furthermore, if he falls into infirmity during the work itself, if the work has proceeded up to the middle, if he did not hear a prohibition through a vision, having recovered a state of health, [then] he follows the beginning [where he left off]. And if he has accomplished less than half, unless it was revealed to him by a spirit, [then] the work will be repeated from the beginning. In addition, working by whatever means neces-

---

22. The title "doctor" is used here as in someone who is highly educated and practiced in ritual magic; the meaning is transferred from the sense of a doctor of philosophy who graduated from a university.

sary to remain at [his] place, if he had moved, [then] the work is relinquished; retiring it, he must complete [it], having retaken [it from its very beginning,] to remain with the proper mental faculty. For whatever reason, if he fell into criminal sin, especially [while] working in the work itself, [then] he must not presume to proceed in the work, unless his penitence has been completed first. For criminal sins are dissimilar, especially if he has lapsed into misery or frailty creeping along with respect to lechery before he proceeded in the work, he must complete a full penitence, unless it was revealed to him in a vision what he ought to do. For concerning whatever criminal sin that has befallen him, penitence must be done first, unless an alleviation was made to him through a vision. For thus, from the twentieth day and beyond up to the completion of the work, it is always to be done with the utmost devotion through the three hours (that is, from morning until noon, from noon to the evening [hour], from the evening [hour] to after twilight). For on all the days from the twentieth day and beyond to those [latter] days the work is done, the visions will appear at night after twilight. And note them all, and accordingly, do what was shown to you in them. And accordingly, do what was revealed to you in the visions for the consummation of the entire work.

[E] *The key of the great work begins, in the name of the almighty eternal Father, Son, and Holy Spirit.*

Since we told you about the work itself in the preceding [section], now we bind tightly together and seal the document with the little key below, so that, having been precluded from every variety of doubts, you must foreknow [the little key], without having not foreseen it, and now it is able to be useful to you to the apposite mandates and discourses. Thus, you must know, by the survivor to the master's work, you having to undertake [the operation], with respect to [possessing] the [desired] faculty, you will have him [as] a helper and supporter. Without him, you do nothing of the work or its license without pride and insincerity, and you must take action purely, chastely, secretly, solitarily, and continuously. But if it comes to the master being banished[23] or to be retired, [then] you are made to be free, and thus, the Lord will be with you. The revelation of the work, the admission of persons, all the ambiguities and the

23. Perhaps from a social group or formerly exiled by the country.

transgression of the mandates, of nearing impulses while you were in the work, are to be put to sleep by all means by you, the visions which will appear divinely to you before the work, in the work, and after the work, you must implement [them] determinedly and keep [them] concealed most secretly. But you will understand in this way, and you will observe solicitiously about the progress of the work from the twentieth day and above.

On the twenty-first day, you do [it] seven times from morning to noon with its intervals, seven times from noon to twilight, and seven times after twilight. On the twenty-second day, you do [it] similarly, except that you do [it] eight times before noon. On the twenty-third day, [you do it] eight times from morning to noon, eight times from noon to twilight, and seven times after twilight. On the twenty-fourth day, [you do it] similarly, except that you do it eight times after twilight. On the twenty-fifth day, [you do it] thirteen times from morning up to the ninth [hour], and twelve times from the ninth [hour] to after twilight with short intervals. On the twenty-sixth day, [you do it] thirteen times from morning to the ninth [hour], and thirteen times from the ninth [hour] to after twilight. On the twenty-seventh day, [you do it] fourteen times[24] from the morning to the ninth [hour], and thirteen times from the ninth [hour] to after twilight, still, never without intervals. On the twenty-eighth day, [you do it] similarly, except that you do it fourteen times from the ninth [hour] to after twilight. On the twenty-ninth day, [you do it] ten times from morning to noon, ten times from noon to twilight, and nine times after twilight. And on the thirtieth day, which is the completion of a lunar month, you do [it] just like in the twenty-ninth day, except that after twilight you do [it] ten times.

After these auspicious days, you will do two days for inspecting books, the arts to be held in memory, neither discussing this art, but assiduously deprecating God, so that, because you have labored so hard for it, you may be able to obtain [it], having truly succeeded. About the rest, it is to be stored for you in the hand of God the almighty through whom, from whom, and out of whom [comes] all things, whose felicity and benediction [exists] in eternity, amen.

---

24. Latin *bis septies,* literally "twice seven times."

All the precepts of the art ends, turning in the direction of the [art's] very efficacy.
[F] You are able to know the entirety beneath this art quickly without a part. This is the entire potent art, nothing of evil is a part to it. The doctor and the disicple must be fortunate continuously.

The work begins with the first [which] is a prayer for memory, the second for eloquence, the third for understanding, the fourth for perseverance, the fifth for particular sciences, the sixth for universals,[25] the seventh for the discretion of all things,[26] the eighth for prose and neume,[27] the ninth for the secret cognition of [poetic] meters,[28] the tenth and last which is for the completion of all things and the sudden, full, and brilliant consummation. But it is to be understood that each prayer has two prologues, one at the beginning and the other at the end, which are to be said before and after, just as it begins in the subsequent prayer; namely, which begins at *Aleph*.

[G] *The first prologue of the first prayer begins Aleph † Alleluya † Alleluya † Alleluya:*

O Holy Lord the Father, the almighty eternal God, the Alpha and the Omega, the highest On, Hely, Heloy, Heyon, Helyothon, Anachetethon,[29] Panton, Craton,[30] whose virtue is totally capable, whose sense has known all, whose being is the highest good, whose whatever good work which you

25. From the logic of philosophy, a universal is what particular quality or qualities certain things have in common.

26. The sixth and seventh prayers are for understanding the philosophical problem of universals and particulars, which deals with a range of metaphysical, logical, and epistemological questions asked by Plato, Aristotle, and Boethius.

27. A *neum* is a technical term from medieval music theory that means a kind of melody, or it can also denote musical notation. The Italian music theorist Guido of Arezzo (c. 991–1033) said, "As in metrics there are letters and syllables, parts and feet, and verses, so in music there are tones, of which one, two, or three join to make a syllable; of these one or two make a neuma (that is, a part of the melody); while one or several parts make a distinction (phrase) (that is, a suitable place for breathing.)" ("Micrologus," xv). Neums were added and defined in formulae in the responsorial singing of church liturgy. See Henry Bewerunge, "Neum," *The Catholic Encyclopedia,* vol. 10 (New York: Robert Appleton Company, 1911).

28. That is, the study of Latin prosody and its different kinds of poetic meters, in which the student silently reflects upon the poetic meter in his mind.

29. Probably a corruption of the Greek epithet *anekphoniton,* which means "the Unpronounceable," which refers to God's name, YHVH (Yahweh or Jehovah).

30. *Panton* plus *craton* equals the Greek *Pantokrator,* which means "Almighty," a title given to God and later to Jesus Christ.

alone make great, miraculous, and inscrutable, whose volition and power no visible or invisible being is able to resist. "O Hel, most fortified king, the most high and pious God, you who are the first and the most novel, and beside you there is no other, the peace of enemies, the true salvation, the way, the life, the truth, Jesus, the Son of the eternal Father, the messenger of great counsel, the Holy Spirit preceding from both, the Paraclete, three and one, the most high"[31] to all creatures, who is very much venerated, adored, feared, and tremendous, the one deity, equal glory, coeternal majesty; look upon [me] today, I beg you, O eternal king of glory, threefold and one God, creator of wonders, the orderer and operator of all things, give to me the magnificent work of your great and ineffable mercy, and to so much of your wonderful glorious abundance, and the venerable sacrament, and the abundance of your superfluent omnipotence; O truthful God of all things, swift, true, and perfect in all things, administer an understanding, an unfailing memory, an expeditious and full eloquence, and having pursued [with you] every necessity with respect to the riches of so great a divine sacrament, for my heart, my soul, [and] my senses gently, powerfully, abundantly, and permanently, you who calls that which does not exist, so to speak, [into] that which does exist, give to me fully and perfectly the knowledge of many merciful sages [or: many mercies and wisdom?] and of your desirable graces, and having petitioned to perceive and to understand abundance, you who are the king of kings and the Lord of lords before and beyond the eternal ages of ages, amen.

[H] *The first prayer for memory begins:*

Aleph,[32] Alche, Phos, Megale, Patir, Ymon, Chere, Caristomem, Patere, Arziel, Meilon, Meray, Ameros, Hecci, Cooton, Ababen, Ruos, Melca, Rece, Eraza, Catafabos, Baruc, Catamcelpha, Emeray, Themon, Laaf, Ioiacra, Baruccata, Eloy, Eloe, Eloa, Fon, Hen, Benpore, Nasaryel, Namayan, Troganos, Camegal, Necotropos, Nicrateyston, Luza, Messyas, Sother, Emmanuel, Sabaoth, Adonay, Iathos, Dabaren, Atras, Buzichere,

---

31. "Oh Hel . . . most high." The passage is quoted from the anonymous *Rhythmus ad Deum, ex Dei nominibus* (*Rhythm for God, Out of the Names of God*). See Pitra, *Spicilegium Solesmense,* 449.

32. *Alef,* the first letter of the Hebrew alphabet.

Boos, Gernes, Measzacyel, Eber, Ebrel, Oon, Loon, Boon, Helion, Helyoton, Anachereton, Pantocraton, Usyon, Sennecherub, Seraphin, Tan, Maxa, Tela, Ragau, Rogel, Taiel, Mozol, Zenay, Iozecra, Matan, Antropon, Uriamagiel, Theocumbos, Nema, Thechiel, Azara, Zenoton, Metri, Yskira, Ranathion, Anothatucle, Pharesay, Epilogos, Fargahal, Aristos, Theothocos, Micromegal, Sambail, Pamoot, Nertenos, Baar, Trabaim, Doxa, Anthama, Theot, Themgeth, amin, amin, amin.

[I] *The second prologue begins after having said the prayer:*

O dispenser of all blessings, the bestower[33] and author of all good things, O Lord God the almighty, O miraculous commiserator of the miserable, the longanimous one, suffering so much, the pious, the benevolent, the mild, the merciful, and the truthful, whose ways [are] [un]searchable,[34] whose judgments [are like] the great abyss,[35] whose all works [are] very good, about whose immeasurable goodness [is] for the good people, and about whose infinite mercy [is] a gift to every creature, endowed and adorned, according to his hope, you who created humankind in your image and likeness, and you wonderfully gave to him many great gifts, and you revoked the lapse by diabolic deceit, I beg you today, O most gentle God, listen to my oration as a prayer to you; O good God, listen to my deprecations for good and pious things in your goodness, propitiously intended, and although, I have sinned, neglected, and have been deliquent, being very much preponderated by human fragility and in many things, nevertheless you, O most pious Father to the prodigal Son, although late returning, confessing, repenting, sighing, and groaning to you, and asks for pardon, have mercy on me, gently and piously; O most pious and most gentle heavenly Father, now receive my prayer kindly and mercifully, and as much as you are the almighty eternal God, you alone who makes great inscrutable things, and there is no one that is able to resist your almighty

33. *Beatitudinum omnium dispensator atque largitor,* this same prayer is later found in the German fifteenth-century prayer book of Bishop Leonhard von Laymingen of Passau (Walters MS W.163, fols. 13v–16v), whose prayers were directed to various saints and had prayers for traveling.

34. Romans 11:33 (NRSV).

35. Psalm 36:6 (NRSV).

will; I beg you with a hard and heavy heart, administer . . .[36] quickly, abundantly, and permanently to the extent of . . . , to me, an ignorant and untaught person, from the fullness of your unfailing treasure and your innumerable wisdom, on account of the glory of your imperious and magnificent name, and on account of your tremendous majesty [and] the honor of an almighty virtue; henceforth, may I always please, praise, bless, glorify, and honor you in word and deed with thought, meditation, and desire, the threefold and one God of all things, the almighty Father, Son, and Holy Spirit, exalted above, and praiseworthy and glorious above in the eternal ages of ages, amen.

[J] *The second prologue of the first prayer ends. The first prologue of the second prayer begins:*
O Creator, lord of all heavenly, earthly, and infernal realms, O Lord, you who are the truth, the great and almighty God of all things, in whose sight all things are naked and open, you who forgets nothing, from whose plenary of grace flowed the gift[37] of an unfailing eloquence into your holy ones, you who are creating peace and forming the good, you who in the beginning divided the light from the darkness,[38] I ask [of you] today, divide the confusion and truth in my senses, and give to me truly and perfectly to understand and to perceive fully the incomparable riches of your graces and wisdom, so that having fully perceived from the unfailing treasure of your innumerable wisdom and your ineffable goodness for the multiple gifts which I desire to be enriched by you, which I desire and which I ask earnestly, insistently, and devotedly; henceforth, I will condemn and despise the prosperity of this world, and I fear none of his adversaries,[39] and the whole you detest, hating it, I will abhor, and that which you love, I will always love, and may I dedicate myself to observe [these vows] diligently for as long as I live, and you, the Father, the Son,

36. The ellipsis acts as a placeholder for the operator to insert his desired goals as it relates to improving his memory, and the second ellipsis is also to be filled in about the extent of that desired goal.

37. Instead of "gift," Vatican Latin 6842 has "fountain."

38. Genesis 1:4.

39. Corrected Latin, *adversarios*. "His adversaries" refers to Satan and his minions.

and the Holy Spirit, the one God, the almighty creator of all things, the redeemer, the governor, the savior of the world, may I love, praise, and bless the magnificence and glory with all my heart and mind, and all the strength of my soul, now and always, in the ages of ages, amen.

[K] *The first prologue of the second prayer ends. The second prayer, which is for eloquence, begins:*

Behenna, Behenna, Behenna, Soon, Euche, Onomas, Metalha, Carpenton, Mecerha, Graman, Sunthir, Penvesu, Nimumer, Nephot, Otheos, Elcana, Sobal, Sobaim, Bose, Senar, Chererap, Esiminam, Ienia, Huet, Penutson, Themsy, Senetsi, Stanaac, Gena, Emtheusa, Haufit, Racheuret, Mecumsit, Delaut, Ropsip, Bicsen, Epalcomosa, Lapirimu, Accup, Hecsenttil, Nuhat, Amina, Nachil, Ydromos, Achite, Mesopon, Semiel, Gammara, Megial, Enos, Echeu, Altherotyl, Raftereni, Huconsin, Teyerheumor, Rassexethfimor, Huhetoutac, Danic, Atysha, Affrut, Amut, Atet, Ufmat, Ethituhet, Phicte, Senrot, Nohimlul, Mepirimi, Epalhic, Eshe, Mehuthe, Nenethem, Teshirahoc, Rofita, Arimi, Eccen, Hel, Ruhama, Cassaa, Senserat, Euher, Otmos, Otselial, Cayaret, Ruhaula, Cemol, Recina, Cenhisue, Ommen, Nehuti, Emho, Sunhetre, Tenartas, Ahvectis, Lototre, Omles, Tohos, Hehot, Reshumthos, Resaat, Mucopnere, Veluesuc, Poshimhic, Nohon, Isimli, Epua, Moxhunsa, Ulhetisfilicati, Tecito, Hicsifu, Utrinca, Heochra, Lapcat, Amin, Senaiel, Manaia, Paracliton, Burgan, Meropmeraria, Zaiaanatan, Tariaquil, Aminos.

[L] *The second prayer ends. The second prologue begins after having said the prayer:*

Behold, O Lord my God, most pious creator and restorer of the human race, I, your servant and your . . . ,[40] the work of your merciful hands, yours bought and redeemed, before the sight of your immeasurable piety, and at the door of infinite mercy and your most benevolent majesty, I stand by, groaning, crying out, deprecating, and asking, and earnestly knocking, and with the whole affection of [my] heart, supplicantly entreat, implore,

40. The ellipsis represents a placeholder for the operator to insert his or her gender as either "son" (*filii*) or "handmaid" (*ancillae*).

and deprecate your inestimable piety of tremendous eternal power with all the efforts of my mind, so that you, O Lord, that you working from on high from your most glorious little habitation of the heavens, I beg [you] to listen mercifully [to me], a poor and unworthy person, look upon [me] gently and kindly, [and] may you want to listen [to me] and to admit [me] as you deem worthy today; O good God, listen and admit my pious prayers and good deprecations inside the most sacred royal court of your most merciful and most abundant exaudition;[41] and now, O most pious God, the inspirer, the exauditor of all good prayers, and the wonderful being of mercy, have mercy on me, your servant, and listen to my entire heart crying out to you to work, and strengthen this . . .[42] within me today that through your Holy Spirit whom you have deemed worthy to work and to strengthen, most gloriously, . . . within your holy apostles and within the multitude of your saints, many times wonderfully; O my Lord God, I beg you turn away your face[43] from the sins, failures, innumerable offenses, and the lack of self-restraint of my youth and old age,[44] and create, O inspector of hearts, within my contrite, clean, and humbled heart[45] [where] your supernal grace [is] perfectly illuminated and enlarged, and may I be able to understand and perceive the permanence, plenary, and supereffluent abundance of your many graces; and you, O Lord, who gives not the spirit by measure,[46] nor takes away the spirit of your sanctity from those who believe and confide in you, augment . . . within me daily, multiply, and strengthen your manifold grace with perfect humility, and on account of the honor of your omnipotent immeasurable piety, pour abundantly and permanently into the vital organ of my heart toward all things; O truthful God, the truly and perfectly spirit of all truth and swift of intelligence,

---

41. An obsolete English word (16th–17th c.) derived from the Latin which means "answers to prayers." Similarly, one who answers prayers is an exauditor.

42. The ellipsis represents a placeholder for the operator to insert any of his own specific desires as it relates to the mental faculty of eloquence. A second ellipsis follows for the same thing but as it was thought to be found within the apostles and saints. A third ellipsis follows for the same thing but now returning back to the operator himself.

43. Psalm 51:11 (NRSV).

44. Psalm 25:7 (NRSV).

45. Psalm 51:9–10 (NRSV).

46. John 3:34 (NRSV).

as much as your entire ways are merciful and true to those who search and understand your testimony and the commandments of your work,[47] give to me by the principal spirit of your tremendous, omnipotent majesty, such great understanding in all things to the extent that I may be able to extend the faculty with respect to the plenary of your mercies, graces, and wisdom, and may I deserve to come before the inerrable glory of heavenly life, you who are above all and within all things in abundance, now and always and in eternity, amen.

[M] *The second prologue of the second prayer ends. The first prologue of the third prayer begins:*

Behold, O Lord my God, the Holy Trinity, the one almighty God of all understanding, the salvific lover, creator, bestower, and guardian, I come today, although an unworthy and vicious[48] sinner in fear and trembling to a servitude that is to be venerated, adored, feared, and honored for your most merciful eternal majesty; therefore, I deprecate, O most high Lord, the omnipotence of your exceedingly tremendous virtue, so that in all things your chain [of servitude] may confer upon me the help of a manifold grace through which it may illuminate, prepare, and strengthen my heart and my soul for prudently understanding the [biblical] interpretations, humbly sustaining [religious observance], and bravely overcoming [sins and vices], because without your nod no leaf from a tree falls to the ground, and human frailty does not stop without your goverance and help. Therefore, good God, lover of goodness, hear my good deprecations and incline your most pious ears of exaudition to my good desire, because you have conferred on me your grace of inspiration, and give to me, according to the multitude of your mercies, and on account of the honor of your omnipotence and the virtue of your imperious and magnificent name, my good petitions, and make . . .[49] in thought, meditation, desire, word, and work; having been well-pleased, your most pious love and most just

47. Latin *operis*.

48. An obsolete English adjective (derived from the Latin *vitiosus*) which pertains to vice and immorality.

49. The ellipsis represents a placeholder for the operator to insert his specific desires as they relate to gaining an understanding of something.

will, deserving that which I adrently and insistently desire and and I pray earnestly [and] devotedly; thereafter, increasing the treasure in the gift of your wisdom, and having attained the multitude of your graces, may I rejoice in you, the only living God and truly my salvation; so that having been replenished with the manifold gift of your benediction, I may confess your great name that is revered[50] and holy, whose honor loves justice, mercy, and truth, now and always in the ages of ages, amen.

[N] *The first prologue of the third prayer ends. The third prayer, which is for understanding, begins, which is neither necessary to be written nor to be spoken, unless having finished first with a confession purely and simply:*

Hemmenna, Halla, Adonay, Ceve, Abaron, Cenay, Theoston, Nocra, Zecrama, Gamar, Enodoron, Ephiphanos, Genesar, Sanalina, Othogalmon, Astromoni, Thegla, Segar, Talmana, Zihic, Athite, Hicsisu, Scieto, Utmenda, Ehocra, Laptac, Heti, Mopillo, Gamno, Micespecorota, Sehet, Esitscio, Sermamvisu, Huhec, Gniophile, Lusuc, Iahim, Huhec, Affec, Thessathas, Lohulan, Rufro, Remia, Misiurat, Thonoc, Ipthahet, Raemeticameirat, Isrofre, Nimor, Caspe, Istiorot, Istenel, Hecersit, Ahuirsub, Hastana, Lielergit, Anissum, Teteptosat, Legset, Zihic, Monis, Eplam, Zehictit, Rasgog, Ehcom, Sopcaham, Ropspi, Hichenes, Hecnirot, Nihubectus, Arepto, Felecti, Eshoc, Rucru, Houlas, Dahac, Olra, Esmiodo, Deiemar, Eheunotho, Geude, Hehocre, Celassem, Cebossut, Horespos, Rotsaos, Hecli, Uthlan, Celecmat, Ustac, Nissep, Erhusit, Huhet, U, U, Themal, Desethl, Ethane, Zeuhet, Ropsiam, Ilotar, Nicsu, Mocthenot, Eptere, Tehilbie, Rencunrut, Taobsar, Hehenhic, Henesa, Muecheusis, Amnisub, Moni, Ehomneor, Bussit, Degamo, Leclusit, Haomre, Erhecsi, Ophatha, Obhic, Numrut, Thotes, Haerna, Desael, Athenuset, Arsut, Niuloter, Opconoci, Matha, Ebre, Ezien, Docsin, Hicmothone, Usimil, Deritton, Acinsus, Ahunto, Etterution, Anues, Sophuhol, Lehahut, Pishe, Rudehet, Thes, Aucus, Aphetir, Ristes, Tehet, Meporat, Heroo, Alma, Sehantia, Sehomur, Efhi, Gomormahu, Torandra, Atropla, Ytheros, Amina.

---

50. Latin *terribile.*

[O] *The third prayer ends. The second prologue begins after the prayer itself is to be said:*

O Holy Lord the Father,[51] the almighty eternal God, O inestimable mercy and immense piety, O Jesus Christ, most pious creator, restorer and regenerator[52] of the human race, the Holy Spirit, the Paraclete, instituting teacher of all the faithful and the most benevolent lover, the eternal vigilant guardian, the Holy Trinity, the one almighty God of all things, you who suspended with three fingers the rock of the earth, having balanced the mountains and hills in a balance,[53] you alone makes great wonders inscrutable,[54] and no one is able to resist your almighty will,[55] whose ways are unsearchable,[56] whose judgments [are like] the great abyss,[57] whose mercies [are] over all your operations, I beg you, look upon the venerable and wonderful sacrament today with respect to the work of your great mercy and to the glory of your abundance which you deemed worthy, and to work and to strengthen this . . .[58] within me today; O God, because you are working in your saints from the holy temple of your supernal Jerusalem, O Lord, do not suffocate me in the faults of my ignorance and youth, and do not judge me on the sins, the innumerable offenses, and the depravity of my old age, but have mercy on me according to the multitude of your mercies that are according to an age,[59] and open my heart, cleanse my conscience, and fill my mind and soul with the grace of a libation of your most gracious mercy and your wisdom to the desirable salvific gifts; therefore, adorn, O Jesus Christ, my Lord God, you who are the Word of the most high Father, the light, the glory, and the creator of the entire fabric of the world, my lips, my mouth, and my tongue, ignite the affluence of your holy words, your mellifluence of eloquence, and

---

51. *Domine Sancte Pater [. . . reparator],* the second prologue to *Hemmenna Halla,* the third prayer of understanding. The first portion of this prayer is later found in the *Ars Notoria* (Version B, NS 138, the prayer of chastity) and even later in Agrippa's *Opera Omnia,* page 659.

52. Latin *regenerator.*

53. Isaiah 40:12 (Vulgate), *quis adpendit tribus digitis.*

54. Psalm 136:4 (NRSV).

55. Esther 4:19, 21 (NRSV with Apocrypha).

56. Romans 11:33, which in turn draws upon Isaiah 40:28 (NRSV).

57. Psalm 36:6 (NRSV).

58. The ellipsis represents the placeholder for the operator to insert his specific desires as they relate to the understanding of something.

59. Psalm 25:6–7 (NRSV).

wisdom, which conquers the malice of this world, open my mouth whose puerile tongue you make capable of [Scholastic] disputation;[60] O most benevolent Lord, the Holy Spirit, the Paraclete, I beg you make [it so], so that the sweetness of your ignited eloquence and the speech of your irreprehensible wisdom may always prosper, abound, and be sweet in my heart and mouth, and [may my opponents] accept me [and my arguments] into [their] hearts and ears; O Holy Trinity of the one God and the Lord of all your beatific love, the sweetest, most maddening, and eternal ardor, also, may it be so and even inhabit within my heart and within my soul for eternity; O almighty eternal Father, do not vacate your manifold grace [and] always . . .[61] within me, O Lord, just as the abundant vine and fruitful olive may bear fruit and abound thus within your holy house, O Lord, and may it offer the most gracious fruit of true salvation in these holy words and good works with respect to your praise, honor, and mercy,[62] and of the many and blessed souls and the salvation of eternal life, you who are the abundance over all and in all things everywhere, now and always, in the eternal ages of ages, amen.

[P] *The second prologue of the third prayer ends. The first prologue of the fourth prayer begins:*

O delight of Angels, the grace of the Archangels, the dignity of the Thrones, the nobility of the Powers, the sublimity of the Virtues, the honor of the Dominions, the fortitude of the Principalities, the excellence of the Cherubim, the charity and dignity of all the heavenly Seraphim, O great and wonderful Adonay, O Holy Lord the Father, O almighty God, author and bestower of all good things, the authority of the patriarchs, the solace of the prophets, the glory of the apostles, the constancy and victory of the martyrs, the justifier and doctor of the confessors, the inviolable and uncontaminated of virgins, the height and crown of all the saints and the inestimable good of

60. Latin adjective *disertas,* literally "capable of arguing and discussing (something)." The historical context suggests the formalized procedure of debate and argumentation in the medieval university, which was based on the philosophical thought of Socrates and Aristotle.

61. The ellipsis represents the placeholder for the operator to insert his specific request as it relates to the mental faculties of understanding, eloquence, and wisdom.

62. Latin *misericordiam.*

your elect, the true rest and highest peace, the entire beatitude and insatiable sweetness and perpetual delight of ineffable joys, today I bend the knees[63] of my body and mind before your holy, ineffable, and exceedingly tremendous almighty majesty, deprecating and expostulating your immense piety of a tremendous domination, as myself, a poor sinner of your great mercy, presuming nothing, and may you amplify the gift of heavenly benediction concerning my confiding[64] merits, and consolidate your manifold grace of charity, as I ask, ardently, devoutly, and insistently about the gift of your benefits, the unfailing treasure of your riches, graces, and wisdom, [since] I will rapidly, fully, and permanently follow as a consequence the abundance [of . . .],[65] you who absconded the profundity of the heavenly mysteries from the wise and prudent sages of this world, when you were revealing [them] to small, mild, and ordinary people;[66] give to me . . ., although an unworthy sinner, seeking to understand your many mercies and manifold grace within me, having desired an exhibition of [your] present benefits, firm and full, having dilated and opted for charity, may [charity] be your consummation of eternal good, wisdom, and grace, the inviolable truth of certitude and the undoubted security of the prized heavenly perception with your cooperation, generosity, and ruling, you who are the threefold and one almighty God, the truth, conquering, ruling, imperially commanding, and making miracles and whatever else you want in heaven and on earth through the infinite ages of ages, amen.

[Q] *The first prologue of the fourth prayer ends. The fourth prayer, which is for perseverance, begins:*

Cnesa, Ospulmo, Niteraf, Ha, Mocenti, Theummen, Lahet, Momomom, Ropsephectum, Pehlahoc, Eputlahet, Antheat, Suneuhet, Tayat, Thamot, Vehuto, Indeat, Rifihiatas, Hen, Biersem, Amumuzaminot, Sephetut, Nunihal, Seret, Ilhotre, Cerschu, Ropspti, Ermanset, Sohothoat,

---

63. Latin *genua.*

64. Latin *confidente.*

65. The ellipsis represents the placeholder for the operator to insert his specific desires as they relate to perseverance. A second ellipsis follows for the same thing.

66. Compare to Matthew 11:25 (NRSV). The Vulgate has *quia abscondisti haec a sapientibus et prudentibus et revelasti ea parvulis.*

Aroemta, Semictur, Arheteo, Thelonheiron, Pernahusel, Phahicrut, Gamen, Consiti, Tay, Racon, Cehue, Manhu, Herlezes, Huhet, Sagiat, Compuri, Ifsur, Uhet, Erla, Geherha, Ahactes, Cluotres, Pihuhersos, Ripmo, Carpthta, Alhat, Ferneset, Roeni, Sobrabohesi, Steherni, Thomic, Lensuc, Etmonam, Micem, Agenelis, Emnobar, Nirbert, Rofdeat, Ricoham, Cheneabstem, Ripus, Tahuham, Nigenhi, Casopmet, Hehuhictor, Sohunda, Cohoropra, Humrin, Thehet, Nuhenton, Moona, Huysub, Hecuhet, Thomit, Pormot, Pehit, Hehet, Sohicos, Parhucur, Rahomsen, Niham, Anna, Amina.

[R] *The fourth prayer of perseverance ends. The second prologue begins after having said the prayer:*
Ha, Ha, Ha, O Lord God, the almighty holy Father, whose name is On and Alpha and Omega, because the angels of the world, [residing] in your presence, are hardly to be discovered [by humankind], nor an infant who is one day old upon the earth is without sin, how much more I, a miserable little man, who has already passed through so many days of this age's worthless and corruptible life, I am not strong [enough] to be without a multitude of sordidness, sins, and faults; therefore, O most merciful Lord, I want and I desire to be cleansed in this way, but[67] there is no one who can make clean any conception from an unclean seed,[68] except you, my true God, you alone who are true, clean from every defect; therefore, O my Lord God, my plasmator[69] and redeemer, you who knows[70] the [human] figment best and well, I come from you not with a troubled body but a totally devoted heart, deprecating and expostulating, as I, a miserable sinner, when you want and as you know, from all my failures, sins, and entire moral contagions, you deemed worthy to cleanse; I know and I confess, O Holy Lord the Father, great, wonderful, almighty God of all things, before the most holy and most just face of your majesty, I do not have thoughts, words, or works without a blemish and without a crime, nevertheless, from the iner-

67. Latin *sed.*
68. A problem according to the Christian doctrine of original sin.
69. An obsolete English noun, which derives from the Latin, and means "one who forms, molds, or fashions (something)."
70. Latin *noscis.*

rable abundance of your mercy and the magnificence of your omnipotence, having confided in the treasure of your immense piety, reserved for all who come to you with their whole heart, although unworthy to the faithful, still I undertake [this operation] with prayers; and you, O Lord, whose Spirit replenished the world, you who has every field of knowledge and you who are supereffluent of true wisdom and the only unfailing fountain, today may you deem worthy to pour gently into the vital organ of my mind the sweetest, delightful, most maddening of your love, the incomparable riches of your manifold wisdom, and your multiform graces, as ardently desired, and may I know and love perfectly, may I speak rightly, and may I do something[71] studiously, and because it may be acceptable to your will for all the days of my life, and may I rejoice in you and in the multitude of your fields of knowledge and wisdom and in the many riches of your graces, which all your creatures bless, adore, and magnify, the eternal and almighty Lord, amen.

[S] *This work is divided, and the four aforesaid prayers are to be said in one lunar month and three others which follow in another lunar month, and the three others in another; that is, through the third lunar month. The prologue of the fifth prayer begins:*

Hoping in you, O God, the fortitude without whom nothing is sacred, nothing is special, and nothing is good, in whose hand are all things, in whose sight nothing is passed by, whose eyes all are naked and open, to whom every heart is open and all desires are spoken, and for whom no secret is hidden, who clothed yourself with confession and decoration, and having put on the light of ineffable brilliance just as a vestment, give to me your wisdom which may always be with me and labor with me; and now you, O Lord God the almighty, send to me today your Holy Spirit from the holy seat of your majesty, who purifies, cleanses, enflames, illuminates, teaches, directs, exercises, governs, reigns, inhabits, protects, visits, and defends my heart, for all the days of my life, declare . . .[72] in

---

71. Latin *quid*. The author is indicating to his reader to fill in this space with a specific desire as it relates to perseverance.

72. The ellipsis represents a placeholder for the operator to insert the desired knowledge of particular sciences to be imbued within him.

whatsoever way upon me today, O Lord my God, your mercy declaring your words to me, because the declaration of those illuminates and gives a little understanding [of it]; therefore, O Lord, augment and strengthen within me a good understanding, so that I may know and do that [which you declare]; O Lord, irrigate and make fertile the aridity of my heart by the water of your spiritual wisdom and affluence of salvific discipline; O Lord my God, I beg you, extend my senses to understanding the salvific sacraments of your mysteries, so that I may grasp it by memory, and implement spontaneously your uncontradictable and irreproachable will in all goodness; O Lord my God, the most merciful [and] miraculous commiserator, have mercy on me, a miserable person, and make miraculous your mercy over me, you who makes whole those who hope in you; O Lord, I beg you turn away your face from the multitude of my sins and do not cast me away from the abundance of your mercies on account of the multitude of my offenses;[73] give to me, having desired for a long time now, your desirable gift of your manifold grace, and grant me, your most delightful wisdom, having wished for joy, how long [it has been since I came] from [being] a sinner and insipid person, [now] having changed your pious and just servant into a wise and good one; open my lips, so that my mouth may prudently and wisely announce[74] the praises of your mighty works and the profound benevolence of the most gracious dignity of your mercy in the church of your sanctity [made] by your mellifluent and ignited holy words by the grace of the Holy Spirit; and may [the announcement] exalt and glorify you, king of kings and Lord of all lords,[75] you who closes and no one opens, you who opens and no one closes, so that by my five senses, in many ways, steadfastly, and perfectly through you, and having been illuminated in you, I may offer the sacrifice of praise to you, a well-pleased [announcement] of my thoughts, meditations, words, and works here [on earth] and in the kingdom of your eternal majesty, on account of the glory of your name, amen.

73. Psalm 51:9, 11 (NRSV).

74. Latin *adnuntiet*.

75. Apocalypse of John 19:16 (Revelation, NRSV).

[T] *The first prologue of the fifth prayer ends. The fifth prayer of the particular sciences begins:*

Luna, Boson, Huhet, Deniheccassit, Oneartar, Abcetes, Iloter, Ritriacrio, Dehetrat, Abhenotisub, Esorimiti, Dehet, Ticsi, Menethicha, Ceptoar, Lumete, Theho, Sohichi, Neuhet, Hennim, Ginahir, Suster, Anhet, Amlomor, Hosopsi, Rambom, Dofutatib, Hois, Cohuhet, Fimen, Vohos, Thehet, Cilema, Arbihem, Theintus, Uhet, Osonset, Chathoesti, Copusol, Theuhet, Sohu, Xilophea, Cassa, Erepti, Rehoncathe, Amhun, Seratum, Itivomer, Luhuhicte, Rossan, Thehethet, Omil, Memisinse, Iuhanbi, Urahet, Tesohumet, Reshaute, Semixit, Repha, Urihos, Acsus, Reprohot, Disricummi, Remor, Renhitimos, Nilahicum, Seset, Uhib, Astha, Uhithesat, Osmecthon, Hicil, Fahas, Resurhetre, Rethan, Rothgie, Tahilba, Ohuce, Retef, Husur, Nigentisub, Heret, Sehepem, Ismutal, Precun, Alinot, Coret, Doholrem, Lihil, Sehe, Repde, Cacigon, Dahilphus, Funtris, Reogora, Itriphion, Cossit, Tehet, Nihicra, Midahan, Pahar, Nimirusta, Senacnerrusub, Thehem, Ziha, Figoon, Illocre, Hahehan, Locilhan, Ahilhi, Housi, Reperinab, Nilheruprut, Vebusur, Abhi, Pingrus, Cehuhet, Aserne, Thomis, Ripno, Cihidis, Cuhuham, Hecsevici, Ahactes, Mohot, Hetremercorrutam, Consit, Espendion, Septiremon, Herehaliha, Huhet, Rahan, Usepti, Uhet, Hicmen, Fobilsi, Tahahec, Cirmoc, Miritimenhat, Raphuphit, Uhecni, Fohunte, Lafinas, Rusges, Uhet, Rephectas, Thehet, Torbecte, Parahan, Lafinis, Teranhetre, Cahasse.

[U] *The fifth prayer ends. The second prologue begins after the prayer is to be said:*
Raaf, the instituting teacher and lover of thoughts, words, and all good works, O God, adjutor of the good and a good director of proficiencies, whose plan [extends] from [the beginning of] eternity up to [the end of] eternity, you who calls those things which are not as those things which are, whose dominion is neither to be estimated at the beginning nor concluded at the end, to whom heaven and earth, sea and infernal realm, and all things which are in them, under them, and around them, obey equally and are a servant to [you] unanimously, whose inestimable piety and inerrable goodness, incomprehensible mercy, unfailing and benevolent omnipotence; O Holy Lord the Father, they magnify, testify, and show

the omnipotence of the eternal Lord. You, O Lord God, the king of the worlds, the only bestower of forgiveness, O Lord, the lover and author of human salvation's indulgences,[76] O Lord, I beg [you], I attend to my supplications and open the eyes of your most pious majesty to my tribulations and my labors and incline your most merciful ears of piety to the most ardent desires of my mind; and you, O Lord my almighty God, the most just Father, to whom alone [belongs] the benediction and brillance, the wisdom and the action of graces, the honor, the virtue, and the fortitude in eternity, today hear my prayer which [comes from] my mouth to you, send to me your most gracious, propitious, copious gift from the temple of your holy majesty, just as your mercy, having helped the helper in all things, and your most protected virtue, having strengthened the defense, and having spoken perseveringly to the copiously eloquent person of the multiple gifts of your many graces, may I always exult in you, my very salvific living God, and may I exalt, bless, and glorify your great [and] holy name, admirable and blessed in eternity, amen.

[V] *The second prologue of the fifth prayer ends. The prologue of the sixth prayer begins:*

O most high lawgiver, the most just preceptor, the wonderful doctor of the best teachers, the laudable teacher of erudition, the amiciable instructor, the joy, the solace, the pleasantness, the defense of sweetness, and the consolation of all existing creatures, O Lord the almighty God, you who are wholly great and wonderful to the universe, upon who the angels desire to look, the eyes of all creatures hope, so that, with the open hand of your abundance you make joyful every gratuitous animal with a benediction, and fill [them] with an innumerable variety of food and an overflowing abundance. O Lord, see and consider my good desires that you gave to me this very grace which is to be inspired, and attend to my labor on account of your piety of mildness, and do not despise, O good master teacher, lover of goodness, to whom the entire good please my good deprecations, not on account of the multitude of my depravities, but on account of the glory

---

76. During the Middle Ages the Catholic faith understood indulgences to be a remission of the punishment of sin; a pardon.

of your name and the almighty honor of your most pious majesty, hear me and give me a suitable, efficacious, and capable heart for understanding the profundity of your mysteries and for thinking about the occult, salvific mysteries of your sacraments, so that, having been filled with the spiritual joy of your most delightful mercy, and having been delighted, may I rejoice to have discovered and acquired the inestimable treasure of your incomparable graces and wisdom; therefore, search my kidneys and my heart,[77] O Lord my God, you who powerfully and mercifully empties out [my] noxious and superfluous [qualities], so that, having been led down the way of your mercy and most pious will, walking before the sanctities[78] of your mandates with an open heart, having cast off the old man with his actions [like a piece of clothing, so that] I may be worthy to put on [clothes] and imitate you, [becoming] a new man, you who restores the old, who reforms the deformed, who renews the corrupt in justice, sanctity, and truth, you who are the way, the truth, and the life, O eternal, incommutable, and blessed God in a generation of generations and in the eternity of times, amen.

[W] *The first prologue of the sixth prayer ends. The sixth prayer, which is for universals, begins:*

Gymel,[79] Pomahuhac, Exemat, Fasem, Epusil, Menhes, Hermohet, Amison, Soichos, Lonhoc, Sermohen, Reuhicron, Sehem, Cehuhe, Memotinret, Uhet, Dinphinde, Muher, Reodam, Cehen, Excrema, Hapticene, Hiham, Exhahuitre, Vohactos, Repcipuhe, Pishu, Ensa, Cenuc, Acir, Oronsit, Cenoc, Amisti, Acinos, Getmi, Thehet, Rucdeliha, Semoc, Asta, Lihit, Rostem, Huhet, Guna, Rosinet, Cloanrnot, Huhet, Thehet, Geham, Sisin, Etar, Cohum, Inhicter, Eheter, Sobum, Desip, Hicsen, Amre, Vehil, Vomol, Retras, Uhet, Tanectes, Liotra, Uhe, Rehet, Lasot, Pothuplos, Cihis, Rentice, Cetil, Nohocsin, Rehet, Lihiphe, Denhicsi,

77. *Renes* means "the kidneys," and *cor* means "the heart," both of which represent the essence or psyche of a person according to the ancient Hebrews. See also *Ars Notoria,* section 117, page 277, footnote 80.

78. Latin *sanctitas.*

79. *Gimel,* the third letter of the Hebrew alphabet. It is also repeated three times to begin section Z.

Lulubivina, Recsin, Tahuhet, Ilnutrasel, Cayat, Tanmet, Pethotre, Ensar, Restiro, Tanhet, Hochusol, Lamisir, Laricsim, Fufuhas, Vitensis, Alho, Uhictur, Veson, Ohuhic, Rehes, Omimom, Demu, Tanhuhec, Etersin, Inpehirhis, Dehe, Fulhimne, Terser, Dehincmesu, Enesa, Nithe, Mocmit, Heerponsit, Taninot, Dehuho, Troshe, Porlthere, Uhicbus, Tohot, Fuhenra, Lapsis, Tosut, Obito, Ilma, Retramor, Lavictur, Robis, Hateron, Poniti, Mehitis, Ebalsus, Ahicius, Ilhurcos, Pentraher, Sison, Tahuhet, Mitinatusut, Rehecma, Libuonrum, Uhecta, Urinehb, Suppearre, Timain, Onhet, Perhoar, On, Vehem, Santo, Cohum, Inhumre, Itamre, Reprumot, Tehet, Epalco, Precim, Rava, Sohamti, Zay, Tamem, Lileurmeth, Pahatin, Seset, Uhet, Olcavihi, Deurocrum, Tehet, Nectiomnen, Decit, Rama, Uhet, Uhicsi, Roya, Ruihuc, Plahicta, Mucposisut, Apce, Huicnesi, Nohos, Utharohet, Nise, Huicbus, Edi, Anhuisset, Armec, Amusub, Ifammot, Amisi, Uhinus, Obumar, Perhicmur, Uhecta, Iaclis, Lohet, Digonitmur, Hosir, Zihic, Ipetasit, Oson, Sihic, Sohon, Inpetrat, Eroptus, Huicambre, Huictetras, Motanhet, Tehomor, Lerm, Uhoc, Cahemol, Tetras, Epactes, Uhet, Sehernat, Hoshuda, Albain, Nahet, Dehinchith, Adia, Sarutrut, Rapte, Huteerba, Amnen, Nuvimta, Asta, Uthorum, amin, amin, amin.

[X] *The sixth prayer for universals ends. The second prologue begins after the said prayer:*

O most merciful commiserator, O God of the miserable, O most mild God, have mercy on me, your servant, you who has taken offense to all faults and are appeased by penitence, you who wonderfully sublimed humankind, having been created in your image and likeness, but having fallen by diabolical suggestion, you who deem [humankind] worthy to call back through miraculous deeds, you who knows to teach humankind knowledge and you alone are able to teach without labor and without delay, you who liberates and no one impedes, you who impedes and no one liberates; O Lord, you whose virtue is total because it is the best, most precious, and admirable, whose every heavenly, earthly, and infernal being obeys and trembles, receive my good deprecations today, O good Lord my God, and hear my good desire that you have freely[80] given to me,

80. Latin *gratiis.*

and fill my heart and conscience according to my pious and good desires, and adorn me with the garments of holy good works for salvation in eternity. O Lord my God, the true light, I beg you, open and illuminate my heart and my understanding by the saving light of your supernal grace for the purpose of thinking about and pursuing zealously the mysteries of your secrets which are to be admired, so that having been decorated by the manifold gift of your generosity and incorporeal gifts of many graces, having been said gloriously, may I exult and rejoice in you, O glorious Lord my God, you having always taught me in every field of knowledge [and] having been perfected, have been discovered the best of teachers, and because you alone, are good, great, and wonderful in all things, fill my heart with your gifts and blessings and with your manifold grace, adorn my senses permanently, you who are almighty, eternal, having been blessed in the ages of ages, amen.

[Y] *The second prologue of the sixth prayer ends. The first prologue of the seventh prayer begins:*

O natural, incommutable, eternal God, through whom all things exist, move, and live, you who made everything out of nothing by your will, you who inestimably searches human thoughts, kidneys, and hearts; O Lord, today look down from your sanctuary and lofty habitation of the heavens over the good desires of my will that you gave me, and give the supplement of perfection of your divine graces to my imperfections, so that by the protection of your many virtues, having been perfectly strengthened in all things, I will so much despise all the lures of this world, so that I may ardently love you, the sole God of all, and do your will in all things; and you, O Lord, you who gives not the spirit by measure, but confers more abundantly and much better than we believe, as much as we ask, I say, O Lord, you change my senses for the better, and give me a new understanding and a new spirit; build and strengthen within the middle of my heart, and having perfectly instructed me in the necessary sciences, and in the doctrines of the good and holy Scriptures, and having been taught eruditely [and] wonderfully through the grace and operation of the omnipotent virtue of your majesty, may I be worthy to speak out about you with the solicitude of all my thoughts, words, and works, you who are

the fountain and origin, the author and bestower of all good things over the magnificent, now and in the ages of ages, amen.

[Z] *The first prologue of the seventh prayer ends. The seventh prayer of all discretions begins.*

Gymel, Gymel, Gymel, Sehepmet, Laphet, Hemni, Cihetrea, Amnen, Uthorum, Nihunta, Asra, Tebi, Recnes, Rubem, Thehet, Prosimsa, Lahitni, Hennia, Huslinem, Hehenham, Tauhet, Feser, Inhat, Sehetra, Cehil, Subhilmen, Enema, Gamhanimun, Neheham, Tenehet, Hemme, Senectiha, Rencit, Namuhet, Tehet, Hucra, Terumdet, Lonhichus, Ehet, Lonheries, Faotrum, Archana, Mohehubo, Tensup, Hecir, Vehinhet, Lusserit, Laberatsub, Hesac, Cohum, Ocmus, Asaarthi, Ficuna, Elasar, Mihecnas, Inpehirro, Ceuhet, Uhictis, Dehimnabirrut, Arsic, Temsub, Tirhe, Mohuc, Tehu, Spohilhis, Oberhentis, Omisinot, Accihiphes, Sevherat, Nohacibuir, Uhocuhet, Nosit, Cuhin, Asepra, Nihon, Consulha, Hiramebilus, Rehefret, Memuc, Foheubu, Orhannos, Remor, Dohimnos, Necum, Uhet, Tohactan, amin, amin, amin.

[AA] *These three aforesaid prayers ought to be said in practice of the work together in one lunar month with the prayer of holy Mary. The second prologue begins after the prayer which is to be said:*

Our Father, you who are in heaven, you alone sanctify, beatify, and rule all things. You know, O Lord my God, because I, your servant and your . . .[81] **am a fragile figment and the work of your hands, therefore, today be propitious to me, a sinner, O Lord, and cleanse my conscience, my mind, and my heart and my soul by the dew of the Holy Spirit, make wonderous and purify by illumination, because you alone are the investigator of all hearts, the founder of everything, the dispenser and judge, the best author and bestower of overflowing abundance of all good gifts, and since without you, mortal infirmity can do nothing, and without your goverance and help, the defense**[82] **and plan does not sustain human mortality; I beg [you], present to my fragility the copious and persevering salvific help, the**

---

81. The ellipsis represents a placeholder for the operator to insert his or her gender as either "son" (*filii*) or "handmaid" (*ancillae*).

82. Latin *praesidio*.

protected defense, the secure refuge, and the continuous subsidary of your graces in everything; O good Lord my God, today be a pious, merciful, and kind exauditor of my good petitions, so that you may fill confidence into me from the plenitude of your many graces and mercies with a supernal grace, console and support [me] continually in all things with the help of your omnipotent majesty, and assiduously provide protection of the good supernal spirits against all the insidious and malignant infestations and unclean spirits, and defend me always and powerfully everywhere; O true light from the true light, I entreat you, O Jesus Christ the savior, expel from me every noxious ignorance of darkness, and replenish and illuminate my heart with the light of your manifold salvific wisdom from caliginosity, and may you deem worthy to endow and to speak to the misery of my heart of the overflowing gifts of your manifold mercies, (some [gifts and mercies] are great and many); O Lord, I ask that . . . ,[83] and I actually desire that . . . , but you, O Lord will be able to give greater and more graces and even the most powerful to the ungrateful, you know[84] to give the best, you conserved [them in order to] to bestow [them]. For you, O Lord the almighty God, you who does not give the spirit by measure, but you know and are able to confer to me better and more abundantly than I believe or than I know to ask. Therefore you are the origin, the beginning, and the creator from whom all good things proceed. O Lord, you are the overflowing dispenser of all of the best gifts, you who gives graces abundantly, and you do not come hastily. O Lord, you are the most maddening,[85] supereffluent, and sole fountain of heavenly paradise, who having wonderfully inundated and irrigated the land of the human heart in the four climates of the globe[86] with the profound salvific water of

---

83. The ellipsis represents a placeholder for the operator to insert his specific desires as they relate to knowing and understanding the metaphysical and philosophical problem of universals and particulars.

84. Latin *noscis.*

85. The sense is that the Lord is the source of divine madness or religious ecstasy, which might be attained through religious practices and granted by angels, not that he is the source of frustration or aggravation.

86. "The land of the human heart in the four climates of the globe" is a poetic metaphor; however, according to medieval worldview, there are actually five terrestrial climates (*climata*), or circles (*circuli*), not four. These five climates span the known world of Europe, Asia, Africa, and the Antipodes (a fourth unknown land). From north to south, there is the Arctic Zone,

wisdom, and you make it to grow and bear fruit, which are pleasing to you in every time of an age, whose tremendous omnipotence of majesty they praise, bless, adore, glorify, and magnify all your creatures through the infinite, ages of ages, amen.

[**AB**] *The second prologue of the seventh prayer ends. The first prologue of the eighth prayer begins:*

O Holy Lord the Father, the almighty eternal God, whom all heavenly, earthly, and infernal creatures tremble all over, dreading, and adorning, look upon me mercifully today, and make with me, on account of your great mercy and compassion, what my soul desires to be given freely by you; O Lord my God, attend and incline most sweetly your ear of piety to the deprecations of my good will which you gave to me. O Lord, consider and look mercifully upon my labor [and] my humility, and vivify[87] **the miseries of the darkness of ignorance, my insipidness, and my imprudence, and may you deem worthy to perlustrate and illuminate [me] powerfully, perseveringly, and mercifully your sevenfold grace with light. O most gracious Lord Jesus Christ, have mercy on me, you who are the way, the truth, and the life,**[88] **direct and justify me in the way of your vivifying wisdom, and give me the truth to understand [and] to love your perfect understanding, and to want and to observe permanently the sciences and teachings which come from you, so that I may deserve both the [mental] faculty and the will within you; O glorious king, to pursue glory, make your mercy heard to me, O most merciful Lord my God, as I rejoice and give thanks in the riches of your graces, mercies, sciences, and in the wisdom of your commandments, and to have my prayer discovered in the sight of the most delightful space of propitiation, and the most gracious place of your most generous exaudition, to whom is the honor, the glory, and the fortitude, to the almighty God, from generation to generation, and in the eternity of the times, amen.**

---

the Northern Temperate Zone, the Equatorial Zone, the Southern Temperate Zone, and the Antarctic Zone. Only the two temperate zones were thought to be inhabitable. These five climates are illustrated in maps of the world (*mappae mundi*). See also chapter V, page 79.

87. Latin *vivifica*.

88. John 14:6.

[AC] *The first prologue ends. The eighth prayer of prose and neumes begins, which is to be said, along with the following others in its lunar month:*
Estachion, Elaf, Gamna, Minon, Ehahidem, Forutuamat, Uhet, Conanmet, Phennihem, Thehet, Pantho, Hemitim, Ceu, Ceetron, Ceuhuc, Etrehet, Cehol, Unaretef, Mahuac, Nauham, Tara, Lunirumin, Licta, Tauhuc, Iuri, Emhomosehet, Lupranaranac, Sahon, Nithe, Repmonem, Zihic, Arox, Dehes, Cihetra, Eorha, Vesilicior, Uhet, Lanecten, Diluchicta, Oreste, Utha, Netehet, Incethore, Karacto, Sishetre, Sehet, Tohat, Deduhetre, Inhutuhem, Rocagia, Tahat, Tehutuhem, Lonhet, Ripmum, Tuspet, Iatal, Craca, Nirsut, Teuhet, Zehuy, Zehunne, Felorem, Namot, Iutum, Zeuhet, Heuhet, Henhet, Erectatim, Lansin, Omil, Docel, Aletra, Huinsi, Daha, Neutham, Tehet, Crepmum, Paetre, Zehet, Suhatre, Pamtipo, Hipheure, Zenehet, Lonbot, Tehet, Tofidenhet, Pahatru, Moilmiu, Macson, Zeuhet, Ithipiendat, Aioles, Denha, Eumhac, Neuhet, Hemin, Haorumon, Nesum, Adhenna, Lupso, Tenehet, Eniha, Nuhuc, Rupsim, Alsepconunis, Mecepra, Zeite, Dirhethus, Haret, Mehem, Niterpirihisca, Pariercum, Cohum, Noma, Usho, Nuhemraham, Amphone, Teheh, Solheurat, Ebailho, Saptor, Dehet, Liocre, Celasem, Parfot, Darhatnus, Nicancas, Cehet, Balanhet, Ponplasut, Aimcelas, Lepna, Zeuhet, Maretui, Refeseren, Preasgia, Erasomu, Culactum, Rehetgetab, Iret, Uhac, Comita, Nopto, Felucithus, Invisis, Iarham, Neresi, Meprat, Elle, Cohum, Hectis, Ihethos, Hen, Nomnac, Anna, Apnerinot, Hauguria, Heexapnit, Ninitho, Suhub, Guritte, Resum, amin, the grace of God, a manifold gift.

[AD] *The eighth prayer ends. The second prologue of the same prayer begins:*
O King of kings, O Lord of all lords, O almighty God, in whose authority all things are situated, of which no one is able to resist [your] will,[89] you who are the creator and governor of worlds, O God, the Alpha and Omega, the beginning and the end, whose eternity has no end, whose beginning has no beginning, whose end has no end, in whose sight every human body will be forgiven, and because you discovered depravity even among your angels,[90] O Lord, and how much more [depravity is] within me, a miserable man,

89. Esther 4:19, 21 (NRSV with Apocrypha).
90. Job 4:18 (NRSV).

who spends time [living] in a muddy and dirty house; I know and confess, almighty God, the benevolent and exceedingly enduring, and the much merciful and truthful God, whom none [can] hide before the eyes of your most just majesty, whose [eyes] search the kidneys and hearts of all; I have no thoughts, words, or works without a crime, the reason for which, O most merciful Lord my God, I deprecate your immense clemency of piety, so that you do not consider my innumerable offenses and my depravities and neither the sins of my youth and my ignorance, but look down upon the multitude of your mercies from are from an age,[91] and the honor of your majesty's most gentle omnipotence, and now make with me mercy which I ask of you and my soul desires ardently to be given freely to it from you, because I do not hope and believe to come before [you] for any of my merits with respect to so many and such gifts which are to be obtained, except only through the sole mercy of your immense piety, the admirable operation of your omnipotent virtue of tremendous power, from whose most affluent mercy, I, your servant and . . . ,[92] your pauper and beggar, having confided in knowledge and wisdom, I presume to ask [you], so that if it especially pleases your majesty or piety, [then] may [it] descend upon me, [your] servant, figment, and the one in need of redemption, having desired for a long time [and] having sought more often the glorious, wonderful, and laudable of your many graces, mercies, and wisdom, lasting with a salvific abundance. Therefore, O most pious and glorious Lord, the king of eternal glory, to whom the Cherubim and Seraphim, and all the heavenly orders, ineffably sing sweet-sounding modulated praises of your mighty works in an inexcogitable[93] exaltation with an indefatigable joy and act jubilant without end, hear me, I beg you, look upon [me] mercifully today, O true God, to my confessions and deprecations, and may the words of goodness and my deprecations be answered in the presence of [your] most glorious, most merciful, exaudible[94] majesty, because you alone are God who in truth performs stupendous and wonderful things; therefore, O most gentle Lord my God, convert my insipid actions

91. Psalm 25:6-7 (NRSV).

92. The ellipsis represents a placeholder for the operator to insert his or her gender as either "son" (*filii*) or "handmaid" (*ancillae*).

93. An obsolete English adjective derived from the Latin which means "unimaginable."

94. The obsolete adjectival form of *exauditio,* meaning "capable of answering prayers."

into the abundance of your manifold grace, and my ignorance into innumerable riches and the gift of your wisdom; convert the tepidness of my heart into a salubrious favor and into the sweetest pleasantness of your beatific and vivifying love; convert my beated breasts[95] into joy, a holy jubilation, and a pious exultation, so that having lost the strength of my heart, my mind, and my conscience, hardened and expelled by the sorrow of my caliginosity, blindness, ignorance, and my insipidness, may I deserve the most beatific joy of your delight, the overflowing salubrious fruitfulness, the light-bearing wisdom and knowledge, and your grace and mercy, and may I deserve to be enriched most affluently here with abundance and to be consoled over your fruitful abundance of mercies by the most blessed consolation in the future with all the saints without end, you who are the author, bestower, and the unfailing plentitude of all good things and the ineffable goodness, whose omnipotence and empire are everlasting, in the ages of ages, amen.

[AE] *The second prologue of the eighth prayer ends. The first prologue of the ninth prayer begins:*

Holy, holy, holy Lord God Sabaoth, whose name [is] Abba,[96] Behem, Ruhos, Alma,[97] Agyos, Otheos, Agyos, Yskyros, Agyos, Athanathos, Eleyson, Ymas,[98] O Lord, you who are the founder and knower of worlds, the shepherd of the eternal, the God who is to be venerated, trembled before, worshipped, adored, you who arranged the heavenly militia of the nine [angelic] orders admirably, and who constituted man a little lower from the angels [in the cosmic hierarchy], crowned over the work of your hands,[99] I adore, praise, bless, and glorify you today and your holy name, because it is above every name. Receive today, O Holy Trinity, my confession and my deprecation, illuminate my heart and conscience, adorn me perfectly and steadfastly by the light of your knowlwdge and teachings; I know and confess, O Lord my God, because you have absconded the

---

95. A sign of sorrow and grief.

96. Aramaic, meaning "father."

97. Latin, meaning "nourishing."

98. "Agyos, Otheos . . . Ymas," Greek, meaning "Holy, God, Holy Strong, Holy Immortal, Have Mercy on Us." This Christian hymn is known as the Trisagion, "Thrice Holy."

99. Psalm 8:5–6, which was also later quoted in Hebrews 2:7 (NRSV).

multitude of your riches of wisdom from the wise and prudent sages of this world, and you have revealed it to the small, simple, and ordinary people[100] with the ineffable dispensation of your mercy. O Lord God almighty, I beg [you], reveal it to me, a little one, an unaged knowledge, and open the eyes of my heart today, so that I may reverently and solicitiously consider and perfectly understand . . . ;[101] may I always be able to grasp [it] by memory, and discuss [it] at length wisely, and may I be able to graciously narrate at length your miraculous [and] mighty works, and may I admire your profound, benevolent, and merciful dignity, your wonderful salvific wisdom, and the doctrines of your holy Scriptures and all good things, so that I may deserve to walk purely and rightly in the way of your commandments, and I will understand [them] in many ways and perfectly with an open heart and may I observe diligently all things pleasing to your will with mindfulness, meditation, desire, word, and deed in all the days of my life, so that in this exile, this life's peregrination,[102] having been placed in misery, I will profit in loving and following you thus to the consummation of this unstable life's course, and having set aside the burden of the corrupted flesh in the confession of your name, may I deserve to be counted in the consortium of your saints, as I praise and bless you without end with them, you who are everywhere in all things with abundance, now and always in eternity, amen.

[AF] *The first prologue ends. The ninth prayer of the secret cognition of [poetic Latin] meters begins:*

Anuen, Negena, Hacti, Cohum, Resit, Iethos, Hen, Noumac, Halma, Panertum, Hanhucriha, Hecse, Aphuit, Inricho, Buhehus, Surehub, Gurhecte, Hermos, Zenehet, Hunna, Tehet, Hunothis, Rutha, Hocmitanhat, Sehorrum, Prohisluti, Atlamis, Rehipien, Cohenotia, Richensi, Liotra, Thehet, Ahugusmor, Dohunnas, Nohon, Eher, Lipcat,

---

100. Compare to Matthew 11:25 (NRSV). The Vulgate has *quia abscondisti haec a sapientibus et prudentibus et revelasti ea parvulis*. The word, *parvulis*, means "little one," such as a child, and the petitioner refers to himself as such in the next sentence.

101. The ellipsis acts as a placeholder for the operator to insert his desired knowledge as it relates to Latin prosody.

102. The archaic English word, "peregrination," ultimately derived from the Latin *peregrinatio,* refers to a person's temporary journey through life on earth.

Herot, Mehen, Hemme, Petihit, Zaiher, Zelahisi, Hunciruhic, Fusenta, Michantair, Hac, Odor, Zeo, Seher, Marecno, Inrocde, Tihumres, Nohon, Ponthi, Inselic, Mohuc, Ripinum, Rucgite, Sontro, Rehethe, Heccidere, Raches, Aloclere, Gammon, Corhe, Tehet, Nicesti, Prehetnis, Heula, Pronufda, Tempeshatre, Hesquimictas, Miefre, Hoshorres, Nohet, Uhet, Cuhet, Tahes, Carmot, Sehet, Iaham, Leptiha, Inhicria, Rephet, Ihob, Thanem, Pealhychi, Uhet, Deso, Exdetharam, Iosehu, Muhucpe, Letsa, Senucdi, Iohvus, Tohet, Sureptes, Concelepsa, Rehep, Tehichos, Amseir, Geranetuum, Uhet, Apmerat, Pameren, Sucelep, Nusenarda, Rohacho, Human, Ihemen, Dioci, Gamnum, Uhet, Imetpoie, Remet, Aspicie, Cocehano, Ehunhe, Hahat, Bahospite, Lesut, Cehete, Hocreo, Dieufus, Centare, Lucus, Cohet, Ihesem, Neuti, Uhet, Sinel, Nacruchue, Uhicheto, Ranuhucri, Trihocnes, Enot, Scohuphophas, Huhet, Zehuhet, Hocte, Nerm, Vetheth, Greset, Crunoc, Ceuthe, Nitraheet, Ronaitur, Rehet, Saluatro, Phahicdis, Pihes, Iphes, Aruthus, Onsit, Henuten, Tehet, Trilipci, Tehol, Intebiher, Inacles, Lihil, Splihimfesor, Glomenar, Aceptee, Fluxit, Poon, Tanan, Denel, Tanhet, Pomot, Seutigia, Cavhat, Cumhectis, Hogamini, Ibeintoi, Recrot, Hence, Pronusdi, Aspius, Muhacles, Misemor, Pahet, Pehetras, Sushu, Eerot, Ehon, Tufit, Coharrum, Crihunna, Exuhoc, Nucra, Resti, Maieshactem, Cahuet, Resoptan, Rucip, Iahasina, Pehaescha, Pusip, Raipna, Ossalmit, Nohon, Genuethos, Nosinoron, Reroptan, Theesha, Sisuhic, Acutonsit, Oron, Brouhe, Pusep, Nechithi, Mihen, Nactis, Pahecat, Finchitus, Humon, Lisut, Thehetabahit, Scouplos, Alhiptare, Seluperi.

[AG] *The ninth prayer ends. The second prologue of this very prayer begins:*
O holy one of the saints, the almighty king of kings, the God of gods, and the Lord of all lords, the ineffable one of glory, the immeasurable one of piety, the exceedingly tremendous majesty, whose ways [are] unsearchable,[103] whose judgments [are like] the great abyss,[104] whose mercy excells over all wonderful works and everything, who stretches out the heavens like a tent, who covers his superior [chambers] on the waters,

103. Romans 11:33, which in turn draws upon Isaiah 40:28 (NRSV).
104. Psalm 36:6 (NRSV).

who makes the spirited winds your angels and the flame of fire your ministers,[105] illuminating[106] every man that you see, you who are the true light, searching, purifying, and illuminating the hearts of men, O most merciful Lord my God, today I beg [you] today, illuminate my senses, my mind, my heart, my soul, and my conscience with the salubrious light of your salvific[107] wisdom; adorn me and all my senses in the manifold gifts of your many graces decently [and] copiously spoken, and open my intellect in this way, O most gentle Lord my God, you who are the key, the doorkeeper, and the door of eternal life, indeed the eternal life and true wisdom itself, and permanently pour into my heart the sevenfold grace of the Holy Spirit, so that having wondered and venerated the mysteries of your secrets with a pious and dignified reverence and the debts of the heart which is to be searched with devotion, I may prevail to understand piously, rightly, truly, quickly and perfectly . . . ,[108] to retain [it] in memory, to discuss [it] worthily, to disclose [its secrets] lucidly, and to love [it] ardently. I beg [you], O most benvolent Holy Spirit, to burn my kidneys and my heart with the sweetest fire of your most delightful and glorious love, so that I may serve you with a sober and chaste body, [and] may I always please you with a clean and contrite heart;[109] and you, O eternal Lord Jesus Christ, O most gentle Son of God almighty, similar to the Father and the Holy Spirit, of infinite mercy, piety, and immense majesty, which no spaces of locations, intervals of times or an age, separate from those who are miserable, today be pious and propitious to me, a sinner, and kindly accomodate your most merciful ears of exaudition to my holy confessions, pious supplications, and good petitions, having been pleased; O good God, whatever good I desire from your immeasurable goodness and from the overflowing commiseration of your infinite mercy, and I ask devoutly, insistently, ardently, and confidently . . . , and I require . . . through the incomprehensible operation of your omnipotent virtue, [and]

105. Psalm 104:2–4 (NRSV).

106. Latin *illuminans.*

107. Latin *salutaris.*

108. The ellipsis acts as a placeholder for the operator to insert his desired knowledge as it relates to Latin prosody. Three more ellipses, intended for the operator's desires, follow later on in this same prayer.

109. Psalm 51:9–10 (NRSV).

may I now deserve to obtain . . . to [its] entirety with swift effect, [you] whose honor and empire lasts without end in the ages of ages, amen.

[AH] *The second prologue of the ninth prayer ends. The first prologue of the tenth prayer begins:*

In honor of the almighty God, Zenocraton, Heudoron, the Alpha and Omega, the beginning and the end, O holy Lord the Father almighty eternal God, always one and the same, you who are everywhere in all things, and you were before all things, and you will be the blessed God in the ages, I deprecate the benevolence and omnipotence of your tremendous majesty, and I invoke the mercy [and] inerrability of your omnipotence, so that you always come before and follow me in the benediction of delightfulness of your many mercies and graces, and may you always make me occupied to have pious works and constantly intend to have good desires; direct my plan and my senses. Vehemently and permanently kindle my heart and my soul with your sweetest vivifying fire and eternal love, powerfully expel the horridness and darkness of my mind's ignorance, and may you illuminate my heart with the salvific light of your wisdom, perlustrate[110] my mind and my conscience continuously, having bedewed [me] with the dew of the Holy Spirit, and perlustrate me with respect to understanding the doctrines and sciences which are coming from you, may you make [me] suitable, worthy, capable, [and] efficacious with respect to the multiple gifts of your graces, and may you redeem [me] with respect to thinking and doing your most pious will in all things, prudently, wisely, strenuously, and indefatigably, henceforth, as long as I live; also may I be able to understand the mandates of your mouth and the sayings of all your prophets, the salvific documents of the holy doctors, and the doctrines of all the good sciences entirely, rightly, truthfully, quickly, and completely, and may I always be able to retain [them] in memory, to discuss [them] wisely, and to observe [them] studiously, in order that you magnify [them] out of the riches of your mercies, sciences, and wisdom; and having spoken abundantly about your most merciful omnipotence, having been exhilarated, with a peaceful mind and a humble heart, I will always exult in you,

110. To purify thoroughly as with a ritual implement, such as the Christian aspergillum.

the sole living God, my true salvation, to whom he always was, is, and always will be, an invincible virtue and the fortitude of omnipotence, the benediction and brilliance, the honor, the praise, and glory, before and beyond the times of the ages, amen.

[AI] *The first prologue of the tenth prayer ends. The tenth prayer begins, which is to the completion of everything:*

Zemon, Tehet, Nepehet, Dardanema, Frusiat, Teci, Morbece, Elashen, Fahat, Evitan, Rasut, Orhot, Desi, Mihetre, Cruhensat, Huhet, Heuroep, Zenhet, Asihe, Cuhemason, Colusta, Uhethet, Hehial, Inhipter, Ehet, Triset, Edicit, Cehicusason, Meihectu, Icil, Namot, Figet, Inpuheme, Navhacta, Haspihiches, Victric, Frihicarum, Fuhenra, Mamoret, Mehoc, Cumtusu, Ehabicdes, Dehipdo, Sanhicne, Tehureo, Camsop, Onhacbit, Macpos, Humdo, Baseras, Exhiher, Euhat, Biffu, Hemre, Rucrus, Cognasit, Uteher, Fresit, Adbotobelre, Flucut, Cumreutscos, Dahanhi, Nocrutna, Sichan, Cafaresu, Exherer, Etdimor, Pahirter, Quehermus, Icilsem, Deserat, Lial, Lila, Gravi, Leuhutum, Defunsa, Relupsa, Zenhet, Umhot, Umdo, Hecsiher, Refrum, Hetrahithus, Loblare, Paharbat, Ilihatsic, Hailhes, Iherum, Conenita, Parasut, Trissit, Cahemomsa, Derotquet, Brahicha, Retras, Retoonahat, Manhu, Luihicdum, Teher, Grehilbus, Heroc, Rehuplit, Hecmuhesa, Ferinohanda, Tehasla, Lamsat, Silanilic, Ganisa, Sosic, Cehespecta, Fahitgat, Ceptore, Pectoher, Combisuha, Tehet, Solles, Pichatre, Masictra, Numten, Peroflat, Hetlumhoc, Susuepdit, Pehilhon, Racu, Sarop, Exahauta, Manhu, Rapten, Uha, Rueprat, Esac, Sican, Tanet, Uhet, Ituum, Tohir, Uhet, Tehet, Meuhet, Suhicuhet, Saracrat, Hecniho, Haubitri, Geraho, Uhec, Losuc, Monsaractur, Tahuitra, Centauhir, Stahupla, Ailhat, Paton, Nonheuhac, Nevafdis, Rafrihithus, Zihic, Ohim, Mun, Nusol, Exreta, Cruoser, Spihucla, nehet, Tonhet, Leblis, Geniha, Libus, Zenet, Iot, Ihet, Reni, Tehes, Muhesam, Gumeso, Racti, Crahetres, Insotes, Sehet, Fahatre, Innostes, Bethin, Hana, Retga, Reharrum, Zehet, Uhet, Uhet, Duminricdis, Mantonuc, Larob, Uson, Niremi, Sonse, Saulhit, Neras, Dahibhas, Haminan, Tisub, Rebas, Hetnum, Seratre, Libar, Vehetres, Heorhas, Hamuha, Hetinot, Vehantu, Hicturum, Inhilmine, Ripmo, Oferissen, Propheptat, Uhet, Dasep, Larhoc, Uhet, Sehermat, Guine,

Hotinum, Cuminsa, Prohic, Delihotre, Maret, Vehenhis, Heurpit, Silnus, Dahan, Ganitha, Viser, Temtanhet, Dehuesto, Crehuphit, Sesin, Onhucla, Macpotonus, Blausut, Dertrat, Tahuhet, Ishum, Definisus, Viramos, Pavebribus, Tersit, Inhuctit, Tehet, Adhomne, Anserit, amin, amin, amin.

[AJ(a)] *The tenth prayer ends. The second prologue begins after the prayer which is to be said:*

Tehet, Zai, the Father, Son, and Holy Spirit, the eternal true God, the almighty creator, the shepherd and the rector of all visible and invisible creatures, I praise, bless, glorify, and magnify you today, although, I, an unworthy and exceedingly sinful person, know, O most pious Lord my God, because no man will be judged in your presence, unless the remission of all sins is granted to him through you, because you discovered the depravity in your angels,[111] how much more [depravity is] within me, a most miserable man, have mercy on the first [man], you discover the depravities by the corruptible weight of multimodal flesh, but you, O God of worlds, wonderful commiserator of mercies, allowing too many mercies and the truth, today look mercifully upon the miseries of my fragility, and have enough mercy on me; O most pious Lord my God, may the eyes of your mercy see my defect and imperfection, and have enough mercy on me, your figment and the one in need of redemption, because you are, seeing beforehand, the founder of human nature, the most pious instructor, the merciful witness, the prudent restorer, the wonderful redeemer, the wise rector, the loving protector, the vigilant guardian, the strong helper, the almighty savior, you who has deemed worthy to call and to admit man to the profundity of your sacraments, not of his merit with goodness, nor of his ingenuity with subtlety, but your gifts with generous gratuity. O Lord, today incline and open your most merciful and most generous ears of exaudition with respect to having always repeated my prayers of ignorance and imprudence, and with respect to the hardness of my heart and the forgetfulness of my mind; O Lord God, the most admirable doctor of the best teachers, hear me and give to me, an ignorant and uneducated person, oblivious and ineloquent, and with a hard and

111. Job 4:18 (NRSV).

heavy heart, a true and upright [heart] with respect to all things, a subtle, quick, capable, [and] full understanding, and a persevering, living, and unfailing memory, an expedient, profluent, mellifluous, and ignited eloquence, and your robust, adorned, and supernal grace, so that, in all the precepts of your commandments, wisdom, teachings of the sciences, and in all the good Scriptures, may I be found fit, useful, stable, strenuous, and indefatigable, and perfect, henceforth; and now for a long time I have desired (whatever)[112] from your innumerable wisdom and from the inestimable abundance of your many mercies and I desire . . . and having often repeated [my] prayers, I have required devoutly, urgently, persistently, and with the total affection of [my] heart . . . by your great mercy and the omnipotent virtue of your most gentle majesty, and I require [it] quickly, fully, and perfectly; now I deserve to obtain [it, and] you, O Holy Trinity, by who all good perfect things exist with abundance, and through which the best gifts are given, but, O Lord, since with respect to these gifts, which are to be obtained, [are] so many, so much, and so excellent, I am [and feel] lesser; the least and none of my merits have helped the [heavenly] helpers, for that reason, I invoke . . . in the [heavenly place] of assistance and because (he/she) is the greatest (or the greater [helper]) for me in assistance,[113] therefore, I invoke with respect to the highest mediator, the honorable name of your tremendous majesty and the ineffable glory of your power, the most holy Tetragrammaton, whose invocation and naming, neither the conjunctions of the syllables nor even the names of letters, I profess to be unworthy, which I offer with the lips or sound through with the voice † Iot † He † Vau † Het †,[114] so that the virtue of your most sacred name may obtain this (very thing) because my desire, my mind, and my devotion cries out in the presence of you.

112. "(Whatever)" is the author's cue to the operator that he may insert his desire here. An ellipsis follows for the same thing, then again, the same desire is to be substituted for "this (very thing)."

113. The ellipsis acts as a placeholder for the operator to insert his patron saint, who helps mediate the final stage of the entire ritual operation.

114. The four Hebrew letters—*Yod, Heh, Vau, Heh*—spelling the most sacred name of God, YHVH, or Jehovah. The same name is also called by its Greek name, the Tetragrammaton (the four-letter name).

[AJ(b)] For I know,[115] O Lord, you who are the ineffable truth, the only, impassable, [and] wonderful operator, for whom nothing fails [and] nothing is impossible, you who wants anything whatsoever, as God, the creator of all things, you who prevails to make . . .[116] wonderfully and incomprehensibly in the twinkling of an eye in the triple world machine with only a nod in a moment, you will permit the invocation of so many of your names [which are] not to be annuled through the earnestness of prayers, labors, and operations; ergo, through this [divine name], so magnificent, so very sacred, so very strong, so glorious, so well-renown and admirable, your name **A † N † E † C † P † H † E † T † O † N †**,[117] that Aaron bore on his forehead,[118] grant me, the one in need of redemption, your servant, you who redeemed the most precious one with your precious, clean, blood,[119] and the desirable and salvific gifts of your many graces, mercies, wisdom, and sciences, which I have desired now for a long time, I wished for continuously, and I asked for so many times. And now, O most pious Lord my God, you who once strengthened the heavens with your word, and you who strengthened the spirited breath of whose mouth, every [spoken] virtue of those [mouths] you deemed worthy to strengthen and to send out [into creation], today may you deem worthy to strengthen and to send out into me the multiplicity of your gifts [and] the everlasting grace, so that through the wonder, virtue, and power of this most sacred of your names and through the incomprehensible operation of your tremendous omnipotent virtue, may I understand . . . rightly, quickly, truly, completely, and may I always grasp [it] by memory, and having been taught, may I discuss [it] at length, may I offer [it] graciously, may I narrate [it] at length pleasingly, wisely, and also easily, and may I know [it] honestly, and may I prevail to teach every wisdom and all the doctrines and sciences which come from you; also, may my speech, reason, discourse, and words be pleasing and accepted by

115. Latin *scio.*

116. The ellipsis acts as a placeholder for the operator to insert his desire, which he asks God to manifest. Another ellipsis for the same thing follows.

117. Greek *Anekphonaton,* transliterated into Latin as *Anecpheton,* meaning "the Unpronounceable," an epithet and reference to the four-letter name of God, YHVH. The seventeenth-century *Lemegeton* presents the name on the ring worn by the operator and also on the Triangle of the Art. The name became corrupted in the transmission of magical texts, being variously misspelled as *Anephexaton, Anepheneton,* and the like.

118. Exodus 28:36–38 (NRSV).

119. Jesus Christ.

everyone and every one who hears them through the operation and the abiding and inhabiting grace of the Holy Spirit within me, having been made mellifluent and ignited within my heart and mouth, and in the ears of all the hearts of my audience, for the purpose of your praise, glory, honor, and of the almighty great name of your tremendous majesty, and to me, and to those who I will want to advise and teach the perpetual salvation. Hear me, O Lord God, the Alpha and Omega, the beginning and the end, appease, attend, and make a miracle of your mercy with me; do not delay any longer for your very own self, and on account of the the glory and honor of your imperial and magnificent name, O Lord my God, because I invoked your wonder-making name over me in the help of my infirmity, because it is blessed, admirable, [and] venerable from an age and in all the ages of ages, amen.

[AK] *Here ends the work of the abovesaid ten prayers, which ought to be said and divided through their own lunar months, and having been worked and celebrated, the prayer of the Blessed [Virgin] Mary, which follows, is to be said at the end of whichever lunar month, and at the end of each lunar month:*

O glorious queen of the angels, O most merciful helper of your devout people, I take refuge in you, help me, since labor [alone] does not suffice, my sins and I impede [myself from attaining my goals] and [my] merits [alone] do not help, and therefore the many, great, [and] incomparable gifts which I desire and ask for, I am not able to obtain them without the greatest [help] and many helpers, from where you [are] in the first place, the first way of grace, the first door of life, the beginning of human salvation, the mother of piety and mercy, I invoke [you] within my [heavenly place of] assistance, especially with respect to your most potent help [placed in front of all others]; I come humbly, devoutly, and confidently today, so that such necessary, salvific, and desirable gifts which I have desired now for long and have asked about so many times, if it pleases God and you, and it expedites my soul through you, O mother of God, O most glorious ever virgin Mary, the pious helper of the miserable faithful, may I deserve to obtain . . .[120] through whom the human race was born

120. The ellpsis acts as a placeholder for the operator to insert his desire, which he asks the Virgin Mary to manifest.

from you, she [who] has the Savior. Also, I invoke you, all the holy Angels and Archangels, the Thrones and Dominions, the Principalities and Powers, the Virtues of the heavens, the Cherubim and Seraphim, all the holy patriarchs and prophets, all the holy apostles and evangelists, all the holy innocents, all the holy confessors and martyrs, all the holy virgins, all the holy monks and hermits, all the holy widows and those who practice the virtue of sexual continence, and all the holy souls, for help and subsidary of my impotence, so that, all you [heavenly beings] of every one of the most efficacious votive urns [placed in front of all others][121] may deem worthy[122] to aid me in all respects, by the most pious suffrages, the most glorious patronages, and the most powerful helpers in all things, and how much may I deserve to be answered by God in my good desires and pious petitions, to the praise, glory, and honor of the Holy Trinity, and all your [heavenly beings][123] and the holy Catholic Church, to the honor, to the benefit, and to the salvation and glory of the perpetual beatitude of my soul, and many others, through the grace, operation, and virtue of the individuated, holy, and omnipotent Trinity, and through all your[124] most gracious and powerful suffrages, amen.[125]

121. Latin *urnis*. Originally, the ancient Romans used urns into which were thrown voting tablets or lots (*suffragia*), just as in the electing of officials during the Roman Republic. Similarly, the Romans used such vessels to cast lots from which were drawn the fate of an individual. Here, the operator conceives the members of the heavenly court as each having their own urn. An operator who hopes to gain the favor of one or several heavenly beings would address his prayer (or, suffrage) to that being, for assistance. It is up to the heavenly being to assist the operator based on what fate or destiny is drawn from the urn.

122. Latin *dignemini*.

123. Latin *vestrorum*.

124. Latin *vestrorum*.

125. This Virgin Mary prayer may have some word agreements with those found in the ninth-century illuminated Utrecht Psalter. The Utrecht Psalter was copied at Canterbury Cathedral by c. 1000 CE, then again, as the Eadwine Psalter of 1155–60, and then again as the Anglo-Catalan Psalter.

Opus Operum, Notae Supplement

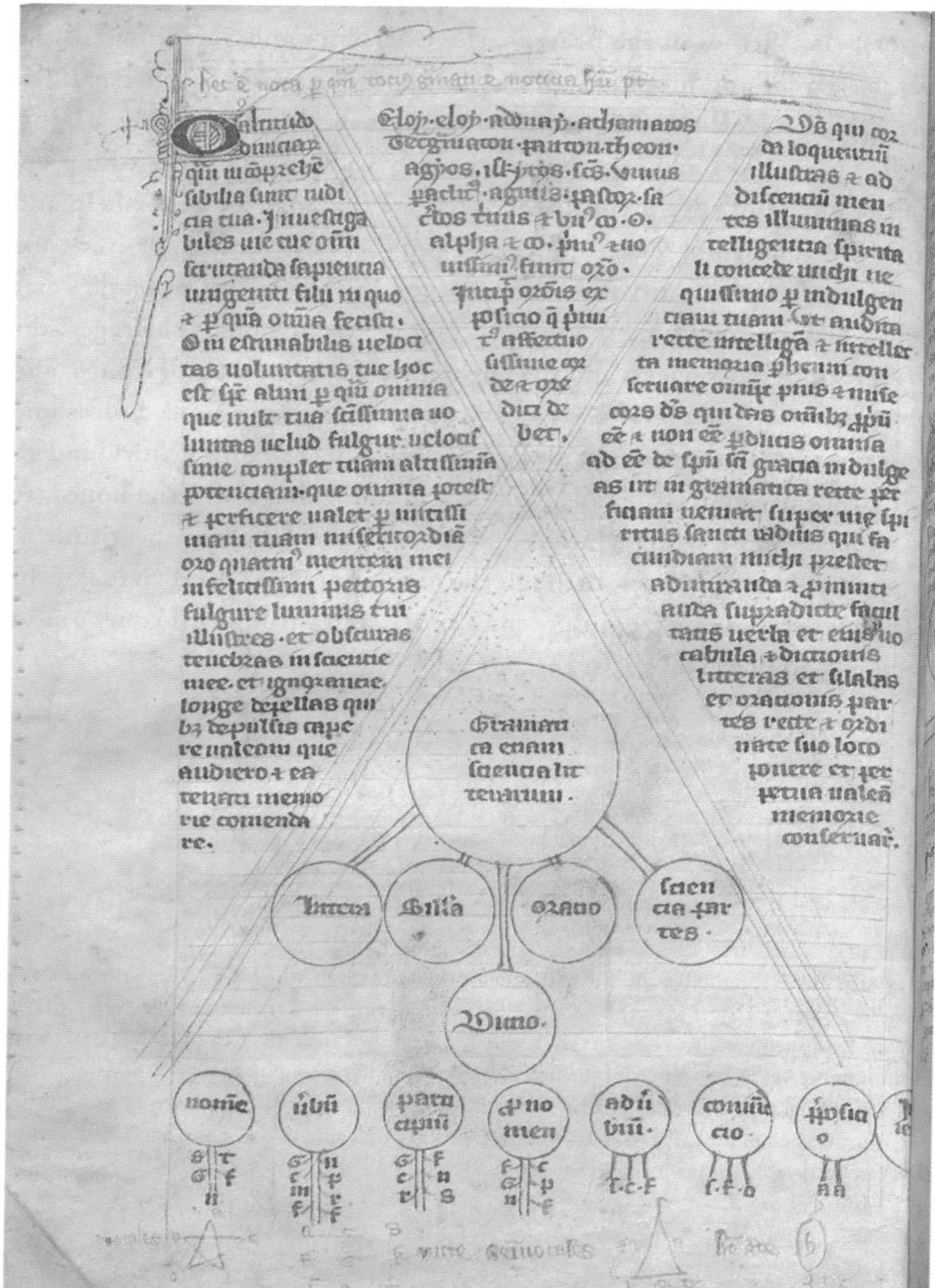

The figure for the entire Art of Grammar (123ab),
BSB CLM 30010, f. 12v

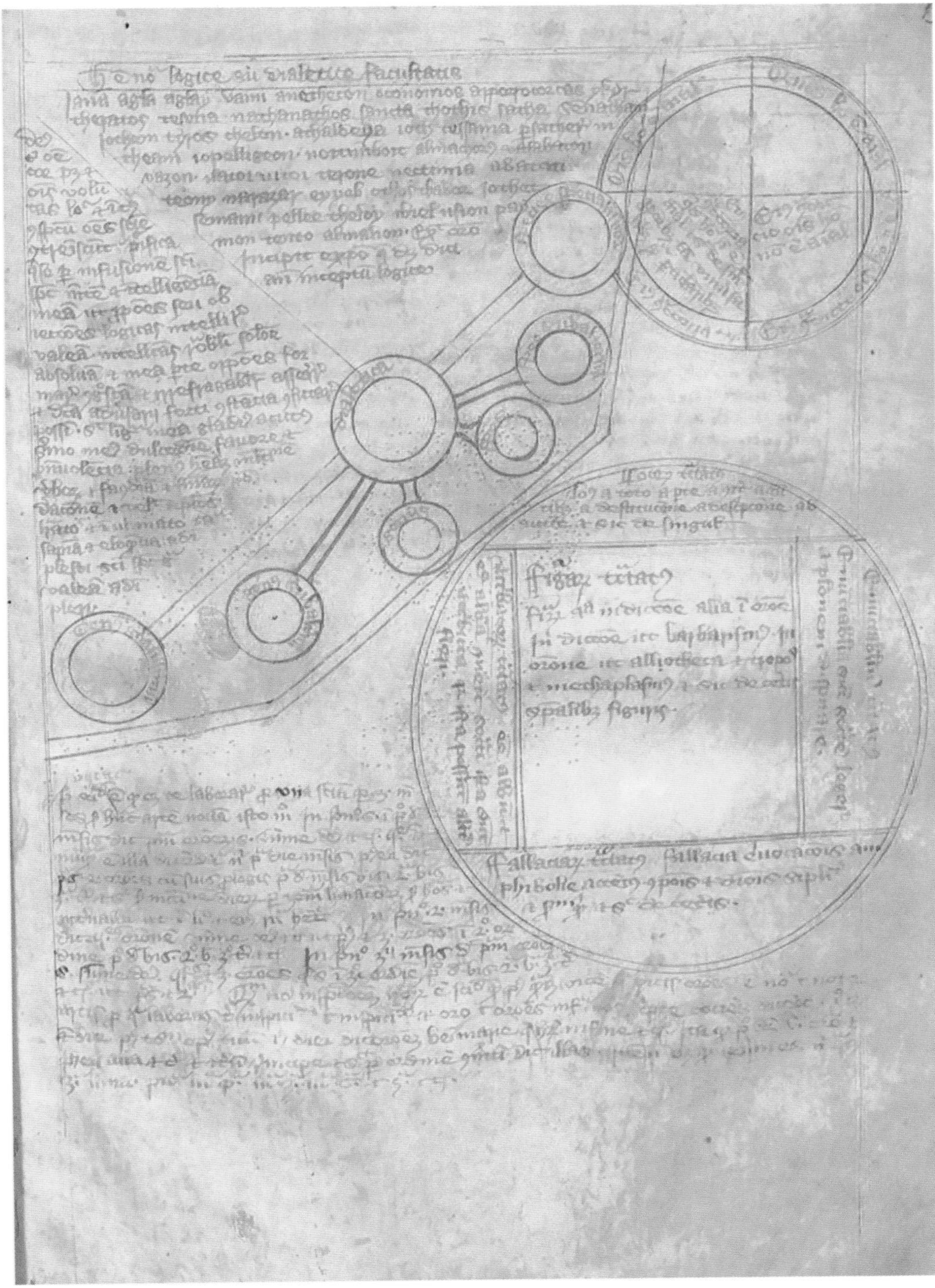

The figure of logic for dialectic skills (4ab),
BSB CLM 30010, f. 13r

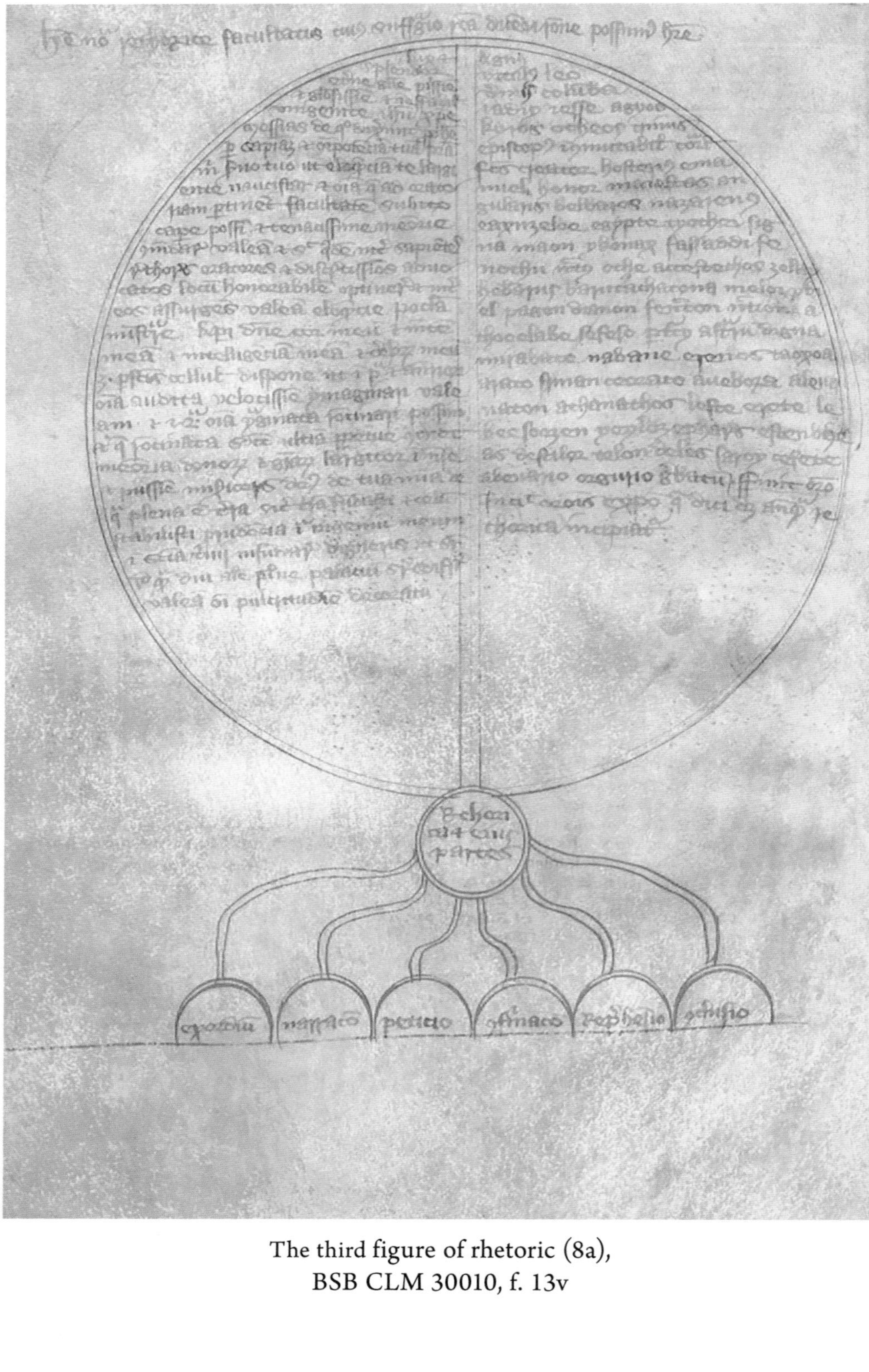

The third figure of rhetoric (8a),
BSB CLM 30010, f. 13v

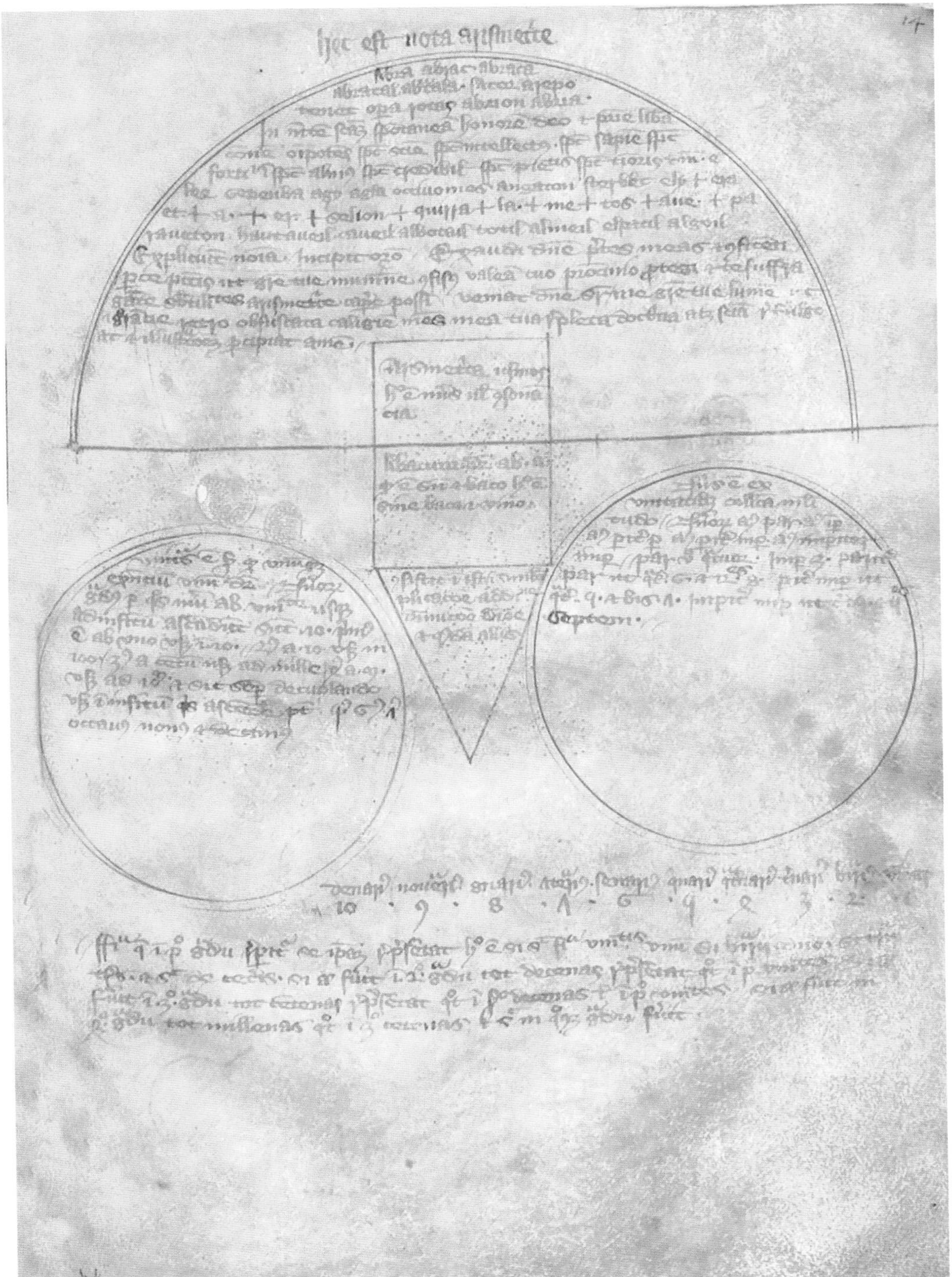

The first figure of arithmetic (12ab),
BSB CLM 30010, f. 14r

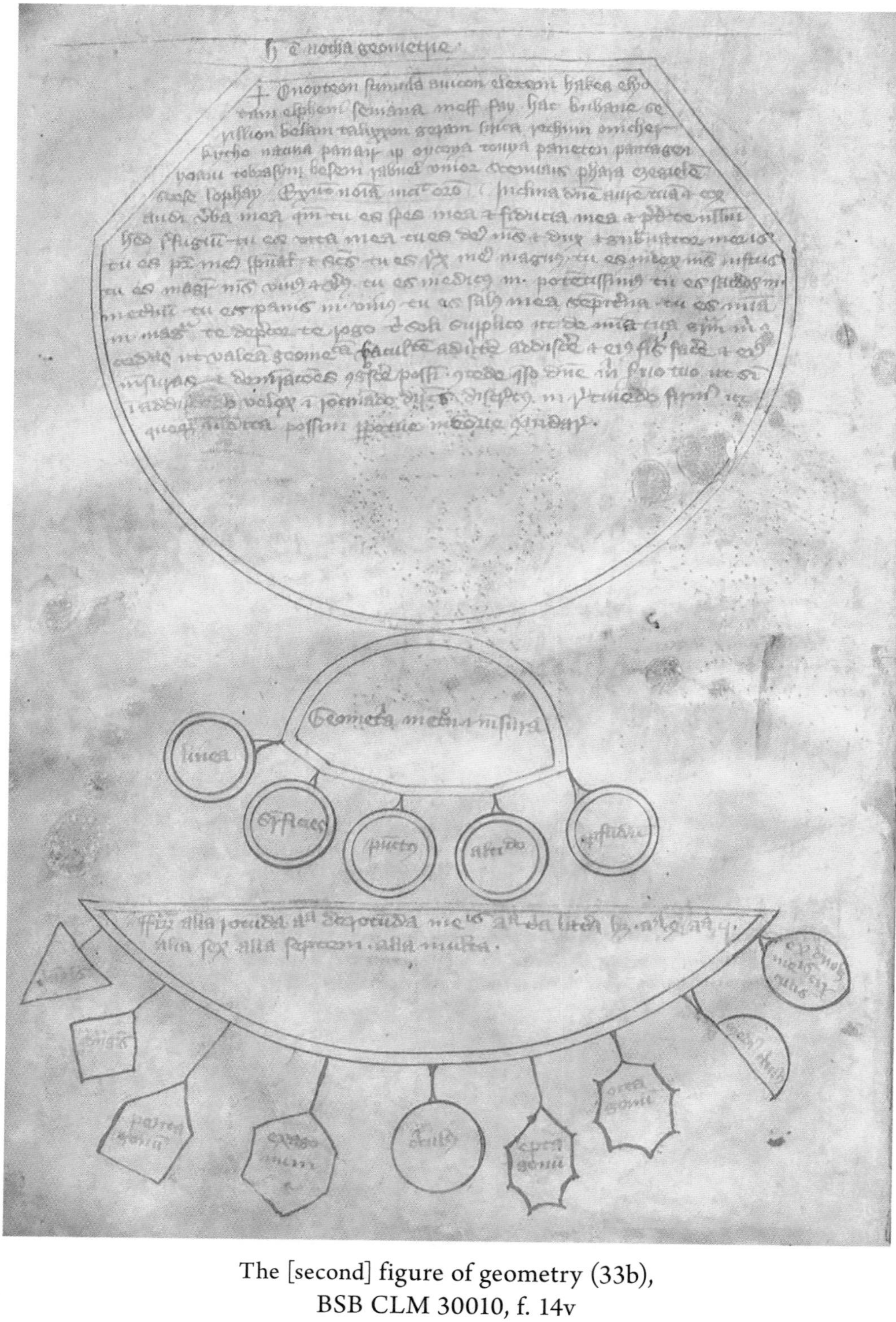

The [second] figure of geometry (33b),
BSB CLM 30010, f. 14v

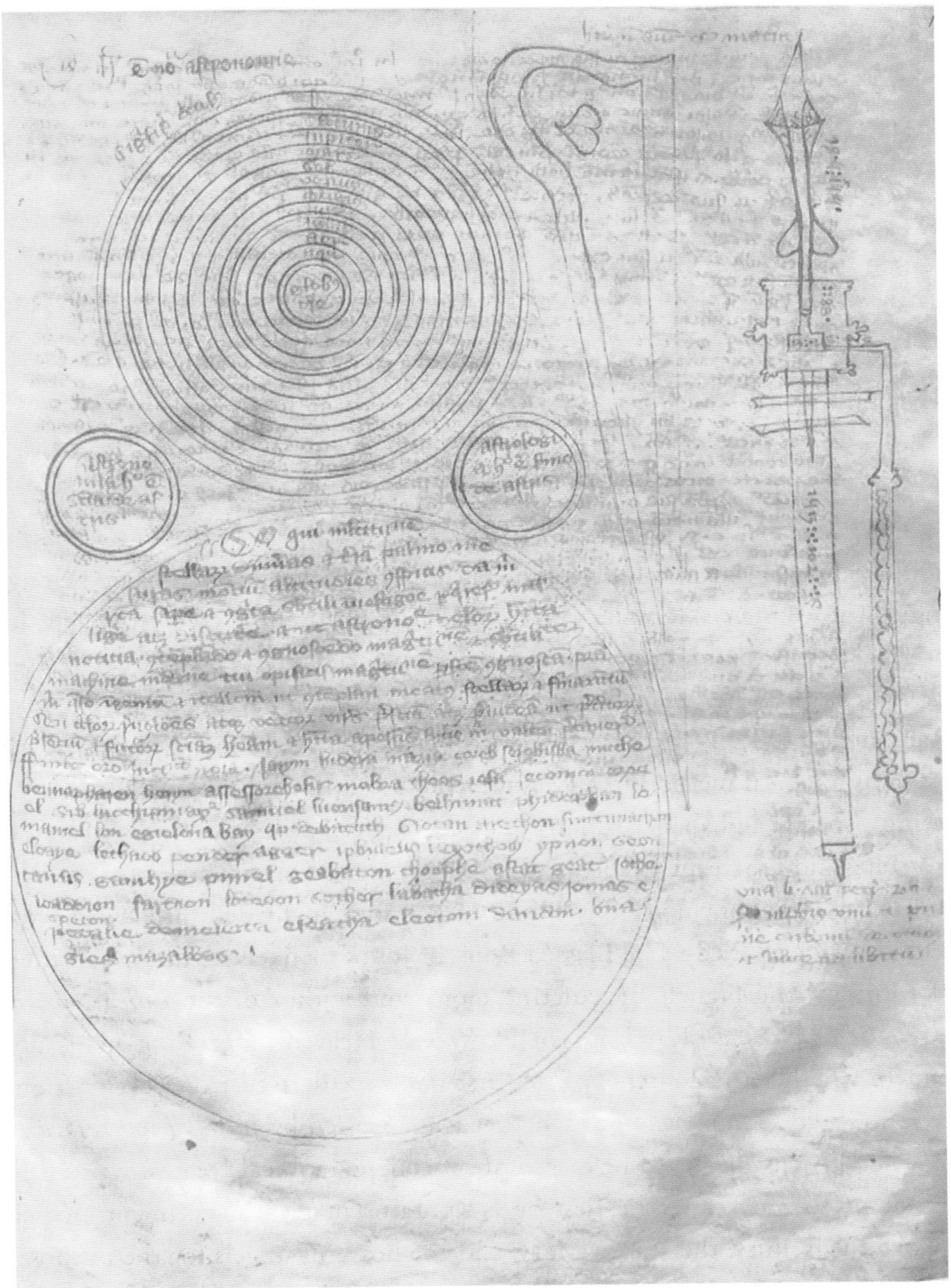

Top left, third figure of astronomy (17b). Lower left, the fifth figure of astronomy (19b), with the prayers *Deus, qui multitudinem stellarum* (NS 89) and *Heloy, Lay, Hobidam* (NS 88).

To the right, there is a *groma,* a Roman surveying instrument which would relate to geometry. It is not found in Ars Notoria at all. BSB CLM 30010, f. 15r

7

Ars Brevis (Short Art)

14th–15th Centuries

The *Ars Brevis* is a mid-fourteenth-century treatise of angelic magic belonging to the *ars notoria* tradition. The title is given by Julien Véronèse, but its original title is found in one of the manuscripts to be the *Ars Notoria Brevis et Bona* (*The Good and Short Notory Art*). This work is not to be confused with Ramon Lull's (1232–1316) *Ars Brevis* (*Short Art*), published in 1308, which explains a logical method to solve problems and answer questions by manipulating a special alphabet set upon geometric figures.[1]

The mid-fourteenth-century treatise of angelic magic presented here is written by an anonymous Catholic author, and it is divided into two books. The first book, titled "The Blessed Book of John," is likely attributed to John of Morginy, the French Benedictine monk and author of the *Liber Florum Caelestis Doctrinae* (The Book of Flowers of Heavenly Teaching). It is not known whether the contents of the first book are derived from lost portions of John's Old Compilation, or whether it is inspired by John's *Liber Florum,* or whether it is meant to be a separate pseudepigraphical treatise written in his name. In any case, the first book contains magical experiments which invoke the Trinity, the Virgin Mary, and the heavenly angels for the purposes of "understanding all the arts and secrets of the entire world," finding hidden treasures, attaining prescience, and renewing the practitioner's senses so that he is capable of composing short treatises with respect to all the arts. The first

1. Yates, "The Art of Ramon Lull," 115–73.

book borrows some prayers from the *Ars Notoria* and the *Opus Operum*. The second book, titled "The Book of Divine Revelation," references the divine revelations received by King Solomon. The second book is almost wholly derivative, containing twenty-two prayers from the *Ars Notoria;* however, none of the magical figures called *notae* are found within the *Ars Brevis*. The entire treatise of the *Ars Brevis* appears somewhat fragmentary or incomplete and shows signs of redaction. The *Ars Brevis* has been classified here into two versions—the Vienna version (V2) and the Sloane version (L2). The book was always found in compilations, accompanying other magical or scientific treatises, including John's *Liber Florum*.

"The Blessed Book of John" presents four magical experiments, each having its own magical figure. There is the experiment for memory; the experiment for the intellect; the experiment for the secrets of Master Albert [Magnus], the bishop of Regensburg; and the experiment for the secrets of God. Each experiment follows the same formulaic ritual procedure with the exception of the figure used, its *ars notoria* prayer, its lesser prayers, and any other respective changes according to that figure. In each experiment, the practitioner is expected to hold fast to the Catholic faith, performing votive masses, fasting, giving alms, offering prayers, and donning vestments. The formulaic ritual procedure consists of the following parts:

1. The votive masses offered each day of the experiment (sections 12–25)
2. The offering of the preamble prayer(s), the *ars notoria* prayer and its magical figure, and the other lesser prayers associated with the figure (section 4–5, 6–7, 42–43, L2.2, L2.3–5, L2.6, L2.7–10, L2.12, V2.2–7)
3. The consecration of the magical figure by the canonical hours (sections 45–52)
4. The consecration of the magical figure by the votive masses (sections 44, 53–55, L2.11)
5. The crucifixion rite (sections 26–34)
6. The consecration of the bedroom using a *lectisternium* and the offering of the prayer *Summe Deus Pater piissime* (sections 56–L2.1, L2.11)
7. The dream incubation for attaining angelic visions for a specific purpose (sections 9, 11, 35, 39–41)
8. The giving of thanks to God the next morning (sections 10, 36–38)

A single experiment lasts for four days in which a single votive mass is offered each day (sections 12–25: i.e., on the first day, the Mass of the Holy Trinity; on the second day, the Mass of the Holy Spirit; on the third day, the Mass of Saint John the Evangelist; and on the fourth day, the Mass of the Blessed Virgin Mary). The *Ars Brevis* presents special additions to the traditional votive masses, which are unique to its own magical experiments. An experiment must begin on the new Moon, but that day may fall on any day of the week, but if it is the Lord's Day (i.e., Sunday), then the practitioner is to double the alms he gives (section 8).

During the Middle Ages, many Catholics owned a devotional prayer book called a book of hours, which was used to pray according to the canonical hours. This common and popular Christian practice is used by the *Ars Brevis* in the consecration of the magical figure (sections 45–52); praying according to the hours can be performed in a single day. Votive masses also played an important role in religious life during the Middle Ages. The devout Catholic would observe the daily mass according to the liturgical calendar year in addition to his own private votive masses, such as for a special intention, or, in this case, these magical experiments. The *Ars Brevis* arose during the era of the Pre-Tridentine Mass (i.e., before 1570) in which there was no standard procedure of the Latin Mass as local traditions prevailed. Votive masses were common practice among the Catholic populace, being offered for a special intention either by the layperson or offered by the local priest. (The modern reader will note that the votive masses referenced here in the *Ars Brevis* are available in English alongside Latin in numerous publications, the most complete being the *1962 Roman Catholic Daily Missal* published by Angelus Press.)

The number of votive masses required for the consecration of the magical figure is either seven (L2 version) or ten (V2 version). For the L2 version, presumably, multiple votive masses are offered in a single day in order to be finished by the end of the fourth day of any given experiment. The L2 version of section 56 suggests that each night the *Summe Deus Pater piissime* prayer is offered, it is to be said ten, seven, or three times, depending on how many votive masses were offered that day. For the V2 version, there is only a single magical figure; therefore, its consecration can take place over the course of an entire week, as indicated by scribal interpolations in the margins of the manuscript.

The prayers are another key component to the *Ars Brevis*. The preamble prayers include *Illuma Domine* and *Ne Derelinquis Nos* (sections 4, L2.6) and *Adiutorium nostrum* (section 5), which sets the operator's intention and initiates the experiment. The *Summe Deus Pater piissime* (sections 57–L2.1) is the preamble given at night after the crucifixion rite and just before the offering of the *ars notoria* prayer, the lesser prayers, and the dream incubation using the magical figure. The L2 version provides the additional preamble, *Alpha et Omega* (section L2.2), drawn from the *Ars Notoria* (Version B).

The *ars notoria* prayers are those prayers which belong to the magical figures. Each of the four magical figures may have originally been associated with one of the *Ars Notoria* prayers, specifically those General prayers. *Phos Megalos* and its Latin prologue, *Lux mundi,* also borrowed from the *Ars Notoria,* belong to the figure of memory according to the L2 version (sections 42–43). *Phos Megalos,* which translates as the "Great Light," is a reference to the Holy Spirit. *Theos Patir* and its Latin prologue, *Te quaeso Domine,* borrowed from the *Ars Notoria,* belong to the figure (sections 6–7). The AGLA figure is divided into four quadrants containing letters which are the abbreviations of divine names; the *Ars Brevis* says the divine name of God, AGLA, is found within the figure. *Theos Pater* translates as "God the Father." In the L2 version, the *Theos Pater* prayer is conflated with another *Ars Notoria* prayer *Ancor, Anacor, Anilos* (section L2.12). The *Tau* cross figure contains in its annulus the angelic names Auctor, Anator, Theos, Danos, Eli, Achos, Phal, Gortino, Otheos, and Otheos, which seems to correspond to the prayer *Ancor, Anacor, Anilos* (*Ars Notoria,* section 29), which already has its association with Jesus Christ in the *Ars Notoria* (Version B), having in front of these angelic names "Jesus, the incomprehensible Son of God." These three magical figures and their prayers would complete the Trinity.

What is problematic about the *Ars Brevis* is that there are four magical figures presented but only three *ars notoria* prayers, leaving the figure of the secrets of Albert Magnus without an *ars notoria* prayer. The conflated *Theos Patir / Ancor, Anacor, Anilos* prayer, found at L2.12, may indicate redaction, such that *Ancor, Anacor, Anilos* once had ritual instructions accompanying its own magical figure.

There is a crucifixion rite (sections 26–34) which instructs the operator to imitate the crucifixion of Christ, in his bedroom, by placing a nail in each hand and standing up against the wall while offering prayers.

The consecration of the bedroom (sections 56–L2.1, L2.11) involves using a *lectisternium,* which was probably a plain white cloth which draped the bed or a table in preparation for the offering of prayers and votive masses. The operator is instructed to bathe, put on vestments, and to asperge the room with holy water and to suffumigate it with incense. These ritual purification practices would cleanse the physical space, making it sacred and inviting to the angel who would come to the operator in a dream.

The dream incubation rite would be set with a special intention, such as answering a difficult question, studying a book, or being able to dispute a topic among one's peers (sections 9, 11, 35, 39–41). The operator is taught to write "*Alpha et omega*" in his right hand. Then he would lie down on his right side in bed with his right hand under his ear and go to sleep. If successful, the operator would receive a dream vision of an angel who would instruct in him in the desired knowledge he sought. The next morning, the operator is instructed to give thanks to God, thereby concluding the experiment (sections 10, 36–38). Presumably, the operator could practice these four experiments successively for each figure.

THE INFLUENCE OF THE *ARS BREVIS* ON WESTERN MAGIC

The *Ars Brevis* inspired its own derivative text, the fifteenth-century *De Arte Crucifixi* attributed to the Hermit Pelagius of Majorca (d. ca. 1480). The crucifixion rite and the dream incubation of the *Ars Brevis* are the central features of the unpublished *De Arte Crucifixi*. Klaasen translates where Véronèse quotes the *De Arte Crucifixi,* in which the crucified Christ visits the operator in a dream:

> And if you proceed well in this operation and do it regularly, there will appear to you, sometimes even when not asked for, the crucified Christ, and he will speak with you, face to face, just like one friend to another, instructing you concerning the truth in many matters, from which you will be able to know the truth of every uncertain question either for you or for someone else. For through this art the past present and future, the counsels and secrets of kings, the rites of spirits, the sins of men, the status of the dead are

known. We [*sic*] will even be able to know hidden thoughts and their actions, the outcome of future things, a hidden treasure, a thief, a robber, health of a friend or enemy. Through this experiment you will easily attain the fullness of the arts, alchemy, medicine, theology, and the remaining sciences and arts, minerals, powers, virtues, the power of stones, the bindings of words, the offices and names and characters of spirits, good and bad, the properties of creatures, and other things in the world that are knowable.[2]

The *De Arte Crucifixi* survives in the following three manuscripts:

- Wolfenbüttel, Herzog August Bibliothek, Cod. Guelf. 912 Novi 4°, f. 82r–86v (badly damaged)
- London, British Library, Harley 181, f. 75r–81r, sixteenth century, Latin
- Vienna, Österreichische Nationalbibliothek, Codex Vindobonensis 11321, f. 131–38, dated to the seventeenth century, German translation

Also, some prayers from the *Ars Brevis* would be copied into the fifteenth-century prayer book of the Polish king Władysław Warneńczyk (*Modlitewnik Władysława Warneńczyka*), belonging to the Jagiellonian dynasty. The king's prayer book despoils John's *Liber Florum* and the *Ars Brevis* prayers for an entirely different magical purpose; that is, a ritual of crystallomancy (BJ 551, fols. 109v–111r). The king's prayer book borrows and adapts the following *Ars Brevis* prayers:

- *Summe Deus Pater piissime,* f. 12v, 20r–20v (*Ars Brevis,* sections 57–L2.1)
- *Lux mundi,* f. 17 (*Ars Brevis,* section 43)
- *Maria vena veniae / Per felicem conceptionem,* f. 27–28r (*Ars Brevis,* sections 22–23)
- *O regina supernorum,* f. 37 (*Ars Brevis,* section 24)
- *Deus qui ecclesiam tuam beati Iohannis,* f. 45v–46v (*Ars Brevis,* section 20)

The ritual of crystallomancy used the prayers to invoke angels to illuminate the crystal so that the practitioner might attain heavenly visions through the

2. Klaasen, *Transformations of Magic;* Véronèse, "La notion d' 'auteur-magicien,'" 119–38.

practice of scrying. The royal prayer book is the earliest evidence that links the *ars notoria* tradition to the ritual of crystallomancy.

The prayer *Ancor, Anacor, Anilos* is also used for crystallomancy in the sixteenth-century magical tome titled the *Book of Oberon,*[3] as well as John Dee and Edward Kelley's Enochian magic crystal ball scrying sessions. Considering that the *ars notoria* tradition had been associated with crystallomancy during the fifteenth and sixteenth centuries, it would then come as no surprise to find the same *Ancor, Anacor, Anilos* prayer in the seventeenth-century magical handbook called the *Lemegeton* (i.e., its first part titled *Ars Goetia*). The *Ars Goetia* is a book of ritual magic meant for the summoning of chthonic spirits and demons. The means of this conjuration was probably by some kind of scrying device, whether it was a water vessel or a crystal. Certainly, the inclusion of the *Ancor, Anacor, Anilos* prayer would support the presence of a crystal in the conjuration of goetic spirits. Furthermore, in the *Ars Goetia,* the prayer is offered as part of the consecration ritual in which the operator dons his priestly vestments. This same consecration ritual is found in the fifteenth-century magical text called the *Clavicula Salomonis* (*The Little Key of Solomon*), and also the *Heptameron,* a sixteenth-century magical treatise spuriously attributed to Peter of Abano (1250–1316).

The *Ars Brevis* is best known for its inclusion in the *Ars Notoria* found in Henry Cornelius Agrippa's *Opera Omnia* (c. 1620), volume 2 (pages 603–60). Robert Turner's English translation (1657) comes from this Latin text. What has not been well understood until now is that the Agrippan Latin text (and consequently its English translation) is a late composite of the *Ars Notoria,* the *Ars Brevis,* and a special blended material of both. The Agrippan Latin text is structured into four main parts: (1) the *Ars Notoria* (sections 1–125, albeit disorganized), (2) the special blended material of the two works, (3) the *Ars Brevis* (sections 1–11, 13–15, 26–33, 35–37, 39–41, 44–52, 56, V2.1, and 57–L2.1),[4] and (4) an addendum to the *Ars Brevis.*[5]

The manner in which the *Ars Notoria* and the *Ars Brevis* were composed

---

3. Harms, Clark, and Peterson, 2015, page 529.

4. Although the Blessed Book of John has significant omissions and the second book of divine revelation is omitted, because those prayers are already present in the first part.

5. *Ars Notoria* (Version B): NS 138, the prayer of chastity, and NS 146, the prayer of reprehension and tacticurnity; the Agrippan Latin text ends with a modified section V2.1 of the *Ars Brevis.*

are obviously distinct, and these distinctions are evident in the Agrippan Latin text. First, the *Ars Brevis* has shown a history of transmitting its contents of the Blessed Book of John in a disorganized manner while also excluding any *Ars Notoria* figures from its second book of divine revelation. These two key characteristics are followed in the Agrippan Latin text (and consequently the Turner translation). Second, the Agrippan Latin text shows dependency on the *Ars Notoria* (Version B) as evidenced by the inclusion of such prayers as *Alpha et Omega* (Version B, variation 1), *Eleminator, Caudones* (Version B, 29b), *Scio enim* (Version B, variation 8), *Conditor omnium* (Version B, variation 12), and *O sapiential Dei Patris incomprehensibilis* (Version B, variation 13). Therefore, such inclusions can safely date the Agrippan Latin text to no earlier than the mid-fourteenth century based on its inclusion of Version B material. The Agrippan Latin text also excludes distinctly Catholic elements such as the worship of the Virgin Mary, the intercession of saints, and votive masses. This is consistent with the scribe[6] of the Sloane 513 manuscript, who crosses out and omits these Catholic elements, even going so far as to say, "Wherever you see 'mass,' relinquish it, and such [Catholic] things of this manner" (section L2.13).[7] These omissions made in the Agrippan Latin text were likely made in the historical context of the Protestant Reformation that swept through Europe during the sixteenth century; thus, the Agrippan Latin text is probably dated no earlier than the sixteenth century. The Agrippan Latin text and its English translator, Robert Turner, continued to influence magical literature well into present times, even being included in editions of the *Legemeton*.

THE MANUSCRIPTS OF THE *ARS BREVIS*

The *Ars Brevis* is found in fourteen witnesses but not all are described here. Their value is unequal, indicating incompleteness, omissions, additions,

6. Probably the late owner John Shaxton.

7. Robert Turner (c. 1626–1666) also makes his own omissions of these Catholic elements, but they are quite minor compared to what was already done by the Agrippan Latin text. In addition, Robert Turner's subtitle to his English translation includes the phrase "shewing the cabalistical key," indicating a direct influence and popularity of Christian Kabbalah on magical literature during his time. The Amsterdam manuscript labeled M 242, a seventeenth-century recension in the tradition of the Agrippan Latin text, also includes Christian Kabbalistic elements and diagrams. See also Belot, *Les Oeuvres,* 28–50.

adaptations, and varied order. The full list of *Ars Brevis* manuscripts can be found in the table in appendix A1.

Because the contents of Amplonianum Collegium, Octave 79, Scot.-Vindobonensis 140 (61), and Sloane 513 are presented in the English translation below, these manuscripts do not require any further discussion. According to Véronèse, Biblioteka Jagiellonian 551 most resembles the form of the manuscript of Vienna (V2), but it has significant omissions. However, it does include some of the *Opus Operum* figures, such as those for grammar and logic. Amplonianum Collegium, Quarto 28a presents a unique opening prayer before the prologue. Véronèse comments that it follows the older versions, for the most part; however, the consecration of the figure is modified and the figure is missing. The manuscript labeled Cr.3.14 held at the Royal Observatory Library also resembles the manuscript of Vienna (=V2) but in a disorderly fashion. Sloane 3008 held at the British Library contains the *Salve virgo mater trinitatis* prayer and does not contain a figure. The sixteenth-century manuscript labeled Latin 4161 is fragmentary, having significant disorganization and omissions (haphazardly, it roughly contains sections 1–60). The treatise contains two magical figures. The first is asserted to be the figure of memory, the circle divided into four quadrants with letters for the abbreviations of angelic names. The second figure, the circle containing the Hebrew *tau* flanked by the Greek *alpha* and *omega,* is identified as the figure of intellect. Latin 4161 and Sloane 513 are significant in their representation of the confusion among scribes as to the correct identity of these magical figures. This confusion is carried forward into the seventeenth century as well.

Agrippa's *Opera Omnia* Latin text is a composite of the *Ars Notoria,* the *Ars Brevis,* and its own special material, which appears to incorporate parts of both. Likewise, the Amsterdam manuscript labeled M 242 held at the Bibliotheca Philosophica Hermetica is similar to the Agrippan Latin text but more disordered and includes other material, most notably a section on obtaining knowledge of alchemy.

The entire *Ars Brevis* tradition is plagued with the problem of correctly identifying three of its four figures, as the manuscripts contest which is which. The names of the four figures are as follows: (1) the figure of memory, (2) the figure of intellect, (3) the figure of the secrets of God, and (4) the figure of the secrets of Master Albert. Only the figure of the secrets of Master Albert is uncontested, as it is exclusively found in Sloane 513. Given this problem, I have decided to give the three contested figures descriptive titles: the AGLA figure, the tau cross figure, and the *Phos Megalos* figure.

In conclusion, the two manuscripts that provide the most content and structure to the *Ars Brevis* ritual experiments appear to be the Vienna manuscript labeled Scot.-Vindobonensis 140 (61) and the London manuscript labeled Sloane 513. Not having access to all these manuscripts, I was not able to create a proper critical Latin edition.

This English translation of the *Ars Brevis,* presented for the first time here, is based on three Latin witnesses, which have been reconstructed into a single Latin edition. Two witnesses come from Véronèse's transcription, as presented within his doctoral dissertation; they come from the two fourteenth-century manuscripts: Erfurt, Wissenschaftliche Bibliothek, Amplonianum Coll., Octavo 79, f. 63–66; and Vienna, Scot.-Vindobonensis 140 (61), f. 140–53v). I have not personally examined these manuscripts. The third witness comes from Tim Lundy's transcription, which is based on the fifteenth-century London manuscript labeled Sloane 513, f. 192–200. The Sloane 513 manuscript presents the four magical figures, special prayers, and ritual instructions not found in Véronèse's transcription; it also has an anti-Catholic scribe who made significant omissions.

After examining, comparing, and editing these things, I have collated the material, forming a single Latin edition of the *Ars Brevis.* From this single Latin edition, I have made the following English translation. Footnotes are placed throughout the English translation to note where one witness ends and another begins. I have also assigned numbered sections to the English translation for the sake of internal references and for future scholars. It is important to understand that the study of the *Ars Brevis* is in its infancy, and no standard form or critical edition has been established.

[The Blessed Book of John]

[The Prologue]

[1] A tested and true experiment with respect to understanding all the arts and secrets of the entire world and all the hidden treasures where they are able to be dug up; thus they are revealed in this notory art by a heavenly angel.[8] This art also talks about future happenings, and the senses returning, capable for composing short [treatises], with respect to all the arts with the necessity of a short time, [as] under an abridgment to the divine mystery. Also it is to be said how one must begin with regard to this work and in what time and what place.

[2] First of all, there are ten precepts to be maintained, and the one operating ought to be pure just like a priest, having made penitence and confession, just as a priest desires to cease from sinning any further, or even if a learned layperson wanted to investigate any such condition, just as it is said, [then] he may proceed, and he will fully investigate anything shown by cooperating with the divine mystery.

[3] And it is to be noted that this operation ought to have a beginning in the new Moon, because the virtue is augmented with the waxing[9] of the Moon in man and in all things generally. The work begins, having been tested [by other past operators] for every thing in the world, and it is for memory.

[The Preamble, **Illuma Domine / Ne Derelinquis Nos***]*

[4] Therefore, when you want to work in the new Moon, first when you inspect the new Moon, say this verse with bent knees, **"O Lord, illuminate your face**

---

8. Amplonianum Coll., Octavo 79, Scot.-Vindobonensis 140 (61), and Sloane 513 begin with the very first sentence and continue onward until otherwise noted. Only Amplonianum Coll., Quarto 28a, begins with the following prayer: "Your love, vehemence, permanence, having been magnified in my heart, and continually enflamed in my soul [while] in your presence, you who are the almighty God, peace, insatiable sweetness, which from eternity . . . the inextinguishable splendor, benediction, clarity, honor, praise and true glory before and beyond the ages of ages, amen." The ellipsis indicates a lacuna, or unintelligible text. Amplonianum Coll., Quarto 28a, truncates the prologue; this manuscript is no longer referenced in the remainder of this English translation.

9. Latin *augmentatio.*

upon us,[10] **and do not abandon us, O Lord our God,"**[11] and say the *Pater Noster*[12] three times.

[The Catholic Vow, Adiutorium nostrum*]*

[5] And with this [preamble prayer], which is to be devoted, you vow never to commit perjury, and that you always want to persevere in the Catholic faith, having done this at night on bent knees before your bed, say: **"Our [heavenly place of] assistance [is established above] in the name of the Lord, he who made heaven and earth,**[13] **and he lives [there as] a person,"** the Lord's prayer, and this prayer:

[The Prayer belonging to the Experiment for the Figure of Intellect]

[6] **"Theos, Patir, Behennos, God of the angels, I invoke you through your most holy angels Elypha, Massay, Gelomicros, Gedebonay, Saromana, Elomerut, and through your archangels whose names are so consecreated, such that they ought not to be uttered by us, which these are De., El., X., P., N., C., K., G., and which human senses can neither speak nor comprehend."**[14]

[7] **"I beg you, O Lord, fortify my conscience by the splendor of your light, illuminate and strengthen my understanding through the Holy Spirit; O Lord, adorn my soul in the sweet perfume, so that having heard, I understand, and having understood, I remember. O Lord, reform my heart; O God, restore my sense; O most pious one, placate my viscera; O calmest one, open my mouth; O most benevolent one, temper my tongue to the praise and glory of your name through your glorious and ineffable name O Lord, you who are the source of goodness and the origin of all piety, have patience and give me memory, true understanding,**

---

10. Psalm 67:1 (NRSV).

11. Psalm 38:21 (NRSV).

12. Matthew 6:9–13 (NRSV).

13. Psalm 124:8 (NRSV). To say that the Lord lives in the heavenly place of assistance (*adiutorium*) as a person (*personam*) is to reference the Trinitarian doctrine of "three persons, one substance."

14. *Theos Pat[e]r* from *Ars Notoria,* section 24.

and let me remember it, you who do not immediately judge the sinner, but feel compassion at the sight of repentance; I, an unworthy one, beg you to wipe away the filthiness of my evil deeds and my crimes, and by the petition of your angels and archangels whom I have mentioned may you make me worthy and efficacious through your glorious majesty, you who are the true God, amen."[15]

[8] *The other precepts follow.*

The following day fast on water and bread and give alms, or if it is the Lord's Day, then double the alms, and if you want cleanliness in heart and soul, [then] you will make an atonement. And if it is a weekday, [you are] to bathe and be clean to put on vestments.

[An Intention for the Dream Incubation Rite, Variation I]

[9] The process follows: therefore, if you want to work concerning some raised difficulty or question, on bent knees, say this prayer, [but] first be purely confessed to God, and [then] say this after confession: **"O Lord, send forth Wisdom, the [female] assistant of your seats, so that [s]he is with me and labors with me,**[16] **so that I may know what is accepted in your presence at every moment, and as the truth of this question, definition, or art is manifest to me."** Say this three times a day.

[The Praise of Thanksgiving Given the Next Morning, Variation I]

[10] And on the following day, when you rise in the morning, give thanks again to God the almighty, saying, **"The glory, the honor, and benediction to him who sits on the throne of the living, forever and ever, amen,"**[17] on bent knees and with clasped hands.

---

15. *Te queso Domine* from *Ars Notoria,* section 25 (Version A) and NS 67 (Version B).

16. Wisdom of Solomon 9:4 (NRSV). Grammatically, the Hebrew word for "wisdom" is חָכְמוֹת (*chokmoth*) and therefore is personified as a female character in the Hebrew Bible. Likewise, the Latin word *assistrix, -tricis,* is used here indicates a female assistant by its suffix *-trix*. However, a Christian interpretation of this passage may suggest that the personified Wisdom here is actually the foretold Jesus Christ. He has the epithet "Wisdom of God" in Luke 11:49 and elsewhere, which would then render this passage as asserting a masculine gender.

17. Apocalypse of John (Revelation) 5:13 (NRSV).

[An Intention for the Dream Incubation Rite, Variation 2]

[11] And if you want to have an acute notion of a book, from where [in any given text] it is treated [and] how [so] from any [kind of] knowledge, [then] this is to be done: open the book, reading within this very [book]; afterward, open to [it] three times, just as it is said, and always when you put yourself to sleep, write in the right palm, ***"Alpha et omega,"*** and you may fall asleep on the right side, the palm which is placed under the ear, and, of course, everything is to be dreamed which you desired, and you will hear a perfect voice informing you about that book or in whatever other [mental] faculty you work. And having done [this] in the morning, open the book, reading within this very [book], and you will immediately have an understanding of its [contents], as if you had been studying in this very [book] with practice for a long period of time, and always to give thanks again to the Lord, just as it is said, and also, always persist in the Catholic faith.

[12] After this work, four Masses,[18] the first of which [is the Mass] of the Holy Trinity on the first day, [which begins] "blessed, [etc.]," through the entire [mass];[19] on the second day, [the Mass] of the Holy Spirit; on the third, [the Mass] of Saint John the Evangelist, [which begins] "in the middle of the church, [etc.]" through the entire [Mass];[20] on the fourth day, [the Mass] of the Blessed Virgin in which we read the Gospel whose end is, "And Mary kept all this in her heart,"[21] and then you must add as follows, **"I, John, keep everything heard, and I remember."** In that mass you have with you a [candle]light that must burn through the entire mass, and one almsgiving [offered] on each day.

---

18. The Mass of the Roman Rite as practiced by the Catholic Church varied greatly from region to region throughout medieval Europe. It was not until the Council of Trent (held between 1545 and 1563) that it became standardized. Also, it is to be noted that the scribe of Sloane 513 strikes out the text from "*Post haec opera quattuor missas . . .*" through to the end of "*de Patre orationem hanc,*" section 12 and the beginning of section 13, and in the margin wrote, "papist," a religious slur for a Roman Catholic whose loyalties are viewed as being aligned with the papacy.

19. The antiphon for the entrance begins with "Blessed be the holy Trinity, *etc.,*" from Tobit 12:6.

20. The introit of the Feast of St. John the Apostle and Evangelist, belonging to the third day of the Octave of Christmas.

21. The Mass of the Immaculate Heart of the Blessed Virgin Mary, which is performed on the Saturday after the second Sunday after Pentecost, and its antiphon for the entrance begins with Psalm 13:6. The *Ars Brevis* identifies this mass by its Gospel reading of Luke 2:41–51 (NRSV).

[First Day, Mass of the Holy Trinity]

[13] But when the Mass of the Holy Trinity is said, and when he or the priest turns to pray in silence,[22] then say this prayer about the Father: **"O Father, craftsman of all creatures, you who founded everything through your ineffable power, excite your power, and come to me who is to be saved, protecting me from all adversity of body and soul."**

[14] And of the Son, say this prayer: **"O Son of the living God, you who are the splendor and the figure 'of light, before whom there is no transmutation nor vicissitude facing an umbration,'[23] from where [it is said in] the Word of God the Most High. You, the Wisdom of the Father,[24] open to me, your unworthy servant, *N.*, a vein of salvific wisdom, so that I may understand and know . . .[25] wisely, may I retain [it] by memory, and to narrate at length all your wondrous works; 'O Wisdom, you who are coming forth from the mouth of the Most High, reaching from end to end strongly and more sweetly, disposing all things, coming to teach me the way of prudence.'"[26]**

[15] Of the Holy Spirit: **"O God, you who gave the Holy Spirit to your disciples, and illuminates their hearts, and you who are deemed worthy to teach [them], 'grant me, your unworthy servant *N.*, the right wisdom in the Holy Spirit, and always to rejoice in its consolation';[27]**

---

22. During the era of the Pre-Tridentine Mass (i.e., before 1570), there was no uniform or standard procedure of the Latin Mass as local traditions prevailed. Thus, the timing of the priest's private prayer also varied, sometimes offered before Communion, sometimes at the Offertory, sometimes at the Secret, and sometimes at the rite's conclusion when the priest leaves the altar.

23. "figure . . . vicissitude," The Letter of James 1:17.

24. That is, Jesus Christ.

25. The ellpisis represents a placeholder for the operator to insert his desired knowledge about something.

26. "O Wisdom . . . prudence." From the "O Antiphons," a collection of seven *Magnificat* antiphons offered at vespers on the final days of Advent, contains one antiphon titled "*O Sapientia*" (O Wisdom), which is cited here. The antiphon comes from the Wisdom of Solomon 8:1. Each antiphon is an epithet for Jesus Christ and references the prophecy of Isaiah about the coming of the Messiah.

27. The quotation comes from the first prayer found within the Mass of the Holy Spirit.

O sevenfold Spirit of grace, by which the heavens were established, 'O [nourishing] Spirit, the mouth of the Lord,' who stabilized every virtue of those [heavens], 'the fountain, origin,[28] and consummation of every thing,'[29] you who are the beloved and truth of the Father, 'give me the rewards of joys, give the gift of graces, break the chains of virtue, bind fast the [bands of the] covenant of peace',[30] you who appeared in the firewood to the disciples of Christ,[31] and you [who] separated those very deific ones with the light of truth—that is, you made [them as] wise men—gently expurgate all the stains of my heart, giving me a docile disposition, a capable intellect, a firm and tenacious memory, and a clear and expedited tongue, so that, deeply rooted in your illuminations, I will know and understand all things seen and heard habitually, [and] I will commit [them] unfailingly to memory by studying, reading, and disputing, so that, in this way, I may be able to discern true from false, justice from injustice; O my God, you prefer [to be] placed before all creatures, and to [be] venerated before everyone; I am, John,[32] an unworthy servant of Christ, and I loved every beauty [and] wisdom beyond salvation, and I propose to have that clean and prosperous . . .[33] in service of the light; listen and present to me . . . in a dream through an influx of your radiant grace, and grant [me] . . . , so that everything may come together with that [dream]."

---

28. Latin idiom *fons et origo,* literally "the fountain and origin," means the source of something.

29. The quoted portion here comes from one of the many troped liturgical phrases used in the Ordinary of the mass. This one comes from the *Kyrie eleison* part of the Mass, although it is used loosely here. The Latin word *alme,* meaning "nourishing," is restored here. The same trope is found later at section L2.8.

30. The quotation "give me . . . the covenant of peace" comes from the Mass of the Holy Trinity and can also be found in the hymn *Plasmator Hominis Deus,* composed by St. Gregory the Great. The Latin quotation reads, "*da gaudiorum praemia da gratiarum munera dissolve litis vincula astringe pacis foedera,*" but the author of the *Ars Brevis* changed *litis* to *virtutis,* as he wants God to release the virtue of heaven upon him.

31. Acts 2:1–4 (NRSV).

32. In ritual magic texts, the operator's name is usually designated by the letter N, indicating that the actual practitioner ought to substitute his name for wherever he reads "*N.*" Here, the name John is a placeholder for the operator's name. This is likely because the unknown author is presenting himself as John of Morigny.

33. The ellpsis is a placeholder for the operator to insert his desired area of knowledge. The second and third ellpses which follow are for the same thing.

[Second Day, Mass of the Holy Spirit]

[16] [But when the Mass of the Holy Spirit is said, and when he or the priest turns to pray in silence,] then say: **"The grace of the Holy Spirit assists me, who makes my heart a little habitation for him, having expelled all my spiritual vices."**

[The Concluding Liturgy of the Masses]

[17] And add below [that], *Te Deum laudamus*[34] through the entire [hymn].
[18] Then say the psalm *Deus misereatur.*[35]
[19] Having said these things and completed [them] devotedly on bent knees. Also, the other precepts and these are to be said [and] observed in the Mass of the Holy Trinity and of the Holy Spirit, but those which follow are to be kept in the Mass of Saint John the Evangelist.

[Third Day, Mass of Saint John the Evangelist]

[20] The first prayer: **"O God, you who has enriched your church with the gifts[36] of blessed John the Apostle and Evangelist, and you commended wonderfully your mother at the cross, listening attentively to the same blessed John, you who opened his mouth in the midst of the church, and filled him with the spirit of wisdom and understanding,[37] the spirit of counsel and fortitude,[38] the spirit of the mouth and recognition; and you filled [him][39] with a holy hope and a spiritual glory, today I commend my**

34. The *Te Deum laudamus* is an early Christian hymn traditionally ascribed to Ambrose or Augustine, although its true authorship is unkown. The *Te Deum laudamus* is sung when the *Gloria in excelsis Deo* is said at Mass.
35. Psalm 67 (NRSV). Véronèse's Latin transcription curiously adds here: "*Hiis dictis et devote peractis flexis genibus dic, 'Posse Pater Filii, da spiritus verum.*'"
36. The royal prayer book of King Wladislas Warnenczk reads, "*dogmatibus,*" meaning "dogmas," at folio 45v.
37. The introit of the Feast of St. John the Apostle and Evangelist, belonging to the third day of the Octave of Christmas.
38. Isaiah 11:2 (NRSV).
39. The royal prayer book of King Wladislas Warnenczk reads, "*inflammasti,*" meaning "you enflamed [him]."

soul to you, and into your hands I commend my spirit,[40] **so that you may make a sign in goodness with me, so that that those who hate me may see it and be destroyed, inasmuch as you, O Lord, have helped me and consoled me;**[41] **having been abandoned, I, John, am a pauper, and you will be a helper to me, an orphan,**[42] **so that, O Lord, what you have withdrawn from me, comes into the new sign and into a speechless wonder,**[43] **by opening my mouth wisely and replenishing me with the spirit of wisdom and understanding, so that I may thrive in the sciences and virtues, and so that my soul always magnifies you, O God the creator, amen.**

[**21**] The prayer and benediction follow: **"O God, you who are Alpha and Omega, the beginning and the end of worlds, O Lord Jesus Christ, who descended from the bosom of the Father into the virginal womb of wonder-making, when you were laid bare on the earth, turned over to men, the blessed John the Apostle and Evangelist reclined upon your breast at [the Last] Supper,**[44] **and thenceforth, he drank from the streams of wisdom and salvific understanding; give me happily to fall asleep in this night and in all others following, so that the streams of salvific wisdom may be watering salubrious things**[45] **for me through the mystery of your angels, and so that my life with all my actions is managed faithfully from these things, to defend [it] and may it be defended on earth, and may the good be directed to their very own proclamations, and after the course of this life, my soul, separated from the soft flesh, may be presented to you, the universal craftsman, apart from every stain clothed about with delightful joy, and so that your glory appeared more sacred when [it was] in this place, and I will put on a glorious stole, through our Lord Jesus Christ."**

---

40. Luke 23:46 (NRSV).

41. Psalm 86:16–17 (NRSV).

42. Psalm 10:14 (NRSV).

43. Sirach 36:6 (NRSVue).

44. John 12:23 (NRSV).

45. "Salubrious things" (*salubria*) may be an indicator to the operator that he may insert his specific request to Jesus Christ.

[Fourth Day, Mass of the Blessed Mary]

[22] The precepts of the Mass of the Blessed Mary.
The first prayer: **"O Mary, the Pardon of Pardons, the Long Flowing Hair of Clemency,[46] the Queen of Virtue, the Rule of Morals, the Ordination of Those Who Conserve, the Order of Those Who Conserve,[47] O Virgin, O Mother, the Queen of Angels, I remind and exhort you through the blessed Annunciation and the continual archangelic salutation, *Ave Maria gratia*.[48]**

[23] And say [this] through the entire [prayer]: **"Through the happy conception[49] the Holy Spirit comes upon you and on behalf of the shadow [of the Most High], because you responded to it humbly, saying to the angel, 'Behold, the handmaiden of the Lord,'[50] through the entire [time]; on account of the most fortunate [and] short period of time, when you gave birth to Jesus Christ, your only-begotten Son, without intercourse with a man and without any pain, whose midwives cradling [his] life [and] the angels standing by announcing the glory of God,[51] and through the three Magi which the star led to your Son, the great king, offered gifts,[52] and through that pain which you were having when you lost your only-begotten Son in the temple,[53] and through that joy which you were having when you found [him] sitting in the midst of the doctors [of philosophy],[54] what you have done for us by the Son of God, so I and the Father, grieving, were wanting you while [Jesus] stood in judgment,[55]**

---

46. Luke 7:36–50 (NRSV).
47. That is, monks and nuns.
48. This was the traditional Catholic prayer to Mary, mother of Jesus, during the Middle Ages. The common modern version of this portion of the prayer is "Hail Mary, full of grace, the Lord is with you. Blessed are you among women, and blessed is the fruit of your womb, Jesus." Luke 1:28 (NRSV).
49. The scribe of Sloane 513 has erased and crossed out the first prayer dedicated to the Virgin Mary through this section 23.
50. Luke 1:35–38 (NRSV).
51. Luke 2:8–20 (NRSV).
52. Matthew 2:1–11 (NRSV).
53. Luke 2:41–45 (NRSV).
54. That is to say, the rabbis. Luke 2:46–51 (NRSV).
55. John 19:26–27 (NRSV). The first person perspective belongs to the disciple whom Jesus loved, who is traditionally thought to be John.

and through the most woeful accounting of the heart at the hour of your Son's Passion, through whose heart the sword of lamentation and sorrow passed; and through the joy [arising] from his resurrection and glorious ascension, hanging over you from above; and through your miraculous assumption into heaven, where you are established above all the choirs of angels, so that you may deem worthy to intercede for me, your miserable and unworthy servant, John, apart from your only-begotten Son our Lord Jesus Christ, whose faith I confess, whose service I am obligated and restrained, so that the wisdom or the very, impetus, [and] salvific river, who is the Wisdom of the Father, vivifies the city of my heart;[56] may the Lord give joy, having been made fruitful, and may the helping grace not depart from me, I, *N.*, a single and poor person, expecting his sorrowful solace; O nourishing Virgin Mary, you who begot Christ, intercede for me."

[24] The second prayer:
"O Queen of the supernals, O Virgin, Mother Mary[57] of our Lord Jesus Christ, having united my hope and consolation, I flee to you, as it were, a fortified place and house of refuge, not without hope of consolation, as much as I hope as much as in the shadow of your wings; come to me in [the heavenly place of] assistance, see the Fall, hear the groaning, stretch out [your] hand, lift the downcast, feed the hungry, give drink to the thirsty, offer consolation to the suffering, and give grace to me, John, your unworthy servant, so that I may know and understand all things heard, and may I be able to commit [them] firmly to memory, and melt hearts of those who hear desiringly, beget the salvific knowledge, so that through your intercession . . .[58] is manifested

56. Latin *civitatem cordis.* A phrase is found in the commentary on the Parable of the Prodigial Son in the thirteenth-century *Gesta Romanorum* (Deeds of the Romans), which is a Latin collection of moral stories. The *Gesta Romanorum* drew from Valerius Maximus's *Factorum ac Dictorum Memorabilium Libri IX* (Nine Books of Memorable Deeds and Sayings), the first-century collection of short stories about morality.

57. The scribe of Sloane 513 erases the Virgin Mary name and epithet, replacing it with "*O Lux mundi Salvator,*" which translates as "O light of the world, the Savior." Realizing the entire prayer is addressed to the Virgin Mary, the scribe preceded to cross out the entire second prayer.

58. The ellipsis acts as a placeholder for the operator to insert his desired knowledge from the Virgin Mary.

within me with the mercy and grace of your Son, our Lord Jesus Christ, and your name be praised in the ages of ages, amen."

[25] And note that you ought to have one wax taper for each mass, until it is smoked out completely, and you ought to give one alms at the mass.

[The Crucifixion Rite]

[26] Having finished these masses and having given alms, at night, when you enter the bedroom chamber you must prostrate yourself before your bed for a long pardon, saying the psalm *Miserere mei, Deus*[59] and the psalm *In te, Domine, speravi,*[60] just as it is said at compline.

[27] Having said these, raise yourself up, and go to the wall of the house, spreading out your hands in the manner of a cross, or having nails[61] against the wall, which you hold in [your] hands, having said this prayer, which follows [below], with total devotion of the mind, *Deus qui [pro nobis miseris peccatoribus crucis patibulum et mortis], etc.*

[28] "O God, you who wanted for us miserable sinners to undergo the punishment of the cross and death, to whom Abraham even immolated his own son Isaac, today I, *N.*, your unworthy servant, alas, a sinner and punished through many evils, immolate and sacrifice my soul and my heart, so that you may infuse and inspire me with the salvific wisdom, you who you infused the spirit of prophecy into your prophets."

---

59. Psalm 51 (NRSV).

60. Psalm 31 (NRSV).

61. Latin *claves,* according to Amplonianum Coll., Octavo 79, and Scot.-Vindobonensis 140 (61); *clavicles fixos,* according to Sloane 513. *Claves* means "keys" and *clavicles fixos* literally means "fitted little keys," suggesting that these are not door keys but small fittings, like nails. The Latin text found in Agrippa's *Opera Omnia* (page 654) has "*duas clavos fixos*" (two fixed keys), and Robert Turner (1657) translates this as "two nayles fixed" in reference to the nails which pierced the hands of Jesus Christ on the cross. Because the operator is performing the ritual action of imitating the crucifixion of Jesus in his bedroom against the wall, then it is sensible to conclude that these are nails. This ritual action recalls those Christian mystics, such as Francis of Assisi, who identified so strongly with Christ that they received the stigmata, the bodily wounds which appear on their bodies and correspond to those same wounds received by Jesus at his crucifixion.

[29] After this say the psalm *Verba mea.*[62]

[30] And add: **"O Lord, he [who] rules me and no one will want me, may he gather me, his unworthy servant, *N.*, [as a shepherd to a sheep] there in the place of pasture; he [who] led me out to the waters of refreshment, he [who] converted my soul, in order to lead me out [to] . . .[63] over the paths of righteousness on account of his holy name;[64] may the evening prayer ascend to you, O Lord, and may your mercy descend upon me, your unworthy servant John, and protect, save, bless, and sanctify me through the little seal of the holy cross; avert the diseases of the body and soul. O Lord, sanctify me by the little seal of the holy cross, so that it may become a little obstacle against his[65] javelins of all my enemies; defend me, O Lord, through the holy wood [of the true Cross] and through the price of your righteous blood."**

[31] Also of the same prayer: **"O God, whose wisdom stabilized the heavens, made firm the earth, and gathered the sea in her own territory, and who created all creatures through simple emanation, and formed man out of this earth in his own image and likeness, he who gave Solomon, the son of King David, an inestimable wisdom, he [who] distributed the knowledge of prophecy to the prophets, he [who] insufflated the miraculous knowledge of prophecy to the prophets, he [who] bestowed fortitude to the apostles, he [who] gave courage to the martyrs, he strengthened the confessors to sanctimony, he [who] conserved the virgins with the flower of virginity, he who exalted and provided his elect from [the beginning of] eternity, and chose many over me, your unworthy servant, John; O Lord God, by giving your mercy to me, a teachable disposition, and understanding, adorned with virtues and sciences, a firm memory and an integral retention, so that whatever [mental] faculties I desire to obtain, I will acquire through your mercy and pursue the domain of influence,**

---

62. Psalm 5 (NRSV).

63. The ellipsis acts as a placeholder for the operator to insert his desired knowledge of something.

64. An adapted Psalm 23:1–3 (NRSV).

65. Satan's.

and may I be able to ineffably please the subservience of your Highness's name."

[32] It follows: **"O Lord, illuminate your face upon me;[66] O my God, hoping in you,[67] come to teach me your virtues,[68] and show your face, and I will be saved."[69]**

[33] And add below the psalm *Ad te, Domine, levavi animam meam, Deus,*[70] excepting this verse, *Confundantur.*[71]

[34] Then add below: **"O Savior, save me, your unworthy servant John, holy birth mother of God, ever Virgin Mary, pray for me, I suppliantly ask you by the prayers of the holy apostles, martyrs, confessors, and holy virgins, so that I may be delivered from all ignorance; may I be deserving to enjoy thoroughly all understanding and memory, now and always, amen."** [Then add] the *Pater noster.*

[The Dream Incubation Rite]

[35] Then it follows, having completed these things at the wall, kneel down in front of the bed, writing on the right palm "*Alpha et Omega.*" Then you may lie yourself down to sleep and you must sleep on your right side, holding the palm under [your] right ear, and you will see the magnificence of God the Most High as you wished.

[The Praise of Thanksgiving Given the Next Morning, Variation 2]

[36] And in the morning, having knelt on your knees in front of the bed, give thanks again to God for these things which he has revealed to you, and you must say this prayer: **"I give thanks to you, O great and won-**

66. Psalm 67:1 (NRSV).
67. Psalm 17:7 (NRSV).
68. Adapted portion of the antiphon *O Sapientia.*
69. Psalm 80:7 (NRSV).
70. Psalm 25 (NRSV).
71. Psalm 25:4 (NRSV).

derful God, who gave salvation and the prosperity of the sciences to me, your unworthy servant *N.*, and strengthen this . . .[72] in every circumstance; you are working at the table, anointing [me with oil], preserving [me]."[73]

[37] Also, another follows from the same: **"I give thanks to you, O immeasurable God, you who has mercy on me, a sinner, when I was not [even] existing near the heavens, you revealed to me . . . ,[74] and when I was ignoring doctrine and wisdom, you informed me with salvific wisdom; I beseech you, grant to your unworthy servant John, O Lord Jesus Christ, so that through this knowledge I may be deserving to be discovered always steadfast in your holy service, amen."**

[38] Then it follows with the completion to the total operation and having finished with devotion every day following, give thanks again to God, having said these prayers last.

[An Intention for the Dream Incubation Rite,
Variation 3]

[39] And when you want to read, whether to study or to dispute, say: **"O Lord, remember your word to your servant in which you gave me hope, this has comforted me in my humanity."**[75]

[40] And add below these prayers: **"O Lord, ruling every dominion, put the right and well-sounding words into my mouth,[76] so that I may inform and instruct others efficaciously to the praise, glory, and honor of your highest [and] glorious name, you who are the Alpha and Omega, blessed in the ages of ages."**

---

72. The ellipsis acts as a placeholder for the operator to insert his desired mental faculty and knowledge of something.

73. Psalm 23:5 (NRSV).

74. The ellipsis acts as a placeholder for the operator to insert his desired knowledge of something.

75. Psalm 119:49–50, Zayin (NRSV).

76. Esther 14:12–13 (NRSV with Apocrypha).

[41] Say under a period of silence: **"Having replenished me 'in new signs and immutable wonders'[77] of the spirit of wisdom, understanding, and eloquence, and 'make my mouth as a sharp sword and my tongue as a chosen arrow,'[78] and strengthen [the words of my mouth] with respect to every wisdom, beget . . . ,[79] melting the hearts of those who hear."**

[The Prayer for the AGLA Figure]

[42] Prayer: **"Yos, Megale, Patyr, Ymmos, Obedel, Ober, Eleod, Geseyes, Ozel, Lecor, Grannal, Zemellam, Lamazar, Gelsamanar, Arasa, Iuson, Sale, Patir, Agiona, Athanos, amin."**[80]

[43] The Latin prayer follows: **"O Light of the world, O immeasurable God, O Father of eternity, the bestower of wisdom, ineffable knowledge, and all spiritual grace; O inestimable Father, dispenser of all things before they happen, knowing [and] making the light from the darkness,[81] 'send forth your hand and touch my mouth,'[82] and 'make that as a sharp sword' for the purpose of explaining your words eloquently; O Lord, 'make my tongue as a chosen arrow'[83] for the purpose of pronouncing wonderful things from memory; O Lord, send forth your Holy Spirit into my heart for the purpose of perceiving and retaining within my soul and to meditate within my conscience, by the oath of your covenant, and by your holy right hand; O pious and holy one, mercifully and piously inspire, teach, instruct, and illuminate the coming in and going out of my senses and my thinking, and teach and correct me, up to the end in your discipline, and let your highest counsel help me through your infinite mercy."**[84]

---

77. Sirach 36:6 (NRSVue).

78. Isaiah 42:9 (NRSV).

79. The ellipsis acts as a placeholder for the operator to insert his desired knowledge of something.

80. The *Phos Megalos* prayer of the *Ars Notoria,* section 10. Sloane 513 presents these *voces magicae* in the margin and indicates that these are the names which encircle the figure of memory.

81. Genesis 1:2–5 (NRSV).

82. Compare the wording to Jeremiah 1:9 (NRSV).

83. Isaiah 42:9 (NRSV).

84. *Te queso Domine,* the Latin prologue prayer of *Ars Notoria,* section 11.

[44] What follows concerns the manner for consecrating the figure which is for memory, and it ought to be consecrated in seven masses by the highest hope, faith, and charity.[85]

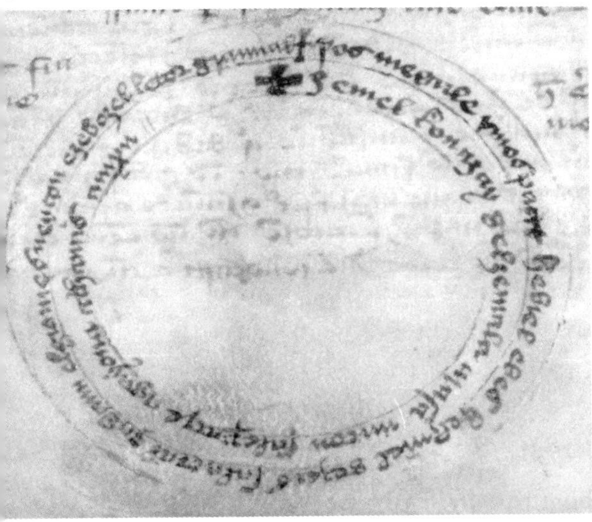

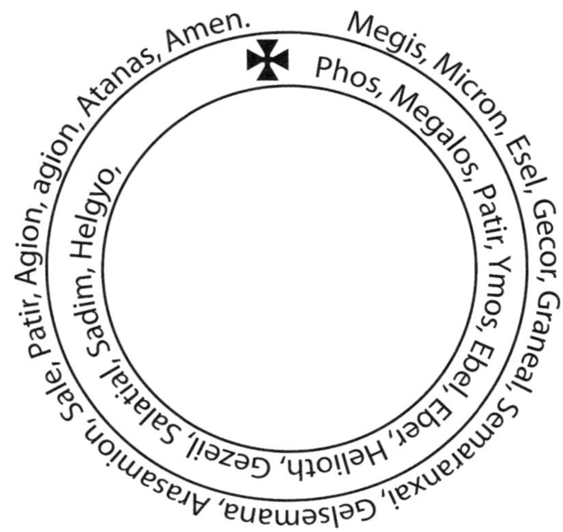

According to the fifteenth-century manuscript Sloane 513, f. 195v, this is the AGLA figure (*left*), which contains the *Phos Megalos* prayer within two concentric circles and an empty center. According to the fourteenth-century manuscripts of Amplonianum Coll., Octave 79, and Scot.-Vindobonensis 140 (61), this is not the AGLA figure. For these two manuscripts, the figure of memory is Figure S4. The figure on the *right* is a modern reconstruction correcting *Yos Megale* to *Phos Megalos* and using the divine names found in *Ars Brevis,* section 42.

85. Here the Erfurt manuscript reads, "He who has the book of blessed John ends; he must proceed accordingly what is taught in it at night. Here begins another book that also teaches about the divine revelation." The book that teaches about the divine revelation refers to those prayers borrowed from the *Ars Notoria*. See the bracketed paragraph at the end of the English translation. Also, Sloane 513, f. 196v, presents an alternative reading of section 44: "This is the figure of intellect and it ought to be consecrated in seven masses, whether in ten or thirteen, with the highest veneration and contrition of the heart with confession, penitence, good works, [and] a devotion with faith, hope, charity, and chastity." After this passage variant, which actually appears to align more closely with section 54, Sloane 513 immediately follows up with section 55 and so on.

[The Consecration of the Figure][86]

[45] And when [the figure] has been consecrated for the purpose of the operation, keep [it] safe and use it in the operation thus. On the first day of the new Moon, having inspected the new Moon, place it under [your] right ear, and it is to be continued on the other nights, and you must inspect it every day.

[46] First, in the early morning hour, the psalm *Qui habitat*[87] is to be said through the entire [psalm], and [then] the Lord's Prayer once, that is *Pater noster,* and [then] the prayer *Theos, Patir,* also once with its litany.[88]

[47] In the first hour of the day, say the psalm *Confitebor,*[89] which is to be read at the evening hour [i.e., vespers], and [then] the Lord's Prayer twice, and [then] the prayer *Theos, Patir* also with its litany twice.

[48] In the third hour, say the psalm *Benedic anima mea Domino,*[90] which you read alone about angels on the Sabbath in the early morning, and [then] the Lord's Prayer thrice, and [then] *Theo, Patyr* with its litany as many times.

[49] In the sixth hour, say the psalm: **"May my deprecation arrive in your presence, O Lord, give me an understanding close to your eloquence;**[91] **may [my] petition enter into your presence, O Lord, give me a memory according to your eloquence; hear my voice according to your mercy, and give me an eloquence according to your judgment, and my lips will utter a hymn when you teach me your justifications and sciences,"** [then say] *Gloria Patri, etc.,*[92] and [then say] the Lord's Prayer nine times, and [then say] *Theos, Patir* [with its litany] as many times.

---

86. From sections 45–53, the two manuscripts which agree here are Vienna, Scot.-Vindobonensis 140 (61), f. 144v–146r; and London, Sloane 513, f. 196r–197r.

87. Psalm 91 (NRSV).

88. Presumably, the litany is the Latin prologue prayer *Te queso Domine* (section 7), borrowed from the *Ars Notoria,* section 25.

89. Psalm 138 (NRSV), followed by a description of when this psalm is typically read in the liturgy; that is, at vespers.

90. Psalm 103 (NRSV), followed by a description of when this psalm is typically read in the liturgy; namely, on Saturday.

91. Psalm 119:169–70 (NRSV).

92. The Minor Doxology.

[50] In the ninth hour, say the psalm *Beati immaculati,*[93] and the Lord's Prayer twelve times, and *Theos Patir* [with its litany] as many times.

[51] In the evening hour, say the psalm *Deus, misereatur nostri,*[94] and the Lord's Prayer fifteen times, and *Theos Patir* [with its litany] as many times.

[52] In the compline hour, say the psalm *Deus Deus meus,*[95] and *Deus in adiutorium meum intende,*[96] and *Te, Deus, laudamus,* and the Lord's Prayer once, *Theos, Patir* once, the other prayer *etc.* once, by prostrating: **"O God, who has made all things by number, weight, and measure,**[97] **from whose number, not even the hair of a man's head falls and escapes, in whose order of points, moments, hours, days, and nights opening [and] having opened the division; likewise, you alone who counts the stars, bestow a constant [and] efficacy to my mind, so that I, *N.*, may love you in this art, that is to say, the cognition [of] . . . ,**[98] **so that I may acknowledge the gift of your piety, amen."**[99]

[53] These are the masses by which the figure of memory is to be consecrated. On Sunday, the first to be said [is the Mass] of the Holy Trinity, having placed the figure under the body;[100] Monday, [the Mass] of the Holy Cross; Tuesday, [the Mass] of the Holy Spirit; Wednesday, [the Mass] of the Blessed Virgin Mary; Thursday, [the Mass] of the Apostles; Friday, [the Mass] of the Angels; Saturday, [the Mass] of All the Saints.

[54] But when it was consecrated, it is to be kept clean in the *sindon,*[101] or another clean dry cloth, and [the consecration ritual] is ended in this [way].

---

93. Psalm 119:1–8, Aleph (NRSV).
94. Psalm 67 (NRSV).
95. Psalm 22 (NRSV).
96. Psalm 70 (NRSV).
97. *Deus qui omnia numero,* an *Ars Notoria* prayer, section 144.
98. The ellipsis acts as a placeholder for the operator to insert his desired knowledge of something.
99. *Ars Notoria,* section 144 and NS 74.
100. That is, under the sacramental bread.
101. The cloth placed under the Eucharist.

This figure ought to be consecrated in ten masses, whether in seven or in three, with the highest veneration and contrition of the heart, confession, penitence, devotion to good works, faith, hope, charity, and chastity.[102]

[55] There are three principal masses, namely, of the Holy Trinity, of the Holy Cross, and of the Holy Spirit. After these are [the Mass] of the Lady, and the others from whichever holy [masses].[103]

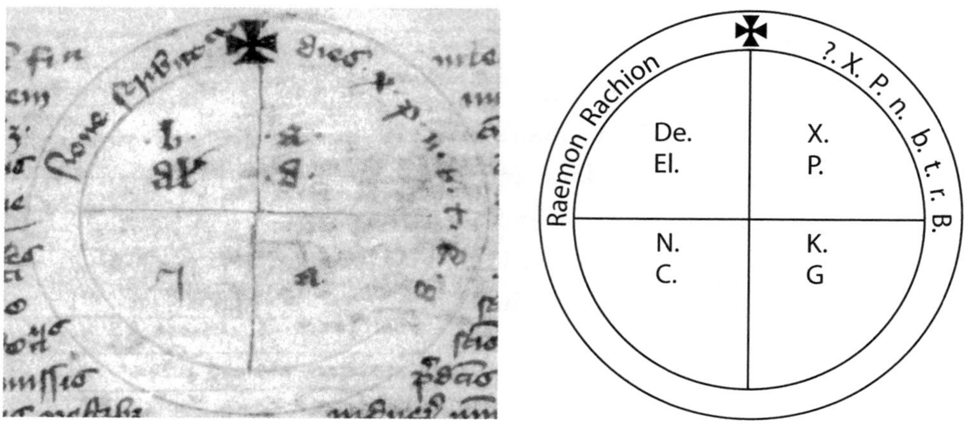

Left: The AGLA figure is accompanied by its notory art prayer, *Theos Pater,* as found in Sloane 513, f. 196v. The AGLA figure is first identified as the figure of intellect, although there is also a later passage which describes this same figure, naming it the figure of memory (Section L2.3). This descriptive passage is crossed-out, presumably by the anti-Catholic scribe, John Shaxton. The figure consists of a circle divided into four quadrants, a Greek monogrammatic cross at the top, and the abbreviated angelic names from *Ars Brevis,* section 6. The figure is described as a circle containing the divine name, AGLA, and the abbreviated angelic names in section L2.3. *Right:* A modern reconstruction of the AGLA figure, which is informed by the list of abbreviated divine names not only from the *Ars Brevis,* but also the *Ars Notoria, Liber Iuratus,* and *Melechet Muscelet.* This reconstruction does not attempt to imitate the original exactly as its imperfections contradict these outside sources and its own clear description that the divine name AGLA is to appear there (*Ars Brevis,* L2.3). Although there is a hidden vestige of the name AGLA, considering the backwards Greek *gamma* in the left lower quadrant, the Hebrew divine name El signaling

102. This passage comes from the Vienna manuscript. Recall the Sloane 513 variant passage that essentially equates to this section. See page 708, footnote 90.

103. This passage comes from the Vienna manuscript. The Sloane 513 variant of this passage reads, "But there are three masses above the principal ones, [that is, the masses] of the Holy Trinity, of the Holy Cross, and of the Holy Spirit; the others can be whichever ones you want."

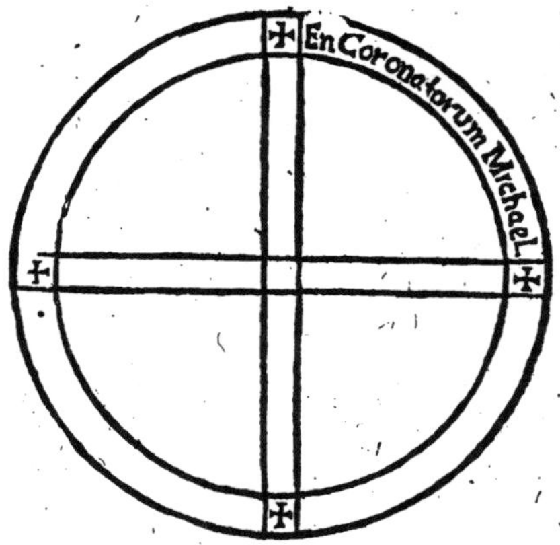

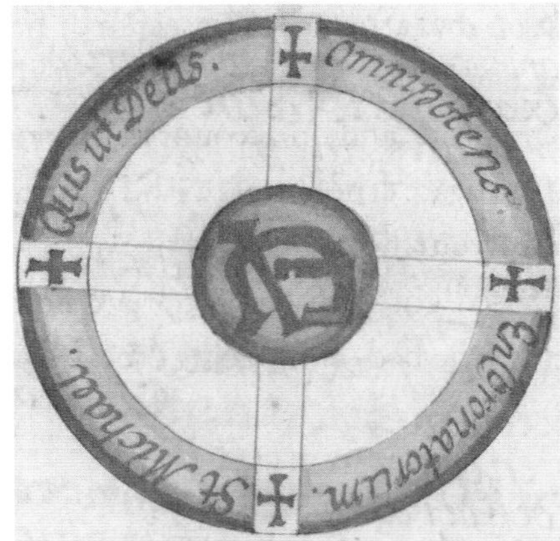

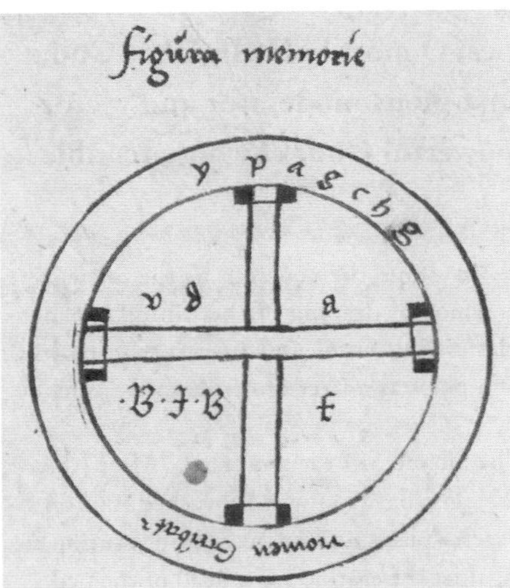

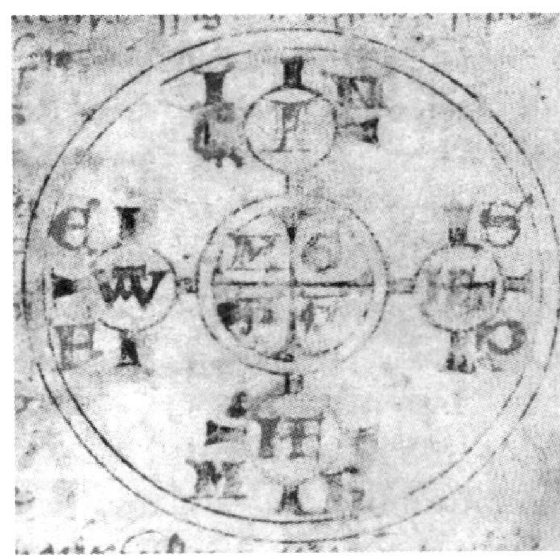

(*cont'd.*) the sound of the Roman letter *l*, and two *a*'s in the other quadrants. (*Liber Florum*, Old Compilation, Book of Figures, III.19, see Fanger and Watson, 382–84). John of Morigny presents the Virgin Mary as the bearer of the gifts of the Holy Spirit and associates intellect with prudence, memory with moral continence, eloquence with justice, and perseverance with fortitude. The next figure comes from BNF Latin 4161, f. 62v, which presents the figure of intellect, but in this manuscript it is identified as the figure of memory. The next figure comes from Agrippa's *Opera Omnia*, p. 657, which omits the letters and adds Greek crosses at the cardinal points and reads, "Michael is crowned" (*Est coronatorum Michael*) in the annulus (notice that Michael is substituted for Mary); it is labeled as the figure of memory. The third figure comes from the seventeenth-century *Tractatus Artis Notoriae* (Amsterdam, BPH, M 242, f. 32), which presents the full inscription along the annulus, reading, "Michael, who like God Almighty, is crowned" (*Quis ut Deus omnipotens, est coronatorum Michael*), and at its center the Hebrew letter *mem* (מ) (*m* stands for Michael). This figure is also identified as the figure of memory.

[56] Now, after it is consecrated, having been said in the masses, then on the last day bathe and put on clean vestments and use a clean *lectisternium*[104] in a secret place, and on account of caution, asperge the place with blessed water. And suffumigate [the place] with frankincense, and place a crucifix on the east side above your head. After it is well arranged, when you come at night with the incense light, at the appropriate hour, [with] no one seeing you, on bent knees before the bed, and [facing] toward the crucifix, say the following prayer:[105]

[The Fourth Night, *Summe Deus Pater Piissime*][106]

[57] O highest God, O most pious Father,[107] O sweetest Jesus Christ, O most gentle Holy Spirit, O sanctifier of the holy ones, O most holy almighty God, O most glorious creator and dispenser, O most pious moderator and rector of all visible and invisible creatures, O most powerful God, of whose terrible

104. Latin *lectisternium,* (etymology: *lectum* + *sternere,* "to drape the couch"), in the ancient Roman sense of the word, meant a cloth used for the ceremonial draping of the dining couch in which a ritual feast is offered to the gods. In the ecclesiastical sense, a *lectisternium* (plural: *lectisternia*) is a clean cloth for the ceremonial draping of a place as an act of consecration, such as the dedication of a chapel.

105. This passage comes from the Vienna manuscript. The Sloane 513 variant reads, "After [the figure] is consecrated in these aforesaid masses, then on the last day, you will be washed, put on clean vestments, which you must use a *lectisternia* at the secret place, and on account of caution, asperge the place with blessed water, and place a crucifix against the east over the head of the bed. After it is placed and well ordered, he must come at night, when having dismissed the hour with the light, no one ought [to be able] to see you coming, and before the bed and kneeling on [your] knees before the crucifix say this prayer: *Summe Deus Pater piissime, etc.,* ten [times], whether seven or three times, according to which masses proceded [it] with the highest devotion, and after the prayer, add below [it] the Lord's prayer thrice, afterward you must inspect the figure with reverence, and then place [it] with the crucifix around [your] own head, and sleep in the place, clothed in clean linen vestaments, invocating divine help, not doubting whatever you asked for you will obtain. This has been tested by many of those who were granted the secrets." Compare these passages also to L2.11 and V2.1.

106. In following the fourfold arrangement of the entire ritual established in the beginning of the treatise, the *Summe Deus Pater piissime* ought to be prayed on the fourth and final night. However, the Vienna manuscript suggests following an entire week, following the consecration of the figure in which a mass is given for each day of the week in section 53. Thus, in its margin it declares that the prayer ought to be read on the fifth day. Also, keep in mind that Sloane 513 has four magical figures, correlating to the established four days (sections 1–25), whereas the Vienna manuscript only has one magical figure.

107. *Summe Deus Pater piissime,* the preamble of *Opus Operum,* C.

and ineffable majesty, almighty exceedingly feared; the heavens, the earth, the sea and the infernal realms and everything, which contains the triple world machine is to be admired and venerated, they tremble and obey.

[58] O invisible God Sabaoth, O strongest and insuperable God, great and immeasurable, whom not any sense can capture, O loveable one above all, O venerable and enerrable or admirable instructor, O invisible teacher of erudition [and] the best masters, O most wise doctor of doctors, the most gentle instructor of simple people, lover of the most benevolent [and] humble people, O God of the sciences, O God and Lord of wisdom, in whom are all the treasures of wisdom and good sciences, who alone wants to teach humankind the wisdom and knowledge of all things [what] you know and are able to do so if you want without labor and without delay, you who are the principal vigilant watcher of the past and future, and assiduous investigator of all hearts through whom we are, live, and die, who sits above the Cherubim looking upon the abyss;[108] you dispose, discern, rule, and direct the universe.

[59] I confess today in the presence of the very holy and tremendous one, the ineffably glorious one with majesty, and in the presence of all the celestial Virtues and Powers, may I make stronger with the glorious one with majesty, praising and blessing you. O Lord and my God, invoking your great name above me because it is above every name; therefore, I deprecate you, O almighty Lord of the highest, who is the adored, honored, and revered God, Adonay, and the admirable dispenser of all beatitudes, [spiritual] heights, and dignities [and] the most generous dispensor of all the best gifts [to whomever you want],[109] so that you would graciously, abundantly, and permanently deem it worthy to pour over me today the multiple gifts of the grace of the Holy Spirit.

[60] And you, the most clement Lord himself, you who deemed worthy to create Adam, the first man, in your image and likeness, having been deemed worthy to enter and to strengthen the temple of my heart, and you want to

108. Book of Daniel, Prayer of Azariah and Song of the Three Holy Children 3:54 (NRSVCE).
109. The bracketed phrase is found in *Opus Operum,* C, but absent from Sloane 513, f. 197r.

lodge . . .[110] into my heart today, descending from the most splendid temple of the most lucid heavens of grace and your omnipotence of ineffable majesty, according to what is worked wonderfully into your saints and faithful ones. O gentlest, most benevolent, eternal, [and] glorious king, send out to me . . . today, (the intelligence)[111] from the admirable and most holy and glorious seat of your majesty's dominion, as you are presenting [it], you alone who makes great miracles for us in this very knowing and subtle art, may I may be made effective interpreting . . . , so that through it, having received [it] with eloquence, memory, and subtlety [and] through the merits of the saints and the intercession of the heavenly Virtues, I may honor you in my knowledge.[112]

[L2.1][113] And now you,[114] the most merciful Lord himself, who once blew 'the little breath of life' into the making of the first man, may you deem it worthy to infuse a full, subtle, persistent, swift, and perfect unfailing memory in all things, a vivacious, tenacious, and efficacious eloquence, [and] a mellifluous, ignited, [and] such an expedited and superfluous tongue within my heart today, so that from the multitude of your benedictions and from the most abundant generosity of your many gifts and your graces copiously spoken; I will despise all things which are to be held in contempt; and you, the only God of all, you who are the true, highest, and ineffable good of every thing, I will ardently love, bless, praise, and glorify, and exalt above all things, the king of kings and the lord of lords in every time and may there always be a praise to [your] magnificent [and] tremendous omnipotence in my mouth at any time, and may the most sweetest

---

110. The ellipsis acts as a placeholder for the operator to insert his desired knowledge of something. A second ellipsis follows for the same thing.

111. The word "intelligence" (*intelligentiam*) acts as a placeholder for the operator to insert his specific desired knowledge. A second ellipsis follows for the same thing. This special request for "intelligence" is found only in the Vienna manuscript labeled Scot.-Vindobonensis 140 (61), f. 145v–146r. The *Opus Operum,* C, presents a request for the sevenfold grace of the Holy Spirit; and Sloane 513, f. 197r, follows this very same request.

112. Erfurt, Amplonianum Coll., Octavo 79, ends, reading, "The book ends without a title," and presents the extended version of this prayer. The Vienna manuscript labeled Scot.-Vindobonensis 140 (61) stops here, but then returns at V2.1 below.

113. L2 section numbering indicates passages that are found in the Sloane 513 manuscript.

114. Sloane 513, f. 197r–v continues the *Summe Deus Pater piissime* prayer just as it appears in *Opus Operum,* C.

ardor of the most maddening, sweetest, and beatific love of you vehemently and permanently enflame endlessly within my heart and within my soul and in eternity in the presence of you, you who are the almighty God of all things, the highest peace, the true wisdom, the insatiable sweetness, the inestimable pleasantness, the ineffable joy, the blessed satiety and glorious end of all good things and beatific desires, for whom he was, is, and always will be from eternity, the invincible virtue, the impassible salvation, the inextinguishable splendor, the benediction and clarity, the honor, the praise and venerable glory, before and beyond all the times of the ages."

[L2.2] + "Alpha and Omega,[115] O almighty God, the beginning of all things without a beginning, the ending without an end, hear today my prayers; O most pious one, neither repay me according to my iniquity nor according to my sins, O Lord my God, but according to your mercy, which is greater than all visible and invisible things. Have mercy on me, O Wisdom of the Father of Christ, the light of the angels, the glory of the holy ones, the hope, the harbor, and the refuge of sinners, the originator of all things and redeemer of human frailties, who holds the weight of heaven and earth, the seas and mountains in the palm of your hand. O most pious one, I deprecate and entreat you, [being] one with the Father, may you illuminate my soul with the ray of light of your most Holy Spirit, may I be able to progress far in this most sacred art, so that I may prevail with respect to the renown of such knowledge and any of all the arts and wisdom with virtue to come before your most Holy Spirit and your name."

[The Magical Figures]

[L2.3a] Note that the entire following figure ought to be about memory,[116] **[L2.3b]** and that figure is that [there] with the extracted series [of letters in the annulus] with a staurogram over, "AGLA, *a, c, r,* [etc.]" which are in the middle. Note that this figure ought to be round and well plain.

115. The first portion of the *Alpha et Omega* prayer taken from the *Ars Notoria* (Variation 1, Version B). The *Alpha et Omega* prayer is just another preamble prayer offered before the central *ars notoria* prayer and its magical figure.

116. Sloane 513 has crossed out this passage.

[L2.4] Also, this figure [is] from the secrets of Master Albert, the powerful ecclesiastical council to the many strong faithful ones of Christ; [it is] a fortunate figure.[117]

[L2.5] The figure ought to be consecrated in nine, seven, or three masses, with the highest devotion and contrition of the heart with confession [and] penitence, devoted to good works with faith [and] hope, and charity and chastity.[118]

[The Preamble, **Ne Derelinquis Nos***]*

[L2.6] Afterward, say, having directed [your] attention to the [heavenly place of] assistance: **"O Lord, God, my salvation and may you not abandon me in my help; O Lord, my God and my salvation, may you not abandon me; O Lord my God do not depart from me."**[119]

[L2.7] "O Wisdom, you who goes forth, out of the mouth of the Most High, reaching from end to end stronger, sweeter, and disposing all things, coming for the purpose of teaching all things to me, *N.*, the Christian way of wisdom,[120] may I love you, O Lord, my fortitude, the Lord, my firmament, my refuge, my liberator and my protector, my horn of salvation and my guardian,[121] and I am a worm and not a man,[122] a disgrace of a man and abjected among the common people. See and look upon me, and have mercy on me. Give the empire to your boy and salvation to me; make [your] Son, your servant. O Lord, make a sign in goodness with me, and they who hate me may see it and they are to be destroyed inasmuch as you, O Lord, have helped me and consoled me."[123]

---

117. The figure of the secrets of Master Albert [Magnus], the Bishop of Regensburg; see the figure on pages 718–19.

118. For Sloane 513, sections 55–56 immediately follow here.

119. Psalm 38:21–22 (NRSV). This is the latter part of the preamble found in section 4.

120. *Sapientia,* one of the seven Great Antiphons, based on Wisdom of Solomon 8:1 (NRSV).

121. Psalm 18:1–2 (NRSV). *Firmamentum,* is the firmament or sky, but it is also understood as "that which upholds or supports, a prop, mainstay" as the sky was once thought to be supported by pillars which sheltered the home of humankind; the Latin word is usually translated as "rock."

122. Psalm 22:6 (NRSV).

123. Psalm 86:16–17 (NRSV).

[L2.8] And on bent knees, say this prayer: **"O nourishing spirit,[124] the mouth of the Lord, the fountain, origin, and consummation of every goodness,[125] gently extinguish the sordidness of my mind, give me a teachable ingenuity, a capable intelligence, a firm memory, and may I grasp an affluent and truthful eloquence, so that I will impetrate to understand a portion [of] . . .[126] through the affluence of your grace from the beginning, the ineffable and inenarrable appearance of the Holy Spirit of the Trinity assisting to the memory of all arts through those of your majesty. O Lord, the producer of every essence, the conservator and rector who liberated Susanna from having been accused of a false crime, Daniel from a lion pit, Abraham from the men of Chaldea, Jacob from the hand of his own brother Esau, David from the hand of Saul, Joseph from the hand of his own brother;[127] renew the figure,[128] having been fortified wonderfully, and may you make wonders with your mercies with me, you who makes [them] salvific; hoping in you, O Lord, show me the rector of the arts, and the most expedite disputator, the highest objector, the debater,[129] the most prompt inspirer, the most discrete dissolutor, the temperate informer,[130] thus having accepted and . . .[131] but on account of the praise and glory of your holy name, so that they fear you, they who see me [and] may they be gladdened, since you, O Lord, you have helped me and consoled me; remember me, O Lord, ruling every dominion, put the right and well-sounding words into my mouth, so that my words are pleasing to those seeing and hearing in my**

---

124. The Latin word *spiritus* is the same word for both "wind" and "spirit." Thus, it makes sense that the wind can blow out and extinguish a flame, in this case, the metaphorical flame of sordidness.

125. One of the many troped liturgical chants found in the ordinary; that is, the liturgical part of the Mass, which is always constant. This one comes from the *Kyrie eleison* part of the Mass.

126. The ellipsis acts as a placeholder for the operator to insert his desire to understanding something.

127. The motif of invoking those biblical figures whom the Lord helped is also found in section V2.6. A parallel passage is also found in Peterson, *Sworn Book of Honorius,* 181–83.

128. That is, the magical figure, presumably the figure of the secrets of Master Albert [Magnus], the Bishop of Regensburg.

129. Latin *argumentator,* the one who argues by reason.

130. These are the roles played by those engaged in a formal Scholastic disputation at a university.

131. The Latin text is unintelligible at the ellipsis.

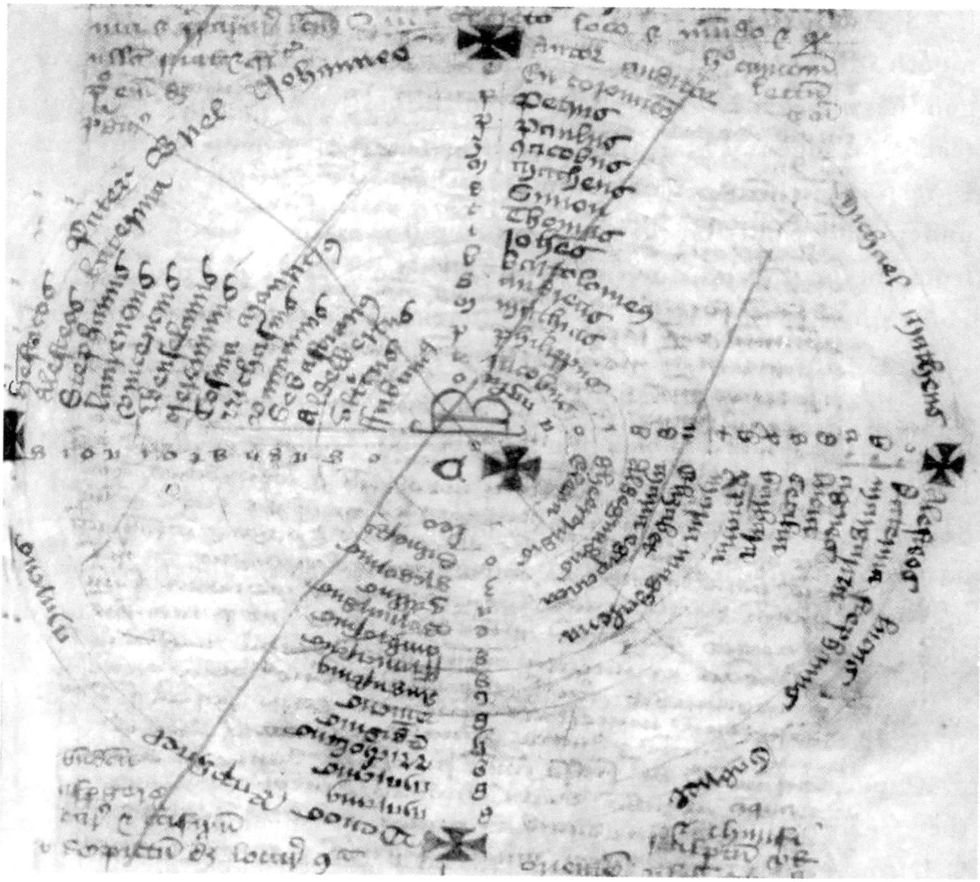

Left: The figure of the secrets of Master Albert [Magnus], the Bishop of Regensburg, according to Sloane 513, f. 198r. *Right:* A reconstruction of the figure. The Sloane 513 folio reveals that the scribe has crossed out the figure. The figure is a circle divided into four quadrants, each containing a list of names, including Christ's disciples, saints, and church fathers. The names of the four evangelists, the four living creatures from Ezekiel's vision, and the four biblical archangels encircle these other names. In each quadrant, the name of the evangelist is associated with one of the four living creatures. In the quadrant belonging to John, there it ought to read "eagle" (Greek αετός), the quadrant belonging to Luke ought to read "ox" (Greek βόδι), the quadrant belonging to Mark ought to read "lion" (Greek λέων) and the quadrant belonging to Matthew ought to read "of man" (Greek ἄνδρός). The illustrator had a poor understanding of Greek, and this deficiency shows in his mistransliteration into Latin. The illustrator also expresses doubt in the arrangment of the male and female names of the saints, whether they ought to be under Luke or John (observe the marginal placement of the names Catherine and Stephen). Under the eagle, John the Evangelist, and the archangel Uriel, are the

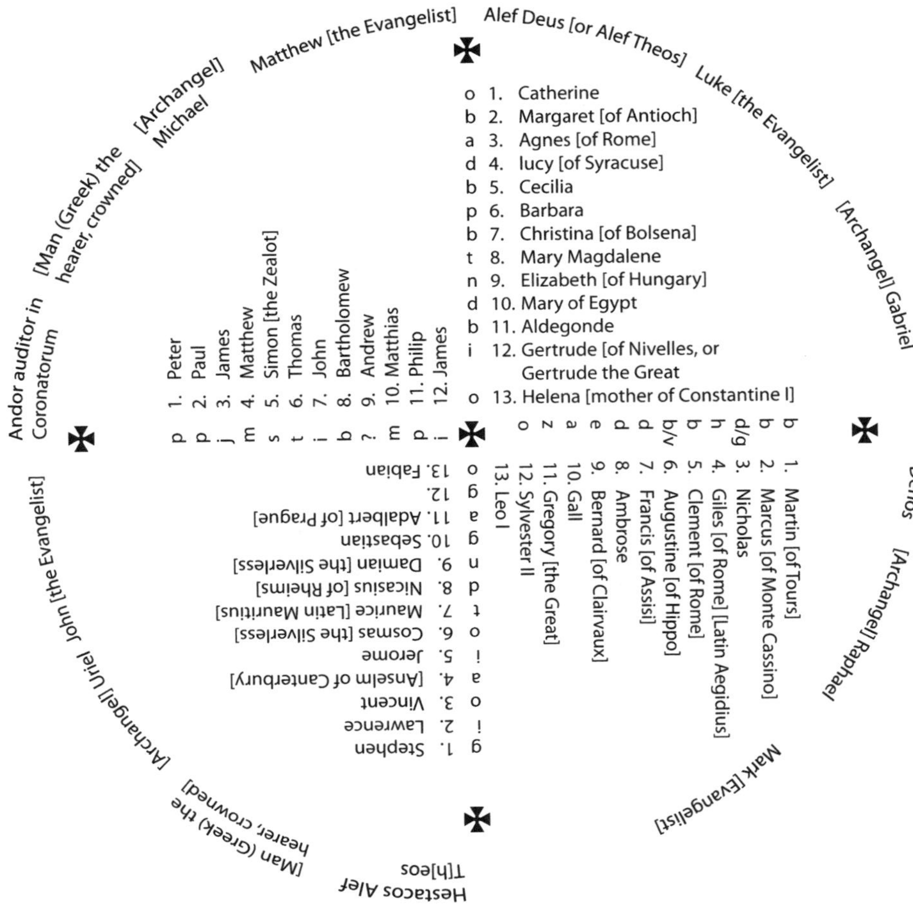

following names: Stephen, Lawrence, Vincent, Anselm of Canterbury(?), Jerome, Cosmas the Silverless (Latinized Greek *anargyroi*), Maurice, Nicasius of Rheims, Damian the Silverless, Sebastian, Adalbert of Prague, an unintelligible name, and Fabian. Under the man ("man the hearer, crowned"), Matthew the Evangelist, and the archangel Michael, are the following names: Peter, Paul, James, Matthew, Simon [the Zealot], Thomas, John, Bartholomew, Andrew, Matthias, Philip, James, Judas. Under the ox, Luke the Evangelist, and the archangel Gabriel, are the following names: Catherine [of Alexandria], Margaret [of Antioch], Agnes [of Rome], Lucy [of Syracuse], Cecilia, Barbara, Christina [of Bolsena], Mary Magdalene, Elizabeth [of Hungary], Mary of Egypt, Aldegonde, Gertrude [of Nivelles, or Gertrude the Great], and Helena [mother of Constantine I]. Under the lion, Mark the Evangelist, and the archangel Raphael, are the following names: Martin [of Tours], Marcius [of Monte Cassino], Nicholas, Giles [of Rome, Latin, *Aegidius*], Clement [of Rome], Augustine [of Hippo], Francis [of Assisi], Ambrose, Bernard [of Clairvaux], Gall, Gregory [the Great], Sylvester II, and Leo I.

presence; O Lord, turn the heart of those in an odium of repugnation for me, and in those who conspire against me; O my God, liberate [me] with [your] hand[132] in eternity, and teach me, *N.*, a Christian, truth, discipline, and knowledge, because, I believe in your commandments;[133] magnify my salvations, and have mercy for me, your Christian servant, and [the salvations] will be taught and unfailing, you who opened the mouth of the blessed apostle and evangelist John in the middle of the church and filled him with the spirit of wisdom and understanding,[134] the spirit of counsel and fortitude, the spirit of knowledge, piety, fortitude, and fear, and the knower of hopeful knowledge, illuminate your face upon me,[135] so that I am able to profit in all things, so that you are to be disseminated as the love of your name toward others who are impious, and you are to be disperged as the fruitful one thorugh the venerable Trinity, through the potency of the Father, the wisdom of the Son, and the virtue of the Holy Spirit, through the triumphing divinity, [and] through a simpler unity, through our Lord Jesus Christ, the admirable incarnation, so that through his interminate, blessed, explicable conception through the Virgin Mary, having been born above a natural one, and through our Lord Jesus Christ, the only begotten conservator, and through the dignified action of his passion and crucifixion, through his death, through the glorious resurrection, through the admirable ascension, through the mission of the spirit Paraclete, through the tremendous judicial day when the one and only retributes according to the quality of our merits, through the vaticinal prophets, through the sanctimony of the patriachs and the first ones of the apostles, through the victory of the martyrs, through the sanctification of the confessors, through the chastity of the virgins, through the merits of all the professing faithful, through the doctrine of the four evangelists, because you inspire me, *N.*, your unworthy Christian servant, to the faculty of the sciences, you who are blessed in the ages of ages, amen.

---

132. Esther 14:12–14 (NRSV with Apocrypha).

133. Psalm 119:66 (NRSV).

134. The introit of the Mass of St. John the Apostle and Evangelist, belonging to the third day of the Octave of Christmas.

135. Psalm 67:1 (NRSV).

[L2.9] Then on bent knees, say *Our Father,* and indeed, may we pray: **O ineffable and inenarrable God, you called the blessed little ones, your apostles, through the circumflexion of the Lord's light with respect to the [heavenly] retinue's procession, and who wonderfully revealed he does not have to speak to man, who certified to Joseph in a dream about future events,**[136] **who [did] not lead [back]**[137] **to Herod in a dream the three kings [who visited] the born Christ with clean offerings, and you [who] intimated through your holy angel Joseph, the guardian of the immaculate Virgin Mary, as he was going, he was received first into Egypt,**[138] **and his mother who, even, you greeted the blessed Mary with a salubrious voice then through the angel Gabriel,**[139] **and you intimated an admirable conception, who certified through Zachariah,**[140] **from the descendants,**[141] **as much as from the voice crying out in the desert;**[142] **having been fortified in a new sign, make wonderful . . .**[143] **which is to be granted as from those angels always in heaven, [the figure] is to be assisted from the same [angels] to me in dreaming visions, knowing [the figure] is to be effected [and] imprinted upon the intellect and memory, and having been impressed, may unforgetfulness be strengthened within me, just as I am able to magnify the magnificence and excellence of your holy name, you whose name is blessed in the ages, amen.**

[L2.10] **O God, whose Moses is placed under a special cloud, and Abraham, destined as he was wandering over the earth and wandering in thought, you who decorated the holy Catherine set against the fifty disputators about deific knowledge,**[144] **you who even wonderfully illuminated the three**

136. Genesis 37 (NRSV).

137. Corrected *reducet* to *reduxisti.*

138. Matthew 2:12–13 (NRSV).

139. Luke 1:26–28 (NRSV).

140. Luke 1:67–79 (NRSV).

141. The genealogies of Matthew 1:1–17 and Luke 3:23–38 (NRSV).

142. Matthew 3:1–3, Mark 1:3, Luke 3:3–6, and John 1:23 (NRSV).

143. The ellipsis acts as a placeholder for the operator to insert his desire as it relates to the magical figure being employed in the ritual.

144. Catherine of Alexandria (c. 287–305) is, according to tradition, a Christian saint who debated about religion with fifty pagan philosophers who were sent by the Roman emperor Maxentius. She won the debate and converted the philosophers to Christianity.

boys, Meshach, Shadrach, and Abednego,[145] you who showed the dreaming Jacob a vision of angels descending and ascending a ladder,[146] you even so wonderfully illuminated the souls of your disciples through the mission of the Holy Spirit, just it was springing forth in the mouth of all their tongues,[147] I am brought to life! Now make wonderful your mercies with me and a sign of light of your face toward . . .[148] which is to be vivified, blessed, well understood, and well imagined, existing and retained better [within my memory], and remembered best, so that having obtained the knowledge [through] the oracle of the holy angels, may I be able to be worthy to undertake . . . , and having undertaken [it], may I be able to disperse [it], and having undertaken [it, it is] to be disseminated to your name. O Lord, having been abandoned, I am a pauper, give me, an orphan, to the Son, the boy of wisdom, your word, the lamp to my feet, [and] the light of the Holy Spirit, and you will be able to be a helper to my paths.[149]

[L2.11; V2.1][150] Having used this figure, it ought to be consecrated first with a pure confession [and] works of mercy. These nine masses are to be said: of the Holy Trinity, of the Holy Cross, of the Holy Spirit, of our Lady, of the Holy Angels, [and] of the [All] Saints. [The place for these masses] will be draped first with a clean *lectisternia* and this [figure] is to be placed [thus]; having bathed and said thrice the Lord's prayer before the bed, then he places the figure under his own head and whatever he may have asked, he will obtain without a doubt if he was worthy to know the secrets.[151]

---

145. Daniel 3 (NRSV).
146. Genesis 28:10–19 (NRSV).
147. Acts of the Apostles 2:1–4 (NRSV).
148. The ellipsis represents a placeholder for the operator to insert his desired knowledge. A second ellipsis follows for the work to be undertaken with the newly acquired knowledge.
149. Psalm 10:14 (NRSV).
150. V2 section numbering indicates passages that are found in the Vienna manuscript.
151. As noted, this passage comes from Sloane 513. The Vienna manuscripts presents its own variant, designated here as V2.1, which reads, "Say this [prayer, *Summe Deus Pater piissime,*] whether nine, seven, or three times according to what masses preceded [it]. And after the prayer add below [it] the *Pater noster* three times. Afterward, look upon the figure with the utmost diligence, the highest reverence. Then place it with the crucifix against your head and you must sleep in a bed of linen, having put on clean vestments [and] having invoked divine help. And do not doubt [it] because whatever you ask for you will obtain. And it has been tested by many who have been granted the secrets of the heavenly kingdom, amen."

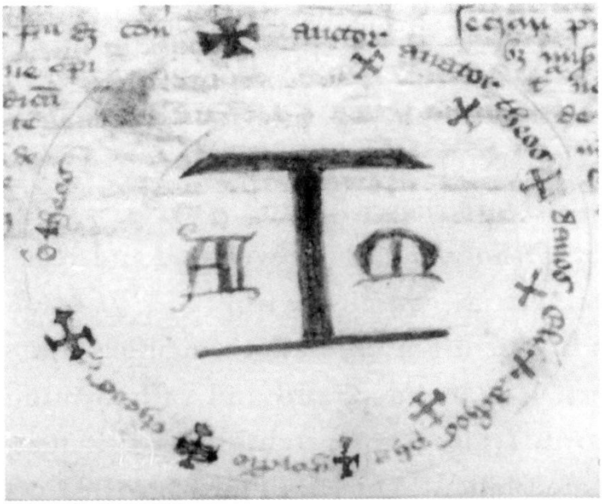

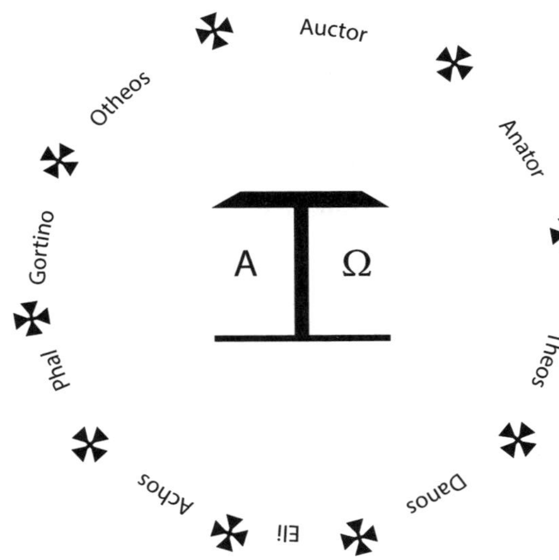

The figure of the secrets of God according to Sloane 513, f. 199v. According to the Erfurt and Vienna manuscripts, this is the figure of memory. This figure contains a central Greek *tau* cross flanked by the Greek letters *alpha* and *omega*. Decorated with crosses the following names are written on the outer band: Auctor, Anator, Theos, Danos, Eli, Achos, Phal, Gortino, Otheos. A couple descriptions of missing figures found in John of Morigny's *Liber Florum* may relate this to magical figure; one reads, "The letters of the great figure, indeed, follows: Tau. Alpha et ω. Ioth. He. Ihs. Vau. Xps. Mary. Holy Spirit. Intellect, fortitudine, counsel, knowledge, piety, fear of the Lord, and wisdom." Another description reads, "The letters of the inexplicable figure of God: Ye. Eu. Ve. Apha. Thau. ω. Father, Word, and Holy Spirit, king of honor." (*Liber Florum*, Old Compilation, Book of Figures, III.19, see Watson and Fanger, "The Prologue to John," 382–84). The next figure is a modern reconstruction. The last figure is from BNF Latin 4161, where it is identified as a figure of intellect.

[L2.12] Say this [prayer] in a secret place. Let it be done with devotion: **Theos Pater Hoemeras through your holy angels Helyph, Amasay, Gerocumeos, Gadebanay, Elamuni through your glorious Archangels of whose names are Scripture and secrets made by God, so that they ought not to be offered by us which are these: Auctor, Anacor, Theos, Anilos, Doner, Clyocles, Phagor, O holy angels, be with me and teach me, *N.*, I beg you, O Lord, illuminate my conscience [to] . . . ,[152] a countenance of splendor, your light in this night, and adorn memory upon my soul over these things which I, *N.*, understand and call to mind about this matter; today, O Lord, I direct my attention to this matter, O most pious God, be placated [about] . . . ,[153] O most gentle one, open my memory and temper my senses kindly over this matter through your ineffable name, you who are the origin of total piety and goodness, have patience with me, and give to me your memory [of] . . . ,[154] which I ask from you in this holy prayer; and bestow to me . . . who did not bubble over praying, may you point [me] toward penitence, having been pitied, you wait, and you retrain my failings and my petitions through your Angels and Archangels about those prefaced things, their virtue, dignity, [and] efficaciousness; may you perfect . . .[155] through your glorious angels, you who are the one and true God, amen, amen, amen.**[156]

[L2.13] (Wherever you see "mass," relinquish it, and such [Catholic] things of this manner.)[157]

---

152. The ellpsis represents a placeholder for the operator to insert his desired knowledge. This desired knowledge is then given the following two epithets.

153. The ellpsis represents a placeholder for the operator to insert what good works he has done to appease God in exchange for his petitioned desires.

154. The ellpsis represents a placeholder for the operator to insert his desired knowledge. The following ellpsis is meant for another kind of desired knowledge.

155. The ellpsis represents a placeholder for the operator to insert a certain mental faculty which he desires to acquire and develop within himself.

156. This prayer joins together *Theos Pater* and *Te queso Domine* of the *Ars Notoria* (sections 24–25) with the angelic names *Auctor, Anacor, Theos, Anilos, Doner, Clyocles, Phagor,* which agree with or bear a strong resemblance to *[Iesu Dei Filius incomprehensibilis] Ancor, Anacor, Anilos* of the *Ars Notoria* (section 29; NS 66–67).

157. Sloane 513 ends here. The manuscript claims it was first owned by Richard Dove, a

[V2.2] The first prayer of memory:[158]

"Hail Virgin, Mother of the Sacred Trinity, the Salvation of the Righteous Ones, the Grace of Sinners, the Glory of the Saints, the Praise of the Perpetual Angels, the Supernal Peace of the Blessed Ones, the Rest of All Heavenly Beings, the Cone of the Poles Lacking an End,[159] the Joy in the Funeral Clothing of Mourners,[160] the Unguent Storeroom to the Miserable,[161] the Treasury of the Poor, the Attendant of the Weak, the Illuminator of the Blind, the Restorer of the Lame, the Medicine of the Sick, the Helm of the Heavens, Lands, Seas, and All Things Contained within Them, the Tabernacle of the Arts, the Fountain of Total Wisdom, the Umbraculum of the Trinity,[162] you are the status of the planets [and] so much of the heavens;[163] the prayer of the Archangels and Angels encircles you, the Weeping of the Virtues, you entreat the Hosts of the Beatitudes with frequent use, look upon us from the top of the circle of eternity and its oracle, the Principalities of the heavens ask of you, the Powers incessantly ask [of you to accomplish their heavenly tasks], passing by quickly, continually, weepingly, the Dominions tremble vehemently [before you], the joined series [of the angelic beings] of the heavens become alarmed [before you], the Cherubim and Seraphim are tame [in your presence], all thirst to adore and praise you; the prediction of prophets keep watch over you, the wisdom of the elect conscribes [you], they describe [you], having spoken of the Evangelists, the minds of the apostles confirm you, the salvific blood of the martyrs preach about you, the chastity of the confessors strengthens

---

Cisterian monk of Buckfast. Following Dove's name, there are the initials "J.S.," which stand for John Shaxton, a later owner of the manuscript, who is otherwise unknown. The Sloane 513 manuscript is a compilation of other treatises with subjects such as mathematics, astronomy, chiromancy, physiognomy, and alchemy.

158. Recall that the Vienna manuscript contains only the Figure of the secrets of God, which it asserts is actually the figure of memory. Sections V1.1–2 immediately follow section 60.

159. An epithet of the Virgin Mary, which describes her as the endless height and depth of the earth's magnetic poles, indicating her place within the heavenly realm.

160. Latin *gaudium in investita moestorum letifera*.

161. John 12:1–11; Mark 14:3–9 (NRSV).

162. The Virgin Mary is thought of as the little shade to the Holy Trinity. Also, the papal coat of arms has an umbraculum, or umbrella, covering the two crossed keys as part of the papal regalia and insignia.

163. Mother Mary, having the title of Queen of the Heavens, is viewed as presenting the astrological forecast to the world.

you [robustly], the moral purity of the virgins adore you, the [. . .][164] of the widows implore you, the number of continents[165] entreat you; what a miserable fool I am! I, *N.*, want to praise you [so much], as if to draw the water of the sea into drops, and to collect [it] in my stomach, [and] to swallow the sky, earth, [and] sea at once; I begin, being able to know . . . ;[166] first, you may dismiss the years, months, days, and hours, [you are][167] of the Trinity, because it is impossible, and such things belong to the past and future, presenting up to the beginning of the world [and] the end of space, each hour of the hours [and] the thousandth millenia of the world, because the celestial bodies and the stars of the heavens are holding the days and are retaining the hours of the days, the mobile and immobile [parts of the cosmos] are holding and retaining the earth with firmness, the volcanic fire, cold heavy ashes, and dust, the coastline of trees, flower branches, fruit, seeds, roots, flowers, the fish of other seas, the deep sea fish, the winged [magnetic] poles [of the earth], the cattle of the lands [and] mountains, the beasts of the fields, the worms of the valleys, the occupation of the Olympians,[168] the plants, [and] herbs, all rational beings themselves are a multitude in those [places], as the Cherubim and Seraphim, your wise parts, are not able to praise a thousandth of a praise up to the end of such a world; [the praise of the Cherubim and Seraphim] was falling short, and your praise was surpassing, from where I ask you weepingly, the most blessed Virgin Mary, whose Son [is] one in the Trinity and threefold in unity, whose fruit of the womb subdued the infernal realm, he shackled the demons, he plundered Egypt, he liberated Israel,[169] and which of the heavens, earth, seas, and all things which are contained within this, and you served to bring to life the creator and the teacher of creatures, I beg you, give me the form of memory [and] the material of eloquence; give, for example, the way of the sciences, the teachings, the liberal arts, and to that,

164. The text is missing.

165. Those who exercise moral and sexual self-restraint as an act of religious devotion.

166. The ellipsis acts as a placeholder for the operator to insert his desired knowledge of something.

167. Corrected Latin transcription from *est* to *es*.

168. That is to say, the celestial bodies and stars of the heavens even have control over the fate of the Olympian deities, astrologically speaking.

169. Exodus 3:22 (NRSV).

the pertinence, my understanding, and all scientific notes; and illuminate the unknown, because you are the fountain of the sciences, the doctrine of wisdom, teach me, I, *N.*, ask [you], and instruct [me], and 'make my mouth as a sharpened sword and my tongue as a chosen arrow.'[170] Strengthen the words of my mouth with respect to every [kind of] wisdom, and melt the hearts of those who hear them and beget [it] longingly,[171] because you who are providing milk to those who give suck, you nurse the hearts of those who feed, you satisfy the eyes of those who desire, and you give all your things to those who invoke; you destroy the mountains [and] you exalt the hills. You are the gift of gifts, the flower of flowers, the lady of ladies, the queen of queens, [the queen] of riches, of the poor, of kingdoms, of princes, of counts, of judges, of the nobles and the ignoble people, of bishops, of priests, of scholars, of the healthy, of the sick, of infants, of boys, of youth, of adolescents, of men, of senility, of virgins, of women, of widows, and grant me the Venusian gifts of the Holy Spirit—intellect, reason, ingenuity, memory, eloquence, and fortune,[172] so that I may be able to draw from the fountains and the torrents of the arts to my mind, and to discuss [any subject matter] with the tongue perfectly, because your name, our Lord Jesus Christ, is blessed in eternity and beyond, amen."

[V2.3] "In the presence of the body and blood of our Lord Jesus Christ, commending me, your servant John, through the virtue of the holy cross and through the holy mystery of the incarnation, resurrection, and Passion, your ascension, so that you may look upon me, your unworthy servant John, [and] may you free and defend [me] from the snares of visible and invisible enemies, from deception and from chains, from javelins and from arrows, from venom and from every pestiferous food and drink, from pain and anguish, from suffering and from death, from shame and from confusion, from fire and water, from vices and from sins, from every fall and rapine, and from harm and from every danger of body and soul;

170. Isaiah 42:9 (NRSV).

171. *Ars Brevis,* section 52.

172. The Venusian gifts of the Holy Spirit are those gifts which come from the Virgin Mary via the Holy Spirit to the believer. For more on the connection between Venus and the Blessed Virgin Mary, see Ferris, "Venus and the Virgin," 252–59.

O Mary, repel all these far away from me, having performed the mysteries of your sufferings and our redemptions through this, you who saves me, I trust [you] fiducially, you hoped to be able to save me through this; therefore, O most merciful God, you who listens to us, they cry out to you; hoping in you, listen to me, a miserable sinner, and just as you must be my necessity, have mercy on me, and dismiss all my sins, and so that your grace for me may carry on and save me from every evil and lead me through into eternal life, amen."

[The Sixth Day][173]

[V2.4] "O my good angel, you who has been given to me in custody as my help in this life's peregrination, may you deign to repel the evil angel from me and the invisible snares through the virtue of our Lord Jesus Christ [and] may you deem worthy to remove *cassatas*[174] far away from me. Deliver my prayers to his pious ears, he who is not an estimator of merits himself, but a bestower of forgiveness, to the extent that he may piously indulge whatever I have sinned, in order that through his very own grace I may deserve to be free, having been justified, from all sins in the land of the living, amen."

[The Sabbath][175]

[V2.5] "Hail Salvation of the World, the Word of the Father, the natural host,[176] the living flesh, the integral deity, the true man, hail the principle of our creation, hail the hope of our redemption, therefore, I give thanks to you, the almighty Father, the pious, praying for their favors to be helped apart from intercession, and for those who are still in purgatory, the Son is to be immolated for the almighty Father, to the extent that the punishment of those [in purgatory] may be quicker and shorter, and for those of us whose sins of flesh and blood are graver still, the opposite; may the body and blood of our Lord Jesus Christ cleanse and wash [away the sins], amen."

173. The Vienna manuscript marks this as the sixth day in its margin.
174. An unidentified word, left untranslated as recorded in Véronèse's transcription.
175. The Vienna manuscript marks this as the Christian Sabbath—that is, Sunday—in its margin.
176. That is, the sacramental bread at Mass.

[V2.6] "O Lord Jesus Christ, you who came into this world on account of us sinners from the bosom of the Father, so that you may redeem us from sin, hear and answer me, an unworthy, obnoxious, and negligent sinner, I know and believe, O holy Lord the Father, that you wanted to live on earth not among the righteous but among the sinners, I confess all my sins to you, I ask for forgiveness from malicious and iniquitable thoughts about everything, whatever is to be wanted in this age; I have sinned [and] I have erred, although I did not deny you, you are a pious Father, I pray to you, kneeling, so that you give to me the remission of all my sins, I praise you, I glorify you, O holy Trinity, I give thanks to you in all my infirmities, because I do not have hope in another except in you, O Lord my God.

"'And I take refuge [with you], O Christ,[177] at the door of your church, and having prostrated with respect to the pledges of your saints, I ask for [your] indulgence; O Lord, I pray and supplicate to you, so that you may grant me on account of your great mercy and your piety to continue in good works until my end, and in that tremendous hour when my soul has been taken up from the body to come before the heavenly kingdom, present to me the right sense, good faith, hope and belief.'

"'O Almighty God, the redeemer of the world, free my soul from the lower infernal realm and from the inextinguishable fire; O God, free me now from this fire of the first man [and] Satan; O my Almighty God, free me from the manison of the impious ones; O my gentle God, free me from eternal anguish; O true light, free me from all evils; O creator of heaven, free my soul from the infernal [one].[178] O Christ, I confide in you, I am the work of your hands, do not abandon me, I ask holy Mary, I ask the twenty-four elders, all the holy patriarchs and prophets, all the holy apostles, the martyrs, confessors, and virgins, all the holy widows and foreigners, and all the orphans and wards, and all the saints and the elect of God, I call upon you for help, so that in this tremendous hour when my soul has stepped out from my body, intercede for me, a most miserable sinner, to [bring me to] God the almighty Father.'

---

177. From this passage on down to the end are a series of prayers. These have been found in the fifteenth-century Burnet Psalter, f. 46v–49r.

178. An alternative translation is "the infernal place."

"I deprecate you, O Michael, the holy archangel of Christ, you who did not undertake [the task] of receiving souls, accepted the authority, so that you may deem worthy to receive my soul when it has stepped out from the body, and deliver it, [i.e., my soul,] from the hand of the enemy, so that [my soul] is able to pass through the gates of the infernal realms and the ways of shadows, so that the lion or the inequitable dragon is not appointed to it,[179] who is accustomed to drag souls into the infernal realm and to lead them through to eternal torment.'[180]

"'I deprecate you, Saint Peter, the first of the apostles, you who accepted the keys of the celestial kingdom, open the doors of paradise for me.'[181]

"O Lord Jesus Christ, the Son of the holy Mary, [my] prayers pour out to you, so that you may act with piety and mercy upon my soul, because I hope in you, O redeemer of the world, so that I will not be repelled away from your face, O Christ, I do not deserve forgiveness, but, for example, grant this . . .[182] to me, disseminate the Holy Trinity to help me, and listen to me, you are the Lord, my great God, you are my just judge, you are my only teacher, you are my most potent medicine, you are my most beautiful love, you are my priest in eternity, you are my true light, my holy delight, my brilliant wisdom, my pure simplicity, my catholic[183] truth, my total concord, my good refreshment, [my] everlasting salvation, my great mercy, my most robust patience, my immaculate victory, my redemption, my resurrection, my perpetual life, light, truth, I deprecate

---

179. An alternative sense is that the petitioner hopes that his own soul is not served up like a dish to the lion or dragon to devour.

180. This prayer is found in the eleventh-century Tiberius Psalter, produced at New Minster, Winchester, held at the Oxford Bodleian Library, MS Douce 296, f. 122v. See Openshaw, "The Battle between Christ and Satan," 52:14–33. The Archangel Michael prayer is also found in the fifteenth-century Burnet Psalter (Aberdeen, University of Aberdeen, Marischal College, Burnet collection, AUL MS 25, f. 47r). During the Middle Ages, particularly the Gothic art period, the Archangel Michael is depicted as participating in the judgment of souls by weighing the good and evil deeds of a soul in a set of scales to determine whether the soul is sent to heaven or hell. There is no biblical basis for Michael to hold this function.

181. This prayer to Saint Peter is also found in the fifteenth-century Burnet Psalter.

182. The ellipsis acts as a placeholder for the operator to insert his desired knowledge of something. A second ellipsis follows for the same thing.

183. Or universal.

you, I supplicate you, I ask you . . . , so that through you I may walk to you, I may come before you, I may rest in you, and I will rise again for you.

"Hear me, O Lord, remembering, O Lord, you vowed to our fathers, just like David, as you must avert your nature away from [me], your servant John, may the angel Michael, the angel Raphael, all the holy Angels, Archangels, Dominions, Principalities, and Powers, Cherubim and Seraphim, and all the holy apostles, martyrs, confessors, virgins, and all the saints be [able to standy by] in assistance to me, Matthew, Luke, Mark, John,[184] Stephen,[185] Lawrence,[186] Martin,[187] Nicolas,[188] Benedict,[189] Bernard,[190] Robert,[191] Catherine,[192] Margaret,[193] Mary Magdalene, and all the saints, intercede for me; O Lord, you formed me from the mud of the earth, you knitted me together with bones and nerves, and you make salvation for me. + Peace + God + Man + Lord + Christ +

---

184. The four Evangelists of the Gospel.

185. Stephen (c. 5–36) was the first Christian martyr who was set to trial for blasphemy and then stoned to death by the Jews according to the Acts of the Apostles.

186. Lawrence (225–258) is a Christian saint who was martyred by the Roman emperor Valerian.

187. Martin of Braga (c. 520–580) was an archbishop of Bracara Augusta in Gallaecia (modern-day Portugal). Gregory of Tours described him as a brilliant self-taught man.

188. Nicolas of Myra (270–343) is a Christian bishop to whom many miracles are attributed.

189. Benedict of Nursia (480–547) is a Christian saint who founded several monastic communities and established his "Rule of Saint Benedict," which is a set of rules that many Christian monks still follow today.

190. Bernard of Clairvaux (c. 1090–1153) is a Christian saint who revitalized Christian monasticism through the emerging Cistercian Order.

191. The identity of this Rupert or Robert is somewhat ambiguous by name; however, based on the order of the listed names of Benedict and Bernard, who are associated with monastic orders, it seems most likely this is Robert of Molesme (1028–1111), who is one of the founders of the Cistercian Order.

192. Catherine of Alexandria (c. 287–305) is a Christian saint and scholar martyred by the Roman emperor Maxentius. Her virginity earned her a respected model of behavior for young women during the Late Middle Ages.

193. Margaret of Scotland (c. 1045–1093), who became queen to Malcolm III of Scotland and helped conform Celtic Christianity to the practices of the Catholic Church, offered charity to orphans and the poor and established ferries to help pilgrims journey to St. Andrews in Fife.

"O Lord, hear my prayer, to you alone have I sinned, and done evil in your sight, and my sins are exceedingly innumerable. I ask for forgiveness, O Lord, for my sins, for my negligence, for vain glory, for carnal concupiscence, for pollution,[194] for payment [to prostitutes], for envy, for detraction, for pride, for sleepiness, for inequitable thoughts, because I come late to your work, I appeared guilty for it, and rarely and unwillingly am I able to dismiss or speak about my sins, I am not able to abscond my iniquities and my acts of malice, because I know and I believe you, Father, the bestower of the remission of sins, do not forsake me, O pious Father, but indulge what I have done wrong, may your holy, lovable, and sweet piety help me, before the gates of the infernal realm apprehend me, pour into me the hand of mercy and the name of your brilliance; O most pious and merciful God, O gentle Father, I praise you, I glorify you, I magnify you, I give thanks to you, you who saved me through the night, command me to save through the day;[195] O holy Lord, make me love you [and] praise you for all the days of my life; O glorious God, you who are just, you alone who are true, who [are] in all things, through which all things are made. O Lord, hear me, just as you heard the three boys in the furnace of burning fire, Shadrach, Meshach, and Abednego;[196] O Lord, hear me, just as you listened to Susanna praying, and you freed her from the hands of unjust witnesses,[197] you have heard me praying, just like you heard Peter at sea[198] and Paul in chains,[199] pierce my soul, and my evils and all my crimes, O Christ my God, if my enemy exalts himself against me, protect me with your arms; I sleep, and my heart is vigilant, your holy angel watches over me day and night. O almighty God, send forth your good Spirit into my heart, who watches over my heart and soul. I have sinned, O Lord, exceedingly in words, in deeds, in your law, in perverse thoughts, my sins are many, and I have been neglecting in the service of God, in my order [of mass]; O kind God, and grant me true piety,

---

194. That is, male ejaculation during sleep.

195. The Burnet Psalter reads, "you who saved me through the day, command me to be saved through the night."

196. Daniel 3.

197. Daniel 13.

198. Matthew 14:30–33.

199. Acts 23–26.

a boastful indulgence,[200] a firm faith, [and] a good perseverance. O Holy Spirit, illuminate me and indulge all my sins for me, here now and in the future age, amen."

[V2.7] Then say the psalm *Benedicite, omnia opera mea, Dominum, etc.,*[201] [and] *Gloria in excelsis Deo, etc.*[202]

200. That is, the forgiveness of sins.
201. The Benedicite, the Song of Creation, is a canticle used as a thanksgiving after Mass, drawing from Daniel 3:35–66, 56–88, and Psalm 148 (KJV).
202. The Greater Doxology. The Latin translates as "Glory to God in the highest!" based on Luke 2:14.

[The Book of Divine Revelation]

The *Ars Brevis* concludes with the second and final book, "the Book of Divine Relevation." This portion consists of twenty-one prayers borrowed from the *Ars Notoria* and a conflated prayer derived from both the *Ars Notoria* and the *Opus Operum* for a total of twenty-two prayers. Since these prayers have already been presented earlier in this book under the *Ars Notoria* and the *Opus Operum,* the reader is directed to read them there. Below are described which prayers the operator is to offer on the days of the ritual.

[The First Day]

On the first day, the operator is to offer *Omnipotens incomprehensibilis* (section 115) and *Adoro te rex regum* (section 116).

[Second Day]

On the second day, the operator is to offer *Confiteor* (section 117), *Pie Deus* (section 119), and *Pie Pater* (section 120).

[Third Day]

On the third day, the operator is to offer *Usyon omnium* (section 141).

The *Ars Brevis* then explains, "This little work is great with these others, which I gave before all the prefaced works without having been offered with some distinction of time, because, it is, nevertheless, understood by the angelic administration."

The *Ars Brevis* continues with listing the following prayers:

Deus qui omnia numero (section 144)
Mediator omnium (section 145)
Deus iustus iudex (section 143)
Extollo sensus (section 121)
Omnium regnorum (section 122)
Deus vivorum (section 123)
Profiteor (section 124)
Domine quia ego servus (section 125)
Domine Sancte Pater [. . . imperfectum] (section 128)

Respice Domine (section 129)
Creator Adonay (section 130)
Sancte Deus (section 135)
Heloy clementissime (section 137)
Omnipotens et misericors (section 138)

Finally, a conflated prayer which combines the opening epithets of God from *Unus magnus* (section 139) with a portion of the *Summe Deus Pater piissime* prayer of *Opus Operum,* C:

"O great, wonderful, eternal God, O angel of the eternal counsel and disposer of all virtues, and ordainer and disposer, adorn my understanding today, and multiply within me discerning reason and thought, as much as you conferred on Adam in offering all creatures names, grant the same judgment of my soul the knowledge and discretion of this art according to your promise."

[Fourth Day]

On the fourth and last day, the operator is to offer *Omnipotens sapientiae* (section 146).

The *Ars Brevis* then concludes with the following passage:

> The teaching of the prayers, as when the seven of the first ones are to be offered: He who wishes to acquire something great of some art, I publish [it] to know the knowledge and wisdom, and if the abovesaid work . . .

With this ellipsis, the *Ars Brevis* abruptly ends.

8

Ars Notoria Abbreviata

(Abridged Notory Art According to Thomas of Toledo)

14th–15th Centuries

This abridged *Ars Notoria,* attributed to Thomas of Toledo, is a fourteenth-century magical treatise in the *ars notoria* tradition. What is particularly remarkable about this treatise is just how short it really is in its length and ritual procedure, and how few demands are placed on the operator. This treatise exhibits the ongoing trend toward minimalism and the ease of use in the *ars notoria* tradition.

The treatise is divided into a prologue and a practical, or executive part (*pas executiva*). The prologue introduces Thomas and his reasoning for composing this treatise. His circle of friends knew he was trained in the *ars notoria* tradition and had requested that he write for them a compendium about it. He explains that the *ars notoria,* as a magical practice, is too costly and too laborious on account of human fragility. He might have been thinking of the costs suffered by Solomon's house servant (section 57) and even Solomon himself (section 134). The glossed version of the *Ars Notoria* had expanded the ritual procedure up to four months and placed high demands on the operator, which is very labor intensive. In considering these barriers to the practice, Thomas decided to compose an abbreviated compendium of the *ars notoria* tradition, but he felt shame for abbreviating it, knowing the depths of its practice. Perhaps he felt the social pressures from his peers to write about it. Before he completed the compendium and delivered it to his circle of friends, he consulted with his teacher, the one who taught him the notory art. His teacher eased his mind, instructing that all that is really required to be successful in the art is to know that the virtue and efficacy of the art is founded on the divine mystery, so implementing three prayers and the figures will suffice. In other words, three heart-felt prayers may be enough to arouse the divine sympathy and elicit action from the angels.[1] With this counsel, Thomas completed his book.

The executive part of the treatise presents the three mediating prayers and ritual instruction. The ritual procedure takes a single month to complete, beginning on either a new Moon or full Moon in the morning. The operator may attain one kind of knowledge per month, choosing from grammar, logic, rhetoric, music, geometry, medicine, astronomy, theology, and jurisprudence. The operator must fast, confess, and avoid sins. There are only four days in which he must fast. He must fast one day of every week: the first day of the first week, the fourth day of the second week, the sixth day of the third week, and the Sabbath of the fourth and last week. On the first day of the ritual, the operator is to go to a secret place to pray in the morning. He is to inspect the figure of his choice, followed by performing the three prayers which are offered at morning, midday, and evening. The next day, the operator repeats the process, while observing those days in which he must fast. Thus, the ternary invocations and inspection of figures continues until the end of the month, at which point, if successful, the operator will have been infused with the worldly knowledge and divine wisdom. There is no mention of attaining a dream visitation from an angel, but this might be presumed by Thomas.

The abridged notory art attributed to Thomas of Toledo is preserved in two manuscripts: (1) Vatican, Vatican Apostolic Library, Palatine collection, Latin 957, folios 92v–94v and (2) Munich, Bayerische Staatsbibliothek, Clm 28858, folios 1–12v. Latin 957 presents two figures (one of which is not labeled), while Clm 28858 presents eleven figures (two of which are not labeled). Clm 28858 appears to have dispersed the instructions throughout the *pars executiva* rather than collect them all at the end; plus, it includes some of the *voces magicae* prayers from the *Ars Notoria*. For example, *Helyscemath* (section 7) is placed before the morning prayer, *Rex invictissime;* and *Lemaac Salmaac* (section 22) is placed before the midday prayer, *O Adonay rex omnium creaturarum*. This presentation may give the false appearance that these Latin prayers are the "prologues" to the *voces magicae* prayers.

1. It is not clear who was Thomas's teacher. Perhaps this "someone" was his own angel, guiding him in the art. Alternatively, it might have been his fellow man and teacher; if so, it is not clear whether Thomas consulted with him in person or in spirit (i.e., telepathically).

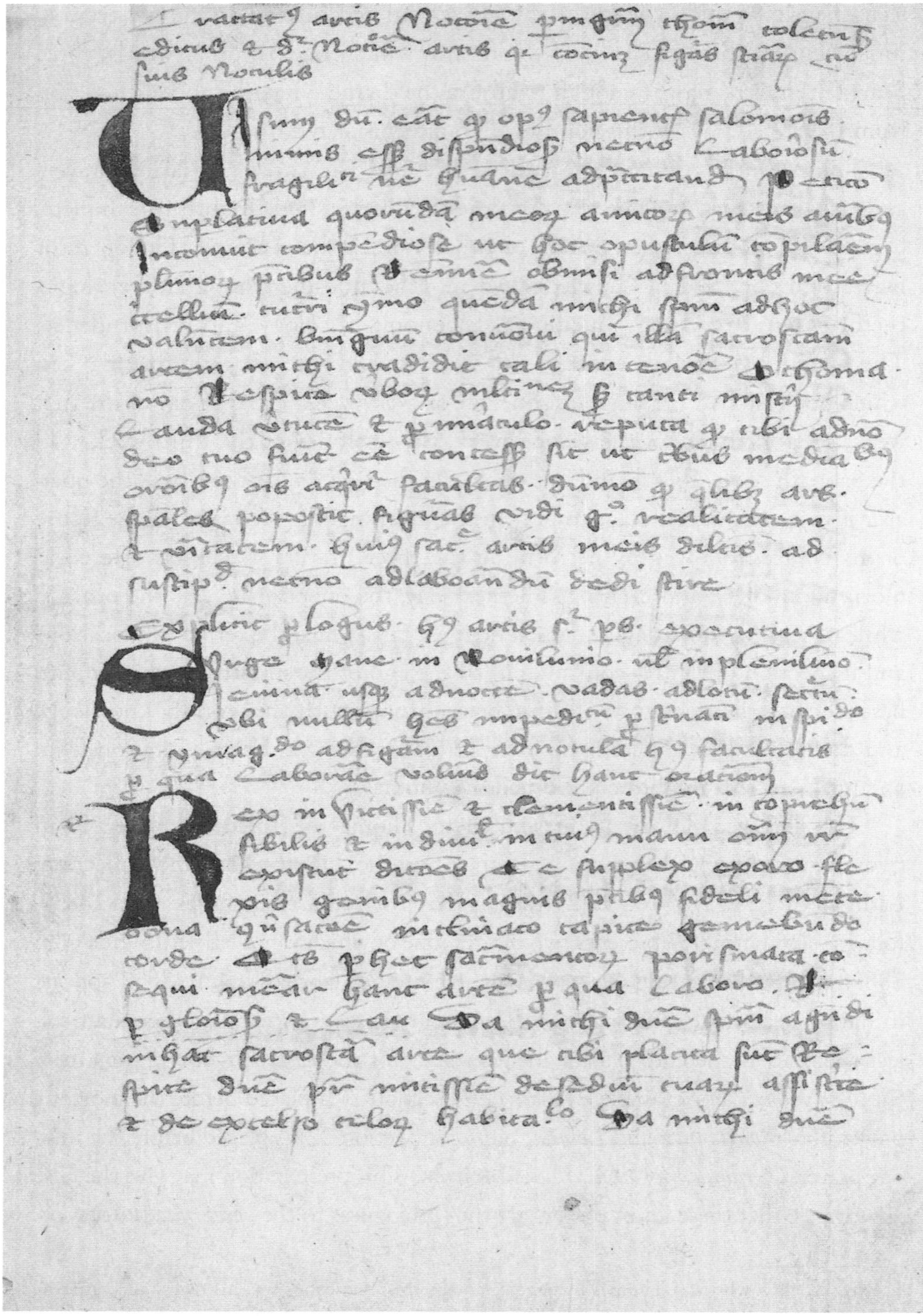

Prologue of Palatine, Latin 957, f. 92v

[Prologue]

[1] [This is] the treatise of the notory art edited according to master Thomas of Toledo, and it is to be called the notory art because it contains the figures of knowledge with its *notulis*. While it was understood that the work of Solomon's wisdom was too costly, and also too laborious for our human fragility to practice, a superlative petition of certain friends of mine spoke thunderously to my ears for a compendium [of Solomon's wisdom], so I was compiling this little work at the requests of many. I omitted [parts of the work of Solomon's wisdom] to remunerate the little circle of tutors in face of my shame; still, I, my very self, called together a certain someone, having a benevolent influence on my spirit, he who had taught me the sacrosanct art by so great an intention, [saying to me], "O Thomas, look not upon the multitude of words, but praise the virtue of so great a mystery, and repute what was to be granted to you by the Lord your God as a miracle,[2] so that every [mental] faculty is to be acquired by three mediating prayers, so long as he asked for the figures to any special art." Ergo I saw the reality and truth of this sacred art with respect to my failures which are to be acknowledged, and indeed, with respect to [the special arts] which are to be labored for [which] I gave to know. The prologue of this art ends, the executing part follows.

---

2. Compare to *Ars Notoria,* section 3 gloss.

[The Ritual of the Abbreviated Notory Art]

[2] Rise up in the morning in the new Moon or in a full Moon, fasting until the night, go to a secret place where [there are] no impeding men, prostrating, with respect to the figure and the *notula* of this faculty, which is to be inspected and imagined, for which you want to labor, say this prayer:

[3] O most invincible and gentle king, incomprehensible and indivisible, in whose hand all things come into being as speech, I pray to you, kneeling on bent knees, with great prayers, a faithful heart, good behavior, bowing my head, [and] sighing in [my] heart, to the extent that I may deserve to understand this art for which I labor [with you] through these porismatic sacraments. O king, through your glorious and praiseworthy name, give to me, O Lord, the spirit of taking actions in this sacrosanct art which are pleasing to you, and look upon [me], O Lord, most mild Father, assist [me] from your seats and the little habitation in the lofty heavens. O Lord, give to me a retaining sense, the grace of being able to speak and write well, eloquence, memory, and perseverance in this excellent art, so that what I remember by heart, or [what] I repeat by mouth, has a foundation rooted within me. O unadorned king, [before who] is to be feared, worshipped, and trembled, my prayer that I, an unworthy [person], *N.*, offer in your majestic almighty presence and through these, your most glorious names, Theos, Patyr,[3] Ymos, Megale,[4] Alleya, Fortisan, Fortison, Almachon, Canay, Gargay, Ypanchon, and through all the impetrations and actions of grace, which have been given to you by all the faithful from the origin of the world, and still, are given up to the consummation of the ages, to the extent that in the praiseworthy and glorious operation of this excellent art, [may I be given] a perspicacious, efficacious, and audacious [faculty] with respect to understanding all things which I will read, just like you. O holy Father, you made King Solomon the most wise, and you taught the example to his descendants in your laudable name, still you made the Ark of the Covenant, a fabrication of the sevenfold wisdom, having been expectorated

3. *Ars Notoria,* section 24.

4. *Ars Notoria,* section 10.

from its own part,[5] and you who deemed worthy to teach him, just like a boy through certain elements with respect to the arts of letters [quickly, typically, the elements of the arts] are to be moved forward with prolixiously and burdensomely for a long time, [but] you will be advanced toward all arts through the increments of these virtues thus [quickly]. Having been elevated from under the fulcrum of this art, may I deserve to understand this art for which I labor [with you] and through your glorious and laudable name, which is blessed in the ages of ages, amen."

[4] *The second or midday prayer:*

"O Adonay, king of all visible and invisible creatures, wonderful disposer, you who granted all things existence, as in their persistent virtue, you who established the heavens and weighed the earth in [your] palm, you positioned the waters, [so that] they do not cross their own boundaries; you who gives virtue, you give to all the gems and herbs the virtue of your entire power to be exercised in them; you did not take away our human fragility of unknowing, each [person] having [their own] profundity, but as a pious dispenser of the mystical sciences, you observed and taught [each person] mercifully, through which man, with the image of the Fallen mold thus, is made similarly effective with respect to intelligence; and in this way, restore within me what I desire in the cleanliness of virtue in this sacrosanct art. Do not bend my heart down into malicious words, lest I may have lost the effect of grace erroneously, [as] I have expended that time and hour in this art. O Lord, give me a perseverant spirit that will lead me powerfully over the quadrangular palace of the seven liberal arts, the others, and the sciences.[6] O Lord, open my throat with respect to undertaking your pure sweet eloquence, and impart to me, just as you imparted [it] to King Solomon of this art; O king [who] has governed

5. The sevenfold wisdom is a reference to the seven gifts of the Holy Spirit. *Expectore,* the Latin participle from the verb *expectoro, -are, -avi, -atum* (etymology: *ex* + *pectus* + *-o,* literally, "to expel from the chest"). Thomas uses the metaphor of expectorating or spitting out the ark to mean that God used a part of his spiritual essence (specifically, from the Holy Spirit) to craft the ark. This required both spit and breath, the essence of creation. In ancient and medieval times, saliva had miraculous and magical properties. See Mark 8:22–26 and John 9:1–12 (NRSV) in which Jesus used his own spittle to restore sight to a blind man.

6. *Ars Notoria,* NS 59.

[all things], O God the mildest Father, make me worthy through these, your holy names, Epharicon, Checal, Loche, Astat, Agyon, Facton, On, Loxo, Ely, Ely, Eloy, Bonos, Adomagos, Bazoduche, Elonos, Panthagecon, Elonosay, to the extent that this art, in which I labor at present, to which I admit the total desire of the heart, may I finally obtain (the concept of the mind),[7] may I be able to rationally explain [it explicitly] in your praise and honor, because you are the one whom every creature praises and adores, fears and dreads in the ages of ages, amen."

[5] *The evening prayer:*

"O King of kings, Lord of lords, glorious and sublime God, I implore you with great obsequiousness and veneration through the profound mysteries of this art which not everyone knows [how to] manifest, but yet you observed [them] for your faithful and loving people from the origin of the world. O Father, the angel of great counsel, the prince of peace, the Father of the future age, these are for every mystery, and the public criers of your magnificent praise, which you have exalted the erudite *prae ceteris*, the magnificence of the sons of man in this art, and you gave them that greatness of the heart [in doing] your miraculous works with respect to a penetrable perspicuousness and clarity, having sent them to us from eternity,[8] may I deliver the vows in your great Church to you Lord God; I pray to you, O Lord, through the virtue of these names of whose efficacy is to be extinguished with fire, and every thing is made in remembrance, and these are their names: Gehar, Niczeron, Nassay, Lanacht, Theos, Clyoram, Elemaleht, Lasornay, Amalydion, Anagona, Ztamburelyon, Algalgal, Sellyach, Semynach, Stelpha, Azaha, Amygday, Lahor, Trualyon. Through these and your other holy names, I deprecate you, O nourishing river, the horse of God the Almighty,[9] and the mercy of the Almighty, may I prevail to define the foundation of this most excellent art to the extent that I am in any way impeded by Satan or some fantastic deception; O Lord, extirpate the old ferment from my heart and body, so that

7. The phrase *conceptum mentis* (the concept of the mind) acts as a placeholder for the operator to insert his desired knowledge according to the figure used in the ritual.

8. *Mittetus qui nobis aeterne.*

9. Epithet of the Holy Spirit. See *Ars Notoria,* NS 13.

I may be made new and efficacious in exercising your commanments and may I become a clever exerciser[10] in all the sciences for which I will have labored through you, O most pious and gentle one, who stands equal in one *ousia*[11] and as triple person of the same parts, through the infinite ages of ages, amen."

[6] *These are the precepts of this most sacred art:*
According to the teachings of this art, if anyone wants to practice this art, he ought to be constant—for example, not for some temporal affair having entered himself into the mysteries, being audacious with respect to [that] which is to be believed—for if he will have hesitated toward the middle of one point, he will not taste the sweetness of this holy art. Also, he must not exercise some, libidinous, and intimate action, for he must see [clearly]; also, he must confess. Also, he must have known that there are four days in one month which are to be fasted, in the first [day of the first week] until nighttime; in the second week, having performed [fasting in] the fourth [day]; in the third week, having performed [fasting on] the sixth [day]; in the fourth week, [having performed fasting on] the Sabbath; he must fast according to one manner, and thus he will obtain one faculty in one month, having moved every doubt far away [himself], just like the manner of conduct, it is in the days and you.

---

10. Latin *concinnus exercitator,* one who practices as a clever speaker and writer. See *Ars Notoria,* section 76, page 254, footnote 166 for the rhetorical sense of *concinnus.*

11. Greek ουσία. Originally, this is a philosophical term from ancient Greek philosophers such as Plato and Aristotle that means "essence" or "substance." It was adapted into Christian theology in the development of the Trinitarian doctrine.

Ars Notoria Abbreviata, *Notae* Supplement

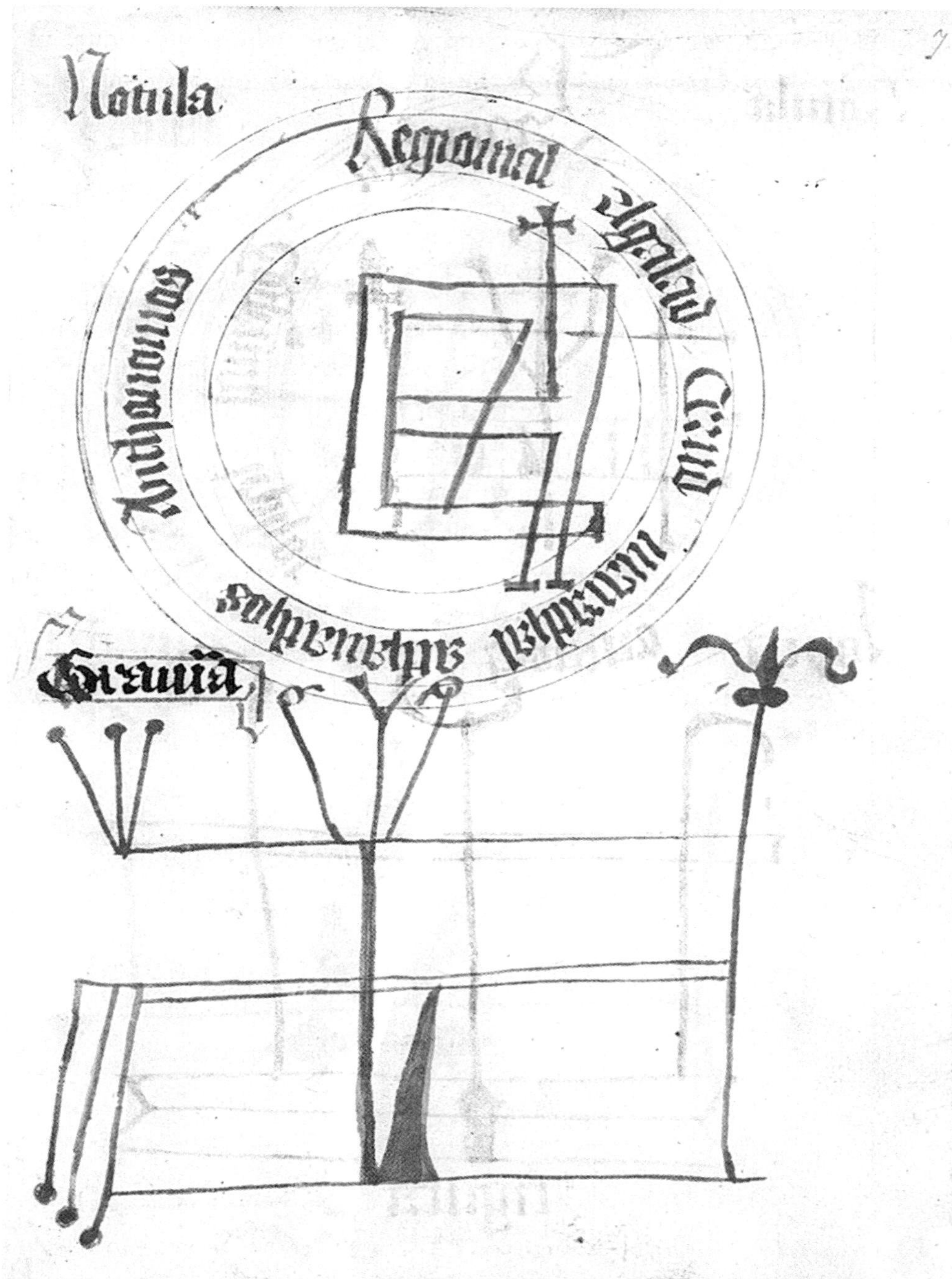

The figure of grammar.
BSB CLM 28858, f. 7r.

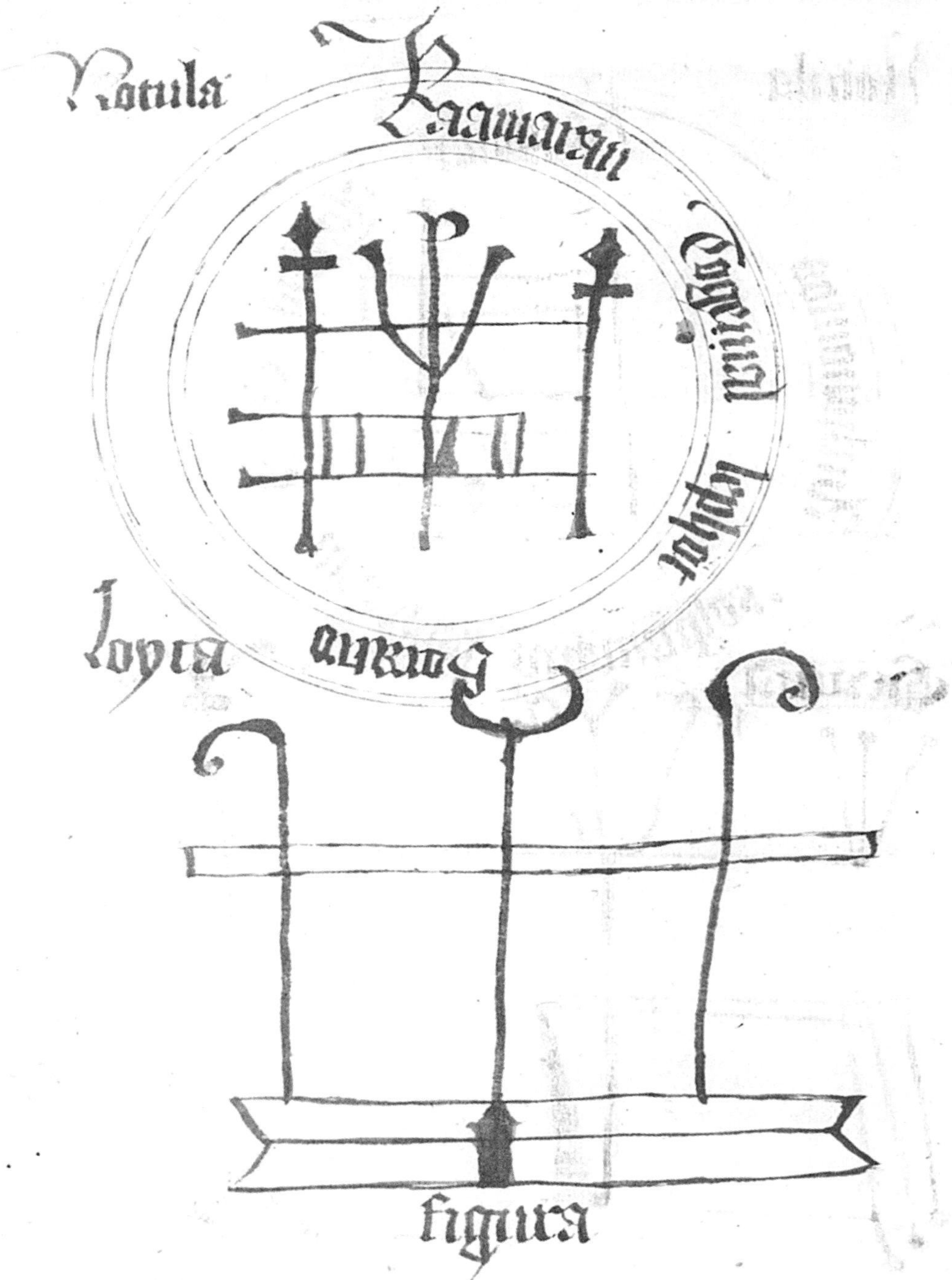

The figure of logic.
BSB CLM 28858, f. 7v.

The figure of rhetoric.
BSB CLM 28858, f. 8r.

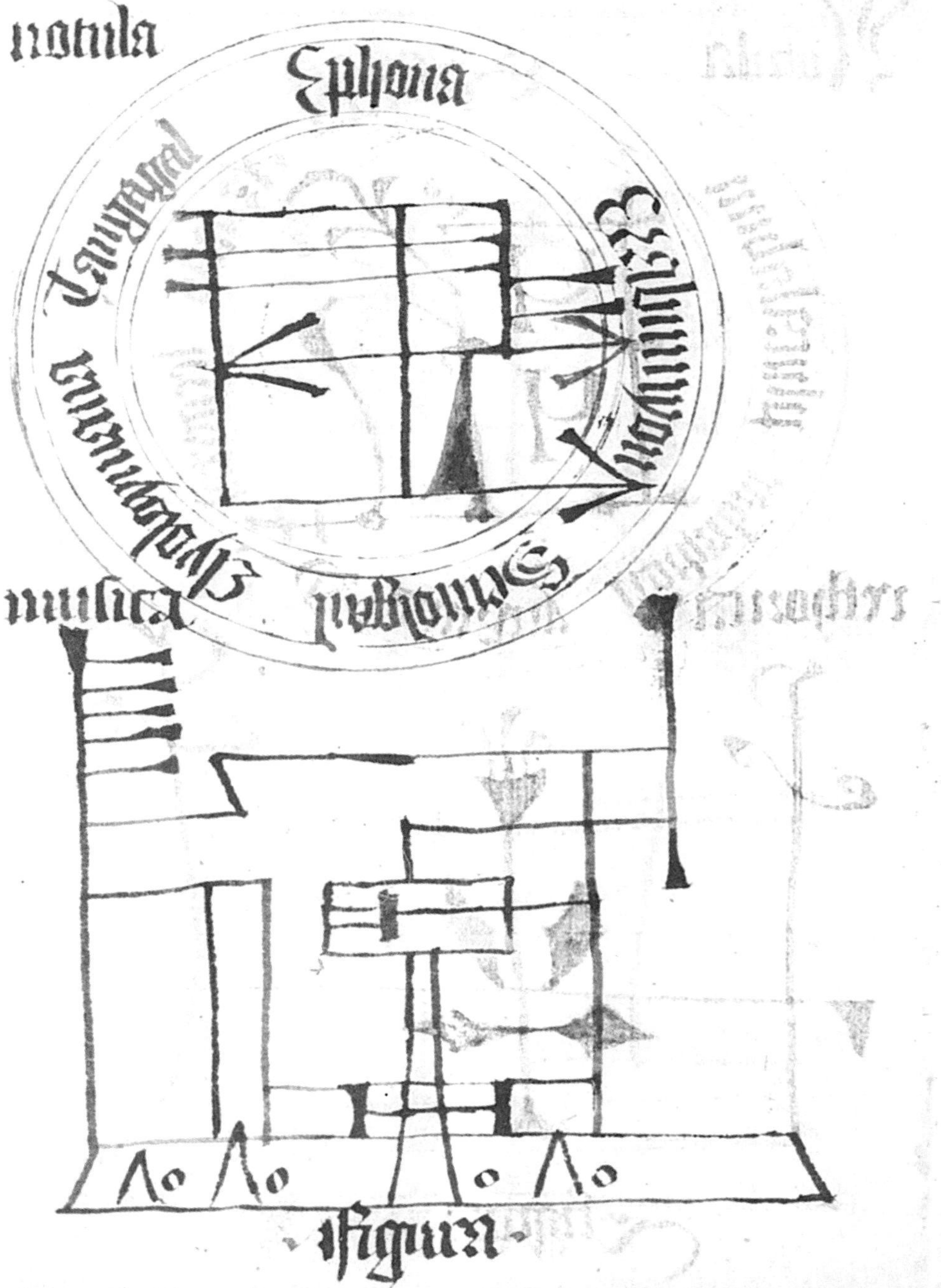

The figure of music.
BSB CLM 28858, f. 8v.

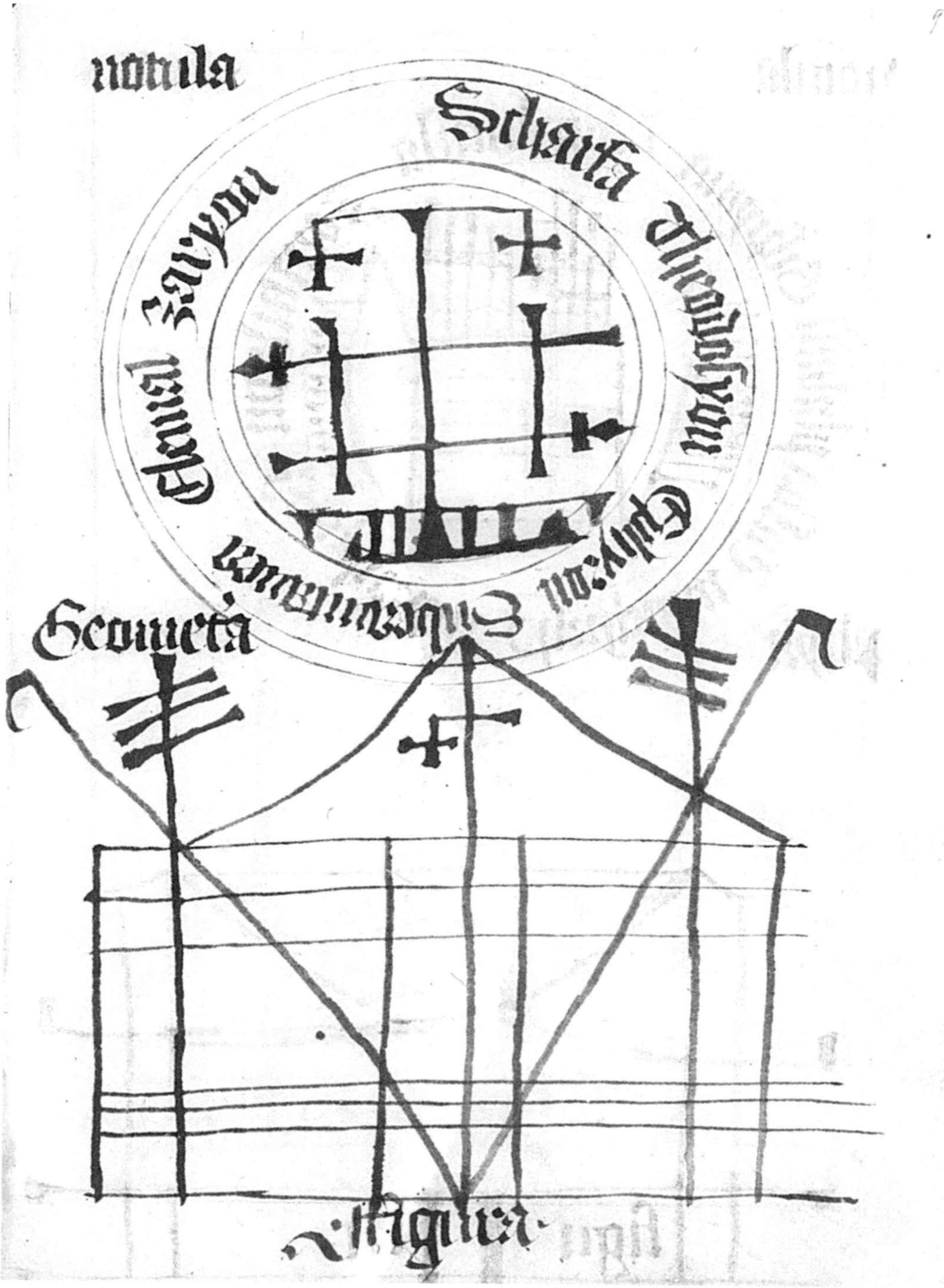

The figure of geometry.
BSB CLM 28858, f. 9r.

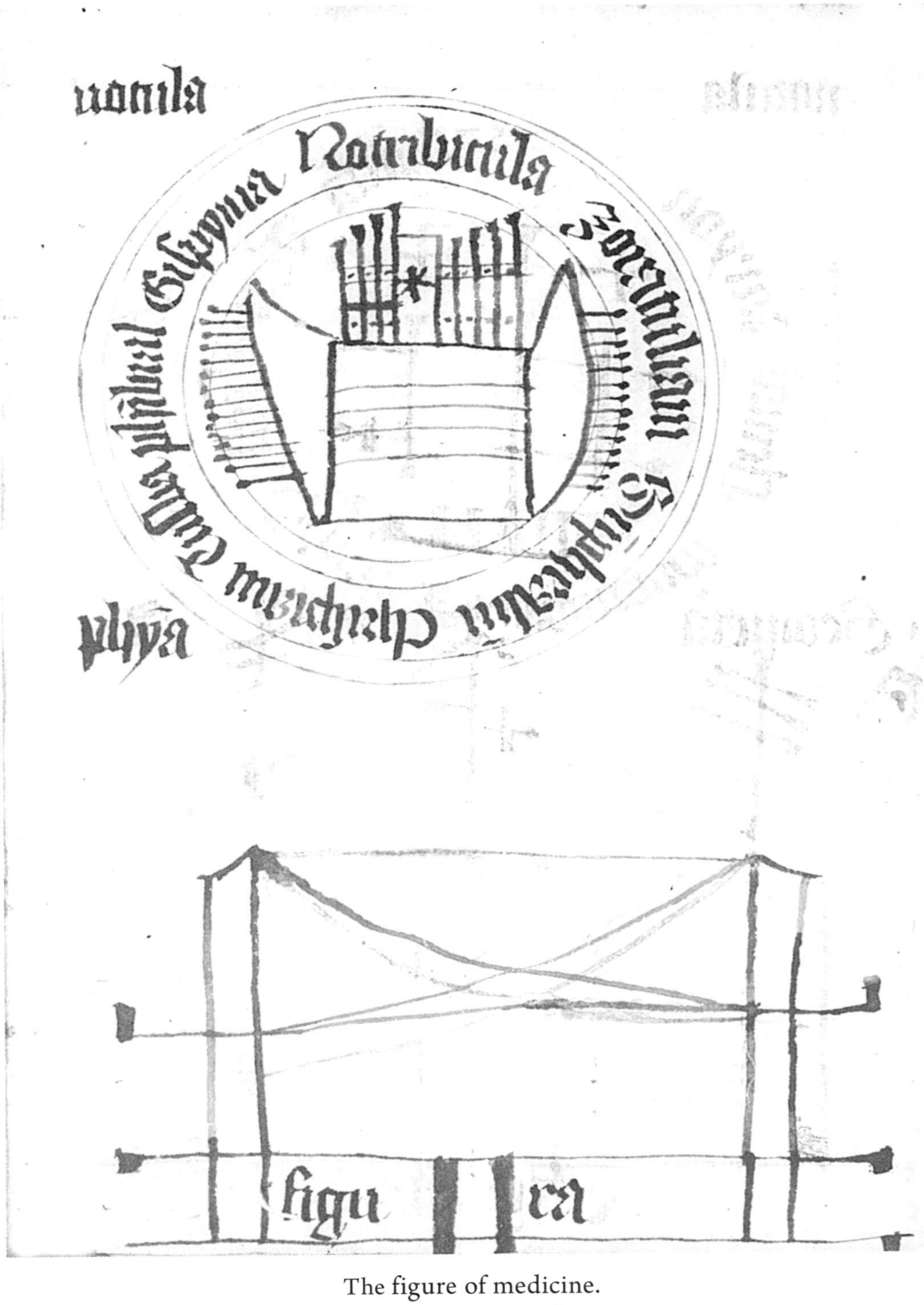

The figure of medicine.
BSB CLM 28858, f. 9v.

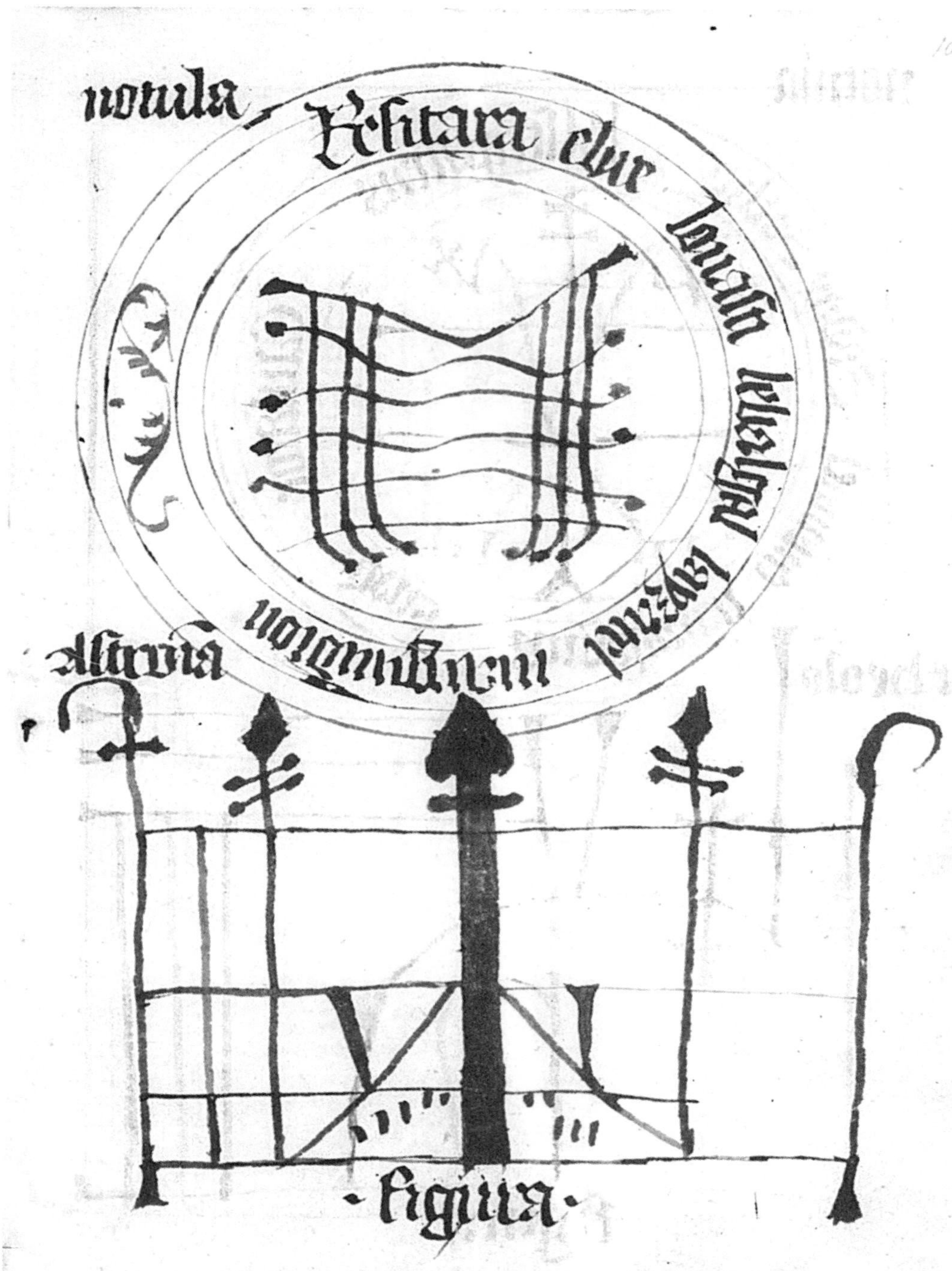

The figure of astronomy.
BSB CLM 28858, f. 10r.

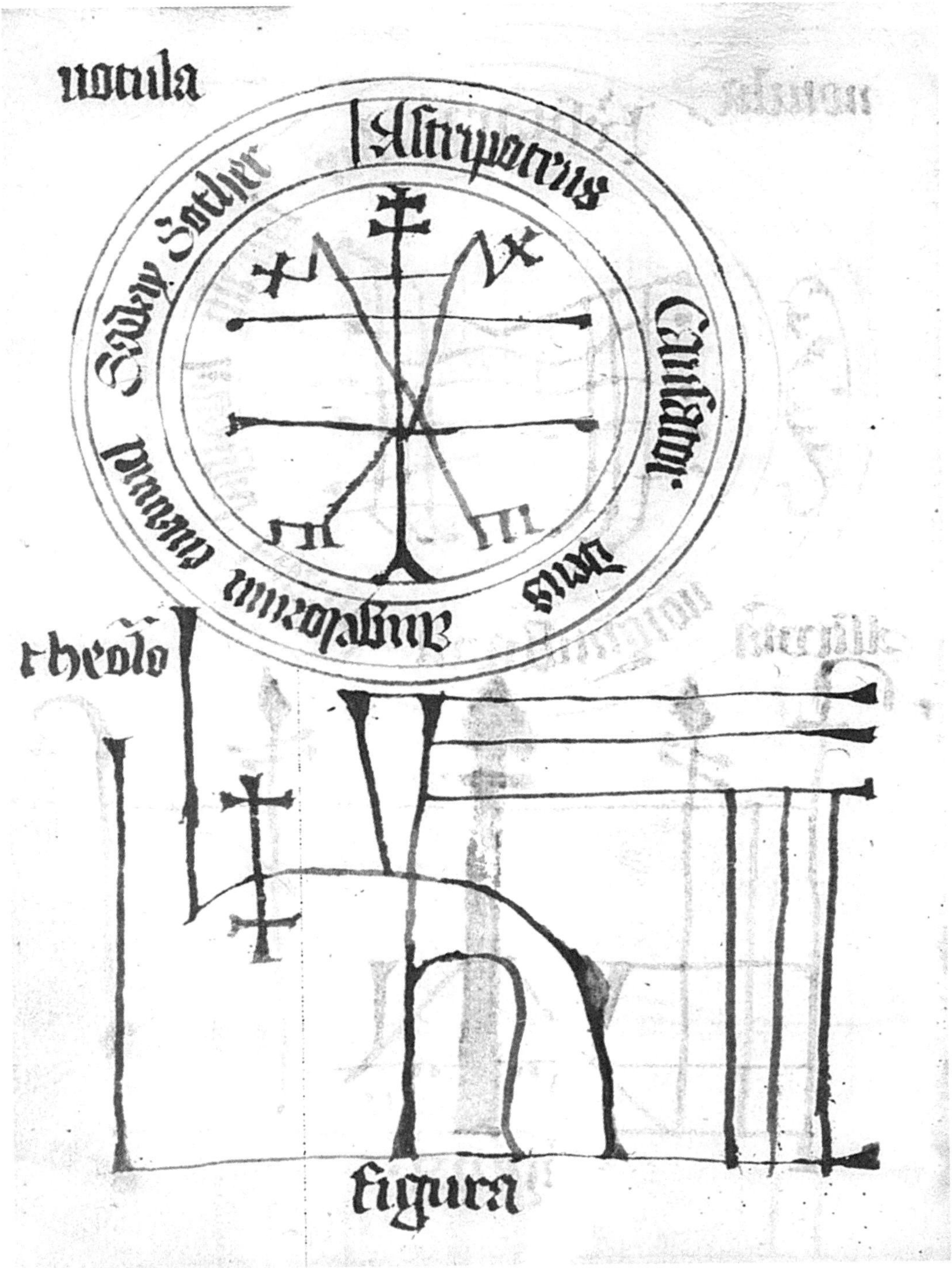

The figure of theology.
BSB CLM 28858, f. 10v.

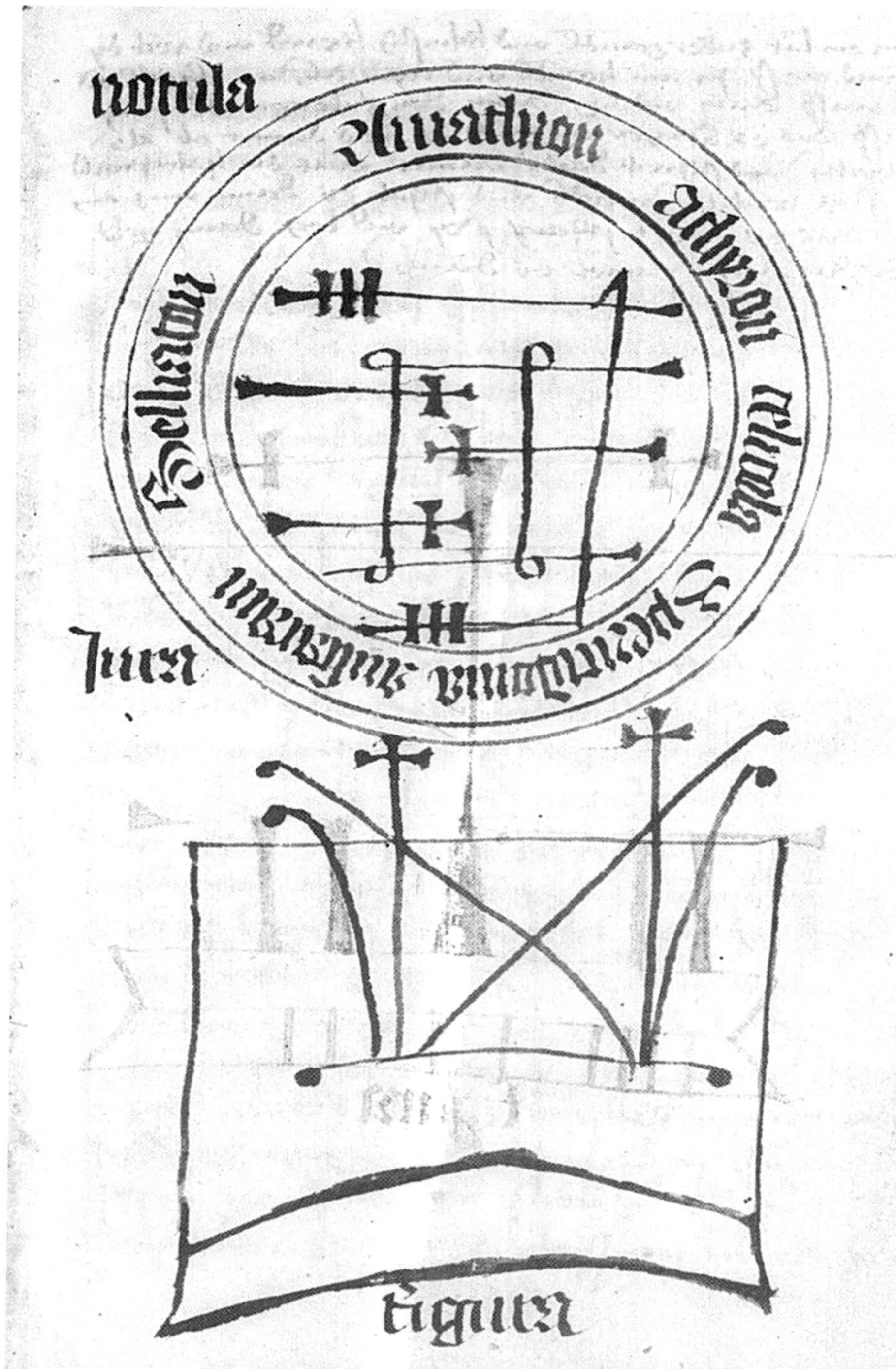

The figure of jurisprudence.
BSB CLM 28858, f. 11r.

9

Ars Paulina (Pauline Art [of Seven Figures])

15th–18th Centuries

The *Ars Paulina,* renamed here as the *Pauline Art of Seven Figures,* is a fifteenth-century magical treatise composed in the *ars notoria* tradition by an anonymous author. The treatise, probably of Italian origin, explains its mythical origins as dating back to the account of Paul of Tarsus, in which he had a divine vision, having been taken up into the third heaven.[1] This magical handbook contains seven figures dedicated to the Holy Trinity, the Virgin Mary, the nine orders of the angelic hierarchy, and the saints in order to attain knowledge of the Holy Scriptures in three months. This magical handbook of seven figures is not to be confused with the seventeenth-century angelic treatise by the same name found in the five-book compilation known as the *Lemegeton.* This seventeenth-century text is for the evocation of celestial and angelic spirits; it is divided into two parts: (1) the angels of the hours of the day and night and their magical seals; and (2) the angels of the zodiac, their seals, and also how to obtain knowledge of one's genius or guardian angel.

The *Ars Paulina* acknowledges that it follows in the footsteps of the *ars notoria* tradition; indeed, the *ars notoria* tradition, as a whole, has shown a history of multiple rewrites and a Christianization of its supposed pagan origins (i.e., the *Flores Aurei*) from the *Ars Nova* to the *Ars Paulina,* which concludes

1. 2 Corinthians 12:1–4 (NRSV).

these practices. The anonymous author or copyist lacks the true definition of what a *nota* actually is, as he postulates its various possible meanings. He appears to have settled on the biblical verse which is to be written within the figure as being the *nota*.

The ritual procedure begins with a prepatory stage involving self-purification practices, including confession, attending Mass, avoiding sins, fasting before the first hour of the day, and assumes an already established practice of prayers according to the canonical hours. The text strongly advises the operator to be confessed before beginning the ritual proper. Next, the operator must fast on bread and water on every Friday for seven weeks. An interim period in which the operator may rest follows between the last Friday to the first day of the new Moon.

The ritual proper begins on the new Moon, beginning with looking at the figure of the Trinity. The operator then reads the biblical versicle, or short prayer, which is associated with the figure; each figure has certain proprieties (i.e., properties) written within each figure; he may also read these as well, and both are to be read three times in each figure. The operator then precedes through the other six figures in a similar manner. Each of the seven figures is dedicated to one of the divine hypostases: (1) the Holy Trinity; (2) God the Father; (3) the Son of God; (4) the Holy Spirit; (5) the Heavenly Virtues, one of the angelic choirs of the ninefold hierarchy; (6) the Virgin Mary; and (7) the Saints. After this is done, the operator is to observe this practice on every Friday following for up to seven Fridays. Then, the operator will enter another interim period of rest, then begin the same procedure on the next new Moon, the second month. Finally, the operator repeats the entire ritual procedure again for a third and final month.

Once the operator has completed the three lunar months, he selects a day in which he goes alone into a secret place, preferrably a church, and says, "Come Holy Spirit, replenish me divinely," at which point the operator is expected to suddenly receive a grand spiritual experience, being blessed with the grace of God and the knowledge of the Holy Scriptures. Following these ritual instructions, *Ars Paulina* appears to come to a close.[2] This is the first published

2. However, the scribe of Latin 3180 did add the *Ars Notoria* prayer *Te queso Domine* along with its instruction as a lesser ritual (sections 25–26).

English translation of the fifteenth-century *Ars Paulina;* it follows the Vatican manuscript labeled Latin 3180, although the Halle and Parisian manuscripts were also consulted. The *Ars Paulina* is found in the following manuscripts:

1. Vatican, Vatican Apostolic Library, Latin 3180, f. 43v–47r, 15th century
2. Halle, Universitäts- und Landesbibliothek Sachsen-Anhalt, 14.B.36, f. 295r–297v, 16th century
3. Paris, Bibliothèque nationale de France, Latin 7170A, f., 16th century, (fragment)
4. Trapani, Biblioteca Fardelliana, Fardelliana 175, f. 50–68, 18th century
5. Leipzig, Stadtsbibliothek 829, 18th century

[*Ars Paulina*]

[1] O Holy Spirit, present to us grace, amen. The *Pauline Art [of Seven Figures]*, having been named after the blessed Paul, begins, having discovered for himself after his rapture, having been crowned [by God], apart from which it is accustomed to being called an *ars notoria,* which the prefaced [treatise, the *Ars Notoria,*] gives the sciences and *notitias,* whether it is accustomed to being called "*notoria*" because through brief notables things or through brief notes[3]—that is, having positioned prayers notably—everything to be said it teaches, and because every wisdom is from the Lord God. Thus, [the *notitia,* or biblical verse,] is to be placed in the first figure of the Trinity with the following prayer.

[2a] The figure of the Holy Trinity must be in the form of divine goodness, may it be in my work; because I begin in his name, my votive prayer and my desire must be finished. **"When you opened up my heart, O Lord, since then I ran the way of your commandments."**[4]

[2b] "O God, whose inerrable power, the inestimable knowledge, incomprehensible majesty, ineffable providence, inevitable judgment, inseparable Trinity, inclining piety is where you breathe [living] essence and no [living] essence is to die, you who lives and reigns as one God in the Father, Son, and Holy Spirit, who [is] everlasting without beginning and without end, in which he is the fountain of all good things, and who [is] the perfection in the Trinity with distinction, you take neither the first nor the last [position]; O eternal king, listen to me with the most simplest thing and acknowledge my prayers, your servant, *N.*, so that I may come before the congregation of your name, incline my heart [up to the heavens] to the infusion of your grace, and give me, your boy, an understanding through the clarity of your holy wisdom, you who lives and reigns as threefold and one in the ages of ages, amen.

---

3. Latin *per brevia notabilia vel per breves notas.*

4. Psalm 119:32, "Heh" (NRSV).

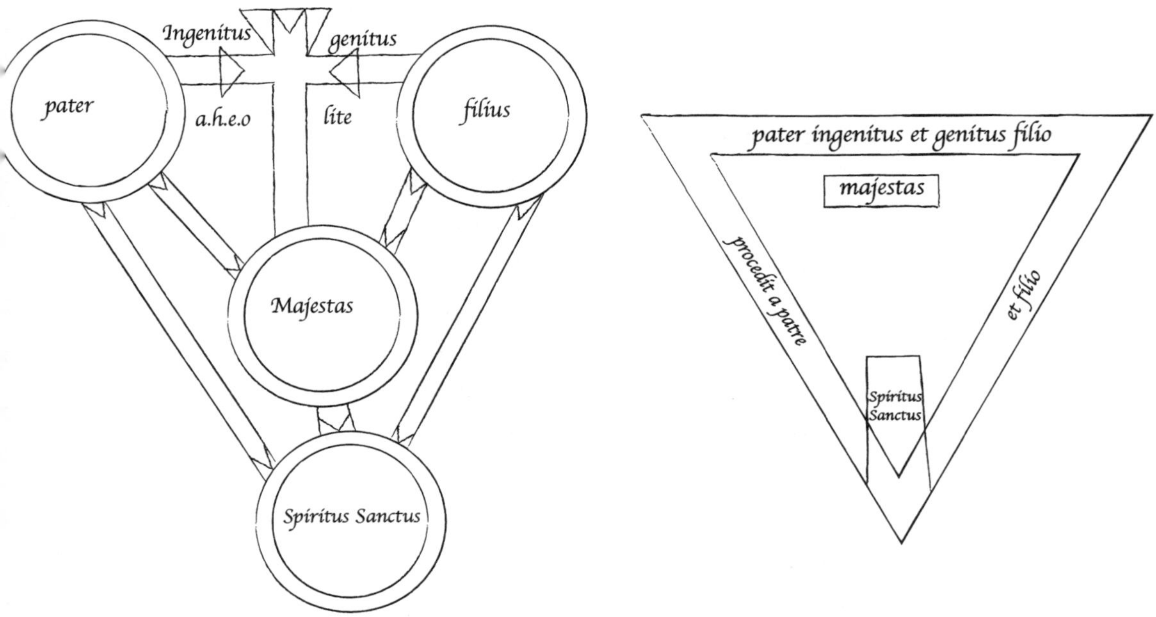

The figure of the Holy Trinity. *Left,* Vat. Lat. 3080. *Right,* Halle 14.B.36.

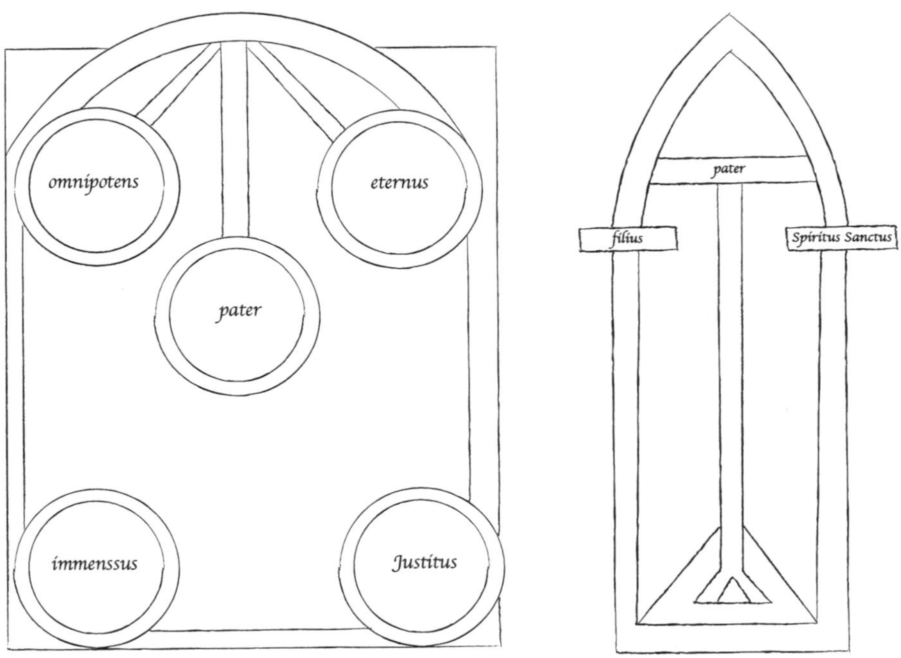

The figure of the Father. *Left,* Vat. Lat. 3080. *Right,* Halle 14.B.36.

[**3a**] Behold the Figure of the Father. The figure of the holy paternity which is the total principal of good, **"Incline your ear, [etc.], amen."**[5]

[3b] O God the almighty Father, you who are the hidden knower, who knew all things before they were made, whose majesty and empire is everlasting in eternity, you who are unbegotten and uncreated, the beginning and end of all creatures, make a sign with me in goodness, and lead me through the path of your commandments, you who are the just and the right judgment; O Lord, make your mercy with your servant, so that the light of your brillance expels the darkness of my mind, having been led through the stain of sins, you who denies no one, humbly deprecating you by whatever means, you alone who does not want to be prayed for [something], but yet you attend or show us to excite [ourselves] toward deprecating you who [are] that exhibition, you who spoke in the person of your Son, speaking, "Ask, and receive, seek and discover, and knock, it is to be opened."[6] Therefore, listen, O Lord, to my call of deprecation, as long as I pray to you, while I raise upward my hands to your holy temple, extend your mercy to knowing you, so that you may give joy, having replenished my heart with the gift of your holiness, you who promised Abraham, your servant and his seed the benediction in the ages of ages. O Lord, open my mouth and implement that . . . ,[7] so that, almighty Father, through your holy scriptures, I your servant, *N.*, may be able to know your congregation, amen.

[**4a**] Behold the figure of the Son of God with the following prayer: **"The figure of God the Father before the substance of the Son out of the virgin or mother of birth in the age of the principal power, goodness, magnitude, eternity, and wisdom, amen."**[8]

5. Psalm 31:2. (NRSV).

6. Matthew 7:7–8.

7. The ellipsis acts as a placeholder for the operator to insert his desired knowledge of the Holy Scriptures.

8. Unidentified source, possibly an adapted prayer from an ordinary of the mass.

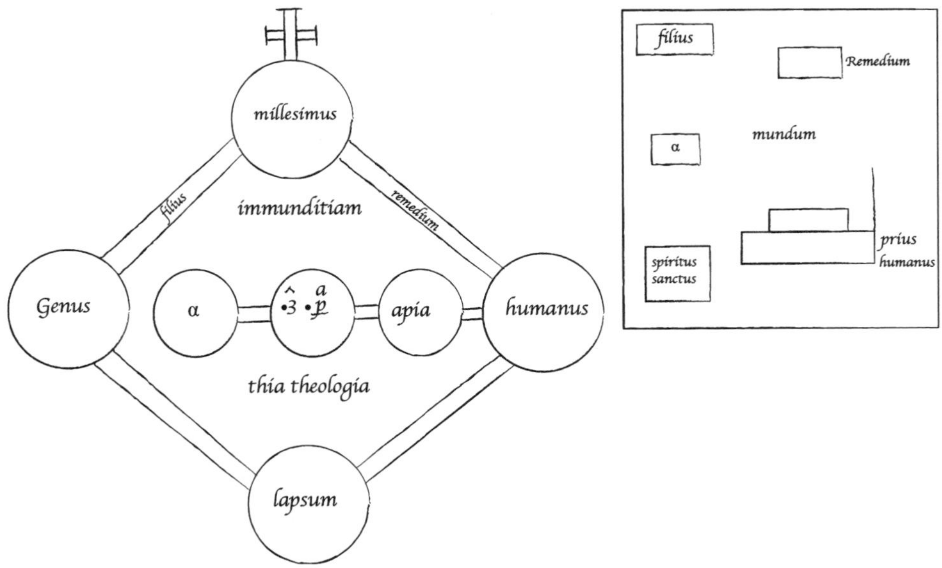

The figure of the Son. *Left,* Vat. Lat. 3080. *Right,* Halle 14.B.36.

[4b] O God, restorer of the human race, you who descended onto the earth, having compassion for our sins from the right hand of God the Father, direct my steps, you who illuminated eyes blind at birth, illuminate the eyes of my heart, which my hope is in you, from the richness of your mercy, not to ever sleep in an ignorant death, you who, wanting to teach the people of Israel, gave Moses the shepherd, afterward you disappear, you are a vision,[9] [and] you are consorted with men; O Lord, see my heart, my humility, and my labor, and open your holy treasures of your wisdom to me, just as you opened to the petitioning Solomon; O Lord, extend your holy arm, and may my free soul, may it not perish; O Lord, pour the dew of your grace for me, your servant, *N.*, and [pour it for] my salvation, make . . .[10] for your . . .[11] through the inspiration of your holy knowledge, amen.

9. Latin *postea interis visus es,* could also be translated as "afterward you die, you are an apparition." This may reference the Gospel accounts of visions of Jesus just after the resurrection: Matthew 14:22–33, 17:1–8; Mark 6:45–52, 9:2–8; John 21:1–14; Luke 9:28–36.

10. The ellipsis acts as a placeholder for the operator to insert his desired knowledge of the Holy Scriptures.

11. The practitioner supplies either "male servant" (*famulum*) or "female servant" (*ancillae*) when speaking the prayer based on his or her sex.

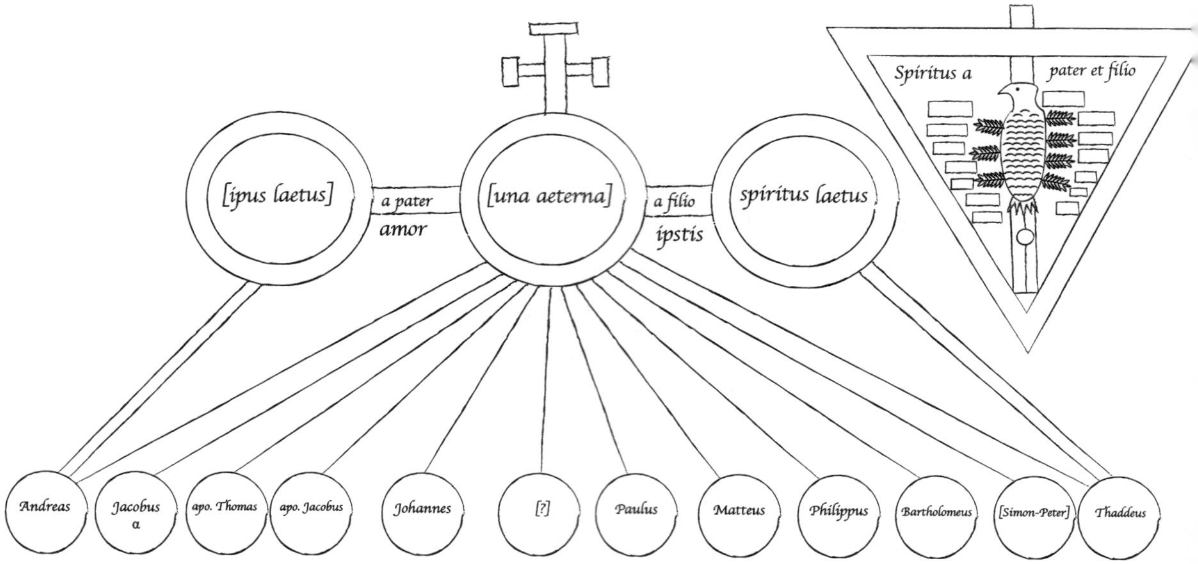

The figure of the Holy Spirit. *Left,* Vat. Lat. 3080. *Right,* Halle 14.B.36.

[5a] Afterward the fourth figure of the Holy Spirit follows through it with the following prayer: **"[Come,] Holy Spirit, [etc.]."**[12]

[5b] O God the Holy Spirit, you who visited the holy apostles by your infusion, and you taught them every kind of language, and you opened [their] senses, so that they understood the Scriptures, and you comforted them, so that no one was frightened, and they were prepared to suffer everything for you, pour into me, your servant, *N.*, and your . . .[13] **your same grace, and breathe into me from where you breathe the [living] essence, and replenish my heart with the knowledge to be kept safe, and restore my sterile ability to speak and write well and eloquence, so that I may attend the congregation of the true Scriptures**[14] **in your love; O Holy Spirit, pour divinely your affected breath into me, amen.**

---

12. *Veni Sancte Spiritus,* also called the Golden Sequence, is a sequence found in the Masses of Pentecost.

13. The practitioner supplies either "son" (*filii*) or "handmaiden" (*ancillae*) when speaking the prayer based on his or her sex.

14. The practitioner studies the Scriptures with his church congregation.

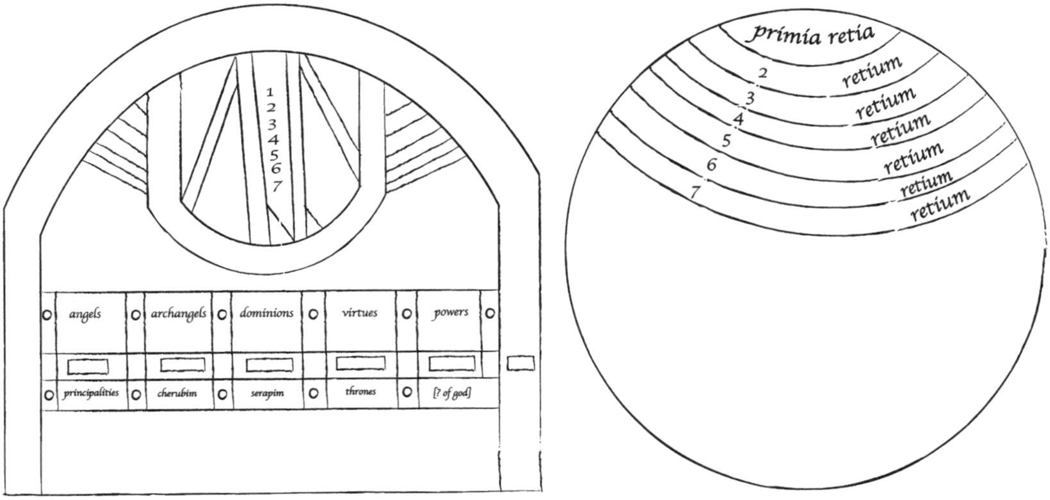

The figure of the Heavenly Virtues. *Left,* Vat. Lat. 3080. *Right,* Halle 14.B.36.

[6a] Behold the following figure of all the holy heavenly Virtues with the following prayer: “[. . .] **the heavenly suffrages lift me up to grace** [. . . , **etc.**], **amen.**”[15]

[6b] O God, you who had become the fabricator of all the Virtues and the orderer of the heavenly spirits, you exercise your disposed secrets and your volitions through their offices; O Lord, look toward me, your servant, *N.*, laboring under darkened ignorances, so that your grace replenishes your goodness and gifts [within me] through the ministration of the heavenly Virtues; that you, O God, are the Lord of the sciences, and may you eruditely instruct (that blessed man),[16] O Lord, and may you teach (that one) about your law; O most gentle Lord, send the angels, the operation of your Virtues, so that I, your servant, *N.*, the participant and strength, seeking to know your knowledge, O God, you who lives and reigns, through the ages of ages, amen.

15. Unidentified source, possibly an adapted prayer from an ordinary of the mass. Latin, “[. . .] *caelestibus suffragiis sublevare me ad gratiam,* [. . . , *etc.*], *amen.*”

16. “(that blessed man)” is a placeholder for the operator to insert his own name. The same goes for “(that one)” in the next clause.

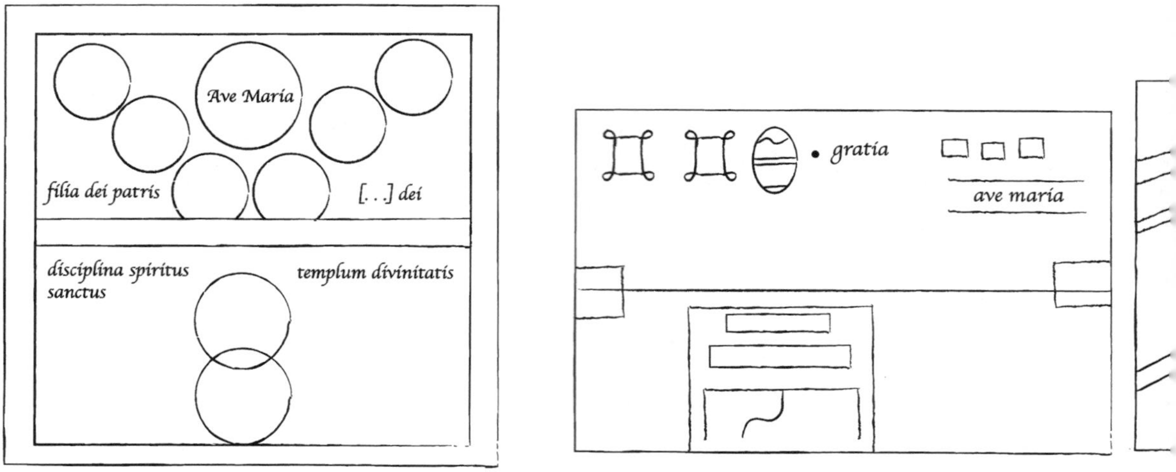

The figure of the Virgin Mary. *Left,* Vat. Lat. 3080. *Right,* Halle 14.B.36.

[7a] Behold the figure of the glorious Virgin Mary: **"O holy birth mother of God, Mary, Virgin mother, irrigate and make abundant my heart with the fountain of plenitude of your grace, and answer me, your servant, *N.*, because my prayer is confided in you."**[17]

[7b] O most holy one of ladies, the mother of God, and you who are the daughter, the consolation of all desolations, and the empress of all goodness, procure mercy for me, your servant, *N.*, in the presence of the Lord and your most holy Son, so that your intimate dew is made abundant with an aspersion upon me, with respect to the acknowledge of your truth, just as you made the prophet Isaiah abundant, amen.

17. *Sancta dei gentrix, Maria, virga mater, irriga et fecunda cor meum fonte plenitudinis gratiae tuae, et exaudi me, famulum tuum, G., quia in te confidit oratio mea.* The scribe of Latin 3180 had a name that began with the letter *G.*

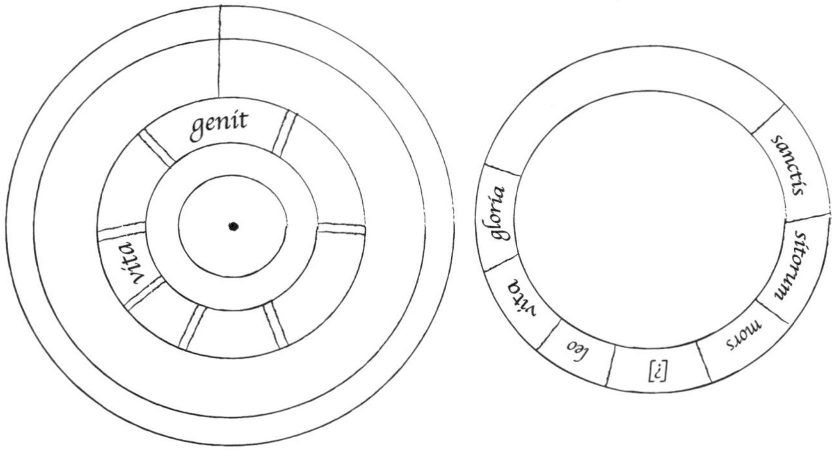

The figure of the Saints. *Left,* Vat. Lat. 3080. *Right,* Halle 14.B.36.

[8a] Behold the seventh and last figure with the following prayer concerning all the saints of the Lord: **"And may the copiousness of true merits with their services pour over me, a sinner. Adore, [O God,] all the [saints'] gifts according to his own, for me, a true servant, *N.*, so that his firewood blazes within my heart, amen."**[18]

[8b] O God, you who are the illuminating splendor of your saints, kindling the heat and inflaming the fire, illuminate my heart, kindle my intellect, enflame my will, direct my imagination or my retention, excite my reason or my reception, strengthen my memory, so that I, your creature, may be deserving to obtain the grace of illumination through the intercession of your saints in the presence of you, may I serve you, my Creator, worthily, having known the truth of all Scriptures; O Lord, you who having spoken [them], and they are made, bid me to be replenished divinely without a delay of time through the gifts of your holy knowledge, the virtue of your mercy, from which every one is given the best, and every gift is made perfect; O Lord, descend and bless me, your creature, and reveal to me, your servant, *N.*, your ways, just as you revealed your heavenly secrets to blessed Paul and blessed John who [laid] over your chest, and you who lives and reigns in the ages of ages, amen.

---

18. *Et veroum meritorum copia, mihi, peccatori, infunda[t] munera sua. Adorate donum omnes secundum cuius pro me famulo vero G, ut lucus sue raditis fulgeat in corde meo, amen.*

[9] Note the precepts from the ordinary of masses to which arts they belong;[19] these are to be observed and kept penitently. First, you must be truly penitent and confessed, and if you were wanting to receive the Eucharist, [then your confession] must be written on a sacred page, because God does not answer sinners. Second, when you begin, you must be on guard against drunkenness, gluttony, and lechery. Third, you must not eat or drink before the first hour of the day, unless you devoutly complete [and] experience all the prayers first. Fourth, if you will fall into mortal sin just short of the very day [of the operation and] if you find a confessor quickly, [then] you must confess quickly, or [if you will fall] to the lesser [sins],[20] just short or less than two days, [then you must confess quickly]; and if you sin mortally at night, [then] you must confess by the early morning before you speak your prayers. Fifth, before you begin this art, you must fast seven Fridays on bread and water.[21] But having completed the seven Fridays, you will rest up to the first day of the new Moon. And in the first new Moon you must begin to look[22] at the first figure; namely, the Trinity. Afterward, you must read the collected [biblical verses] of that figure and its propriety[23] with devotion, then the prayer in the first hour of the day. Still, note that you must read nothing from the writings within the figure,[24] and thus, you will observe according to the proprieties and mandates three times in any figure, and thus you will observe through the seven days continuously, and you will rest up to the other new Moon, and thus [what] you acknowledge in the first Moon, you will observe continuously through the seven days. And you will perform [these things according to the rules] for the third time you undergo [the ritual] in the third Moon. And having completed the three lunar months, you must elect for you one day you want for yourself, and in that day

19. These are the biblical versicles and short prayers found in the caption to each figure.

20. Latin idiom *adminus,* which literally means "to the lesser"; that is to say, the less severe or milder sins.

21. That is, the operator is to fast on bread and water on every Friday for seven weeks as a part of self-purification prior to the ritual proper. Then there is an interim period of rest between the last fast and the new Moon.

22. Latin *osculari,* not the verb *inspicio* as found in the *Ars Notoria.*

23. An obsolete English word derived from the Latin, which means the particular property or essence of someone or some thing.

24. This command runs contradictory to the previous sentence. Perhaps this instruction is carried down from the *ars notoria* tradition in which it was prohibited to speak the *voces magicae* written within the figures.

at the third hour you must be in the most secret place (if it is possible, this takes place in a church), and then you must begin to say on bent knees, **"Come Holy Spirit, replenish me divinely,"** and you must say [it] thrice, and rise up in the name of the Lord, and immediately the grace of God will encircle you, and you will have your full effect. And in this way, you will immediately understand the divine Scripture through your very own self after the seven days, and you will be totally full with sublimity, understanding, and eloquence, so that you will marvel about yourself, and [wonder] if you are born again. Thanks be to God, amen.

Appendices

APPENDIX 1

Manuscripts and Editions

This appendix contains tables which inventory the manuscripts and editions of the *ars notoria* tradition. The first table lists the manuscripts and editions of the *Ars Notoria*. The second table inventories the manuscripts of the *Opus Operum*. The third table lists the manuscripts and editions belonging to the *Ars Brevis*. The fourth table gives the manuscripts of the abridged notory art attributed to Thomas of Toledo. The fifth table shows the manuscripts belonging to the *Ars Paulina* (i.e., *The Pauline Art [of Seven Figures]*). The sixth and final table catalogs those witnesses identified as belonging to the *ars notoria* tradition but have not been studied; this final table is meant for those who wish to pursue further in-depth scholarship of the *ars notoria* tradition. For those interested in the extant manuscripts of John of Morigny's *Liber Florum Caelestis Doctrinae*, see Fanger and Watson (2015).

The *Ars Notoria* Manuscripts table examines the extant witnesses from the first half of the thirteenth century up to the nineteenth century. This table includes new additional witnesses and updated research, following after the lists from Thorndike, Klaassen, Véronèse, and Skinner and Clark. Although Véronèse admits to problems with the exact accounting of the extant manuscripts, he makes a general inference that the *ars notoria* tradition became established in the thirteenth century, rose in popularity in the fourteenth century when there was a proliferation of derivative works, and then showed a steady decline after the fifteenth century.[1] This is evident in studying the table.

1. Véronèse, "L'Ars notoria au Moyen Age," 1:32–35.

The table is laid out in four columns (from left to right): title, date and provenance, library information, and version. The title is usually what is written in the witness; if not, I have simply identified it as "*Ars Notoria*" or left it as untitled. The date and provenance is the best estimate provided by informed scholars such Véronèse himself or the library who houses the witness in question. Sometimes the date is written in the manuscript, including the month and date.

The library information presents the details of a manuscript or edition. These details include the city in which the witness is currently located, the library or institution in which the witness is housed, the name of the collection to which that witness belongs, the witness's shelf number or call number, and the folios or pages on which the *Ars Notoria* text can be found. The collection is typically named after the donor, patron, or other prominent figure associated with the library or institution (e.g., Hans Sloane). The folio is identified according to whether it is recto (r), the front page or the right-hand side of an open book; or verso (v), the back page or the left-hand side of an open book.

For example, the first *nota* of grammar is found in Paris, BnF Latin 7152, f. 12. The city of provenance is Paris, "BnF" stands for the Bibliothèque nationale de France (National Library of France), "Latin 7152" is the call number, and "f. 12" (folio 12) means it is found on page 12 on the recto side of the page (the "r" is dropped customarily).

The final column presents to which version the *Ars Notoria* witness belongs. Véronèse's classification system has three possible designations—Version A, A2, or B. I am also classifying those witnesses which contain both the *Ars Notoria* and the *Opus Operum* (its text and/or its figures) as Version A2.[2] I have also extended Véronèse's classification system to the later manuscripts. Here, I am proposing a fourth version, Version C, to denote those *Ars Notoria* witnesses which present two or more of the following characteristics: (1) reveals special material not found in the previous three versions, (2) contains no *Ars Notoria* figures, (3) presents Christian Kabbalistic or other magical figures and (4) has *Ars Notoria* sections presented in a disorganized manner.. These witnesses are

2. The Parisian manuscript labeled NAL 1565 is classed as a Version A2 manuscript for its *Opus Operum* figure; however, it also exhibits Version B–style figures, specifically the first figure of grammar (f. 14), the four wheels of knowledge (f. 15v–a), and the second figure of rhetoric (f. 16).

typically those which join the *Ars Notoria* with the *Ars Brevis* and may include additional esoteric and magical interests; they are often dated to the sixteenth and seventeenth centuries.

Question marks indicate uncertainty about that particular quality within the table. The manuscripts Véronèse used in creating his critical edition is marked by a single asterisk in the "Version" column of the table. Some manuscripts include the names of their owners; these are also found in the "Library Information" column.

ARS NOTORIA MANUSCRIPTS

Title	Date and Provenance	Library Information	Version
Flores Aurei, sive Ars Notoria	1225, northern Italy	Yale, University Library, Mellon 1, f. 1–18v	A*
Untitled	Early 13th century, Italy	Paris, BnF Latin 7373, f. 176, (fragment, first figure of rhetoric)	A
Ars Notoria	1225, northern Italy	Erfurt, Wissenschaftliche Bibliothek, Amplonianum Collegium, Quarto 380, f. 49–64v (no *notae*)	A*
Ars Notoria	1239, northern Italy	Paris, BnF Latin 7152, f. 1–22	A2*
Ars Notoria	1250, Italy?	London, British Library, Sloane 1712, f. 1–22v	A, A2*
Ars Notoria	Third quarter of the 13th century (1250–1260),	Turin, Biblioteca Nazionale, E.V.13, f. 1–31v	A*
Ars Notoria	Late 13th century	Vienna, Österreichische Nationalbibliothek, Cod. 15482, 1–14v	A2
Untitled	13th–14th centuries	Oxford, Bodleian Libraries, Digby 218 part 7, f. 109 (fragment, four figures)	A

*Manuscripts used by Véronèse for his critical edition.

ARS NOTORIA MANUSCRIPTS (*cont'd.*)

Title	Date and Provenance	Library Information	Version
Untitled	13th century	Klosterneuburg, Augustiner-Chorherrenstift, CC 221, f. 1r–15v (fragment, eight figures)	A
Ars Notoria	13th–14th centuries	Klosterneuburg, Augustiner-Chorherrenstift, CC 759, f. 169–75	A
Ars Notoria	13th–14th centuries	Vienna, Österreischiche Nationalbibliothek, cod. 15482, f. 1–14v	A2
De Arte Notoria	13th–15th centuries	Vorau (Styria), Stift Vorau. Bibliothek, Codex Voraviensis 186 (CCCXIX), item 11, f. 188v–191r, 1v–2v (fragment)	?
Ars Notoria	14th century	Graz, Universitätsbibliothek 1016, f. 47v–71v	A2
Apollonii Flores Aurei	14th century	Leiden, Bibliotheca Universitatis Leidensis, Codices Vulcaniani, 45, f. 12–25v	A2
Apollonius Flores Aureos ad Eruditionem	14th century	Munich, Bayerische Staatsbibliothek, CLM 268, f. 1–16v	A
Ars Notoria	14th century	Vatican, Biblioteca Apostolica, Vatican Latin 6842, f. 8rb–23v	A2
Ars Notoria	1340–1350	Vatican, Biblioteca Apostolica, Vatican Latin 3185, f. 1–26v	A
La Art de Memoire	14th century	Paris, BnF NAL 1565, f. 1–20	A2, B
Ars notoria (tractatus de arte notoria Salomonis)	14th century	Erfurt, Wissenschaftliche Bibliothek, Amplonianum Coll., Octavo 84 (= Math 14), f. 96–107v	A2
Salomonis verissimus et sanctissimus Almandel, auctore Apollonio	14th century	Wolfenbüttel, Herzog August Bibliothek, Cod. Guelf. 47.15 Aug. Quarto, f. 1–35	A2

ARS NOTORIA MANUSCRIPTS (*cont'd.*)

Title	Date and Provenance	Library Information	Version
Apollonii Flores Aurei	Second quarter of the 14th century, Germany	Munich, Bayerische Staatsbibliothek, CLM 276, fols. 1–26	A
Ars Notoria	Second quarter of the 14th century, northern Italy	Kremsmünster, Austria. Stifsbibliothek, CC 322, f. 1–25	B*
Ars Notoria	14th century, France?	Bernkastel-Kues, Germany, Hospitalsbibliothek, 216, f. 1–45	B*
Ars Notoria	14th century	Krakow, Jagiellonian Biblioteka, 2076, f. IIr–v (fragment)	B
Dogma Artis Notoriae, sive Eruditio Praeceptores Eadem	Second quarter of the 14th century, Germany	Munich, Bayerische Staatsbibliothek, CLM 276, f. 39v–47v (glosses)	B
Ars Notoria	Second quarter of the 14th century, Bologna, Italy	Paris, Bnf Latin 9336, f. 1–28v	B*
Ars Notoria	c. 1401–1450	Weimar, Herzogin Anna Amalia Bibliothek, f. 374/2, f. 2ra–10rb (gloss), 10va–27v (base text)	B
Flores Aueris, Ars memorativa	1431	Prague, National Library of the Czech Republic, 267 (I. F. 35), f. 464v–76v, 477–84 (Frater Matheus Beran)	A
Ars Notoria	15th century	Florence, Biblioteca Medicea Laurenziana, Plut. 89, Sup. 35, f. 151–53 (fragment)	A2
Ars Notoria	Mid-15th century	Edinburgh, Royal Observatory Library, MS Cr.3.14, f. 23–30	A2
Flores Aurei et eruditionem (Recueil d'astrologie)	15th century, southeastern France?	Carpenteras, Bibliotheque Municipale, 0341, f. 1–51	A
Ars Notoria	15th century, Flanders?	Oxford, Bodleian Libraries, Bodley 951 [Bodleian, Ashmole 2871], f. 1–19v	B*

ARS NOTORIA MANUSCRIPTS (*cont'd.*)

Title	Date and Provenance	Library Information	Version
Sacratissima Ars Notoria	16th century (1554)	Paris, BnF Latin 7153, f. 1–192v	B
Sacratissima Ars Notoria	16th century (1550–1560)	Paris, BnF Latin 7154, f. 3–100v	B
?	16th century	London, British Library, Harley 181, f. 1–74v (composite)	B
?	16th century	Prague, National Library, 1866, f. 52–55v (fragment)	B?
Liber de Arte Notoria	16th century	Paris, BnF 7170A, f. 1–6v (fragment)	B
?	1567	London, British Library, Sloane 3846, f. 23v–24v (fragment)	B?
Ars Notoria	16th century	Halle, Landesbibliothek, Sachsen-Anhalt, 14. B. 36, f. 307r–343v (composite of *Ars Notoria* and *Ars Brevis*)	C
?	Late 16th century	Oxford, Bodleian Libraries, Ashmole 1515, f. 4–10, 23–40 (fragment; Latin, English)	B
Ars Notoria	1567–1600 Italy	Berlin, Staatsbibliothek zu Berlin, MS Lat. Fol. 326, 142 sheets	B
Liber de Arte Memorativa	1600, London	Jerusalem, National Library of Israel, Yahuda Var. 34, f. 1–31v; Simon Forman	B
?	16th–17th centuries	Raleigh, North Carolina, 39; Rev. A. B. Hunter, f. 1–24 (composite)	B?
Liber de Arte Memorativa sive Notoria	1600, June 28	Cambridge, Trinity College, O.9.7 (James number 1419), p. 7-114, (composite; Simon Forman)	B

ARS NOTORIA MANUSCRIPTS (*cont'd.*)

Title	Date and Provenance	Library Information	Version
Liber de Arte memorativa Ars Notoria	1601	Oxford, Bodleian Libraries, Jones 1 [Bodleian 8908], f. 6–85v	B
Fragment in *Sefer Mafteah Shelomoh*	17th century, Amsterdam	London, British Library, Oriental 14759, f. 1r–4v, 52r–53v (fragment in the Hebrew version of the *Key of Solomon;* has ten *Ars Notoria* figures)	B
Ars Notoria	c. 1620	Found within Henry Cornelius Agrippa, *Opera Omnia,* pages 603–60 (composite; Latin, *Ars Notoria* and *Ars Brevis*)	C
Ars Notoria Salomonis	17th century	London, British Library, Sloane 3648, f. 33–47 (composite of *Ars Notoria* and *Ars Brevis;* English)	C
The Notory Art of Solomon	17th century	London, British Library, Harley 6483, f. 280 (composite; English, Robert Turner trans.)	C
Ars Notoria Salomonis	17th century	London, British Library, Sloane 3825, f. 148–179 (composite; English)	C
Ars notoria	1826, April 26	Glasgow, University Library, Ferguson 50, p. 1–138 (composite; French)	C?

OPUS OPERUM MANUSCRIPTS

Title	Date	Library Information
Opus Operum	1250, Italy?	London, British Library, Sloane 1712, f. 22vb–37
Opus Operum	13th–14th centuries	Vienna, Österreichische Nationalbibliothek, Cod. 15482, (fragment)
Ars Notoria Salomonis (Opus Operum)	Early 14th century	Leiden, Bibliotheca Universitatis Leidensis, Codices Vulcaniani, 45, f. 1–11v
Opus Operum	14th century	Vatican, Biblioteca Apostolica, Vatican Latin 6842, f. 1–8r (no figures)
Ars Notoria que Nova Ars Appellavit (Opus Operum)	14th century	Munich, Bayerische Staatsbibliothek, Clm 30010, f. 1–16.
Opus Operum	Second quarter of the 14th century, Germany	Munich, Bayerische Staatsbibliothek, Clm 276, fols. 26br–39r (no figures)
Opus Operum	1601	Oxford, Bodleian Libraries, Jones 1 [Bodleian 8908], f. 6–85v
Ars Notoria Salomonis (Opus Operum)	17th century	Munich, Bayerische Staatsbibliothek, Clm 17711, f. 332r–376v (composite)

ARS BREVIS MANUSCRIPTS

Title	Date	Library Information
Ars notoria brevis et bona (Ars Brevis)	c. 1350	Erfurt, Wissenschaftliche Bibliothek, Amplonianum Coll., Octavo 79, f. 63–66 (one figure)
Ars Brevis	1377	Vienna, Österreichische Nationalbibliothek, Scot.–Vindobonensis 140 (61), f. 140–153v (one figure)
Ars Brevis	15th century	Krakow, Biblioteka Jagiellonian, 551, f. 117v

ARS BREVIS MANUSCRIPTS (*cont'd.*)

Title	Date	Library Information
Ars Brevis	15th century	Erfurt, Amplonianum Coll., Dep. Req. Approx. Quarto 028a, f. 38 (37)–42v (41v)
Ars Brevis	15th century	Edinburgh, Royal Observatory Library, Cr.3.14 (fragment)
Ars Brevis	15th century	British Library Sloane 513, f. 192–200 (Richard Dove, monk of Buckfastleigh; John Shaxton; four figures)
Tractatus de Arte Notoria, cum figura Theologiae	15th century London	British Library, Sloane 3008, fol. 66–68 (fragment of *Salve virgo mater trinitatis,* no figures)
Ars Notoria	16th century	Paris, Bibliothèque nationale de France, Latin 4161, f. 62v–66v (incipit at 63r; two figures)
Ars Notoria Salomonis	16th century	London, British Library, Sloane 3853, f. 159v–174v
?	1623	Cambridge, Trinity College, R.16.26, f. 3–22 (composite)
Liber de Arte memorativa Ars Notoria, Opus Operum	1601	Oxford, Bodleian Libraries, Jones 1 [Bodleian 8908], f. 6–85v; (composite?) Simon Forman
Ars Notoria Salomonis	c. 1620	Lyons, [Lugduni] Beringi Fratres, H. C. Agrippa, *Opera Omnia,* 2:603–660 (there are several printed editions, most notably the one held in Vienna at the ONB and there is the Strasburg, Zetzner edition, 1605B; composite of *Ars Notoria* and *Ars Brevis*, Version C).
Tractatus Artis Notoriae, Apollonius Flores Aureos	17th century	Amsterdam, Stichting het Wereldhart, Bibliotheca Philosophica Hermetica (BPH) M 242, f. 1–153 (composite of *Ars Notoria* and *Ars Brevis*, Version C)

MANUSCRIPTS OF THE ABRIDGED NOTORY ART OF THOMAS OF TOLEDO

Title	Date	Library Information
Tractatus Artis Notoriae	End of 14th century	Vatican, Biblioteca Apostolica, Pal. Lat. 957, f. 92v–95r; Thomas of Toledo (text plus *nota* of rhetoric)
Ars Notoria Salomonis Abbreviata	Late 15th century	Munich, Bayerische Staatsbibliothek, CLM 28858, f. 1–11v (text plus nine identified *notae*)

ARS PAULINA MANUSCRIPTS

Title	Date	Library Information
Ars Paulina	15th century	Vatican, Vatican Apostolic Library, Latin 3180, f. 43v–47r
Recorded as *Ars Notoria* but is actually *Ars Paulina*	16th century	Halle, 14.B.36, fol. 295r–305
Liber Visionum et Ars Paulina	16th century	Paris, BnF Latin 7170A, f. 9–10v
Ars Paulina	18th century	Leipzig, Stadtbibliothek 829 (not consulted)
Ars Notoria et Paulina	18th century	Trapani, Fardelliana (VII.C.35), 175, f. 50–68 (not consulted)

UNEXAMINED MANUSCRIPTS

Title	Date	Library Information
Eiusdem tractatus de quibusdam animalibus et eorum virtutibus et secretis, Meudus agenda &c., Lune oculum &c., Agitur hic de secretis superstitiosis. N.B. Extant praeterea in folio 1,57 et 58 orationes quaedam ad Deum et B Michaelem	1395	Florence, Bibliotheca Ambrosiana, B 8 Sup., part 6d, f. 57v–58 (Latin prayers addressed to God and Archangel Michael)
Kabbalistic composite manuscript	15th century	Düsseldorf, Universitäts- und Landesbibliothek Düsseldorf, K07:073
Unknown	15th century	Oxford, Merton College, Medieval 999
Unknown	15th century	Copenhagen, Kongelige Bibliotek Gl. Kgl. Samlung, S 3499, f. 51r–59v (German prayers)
Unknown	16th century	Kassel, Universitätsbibiothek, Quarto Chem. 96, f. 135–162 (no *notae*)
Ars Nova (?), Ars Notoria (Ars Paulina), Ars Notoria (Ars Brevis)	16th century	Halle, Landesbibliothek, Sachsen-Anhalt, 14. B. 36, f. 275r–294v (not recognizable), f. 295r–305r (*Ars Paulina*), f. 307r–343v (*Ars Brevis*)
Liber de arte memorativa sive notoria	1600	Cambridge, Trinity College MS O.9.7.
Artista de Carrenscrux, Sacer libellus arcanorum pro memoria ac arte notoria	1748	Vienna, Österreichische Nationalbibliothek, 11340, f. 39v (Elias frater OFM)
Ars Notoria Appolonii (sic)	14th–15th centuries	Eisleben, Turmbibliothek der Andreaskirche, MS 969, 20 register entry, f. 272–75
Ars Notoria?	Unknown	Florence, Biblioteca Medicea Laurenziana, Plut. 17, Cod. III., f. 156

APPENDIX 2

MAGICAL FIGURES OF THE *ARS NOTORIA*

The table starting on page 783 presents all the magical figures of the *Ars Notoria*. There are four columns in the table (from left to right): the identification tag, an example figure, the subject matter related to the figure, and finally a column that lists the manuscripts in which that figure is found. First, the identification tags are modeled after the numbering of the figures as found in the *Ars Notoria* (BnF Latin 7153), which runs from 1 to 41; any figures not numbered according to this model will begin at 42, then 43, and so on. At present, only the figure of exceptives has been designated as the 42nd figure, the very last figure according to this identificaiton scheme. This means there are only 42 unique figures of the *Ars Notoria*. Next, the 42 figures are divided into two groups of manuscripts—Version A (thirteenth to fourteenth centuries) and Version B (fourteenth to sixteenth centuries). By my definition, there are no *Ars Notoria* figures in Version C. The identification tag consists of a number and a letter. The letter *a* corresponds to all manuscripts belonging to Version A; likewise, the letter *b* corresponds to all manuscripts belonging to Version B. The reader will notice the shift in the appearance of the figures as the tradition transitions from Version A to Version B; this stage designates the figure as belonging to the Version A2 tradition. Such a figure has been assigned as "*a*–2." The column labeled "Example Figure" shows a figure that is representative of that particular figure found across all such manuscripts containing that figure, such as the fifth figure of astronomy from BnF Latin 7153, f. 150 as the best exemplar. In some cases, either Version A or Version B does not supply a figure, so they are marked as "No figure." In other words, a certain figure may be found in Version A but not in Version B and vice versa. The next column, labeled "Subject," identifies the subject matter (e.g., grammar, logic, etc.) that is associated with that particular figure. The last column, labeled "Manuscript," lists all the manuscripts in which a particular figure is found. Again, in certain cases where Version A or Version B does not supply a figure, the Manuscript column is marked as not applicable (N/A). For the library information listed there, the cities are omitted, and the institution names, collections, and call numbers are oftentimes abbreviated. The figures associated with the *Opus Operum* are also included in this table.

Among the manuscripts of the *Ars Notoria,* some of the figures are mislabeled. Many of these discrepencies, but not all, are mentioned here. Yale 1 Mellon f. 16v–q, BnF Latin 7152 f. 20–a, Sloane 1712 f. 20v–e, and Vat. Lat. 3185 f. 23v–b are mislabeled as a "fifth" figure of the general sciences. The text does not present a fifth figure of the general sciences, only four. In Clm 276, the figure becomes identified as "the *nota* of the moving stars," which is an alternate title for the third figure of astronomy. For Vatican Latin 6842, the same figure, consisting of concentric rings, is labeled as the figure of music. Version A has a triangular figure labeled as the figure of music, and this is correct, for its triangular design is sensible when considering Plato's Lambda, which teaches about the musical scale.

Clm 276, f. 14v, incorrectly numbered the second, third, and fourth *notae* of philosophy. The second is incorrectly numbered as the third, the third is incorrectly numbered as the fourth, and the fourth is incorrectly numbered as the second.

Clm 276, f. 17, incorrectly numbered the third *nota* of the general sciences as the second *nota* of the general sciences.

Clm 276, f. 18, is labeled as both the first figure of theology and the figure of justice, peace, and fear; actually, the figure of justice, peace, and fear is missing entirely. Clm 26, f. 19, incorrectly numbered the fifth figure of theology as the fourth.

Mellon 1, Latin 7152, Sloane 1712, Clm 276, and Vat. Lat. 6842 all consistently mislabel the first figure of philosophy (25a) as the second figure of theology, saying it is "inexpressible by men." Certainly, the notory art brings confusion between the two disciplines of philosophy and theology since some viewed philosophy as the "handmaiden" to Christian theology, beginning with the second-century church father Clement of Alexandria. In Version A manuscripts, the scribes present the *voces magicae* prayer belonging to the first figure of philosophy, *Ezethomos* (written as *Logemoth Zalamaton* or *Lezemoth Zalamaton*), in a rectangular box with bars drawn across it but lacks the figure. Vat. Lat. 6842 misidentifies this prayer as belonging to the figure of medicine (f. 21). These manuscripts assert that the first figure of philosophy is also called the *figura terroris* (the figure of terror, or the figure of awe). An additional *voces magicae* prayer follows, of which it is said that man is not permitted to offer, but Solomon offered it seven times before the angel over the golden altar, which he had offered in peacemaking in the house of the Lord (i.e., Mount Gibeon).

ID	Example Figure	Subject	Manuscript
		Grammar	
1a	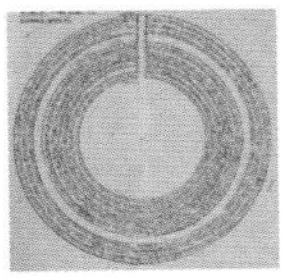	First Figure of Grammar	Mellon 1, f. 10v BnF Latin 7152, f. 12 Sloane 1712, f. 14v CLM 276, f. 8 Turin EV 13, f. 1 Vat. Lat. 6842, f. 16
1b		First Figure of Grammar	BnF Latin 9336 f. 18 Yar Vah 34, f. 9 BnF Latin 7154, f. 59 BnF Latin 7153, f. 131
2a		Second Figure of Grammar	Mellon 1, f. 11 BnF Latin 7152, f. 12v Sloane 1712, f. 15 CLM 276, f. 8v Vat. Lat. 6842, f. 16v
2b		Second Figure of Grammar	BnF Latin 9336, f. 18v Yar Vah 34, f. 8v BnF Latin 7154, f. 61v, 77 BnF Latin 7153, f. 132
3a		Third Figure of Grammar	Mellon 1, f. 11v BnF Latin 7152, f. 13 Sloane 1712, f. 15v CLM 276, f. 9 Vat. Lat. 6842, f. 17
3b		Third Figure of Grammar	BnF Latin 9336, f. 19 Yar Vah 34, f. 10 BnF Latin 7154, f. 63 BnF Latin 7153, f. 133

ID	Example Figure	Subject	Manuscript
123a–2	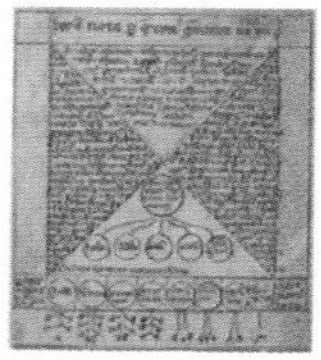	The Entire Art of Grammar	BnF Latin 7152, f. 13v Sloane 1712, f. 36 Turin EV 13, f. 6
		Logic/Dialectic	
4a	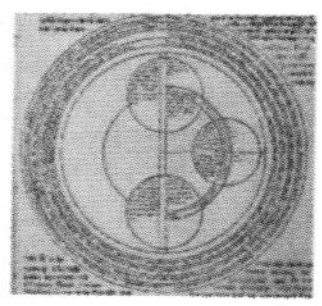	First Figure of Logic/ Dialectic	Mellon 1, f. 12 BnF Latin 7152, f. 14 Sloane 1712, f. 16v CLM 276, f. 9v Vat. Lat. 6842, f. 17v
4a–2		Figure of Logic for Dialectic Skills	BnF Latin 7152, f. 14v Sloane 1712, f. 36v
4b		First Figure of Logic/ Dialectic	BnF Latin 9336 f. 19v Yar Vah 34, f. 10v BnF Latin 7154, f. 64v BnF Latin 7153, f. 134
5a		Second Figure of Logic/ Dialectic	Mellon 1, f. 12v BnF Latin 7152, f. 15 Sloane 1712, f. 17v CLM 276, f. 10 Vat. Lat. 6842, f. 18
5b		Second Figure of Logic/ Dialectic	Sloane 1712, f. 36v–a BnF Latin 9336, f. 20 Yar Vah 34, f. 12 BnF Latin 7154, 66v BnF Latin 7153, f. 135v–136

ID	Example Figure	Subject	Manuscript
Rhetoric			
6a		First Figure of Rhetoric	Mellon 1, f. 13 BnF Latin 7152, f. 15v Sloane 1712, f. 18 CLM 276, f. 10v Vat. Lat. 6842, f. 18v BnF Latin 7373, f. 176
6b		First Figure of Rhetoric	BnF Latin 9336, f. 20v Yar Vah 34, f. 13 BnF Latin 7154, f. 69 BnF Latin 7153, f. 7153
7a	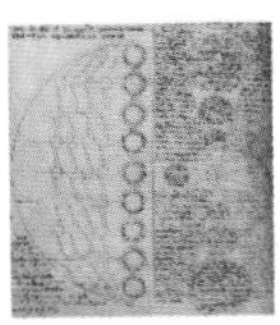	Second Figure of Rhetoric	Mellon 1, f. 13v BnF Latin 7152, f. 16 Sloane 1712, f. 18v–a CLM 276, f. 11, 11v Vat. Lat. 6842, f. 19, 19v
7b		Second Figure of Rhetoric	BnF Latin 9336, f. 23 Yar Vah 34, f. 12v BnF Latin 7154, f. 70v BnF Latin 7153, f. 138
8a	No Image	Third Figure of Rhetoric	n/a
8a–2	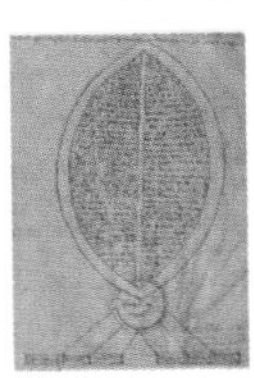	Third Figure of Rhetoric	BnF Latin 7152, f. 16v Sloane 1712, f. 36v–b
8b		Third Figure of Rhetoric	BnF Latin 9336, f. 23v Yar Vah 34, f. 14 BnF Latin 7154, f. 72 BnF Latin 7153, f. 139

ID	Example Figure	Subject	Manuscript
9a		Fourth Figure of Rhetoric	Mellon I, f. 14–b Sloane 1712, f. 19–a CLM 276, f. 12 Vat. Lat. 6842, f. 20
9b		Fourth Figure of Rhetoric	BnF Latin 9336, f. 21 Yar Vah 34, f. 13v BnF Latin 7154, f. 73v BnF Latin 7153, f. 140
Medicine			
10a	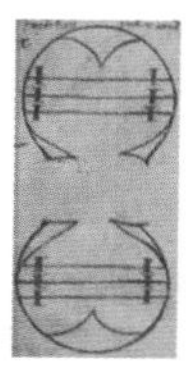	Figure of Medicine	Mellon I, f. 16v–t BnF Latin 7152, f. 20–d Sloane 1712, f. 20v–h CLM 276, f. 18–a Vat. Lat. 6842, f. 22–i
10b	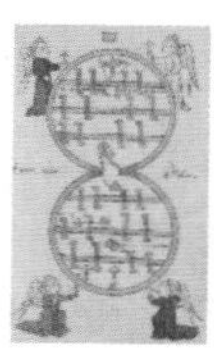	Figure of Medicine	BnF Latin 9336, f. 21v–a Yar Vah 34, f. 15 BnF Latin 7154, f. 74v BnF Latin 7153, f. 141
Music			
11a		Figure of Music	Mellon I, f. 16v–r BnF Latin 7152, f. 20–b Sloane 1712, f. 20v–f CLM 276, f. 17v–b Vat. Lat. 6842, f. 22–g
11a–2	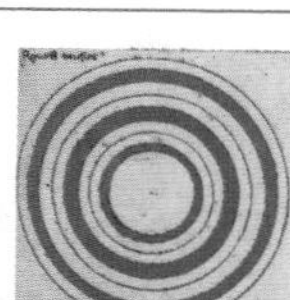	Figure of Music	Vat. Lat. 6842, f. 22–f

ID	Example Figure	Subject	Manuscript
11b		Figure of Music	BnF Latin 9336, f. 21v–b Yar Vah 34, f. 14v BnF Latin 7154, f. 75v BnF Latin 7153, f. 142
		Arithmetic	
12a		First Figure of Arithmetic	Mellon 1, f. 14v–a BnF Latin 7152, f. 18–a Sloane 1712, f. 19v–a CLM 276, f. 13 Vat. Lat. 6842, f. 20v–b
12a–2	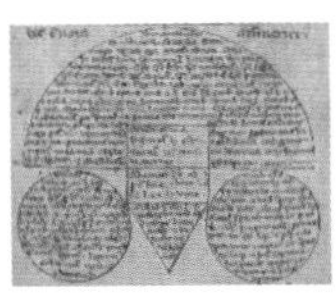	First Figure of Arithmetic	Sloane 1712, f. 36v–c Turin EV 13, f. 21
12b		First Figure of Arithmetic	BnF Latin 9336, f. 24–a Yar Vah, f. 16–a BnF Latin 7154, f. 76v BnF Latin 7153, f. 143
13a	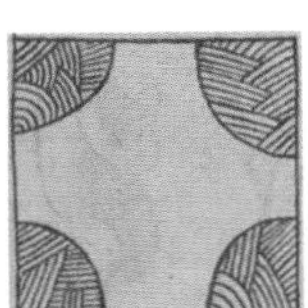	Half Figure of Arithmetic	Mellon 1, f. 14v–b BnF Latin 7152, f. 18–b Sloane 1712, f. 19v–b CLM 276, f. 13v Vat. Lat. 6842, f. 21–a
13b		Half Figure of Arithmetic	BnF Latin 9336, f. 24–b Yar Vah 34, f. 16–b BnF Latin 7154, f. 77 BnF Latin 7153, f. 145
14a	No Image	Second Figure of Arithmetic	n/a

ID	Example Figure	Subject	Manuscript
		Arithmetic	
14b	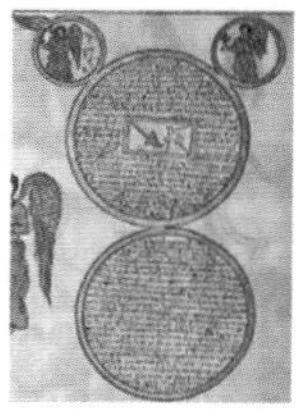	Second Figure of Arithmetic	BnF Latin 9336, f. 24–c Yar Vah 34, f. 16–c BnF Latin 7154, f. 78 BnF Latin 7153, f. 145
		Astronomy	
15a		First Figure of Astronomy (of Wonders)	Mellon 1, f. 16v–x BnF Latin 7152, f. 20v–a Sloane 1712, f. 21–a CLM 276, f. 17v–e Vat. Lat. 6842, f. 22v–b, f
15b		First Figure of Astronomy	BnF Latin 9336, f. 24v–a Yar Vah 34, f. 15v–a BnF Latin 7154, f. 79 BnF Latin 7153, f. 146
16a	No Image	Second Figure of Astronomy	n/a
16b		Second Figure of Astronomy	BnF Latin 9336, f. 24v–b Yar Vah 34, f. 15v–b BnF Latin 7154, f. 79v BnF Latin 7153, f. 147
17a	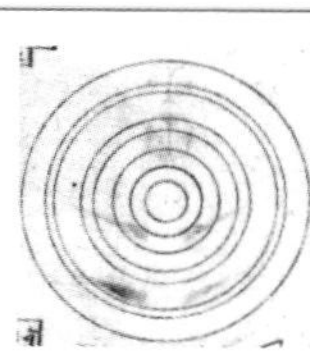	Third Figure of Astronomy (of the Moving Stars)	Mellon 1, f. 16v–q BnF Latin 7152, f. 20–a Sloane 1712, f. 20v–e CLM 276, f. 17v–b
17b		Third Figure of Astronomy	Sloane 1712, f. 37 BnF Latin 9336, f. 22–a Yar Vah 34, f. 17–a BnF Latin 7154, f. 80v BnF Latin 7153, f. 148

ID	Example Figure	Subject	Manuscript
18a	No Image	Fourth Figure of Astronomy	n/a
18b	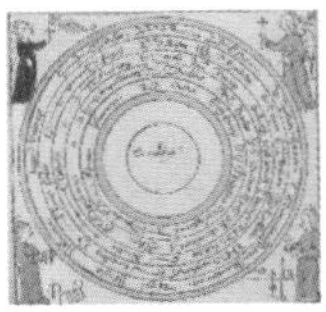	Fourth Figure of Astronomy	BnF Latin 9336, f. 22–b Yar Vah 34, f. 17–c BnF Latin 7154, f. 81 BnF Latin 7153, f. 149
19a	No Image	Fifth Figure of Astronomy	n/a
19b		Fifth Figure of Astronomy	BnF Latin 9336, f. 22–c Yar Vah 34, f. 17–b BnF Latin 7154, f. 82 BnF Latin 7153, f. 150
20a	No Image	Sixth Figure of Astronomy	n/a
20b	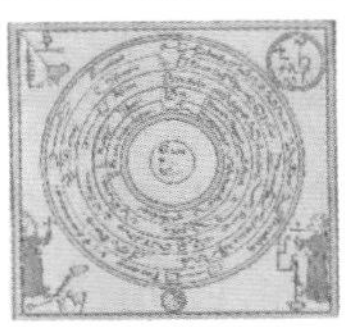	Sixth Figure of Astronomy	BnF Latin 9336, f. 22–d Yar Vah 34, f. 17–d BnF Latin 7154, f. 82v BnF Latin 7153, f. 151
General Sciences			
21a		First Figure of the General Sciences (Figure of God)	Mellon 1, f. 16–m BnF Latin 7152, f. 19v–c Sloane 1712, f. 20v–a CLM 276, f. 17–a Vat. Lat. 6842, f. 22–b
21b		First Figure of the General Sciences (Figure of God)	BnF Latin 9336, f. 22v–a Yar Vah 34, f. 16v–a, 19 BnF Latin 7154, f. 83v BnF Latin 7153, f. 152
22a		Second Figure of the General Sciences	Mellon 1, f. 16–n BnF Latin 7152, f. 19v–d Sloane 1712, f. 20v–b CLM 276, f. 17–b Vat. Lat. 6842, f. 22–d

ID	Example Figure	Subject	Manuscript
22b		Second Figure of the General Sciences	BnF Latin 9336, f. 22v–b Yar Vah 34, f. 16v–b, 18v BnF Latin 7154, f. 84 BnF Latin 7153, f. 153
23a		Third Figure of the General Sciences (*Nota* of Awe)	Mellon 1, f. 16–o BnF Latin 7152, f. 19v–e Sloane 1712, f. 20v–c CLM 276, f. 17–c Vat. Lat. 6842, f. 22–e
23b		Third Figure of the General Sciences (*Nota* of Awe)	BnF Latin 9336, f. 22v–c Yar Vah 34, f. 16v–c, 22 BnF Latin 7154, f. 84v BnF Latin 7153, f. 154
24a		Fourth Figure of the General Sciences	Mellon 1, f. 16–p BnF Latin 7152, f. 19v–f Sloane 1712, f. 20v–d CLM 276, f. 17–d Vat. Lat. 6842, f. 22–a
24b		Fourth Figure of the General Sciences	BnF Latin 9336, f. 27–a Yar Vah 34, f. 18 BnF Latin 7154, f. 85 BnF Latin 7153, f. 155
		Philosophy	
25a		First Figure of Philosophy (Inexpressible by Men)	Mellon 1, f. 17–b BnF Latin 7152, f. 21–a Sloane 1712, f. 21v–a CLM 276, f. 18v–a Vat. Lat. 6842, f. 23–a

ID	Example Figure	Subject	Manuscript
25b	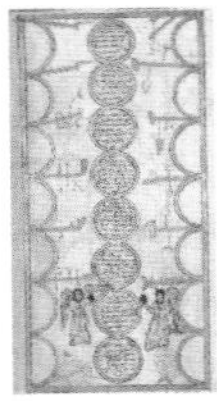	First Figure of Philosophy	BnF Latin 9336, f. 27–b Yar Vah 34, f. 17v BnF Latin 7154, f. 86 BnF Latin 7153, f. 156
26a	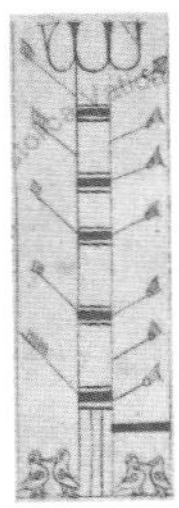	Second Figure of Philosophy	Mellon 1, f. 15–a BnF Latin 7152, f. 18v–a Sloane 1712, f. 19v–d CLM 276, f. 14v–a Vat. Lat. 6842, f. 21–e
26b	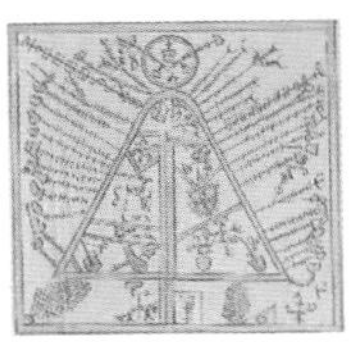	Second Figure of Philosophy	BnF Latin 9336, f. 27v–a Yar Vah 34, f. 23–a BnF Latin 7154, f. 86v BnF Latin 7153, f. 157
27a		Third Figure of Philosophy (*Nota* of Awe)	Mellon 1, f. 15–g BnF Latin 7152, f. 18v–b Sloane 1712, f. 20–a CLM 276, f. 14v–c Vat. Lat. 6842, f. 21–d
27b		Third Figure of Philosophy (*Nota* of Awe)	BnF Latin 9336, f. 27v–b Yar Vah 34, f. 23–b BnF Latin 7154, f. 87 BnF Latin 7153, f. 158
28a	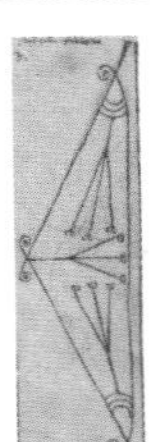	Fourth Figure of Philosophy	Mellon 1, f. 15–h BnF Latin 7152, f. 18v–c Sloane 1712, f. 20–b CLM 276, f. 14v–b Vat. Lat. 6842, f. 21–c

ID	Example Figure	Subject	Manuscript
28b		Fourth Figure of Philosophy	BnF Latin 9336, f. 25–a Yar Vah 34, f. 23v–a BnF Latin 7154, f. 87v BnF Latin 7153, f. 159
29a	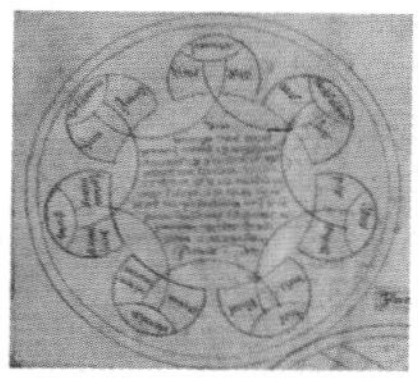	Fifth Figure of Philosophy	Mellon 1, f. 15v–j BnF Latin 7152, f. 17–a, 19–a Sloane 1712, f. 20–c CLM 276, f. 15v–a Vat. Lat. 6842, f. 21–a, 21–b, 22–h
29b		Fifth Figure of Philosophy	BnF Latin 9336, f. 25–b Yar Vah 34, f. 23v–b BnF Latin 7154, f. 88 BnF Latin 7153, f. 160
30a		Sixth Figure of Philosophy (*Nota* of Awe, *Nota* of God)	Mellon 1, f. 15v–k BnF Latin 7152, f. 17–b, 19–b Sloane 1712, f. 20–d Vat. Lat. 6842, f. 21–c
30b	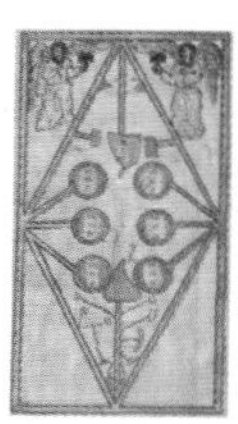	Sixth Figure of Philosophy	BnF Latin 9336, f. 25–c Yar Vah 34, f. 23v–c BnF Latin 7154, f. 89 BnF Latin 7153, f. 161
31a	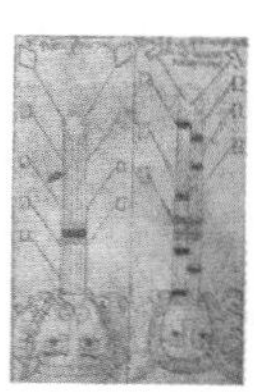	Seventh Figure of Philosophy	Mellon 1, f. 16–l BnF Latin 7152, f. 19v–a, b Sloane 1712, f. 20–e, f CLM 276, f. 16v–a Vat. Lat. 6842, f. 22–c

ID	Example Figure	Subject	Manuscript
31b		Seventh Figure of Philosophy	BnF Latin 9336, f. 25v–a Yar Vah 34, f. 24–a BnF Latin 7154, f. 90 BnF Latin 7153, f. 162
		Geometry	
32a	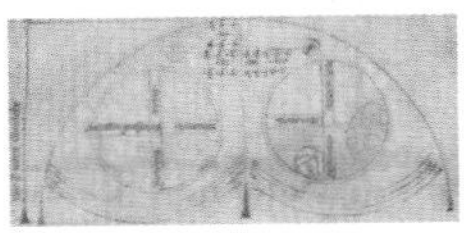	First Figure of Geometry	Mellon 1, f. 14–a Sloane 1712, f. 19–b CLM 276, f. 12v Vat. Lat. 6842, f. 20v–a
32b		First Figure of Geometry	BnF Latin 9336, f. 25v–b Yar Vah 34, f. 24–b BnF Latin 7154, f. 91 BnF Latin 7153, f. 144
33a	No Image	Second Figure of Geometry	n/a
33a–2	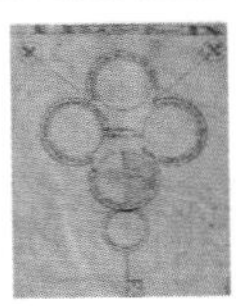	Second Figure of Geometry	BnF Latin 7152, f. 22v
33b		Second Figure of Geometry	Sloane 1712, f. 37–a BnF Latin 9336, f. 26–a Yar Vah 34, f. 24v BnF Latin 7154, f. 92 BnF Latin 7153, f. 164 Turin MS EV 13, f. 16v
		Theology	
34a	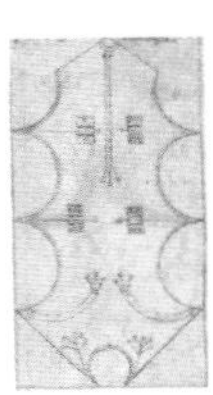	First Figure of Theology	Mellon 1, f. 16v–z BnF Latin 7152, f. 20v–c Sloane 1712, f. 21–c CLM 276, f. 18–b Vat. Lat. 6842, f. 20v–c, g

ID	Example Figure	Subject	Manuscript
34b		First Figure of Theology	BnF Latin 9336, f. 26–b Yar Vah 34, f. 25 BnF Latin 7154, f. 93v BnF Latin 7153, f. 165 Vat. Lat. 6842, f. 22v–c, g
35a	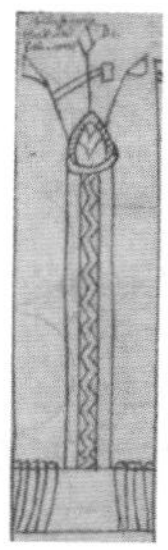	Second Figure of Theology	Mellon 1, f. 17–a BnF Latin 7152, f. 20v–d Sloane 1712, f. 21–d CLM 276, f. 16–b Vat. Lat. 6842, f. 20v–e
35b		Second Figure of Theology	BnF Latin 9336, f. 26v–a Yar Vah 34, f. 26v–a BnF Latin 7154, f. 94v BnF Latin 7153, f. 166
36a		Third Figure of Theology	Mellon 1, f. 17–c BnF Latin 7152, f. 21–b Sloane 1712, f. 21v–b CLM 276, f. 18v–b Vat. Lat. 6842, f. 23–b
36b		Third Figure of Theology	BnF Latin 9336, f. 26v–c Yar Vah 34, f. 26v–b BnF Latin 7154, f. 95v BnF Latin 7153, f. 167
37a	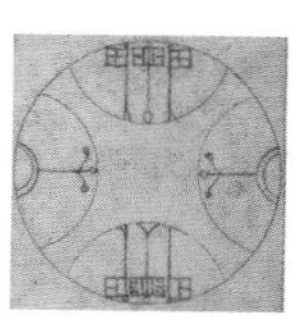	Fourth Figure of Theology	Mellon 1, f. 17–d BnF Latin 7152, f. 21–c Sloane 1712, f. 21v–c CLM 276, f. 18v–c Vat. Lat. 6842, f. 23–c

ID	Example Figure	Subject	Manuscript
37b		Fourth Figure of Theology	BnF Latin 9336, f. 26v–b Yar Vah 34, f. 25v BnF Latin 7154, f. 96v BnF Latin 7153, f. 168
38a	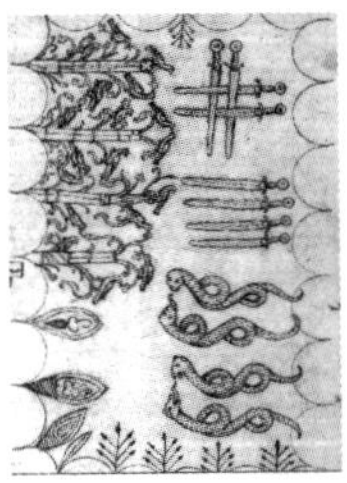	Fifth Figure of Theology, the Ineffable *Nota*	Mellon 1, f. 17v BnF Latin 7152, f. 21v Sloane 1712, f. 22 CLM 276, f. 19 Vat. Lat. 6842, f. 23v
38b		Fifth Figure of Theology, the Ineffable *Nota*	BnF Latin 9336, f. 28–a Yar Vah 34, f. 28 BnF Latin 7154, f. 97v BnF Latin 7153, f. 169
Virtues			
39a	No Image	Figure of Chastity	n/a
39b		Figure of Chastity	BnF Latin 9336, f. 28–b Yar Vah 34, f. 20, 29v BnF Latin 7154, f. 98v BnF Latin 7153, f. 170
40a	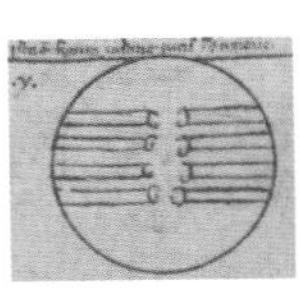	Figure of Justice, Peace & Fear	Mellon 1, f. 16v–y BnF Latin 7152, f. 20v–b Sloane 1712, f. 21–b Vat. Lat. 6842, f. 22v–d

ID	Example Figure	Subject	Manuscript
40b		Figure of Justice, Peace & Fear	BnF Latin 9336, f. 28v Yar Vah 34, f. 19v, 29v BnF Latin 7154, f. 99v BnF Latin 7153, f. 171
41a	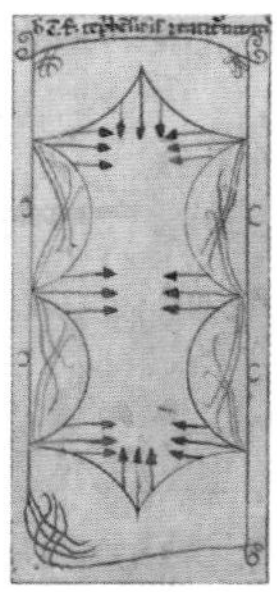	Figure of Reprehension & Taciturnity	Mellon 1, f. 16v–s BnF Latin 7152, f. 20c Sloane 1712, f. 20v–g CLM 276, f. 17v–d
41b	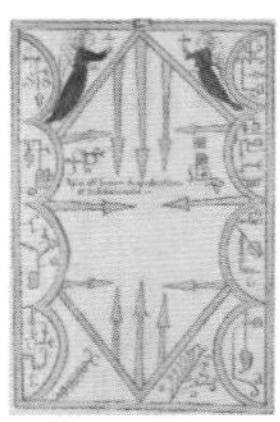	Figure of Reprehension & Taciturnity	BnF Latin 9336, f. 28v–b Yar Vah 34, f. 21, 29 BnF Latin 7154, f. 100v BnF Latin 7153, f. 172
		Exceptives	
42a		Figure of Exceptives (divinatory magic)	Mellon 1, f. 16v–v BnF Latin 7152, f. 20–e Sloane 1712, f. 20v–i CLM 276, f. 16–b, 17v–c Vat. Lat. 6842, f. 22–a
42b	No Image	Figure of Exceptives (divinatory magic)	n/a

APPENDIX 3

AUTHORSHIP OF THE *ARS NOTORIA*

As noted in chapter I, the *Ars Notoria*'s author remained anonymous, and by attributing four important authors to the *Ars Notoria,* he also established credibility, veracity, and reliability for the text.

Because so little can be said of the true author or authors, it is best to turn to the four pseudepigraphical authors—King Solomon, Apollonius of Tyana, the prophet Mani, and Euclid of Thebes[1]—and what that can tell us about the origin of the art of acquiring knowledge of all the sciences in a short amount of time.

KING SOLOMON OF ISRAEL

The author of the *Ars Notoria* chose King Solomon (r. 970–931 BCE) as one of the four authorities for two main reasons. First, Solomon was renowned for his wisdom and knowledge in ancient times.[2] Second, Solomon already had a medieval reputation as a legendary magician and author of books of magic. The true author mentions certain books that were attributed to Solomon from which the notory art came; thus, the true author saw himself as passing on a Solomonic tradition, and thereby stamping Solomon's seal of approval upon this book that this is genuine magic. Further discussion of the texts attributed to Solomon can be found in appendix A7.

1. *Ars Notoria,* sections 1 and 147.
2. 1 Chronicles 1:1–13; 1 Kings 3:3–15

MANI

The book mentions the Iranian prophet Mani, the founder of the now extinct world religion called Manichaeanism, as one of the four great experimenters on the notory art. The Catholic Church named several religious movements as Manichaean, including that of the Cathars. The *Liber De Duobus Principiis* (*Book of the Two Principles*) is a collection of polemical and expository texts written by an anonymous Cathar in northern Italy, probably between 1235 and 1241. The author was a disciple of John of Lugio, a leader of absolute dualists who called themselves Albanenses. Pope Innocent III (papacy 1198–1216) led the Albigensian Crusade (1209–1229) against the Cathars in southern France. The *Ars Notoria*'s reference to Mani is best understood in this historical context, not actually going back to the historical prophet and the time in which the religion was still a living tradition. By the thirteenth century, Manichaeanism had been extinct for about six hundred years, as much of its material evidence had been destroyed; therefore, no one in medieval Europe would have had access to original source books, nor would they have the necessary language proficieny to offer any substantial knowledge of Manichaeanism. This is further supported by the fact that no other information is divulged about Mani in the *Ars Notoria* other than his name. By mentioning Mani, the author of the *Ars Notoria* is evoking those heretics who stand against the Catholic Church; this attitude is also found in the *Sworn Book of Honorius,* authored supposedly by Honorius, the son of Euclid of Thebes. In fact, the *Ars Notoria* may be invoking the name of Mani as not as the third-century prophet but as the contemporaneous founder of any one of the heretical sects.

Historical Manichaeanism flourished in the Byzantine city of Harran until the Arabs took over in the tenth century. Harran was a hub for Hermeticism, alchemy, and astrology, all of which were also associated with Apollonius of Tyana, another key figure in the notory art. It is possible that Pseudo-Apollonius's writings on astral magic were known there. The Pseudo-Apollonius writings on astral magic and the notory art were transmitted by the Arabs to Latin Europe; these were the only writings known at the time to portray Apollonius in a positive light. These writings rely on a Hermetic-Neoplatonic worldview. The *Ars Notoria* places a Christian veneer over this pagan worldview.

Another key historical figure is Iamblichus of Chalcis, a Syrian Neoplationist of Arab origin who wrote a Greek treatise on theurgy; his work can be found in the undertones of the magic of the notory art. In all three cases for Mani, Apollonius, and Iamblichus, it is doubtful any Latin scribe in the West would have had the language proficiency and access to the Syriac, Arabic, Greek, and Latin sources that provide the crucial knowledge to even link and associate these personalities to the *Ars Notoria.*

The true author's sources for the elaborate prayer regimen also suggest Byzantine roots, including the Greek Orthodox hymn known as the Trisagion and the expression "Lord, have mercy" (*Kyrie Eleison*). Version B manuscripts prescribe to the operator to drink saffron and rosewater tea, which are ingredients of Persian origin that would have reached the Byzantine Empire via the Silk Road. Byzantine influence may be seen in the magical figures, too. The fifth *nota* of theology illustrates Solomon's temple such that it recalls an actual throne of Solomon with elaborate automatons at the Byzantine court in the Great Triklinos of the Magnaura Palace, the hall where the emperor and his officials received foreign embassies.[3]

EUCLID OF THEBES

Euclid of Thebes is not to be confused with either the Greek Socratic philosopher Euclid of Megara (c. 435–365 BCE) or the Greek founder of geometry, Euclid of Alexandria (fl. 300 BCE). There is no indication that these later two Euclids had reputations as being magicians or wrote about magic. Euclid of Thebes is said to be the father of Honorius, the supposed author of the *Liber Iuratus Honorii* (*Sworn Book*). According to the prologue of the *Liber Iuratus Honorii,* when the master magicians found themselves under persecution by the church, the masters from Naples, Athens, and Toledo convened to hold a council in which it was determined that "Honorius, son of Euclid, master of Thebes, where that art at the time was established . . . would labor on our behalf" to write ninety-three chapters, forming an abridgment, from the seven books of the magical art. The four cities—Naples, Athens, Toledo, and Thebes (Egypt)—represent four distinct cultural centers of magic in the known world.

3. For more details, see chapter V, "Analysis of the Figures."

The contemporary scholar Joseph Peterson argues that the city of Thebes mentioned here refers to the one in Greece, not Egypt.[4] Even so, it is still plausible that Thebes of Egypt is the intended city, but more evidence is needed to support either conclusion.

As King Solomon and Apollonius of Tyana are considered the first pairing of prominent historical figures who led to the composition of the *Ars Notoria,* Mani and Euclid of Thebes ought to be considered the second pairing of contemporaneous figures who experimented with it. Neither Mani or Euclid of Thebes are given any credit for any material found within the *Ars Notoria*. Yet, they are associated with the notory art because it is said that they had tested it (*probatum est*) in their own magical experiments (section 1). In this way, the names of Mani and Euclid of Thebes evoke the contemporary religious movements, magio-religious practices, and illicit writings which opposed the Catholic Church during the thirteenth century. The name Euclid of Thebes calls to mind the fourteenth-century magical treatise the *Liber Iuratus Honorii,*[5] which is dependent upon the many prayers found in the *Ars Notoria* (Version B).[6] Unfortunately, there is no further information available about the identity of Euclid or Honorius beyond the *Ars Notoria* and the *Liber Iuratus.*

APOLLONIUS OF TYANA

Finally, the *Ars Notoria*'s authorial attribution to Apollonius of Tyana (the commentator to King Solmon's Hebrew writings) and the list of the seven exceptives, or systems of divination, likely reference source texts that hold Arabic origins. For Apollonius of Tyana, there are pseudepigraphical texts on astral magic whose titles are Arabic and Greek. For the seven divinations, the *Alchandreana* corpus, a tenth-century collection of astrological and prognosticative Latin texts based on Arabic, Hebrew, and Latin sources, is a strong candidate for the

4. Peterson, *Sworn Book of Honorius*, 12.

5. Specifically, the London version. Jan R. Veenstra proposes "a hypothetical Honorius text that Ganell uses presents a purification ritual that liturgically relies on a book called the *Liber trium animarum* and that incorporates a set of one hundred divine names. (To the compiler of the London Honorius, the *Liber trium animarum* was unknown, so he copied the prayer numbers but was compelled to come up with a new liturgy that he derived mainly from the *Ars Notoria*)." From Fanger, *Invoking Angels,* 159.

6. See Skinner and Clark, *Ars Notoria,* 44 and appendix 3.

author's knowledge of the forbidden arts. Similarly, the Pseudo-Aristotelian chiromantic treatise translated by John of Seville indicates Arabic origins. The key question is whether the true author had access to these Greek, Arabic, and Syriac sources or only encountered them after they had already been translated into Latin and made accessible to medieval Europeans. Even so, some of these sources were not translated in time for the arrival of the *Ars Notoria,* and some were not even translated at all.

An overview of the works attributed to Apollonius can be found in appendix A6.

APPENDIX 4

Medieval Computations of Time

This appendix serves as a reference for timing the ritual procedure of the *Ars Notoria* according to the divisions of time familiar to its authors and medieval practitioners.

TIMING ACCORDING TO ASTRONOMICAL CALCULATIONS

In Michael Scot's *Liber Introductorius* (*Introduction*), he says that the practitioners of the notory art owe more to the stars than they are ready to admit.[1] The *Ars Notoria* places a strong emphasis on the days of the Moon, or lunations, and, based on its claim of authorship and authority belonging to Apollonius of Tyana, to whom are attributed several astral magic treatises, it seems plausible to at least consider the fact that ritual timing according to the Moon may originate from the Arabic fascination with astral magic and lunar mansions. Another rationale for aligning the notory art ritual to the Moon may come from the belief that, astrologically speaking, the waxing and waning of the Moon, which governs moisture and humidity, has a direct effect upon the human body's own fluids, causing them to ebb and flow accordingly. Thus, if the operator aligns his own actions according to the Moon, he would benefit from this ebb and flow, making his ritual experiment successful.

1. Bodleian 266, fols. 2 and 20v; from Thorndike, *History of Magic,* 2:321.

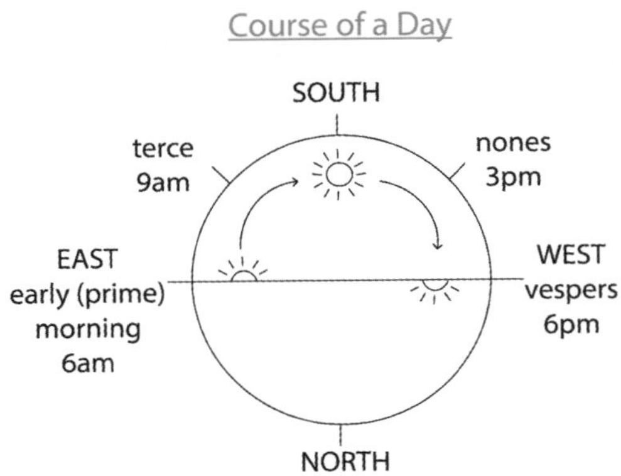

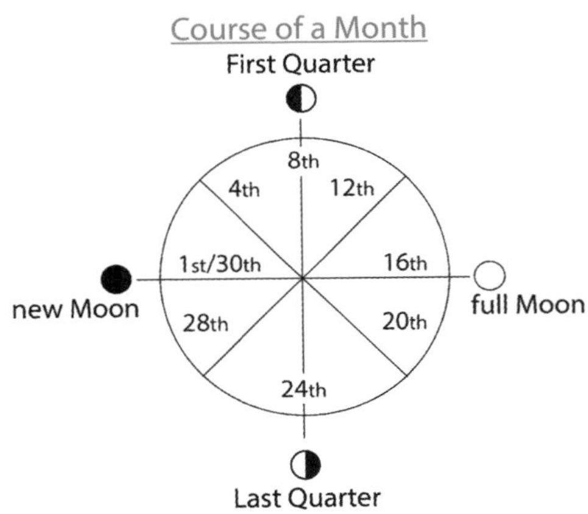

TIMING ACCORDING TO CHRISTIAN PRACTICE

Throughout its ritual instructions, the *Ars Notoria* makes frequent mention of hours by which to pray at certain times of the day. These are the canonical hours that for centuries in Europe marked the divisions of the day that specified the times Christians would pray. The canonical hours are also called the Liturgy of the Hours, and traveling Christians would often carry a book of hours, in which were written devotional prayers for certain canonical hours. The following table reflects the canonical hours observed during medieval times.

THE CANONICAL HOURS

Canonical Hour	Solar Hour	Approximate Clock Time
Matins, or Vigil	Night	2:00 a.m. or 5:00 a.m.
Lauds	Dawn prayer	5:00 a.m.
Prime	First hour, sunrise	6:00 a.m.
Terce	Third hour, midmorning	9:00 a.m.
Sext	Sixth hour, noon	12:00 p.m.
Nones	Ninth hour, midafternoon	3:00 p.m.
Vespers	Evening hour, sunset	6:00 p.m.

An ecclesiastical lunar month contains twenty-nine or thirty days. The first day of a lunar month is the ecclesiastical new Moon and is equated with a new crescent Moon. The ecclesiastical new Moon can be any day from the day of the astronomical new Moon to two days later. An ecclesiastical full Moon is the fourteenth day from the start of the ecclesiastical lunar month. The epact (Latin *epactae,* from Greek *epaktai hemerai,* meaning "added days") is the number of days by which a solar year exceeds twelve lunar months, usually by eleven days; it is also used in computations to determine the date of Easter.

TIMING ACCORDING TO ANCIENT TRADITION AND SUPERSTITION

Egyptian Days and Hours

A form of calendar prognostication, Egyptian days signify misfortune and bad luck. Certain activities were avoided on these days. There were twenty-four Egyptian days in the year, two each month. However, there was no standard for how many Egyptian days there were, nor was there a standard for their calculation. Medieval Europe had inherited Egyptian days and hours from the ancient pagan world. The astronomer Johannes de Sacrobosco (c. 1195–1256), the author of the widely used medieval textbook called the *Sphere,* provided a mnemonic aid called *Armis Gunfe* for remembering when Egyptian days fell in the Julian calendar that was widely known from the thirteenth to sixteenth centuries. He linked the Ten Plagues from the book of Exodus to these ten days, then added that there must have been fourteen minor plagues to account for a total of twenty-four days. The Egyptian days according to Sacrobosco are listed below with their dangerous hours in parentheses.

January: 1 (11), 25 (6)
February: 4 (8), 28 (10)
March: 1 (1), 28 (2)
April: 10 (1), 20 (11)
May: 3 (6), 25 (10)
June: 10 (18), 16 (4)
July: 13 (12), 22 (11)
August: 1 (1), 20 (7)
September: 3 (17), 21 (4)
October: 3 (5), 22 (9)
November: 5 (8), 28 (5)
December: 7 (1), 22 (6)

For further information, see Don C. Skemer's "*Armis Gunfe:* Remembering Egyptian Days," 75–106.

APPENDIX 5

The *Enlightened Work* from the Wisdom of Solomon

Lost Ancient Hebrew Book or Hebrew Version of the Ars Notoria

A fourteenth-century Hebrew treatise could be evidence of another branch of the *Ars Notoria* tradition: מלאכת מושכלת מחכמת שלמה הע"ה. The work, translated as *The Enlightened Work from the Wisdom of Solomon,* contains ritual magic instructions that bear a strong resemblance to the *Ars Notoria.* The Hebrew treatise is held at St. Petersburg at the Institute of Oriental Manuscripts of the Russian Academy of Sciences with shelf number B 247, and the treatise itself is found on folios 90v–94r. The manuscript is identified as of Italian origin dated to the seventeenth century and contains other Hebrew and magic-related texts. Rabbi Yosef M. Cohen, who has graciously offered his preliminary study of this Hebrew treatise, has identified it to be a copy of an older Hebrew original. The treatise opens:

> This precious and desirable book, the *Enlightened Work from the Wisdom of Solomon* (of blessed memory) was composed by one of the sages. This became revealed via the glorious and holy Solomon, son of Nathan, the son of Nathan the Angerien, from the renowned city of Angers in the year 5153[1] *anno mundi* who was wise in all particulars and generalities. He authored another treatise titled *Melechet HaZikaron* [*The Art of Memory*]. Both enquire and elucidate the wisdom and workings of enlightenment.

1. 1392 CE by the Gregorian calendar.

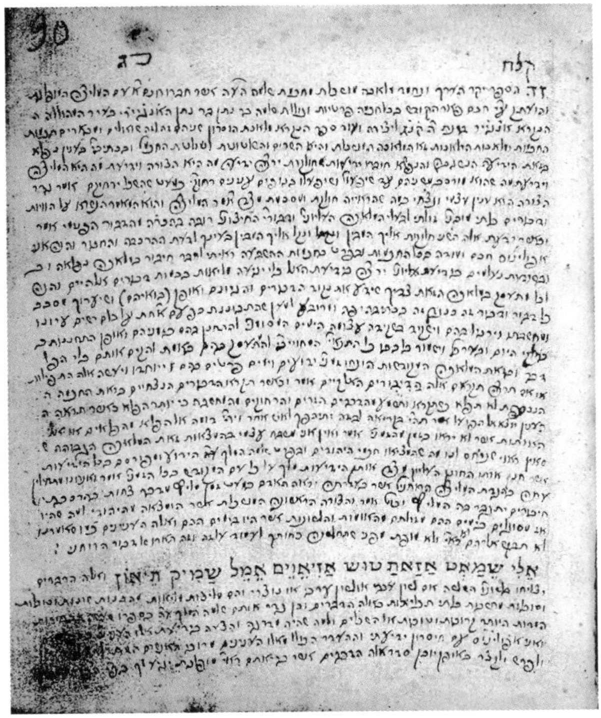

Manuscript B 247, f. 90v, the first page of
The Enlightened Work from the Wisdom of Solomon.

The treatise identifies a Jewish sage from the French city of Angers as having composed this work from writings attributed to Solomon. The treatise has a single known historical attestation from Yohanan Alemanno (c. 1435–died after 1504 following the mythical story of the *Ars Notoria,* the treatise also mentions Apollonius of Tyana as reading from the book of the Jews about King Solomon. Just like the *Ars Notoria,* the treatise describes the same favorable days of the Moon (4th, 8th, 12th, 16th, 20th, 23th, 26th, and 30th) to be "good days that King Solomon (of blessed memory) considered are appropriate times to perform these operations; for these are either renowned from the tradition [Kabbalah], or from Godly wisdom, or from the spiritual powers and supernal angels." Finally, the treatise contains all twelve *voces magicae* prayers that belong to the General prayers found in the *Ars Notoria* (i.e., from *Hely Semat* to *Hely Lehem,* according to Version A). There is a thirteenth and final prayer, which begins "*Yaimos yaiaizaibael yozoza ala anaton aeial acamaarlatamos aizomaeitaeal mabias zaeitarious, etc.,*" and it has not yet been identified. The text definitively ends here. There are no figures in the treatise.

Of the twelve known General prayers found in this Hebrew treatise, *Theos Patir Heenminos* (*Ars Notoria,* section 24), is the most interesting for its tantalizing hint at the possibility of an old Hebrew source for both the *Ars Notoria* and the *Liber Iuratus Honorii* (*The Sworn Book of Honorius*), the fourteenth-century handbook of ritual magic. The *Theos Patir Heenminos* prayer reads:

> Theos, Patir, Heenminos, through your most holy angels, Elypha, Masan, Gelomioos, Gedehantrai, Sasaramana, Elomuid, and through your archangels, whose names are made secret by God, so that they ought not be offered by us which are these: DE. EL. X. P. N. H. O. R. G., and the rest, some of which are not sufficient to comprehend by human senses.[2]

The abbreviations "DE. EL. X. P. N. H. O. R. G." represent the angelic names which have been kept secret out of holy reverence. What are these angelic names? Both the *Ars Notoria* (Version B) and *Liber Iuratus,* which relies on Version B, spells out these abbreviated angelic names. Version B, section 24, reads (the angelic names are underlined):

> **O most high God, O invisible God, Theos, Pat[e]r, Gehemnos, Lehemnyhos, we ask you, Ymos, through your most holy angels who are Michael (that is, "the house of God") Gabriel (that is, "the strength of God") Raphael (that is, "the medicine of God") Seraphim (that is, "the burning one") Cherubim (that is, "the fullness of knowledge"), Helypha, Masay, Cherubyn, Ielonucios, Gadabany, Zedabanay, Gederanay, Saramany, Loniteci, Lotrosi, Gerohanathon, Zahamany, Lomyht, Gedanabasy, Seremanay, Secemanay, Heulothant, Helomyht, Heuloramiht, Samanazay, Gedebandy, by the fullness of knowledge, we humbly ask you, O Cherubim and Seraphim, and you, O Jesus Christ, through all your glorious holy**

---

2. *Ars Notoria,* section 24 (Version A). Compare also *Ars Brevis,* section 6, which lists the abbreviated letters as De., El., X., P., N., C., K., and G. Also, the *Ars Brevis* has the figure of intellect, which contains a series of letters within it.

angels, whose names are consecrated by God, which no mortal is permitted to pronounce, which are these, Deyhel, Dehel, Depymo, Deyn, Hel, Exluso, Depymon, Helynon, Exmegon, Paryneos, Exmegan, Pheheneos, Navagen, Hosiel, Oragon, Garbona, Rachion, Monyham, Megon, Hamos, and those are which human sense cannot and will not be able to comprehend.

The *Enlightened Work* has the same prayer, which reads in the original Hebrew:

טֵאוֹשׁ פַּטִיר קוֹנִמוּס אֵישְׁקְנֵיסִמוּס אַנְיִילוֹשׁ טֵאוֹשׁ אֵלִיפַּנַאמַשַׁן
מַשַׁאִן סֵילִימַנַטוֹס גִילִימֵינְטוֹשׁ סֵגֵדֵי כַּמַאִן שַׁרַאמַנַא אֵילוֹמִינוֹר אַנְרַא
שַׁאלִיבְטַמַנַא [שַׁאלִיכְטַמַנַא] פֵּיר אַרַקַא נְיִילוֹשׁ טוֹאוֹשׁ

The Romanized transliteration of this prayer reads, "*Theos patir konimus aesknaisimos aniilos theos aelipanamasan masain salimanatos gilimantos saigaidai camain saramana aelominor anra salibtamana* [varia lectio: *salictamana*] *pair araca niilos tauous,*" and includes a list of angel names. The table on the following page shows these names, both spelled out and abbreviated, in a comparative study across the treatises.

It is clear that angelic names found in the *Ars Notoria* (Version B) and *Liber Iuratus* largely agree with those found in the *Enlightened Work*. The abbreviations of the *Ars Notoria* are also supported. Both Version B and *Liber Iuratus* appear to have accumulated a second partial listing of names another reading variation.

What is the common source for these angelic names? Did Version B have a source of angelic names to which Version A refers? Was that source originally written in Hebrew? Was that source known to the supposed fourteenth-century Solomon, son of Nathan, the son of Nathan the Angerien? Was the source of angelic names derived from of one of the "ancient Hebrew books," a key source of the *Ars Notoria*? Or was the *Enlightened Work* simply a Latin-to-Hebrew translation of the *Ars Notoria*? For now, these questions go unanswered but are worthy of a pause for contemplation.

COMPARISON OF ANGELIC NAMES

Ars Notoria (section 24, Version A)	*Ars Notoria* (section 24, Version B)	*Liber Iuratus Honorii*	*The Enlightened Work*
DE	Deyhel, Dehel, Depymo, Deyn; Depymon	Deihel, Dehel, Depymo, Dein; Depymon	–
EL	Hel; Helynon	Hel; Helynon	אֱלַמוֹן Ailamon
X	Exluso; Exmegon; Exmegan,	Exluso; Exmogon, Exmegan	אִיכְמֵגוֹן Eicimagon
P	Paryneos; Pheheneos	Parineos; Pheleneos	פַּרַמֵיאוֹשׁ Paramaeos
N	Navagen	Nauagen (or Navagen)	בוֹמַאגֵין Bomagain
H	Hosiel	Hosyel (Hosiel)	אוֹשִׁיאֵל Osiel
O	Oragon	Dragon (or Oragon)	אוֹרַגוֹן Oragon
R	Rachion	Rathion (or Rachion)	רֵמַאוֹן Raemon; רֵיאִימוֹן Raieimon
G	Garbona	Garbona	גַדְבוֹנא Gadbona
–	Monyham, Megon, Hamos	Monyham, Megonhamos	–

APPENDIX 6

Works Attributed to Apollonius

The Heir to Hermes Trismegistus

In late antiquity, it is said that Apollonius, the purported commentator of the notory art, left behind three works, all of which are now lost. Concerning the first, Philostratus describes that during Apollonius's travels, Apollonius met wise Indians with whom he had deep conversations, which led to writing his treatise titled *On Astrology*. Philostratus quotes Damis, Apollonius's traveling companion, saying:

> Apollonius alone, Damis says, conducted secret discussions with Iarchas in which they considered astral prophecy, discussed prediction, and treated sacrifices and the appellations pleasing to the gods. From this source, he says, Apollonius derived his four books on planetary prophecy (a work also mentioned by Moeragenes), and also what he wrote about sacrifices, and how to sacrifice to each of the gods appropriately and acceptably.[1]

Philostratus goes on to speak about Apollonius's other treatise, *On Sacrifices,* saying, "But the work *On Sacrifices* I have found in many sanctuaries, many cities, and the homes of many wise men."[2] This same treatise is also mentioned by the Neoplatonic philosopher Porphyry of Tyre (c. 234–305 CE)[3]

1. Philostratus, *Life of Apollonius,* 3.41.
2. Philostratus, *Life of Apollonius,* 3.41.
3. Porphyry of Tyre, *On Abstinence,* 2.34.

and the church father Eusebius of Caesarea (260/265–339/340 CE). Eusebius cites Apollonius:

> In this way, then, I think, one would best show the proper regard for the deity, and thereby beyond all other men secure His favor and good will, if to Him whom we called the First God, and who is One and separate from all others, and to whom the rest must be acknowledged inferior, he should sacrifice nothing at all, neither kindle fire, nor dedicate anything whatever that is an object of sense—for He needs nothing even from beings who are greater than we are: nor is there any plant at all which the earth sends up, nor any animal which it, or the air, sustains, to which there is not some defilement attached—but should ever employ towards Him only that better speech, I mean the speech which passes not through the lips, and should ask good things from the noblest of beings by what is noblest in ourselves, and this is the mind, which needs no instrument. According to this therefore we ought by no means to offer sacrifice to the great God who is over all.[4]

This quotation embodies the theurgic idea that humankind can achieve union with God through the intellect (*nous*), which for the neo-Pythagoreans included geometric and mathematical concepts of an esoteric nature. Apollonius's third book, a biography of Pythagoras and his doctrines, is thought to have influenced the writings of Iamblichus and Porphyry of Tyre.

Apollonius is known as Balinus (or Balinas, Belenus, or Abuluniyus) in Arabic and was called a *Sahib at-tilasmat,* a "Master of the Talismans." A number of treatises on Hermetic philosophy and astral magic were falsely attributed to Apollonius of Tyana, and they span Greek, Arabic, and Latin traditions. This collection of tracts belongs to the Pseudo-Apollonius corpus. A single, published, astral magic treatise attributed to Pseudo-Apollonius is sometimes published and distributed as a series of separate tracts, thereby accounting for multiple titles. Some works of Hermes have been falsely ascribed to Apollonius as well; this is likely due to the fact that Apollonius is

4. Eusebius, *Preparation for the Gospel,* 4.13.

seen as Hermes's heir. Little scholarly attention has been given to the works falsely attributed to Apollonius of Tyana; what is known has all been gathered together and reviewed here. Aside from *Flores Aurei* (*Golden Flowers*), these works are explored below.

The Arabic work titled *Kitab Balaniyus al-Hakim fi'l- 'llal, Kitab Sirr al-khaliqa wa-san 'at al-tabi'a* (*The Book of Balinas the Wise: On the Causes, or, the Book of the Secret of Creation*), dated circa 813–833 CE, was translated into Latin by Hugo of Santalla in the twelfth century as *De Secretis Naturae* (*On the Secrets of Nature*). The Arabic work may be based on an original written in Syriac or Greek.[5] The book consists of six sections: (1) "On the Creator and His Creatures," (2) On Celestial Bodies and Meteorology," (3) "On Minerals," (4) "On Plants," (5) "On Animals," and (6) "On Humans," and these describe the nature and names of God and provide a systematic description of universal causality from the origin of the cosmos to minerals, stones, plants, animals, and finally, man. The book tells the story of Apollonius going into the crypt of Hermes and finding the *Tabula Smaragdina* (*Emerald Tablet*), which supposedly explains the basic principle of alchemy, and which is summed up in the axiom "As above, so below."[6] The text propounds the Neoplatonic hierarchy of being in the mouth of Apollonius.[7]

The book *De Angelica Factura* or *De Angelica Factione* (*On Making Angelic Things*) is attributed to Apollonius of Tyana and cited by the Italian

---

5. The scholar Ursula Weisser asserts that the Arabic translation was made by Sagiyus (or Sajiyus), a Byzantine priest of Nablus, from a now lost Greek original written in the sixth century CE. See Weisser, ed., *"Buch uber Geheimnis der Schöpfung."* Mohammad Karimi Zanjani Asl reports another scholarly perspective that Sagiyus is the same Sergius of Reshaina (d. 536), a physician, Monophysite Christian priest, and translator of medical works from Greek to Syriac that would later be translated into Arabic during the Abbasid Caliphate. See Mohammad Karimi Zanjani Asl, "Sirr al-khaliqa and Its Influence in the Arabic and Persianate World, 435–73.

6. Ebeling, *The Secret History of Hermes Trismegistus,* 46–47, 49. The tablet later appeared in a ninth-century book titled *Kitab Sirr al-Asar* (*Book of the Secret of Creation and the Art of Nature*), which would be translated into Latin as the Pseudo-Aristotelian book *Secretum Secretorum* (*Secret of Secrets*) by John of Seville in 1140. The tablet also appeared later in the *Kitab Ustuqus al-Uss al-Thani* (*Second Book of the Elements of Foundation*) attributed to the alchemist Geber (Jabir ibn Hayyan, 722–815). See Houtsma et al., *E. J. Brill's First Encyclopaedia of Islam,* X:594. See also Hauck, *The Emerald Tablet,* chapter 2.

7. On the Neoplatonic hierarchy of being, see the Latin *Asclepius* 6 and 38. See also *Corpus Hermeticum* III, 1–3; X, 7–8, 44–45, and 116–17.

university professor and magician Cecco d'Ascoli (1257–1327) in his commentary on the *Sphere of the Cosmos* by John de Sacrobosco. Cecco explains both astronomical concepts and describes a cosmology filled with angels and demons, using technical terms that apply to both the scientific world and the magical one. He cites Apollonius about *tropici,* a term that holds both its astronomical sense and is supplied with a magical sense, saying:

> Because just as you ought to understand that, the tropics are to be learned about on two accounts: one, by the measure for circles written by the Sun, that this authority accepts, another measure according to a hierarchy of certain [spirits] divided up for which they are to be called the tropics, that is, the Tropos [the Prince of the spirits,] turned [them] according to a command, which is the first of these, as Apollonius said in the book *On Making Angelic Things,* "Just as the light of the heavens of the world revolves its motion more, the tropic [spirits] are to be turned according to the Tropos command."[8]

In the astronomical sense, the tropics are the two extreme circles of latitude of the earth at which the Sun can be seen directly overhead, at its most northerly (the Tropic of Cancer) and its most southerly (the Tropic of Capricorn). The part of the earth that lies between these two circles is called the Tropics. In the magical sense, the *tropici* are spirits within a hierarchy who obey their prince, called Tropos (from the Greek, meaning "a turning," or the point where the Sun turns and goes back in the opposite direction; for example, the Sun turning south after reaching the Tropic of Cancer).

The Book of Wisdom (Greek *Biblos Sophias;* Arabic *Miftah al-hikma*) is a twelfth-century Greek astral magic treatise that dates to the fifth century but survives only as early as the fifteenth century. The work lists the names of the seasons, the hours, the Sun, the Moon, heaven and earth by which one could make talismans to have an effect upon man and nature. The Latin versions are

---

8. My translation from the Latin quotation in Emanuele Fontana, "Cecco D'Ascoli: Cultura, Scienza e Politica nell'Italia del Trecento," Convegno Internazionale (Ascoli Piceno, 2–3 Dicembre 2005), *Rivista Di Storia Della Chiesa in Italia* 61, no. 2 (2007): 602–7, http://www.jstor.org/stable/43050417. See also Thorndike, *The Sphere of Sacrobosco,* 395.

De Viginti Quattuor Horis (*Of the Twenty-Four Hours*), *De Quattuor Imaginibus Magnis (Ab Aliis Separatis)* (*On the Four Great Images [Separated from the Others]*)[9] *De Discretione Operis Differentia ex Iudiciis Hermetis de Intentione Huius Operis* (*On the Discretion of Works Different from the Hermetic Judgments by the Intention of This Work*), and *De Imaginibus Diei et Noctis* (*On the Images of the Day and Night*).[10] The Arabic version is called the *Kitab talasim Balinas al-akbar* (*Great Book of Balinas's Talismans*). The Arabic version may have the alternative title *Kitab Hurmus alladhi tarjamahu Balinas min qibal al-nayranjat* (*The Book of Hermes Translated by Apollonius, Regarding Talismans*), which was the main source for the philosopher Fakhr al-Din al-Razi (d. 1209–1210).[11]

The Arabic version seems to share strong similarities with at least three other Arabic magic handbooks. The first of these is the *Mushaf al-qamar* (*Codex of the Moon*), which has a Latin version called *Liber Imaginum Lunae* (*Book of Moon Images*) that survives in fourteenth-century manuscripts. It describes Apollonius as pupil to his master, Hermes, and provides instructions for performing astral magic, specifically the making of lunar mansion talismans. The material is found in the *Book of the Moon* (Latin *Liber Lunae,* Hebrew *Sepher ha-Levanah*).[12] The second Arabic magic handbook is *Kitab al-Ahjar 'ala ra'y Balinas* (*The Book of Stones according to the Opinion of Balinas*),[13] which is found in the medieval alchemist Jabir ibn Hayyan's collection of 144 alchemical treatises known as *Kutub al-Mawazin* (*The Books of Balances*) and then also in the *Picatrix.*

---

9. *Speculum Astronomiae* (Mirror of Astronomy), chapter 11, lists the book titled *De Quattuor Imaginibus Magnis.*

10. Marathakis, trans., *The Book of Wisdom of Apollonius of Tyana*. See also Page, *Magic in the Cloister,* 75.

11. Gardiner, "Books on Occult Sciences," 1:735–65.

12. *Speculum Astronomiae,* chapter 11. See also Karr, ed., and Nachshon, trans., *Liber Lunae.*

13. This work may also be known as *Kitab Ablus al-hakim* (*The Book of the Sage Ablus*), in which Ablus is an alternate Arabic spelling for Apollonius, which is referenced in Pseudo-Majriti's *Ghayat al-hakim,* the Arabic astral magic treatise whose Latin version, the *Picatrix,* describes as the *Lapidary of Mercurius,* the *Book of Apollonius*. The *Book of the Images of Mercury* is originally attributed to Hermes Trismegistus as pointed out in chapter 11 of the *Speculum Astronomiae,* but in the *Picatrix,* it belongs to his student Apollonius. See Attrell and Porreca, trans., *Picatrix: A Medieval Treatise,* 104. See also Syed Nomanul Haq, *Names, Natures and Things,* 81–108. *The Book of Stones* may be found in the *Picatrix,* book 2, chapter 10.

The third belongs to the Arabic magic tradition and is known as the *Kitab al-Khawass* (*Book of Occult Virtues*), which describes talismans made from organic matter then shaped into an effigy or placed inside a pot. This tradition is cited in the Arabic book on cosmography titled *'Aja'ib al-makhluqat wa ghara'ib al-mawjudat* (*Marvels of Creatures and Strange Things Existing*) by Zakariya al-Qazwini (1203–1283), a Persian astronomer, geographer, and physician. It is also found in the *Kitab Mujarrabat al-Khawass* of Abu l-'Ala' ibn Zuhr (c. 1060–1131), a member of the great medical family called the Avenzoars, who was probably born in Seville and later moved to Cordova.[14] His book is structured according to the Arabic letters such that each element of nature (animal, vegetable, or mineral) appears in the chapter of the letter with which its Arabic name begins.[15] Abu Bakr al-Razi borrows from it in his *Kitab al-Khawass,* presenting fourteen talismans against obnoxious creatures such as flies and mice.[16]

The *Liber De Septem Figuris Septem Planetarum* (*On the Seven Figures of the Seven Planets*), falsely attributed to Apollonius of Tyana, describes engraving seven magic squares onto metal plates. Each magic square is associated with one of the seven planets; these metal plates act as planetary talismans. A magic square is a set of numbers arranged in a grid that gives the same total when added in a straight line, whether vertically, horizontally, or diagonally.[17] Magic squares related to the seven planets first appear in the *Kitab tadbirat al-kawakib* (*Book on the Influences of the Planets*) by the Arab Muslim astrologer and astronomer Arzachel (or Abu Ishaq Ibrahim al-Zarqali) (1029–1087), which was then translated into Latin by John of Seville; the magic squares later appear in the works of Ahmad ibn 'ali al-Buni and then again in the thirteenth-century Alfonsine treatise labeled as the

---

14. Like the other mythical accounts of discovery, Abu al-'Ala ibn Zuhr tells the story of Alexander the Great, who traveled among the Egyptian temples in Syria and found a small metallic effigy containing hellebore and sulphur that was used to keep flies away. As already discussed here and elsewhere, it can be seen that the Hermetic tradition carries a line of transmission, including Apollonius of Tyana, Aristotle, and his student Alexander the Great.

15. This organizing structure is also found in the natural magic treatise the *Kyranides* and other ancient medical treatises. The book contains many references, including Hippocrates, Dioscorides, Aristotle, Plato, Galen, etc., which may be a source for the *Picatrix.*

16. Raggetti, "Apollonius of Tyana's Great Book of Talismans," 155–82.

17. Page, *Magic in the Cloister,* 76.

Libro de Astromagia (*Book of Astral Magic*) translated into Castilian.[18]

The *Risalat al-Sihr* (*Treatise on Magic*) is mentioned several times in the *al-Mudkhal al-Kabir ila 'ilm af 'al al-Ruhaniyat waw Talassimat* (*Great Introduction to the Treatise on Spirits and Talismans*) that was translated by Hunayn ibn Ishaq. *Risalat al-Sihr* may be the same treatise mentioned by Cecco d'Ascoli who attributes the books *De Hyle* and *De Arte Magica* to Apollonius in his commentary on the *Sphere of the Cosmos* by John de Sacrobosco. Cecco quotes Apollonius, saying, "And Apollonius used to introduce in his *Arte Magica,* 'A doctor without stars and the necromancer without bones of the dead is like an image not vivified by spirits.'" And he also says, "The greater horizon of separate things enter into the lesser one [which is where our souls are said to reside]." Also, Cecco quotes Apollonius, saying, "Apollonius understands [it] in his book, *De Hyle,* where he speaks verbatim thus, 'as the sphere of the heavens is composed out of the great and small character of the circles, the nature of things which come into being out of the elements of the world, the angelic operation is to be employed to this effect.'"[19]

Also relevant are two works called *Risala fi Ta'thir al-Ruhaniyat fi l-Murakkabat* (*Treatise on the Influence of the Spirits on the Composite Things*) and *al-Mudkhal al-Kabir ila 'ilm af 'al al-Ruhaniyat waw at-Talassim* (*Great Introduction to the Treatise on Spirits and Talismans*). Both were translated by Hunayn ibn Ishaq (Latin *Iohannitius*) (809–873), an Arab Nestorian Christian translator who worked with a group of translators (including Thabit ibn Qurra) to translate Greek and Persian texts into Arabic and Syriac. Hunayn ibn Ishaq worked under the reign of both Al-Ma'mun (r. 813–833) and Al-Mu'tasim (r. 833–842), two Abbasid caliphs who are mentioned in the mythical accounts of two other treatises, the Pseudo-Aristotelian chiromantic treatise and the *The Book of the Treasure of Alexander.*[20] It is possible Hunayn ibn Ishaq is the intended translator in those mythical accounts. The first book, *Risala fi Ta'thir*

---

18. Comes, "The Transmission of Azarquiel's Magic Squares," in *Medieval Textual Cultures,* Wallis and Wisnovsky, eds., 159–198.

19. Thorndike, *The Sphere of Sacrobosco,* 393–95. Another reputed work attributed to Belenus is *Tilasmat mirrikh al-Hind* (*The Talisman of Mars*) (see Bodleian Library MS. Persian D. 100 [cat. Nr. 2749/1]), but I do not have access to the manuscript or knowledge of Persian to identify it.

20. For the Pseudo-Aristotelian chiromantic treatise, see chapter III, "Knowledge of the *Ars Notoria.*" For *The Book of the Treasure of Alexander,* see Frisvold, Nicholaj de Mattos, trans., and Christopher Warnock, ed., *The Book of the Treasure of Alexander,* 2010.

al-Ruhaniyat fi l-Murakkabat, is unknown; the second, *al-Mudkhal al-Kabir ila 'ilm af'al al-Ruhaniyat waw at-Talassim,* may be the same *Book of Spirits and Images* referenced in the *Picatrix* that contains the material already mentioned about *The Book of Stones according to the Opinion of Balinas.*[21]

21. For all these Pseudo-Apollonius works, see Mohammad Karimi Zanjani Asl, "Sirr al-khaliqa and Its Influence in the Arabic and Persianate World," 435–73. Mohammad Karimi Zanjani Asl does fail to follow up on some of his sources, as some treatises he attributes to Pseudo-Apollonius are in fact attributed to others or bear some other kind of relation; all known Pseudo-Apollonius works are listed here.

APPENDIX 7

WORKS ATTRIBUTED TO SOLOMON

King Solomon had many works falsely ascribed to him. Owing to his love for wisdom, Solomon is said to have written the biblical books Proverbs, Ecclesiastes, Song of Songs, and the apocryphal text called the Wisdom of Solomon. Solomon's portrayal as a legendary magician who wrote many books of magic begins around the time of the early Christian Church. The first extant manual comes from a Greek text of late antiquity called the *Testament of Solomon* (c. first to fourth century CE). The *Testament of Solomon* tells the story of a magical ring given to Solomon by the archangel Michael by which he could command spirits. The text also acts a registry of spirits from which a practicing magician can draw for his own ends. The *Testament* might have been influenced by some of the rituals in the collection of magical rituals called the *Greek Magical Papyri* (or *PGM*; c. second century BCE to fifth century CE) that makes references to Solomon as a magician. The *PGM* describes an exorcism of those possessed by demons in which Solomon's seal is used as a phylactery that is "terrifying to every *daimon*" and forces them to tell the truth.[1] Also, the *PGM* reveals a successful scrying procedure called "Solomon's fall" in which the magician puts the scryer into a trance, which causes him (or her) to fall down.[2]

The *Liber de umbris idearum* (*Book from the Shadow of the Ideas*) is falsely attributed to Solomon by the Italian astrologer and physician Cecco d'Ascoli (1257–1327) in his commentary upon the *Sphere of Sacrobosco*. This astral magic

1. Betz, ed., *The Greek Magical Papyri,* IV.3014–17, 3040–41.
2. *PGM* IV.850–929.

treatise "gave instructions on how to construct astronomical images in order to receive responses from demons."[3] This book's title was later appropriated by Giordano Bruno for his treatise on the Hermetic art of memory.

The *Speculum Astronomiae* (*Mirror of Astronomy*), posthumously attributed to the German Catholic philosopher and theologian Albertus Magnus (before 1200–1280), condemns the following five books attributed to Solomon:

> *De Quattuor Annulis* (*Concerning the Four Rings*), which is falsely attributed to four of Solomon's disciples who are named Fortunatus, Eleazar, Macarus, and Toz the Greek. The book contains suffumigations, construction of the pentacles, the duties of the assistants, and the design of the "gates" for the magic circle that resemble elements of the *Heptameron,* a medieval book of angelic magic attributed to Peter of Abano (1250–1316). Véronèse asserts that *De Quattuor Annulis* was known to Michael Scot and William Auvergne as *Idea of Solomon*. *De Quattuor Annulis* was also condemned by the abbot Johannes Trithemius of Sponheim in his 1508 work *Antipalus Maleficiorum* (*Against the Underworld Swamp Waters of Malefic Spirits*).[4]

3. Cornish, *Reading Dante's Stars,* 105. Cecco's commentary is available in Thorndike, *The Sphere of Sacrobosco,* 406.

4. Vaticana, Pal. Lat. 1196 (thirteenth to fourteenth centuries); Florence Italy, BN, II. III.214, fol. 26v–29v, which is an abridged and incomplete version from the fifteenth century; Florence Italy, Biblioteca Medicea Laurenziana, Plut. 89 Sup. 38, fol. 211–24v (dated 1494), *s.a. Fasciculus rerum geomanticarum*; Amsterdam BPH 114, 39–70, which has been renamed Coxe 25 and held in a private collection; Paris, BnF Latin 7349, fol. 99–101 (fifteenth century). From Boudet, *Entre science et nigromance,* 146, fn 98–99. See also Firenze Naz. Palatine 1022 (sixteenth century), which has *Anelli de Pietro d'Abbano* (*The Rings of Peter de Abano*). The literary interrelationship between *De Quattuor Annulis* and *Idea Saolomonis* is uncertain. *De Officiis Spirituum* (*On the Offices of Spirits*), also known as *Liber Officiorum Spirituum* (*The Book of the Office of Spirits*), which was the main source for Johann Weyer's *Pseudomonarchia Daemonum* and the *Ars Goetia,* references *De Quattuor Annulis.* See Véronèse, "Pietro d'Abano magicien," 309–10 (via Joseph Peterson's Esoteric Archives website). The title to Trithemius's work, *Antipalus Maleficiorum,* has been mistranslated in other previous publications. The Latin word *antipalus* is broken down into two parts: *anti,* meaning "against," and *palūs,* meaning "swamp," but more specifically in the context of the swampy waters of the Underworld. The confusion had arose over the word *palūs,* which had been mistaken for *pālus,* which means "a post, stake, or the wooden practice sword of the Roman gladiators." The placement of the macron over the vowel has led to mistranslations. Trithemius's reference to Underworld waters is further supported by necromantic lore in which the necromancer practices scrying using a rushing river or water vessel to contact the dead from the Underworld, just like Odysseus did in the *Odyssey* (books 10–11).

De Novem Candariis (*Concerning the Nine Pentacles*).[5] This book describes the making of pentacles (*candaria*),[6] which forms part of a greater ritual. The pentacles are meant to be worn by the operator as a sign and confirmation of his authority over spirits and his power to command them. The pentacles may be intended to be worn like the priestly breastplate of Aaron as described in Exodus. The pentacles of this book are the predecessors to those found in the *Magical Treatise of Solomon* and the ones missing from the *Clavicula Salomonis* (*Key of Solomon*).

De Tribus Figuris Spirituum (*Concerning the Three Figures of the Spirits*).[7] The title is said to refer to the three princes of the four regions of the world; presumably these are Satan, Lucifer, and Belzebuth, which were transmitted to later books of magic, such as the *Key of Solomon* (Universal Treatise Family), and the *Grimorium Verum* (a pseudo-Latin book title meant to translate as the *True Grimoire*). There is a mention of treatise titled *Hierarchy,* which is listed among other Solomonic magic treatises in Johannes Hartlieb's *Book of All Forbidden Arts,* and may possibly relate to *De Tribus Figuris Spirituum.*[8]

De Figura Al-mandal (*On the Al-mandel Figure*).[9] The twelfth-century book describes a one-foot square altar made of either metal or wax with certain names and figures engraved upon it with a candle at each of its

5. Thorndike mistranslates *candaria* as "candle" in his *History of Magic and Experimental Science,* 2:280. British Museum, Sloane 3851, fols. 68–75. As for the number of pentacles, the French MS W4664 and BnF MS 14787 list twelve pentacles.

6. The Latin word for "pentacle" is *candaria,* deriving from the Latin *cantharias,* meaning a "beetle." This in turn comes from the Greek *kantharos,* meaning "scarab" (or "dung beetle"), and by extension a gem shaped as a scarab. Egyptians carved scarabs, which were used as talismans; hence, the scarab form is more relevant to its function than its gem substrate. In necromancy, a certain stone is used to bind the ghost so that it obeys the necromancer's commands. Interestingly enough, there are nine pentacles, and the number nine bears an esoteric significance in necromancy. The *De Novem Candariis* is found in BnF It. 1524, *Clavicula Salomonis,* dated 1446 (another manuscript in the Toz Graecus family and the Hebrew *Maphteah Shelomoh*); also, Coxe 25 in a private collection, the Ghent MS in Latin of the sixteenth century, and *Summa Sacre Magica* of the fourteenth century.

7. Véronèse has identified Sloane 3850, f. 69v–75 as the only known extant exemplar.

8. Kieckhefer, trans., *Hazards of the Dark Arts,* 33.

9. Boudet and Véronèse have identified two essential versions of the *Al-mandal* (Version F and Almadel). See Véronèse, *L'Almandal et l'Almadel latins au Moyen Age.* Véronèse claims the book of magic was translated from Arabic into Latin. See also Peterson, *The Lesser Key of Solomon.*

corners. After suffumigations and invocations, the operator may receive the help of spirits. This book of magic is also mentioned by William of Auvergne (1228–1249), Antonio da Montolmo (fl. fourteenth century), Johannes Trithemius (1462–1516), Heinrich Cornelius Agrippa (1486–1535), and Johann Weyer (1515–1588), so it must have been widely distributed.[10]

De Sigillis Ad Daemoniacos (*On the Sigils with Regard to the Demons*). The incipit begins "*Caput sigilli gendal et tanchil,*" but the contents of this work are unknown, and there are no known extant manuscripts.[11]

The author of the *Mirror of Astronomy* also mentions a Hebrew book of Raziel that he calls *The Liber Institutionis* (*Book of Learning*), but today it is known by its Latin translation, *Liber Razielis,* which was structured in the form of seven books commissioned by Alfonso in 1259. The Latin *Liber Razielis* is composed of the following seven books: (1) *Liber Clavis* (*Book of the Key*), concerning astrology; (2) *Liber Ala* (*Book of the Wing [or Tree Hollow or Animal Limb]*), concerning natural magic about stones, herbs, and beasts; (3) *Liber Thymiama* (*Book of Incenses*); (4) *Liber Temporum* (*Book of Times*), concerning times ruled by spirits; (5) *Liber Munditiae et Abstinentiae* (*Book of Cleanliness and Abstinence*); (6) *Liber Sameyn* (*Book of the Heavens,* from the Hebrew *samaim*), concerning the names of the heavens and their angels;[12] and (7) *Liber Magice* (*Book of Magic*), concerning astral magic. Another version of the seventh book is the *Liber Virtutis* (*Book of Virtue*), which is an abridged version of *Liber Semaforas,* concerning names of power. These seven books were said to have been gathered together by Solomon and to which other related texts were added as appendices.

Other books attributed to Solomon and appended to *Liber Razielis* include the following: (1) *Glosae Semiphoras* (*Semiphoras Glosses*), by Zadok of Fez, the Jewish high priest of Israel during Solomon's reign; (2) *Verba in Operibus Razielis* (*Words in the Works of Raziel*), attributed to Abraham of Alexandria, the Syrian Coptic Orthodox pope (d. 978); (3) *Flores* (*Flowers*), attributed to Philopater Mercurius (Abu Sayfayn) of the Babylon Fortress in Cairo who was

10. Weill-Parot, "Cecco D'Ascoli and Antonio da Montolmo," 234.
11. *Speculum Astronomiae,* chapter 11.
12. See Morgan, *Sepher Ha-Razim.*

a third-century Christian saint and martyr; (4) *Capitulum Generale Sapientium Aegypti pro Operibus Magicae* (*The Chapter of the General Wise Sages of Egypt for Works of Magic*); (5) *Tabulae et Karacteres et Nomina Angelorum Gaudium* (*Tables, Characters, and Names of Joyous Angels*), (6) *Book of Toz the Greek,* also called *Liber Theysolius,* or *Liber super Perfectione Operis Razielis* (*Book Concerning the Completion of the Work of Raziel*), which is about attaining a familiar spirit; (7) *Liber Imaginum Sapientium Antiquorum* (*Book of Images of the Ancient Wise Sages*); and (8) *Imagines super septem dies Hebdomade et Sigilla Planetarum* (*Images Concerning the Seven Days of the Week and Planetary Sigils*), which can be found in Vatican Library VRL 1115.[13]

Solomon wrote a collection of prayers that he received from the angel and became known as the *Liber Florum Doctrinae Caelestis* (*Book of Flowers of Heavenly Teaching*).[14] According to the *Ars Notoria*'s own mythical account, this book would be reworked by Pseudo-Apollonius as *Flores Aurei;*[15] based on textual analysis, the book was reworked again and later became the present form of the *Ars Notoria.* According to the *Ars Notoria,* there are five books on the necromantic art attributed to Solomon. Plus, there is his *Liber Florum Doctrinae Caelestis,* which is his compilation of the divinely revealed books, *Eniclyssoe, Gemeliot,* and *Lengemath.* The glossed version of the Ars *Notoria* mistakes *Ydea Salomonis* for *Lengemath.*

The *Liber Florum Doctrinae Caelestis* is a key source for the *Flores Aurei* which, according to the mythical story, was "a volume about a magnitude of qualities" containing the Greek and Hebrew words and prayers Solomon wrote following his divine visitation with the angel Pamphilius. The referenced

13. See Sophie Page "Uplifting Souls: The Liber de essentia spirituum and the Liber Razielis," in Fanger, ed., *Invoking Angels,* 79–112. See also Page, "Magic and the Pursuit of Wisdom," 41–70. Also, Hartlieb makes a passing reference to an *Opus Urionis* in the *Liber Razielis.* Kieckhefer, trans., *Hazards of the Dark Arts,* 37. This appears to be a misspelling of *Opus Visionis [Divine],* which comes from Berengario Ganell's *Liber Iuratus* (two chapters after book 4). Therein is found a unique piece of the *Liber Iuratus* which says, "there is a list of six 'works of God' that can be performed after the consecration [of the *sigillum Dei*]; the first of these is the *opus visionis divine.*" See Veenstra in *Invoking Angels,* 155. On a side note, it is worth pointing out the parallel between the Solomonic and Raziel traditions in regard to their divine revelations. Adam receives divine knowledge from Raziel and then sins, entering a fallen state, just as Solomon receives divine knowledge from Pamphilius, and then sins, weakening his sons and kingdom.

14. *Ars Notoria,* sections 34, 38 and their glosses.

15. *Ars Notoria,* section 2 gloss.

passage also mentions that Solomon had written a corpus of writings based on this revealed book. The "magnitude of qualities" is a reference to the philosophical concept of hylomorphism.[16] The *Ars Notoria* explains the "qualities of the most sacred Greek and Hebrew words and of the prayers."[17]

Eniclyssoe may be a source for the mythical origin story and the *voces magicae* found in the *Ars Notoria*.[18]

Gemeliot, which contains the arts and sciences, as well as an extended quotation regarding the encounter between Solomon and the angel about grammar and rhetoric.[19]

Lengemath, also called the "restoration of languages," is said to contain a prayer of eloquence whose incipit is *Gemoht Gehel*.[20] Unfortunately, the Pseudo-Solomonic works the *Liber Florum Doctrinae Caelestis, Eniclyssoe, Gemeliot,* and the *Lengemath* are lost and otherwise unattested.

Lemegeton, or the *Lesser Key of Solomon,* is attributed to Solomon because it is a book that contains the names of spirits whom Solomon summoned and with whom he conversed. The book attests to an early thirteenth-century recension of our seventeenth-century extant *Lemegeton,* which is a compilation of five separate books, but there is no known manuscript to prove its thirteenth-century existence. Although nothing is further said about the contents of this early recension, except that it mentions the notory art and records the *Lamehc Leynac* prayer.[21]

Ydea Salomonis (the *Idea of Solomon*) is mentioned by the translator and astronomer Michael Scot (c. 1236) in the prologue of the *Liber Introductorius.* Also, the bishop of Paris, William of Auvergne (c. 1180–1249), in his *De Legibus* (*On Laws*) condemns the book, saying that there is no divinity in the pentagon, the rings, and the seals, and the nine pentacles of Solomon all of which lead to demonolatry, concluding, "As for that horrible image called the

16. Jung, "Intension and Remission of Forms." https://doi.org/10.1007/978-94-024-1665-7_243.

17. *Ars Notoria,* section 34 gloss. This "magnitude of qualities" of the Greek and Hebrew words would bear relation to the notary art of shorthand writing called Tironian notes that is discussed in chapter 4.

18. *Ars Notoria,* sections 8 and 8 gloss

19. *Ars Notoria,* sections 73–76.

20. *Ars Notoria,* section 62.

21. *Ars Notoria,* section 20b and section 21 gloss.

Idea Salomonis et entocta, let it never be mentioned among Christians."[22] *Idea Salomonis* is listed among other condemned texts on magic in the *Speculum Astronomiae*. According to the gloss of the *Ars Notoria,* the *Helyscemaht* and/or the *Assaylemaht* prayer is found there.[23]

22. Michael Camille, "Visual Art in Two Manuscripts of the *Ars Notoria,*" in Fanger, ed. *Conjuring Spirits,* 112.

23. *Ars Notoria,* section 8 gloss and section 16 gloss.

APPENDIX 8

Annotated Bibliography of Medieval Scholarship

This is a list of the most popular literary works on the seven liberal arts, philosophy, and theology that were read by the medieval student of Latin Europe. This list is by no means exhaustive; however, it should give the reader a foundation in understanding the intellectual environment of the medieval world in which the *Ars Notoria* arose. The chief introductory text to the seven liberal arts is Martianus Capella's *De Nuptiis Philologiae et Mercurii* (*The Marriage of Philology and Mercury*). Other notable works include the writings of Alcuin, Boethius's many works, Isidore of Seville's *Etymologiae,* and Thierry of Chartres's *Heptateuch.*

GRAMMAR

On the Latin Language

Aelius Donatus, a fourth-century Roman rhetorician and grammarian, wrote two treatises on Latin grammar, *Ars Maior* (*The Greater Art*) and *Ars Minor* (*The Lesser Art*), which became the mainstay schoolbooks for learning Latin in the Middle Ages. Donatus's most notable commentators included Remigius of Auxerre and Isidore of Seville.

Dionysius Cato, who lived in the third or fourth century CE, wrote the *Distichs of Cato* for instructing in the Latin language and morality.

Diomedes Grammaticus, another Latin grammarian who lived in the late fourth century CE, wrote an *Ars Grammatica* in three books.

Priscian, who lived in the sixth century CE, wrote the *Institutiones Grammaticae* (*Institutions of Grammar*) and the *Institutio De Nomine Pronomine Verbo* (*Instruction on the Noun, Pronoun, and Verb*), which became the two standard textbooks for learning Latin during the Middle Ages.

On Poetry

Vergil, the ancient Roman poet of the *Aeneid,* was studied for its dactylic hexameter in Latin prosody, grammar, and rhetoric. Maurus Servius Honoratus, an Italian of the late fourth century and early fifth century, was a grammarian and commentator, having written commentaries on Vergil's *Aeneid* and *Eclogues.*

The *Metamorphoses* of Ovid is a Latin narrative poem that has had a profound influence on Western culture for centuries.

Horace, the Roman lyric poet of the first century BCE, was studied for attaining knowledge of the trivium. His *Satires* and *Epistles* were given the most attention during the Middle Ages.

Statius, the first-century Roman poet, wrote the Latin epic poem titled *Thebaid* about the civil war between the brothers Eteocles, king of Thebes, and Polynices, leader of the army from Argos who fought to claim his share of royal power following the abdication of Oedipus. This was another poem for studying lines of dactylic hexameter.

Juvenal (fl. late first and early second century CE), a Roman poet who is best known for his *Satires.*

Bede, a seventh-century English Benedictine monk, wrote the *De Arte Metrica* (*Metrical Art, or Art of Poetry*) and *De Schematibus et Tropis* (*On Schemes and Tropes*) to instruct students in the fundamentals of grammar and poetry.

LOGIC/DIALECTIC

The main authority on logic during the Middle Ages was Aristotle. Aristotle's six works on logic—*Categories, On Interpretation, Prior Analytics, Posterior Analytics, Topics,* and *Sophistical Refutations*—were known collectively as the *Organon*. From the collapse of the Western Roman Empire in the fifth century up until the first part of the twelfth century, the Latin West only had access to Aristotle's *Categories* and *On Interpretation,* these having been translated by

Gaius Marius Victorinus. The following list is what became known as the "old art" (*ars vetus*) or the "old logic" (*logica vetus*):

Aristotle's *Categoriae* (*Categories*)
Aristotle's *De Interpretatione* (*On Interpretation*)
Porphyry of Tyre's *Isagoge* (*Introduction*)[1]
Pseudo-Hermes Trismegistus's *De Sex Rerum Principiis* (*On the Six Principles*)[2]

Boethius's commentaries on these three writings:

- *In Porphyrius's Isagoge,* first and second editions
- *In Aristotelis Categorias* (*In Aristotle's Categories*)
- *In Aristotelis Perihermeneias* (*In Aristotle's Interpretation,* first and second editions)

Boethius's logical monographs:

- *Introductio Ad Syllogismos Categoricos,* or *Antepraedicamenta* (Boethius's *Introduction to the Categorical Syllogism*)[3]
- *De Syllogismis Categoricis* (*On Categorical Syllogisms*)
- *De Hypotheticis Syllogismis* (*On Hypothetical Syllogisms*)
- *De Divisione* (*On Division*)
- *De Differentiis Topicis* (*On Topical Differences*)

Peter Abelard, a twelfth-century philosopher and theologian, wrote *Logica Ingredientibus* (*Logic for Beginners*), *Dialectica* (*Dialectic*), and *Logica: Nostrorum Petitioni Sociorum* (*Logic: To the Response of Our Associates*), which were commentary on the old logic.

The "new logic" (*logica nova*) consisted of four works of Aristotle:

1. The medieval student's introduction to the study of logic, which examined Aristotle's *Categoriae.*
2. *De Sex Rerum Principiis* was attributed to Gilbert de la Porree and added later to the old logic in the twelfth century.
3. This work was an introduction to Aristotle's logic but was a revision left unfinished.

Analytica Priora (*Prior Analytics*)
Analytica Posteriora (*Posterior Analytics*)
Topica (*Topics*)
De Sophisticis Elenchis (*Sophistical Refutations*)[4]

RHETORIC

Aristotle's *Rhetoric* deals with the art of persuasion and dates from the fourth century BCE.

Marcus Tullius Cicero, the first-century BCE Roman statesman, orator, lawyer, and philosopher, wrote *De Inventione* (*On Invention*), which was the primary textbook of rhetoric and became known as the "First Rhetoric" in the Middle Ages. Gaius Marius Victorinus wrote a fourth-century commentary on Cicero's *De Inventione,* called *Commenta in Ciceronis Rhetorica,* teaching the relationship between rhetoric and logic, the theory of genus and species, and explaining terminology.

Cicero's *De Oratore* (*On the Orator*) was a dialogue written on rhetoric and philosophical concepts, and the art of memory is credited to Simonides of Ceos.

The unknown author of *Rhetorica ad Herennium* (*Rhetoric: For Herennius*), also called the "second" or "new rhetoric," has been used as the primary textbook on the art of persuasion, dating from the first century BCE. This treatise was formerly attributed to Cicero. Thierry of Chartres (1100–1150) wrote commentaries on *Rhetoric: For Herennius* and Cicero's *On Invention.*

Quintilian's *Institutio Oratoria* (*Institutes of Oratory*) is a first-century CE twelve-volume textbook on the foundational education and development of the orator himself.

Seneca the Younger, the first-century Roman Stoic philosopher, wrote *Epistulae Morales ad Lucilium* (*Moral Letters to Lucilius*), which was studied by students of rhetoric and ethics during the Middle Ages.

Cassiodorus, a sixth-century Roman statesman and scholar of antiquity, wrote *Expositio Psalmorum* (*Exposition of the Psalms*) in an attempt to join Roman rhetoric to the Psalms. In his *Institutiones* (*Institutions*), he discusses

4. Boethius translated *Analytica Priora, Topica,* and *De Sophisticis Elenchis.* James of Venice translated the *Posterior Analytics.*

the liberal arts and provides a short treatment of grammar. Between the famous church father Augustine of Hippo and Cassiodorus, the Christian Church reluctantly accepted the notion of studying the intellectual culture of their pagan predecessors for investigating the truth wherever it can be found and, of course, having one's education guided by the Christian Scriptures.

ARITHMETIC

On Number Theory

Nicomachus of Gerasa's (60–120 CE) *Arithmetike Eisagoge* (*Introduction to Arithmetic*) contains philosophical ideas drawn from Pythagoras and Plato in relation to mathematics. Boethius's *De Institutione Arithmetica* (*On Arithmetic*) is an adapted Latin translation of Nicomachus's Greek work and was widely used among medieval students. Thierry of Chartres wrote a commentary on Boethius's teaching of arithmetic.

On the Arabic Numeral System

Leonardo of Pisa (c. 1170–c. 1240/1250), posthumously known as Fibonacci, wrote the *Liber Abaci* (*The Book of Calculation*), which describes the Hindu-Arabic numeral system that was Europe's introduction to the system that came to replace the Roman numeral system.

MUSIC

Music of the spheres was a philosophical concept developed by Pythagoras that considers the proportions in the movements of the seven classical planets as a form of music; this was not an audible sound but rather a harmonic, mathematical, and religious concept.

Ptolemy's *Harmonikon* (*Harmonics*) studies the musical scale and then applies musical intervals to the human soul and celestial bodies, describing a cosmic harmony. Porphyry of Tyre contributed a commentary upon Ptolemy's *Harmonics.*

Nicomachus of Gerasa's *Encheiridion Harmonikes* (*Manual of Harmonics*) gives the first detailed account of the music of the spheres.

Boethius's *De Institutione Musica* (*On Music*) presents three branches of medieval music—universal music, human music, and music made by singers and instrumentalists. *On Music* is based on the *Manual of Harmonics* by Nicomachus of Gerasa and on Ptolemy's *Harmonics.*

GEOMETRY

In Plato's *Timaeus,* the Platonic solids—the tetrahedron, cube, octahedron, dodecahedron, and icosahedron—are regular convex polyhedrons. Plato theorized that the four classical elements were made of these solids.

Euclid of Alexandria, the Greek mathematician who flourished between the mid-fourth to mid-third century BCE, wrote *Elements,* one of the most influential works in the history of mathematics. Boethius's lost *Ars Geometriae* (*Art of Geometry*) was based on Euclid's *Elements;* there were also extracts from both Euclid's and Boethius's works that were used for education during the Middle Ages.

There were many translations of and commentaries on Euclid's *Elements.*[5] Most notably, Boethius wrote a Greek to Latin translation, *De Institutione Geometrica,* which is now lost. Adelard of Bath (c. 1080–c. 1152), an English natural philosopher, provided a Latin translation. Gerard of Cremona (c. 1114–1187), one of the Toledo School of Translators, also translated Euclid's *Elements.* Campanus of Novara (c. 1220–1296) wrote the most influential Latin edition of Euclid's treatise. Porphyry of Tyre wrote a commentary.

Archimedes, the third-century BCE Greek mathematician wrote *Kuklou Metrēsis* (*On the Measurement of the Circle*), which was translated from Arabic to Latin by Gerard of Cremona.

Banu Musa were three Persian brothers of the ninth century whose work, the *Kitab marifat masakhat al-ashkal* (*Book on the Measurement of Plane and Spherical Figures*), was translated from Arabic to Latin by Gerard of Cremona, given the title *Liber Trium Fratum De Geometria,* and was quoted by European authors.

Hugh of St. Victor wrote *Practica Geometriae* (*Practical Geometry*), which makes the distinction between the theoretical and practical aspects of geometry,

---

5. A first *nota* of rhetoric is found within a thirteenth-century copy of Euclid's *Elements* held at the Bibliothèque nationale de France, Latin 7373, f. 176.

acting as a textbook on surveying. He divides practical geometry into altimetry, planimetry, and cosmimetry (i.e., the measurement of the world).

ASTRONOMY AND ASTROLOGY

Plato's *Timaeus* explores the nature of the physical world made up of the four classic elements and the eternal world of forms. Plato proposes the existence of a demiurge, or a god, who causes things to manifest and also a World-Soul that is composed of Sameness, Difference, and Existence to explain people's perception of reality.

Cicero's *Somnium Scipionis* (*Dream of Scipio*) is presented in the sixth book, *De Re Publica* (*On the Commonwealth*), which tells a fictional dream vision of the Roman general Scipio Aemilianus that describes the ancient view of cosmology and the music of the spheres. Macrobius's *Commentarii in Somnium Scipionis* (*Commentary on the Dream of Scipio*) was known to Boethius and influenced learning during the Middle Ages.

Claudius Ptolemy, the second-century Greek astronomer and astrologer, wrote the *Almagest,*[6] which explained the apparent motions of the stars and planets from a geocentric model of the universe. The *Almagest* would hold authority in the field of science until Copernicus. Ptolemy also wrote *Apotelesmatika* (*Astrological Outcomes*), also called *Tetrabiblos* (*Four Books*), which was an astrological text influential to Albertus Magnus, Thomas Aquinas, the universities of learning, and the medieval medical profession.

Mashallah ibn Athari, an eighth-century Persian Jewish astronomer wrote *De scientia motus orbis* (*Of the Knowledge of Moved Orbs*), which was a popular Aristotelian cosmological treatise aimed at the layman. His other works are famous as the source of Chaucer's knowledge about astrolabes.

Alfraganus's ninth-century *Kitāb fī Jawāmiʿ ʿIlm al-Nujūm* (*Compendium of the Science of the Stars*, or *Elements of Astronomy on the Celestial Motions*), was a summary of Ptolemy's *Almagest* combined with revised calculations from earlier Islamic astronomers. His work was translated into Latin by John of Seville in 1135 and Gerard of Cremona prior to 1175.

---

6. Gerard of Cremona's Latin translation was the most popular. Boethius wrote *De Institutione Astronomica* based on Ptolemy, but this work is now lost.

Pseudo-Ptolemy's *Centiloquium* consisted of one hundred aphorisms about astrology and was known in the tenth century CE when a commentary was written on it by the Egyptian mathematician Ahmad ibn Yusuf al-Misri.

Albumasar (787–886), the Islamic astronomer and astrologer, wrote *Kitāb al-mudkhal al-kabīr* (Latin translation provided by John of Seville and titled *Introductorium in Astronomiam;* i.e., *The Abbreviation of the Introduction to Astrology*) made from his *Great Introduction.*

The Toledan Tables were astronomical tables, called ephemerides, used to predict the movements of celestial bodies relative to the fixed stars. The tables were partly based on the work of Arzachel (a.k.a. al-Zarqali) and translated from the Arabic into Latin by Gerard of Cremona around 1175.

Bernardus Silvestris's *Cosmographia* (*Cosmography*), also called *De Mundi Universitate* (*On the Totality of the World*), is a Platonist allegory about the creation of the universe.

Johannes de Sacrobosco was a thirteenth-century British monk who wrote an introduction to astronomy titled *De Sphaera Mundi* (*The Sphere of the Cosmos*) around 1230. It was based heavily on Ptolemy's *Almagest* and drew from Islamic astronomy.

Guido Bonatti was an Italian astrologer and adviser to Frederick II, the Holy Roman emperor, and was the author of the *Liber Astronomiae* (*Book of Astronomy*) around 1277. It was reputed to be "the most important astrological work produced in Latin in the thirteenth century."

MEDICINE

Marcus Manilius, a first-century astrologer, wrote an epic poem titled *Astronomica,* which describes medical astrology, or iatromathematics, in which zodiac signs held rulership over certain parts of the body.

Hippocrates (c. 460–370 BCE) was a Greek physician and considered the "Father of Medicine," whose lasting contribution resides in the Hippocratic corpus. His collection of writings amounts to about sixty treatises on various medical topics in the form of textbooks, lectures, research notes, and philosophical essays.

Galen was a prolific second-century Roman author and physician of medicine whose corpus of Greek writings was the bedrock of medieval medicine, with some treatises translated into Arabic and Latin. He may have written more than five hundred treatises, working from the theory of the four humors. Galen's *Ars Medica* would inspire a collection of medical texts gathered by the ninth-century physician Hunayn bin Ishaq (Latin *Iohannitius*) that would later become the *Articella,* a collection of medical works made up of the following texts: *Isagoge Ioannitii ad Tegni Galieni* (Hunayn's *Introduction to the Art of Galen*); Hippocratic *Aphorisms;* Theophilus's *Prognostics* and *Urines;* and Philaretus's *Pulses.* The *Articella* would become the central textbook during the heyday of the *Ars Notoria.*

Avicenna was an eleventh-century Persian physician who is considered the "Father of Early Modern Medicine." His encyclopedic work titled *Canon Medicinae* (*The Canon of Medicine*) was translated into Latin by Gerard of Cremona.

Pliny the Elder was a first-century Roman author and natural philosopher who wrote the encyclopedic *Naturalis Historia* (*Natural History*), which contained information on drugs and medicine.

Pedanius Dioscorides was a first-century Greek physician who wrote *De Materia Medica* (*On Medical Material*), which was a pharmacopoeia of herbal medicine that was widely read during the Middle Ages.

The eleventh-century physician Constantine the African emigrated to southern Italy, where he translated the Arabic medical texts of Razes, Ibn Imran, Ibn Suleiman, and Ibn al-Jazzar into Latin. His Latin translations were used as textbooks during the Middle Ages.

PHILOSOPHY

The two main philosophers of the Western world were Plato and Aristotle. During the third to sixth centuries, commentaries on Plato's works were written by a number of philosophers called Neoplatonists. During the twelfth and thirteenth centuries, the Arabs transmitted the Greek works of Aristotle to Europe, which were translated into Latin and disseminated among teachers, students, and universities. There were many commentaries on both philosophers. With the rediscovery of Aristotle, commentaries on Aristotle were the most current for the times.

Plato

Plato's *Timaeus* (the first part of a projected trilogy of *Timaeus, Critias,* and *Hermocrates*) discusses his views on the nature of the physical world, the demiurge, the perfect world of forms, the World-Soul, the creation of the seven classic planets, the ecliptic, and the four elements. Plato's *Timaeus* was the only work translated into Latin—thanks to Cicero and Calcidius—that was available to medieval Europe. It was not until the fifteenth century when Marsilio Ficino began providing Latin translations that Europe started to gain access to Plato's philosophical corpus.

Aristotle

Physics, or natural philosophy, was the practice of studying nature and the physical universe. For Aristotle, physics encompassed fields of knowledge that we would now call the philosophy of mind, sensory experience, memory, anatomy, and biology. Aristotle's works on natural philosophy included his *Physica* (*Physics*), *De Caelo* (*On the Heavens*), *De Generatione et Corruptione* (*On Generation and Corruption*), *Meteorologica* (*Meteorology*), *De Mundo* (*On the Universe*),[7] and *De Anima* (*On the Soul*).

Aristotles's *Metaphysics* is called the "first philosophy" and addresses the philosophical problems that arise in understanding abstract concepts such as cause, matter, form, time, and space. Al-Kindi's *De Quinque Essentiis* (*On the Five Essences*) was an accessible commentary thanks to the translation work of Gerard of Cremona.

Aristotle's *Parva naturalia* (*Little Physical Treatises*) included *Sense and Sensibilia; On Memory and Reminiscence; On Sleep; On Dreams; On Divination in Sleep; On Length and Shortness of Life; On Youth, Old Age, Life and Death, and Respiration; On Breath; History of Animals; Parts of Animals; Movement of Animals; Progression of Animals;* and *Generation of Animals.*

Aristotles's practical philosophy covered the matter of ethics. His most notable works include *Nicomachean Ethics, Great Ethics, Eudemian Ethics,* and *On Virtues and Vices.*

---

7. *On the Universe* is now considered spurious by the twentieth-century scholar André-Jean Festugière.

Neoplatonism

Proclus's important work titled *Elementatio Theologica* (*Elements of Theology*) was translated from Greek into Latin by William of Moerbeke.

Boethius's *De Consolatione Philosophiae* (*Consolation of Philosophy*) was written while Boethius was imprisoned and awaiting his execution. It was one of the most influential works during the Middle Ages. Boethius brought an understanding of Plato and Neoplatonic concepts to a large audience along with Christian ethical messages.

THEOLOGY

The Vulgate Bible was the Latin translation of the Bible and was part of the foundational teachings in both schools and churches. It differs from modern Bibles in names and numbering of its books.

Peter Comestor, a French theologian and university administrator, wrote the famous twelfth-century *Historia Scholastica,* an abridgment and gloss to the Bible that was a significant secondary source that was translated into every major Western European language.

Patristic writings and Christian apologetics were part of one's studies in theology, including the works of Tertullian, Justin Martyr, Clement of Alexandria, Augustine of Hippo, and Jerome of Stridon.

Anselm of Canterbury (1033–1109) was a Benedictine monk who has been called the father of Scholasticism and whose works embodied the phrase "faith seeking understanding." His most notable work is the *Proslogion* (*Discourse*), which provides the ontological argument for God's existence.

Anselm of Laon (d. 1117) was a French theologian whose *Glossa Ordinaria* (*Ordinary Gloss*) presented patristic and early medieval interpretations of biblical scripture in an accessible and easily referenced fashion.

Hugh of St. Victor (c. 1096–1141) was a Saxon canon regular and theologian who believed that philosophy and the liberal arts serve theology, just as was thought by Augustine and Clement of Alexandria. His most significant works include *De Sacramentis Christianae Fidei* (*On the Sacraments of the Christian Faith*), *Didascalion* (*On the Study of Reading*), and *In Hierarchiam Celestem Commentaria* (*Commentary on the Celestial Hierarchy*).

Bernard of Clairvaux was a twelfth-century French abbot whose most famous works included *De Diligendo Dei* (*On Loving God*), which details seven stages of ascent to achieving union with God, and *Sermones super Cantica Canticorum* (*Sermons on the Song of Songs*).

Hildegard of Bingen was a twelfth-century German Benedictine abbess and Christian mystic who is best known for her visionary treatise *Scivias* (*Know the Ways*), her *Liber Vitae Meritorum* (*Book of Life's Merits*), and her *Liber Divinorum operum* (*Book of Divine Works*).

Peter Lombard was a twelfth-century Scholastic theologian who wrote *Libri Quattuor Sententiarum* (*The Four Books of Sentences*), which was essentially a collection of patristic writings arranged along with biblical scriptures, that became the standard textbook of medieval theology.

Finally, Pseudo-Hermes or Pseudo-Aristotle was the author of *Liber Viginti Quattuor Philosophorum* (*The Book of Twenty-Four Philosophers*), which proposes twenty-four definitions of God in order to answer the question "What is God?" This little work from the twelfth century was translated by Hugo of Santalla.

MECHANICS

The relevant literature on the mechanical arts includes a Pseudo-Aristotelian treatise titled *Problemata Mechanica* (*Mechanical Problems*), the *Mechanics* of the Greco-Egyptian engineer Hero of Alexandria (c. 10–70 CE), and book 8 of the *Synagoge* (*Collection*) written by the Greek mathematician Pappus of Alexandria, all of which were known in both the ancient Greek and medieval Arab worlds.

Also important at the time was Jordanus de Nemore and his *Scientia de Ponderibus* (*Science of Weights*).

BIBLIOGRAPHY

PRIMARY SOURCES FOR *ARS NOTORIA*, VERSIONS A & A2

Apollonius of Tyana. *Ars notoria, sive Flores aurei,* c. 1225. Mellon MS 1, f. 1–36. Yale University, Beinecke Rare Book and Manuscript Library, New Haven, Conn.

———. *Expositiones Apollonii ad cognitiones scientiarum quas Flores aureos appellavit,* 1239. Latin 7152, f. 1–22. Bibliotheque nationale de France, Paris.

———. *Flores Aurei* (f. 1–39), *Ars Notoria* (f. 39v–47v), end of the 15th century. Clm 276. Bayerische Staatsbibliothek, Munich.

Ars Notoria, First quarter of the 14th century. Latin 6842. Biblioteca Apostolica, Vatican City.

Ars notoria Salomonis, second half of the 13th century or first half of the 14th century. MS Sloane 1712, f. 1–22v. British Library, London.

Ars notoria, first quarter of the 15th century. Amplonius Ratinck de Berka 4° 380, f. 49–64v. Stadt-und Regionalbibliothek, Erfurt, Germany.

Ars notoria Salomonis, second half of the 13th century or first half of the 14th century. MS Sloane 1712, f. 1–22v. British Library, London, United Kingdom.

Notae atrium liberalium (Ars notoria), third quarter of the 13th century. E.V. 13, f. 1–31v. Biblioteca Nazionale Universitaria di Torino, Turin, Italy.

PRIMARY SOURCES FOR *ARS NOTORIA*, VERSION B

Ars notoria de Salomone (Sacratissima ars notoria), 15th century. Latin 7153, f. 1–172. Bibliotheque nationale de France.

Liber de Arte Memorativa, 1600. Yahuda Var. 34, f. 1–31v. National Library of Israel, Jerusalem.

Sacratissima ars notoria, 1360–1375. Latin 9336, f. 1–29. Bibliotheque nationale de France, Paris.

Sacratissima ars notoria, 16th century. Latin 7154, f. 1–100. Bibliotheque nationale de France, Paris.

First quarter of the 15th century. Bodley 951 (19 fol.). University of Oxford, Bodleian Library, Oxford, UK.

Second quarter of the 14th century. CC 322 (25 fol.). Kremsmunster Abbey (Stifsbibliothek), Kremsmunster, Austria.

14th century. MS 216, f. 1–43. St. Nikolaus von Kues Hospitalsbibliothek, Bernkastel-Kues, Germany.

PRIMARY SOURCES FOR *OPUS OPERUM*

Opus Operum, second half of the 13th century or first half of the 14th century. MS Sloane 1712. British Library, London.

Opus Operum, first quarter of the 14th century. Vulcanius 45. Universiteitsbibliotheek, Leiden, Netherlands.

Opus Operum, first quarter of the 14th century. Latin 6842. Biblioteca Apostolica, Vatican City.

Opus Operum, end of the 15th century. Clm 276. Bayerische Staatsbibliothek, Munchen, Germany.

PRIMARY SOURCE FOR ARS BREVIS

Richard Dove of Buckfast. Ars Notoria, c. 15th century. Sloane 513, f. 192-200. British Library, Hans Sloane collection, London.

14th century. Amplonianum Coll., Octavo 79, f. 63-66. Wissenschaftliche Bibliothek, Erfurt.

14th century. Scot.-Vindobonensis 140 (61), f. 140-53v. Österreichische Nationalbibliothek, Vienna.

PRIMARY SOURCES FOR ARS NOTORIA ABBREVIATA

Ars Notoria Salomonis (abbreviated), End of 15th century. Clm 28858, f. 1-12v. Bayerische Staatsbibliothek, Munich.

Ars Notoria Salomonis (abbreviated), End of 14th century. Palatine Latin 957, f. 92v-94v. Biblioteca Apostolica, Palatine collection, Vatican.

PRIMARY SOURCE FOR ARS PAULINA

Ars Paulina, 15th century. Latin 3180, f. 43v-47r. Biblioteca Apostolica, Vatican.

SECONDARY SOURCES

Adolph Rusch of Strassburg. *Biblia Latina cum glossa ordinaria: Facsimile reprint of the Editio Princeps* (1480/1481), 4 vols. With an introduction Karlfried Froehlich and Margaret T. Gibson. Turnhout: Brepols, 1992.

Aelianus, Claudius. *Various History.* Translated by Thomas Stanley, 2nd edition. London: George, 1670.

Aeschylus. *Persians.* Translated by Herbert Weir Smyth. Cambridge: Harvard University Press, 1926.

Agrippa, Henry Cornelius. *De occulta philosophia libri tres.* Edited by Vittoria Perrone Compagni. Leiden: Brill, 1992.

———. *Fourth Book of Occult Philosophy: The Companion to Three Books of Occult Philosophy.* Translated by Robert Turner. Edited by Donald Tyson. Woodbury: Llewellyn, 2009.

———. *Opera Omnia,* II. Lyons: Beringos Fratres, c. 1620, 603–60.

———. *Three Books of Occult Philosophy.* Translated by James Freake. Edited by Donald Tyson. Llewellyn's Sourcebook Series. Woodbury, Minn.: Llewellyn, 1993.

Alcuin of York. *Dialogue on Dialectics.* Bavarian State Library, Clm Codex Latin 19437, f. 43.

Alfaye, Silvia. "*Sit Tibi Terra Gravis:* Magical-Religious Practices Against Restless Dead in the Ancient World." *Formae Mortis: El transito de la vida a la muerte en las sociedades antiguas,* (2009): 181–216.

Alfonsi, Peter. *Dialogue Against the Jews (Fathers of the Church: Medieval Continuations).* Translated by Irven M. Resnick. United Kingdom: Catholic University of America Press, 2006.

Anderson, Wendy Love. *The Discernment of Spirits: Assessing Visions and Visionaries in the Late Middle Ages.* Spatmittelalter, Humanismus, Reformation, no. 63. Tubingen: Mohr Siebeck, 2011.

Apuleius. *Apologia.* Translated by H. E. Butler. Glouchester, UK: Book Depository, 2008.

———. *The Golden Ass.* Translated by E. J. Kenney. New York: Penguin Books, 2004.

Aquinas, Thomas. *The Summa Theologiae of St. Thomas Aquinas.* Translated by Fathers of the English Dominican Province, 2nd revised ed., 1920. Online edition 2017 by Kevin Knight. *Nihil Obstat.* F. Innocentius Apap, O.P., S.T.M., Censor. Theol.,

Imprimatur. Edus. Canonicus Surmont, Vicarius Generalis. Westmonasterii. *Nihil Obstat.* F. Raphael Moss, O.P., S.T.L. and F. Leo Moore, O.P., S.T.L., *Imprimatur.* F. Beda Jarrett, O.P., S.T.L., A.M., Prior Provincialis Angliae.

Ascheri, Mario. *The Laws of Late Medieval Italy (1000-1500): Foundations for a European System.* Leiden: Koninklijke Brill, 2013.

Asl, Mohammad Karimi Zanjani, "Sirr al-khaliqa and Its Influence in the Arabic and Persianate World: 'Awn b. al-Mundhir's Commentary and Its Unknown Persian Translation." *Al-Qantara,* XXXVII 2, July–December 2016: 435–73.

Attrell, Dan. *Picatrix: A Medieval treatise on Astral Magic, Magic in History.* Translated by David Porreca. University Park: Pennsylvania State University Press, 2019.

Augustine of Hippo. *De Civitate Dei.* The Latin Library website.

Avicenna. *A Treatise on the Canon of Medicine of Avicenna.* Translated by Oskar Cameron Gruner. New York: AMS Press, 1973.

Bednarski, Steven. *A Poisoned Past: The Life and Times of Margarida de Portu, a Fourteenth-Century Accused Poisoner.* Tonawanda: University of Toronto Press, 2014.

Betz, Hans Dieter, ed. *The Greek Magical Papyri in Translation Including the Demotic Spells,* 2nd edition. Chicago: University of Chicago Press, 1992.

Bishr, Sahl Ibn. *The Introduction to the Science of the Judgments of the Stars.* Translated by James Herschel Holden. Tempe, Ariz.: American Federation of Astrologers, 2008.

Bladel, Kevin Van. *The Arabic Hermes: From Pagan Sage to Prophet of Science, Oxford Studies in Late Antiquity.* New York: Oxford University Press, 2009.

Boethius. *Commentaries on Isagoge.* Edited by Samuel Brandt. *Corpus scriptorum ecclesiasticorum latinorum,* vol. 48. Vienna/Leipzig: Tempsky/Freitag, 1906.

———. *The Consolation of Philosophy.* Translated by Victor Watts, revised edition. New York: Penguin Books, 1999.

———. *On the Holy Trinity (De Trinitate).* Translated by Erik C. Kenyon. N.p.: self-pub., 2004.

"The Book: Scrolls in the Age of the Book." Harvard University; HarvardX on edX website. Video. Instructors Kelly, Thomas Forrest, and Timothy M. Baker. Accessed on August 1, 2019.

The Book of Wisdom of Apollonius of Tyana: Apotelesmata Apollonii. Translated by Ioannis Marathakis. Self-published, 2020.

Boudet, Jean-Patrice. *Entre science et nigromance: astrologie, divination et magie dans l'occident medieval, XIIe–XVe siècle.* Paris: Publications de la Sorbonee, 2006.

———. '*L'ars notoria* au Moyen Age: une resurgence de la theurgie antique?' *La Magie Actes du colloque international de Montpellier,* March 1999. Montpellier, 2000, 173–91.

Boustan, Ra'anan S. "Israelite Kingship, Christian Rome, and the Jewish Imperial Imagination: Midrashic Precursors to the Medieval 'Throne of Solomon.'" In *Jews, Christians, and the Roman Empire: The Poetics of Power in Late Antiquity*. Edited by Natalie B. Dohrmann and Annette Yoshiko Reed. Philadelphia: University of Pennsylvania Press, 2013.

Boys-Stones, George, Jas Elsner, Antonella Ghersetti, Robert Hoyland, Ian Repath, and Simon Swain, editors. *Seeing the Face, Seeing the Soul: Polemon's Physiognomy from Classical Antiquity to Medieval Islam*. New York: Oxford University Press, 2007.

Budge, E. A. Wallis, trans. and ed. *Syrian Anatomy, Pathology and Therapeutics, or "The Book of Medicines,"* vol. 2. New York: Oxford University Press, 1913.

Burnett, Charles. "The Eadwine Psalter and the Western Tradition of the Onomancy in Pseudo-Aristotle's 'Secret of Secrets.'" *Archives D'histoire Doctrinale Et Littéraire Du Moyen Âge* 55 (1988): 143–67.

———. "'Give Him the White Cow,' Notes and Note-Taking in the Universities in the Twelfth and Thirteenth Centuries." *History of the Universities* 14, 1998: 1–30.

———. *Magic and Divination in the Middle Ages: Texts and Techniques in the Islamic and Christian Worlds*, Collected Studies Series. Aldershot: Variorum Ashgate, 1996.

Burton, Simon J. G., Joshua Hollmann, and Eric M. Parker. *Nicholas of Cusa and the Making of the Early Modern World*. Boston: Brill, 2019.

Bylebyl, Jerome J. "The Medical Meaning of Physica." *Osiris* 6 (1990): 16–41.

Cadden, Joan, David Lindberg, and M. Shank. "The Organization of Knowledge: Disciplines and Practices." In *The Cambridge History of Science*. Edited by David C. Lindberg and Michael H. Shank. Cambridge: Cambridge University Press, 2013, chapter 9, 240–67.

Carruthers, Mary. *The Book of Memory: A Study of Memory in Medieval Culture*. 2nd edition. Cambridge: Cambridge University Press, 2008.

Chadwick, H. *Pseudo-Athanasii de Trinitate libri x-xii: Expositio fidei catholicae, Professio arriana et confession catholica, De Trinitate et de Spiritu Sancto. Recognovit brevique adnotatione critica instruxit* Manlius Simonetti. Bologna: Cappelli, 1956, 148. *The Classical Review,* volume 8, issue 1. March 1958, 86. Published online by Cambridge University Press: February 13, 2009.

Cicero, *Pro Cluentio* VI.15, The Latin Library website.

Comes, Rosa. "The Transmission of Azarquiel's Magic Squares in Latin Europe." In *Medieval Textual Cultures: Agents of Transmission, Translation and Transformation*. Edited by F. Wallis and R. Wisnovsky. Berlin/Boston: De Gruyter, 2016.

Comparetti, Domenico. *Vergil in the Middle Ages*. Princeton: Princeton University Press, 1997.

Copeland, Rita, and Ineke Sluiter, ed. *Medieval Grammar and Rhetoric: Language Arts Literary Theory, AD 300 – 1475*. Oxford: Oxford University Press, 2009.

Doquang, Mailan S. *The Lithic Garden: Nature and the Transformation of the Medieval Church*. New York: Oxford University Press, 2018.

Duling, D. C., trans. *Testament of Solomon*. In *The Old Testament Pseudepigrapha,* 2 vols. Garden City: Doubleday, 1983.

Dupebe, Jean. "*L'Ars notoria* et la polemique sur la divination et la magie." In *Divination et controverse religieuse en France au XVIe siècle*. Paris: L'E.N.S. de Jeunes Filles, 1987, 122–34.

Dykes, Benjamin N. *A Compilation on the Science of the Stars*. Minneapolis: Cazimi Press, 2015.

Ebeling, Florian. *The Secret History of Hermes Trismegistus: Hermeticism from Ancient to Modern Times*. Translated by David Lorton. Ithaca: Cornell University Press, 2007.

Edge, Joanne. "Licit Medicine or 'Pythagorean Necromancy'? The 'Sphere of Life and Death' in Late Medieval England," 87:238. *Historical Research,* Institute of Historical Research, 2014: 611–32.

———. "Nomen Omen: the 'Sphere of Life and Death' in England, c. 1200–c. 1500." PhD diss., University of London, 2014.

Eknoyan, Garabed. "The Kidneys in the Bible: What Happened." *Journal of the American Society of Nephrology,* December 2005, 16 (12): 3464–471.

Erasmus, Desiderius. *The Colloquies of Erasmus*. Translated by Nathan Bailey. Edited by E. Johnson. 2 vols. London: Reeves and Turner, 1878.

Eusebius. *Preparation for the Gospel* Translated by E. H. Gifford. Oxford: Clarendon Press, 1903

Evans, Elizabeth C. "Galen the Physician as Physiognomist." *Transactions and Proceedings of the American Philological Association* 76 (1945): 287–98.

Faivre, Antoine. *Eternal Hermes: From Greek God to Alchemical Magus*. Translated by Joscelyn Godwin. Grand Rapids: Phanes Press, 1995.

Falk, Sebastian L. D. "Improving Instruments: Equatoria, Astrolabes, and the Practice of Monastic Astronomy in Late Medieval England." PhD. diss., University of Cambridge, 2016.

Fanger, Claire. "Sacred and Secular Knowledge Systems in the 'Ars Notoria' and the 'Flowers of Heavenly Teaching' of John of Morigny." In *Die Enzyklopadik der Esoterik*. Edited by Andreas B. Kilcher and Philipp Theisohn. Paderborn: Wilhelm Fink, 2010, 157–76.

Fanger, Claire, *Conjuring Spirits: Texts and Traditions of Medieval Ritual Magic*. Magic in History. University Park: Pennsylvania State University Press, 1998.

———. *Rewriting Magic: An Exegesis of the Visionary Autobiography of a Fourteenth-Century French Monk*. Magic in History. University Park: Pennsylvania State University Press, 2015.

———. ed. *Invoking Angels: Theurgic Ideas and Practices, Thirteenth to Sixteenth Centuries.* Magic in History. University Park: Pennsylvania State University Press, 2012.

Ferris, Sumner. "Venus and the Virgin: The Proem to Book III of Chaucer's 'Troilus and Criseyde' as a Model for the Prologue to the "Prioress's Tale." *The Chaucer Review* 27, no. 3 (1993): 252–59.

Fine, Steven. *Art and Judaism in the Greco-Roman World: Toward a New Jewish Archaeology*. New York: Cambridge University Press, 2010.

Fludd, Robert. *Fasciculus Geomanticus: in quo varia variorum opera geomantica continentur*. 2nd edition. Verona: n.p., 1704.

Forshaw, Peter J. "The Occult Middle Ages." In *The Occult World*. Edited by Christopher Partridge. New York: Routledge, 2016, chapter 2: 34–48.

Frisvold, Nicholaj de Mattos, trans., and Christopher Warnock, ed., *The Book of the Treasure of Alexander*. Iowa City: Renaissance Astrology, 2010.

Garipzanov, Ildar H. *The Symbolic Language of Royal Authority in the Carolingian World (c. 751–877)*. Brill's Series on the Early Middle Ages. Boston: Brill, 2008.

Gellius, Aulus Cornelius. *Attic Nights, Volume 1: Books 1–5*. Translated by J. C. Rolfe. Loeb Classical Library, 195. Cambridge: Harvard University Press, 1927.

Giglioni, Pierangela, ed. "*Tractatus contra divinatores et sompniatores" di Agostino d'Ancona: introduzione ed edizione del testo*. Vol. 48 (1985): 5–111.

Godwin, Joscelyn. *The Harmony of the Spheres: A Sourcebook of the Pythagorean Tradition in Music*. Rochester, Vt.: Inner Traditions, 1993.

Goldstein, Miriam. "Early Jewish-Christian Polemic in Arabic: *Judeo-Arabic Versions of Toledot Yeshu*." *Ginzei Qedem* 6 (2010): 9–42.

Greer, John Michael, trans., with commentary by Christopher Warnock. *Astral High Magic: De Imaginibus of Thabit Ibn Qurra*. Iowa City: Renaissance Astrology, 2011.

Greer, John Michael, and Christopher Warnock, trans. *The Picatrix*. Liber Atratus and Rubeus Editions. N.p.: Adocentyn Press, 2010–2011.

Gregory, Timothy E. *A History of Byzantium*. 2nd edition. Malden: Wiley-Blackwell, 2010.

Guénin, Louis-Prosper, and Guénin, Eugène Guénin. *Histoire de la sténographie dans l'antiquité et au moyen-âge; les notes tironiennes*. Paris: Hachette, 1908.

Haines, John. *The Notory Art of Shorthand (Ars notoria notarie): A Curious Chapter in the History of Writing in the West*. Dallas Medieval Texts and Translations 20. Walpole: Peeters, 2014.

Hansson, Sven Ove, ed. *The Role of Technology in Science: Philosophical Perspectives.* Philosophy of Engineering and Technology, book 18. Stockholm: Springer, 2015.

Haq, Syed Nomanul. *Names, Natures and Things: The Alchemist Jábir ibn Hayyán and his Kitáb al-Ahjár* (Book of Stones). Boston Studies in the Philosophy of Science, vol. 158. Dordrecht: Kluwer Academic Publishers, 1994.

Harms, Daniel, Clark, James R., Peterson, Joseph H., *The Book of Oberon: A Sourcebook of Elizabethan Magic.* Woodbury, Minn: Llewellyn Publications, 2015.

Hauck, Dennis William. *The Emerald Tablet: Alchemy for Personal Transformation.* New York: Penguin/Arkana, 1999.

Herodotus. *Histories* 2.75.1–4. Translated by A. D. Godley. London: Loeb Classical Library, 4 volumes, 1920–1925.

Hippolytus. *Refutation of All Heresies* Translated by J.H. MacMahon. From *Ante-Nicene Fathers,* Vol. 5. Edited by Alexander Roberts, James Donaldson, and A. Cleveland Coxe. Buffalo, NY: Christian Literature Publishing Co., 1886.

Hirsch, Emil G., Ira Maurice Price, Wilhelm Bacher, M. Seligsohn, Mary W. Montgomery, and Crawford Howell Toy. "Solomon." In Isidore Singer et al., eds. *The Jewish Encyclopedia.* New York: Funk & Wagnalls, 1901–1906.

Hogendijk, Jan P. "On Euclid's Lost *Porisms* and Its Arabic Traces." *Bollettino Di Storia Delle Scienze Matematiche,* vol. 7. February 1987, 93–115.

Homer. *The Odyssey.* Translated by Emily Wilson. New York: W. W. Norton, 2018.

Houtsma, M. Th., Russel Arnold, Basset, Hartmann, Gibb Camilla, Heffening, Levi-Provencal, Wensinck, eds. *E. J. Brill's First Encyclopaedia of Islam, 1913–1936.* 9 vols. New York: Brill, 1993.

Hugh, St. Victor. *Didascalicon, sive De Studio Legendi.* Charles Henry Buttimer. Washington DC: Catholic University Press, 1939.

Humphries Jr., Thomas L. *Ascetic Pneumatology from John Cassian to Gregory the Great.* New York: Oxford University Press, 2013.

Isidore of Seville. *Etymologies.* Translated by Stephen A. Barney, W. J. Lewis, J. A. Beach, and Oliver Berghof with the collaboration of Muriel Hall. Cambridge: Cambridge University Press, 2006.

James, M. R., ed. *The New Testament Apocrypha.* Berkeley: The Apocryphile Press, 2004.

John of Morigny. *Liber Florum Celestis Doctrine: The Flowers of Heavenly Teaching.* Studies and Texts, ST 199. Edited by Claire Fanger and Nicholas Watson. Toronto: Pontifical Institute of Mediaeval Studies, 2015.

John of Sacrobosco. *On the Sphere.* Quoted in Edward Grant, *A Source Book in Medieval Science.* Cambridge: Harvard University Press, 1974.

John of Salisbury. *Ioannis Saresberiensis Policraticus I–IV.* Edited by K. S. B. Keats-Rohan. *Corpus Christianorum Continuatio Mediaeualis,* 118. Turnhout: Brepols, 1993.

Jones, Alexander, ed., trans. *Pappus of Alexandria: Book 7 of the Collection.* Sources in the History of Mathematics and Physical Sciences 8, 2 vols. New York: Springer, 1986.

Joost-Gaugier, Christiane L. *Measuring Heaven: Pythagoras and His Influence on Thought and Art in Antiquity and the Middle Ages.* Ithaca: Cornell University Press, 2006.

Josephus, Flavius. *Jewish Antiquities* in *The Works of Flavius Josephus.* Translated by William Whiston, A.M. London: Lackington, Allen, and Co., 1895.

Jung, Elzbieta. "Intension and Remission of Forms." In *Encyclopedia of Medieval Philosophy.* Edited by H. Lagerlund. Dordrecht: Springer, 2020.

Juste, David. *Les Alchandreana primitifs: Etude sur les plus anciens traits astrologiques latins d'origine arabe (Xe siècle).* Brill's Studies in Intellectual History. Boston: Brill, 2007.

———. "Non-transferable Knowledge: Arabic and Hebrew Onomancy into Latin." *Annals of Science* 68:4 (2011): 517–29.

———. *"Pseudo-Ptolemy, De imaginibus super facies signorum" Ptolemaeus Arabus et Latinus. Works.* Ptolemaeus Arabus et Latinus website. Accessed November 28, 2020.

———. *"Pseudo-Ptolemy, Liber de impressionibus imaginum, anullorum et sigillorum secundum facies duodecim signorum zodiaci" Ptolemaeus Arabus and Latinus. Works.* Ptolemaeus Arabus et Latinus website. Accessed November 28, 2020.

———. *"Pseudo-Ptolemy, Canon Ptolemei et Pictagore de diversis eventibus secundum naturas planetarum". Ptolemaeus Arabus et Latinus. Works.* Ptolemaeus Arabus et Latinus website. Accessed November 28, 2020.

———. *"Pseudo-Ptolemy, Archanum magni Dei de reduction geomancie". Ptolemaeus Arabus et Latinus. Works.* Ptolemaeus Arabus et Latinus website. Accessed November 28, 2020.

Juvenal, *Satires.* The Latin Library website.

Kärkkäinen, Pekka. *Internal Senses* in *Encyclopedia of Medieval Philosophy.* Edited by H. Lagerlund. Dordrecht: Springer, 2011.

Karr, Don, ed., and Calanit Nachshon, trans. *Liber Lunae: Book of the Moon & Sepher ha-Levanah.* Singapore: Golden Hoard, 2011.

Kieckhefer, Richard. *Magic in the Middle Ages.* Canto Classics. 3rd ed. New York: Cambridge University Press 2022.

———. *Forbidden Rites: A Necromancer's Manual of the Fifteenth Century.* Magic in History Sourcebook series. University Park: Pennsylvania State University Press, 1998.

———, trans. *Hazards of the Dark Arts: Advice for Medieval Princes on Witchcraft and Magic*. Magic in History Sourcebooks series. University Park: Pennsylvania State University Press, 2017.

Klassen, Frank. *The Transformations of Magic: Illicit Learned Magic in the Later Middle Ages*. Magic in History Sourcebooks series. Pennsylvania State University Press, 2013.

Klutz, Todd, ed. *Magic in the Biblical World: From the Rod of Aaron to the Ring of Solomon*. The Library of New Testament Studies. New York: T & T Clark International, 2004.

Kunitzsch, Paul. *Sic Itur Ad Astra: Studien Zur Geschichte Der Mathematik und Naturwissenschaften*. Wiesbaden: Harrassowitz Verlag, 2000.

Laetus, Julius Pomponius. *De Proprietate Sermonum. - Pompeius Festus, De Verborum Significatione. - Varro, De Lingua Latina*. Edited by Franciscus Rolandellus. N.p.: Giovanni Angelo Scinzenzeler, 1500.

Lang, Benedek. *Angels around the Crystal: The Prayer Book of King Wladislas and the Treasure Hunts of Henry the Bohemian* in *Aries*, vol. 5, no. 1:7. Leiden: Koninklijke Brill NV, 2005.

———. *Unlocked Books: Manuscripts of Learned Magic in the Medieval Libraries of Central Europe*. Magic in History Sourcebooks series. University Park: Pennsylvania State University Press, 2008.

Lawrence-Mathers, Anne, and Carolina Escobar-Vargas. *Magic and Medieval Society*. Abingdon: Routledge, 2014.

Lecouteux, Claude. *A Lapidary of Sacred Stones: Their Magical and Medicinal Powers Based on the Earliest Sources*. Rochester, Vt.: Inner Traditions, 2012.

———. "Les Grimoires et Leurs Ancetres." In *L'univers du livre medieval. Substance, lettre, signe*. Edited by Karin Ueltschi. Paris: Champion, 2014.

Leopold of Austria. *Compilatio de Astrorum Scientia Decem Continens Tractatus*. Augsburg: E. Ratdolt, 1489.

LePree, James Francis, and Ljudmila Djukic, eds. *The Byzantine Empire: A Historical Encyclopedia*. Santa Barbara: ABC-Clio, 2019.

Levin, Flora R., trans. and ed. *The Manual of Harmonics of Nicomachus the Pythagorean*. Grand Rapids: Phanes Press, 1994.

Lind, Michael. "Why the Liberal Arts Still Matter." *The Wilson Quarterly* vol. 30, no. 4 (Autumn 2006), Washington D.C.: Woodrow Wilson International Center for Scholars.

Linden, Stanton J. ed., *The Alchemy Reader: From Hermes Trismegistus to Isaac Newton*. Cambridge: Cambridge University Press, 2003.

Lucan. *Pharsalia*. Masters of Latin Literature. Translated by Jane Wilson. Ithaca: Cornell University Press, 1993.

Luibheid, Colm, and Paul Rorem trans.; and Rene Roques, Jaroslav Pelikan, Jean Leclercq, and Karlfried Froehlich, eds. *Pseudo-Dionysius: The Complete Works*. The Classics of Western Spirituality. New York: Paulist Press, 1987.

Lydus, Johannes. *The Months (de Mensibus)*. Translated by Mischa Hooker, presented by Roger Pearse. 2013–2014.

Lyons, Malcolm C. trans. *The Arabian Nights: Tales of 1,001 Nights*. 3 vols. New York: Penguin Classics, 2008.

Magdalino, Paul, and Maria Mavroudi. *The Occult Sciences in Byzantium*. Geneva: La Pomme d'or, 2006.

Majercik, Ruth, trans. *The Chaldean Oracles*. Platonic Texts and Translations Series. 2nd ed. Bream: The Prometheus Trust, 2013.

Malan, Solomon Caesar, ed. *The Book of Adam and Eve: Also Called the Conflict of Adam and Eve with Satan: A book of the Early Eastern Church, Translated from the Ethiopic, with Notes from the Kufale, Talmud, Midrashim, and Other Eastern Works*. London: Williams and Norgate, 1882.

Marchese, Francis. "Medieval Information Visualization." Institute of Electrical and Electronics Engineers Conference paper, 2013.

Masi, Michael, trans. *Boethian Number Theory: A Translation of the De Institutione Arithmetica*. Amsterdam: Rodopi B. V., 1983.

Mathers, Samuel Liddell MacGregor, trans. *The Key of Solomon the King*. Newburyport: Red Wheel/Weiser, 2016.

Mews, Constant J. *Abelard and Heloise*. Great Medieval Thinkers. New York: Oxford University, 2005.

Mitchell, Laura Theresa. "Cultural Uses of Magic in Fifteenth-Century England." PhD diss., University of Toronto, 2011.

McCluskey, Stephen C. *Astronomies and Cultures in Early Medieval Europe*. New York: Cambridge University Press, 1998.

Morgan, Michael. *Sepher Ha-Razim: The Book of Mysteries*. Chico: Society of Biblical Literature, 1983.

Nicomachus of Gerasa. *Introduction to Arithmetic*. Translated by Martin Luther D'Ooge, Frank Egleston Robbins, and Louis Charles Karpinski. New York: MacMillan, 1926.

Ogden, Daniel. "Lay That Ghost: Necromancy in Ancient Greece and Rome." *Archaeology Odyssey* 5:4 (July/August 2002), republished by *Biblical Archaeology* in *Bible History Daily*, October 31, 2017. Biblical Archaeology Society website.

———. *Greek and Roman Necromancy*. Princeton: Princeton University Press, 2004.

———. *Magic, Witchcraft and Ghosts in the Greek and Roman Worlds: A Sourcebook*. New York: Oxford University Press, 2009.

Openshaw, Kathleen. "The Battle between Christ and Satan in the Tiberius Psalter." *Journal of the Warburg and Courtauld Institutes* 52. 1989.

Otisk, Marek. "The Definitions of Number in Boethius' Introduction to Arithmetic," 14 (2022): 16–26.

Owen, Thomas, trans. *Geoponika: Agricultural Pursuits*. 2 vols. London: W. Spilsbury, 1805.

Pack, Roger A. "A Pseudo-Aristotelian Chiromancy." *Archives D'histoire Doctrinale Et Littéraire Du Moyen Âge* 36 (1969): 189–241.

———."Aristotle's Chiromantic Principle and Its Influence." *Transactions of the American Philological Association (1974–)* 108 (1978): 121–30.

———."Pseudo-Aristoteles: Chiromantia." *Archives D'histoire Doctrinale Et Littéraire Du Moyen Âge* 39 (1972): 289–320. Accessed February 17, 2020.

Pack, R. A., and R. Hamilton. "Rodericus de Majoricis Tractatus Ciromancie." *Archives d'histoire Doctrinale et Littéraire Du Moyen Âge 38* (1971): 271–305.

Paetow, Louis John. *A Guide to the Study of Medieval History for Students, Teachers, and Libraries*. Berkeley: University of California Press, 1917.

Page, Sophie. *Magic in the Cloister: Pious Motives, Illicit Interests, and Occult Approaches to the Medieval Universe*. Magic in History Sourcebooks series. University Park: Pennsylvania State University Press, 2013.

———. *Magic in Medieval Manuscripts*. Buffalo: University of Toronto Press, 2017.

Pearson, Birger A., trans., and Marvin Meyer, ed. *Testimony of Truth*. In *The Nag Hammadi Scriptures: The International Edition*. New York: HarperCollins, 2007.

Peterson, Joseph H., ed. *John Dee's Five Books of Mystery: Original Sourcebook of Enochian Magic*. Boston: Weiser Books, 2002.

———. *The Lesser Key of Solomon: Detailing the Ceremonial Art of Commanding Spirits Both Good and Evil*. York Beach: Weiser Books, 2001.

———. *Liber Trium Animarum: The Book of Three Souls*. Kasson, Minn.: Twilit Grotto, 2022.

———, ed. and trans. *The Sworn Book of Honorius: Liber Iuratus Honorii*. Lake Worth: Ibis, 2016.

Philosophy of Solomon. British Museum, Royal 7-D-II, fols. 3–10.

Philostratus. *On Heroes*. Translated by Ellen Bradshaw Aitken and Jennifer K. Berenson Maclean. Harvard University Center for Hellenic Studies website.

———. *The Life of Apollonius of Tyana*. Edited and translated by Christopher P. Jones. 2 vols., Loeb Classical Library. Cambridge: Harvard University Press, 2005, 16–17.

Pitra, Jean Baptiste François. *Spicilegium Solesmense complectens Sanctorum Patrum scriptorumque ecclesiasticorum anecdota hactenus opera selecta e graecis orientalibusque et latinis codicibus: Tomus tertius in quo praecipui veteres auctores de re symbolica proferuntur et illustrantur,* vol. 3. Paris: Firmin Didot Fratres, 1855.

Plato. *Euthydemus.* Translated by Gregory A. McBrayer and Mary P. Nichols. Indianapolis: Focus, 2012, 275.

Plato. *Theaetetus* in *Plato in Twelve Volumes,* Vol. 12 translated by Harold N. Fowler. Cambridge, MA: Harvard University Press; London,: William Heinemann Ltd. 1921.

Pliny the Elder. *The Natural History.* Translated by John Bostock and Henry T. Riley. London: Taylor and Francis, 1855.

Plutarch. *Parallel Lives: Demosthenes and Cicero. Alexander and Caesar.* Edited by Bernadotte Perrin. Loeb Classical Library, vol. 7. Cambridge: Harvard University Press, 1919.

Polloni, Nicola. "Gundissalinus and Avicenna: Some Remarks on an Intricate Philosophical Connection." *Documenti e Studi sulla Tradizione Filosofica Medievale* 28 (2017): 515–52.

Polo, Marco. *The Most Noble and Famous Travels of Marco Polo, Together with the Travels of Nicolao de Conti.* Translated by John Frampton with commentary by N. M. Penzer. 2nd edition. London: Adam and Charles Black, 1937.

Porphyry of Tyre. *Isagoge.* Translated by Octavius Freire Owen.

———. On Abstinence. Translated by Gillian Clark. New York: Cornell University Press, 2000.

Quia nobilissima scientia astronomiae, a mid-14th-century treatise. Cambridge University Library Gg. VI.3, ff. 217v–220v; and Oxford, Bodleian Library, Digby 57, ff. 130r–132v.

Quintilian. *Institutio Oratoria.* Cambridge, Mass.: Harvard University Press, 1920.

Rafiabadi, Hamid Naseem, ed. "Islam, Christians, and the West." In *Quia nobilissima scientia astronomiae.* New Delhi: Sarup and Sons, 2003.

Radner, Karen. "The Winged Snakes of Arabia and the Fossil Site of Makhtesh Ramon in the Negev." *Wiener Zeitschrift Für Die Kunde Des Morgenlandes* 97 (2007): 353–65.

Ragai, Jehane. "The Philosopher's Stone: Alchemy and Chemistry." *Alif: Journal of Comparative Poetics* no. 12 (1992): 58–77.

Raggetti, Lucia. "Apollonius of Tyana's Great Book of Talismans." *Nuncius* 34, issue 1, Lieden: Brill, 2019, 155–82.

Rakhshandah H., and Hosseini M. "Potentiation of pentobarbital hypnosis by *Rosa damascena* in mice." *Indian Journal of Experimental Biology* 44, no.11 (Nov. 2006):910–12. PMID: 17205713.

Rautman, Marcus Louis. *Daily Life in the Byzantine Empire.* Westport: Greenwood, 2006.

Reinink, A.W., and Jeroen Stumpel, eds. *Memory & Oblivion: Proceedings of the XXIXth International Congress of the History of Art held in Amsterdam, 1–7 September 1996*, vol. 1. Springer-Science+Business Media, B.V., English edition, Robert Simon, 1999.

Ritner, Robert K. "Necromancy in Ancient Egypt." In Leda Jean Ciraolo and Jonathan Lee Seidel eds. *Magic and Divination in the Ancient World*. Ancient Magic and Divination, 2. Leiden: Brill/Styx, 2002, 89–96.

Rose, Valentin. "Ars Notaria." In *Hermes*. N.l., Franz Steiner Verlag, 1874, 303–26.

Russo, Lucio, and Silvio Levy trans. *The Forgotten Revolution: How Science Was Born in 300 BC and Why It Had to Be Reborn*. Berlin: Springer, 2004.

Saparmin, N. binti. (2019). "History of Astrology and Astronomy in Islamic Medicine." *International Journal of Academic Research in Business and Social Sciences* 9, no. 9 (2019): 282–96.

Scholem, Gershom. "Chiromancy (Palmistry)." In *Encyclopedia Judaica*, vol. 5. Jerusalem: Keter, 1972, cols. 477–79.

Scot, Michael. *Liber Introductorius*. Munich, Bayerische Staatsbibliothek, Hs CLM 10268, MS M., first quarter of the 14th century, f. 1–146.

Seneca the Elder. *Controversiae* III, 8. *Oratorum et rhetorum sententiae divisions colores*.

Sepher Maphteah Shelomoh, Hebrew *Book of the Key of Solomon*; British Library, MS Oriental 14759, dating to 1700 or before.

Shavit, Yaacov. *An Imaginary Trio: King Solomon, Jesus, and Aristotle*. Boston: Walter De Gruyter, 2020.

Shaw, Gregory. "Neoplatonic Theurgy and Dionysius the Areopagite." *Journal of Early Christian Studies* (Winter). John Hopkins University Press, 1999: 573–99.

———. *Theurgy and the Soul: The Neoplatonism of Iamblichus*. 2nd edition. Kettering: Angelico Press/Sophia Perennis, 2014.

Shelby, Lon R. "The Geometrical Knowledge of Mediaeval Master Masons." *Speculum* 47, no. 3 (July 1972): 395–421. Published by The University of Chicago Press on behalf of the Medieval Academy of America.

Skemer, Don C. "'Armis Gunfe': Remembering Egyptian Days." *Traditio* 65 (2010): 75–106.

Skinner, Stephen. *Geomancy in Theory and Practice*. Singapore: Golden Hoard, 2011.

———. *Techniques of Graeco-Egyptian Magic*. Singapore: Golden Hoard, 2014.

———. *Techniques of Solomonic Magic*. Singapore: Golden Hoard, 2015.

———. Personal communication.

Skinner, Stephen, and Don Karr. *Sepher Raziel: Liber Salomonis*. Sourceworks of Ceremonial Magic, vol. 6. Singapore: Golden Hoard, 2010.

Skinner, Stephen, and Daniel Clark. *Ars Notoria: The Grimoire of Rapid Learning by Magic*. Sourceworks of Ceremonial Magic, vol. 11. Singapore: Golden Hoard, 2019.

Smith, Andrew, trans. *Boethius: On Aristotle, On Interpretation 1–3* and *4–6*. Edited by Richard Sorabji. New York: Bloomsbury, 2011.

Spargo, John Webster. *Virgil the Necromancer: Studies in Virgilian Legends*. Harvard Studies in Comparative Literature. London: Milford, 1934.

Stahl, William Harris, trans. and ed. *Commentary on the Dream of Scipio by Macrobius*. Records of Western Civilization. New York: Columbia University Press, 1990.

Stahl, William Harris, Richard Johnson, and E. L. Burge, trans. and eds. *Martianus Capella and the Seven Liberal Arts,* vol. 2. The Marriage of Philology and Mercury, no. 84, Records of Western Civilization. New York: Columbia University Press, 1977.

Statius. *Thebaid*. Translated by Jane Wilson Joyce. Ithaca: Cornell University Press, 2008.

Tanner, Heather J. *Medieval Elite Women and the Exercise of Power, 1100–1400: Moving beyond the Exceptionalist Debate*. Palgrave MacMillan: Columbus, 2019.

Tardieu, Michel. *Manichaeism*. Translated by M. B. DeBevoise with introduction by Paul Mirecki. University of Illinois Press: Chicago, 2008.

Taylor, Barnaby. *Lucretius and the Language of Nature*. Oxford Classical Monographs. New York: Oxford University Press, 2020.

Thorndike, Lynn. "Chiromancy in Mediaeval Latin Manuscripts" *Speculum* 40, no. 4 (1965): 674–706. Accessed December 13, 2020. https://doi.org/10.2307/2851404.

———. *A History of Magic and Experimental Science,* 8 vols. New York: Columbia University Press, 1923–1958.

———. "The Latin Pseudo-Aristotle and Medieval Occult Science." *The Journal of English and Germanic Philology* 21, no. 2 (1922): 229–58. Accessed August 30, 2020.

———. *The Sphere of Sacrobosco and Its Commentators*. Chicago: University of Chicago Press, 1949. http://www.jstor.org/stable/27702640.

———. "An Unidentified Work by Giovanni Da'Fortana: Liber De Omnibus Rebus Naturalibus." *Isis* 15, no. 1 (1931): 31–46.

Torijano, Pablo A. *Solomon the Esoteric King: From King to Magus, Development of a Tradition*. Lieden: Brill, 2002.

Trachtenberg, Joshua. *Jewish Magic and Superstition*. New York: Behrman's Jewish Book House, 1939.

Tuczay, Christa Agnes. "The Book of Zabulon—A Quest for Hidden Secrets: Intertextuality and Magical Genealogy in Middle High German Literature, with an Emphasis on Reinfried von Braunschweig." In *Magic and Magicians in the Middle Ages and the Early Modern Time: The Occult in Pre-Modern Sciences, Medicine, Literature, Religion, and Astrology.* Edited by Albrecht Classen. Boston: De Gruyter, 2017, 397–422.

Tunison, Joseph Salathiel. *Master Virgil: The Author of the Aeneid as He Seemed in the Middle Ages.* A Series of Studies, 2nd ed. Cincinnati: R. Clarke, 1890.

Turner, Robert, trans. *Ars Notoria: The Notory Art of Solomon.* London: Cottrel, 1657.

Veenstra, Jan. *Magic and Divination at the Courts of Burgundy and France: Text and Context of Laurens Pignon's Contre Les Devineurs (1411).* Brill's Studies in Intellectual History. New York: Brill, 1998.

Véronèse, Julien. "Contre la divination et la magie a la cour: trois traits addresses a des grands aux XIVe et XVe siecles." Micrologus. Nature, Sciences and Medieval Societies, Brepols/SISMEL, 2008, I saperi nelle corti / Knowledge at the Courts, XVI.

———. "La notion d' 'auteur-magicien' a la fin du Moyen Age: Le cas de l'ermite Pelagius de Majorque (†v. 1480)." In *Medievales: Langues, Textes, Histoire* 51 (Autumn). Vincennes: Presses universitaires de Vincennes, 2006, 119–38.

———. *L'Ars notoria au Moyen Age: Introduction et edition critique.* Micrologus library, 21. Firenze: Sismel—Galluzzo, 2007.

———. "L'Ars notaria au Moyen Age et a l'epoque modern: etude d'une tradition de magie theurgique, XIIe–XVIIes," these de doctorat d'histoire de Paris-X, 2004, 2 vols.

———. *L'Almandal et l'Almadel latins au Moyen Âge: Introduction et éditions critiques.* Florence: SISMEL Edizioni del Galluzzo, 2012.

———. "La transmission groupée des textes de magie 'salomonienne' de l'Antiquité au Moyen Âge. Bilan historiographique, inconnues et pistes de recherche." In *L'antiquite tardive dans les collections medievales: textes et representations, Vie–XIVe siècle,* S. Gioanni et B. Grevin. Rome: Ecole francaise de Rome, 2008, 193–223.

———. "Les Anges dans l'Ars notoria: revelation, processus visionnaire et angelologie." *Melanges de l'Ecole francaise de Rome: Moyen Age* 114, no. 2. Rome: Ecole francaise de Rome, 2002, 813–49.

———. "God's Names and Their Uses in the Books of Magic attributed to King Solomon." *Magic, Ritual, and Witchcraft* 5, no. 1 (Summer 2010).

———. "Pietro d'Abano magicien à la Renaissance : le cas de l'Elucidarius magice (ou Lucidarium artis nigromantice)." In Médecine, astrologie et magie entre Moyen Âge et Renaissance: autour de Pietro d'Abano, dir. J.-P. Boudet, Fr. Collard et N. Weill-Parot, Florence, Sismel-Edizioni del Galluzzo, Micrologus Library (50), 2013 295–330.

Virgil. *The Aeneid.* Translated by Robert Fagles with introduction by Bernard Knox. New York: Penguin Books, 2006.

Virgilii Cordubensis Philosophia ex Vetustisimo Codice Papyraceo. Biblioteca Nacional de Espana, MS 6463, 1753.

Waterfield, Robin, trans. *Theology of Arithmetic.* Grand Rapids: Kairos Book, Phanes Press, 1988.

Watson, Nicholas, and Claire Fanger. "The Prologue to John of Morigny's *Liber Visionum:* Text and Translation." Esoterica 3 (200) 108–217.

Weill-Parot, Nicolas. "Cecco d'Ascoli and Antonio da Montolmo: The building of a 'nigromantical' cosmology and the birth of the author-magician." In *The Routledge History of Medieval Magic.* The Routledge Histories. Edited by Sophie Page and Catherine Rider. New York: Routledge Taylor & Francis Group, 2019.

Weisser, Ursula, ed. *"Buch uber Geheimnis der Schopfung und die Darstellung der Natur" von Pseudo-Apollonios von Tyana.* Aleppo: Institute for the History of Arabic Science, 1979.

William of Auvergne. *De Legibus* (1228–30), chapter 24.

Witt, Ronald. Medieval "Ars Dictaminis" and the Beginnings of Humanism: A New Construction of the Problem*. *Renaissance Quarterly, 35,* issue 1, 1982.

Yates, Frances A. "The Art of Ramon Lull: An Approach to It through Lull's Theory of the Elements." *Journal of the Warburg and Courtauld Institutes* 17, no. 1/2 (1954): 115–73. Accessed May 2, 2021. https://doi.org/10.2307/750135.

———. *Frances Yates: Selected Works, Volume III, The Art of Memory.* New York: Routledge, 1966.

Yonge, C. D., trans. *The Orations of Marcus Tullius Cicero,* vol. 4. London: Bell and Sons, 1913–21.

Zambelli, Paola. *The Speculum Astronomiae and Its Enigma: Astrology, Theology and Science in Albertus Magnus and His Contemporaries.* Boston Studies in the Philosophy of Science, vol. 135. Dordrecht: Springer-Science+Business Media, B.V., 1992.

Ziolkowski, Jan M. and Michael C. J. Putnam, ed., *The Virgilian Tradition: The First Fifteen Hundred Years,* (New Haven: Yale University Press, 2008).

Ziolkowski, Jan. "Virgil the Magician." In *Dall'antico Al Moderno: Immagini del Classico Nelle Letterature Europee*. Edited by Piero Boitani and Emilia Di Rocco. Roma: Edizioni Di Storia E Letteratura, 2015, 59–75.

Zironi, Alessandro. "Disclosing Secrets: Virgil in Middle High German Poem." In *Obscurity in Medieval Texts*. Vol. 30. Edited by Lucie Dolezalova, Jeff Rider, and Alessandro Zironi. Krems: *Medium aevum quotidianum* 2013.

Index of Prayers

This index presents the standardized prayer incipits.
Below these main entries are the subentries of all its variations.
An asterisk indicates a Latin prologue to a prayer.

GENERAL INDEX

logique
rethorique
musique